INTERMEDIATE ACCOUNTING

VOLUME 2

SEVENTH EDITION

Thomas H. Beechy
Schulich School of Business
York University

Joan E. Davison Conrod
Faculty of Management
Dalhousie University

Elizabeth J. Farrell
Schulich School of Business
York University

Ingrid McLeod-Dick
Schulich School of Business
York University

Intermediate Accounting
Volume 2
Seventh Edition

The Internet addresses listed in the text were accurate at the time of publication. The inclusion of a Web site does not indicate an endorsement by the authors or McGraw-Hill Ryerson, and McGraw-Hill Ryerson does not guarantee the accuracy of the information presented at these sites.

ISBN-13: 978-1-25-910802-0

ISBN-10: 1-25-910802-3

1 2 3 4 5 6 7 8 9 0   TCP   1 9 8 7 6

Printed and bound in Canada.

Care has been taken to trace ownership of copyright material contained in this text; however, the publisher will welcome any information that enables them to rectify any reference or credit for subsequent editions.

Portfolio and Program Manager: Karen Fozard

Product Manager: Keara Emmett

Executive Marketing Manager: Joy Armitage Taylor

Product Developer: Lindsay MacDonald

Senior Product Team Associate: Stephanie Giles

Supervising Editor: Jessica Barnoski

Photo/Permissions Editor: Photo Affairs, Inc.

Copy Editor: Karen Rolfe

Plant Production Coordinator: Sarah Strynatka

Manufacturing Production Coordinator: Emily Hickey

Cover Design: Mark Cruxton

Cover Images: (Globe and money) © Vstock LLC/Getty Images RF; (Skyscrapers) © Arpad Benedek/Getty Images RF; (Canadian flag) © BjArn Kindler/Getty Images RF; (Tablet, pen, keyboard) © John Lamb/Getty Images RF

Interior Design: Lightbox Visual Communications Inc.

Composition: MPS

Page Layout: SPi Global

Printer: Transcontinental Printing Group

About the Authors

Thomas H. Beechy, York University

Thomas H. Beechy is Professor Emeritus of Accounting at the Schulich School of Business, York University. He also is the Schulich Director of International Academic Development. Professor Beechy holds degrees from the George Washington University (BA), Kellogg School of Management at Northwestern University (MBA), and Washington University (DBA). Professor Beechy was employed as a case writer for the Kellogg School, following which he taught at Illinois Institute of Technology for 10 years. He has been a professor at York University since 1971, teaching in BBA, MBA, IMBA and EMBA programs. Professor Beechy has been a leader in Canadian accounting education, emphasizing the importance of prescriptive case analysis for developing students' professional judgement. He has been an active researcher and advocate in Canadian in both business and nonprofit financial accounting realms.

Joan E. Davison Conrod, Dalhousie University

Joan Davison Conrod is a Professor of Accounting in the Rowe School of Business at Dalhousie University. Her teaching excellence has been recognized through awards such as the 2013 3M National Teaching Fellowship, the Dalhousie University Alumni Award for Teaching Excellence, and the AAU Distinguished Teacher award. Joan is an active member of the University community and has served on the Dalhousie University Senate and the Board of Governors. She is a past president of the Canadian Academic Accounting Association. Joan has a lengthy history of involvement in professional accounting education, a contributing factor in her FCPA designation. She taught financial and managerial accounting courses to professional accounting students across Canada, but particularly in Atlantic Canada, for 20 years. She has served on CA education committees at the local, regional, and national levels. Her publications include the text *Advanced Financial Reporting* for CPA-Canada, and a variety of case material and other publications.

Elizabeth J. Farrell, York University

Elizabeth J. Farrell is an adjunct professor and has taught at the Schulich School of Business for many years. She was awarded her FCPA, FCA from the Institute of Chartered Accountants of Ontario in 2013. In recognition of her excellence in teaching, she was awarded the Seymour Schulich Award for Teaching Excellence in 1999, 2003, and 2010 and was nominated for the award in 2004, 2005, 2006, 2007, 2008, 2012, and 2015. She was awarded the John Peace teaching faculty award in 2001 and 2012. She has taught financial accounting courses for over 20 years. Liz served as assistant coordinator of the Institute of Chartered Accountants of Ontario's School of Accountancy, where she also had served as a seminar leader for many years. She served as a member of the competency map committee. She has taught executive development courses for the Schulich Executive Education Centre (SEEC), as well as professional development courses for the CPA Ontario and for CPA firms. In addition to being a co-author of *Intermediate Accounting*, she has worked on an accounting case analysis software package; study guides; an IFRS Property, Plant, and Equipment, Intangible Assets and Impairment professional development course; *IFRS—Leases; ASPE—A Comparison to IFRS*; Researching and Documenting an Accounting Issue; and a variety of case material and other publications. She was one of the lead authors for the assurance elective module for the CPA PEP program. She also serves as a Board member for a not-for-profit organization.

Ingrid McLeod-Dick, York University

Ingrid McLeod-Dick is an adjunct professor and has taught at the Schulich School of Business for many years in its BBA, MBA, and EMBA programs. In recognition of her excellence in teaching, she received the John Peace part-time faculty teaching award in 2000 and was nominated for the Seymour Schulich Award for Teaching Excellence in 2000 to 2007 and 2012. She was awarded her FCA from the Ontario Institute of Chartered Accountants in 1994. Ingrid also served as a seminar leader for many years for the Institute of Chartered Accountants of Ontario's School of Accountancy. She currently teaches professional development courses for the ICAO. Her publications include the IFRS Financial Presentation and Disclosure course, and she is a contributing author to *Guides to International Financial Reporting Standards in Canada*, as well as a variety of case material for the PEP program for CPA Canada.

Brief Table of Contents—Volume 2

Table of Contents—Volume 2

Preface

Welcome to the complex Canadian GAAP reporting environment! The vast majority of Canadian public companies prepare financial statements that comply with International Financial Reporting Standards (IFRS), as set by the International Accounting Standards Board (IASB) and contained in the *CPA Canada Handbook, Part I*. In contrast, Canadian private companies may choose to comply with either IFRS or Canadian Accounting Standards for Private Enterprise (ASPE), as contained in the *CPA Canada Handbook, Part II*. These two sets of GAAP are similar in many respects but quite different in other respects. This duality presents a huge challenge to accountants, managers, and financial statement users.

Clearly, accounting standards are ever expanding, and change is the norm; you might find the expanding universe of accounting knowledge to be intimidating. Intermediate accounting is the essential course for developing both the technical skills and the professional judgement that you need to succeed. We believe that neither technical knowledge nor professional judgement is sufficient on its own; it is the blend of the two that represents the value added by a professional accountant.

So that is what *Intermediate Accounting* will do for you: provide complete, appropriate technical knowledge while also developing your professional judgement. Both these elements are described in the broad range of topics in this book. We clearly explain the standards, identify patterns, explore the impact of alternatives on users and uses of financial statements, and look forward to further changes that are on the horizon. Throughout this book, we stress the importance of ethical standards—an accountant must learn to recognize and respond appropriately in potentially challenging situations.

In selecting material to include in this book, we have assessed the realities of Canadian business practice and the choices that are currently available. We have a distinctly Canadian agenda, looking at the issues that matter in Canadian business. We are clear in our treatment of the body of knowledge. Our coverage does not get bogged down in the (sometimes twisted) past history of a given issue, nor does it speculate needlessly on what might or might not happen in the future. Our emphasis is on preparing you to apply the standards now in place, providing an overview of some expected changes, and moving to develop the necessary judgemental skills to apply those standards wisely and effectively. These same judgemental skills will serve you equally well even when standards change in the future, as they undoubtedly will.

After you master the contents of *Intermediate Accounting*, you will be able to account for the wide range of events and transactions found in this unique and challenging economic environment. We are proud that this book is now in its seventh edition. Many thousands of students have started their substantive study of the corporate reporting environment with this book. In addition, many people have supported the evolution of this book over the last 25 years, and we are very grateful for their encouragement and continued goodwill.

IFRS and ASPE

A Canadian agenda means that we all must master international standards. Every chapter is based first and foremost on IFRS. Differences between ASPE and IFRS are explained in a separate section, to provide clarity regarding one set of standards as compared with the other. Assignment material reflects both IFRS and ASPE so that applications reflect the dual GAAP environment.

Technical Knowledge

Accountants have to be able to account for things! The seventh edition provides a level of expertise that must become part of every accountant's body of knowledge: how to record a receivable, capitalize a lease, account for a pension, or prepare a statement of cash flows. Some of the transactions that we must account for are very complex, and the specific rules must be mastered. An affinity for numbers is important.

Professional Judgement

Professional judgement, it is often said, is the hallmark of a profession. There are often different ways to account for the same transaction. Professional accountants must become expert at sizing up the circumstances and exercising judgement to determine the appropriate accounting policy for those circumstances.

Once an accounting policy has been established, management almost always must make accounting measurement estimates before the numbers can be recorded. Accounting estimates require the exercise of professional judgement.

Professional judgement is not acquired overnight. It is nurtured and slowly grows over a lifetime. In this book, we begin the development process by explicitly examining the variables that companies consider when evaluating their options, and the criteria that accountants use to make choices. Many opportunities to develop and improve judgement are provided in the case material.

Accuracy

The text has been extensively reviewed and proofread prior to publication. Chapter material has been reviewed by professional accountants. All assignment materials have been solved independently by multiple individual "assignment checkers" in addition to the authors. Nevertheless, errors may remain, for which we accept full responsibility. If you find errors, please email the authors at **j.conrod@dal.ca, efarrell@schulich.yorku.ca,** or **ing.mcleod@sympatico.ca.** Your help will be greatly appreciated.

Topical Review Identifying Key Changes

Chapter 1

The book starts by exploring the multiple accounting frameworks in use in Canada for public companies and private companies—IFRS standards for public companies, IFRS or ASPE or DBA for private companies. The chapter then explores the issue of international comparability and the difference between nations in their acceptance of IFRS—whether a nation adopts, adapts, or harmonizes with IFRS. While companies in different countries may use IFRS, the financial reports still embed significant differences that arise from differences in nations' economic, business, and sometimes even religious practices.

After establishing the multiple GAAP frameworks, our attention turns to the basis of application of any framework. Before we can make judgements on choosing accounting policies and making accounting estimates, we must understand the many possible (and often conflicting) objectives underlying a company's financial reporting. Thus, the second major theme of the first chapter is how the many different factors and influences shape a company's financial reporting. This is fundamental material that supports professional judgement.

Chapter 1 has been extensively revised and rewritten for this edition, with new exhibits to further clarify the material.

Chapter 2

The primary focus of Chapter 2 is on the accounting choice process, emphasizing underlying assumptions, qualitative characteristics, and measurement methods. Having set the basic reporting framework in Chapter 1, Chapter 2 further develops the theme of professional judgement. This chapter explains the basic assumptions underlying financial reporting and then moves on to develop the qualitative characteristics that must be considered when developing professional approaches to accounting issues.

Ethical issues are strongly emphasized in this chapter, as they are throughout the book. After discussing the broad recognition issues for revenue and expense, the chapter then sets out the elements of financial reporting. The increased incidence of fair value measurement within IFRS requires that the traditional distinction between "revenue" and "gains" be modified.

By the end of Chapter 2, all of the factors and elements underlying the exercise of professional judgement have been laid out and clarified. These factors and elements underlie the professional judgements that students must make as they move through the text, particularly in the case material at the end of each chapter.

Chapter 3

Chapter 3 discusses the nature of income and the difference between the economic and accounting concepts of income. The statement of comprehensive income is explained, and emphasizes the distinction between operating income and comprehensive income. The general presentation approach is explained, along with format variations that are accepted in practice.

Chapter 3 contains the book's primary discussion of asset disposals, discontinued operations, and restructuring. Discontinued operations is just one part of a broader issue of asset disposals. We have introduced asset disposals in this chapter to provide a clearer context for understanding discontinued operations. We discuss and provide examples of all forms of asset disposals, including abandonment, sales of individual assets, sale of asset groups, and discontinued operations. Because asset disposals are often connected with restructurings, we also present the criteria and reporting requirements for restructuring plans as well as the requirements for reporting constructive obligations that frequently accompany restructurings.

The chapter ends with a discussion of ASPE and the ways in which the reporting requirements for private enterprises using ASPE differ from enterprises reporting under IFRS.

Chapter 4

This chapter begins with a general discussion of the purpose and limitations of the statement of financial position. This discussion includes an explanation of the different ways in which the assets, liabilities, and shareholders' equity can be presented, depending on the individual regional practice.

Specific individual items on the statement are then discussed. IFRS requires certain items to be reported on the face of the statement but does not prescribe a specific format.

The next section discusses and illustrates the statement of changes in equity. We illustrate that the statement of changes in equity (SCE) includes not only the "normal" shareholder accounts (e.g., share equity and retained earnings) but also each of the various components of other comprehensive income.

In the fourth section, we have expanded the overview of accounting changes, including changes in estimate, changes in accounting policy, and error correction. Accounting changes are pervasive, and this section prepares students to understand accounting changes as they move through the specific topics that comprise the rest of the book. A full discussion of accounting changes is reserved for the end of the book, Chapter 21 (in Volume Two).

The final section is a discussion of disclosure notes. This section reflects the current disclosure requirements of IFRS, including related party transactions, segment reporting, contingencies, and guarantees.

Chapter 5

The statement of cash flows (SCF) is dealt with in sequence, as a primary financial statement. The chapter deals with the mechanics of statement preparation, using both a format-free approach and the T-account method. The journal-entry-based worksheet approach is included in an appendix. Coverage is linked to the reporting example of International Forest Products, to emphasize IFRS presentation issues and judgemental presentation choices. Presentation of investment revenue cash flow, interest, and dividends paid is discussed and illustrated in a separate section. Statement of cash flows (SCF) issues are reviewed in every subsequent chapter of the book. Plus, there is a comprehensive SCF review at the end of Volume Two.

Chapter 6

Revenue is one of the most judgemental areas of accounting policy choice and new standards requiring a contract-based approach must be adopted by 2018 although earlier adoption is permitted. For the seventh edition of the book, this chapter reflects the new standard for revenue recognition under IFRS and specifically outlines the five criteria required for revenue recognition. A consistent approach is used to apply these criteria to determine the appropriate revenue recognition for various types of transactions. Specifically, the chapter provides examples of revenue transactions, including sales with rights of return or warranty agreements, bill and hold arrangements, consignments, and licensing fees. Transactions involving multiple deliverables are explained, with examples of loyalty point programs and franchisee fees provided. In accounting for long-term contacts, examples illustrate contracts requiring revenue to be recognized at a single point in time and contracts requiring revenue to be recognized over time.

Biological assets and agricultural produce are also discussed in the chapter. Barter transactions and exchanges of similar and dissimilar goods or services are important but challenging aspects of accounting. The chapter puts these transactions into a broader context and illustrates, based on IFRS, just how each of the various types of non-monetary exchanges should be measured and reported.

The chapter also details the revenue recognition standard under ASPE, which is now different than under IFRS. ASPE still requires an earning-based approach be used for revenue recognition. Significant differences are explained and examples provided where necessary. In addition, there is a brief discussion on the accounting treatment of related party transactions and non-monetary transactions under ASPE.

Chapter 7

This chapter now deals with two important financial instruments: cash and receivables. Coverage of payables has been shifted to Volume Two. Classification and valuation decisions are central to the coverage of cash and receivables. New to this edition are the new impairment guidance and revised financial asset classifications in IFRS 9. Important topics, such as foreign currency translation (a must, in this age of globalization) and the IFRS rules governing the transfer of receivables, are incorporated. Material on bank reconciliations is in an Appendix, and coverage of present and future value calculations is available online on Connect, as is a more extensive set of compound interest tables.

Chapter 8

This chapter conforms to the IFRS approach applying lower of cost and market valuation methods wherein the IFRS defines "market" as net realizable value. Also, we explain the process for writing inventory back up if NRV recovers before the inventory is sold.

This chapter provides focus on many accounting issues with respect to inventory: items to include or exclude, lower of cost or NRV valuation, onerous contracts, errors, and estimation techniques.

Inventory valuation raises the possibility of unethical behaviour. Therefore, the chapter includes discussion of the ethical issues surrounding inventory valuation and accounting.

Chapters 9 and 10

Accounting for fixed assets and intangible assets is challenging in the IFRS context. There are three possible models to consider depending on the type of asset: the fair value model, the revaluation model, and the cost model. Also, component accounting and depreciation add complexities to the accounting for fixed assets. Impairment testing and reversals will create more volatility in earnings using IFRS. These chapters systematically look at acquisition, amortization, impairment, and disposal considering both the IFRS and ASPE. The appendices cover the complexities related to investment property, government assistance, capital cost allowance, and the revaluation model.

Chapter 11

This chapter reflects coverage of IFRS 9, effective in 2018 but available for early adoption. Accounting for passive investments, including amortized cost, fair value through profit and loss, and fair value through other comprehensive income are explained and illustrated for bond and equity investments. Accounting for investment revenue and impairment is also discussed with many numeric examples provided. The classification of strategic investments based on the level of control and influence is examined as related to associates, joint arrangements and subsidiaries. The accounting methods for strategic equity investments including cost, equity method, and consolidation are briefly addressed. Both policy and numeric issues are thoroughly explored. The chapter includes a number of helpful diagrams and figures to help clarify the roadmap through this complex territory. ASPE alternatives are very different in this area, and the choices are documented, described and illustrated where necessary.

Volume One Appendix—Fundamentals: The Accounting Information Processing System

The Appendix reviews the accounting cycle from the original transaction to the journals, trial balance, and preparation of financial statements. Examples of adjusting journal entries are discussed as well as subsidiary ledgers and worksheet applications. Extensive examples are used to illustrate the accounting cycle.

Chapters 12 and 13

There are two chapters on liabilities to start Volume Two. Chapter 12 deals with operating payables, as well as notes payable and provisions. The chapter includes some examples of liability measurement that require discounting. We hope that this shorter chapter is an appropriate way to start off a new term! This chapter fully reflects IFRS and ASPE standards in the area.

Chapter 13 delves into long-term debt, using bonds as an example. The chapter relies on discounted cash flow models for liability measurement, accompanied by the effective-interest method of amortization. Straight-line amortization is illustrated in the ASPE section. Various valuation and measurement complexities are covered, including the effect of upfront fees and derecognition scenarios. This chapter includes a section on the capitalization of borrowing costs.

Chapter 14

This chapter deals with straightforward shareholders' equity issues. Multicolumn presentation of the shareholders' equity statement, consistent with International Accounting Standard 1 (IAS 1), is completely incorporated. Classification and presentation of amounts in accumulated other comprehensive income, (e.g., from fair-value-through-other-comprehensive-income (FVTOCI) investments, and certain foreign currency gains/losses) is included, and is supported by assignment material. Summary charts have been incorporated, where appropriate.

Chapter 15

One major topic in this chapter is classification: debt versus equity, compound financial instruments, and the like. Classification is based on the substance of a financial instrument rather than its legal form. A major section covers the IFRS approach to share-based payments, emphasizing the estimates needed for measurement and forfeitures. Basic patterns for option accounting are established. Finally, the material on derivative instruments is included in this chapter. While many of the complexities of derivatives are appropriately left to advanced accounting courses, this introduction is vital. We think that the material is clear and understandable, at an appropriate level for Intermediate courses.

Chapters 16 and 17

Accounting for income tax remains two separate chapters, to acknowledge that many instructors prefer to spend two blocks of time on this most challenging area. The Chapter 16 material establishes a three-step process for typical situations. The focus of Chapter 17 remains accounting for the tax effect of losses—carrybacks and carryforwards. This is difficult material for students, but the Chapter 17 problems incorporate the prior-chapter material and allow solid reinforcement of the steps associated with tax accounting. The ASPE section explains the taxes payable method that is available for private enterprises.

Chapter 18

The chapter itself deals with the current IFRS lease accounting requirements. The new lease accounting standard requres all leases longer than one year to be capitalized, although classes of low-value assets can be excluded. This new standard will not become effective before 2019. Accordingly, the new lease standard is presented in the Appendix, supported by appropriate assignment material.

Chapter 19

Pensions and other post-retirement benefits are highly complex arrangements, with correspondingly complex accounting treatment. The current IFRS standard is emphasized, wherein three elements are identified and recorded. ASPE coverage is included. This chapter also includes an example of accounting for other post-retirement benefits and appropriate coverage of defined contribution plans, since the latter are gaining in popularity.

Chapter 20

Earnings per share material includes an explanation of basic and diluted earnings per share (EPS). IFRS terminology is used throughout. The procedural steps associated with organizing a complex EPS question are emphasized to provide more comfort and support in this complicated area. There are a variety of useful summary figures and tables.

Chapter 21

Accounting policy changes and error corrections require restatement of one or more prior years' financial statements. Restatement is surely an important topic, given the number of fraud-based restatements reported in the public press in recent years. Also, the ongoing changes in accounting standards means that companies must often restate their accounts. This chapter deals with the theory and mechanics related to such restatement, reflecting current IFRS standards.

Chapter 22

The text concludes with a review of financial statement analysis and emphasizes the importance of accounting policy choice and disclosure in the analysis of published financial statements. The chapter provides an in-depth discussion related to the type of information to gather specifically to assist with the analysis. Each of the ratios described in the chapter are calculated for the same sample company, and the results are analyzed, taking into consideration the entity's business and industry. There is an extensive case illustration, showing restatements, which demonstrates the importance of accounting policy choice.

Volume Two Appendix—Statement of Cash Flows

SCF topics have been explained in each chapter of the text, and students have had assignment material to reinforce each topic. However, some instructors prefer to end the course with a comprehensive review of SCF topics, as review and reinforcement. This Appendix gathers material that will support this approach. The Appendix is based on a T-account analysis, and has an appropriate range of assignment material.

Pedagogical Walkthrough

Introduction

Each chapter has an introduction that explains the objectives of the chapter in narrative form.

Concept Review

Throughout each chapter concept review questions are included. Students can stop and think through the answers to these basic questions, covering the previously explained material. This helps comprehension and focus! Answers to these questions can be found online on Connect.

CONCEPT REVIEW

1. What is the definition of "current" for current assets and current liabilities?
2. Why might some of a company's major "assets" not appear on the SFP?
3. What interpretive problems arise from the fact that the financial statements of public companies are consolidated?

Figures and Tables

Where appropriate, chapter material is summarized in figures and tables to establish the patterns and help reinforce material.

EXHIBIT 6-1

THE REVENUE RECOGNITION PROCESS

Performance complete, but **conditional right** to consideration	Received consideration but performance not yet completed	Performance complete and **unconditional right** to consideration
Goods and services transferred but receipt of consideration is conditional (e.g., delivering another **distinct** performance obligation)	Payment received (or receivable) before goods and services are transferred	Goods and services transferred and unconditional right to consideration
↓	↓	↓
DR Contract Asset/Accrued Receivable CR Revenue	DR Accounts Receivable (or Cash) CR Contract Liability/ Unearned Revenues	DR Accounts Receivable (or Cash) CR Revenue
↓	↓	
Conditions are met and now unconditional right to consideration	Performance is completed (goods and services are transferred)	
DR Accounts Receivable/Cash CR Contract Asset/Accrued Receivable	DR Contract Liability/Unearned Revenue CR Revenue	

Ethical Issues

Many chapters discuss accounting issues that raise ethical concerns. These concerns are highlighted in the chapter. Where ethical issues are particularly problematic, we have included a separate "Ethical Issues" section to help students focus on the ethical aspects of policy choice.

Ethics assignment material has also been incorporated into the case material. Essentially, when an accountant makes a recommendation on a contentious choice of accounting policy, ethics are tested. Students exercise true-to-life ethical judgement when they have to make a tough judgement call and recommend an accounting policy that is "good" for one group but "bad" for another. These ethical overtones are highlighted in the case solutions to help instructors draw them out in discussion and evaluation.

ETHICAL ISSUES

Choice of accounting policy must be based on the facts, the user environment, and the competitive situation. Policies chosen to manipulate certain measurements, or foster erroneous conclusions by financial statement users, are not acceptable. However, accountants must be aware of the implications of choosing a certain policy. A decision to capitalize costs, and amortize them over the period of use instead of immediate expensing, will effectively transfer the cash outflow out of operating activities and show the outflow under investing activities.

Looking Forward

Standards are constantly evolving and changing! To help keep abreast of forthcoming probable changes, at the end of each chapter we provide a discussion of key anticipated changes in IFRS and/or ASPE standards.

Accounting Standards for Private Enterprises

At the end of each chapter, there is a section that expands on essential items to understand for Accounting Standards for Private Enterprise (ASPE) in Canada. These sections include numeric examples, where appropriate. The ASPE sections provide students and instructors with a detailed, but easy-to-use guide to these important standards.

Accounting Standards for Private Enterprises

 Balance Sheet

Canadian ASPE continues to use the title *balance sheet*, but use of that title is not required. *Statement of financial position* remains an acceptable alternative. The general format of the balance sheet is the same as for IFRS. *CPA Canada Handbook, Part II*, section 1521, contains a list of items that should be "separately presented." Some of these will usually appear on the face of the balance sheet, but some may be disclosed in the notes. The only items in the list that do not specifically appear in IFRS are:

- Prepaid expenses
- Obligations under capital leases
- Asset retirement obligations

Relevant Standards

At the end of each chapter, we provide a comprehensive list of the IASB and ASPE standards that are relevant to the material in that chapter. We have not quoted the standards directly in chapter material, and we have not provided paragraph references to either the IASB publications or *CPA Canada Handbook*. This omission is intentional—the two sources are harmonized but may use different words. Also, the IASB makes "annual improvements" that change the wording of some standards. Our focus is on the application of standards, not the technicalities of the wording.

RELEVANT STANDARDS

CPA Canada Handbook, Part I (IFRS):

- IAS 1, Presentation of Financial Statements
- IAS 8, Accounting Policies, Changes in Accounting Estimates and Errors
- IAS 24, Related Party Disclosures
- IAS 10, Events after the Reporting Period
- IAS 37, Provisions, Contingent Liabilities and Contingent Assets
- IFRS 8, Operating Segments

Summary of Key Points

A summary of key points concludes each chapter. This provides a list of the key ideas and reinforces the chapter material.

Key Terms

Each chapter concludes with a list of key terms used and explained in the chapter.

Review Problems

From Chapter 3 onward, we provide at least one self-study review problem, with the solution. This provides an opportunity to practise the primary aspects of that chapter's content.

Cases

More than 60 cases are included in *Intermediate Accounting*, and there is at least one new case in every chapter in the seventh edition. The cases portray realistic situations, usually with multiple financial reporting implications. Students must put themselves into the situation and grapple with the facts to arrive at the most appropriate accounting policies for the circumstances. A blend of professional judgement and technical skills is needed to respond to a case. Case coverage is not limited to "one chapter" bites but often integrates material learned to date. For those trying to build a base of professionalism, the use of cases consistently over the term is highly recommended. Cases can be assigned for class debriefing, class presentations, or written assignments.

Technical Review

In this edition, we have added five new Technical Review exercises at the end of each chapter, preceding the somewhat more demanding assignment material. These Technical Review Exercises are directive, brief, and quantitative and encourage students to ensure they understand the chapter's basic quantitative aspects. We have provided ten such exercises in total in each chapter (except in the introductory chapters) these are more conceptual than numerical in nature, and technical review is not the focus.

Assignment Material

There is an extensive range of assignment material at the end of each chapter. The assignments provide the opportunity to "learn by doing."

The Technical Review Exercises, in addition to a wealth and variety of assignments, are available online on Connect; the Connect logo identifies these questions. The Connect problems allow web-based iterations of the problem for assessment, immediate feedback, and extra practice.

★

Stars accompany each assignment to indicate length, with one star indicating a shorter assignment and three stars indicating a longer assignment.

To help students practise on their own, we have selected a few assignments from each chapter and put their solutions online. These selected assignments are highlighted by the icon below the question.

Excel® templates for selected assignments provide an introduction to basic spreadsheet applications. These assignments are identified with the icon above the question and are available online.

Market-Leading Technology

▪ connect

Learn without Limits

McGraw-Hill Connect® is an award-winning digital teaching and learning platform that gives students the means to better connect with their coursework, with their instructors, and with the important concepts that they will need to know for success now and in the future. With Connect, instructors can take advantage of McGraw-Hill's trusted content to seamlessly deliver assignments, quizzes and tests online. McGraw-Hill Connect is the learning platform that continually adapts to each student, delivering precisely what they need, when they need it, so class time is more engaging and effective. Connect makes teaching and learning personal, easy, and proven.

Connect Key Features:

SmartBook®

As the first and only adaptive reading experience, SmartBook is changing the way students read and learn. SmartBook creates a personalized reading experience by highlighting the most important concepts a student needs to learn at that moment in time. As a student engages with SmartBook, the reading experience continuously adapts by highlighting content based on what each student knows and doesn't know. This ensures that he or she is focused on the content needed to close specific knowledge gaps, while it simultaneously promotes long-term learning.

Connect Insight®

Connect Insight is Connect's new one-of-a-kind visual analytics dashboard—now available for instructors—that provides at-a-glance information regarding student performance, which is immediately actionable. By presenting assignment, assessment, and topical performance results together with a time metric that is easily visible for aggregate or individual results, Connect Insight gives instructors the ability to take a just-in-time approach to teaching and learning, which was never before available. Connect Insight presents data that helps instructors improve class performance in a way that is efficient and effective.

Simple Assignment Management

With Connect, creating assignments is easier than ever, so instructors can spend more time teaching and less time managing. Instructors can:

- Assign SmartBook learning modules;
- Draw from a variety of text-specific Technical Review Exercises, Assignments, and test bank questions to assign online;
- Edit existing questions and create their own questions; and
- Streamline lesson planning, student progress reporting, and assignment grading to make classroom management more efficient than ever.

Smart Grading

When it comes to studying, time is precious. Connect helps students learn more efficiently by providing feedback and practice material when they need it, where they need it. Instructors can:

- Automatically score assignments, giving students immediate feedback on their work and comparisons with correct answers;
- Access and review each response; manually change grades; or leave comments for students to review;
- Track individual student performance—by question, assignment or in relation to the class overall—with detailed grade reports;
- Reinforce classroom concepts with practice tests and instant quizzes; and
- Integrate grade reports easily with Learning Management Systems including Blackboard, D2L, and Moodle.

Instructor Library

The Connect Instructor Library is a repository for additional resources to improve student engagement in and out of the class. It provides all the critical resources instructors need to build their course. Instructors can:

- Access Instructor resources;
- View assignments and resources created for past sections; and
- Post their own resources for students to use.

Acknowledgements

Our initial draft of this edition was reviewed by several colleagues with expertise in IFRS. Our manuscript benefited significantly from the comments and suggestions from Judy Cumby, FCPA, FCA; Marisa Morriello, CPA, CA; and Jessica Di Rito. Many other reviewers had contributed valuable comments on the previous editions, which informed our decisions about coverage and approach for the seventh edition.

We are grateful to the team members who exhaustively checked the assignment material and the solutions, including Eric McTaggart; Amy Pike; Li Chen; Jessica Di Rito, CPA, CA; Marcella Agustina; Marisa Morriello, CPA, CA; Balpreet Singh; and Cara Chesney, CPA,CA. The residual errors are our responsibility, but these expert individuals have significantly improved our accuracy. A special thanks to Karla Benata.

We appreciate the permissions granted by the following organizations to use their problem and case material:

- The Chartered Professional Accountants of Canada;
- The Chartered Professional Accountants of Ontario;
- The Atlantic School of Chartered Accountancy;
- The American Institute of Certified Public Accountants; and
- Brookfield Asset Management Incorporated.

We are grateful to the people at McGraw-Hill Education who guided this manuscript through the development process. We appreciate the support of Keara Emmett, our Product Manager; Lindsay MacDonald, our Product Developer; and the production team, led by Crystal Shortt and including Jessica Barnoski, Sarah Strynatka, and Emily Hickey, who have all contributed in significant ways to this final product. And, of course, Karen Rolfe, freelance copy editor, has become a welcome and active partner in this enterprise.

On a personal level, we would like to thank our friends and family members for their support and encouragement throughout the lengthy process of bringing this book to fruition, especially, in Toronto—Brian McBurney; in Halifax—Andrew, Yen, Meredith, and Daniel Conrod; in Richmond Hill—Ed Farrell, Catherine, Michael, and Megan Farrell; and in Collingwood—Michael Dick and Kenneth Dick.

CHAPTER 12

Financial Liabilities and Provisions

INTRODUCTION

What is a liability? The answer might seem rather obvious: an amount owed from one entity to another. In fact, many liability situations, especially those related to financial liabilities, are straightforward from an accounting perspective. However, when liabilities are estimated or uncertain, they can present accounting challenges. For instance:

- Does a liability exist if there is no legal liability but the company has announced a particular commitment or plan of action?
- How is a liability measured if the obligation is for services, not a set amount of money?
- How can a liability be measured if the amount of cash to be paid is based on future events?

Liability financing is an integral part of the capital structure of many companies. For example, Canadian Tire Corporation Limited is a Canadian company that offers a range of general merchandise and also apparel, sporting goods, petroleum, and financial services to consumers. The company reported total assets of $14.5 billion in 2014. Of this amount, $5.6 billion, or 33%, was financed through shareholders' equity, with the balance, $8.9 billion, or 67%, provided by debt in various forms. A sizable portion of the debt represents deposits from the financial services segment ($2.2 billion, or 15% of total assets) and trade payables represent 14% of assets ($2 billion). There are also long-term loans of $2.1 billion, or 14% of total assets. The balance is allocated to non-controlling interest.

This chapter reviews common liabilities, including both financial liabilities and provisions. Financial statement classification and disclosure are reviewed. Long-term debt is covered in Chapter 13. Chapter 14 deals with accounting for share equity. Then, Chapter 15 addresses coverage returns to debt arrangements, those that have some attributes of debt and some attributes of equity. Innovative financial markets have introduced significant complexities into the accounting world!

LIABILITY DEFINITION AND CATEGORIES

According to the conceptual framework, a liability is defined as a *present obligation* of the entity *arising from past events*, the settlement of which is expected to result in an *outflow* of economic benefits. Settlement could be accomplished through *future transfer or use of assets, provision of services, or other yielding of economic benefits*. These characteristics can be simplified for practical purposes by remembering that a liability:

- Is an expected *future* sacrifice of assets or services;

- Constitutes a *present* obligation; and

- Is the result of a *past* transaction or event.

Note that there are three time elements in the definition: a *future* sacrifice, a *present* obligation, and a *past* event. All three elements are necessary for a liability to be recognized. It is not possible to create a liability from an anticipated future event, such as expected future operating losses. There must be some past transaction that is identifiable as an **obligating event**, which is an event that creates an obligation where there is no other realistic alternative but to settle the obligation.

Constructive Obligations

Some liabilities are **legal obligations**, or liabilities that arise from contract or legislation. Most liabilities are legal obligations, including trade payables and borrowings. Other liabilities are **constructive obligations**, where a liability exists because there is a pattern of past practice or established policy. A company can create a constructive obligation if it makes a public statement that the company will accept certain responsibilities *because the statement creates a valid expectation that the company will honour those responsibilities*. Others rely on this representation. Thus, a liability can be created when a company reacts to moral or ethical factors.

ETHICAL ISSUES

A company has announced a voluntary product recall that will take several months to complete. Customers have been offered a replacement product or repair on the original unit. The recall was prompted by the company's code of ethics to support its product integrity and customer base. The recall is voluntary in that the defect is not covered by warranty, and no legislation exists to force the company to act. In this case, clear communication to another party establishes the obligation. A constructive liability exists and the *anticipated costs of the recall must be accrued*.

Categories of Liabilities

Accounting for liabilities depends on whether the liability fits into one of two categories:

- Financial liabilities; or
- Nonfinancial liabilities.

A **financial liability** is a *financial instrument*. A financial liability is a contract that gives rise to a financial liability of one party and a financial asset of another party. That is, one party has an account payable and the other party has an account receivable. Another example is a loan payable and a loan receivable. The two elements are mirror images of each other.

A **nonfinancial liability** can be defined by what it is *not*—any liability that is not a financial liability is a nonfinancial liability. A non-financial liability has no offsetting financial asset on the books of another party. **Provisions,** or liabilities that have uncertainty surrounding timing or amount, are a major category of non-financial liabilities.

Examples of nonfinancial liabilities include:

- Revenue received in the current period but not yet earned (i.e., unearned revenue); or

- Cash outflows that are expected to arise in the future but that are related to transactions, decisions, or events of the current period (e.g., a decommissioning obligation).

Categories of Financial Liabilities

Financial liabilities themselves fall into two categories. *Classification determines the subsequent measurement of the financial liability.*

Most liabilities fall in the *other financial liabilities* category. The FVTPL liability category is meant primarily for liabilities that will be sold or transferred in the short term. In other circumstances, management may designate liabilities as FVTPL. This might be appropriate, for example, if various hedging strategies were in place and management wished to have both hedged asset and liability in the same category for valuation purposes.

FVTPL for liabilities is similar to assets discussed in earlier chapters with the exception of subsequent measurement of liabilities designated in FVTPL. For those liabilities the fair value change related to changes in credit risk are recognized in OCI with the remainder of fair value changes recognized in earnings. The exception to this is if this would create or increase an accounting mismatch, then all of the changes would go into earnings.

Specifically, the alternatives can be summarized as follows:

Classification	Summarized Classification Criteria	Initial Valuation	Subsequent Valuation
1. "Other" financial liabilities	Most financial liabilities; all those except those in category 2, below	Fair value, which is the transaction value and establishes the cost of the financial instrument Capitalize: Transaction costs, if any	Cost (Amortized cost)
2. Fair value through profit or loss (FVTPL)	May be FVTPL if: a. The liability will be sold in the short term; or b. Designated FVTPL by management to avoid an accounting mismatch (related/hedged financial instruments are FVTPL)	Fair value, which is the transaction value and establishes the cost of the financial instrument. Expense transaction costs, if any.	a. Fair value; gains and losses in earnings b. Fair value; change in fair value due to changes in credit risk in OCI remainder in earnings

Measurement of Other Financial Liabilities

Other financial liabilities are initially measured as the fair value of the consideration received and capitalized transaction costs (which reduces the liability) and then carried at this value (which is cost), or amortized cost, over their lives. That is, the initial fair value is (generally) the stated amount of the transaction, or the transaction price.[1] For example, a company receives an invoice for the fair value of goods shipped by a supplier; the goods are the consideration, and their invoice price is the fair value of the liability.

---

1. The *stated amount* of the transaction might not be *fair value* if the transaction is a related party transaction.

Discounting

Liabilities of all categories must be valued at the present value of cash flows—commonly called **discounting**—where the time value of money is material. The discount rate chosen must reflect the current market interest rate, specific to the risk level of the liability. Note, however, that if the amount and timing of cash flows is highly uncertain, then discounting is not possible and undiscounted amounts are recorded. When liabilities are discounted, interest expense on the discounted liability is recorded as time passes. Discounting will be illustrated later in the chapter.

Reporting Example

Included in its significant accounting policy disclosure, Canadian Tire reports information about the valuation of financial liabilities. These liabilities are valued at amortized cost. Provisions, which are non-financial liabilities, are measured based on best estimate and are discounted, if the effect of discounting is material.

The Company's ... financial liabilities are generally classified and measured as follows:

Asset/Liability	Category	Measurement
Bank indebtedness	Other liabilities	Amortized cost
Deposits	Other liabilities	Amortized cost
Trade and other payables[2]	Other liabilities	Amortized cost
Short-term borrowings	Other liabilities	Amortized cost
Loans payable	Other liabilities	Amortized cost
Long-term debt	Other liabilities	Amortized cost

Provisions

A provision is recognized if, as a result of a past event, the Company has a present legal or constructive obligation that can be estimated reliably and it is probable that an outflow of economic benefits will be required to settle the obligation. The amount recognized as a provision is the best estimate of the consideration required to settle the present obligation at the end of the reporting period, taking into account risks and uncertainty of cash flows. Where the effect of discounting is material, provisions are determined by discounting the expected future cash flows at a pre-tax rate that reflects current market assessments of the time value of money and the risks specific to the liability.

...

Source: Canadian Tire Corporation, Limited 2014 Annual Report, www.sedar.com, posted 26 February 2015. *Note:* This is not a complete replication of all financial assets and liabilities. For the complete listing, please see pp. 72, 77 of the 2014 Annual Report at http://corp.canadiantire.ca/EN/Investors/Documents/2014%20Annual%20Report-EN.pdf

[2] *Includes derivatives that are classified as FVTPL or are effective hedging instruments, and measured at fair value .*

COMMON FINANCIAL LIABILITIES

Common financial liabilities are reviewed in the section that follows. These financial liabilities are all classified as *other financial liabilities* and are initially measured as the fair value of the consideration received plus capitalized transaction costs, if any, and then are carried at this value (which is the transaction value) over their lives.

Accounts Payable

Accounts payable—more descriptively, **trade accounts payable**—are obligations to suppliers arising from the firm's ongoing operations, including the acquisition of merchandise, materials, supplies, and services used in the production and sale of goods or services. Current payables that are not trade accounts payable (e.g., income tax payable and the current portion of long-term debt) should be reported separately from accounts payable. In determining the amount of the liability, it is necessary to adjust for purchase discounts, allowances, and returns, as is done for accounts receivable. Of course, a company does not record an allowance for anticipated nonpayment, since it is the payer!

Notes Payable

Notes payable often result from borrowing from a lender. Other notes payable are from suppliers, as part of the terms of a purchase agreement. Notes payable are a written promise to pay a specified amount at a specified future date (or a series of amounts over a series of payment dates). Some notes formalize **collateral security** for the lender, assets of the borrower that the secured lender can seize if the note goes into default.

The **stated interest rate** in a note may not equal the market rate prevailing on obligations involving similar credit rating or risk. The **market interest rate** is the rate accepted by two parties for loans of equal profile—identical amounts, with identical credit risk, terms, and conditions.

Notes may be categorized as **interest-bearing** or **non-interest-bearing** notes. Interest-bearing notes specify the interest rate to be applied to the face amount in computing interest payments. Non-interest-bearing notes do not state an interest rate but command interest through the difference between cash lent and (higher) cash repaid. Notes with stated interest rates below market rates may be used by suppliers as a sales incentive.

Notes payable are initially valued at fair value, which is often simply the loan amount. *If the note carries a stated interest rate equal to market interest rates or has a very short term, then valuation issues are immaterial and stated values are used.* If the stated and market interest rates are different, and term is more than a year (i.e., not short), then present value—discounting—must be used to establish initial fair value. When discounting is used, the *market interest rate is used to value the note and the transaction. The market rate is also used to measure interest expense*. Discounting is illustrated in a later section of this chapter.

Example: Interest-bearing note at market interest rate

On 1 May 20X4, Sun Co. borrowed $120,000 from Dominion Bank. The note has a two-year term, and requires that interest of 4% be paid each 30 April, with the principal payable on 30 April 20X6. *The stated and market interest rates are equal.* The entries over the life of the loan:

Initial entry:

Cash	120,000	
Notes payable		120,000

Interest is accrued at the 31 December year-end:

Interest expense ($120,000 × 4% × 8/12)	3,200	
Accrued interest payable		3,200

Interest is further recorded, and also paid, on 30 April:

Interest expense ($120,000 × 4% × 4/12)	1,600	
Accrued interest payable	3,200	
Cash		4,800

Identical interest entries are repeated for the second year of the loan and then the principal is repaid on 30 April 20X6.

Loan Guarantees

A loan guarantee requires the guarantor to pay the loan principal and interest if the borrower defaults. This is a *financial liability* of the guarantor. The financial instruments rules require that loan guarantees be recorded at their *fair value*. Assume that a loan guarantee for $500,000 is issued for a related company, but there is only a 10% chance that it will have to be honoured. The 10% probability means that the guarantee has a positive fair value of $50,000 ($500,000 × 10%) and must be recorded at this amount, with an expense recognized. Timing must be considered to evaluate the need for discounting. *Loan guarantees would not be recorded if there was a 0% chance of payout.* Extensive disclosure of guarantees is also required, including the maximum potential future payment, the identity of the other party, and collateral, if any.

Cash Dividends Payable

Cash dividends declared but not yet paid are reported as a current liability if they are to be paid within the coming year or operating cycle. Declared dividends are reported as a liability between the date of declaration and payment because declaration gives rise to an enforceable contract.

Liabilities are not recognized for undeclared dividends in arrears on preferred shares or for any other dividends not formally declared by the board of directors. Dividends in arrears on cumulative preferred shares should be disclosed in the notes to the financial statements. These dividends must be paid before any common dividends can be paid.

Monetary Accrued Liabilities

Examples of monetary accrued liabilities include wages and benefits earned by employees, interest earned by creditors but not yet paid, and the costs of goods and services received but not yet invoiced by the supplier. Accrued liabilities are recorded in the accounts by making adjusting entries at the end of the accounting period.

Advances and Returnable Deposits

A company may receive advances or cash deposits from customers as guarantees for payment of future obligations or to guarantee performance on a contract or service. Deposits may also be made as guarantees in case of noncollection or for possible damage to property. For example, deposits required from customers by gas, water, electricity, and other public utilities are liabilities of such companies to their customers. Employees may also make returnable deposits to ensure the return of keys and other company property, for locker privileges, and for club memberships.

Advances from customers and deposits should be reported as current or long-term liabilities, depending on the time involved between date of deposit and expected termination of the relationship. If the advances or deposits are interest bearing, an annual adjusting entry is required to accrue interest expense and to increase the related liability.

Assume that Harcourt Ltd. receives $5,000 from a customer, as a deposit for merchandise with a retail value of $18,500. When the deposit is received:

Cash	5,000	
Customer deposit liability		5,000

When the sale takes place:

Cash ($18,500 – $5,000)	13,500	
Customer deposit liability	5,000	
Revenue		18,500

If for some reason the sale were not to be completed, the customer typically has recourse to the company for refund or alternative product arrangement. The terms of these arrangements are set by contract when the deposit is accepted.

Taxes

Provincial and federal laws require businesses to collect certain taxes from customers and employees for remittance to governmental agencies. These taxes include sales tax, income tax withheld from employee paycheques, property tax, and various payroll taxes. Similar collections are made on behalf of unions, insurance companies, and employee-sponsored activities. Collections made for third parties increase both cash and current liabilities. The collections represent liabilities that are settled when the funds are remitted to the designated parties. Common examples of such taxes follow.

Sales Taxes

Companies are required to collect sales taxes from customers and remit them to the appropriate government agency. Taxes include the goods and services tax (GST) and, in most provinces, provincial sales taxes (PST), or both together—the harmonized sales tax (HST). Revenues are recorded net of GST/HST collected, and purchases of goods and services are recorded net of any GST/HST recoverable. Any GST/HST that is not recoverable is accounted for as a component of the cost of the goods or services to which it relates. On the other hand, *PST is never refundable*, and PST paid is part of the cost of whatever was bought: capital assets or inventory, for example.

GST/HST is remitted periodically, net of GST/HST paid on purchases. The *net amount* of GST/HST payable or receivable should be carried as a liability or asset, as appropriate. Typical entries, with 5% GST and assuming 8% provincial sales tax and $500,000 of sales, are as follows:

1. At date the tax is assessed (point of sale):		
Cash and accounts receivable	565,000	
Sales revenue		500,000
GST payable ($500,000 × 5%)		25,000
PST payable ($500,000 × 8%)		40,000

Assume that $300,000 of inventory was purchased, subject to GST and PST. *Note that PST is part of the cost of inventory, but GST is a recoverable amount.*

2. At inventory purchase:		
Inventory ($300,000 × 1.08)	324,000	
GST payable ($300,000 × 0.05)	15,000	
Cash or accounts payable ($300,000 × 1.13)		339,000

Taxes are remitted:

3. At date of remittance to taxing authority:		
GST payable ($25,000 − $15,000)*	10,000	
Cash		10,000
PST payable	40,000	
Cash		40,000
*GST remitted is reduced by GST paid on purchased goods and services.		

If the company were in an HST jurisdiction, there would be no PST and all HST is accounted for exactly as for GST: The HST amount is a liability when collected, but HST paid on purchases reduces the subsequent remittance.

Payroll Taxes

Employers act as a collection agent for certain taxes and payments. They withhold appropriate amounts from their employees and remit money to the appropriate party shortly thereafter; a liability exists in the meantime. Common withholdings include:

- *Personal income tax.* An employee's personal federal and provincial tax are deducted at source and remitted regularly (at least monthly) to the federal government. At the end of the year, the employee receives a record of deductions, and determines, on his or her annual tax return, who owes whom and how much.

- *Canada Pension Plan (CPP)*. Employees have to pay a percentage of their salary to the CPP; employers have to match this amount dollar for dollar, up to a stated maximum.

- *Employment Insurance (EI)*. Employees have to pay a percentage of their salary to secure EI benefits; the employer must pay 1.4 times the employees' contributions as its share, up to a stated maximum.

- *Insurance premiums, pension plan payments, union dues, etc.* A variety of employee benefits, such as group insurance, medical insurance, and pension plans, require that employees pay all or a portion of the premiums; these are deducted at source. If stipulated in labour agreements, union dues are also deducted at source. Other deductions may include charitable donations and parking fees. All of these are remitted to the appropriate party after deduction.

Payroll deduction accounting is illustrated in Exhibit 12-1.

EXHIBIT 12-1

ILLUSTRATION OF PAYROLL DEDUCTIONS

Thor Company reported the following payroll information for January 20X5:

Gross wages		$100,000
Deductions:		
Income tax	$ 20,000	
Canada Pension Plan	2,250	
Employment Insurance	2,100	
Union dues	1,400	
Charitable contributions	1,600	27,350
Net pay		$ 72,650

To record salaries and employee deductions:

Salary expense	100,000	
Employee income tax payable		20,000
CPP payable		2,250
EI payable		2,100
Union dues payable		1,400
Charitable contributions payable		1,600
Cash		72,650

To record payroll expenses payable by the employer:

Salary expense	5,190	
CPP payable (matching payment)		2,250
EI payable ($2,100 × 1.4)		2,940

To record remittance of payroll deductions (composite entry):

Employee income tax payable	20,000	
CPP payable	4,500	
EI payable	5,040	
Union dues payable	1,400	
Charitable contributions payable	1,600	
Cash		32,540

Property Taxes

Property taxes paid directly by a company are based on the assessed value of real property. Unpaid taxes constitute a lien on the assessed property. Property taxes are based on the assessed value of the property, which may or may not correspond to market value, and the mill rate (tax rate per thousand dollars of assessed value).

Estimates are needed for monthly property tax accruals because tax rates are usually set by the taxing authority partway through the fiscal year. When corrections are needed, prior fiscal years are *not* restated—changes in these estimates are lumped into the current year.

Conditional Payments

Some liabilities are established on the basis of a firm's periodic income. They are either legal liabilities or constructive liabilities, but their amount cannot be firmly established until year-end. However, in order for monthly or quarterly financial statements to be complete, the liabilities must be estimated whenever interim statements are prepared. Until paid, they represent current liabilities of the organization.

Income Tax Payable

Interim reports require a provision for both federal and provincial tax liabilities, so estimates are required. The estimated liability should be reported as a current liability based on the firm's best estimates. After year-end, the tax return is prepared and the estimate is adjusted for the year-end financial statements before the books are finally closed. Periodic installment payments are required. Accounting for corporate income tax is reviewed in Chapters 16 and 17.

Bonuses

Many companies pay cash bonuses, which depend on earnings. These are estimated at interim periods, but calculated "for real" at the end of the fiscal year. Calculations must be made in accordance with established formulas or the authorization of the board of directors. Bonuses can be material—both to the company and to the employee, so it is important that they are properly approved and recorded. Compensation arrangements are covered in more depth in Chapter 15.

FOREIGN CURRENCY PAYABLES

If a company has accounts or notes that are payable in foreign currencies, they must be *restated to Canadian dollars* at the current exchange rate at the year-end date. When the payable is first recorded, the then-current exchange rate is used. For example, suppose that Talud Ltd. buys inventory from a supplier in England for £5,000 when the **spot rate** (current exchange rate) was £1 = Cdn$2.20. The purchase would be recorded as follows:

Inventory	11,000	
Accounts payable (£5,000 × Cdn$2.20)		11,000

The payable is stated (or *denominated*) in pounds, not in dollars. The inventory is recorded at the Canadian dollar equivalent of the sales price. However, when Talud pays the account, it will pay £5,000, not Cdn$11,000. The cash payment must be recorded at the current exchange rate. Suppose that Talud pays when the exchange rate is £1 = Cdn$2.10. Talud will pay only Cdn$10,500 when it obtains £5,000. The exchange gain is recognized in earnings.

Accounts payable	11,000	
Foreign exchange gains and losses		500
Cash (£5,000 × Cdn$2.10)		10,500

Exchange Gain or Loss

The difference between the Canadian equivalent of the payable and of the cash paid is recorded in an *exchange gain or loss* account. Exchange gains and losses are netted in this account over the period, and the net balance is reported in earnings. It is important to understand that changes in the exchange rate following the initial transaction *do not affect the amount initially charged to inventory.* In the Talud example above, the Cdn$11,000 inventory amount is not affected by the subsequent exchange rate change. *Historical cost is determined by the exchange rate at the date of the purchase transaction.*

Year-End

Assume instead that at Talud's year-end date, the payable (recorded at Cdn$11,000) is still outstanding. The payable must be translated at the then-current exchange rate. If the exchange rate at the year-end date is £1 = Cdn$2.25, the value of the account payable will be Cdn$11,250 (£5,000 × Cdn$2.25). The increase of $250 in the Canadian equivalent of the £5,000 balance would be recorded as follows:

Foreign exchange gains and losses	250	
Accounts payable (Cdn$11,250 – Cdn$11,000)		250

When the account payable is paid on its due date, a further exchange gain or loss is recorded if the exchange rate is no longer £1 = Cdn$2.25.

CONCEPT REVIEW

1. What is the recorded value of a capital asset costing €100,000 that is purchased by a Canadian company when the exchange rate is €1 = Cdn$2.10 and paid for when €1 = Cdn$1.95?
2. What total amount of exchange gain or loss is recorded in the transaction in question 1?

NON-FINANCIAL LIABILITIES: PROVISIONS

Provisions are the major category of nonfinancial liability. A provision is defined as *a liability of uncertain timing or amount*. Provisions can be caused by both legal and constructive obligations. Remember that since liabilities are "expected" outflows, some degree of uncertainty can exist.

Financial liabilities, such as payables and accruals, have a high degree of certainty. A liability that has *some uncertainty about the amount or the timing*, but is judged to be "more likely than not"—that is, the liability is probable but not completely certain—is recognized as a liability called a *provision*. A liability that is judged to have a lower degree of certainty and falls below the "more likely than not" threshold—that is, a liability that is *not probable*—is called a **contingency** and is not recognized; information about contingencies is included in the disclosure notes. That is:

Degree of Certainty	Classification
Completely certain	Financial liabilities: Payables, accruals (recorded)
Probable	Provision (recorded)
Not probable	Contingency (disclosed)

Measurement of a Provision

When a liability is characterized by a degree of uncertainty, the uncertainty often is centred on the amount involved. A reasonable estimate must be obtained. The amount recognized as a provision is the *best estimate of the expenditure required to settle the present obligation* at the end of the reporting period.

First, to be recorded, there must be a *probable payout,* or a probability of payout must be more than 50%. Provisions are then recorded at the *best estimate*. This is the amount that would be rationally paid to settle the obligation at the reporting date, if such a payment were possible. The **most likely outcome** (highest probability alternative) should be considered. If there is a range of outcomes, the **expected value** (the sum of outcomes multiplied by their probability distribution) is also a factor to be considered. If each point in the range is equally likely, the midpoint of the range would be recognized.

For example, assume that there is a large population of items, each with a probability attached. *Expected value* should be used for valuation. A company might have 50 legal claims outstanding, each with a $10,000 potential claim. If 30% are judged to be likely to end with no cost to the company, and 70% end with a $10,000 payout, some payout is certain (>50%). The amount to be recorded is the *expected value* of $350,000 [(50 × 30% × $0) + (50 × 70% × $10,000)]. *Expected value is the best estimate for a large population scenario.*

If there is a small population, then the most likely outcome may be the best estimate. For example, assume that there are three legal claims outstanding against a company, each for $100,000. There is a 30% chance that the company will have to make a payment on one lawsuit, a 50% chance for two payouts, and a 20% chance for three payouts. Some payout is certain. The *most likely outcome* is two lawsuits because the probability of that outcome is highest, at 50%. This means that the company should accrue $200,000. The *expected value* is $190,000, which is close, and provides support for the $200,000 accrual [(30% × $100,000) + (50% × $200,000) + (20% × $300,000)]. *For a small population, the most likely outcome is often recorded as the best estimate.*

However, the *most likely outcome* is not always close to the *expected value,* especially in a small population. Assume now that there is a 40% chance that the company will have to make a payment on one lawsuit, a 30% chance for two payouts, and a 30% chance for three payouts. The most likely (40%) outcome is a $100,000 payment, but the expected value is $190,000 [(40% × $100,000) + (30% × $200,000) + (30% × $300,000)]. In this case, there are considerable odds (the cumulative probability is 60%) that either two or three lawsuits will have to be paid, and a $100,000 accrual is not enough. Therefore, $200,000 should be accrued; there is only a 40% chance that the payout would be less than this amount. *For a small population, the expected value can provide evidence to support an accrual of a particular outcome, even if it alone is not the most likely.*

Summary

A provision must be probable to be recorded. Then the *best estimate* to record for a provision is:

Population	Best Estimate	Adjusted For
Large population	Expected value	Discounted for time value of money
Small population	Most likely outcome, with judgement, considering: 1. Expected value; and 2. Cumulative probabilities	Discounted for time value of money

Re-Estimate Annually

If a provision is estimated, then the amounts are re-estimated at each reporting date. The change in any recorded amount is expensed in the year. For example, if the estimate of a payout is originally $35,000, then this amount is recorded. If the estimate increases from $35,000 to $50,000 in a later year, an additional $15,000 of expense is recorded *in the year that the estimate changed.* On the other hand, if the estimated payment were to decline to $5,000, a *recovery* (negative expense) would be recorded in the period that the estimate changed.

Discounting

Provisions must be discounted where the time value of money is material. The discount rate chosen must reflect current market interest rates, and the risk level specific to the liability. For a reporting example, refer again to the note disclosure provided by Canadian Tire, presented earlier in this chapter, where the company stated that discounting is used where material. Discounting is illustrated later in this chapter.

Exception

If the amount and timing of cash flows is highly uncertain, *discounting cannot be accomplished in a meaningful fashion* and amounts are recorded on an undiscounted basis. Since provisions are by their nature uncertain amounts, discounting may often be impractical.

Contingency

When a liability situation gives rise to a *contingency*, it is not recognized but instead is included in the disclosure notes. No financial statement liability element is recorded. In general, contingencies exist when:

- The obligation is possible but not probable;

- There is a present obligation but no economic resources are attached; or

- There is a present obligation but *rare circumstances* dictate that an estimate cannot be established.

Contingent Assets

While on the subject of contingencies, note that an asset is not recorded until a company is *virtually certain* of the related benefits to be obtained. At that point it is an asset, not a contingent asset. *Virtual certainty is* a much higher degree of certainty than just *certainty*. *Contingent assets* are assets that arise from past events but whose existence must be confirmed by a future event that is not wholly in the control of management. If a company is suing a supplier, for instance, no amount is recorded for the claimed amount, even if it is likely that the company will win and the amount can be estimated. In fact, a winning court judgement would not be recorded until it seems virtually certain that the *amount will be paid*. Disclosure is the appropriate route.

Prohibited Practices

In the past, some companies have attempted to smooth earnings through the creation and reversal of provisions. For example, an expense and a liability might be recorded in years when earnings were high (e.g., "provision for future losses") just to lower earnings, and then reversed in a year when earnings were low to raise earnings. This practice is not permitted by accounting standards.

Finally, it is not permissible to use a provision set up for one purpose to offset expenditures for another purpose. For example, only environmental remediation expenditures can be used to reduce the environmental remediation provision.

CONCEPT REVIEW

1. What is a *provision* versus a *contingency*?
2. How is an expected value obtained for a provision?
3. Why might a multiyear, non-interest-bearing provision *not* be discounted?

EXAMPLES OF PROVISIONS

Lawsuits

If a company is being sued by another party, the company may be found guilty and ordered to pay money or otherwise make restitution to the plaintiff. Alternatively, the courts may find the company not guilty. Court decisions are subject to appeals, and the process may last for years. The defendant and the plaintiff may agree in the meantime to an out-of-court settlement.

Based on the certainty of payout, an unsettled court case may result in a provision (probable payout) or a contingency (not probable). Probability is assessed by the legal team, and the accountant and auditor may rely on the opinion of these experts. Note, though, that a constructive liability may be present if a company has announced that a settlement is being sought. A contingency may be present if there is a probable payout but the amount cannot be estimated; this inability to measure the payout should be rare. That is:

First:	Then, Either/Or:	
Ability to Measure Degree of Certainty	Measurable	Not Measurable
Certain (Probable)	Provision (recorded)	Contingency (disclosed) (rare situation)
Not certain (Not probable)	Contingency (disclosed)	Contingency (disclosed)

In general, defence teams are NOT often willing to admit that their clients are *likely to lose* a lawsuit, although obviously there is a loser and a winner in every case. Therefore, recorded provisions are relatively rare unless the company has decided to settle out of court. Instead, disclosure of contingencies relating to lawsuits is common, despite accounting standards regarding probability and measurability.

ETHICAL ISSUES

Assume that a company is being sued by an ex-employee for $500,000 for wrongful dismissal. The company is defending itself actively but has privately admitted that a settlement of $200,000 would be acceptable. Should the $200,000 be recorded? Making it known would provide information to the plaintiff and possibly hurt the company's bargaining position in discussions to end the lawsuit. On the other hand, leaving the $200,000 out of the financial statements understates probable liabilities and overstates profits.

The company is ethically required to follow appropriate reporting but is equally ethically bound to serve its shareholders' best interests. Recording the $200,000 is appropriate. If disclosure is expected to prejudice the position of the company in a dispute with another company, the expense and the liability may be grouped with other items to avoid granting additional information to the plaintiff. The omission of disclosure must be explained.

Reporting Example

The Nestlé Group has a recorded provision for outstanding lawsuits but also has contingencies. Information from the disclosure notes is as follows (in millions of Swiss francs (CHF); note that disclosure of litigation is restricted in the best interests of the company, and measurement is problematic:

Provision for Litigation	
At 31 December 2013	2,246
Currency retranslations	(67)
Provisions made in the period	488
Amounts used	(92)
Unused amounts reversed	(94)
Reclassified as held for sale	(4)
Modification on the scope of consolidation	59
At 31 December 2014	2,670

Litigation

Litigation provisions have been set up to cover tax, legal and administrative proceedings that arise in the ordinary course of the business. These provisions cover numerous separate cases whose detailed disclosure could be detrimental to the Group interests. The Group does not believe that any of these litigation proceedings will have a material adverse impact on its financial position. The timing of outflows is uncertain as it depends upon the outcome of the proceedings. In that instance, these provisions are not discounted because their present value would not represent meaningful information. Group Management does not believe it is possible to make assumptions on the evolution of the cases beyond the balance sheet date.

...

12.2 Contingencies

The Group is exposed to contingent liabilities amounting to a maximum potential payment of CHF 2012 million (2013: CHF 1669 million) representing potential litigations of CHF 1914 million (2013: CHF 1658 million) and other items of CHF 98 million (2013: CHF 11 million). Potential litigations relate mainly to labour, civil and tax litigations in Latin America.

Contingent assets for litigation claims in favour of the Group amount to a maximum potential recoverable of CHF 176 million (2013: CHF 51 million).

Source: Nestlé Group, 2014 Consolidated Financial Statements, www.nestle.com, retrieved 7 January 2016.

Executory Contracts and Onerous Contracts

Companies often have contracts outstanding that require them to pay another party in the future, after the other party has performed some service or act. These contracts are known as **executory contracts** because they do not become liabilities until they have been *executed* by one party or the other. The contracts commit the enterprise to a future expenditure, but they are not *liabilities* until the other party has performed the service or act specified in the contract. Examples are employee contracts for future employment, contracts for future delivery of goods and services, and most unfilled purchase orders.

If the unavoidable costs of meeting the contract exceed the economic benefits under the contract, then the contract is classified an **onerous contract**. A *provision* must be recorded with respect to the onerous contract, for the lesser of the costs to fulfill the contract and the costs from cancellation.

For example, assume that a company has agreed to purchase 10,000 kg of ore at a price of $1.00 per kg. The price in today's market is $0.80 per kg. A provision must be recorded for the expected loss of $2,000 [10,000 kg × ($1.00 − $0.80)]:

Loss on purchase commitment	2,000	
Provision for loss on purchase commitment		2,000

If the ore is then purchased when the price is $0.95 per kg, there is a partial loss recovery, and the inventory is recorded at its fair value:

Ore inventory	9,500	
Provision for loss on purchase commitment	2,000	
Loss recovery on purchase commitment		1,500
Accounts payable		10,000

Restructuring

A *provision for restructuring* is an estimate of the money that will be paid out in connection with a future restructuring program. A restructuring program is a plan of action that is planned and controlled by management, which materially changes the scope of the business undertaken by the entity, or the manner in which the business is conducted. Examples include the sale or termination of a line of the business, closure or relocation of operations in a country or region, change in management structure, and the like.

A liability will be recorded if the entity has a detailed formal plan for the restructuring *and* has started to implement the plan or otherwise announced the specifics of the plan to those who will be affected. An announcement that creates a provision must include major specific facts and details that raise valid expectations that the restructuring will take place.

Common elements of restructuring provisions are employee termination costs and costs to end contracts. A more detailed review of impairment implications, including any impairment of assets triggered by such a decision, is found in Chapters 3 and 10.

Warranty

This discussion deals with warranties that provide assurance that the product will meet agreed-upon specifications and the warranty is not sold separately. There is no distinct service provided. The *cost deferral method* is used for these warranties.[2] A warranty is often a *legal liability*, specifically awarded to the customer in the sale contract as protection against damaged goods. Warranties may also be in force as *constructive obligations* based on a company's announced intentions.

Cost Deferral—Example

To illustrate accounting for warranties, assume that Rollo Ltd. sells merchandise for $200,000 during 20X2. Rollo's merchandise carries a two-year unconditional warranty for parts and labour, and the cost deferral method is appropriate. Rollo's past experience has indicated that warranty costs will approximate 0.6% of sales. Payout is certain and the amount estimated is an expected value. The entry to record sales and the warranty obligation in 20X2 will be as follows:

Accounts receivable	200,000	
Sales revenue		200,000
Warranty expense	1,200	
Provision for warranty		1,200

If, in 20X3, Rollo incurs costs of $350 to repair or replace defective merchandise, the cash outflow is charged to the liability account:

Provision for warranty	350	
Cash (and other resources used)		350

The expense for the year *is not the amount paid*; the expense is the *total of all expected future claims*. The balance in the provision for warranty account will be an $850 credit. The provision will be carried forward from year to year, adjusted each year for management's estimate of the future warranty costs. As is the case for all accounting estimates, the estimate of annual warranty cost and the outstanding liability may be changed in the light of new experience or as the result of changed product design.

---

2. If warranties are sold as a separate service contract, the *revenue deferral method* is used. Refer to Chapter 6 for a discussion of these circumstances.

In 20X3, Rollo sells another $240,000 worth of merchandise. Rollo now plans to use an estimate of 0.4% of sales for warranties, and believes that it should have used this estimate in the prior year, as well. The current-year expense is $560, which is $960 for this year ($240,000 × 0.4%), less a $400 adjustment to decrease last year's accrual [$200,000 × (0.6% − 0.4%)]. The $400 correction is made this year, and *changes the current year expense*. Correction is not done retrospectively. An amount of $500 is spent on claims in 20X3, some for product sold in 20X2 and some related to goods sold in 20X3. After these entries, the provision for warranty will have a credit balance of $910 ($850 + $560 − $500).

Accounts receivable	240,000	
Sales revenue		240,000
Warranty expense ($960 − $400)	560	
Provision for warranty		560

Provision for warranty	500	
Cash (and other resources used)		500

If, in any year, the charges to the provision for warranty work done are higher than the balance in the provision account, the provision account will *temporarily* go into a debit balance until the year-end adjustment is made. The temporary existence of a debit balance simply indicates that the expense has not yet been accrued. The ending provision for warranty must be reviewed for reasonableness, though. If costs are creeping up, the provision will have a low balance, and the estimate that is accrued each year may need upward revision. On the other hand, if the provision credit balance builds up over time, the rate should be revised downward. Sometimes, the "excess" in a particular year may not call for an increase in the regular estimate if it is a one-time occurrence.

The provision for warranty is a current liability if the warranty is for one year or less. If the warranty is for a longer period, the provision should be split between current and long-term portions and the need for discounting should be considered.

Warranty as a Constructive Liability

A warranty obligation that provides assurance that the product will operate as intended and meet specifications may be a *constructive liability for repair or replacement because of actions or statements of the company*. For example, if a hazard is identified because of a product defect, a company may put a repair, replacement, or refund program in place that exceeds its legal responsibilities. This may be done to preserve the company's reputation, or simply to avoid future court action. This constructive liability is recorded as a provision, along with an expense, when it arises—the announcement of the program. Expected value is used for valuation, and the provision must be regularly reviewed to ensure valuation is reasonable.

Restoration and Environmental Obligations

Provisions are often created with respect to environmental obligations, as discussed in Chapter 9. If there are legislative remediation requirements, then the cost of the required activities must be estimated and accrued. If legislative requirements are *pending,* the provision is accrued only if there is **virtual certainty** that the legislation will be enacted. On the other hand, the liability may be a constructive liability, which must be accrued absent legislative requirements. For example, if a company has a published policy concerning environmental cleanup activities, or otherwise accepts responsibility for remediation in a public forum, then a provision for expected costs must be recorded. Lengthy time periods are common in this area, and discounting is usually required. An example is included with the section on discounting later in the chapter.

Sales Returns and Refunds

A company may allow merchandise to be returned for a cash refund or a credit on account. This may be a legal obligation, in accordance with stated return policies, or a constructive obligation based on past practice. If returns are predictable, the obligation must be estimated and recorded at the time of the sale.[3] At any reporting date, the provision for sales returns must be reviewed for reasonableness, taking into account usage and recent transaction history.

Coupons and Gift Cards

Coupons are often used as sales incentives. A provision for outstanding coupons may be recorded, but only in limited circumstances. The key to a coupon offer is whether economic benefits are transferred. If the product is still sold at a profit, even after the coupon, then no economic benefits are deemed to transfer and the provision has no accounting value. If, on the other hand, retailers or customers are reimbursed in cash for coupons or if products are sold at a loss, then a provision is appropriate. Note also that if the company reserves the right to cancel the coupons at any time, then there is no enforceable obligation. A reliable measurement for the provision includes estimating the take-up rate for the coupons; the **breakage** (unused) rate can be estimated based on past history or other valid evidence.

For example, assume 1,000 customers buying an appliance are given a coupon for a $10 cash rebate if proof of purchase is submitted. A liability exists because of the promise to pay cash, and the liability is a provision because the amount must be estimated. Based on past experience, 40% of the coupons will be submitted. The amount recorded is an expected value of $4,000 ($10 refund × 40% take-up rate × 1,000 coupons). The following entry would be made when the sale of 1,000 units is recorded:

Sales discounts	4,000	
Provision for coupon refund		4,000

If 370 coupons are honoured, and the remainder expire:

Provision for coupon refund	4,000	
Cash (370 coupons × $10 refund)		3,700
(Recovery of) sales discounts		300

Many companies sell gift cards to customers. Issuance of these cards creates an unearned revenue liability. The cards usually have an unlimited life due to provincial legislation and thus represent an indefinite legal liability. However, if the entity believes that some cards will be unused and can gather evidence to estimate *breakage*, then the liability becomes an estimate and thus is a provision. Discounting might be appropriate if the time period is long.

Loyalty Programs

A common sales incentive is a customer loyalty program, where the customer is awarded loyalty points, which can then be used to obtain free (or discounted) goods or services. There are many ways that these programs can be structured.

A loyalty program is an example of a sales contract involving multiple deliverables, as we saw in Chapter 6. No separate expense is recognized—*the loyalty program is an allocation of original revenue*. That is, the sale transaction with the customer has multiple parts, and the value of the award credits is one such part. An *unearned revenue* account, sometimes called a *provision for rewards*, is created. This provision is measured according to the value of the awards to the customer, not the cost of the goods to the company.

---

3. See also the Chapter 6 discussion of uncertainties associated with transactions that trigger revenue recognition.

For example, assume that a sale of $65,000 to customers carries with it loyalty points that allow acquisition of product with a fair value of $5,000. This $5,000 estimate assumes some breakage of points awarded. The following entry would be made when the sale is recorded:

Cash	65,000	
Sales revenue		60,000
Provision for loyalty program rewards		5,000

The provision is reduced when the loyalty points are redeemed and revenue is recognized.

Reporting Example

Canadian Tire offers loyalty points to shoppers and records a provision with respect to the program. This policy is described in Note 3, Significant accounting policies:

> ### Customer loyalty
>
> An obligation arises from the My Canadian Tire 'Money' customer loyalty program when the Company issues e-Canadian Tire 'Money' and when the Dealers pay the Company to acquire paper-based Canadian Tire 'Money', as the Dealers retain the right to return paper-based Canadian Tire Money to the Company for refund in cash. These obligations are measured at fair value by reference to the fair value of the awards for which they could be redeemed and based on the estimated probability of their redemption. The expense is recorded in selling, general and administrative expense in the consolidated statements of the income.
>
> Source: Canadian Tire Corporation, Limited 2014 Annual Financial Statements, www.sedar.com, posted 26 February 2015.

Repairs and Maintenance

Repairs and maintenance are expenses of the year in which the repair or maintenance activity occurs. Such costs are not accrued to smooth out earnings, even when they are "lumpy." For example, assume that a cargo vessel must be painted every five years. The cost of painting is simply an expense of year five. The company may *not* accrue one-fifth of the cost each year and establish a provision for maintenance. Essentially, no obligating event has taken place after one year or even four years; the decision to paint is still in the future.

As another example, assume that a company has a contractual obligation to overhaul a leased aircraft every five years. Again, no provision is set up prior to the overhaul because there has been no obligating event. After an obligating event, the end of the fifth year, the company has no ability to avoid the overhaul. Before the end of the fifth year, the company could avoid the overhaul by selling the aircraft. When the overhaul is done, the cost is capitalized and then depreciated over the next five years. Similarly, if a lease requires maintenance activity after 1,000 hours of use, no obligating event occurs until the 1,000th hour is clocked. Up to that point in time, management could decide to leave the asset idle to avoid the maintenance activity.

Self-Insurance

Companies may choose to self-insure for known risks. Many large companies self-insure for fire and theft losses, meaning that they carry no external insurance. The cost of claims is assumed to be lower, over time, than the cost of insurance and so the choice is a rational business decision. Self-insurance does, however, retain certain risks for the company.

A provision for estimated losses must be established for *events (fire and theft) taking place prior to the reporting date*, but also for *loss events that have happened during the year but are not yet known*, such as undiscovered damage. Such damage might be discovered after the year-end, and it must be accrued. This allows for a reasonable delay based on known events. The amount is a provision because it is estimated.

However, companies may not record a provision in excess of the cost of estimated incidents in the year. A company may wish to do this to smooth the expense between years with low losses and years with high losses. *A provision must be justified based on a loss event.* If there is no such event, no accrual can be made, even if the odds suggest that a future year will have heavier incidence of loss events.

Compensated-Absence Liabilities

The Canada Labour Code requires that employees receive paid vacations and holidays. The expense for salaries and wages paid during these absences from work is recognized in the current year. *When employees can carry over unused time to future years*, any expense due to compensated absences must be recognized (accrued) in the year in which it is earned. The accrual is based on the additional amount that the entity expects to pay as a result of the unused entitlement accumulated at the year-end date.

An adjusting entry must be made at the end of each fiscal year to accrue all of the compensation cost for the vacation and medical leave time that is carried over. An expense and a current liability are recorded. When the time is taken, the liability account may be debited at the time the employee is paid. Alternatively, the liability may be adjusted only at year-end. Either approach will recognize the cost of the compensated absences as an expense in the period earned rather than when taken.

For example, consider the carryover of vacation time of the Conway Company, which has 500 employees. Each employee is granted three weeks paid vacation time each year. Vacation time, up to a maximum accumulation of four weeks, may be carried over to subsequent years prior to termination of employment. At the end of 20X5, the end of the annual accounting period, personnel records revealed the following information concerning carryover vacation amounts:

Carryovers from 20X5*				
Number of Employees	**Weeks per Employee**	**Total Weeks**	**Salary per Week**	**Total Accrual**
10	2	20	$ 1,500	$30,000
3	1	3	2,000	6,000
				$36,000

*These are carryovers from 20X5 to future years.

Disregarding payroll taxes, which are excluded here to simplify the analysis, the indicated entries are as follows:

31 December 20X5—adjusting entry to accrue vacation salaries not yet taken or paid		
Salary expense	36,000	
Provision for compensated absences		36,000

During 20X6, vacation time carryover is taken and salaries paid (all employees took their carried-over vacation time, except for one person who still carried over two weeks, valued at $1,500 per week)

Provision for compensated absences	33,000	
Cash ($36,000 – $3,000)		33,000

The balance remaining in the liability account is $3,000: two weeks at $1,500 per week.

This illustration assumes that there was no change in the rate of pay from 20X5 to 20X6 (when the carryover was used) for those employees who had the carryover. If there were rate changes, the pay difference would be debited (if an increase) or credited (if a decrease) to salary expense during 20X6.

This item is a liability only if a company allows employees to *carry over vacation entitlements:* many do not, and no liability exists. Most financial institutions, for example, require employees to take all their vacation entitlements before the end of each calendar year; it is important to their internal control systems to have someone else go in and do the employee's job regularly so that the employee cannot hide suspicious activities indefinitely.

Summary

Refer to the following chart as a summary:

Possible Financial Statement Element—Provision	Record?
Lawsuits	Yes—if certain and measurable No—if not certain; classified as a contingency if not certain or if certain but not measurable (rare)
Executory contracts	No—wait and record only on delivery
Onerous contracts	Yes—record estimated loss
Restructuring	Yes—if formal plan that has been implemented or communicated
Warranty	Yes—accrue provision when the warranty contract provides assurance the product will meet agreed-upon specifications and the warranty is not sold separately. Yes—accrue provision if constructive liability (*Note:* In some circumstances, revenue deferral is used.)
Restoration and environmental	Yes—record if constructive or legislative; estimate must be made
Sales returns	Yes—record if predictable—constructive or contractual; estimate must be made
Coupons and gift cards	Yes—if distribution of economic benefits involved (cash or products issued at a loss); breakage rate to be estimated No—if cancellable or non-cash and represent a small discount so that products still sold at a profit
Loyalty programs	Yes—assign fair value and allocate unearned revenue on initial sale; breakage rate to be estimated Multiple deliverables approach used

Repairs and maintenance	No—normally accounted for in the year of the repair or maintenance activity Yes—if an obligating event (under contract) takes place
Self-insurance	Yes—for losses experienced and for expected losses where the incident has happened No—no general provision designed for smoothing permitted
Compensated absence	Yes—accrue for rights carried over to subsequent fiscal year

CONCEPT REVIEW

1. What is an onerous contract?
2. Why does selling a product with a warranty attached give rise to a provision?
3. When is a provision for coupons recorded?
4. When is a provision for self-insurance recorded?

THE IMPACT OF DISCOUNTING

Liabilities must be discounted where the time value of money is material. This will affect multiyear liabilities that bear no interest rate (i.e., are interest-free), or multiyear liabilities that have interest rates below market interest rates. Remember, though, the following:

- As a matter of convenience, and materiality, liabilities with an initial term of less than one year are not discounted.

- If the timing or amounts of liabilities are uncertain, then discounting is not practical and is not required.

Common examples of liabilities that must be discounted are low-interest loans, perhaps provided as sales incentives by suppliers, and environmental liabilities.

Calculation of Present Value

The **nominal interest rate** is the interest rate stated for a liability; the nominal rate might be zero. The **effective interest rate**, or **yield**, is the *market interest rate, for debt of similar term, security, and risk*. Using the effective interest rate as the discount rate, the discounted amount, or **present value**, (P) is calculated as:[4]

$P = [I \times (P/A, i, n)] + [F \times (P/F, i, n)]$, where

P = fair value of the loan; issuance proceeds on issuance date

I = dollar amount of each period's interest payment, if any, or

= nominal rate, if any, times the loan face value

F = maturity value of the loan

n = the number of periods to maturity

i = the market interest rate

---

4. A review of present value calculations is included on Connect, if practice is needed.

That is, the maturity amount and the interest amount—the entire cash flow stream associated with the liability—must be discounted to present value using the market interest rate.

When a liability pays the effective market interest rate, the discounted amount is equal to the maturity amount and there is no need to discount. When the nominal and market interest rates are different, the discounted amount will differ from the maturity amount, and there are accounting implications.

Examples of liabilities that must be discounted follow.

Example 1: No-Interest Note Payable

Assume that Radial Information Ltd. has purchased equipment and signed a note payable for $18,000 on 1 April 20X8. If Radial had agreed to pay $18,000 for the equipment in six months' time, with no additional interest, the liability and the capital asset would be recorded at $18,000, with no discounting because the interest-free period is short.

Assume now that the note payable is due in three years' time, with no additional interest. Discounting is required because the time span is longer. Assume also that Radial could borrow a similar amount over three years from a financial institution at a 9% interest rate. Assuming annual compounding, the present value[5] of the liability is $13,900 [$18,000 × (P/F, 9%, 3)]. This is the value at which the equipment and the liability will be recorded. The liability will increase by 9% interest on the outstanding balance each year and be equal to $18,000 at maturity. The **effective interest method** is used to measure interest expense and the growth of the liability. This series of events and transactions is recorded as follows:

| Equipment | 13,900 | |
| Note payable, net | | 13,900 |

In subsequent periods, interest expense is recorded, and then the liability is paid:

Year 1 interest:

| Interest expense ($13,900 × 9%) | 1,251 | |
| Note payable, net | | 1,251 |

Year 2 interest:

| Interest expense [($13,900 + $1,251 = $15,151) × 9%] | 1,364 | |
| Note payable, net | | 1,364 |

Year 3 interest and payment:

| Interest expense [($15,151 + $1,364 = $16,515) × 9%] | 1,485 | |
| Note payable, net | | 1,485 |

---

5. Present value tables are appended at the end of the text and illustrate the notation used throughout this text.

| Note payable ($16,515 + $1,485) | 18,000 | |
| Cash | | 18,000 |

The interest calculations may be organized in a table:

	(1) Opening Net Liability	(2) Interest Expense at Market Rate (1) × 9%	(3) Closing Net Liability (1) + (2)
Year 1	$13,900	$1,251	$15,151
Year 2	15,151	1,364	16,515
Year 3	16,515	1,485	18,000

Use of a discount account

When the discounted account is a formal note payable, with a specified maturity value, the note payable is usually recorded at its maturity value. A discount account is used to revalue the note to its discounted amount. The discount account is a contra account to the note payable, and is netted with the liability on the SFP. Interest is then recognized by **unwinding**—or reducing—the discount. Returning to Example 1 above, the entries, if a discount account were used:

Equipment	13,900	
Discount on note payable ($18,000 – $13,900)	4,100	
Note payable		18,000

As before, the liability is reported *net* on the SFP at $13,900 ($18,000 − $4,100). The presence or absence of a discount account does not change the net value reported on the statement of financial position (SFP).

Year 1 interest:

| Interest expense | 1,251 | |
| Discount on note payable | | 1,251 |

The liability is reported on the SFP *net* at $15,151 [$18,000 − $2,849 ($4,100 − $1,251)]. This is the same amount as is reflected in the net method.

Year 2 interest:

| Interest expense | 1,364 | |
| Discount on note payable | | 1,364 |

The liability is reported net on the SFP *net* at $16,515 [$18,000 − $1,485 ($2,849 − $1,364)]. Again, this is identical to the net method.

Year 3 interest and payment:

Interest expense	1,485	
Discount on note payable		1,485

Note payable	18,000	
Cash		18,000

There are no reporting or measurement implications that arise from use of a separate discount account. Use of a discount account is common practice for notes payable but is not used for (estimated) provisions, since provisions lack a specified maturity value.

Interest accrual

If the fiscal year is different from the date of the note, accruals must be made at the year-end to record interest incurred. To illustrate this interest accrual, assume that the year-end is 31 December, or 9/12 of the year. The $1,251 interest that relates to the first 12 months of the loan is recorded as time progresses. The accrual entry for nine months of interest at the end of Year 1, using the gross method:

Interest expense ($1,251 × 9/12)	938	
Discount on note payable		938

Entry on loan anniversary date, 31 March:

Interest expense ($1,251 × 3/12)	313	
Discount on note payable		313

The entire first 12 months' interest of $1,251 must be recorded before interest is recalculated (i.e., before compounding), in order to correspond to compounding periods. Tracking the interest calculation with a table helps with the accuracy of the calculations.

Example 2: Note Payable with Different Market and Stated Rate

Assume that Baylor Co. purchases inventory on 1 April 20X2 and agrees to pay the vendor $12,000 on 31 March 20X4, plus annual interest at 4% each 31 March. The market interest rate for similar term and security is 10%. Assume also that the inventory purchased does not have a readily determinable market value. To value the transaction, it is necessary to calculate the present value of the note, including both principal and interest:

Present value of maturity amount: $12,000(P/F, 10%, 2) =	$ 9,917
Present value of the nominal interest payments: $480(P/A, 10%, 2) =	833
Present value of the note at 10%	$10,750

The note may be recorded gross (with a discount) or net. The two methods are illustrated below.

1 April 20X2:	Gross		Net	
Inventory (1)	10,750		10,750	
Discount on note payable	1,250		—	
Note payable		12,000		10,750

(1) If the note were a cash loan, this debit would be to cash.

Under either method, the *net book value* of the note is $10,750, the present value.

The interest calculation may again be organized in a table, which now includes cash paid and the discount:

	(1) Opening Net Liability	(2) Interest Expense 10% Market Rate (1) × 10%	(3) Interest Paid 4% Stated Rate $12,000 × 4%	(4) Discount Amortization (2) − (3)	(5) Closing Net Liability (1) + (4)
Year 1	$10,750	$1,075	$480	$595	$11,345
Year 2	$11,345	1,135	480	655	12,000

The net notes payable balance—columns 1 and 5—*is always the present value of remaining payments*. For example, the $11,345 balance is the present value on 31 March 20X3 of the remaining payment (principal plus interest), a payment that is due on 31 March 20X4.

$12,480(P/F, 10%, 1) = $11,345

If the fiscal year corresponded with the dates of the note, the interest and payment information from this table would correspond directly to the interest entry, that is, for the first payment:

31 March 20X3:	Gross		Net	
Interest expense	1,075		1,075	
Discount on note payable		595		—
Note payable		—		595
Cash		480		480

For the second payment and principal repayment:

31 March 20X4:	Gross		Net	
Interest expense	1,135		1,135	
Discount on note payable		655		—
Note payable		—		655
Cash		480		480
Note payable	12,000		12,000	
Cash		12,000		12,000

Interest accrual

If the fiscal year is different from the date of the note, accruals must be made that also include discount amortization. To illustrate, assume that the year-end is 31 December, or 9/12 of the year. The entry at the end of the fiscal year, using the gross method:

Interest expense ($1,075 × 9/12)	806	
Accrued interest payable ($480 × 9/12)		360
Discount on note payable ($595 × 9/12)		446

The accrual entry records a portion of the discount and the cash interest payable. The amounts recorded are 9/12 of each of the lines in the interest table that correspond to the first year.

The entry on cash payment, 31 March, picks up the elimination of interest payable, the remaining three months of interest expense, three months of discount amortization, and the cash payment:

Interest expense ($1,075 × 3/12)	269	
Accrued interest payable	360	
Discount on note payable ($595 × 3/12)		149
Cash		480

Example 3: Provision for Lawsuit

Assume that a provision of $200,000 is recorded for a lawsuit, on the expectation that the amount will be paid in two years' time. Timing can be estimated with certainty. The company can borrow for general operating purposes over this term at an interest rate of 8%. The discounted amount represents the maturity amount only, since there is no interest. A discount account is not used; the provision is recorded net.

The discounted amount is $171,468 [$200,000 × (P/F, 8%, 2)], and is recorded as follows:

Loss on litigation	171,468	
Provision for litigation		171,468

In subsequent periods, interest expense is recorded, and then the liability is paid:

Year 1 interest:

Interest expense ($171,468 × 8%)	13,717	
Provision for litigation		13,717

Year 2 interest and payment:

Interest expense [($171,468 + $13,717) × 8%]	14,815	
Provision for litigation		14,815

Provision for litigation ($171,468 + $13,717 + $14,815)	200,000	
Cash		200,000

The calculations may be organized in a table:

	(1) Opening Net Liability	(2) Interest Expense at Market Rate (1) × 8%	(3) Closing Net Liability (1) + (2)
Year 1	$171,468	$13,717	$185,185
Year 2	$185,185	14,815	200,000

Example 4: Provision with Estimate Change

Assume that on 2 January 20X5 HDL Ltd. purchases a transmission tower for $1,300,000, which it installs on the roof of its leased premises. This is recorded as an asset. HDL is required by the terms of the building lease to remove the tower at the end of six years. The estimated cost of removal is $50,000.

To recognize the liability, the $50,000 must be discounted at an interest rate for borrowing with similar term and security. This rate is assumed to be 6%:

$$P = \$50,000 × (P/F, 6\%, 6) = \$35,248$$

The retirement obligation is added to the cost of the transmission tower, and a provision is recorded:

| Transmission tower | 35,248 | |
| Decommissioning obligation | | 35,248 |

The cost of the transmission tower is the acquisition cost plus the decommissioning obligation amount, or $1,335,248. This asset, including the decommissioning amount, will be depreciated over its six-year life. HDL must also accrue interest expense on the decommissioning obligation each year, using the 6% interest rate. For 20X5, the accrual will be:

| Interest expense ($35,248 × 6%) | 2,115 | |
| Decommissioning obligation | | 2,115 |

At the end of 20X5, the book value of the obligation will be $35,248 + $2,115 = $37,363. As in other examples, a table can be used to organize the calculations:

	(1) Opening Net Liability	(2) Interest Expense at Market Rate (1) × 6%	(3) Closing Net Liability (1) + (2)
20X5	$35,248	$2,115	$37,363
20X6	37,363	2,242	39,605
20X7	39,605	2,376	41,981
20X8	41,981	2,519	44,500
20X9	44,500	2,670	47,170
20X10	47,170	2,830	50,000

Remeasurement

HDL must adjust the amount of the obligation—and adjust the asset value—if there is:

- A change in the amount or timing of the expected retirement obligation cash flows; or
- A change in the discount rate to reflect current market rates.

In HDL's case, the timing could change if the lease term is extended. The estimated cost of removal is quite likely to change over time because of technology changes and cost component changes driven by increasing or decreasing prices.

When an estimate changes, *interest for the year is first recorded based on estimates in place at the beginning of the period.* Any adjustment caused by estimate changes is then recorded, but not to interest expense—this is an adjustment to the asset and decommissioning liability account.

Assume that the appropriate interest rate was revised to 5% at the end of 20X6. The other major assumptions—$50,000 amount to be paid, and the date of tower removal—have not changed.

First, 20X6 interest is recorded at the old rate of 6%:

Interest expense (see table above)	2,242	
Decommissioning obligation		2,242

The decommissioning obligation now has a balance of $39,605, per the table above.

Reflecting the new interest rate, the decommissioning obligation is recalculated as:

$$\$50,000 \times (P/F, 5\%, 4) = \$41,135$$

An increase of $1,530 ($41,135 − $39,605) is needed, reflecting the lower interest rate. *This is adjusted to the asset and liability accounts.*

Transmission tower	1,530	
Decommissioning obligation		1,530

At the end of 20X6, HDL's decommissioning obligation is as follows:

Initial recognition, 2 January 20X5	$35,248
Interest, 31 December 20X5	2,115
Interest, 31 December 20X6	2,242
Balance of original estimated obligation	39,605
Adjustment, 20X6	1,530
Balance, 31 December 20X6	$ 41,135

Future years will reflect interest expense at the rate of 5%. The table is as follows:

	(1) Opening Net Liability	(2) Interest Expense at Market Rate (1) × 5%	(3) Closing Net Liability (1) + (2)
20X7	$41,135	$2,057	$43,192
20X8	43,192	2,160	45,352
20X9	45,352	2,268	47,620
20X10	47,620	2,380	50,000

Suppose that at the end of 20X7, HDL decides that the cost of removing the tower will be $45,000 and that the appropriate interest rate is now 7%. Following the same patterns as in 20X6, interest is first recorded using the 5% rate that was deemed appropriate in the prior year:

| Interest expense (see table above) | 2,057 | |
| Decommissioning obligation | | 2,057 |

The decommissioning obligation now has a balance of $43,192, per the table above.

Reflecting the new cost estimate and interest rate, the decommissioning obligation is recalculated as:

$$\$45,000 \times (P/F, 7\%, 3) = \$36,734$$

A decrease of $6,458 ($36,734 − $43,192) is needed, reflecting the revised estimates. This is adjusted to the asset account. As a result, at the end of 20X7, HDL's decommissioning obligation has a balance of $36,734.

| Decommissioning obligation | 6,458 | |
| Transmission tower | | 6,458 |

Changes to estimates and interest rates are common, and as result, changes to these liability accounts and the related assets are common. Annual depreciation on the transmission tower reflects these changing values!

Reporting Example

Interfor Corporation records a provision regarding its obligation to reforest areas harvested under various timber rights. The disclosure notes include detailed information about the change to the provision for the year. In 2014, the beginning and ending balances were both over $32 million but many changes occurred over the year. The company recognized $11 million as reforestation expense during the year and had expenditures for a similar amount. There were also changes related to accretion (interest) expense or unwinding of the discount of $0.5 million and changes in estimated future costs of $0.4 million. Note that the $32 million balance is reported $9 million as a current liability and $23 million as a long-term liability, reflecting the estimated timing of the expenditures.

12. Reforestation liability:

The Company has an obligation to reforest areas harvested under various timber rights. The obligation is incurred as logging occurs and the fair value of the liability for reforestation is determined with reference to the present value of estimated future cash flows required to settle the obligation.

Changes in the reforestation liability for the years ended December 31 are as follows:

	2014	2013
Reforestation liability, beginning of year	$ 32,416	$ 28,485
Reforestation expense on current logging and market logging agreements	11,264	13,283
Liabilities assumed with timber acquisition	—	2,279

Reforestation expenditures	(11,770)	(11,341)
Unwind of discount	529	441
Changes in estimated future reforestation expenditures	457	(731)
	$ 32,896	$ 32,416
Consisting of:		
Current reforestation liability	$ 9,797	$ 11,754
Long term reforestation liability	23,099	20,662
	$ 32,896	$ 32,416

The total undiscounted amount of the estimated future expenditures required to settle the reforestation obligation, adjusted for inflation, at December 31, 2014 is $34,628,000 (2013 – $35,060,000). The reforestation expenditures are expected to occur over the next one to fifteen years and have been discounted at a long term risk-free interest rate of 2% (2013 – 3%). Reforestation expense resulting from obligations arising from current logging are included in Production costs for the year and expense related to the unwinding of the discount is included in Finance costs.

Source: Interfor Corporation 2014 Annual Financial Statements, www.sedar.com, posted 12 February 2015.

CONCEPT REVIEW

1. Why might an asset purchased for $20,000 but paid for in five years' time be recorded at a lower amount?
2. What is discounting? What does it mean to unwind a discount?
3. What interest rate must be used to discount a low-interest note payable?
4. If an estimate changes on a discounted provision for environmental cleanup for a resource property, what two accounts are affected?

CLASSIFYING LIABILITIES

Most companies segregate their liabilities using the current and long-term categories. Working capital, or current assets less current liabilities, is a traditional measure of short-term liquidity and is often the subject of loan covenants. For this reason, classification of liabilities is an important issue.

A **current liability** is one that will be settled *within the next operating cycle or the next 12 months*. The operating cycle is the time between acquisition of assets for processing and their realization in cash. If the operating cycle is not clearly identifiable, it is assumed to be 12 months. For most companies, the effective guiding time period is the 12-month requirement. A **long-term liability** has a due date past this time window.

Some companies lack a clearly defined operating cycle and thus do not use a current/noncurrent distinction. These companies are required to present liabilities (and assets) in order of liquidity but do not make a "cut" between current and long term. For example, financial institutions normally categorize their assets and liabilities according to order of liquidity but do not segregate financial statement elements on the basis of **maturity date**.

In North America, current liabilities normally are listed in descending order based on the strength of the creditors' claims. In other countries, this may be reversed. Either approach is acceptable.

Classification of Notes Payable

Notes payable may be long-term liabilities or current liabilities. Classification depends on the terms of the loan. Loans are current liabilities if:

1. *Loans are due on demand.* Demand loans are payable on demand, or after a short delay of 7 to 30 business days to arrange alternative financing. These loans are legally current liabilities and must be classified as such, even if a demand for payment within the current year is not expected.

2. *Loans are due within the next year.* If a loan has a due date within the next 12 months, it is a current liability, even if the company expects to renegotiate the loan. That is, a 20-year note payable will be long term until year 19, and then it will be a current liability. The liability is current even if the company plans to refinance in year 20 with a new long-term bond.

   If debt is partially due within the next year, the current portion must be reclassified. For example, consider the classification of this $500,000 liability, of which $100,000 must be repaid in the year to come:

Current liabilities: Current portion of notes payable	$100,000
Long-term liabilities: Notes payable ($500,000 less current portion: $100,000)	$400,000

3. *Long-term debt is in violation of covenants and thus can be called by the lender at any time.* Since the lender could demand repayment, the loan is current. A company might be in arrears on loan terms, such as the requirement to pay interest on time, or may have violated covenants, such as the maximum debt-to-equity ratio on the financial statement date. If the lender has agreed *before year-end* to new terms, then the loan may remain as long term. The loan is also long term if the lender has agreed to a 12-month grace period, from the year-end date, to renegotiate the loan. However, if such agreements are reached *after year-end*, then the loan must reflect its *status at year-end* and would be classified as a current liability.

Short-Term Obligations with an Arrangement for Refinancing

A company may wish to reclassify liabilities from current to long term to improve the reported working capital position. This reclassification is not to be taken lightly—a large reclassification has a material impact on the financial statements.

Intention to restructure a short-term loan as a long-term loan is not enough to justify reclassification. However, it may happen that a company enters into an arrangement for refinancing debt prior to actually restructuring the obligation. A *contractual arrangement* may be relied on to support classification of short-term obligations as long-term debt, as long as it is, indeed, a legal contract with a reputable party. *This agreement must be in place at the year-end date.* An agreement entered into after this date cannot be used as a basis to reclassify. If a short-term obligation is to be excluded from current liabilities under a future financing agreement, note disclosure of the details would be appropriate.

Classification of Provisions

Provisions are classified as current or long term based on the timing of expected future cash flows. However, classification must be first based on the legal terms of the provision. For example, assume that customers must make a deposit for containers, refundable 30 days after the container is returned. Most customers are continuing customers, and the deposits are "rolled over" from one shipment to the next, with the result that years go by with no refunds made. Regardless of the expected cash flow, the deposit liability is current because the customer has the right to a refund after 30 days.

DISCLOSURE AND STATEMENT OF CASH FLOWS

Disclosures for Financial Liabilities

Accounting standards require disclosure of information that will allow users to evaluate the significance of financial instruments in an evaluation of financial position and performance. Financial instrument disclosure is extensive; this recap provides the highlights only. Companies must disclose:

1. The *carrying amounts* for financial instruments in each category. For some categories, this is amortized cost or cost. For others, carrying value is fair value.

2. Regardless of what is used for carrying value, disclosure must be made of fair value, and a description of the methods used to estimate fair value. For many of the financial instruments in this chapter, cost and fair value are identical.

3. The important components of each financial statement category. For example, trade payables versus income tax payable must be shown separately, as must various notes payable.

4. Information related to the legal terms of the liability, including maturity date, interest rate, collateral, and so on.

5. Any defaults and breaches of notes payable, including any resolution of the default issues and the carrying amount of the related loan.

6. Various revenue and expense amounts, including interest expense.

7. Information on exposure to various sources of risk, as appropriate. Risks might include credit, risk, liquidity risk, and market risk. Objectives, policies, and processes for managing risk must be disclosed. Such disclosure is extensive and includes both qualitative and quantitative elements.

8. Accounting policy information is required as a matter of course for all financial statement elements.

Disclosures for Provisions and Contingencies

Provisions must be shown in a separate category from payables and accruals, and the nature of each recorded liability explained. In fact, extensive disclosure for each class of obligations is required to improve transparency in an area that is dominated by judgement. In particular, companies must disclose a reconciliation, or *a continuity schedule* (opening balance to closing balance), that explains the movement in each *class* of provisions. Unrecorded amounts, that is, contingencies, must be described completely, along with a discussion of their nature and an estimate of their financial effect, if practicable.

The continuity schedule for provisions of Canadian Tire Corp. is shown below. This schedule reports opening and closing balances for five provisions, as well as the source of changes during the year. Provisions are set up primarily for sales and warranty returns, site restoration and decommissioning, onerous contracts, and customer loyalty. Customer loyalty relates to the cash value of Canadian Tire "money" (coupons) between Canadian Tire and their dealers. Note that two provisions, sales and warranty returns, and site restoration and decommissioning, are discounted; each of these reports "unwinding" of the discount. The site restoration and decommissioning provision has also been increased because of a change in the discount rate. The disclosure note also indicates the dollar value of provisions reported as current versus long term on the SFP.

21. Provisions

The following table presents the changes to the Company's provisions:

Provisions

A provision is recognized if, as a result of a past event, the Company has a present legal or constructive obligation that can be estimated reliably and it is probable that an outflow of economic benefits will be required to settle the obligation. The amount recognized as a provision is the best estimate of the consideration required to settle the present obligation at the end of the reporting period, taking into account risks and uncertainty of cash flows. Where the effect of discounting is material, provisions are determined by discounting the expected future cash flows at a pre-tax rate that reflects current market assessments of the time value of money and the risks specific to the liability.

Sales and warranty returns

The provision for sales and warranty returns relates to the Company's obligation for defective goods in current store inventories and defective goods sold to customers that have yet to be returned, as well as after sales service for replacement parts. Accruals for sales and warranty returns are estimated on the basis of historical returns and are recorded so as to allocate them to the same period the corresponding revenue is recognized. These accruals are reviewed regularly and updated to reflect Management's best estimate; however, actual returns could vary from these estimates.

2014

(C$ in millions)	Sales and warranty returns	Site restoration and decommissioning	Onerous contracts	Customer loyalty	other	Total
Balance, beginning of year	$ 109.5	$ 32.4	$ 3.2	$ 71.2	$ 18.0	$ 234.3
Charges, net of reversals	252.5	5.7	1.1	123.8	14.0	397.1
Utilizations	(247.4)	(5.8)	(3.4)	(115.1)	(16.9)	(388.6)
Unwinding of discount	1.0	0.6	0.2	—	—	1.8
Change in discount rate	—	5.5	—	—	—	5.5
Balance, end of year	$ 115.6	$ 38.4	$ 1.1	$ 79.9	$ 15.1	$ 250.1
Current provisions	112.2	6.0	0.7	79.9	7.2	206.0
Long-term provisions	$ 3.4	$ 32.4	$ 0.4	$ —	$ 7.9	$ 44.1

Site restoration and decommissioning

Legal or constructive obligations associated with the removal of underground fuel storage tanks and site remediation costs on the retirement of certain property and equipment and with the termination of certain lease agreements are recognized in the period in which they are incurred when it is probable that an outflow of resources embodying economic benefits will be required and a reasonable estimate of the amount of the obligation can be made. The obligations are initially measured at the Company's best estimate, using an expected value approach, and are discounted to present value.

Onerous contracts

A provision for onerous contracts is recognized when the expected benefits to be derived by the Company from a contract are lower than the unavoidable costs of meeting its obligations under the contract. The provision is measured at the present value of the lower of the expected cost of terminating the contract or the expected net cost of continuing with the contract.

Customer loyalty

An obligation arises from the My Canadian Tire 'Money' customer loyalty program when the Company issues e-Canadian Tire 'Money' and when the Dealers pay the Company to acquire paper-based Canadian Tire 'Money', as the Dealers retain the right to return paper-based Canadian Tire Money to the Company for refund in cash. These obligations are measured at fair value by reference to the fair value of the awards for which they could be redeemed and based on the estimated probability of their redemption. The expense is recorded in selling, general and administrative expense in the consolidated statements of the income.

Source: Canadian Tire Corporation, Limited 2014 Annual Consolidated Financial Statements, www.sedar.com, posted 26 February 2015.

Statement of Cash Flows

With respect to liabilities and the issues in this chapter, the following reporting must be observed when preparing statement of cash flows (SCF):

- Changes in liabilities and provisions that are related to earnings are adjusted in operating activities.

- Cash changes in borrowings, both new loans and repayments, are reported in financing activities on the gross basis (cash proceeds and repayments presented separately).

- Non-cash changes in borrowings, such as notes payable issued for assets, are non-cash transactions and are excluded from the SCF. Non-cash transactions are described in disclosure notes.

- Interest that is represented by unwinding a discount is a non-cash expense and is added back in operating activities.

- Cash paid for interest can be reported either in operating activities or financing activities, and excludes any portion of interest caused by unwinding a discount.

Example

As an example, consider the following liability accounts of Milo Resources Ltd.:

	20X5	20X4
Trade accounts payable	$1,706,300	$1,423,000
Provision for legal	260,000	—
Decommissioning obligation	245,000	210,000
Notes payable, 8%	200,000	—
Notes payable, net, 9%	68,500	—

Additional information:

- Provision for legal is based on three outstanding court cases. No cash was paid this year. The amount is not discounted due to uncertainty of timing of cash flows.

- The decommissioning obligation relates to a mining property. The $35,000 change in this account this year is due to interest ($17,000) and also due to a change in estimate ($18,000).

- The 8% notes payable were issued at market interest rates in early 20X5.

- The 9% note payable reflects market interest rates at issuance but is in fact a no-interest, five-year note payable arranged with a supplier in early 20X5, for a piece of equipment. The note was originally recorded at its discounted amount of $65,000. Interest of $3,500 was recorded in 20X5.

Milo Resources uses the indirect method of presentation in the operating activities section of the SCF, and classifies interest paid in the operating activities section.

As a result of these transactions, the SCF would report:

1. In operating activities, as an add-back, change in non-cash working capital, trade accounts payable, +$283,300.
2. In operating activities, as an add-back, non-cash expense for legal, +$260,000.
3. In operating activities, as an add-back, non-cash expense for interest on decommissioning obligation, +$17,000. The other $18,000 change in this account is not shown on the SCF, because it is a non-cash "acquisition"/addition to the mining property. Non-cash transactions are disclosed.
4. In financing, issuance of 8% notes payable, +$200,000.
5. The $65,000 issuance of 9% notes payable is a non-cash acquisition of equipment and is not shown on the SCF. The transaction is described in a disclosure note.

6. The company would show, in operating activities, as an add-back, non-cash expense for interest 9% notes payable, +$3,500.

7. Cash paid for interest on the 8% note, $16,000 ($200,000 × 8%) is shown as an outflow in operating activities, already included in earnings, so no adjustment is needed.

In operating activities, one must examine sources of revenue and expense that do not reflect the underlying cash flow, and make appropriate adjustments. This includes changes in current liability accounts, and interest expense that represents unwinding a discount. Finally, issuing notes payable for cash and repaying notes for cash are financing transactions.

Looking Forward

Definition—Proposed Change

As part of a review of the conceptual framework, the International Accounting Standards Board (IASB) is reconsidering the definition of financial elements, including the definition of a liability. The definition under consideration is that a liability is "a present obligation for which the entity is the obligor." This definition removes the requirement that the liability relates to a past event but retains the requirement that there be a *present obligation*. In particular, a present economic obligation exists when a company is committed to a specific action that is capable of resulting in cash outflows, and there is a mechanism to enforce the economic obligation against the entity. If such a change is made, there would be a ripple effect through reporting standards.

Accounting Standards for Private Enterprises

 Accounting Standards for Private Enterprise (ASPE) and the International Financial Reporting Standards (IFRS) for financial liabilities are largely similar. Much of the similarity stems from the common financial instruments rules, which were developed as a joint project between the IASB, Canada, and the United States.

For nonfinancial liabilities, there is less direct alignment. In fact, ASPE contains no comprehensive standards governing accounting policy for non-financial liabilities. The term "provision" is not used under ASPE; IFRS standards use this term for liabilities that are *uncertain as to timing or amount*. Under ASPE, such estimated liabilities are recognized if they *meet the liability definition, if they are measurable, and if future economic sacrifices are probable*. The outcome of applying this approach is largely consistent with IFRS; for example, restructuring liabilities are recorded, warranty liabilities are recorded and so on.

There are some differences with ASPE, where IFRS standards contain specific guidance for provisions, for example, with respect to measuring the amount to record (expected value versus most likely outcome) and choice of discount rate, if needed. In ASPE if there is a range and if each point in the range is equally likely the lower value is used in the range.

Constructive liabilities are not recorded under ASPE. Accordingly, in areas such as decommissioning obligations (in ASPE called asset retirement obligations), only legal liabilities are recognized.

There are no standards for customer loyalty points under ASPE. The IFRS approach explained in this chapter may be adopted or not.

When comparing IFRS and ASPE, the term "contingent liabilities" has a different meaning. An ASPE contingent liability is one that will result in the outflow of resources only *if* another event happens. ASPE accounting treatment for contingencies follows the following grid:

Measurability:

Probability:	Measurable	Not Measurable
Likely	Record (plus disclose if amount recorded is uncertain).	Disclose in the notes.
Undeterminable	Disclose in the notes.	Disclose in the notes.
Not Likely	Do not record or disclose unless material.	Do not record or disclose unless material.

Under ASPE, a *contingent liability is either recorded or disclosed*; under IFRS, the liability is deemed a contingency only if it is *disclosed and not recorded*. Under IFRS, the liability is a *provision* if it is recorded. This is a different use of the word "contingency."

Under both sets of standards, the general framework is the same—some situations result in only a disclosure note, and other situations in a recorded liability, depending on the likelihood and measurability of the outflow of economic resources. In addition, though, the specifics of the criteria established under IFRS and ASPE may dictate somewhat different results.

In ASPE a contingent gain is never recorded.

Straight-line discount amortization Under ASPE, use of the effective interest method is not required. The **straight-line method** can be used to amortize the discount and measure interest expense.

Example Return to the example in the chapter, where Baylor Co. purchases inventory of 1 April 20X2 and agrees to pay the vendor $12,000 on 31 March 20X4, plus annual interest at 4% each 31 March. The present value of the note payable is $10,750, discounted at the market interest rate of 10%.

The interest calculation, based on straight-line amortization, reflects equal amounts of discount amortization in each year. The original discount is $1,250 ($12,000 – $10,750). This is $625 ($1,250 ÷ 2) per year, over the two-year term of the loan. Interest expense is then cash paid plus the discount amortization, or $1,105 ($625 + $480). The calculations can be organized in a table:

	(1) Opening Net Liability	(2) Interest Expense (3) + (4)	(3) Interest Paid 4% Stated Rate $12,000 × 4%	(4) Discount Amortization Straight-Line	(5) Closing Net Liability (1) + (4)
20X3	$10,750	$1,105	$480	$625	$11,375
20X4	$11,375	1,105	480	625	12,000

The straight-line method produces the same interest amount each period but shows a varying *rate* of interest period by period (i.e., "interest ÷ opening net liability" will vary). It is less accurate for this reason, and is not permitted under IFRS standards. However, it is much simpler and may yield results that are not materially different from the effective interest method.

Classification and disclosure A company may wish to reclassify liabilities from current to long term to improve the reported working capital position. If a long-term loan is coming due but is being renegotiated, IFRS requires that a legally enforceable agreement be in place *by the end of the fiscal year (the reporting date)* if the loan is to be classified as long term. Under ASPE, classification of such a loan as long term would be permitted if renegotiation resulted in agreement by the *date the financial statements are released*.

Finally, disclosure is less onerous in all areas under ASPE compared with IFRS. For example, no reconciliations or continuity schedules are required.

RELEVANT STANDARDS

CPA Canada Handbook, Part I (IASB):

- IAS 1, Presentation of Financial Statements
- IAS 21, The Effects of Changes in Foreign Exchange Rates
- IAS 37, Provisions, Contingent Liabilities and Contingent Assets
- IFRS 7, Financial Instruments: Disclosures
- IFRS 9, Financial Instruments

CPA Canada Handbook, Part II (ASPE):

- Section 1510, Current Assets and Current Liabilities
- Section 1651, Foreign Currency Translation
- Section 3110, Asset Retirement Obligations
- Section 3280, Contractual Obligations
- Section 3290, Contingencies
- Section 3856, Financial Instruments
- AcG-14, Disclosure of Guarantees

SUMMARY OF KEY POINTS

1. Liabilities are present obligations of a company resulting from past events, the settlement of which is expected to result in the outflow of economic benefits. Liabilities may be nonfinancial or financial and may result from legal obligations or constructive obligations.

2. Accounts and notes payable are *financial liabilities* that are classified as *other payables*, and carried at amortized cost and discounted, if needed. In some circumstances, such financial liabilities are classified as FVTPL and carried at fair value.

3. Nonfinancial liabilities include provisions, which are liabilities of *uncertain timing or amount*. Provisions are recorded if there is a present obligation as a result of a past event, the outflow of resources is probable, and an estimate can be made. If the potential provision is *not probable or is not measurable*, then it is a *contingency* and is not recorded but is disclosed.

4. Common liabilities include accounts, notes, accruals, property taxes, cash dividends, taxes, bonuses, and other payables.

5. Transactions that are denominated in a foreign currency are recorded at the exchange rate that exists at the transaction date. Monetary balances (i.e., cash, receivables, and payables) are restated to the exchange rate that exists on the year-end date. Exchange gains and losses are recognized in earnings.

6. Provisions are recorded at the best estimate, discounted if needed, and are re-estimated each reporting period. Best estimate may be the expected value (large populations) or the most likely outcome informed by expected value and cumulative probability (small populations).

7. Examples of provisions include lawsuits, onerous contracts, restructuring, warranties, restoration and environmental obligations, sales returns, coupons, loyalty programs, repairs and maintenance, self-insurance, and compensated absences. Accounting policy for these elements is summarized in a chart in the chapter.

8. Discounting is required to value a liability if it is long term and is a non-interest-bearing liability or if it is interest-bearing but the interest rate is below or above the market interest rate. Subsequent interest expense is measured using the market interest rate and will involve unwinding the discount or premium.

9. Using the effective interest method as applied to a discounted liability, interest expense is the product of the market rate at issuance and the net discounted balance in the liability at the beginning of the period. Interest is accrued with the passage of time.

10. Common situations where discounting is required include non-interest-bearing notes payable, low-interest loans, and non-interest-bearing provisions.

11. Discounted notes payable may be recorded in the books net of the calculated discount, or the discount can be recorded using the gross method, where there is a separate contra account for the discount.

12. When a provision is discounted, interest is recognized as time passes. If estimates of future cash flows change in amount or timing, or the market interest rate changes, interest is accrued on the provision for the period first and then the carrying value is adjusted to the revised present value.

13. Liabilities are current when they are due within the next operating cycle or 12 months; this includes the current portion of a long-term liability. If refinancing arrangements are in place before the end of the year, a liability to be refinanced may be classified as long term.

14. Extensive disclosure is required for financial liabilities, including carrying value, fair value, details of contractual requirements, and continuity schedules for provisions, in addition to information on credit risk, liquidity risk, and market risk. Disclosure for provisions includes a description of the provision, and a continuity schedule that shows how the liability changed over the fiscal year.

15. ASPE does not require that constructive liabilities be recorded and thus results in lower levels of liabilities in certain circumstances. ASPE also allows straight-line amortization of a discount. Other differences between IFRS and ASPE include the definition of the term "contingency," and details governing measurement and classification in specific situations.

Key Terms

breakage
collateral security
constructive obligations
contingency
current liability
discounting
effective interest method
effective interest rate
executory contracts
expected value
financial liability
interest-bearing
legal obligation
long-term liability
market interest rate

maturity date
most likely outcome
nominal interest rate
non-interest-bearing
nonfinancial liability
obligating event
onerous contract
present value
spot rate
stated interest rate
straight-line method
trade accounts payable
unwinding
virtual certainty
yield

Review Problem 12-1

The following selected transactions and events of Oakland Ltd. were completed during the accounting year just ended, 31 December 20X5. Interest rates reflect market rates unless indicated.

a. On 1 June, the company borrowed $55,000 in cash from the bank on a demand basis. The interest rate was 6%, to be paid on the anniversary date of the loan.

b. Merchandise was purchased on account; a $30,000, one-year, 7% interest-bearing note, dated 1 April 20X5, was given to the supplier. Interest is paid when the amount is due on 1 April 20X6.

c. Merchandise was purchased on account; a two-year, $16,000, 1% note dated 1 February 20X5 was given to the supplier. Interest is due annually on 1 February. The going interest rate for this term and risk was 7%. Use the gross method to record the note payable.

d. A supplier delivered goods on account costing US$20,000. The exchange rate was US$1 = Cdn$0.98 at that time.

e. Oakland has been sued by a customer for $500,000. The legal team confidently believes that there is an 80% chance that Oakland will successfully defend itself.

f. New legislative requirements came into force at the beginning of this year regarding environmental remediation. Oakland believes it will have to pay $80,000 in eight years' time when the company vacates leased premises. The going interest rate for this term and risk was 7%.

g. Payroll records showed the following. Amounts are unpaid:

		Employee		
Gross Wages	Income Tax	EI	CPP	Union Dues
$120,000	$32,000	$6,100	$5,500	$2,500

h. The employer portion of EI and CPP are recorded.

i. Remittances were income tax, $31,350; EI, $10,250; CPP, $9,720; union dues, $1,480.

j. Cash dividends declared but not yet paid were $22,500.

k. Accrue appropriate interest at 31 December, and adjust the foreign-denominated payable to the year-end rate, US$1 = Cdn$0.96.

Required:

1. Give the entry or entries for each of the above transactions and events, if needed.
2. Prepare a list (title and amount) of the liabilities of Oakland at 31 December 20X5.

REVIEW PROBLEM 12-1—SOLUTION

Requirement 1

a. Bank demand loan:

Cash	55,000	
Note (or loan) payable, 6%		55,000

b. Purchased merchandise (1 April 20X5):

Inventory	30,000	
Note payable, 7%		30,000

c. Purchased merchandise (1 February 20X5):

Inventory	14,264	
Discount on notes payable	1,736	
Note payable, 1%; yield 7%		16,000

$16,000 (P/F, 7%, 2) + $160 (P/A, 7%, 2) = $14,264

d. US–denominated liability:

Inventory	19,600	
Accounts payable ($20,000 × $0.98)		19,600

e. No entry. Small population and most likely outcome is no payout. Disclosure if amount is material.

f. Decommissioning obligation:

Leased premises or other asset	46,561	
Decommissioning obligation		46,561

$80,000 (P/F, 7%, 8) = $46,561

g. To record salaries and employee deductions:

Salary expense	120,000	
Employee income taxes payable		32,000
EI payable		6,100
CPP payable		5,500
Union dues payable		2,500
Cash		73,900

h. To record payroll expenses payable by the employer:

Salary expense	14,040	
CPP payable		5,500
EI payable ($6,100 × 1.4)		8,540

i. To record remittance of payroll deductions:

Employee income taxes payable	31,350	
EI payable	10,250	
CPP payable	9,720	
Union dues payable	1,480	
Cash		52,800

j. Cash dividends declared but not yet paid:

Retained earnings (or dividends)	22,500	
Cash dividends payable		22,500

k. Year-end adjustments:

Interest expense	1,925	
Interest payable		1,925
$\$55,000 \times 0.06 \times 7/12$		
Interest expense ($\$30,000 \times 0.07 \times 9/12$)	1,575	
Interest payable		1,575
Interest expense ($\$14,264 \times 0.07 \times 11/12$)	915	
Discount on note payable		768
Interest payable ($\$160 \times 11/12$)		147
Accounts payable	400	
Exchange gain		400
($\$20,000 \times \$0.96$) = $\$19,200$ versus $\$19,600$ recorded		
Interest expense	3,259	
Decommissioning obligation		3,259
($\$46,561 \times 0.07$)		

Requirement 2

Liabilities:

Note (loan) payable	$55,000
Accounts payable (US)	19,200
Interest payable ($1,575 + $1,925 + $147)	3,647
Employee income tax payable	650
EI payable	4,390
CPP payable	1,280
Union dues payable	1,020
Cash dividends payable	22,500
Note payable ($16,000 − ($1,736 − $768)	15,032
Note payable, 7%	30,000
Decommissioning obligation ($46,561 + $3,259)	49,820

CASE 12-1

SKI INC.

Ski Inc. (SI) is a public company that has been in business since the 1980s. It owns and operates over 20 ski clubs across Canada. SI also owns and operates ski shops where customers can rent or buy ski equipment. SI has a bonus plan based on net income.

SI started operations with one ski club and continued to expand through purchasing existing ski clubs. SI has a bank loan with Canadian Bank. SI had a tough year last year in 20X5 with its first-ever taxable loss of $400,000 due to low snowfalls and lower than normal guest revenues. SI needed to increase its financing with the bank and now the bank requires a minimum current ratio be maintained.

You have recently been hired as an accounting consultant to assist SI's board of directors. You have been asked to develop appropriate accounting policies for events that have occurred during 20X5. The board has asked that you explain fully your analysis for your recommendations. SI has a December 31 year-end. The incremental borrowing rate for SI is 8%.

1. SI's ski clubs are very popular and have a wait list for memberships. Potential members can pay a $500 nonrefundable fee to obtain a spot on the wait list for a membership. The average time on the wait list is three to five years. Once a membership spot becomes available, the $500 is deducted from the initiation

fee. Members are required to pay a $10,000 initiation fee to join the club. In addition, they pay an annual fee of $2,000, which is due September 1 for the following ski season. Members can bring guests to the club. They make a reservation for the guest. The guests pay by credit card on the day they ski. If a guest does not show up, the member is charged the fee.

2. In the summer of 20X5, SI offered two special promotions to try to increase guest revenue. The first was that guests can buy a special pass for a flat fee of $100, which includes a ski pass for the day and a free lesson for any time within the next year. The cost of the ski pass on its own is $80 and the cost of the lesson is $50 on its own. The second is that SI distributed 200 coupons in the surrounding area for $5 of a lift pass.

3. SI purchased a new high-speed chair lift in 20X5. The manufacturer of the ski lift offered a 0% loan as an incentive to purchase. The chair lift cost $2.5 million and the loan is due in two years.

4. In 20X5, a guest slipped on ice and was injured in the parking lot of the ski club. The guest sued SI for damages. Lawyers for SI say the case has no merit based on past lawsuits. The board has decided to settle the lawsuit to avoid negative publicity. The estimated range for the payment is between $200,000 and $300,000.

5. SI leases some of its premises for its ski shops. In 20X5, SI decided to close one of those locations and open a shop in the on-hill ski lodge. SI must continue paying lease payments of $10,000 a month for the next two years until the end of the lease. SI has been able to sublease the location for $5,000 a month.

6. In 20X5, SI installed new gasoline storage tanks at a number of its resorts. SI decided to store gas at the ski hill, which is more convenient. The gas is used to operate trucks, snowmobiles, and equipment to groom the ski hills. The cost to purchase the tanks was $10 million. Government legislation requires that these tanks be replaced in 15 years. The estimated cost to remove and replace the tanks is $2.5 million.

Required:

As the accounting consultant, prepare the requested report.

CASE 12-2

PRESCRIPTIONS DEPOT LTD.

Prescriptions Depot Ltd. (PDL) is a national chain of drug stores, some company owned and some operated as franchises. The company reported $5.4 billion in revenue in the most recent fiscal year, and net earnings of $295 million. Gross profit was in the range of 20% but is different for various product lines. Some products are essentially grocery items, and gross margin is minimal. Other products sell with a 30%–40% profit margin. Prescription drugs also generate a range of profit margins, but industry averages are 15%–25% gross margin. Company reporting objectives are focused around increasing earnings. PDL realizes, though, that many market analysts carefully look for trends in sales growth, particularly year-over-year same-store sales growth. The company is not public but wishes to comply with IFRS, since medium-term plans include a public offering.

You are a new analyst in the company's performance reporting department. You have been asked to review accounting policy for several issues.

PDL accepts vendor "cents off" coupons, which involve small discounts to the retail price of a given product. PDL records the sale to the customer at the net cash received. PDL remits the coupons to the vendor and reduces the amount otherwise owing to the vendor and the cost of inventory by the coupon amount. For example, assume that

PDL has accepted 5,000, $1 coupons for shampoo. Sale of the shampoo has a retail value of $25,000, but PDL reports the sale at the $20,000 amount of cash collected from the customer ($25,000 less the $5,000 in coupons). If PDL owes the vendor $98,000, PDL then pays only $93,000, and PDL records $93,000 as the cost of the product.

PDL has also issued certain coupons for cash refunds, a cash payment directly to the end consumer from PDL and not through a vendor arrangement. For example, in one promotion, any customer who purchased $500 of home health care merchandise on a given weekend would, after filing the appropriate form and receipts, receive a $35 cash refund. A six-week period is provided for the documents to be filed, and then the offer expires. The volume of these refunds has been low, but PDL may be more active with these promotions in the future. The refund was recorded as a reduction to cash and a reduction to sales, when the refund was issued.

The company has a loyalty points program, wherein customers with membership cards earn five loyalty points for every dollar spent in the store. Higher points per dollar are assigned to prescription drug sales. Once points accumulate, customers can redeem the points at various levels/values for full or partial payment on merchandise purchases. At various times, sales incentives are offered, such as "double points" awarded to large one-time purchases. At other times, to trigger redemption, redeemed points are given bonus values. Some points are never redeemed, but the collection and redemption levels are healthy, and PDL is convinced that customer loyalty is significantly enhanced by the program.

When points are granted in conjunction with a sale transaction, the sale is recorded for the full amount of the sale. An estimate of the cost of goods to be obtained through point redemption is recorded at the same time. For example, a sale of $100 is recorded, along with its $75 cost of goods sold. Points are issued that are expected to be redeemed for goods with a retail price of $4 and a cost of $3. Accordingly, a $3 expense and liability is recorded at the same time as the sale. When points are redeemed, inventory is reduced, at its $3 cost, and the liability is reduced. The overall liability balance is carefully reviewed each quarter, and adjusted up or down for shifts in cost expectations, redemption levels, and changes to the percentages redeemed under "bonus" conditions.

PDL rents many of its premises, under three- to five-year lease contracts. Typically, the lessor undertakes renovations for PDL to make the premises suitable for occupancy as a retail drugstore. However, PDL itself installs a behind-the-counter set-up in the pharmacy area. This includes an area for secure drug storage, drug disposal, "sharps" (needle) disposal, and secure data transmission and storage devices. These are all designed to meet legislative or industry standards, and the set-up is built to exacting standards to ensure drug safety and patient confidentiality. PDL is then responsible for the removal of this set-up when and if it vacates at the end of a lease term.

Required:

As the analyst, prepare a report that identifies the accounting issues with your analysis and recommendations.

CASE 12-3

CAMANI CORP.

Camani Corp. (CC) is involved in the production, distribution, and marketing of consumer products that encompass a broad range of items, from hair care products, to cosmetics and perfume, to vitamins and supplements. CC has been hard hit by the recent economic downturn, during which consumer spending has been curtailed. The financial results of the current year, 20X3, are critical for all stakeholders and will reflect on the viability of the existing strategic model. The executive team will receive a healthy "return to profitability" bonus if 20X3 earnings are positive, after two years of losses.

You are a member of the board of directors of CC and sit on the audit committee. You have a fair understanding of financial statements and take some pride in your technical proficiency. You have just left an audit committee meeting, where a 20X3 summarized draft SFP and a summarized draft statement of earnings has been presented (Exhibit 1). Earnings are positive. However, you are concerned that no SCF has yet been prepared. You also are concerned that some of the estimates and policy decisions made might have been affected by management's desire to show positive 20X3 earnings (Exhibit 2).

EXHIBIT 1

CAMANI CORPORATION

Summarized Draft 20X3 Statement of Financial Position

At 31 December (in thousands)	20X3	20X2
Cash	$ 2,340	$ 1,680
Accounts receivable	16,780	13,040
Inventory	61,920	54,970
Prepaids	542	455
Land	5,860	5,860
Plant and equipment (net)	19,720	18,650
Other assets	650	290
Total debits	$107,812	$94,945
Liabilities		
Accounts payable and accrued liabilities	47,388	42,867
Long-term debt	53,527	46,200
Equity		
Common shares	5,640	5,235
Retained earnings	1,257	643
Total credits	$107,812	$94,945

Summarized Draft Statement of Earnings

For the year ended 31 December 20X3	
Sales revenue	$104,910
Cost of goods sold	(66,230)

Depreciation expense	(3,900)
Operating, administration, financing and marketing	(33,245)
Earnings and comprehensive income	$ 1,535

EXHIBIT 2

CAMANI CORPORATION

Policy and Estimate Information, 31 December 20X3

1. Legal issues

   In 20X3, as in prior years, CC is a defendant in a range of small lawsuits, primarily resulting from customer issues but also with several suppliers. These lawsuits are often settled out of court, and payments in prior years for individual cases have been in the $20,000 to $100,000 range. At the end of 20X3, an accrual of $830 was made based on expected value and the following "probability as recorded" (second column) assessment to determine expected value:

Total Payment (in thousands)	Probability as Recorded	Alternative Probability
$ 100	10%	0%
500	30	20
700	30	30
1,200	20	30
2,200	10	20

   Another assessment of the probability might be as listed in the "alternative probability" column, above.

2. Depreciation policy

   CC reviewed estimates of useful life and residual values for depreciable assets in 20X3. Based on this review, the depreciation amount of $3,900 was recorded. If prior year estimates and amounts had been used, depreciation would have been in the range of $4,100.

3. Technology services

   CC had recorded $1,200 as an estimate for technology services rendered to date by a supplier. The supplier has a $4,000 contract, and CC estimated that this contract was 30% complete. Another suggestion is that the project is 45% complete.

4. Inventory valuation

   CC has significant inventory on hand at the end of 20X3. This inventory is valued after a writedown to lower of cost or market. The writedown in 20X3 was $2,350. This is the lowest writedown in the company's history, although it is justified by a thorough analysis of sales values and volumes. If percentage writedowns were similar to those in prior years, the writedown would have been in the range of $3,125.

5. Restructuring

CC is contemplating the restructuring of its sales and marketing group, to improve efficiency and reduce costs. The tentative plan involves downsizing one group of sales people in 20X4; likely severance costs would be in the range of $500. No accrual has been made in the books because the program has not yet been approved or announced.

6. Environmental liability

CC has an environmental liability for premises remediation at one rental location. When CC vacates this location, construction will be required to return the site to its previous condition. Accordingly, the $400 cost of this, at its present value of $306 (4 years, at 7%), was recorded as a long-term liability as of 1 January 20X3. Interest of $21 (a non-cash expense) was recorded in 20X3, along with straight-line depreciation over four years. Another estimate of the interest rate would be 5%.

Note: In all assignment material in this text, assume a 31 December fiscal year-end unless advised otherwise.

Therefore, you have decided to do some analysis of your own. First, you want to calculate cash flow from operating activities for the draft set of financial statements that have been presented. Second, you feel you could learn about the sensitivity of the results if you adjust the financial statements for estimates and policies that you believe are aggressive. Finally, you plan to recalculate cash from operating activities based on your revised financial statements. You know you will need to write a brief report around your analysis so that you can refer it on to the chair of the audit committee for discussion at your next meeting.

Required:

Prepare the suggested analysis and report. Note that CC includes dividend payments to its shareholders as an operating cash flow. There is no income tax.

TECHNICAL REVIEW

connect

TR12-1 Financial Liabilities and Provisions (IFRS):

1. Provisions include legal and constructive obligations.
2. Amortized cost uses either effective interest method or straight-line method.
3. The foreign currency gain or loss for a note payable is recognized in OCI.
4. For estimating provisions with a range, the mid-point of the range is used.
5. A mortgage due within the next year is classified as a long-term liability if refinancing is completed by the date the financial statements are completed.

Required:

Identify whether each statement is true or false.

connect

TR12-2 Financial Liabilities and Provisions (ASPE):

1. Provisions include legal and constructive obligations.

2. Amortized cost uses either effective interest method or straight-line method.

3. The foreign currency gain or loss for a note payable is recognized in net income.

4. When estimating provisions with a range, the mid-point of the range is used.

5. A mortgage due within the next year is classified as a long-term liability if refinancing is completed by the date the financial statements are completed.

Required:

Identify whether each statement is true or false.

connect

TR12-3 Provision—Measurement:

Consider the following three cases:

Case 1   A company has four legal claims outstanding, each for $100,000. There is a 10% chance that one claim will be paid out, a 10% chance that two will be paid out, a 5% chance for three, and a 5% chance for four payouts.

Case 2   A company has four legal claims outstanding, each for $100,000. There is a 10% chance that one claim will be paid out, a 60% chance that two will be paid out, a 5% chance for three, and a 15% chance for four payouts.

Case 3   A company has four legal claims outstanding, each for $100,000. There is a 30% chance that one claim will be paid out, a 20% chance that two will be paid out, a 20% chance for three, and a 20% chance for four payouts.

Required:

For each case, decide if *some* payout is *likely* or *not likely*. Compare the most likely outcome with the expected value, and explain the amount that must be recorded.

connect

TR12-4 Guarantee:

Best Ltd. has guaranteed a $800,000 loan of Grand Ltd., a customer. There is security valued at $500,000—assets of Grand—registered against the loan. Best estimates that there is a 30% chance that it will be required to step in and pay $300,000 on the loan this coming year.

Required:

Calculate the liability Best must record, if any.

connect

TR12-5 Provision—Warranty:

Helpi Auto Parts Ltd. offers a six-month warranty on parts that the company has installed. This warranty ensures that parts are working as intended. The warranty covers the cost of parts, plus labour for repairs. Warranty costs are estimated to be 1.5% of sales for parts plus 3% of sales for labour. On 1 April, the warranty liability had a $16,400 credit balance. Warranty work in April consumed $8,700 of parts and $14,000 of labour. Sales amounted to $550,000 in April.

Required:

1. What amount of warranty expense should be recorded in April?
2. What is the balance in the warranty provision at the end of April?

connect

TR12-6 Foreign Currency:

A company has an account payable to a U.S. company, a supplier of inventory, in the amount of US$150,000. The payable was incurred when the exchange rate was US$1 = Cdn$.75. At year-end, the rate is $.72.

Required:

1. What amount of inventory is recorded?
2. What amount of exchange gain or loss will the company report for the year?

connect

TR12-7 Note Payable:

On 1 October 20X6, Halpern Co. borrowed $120,000 from Canada Bank. The note has a two-year term, and requires that interest of 9% be paid each 30 September, with the principal payable 30 September 20X8.

Required:

Provide all entries for the note from 20X6 to 20X8.

≣ connect

TR12-8 Discounting—Note Payable:

Materials Ltd. purchases inventory on 1 April 20X7 and agrees to pay the vendor $250,000 on 31 March 20X9, plus annual interest at 2% each 31 March. The market interest rate for similar term and security is 7%. Assume also that the inventory does not have a readily determinable market value.

Required:

1. Calculate the present value of the note payable.
2. Prepare a table that shows the balance of the note payable and interest expense over the life of the note.

≣ connect

TR12-9 Discounting—Provision:

On 2 January 20X8, Keen Mining Ltd. commenced a mining operation. Keen is required by the terms of provincial legislation to remediate the mine site when mining is completed, likely in 10 years' time. This means that a provision for decommissioning must be recorded. Keen estimates that decommissioning will cost $420,000 in 10 years. A reasonable market interest rate is 6%.

Required:

1. Calculate the present value of the decommissioning obligation on January 2, 20X8.
2. Prepare a table that shows the balance of the obligation for three years (only).
3. Assume that at the end of 20X10, Keen estimates that the cost of remediation will be $490,000, and that interest rates are now in the range of 8%. Calculate the interest expense for 20X10, the new present value, and the adjustment to the obligation for the change in estimates.

≣ connect

TR12-10 Classification Liabilities:

Identify if the following liabilities would be classified as current or non-current. Assume a December 31 year-end.

1. Demand loan
2. Accounts payable
3. Mortgage due in Feb. not refinanced by Dec 31
4. Loan covenant violation that the banker waived the right to collect by Dec 31.
5. Payroll taxes

Required:

Identify if the following liabilities would be classified as current or non-current.

★ A12-1 Common Financial Liabilities:

Dash Ltd. engaged in various transactions during the month of September:

a. Bought $5,200 of office supplies on account.

b. Borrowed $30,000 for the Big Bank at the beginning of the month and agreed to pay the loan back in one year, plus interest at 10%. This is the market interest rate.

c. Bought inventory for resale with an invoice price of $143,000.

d. The September hydro bill for $2,600 arrived but is not due until October.

e. Declared a cash dividend of $1.5 per preferred share and $0.50 per common share, payable 16 October. There are 4,000 preferred shares and 10,000 common shares outstanding.

f. Returned goods with an invoice price of $35,200 to the supplier in (c).

g. Paid the supplier in (c) 50% the net amount owing.

h. Accrued interest on the bank loan at the end of the month.

i. Accrued monthly rent of $2,400 for September, to be paid in October.

Required:

1. Journalize each of the above transactions in general journal form. Use a general accounts payable account in journal entries except for loans, interest, and dividends payable.

2. List the liability accounts and amounts that result from your entries in requirement 1.

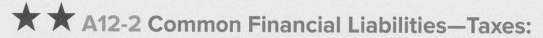

★★ A12-2 Common Financial Liabilities—Taxes:

Hogarth Ltd. had the following transactions in February 20X8:

a. Recorded sales of $3,600,000, plus GST of 5%.

b. Recorded sales of $12,400,000, plus GST of 5%.

c. Bought equipment for $1,250,000, plus GST of 5%.

d. Recorded the bimonthly payroll of $85,800. CPP deductions were $1,200, EI deductions were $1,400, and income tax withheld amounted to $7,400. (Employer portions of payroll taxes are recorded only at the end of the month.)

e. Recorded sales of $2,800,000, plus GST of 5%.

f. Bought inventory for $12,200,000, plus GST of 5%.

g. Recorded the bimonthly payroll. The amounts were identical to the prior bimonthly payroll.

h. Recorded the employer portion of payroll expenses for the entire month.

i. Remitted payroll taxes for the month.

j. Remitted net GST for the month.

Required:

Provide journal entries to record all transactions. Assume transactions with customers and suppliers were for cash.

★ ★ A12-3 Common Financial Liabilities—Taxes:

Hendrie reported opening balances as at 1 June 20X8:

GST payable	$43,000 (cr.)
Income tax deductions payable	2,600 (cr.)
CPP payable	1,900 (cr.)
EI payable	800 (cr.)

The company had the following transactions in June 20X8:

a. Collected $708,000 of GST on sales to customers.
b. Recorded the bimonthly payroll, which included CPP deductions of $2,800, EI deductions of $2,400, and income tax withheld of $21,400.
c. Recorded the second bimonthly payroll. The payroll included CPP deductions of $3,000, EI deductions of $2,800, and income tax withheld of $23,400.
d. Bought capital assets of $1,920,000, plus GST of 5%.
e. Recorded the employer portion of payroll expenses for the entire month.
f. Paid $533,000 GST to the Receiver General for Canada.

Required:

Calculate the balances in the four accounts listed above as at 30 June 20X8. There were no payments on account during the month.

A12-4 Foreign Currency Payables:

Golden Ltd. had the following transactions in 20X5:

a. Bought goods on 1 June from Brit Ltd. for 70,000 euros, with payment due in four months' time.
b. Bought goods from New York Sales Corp. on 15 June for US$150,000; payment was due in one month.
c. Bought goods from London Ltd. on 15 July for 20,000 euros; settlement was to be in two months.
d. Paid New York Sales Corp. on 15 July.
e. Paid London Ltd. on 15 September.
f. Paid Brit Ltd. on 1 October.

EXCHANGE RATES:

Canadian Equivalencies	Euros	US$
1 June	2.11	1.07
15 June	2.19	1.11
15 July	2.13	1.17
15 September	2.20	1.03
1 October	2.17	1.06

Required:

Prepare journal entries for the above transactions.

 Solution

 connect

★ ★ A12-5 Common Financial Liabilities and Foreign Currency:

Data regarding Petrilla Corp. in March 20X9:

Selected opening balances:	GST payable	$62,800 (cr.)
	CPP payable	3,900 (cr.)
	EI payable	5,200 (cr.)
	Income tax deductions payable	16,320 (cr.)

a. Cash sales for the period, $980,000 plus 5% GST.

b. Monthly payroll, $117,000; less EI, $3,800; CPP, $2,200; income tax, $12,200. The employer portion of payroll taxes was also recorded.

c. Inventory purchases on account, $1,520,000 plus 5% GST.

d. Cash sales, $3,140,000, plus 5% GST.

e. Sales to U.S. customer on account, US$176,000. There was no GST on the sale. The U.S. dollar was worth Cdn$1.03 on this date.

f. The U.S. customer paid US$140,000 on account, when the U.S. dollar was worth $1.07. The remaining amount will be paid in June.

g. GST owing was remitted.

h. Sixty percent of the amount owing to suppliers in (c) was paid.

i. At the end of the month, the U.S. exchange rate was Cdn$1.06.

Required:

1. Journalize all transactions listed above.
2. List the accounts and amounts that would appear on the 31 March statement of financial position. Exclude cash and inventory.

★ ★ A12-6 Provisions:

The following items pertain to possible provisions:

a. The ABC Mining Co. has announced that it will restructure its Atlantic Canada operations and lay off 80% of workers in the area. The employees affected are informed and given six months' notice and promised generous severance packages at the end of six months.

b. Siam Services Ltd. has 500 coupons outstanding that allow customers a $10 cash rebate from a $120 purchase price for a computer monitor. Customers must submit documentation to prove cash purchase. Approximately 65% of the coupons will be submitted by customers for payment.

c. The board of directors for the Dillon Timber Co. has decided to lay off 10% of its Canadian workforce. The plan is still in the proposal stage, and it is not clear which workers will be affected. The cost is likely to be in excess of $5 million.

d. The Sweet Mining Co. has a legislative requirement for site environmental remediation in its northern Manitoba operations. This remediation must be performed when the mineral resources are depleted and the site is closed to active mining, likely in four years.

e. Ming Metals Ltd. has announced that it plans to perform site environmental remediation at its active Quebec mine site. This remediation is in excess of provincial legislative requirements and will be performed when the mineral resources are depleted and the site is closed to active mining, likely in four years.

f. Jackson Ltd. has signed a lease with another company to rent a facility for three years at a cost of $27,000 per year.

g. On the leased premises per (f), Jackson will erect a transmission tower, at its own expense, on the building roof. At the end of the lease term, Jackson must remove the tower under the terms of the lease, and removal is expected to cost $50,000.

h. A customer has sued the Kerman Co. for $2 million. The company may lose but may well offer to settle the suit for $400,000 in the next six months. The customer may or may not accept the settlement. The amount would have a significant impact on the company's financial position.

i. A prior employee has sued Luong Ltd. for $500,000 for health-related issues that the employee claims were caused by working conditions. The company will likely successfully defend itself. However, the amount is material and if the lawsuit is successful, other employees will likely also sue.

j. The Y34 Co. has guaranteed the $10 million loan of another company. This amount is material. The other company has a poor credit rating, and there is a 40% chance of having to make a $10 million payment under the guarantee.

k. The Week Co. has been audited by Canada Revenue Agency, resulting in a tax assessment for $1.5 million, an amount that would have a significant impact on the company's financial position. The company has appealed the decision and feels it has a good case.

Required:

For each of the above items, indicate whether the appropriate accounting treatment is to record a liability in the statement of financial position and report a loss in earnings, or whether there is no liability to be recognized.

★ ★ A12-7 Provisions:

The following items pertain to the 20X9 operations of Fillet Information Services Ltd.:

a. The company issued a purchase order for manufacturing equipment with an invoice price of $850,000, to be installed next year.

b. The company issued a purchase order for $200,000 of a commodity to be delivered next year. The price of this commodity subsequently declines to $160,000, but Fillet is committed to pay $200,000.

c. Fillet borrows $100,000 in US dollars when the exchange rate is US$1 = Cdn$1.10. At year-end, the exchange rate is US$1 = Cdn$1.05.

d. A lawsuit for $2 million was brought against Fillet by a customer for lost profits after an information system failure. Lawyers estimate that there is only a 5% chance that the lawsuit will result in a $2,000,000 payment, but there is a 65% chance that there will be a $500,000 payment, and a 30% chance that the lawsuit will be dismissed with no payment.

e. Fillet has guaranteed a $550,000 bank loan taken out by another company; there is only a 10% chance that Fillet would have to make a payment under this guarantee. If any payment were made, it would not be the full amount; it would be only $300,000 because of other security held for the loan.

f. Fillet has issued 1,000 coupons allowing customers to get a $100 cash rebate from Fillet when they purchase a $1,000 technology hardware and software bundle from a retailer. Based on past history, only 10% of these coupons will be used. The technology bundle will still sell at a profit.

g. Fillet participates in a loyalty points program, where customers with certain loyalty point levels may receive free merchandise from Fillet's regular product and service line.

Required:

Explain how each of these items will affect the financial statements of Fillet at year-end 20X9.

★ ★ A12-8 Provisions:

The following items pertain to possible provisions:

a. A company uses a part manufactured in Germany in its automobile manufacturing plant. There has been a concern about the failure of this part in cars manufactured in Germany. No failures have occurred to date in Canada. The company decided to do a voluntary recall of all cars manufactured with this part. The recall is 40% complete and has cost $1,200,000 to date.

b. A company self-insures for floods. That is, it pays no insurance but is liable to replace assets lost through flood damage. No losses have been incurred this year, but there have been $200,000 of losses in most other years, and the company is concerned that there might well be $400,000 of losses next year, evening out the pattern.

c. A company offers a three-year guarantee over parts and labour for products sold to ensure that parts work as expected. There were no payments this year, and only 5% of products sold this year are expected to need repairs in the next year. The cost of this work would be in the range of $100,000.

d. A company has been sued by a customer for $1,000,000. The customer slipped on ice coming out of the store and claims the store did not put salt down or clear the stairs properly. The company's lawyer has indicated that there is a 10% chance that the company will lose the lawsuit based on past history. The company, though, has decided to settle to avoid negative publicity. The costs of settling are estimated to range between $250,000 and $500,000.

e. A company is required by legislation to undertake environmental remediation for a mining site that is currently active. The site will not be cleaned up until the mine closes, which is now scheduled for 2032. It is not certain how much the cleanup will cost at that time, or how long it will take.

Required:

In each of the above cases, indicate whether a liability is recorded or not. If recording is required, give the amount, or explain how it will be estimated.

  # A12-9 Provision Measurement:

Mapplebeck Company Ltd. is gathering evidence to support an accrual for legal claims. Three lawsuits are outstanding:

Claim 1 is a lawsuit from an employee for $750,000. According to the legal team, there is a 10% chance that it will have to be paid in full and a 90% chance that it will be dismissed.

Claim 2 is a lawsuit from a supplier for $5,000,000 for breach of contract. According to the legal team, there is a 70% chance that it will have to be paid out in full and a 30% chance that it will be dismissed.

Claim 3 is a lawsuit from a customer for $1,600,000. According to the legal team, there is only a 30% chance that it will be dismissed in court. Accordingly, the company has made a settlement offer of $1,000,000 to the plaintiff, but the plaintiff has not yet responded to the settlement offer. The legal team believes there is a 40% chance the settlement will be accepted. If it is not accepted, the action will go to court, with a 30% chance of dismissal and a 70% chance of an $1,600,000 payout.

Required:

For each case, indicate the amount that should be recorded as a liability for the lawsuit. Assume that the payment period is relatively short so that discounting is not needed.

★ A12-10 Provision Measurement:

Fresh Products Ltd. is gathering evidence to support an accrual for warranty claims. The warranty is offered on three products sold to ensure that they operate as expected.

For Product 1, there are 75 warranty claims outstanding. One-third have a potential value of $1,000 each (90% of these will be paid, based on past history), one-third have a potential value of $5,000 each (70% of these will be paid), and one-third have a potential payout of $12,000 each (60% will be paid). The claims that are not paid are likely to be dismissed because of an expired warranty or incorrect statement of damages.

For Product 2, there are only nine claims outstanding; however, all are large, at $50,000 each. The experienced claims adjustor reviewing the files is completely confident that eight will be dismissed without any payment. For the remaining claim, there is a 60% chance that it will have to be paid in full and a 40% chance that it will be dismissed.

Product 3 has only one potential claim outstanding. The claim is for $1,000,000, and the adjustor believes that there is a 60% chance it will be dismissed, a 10% chance it will result in a payout of $1,000,000, and a 30% chance that there will be a payout of $200,000.

Required:

Indicate the amount that should be recorded as a warranty provision for each product.

 connect

★ A12-11 Provisions—Compensated Absences:

Tunacliff Mowers allows each employee to earn 15 fully paid vacation days each year. Unused vacation time can be carried over to the next year; if not taken during the next year, it is lost. By the end of 20X5, all but 3 of the 30 employees had taken their earned vacation time; these 3 carried over to 20X6 a total of 20 vacation days. These 20 days represented total 20X5 salary of $6,000. During 20X6, each of these three used their 20X5 vacation carryover; none of them had received a pay rate change from 20X5 to the time they used their carryover. Total cash wages paid: 20X5, $700,000; 20X6, $740,000.

Required:

1. Give the entries for Tunacliff related to vacations during 20X5 and 20X6. Disregard payroll taxes.
2. Compute the total amount of wage expense for 20X5 and 20X6. How would the vacation time carried over from 20X5 affect the 20X5 statement of financial position?

★ A12-12 Provisions—Warranty:

Review the financial statement extract provided below:

(amounts in thousands)	Provision for Warranty
Balance, 1 January 20X5	$1,062
Additional provision created	1,164
Utilized during the year	(690)
Unwinding of discount	80
Balance, 31 December 20X5	$1,616

Required:

1. In general, what is a provision?
2. Is this a current or both current and long-term warranty provision?
3. The provision for warranty might be a legal liability or a constructive liability. What is the meaning of "constructive liability" compared to a "legal liability"?
4. What is the meaning of the $1,164 "additional provision created"?
5. How would the $1,164 be measured, assuming a large population of potential claims?
6. What is the meaning of the $690 "utilized during the year"?
7. What is the meaning of the $80 "unwinding of discount"?

connect

★ ★ A12-13 Provisions—Warranty:

Consumer Corp. sells dishwashers and washing machines that come with a two-year unlimited warranty on parts and labour for repairs. The warranty is intended to assure customers that the appliances will operate as advertised. The warranty is expected to cost 2% of sales in the first year and 4% of sales in the second year, for a total of 6%. The provision for warranty has a credit balance of $145,000 at the beginning of 20X5. The following events and decisions relate to the warranty:

20X5	Sales revenue of $4,600,000 was generated from products covered by the warranty. Both the sale and the warranty provision must be recorded.
20X5	Warranty work consumed parts inventory with a cost of $9,000, and labour of $22,000.
20X6	Sales revenue from products covered by the warranty were $6,100,000. Both the sale and the warranty provision must be recorded.
20X6	Sales revenue of $6,100,000 was generated from products covered by the warranty. Warranty work consumed parts inventory with a cost of $126,000, and labour of $289,000
20X6	Year-end review indicated that the percentage used as an estimate for warranty work in 20X5 and 20X6 should have been a total of 8% of sales, rather than 6%.
20X6	Because of a specific prevalent defect to a seal discovered during repairs in 20X6, the company announced that it would cover repairs for this specific defect for a third year for all sales of product made in 20X5 and 20X6. The cost of this work was estimated to be 1% of sales. This is in excess of the percentage increase described above. Products were re-engineered to eliminate the defect starting in 20X7.

Required:

1. Prepare journal entries for the events listed above. Because of uncertainty of estimates, no discounting is to be applied.
2. Calculate the balance of the provision for warranty at 31 December 20X5 and 20X6.

★ ★ A12-14 Provisions—Warranty:

Garage Hardware Ltd. provides a product warranty for defects on two major lines of items sold since the beginning of 20X5. Line A carries a two-year warranty for parts and service, while Line B carries a three-year warranty for parts and service. The warranty cannot be purchased separately, and is intended to provide assurance to customers that the products will operate in accordance with the specifications provided. Garage contracts with a local service company to service the warranty on Line A, at a cost of $75 per unit payable at the date of sale. Garage performs its own warranty work for Line B. On the basis of experience, Garage estimates that warranty work costs 3% of sales for parts and 7% for labour and overhead for the entire three years; this cost is expected to be incurred 25% in Year 1, 10% in Year 2, and 65% in Year 3.

Data is as follows:

	20X5	20X6	20X7
Sales in units, Line A	700	1,000	none
Sales price per unit, Line A	$ 610	$ 660	
Sales in units, Line B	600	800	none
Sales price per unit, Line B	$ 700	$ 750	
Actual warranty outlays, Line B			
Parts	$3,000	$ 9,600	$12,000
Labour and overhead	7,000	22,000	30,000

Required:

1. Prepare journal entries for annual sales, expense, and warranty transactions for 20X5 to 20X7, inclusive. Because of uncertainty of estimates, no discounting is to be applied.
2. How much is warranty expense in each year from 20X5 to 20X7?
3. What is the balance in the provision for warranty at 31 December 20X5, 20X6, and 20X7?
4. What warranty work is left to do at the end of 20X7?

★★ A12-15 Discounting—No-Interest Note:

Bay Lake Mining Ltd. purchases earth-moving equipment on 1 August 20X6 and signs a three-year note with the supplier, agreeing to pay $425,000 on 31 July 20X9. There is no interest in the note. The equipment purchased does not have a readily determinable market value.

Required:

1. Does Bay Lake Mining Ltd. actually have a no-interest loan? Explain.
2. Calculate the present value of the note payable, using an interest rate of 6%.
3. Explain the factors that would be considered in determining the 6% discount rate.

4. Prepare a table that shows the balance of the note payable and interest expense over the life of the note.

5. Provide all entries for the note for 20X6 and 20X7. Record adjusting entries at the end of the fiscal year and on the anniversary date of the loan. Use the gross method.

6. Show the note payable (accounts and amounts) as it would be included on the statement of financial position at 31 December 20X6 and 20X7.

 ## A12-16 Discounting—Low-Interest Note:

Infinite Solutions Ltd. purchases inventory on 1 September 20X7 and signs a note with the supplier, agreeing to pay $90,000 on 31 August 20X9, plus annual interest at 2% each 31 August. The market interest rate for similar term and security is 8%. Assume also that the inventory purchased does not have a readily determinable market value. The company has a December 31 year end.

Required:

1. Calculate the present value of the note payable.

2. Prepare a table that shows the balance of the note payable and interest expense over the life of the note using the effective interest method.

3. Provide all entries for the note from 20X7 to 20X9. Use the gross method.

 ## A12-17 Discounting—Low-Interest Note:

On 1 January 20X9, a borrower signed a long-term note, face amount, $1,600,000; time to maturity, three years; stated rate of interest, 2%. The effective rate of interest of 6% determined the cash received by the borrower. The principal of the note will be paid at maturity; stated interest is due at the end of each year.

Required:

1. Compute the cash received by the borrower.

2. Give the required entries for the borrower for each of the three years. Use the effective interest method.

A12-18 Discounting—Provision:

In late September 20X6, Boothe Ltd. established a provision of $500,000 for a legal matter. The company expects the amount will be paid in late September 20X8. Timing can be estimated with certainty.

Required:

1. Why is discounting required?
2. Calculate the present value of the provision, using an interest rate of 7%.
3. Explain the factors that would be considered in determining the 7% discount rate.
4. Prepare a table that shows the balance of the provision and interest expense over the life of the liability.
5. Provide all entries for the provision for 20X6 through 20X8. Record adjusting entries at the end of the fiscal year and on the anniversary date of the provision. The estimated amount was paid to the plaintiff on 30 September 20X8.
6. Show the provision as it would be included on the statement of financial position at 31 December 20X6 and 20X7.
7. Explain how the accounting for this provision would change if the amounts and timing of cash outflows were highly uncertain.

eXcel

★ ★ A12-19 Discounting—Provision:

Silver Linings Ltd. commenced a mining operation in early 20X5. The company is required by the terms of provincial legislation to remediate the mine site when mining is completed, likely in five years' time. Silver Linings Ltd. estimates that this will cost $2,700,000. A reasonable market interest rate is 8%.

Required:

1. Calculate the present value of the decommissioning obligation.
2. Prepare a table that shows the balance of the provision and interest expense over the life of the liability.
3. Assume that at the end of 20X6, the company re-estimates that the cost of remediation at $3,400,000. Other assumptions are unchanged. Calculate the interest expense for 20X6, the new present value, and the adjustment to the obligation for the change in estimates. Also prepare a table that shows the balance of the provision and interest expense over the life of the liability.
4. Assume that at the end of 20X8, the company re-estimates that the cost of remediation at $2,900,000, and the market interest rate is now 7%. Calculate the interest expense for 20X8, the new present value, and the adjustment to the obligation for the change in estimates.
5. Calculate the balance of the decommissioning obligation at each 31 December, from 20X5 to 20X8.

eXcel

★ ★ A12-20 Discounting—Provision:

Homespun Resources Ltd was incorporated in 20X2 and is a mining operation operating in northern Alberta. The company is required by the terms of provincial legislation to remediate mine sites when mining is completed. The following events and decisions with respect to operations relate to Homespun's decommissioning obligations:

January 20X2	Commenced mining on Site 1; expected duration of operations is three years, and site remediation is expected to be $500,000 at that time. Decommissioning obligation is recorded. A reasonable interest rate is 7%.
30 September 20X2	Commenced mining on Site 2; expected duration of operations is five years, and site remediation is expected to be $1,200,000 at that time. Decommissioning obligation is recorded. A reasonable interest rate is 7%.
31 December 20X2	Interest on decommissioning obligation for Site 1 and Site 2 is recorded.
30 September 20X3	Interest on decommissioning obligation for Site 2 is recorded, on the anniversary date of the mine opening.
31 December 20X3	Interest on decommissioning obligation for Site 1 and Site 2 is recorded. Site 1 is now estimated to close in two years' time (rather than the one remaining year expected) and remediation costs are anticipated to increase by 30%.
30 September 20X4	Interest on decommissioning obligation for Site 2 is recorded, on the anniversary date of the mine opening. Site 2 is now estimated to close in two years (rather than the three remaining years expected) and remediation is now estimated at $900,000.
31 December 20X4	Interest on decommissioning obligation for Site 1 and Site 2 is recorded.

Required:

1. Prepare journal entries for the events listed above.
2. Calculate the balance of the decommissioning obligation at each 31 December, from 20X2 to 20X4.

A12-21 Classification and Statement of Cash Flows:

GYO Ltd. reports the following amounts on its statement of cash flows:

	20X5	20X4
Trade accounts payable	$1,706,300	$1,423,000
Dividends payable	50,000	—
Provision for restructuring	260,000	—
Provision for coupon refunds	45,000	10,000

Decommissioning obligation	52,500	46,500
Note payable, 8%	400,000	—
Note payable, net, 6%	68,500	—

Other information:

- The 8% note payable is a bank loan due in 20X6, but negotiations for its renewal are taking place. Interest of $32,000 was paid at year-end.

- The provision for restructuring is based on the company's plan to reduce its workforce in 20X6, according to a plan approved by the board of directors. The provision for restructuring is the estimated severance amounts that will be paid to employees affected by the restructuring.

- The decommissioning obligation relates to a leased premises that must be remediated at the end of the lease term in 20X9. The change in this account this year is due to interest.

- The 6% note payable reflects market interest rates at issuance but is, in fact, a no-interest, five-year note payable arranged with a supplier, for a piece of equipment. The note was originally recorded at its discounted amount of $89,000. Interest of $4,000 was recorded in 20X5.

- Dividends of $140,000 were declared during the year.

GYO uses the indirect method of presentation in the operating activities section of the statement of cash flows and follows the policy of reporting dividends paid in financing activities. Interest paid is included in operating activities.

Required:

1. For each item above, indicate whether the balance would be reported as a current or a long-term liability. For the 8% note payable, what condition must be met by year-end to ensure that the note may be classified as long term?

2. List the items as they would appear on the statement of cash flows in 20X5. Include the amount, description, and classification.

 connect

★ ★ A12-22 Statement of Cash Flows:

Sing Imports Corp. reports the following amounts on its statement of cash flows:

	20X2	20X1
Trade accounts payable	$506,300	$699,600
Dividends payable	10,000	25,000
Provision for litigation	260,000	100,000

Decommissioning obligation	112,700	106,000
Note payable, 5%	400,000	600,000
Note payable, net, 6%	66,500	62,100

Other information:

- Dividends of $100,000 were declared during the year.
- The provision for litigation is based on outstanding legal claims. The amount is not discounted because of uncertainty of cash flow amounts and timing. The provision was increased this year because of new lawsuits filed against the company.
- The decommissioning obligation relates to a leased premises that must be remediated at the end of the lease term. The change in this account this year is due to unwinding the discount.
- The 5% note payable is a bank loan at market interest rates. Interest of $30,000 was paid at year-end.
- The 6% note payable reflects market interest rates at issuance but is, in fact, a no-interest, multi-year liability associated with inventory purchase. The change in the account relates to unwinding the discount.

Sing uses the indirect method of presentation in the operating activities section of the statement of cash flows and follows the policy of reporting dividends paid in financing activities; interest paid is included in operating activities.

Required:

List the items as they would appear on the statement of cash flows in 20X2. Include the amount, description, and classification.

 ## A12-23 Liabilities—ASPE:

Gaudet Industries Ltd. has a $5,000,000 note payable outstanding. The terms of the note require repayment of principal on 30 June 20X2. The company is now finalizing the financial statements for the year ended 31 December 20X1. In January 20X2, before the financial statements are released, the company comes to an agreement with the lender to refinance the liability, with the new due date 30 June 20X5.

Gaudet also has committed to donate $200,000 to support the provincial snowboarding association race programs for the year. No donation agreement has yet been signed, but a public announcement has been made, and the company and snowboarding association have met and agreed to the races the funding will support for the season, and promotion of Gaudet Industries Ltd. through its website.

Required:

1. If Gaudet complies with IFRS, will this note payable be classified as current or long-term liability as at 31 December 20X1?
2. If Gaudet complies with IFRS, will the $200,000 amount be recorded as a liability? Explain.
3. Repeat requirements 1 and 2, assuming that Gaudet complies with ASPE.

 **A12-24 Liabilities—ASPE:**

Return to the facts of A12-16.

Required:

1. Repeat the assignment question, using straight-line amortization of the discount.
2. Which method of discount amortization provides the more accurate measure of interest expense? Why does ASPE allow use of straight-line amortization?

 **A12-25 Liabilities—ASPE:**

Return to the facts of A12-17.

Required:

1. Repeat the assignment question, using straight-line amortization of the discount.
2. Which method of discount amortization provides the more accurate measure of interest expense? Why does ASPE allow use of straight-line amortization?

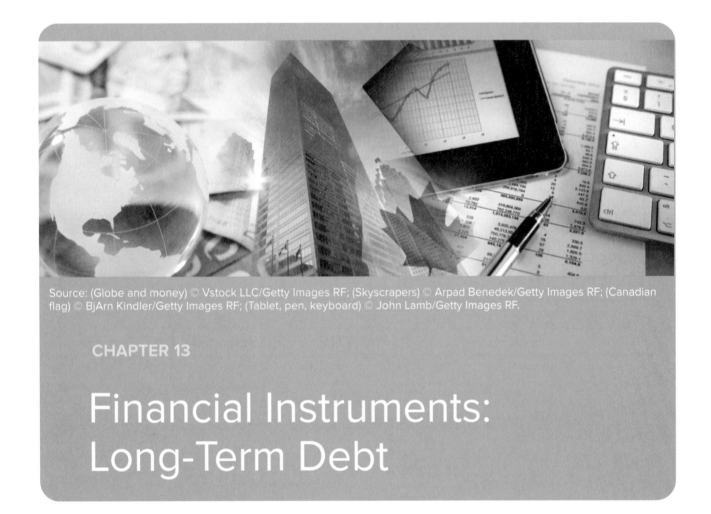

Source: (Globe and money) © Vstock LLC/Getty Images RF; (Skyscrapers) © Arpad Benedek/Getty Images RF; (Canadian flag) © BjArn Kindler/Getty Images RF; (Tablet, pen, keyboard) © John Lamb/Getty Images RF.

CHAPTER 13

Financial Instruments: Long-Term Debt

INTRODUCTION

Long-term debt is a significant source of financing for many companies. The lender becomes a significant stakeholder in the company for a lengthy period of time. Obviously, the lender is an important user of the financial statements. The terms of these loans, including the requirement to pay not only interest and principal but also terms regarding security and covenants, are meant to limit, or at least define, the risks that the lender accepts. In all cases, some risk remains; lenders will use the financial statements as well as other information to evaluate the liquidity, solvency, and financial performance of the companies in which they have invested.

Hydro One Inc. is responsible for the transmission and distribution of electricity to customers in Ontario. In 2014, the company reported over $22 billion in total assets and a massive $8.9 billion in long-term debt. It has 25 different financial instruments listed as long-term debt, with various interest rates, due dates, and conditions. Obviously, the company has a large group of lenders, and its financial statements are carefully scrutinized by all.

Reporting long-term debt in the financial statements requires appropriate accounting for issuance and retirement. In addition, derecognition prior to maturity can create major changes in the financial statements. Measurement of annual interest cost is critical, and there are some circumstances that require borrowing costs to be capitalized rather than expensed. Remember, debt transactions often involve millions of dollars at a time. As a result, in all accounting measurements and policies, the amounts are material, and the stakes are high.

This chapter reviews common sources of debt financing. The technical elements of accounting for long-term debt—issuance, interest measurement, and derecognition—are reviewed using bonds payable as a base. Chapter 14 moves on to equity transactions, but Chapter 15 returns to more complex debt arrangements that combine attributes of both debt and equity.

SOURCES OF FINANCING

The discussion that follows provides a review of common forms of financing, which are summarized in Exhibit 13-1.

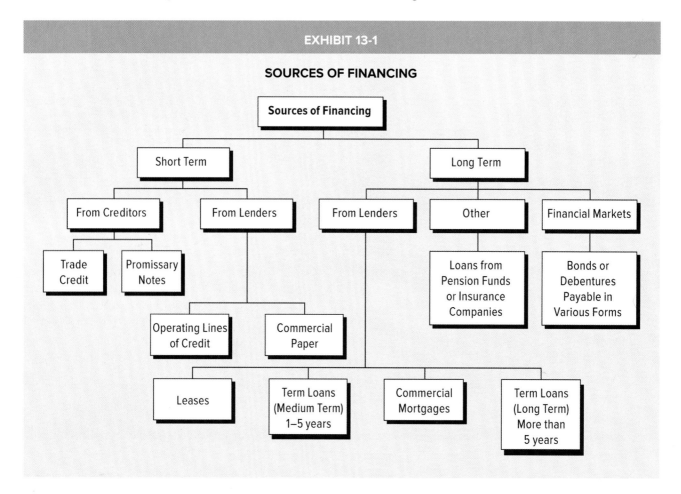

EXHIBIT 13-1

SOURCES OF FINANCING

Short-Term Financing

Trade Credit

The most obvious source of short-term financing is through the trade credit extended by suppliers. Some corporations use trade creditor financing to its fullest extent as a source of "interest-free" financing, sometimes stretching the ethical boundaries of business practice. For example, large corporations may rely on their purchasing power and their "clout" as big customers of smaller suppliers to put off paying their trade accounts payable.

Some purchases are made by signing promissory notes that obligate the company to pay a supplier (or an intermediary, e.g., a financial institution) at or before a given date. Promissory notes are legally enforceable negotiable instruments. The notes may bear interest, or they may be non-interest-bearing. The use of notes for trade purchases is particularly common in international trade, since the financial institutions that act as intermediaries are better placed to enforce payment.

Short-Term Bank Loans

Like individuals, Canadian business entities borrow from chartered banks. Lending arrangements can be classified according to term and security.

Short-term loans to business entities usually take the form of **operating lines of credit**. These loans are granted to help finance working capital and typically are secured by a lien or charge on accounts receivable and inventory. There normally is a gap between the time that cash is paid to suppliers for inventory and the time that money is received from customers who, in the end, buy the inventory. Businesses can use equity funds to finance this cash flow, but receivables and inventories are reasonable collateral for loans, and it is typically cheaper to borrow for this purpose. The interest rate on bank lines of credit is usually flexible and is based on the cost of funds for the financial institution.

There is typically a limit on working capital loans, expressed as a percentage of the collateral base. For example, a business may have an operating line of credit (also called a **credit facility**) that allows the company to borrow up to 75% of the net realizable value of accounts receivable and 50% of the book value of inventory. These loans will increase and decrease in seasonal businesses, following the ebb and flow of the business cycle.

Operating lines of credit are due on *demand*, which means that if the lender gives the borrower appropriate notice, usually a few business days, the loans must be repaid immediately. In practice, repayment is not normally demanded unless the amount of collateral declines or the company otherwise violates some aspect of the loan agreement.

Despite their "due on demand" status, lines of credit often are a permanent fixture in a company's financial structure. The credit facility may be attached to the business's current account (i.e., the business chequing account) and drawn on as an *overdraft*. Companies use such loans as part of their cash management strategies.

Large corporations that have good credit ratings can issue *commercial paper*, which is a type of short-term promissory note that is sold (through a financial intermediary, again usually a bank) in open markets. The issuer of commercial paper does not know who the purchaser is, and settlement at the due date is through the financial intermediary.

Commercial paper is meant to be issued by only very stable companies. In the liquidity crunch that spiked in 2007, some asset-backed commercial paper (ABCP) turned out to be highly risky because the issuers lacked liquid resources to repay the loans. Under a court-supervised restructuring program, ABCP obligations were replaced with notes payable of varying maturities, some reasonably long term. One of the criteria for issuing ABCP is an excellent credit rating; the credit rating agencies were severely criticized for their role in the ABCP episode because hindsight showed that the issuers were not as stable as needed.

A final type of short-term financing that merits mention is the sale or assignment of a company's receivables to a financial institution. This represents another way current assets can be used as a source of short-term financing.

Long-Term Financing

Long-term loans are often an attractive means of financing for the borrower compared with either short-term debt or equity. These loans are appealing because:

- Short-term financing may not be available from period to period, and the cost may be higher than for long-term debt;
- Long-term lenders are not shareholders, and do not acquire voting privileges over the borrower, so issuance of debt causes no ownership dilution;
- Debt capital is obtained more easily than equity capital for many companies, especially private companies;
- Interest expense, unlike dividends, is tax deductible; and
- A firm that earns a return on borrowed funds that exceeds the rate it must pay in interest is using debt to its advantage and is said to be successfully levered (or leveraged).

Leverage is risky. If sales or earnings decline, interest expense becomes an increasing percentage of earnings. Business failure may be the result of carrying high debt levels in expectation of high sales and profits. If sales and profits (and operating cash flows) do not materialize, overlevered companies soon find themselves in financial difficulty. Firms often attempt to restructure their debt by extending maturity dates or requesting a reduction in principal or interest.

Debt is an attractive investment for *investors (lenders)* because it provides legally enforceable debt payments, eventual return of principal, and a priority claim to assets if the corporation restructures its debt or if it goes into receivership or bankruptcy. Creditors can further reduce their risk by extending secured debt, where the obligation is contractually tied to specific assets that the creditor can seize in the event of the debtor's default.

Long-term debt can take a wide variety of forms, including:

- Bank loans;
- Notes payable;
- Mortgages;

- Other asset-backed loans;
- Publicly issued bonds, secured or unsecured; and
- Long-term leases.

Long-term leases are the subject of Chapter 18. Other forms of financing are discussed in this chapter. More inventive forms of financing that have at least some of the characteristics of long-term debt are discussed in Chapter 15.

Long-Term Bank Financing

Long-term loans could be *term loans* or *commercial mortgages*. **Term loans** might better be characterized as *medium-term* loans because they are usually for periods of 1.5 to 5 years. Banks will lend for this medium term if there is appropriate collateral, such as tangible capital assets (e.g., equipment, land, or buildings). Land and buildings would also qualify for longer-term loans. Security is lodged in the form of a claim on the item of property, plant, or equipment. At the end of the loan term, after all the payments have been made, the security is released. The repayment terms of medium-term loans can be structured in either of two ways:

1. *Blended payments.* The interest rate is fixed at the beginning of the loan term, and regular equal annuity payments are made, which include both principal and interest. For example, a $1,000,000, five-year loan at an interest rate of 7% could be repaid in five annual instalments of $243,891 [$1,000,000 ÷ (P/A, 7%, 5)]. Each payment includes some interest and some principal.

2. *Designated monthly principal payments, plus accrued interest on the outstanding balance.* The interest rate may be *fixed* at the beginning of the loan term or may *float* with prime interest rates. The borrower makes an interest payment at the end of every month, based on the loan balance for that month and the interest rate in effect. In addition, the borrower and lender work out a repayment scheme for the principal that will fully repay the loan by the end of its term. The payment terms may require equal monthly, quarterly, or semi-annual principal payments (plus interest), or lump-sum payments following a busy season. Sometimes there is a large final lump-sum payment required; this is known as a *balloon payment.*

For accounting purposes, interest is accrued as time passes and is paid when due. If principal and interest payments are *blended*, the portion of each payment that represents principal is recorded as a reduction of the loan. Alternatively, if designated lump-sum principal payments are made, these are recorded as a direct reduction of the loan. Medium-term loans are classified as long term on the borrower's statement of financial position, although the principal portion due within one year or operating cycle is classified as a current liability.

Long-Term Loans

Long-term loans, *in the eyes of the lenders*, are loans with repayment terms extending beyond five years. Financial institutions typically grant such loans as *asset-based financing* or as *commercial mortgages*. Commercial mortgages are secured against land and buildings and involve regular blended payments (e.g., monthly or bimonthly). The amortization period of such loans could be for as long as 25 years, but the term, or the lender's commitment to extending the loan at the given interest rate arrangement, is usually a shorter period. The term normally will not exceed five years and may be shorter. The lender is under no obligation to renew the loan at the end of the term if it is not satisfied with the creditworthiness of the borrower.

When a long-term loan is extended at a fixed interest rate, the interest rate is fixed only for the term of the loan, not for the entire amortization period. The interest rate is reset at the beginning of each term. For example, a business could arrange a 25-year (amortization period) mortgage with a five-year term. Blended payments would be devised to repay all principal after 25 years, but the interest rate would be reset after every five years. The blended payments would be recalculated and could go up if interest rates increased or down if rates decreased.

For example, assume that Medical Arts Building Ltd. reported a mortgage in its 30 September 20X9 disclosure notes as follows:

6.75% mortgage loan, repayable at $18,880 per month, including principal and interest, due 1 April 20X11 $2,213,335

Security for the mortgage consists of land and buildings, an assignment of insurance proceeds, and a general assignment of rents and leases.

The end of the *term* is 1 April 20X11, but *the amortization period* is 25 years. The mortgage would not be fully repaid at the end of the *term*, since the $18,880 blended monthly payments are not high enough to achieve this. Repayment amounts and interest rates would be renegotiated at the end of each term.

Long-term loans with a floating interest rate can also be arranged. Floating-rate loans normally provide for an adjustment of the interest rate (and the monthly payment) at six-month intervals. The blended payments for the next six months are recalculated at that time. Like fixed-rate loans, the term of a floating-rate loan is limited so that the lender can periodically reassess the risk of the loan.

Other Sources of Long-Term Debt

For small and most medium-sized private companies, the chartered banks are the major source of financing. However, large companies (both public and private) have other sources of financing available. Larger corporations can arrange loans with life insurance companies or pension funds, which have money to invest for long periods of time.

Bonds or Debentures Payable

A bond (or **debenture**) is a debt security issued by a corporation or government to secure large amounts of capital on a long-term basis. A bond represents a formal promise by the issuing organization to pay principal and interest in return for the capital invested.

A formal bond agreement, known as a **bond indenture**, specifies the terms of the bond and the rights and duties of both the issuer and the bond holder. The indenture specifies any restrictions on the issuing company, the dollar amount authorized for issuance, the interest rate and payment dates, the maturity date, and any conversion and call privileges. An independent trustee is appointed to protect the interests of both the issuer and the investors. The trustee (usually a financial institution) maintains the necessary records and disburses interest and principal. The investors receive bond certificates, which represent the contractual obligations of the issuer to the investors.

Debt Covenants

Debt agreements often restrict the operations and financial structure of the borrower to reduce the risk of default. **Debt covenants** are restrictions placed on a corporation's activities as a condition of maintaining the loan. If the covenants are broken, the lender has the right to call the loan: The lender can demand immediate repayment of the principal. Bankers also refer to covenants as *maintenance tests*. Restrictions can be either accounting based or behavioural (restricted actions). Examples of each type are as follows:

Accounting-based Covenants

- Maximum debt to equity ratio or debt-to-assets (often called debt-to-capitalization);
- Minimum current ratio; and
- Minimum interest coverage ratio, often based on **EBITDA** (earnings before interest, tax, depreciation, and amortization).

Restricted Actions

- Limitations on the issuance of additional debt without the permission of the lender;
- Restrictions on dividend payments;
- Prohibition or restriction on the redemption or retirement of shares;
- Limitations on the ability of the company to pledge assets as security for other purposes;
- Requirement that current management or key employees remain in place; and
- Limitations on transfer of control.

Reporting Example

The following information has been extracted from the financial statements of Bombardier Inc. These disclosures come from Note 26, Long-Term Debt; and Note 30, Credit Facilities. These notes also include extensive disclosures, not repeated here, on the terms and condition of debt. Note the wide range of financing sources that the company uses and the company's debt covenants for its credit facilities.

26. LONG-TERM DEBT

Long-term debt was as follows, as at:

	Amount in currency of origin	Currency	Contractual[1]	Interest rate After effect of fair value hedges	Maturity	December 31 2014 Amount	December 31 2013 Amount	January 1 2013 Amount
Senior notes	750	USD	4.25%	n/a	Jan. 2016	$ 746	$ 742	$ —
	650	USD	7.50%	3-month Libor + 4.19	Mar. 2018	686	695	724
	600	USD	4.75%	n/a	Apr. 2019	593	—	—
	850	USD	7.75%	3-month Libor + 4.14	Mar. 2020	922	915	978
	780	EUR	6.13%	3-month Euribor + 2.87[6]	May 2021	1,110	1,187	1,183
	500	USD	5.75%	3-month Libor + 3.37	Mar. 2022	504	478	492
	1,200	USD	6.00%	3-month Libor + 3.56	Oct. 2022	1,219	—	—
	1,250	USD	6.13%	3-month Libor + 3.50	Jan. 2023	1,277	1,200	—
	785[5]	EUR	7.25%	3-month Libor+ 4.83	n/a	—	1,171	1,162
Notes	250	USD	7.45%	n/a	May 2034	248	248	247
	162	USD	6.30%	3-month Libor + 1.59	n/a	—	164	171
Debentures	150	CAD	7.35%	n/a	Dec. 2026	129	140	150
Other[2]	Various[3]	Various	Various[3]	n/a	2015-2026	249	263	298
						$ 7,683	$ 7,203	$ 5,405

Of which current[4]	**$ 56**	$ 215	$ 45
Of which non-current	**7,627**	6,988	5,360
	$ 7,683	$ 7,203	$ 5,405

30. CREDIT FACILITIES

Letter of credit facilities

The letter of credit facilities and their maturities were as follows, as at:

	Amount committed	Letters of credit issued	Amount available	Maturity
December 31, 2014				
BT facility	**$ 4,249** [1]	**$ 3,573**	**$ 676**	**2018** [2]
BA facility	**600**	**261**	**339**	**2017** [3]
PSG facility	**600**	**327**	**273**	**2015** [4]
	$ 5,449	**$ 4,161**	**$ 1,288**	
December 31, 2013				
BT facility	$ 4,827 [1]	$ 4,132	$ 695	2018
BA facility	600	403	197	2016
PSG facility	600	393	207	2014 [4]
	$ 6,027	$ 4,928	$ 1,099	
January 1, 2013				
BT facility	$ 4,486 [1]	$ 3,291	$ 1,195	2017
BA facility	600	430	170	2015
PSG facility	900	339	561	2013 [4]
	$ 5,986	$ 4,060	$ 1,926	

Financial covenants

The Corporation is subject to various financial covenants under the BA and BT letter of credit facilities and the two unsecured revolving credit facilities, which must be met on a quarterly basis. The BA letter of credit and revolving credit facility include financial covenants requiring a minimum EBITDA to fixed charges ratio, as well as a maximum net debt to EBITDA ratio, all calculated based on an adjusted consolidated basis i.e. excluding BT. The BT letter of credit and BT revolving credit facility include financial covenants requiring minimum equity as well as a maximum debt to EBITDA ratio, all calculated based on BT stand-alone financial data. These terms and ratios are defined in the respective agreements and do not correspond to the Corporation's global metrics as described in Note 31 – Capital management or to the specific terms used in the MD&A. In addition, the Corporation must maintain a minimum BT liquidity of €600 million ($728 million) and a minimum BA liquidity of $500 million at the end of each quarter. These conditions were all met as at December 31, 2014 and 2013 and January 1, 2013.

The Corporation regularly monitors these ratios to ensure it meets all financial covenants, and has controls in place to ensure that contractual covenants are met.

Source: Bombardier Inc., or its subsidiaries, 2014 Audited annual financial statements, pages 157, 164, 165, www.sedar.com, posted 12 February 2015.

CONCEPT REVIEW

1. What assets are most commonly used as security for operating lines of credit?
2. What are the advantages of long-term debt over equity financing?
3. What is the difference between the *term* and *amortization period* for a commercial mortgage?
4. What is a debt covenant?

DEBT ISSUANCE AND INTEREST EXPENSE

Accounting for long-term debt will be illustrated in the context of bonds payable, since bonds are a common form of long-term debt.

Classification

Bonds payable are *financial instruments* and are classified as *other financial liabilities. A bond is initially valued at fair value,* which is the cash received, netted with transaction costs. A bond is then carried at this value (which is cost on the date of acquisition) and then at *amortized cost* over its term. That is, the initial fair value is the cash received when the bond is issued, which is based on a present value model. Transaction costs, such as upfront fees, are capitalized or netted with this amount, which reduces the amount. If this amount is not the par value, or maturity value, the difference is amortized and recorded over the life of the bond.

Bond Valuation

Fair value is established as the present value of all future cash payments discounted using the *effective interest rate,* also called the *market yield rate,* or the **incremental borrowing rate (IBR)**. The effective interest rate is *the borrower's interest rate for additional debt of similar term and risk.* Discounting was illustrated in Chapter 12 and is an important valuation model for long-term liabilities, such as bonds.

Remember that the *nominal interest rate* is the interest rate stated in the bond agreement. The **effective interest rate**, or **yield**, is the true cost of borrowing. The discounted amount, which is fair value and the proceeds on issuing a bond payable, is:

$P = [I \times (P/A, i, n)] + [F \times (P/F, i, n)]$, where

P = fair value of the bond payable; issuance proceeds on issuance date;

I = dollar amount of each period's interest payment, or

  = nominal rate × the bond face value

F = maturity value of the bond

n = the number of periods to maturity

i = the market interest rate

When a bond pays the effective market interest rate, the bond will be issued for its face value or par value, or maturity amount. When the nominal and market interest rates are different, price of the bond (issue proceeds) will be greater or less than the maturity amount, and a premium or discount will be recognized.

Fair Value after Issuance

After issuance, the bond may be bought and sold between different investors. The bond will trade at its *current fair value*. This is a discounted amount, using a market yield rate that reflects updated assessment of both *company risk* and *market yield*. The number of interest periods, *n*, reflects the *remaining* life of the bond. If the yield rate, *i*, rises, the discounted amount will decline, and if the yield rate decreases, the discounted amount will be higher.

Measurement of Interest Expense

Accounting for long-term debt is straightforward if the effective interest rate and the nominal interest rate are the same. If these two rates are the same, the liability is issued at its maturity value. Interest is accrued as time passes, and interest payments are accounted for as cash is disbursed. Cash amounts correctly state the liability amount and interest expense.

If the nominal interest rate is *different* from the market interest rate at the time the note is issued, the *discount rate* is used to measure interest expense over the life of the liability. The initial discount or premium is reduced to zero, or *amortized to interest expense*, over the life of the liability. This is also called *unwinding* the discount or premium. The net liability is carried on the statement of financial position (SFP) at amortized cost or par value combined with the discount or premium.

Example

To illustrate accounting for bonds payable, assume that on 1 January 20X5, Gresham Ltd., a calendar-year firm, issues $100,000 of 7% debentures dated 1 January 20X5, with interest paid each 31 December. The bonds mature on 31 December 20X9. Note the simplifying assumptions: This bond is for only a five-year term and pays interest *annually* at the end of Gresham's fiscal year.

1. The **face value** or *par value* (also called *maturity*, or *principal value*) of a bond is the amount payable when the bond is due ($100,000 for Gresham).

2. The **maturity date** is the end of the bond term and the due date for the face value (31 December 20X9, for Gresham).

3. The **nominal interest rate** (also called the *coupon, stated,* or *contractual rate*) is the rate that determines periodic interest payments. For Gresham, the nominal rate is 7%, paid annually.

4. The **interest payment dates** are the dates the periodic interest payments are due (31 December for Gresham). Gresham pays $7,000 interest on the $100,000 bond on each 31 December regardless of the issue price or market rate of interest at date of issue.

5. The **bond date** (authorization date) is the earliest date the bond can be issued and represents the planned issuance date of the bond issue (1 January 20X5 for Gresham).

Three situations will illustrate accounting for bonds, under different effective interest rate assumptions. (Always assume that the effective interest rate is quoted for compounding periods identical to those offered by the bond unless told otherwise.)

- Situation A: Effective interest rate = 7%
- Situation B: Effective interest rate = 6%
- Situation C: Effective interest rate = 8%

Situation A

The bond will sell at face value because the market and stated interest rates are both 7%. The price of the bonds will be equal to the present value of the future cash flows at the market rate of 7%:

$$\text{Issue price} = [\$100,000 \times (P/F, 7\%, 5)] + [(\$100,000 \times 7\%) \times (P/A, 7\%, 5)]$$
$$= \$100,000$$

When the bonds are issued, the issuer records a long-term liability, and interest is recorded as time passes. The bond is repaid at maturity.

1 January 20X5—issue bonds		
Cash	100,000	
Bonds payable		100,000
31 December each year, 20X5 through 20X9—interest payment		
Interest expense	7,000	
Cash ($100,000 × 7%)		7,000
31 December 20X9—bond maturity		
Bonds payable	100,000	
Cash		100,000

Interest expense for bonds issued at face value equals the amount of the interest payment. The book value of the bonds remains $100,000 to maturity. Changes in the fair market value of the bond, *caused by changes in the yield rate subsequent to the issuance date*, are not recognized in the financial statements but are disclosed.

Situation B

The market rate of interest is 6%; the bonds sell at a premium.

$$\text{Issue price} = [\$100,000 \times (P/F, 6\%, 5)] + [(\$100,000 \times 7\%) \times (P/A, 6\%, 5)]$$
$$= \$104,213$$

The bonds sell at a *premium* because they pay a stated rate that exceeds the market rate on similar bonds. The initial $4,213 premium is recorded in an account titled *premium on bonds payable*, which is shown with the bonds payable account on the statement of financial position.[1] The following entry is made to record the issue:

---

1. If a premium or discount is recorded separately, recording follows the *gross method*. The premium or discount is shown with the bond on the SFP. Alternatively, the *net method* may be used. Under the net method, one account may be used for both the par value and the premium or discount, mimicking the financial reporting treatment in the general ledger. Text examples will reflect the gross method.

1 January 20X5—issue bonds		
Cash	104,213	
Bonds payable		100,000
Premium on bonds payable		4,213

Total interest expense over the term of a bond is *not* equal to total cash interest when a bond is sold at a premium or discount. Instead, interest expense must equal the total cash payments required by the bond (face value and interest) less the aggregate issue price. Total interest expense is shown by this calculation:

Face value	$100,000
Total cash interest: 7% × $100,000 × 5 years	35,000
Total cash payments required by bond	135,000
Issue price	104,213
Total interest expense over bond term ($35,000 − $4,213)	$ 30,787

Gresham received $4,213 more than face value at issuance but will pay only face value at maturity. Therefore, the effective rate is less than the stated rate, and total interest expense for Gresham over the bond term is *less* than total interest paid.

Premium or Discount Recognition

The premium or discount must be completely recognized (*unwound* or *amortized*), over the bond term using the *effective-interest method*, so that net book value equals face value at maturity. Amortized premium reduces periodic interest expense to an amount less than interest paid, and amortized discount increases interest expense over the cash interest paid. The net bond liability equals face value *plus* the remaining unamortized bond premium or *less* the remaining unamortized bond discount. The following entries illustrate unwinding a premium:

31 December 20X5		
Interest expense ($104,213 × 6%)	6,253	
Premium on bonds payable	747	
Cash ($100,000 × 7%)		7,000
The carrying value of the bond is now $103,466		
($104,213 − $747)		
31 December 20X6		
Interest expense ($103,466 × 6%)	6,208	
Premium on bonds payable	792	
Cash		7,000
The carrying value of the bond is now $102,674		
($103,466 − $792)		

Interest expense under the effective-interest method is the product of the effective interest rate (6%) and the net liability balance at the beginning of the period. In effect, the company returns part of the original "excess" proceeds with each interest payment. In 20X5, this amount is $747, which reduces the net bond liability at the beginning of 20X6. Consequently, 20X6 interest expense is less than that for 20X5.

The bonds are listed on the 31 December 20X6 SFP as a long-term liability:

Bonds payable	$100,000
Premium on bonds payable ($4,213 − $747 − $792)	2,674
Net book value of bonds payable	$102,674

Proof of Book Value

The book value of the bonds at 31 December 20X6 is the present value of remaining cash flows *using the effective interest rate at the date of issuance:*

$$PV_{31/12/20X6} = [\$100,000 \times (P/F, 6\%, 3)] + [(\$100,000 \times 7\%) \times (P/A, 6\%, 3)]$$
$$= \$102,674$$

Amortization Table

An amortization table is often prepared to support bond accounting. The table gives all the data necessary for journal entries over the term of the bond and each year's ending net liability balance. An amortization table is shown in Exhibit 13-2.

EXHIBIT 13-2

AMORTIZATION TABLE FOR GRESHAM LIMITED BONDS

Situation B—Bonds Sold at Premium; Effective-Interest Amortization

Date	Interest Payment at 7%	Interest Expense at 6%	Premium Amortization[1]	Unamortized Premium[2]	Net Bond Liability[3]
1 Jan. 20X5				$4,213	$104,213
31 Dec. 20X5	$ 7,000	$ 6,253	$ 747	3,466	103,466
31 Dec. 20X6	7,000	6,208	792	2,674	102,674
31 Dec. 20X7	7,000	6,160	840	1,834	101,834
31 Dec. 20X8	7,000	6,110	890	944	100,944
31 Dec. 20X9	7,000	6,056	944	0	100,000
	$35,000	$30,787	$4,213		

[1] Interest payment − Interest expense

[2] Previous unamortized premium − Current period's amortization

[3] $100,000 face value + Current unamortized premium

Situation C

The market rate of interest is 8%; the bonds sell at a discount.

$$\text{Issue price} = [\$100{,}000 \times (P/F, 8\%, 5)] + [(\$100{,}000 \times 7\%) \times (P/A, 8\%, 5)]$$
$$= \$96{,}007$$

The Gresham bonds sell at a discount in this case because the stated rate is less than the yield rate on similar bonds. The discount is recorded in the discount on bonds payable account, a contra-liability valuation account, which is subtracted from bonds payable to yield the net liability. The entries for the first two years after the bond issuance follow, along with an amortization table (Exhibit 13-3) and the relevant portion of the SFP after two years.

EXHIBIT 13-3

AMORTIZATION TABLE FOR GRESHAM LIMITED BONDS

Situation C—Bonds Sold at Discount: Effective-Interest Amortization

Date	Interest Payment at 7%	Interest Expense at 8%	Discount Amortization[1]	Unamortized Discount[2]	Net Bond Liability[3]
1 Jan. 20X5				$3,993	$ 96,007
31 Dec. 20X5	$ 7,000	$ 7,681	$ 681	3,312	96,688
31 Dec. 20X6	7,000	7,735	735	2,577	97,423
31 Dec. 20X7	7,000	7,794	794	1,783	98,217
31 Dec. 20X8	7,000	7,857	857	926	99,074
31 Dec. 20X9	7,000	7,926	926	0	100,000
	$35,000	$38,993	$3,993		

[1] Interest expense – Interest payment

[2] Previous unamortized discount – Current period's amortization

[3] $100,000 face value – Current unamortized discount

Journal entries:

1 January 20X5—issue bonds		
Cash	96,007	
Discount on bonds payable	3,993	
Bonds payable		100,000

31 December 20X5—interest expense		
Interest expense ($96,007 × 8%)	7,681	
Discount on bonds payable		681
Cash ($100,000 × 7%)		7,000
31 December 20X6—interest expense		
Interest expense [($96,007 + $681) × 8%]	7,735	
Discount on bonds payable		735
Cash ($100,000 × 7%)		7,000

SFP presentation:

31 December 20X6	
Bonds payable	$100,000
Discount on bonds payable ($3,993 − 681 − 735)	(2,577)
Net book value of bonds payable	$ 97,423

Summary

Exhibit 13-4 summarizes several aspects of bond accounting. The exhibit relates to bonds with semi-annual interest payments, which is the usual situation.

EXHIBIT 13-4

SUMMARY TABLE: ACCOUNTING FOR BONDS ASSUMING SEMI-ANNUAL INTEREST PAYMENTS

Fair value of bonds = Present value of the cash flow to the investor
= Discounted principal payments + Discounted interest payment annuity
= [(Face value) × (P/F, i, n)] + [(Face value × s) × (P/A, i, n)]

Where: i = effective interest rate *per six-month period*
n = number of semi-annual periods in bond term
s = stated (nominal) interest rate per six-month period

Discount or premium =

When effective rate (i) exceeds stated rate (s):

Initial discount = Face value − Price of bond issue

When stated rate (s) exceeds effective rate (i):

Initial premium = Price of bond issue − Face value

Net book value of bonds = Face value *plus* unamortized premium or *minus* unamortized discount

As Maturity Approaches:	Premium	Discount
The unamortized amount	Declines	Declines
The net book value	Declines	Increases
Annual interest expense, using	Declines	Increases effective-interest method

Interest Measurement:

Effective-Interest Method

Calculations:

Calculation of interest expense	Effective rate × Net carrying value of bond
Calculation of discount or premium amortization	Difference between cash paid and expense

Patterns:

Annual interest expense	Changes each year
Annual interest expense as a	Constant over term

percentage of beginning *book value* of the bond (interest rate)

Interest Payment Dates Different from Statement Dates

In the preceding situations, all specified interest payment dates coincided with the fiscal year-end. However, this coincidence is not frequent in practice. When the end of a fiscal period falls between interest payment dates, it is necessary to accrue interest from the last (previous) interest payment date, and to bring the bond discount/premium amortization up to date.

For example, assume the facts for Situation C for Gresham Ltd. bonds, except that the fiscal year-end is 30 September. The bonds are issued on the bond date, 1 January 20X5, and interest is payable annually on 31 December. On 30 September 20X5, interest must be accrued and the discount amortized:

30 September 20X5—interest accrued		
Interest expense ($7,681 (first full year's expense) × 9/12)	5,761	
Accrued interest payable ($100,000 × 7% × 9/12)		5,250
Discount on bonds payable [$681 (first full year's amortization) × 9/12]		511

The amortization is derived from the table in Exhibit 13-3 and is allocated evenly over the period between interest dates. The loan balance is not recalculated and included in the table (i.e., not recompounded) because *compounding is tied to interest dates and not to reporting periods*. That is, the table is always based on the *bond's* dates and terms. Then it is necessary to adjust calculations to fit the fiscal year.

When the interest is paid on 31 December, the following entry is made, assuming that the interest accrual has not been reversed:

31 December 20X5—interest payment		
Interest expense ($7,681 × 3/12)	1,920	
Accrued interest payable	5,250	
Discount on bonds payable ($681 × 3/12)		170
Cash		7,000

Delayed Issuance and Issuance Between Interest Payment Dates

In the previous examples, bonds were issued on their original issue date, an assumption chosen to emphasize the accounting principles regarding effective interest rates and bond amortization. However, bonds are not necessarily issued on their initial issue date. Market conditions or company plans may change the issuance date from the original intent. Bonds that are sold at some time later than their initial issue date are sold at a price that reflects the future cash flows discounted to the actual date of sale.

Delayed Issuance

Suppose that the Gresham Ltd. bonds are sold on 1 January 20X6 instead of on their bond date of 1 January 20X5. This *is* an interest payment date, although one year late. The price of the bonds will be the present value of the future cash flows from interest ($7,000 per year for *four* years) and principal ($100,000 received *four* years hence). If the market rate of interest is 8% (Situation C), the price of the bonds will be:

$$\text{Issue price} = [\$100,000 \times (P/F, 8\%, 4)] + [(\$100,000 \times 7\%) \times (P/A, 8\%, 4)]$$
$$= \$96,688$$

This price can be verified by referring to the net bond liability shown in Exhibit 13-3 for 31 December 20X5. The discount will be amortized over the four years remaining until maturity.

Between Interest Dates

The delayed issuance of a bond may not coincide with an interest date, and issuance may occur *between interest dates*. In this case, the bond issue price cannot be directly calculated as a present value figure, since the present value figure must be at a particular interest date. Instead, the present value of the bond must be calculated as of the two interest dates *around* the issuance date (one before, one after). The difference between these two values is then pro-rated to the issuance date. Alternatively, some calculators and spreadsheet models allow numbers other than whole numbers to be entered as n (e.g., $n = 14.75$; 14 years and 9 months.)

For example, if the Gresham bonds in Exhibit 13-3 were issued on 1 March 20X5 when the effective-interest rate was 8%, the proceeds would be $96,121. This is the $96,007 present value on 1 January 20X5 ($n = 5$) plus $114, which is 2/12 of the $681 difference between the present value of the bond on 1 January 20X5 and the $96,688 present value on 31 December 20X5 ($n = 4$). *The present value has to be calculated twice and the difference pro-rated.*

Accrued Interest

When bonds are sold between interest dates, interest accrued since the last interest date is also collected in cash. Accrued interest is added to the price because the holder of the bonds on any interest date *receives the full amount of interest* since the last interest date, even if the investor held the bonds for a shorter period.

Example

Assume that the Gresham Ltd. bonds are sold on 1 June 20X5, five months after the bond date but seven months before the next interest date. The holders of the bonds on 31 December 20X5 will receive the full 12-month interest payment of $7,000 despite the fact that they held the bonds for only 7 months. To compensate for the fact that they have earned only 7 months' interest but will receive 12 months' interest, they *pay the issuing company for interest for the five-month period that they did not hold the bonds.*

On 1 June 20X5, Gresham would receive net proceeds of $96,291 for the bond, plus accrued interest of $2,917. Note that:

- The $96,291 proceeds is calculated as $96,007 plus 5/12 of the $681 difference between the two surrounding present values; and
- Interest of $2,917 is five months' accrued interest ($100,000 × 7% × 5/12).

The bond issuance will be recorded by Gresham Ltd. as follows:

1 June 20X5—initial issuance of bonds		
Cash ($96,291 + $2,917)	99,208	
Discount on bonds payable ($100,000 − $96,291)	3,709	
Interest payable ($100,000 × 7% × 5/12)		2,917
Bonds payable		100,000

Initial Discount Amortization

After a bond is issued between interest dates, the initial discount amortization recognized will be the amount needed to get the bond to the "end point" in the amortization schedule at the end of the relevant period. For this bond, the issuance proceeds were $96,291, and the 20X5 period ends with an amortized value of $96,688 in the table. Therefore, amortization of $397 is needed ($96,688 − $96,291).

When the company pays the $7,000 interest on 31 December 20X5, the entry to record the interest payment and the discount amortization will be as follows:

31 December 20X5—payment of interest and amortization of discount		
Interest expense	4,480	
Interest payable	2,917	
Cash		7,000
Discount on bonds payable ($96,291 − $96,688)		397

The $4,480 recorded as interest expense is seven months' expense.

Alternative Interest Expense Treatment

When the bonds were issued, the accrued interest portion of the proceeds could have been credited to *interest expense* instead of interest payable; the debit for the payment of interest on 31 December would then be recorded entirely to interest expense. The result is still $4,480 in interest expense after the first payment (i.e., a debit of $7,397 and a credit of $2,917 equals $4,480.) The entries would appear as follows; they are identical to those shown above, except where highlighted.

1 June 20X5		
Cash	99,208	
Discount on bonds payable	3,709	
Interest expense		2,917
Bonds payable		100,000
31 December 20X5		
Interest expense	7,397	
Cash		7,000
Discount on bonds payable		397

The choice of approach is up to the company; the second entry is more straightforward under this approach, which is helpful. However, the credit to interest expense in the initial entry is counter-intuitive. The (temporary) credit balance in interest expense would have to be reclassified if financial statements were prepared in the period between issuance and first interest payment.

Observations on Bond Amortization

A bond discount or premium is unwound over the life of the bond to measure the "true" cost of debt. Remember that the cost of debt is a sensitive issue for many companies. However, premium and discount amortization represent an arbitrary allocation, departing (as all interperiod allocations do) from the underlying cash flow of the transaction.

This chapter emphasizes the use of the effective-interest method of amortization. The effective-interest method is the method required by international financial reporting standards because it best reflects the underlying basis of valuation for long-term debt. It also is the method used in other major areas of long-term liability accounting, such as lease accounting (see Chapter 18) and pension accounting (see Chapter 19). The inherent advantage of the effective-interest method is that it provides a measure of interest expense (and liability valuation) that reflects the present value process by which the liability was originally valued and recorded. The effective-interest method of amortization achieves a constant *rate* of interest expense over the life of the bond.

The premium or discount can also be unwound using a *straight-line pattern*. This method is simpler and results in a constant *dollar amount* of interest expense each year. This interest expense represents a *different rate* each period (i.e., the interest expense divided by the liability balance is not constant.) This can be a troubling inconsistency when borrowing rates are sensitive.

Straight-line may be used under ASPE. The straight-line approach was illustrated in Chapter 12 and is illustrated again in this chapter in the ASPE section.

Remember also that accounting measurement is based on the *historical* interest rate and fair value as of the date of issuance. Amortization does not reflect *current* market interest rates or fair values.

Fair Value of the Bond

Bonds are an investment for lenders and may be sold before the maturity date. The bond will have a fair value that reflects a revised present value. Discounting uses *a revised yield rate* that reflects not only current market yield rates but also any new information about company risk. The number of interest periods used, *n*, reflects the *remaining* life of the bond.

Return to Situation C, where the Gresham 7% bond was issued to yield 8% in 20X5; proceeds were $96,007. After two years, on 31 December 20X6, it is reported on the SFP for $97,423 (refer to Exhibit 13-3). If the yield rates increase to 9%, the bond will have a fair value of $94,937:

$$\text{Fair value} = [\$100,000 \times (P/F, 9\%, 3)] + [(\$100,000 \times 7\%) \times (P/A, 9\%, 3)]$$
$$= \$94,937$$

Note that cash flows—principal and interest—have not changed. The term, *n*, is different, and is now three periods rather than five. The discount rate used is now the revised market yield rate, or 9%.

This is the value that one investor would pay another to purchase this bond. *This fair value is not recorded in Gresham's financial statements but must be disclosed.*

Debt Issuance Costs

Debt issuance costs include not only upfront fees, underwriting charges, and commissions but also legal, accounting, engraving, printing, registration, and promotion costs. These costs are paid by the issuer and reduce the *net proceeds* from the debt issue. This increases the overall cost, or the effective interest rate, for the issuer.

International accounting standards require that debt issuance costs be recorded and amortized on an effective-interest basis, as is any debt discount.[2] The amount acts as an additional discount, or reduction of a premium. Unwinding this account results in additional interest expense. Alternatively, it may be included in "other financing expense." On the SFP, companies should present unamortized debt issuance cost as a contra account to long-term liabilities.

Example

Upfront fees and underwriting fees can be substantial. In effect, the fee increases the loan's effective-interest rate. For example, assume that a firm issues a $5 million dollar, 10-year 5% bond with annual interest payments. Underwriting costs, paid at the beginning of the loan term (up front) are $368,000. The bond sells at par, and the firm will receive the net proceeds, or $4,632,000 ($5,000,000 − $368,000), on issuance.

The effective interest rate inherent in the cash flow pattern, including the fee, has to be calculated to determine the effective interest rate charged. The payments are $368,000 at the beginning of the loan, $250,000 at the end of each year ($5,000,000 × 5%), and then the principal after 10 years. That is,

$$\$5,000,000 = \$368,000 + [\$250,000 \times (P/A, i, 10)] + [\$5,000,000 \times (P/F, i, 10)]$$

The next step is to solve for *i*. Since the cash flow streams are uneven, this calculation must be done with a financial calculator or computer spreadsheet with the IRR function. The discount rate that will equate the cash flow streams to the principal amount of $5,000,000 is 6%.

---

2. The discussion relates to liabilities carried at amortized cost. If liabilities are classified as fair-value-through-profit-and-loss (FVTPL), these costs are expensed immediately.

Accounting for the transaction, for the first two years, is as follows:

On issuance		
Cash	4,632,000	
Deferred financing cost	368,000	
Bond payable		5,000,000
At the end of the first year, to record interest expense		
Interest expense ($4,632,000 × 6%)	277,920	
Deferred financing cost		27,920
Cash ($5,000,000 × 5%)		250,000
At the end of the second year, to record interest expense		
Interest expense [($4,632,000 + $27,920) × 6%]	279,595	
Deferred financing cost		29,595
Cash		250,000

Note that interest expense is measured using the effective-interest method. Subsequent years would follow this pattern, and, after the 10th interest payment, the balance in the deferred financing cost account is zero.

CONCEPT REVIEW

1. For a bond to sell at par, what must be the relationship between the nominal rate and the effective rate of interest? At a discount? At a premium?
2. When a bond is issued at a discount, why is interest expense higher than cash paid?
3. What happens to the fair value of an issued, outstanding bond when the yield rate increases? Is this reflected in the financial statements?
4. When there are upfront fees charged as a result of the issuance of a bond payable, is there an immediate expense? What happens to the effective interest rate?

DEBT DENOMINATED IN A FOREIGN CURRENCY

Many Canadian companies borrow from foreign lenders; most commonly, from U.S. lenders. These transactions are channelled through U.S. banks and other financial institutions and through the U.S. bond markets. Corporations also borrow in other currencies, such as euros, Japanese yen, and so on.

Exchange Risk

The most obvious point about these loans is that the borrowing company has exchange risk, caused by exchange fluctuations. For example, if a company borrows US$100,000 when the exchange rate for US$1.00 is Cdn$1.05, the company will receive Cdn$105,000. If the exchange rate changes to US$1.00 = Cdn$1.12 by the time that the debt must be repaid, the company will have to pay Cdn$112,000 to buy US$100,000 for debt principal repayment and thus will have to repay more than it borrowed. This $7,000 difference ($105,000 less $112,000) is called an *exchange loss*, and it is equal to the change in the exchange rates multiplied by the principal: ($1.05 − $1.12) × US$100,000.

Note that exchange rates can be expressed in U.S. dollar equivalencies, as shown above, where US$1.00 = Cdn$1.05, or can be described as Canadian dollar equivalencies, Cdn$1.00 = US$0.9524 (i.e., $1.00 ÷ $1.05). There are also differences between buying and selling exchange rates, as quoted by exchange brokers or banks; the brokers make an element of profit on the spread between the buying and selling rates. *Rates for buying exchange should be used for liabilities.*

Hedging

Companies may take a number of actions to reduce their risk of losses (and gains) from changes in exchange rates. **Hedges** reduce risk and typically involve arranging equal and offsetting cash flows in the desired currency. Hedges are a protective measure. Hedging will be explored in Chapter 15.

Accounting for Exchange Rate Fluctuations

As we saw in Chapter 12, the basic principle underlying valuation of foreign currency monetary liabilities is that they should be reported on the SFP in the equivalent amount of reporting currency (normally, Canadian dollars for Canadian companies) at the **spot rate** on the *reporting date*. The loan principal is originally translated into Canadian dollars on the day it is borrowed at the current, or spot, exchange rate. At every subsequent reporting date, the loan is *remeasured* at the spot rate. If exchange rates have changed, an exchange gain or loss will result. This gain or loss is *unrealized*. *The exchange gain or loss is included in earnings in the year in which it arises.*

Exhibit 13-5 illustrates accounting for a long-term loan, whose Canadian dollar equivalent is $545,000 when borrowed and $565,000 when retired. When the Canadian dollar equivalent goes up during the life of the bond, a loss is recorded. When the Canadian dollar equivalent goes down, a gain is recorded.

EXHIBIT 13-5

EXCHANGE GAINS AND LOSSES ON LONG-TERM DEBT PRINCIPAL

Data:

Four-year term loan, US$500,000

Funds borrowed 1 January 20X6; due 31 December 20X9

Exchange rates:

1 January 20X6	US$1 = Cdn$1.09
31 December 20X6	US$1 = Cdn$1.10
31 December 20X7	US$1 = Cdn$1.12
31 December 20X8	US$1 = Cdn$1.08
31 December 20X9	US$1 = Cdn$1.13

Entries:

Note: Entries are for principal only.

1 January 20X6—to record receipt of loan proceeds		
Cash ($500,000 × $1.09)	545,000	
Long-term debt		545,000
31 December 20X6—to record adjustment to spot rate		
Exchange loss	5,000	
Long-term debt [$500,000 × ($1.09 – $1.10)]		5,000
31 December 20X7—to record adjustment to spot rate		
Exchange loss	10,000	
Long-term debt [$500,000 × ($1.10 – $1.12)]		10,000
31 December 20X8—to record adjustment to spot rate		
Long-term debt [$500,000 × ($1.12 – $1.08)]	20,000	
Exchange gain		20,000
31 December 20X9—to record adjustment to spot rate		
Exchange loss	25,000	
Long-term debt [$500,000 × ($1.08 – $1.13)]		25,000
31 December 20X9—to repay loan		
Long-term debt ($500,000 × $1.13)	565,000	
Cash		565,000

Summary:

Canadian dollar cash borrowed	$ 545,000
Canadian dollar cash repaid	565,000
Exchange loss over the life of the loan	$ 20,000

Accounting recognition of loss:

20X6	$ 5,000 (dr.)
20X7	10,000 (dr.)
20X8	20,000 (cr.)
20X9	25,000 (dr.)
Total	$20,000 (dr.)

The effect of an exchange fluctuation appears in earnings in the year of the change in rates. This makes it easier for financial statement users to determine the impact of an exchange rate fluctuation on the company's financial position. Of course, it also makes earnings fluctuate if exchange rates are volatile. Note the volatility year-by-year in Exhibit 13-5 for the exchange gain or loss. Sizable gains are followed by sizable losses.

Interest Expense

Annual interest, also denominated in the foreign currency, is accrued using the exchange rate in effect during the period—the *average exchange rate*. When it is paid, cash outflows are measured at the exchange rate in effect on that day. The difference between the expense and the cash paid is also an exchange gain or loss.

For example, if the US$500,000 loan had an interest rate of 7%, and exchange rates were US$1.00 = Cdn$1.08 on average over the first year, the interest expense accrual would be recorded as follows:

Interest expense ($500,000 × 7% × $1.08)	37,800	
Interest payable		37,800

At year-end, the exchange rate is $1.10, and the interest is paid:

Interest payable	37,800	
Exchange loss	700	
Cash ($500,000 × 7% × $1.10)		38,500

If the interest is not due at year-end, the interest payable account is adjusted to the year-end spot rate, and again an exchange gain or loss is recognized.

CONCEPT REVIEW

1. A Canadian company borrows US$1,000,000 when the exchange rate is Cdn$1.03. The exchange rate is $0.99 at the end of the fiscal year. How much long-term debt is reported on the statement of financial position? How much is the exchange gain or loss?
2. A loan requires that US$10,000 be paid in interest annually, at the end of each fiscal year. The average exchange rate is US$1 = Cdn$1.02, and the year-end rate is US$1 = Cdn$0.99. How much interest expense and exchange gain is recorded?

CAPITALIZATION OF BORROWING COSTS

Borrowing costs are normally expensed. However, any such cost that is *directly attributable to the acquisition, construction, or production of a qualifying asset* forms part of the cost of that asset and *must be capitalized*. This is consistent with the general principal that all acquisition costs, including all costs of getting the asset ready to use, are appropriately part of its capital cost. Capitalization is limited, though, by the fair-value cap imposed through impairment tests. That is, the maximum asset value is fair value regardless of the component costs.

Qualifying Assets

Borrowing costs can be capitalized for **qualifying assets**, which are limited to nonfinancial assets, such as inventories, intangible assets, machinery, and office or manufacturing facilities. Borrowing costs cannot be capitalized on financial assets, such as investments.

Borrowing costs are to be capitalized if the assets are a qualifying asset, which take substantial time to get ready for intended use or sale. There must be a time delay for construction, customization, or shipping. For example, inventory that is manufactured over a short period of time is not eligible for borrowing cost capitalization. Also, if an asset is ready for its intended use (or resale) when it is acquired, no borrowing costs can be capitalized. If an asset is purchased and the shipping time is lengthy, then borrowing costs are capitalized for the shipping period.

Borrowing costs need not be capitalized on inventory if the inventory is carried at fair value (e.g., agricultural produce), or if borrowing costs relate to inventories that are *manufactured in large quantities on a regular basis.* For these two cases, companies may choose whether to capitalize or not, depending on their reporting objectives and circumstances.

Borrowing Costs Defined

Borrowing costs to be capitalized include interest, measured using the effective-interest method, plus any other cost that an entity incurs in connection with the borrowing of funds. This includes expensed upfront fees, and foreign currency adjustments. **Imputed interest** on equity is not eligible for capitalization.

Capitalized borrowing costs might be those that are specific to the acquisition transaction. If there is a specific loan in place to finance the acquisition, identifying borrowing costs is straightforward. If a qualifying asset is purchased from *general borrowings* rather than with a specific loan, then the calculations are more complex because it is harder to associate the borrowing with the acquisition. If this is the case, *the average borrowing rate is calculated on the total of general borrowings,* and this rate is applied to the specific expenditures made, for the time period involved.

Capitalization begins when the following three criteria are all met:

- When money is borrowed*; and*
- A payment is made on an asset; *and*
- Activities begin that will make the asset ready to use.

Capitalization ends when the asset is put into use or is ready for its intended purpose. If *substantially all* the activities to get the asset into use are completed, then capitalization should cease. Finally, capitalization stops if the work is not progressing—if work is stopped because of a strike or other delay that is an unplanned work stoppage, capitalization is not permitted for the idle period. It would restart when the strike is over.

Capitalization Calculations

Hercules Ltd. has purchased a custom piece of machinery overseas, with the following payments made:

1 February payment	$340,000	Hercules buys the equipment but contracts the supplier for customization.
		Customization work commences.
31 March payment	50,000	Customization is complete and equipment is shipped.
31 August final payment	40,000	Equipment arrives, is tested, and is accepted; the equipment is placed in use on this date.
Total cost	$430,000	

The company had no specific loan for this acquisition but paid for the equipment out of general borrowed money. The company's capital structure and borrowing costs for the year:

	Average Balance	Borrowing Cost
Operating line of credit	$ 500,000	$ 31,000
Term bank loan	2,300,000	119,000
Long-term loan	5,200,000	210,000
Mortgage loan for manufacturing facility	4,800,000	185,000
Equity financing	8,500,000	—

The capitalization rate is based on the general loans, *excluding the mortgage loan specific to the manufacturing facility* and excluding any (imputed) cost of capital for equity financing. The mortgage loan is excluded because it is not *general borrowing*, and its specific purpose is not related to the machinery.

This produces a rate of 4.5% ($31,000 + $119,000 + $210,000)/($500,000 + $2,300,000 + $5,200,000). This rate is then used to calculate the borrowing cost that can be capitalized for the months between purchase and first use of the asset:

Payment	Calculation	Capitalizable Borrowing Costs
1 February payment	$340,000 × 7/12 × 4.5% (1 February–31 August)	$8,925
31 March payment	$50,000 × 5/12 × 4.5% (31 March–31 August)	938
31 August final payment	$40,000 × 0/12 × 4.5% (31 August–31 August)	—
		$9,863

The capitalization period includes the shipping period, the installation period, and the testing period, and ends when the machinery is put in service.

If the interest had previously been expensed, the following adjusting entry would now be made:

Equipment	9,863	
Interest expense		9,863

Timing

Depreciation for the equipment is based on its total cost, which now includes interest and accordingly is higher than if the interest had not been capitalized. In the end, interest is expensed either way—*up front* if no capitalization were appropriate, or *over time*, through depreciation after capitalization. With capitalization, though, the cost of the asset is more completely captured, and the cost of acquisition is reflected with more accuracy.

DEBT RETIREMENT

Derecognition

When debt is recorded in the accounts, it is *recognized*. When it is removed from the accounts, it is **derecognized** or *extinguished.* The vast majority of financial liabilities, both current and long term, are derecognized because the company *pays the amount of the liability* to the creditor or bond holder at maturity. Sometimes, debt is repaid and derecognized before its maturity, either by arrangement with the debt holder or through open-market transactions.

Derecognition at Maturity

Debt retirement at maturity is straightforward. By the time the debt reaches full maturity, all the related discount or premium is fully amortized, thereby making the carrying value of the debt equal to its face value. As well, any debt issue cost will be fully amortized.

For example, assume that a company pays the full amount of an outstanding $5,000,000 bond at maturity. The entry to record extinguishment of the debt is:

| Bonds payable | 5,000,000 | |
| Cash | | 5,000,000 |

There are no gains or losses to be recorded. Any costs incurred to retire the bond (e.g., trustee management fees, clerical costs, or payment fees) will be charged immediately to expense.

Derecognition Prior to Maturity

Borrowers will sometimes retire debt before maturity. Retirement of debt may be motivated by a wish to improve the debt to equity ratio, facilitate future debt issuances, and eliminate debt covenants.

Bonds may be purchased on the open market at any time. In an open-market purchase of bonds, the issuer pays the fair value of the bond (which is the present value using current market interest rates), as would any investor buying the bonds. Alternatively, the terms for early retirement might be set out in the original bond indenture. Bonds may be **redeemable**, which means that the *borrower* may pay back the loan using a **call option** that sets a *specific price* at a specific time prior to maturity. *Investors can force repayment* of a bond if the bond is **retractable**.

If bonds carry a call privilege, the issuer may retire the debt by paying the call price, or redemption price, during a specified period. Typically, the **call price** exceeds face value by a certain percentage (e.g., 5%), which may decline each year of the bond term. If the call premium were 5%, a $100,000 bond would be redeemed for a payment of $105,000, plus accrued interest, if any.

Fair Value and the Gain or Loss

A major factor in retiring bonds before maturity is the change in fair value that is caused when market yield rates change. Open market retirement prices are based on this fair value. When interest rates increase, the fair value of an existing liability will decline because the yield rate has increased. The fair value will then rest below book value. However, the only way to *record* this change in value is to repay the bond.

Examine the following cases, relating to a $500,000, 5% bond, originally sold to yield 6%, that pays interest semi-annually and has 18 periods left to maturity:

	Case 1 (Yield Rate Now 7%)	Case 2 (Yield Rate Now 4.5%)
Bond carrying value—amortized cost	$465,616	$465,616
Bond fair value—present value	$434,052	$518,335
Based on market interest rates	(7% yield)	(4.5% yield)
Retirement price	Fair value	Fair value
Gain or loss recorded	Gain of $31,564	Loss of $52,719

If market interest rates *increase* (causing bond prices to *fall*), firms could retire existing bonds by buying them on the open market, triggering a gain and immediate higher earnings. For example, in Case 1, market interest rates are now 7%, and this bond, with a book value of $465,616, can be retired on the open market for $434,052. A gain of $31,564 is recorded. Since a replacement bond will have the same fair value as the old bond, this *economic decision* is value-neutral. However, it has distinct *accounting implications* because the gain is recorded.

If interest rates *decrease* (causing bond prices to *rise*), firms would retire existing bonds at a loss, and earnings will fall in the retirement period. For example, in Case 2, market interest rates are now 4.5%, and a bond with a book value of $465,616 can be retired on the open market for $518,335. A loss of $52,719 is recorded.

In both cases, the retirement decision results in recording a gain or loss that *reflects the changed fair value of the bond.* Of course, *whether the retirement happens or not, the fair value of the bond has still changed,* which has a natural impact on the value of the firm as a whole.

Now, consider the impact of a call provision. A call provision at the company's option protects the company from a change in fair value caused by a decline in interest rates. If the $500,000 bond above specified that the company could call the bond for 102% of par, the highest value to be paid out would be $510,000. This fair value has an implicit yield rate of approximately 4.7% when $n = 18$ and caps the fair value of the liability at this level. If market rates fell below 4.7%, the company would have an economic, if not an accounting, incentive to retire. The real frustration is that retirement at $510,000 would still trigger an accounting loss; this is the result when the accounting system is based on amortized cost rather than fair value.

ETHICAL ISSUES

Some companies will enter into retirement transactions simply to trigger the gain or loss. Some might wish a boost to earnings in the current year (Case 1), while others will be looking to trigger a loss in the current year (Case 2). These companies may have various incentive contracts that provide motives for such activities. For example, a bonus based on earnings might trigger a repurchase as in Case 1. A company in a loss year, in which there will be no bonuses, may trigger a loss as in Case 2 to "clear the deck" for lower interest costs in the subsequent years and improve the chance of a bonus at that time.

Recording Derecognition Prior to Maturity

Accounting for debt retirement prior to maturity involves the following:

- Update interest expense to the retirement date, through recording interest payable, discount or premium amortization, and related debt-issue costs;
- Remove the liability accounts, including the appropriate portion of the unamortized premium or discount and bond issue costs;
- Record the transfer of cash, other resources, or the issuance of new debt securities; and
- Record a gain or loss.

Classification of the Gain or Loss

A gain or loss on bond retirement is classified either as an *ordinary* gain and loss or as a separate line item, depending on its frequency and the circumstances surrounding the transaction. A gain or loss is *deferred and amortized* over the term of any "replacement" debt, *if* and *only if* the transaction is a *substitution or modification of debt*. This circumstance is explained later in this section.

Example

As a basis for an example, Exhibit 13-6 repeats a portion of the amortization table for the Gresham bonds from Exhibit 13-2. Assume that interest rates have increased since the bonds were issued and that on 1 March 20X6, Gresham repurchases 20% ($20,000 face value) of the bonds on the open market at 90. The price decline reflects increased market interest rates. Gresham has undertaken this transaction because the company has idle funds and wishes to improve (reduce) its debt-to-equity ratio.

EXHIBIT 13-6

OPEN-MARKET EXTINGUISHMENT

Gresham Limited Bonds

Data:

Issue date: 1 January 20X5	Total face value: $100,000
Stated (nominal) interest rate: 7% per annum	Bond date: 1 January 20X5
Interest payment date: 31 December	Yield rate at issuance: 6% per annum
Maturity date: 31 December 20X9	
Bond repurchase date: 1 March 20X6	Bond repurchase price: 90
Bond face value extinguished: $20,000	

Partial Amortization Table

Date	Interest Payment at 7%	Interest Expense at 6%	Premium Amortization	Unamortized Premium	Net Bond Liability
1 Jan. 20X5				$4,213	$104,213
31 Dec. 20X5	$7,000	$6,253	$747	3,466	103,466
31 Dec. 20X6	7,000	6,208	792	2,674	102,674

Entries:

1 March 20X6—update interest and premium amortization on portion retired

Interest expense (6% × $103,466 × 2/12 × 20% of the bond)	207	
Premium on bonds payable	26	
Interest payable ($20,000 bonds being redeemed × 7% × 2/12)		233

1 March 20X6—record purchase of bonds; eliminate relevant accounts and recognize gain

Bonds payable	20,000	
Premium on bonds payable ($3,466 unamortized bond premium × 20% redeemed) − $26 amortized in previous entry	667	
Interest payable	233	
Cash ($20,000 × 90% purchase price) + $233 interest payable		18,233
Gain on bond redemption		2,667

The $2,667 gain on bond retirement is the difference between the net book value of the bond and the cash paid on retirement. Brokerage fees and other costs of retiring the bonds decrease the gain or increase the loss.

Extinguishment does not affect the accounting for the remaining 80% of the bond issue; 80% of the values in the amortization table would be used for the remaining bond term.

Defeasance

A transaction called a **defeasance** may be used to engineer derecognition of a bond liability without formally repaying it; repayment is often not appealing to the investor. To set the stage for a defeasance, the original bond indenture will contain a provision that permits the corporation that issued the bonds to transfer investments into an irrevocable, trusteed fund. The trustee is then responsible for interest and principal payments on the debt, using money generated by the investments.

If and when such a trust is set up and fully funded according to terms in the bond indenture, accounting standards allow the liability to be derecognized.

The bonds still exist, but the trust assumes all responsibility for them, and the issuer has no further liability. Furthermore, the investor has consented to the transaction as part of the original bond indenture.

The entry to record a defeasance is a debit to the liability account and credit to cash or investments, with a gain or loss recorded for any difference in amounts.

Example

Assume that a bond with a par value of $100,000 and remaining unamortized premium of $6,000 is *defeased* according to the terms of the bond indenture for $92,600. The $92,600 is the present value of the bond payments, discounted at market rates, or the investment required in interest-bearing securities that will yield interest and principal amounts sufficient to cover the required future cash flows for the bond.

Note that market yields must have increased to the extent that investments of $92,600 generate sufficient cash over time to both pay the bond interest and repay principal at maturity. The following entry would be made:

Bonds payable (par value)	100,000	
Premium on bonds payable (remaining balance)	6,000	
Cash		92,600
Gain on bond defeasance		13,400

Taking the liability off the books in essence nets the liability with the investments segregated for liability repayment. Netting is not allowed unless very stringent criteria are met, and an important criterion for netting is that the *borrower has a legal release from the creditor.* The agreement in the bond indenture establishes this release.

In-Substance Defeasance

In-substance defeasance establishes a trust for bond interest and principal repayment, *even though the original bond indenture is silent on the possibility.* In essence, it establishes the trust without creditor permission (or perhaps without even creditor knowledge of the arrangement). In the past, an in-substance extinguishment would be recorded, derecognizing the bonds and recognizing a gain or loss, if certain criteria were met.

Under current accounting standards, this is no longer allowed because there is no legal release provided by the creditor. Accordingly, the company would record a separate investment account if funds were transferred to the trustee, and then would continue to report the liability and the separate investment.

The concern about in-substance defeasance

Standard setters had many reasons to be concerned about in-substance defeasance transactions recorded as extinguishments.

ETHICAL ISSUES

Companies demonstrated a tendency to set up an in-substance defeasance if interest rates increased. The increase in interest rates reduced the amount of investment needed to fully service the related debt, (i.e., reduced the fair value of the debt). This defeasance transaction resulted in a gain for the company. The transaction might have been used primarily to manipulate earnings.

Another concern of standard setters is that the borrowing company would have debt legally outstanding that is not reported on the SFP. This situation does not appeal to the basic *representational faithfulness* of financial reporting.

Standard setters were also concerned that something might go awry with the trust or the debt to make the in-substance defeasance economically or legally unsuccessful. For example, if the debt were subject to financial statement covenants, and the covenants were breached, then the debt might come due immediately. Alternatively, assets in the fund may lose value unexpectedly. If either of these things happened, the investments in the trusteed fund would not be sufficient to make all required payments.

For all these reasons, *debt may not be derecognized as a result of an in-substance defeasance.*

Substitution or Modification of Debt

A company may go to an existing lender, and essentially *repay a loan and reborrow in one transaction,* replacing an existing loan prior to its due date. As for an early retirement, the motive may be a desire to borrow at a different interest rate, record movement in fair value of the existing obligation, or release a restrictive covenant. This is called a **substitution of debt** or **modification of debt**.

If the exchange results in significantly different terms, the company must record an extinguishment (loan retired at a gain or loss), and a new loan, with the two transactions accounted for independently. This will be the case as long as the present value of the new loan arrangement is at least 10% different than the present value of the old loan arrangement, including fees and transaction costs. The presence of a 10% difference implies that there has been a change in the *substance* of the agreement. Any remaining unamortized fees and any fees incurred on extinguishment are expensed.

On the other hand, if there is less than a 10% difference in present value, no gain or loss on retirement is recorded. Balances of the old loan are rolled to the new loan. Any additional fees from such a substitution or modification would be added to any remaining unamortized fees from the original debt and amortized over the remaining term of the modified liability.

CONCEPT REVIEW

1. Under what circumstances is the change in the fair value of a bond liability recorded in the financial statements?
2. What is a retractable bond?
3. How is a gain or loss on retirement of bonds calculated?
4. What are the accounting implications of a defeasance transaction? An in-substance defeasance?

STATEMENT OF CASH FLOWS AND DISCLOSURE

Changes in long-term debt trigger disclosure on the statement of cash flows (SCF), and also require significant disclosure so that financial statement readers will appreciate the future cash flow implications as well as the agreed-upon terms and conditions.

Statement of Cash Flows

The SCF will reflect cash paid and cash received. The presence of multiple accounts related to a particular liability can complicate analysis in the area. For example, consider the accounts of Hilmon Ltd.:

	20X5	20X4
Bonds payable, 5%	$5,000,000	0
Discount on sbonds payable	246,000	0
Interest payable	125,000	$ 25,000
Bonds payable, 4 1/2%	0	2,000,000
Discount on bonds payable	0	18,000

During the year, the 5% bonds were issued for $4,750,000. The 4½% bonds were retired for 102. Interest expense was $252,000, and a loss was reported on retiring the 4½% bond. Discount amortization was recorded during the period—$4,000 on the discount for the 5% bond and $2,000 on the discount for the 4½% bond before retirement.

These transactions would appear on the SCF as follows:

1. In the financing section, an inflow of cash from issuing the 5% bond, $4,750,000, is reported. The proceeds are reported at their actual cash amount, and par value is not separately reported.

2. In the financing section, an outflow of cash from retiring the 4½% bond, $2,040,000 ($2,000,000 × 102%), is reported. Again, the par value of the bond is irrelevant, as is the carrying value. It is the cash flow that is important. It is *not acceptable* to net an issuance with a disposal or lump several issuances and disposals together. Transactions are to be shown separately.

3. In the operating activities section, reported using the indirect method, the loss on the bond retirement must be added back to earnings. This loss is $56,000. (The carrying value of the bond on the day of retirement was $1,984,000, including the discount but after this year's $2,000 discount amortization. The cost of bond retirement was $2,040,000; the difference is the $56,000 loss.)

4. In the operating activities section, interest expense of $252,000 is added back.

5. On the SCF, interest paid can be classified as an operating activity or a financing activity. The cash paid for interest is $146,000 (the expense, $252,000 less $6,000 of discount amortization and also reduced for the increase in interest payable of $100,000).

Disclosures for Long-Term Liabilities

Most liabilities are financial instruments, and significant disclosure is required. This disclosure was reviewed in Chapter 12. Remember that, among many other elements of disclosure, a company must disclose accounting policies used for liabilities, the *fair value* of each class of financial liability, and the method used to establish fair value (discounted cash flow, most likely).

Required disclosure for long-term debt also includes information primarily related to the terms of the debt contract, security, and future cash flows. Some of the highlights are:

*   The title of the issue, interest rate, interest expense on long-term debt in total, maturity date, amount outstanding, assets pledged as collateral, sinking fund—if any, and redemption or conversion privileges;

*   The aggregate amount of payments required in the next five years to meet sinking fund or retirement provisions;

*   If the debt is denominated in a foreign currency, then the currency in which the debt is to be repaid;

*   Secured liabilities must be shown separately, and the fact that they are secured must be disclosed; and

*   Details of any defaults of the company in principal, interest, sinking fund, or redemption provisions, carrying value of loans payable in default, and any remedy of the default that was undertaken by the financial statement completion date.

It is also interesting to note the requirement to disclose objectives, policies, and processes for managing risk and managing capital must be disclosed. Information must be disclosed to allow assessment of the significance of liabilities for the company's financial position and performance. Such disclosure is extensive, and includes both qualitative and quantitative elements.

Reporting Example

Exhibit 13-7 includes *selected* disclosures related to capital disclosure and fair value of financial instruments for Bombardier Inc.

EXHIBIT 13-7

SELECTED NOTE DISCLOSURE, BOMBARDIER INC.

2. SUMMARY OF SIGNIFICANT ACCOUNTING POLICIES

...

Financial Instruments

...

e)   **Other than HFT financial liabilities**

Trade and other payables, long-term debt, government refundable advances, vendor non-recurring costs, sale and leaseback obligations and certain other financial liabilities are classified as other than HFT liabilities and are measured at amortized cost using the effective interest rate method.

...

31. CAPITAL MANAGEMENT

The Corporation's capital management strategy is designed to maintain strong liquidity and to optimize its capital structure in order to reduce costs and improve its ability to seize strategic opportunities. The Corporation analyzes its capital structure using global metrics, which are based on a broad economic view of the Corporation. The Corporation manages and monitors its global metrics such that it can achieve an investment-grade profile.

The Corporation's objectives with regard to its global metrics are as follows:

- adjusted EBIT to adjusted interest ratio greater than 5.0; and
- adjusted debt to adjusted EBITDA ratio lower than 2.5.

Global metrics – The following global metrics do not represent the ratios required for bank covenants. A reconciliation of the global metrics to the most comparable IFRS financial measures are provided in the Non-GAAP financial measures section of the MD&A for fiscal year 2014.

	2014	2013
Adjusted EBIT[1]	$ 1,262	$ 967
Adjusted interest[2]	$ 401	$ 346
Adjusted EBIT to adjusted interest ratio	3.1	2.8
Adjusted debt[3]	$ 8,401	$ 7,912
Adjusted EBITDA[4]	$ 1,775	$ 1,454
Adjusted debt to adjusted EBITDA ratio	4.7	5.4

[1] Represents EBIT before special items plus interest adjustment for operating leases, and interest received as per the supplemental information provided in the consolidated statements of cash flows, adjusted, if needed, for the settlement of fair value hedge derivatives before their contractual maturity dates.

[2] Represents interest paid as per the supplemental information provided in the consolidated statements of cash flows, plus accretion expense on sale and leaseback obligations and interest adjustment for operating leases.

[3] Represents long-term debt adjusted for the fair value of derivatives (or settled derivatives) designated in related hedge relationships plus sale and leaseback obligations and the net present value of operating lease obligations.

[4] Represents adjusted EBIT plus amortization and impairment charges of PP&E and intangible assets and amortization adjustment for operating leases.

In addition to the above global level metrics, the Corporation separately monitors its net retirement benefit liability which amounted to $2.5 billion as at December 31, 2014 ($2.0 billion as at December 31, 2013). The measurement of this liability is dependent on numerous key long-term assumptions such as current discount rates, future compensation increases, inflation rates and mortality rates. In recent years, this liability has been particularly volatile due to changes in discount rates. Such volatility is exacerbated by the long-term nature of the obligation. The Corporation closely monitors the impact of the net retirement benefit liability on its future cash flows and has introduced significant risk mitigation initiatives in recent years in this respect.

In order to adjust its capital structure, the Corporation may issue or reduce long-term debt, make discretionary contributions to pension funds, repurchase or issue share capital, or vary the amount of dividends paid to shareholders.

See Note 30 – Credit facilities for a description of bank covenants.

33. FAIR VALUE OF FINANCIAL INSTRUMENTS

...

Long-term debt – The fair value of long-term debt is estimated using public quotations, when available, or discounted cash flow analyses, based on the current corresponding borrowing rate for similar types of borrowing arrangements.

...

13. FINANCIAL INSTRUMENTS

Carrying amounts and fair value of financial instruments

The classification of financial instruments and their carrying amounts and fair value of financial instruments were as follows as at:

| | FVTP&L | | | | | Total | |
	HFT	Designated	AFS	Amortized cost[1]	DDHR	carrying value	Fair value
December 31, 2014							
Financial liabilities							
Trade and other payables	$ —	$ 18	n/a	$ 4,198	$ —	$ 4,216	$ 4,216
Long-term debt[2]	—	—	n/a	7,683	—	7,683	7,692
Other financial liabilities	73	172	n/a	719	592	1,556	1,655
	$ 73	$ 190	n/a	$ 12,600	$ 592	$13,455	$13,563

Source: Bombardier Inc., or its subsidiaries, 2014 Audited annual financial statements, pages 114, 117, 119, 137, 138, 165, 170, 171, www.sedar.com, posted 12 February 2015.

Note that the company reports that it uses the effective interest method in the accounting policy disclosure note. Bombardier defines the term *capital* under capital disclosures, and provides its targets for global metrics. The company also reports cost versus fair value of financial liabilities in a separate note. Long-term debt has an amortized cost of approximately $7.7 billion; this is also its fair value, which implies that interest rates have been stable. Discounting is used to establish the fair value of long-term debt.

Looking Forward

No changes are being considered at this time.

Accounting Standards for Private Enterprises

 ASPE and IFRS standards for long-term liabilities are similar. There are some differences in terminology and approach, but the impact of these differences is not significant in the bigger picture. Much of the similarity stems from the common financial instruments rules, which were developed as a joint project between the IASB, Canada, and the United States. Since these standards govern the accounting model for a significant section of the financial statements, the similarity of standards between these major jurisdictions provides a fair bit of common ground. There are several major differences, however.

Capitalization of Borrowing Costs

Capitalization of borrowing costs *is not required* for private enterprises as it is under IFRS. Companies may choose to capitalize or not, although imputed interest on equity financing may *not* be capitalized. If companies follow a policy of capitalization, ASPE includes no guidelines governing the kinds of borrowing costs to be capitalized, commencement and completion dates, or determining the costs of general borrowing pools. Companies must disclose policy in the area and the extent of interest capitalized.

In this area, as in most other areas, disclosure is less onerous under ASPE compared with IFRS.

Straight-Line Amortization

As we noted in Chapter 12, ASPE allows the use of the straight-line method to unwind a discount or premium. Straight-line amortization is also permitted for upfront costs. The effective interest method *is permitted but is not required.*

Refer to Exhibit 13-8, which repeats the amortization table for Situation B for the Gresham bonds reviewed earlier in the chapter. These bonds sold at a premium of $4,213, reflecting the fact that the bonds paid interest at 7%, but the market yield was lower, at 6%. When straight-line amortization is used to unwind the premium, premium amortization is set at $843 per year. This is the premium divided by the five-period term of the bond. Interest expense is then the combination of interest paid, $7,000, less the premium amortization. The expense is the same amount each period.

EXHIBIT 13-8

AMORTIZATION TABLE FOR GRESHAM LIMITED BONDS

Situation B—Bonds Sold at Premium; Straight-Line Amortization

Date	Interest Payment at 7%	Interest Expense[1]	Premium Amortization[2]	Unamortized Premium[3]	Net Bond Liability[4]
1 Jan. 20X5				$4,213	$104,213
31 Dec. 20X5	$ 7,000	$ 6,157	$ 843	3,370	103,370

Date	Interest Payment at 7%	Interest Expense[1]	Premium Amortization[2]	Unamortized Premium[3]	Net Bond Liability[4]
31 Dec. 20X6	7,000	6,157	843	2,527	102,527
31 Dec. 20X7	7,000	6,157	843	1,684	101,684
31 Dec. 20X8	7,000	6,158	842	842	100,842
31 Dec. 20X9	7,000	6,158	842	0	100,000
	$35,000	$30,787	$4,213		

[1] $7,000 – $843

[2] $4,213 ÷ 5; rounded

[3] Previous unamortized premium – Current period's amortization

[4] $100,000 face value + Current unamortized premium

Compared with the effective-interest method, interest expense is not as accurately measured. Interest expense should be 6% each period, reflecting the yield rate. However, for example, in 20X5 interest expense is $6,157, or 5.95% of the opening liability balance of $104,213. In 20X9, interest expense of $6,158 is 6.1% of the opening liability balance of $100,842. These measurement differences seem small, but may be significant in certain circumstances.

Exhibit 13-9 contrasts the two amortization methods.

EXHIBIT 13-9

COMPARISON OF STRAIGHT-LINE AND EFFECTIVE-INTEREST AMORTIZATION

	Effective Interest	Straight-Line
Calculations:		
Calculation of interest expense	Effective rate × Net carrying value of bond	Cash paid + Discount amortization or – Premium amortization
Calculation of discount or premium amortization	Difference between cash paid and expense	Discount or premium ÷ Period that bond is outstanding

Patterns:		
Annual interest expense	Changes each year	Constant over term
Annual interest expense as a percentage of beginning book value (interest rate)	Constant over term	Changes each year

RELEVANT STANDARDS

CPA Canada Handbook, Part I (IFRS):

- IAS 1, Presentation of Financial Statements
- IAS 21, The Effects of Changes in Foreign Exchange Rates
- IAS 23, Borrowing Costs
- IFRS 7, Financial Instruments: Disclosure
- IFRS 9, Financial Instruments

CPA Canada Handbook, Part II (ASPE):

- Section 1510, Current Assets and Current Liabilities
- Section 1651, Foreign Currency Translation
- Section 3856, Financial Instruments

SUMMARY OF KEY POINTS

1. Debt financing introduces financial leverage in a company's capital structure, and increases financial risk.
2. Short-term financing is available through trade credit, promissory notes, and short-term bank loans of various kinds.
3. Long-term financing can be sourced through financial institutions or capital markets. Common loan vehicles are term loans, commercial mortgages, and bonds.
4. Long-term debt often involves debt covenants to provide reassurance and recourse to lenders. Covenants include accounting-based covenants and restricted actions.
5. Long-term debt is usually classified as a financial liability, in the *other financial liabilities* category, and is carried at amortized cost. Bonds payable are a classic example of long-term debt instruments that specify the face value paid at maturity and the stated interest rate payable according to a fixed schedule.

6. The recorded value at date of issuance for long-term debt is the present value of all future cash flows discounted at the current market rate for debt securities of equivalent risk. The net book value of long-term debt at a reporting date is amortized cost, which is the present value of all remaining cash payments required, discounted at the market rate at issuance.

7. Using the effective interest method, interest expense is the product of the market rate *at issuance* and the net balance of the liability (including the premium or discount) at the beginning of the period. Interest is accrued with the passage of time.

8. The price of a bond at issuance is the present value of all future cash flows discounted at the current market rate of interest for bonds of similar risk. Bonds are sold at a premium if the stated rate exceeds the market rate and at a discount if the stated rate is less than the market rate. The price of a bond issued between interest dates is based on a pro-rata calculation of present values at interest dates.

9. Accrued interest is paid by the investor when a bond is issued between interest dates; the investor is then entitled to a full interest payment on the next interest payment date. The issuer records accrued interest received as a credit to interest payable, which is repaid on the next interest payment date.

10. Debt issue costs and upfront fees are sometimes involved in the issuance of debt. Such fees are a cost of borrowing and are charged to interest expense over the life of the loan. This increases the effective interest cost of the loan.

11. Long-term loans may be denominated in a foreign currency, which causes exchange gains or losses when exchange rates fluctuate. Exchange gains and losses are reported in earnings.

12. Borrowing costs can be capitalized on eligible nonfinancial assets if there are costs relating to loans for the period of time to acquire, construct, or produce such an asset. Costs of specific loans or general borrowing can be capitalized, subject to a fair value cap.

13. Bonds retired, or derecognized, at maturity are recorded by reducing the liability and the asset given in repayment. No gain or loss arises. Bonds retired/derecognized before maturity, through call, redemption, or open market purchase, typically involve recognition of a gain or loss as the difference between the book value of the debt (including all related accounts, such as unamortized premium or discount, and upfront fees) and the consideration paid.

14. A defeasance is an arrangement whereby the debtor irrevocably places investments in a trust fund for the sole purpose of using those resources to pay interest and principal on specified debt. The creditor agrees to this and legal release is given. A defeasance is recognized on the books and results in derecognition of the liability.

15. If a bond is subject to a substitution or modification of terms, an extinguishment (with a gain or loss) must be recognized and a new loan recorded if the present value of the new arrangement is 10% different from the old arrangement.

16. Disclosures for long-term debt include significant disclosure related to accounting policy, nature and extent of risks, as well as fair value. Other disclosure relates to the terms of debt contracts, including the major conditions and cash flows agreed to in the loan contract.

Key Terms

bond date	**debt issuance costs**
bond indenture	**defeasance**
call option	**derecognized**
call price	**EBITDA**
credit facility	**effective interest rate**
debenture	**face value**
debt covenants	**hedges**

imputed interest	operating line of credit
in-substance defeasance	qualifying asset
incremental borrowing rate (IBR)	redeemable
interest payment dates	retractable
long-term loans	spot rate
maturity date	substitution of debt
modification of debt	term loan
nominal interest rate	yield

Review Problem 13-1

On 1 August 20X6, Pismo Corp. issued bonds with the following characteristics:

- **a.** $50,000 total face value
- **b.** 12% nominal rate
- **c.** 16% yield rate
- **d.** Interest dates are 1 February, 1 May, 1 August, and 1 November
- **e.** Bond date is 31 October 20X5
- **f.** Maturity date is 1 November 20X10

Required:

1. Provide all entries required for the bond issue through 1 February 20X7 using the effective interest method. The company has a 31 December year-end.
2. On 1 June 20X8, Pismo retired $20,000 of bonds at 98 through an open market purchase. Provide the entries to update the bond accounts in 20X8 (entries have been completed through 1 May 20X8) for this portion of the bond and to retire the bonds.
3. Provide the entries required on 1 August 20X8.

REVIEW PROBLEM 13-1—SOLUTION

1. *1 August 20X6—issue bonds*

Cash	43,917[1]	
Discount on bonds payable ($50,000 − $43,917)	6,083	
Bonds payable		50,000

[1] Four and one-quarter years, or 17 quarters, remain in the bond term:
$43,917 = [$50,000 × (P/F, 4%, 17)] + [($50,000 × 3%) × (P/A, 4%, 17)]

1 November 20X6—interest payment date

Interest expense	1,757[1]	
Discount on bonds payable		257
Cash		1,500[2]

[1] $1,757 = $43,917 × 4%

[2] $1,500 = $50,000 × 3%

31 December 20X6—adjusting entry

Interest expense	1,178[1]	
Discount on bonds payable		178
Interest payable		1,000[2]

[1] $1,178 = ($43,917 + $257) × 4% × (2/3 of quarter)

[2] $1,000 = $1,500 × 2/3

1 February 20X7—interest payment date

Interest expense	589[1]	
Interest payable	1,000	
Discount on bonds payable		89
Cash		1,500

[1] $589 = ($43,917 + $257) × 4% × (1/3 of quarter)

2. On 1 May 20X8, the remaining term of the bonds is 2½ years, or 10 quarters, and the $20,000 of bonds to be retired have the following book value:

$$\$18,378 = [\$20,000 \times (P/F, 4\%, 10)] + [(\$20,000 \times 3\%) \times (P/A, 4\%, 10)]$$

On 1 May 20X8, the remaining discount on the portion of bonds to be retired is therefore $1,622 ($20,000 − $18,378).

1 June 20X8—update relevant bond accounts before retirement

Interest expense	245[1]	
Discount on bonds payable		45
Cash		200[2]

1 June 20X8—remove relevant bond accounts

Bonds payable	20,000	
Loss, bond extinguishment	1,177	
Discount on bonds payable		1,577[3]
Cash (.98 × $20,000)		19,600

[1] $245 = $18,378 × 4% × 1/3 (one month of the three-month period) (or 16% × 1/12)

[2] $200 = $20,000 × 3% × 1/3 (or 12% × 1/12)

[3] $1,577 = $1,622 − $45

3. On 1 May 20X8, the remaining term of the bonds is 2½ years, or 10 quarters, and the remaining $30,000 of bonds have the following book value:

$$\$27,567 = \$30,000 \ (P/F, 4\%, 10) + [(\$30,000 × 3\%) × (P/A, 4\%, 10)]$$

On 1 May 20X8, the remaining discount is therefore $2,433 (i.e., $30,000 − $27,567).

1 August 20X8—interest payment date

Interest expense	1,103[1]	
Discount on bonds payable		203
Cash		900[2]

[1] $1,103 = $27,567 × 4%

[2] $900 = $30,000 × 3%

CASE 13-1

FORESTRY INC.

Forestry Inc. (FI) is a private company that operates in the forest products business. It has two divisions. The first division is the forest operations where the company owns and grows large tracts of timber. The second division is the sawmill operations where it manufactures lumber and building materials. FI has a stock option plan to compensate its top employees based on net income.

At the start of 20X5 FI had a bank loan with Canadian Big Bank. FI is restricted from declaring dividends until this loan is repaid.

Last year the owners were approached by a public company to buy the shares of the corporation. The owners are considering this offer as well as going public and offering more shares to investors as a public company. The shares currently are owned only by the owners, a few private investors and employees through the stock option plan.

You have recently been hired to develop new accounting policies for FI's 31 December year-end. You have been asked by the board to discuss alternatives and provide recommendations on the appropriate accounting policies for events that have occurred during 20X5. In addition, the board would like to know the impact on their accounting policies if they decided to adopt IFRS for these issues and their financial statements. Where possible, you have been asked to quantify the impact of the accounting policies. The incremental borrowing rate for FI is 10%.

1)   In 20X5, FI was able to renegotiate its bank loan and replace it with a new loan without a restrictive covenant. The new bank requires annual audited financial statements. The loan is payable immediately if FI exceeds a debt to equity ratio of .65. At the end of 20X5 the debt to equity ratio was .60. The old loan had unamortized transaction costs and financing fees of $800,000. The transaction costs and financing fees associated with the new loan are $1.2 million. The new loan is substantially larger than the old loan to assist with the construction of a new sawmill facility.

2)   In 20X5, a lawsuit was filed by residents near one of the timberlands that were sprayed with pesticide to prevent a beetle infestation. The residents claim that the pesticides contain a cancer-causing ingredient. FI consulted its lawyers who agree that medical studies support those claims.

3)   Construction of the new sawmill started in February 20X5. At the end of 20X5 costs of $6 million had been incurred. Construction is anticipated to take until November 20X6. Construction costs are estimated to be $100 million. In October 20X5, one of the trades went on a strike. The strike shut down construction and lasted two months.

4)   FI has long-term supply contracts with a number of large building centres where the company is required to deliver a set amount of lumber each month. If the minimum quantity of lumber is not delivered, FI is required to pay a penalty. In 20X5, FI has not been able to fulfill all orders because of a shortage of lumber due to a beetle infestation; FI anticipates incurring penalty costs of $250,000 until the new sawmill is completed. Once the new plant is completed, FI anticipates being able to meet the demands of its long-term supply contracts and regular customers.

5)   FI sells its lumber to local building centres as well as through agents. FI is paid for the lumber 30 days after delivery. FI uses an agent to sell its lumber overseas. FI pays a set fee to the agent. The agent sells the lumber and deposits the money electronically in FI's account net of its fee.

6)   Government legislation requires FI to reforest all lands in 15 years when the timber is harvested. FI estimated the cost will be $2.5 million to reforest the timber harvested in 20X5.

7)   FI discovered a beetle infestation at the sawmill when employees went to convert the timber into lumber. FI anticipates that $5 million of timber was infested. The timber could not be used for lumber but it could be sold to be processed into wood chips for fuel. The estimated value of the timber being sold for wood chips is $1 million.

8)   FI issued bonds for $10,000,000 on 1 January 20X5, to help fund the construction of the new sawmill. The five-year bond pays interest of 8% semi-annually each 30 June and 31 December.

Required:

Prepare the report for the board.

CASE 13-2

HUY PUBLICATIONS LTD.

Huy Publications Ltd. (HPL) operates in the highly competitive printing business, a sector known for its high rate of business failures. While HPL has had some rough financial years in the past, it now owns state-of-the-art printing facilities—financed through government-guaranteed debt—that have stabilized the company's position. HPL is controlled by Jack Huy and his two sons, but there are several other shareholders who were brought into the company when additional share capital was necessary for survival.

In March 20X2, HPL completed negotiations for a 10-year, $14,600,000 loan. Senior management was meeting to evaluate the three alternatives:

1. A 10-year $14,600,000 long-term loan from the Canadian Bank. The loan has the following terms:

   a. The interest rate is 8.2%, compounded annually. The interest rate is fixed for the life of the loan and is paid at the end of each year.

   b. Principal is to be repaid in one lump sum at the end of 10 years.

   c. The bank will charge a $19,000 upfront administrative fee.

   d. HPL will be required to move all banking activities of the company to the Canadian Bank (from the Ottawa Bank, its current financial institution.) This will cost HPL $5,500 in fees, either at Canadian or Ottawa.

   e. HPL will agree to a maximum debt to equity ratio of 2-to-1 and pay no dividends in excess of 30% of reported earnings during the life of the loan. Ratios are based on audited financial statements.

   f. Loan security is a second mortgage on HPL's printing facilities and personal guarantees from the principal shareholders of HPL.

2. A 10-year $14,600,000 long-term loan from the Ottawa Bank. The loan has the following terms:

   a. The interest rate is 6.5%, compounded annually, for the first five years of the loan. The interest rate for the second five years is to be established at the beginning of the second five-year term based on prime interest rates at that time. Interest is due at the end of each year.

   b. The bank will charge a $110,000 upfront administration fee.

   c. HPL will agree to issue no new long-term debt over the life of the loan, without the express permission of Ottawa, and maintain dividend declarations to common shareholders at no more than current levels (approximately 10%–15% of earnings).

   d. The loan will be secured by a second mortgage on HPL's printing facilities and a floating charge on all corporate assets.

   e. Principal is due at the end of the loan term.

3. A 10-year, $14,600,000 bond payable from a pension fund. The bond has the following terms:

   a. The interest rate is fixed at 8%, compounded semi-annually over the life of the bond. Interest is due every six months.

   b. The bond is secured by the general credit rating of HPL.

   c. HPL will agree to the following conditions:

      i. The current ratio will not go lower than 3-to-1.

      ii. The debt to equity ratio will not exceed 2.5-to-1.

      iii. No dividends will be paid to common shareholders unless the current ratio is 3.5 to 1 after declaration. (All ratios are based on audited financial statements.)

      iv. No common shares will be issued or repurchased without the written permission of the lender.

      v. No changes to management will take place without informing the lender.

      vi. The lender will be given a seat on the HPL board of directors for the life of the bond.

      vii. The bond will involve $227,500 in legal and other costs at inception, to be paid by HPL.

Required:

Prepare a preliminary evaluation of the financing decisions for senior management.

CASE 13-3

DRY CLEAN DEPOT LTD.

"Kevin, it's such a relief to get this $2,000,000 of financing in place at a reasonable cost. We finally have the go-ahead for that new equipment! If we order now, we'll have it in place and operating next year this time, what with production, shipping, installation, and testing. We'll have to use some of our own money for this, but we'll now be able to pay for it." Max Benstead was excited as he called you, Kevin Mohammed, into his office.

Max is the CFO of Dry Clean Depot Ltd. (DCDL), a company with a chain of 40 dry cleaning stores in Southern Ontario. DCDL's retail stores are leased, under three- to five-year leases, in various malls and store-front locations. Each pod of retail outlets is served by one larger hub location where the dry-cleaning operation is performed; clothes are transported to and from the hub locations daily.

The new loan has the following terms:

Principal:	$2,000,000
Term:	Ten years; money to be advanced in one payment, immediately, net of upfront fees
Security:	First charge on machinery, inventory, and accounts receivable
Upfront fees:	$377,000
Interest:	$90,000 paid at the end of each year
Covenants:	No dividends in excess of $100,000 per annum;
	Maximum 2-to-1 debt to equity ratio;
	Minimum cash balance of $500,000 on deposit required at all times

You are a professional accountant, reporting to Max, and he has asked you to analyze any accounting implications of the new loan, along with some other issues in relation to accounting policies for the areas that Max has listed (Exhibit 1). He has requested a brief report on his desk tomorrow.

EXHIBIT 1
DCDL
Additional Information

1. DCDL is a tenant at a retail location in Sudbury, one of its drop-off locations. Two years of the five-year lease will have expired as of the end of this fiscal period. DCDL has been disappointed with the sales volume at this location and has decided to vacate the premises at the end of this year, even though it will still be responsible for the $27,500 annual rent payments for a further three years. The landlord has been informed of this decision. After considerable effort, DCDL has

located an acceptable alternate tenant for the premises, but rent terms reflect the downturn in rental markets. This subtenant has signed a contract with DCDL, agreeing to pay $5,000 for the first year of the remaining lease period, with second- and third-year rent equal to $5,000 plus 10% of sales reported by the subtenant in excess of $150,000.

2. Dry cleaning involves a cleaning process that uses an organic solvent, typically perchloroethylene (called "perc") rather than water. Perc is classified as a hazardous air contaminant and it must be handled as a hazardous waste. In particular, special precautions for storage, use, and disposal are required to prevent perc from getting into any underground drinking water supply system. The landlords house dry-cleaning operations, rather than drop-off depots, and require premise inspections and core soil samples on surrounding property to be completed regularly. DCDL is responsible for site remediation in the event of contamination under the terms of all such leases. One of the eight operating sites under lease appears to have some contamination and may have to have remediation work performed. Additional tests are underway to determine the nature and extent of the issue. If there are indeed contamination issues, DCDL has agreed with the landlord that remediation will take place when the lease ends in two years' time, and DCDL will move its cleaning operation at that time. DCDL will not move if there is no contamination issue. The cost of remediation might be in the $250,000 to $500,000 range.

3. Starting in March of the current year, DCDL began offering customers the option of buying a prepaid card for dry-cleaning services. The plastic cards can be loaded with "dry-cleaning dollars" and offer a discount to encourage use. It costs $100 for a card that can be used for $120 of services. During the year, when a card is sold, a liability for $120 is recognized, and the $20 discount is entered in an account called *promotion expense*. The cards have no expiration date, in accordance with provincial legislation. To date, cards with a face value of $468,000 have been issued, and an expense of $78,000 has been recorded. Services with a retail value of $342,000 have been paid for through the cards. When the card is used, the retail value of the sale is transferred to revenue. Max is expecting that somewhere between 5% and 10% of the value on the cards will never be used, between cards that are lost or neglected, or with customers relocating.

4. DCDL is planning to purchase replacement dry-cleaning equipment, with enhanced efficiency and perc recycling abilities. This equipment resembles a large front-load washing machine, and acts as both a washer and a dryer. New technology is capable of extracting 99.99% of perc for re-use, in half the time that the existing models use. This will increase efficiency, allowing either more volume or fewer operating locations. The invoice price of equipment is $2,450,000, all of which is due when the order is placed. Equipment is custom-made to exacting specifications that are unique for each case. After a six-month lead time for custom production, equipment will be shipped from the manufacturer in the Pacific Rim. Shipping will cost approximately $34,000. Shipping will take three months. Import duties will likely amount to 20% of invoice price. DCDL expects to pay $17,000 to have the equipment installed and another $21,000 for labour and supplies during the one-month testing phase.

DCDL has revenues of approximately $7,000,000, and an average gross profit rate of 60%. Operating costs, including occupancy and labour, are high. The company complies with IFRS, despite being a private company. Max influenced this decision, knowing that the company might be part of a public offering in the future, but also because Max wished to develop expertise in IFRS applications to enhance his own personal skills profile.

Required:

Write the report.

TECHNICAL REVIEW

 connect

TR13-1 Financial Instruments: Long-Term Debt (IFRS):

1. Bonds are usually classified in other liabilities.
2. Transaction costs always reduce the value of the financial liability.
3. The cash received will be more than the face value of the bond if a bond is issued at a premium.
4. Amortization of a discount on bonds payable will reduce interest expense.
5. Borrowing costs are capitalized for a qualifying asset.

Required:

Identify whether each statement is true or false.

 connect

TR13-2 Financial Instruments: Long-Term Debt (ASPE):

1. Bonds must be measured using amortized cost.
2. Straight-line amortization is used for amortized cost.
3. Transaction costs are expensed for financial liabilities.
4. Borrowing costs include both interest from specific and general loans.
5. Borrowing costs may be capitalized for a self-constructed asset.

Required:

Identify whether each statement is true or false.

 connect

TR13-3 Debt Present Value:

Loschiavo Ltd. was authorized to issue $1,000,000 of 5-year, 8% bonds payable on 1 January 20X2. The bonds are due on 31 December,20X6. Interest payments dates were 30 June and 31 December. The bond was sold to yield 10%.

Required:

1. Provide the journal entry for issuance of the bond.
2. Provide the journal entries for interest expense for 20X2 assuming the effective interest method of amortization.
3. Provide the journal entries for interest expense for 20X2 assuming the straight-line method of amortization.

connect

TR13-4 Debt Present Value:

Prentice Ltd. was authorized to issue $5,000,000 of 10-year, 6% bonds payable on 1 August 20X2. The bonds are due on 31 July 20X12. Interest payments dates were 31 July and 31 January. The bond was sold to yield 8%.

Required:

1. Calculate the proceeds from issuance.
2. Calculate the proceeds from issuance if the yield rate is 5% and the bond is issued on 1 August 20X4, still with a maturity date of 31 July 20X12.
3. Calculate the proceeds from issuance if the yield rate is 8%, and the bond is issued between interest dates, on 1 October 20X2, still with a maturity date of 31 July 20X12. Exclude accrued interest.

connect

TR13-5 Interest Expense—Straight-Line:

Cumming Corp. issues a $6,000,000, 5% bond on 1 April 20X3. At this time, market interest rates are in the range of 6%. The bond had a 10-year life from 1 April 20X3, and paid interest semi-annually on 31 March and 30 September.

Required:

1. Calculate the proceeds that would be raised on bond issuance.
2. Prepare an amortization table using the straight-line method of amortization. Complete the first four payments *only*.

connect

TR13-6 Interest Expense—Effective Interest:

Use the facts from TR13-5.

Required:

1. Prepare an amortization table using the effective interest method of amortization. Complete the first four payments *only*.

connect

TR13-7 Debt Issuance Costs:

Power Solutions Ltd. issues a $10,000,000, five-year, 4.5% bond with semi-annual interest payments. Underwriting costs, paid up front, are $640,000. The bond sells at par.

Required:

1. How much cash does Power receive when the bond is issued?
2. What is the effective interest rate on the bond (rounded)?
3. Prepare an amortization table using the effective interest method of amortization. Complete the first four payments *only*.

∎ connect

TR13-8 Borrowing Costs:

Li Corp. purchased a container load of antiques for resale at an invoice cost of $1,200,000. The goods were paid for when they were shipped in early June. The container arrived in Canada at the end of August, and then at Li's location, by rail, at the end of September. The goods were then available for sale. Freight costs of $126,000 were paid in October. Li has recorded $174,000 of total interest expense from $2,900,000 of general borrowing over the year.

Required:

Prepare the adjusting journal entry to capitalize borrowing costs on inventory at year-end December 31.

∎ connect

TR13-9 Debt Retirement:

On 31 December 20X7, a company has the following bond on the statement of financial position:

Bond payable, 7%, interest due semi-annually on 31 Dec. and 30 June; maturity date, 30 June 20X11	$10,000,000
Premium on bonds payable	84,000
	$10,084,000

On 28 February 20X8, 20% of the bond was retired for $2,200,000 plus accrued interest to 28 February. Interest was paid on this date only for the portion of the bonds that were retired. Premium amortization was recorded on this date in the amount of $800, representing amortization on the retired debt only.

Required:

Provide the entries to record the bond interest on 28 February and the bond retirement.

connect

TR13-10 Foreign Exchange:

Leader Inc. has the following foreign financing:

The company borrowed US$325,000, for five years, when US$1.00 = Cdn$1.01. The exchange rate at the end of the first year is US$1.00 = Cdn$1.03, and at the end of the second year is US$1.00 = Cdn$0.98. Assume the debt was raised at par. Ignore interest.

Required:

How much exchange gain or loss would be shown in earnings in the second year?

ASSIGNMENTS

 A13-1 Sources of Financing:

The following are possible sources of financing:

> Operating line of credit
> Commercial paper
> Term loan
> Commercial mortgage
> Long-term bond payable
> Equity financing

Required:

Explain the circumstances under which each source of financing is a logical suggestion. (*Hint:* This is often based on the security required.)

 A13-2 Sources of Financing:

The following are possible sources of financing:

> Operating line of credit
> Commercial paper
> Term loan
> Commercial mortgage
> Long-term bonds payable
> Equity financing

Consider each of the following cases:

Case A   The company's primary assets are land and buildings.
Case B   The company is a large public company with significant tangible assets and a need for millions of dollars in long-term financing.
Case C   The company's primary assets are intangible and earnings are erratic.
Case D   The company requires short-term financing and has sizeable inventory and account receivable balances.

Required:

For each case, suggest a logical source of financing. Explain.

A13-3 Sources of Financing:

The following are possible sources of financing:

> Operating line of credit
> Commercial paper
> Term loan
> Commercial mortgage
> Long-term bonds payable
> Equity financing

Consider each of the following cases:

Case A   The company is a large public company with significant tangible assets, an excellent credit rating, and a need for short-term loans at low cost.
Case B   The company has significant tangible assets that are all pledged as security for other loans, and the industry sector is very risky.
Case C   The company's primary assets are machinery and equipment.
Case D   The company's primary assets are accounts receivable.

Required:

For each case, suggest a logical source of financing. Explain.

connect

★ A13-4 Debt Issuance—Fair Value:

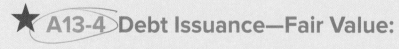

Harrison Ltd. issued $4,000,000 of bonds payable on 30 April 20X0. The bonds are due on 30 April 20X8, and bear interest at 4.5% per annum, payable every 30 October and 30 April. The bonds were issued to yield 5% per annum. Harrison's fiscal year ends on 31 December. Harrison uses the effective interest method of amortization.

Required:

1. Calculate the proceeds from issuance.
2. Calculate the proceeds from issuance if the yield rate is 4% and the bond is issued on 30 October 20X2, still with a maturity date of 30 April 20X8.
3. Calculate the proceeds from issuance if the yield rate is 8%, and the bond is issued on 30 April 20X1, still with a maturity date of 30 April 20X8.
4. Assume that on 30 October 20X5 the market rate of interest is 10% for notes of similar risk and maturity. Determine:
   a. The book value (including unamortized discount/premium) that will be shown on the statement of financial position at that date assuming the bond was issued as in requirement 1.
   b. The fair value that will be disclosed in the notes.

★ A13-5 Debt Issuance—Interest Expense:

Sanderson Corp. issued $20,000,000 of bonds payable on 1 June 20X5. The bonds are 10-year bonds, and bear interest at 5.5% per annum, payable semi-annually each 31 May and 30 November. The bonds were issued to yield 6% per annum.

Required:

1. Calculate the proceeds from issuance and interest expense and interest paid for the first six months that the bond is outstanding.
2. Calculate the proceeds from issuance if the yield rate is 8% and the bond is issued on 1 June 20X7, still with the original maturity date. Also calculate interest expense and interest paid for the first six months that the bond is outstanding.
3. Calculate the proceeds from issuance if the yield rate is 4% and the bond is issued on 30 November 20X9, still with the original maturity date. Also calculate interest expense and interest paid for the first six months that the bond is outstanding.
4. Explain why interest expense is different in requirements 1 to 3, even though interest paid is identical.

eXcel

A13-6 Interest Expense:

Mathieson Co. issues a $10,000,000, 6 ½ % bond on 1 October 20X4. At this time, market interest rates are in the range of 6%. The bond had a 10-year life from 1 October 20X4, and paid interest semi-annually on 31 March and 30 September.

Required:

1. Calculate the proceeds that would be raised on bond issuance.
2. Prepare an amortization table using the effective interest method of amortization. Complete the first four payments *only*.
3. Prepare journal entries for 20X4 and 20X5, using the effective interest method. ABC has a 31 December fiscal year-end.

★ ★ A13-7 Interest Expense:

On 30 September 20X1, Golf Mania Co. issued $3 million face-value debentures. The bonds have a nominal interest rate of 10% per annum, payable semi-annually on 31 March and 30 September, and mature in 10 years, on 30 September 20X11. The bonds were issued at a price to yield 8%. Golf Mania Company's fiscal year ends on 30 September and the company uses the effective interest method.

Required:

1. Determine the price at which the bonds were issued.
2. Prepare journal entries to record the issuance of the bonds, payment of interest, and all necessary adjustments for the first two years (i.e., through 30 September 20X3).
3. Compute the amount of unamortized bond premium remaining on 1 October 20X7 reflecting the effective interest method, without preparing an amortization schedule. (*Note:* At any point in time, the book value of the bonds is equal to the present value of the remaining cash flows.)
4. Calculate the amount of premium amortization, for the six months ending 31 March 20X8.

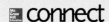

★ ★ A13-8 Interest Expense:

Hambelton Ltd. issued $4,000,000 of 5% bonds payable on 1 September 20X9 to yield 4%. Interest on the bonds is paid semi-annually and is payable each 28 February and 31 August. The bonds were dated 1 March 20X8, and had an original term of five years. The accounting period ends on 31 December. The effective-interest method is used.

Required:

1. Determine the price at which the bonds were issued.
2. Prepare a bond amortization table for the life of the bond.
3. Prepare journal entries to record the issuance of the bonds, payment of interest, and all necessary adjustments through to the end of 20X10.
4. Calculate the interest expense that would be recorded in each of 20X9 and 20X10.
5. Show how the bond would be presented on the statement of financial position as of 31 December 20X9 and 20X10.

★ ★ A13-9 Bond Issuance and Interest Expense:

The following partial amortization table was developed for a 5.4%, $800,000 5-year bond that pays interest each 30 September and 31 March. The table uses an effective interest rate of 5%. The bond was dated 1 April 20X1.

Amortization Schedule, Effective-Interest Method:

Interest Period	Cash Interest	Interest Expense	Premium Amortization	Balance Unamortized Premium	Carrying Amount of Bonds
Opening				$14,003	$814,003
1 (30 Sept. 20X1)	$21,600	$20,350	$1,250	12,753	812,753
2	21,600	20,319	1,281	11,472	811,472
3	21,600	20,287	1,313	10,159	810,159
4	21,600	20,254	1,346	8,813	808,813
5	21,600	20,220	1,380	7,433	807,433
6	21,600	20,186	1,414	6,019	806,019
7	21,600	20,150	1,450	4,569	804,569

Required:

1. Assume that the bond was issued on 1 April 20X1. Prepare all entries for 20X1 and 20X2. The fiscal year ends on 31 December.

2. Show how the bond would be reported on the statement of financial position as of 31 December 20X2 consistent with the entries in requirement 1.

 **A13-10 Bond Issued Between Interest Dates:**

Randy Corp. issued $200,000 of 7.6% (payable each 28 February and 31 August), 4-year bonds. The bonds were dated 1 March 20X4, and mature on 28 February 20X8. The bonds were issued (to yield 8%) on 30 September 20X4, for appropriate proceeds plus accrued interest. The accounting period ends on 31 December.

Required:

1. Calculate the present value of the bond first assuming that it was issued on an interest date, 1 March 20X4.

2. Prepare an amortization schedule using the effective interest method of amortization.

3. Calculate the proceeds of the bond reflecting the fact that it was actually issued on 30 September 20X4. Also calculate the accrued interest.

4. Give entries from the 30 September 20X4 date of issuance through 28 February 20X5. Base amortization on (2) above. Credit the accrued interest collected on 30 September 20X4 to interest payable in the initial journal entry.

Solution

eXcel

connect

★ ★ A13-11 **Bond Issued Between Interest Dates:**

Return to the facts of Assignment 13-9. The bond is now issued on 1 August 20X1.

Required:

1. Calculate the issuance proceeds of the bond and accrued interest.
2. Record all entries associated with the bond for 20X1 and 20X2.
3. Calculate interest expense for 20X1 and determine the net balance of bonds payable as of 31 December 20X1.

★ ★ A13-12 **Bond Issued Between Interest Dates:**

Arbuckle Ltd. issued $80,000 of four-year, 7% bonds dated 1 December 20X5. Interest is payable semi-annually on 31 May and 30 November. The bonds were issued on 1 February 20X6. The effective interest rate was 8%.

Required:

1. Calculate the present value of the bond assuming that it had been issued on 1 December 20X5.
2. Prepare a bond amortization schedule. Use the effective-interest method of amortization.
3. Calculate the proceeds of the bond reflecting the fact that it was issued on 1 February 20X6. Also calculate the accrued interest.
4. Based on your calculations in (3), how much amortization is included in interest expense for the period ended 31 May 20X6?

eXcel

★ A13-13 **Debt Issuance Costs:**

A 3% loan was granted to Simeoni Ltd. in 20X2. The principal amount was $8,000,000 and the term was three years. Interest is paid at the end of each year. In addition, the lender charged an upfront fee of $435,700 for evaluating the loan application. Simeoni plans to expense this as a financing fee in 20X2. Management was delighted to get a 3% loan because other financial institutions had bid a much higher interest rate for the same terms and security.

Required:

1. Did Simeoni get a 3% loan? Explain, and calculate the effective interest rate associated with the loan.
2. What is the appropriate accounting treatment of the upfront fee? When is it expensed?
3. Give the required entries for Simeoni over the life of the loan.

 connect

★ A13-14 Debt Issuance Costs:

On 1 January 20X8, a borrower arranged a $1,000,000 three-year 2% bond payable, with interest paid annually each 31 December. There was an upfront fee of $106,920, which was deducted from the cash proceeds of the loan on 1 January 20X8.

Required:

1. Calculate the effective interest rate associated with the loan. What net amount is received on 1 January 20X8?
2. Calculate the interest expense reported by the borrower for each year.

 connect

★ A13-15 Foreign Currency:

On 1 May 20X9, All-Man Imports Ltd. (AML) obtained a five-year loan from a major New York bank. The loan is for US$20,000,000, bears interest at 6% per annum (paid annually on the loan anniversary date), and matures on 31 December 20X14. AML reports in Canadian dollars. At the date the note was issued, the exchange rate was US$1.00 = Cdn$0.99. On 31 December 20X9, the exchange rate was US$1.00 = Cdn$0.95, and the average exchange rate for the last 8 months of the year was US$1.00 = Cdn$0.98.

Required:

1. Prepare the journal entry to record the loan on 1 May 20X9.
2. What amounts relating to the loan will appear on AML's statement of financial position on 31 December 20X9? What amounts are included in earnings for 20X9?

★ A13-16 Foreign Currency:

In order to take advantage of lower U.S. interest rates, Zhang Ltd. borrowed $8 million from a U.S. bank on 1 May 20X2. Annual interest, at 7¼%, was due each subsequent 1 May, with lump-sum principal due on 1 May 20X5. Zhang Ltd. has a 31 December year-end. Exchange rates were as follows:

	US$1 =
1 May 20X2	Cdn$1.09
31 December 20X2	1.12
1 May 20X3	1.14
31 December 20X3	1.10
Average, 1 May 20X2 – 31 December 20X2	1.11
Average, 1 January 20X3 – 31 December 20X3	1.09

Required:

1. Calculate the loan principal that would appear on the 31 December 20X2 and 20X3 statement of financial position and the related exchange gain or loss in 20X2 and 20X3.

2. Calculate interest expense for the years ended 31 December 20X2 and 20X3. Why would there be an exchange gain or loss related to interest expense? Calculate this gain or loss for the year ended 31 December 20X2.

 Solution

★ (A13-17 Borrowing Costs:

Compass Direction Ltd. has constructed a warehouse facility, paying $560,000 for land on 1 February 20X2, $500,000 to a contractor in late March 20X2, another $2,000,000 in late August 20X2, and finally $1,200,000 in late November 20X2. The warehouse was put into use in early December 20X2. The company had one construction loan, a note payable for $1,700,000. This money was borrowed in late August 20X2. The rest of the acquisition was financed through general borrowing. The company's capital structure and borrowing costs for the year:

	31 December Balance (stable over year)	Borrowing Cost for Year
Operating line of credit	$1,200,000	$ 84,000
Term bank loan	4,300,000	280,000
Long-term loan, warehouse facility (commencing in late August)	1,700,000 (from late August to year-end)	35,500
Mortgage loan for manufacturing building	2,500,000	125,000
Equity financing	3,500,000	—

Required:

1. Calculate the cost of general borrowing, and indicate when the capitalization period ends for borrowing costs.
2. Calculate the borrowing cost that is to be capitalized as part of the warehouse asset.

★ ★ A13-18 Borrowing Costs:

Jerrow Corp. has recorded $520,000 of total interest expense from $9,500,000 of general borrowing, which consists of short-term bank debt of $1,500,000 and an $8,000,000 bond payable. Other financing for the company's $14 million operation was sourced through equity financing, which has an approximate cost of 18%.

In March 20X2, Jerrow acquired inventory for resale at an invoice cost of $730,000. The goods were paid for when they were shipped in early March. Due to delays in shipping, the goods arrived in late November and were then available for sale, although they were still unsold at 31 December, the year-end.

In June 20X2, the company contracted for construction of a storage facility, which was nearing completion by the end of 20X2. Payments on the facility were $500,000 in late July, $400,000 in late October, and $1,200,000 in early December. One final payment of $200,000 is expected sometime in January after final inspection is completed. The company borrowed $1,000,000 in early December for this project, at an annual interest rate of 7%. No interest on this loan had been paid or recorded at 31 December, the year-end. This project is financed through the specific loan and general cash balances.

Required:

1. What accounting policy must Jerrow adopt for borrowing costs related to inventory and the storage facility under construction?

2. Prepare the adjusting journal entry to capitalize borrowing costs on inventory and the storage facility at year-end.

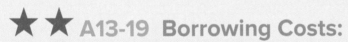 **A13-19 Borrowing Costs:**

Early in 20X1, Nitro Demolition Ltd. borrowed money to partially finance the acquisition of a bulldozer. The loan was a five-year, $90,000 loan, secured by a first charge on the bulldozer and the guarantee of the company president. The interest rate was 2%, with interest paid annually at the end of each year. An upfront fee of $15,165 was charged on the loan.

The money was borrowed on 15 January, and the bulldozer was ordered and paid for on this date. It was delivered on 30 June 20X1. The invoice price of the equipment was $180,000. It was then customized at a cost of $15,000 in July. Staff training and testing on the equipment was completed in August at a cost of $10,000, and the machine was operational in early September 20X1.

In addition to the loan for this equipment, the company had the following capital structure and borrowing costs for the year:

	Average Balance	Borrowing Cost
Operating line of credit	$3,000,000	$160,000
Term bank loan	1,500,000	95,000
Mortgage loan for manufacturing facility	5,000,000	305,000
Equity financing	3,500,000	—

Required:

1. Provide journal entries to record the $90,000 loan on 15 January. What is the effective cost of this financing (round to the nearest whole percent)? How much cash is received?

2. Calculate the total cost of the equipment, including capitalized borrowing costs. Round the percentage cost of general borrowing to two decimal places.

★ ★ A13-20 Debt Retirement—Open Market Purchase:

On 1 July 20X2, Hendrie Corp. issued $6,000,000 of 5% (payable each 30 June and 31 December), 10-year bonds payable. The bonds were issued to yield 6%. The company uses effective interest amortization for the discount.

Due to an increase in general interest rates, these bonds were selling in the market at the end of June 20X5 at an effective rate of 8%. Because the company had available cash, $2,400,000 (face amount) of the bonds were purchased in the market and retired on 1 July 20X5. This repurchase took place after the 30 June interest payment was made and recorded.

Required:

1. Give the entry by Hendrie to record issuance of the bonds on 1 July 20X2.
2. Give the entry by Hendrie to record the retirement of $2,400,000 of the debt on 1 July 20X5. How should the gain or loss be reported on the 20X5 financial statements of Hendrie?
3. Was the retirement economically favourable to the issuer, investor, or neither?

★ ★ A13-21 Debt Retirement:

The following cases are independent:

Case A   On 1 January 20X5, Radar Co. issued $200,000 of bonds payable with a stated interest rate of 12%, payable annually each 31 December. The bonds matured in 20 years and had a call price of 103, exercisable by Radar at any time after the fifth year. The bonds originally sold to yield 10%.

On 31 December 20X16, after interest was paid, the company called the bonds. Radar uses effective interest amortization; its accounting period ends 31 December.

Required:

Give the entry for retirement of the debt.

Case B   On 1 January 20X2, Nue Corp. issued $200,000 of 10%, 10-year bonds to yield 11%. Interest is paid each 31 December, which also is the end of the accounting period. The company uses effective interest amortization. On 1 July 20X5, the company purchased all of the bonds at 101 plus accrued interest.

Required:

1. Give the issuance entry.
2. Give all entries on 1 July 20X5.

★ ★ A13-22 Debt Retirement:

The following two cases are independent.

Case A   At 31 December 20X3, QML Ltd. reports the following on its statement of financial position:

Bonds payable, due 30 June 20X16, 6%, interest payable annually on 30 June	$15,000,000
Discount on bonds payable	186,750
Deferred upfront costs	53,550

Accrued interest payable of $450,000 was recorded on 31 December 20X3 ($15 million × 6% × 6/12) and the bond discount was correctly amortized to 31 December 20X3. On 1 March 20X4, 60% of the bond issue was bought back in the open market and retired at 98 plus accrued interest.

Required:

Provide the entries to record the interest and the retirement. Record interest and amortization only on the portion of the bond that is retired on 1 March 20X4; amortization of $429 must be recorded for the upfront costs and $1,494 on the discount.

Case B   On 31 December 20X7, Dartmouth Co. has the following bond on the statement of financial position:

Bond payable, 8%, interest due semi-annually on 31 March and 30 September; maturity date, 30 September 20X10	$12,000,000
Discount on bonds payable	(88,000)
	$ 11,912,000

Accrued interest payable of $240,000 was recorded on 31 December 20X7 ($12 million × 8% × 3/12) and the bond discount was correctly amortized to 31 December 20X7. On 31 March 20X8, semi-annual interest was paid and the bond discount was amortized by a further $8,000. Then, 30% of the bond was retired at a cost of $3,515,000 (exclusive of interest).

Required:

Provide the entries to record the bond interest and retirement on 31 March 20X8.

★ ★ A13-23 Debt Retirement:

At 31 December 20X8, Northern Resources Ltd. reports the following on its statement of financial position:

Bonds payable, 5%, interest payable semi-annually on 30 June and 31 December	$9,000,000
Discount on bonds payable	448,000
	$8,552,000

The effective interest rate, or market interest rate, was 6% on issuance. On 1 March 20X9, 30% of the bond issue was bought back in the open market and retired at 101 plus accrued interest. The following table relates to 20X9 (numbers have been rounded):

	Amortization Schedule, Effective Interest Method				
Interest Period	Cash Interest	Interest Expense	Discount Amortization	Balance Unamortized Discount	Carrying Amount of Bonds
reporting date (above)				$448,000	$8,552,000
1	$225,000	$256,565	$31,565	416,435	8,583,565
2	225,000	257,505	32,505	383,930	8,616,070

Required:

Provide the entries to record:

1. Interest paid to the date of retirement on the 30% of bond retired.
2. Bond retirement.
3. Interest on 30 June 20X9 for the portion of the bond still outstanding.

★ ★ ★ A13-24 Debt Issuance and Retirement—Accrued Interest:

On 1 June 20X5, Lush Corp. issued $40,000,000 of 7.5% bonds, with interest paid semi-annually on 30 April and 31 October. The bonds were originally dated 1 November 20X4, and were 15-year bonds. The bonds were issued to yield 8%; accrued interest was received on issuance. The company uses the effective-interest method to amortize the discount. On 31 December 20X5, 10% of the bond issue was retired for 99 plus accrued interest.

Required:

1. Calculate the issue proceeds and the accrued interest. (*Note:* Begin by calculating the present value of the bond at 1 May and 1 November 20X5.)
2. Provide the journal entry for 1 June 20X5.

3. Provide the journal entry at 31 October 20X5.
4. Provide the journal entry(ies) at 31 December 20X5.

 ## A13-25 Debt Issuance—Defeasance:

Pasquali Ltd. issues $600,000 of 9% bonds on 1 July 20X1. Additional information on the bond issue is as follows:

Bond date	1 January 20X1
Maturity date	1 January 20X11
Yield rate	12%
Interest payment dates	30 June, 31 December

Required:

1. Record the bond issue and the first interest payment under the effective-interest method.
2. On 1 August 20X6, the company defeased 30% of the bonds for the market price of 103 plus accrued interest. Record the entries necessary to update the portion of the bond issue defeased (interest from 30 June 20X6) and to record the defeasance.
3. What critical element of a defeasance allows it to be recorded with derecognition of the bond? Contrast this to in-substance defeasance.
4. Have interest rates risen or fallen between the issuance of the bonds and the defeasance? (Assume no significant change in the company's risk.)
5. Discuss the nature of the gain or loss recorded in (2).
6. Record the entry to accrue interest expense on 31 December 20X6, on the remaining bonds.

 ## A13-26 Partial Statement of Cash Flows:

The following balances are from the statement of financial position of Merit Ltd.

Account	20X9	20X8
Bonds payable, 7%	$17,000,000	$20,000,000
Discount on bonds payable	116,800	152,500
Bonds payable, 6.5%	4,000,000	10,000,000
Discount on bonds payable	21,300	61,500
Bonds payable, 7.25%	5,000,000	0
Discount on bonds payable	132,000	0

Additional information:

a. A portion of the 7% bond payable was retired at 101. Discount amortization of $14,700 was recorded during the year.

b. A portion of the 6.5% bond payable was retired at 97.5. Discount amortization of $5,200 was recorded during the year.

c. The 7.25% bond was issued in 20X9 in exchange for land. Discount amortization of $17,200 has been recorded during the year.

d. Interest expense was $2,110,000 for the year.

Required:

1. Prepare statement of cash flows items in financing activities related to the bond issuance and retirement.
2. Calculate the cash paid for interest in 20X9.
3. Calculate the gain or loss on bond retirements in 20X9.

 connect

★ ★ A13-27 Partial Statement of Cash Flows:

Comparative SFP balances from Forsythe Solutions Corp.:

	20X2	20X1
Interest payable	$ 62,500	$ 49,000
Bonds payable, 5%	8,000,000	0
Discount on bonds payable	196,000	0
Bonds payable, 6%	0	20,000,000
Discount on bonds payable	0	603,000

Additional information:

- The 5% bonds were issued for $7,800,000.
- The 6% bonds were retired for 102. Discount amortization prior to retirement was $54,000.
- Interest expense in 20X2 on both bonds was $625,000, including discount amortization.

Required:

1. Prepare statement of cash flows items in financing activities related to the bond issuance and retirement.
2. Calculate the amount of cash paid for interest in 20X2.
3. Calculate the gain or loss on bond retirement in 20X2.

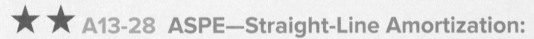

A13-28 ASPE—Straight-Line Amortization:

Return to the facts of Assignment 13-6.

Required:

1. Calculate the proceeds that would be raised on bond issuance.

2. Prepare an amortization table using the straight-line method of amortization, permitted under ASPE standards. Complete the first four payments *only*.

3. Prepare journal entries for 20X4 and 20X5, using the straight-line method. ABC has a 31 December fiscal year-end.

4. Why is the effective-interest method preferable to the straight-line method? What is the advantage of the straight-line method? Why does ASPE allow the straight-line method?

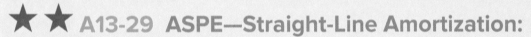

A13-29 ASPE—Straight-Line Amortization:

Return to the facts of Assignment 13-9.

Required:

1. Prepare a bond amortization table, as provided in Assignment 13-9, using the straight-line method, permitted under ASPE standards. Include only seven payments in the table.

2. Assume that the bond was issued on 1 April 20X1. Prepare all entries for 20X1 and 20X2. The fiscal year ends on 31 December.

3. Show how the bond would be reported on the statement of financial position as of 31 December 20X2, consistent with the entries in requirement 2.

4. Calculate, for period 1 and 7, interest expense as a percentage of the opening bond liability. Explain why this is not the yield rate of 5%.

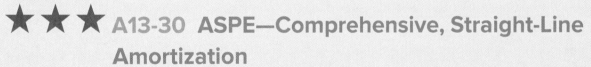

A13-30 ASPE—Comprehensive, Straight-Line Amortization

Fast Transportation Co. sold $1,500,000 of five-year, 12% bonds on 1 August 20X2. Additional information on the bond issue is as follows:

Bond date	1 February 20X2
Maturity date	31 January 20X7
Yield rate	10%

Interest payment dates	31 July and 31 January
Bond discount/premium amortization	Straight-line method
Proceeds on issuance	$1,606,617

Required:

1. Record the bond issuance on 1 August 20X2.

2. Prepare the adjusting journal entry on 31 December 20X2.

3. Give the entry to record the interest payment on 31 January 20X3.

4. On 31 July 20X5, after interest is paid, Fast purchases and retires 40% of the bond issue at 98. Record the bond retirement.

5. What item(s) will appear on the statement of cash flows with respect to the retirement? Indicate the amount and the section.

6. How will the remaining bond appear on the statement of financial position directly after the retirement?

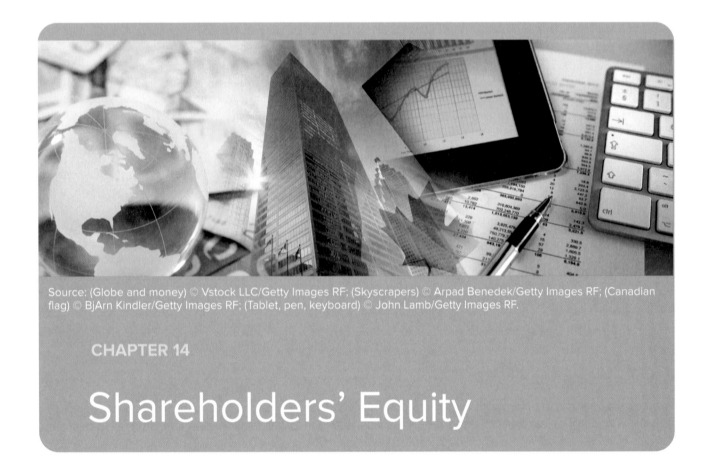

CHAPTER 14

Shareholders' Equity

INTRODUCTION

Shareholders' equity represents the difference between the assets and liabilities of an entity. Equity is the *residual interest* in net assets because it is what is left when liabilities are subtracted from assets—the residual. Equity is therefore sometimes referred to as **net assets**. Equity has various components, or sources. Generally, shareholders' equity includes the *net contribution to the firm by the owners*, called *contributed capital*, plus the firm's *cumulative earnings retained* in the business.

Bombardier Inc. is a Canadian-based mining company involved in manufacturing transportation equipment including aircraft and rail transportation equipment. The company reported total assets of $27.61 billion in 2014, and approximately $27.56 billion in liabilities. The balance is financed through equity. Equity of Bombardier has several components. Equity includes $1.728 billion of share capital (both preferred and common shares), contributed surplus from stock-based compensation totalling $92 million; $(268) million in accumulated other comprehensive income, $1.151 billion in other retained earnings, ($2.661) billion in retained earnings related to remeasurements from the defined benefit plan, and $13 million in non-controlling interest. The notes disclose that the share capital relating to common shares includes both Class A and Class B shares. Like many family-owned private companies that went public, Bombardier has multiple voting shares. Its Class A common shares have 10 votes per share and its Class B common shares have one vote per share. Other retained earnings represents cumulative net earnings less dividends.

This chapter examines accounting issues related to contributed capital, particularly issuance and retirement of share capital. Accounting and disclosure for retained earnings is covered, including accounting for dividends. Other components of shareholders' equity are also discussed, with special attention given to accumulated other comprehensive income.

THE CORPORATE FORM OF ORGANIZATION

The whole topic of accounting for shareholders' equity applies specifically to corporations; only corporations can have shareholders and shareholders' equity. Partnerships and sole proprietorships have ownership interests but not share capital. A corporation may be formed either provincially or federally, and there is legislation governing the rights and responsibilities associated with incorporation. The discussion in this text is based on the federal *Canada Business Corporations Act (CBCA)*, with occasional references to provincial legislation.

Private versus Public Corporations

Private Companies

Corporate entities may be either private or public. The vast majority of corporations in Canada are private, many of which are quite small. However, approximately half of the corporations on the *Financial Post*'s list of the 500 largest Canadian corporations are private. **Private companies** have a limited number of shareholders (generally limited to a maximum of 50 by the provincial securities acts). Shares cannot be traded on public markets. Private companies often have a **shareholders' agreement** that describes the ways in which shareholders can transfer their shares as well as other rights and responsibilities of the shareholders.

Private companies in Canada may choose to adopt Accounting Standards for Private Enterprise (ASPE), avoiding the more complex IFRS standards. Such a choice is based on the users of financial information and their needs.

Public Companies

Public companies are those whose securities, either debt or equity, are traded on stock exchanges. Public companies must, in addition to the reporting requirements required by IFRS, comply with the extensive reporting requirements of the particular stock exchange or exchanges on which the companies' securities trade.

Share Capital

Share capital, represented by share certificates, represents ownership in a corporation. Shares may be bought, sold, or otherwise transferred by the shareholders without the consent of the corporation unless there is an enforceable agreement to the contrary.

Common Shares

A corporation may be authorized to issue several different **classes of shares**, each with distinctive rights. That is, different types of shares may be created, each with differing rights and privileges. Dividend entitlements and voting rights are characteristics that might be altered among classes. At least one class of shares must be **common shares**, which have the right to vote and the right to receive the residual interest in the net assets of the company on dissolution. Voting rights include the power to vote for the members of the board of directors. Common shareholders are entitled to dividends *only as declared*, and they are at risk if the board of directors chooses to reduce or eliminate a dividend.

Preferred Shares

Preferred shares are so designated because they confer certain preferences over common shares. The most common feature of preferred shares is a priority claim on dividends declared, usually at a stated rate or amount. Characteristics of preferred shares often involve the following:

- *Limited or nonexistent voting rights.* Typically, preferred shares are nonvoting. They may be given voting rights in certain circumstances, such as when preferred dividends have not been paid or during a vote on a takeover bid.

- *Dividend priority.* A corporation generally has no obligation to declare any type of dividend. When the board of directors does declare a dividend, preferred shareholders may have preference, which means that they get their preferred dividend before any common dividend. The dividend rate on preferred shares must be specified, usually as a dollar amount per share, such as $1.20 per share. Alternatively, the dividend may be described as a percentage or rate, such as 8¼%, 6%, or floating rate (i.e., tied to prime interest rates). When the dividend rate is a percentage, it must refer to some sort of stated principal or par value for the share, which is a reference price, such as $25. This reference value has no special economic significance.

- *Cumulative dividends.* Preferred shares may have the right to receive cumulative unpaid past dividends (called **dividends in arrears**) in the current year before any common dividends can be paid.

- *Participating dividends.* Preferred shares may have the right to share additional dividends with common shares once the annual dividend has been paid to the preferred shareholders and the common shareholders receive some kind of base return.

- *Assets upon liquidation.* In case of corporate dissolution, preferred shares may have a priority over the common shareholders on the assets of the corporation up to a stated amount per share.

- *Conversion.* Preferred shareholders may have the right to convert to common shares or to another class of preferred shares with different entitlements.

- *Guarantee.* Preferred shareholders may have a guaranteed return of their invested principal at some point in time through redemption or retraction provisions.

The accounting implications of these terms will be explored in later sections of this chapter and the next.

Special Terms and Conditions

While "classic" common and preferred shares abound, so do more unique examples. In Canada, preferred issues may be structured to look a lot like debt—they pay a dividend related to interest rates and provide for repayment at a specific point in time. These preferred shares are designed to be sold to investors who not only want the preferential tax treatment given to dividend (versus interest) payments but also want some of the security provided by debt. The result is not permanent equity investment. We will take a closer look at these types of preferred shares in the next chapter.

Some companies issue common shares that have *multiple* votes or, at the opposite end of the spectrum, *limited or no voting* rights. These shares are called **special shares** or **restricted shares**. For example, consider our example at the start of the chapter of Bombardier Inc. The company has two classes of common shares outstanding, with equal dividend rights and equal claim to net assets on dissolution. However, the 314 million Class A shares each have 10 votes each, or voting power of 3.1 billion votes, and ownership is concentrated in the Bombardier family. In contrast, the 1.4 billion Class B shares have 1 vote each, or voting power of 1.4 billion votes. Combined, there are 4.5 billion votes, 69% attributable to the Class A shares. However, the Class A shares can be converted at any time into Class B shares and, indeed, since Class A shares are not traded, must be converted if the shareholder wishes to divest. Class B shares are convertible into Class A shares in the event of a takeover bid that is first approved by the Bombardier family shareholders or if the Bombardier family shareholdings slip below 50% of total Class A shares.

Note that the multiple voting shares are designed to allow the holders to *exercise voting control* but only while the company is in steady state with respect to ownership.

Par Value versus No Par Value Shares

Par value shares have a designated dollar amount per share, as stated in the articles of incorporation and as printed on the face of the share certificates. Par value shares may be either common or preferred. The CBCA and most provincial business corporation acts *prohibit the use* of par value shares, but several provincial jurisdictions permit their issuance (e.g., Quebec, Nova Scotia, and British Columbia).

Par value shares issued initially above par are said to have been issued at a **premium**. Issuing shares below par is not permitted under legislation. When par value shares are issued at a premium, only the par value is assigned to the share account. Any excess is allocated to the premium on share capital account, which is a *separate component of contributed capital.* Par values are usually set very low, and thus a major portion of the proceeds on issuance is classified as the premium. The classification of issuance proceeds in two separate accounts within the equity section, instead of one, has no *economic significance.* The *legal significance* is that par value represents legal capital, which cannot be distributed back to shareholders unless creditors formally approve. Contributed capital, on the other hand, may be distributed with the approval of the board of directors.

No-par shares do not carry a designated or assigned value per share. This means that all consideration (or value) received on issuance of the securities is classified in the share capital account. This reflects the economic substance of the transaction; that is, the shares were issued for a specific value. All consideration received is therefore legal capital.

Terms Related to Share Capital

The following terms are used to describe important aspects of share capital:

- *Authorized share capital.* The maximum number of shares that can be legally issued. Under the CBCA, a corporation is entitled to issue an unlimited number of shares, so there is no legal maximum. However, the corporation may choose to place a limit on authorized shares. Such a limit must be stated in the articles of incorporation and can be changed at a later date by application to the appropriate ministry for an amendment to the corporation's articles of incorporation. Some provincial legislation establishes a maximum.

- *Issued share capital.* The number of shares that have been issued to shareholders to date.

- *Outstanding share capital.* The number of shares that have been issued and are currently owned by shareholders. *Issued shares will be higher than outstanding shares if there are treasury shares outstanding. Shares that have been repurchased from shareholders and retired are considered to be neither issued nor outstanding.*

- *Treasury shares.* Shares that are reacquired by the corporation, and held pending resale. Treasury shares are *issued* but not *outstanding*.

- *Subscribed shares.* Unissued shares set aside to meet subscription contracts (i.e., shares "sold" on credit and not yet paid for). Subscribed shares are usually not issued until the subscription price is paid in full in accordance with legislative requirements.

CONCEPT REVIEW

1. What is the essential difference between a public and a private corporation?
2. What is the most common preference right of preferred shares over common shares?
3. What are restricted shares?
4. What are treasury shares?

ISSUANCE OF SHARE CAPITAL

Accounting for shareholders' equity emphasizes source; therefore, if a corporation has more than one share class, separate accounts must be maintained for each. If there is only one share class, an account entitled *share capital* may be used. In cases where there are two or more classes, account titles associated with the shares are used, such as *Common Shares; Class A shares; Preferred Shares, $1.25*; The dollar amounts listed with no-par preferred shares indicate the dividend entitlement.

Authorization

The CBCA or the articles of incorporation will authorize an unlimited (or, less frequently, a limited) number of shares. This authorization may be recorded as a *memo entry* in the general journal and in the ledger account by the following notation:

Common shares—No-par value (authorized: unlimited shares)		

Shares Issued for Cash

When shares are issued, a share certificate, specifying the number of shares represented, is prepared for each shareholder. This may be done in electronic form, with a brokerage house acting as an intermediary/custodian for the investor. Companies keep track of the number of shares held by each shareholder in a shareholder ledger, a subsidiary ledger to the share capital account.

In most cases, shares are issued for cash. The issuance of 10,000 common shares, no-par, for cash of $10.20 per share would be recorded as follows:

Cash	102,000	
Common shares, no-par value (10,000 shares)		102,000

Note that the common share account is credited for the total proceeds received. Had the shares been assigned a $1 per share par value, the proceeds would be divided between par value and premium:

Cash	102,000	
Common shares, $1 par (10,000 shares)		10,000
Contributed capital: premium on common shares		92,000

The $10,000 common share amount and the premium on common shares are separate equity accounts.

Shares Issued on a Subscription Basis

Prospective shareholders may sign a contract to purchase a specified number of shares on credit, with payment due at one or more specified future dates. Such contractual agreements are known as **stock subscriptions**, and the shares involved are called *subscribed share capital. Shares are not issued until fully paid, according to the terms of incorporation legislation.* Because financial statement elements have been created by a legal contract, accounting recognition is necessary. The purchase price is debited to stock subscriptions receivable, and share capital subscribed is credited.

To illustrate, assume that 120 no-par common shares of BT Corp. are subscribed for at $40 by J. Tan. The entry by BT would be as follows:

Stock subscriptions receivable—common shares (Tan)	4,800	
Common shares subscribed, no-par (120 shares)		4,800

The receivable will be paid in three $1,600 instalments. Assume the third and last collection on the above subscription is received. The entries would be as follows:

To record the collection		
Cash	1,600	
Stock subscriptions receivable—common shares (Tan)		1,600
To record issuance of shares		
Common shares subscribed, no-par (120 shares)	4,800	
Common shares, no-par (120 shares)		4,800

A credit balance in common shares subscribed reflects the corporation's obligation to issue the 120 shares on fulfillment of the terms of the agreement by the subscriber. This account is reported in shareholders' equity on the statement of financial position along with the related share capital account.

There are two alternative ways to present stock subscriptions receivable. Some argue it should be classified as an asset: a current asset if the corporation expects current collection; otherwise, a noncurrent asset under the category *other assets*. Others argue it should be offset against the common shares subscribed account in the shareholders' equity section of the statement of financial position. That is, the amount receivable is shown as a contra account in equity. This presentation ensures that the *net* equity balances reflect only paid-in amounts as capital; promises of future payment are recorded but netted out. *Presentation as a contra account is industry practice,* as it maintains the integrity of the equity elements of financial statements.

Default on Subscriptions

When a subscriber defaults after partial fulfillment of the subscription contract, certain complexities arise. [1] In case of default, the corporation may decide to (1) return all payments received to the subscriber; (2) issue shares equivalent to the number paid for in full, rather than the total number subscribed; or (3) keep the money received with no shares issued. The first two options involve no disadvantage to the subscriber, although the corporation may incur an economic loss if share prices have dropped. The third option is not common, although legislation generally does not prevent it. The first two options are illustrated below, using the J. Tan example, above. Assume that Tan made the first payment but subsequently defaulted on the arrangement.

Alternative 1—return all payments

To record the collection		
Cash	1,600	
Stock subscriptions receivable—common shares (Tan)		1,600
To record cash payment and reversal of commitment		
Common shares subscribed, no-par (120 shares)	4,800	
Stock subscriptions receivable—common shares (Tan)		3,200
Cash		1,600

Alternative 2—issue pro-rata shares

To record the collection		
Cash	1,600	
Stock subscriptions receivable—common shares (Tan)		1,600
To record share issuance and reversal of balance of commitment		
Common shares subscribed, no-par (120 shares)	4,800	
Stock subscriptions receivable—common shares (Tan)		3,200
Common shares, no-par (40 shares)		1,600

---

1. A subscription agreement is a legal contract. The corporation may choose to take the subscriber to court to enforce payment and thus avoid default. This section deals with the treatment if the corporation allows the subscriber to avoid the contract commitment.

Non-Cash Issuance of Share Capital

Corporations sometimes issue share capital for non-cash consideration. These transactions are also called *share-based payments*. Companies may pay for goods or services with shares, or acquire long-term assets.

When shares are issued for non-cash assets or services or to settle debt, the transaction should be recorded at the *fair value of the assets received*, assuming that this value can be reliably determined. The fair value of the equity shares issued cannot be used to value the transaction unless the fair value of the assets *cannot be determined*. This should be a rare occurrence. Logically, though, all evidence should be considered, including the value of shares in recent similar transactions.

To illustrate, assume that Bronex Corp. issued 136,000 Class A no-par shares in exchange for land. The land was appraised at $420,000, while the shares, based on several prior transactions in the shares, were valued at $450,000. The transaction would be valued at $420,000, which is the more conservative value, but in the range of the implied value of the shares. The entry is:

Land	420,000	
Share capital, Class A no-par value (136,000 shares)		420,000

Basket Sale of Share Capital

A corporation usually issues each class of its share capital separately. However, a corporation may issue two or more classes for one lump-sum amount (often referred to as a *basket sale*).

When two or more classes of securities are issued for a single lump sum, the total proceeds must be allocated logically among the several classes of securities. The two methods used in such situations are (1) the *proportional method*, in which the lump sum received is allocated proportionately among the classes of shares on the basis of the relative fair value of each security, and (2) the *incremental method*, in which the fair value of one security is used as a basis for that security and the remainder of the lump sum is allocated to the other class of security. When there is no fair value for any of the issued securities, proceeds may be allocated arbitrarily.

To illustrate, assume Vax Corp. issued 1,000 no-par common shares, and 500 no-par preferred shares, in three different situations:

Situation 1—Proportional method

The common shares were selling at $40 per share and the preferred at $20. Assume the total cash received is $48,000, which has been approved by the board of directors. Because reliable fair values are available for both share classes, the proportional method is preferable as a basis for allocating the lump-sum amount, as follows:

Proportional allocation

Fair value of common (1,000 shares × $40)	$40,000 = 4/5 of total
Fair value of preferred (500 shares × $20)	10,000 = 1/5
Total fair value	$50,000 = 5/5

Allocation of the lump-sum sale price of $48,000

Common ($48,000 × 4/5)	$38,400
Preferred ($48,000 × 1/5)	9,600
Total	$48,000

The journal entry to record the issuance:

Cash	48,000	
Common shares, no-par (1,000 shares)		38,400
Preferred shares, no-par (500 shares)		9,600

Situation 2—Incremental method

The common shares were selling at $40; a market for the preferred has not been established. Because there is no market for the preferred shares, the fair value of the common ($40,000) must be used as a basis for the entry:

Cash	48,000	
Common shares, no-par (1,000 shares)		40,000
Preferred shares, no-par (500 shares)		8,000

Situation 3—Arbitrary allocation

When there is no established market for either class of shares, an arbitrary allocation is used. In the absence of any other logical basis, a temporary allocation may be made by the board of directors. If a fair value is established for one of the securities within a year, a correcting entry based on such value would be made.

Share Issue Costs

Corporations often incur substantial expenditures when they issue shares in a public offering. These expenditures include registration fees, underwriter commissions, legal and accounting fees, printing costs, clerical costs, and promotional costs. These expenditures are called **share issue costs**. If the share issuance is planned but then abandoned, the costs are expensed. The costs of a successful share issuance are included "in equity"; they are not expensed. Two methods of accounting for share issue costs are found in practice:

1. *Offset method.* Under this method, share issue costs are treated as a reduction of the amount received from the issuance of the related share capital. The rationale to support this method is that these are one-time costs that cannot be reasonably assigned to future periodic revenues and that the net cash received is the actual appropriate measure of capital raised. Therefore, under this method, share issue costs are debited to the share capital account.

2. *Retained earnings method.* Companies will charge share issue costs directly to retained earnings. Retained earnings are reduced as a result. This reduces common equity but records the gross proceeds received from the issuance of shares to the share capital account.

Both methods are found in practice, although the offset method is more common.

RETIREMENT OF SHARE CAPITAL

A company can buy back any of its shares, preferred or common, at any time, if they are offered for sale. Such a sale can be a private transaction, or a public (stock market) transaction. Legislation provides conditions (typically solvency tests that must be met subsequent to the purchase) for the purchase and cancellation of outstanding shares. Corporations that intend to buy back their own shares must file their plans with the relevant securities commissions; the plan is known as a **normal course issuer bid**.

Shares may also be bought back according to the terms of the shares themselves. Some preferred shares are *retractable*, which means that at the option of the shareholder and at a contractually arranged price, a company is required to buy back its shares. Other preferred shares are **callable**, or *redeemable*, which means that there are specific buyback provisions at the option of the company. In either of these transactions, the company deals directly with the shareholder.

Reasons for Share Retirement

Why is repurchase of shares a good strategy for the company? The company may want to:

- *Increase earnings per share* (EPS). EPS is the ratio obtained by dividing earnings by outstanding shares. EPS is considered a critical indication of a company's earnings performance and future prospects and is closely watched by financial markets. Idle cash, earning minimal interest income, can be spent to retire shares that will reduce the denominator (number of shares outstanding) of the EPS ratio. Because of the negligible return given up, this will not hurt the numerator (earnings) in a proportional fashion. Accordingly, EPS will rise, and the market price per share should rise as well.

- *Provide cash flow to shareholders in lieu of dividends.* A repurchase offer enables those shareholders who want to receive cash to do so through offering all or part of their holdings for redemption. There may be tax advantages of this form of payout because the recipient will pay taxes on capital gains on the shares rather than tax on ordinary dividend income. Those shareholders who do not wish to receive cash at the time can continue to hold their shares.

- *Acquire shares when they appear to be undervalued.* A corporation with excess cash may feel that buying undervalued shares for cancellation will benefit the remaining shareholders. These transactions also help make a market (i.e., provide a buyer) for the shares.

- *Buy out one or more particular shareholders and thwart takeover bids.*

- *Reduce future dividend payments by reducing the shares outstanding.*

ETHICAL ISSUES

Companies must exercise extreme caution in transactions involving their own shares because of the opportunity that the corporation has to use insider information to the detriment of a selling shareholder. For example, an oil company with inside knowledge of a profitable oil discovery could withhold the good news and acquire shares at an artificially low market price. This would unfairly deprive the selling shareholder of true fair value. For these reasons, security laws prohibit corporations from engaging in deceptive conduct, including acts related to transactions involving their own shares. Continuous disclosure of information is also required. Companies require regulatory approval to repurchase shares, often through a *normal course issuer bid,* which establishes the extent and the intent for share repurchase and retirement.

Accounting for Retirement

There are no standards issued by the IASB that describe appropriate policy to follow when a company purchases and retires its own shares. Legislation dictates accounting treatment. Existing Canadian practice is described below.

When shares are purchased and immediately retired, *contributed capital* allocated to the shares is removed from the accounts. Where the reacquisition cost of the acquired shares is different from the average original issuance price (i.e., the *paid-in* capital), the cost is allocated as follows for no-par shares:

Condition	First, DEBIT	Then	
		CREDIT	DEBIT
When the reacquisition cost is *lower* than the average price per share issued to date	Share capital, at the *average paid-in value* per issued share	Other contributed capital from share retirement	n/a
When the reacquisition cost is *higher* than the average price per share issued to date	Share capital, at the *average paid-in value* per issued share	n/a	1. Other contributed capital that was created by earlier cancellation or resale transactions *in the same class of shares,* if any; then 2. Retained earnings.

The effect of this approach is to ensure that a corporation records *no change in earnings* (i.e., no gain or loss in earnings) from buying back its own shares. If a company could record gains and losses from transactions in its own shares, the potential for income manipulation is obvious.

Illustration: Case 1

Assume that Sicon Corp. has 200,000 no-par common shares outstanding. There is $1 million in the common share account, the result of an average issuance price per share of $5. The contributed capital account from previous retirement transactions of common shares has a $7,200 credit balance. The corporation acquired and retired 10,000 shares at a price of $6.25 per share. The specific shareholder who sold these shares back to Sicon had originally paid $4 per share. The transaction would be recorded as follows:

Common shares (10,000 shares)		
[($1,000,000 ÷ 200,000) × 10,000]	50,000	
Contributed capital, common share retirement	7,200	
Retained earnings ($62,500 − $50,000 − $7,200)	5,300	
Cash (10,000 × $6.25)		62,500

The first step in constructing this journal entry is to compare the cash paid to retire the shares ($62,500) with the *average* initial issuance price to date ($50,000). The specific issue price of these shares ($4) is irrelevant. The corporation paid $12,500 more to retire these shares than the average original proceeds. The $12,500 is debited first to contributed capital from prior common share retirements until that account is exhausted. *This contributed capital account may never have a debit balance.* Retained earnings is debited for the remainder. The effect of this transaction is to reduce paid-in capital by $57,200, retained earnings by $5,300, and total shareholders' equity by $62,500. *No loss is recorded in earnings.* Assets are reduced by $62,500.

Illustration: Case 2

If the shares were reacquired for $4.25 per share, the entry to record the transaction would be:

Common shares (10,000 shares)		
[($1,000,000 ÷ 200,000) × 10,000]	50,000	
Contributed capital, common share retirement		
($50,000 – $42,500)		7,500
Cash (10,000 × $4.25)		42,500

Total shareholders' equity and paid-in capital go down by $42,500 ($50,000 less $7,500), reflecting the fact that the corporation paid less to repurchase the shares than the average issuance price to date. No gain is recorded. Assets are reduced by $42,500.

The price paid for the shares may be the current market price or a price agreed on when the shares were originally issued, as is the case for redeemable or retractable shares. In all cases, the entries follow the same pattern: Retirement price is compared with the average issuance price to date, and the difference is a capital amount.

Note that the contributed capital account involved in the above example was identified as contributed capital, common share retirement. Subsequent common share retirements will increase or decrease this account. However, if there are retirements of any other class of shares (e.g., preferred shares), then a *separate contributed capital account* would have to be set up. These contributed capital accounts are used only for transactions involving the *same class of shares*.

Reporting Example

Metro Inc. provides an example of shares redeemed in its 2015 financial statements. In this example, Metro reduced common shares by $30.1 (thousand) in 2014 ($49.8 in 2013).

22. CAPITAL STOCK

The authorized capital stock of the Corporation was summarized as follows:

- unlimited number of Common Shares, bearing one voting right per share, participating, without par value;

- unlimited number of Preferred Shares, non-voting, without par value, issuable in series.

In 2015, the Corporation carried out a 3-for-1 stock split of its Common Shares. All information pertaining to shares have been retroactively restated to reflect the effect of the stock split.

Common Shares issued

The Common Shares issued and the changes during the year were summarized as follows:

	Number (Thousands)	
Balance as at September 28, 2013	274,944	640.4
Shares redeemed for cash, excluding premium of $409.9	(21,278)	(49.8)
Stock options exercised	565	8.6

Balance as at September 27, 2014	**254,231**	**599.2**
Shares redeemed for cash, excluding premium of $387.9	**(12,676)**	**(30.1)**
Stock options exercised	**730**	**9.9**
Balance as at September 26, 2015	**242,285**	**579.0**

Source: Metro Inc., 2015 Annual Financial Statements, www.sedar.com, posted 17 December 2015

Conversion of Shares

Shares of any class may include the provision that they may be converted, at particular times and/or in particular quantities, into shares of another class. For example, preferred shares may be convertible into common shares. Conversions are accounted for at *book value,* with an equal decrease to one share class and increase to another. For example, if 20,000 no-par preferred shares, issued for an average of $36.70 per share, were to convert according to pre-established terms to 60,000 no-par common shares (i.e., 3-for-1):

Preferred shares (no-par, 20,000 shares)		
(20,000 × $36.70)	734,000	
Common shares (no-par, 60,000 shares)		734,000

TREASURY STOCK

A firm may buy its own shares and hold them for eventual resale. This is called **treasury stock**. *Such shares may not vote at shareholder meetings or receive dividends.* The CBCA (and provincial legislation modelled after the act) provides that corporations that reacquire their own shares must immediately retire those shares. Thus, corporations may not engage in treasury stock transactions in most Canadian jurisdictions. However, there are some circumstances where shares may be purchased and held in trust before they are distributed to an employee under a share compensation arrangement. Some provincial legislation also allows companies to hold treasury stock. Treasury shares are far more common in other countries, where corporations regularly engage in treasury stock transactions, subject to the insider trading rules of the various stock exchanges.

The key to a treasury stock acquisition is that reacquired shares may be reissued. The company may eventually reissue the shares to raise additional capital—a process far faster/simpler through the issuance of treasury stock than a new share issue. The shares may also be used for stock dividends, employee stock option plans, and so on. A corporation that is permitted to engage in treasury stock transactions may have additional flexibility over one not so permitted. However, the importance of this aspect of treasury shares has decreased in recent years due to the prevalence of **shelf registration**, which is a standing approval from the securities commissions to issue more shares as needed.

Accounting for Treasury Stock

Canadian practice regarding policy for the acquisition and resale of treasury stock is presented in this discussion because there are no standards issued by the IASB in this area.

When a company buys treasury stock, the cost of the shares acquired is debited to a treasury stock account, which appears as a *deduction* at the end of the shareholders' equity section. When the shares are resold, the treasury stock account is credited for the average cost, and the difference, which is the "gain or loss," affects various equity accounts. The "gain or loss" is not reported in earnings; a firm cannot improve reported earnings by engaging in capital transactions with its own shareholders.

When treasury stock is reissued at a price in excess of its cost, the excess should be recorded as contributed capital in a separate contributed capital account. Where the shares are reissued at less than their cost, the deficiency should be charged to contributed capital, if any, then retained earnings. The rules are as follows:

Condition	First, CREDIT	Then	
		CREDIT	**DEBIT**
When the reissue price is *higher* than the average price per share	Treasury stock, at the *average price per share*	Other contributed capital from treasury stock transactions	n/a
When the reissue price is *lower* than the average price per share	Treasury stock, at the *average price per share*	n/a	1. Other contributed capital from treasury stock transactions, if any; then 2. Retained earnings.

This method of accounting for treasury stock is called the **single-transaction method**. The treatment is the same as that used for share retirement. An example will illustrate the sequence of entries.

1. To record the initial sale and issuance of 10,000 common shares at $26 per share:

Cash (10,000 shares × $26)	260,000	
Common shares (10,000 shares)		260,000

2. To record the acquisition of 2,000 common treasury shares at $28 per share:

Treasury stock, common (2,000 shares × $28)	56,000	
Cash		56,000

Note: The cash price paid is always the amount debited to the treasury stock account.

3. To record reissuance of 500 treasury shares at $30 per share (above cost):

Cash (500 shares × $30)	15,000	
Treasury stock, common (500 shares at cost, $28)		14,000
Contributed capital from treasury stock transactions		1,000

Note: Had this reissuance been at cost ($28 per share), no amount would have been entered in the contributed capital account. If treasury shares are bought in a series of acquisitions at different prices, weighted average cost is used on disposition.

4. To record the acquisition of 1,000 common treasury shares at $35 per share:

Treasury stock, common (1,000 shares × $35)	35,000	
Cash		35,000

Acquisition changes the average cost in treasury stock: There is now $77,000 ($56,000 − $14,000 + $35,000) in the treasury stock account for 2,500 shares; this is a weighted average of $30.80 per share.

5. To record the reissuance of another 500 treasury shares at $19 per share (below cost):

Cash (500 shares × $19)	9,500	
Contributed capital from treasury stock transactions*	1,000	
Retained earnings	4,900	
Treasury stock, common (500 shares at average cost, $30.80)		15,400
*The debit is limited to the current balance in this account (see entry [3]); any remainder is allocated to retained earnings.		

Assuming entries (1) through (5), and a beginning balance in retained earnings of $40,000, the statement of financial position will reflect the following:

Shareholders' Equity

Contributed capital

Common shares, 10,000 shares issued, and 8,000 shares outstanding; 2,000 shares are held as treasury stock	$260,000
Retained earnings ($40,000 – $4,900)	35,100
Total contributed capital and retained earnings	$295,100
Less: Treasury stock, 2,000 shares at cost	61,600
Total shareholders' equity	$233,500

Reporting Example

Metro Inc. provides an example of treasury shares in its 2015 financial statements. In this example, Metro shows treasury shares as a reduction in equity.

Equity		
Capital stock *(note 22)*	**579.0**	599.2
Treasury shares *(note 22)*	**(18.5)**	(15.2)
Contributed surplus	**18.0**	15.8
Retained earnings	**2,059.7**	2,068.6
Accumulated other comprehensive income	**5.2**	0.2
Equity attributable to equity holders of the parent	**2,643.4**	2,668.6
Non-controlling interests	**13.8**	15.5
	2,657.2	2,684.1

Source: Metro Inc., 2015 annual financial statements, www.sedar.com, posted 17 December 2015.

RETAINED EARNINGS

Retained earnings represents accumulated net earnings or net loss, error corrections, and retrospective changes in accounting policy, if any, less accumulated cash dividends, stock dividends, and other amounts transferred to contributed capital accounts. If the accumulated losses and distributions exceed the accumulated gains, a **deficit** will exist (i.e., a debit balance in retained earnings).

The following items directly affect retained earnings:

Decreases (debits)

- Cash and other dividends;
- Stock dividends;
- Share retirement and treasury stock transactions when cash paid exceeds average cost;
- Share issue costs;
- Spinoff of investment to shareholders;
- Adjustments related to complex financial instruments, such as hybrid financial instruments (see Chapter 15);
- Error correction (may also be a credit) (see Chapter 21); and
- Effect of a change in accounting policy applied retrospectively (may also be a credit) (see Chapter 21).

Increases (credits)

- Earnings (will be a debit if a net loss); and
- Removal of deficit in a financial reorganization.

Appropriations and Restrictions of Retained Earnings

Appropriated retained earnings and restricted retained earnings formally constrain a specified portion of accumulated earnings for a specified reason. Retained earnings are appropriated and restricted primarily to reduce the amount of retained earnings that financial statement readers might otherwise consider available to support a dividend declaration. Constrained retained earnings are sometimes called a *reserve*. **Appropriated retained earnings** are the result of discretionary management action. **Restricted retained earnings** are the result of a legal contract or corporate law.

The following are examples of some of the ways in which appropriations and restrictions of retained earnings may arise:

- To fulfill a contractual agreement, as in the case of a debt covenant restricting the use of retained earnings for dividends that would result in the disbursement of assets;
- To report a discretionary appropriation of a specified portion of retained earnings in anticipation of possible future losses; or
- To fulfill a legal requirement, as in the case of a provincial corporate law requiring a restriction on retained earnings equivalent to the cost of treasury stock held.

An appropriation of retained earnings *does not involve any segregation of assets.* Retained earnings appropriations are just accounting entries that divide existing retained earnings into multiple accounts. If management actually sets aside funds for a specific purpose, restricted cash investments will be reported as an asset.

Appropriation or restriction of retained earnings is formally made by transferring (debiting) an amount from retained earnings to (crediting) an appropriated retained earnings account. The entry has no effect on assets, liabilities, or total shareholders' equity. When the need for an appropriation or restriction no longer exists, the appropriated balance is returned to the unappropriated retained earnings account. Both appropriations and restrictions are rarely seen in practice; it is far more common to have a covenant in a lending arrangement specifying that the company must maintain a certain level of retained earnings.

DIVIDENDS

Nature of Dividends

A dividend is a distribution of earnings to shareholders in the form of assets or shares. A dividend typically results in a credit to the account that represents the item distributed (cash, non-cash asset, or share capital) and a debit to retained earnings.

Some corporate legislation and bond covenants place restrictions on the amount of assets and/or retained earnings that may be used for dividends. These constraints recognize the effects of dividends; that is, dividends require (1) a disbursement of assets and (2) a reduction in retained earnings, by the same amount. The company must have both assets and retained earnings to be eligible to declare/distribute dividends. Under the CBCA, a liquidity test must also be met: Dividends may not be declared or paid if the result would be that the corporation became unable to meet its liabilities as they came due or if the dividend resulted in the realizable value of assets being less than liabilities plus stated capital. In addition, dividends may not be paid from *legal capital (share capital)* without specific creditor approval.

Relevant Dividend Dates

Four dates have legal significance for dividends:

Declaration Date

On the **declaration date**, the corporation's board of directors formally announces the dividend declaration. The courts have held that formal declaration of a cash or property dividend constitutes an enforceable contract between the corporation and its shareholders. Therefore, on the dividend declaration date, such dividends are recorded and a liability (i.e., dividends payable) is recognized.

Record Date

The **record date** is the date on which the list of *shareholders of record,* who will receive the dividend, is prepared. Usually, the record date follows the declaration date by two to three weeks, to allow for changes in share ownership to be recorded. No entry is made in the accounts on the record date, but the shareholder list will determine the names on the eventual dividend cheques.

Ex-Dividend Date

An investor who holds (buys) shares on or after the **ex-dividend date** *does not* receive the dividend. Technically, the ex-dividend date is the day following the record date, but, to provide time to record the transfer of shares, the effective ex-dividend date is usually several days prior to the date of record. Thus, the investor who holds shares on the day prior to the stipulated ex-dividend date receives the dividend.

Payment Date

This date is determined by the board of directors and is usually stated in the declaration. It is the date on which dividends are paid or distributed to the shareholders of record. The **payment date** typically follows the declaration date by four to six weeks. At the date of payment, the liability recorded at date of declaration is debited, and the appropriate asset account is credited.

Note that of these four dates, the only ones that affect the accounting records of the company that declares the dividend are (1) the declaration date and (2) the payment date. The other two dates are significant for investors but not for accounting.

Cash Dividends

Assume the board of directors of Bass Co., at its meeting on 20 January 20X2, declares a dividend of $0.50 per common share, payable 20 March 20X2, to shareholders of record on 1 March 20X2. Assume that 10,000 no-par common shares are outstanding.

At declaration date—20 January 20X2		
Common dividends declared* (10,000 shares × $0.50)	5,000	
Cash dividends payable		5,000
*Later closed to retained earnings; alternatively, retained earnings may be debited directly		
At payment date—20 March 20X2		
Cash dividends payable	5,000	
Cash		5,000

Cash dividends payable is reported as a current liability.

Preferred shares typically have first preference on amounts declared as dividends. Assume that Bass, in addition to the 10,000 common shares mentioned above, also has 5,000 $1.20 preferred shares outstanding. The board of directors declared dividends totalling $10,000, with the same declaration and payment dates as in the previous example. The first $6,000 will go to the preferred shareholders (5,000 shares × $1.20 per share); the remaining $4,000 will be distributed to the common shareholders at the rate of $0.40 per share ($4,000 ÷ 10,000 shares). Entries will be as follows:

At declaration date—20 January 20X2		
Preferred dividends declared*	6,000	
Common dividends declared*	4,000	
Cash dividends payable, preferred (5,000 × $1.20)		6,000
Cash dividends payable, common (10,000 × $0.40)		4,000
*Later closed to retained earnings; alternatively, retained earnings may be debited directly		
At payment date—20 March 20X2		
Cash dividends payable, preferred	6,000	
Cash dividends payable, common	4,000	
Cash		10,000

If Bass were to have declared $5,000 of dividends, the preferred shareholders would have received it all. They have preference for the first $6,000 each year.

In corporate reporting, it is important to distinguish the portion of the dividend attributable to the preferred shares versus the common. Accordingly, these are recorded separately in the accounts.

Cumulative Dividends on Preferred Shares

Cumulative preferred shares provide that dividends not declared in a given year accumulate at the specified rate on such shares. This accumulated amount must be paid in full if and when dividends are declared in a later year *before any dividends can be paid on the common shares.* If cumulative preference dividends are not declared in a given year, they are said to have been *passed* and are called *dividends in arrears* on the cumulative preferred shares.

If only a part of the preferred dividend is met for any year, the remainder of the cumulative dividend is in arrears. Cumulative preferred shares carry the right, on dissolution of the corporation, to dividends in arrears to the extent that the corporation has retained earnings. However, different provisions for dividends in arrears may be stipulated in the articles of incorporation and bylaws.

Dividends in arrears are not liabilities. Since preferred shareholders cannot force the board of directors to declare dividends, dividends in arrears do not meet the definition of a liability. Dividends in arrears for cumulative preference shares must be disclosed in the notes to the financial statements.

Participating Dividends on Preferred Shares

Participating preferred shares provide that the preferred shareholders participate above the stated preferential rate on a pro rata basis in dividend declarations with the common shareholders. This works as follows:

- First, the preferred shareholders receive their preference rate.
- Second, the common shareholders receive a specified matching dividend *if the amount declared is high enough.*
- *If the total declared dividend is larger than these two amounts,* the excess is divided on a pro rata basis between the two share classes.

The pro rata distribution may be based simply on the respective number of shares outstanding, the two classes' *total* base level dividends, or the respective *total* capital balances. Participation terms often reflect relative capital invested and must be specified in the articles of incorporation and stated on the share certificates.

Reporting Example

An example of a company that has participating shares is Power Corporation of Canada, a diversified international management and holding company active in financial services, communications, and a variety of other business sectors. Total assets are $378 billion. In its capital structure, Power Corporation reports subordinated voting shares, which are common shares; nonparticipating preferred shares; and participating preferred shares with the following terms:

PARTICIPATING SHARES

Participating Preferred Shares are entitled to ten votes per share; and, subject to the rights of holders of the First Preferred Shares to a non-cumulative dividend of 0.9375¢ per share per annum before dividends on the Subordinate Voting Shares and the further right to participate, share and share alike, with the holders of the Subordinate Voting Shares in any dividends that may be paid with respect to the Subordinate Voting Shares after payment of a dividend of 0.9375¢ per share per annum on the Subordinate Voting Shares.

Source: Power Corporation of Canada, 2014 annual financial statements, www.sedar.com, posted 18 March 2015.

The preferred shares are noncumulative but participate in dividends with common shares after both classes receive a base dividend.

Partially versus Fully Participating

Shares may be *partially participating* or *fully participating*. If partially participating, preferred shares may participate in dividend declarations in excess of their preference rate, but the participation is capped at a certain level. Dividends above this level accrue solely to the common shareholders. Fully participating shares, on the other hand, share in the full extent of dividend declarations.

For example, a corporation may issue preferred shares entitled to a dividend of $0.50, with participation up to $0.70 after common shareholders receive $0.25 per share. The $0.25 dividend to the common shareholder is the matching dividend, and it is specified in the articles of incorporation. It is meant to provide a certain rate of return on the common shares in the initial allocation and acknowledges that the share classes are of different relative size and value. In this case, participation with the common shareholders is limited to the additional $0.20 above the regular $0.50 rate.

Example

The following three cases, A, B, and C, illustrate various combinations of cumulative versus noncumulative rights and of participating versus nonparticipating rights. Assume that Mann Corp. has the following share capital outstanding:

Preferred shares, no-par, dividend entitlement, $0.50 per share; 10,000 shares outstanding	$250,000
Common shares, no-par, 40,000 shares outstanding	200,000

Case A

Preferred shares are noncumulative and nonparticipating; dividends have not been paid for two years; dividends declared, $28,000.

	Preferred	Common	Total
Step 1—Preferred, current ($0.50 × 10,000)	$5,000		$ 5,000
Step 2—Common (balance)	_____	$23,000	23,000
Total	$5,000	$23,000	$28,000

Because the preferred shares are noncumulative, preferred shares may receive dividends only for the current year regardless of the fact that dividends were missed in two previous years.

Case B

Preferred shares are *cumulative* and *nonparticipating;* dividends are two years in arrears; total dividends declared, $28,000.

	Preferred	Common	Total
Step 1—Preferred in arrears ($0.50 × 10,000 × 2)	$10,000		$10,000
Step 2—Preferred, current ($0.50 × 10,000)	5,000		5,000
Step 3—Common (balance)	_____	$13,000	13,000
Total	$15,000	$13,000	$28,000

Preferred shares receive their dividends in arrears and the current dividend before the common shares receive any dividend.

Case C

Preferred shares are cumulative, two years in arrears and fully participating after common shares have received $0.25 per share. *Participation is based on the respective total base dividend for one year.* Total dividends declared in this case are $37,000. Participation is based on one year's dividends: Preferred shares are entitled to $0.50 per share ($5,000 total), and common will receive $0.25 per share ($10,000 total). The base dividend is $15,000 (i.e., $5,000 + $10,000). Payment of dividends in arrears does not affect this calculation, which is based on *one* year's base dividend. Participation is 1/3 ($5,000/$15,000) for the preferred and 2/3 ($10,000/$15,000) for the common.

	Preferred	Common	Total
Step 1—Preferred, in arrears ($5,000 × 2)	$10,000		$10,000
Step 2a—Preferred, current (10,000 × $0.50)	5,000		5,000
b—Common, matching (40,000 × $0.25)		$10,000	10,000
c—Extra dividend, participating 1/3 : 2/3	4,000	8,000	12,000*
Totals	$19,000	$18,000	$37,000

*Extra dividend available: $37,000 − $10,000 − $5,000 − $10,000 = $12,000.

Had the preferred shares been *partially* participating, say, to a *total* of $0.75 per share, then the current year (excluding arrears) preferred dividend would have been limited to $7,500, and participation would have been a maximum of $2,500 ($7,500 − $5,000). The common shares would then have received more of the final $12,000 layer of dividends ($9,500, or $12,000 − $2,500).

In the absence of an explicit stipulation in the articles of incorporation or bylaws, preferred shareholders have no right to participate in dividends with common shares beyond their stated dividend rate.

Property Dividends

Corporations occasionally pay dividends with non-cash assets. Such dividends are called **property dividends**, or *dividends in kind.* The property may be an investment in the securities of other companies held by the corporation, real estate, merchandise, or any other non-cash asset designated by the board of directors. The dividend is recorded at the fair value of the assets distributed, and a gain (or loss) is recorded for the difference between book value and fair value of the asset.

Liquidating Dividends

Liquidating dividends are distributions that are a return of the amount received when shares were issued, rather than assets acquired through earnings. Owners' equity accounts *other than retained earnings* are debited. Since such dividends reduce contributed capital, they typically require creditor approval.

Liquidating dividends are appropriate when there is no intention or opportunity to conserve resources for asset replacement. A mining company might pay such a liquidating dividend when it is exploiting a nonreplaceable asset. Mining companies sometimes pay dividends on the basis of "earnings plus the amount of the deduction for depletion." Shareholders must be informed of the portion of any dividend that represents a return of capital, since the liquidation portion of the dividend is not income to the investor and is usually not taxable as income; it reduces the cost basis of the shares.

When accounting for a liquidating dividend, the debit would not go to retained earnings. For example, share capital might be debited. However, any other contributed capital accounts would be debited and eliminated before share capital would be reduced.

Scrip Dividends

A corporation that has a temporary cash shortage might declare a dividend to maintain a continuing dividend policy by issuing a **scrip dividend**. The dividend takes the form of a certificate issued. This certificate is essentially a form of a promissory note, which will be repaid in cash on its due date. This form of dividend is also called a *liability dividend*.

Stock Dividends

A stock dividend is a proportional distribution to shareholders of additional shares of the corporation. A stock dividend does not change the assets, liabilities, or total shareholders' equity of the issuing corporation. It does not change the proportionate ownership of any shareholder. It simply increases the number of shares outstanding.

For instance, assume that Early Broadcasting Ltd. has 120,000 common shares outstanding. One shareholder, J.S. Brown, owns 12,000 shares, or one-tenth of the shares. The corporation declares and issues a 10% stock dividend. This has the following effect on share capital:

	Before Dividend		After Dividend*	
Total shares outstanding	120,000	*100%*	132,000	*100%*
Brown's shareholding	12,000	*10%*	13,200	*10%*

*Previous outstanding total × 110%.

Brown's relative ownership percentage has not changed. If the shares sold for $20 per share before the dividend, what will happen to that market value after the split? Logically, it should decline.

	Before	After	
A. Total market value of the company (120,000 × $20)	$2,400,000	$2,400,000	(i.e., no change)
B. Shares outstanding	120,000	132,000	
Price per share (A ÷ B)	$20	$18.18	
Brown's total market value			
12,000 × $20.00	$ 240,000		
13,200 × $18.18		$ 240,000	

What will really happen to the market price of the shares in this situation? The answer is unclear. Often, there is a smaller decrease in market price than the size of the stock dividend would seem to dictate. That is, market value might fall to $18.50 rather than $18.18. Some believe that this is a market reaction to other factors (e.g., an anticipated increase in cash dividends that historically follows a stock dividend). Because of the complexity and sophistication of the stock markets, it is very difficult to determine why a share price does or does not change on a given day. However, it is generally recognized that if a company doubles its outstanding shares through a stock dividend, the market price will reduce by approximately one-half.

In the books, a stock dividend can cause the transfer of an amount from retained earnings to the contributed, or paid-in, capital accounts (i.e., share capital). Therefore, it changes only the internal account balances of shareholders' equity and not the total shareholders' equity.

Reasons for a Stock Dividend

Numerous reasons exist for a company to issue a stock dividend:

- To reveal that the firm plans to permanently retain a portion of earnings in the business. The effect of a stock dividend, through a debit to retained earnings and offsetting credits to permanent capital accounts, is to raise contributed capital and reduce retained earnings. This will shelter this amount from expectations of future declaration of cash or property dividends.
- To increase the number of shares outstanding, which reduces the market price per share and tends to increase the trading of shares in the market. Theoretically, a broader range of investors can afford investments in equity securities if the unit cost is low.
- To signal a planned future increase in cash dividends. As stated above, such a sequence of events has been historically validated, and the expectation of improved future cash flow tends to lift share price.

Dividend Reinvestment Plan

A **dividend reinvestment plan (DRIP)** allows shareholders to choose between a cash dividend and a stock dividend. The terms of this might appear as follows:

> Common shareholders may elect to have their cash dividends reinvested in common shares of the Company in accordance with the Company's Shareholder Dividend Reinvestment and Share Purchase Plan. Under the Plan, the Board of Directors determines whether the common shares will be purchased on the stock market or issued by the Company from treasury shares.

For example, Pengrowth Energy Corporation reported increases in capital due to its dividend reinvestment plan.

12. SHAREHOLDERS' CAPITAL

Pengrowth is authorized to issue an unlimited number of common shares and up to 10 million preferred shares. No preferred shares have been issued.

(Common shares in 000's)	2014 Number of common shares	Amount	2013 Number of common shares	Amount
Balance, beginning of year	522,031	$4,693.1	511,804	$4,634.8
Share based compensation (cash exercised)	257	1.6	336	2.1
Share based compensation (non-cash exercised)	1,985	13.2	1,260	11.3
Issued for cash under Dividend Reinvestment Plan ("DRIP")	9,165	51.8	8,631	44.9
Balance, end of year	533,438	$4,759.7	522,031	$4,693.1

DIVIDEND REINVESTMENT PLAN

Pengrowth's Dividend Reinvestment Plan ("DRIP") entitles shareholders to reinvest cash dividends in additional shares of Pengrowth. Under the DRIP, the shares are issued from treasury at a 5 percent discount to the weighted average closing price as determined by the plan.

Source: Pengrowth Energy Corporation, 2014 annual financial statements, www.sedar.com, posted 26 Feb 2015.

Accounting Issues Related to Stock Dividends

One major issue in accounting for stock dividends is the value that should be recognized. The shares issued for the dividend could be recorded at fair value, at stated (or par) value, or at some other value.

There are no specific accounting standards on these issues, but the CBCA requires shares to be issued at fair market value. In Ontario, on the other hand, legislation specifically permits the board of directors to capitalize any amount it desires. When the shareholder has the choice between cash and shares, it seems most logical to record the full fair value of the dividend. We will examine three alternatives: fair value, stated value, and memo entry.

Fair-Value Method

The board of directors would require capitalization of the current fair value of the additional shares issued. The fair value of the stock dividend should be measured on the basis of the market price per share on the declaration date.

Assume that Markholme Corp. has 464,000 common shares outstanding, originally issued for $2,784,000. The company declares and distributes a 5% common stock dividend on 1 July 20X2 and determines that an appropriate fair value is $7.25 per share. The following entry will be recorded:

Stock dividend (or, retained earnings)		
(464,000 × 5% = 23,200 × $7.25)	168,200	
Common shares, no-par (23,200 shares)		168,200

Stated-Value Method

The board of directors in certain jurisdictions may decide to capitalize a stated amount per share—average paid in per share to date, or par value, if applicable. Strong arguments can be made for some sort of stated value (i.e., not fair value) because (1) the corporation's assets, liabilities, and total shareholders' equity are not changed; and (2) the shareholders' proportionate ownership is not changed. If the market price per share is proportionately reduced by the stock dividend, then it is clear that the shareholders have received nothing of value and should not be encouraged to believe that they have. In these circumstances, capitalization should be limited to legal requirements.

If Markholme, explained above, declares the same 5% stock dividend but the board of directors determines that the average amount paid in to date for the outstanding common shares is to be used, then $6 ($2,784,000 ÷ 464,000) will be used to determine the capitalization amount. The entry will be identical, except the amount recognized will be $139,200 (464,000 × 5% × $6).

Memo Entry

Since a large stock dividend may be issued for the primary purpose of reducing market price per share, it is obvious at least in this case that the shareholder has received nothing of value. A memo entry may be recorded to identify the number of shares issued, outstanding, and subscribed. No change is made in any capital account. This parallels the treatment of a stock split, to be discussed later in this chapter. Large stock dividends are often called *stock splits effected as a stock dividend*.

For example, in March 2006, the Royal Bank of Canada announced a 100% stock dividend. If a shareholder owned 100 shares before the dividend, the shareholder had 200 shares afterward. The stock dividend was accounted for with a memo entry. However, this treatment may also be used for small stock dividends. Markholme, above, could record a memo entry documenting the distribution of 23,200 (464,000 × 5%) shares.

Timing of Recognition

Fundamentally, a stock dividend is recorded as a debit to retained earnings and a credit to the share capital account. However, unlike a cash dividend, a stock dividend *can be revoked prior to the issuance date*. As a result, many companies do not record the dividend on the declaration date but instead record it on the issuance date. Either recording approach can be used.

Example

Marvel Corp., which has 100,000 common shares outstanding, declares a 10% common stock dividend. The board of directors directs that the dividend be recorded at fair value. A total of 10,000 no-par common shares are issued. The fair value is $5 per share. The entries are as follows:

Alternative 1: Originating Entry at Declaration		
Declaration date		
Stock dividends (or, retained earnings)	50,000	
Stock dividends distributable*		50,000
*Reported as a credit in shareholders' equity until issuance.		
Issuance date		
Stock dividends distributable	50,000	
Common shares, no-par (5,000 shares)		50,000

Alternative 2: Originating Entry at Issuance		
Declaration date		
No entry		
Issuance date		
Stock dividends (or, retained earnings)	50,000	
Common shares, no-par (5,000 shares)		50,000

The differences between these two approaches are trivial. The stock dividends distributable account is not a liability because it does not involve settlement by the future transfer of assets (cash etc.) It is an obligation to issue equity and is properly classified in shareholders' equity. Note disclosure would accompany both alternatives.

Special Stock Dividends

When a stock dividend is of the same class as that held by the recipients, it is called an *ordinary stock dividend* (e.g., common shares issued to the owners of common). When a class of share capital other than the one already held by the recipients is issued, such a dividend is called a *special stock dividend* (e.g., preferred shares issued to the owners of common). In this case, the fair value of the preferred shares issued as a dividend should be recorded.

Fractional Share Rights

When a stock dividend is issued, many shareholders will own an "odd" number of shares and will be entitled to a fraction of a share. For example, when a firm issues a 5% stock dividend and a shareholder owns 30 shares, the shareholder is entitled to 1.5 shares ($30 \times 5\%$). When this happens, the firm may issue *fractional share rights* for portions of shares to which individual shareholders are entitled. It is also quite common for the company to write a cheque for the fair value of the fractional entitlement.

To demonstrate, suppose Moon Co. has 1,000,000 outstanding no-par common shares. Moon issues a 5% stock dividend. The fair value of the common shares is $80 per share, and this value will be used to record the stock dividend. The number of shares to be issued is 5% of the number of shares outstanding ($1,000,000 \times 5\%$), or 50,000 shares.

Assume the distribution of existing shares is such that 42,000 whole or complete shares can be issued. The firm will issue fractional share rights for the remaining 8,000 shares. Each fractional share right will entitle the holder to acquire 5%, or 1/20, of a share. Since there are 8,000 shares yet to be issued, there will be $8,000 \times 20$, or 160,000 fractional share rights issued. A market will develop for the fractional share rights, with each having a fair value of approximately 1/20 of a whole share ($80 \div 20$), or $4. Shareholders can buy or sell fractional share rights to the point where whole shares can be acquired. A holder will have to turn in 20 fractional share rights to receive one common share.

The entry for recording the issuance of the stock dividend and fractional share rights is as follows:

Stock dividends (or, retained earnings)		
(50,000 × $80)	4,000,000	
Common shares, no-par (42,000 shares × $80)		3,360,000
Common share fractional share rights		
(8,000 shares; 160,000 rights) (8,000 × $80)		640,000

When rights are turned in for redemption in common shares, the common share fractional share rights account is debited and common shares are credited. Suppose, for example, that 150,000 fractional share rights are turned in for 7,500 common shares ($150,000 \div 20$). The entry to record the transaction would be:

Common share fractional share rights	600,000	
Common shares, no-par (7,500 shares × $80)		600,000

If the remaining rights are allowed to lapse, the corporation would record contributed capital:

Common share fractional share rights	40,000	
Contributed capital, lapse of share rights		
(500 × $80)		40,000

Cash Alternative

An alternative to the issuance of fractional share rights is to make a cash payment to shareholders for any fractional shares to which they are entitled. The shareholder above who owns 30 shares and is entitled to 1.5 shares will receive one share from the firm and a cash payment of $40 ($80 per share × .5 shares), representing the value of the one-half share at current fair value. The entry to record the cash payment is a debit to retained earnings and a credit to cash. This procedure is simpler for the shareholder because there is no need to buy or sell fractional shares.

If cash were offered for fractional shares, the stock dividend would be recorded, in summary form, as follows:

Stock dividends (or retained earnings) (50,000 × $80)	4,000,000	
Common shares, no-par (42,000 shares)		3,360,000
Cash (8,000 shares × $80)		640,000

This alternative clearly has cash flow implications for the company, but it avoids the complications of dealing with fractional shares for all concerned.

Summary

Dividends and distributions are summarized as follows:

Type	Shareholder Receives	Recorded At	Watch Out For
Cash	**Cash**	**Exchange amount; cash**	**Amount allocated to common versus preferred shares**
Property	Some company asset as designated by the board of directors: inventory, investments, etc.	Fair value of property received; gain or loss recorded on declaration	—
Scrip	Promissory note	Exchange amount; as stated	Shareholders get a receivable; company sets up a liability
Stock	Shares	May be recorded at fair value, book value, or an arbitrary value May also be recorded as a memo entry only	May issue fractional shares for part shares or May issue cash for part shares
Stock split (see next section)	Shares	n/a	Memo entry only; not recorded

CONCEPT REVIEW

1. Of the four dates pertaining to cash dividends, which dates require accounting entries? What are the entries?
2. What effect does a cash dividend have on shareholders' equity? How does the effect of a stock dividend differ from that of a cash dividend?
3. What is a participating preferred dividend?

STOCK SPLITS

A **stock split** is a change in the number of shares outstanding with no change in the recorded capital accounts. A stock split usually increases the number of shares outstanding by a significant amount, such as doubling or tripling the number of outstanding shares. Shares that sell at high market values are perceived to be less marketable, especially to smaller investors. Therefore, the primary purpose of a stock split is to increase the number of shares outstanding and decrease the market price per share. In turn, this may increase the market activity of the shares. By increasing the number of shares outstanding, a stock split also reduces earnings per share.

For example, Bell Canada Enterprises has split its shares three times since the company's inception:

- 1 October 1948, 4-for-1;
- 26 April 1979, 3-for-1; and
- 15 May 1997, 2-for-1.

An investor who owned 100 shares in 1948 would own 2,400 shares $[([100 \times 4] \times 3) \times 2]$ after the third split. These shares represent the same proportional share of the total company.

In contrast, a **reverse split** decreases the number of shares. It results in a proportional *reduction* in the number of shares issued and outstanding and an increase in the average book value per share. Reverse splits may be used to increase the market price of shares with a low market value per share. For example, Domtar Paper (Canada) Inc. implemented a 1-for-12 reverse split in 2009, with fractional shares distributed in cash:

> As a result of the reverse stock split, every 12 shares of the Company's issued and outstanding exchangeable shares at the Effective Time have been automatically combined into one issued and outstanding exchangeable share, without any change in the par value of such shares, subject to the elimination of fractional shares resulting from the reverse stock split which have been aggregated and sold into whole shares on the open market by the Company's transfer agent with proceeds of such sales allocated to the record holders' respective accounts pro rata in lieu of fractional shares.

Accounting for Stock Splits

In a stock split, *a memo entry is recorded*. No consideration has been received by the corporation for the issued shares. Shares issued, outstanding, and subscribed are changed, as is par value, if any. The following dollar amounts are *not* changed:

1. Share capital account;
2. Additional contributed capital accounts;
3. Retained earnings; and
4. Total shareholders' equity.

Consider a 200%, or 2-for-1, stock split (two new shares for each old share), and compare it with a 100% stock dividend (one additional share for each share already outstanding). For example, assume Technology Corp. has 40,000 shares outstanding, which were issued initially at $10 per share. The current balance of retained earnings is $450,000. A 100% stock dividend and a 200% stock split accomplish the same things in economic terms in that they double the outstanding shares but halve the market value per share. However, the two transactions can appear differently on the books if the dividend is recorded but the split is reflected through a memo only. The difference is shown in Exhibit 14-1, where the stock dividend is recorded at $10 per share, and the split is accorded memo treatment.

EXHIBIT 14-1

TECHNOLOGY CORPORATION

Stock Dividend and Stock Split Compared

	Total Prior to Share Issue	Total After 100% Stock Dividend	Total After 2-for-1 Stock Split
Initial issue 40,000 × $10 =	$400,000		
100% stock dividend: (40,000 + 40,000) × $10 =		$800,000*	
Two-for-one stock split: 80,000 × $5			$400,000
Share capital	$400,000	$800,000*	$400,000
Retained earnings	450,000	50,000*	450,000
Total shareholders' equity	$850,000	$850,000*	$850,000

*Retained earnings capitalized: 40,000 shares × $10 = $400,000 (entry: debit retained earnings, $400,000; credit share capital accounts, $400,000.) After the stock dividend, share capital equals $800,000, which is $400,000 + $400,000. Retained earnings is $450,000 − $400,000, or $50,000.

In Exhibit 14-1, note that the stock dividend, recorded at $10 per share, changes both share capital and retained earnings. The stock split, however, changes neither of these amounts. *Total* shareholders' equity is unchanged by both the stock dividend and the stock split.

Commentary

Remember that the shareholder is left in the same position whether there is a 200% stock split or a 100% stock dividend—two shares will be owned for every one share previously held. Similarly, the market price of the shares should be the same whether the transaction is described as a split or a dividend.

This similarity of results makes the different accounting methods suspect, since there are alternatives available for transactions that are basically the same. This hardly seems to promote the idea of *substance over form*. Accordingly, *memo treatment* of a large stock dividend is the preferable approach because it produces the same result as the memo treatment for a stock split.

Adjustments Required for Stock Splits

When a stock is split, the per-share values all change. For example, in a 2-for-1 split, the paid-in value per share is halved. If Sincon Corp. has 40,000 outstanding shares and total contributed capital of $800,000, the average issue price is $20. After a 2-for-1 split, the company will have 80,000 shares, and the average issue price drops to $10 per share.

Similarly, other per-share amounts, such as earnings per share (EPS), will change. Suppose that Sincon had EPS of $3 before the split and paid dividends of $2 per share. The equivalent EPS after the split will be $1.50. To pay dividends after the split that are equivalent to the dividend rate before the split, Sincon needs to pay only $1—but on twice as many shares.

Because of the change in number of shares in a stock split (or a reverse split), the company must recalculate all prior years' per-share amounts so that they will be comparable with post-split per-share amounts. Earnings per share and dividends per share must be restated.

Conversion rights for senior securities must also be adjusted. If preferred shares are convertible into three common shares prior to a 2-for-1 common share split, the preferred shares will be convertible into six common shares after the split.

Implementation

A stock split is implemented by either:

1. Calling in all of the old shares and concurrently issuing the split shares, or
2. Issuing the additional split shares with notification to shareholders of the change in outstanding shares.

It is more common simply to issue additional shares. If the shares have an assigned par value, share certificates must be replaced to reflect revised par value.

ADDITIONAL CONTRIBUTED CAPITAL

Contributed capital is created by a number of events that involve the corporation and its shareholders. Several accounts for additional contributed (paid-in) capital were introduced in this chapter, such as contributed capital on share repurchase.

Donated Capital

Sometimes a corporation will receive a donation of assets, which creates **donated capital**. An example would be a donation of land from a shareholder. In this case, the corporation records the donated asset at its fair market value, with a corresponding credit to donated capital. The donation is viewed by the accounting profession as a capital contribution rather than as an earnings item (i.e., it is not a gain.) Donated capital appears in shareholders' equity as additional contributed capital. It must be described as to source.

Other

Shares may also be donated back to a company. Corporate legislation typically requires that such shares be retired, and the retirement entry is similar to the examples given earlier, except that there is no cash consideration given—the entire paid-in value of the shares (at average cost) is transferred to an additional contributed capital account. If the shares can be legally held and reissued, the shares may be accounted for as treasury shares.

Exhibit 14-2 summarizes some of the transactions that may cause increases or decreases in additional contributed capital.

EXHIBIT 14-2

TRANSACTIONS THAT MAY CHANGE ADDITIONAL CONTRIBUTED CAPITAL

Increase

1. Receipt of donated assets
2. Retirement of shares at a price less than average issue price to date
3. Issue of par value shares at a price or assigned value higher than par
4. Treasury stock transactions, shares reissued above cost
5. Stock option transactions (see Chapter 15)

Decrease

1. Retirement of shares at a price greater than average issue price to date, when previous contributed capital has been recorded
2. Treasury stock transactions, shares issued below cost, when previous contributed capital has been recorded
3. Financial restructuring

ACCUMULATED OTHER COMPREHENSIVE INCOME

Accumulated other comprehensive income (AOCI) are equity accounts that accumulate gains and losses that are part of *other comprehensive income* but not part of *earnings*. AOCI reflect the *cumulative amounts* of the items that are added to or subtracted from earnings to arrive at comprehensive income. These cumulative gains and losses are often *unrealized* but may also be *realized* amounts. AOCI is a component of shareholders' equity.

Example

Assume the following facts for AgriCorp Ltd., a company with investments carried at fair value, with unrealized gains and losses recorded in other comprehensive income (OCI). That is, the company holds investments classified as fair-value-through-other-comprehensive-income (FVTOCI) investments:

	20X2	20X3	20X4
FVTOCI investments			
Cost; purchased in January 20X2	$100,000		
Fair value, end of year	$130,000	$110,000	$160,000
Earnings	$345,000	$287,000	$371,000

Based on this information, comprehensive income is as follows:

	20X2	20X3	20X4
Earnings	$345,000	$287,000	$371,000
Other Comprehensive Income: Change in fair value			
($130,000 – $100,000)	30,000		
($110,000 – $130,000)		(20,000)	
($160,000 – $110,000)			50,000
Comprehensive income	$375,000	$267,000	$421,000

Accumulated other comprehensive income (AOCI) would be:

	20X2	20X3	20X4
Shareholders' equity			
AOCI caused by FVTOCI investments			
($130,000 − $100,000)	$30,000		
($110,000 − $100,000), or ($30,000 − $20,000)		$10,000	
($160,000 − $100,000), or ($10,000 + $50,000)			$60,000

This example has ignored income tax implications. Elements that are taxable, either in the current period or in the future, have tax assigned to them when recognized and are reported net of tax in other comprehensive income and in AOCI. Reporting issues related to income tax are explored in later chapters of this text.

Sources of Accumulated Other Comprehensive Income

Standard setters dictate the items that create *other comprehensive income (OCI)* and AOCI. Items in OCI need to be presented based on whether they are reclassified to profit or loss or stay in AOCI. There are a limited number of items at present, although the list seems to keep growing:

- Gains and losses on FVTOCI (equity) financial instruments (see Chapter 11);
- Gains and losses on FVOCI (debt) financial instruments (see Chapter 11);
- Revaluation of property, plant, and equipment to fair value (see Chapter 10);
- Gains and losses on cash flow hedging instruments (see Chapters 13 and 15);
- Change in fair value due to credit risk for financial liabilities designated at FVTPL (see Chapter 12);
- Actuarial revaluations and certain experience gains and losses related to defined benefit pensions (see Chapter 19); and
- Translation gains and losses on foreign operations whose functional currency is a foreign currency rather than the presentation currency.

Standards require these amounts to be shown separately in AOCI.

Translation Gains and Losses on Foreign Operations

The final item in AOCI listed above is the **cumulative foreign currency translation account**. This item represents unrealized gains and losses that arise from a certain type of foreign currency exposure.

In Chapter 13, accounting for a liability denominated in a foreign currency was reviewed; gains and losses caused by changes in foreign exchange rates are included in earnings as they arise, and no reserve is involved. However, many corporations have subsidiaries in one or more foreign countries. The basic operations of these foreign subsidiaries are carried out in a currency other than the Canadian dollar, and their separate entity financial statements are reported in the host country foreign currency. For the parent company to prepare consolidated financial statements, the foreign operation's *foreign currency* financial statements must be translated into the parent's *presentation currency*. The process of translation is a topic for advanced accounting courses and is not discussed here.

However, in general terms, translation of foreign operations gives rise to an overall exchange gain or loss. If the foreign operation has revenues and expenses primarily in the foreign currency, the subsidiary has a **functional currency** that is the foreign currency. The exchange gains and losses that arise from translating the financial statements of such foreign operations do not flow through earnings, but instead, the annual amounts are included in other comprehensive income. The cumulative amount is in AOCI. Alternatively, if the foreign subsidiary's cash flows are dominated by sales and expenses that are not in the subsidiary's domestic currency, then remeasurement is required and exchange gains and losses are part of earnings.

THE STATEMENT OF CHANGES IN EQUITY, OTHER DISCLOSURE, AND THE STATEMENT OF CASH FLOWS (SCF)

The details of the components of equity are shown in a statement of changes in equity. Items in AOCI can be shown either on the statement of changes in equity or in the disclosure notes. That is, it is possible to show only a single line for AOCI on a statement of changes in equity or with the break-down shown in the notes.

The Statement of Changes in Equity

Exhibit 14-3 illustrates the general format of a statement of changes in equity. Numbers have been assumed. Each company will tailor this statement to its own shareholders' equity accounts and transactions. There are columns for each account within equity. The statement starts with opening dollar balances, and has a line item for each source of change to an account, resulting in the end-of-year balance.

EXHIBIT 14-3

STATEMENT OF CHANGES IN EQUITY—GENERAL FORMAT

(in thousands) (numbers assumed)	Preferred Shares	Common Shares	Retained Earnings	Accumulated OCI FVTOCI Investments	Total Equity
Balance at 1 January 20X1	$2,000	$4,800	$13,600	$700	$ 21,100
Comprehensive income	—	—	2,300	150	2,450
Shares issued for cash	500	900	—	—	1,400
Share buyback	—	(350)	(200)	—	(550)
Share issue costs	—	—	(100)	—	(100)
Dividends to shareholders		—	(600)	—	(600)
Shares issued under DRIP program*	—	250	—	—	250
Balance at 31 December 20X1	$2,500	$5,600	$15,000	$850	$23,950

*Since there were $600 of dividends, and $250 of shares issued under a DRIP program, cash dividends must be $350.

Note that *comprehensive income* affects retained earnings (for the amount of earnings) *and AOCI* (for the unrealized amounts that are part of other comprehensive income but not earnings, here assumed to be caused by FVTOCI investments). Some companies will add extra columns to include the *number of shares* for common and preferred shares, in addition to the dollar amount.

Other Disclosure

For each class of share capital, the legal rights, preferences, and restrictions must be described in the disclosure notes. This includes all authorized share classes, whether shares are issued or not. The number of shares issued and fully paid at year-end must be disclosed, as well as shares issued and not fully paid (shares subscribed). The *number of shares* issued, repurchased, and retired during the year must be disclosed, if this information is not in the statement of changes in equity.

Companies must disclose their objectives, policies, and processes for *managing capital.* This includes their definition of capital, which obviously includes equity but also may include some forms of debt. If there are externally imposed capital requirements, these requirements and compliance with the requirements must be disclosed.

The Statement of Cash Flows (SCF)

Transactions affecting equity accounts must be reflected on the statement of cash flows (SCF). However, non-cash transactions are excluded from the SCF and separately listed in the disclosure notes. The following items are common on the SCF:

- Net earnings, which increase retained earnings, are listed as the first item in operating activities, assuming that the indirect method is used to present operating activities.
- Dividends are a cash outflow, adjusted for any change in dividends payable. Dividends may be classified in financing activities or in operating activities, a policy choice to be made by the company.
- Stock dividends and stock splits are non-cash transactions.
- Shares issued for cash are listed as an inflow in financing activities.
- Cash collected on subscriptions receivable are listed in financing activities.
- Purchase and sale of treasury stock creates cash flow, listed in financing activities as an outflow or an inflow.
- Shares bought back and retired are listed as an outflow in financing activities at their total cash amount, whether recorded in share capital, contributed capital, or retained earnings.
- Non-cash transactions include shares issued for assets other than cash, many changes in OCI that are based on unrealized changes in fair value, appropriations, and the like. These items are disclosed rather than listed on the SCF.

In all cases, the transaction affecting equity accounts should be recreated, and the cash impact determined. This cash flow is then listed on the SCF.

Example

Return to the statement of changes in equity shown in Exhibit 14-3. Based on the information shown, the following items would be included on an SCF:

- In operating activities, earnings, $2,300;
- In financing activities, issued common shares for cash, $900;
- In financing activities, issued preferred shares for cash, $500;
- In financing activities, paid share issue costs, ($100);
- In financing activities, bought back shares, ($550); and
- In financing activities, or operating activities, paid dividends, $(350) ($600 − $250).

Non-cash transaction: issued shares of $250 under a dividend reinvestment program.

Reporting Example

Exhibit 14-4 shows the statement of changes in shareholders' equity for Brookfield Asset Management Inc., a Canadian public company operating worldwide. The company operates assets including property, renewable energy, infrastructure, and private equity.

EXHIBIT 14-4

BROOKFIELD ASSET MANAGEMENT INCORPORATED

CONSOLIDATED STATEMENTS OF CHANGES IN EQUITY

YEAR ENDED DECEMBER 31, 2014 (MILLIONS)	Common Share Capital	Contributed Surplus	Retained Earnings	Ownership Changes[1]	Accumulated Other Comprehensive Income			Common Equity	Preferred Equity	Non-controlling Interests	Total Equity
					Revaluation Surplus	Currency Translation	Other Reserves[2]				
Balance as at December 31, 2013	$2,899	$159	$7,159	$2,354	$5,165	$190	$(145)	$17,781	$3,098	$26,647	$47,526
Changes in year:											
Net income	—	—	3,110	—	—	—	—	3,110	—	2,099	5,209
Other comprehensive income	—	—	—	—	1,094	(670)	(123)	301	—	110	411
Comprehensive income	—	—	3,110	—	1,094	(670)	(123)	3,411	—	2,209	5,620
Shareholder distributions											
Common equity	—	—	(388)	—	—	—	—	(388)	—	—	(388)
Preferred equity	—	—	(154)	—	—	—	—	(154)	—	—	(154)
Non-controlling interests	—	—		—	—	—	—	—	—	(2,428)	(2,428)
Other items											
Equity issuances, use of redemptions	132	(18)	(69)	—	—	—	—	45	451	2,505	3,001
Share-based compensation	—	44	(7)	—	—	—	—	37	—	16	53
Ownership changes	—	—	51	(375)	(126)	39	(168)	(579)	—	596	17
Total change in year	132	26	2,543	(375)	968	(631)	(291)	2,372	451	2,898	5,721
Balance as at December 31, 2014	$3,031	$185	$9,702	$1,979	$6,133	$(441)	$(436)	$20,153	$3,549	$29,545	$53,247

1. Includes gains or losses on changes in ownership interests of consolidated subsidiaries
2. Includes available-for-sale securities, cash flow hedges, actuarial changes on pension plans and equity accounted other comprehensive income, net of associated income taxes

Source: Brookfield Asset Management Inc., 2014 Annual Financial Statements, www.sedar.com, posted 27 March 2015.

The statement begins with the share capital account column; the statement shows that shares were issued during the period for $132 (all amounts in millions). Next is the contributed surplus account column showing changes under the terms of stock options and that shares were repurchased. The next account column is retained earnings, which is adjusted for net income, dividends distributed, and other items. The next account column relates to ownership changes during the year. The next three columns relate to AOCI. An alternative presentation would have been to show one column for AOCI and show the detailed breakdown in the notes to the financial statements. The first column related to AOCI is revaluation surplus for adjustments to fair value from using the revaluation model for some of the company's assets. The second column related to AOCI is due to foreign currency translation adjustments. The final column related to AOCI includes other reserves. The next two columns relate to common and preferred equity. The final column relates to non-controlling interest.

CONCEPT REVIEW

1. How do a stock split and a stock dividend differ in their impact on the shareholders' equity accounts?

2. Identify at least two ways in which a corporation can obtain contributed capital other than by the issuance of new shares.

3. What items create unrealized gains and losses that give rise to AOCI reported in equity?

Looking Forward

Shareholders' equity issues are not now on the agenda of either the IASB or the Canadian AcSB. However, the definition of *accumulated other comprehensive income* and the circumstances under which it is recognized and derecognized are being deliberated as part of a review of the conceptual framework.

Accounting Standards for Private Enterprises

There are very few differences between public and private companies in the area of accounting for equity interests. However, private companies are *required* to follow the standards governing share retirement and treasury stock transactions as described, specifically in terms of subscription receivable and share issuance costs (must be contra-share capital account, i.e., reported as a debit balance netted from share capital). The IASB has no standards in this area; the chapter material is presented as a logical approach, but not the required approach, for public companies.

Shares with special terms and conditions are frequently encountered in private companies. This is caused by opportunities for tax planning, the need to balance competing shareholder interests, and various succession and incentive plans. Disclosure of the terms and conditions of shares is just as important for private companies as for public companies.

When shares are issued for non-cash consideration, a private company will value the transaction at the fair value of the shares given up, unless the valuation of the shares is problematic. If the fair value of the assets is more clearly determinable, then this value should be used. The IASB standards *require that the fair value of the assets received* be used to value the transaction.

For private companies, net income is reported, but there is no reporting of comprehensive income. There are no unrealized amounts that must be included in such a measure. For example, the investment category FVTOCI does not exist for private companies. If there are specific unrealized amounts that are excluded from net income, such as unrealized gains and losses from a foreign subsidiary, they are allocated directly to a separate equity account and are not recognized first through comprehensive income.

The approach to classifying foreign subsidiaries is different under ASPE. While IFRS relies on identification of a functional currency, ASPE requires foreign subsidiaries to be classified as self-sustaining or integrated, based on the nature and extent of parent company relations and transactions. Self-sustaining subsidiaries cause unrealized exchange gains and losses in equity, while integrated operations cause exchange gains and losses recorded in earnings.

Finally, a private company has no requirement to prepare a comprehensive statement of changes in equity. Only a retained earnings statement is included with the financial statements. The changes in other equity accounts may be included in the disclosure notes.

RELEVANT STANDARDS

CPA Canada Handbook, Part I (IASB):

- IAS 1, Presentation of Financial Statements
- IFRS 2, Share-based Payments
- IFRIC 17, Distributions of Non-cash Assets to Owners

CPA Canada Handbook, Part II (ASPE):

- Section 3240, Share Capital
- Section 3251, Equity
- Section 3260, Reserves
- Section 3831, Non-monetary Transactions

SUMMARY OF KEY POINTS

1. Equity is a residual amount on the statement of financial position but has various component elements. The major sources are contributed capital from shareholders and earnings.
2. Ownership claims are represented by shares. Different share classes have different contractual rights; the two basic types of shares are common and preferred. Preferred shares have one or more contractually specified preferences over common shares, while common shares generally are voting and have a residual claim to the firm's assets.

3. In conformity with legislative requirements, most shares issued are no-par shares. The entire amount of consideration received on the issuance of no-par shares is recorded in the share capital account.

4. Authorized capital represents the total number of shares that legally can be issued. Issued shares are the number of shares that have been issued to shareholders to date. Treasury stock exists when outstanding shares are reacquired by the corporation and are held pending resale. Outstanding shares are those currently held by shareholders. Subscribed shares are unissued shares that must be used to meet subscription contracts.

5. When a corporation issues shares for assets or for services, the fair value of the goods or services received is used to value the transaction. If shares are issued as a basket, the proportional or incremental method could be used to value the transaction, based on information available.

6. Share issue costs are either offset against the proceeds received, resulting in the net proceeds being recorded in share capital, or deducted from retained earnings.

7. When shares are retired, an amount of share capital relating to the shares is first removed at average cost. If the remaining balance is a credit, it is used to increase a contributed capital account on share retirement. If the remaining balance is a debit, it is debited to existing contributed capital account from prior retirements in this class of shares, if any, and any remaining balance is debited to retained earnings.

8. Treasury stock is debited to a contra shareholders' equity account titled "treasury stock," at cost. When the stock is resold, the difference between the acquisition price and the resale price is accounted for using the same rules as retirements.

9. Retained earnings represents the accumulated profit or loss, less dividends declared since the inception of the corporation, and certain adjustments arising from share retirement, error correction, and changes in accounting policy.

10. Dividends are distributions to shareholders and may be in the form of cash, non-cash assets, debt, or the corporation's own shares.

11. Dividends are allocated to the various share classes based on their respective contractual claims. If preferred shares are cumulative and dividends are not paid in full in a given year, dividends declared in a later year are first paid to the preferred shares for the amount in arrears (plus their current dividend) before any amount is allocated to common shares. If preferred shares are participating, they receive a base dividend, then the common shares receive a base dividend; any dividend declared over the base is allocated between the two share classes.

12. Stock dividends are proportional issuances of additional shares. Stock dividends may be recorded at fair value, at a stated amount, or in a memo entry. In general, small stock dividends are recorded at fair value, while large dividends are recorded in a memo entry.

13. Fractional shares are issued when a shareholder would receive a portion of a share as a result of a stock dividend. Fractional shares are recorded in a shareholders' equity account that may lapse and create contributed capital or may be turned in for whole shares, creating share capital. Alternatively, the company may pay out money in lieu of fractional shares.

14. A stock split is a change in the number of shares outstanding accompanied by an offsetting change in value per share. A memo entry reflects the changed number of outstanding shares.

15. Accumulated other comprehensive income (AOCI) within equity is caused by cumulative amounts designated by standard setters as part of other comprehensive income.

16. Companies are required to disclose the components of shareholders' equity, along with a statement that shows the change in each account within shareholders' equity during the year. Complete disclosure of the terms of shares is also required.

Key Terms

accumulated other comprehensive income

appropriated retained earnings

callable

classes of shares

common shares

cumulative foreign currency translation account

declaration date	public companies
deficit	record date
dividend reinvestment plan (DRIP)	restricted retained earnings
dividends in arrears	restricted shares
donated capital	reverse split
ex-dividend date	scrip dividend
functional currency	share issue costs
net assets	shareholders' agreement
no-par shares	shelf registration
normal course issuer bid	single-transaction method
par value shares	special shares
payment date	stock split
preferred shares	stock subscriptions
premium	treasury stock
private companies	
property dividends	

Review Problem 14-1

On 2 January 20X1, Greene Corp. was incorporated in the province of Ontario. It was authorized to issue an unlimited number of no-par value common shares, and 10,000 shares of no-par, $8, cumulative and nonparticipating preferred shares. During 20X1, the firm completed the following transactions:

8 Jan.	Accepted subscriptions for 40,000 common shares at $12 per share. Down payment on the subscribed shares totalled $150,000.
30 Jan.	Issued 4,000 preferred shares in exchange for the following assets: machinery with a fair market value of $35,000, a factory with a fair market value of $110,000, and land with an appraised value of $295,000.
15 Mar.	Machinery with a fair market value of $55,000 was donated to the company.
25 Apr.	Collected the balance of the subscriptions receivable and issued common shares.
30 June	Purchased 2,200 common shares at $18 per share. The shares were retired.
31 Dec.	Closed the income summary to retained earnings. The income for the period was $198,000.
31 Dec.	Declared sufficient cash dividends to allow a $1 per share dividend for outstanding common shares. The dividend is payable on 10 January 20X2 to shareholders of record on 5 January 20X2.

Required:

1. Prepare the journal entries to record the above transactions.
2. Prepare a multicolumn statement of changes in equity that explains the change in each equity account.
3. Prepare the shareholders' equity section of the SFP for Greene at 31 December 20X1.

REVIEW PROBLEM 14-1—SOLUTION

Account for subscription of common shares		
Cash	150,000	
Stock subscription receivable	330,000	
Common shares subscribed (40,000 shares)		480,000
Issue preferred shares in exchange for assets; recorded at fair market value of the assets		
Machinery	35,000	
Factory	110,000	
Land	295,000	
Preferred shares (4,000 shares)		440,000
Record receipt of donated assets		
Machinery	55,000	
Contributed capital—donations		55,000
Record receipt of cash for subscribed shares and issuance of shares		
Cash	330,000	
Stock subscription receivable		330,000
Common shares subscribed (40,000 shares)	480,000	
Common shares (40,000 shares)		480,000
Record acquisition and retirement of common shares		
Common shares ($480,000 ÷ 40,000) × 2,200	26,400	
Retained earnings	13,200	
Cash ($18 × 2,200)		39,600

Close the income summary		
Income summary	198,000	
Retained earnings		198,000
Record dividends declared		
Preferred dividends declared (or retained earnings)	32,000	
Common dividends declared (or retained earnings)	37,800	
Dividends payable, preferred shares		32,000
Dividends payable, common shares		37,800
Preferred dividend: 4,000 shares × $8		
Common dividend: 37,800 shares × $1		

GREENE CORPORATION

Changes in Shareholders' Equity for the Year Ended 31 December 20X1

	Preferred shares	Common shares	Common shares subscribed	Donated Capital	Retained earnings	Total equity
Balance at 1 January 20X1	$ —	$ —	$ —	$ —	$ —	$ —
Earnings and comprehensive income					198,000	198,000
Shares subscribed			480,000			480,000
Shares issued	440,000	480,000	(480,000)			440,000
Share buyback		(26,400)			(13,200)	(39,600)
Donation of assets				55,000		55,000
Dividends to preferred shareholders					(32,000)	(32,000)
Dividends to common shareholders					(37,800)	(37,800)
Balance at 31 December 20X1	$440,000	$453,600	—	$55,000	$115,000	$1,063,600

GREENE CORPORATION

Shareholders' Equity at 31 December 20X1

Contributed capital	
Share capital	
Preferred shares, no-par, $8, cumulative and non-participating (10,000 shares authorized, 4,000 shares issued)	$ 440,000
Common shares, no-par (unlimited shares authorized, 37,800 shares issued and outstanding)	453,600
Other contributed capital	
Donation of machinery	55,000
Total contributed capital	$ 948,600
Retained earnings	115,000
Total shareholders' equity	$1,063,600

CASE 14-1

WINERY INC.

Winery Inc. (WI) is a private corporation formed in 20X5. Prior to 20X5, WI had been operating as a partnership owned by the Verity family. Due to their success and desire to expand they have made the decision to incorporate so that they will have additional sources of financing. They are just establishing their accounting policies for their first year-end as a corporation. Their previous financial statements as a partnership were used for filing their tax returns and management purposes. They were not audited or reviewed.

WI grows grapes and produces wines in Ontario. It also produces beer, spirits, and juices. WI has a small store on the property where it operates winery tours and sells wine. WI incorporated to raise additional capital to expand its operations by building a new building for the winery operations that has 50% additional capacity and a larger store.

In 20X5, to finance the expansion of the winery, WI obtained a bank loan with Big Bank. Previously, when WI operated as a partnership, the bank had provided the company with a line of credit and the owners had provided personal guarantees. The loan now has the personal guarantees removed and instead the bank requires annual audited financial statements and has a financial covenant that stipulates a maximum debt to equity ratio.

You have recently been hired to develop new accounting policies for WI's 31 December year-end. Previously, the partnership used the cash basis of accounting. The owners know this will no longer be suitable for their corporation. You have been asked by the owners to discuss alternatives and provide recommendations on the appropriate accounting policies for events below that have occurred during 20X5. WI has a tax rate of 34% and an incremental borrowing rate of 10%.

1. The Verity family was issued Class A shares that have 10 votes per share. Other private investors were issued Class B shares with one vote per share. Investors were allowed to purchase the Class B shares in installments over the next four years. All shares must be fully paid in 20X9.

2. WI issued preferred shares in 20X5 to private investors. Instead of cash dividends, shareholders will receive bottles of wine as dividends.

3. In the past, income taxes were paid by the partners (partners taxed personally) not by the corporation. WI anticipates a taxable loss of $500,000 this year due to the expansion.

4. WI initiated a stock option plan in 20X5. Stock options will be granted if employees reach a targeted level of sales for the year.

5. WI incurred $80,000 of costs in 20X5 to develop a website for the company. This included acquired software, costs to register the Internet domain name, research ideas on the style of the website, graphic design, consulting fees, training, and monthly updates on prices.

6. A customer can purchase WI's wine in the store at the winery and, starting in 20X5, through the new website. A customer can become a member of WI's new wine club. To join the club, a $200 annual fee is paid. In return, the member is shipped one bottle of wine a month. As part of the annual fee, members receive a free subscription to the Wine Digest, which could be purchased on its own. If the member likes the wine, he or she can then order a case through the website at a 10% discount.

7. The new winery was completed by the beginning of the summer of 20X5. The old winery has been declared a heritage site that cannot be torn down. This has been converted into two stores, which were rented out to two separate tenants with a two-year lease. One store sells local crafts and the other is a farmers market. Lease payments are a small fee of $100 a month plus 10% of revenues. Once WI has enough cash, the company wants to convert this building into a restaurant.

8. Due to the expanded capacity of its new winery, WI did not have enough grapes for production needs. WI entered into an agreement to purchase some grapes from Chile for production. To protect the company from foreign exchange fluctuations, WI entered into a hedge.

9. For tax planning purposes when converting to a corporation, WI issued term preferred shares to the owners. These shares have a cumulative dividend of 10% and a mandatory repayment date in 10 years. Any unpaid dividends must be repaid at that date.

Required:

Prepare the report requested.

CASE 14-2

CONSTANCE INC.

Constance Inc. (CI) is a small private company located in Miramichi, New Brunswick. CI was incorporated in late 20X0 and has 10 common shareholders, consisting of two founders and eight of the founders' friends and relatives. At the time of CI's incorporation, each shareholder was issued 200,000 common shares. In 20X1, CI completed development of technology that has the potential to revolutionize online clothing shopping. The technology, patented in 20X1 as *Check Me Out*, was sold to one major online clothing retailer in 20X1. During fiscal 20X2, an additional seven on-line clothing retailers purchased the technology. However, now, in early 20X3, cash is tight at CI. Current investors do not have the personal resources to invest further, yet CI desperately needs more cash to market and sell *Check Me Out* to clothing retailers. Bank loans are not an option for financing because of the perceived risk of CI. CI's founders believe that a takeover by a large technology company or on-line retailer is the best outcome for all.

Check Me Out enables a shopper to upload personal photographs to a clothing retailer's website, once the retailer is a client of *Check Me Out*. These photographs are translated into a 3-D image of the shopper. The shoppers can then virtually "try on" the retailer's clothing and view the resulting images from almost 100 different angles. The technology has received positive feedback, and CI's owners are confident that CI will be a success. Large technology firms have started to show interest in CI as a takeover target. Shareholders are hoping that something firms up in this regard in the next 6 to 12 months.

The founders of CI are not knowledgeable in the area of financial accounting. They realize the importance of understandable financial statements and want to make sure all applicable accounting standards are followed. For this reason, they engage the firm of Martin and Leaves Public Accountants to advise on accounting transactions in the 20X3 fiscal year. You are a co-op student working at Martin and Leaves, with a strong handle on intermediate accounting topics. For this reason, you have been asked to evaluate several issues raised by CI and prepare a memo detailing your analysis, additional information needed, and your recommendations. CI prepares its financial statements in accordance with IFRS. You know that potential purchasers of CI will be very interested in reported EBITDA (earnings before interest, tax, depreciation, and amortization).

Issue 1: In January 20X3, CI's founders attended several trade shows to promote *Check Me Out*. The cost to attend these trade shows was quite high. Since CI did not have the cash to pay for these trips, a CI shareholder cashed in several hundred thousand loyalty points earned through a credit card to cover the flights and hotels. In exchange, CI issued 10,000 common shares to the shareholder. CI is unsure as to how to record this transaction. The shares issued might be worth $25,000, based on informal discussions with a technology company that has expressed interest in acquiring CI.

Issue 2: CI is currently engaged in a legal case over the patent for *Check Me Out*. Mark Ramsey, the ex-boyfriend of one of CI's founders, has filed suit against CI. Ramsey claims that *Check Me Out* was his idea. He is suing CI for $2,500,000. CI claims that the suit is preposterous and completely impossible to prove. Nothing has been recorded in the financial statements with respect to this lawsuit. Legal advice has yet to be sought.

Issue 3: On 1 March 20X3, CI declared a 10% stock dividend. The purpose of this was to appease the shareholders while they wait for a return on their investments. The stock dividend has yet to be issued.

Issue 4: In an effort to further market *Check Me Out* and create an additional revenue stream, CI developed an app for mobile phones during the first quarter of 20X3. This app is called *Check Me Out Mobile*. The most unique feature of this app is that it allows shoppers to virtually try on clothing while in a physical storefront. The app can display virtual images of the shopper wearing items on display in the store. The app can combine items from the store, other stores where the shopper has uploaded data, and the shopper's own closet. The app will be promoted with the slogan, "It's like having a stylist living in your phone," because of the variety of outfit alternatives that can be displayed.

A retailer does not have to be a *Check Me Out* client for shoppers to use the app in their store. However, functionality is greatly enhanced when the retailer is a client. For example, a retailer that is *Check Me Out* enabled will have codes displayed on clothing tags that can be scanned and quickly "tried on" by customers. If a retailer is not *Check Me Out* enabled, a shopper will have to take a picture of the clothing item to enter the item in their virtual wardrobe.

Costs of $150,000 were incurred to create the app. The breakdown of these costs, which are reported under intangible assets on CI's balance sheet, is as follows:

Market research	$25,000
Design of prototype	$35,000
Testing and refinement	$40,000
Advertising	$50,000

The app will go on sale on 1 April 20X3. Based on market research conducted, and the positive word-of-mouth that has been generated through various social media marketing campaigns, it is expected that initial sales of this product will be strong. CI forecasts sales of approximately $100,000 during fiscal 20X3. Beyond that, it is difficult to speculate what will happen. CI suspects that the long-term success of the app is dependent on whether clothing retailers continue to adopt *Check Me Out*.

Required:

Prepare the report requested.

(Laura Cumming, used with permission)

CASE 14-3

TOPSAIL LTD.

Topsail Ltd. (Topsail) was founded 10 years ago by Dave Jetson, a carpenter and entrepreneur. Topsail is a growing construction company, building houses and doing major renovations for residential customers throughout the greater Moncton area. Dave is the president and sole common shareholder of the company.

Topsail approached its credit union in early 20X1 to increase its long-term debt to finance the purchase of equipment. A great deal of Topsail's equipment had been showing the strain of increased use and its efficiency was slipping. The credit union agreed to finance this purchase using the new equipment as collateral but has imposed a reasonably stringent debt to equity covenant. The credit union also requires audited financial statements. In the fall of 20X1, Dave met Carlie Smith, a partner with Morash and Bruce, Professional Accountants LLP (MB), at a mutual friend's dinner party. He phoned her a week later because he decided to hire MB to help him out on various matters. You work as a staff accountant at MB.

Topsail has a fiscal year-end of 31 December 20X1. The credit union will require an audit. Prior statements have not been audited and have been prepared solely for preparation of Topsail's tax return. Earnings in recent years have averaged $300,000. Dave has already appointed another public accounting firm as Topsail's auditor; he wants advice from MB on identifying and setting accounting policy issues. Carlie took notes on the call and has turned the notes over to you for analysis (Exhibit 1).

EXHIBIT 1

Notes from Phone Conversation with Dave Jetson

Topsail received an order from a recurring customer, Skyline, for custom-built cabinets for its new large retail store in Dieppe. Topsail completed the cabinets on 30 November, well ahead of the contract delivery date of 9 December. Topsail had received a $100,000 deposit for the cabinets in early October, with the balance of the contract of $150,000 to be paid upon delivery and acceptance of the cabinets by Skyline. In early December, Skyline notified Topsail that it could not take delivery of the cabinets until 15 January 20X2 due to the unexpected delay in the opening of the company's new store. Dave has heard a rumour that the reason for the delay in opening was because of Skyline's inability to arrange financing for inventory.

Over the years, Topsail has acquired an extensive range of machinery and equipment, ranging from small hand-held pieces to its most costly piece of equipment, a top-of-the-line insulation blowing machine, purchased five years ago for $45,000 that now has a net book value of $30,000. A similar but more efficient machine will become available in February 20X2. Topsail plans to replace the aging equipment when this new product comes on the market. Dave anticipates being able to sell the existing piece of equipment for $10,000.

In March 20X1, Dave spent $20,000 on an extensive advertising and marketing campaign to generate additional business for Topsail. This expenditure was set up as an intangible asset.

Dave mentioned that a former Topsail client, Bob Swaine, is suing the company for failure to finish the basement in his new home, which was purchased from Topsail. Despite there being no mention of completion of a basement in the sale contract, Bob thought all new homes came totally finished. Topsail's lawyer is quite certain the case will be thrown out of court.

Dave recently issued Topsail preferred shares in the amount of $25,000 to one of his key employees, Doug Smith. The shares have a rate of return of 7% per annum and are cumulative, redeemable, and retractable in two years' time at face value plus dividends in arrears, if any.

Dave used this money to help finance a $120,000 acquisition of common shares in Abel Electricity Ltd., owned by a group of electricians providing electrical services to Topsail and a number of other contractors in the Moncton area. Abel is the sole provider of electrical services to Topsail. Dave explained "Thank goodness I have pull with Abel, since I use their services all the time, especially now that my business is growing! I would have paid about $10,000 more for the work the company did this year if I had dealt with any other electrical company. Plus we did that swap, which is a big help with cash flow."

Dave reported that he swapped a used van that still worked but was no longer being used by Topsail in exchange for 100 hours of electrician time from Abel. Abel was all too happy to offer this service, since its cash flow has been sporadic and the bank had been threatening to cut its line of credit. Abel's income has continued to grow but the company seems to have trouble collecting receivables from customers on a timely basis. Dave said "I sure hope this investment pans out. I figure the initial $120,000 I paid for the shares will be worthwhile in the future. After all, Abel had income of over $200,000 last year, and it's only Abel's fourth year of operation!" Dave owns 25% of the shares of Abel.

Dave has not declared any dividends this year but usually takes out a mix of salary and common share dividends as recommended by his tax advisor. He will declare the common dividend soon but plans to wait for all the dividends on the preferred shares when they come due in two years' time. He has cleared this with Doug Smith, who agreed, because Doug figures that he can avoid paying income tax on the dividends for a couple of years under this scheme.

Required:

Prepare a report for Carlie to use as the basis for advice to Dave on financial reporting issues.

(Tammy Crowell, used with permission)

connect

TR14-1 Shareholders Equity:

1. Cumulative preferred shares are required to receive dividends every year.
2. Par value shares cannot be issued below par.
3. Issued shares will be higher than outstanding shares if there are treasury shares outstanding.
4. Share issue costs are always treated as a reduction of the amount received from issued share capital.
5. Revaluation surpluses from the revaluation model for a building is an item in AOCI.

Required:

Identify whether each statement is true or false.

connect

TR14-2 Subscription Shares:

On 1 January 20X5 100,000 shares of ABC Corp. are subscribed by Lucas Mapplebeck for $50 per share. The shares will be paid for in four equal instalments due every six months. The first instalment is due 1 July 20X5.

Required:

1. Assume all payments are made. Provide all journal entries for the subscription shares.
2. Assume Lucas Mapplebeck defaults on the last payment. Pro-rata shares are issued by ABC.
3. Assume Lucas Mapplebeck defaults on the last payment. All payments made are returned by ABC.

connect

TR14-3 Share Retirement:

On 1 January 20X5, AlbaCore Ltd. reported the following in shareholders' equity:

Preferred shares, no-par value; authorized, unlimited shares; issued, 100,000 shares	$2,500,000
Common shares, no-par value; authorized, unlimited shares; issued, 620,000 shares	4,960,000
Contributed capital on retirement of preferred shares	30,000
Retained earnings	3,850,000

The company acquired and retired shares in the following sequence during 20X5:

1. Retired 20,000 common shares at $12 per share.
2. Retired 30,000 common shares at $6 per share.
3. Retired 10,000 preferred shares at $30 per share.
4. Retired 5,000 preferred shares at $22 per share.

Required:

1. Prepare journal entries for the share retirement transactions.
2. Calculate the balances in each equity account, after the effects of the transactions in requirement 1.

■ connect

TR14-4 Treasury Stock:

At the end of 20X8, Minnow Reserves Corp. reported the following in shareholders' equity:

Preferred shares, no-par value; authorized, unlimited shares; issued, 50,000 shares	$1,250,000
Common shares, no-par value; authorized, unlimited shares; issued, 1,500,000 shares, outstanding, 1,450,000 shares	3,000,000
Contributed capital on treasury stock transactions	10,000
Retained earnings	2,600,000
Treasury stock, 50,000 common shares	(250,000)

The company had treasury stock transactions in the following sequence during 20X9:

1. Purchased 100,000 common shares as treasury stock at $8 per share.
2. Reissued 40,000 treasury shares at $9 per share.
3. Reissued 50,000 treasury shares at $4 per share.

Required:

1. Prepare journal entries for the treasury stock transactions.
2. Calculate the balances in each equity account, after the effects of the transactions in requirement 1.

■ connect

TR14-5 Retained Earnings:

Item	Increase/Decrease
1. Dividends	_____
2. Earnings	_____
3. Share issue costs	_____
4. Loss	_____
5. Spinoff of investment to shareholders	_____

Required:

Indicate if each item would increase or decrease retained earnings.

connect

TR14-6 Types of Dividends:

Description	Type of Dividend
1. Pay dividend with non-cash item	A. Script dividend
2. Dividend takes form certificate issued (promissory note)	B. Stock dividend
3. If dividends not declared the dividend is missed	C. Noncumulative shareholder dividend
4. Distribution to shareholders of additional shares	D. Cumulative shareholder dividend
5. If dividends not declared dividends in arrears	E. Property dividend

Required:

Match the description with the type of dividend.

connect

TR14-7 Dividends:

On 31 December 20X5, Watercress Properties Ltd. reported the following in shareholders' equity:

Preferred shares, no-par value; $1.00 dividend, authorized, unlimited shares; issued, 75,000 shares	$1,875,000
Common shares, no-par value; authorized, unlimited shares; issued, 300,000 shares	3,900,000
Retained earnings	6,100,000

Dividends of $405,000 are declared in 20X6. Consider the following three cases:

	Preferred Cumulative?	Dividends Last Paid in	Preferred Participating?
Case A	No	20X2	No
Case B	Yes	20X3	No
Case C	Yes	20X5	Yes, after common receive $0.50 per share; participation based on relative dividends at base level

Required:

Calculate dividends to be paid to preferred and common shares in each case.

■ connect

TR14-8 Stock Dividends:

On 1 January 20X5, Dolphin Operations Ltd. reported the following in shareholders' equity:

Common shares, no-par value; authorized, unlimited shares; issued, 2,400,000 shares	$ 7,200,000
Retained earnings	24,900,000
	$32,100,000

In 20X5, the company declared and issued a 10% stock dividend. The stock dividend was to be valued at $5 per share. The dividend resulted in a number of full shares being issued, but also there were 8,000 shares to be issued as fractional shares.

Required:

1. Prepare all journal entries for the stock dividend in 20X5. The dividend is recorded when issued. Fractional share rights are issued for fractional shares. One month after issuance, 60% of the rights are exercised and 40% lapse.
2. Repeat requirement 1, assuming cash is distributed in lieu of fractional shares.
3. Calculate the balances in the equity accounts, after the effects of the transactions in requirement 1. What do you notice about the total?

■ connect

TR14-9 AOCI:

On 31 December 20X6, Wave Exploration Ltd. reported the following in shareholders' equity:

Retained earnings	900,000
Accumulated other comprehensive income re: FVTOCI investments	50,000
Accumulated other comprehensive income re: foreign currency	(230,000)

Comprehensive income for 20X7 is as follows:

Earnings	$287,000
Other Comprehensive Income:	
Change in fair value of FVTOCI investments	(35,000)
Foreign exchange gain on foreign subsidiary	20,000
Comprehensive income	$272,000

Required:

1. Calculate the balance in each equity account, reflecting disposition of 20X7 comprehensive income.
2. Explain the meaning of each account. What would make each account increase or decrease?

connect

TR14-10 AOCI:

Item	Increase/Decrease
1. Unrealized gain on FVTOCI investment	_____
2. Foreign exchange loss on foreign subsidiary	_____
3. Net actuarial gain on defined benefit plan	_____
4. Revaluation increase on building	_____
5. Loss on cash flow hedge	_____

Required:

Indicate if each item would increase or decrease AOCI.

A14-1 Corporate Accounts:

The following accounts are taken from the general ledger of GRL Trading Ltd. on 31 December 20X1:

Preferred shares, no-par value, $3, unlimited number authorized, cumulative, and fully participating; 27,000 shares issued and outstanding	$ 84,000
Bonds payable, 6%	250,000
Stock subscriptions receivable, common shares	1,500
Common shares, no-par, unlimited number authorized; 45,000 shares issued and 44,900 outstanding	675,000
Discount on bonds payable	3,000
Retained earnings	326,500
Treasury shares, 100 common shares	4,300
Unrealized exchange gain on translation of foreign subsidiary's financial statements	75,250
Fractional common share rights	4,600
Contributed capital on common share retirement	9,450
Common shares subscribed, 100 shares	4,500

Required:

1. Prepare the shareholders' equity section of the SFP at year-end. Assume accounts have normal (i.e., debit or credit) balances.
2. Explain the meaning of each account in equity.

 connect

★ **A14-2 Share Issuance:**

Holimont Ltd. (HL) has unlimited no-par common shares authorized. The following transactions took place in the first year:

a. To record authorization of shares by board of directors (memorandum).
b. Issued 100,000 shares at $20; collected cash in full and issued the shares. Share issue costs amounted to $60,000. Treat this amount as a reduction of the common share account.

c. Received subscriptions for 50,000 shares at $30 per share; collected 60% of the subscription price. The shares will not be issued until collection of cash in full.

d. Issued 400 shares to a lawyer in payment for legal fees related to trademark registration. The lawyer estimates that the legal services provided would have been worth $12,000.

e. Issued 20,000 shares and assumed an $60,000 mortgage in total payment for a building with a fair value of $280,000.

f. Collected balance on subscriptions receivable in (c).

Required:

Journalize the above transactions. Or indicate if no journal entry.

★ ★ A14-3 Share Issuance:

Cranberry Ltd. (CL) was incorporated in 20X6. Unlimited no-par common shares were authorized. IFRS was chosen for external reporting. During the first week, the company had the following share transactions:

a. The company issued 80,000 shares to the group of four people who were instrumental in organizing the company and who will sit on the board of directors: Paula Davidge, Robert Bowyer, Caroline Bell, and David Scarlett each received 20,000 shares.

b. Paula Davidge will be the chair of the board. In exchange for 460,000 shares, she contributed land, appraised at $400,000, and a building that is appraised at $1,900,000. This will be the site of the operations of CL.

c. Robert Bowyer signed a subscriptions agreement to pay $1,160,000 to the company in exchange for 200,000 shares. He will pay the money in equal instalments over the next five years.

d. Caroline Bell received 350,000 shares for the assets of the company she was running prior to the incorporation of CL; this company will now be part of CL's operations. Machinery was estimated to be worth $300,000 to $400,000, customer lists were estimated to be worth $1,200,000 to $1,500,000, but there was also goodwill implicit in the number of shares issued.

e. David Scarlett invested $500,000 cash in exchange for 100,000 shares.

Required:

Discuss the valuation of each of the share transactions. Include a recommendation for each transaction.

★ ★ A14-4 Share Issuance; Subscriptions:

Flowers Inc. (FL) reported the following in shareholders' equity at the end of 20X6:

Common shares, no-par value; authorized, unlimited shares; issued, 610,000 shares	$ 2,806,000
Retained earnings	3,950,000
	$6,756,000

The company signed an agreement with Containers Ltd. (CL) in early 20X7, wherein CL agreed to purchase 267,500 common shares for $1,070,000. CL paid $70,000 on signing the contract, and agreed to pay $250,000 per year in each of the following four years. No shares were to be issued until all money was paid.

Required:

1. Journalize the share subscription agreement, and the initial payment. Then, calculate the balances in all equity accounts, reflecting the entries. Subscriptions receivable is a contra account in equity.

2. Justify treating subscriptions receivable as a contra equity account.

3. In each of the three cases described below, journalize all transactions. Then, calculate the balances in all equity accounts, reflecting the entries.
   a. CL makes all payments on schedule and shares are issued after the final payment.
   b. CL makes the initial payment and the first annual payment and then cancels the agreement, with the permission of FL. FL issues no shares but is entitled to keep the money paid to date as part of the cancellation agreement.
   c. CL makes the initial payment and the first annual payment and then cancels the agreement, with the permission of FL. FL issues shares for the cash paid to date.

 ## A14-5 Share Retirement:

During 20X5, Walter Ltd. retired 4,000 common shares and 2,000 preferred shares, respectively. Earnings was $100,000 in 20X5, and dividends declared, $40,000. The comparative equity accounts for 20X4 and 20X5:

Balances 31 December	20X5	20X4
Preferred shares	360,000	460,000
Common shares	$1,200,000	$1,400,000
Contributed capital, retirement of preferred shares	54,000	0
Retained earnings	270,000	240,000

Required:

1. What was the original issue price of the common shares? The preferred?

2. What amount was paid for the common shares retired? The preferred? (*Hint:* Reconstruct the journal entries to record the retirement.)

 ## A14-6 Share Retirement:

At the beginning of 20X1, the accounting records of Friends Corp. reported the following:

Preferred shares, 6,000 shares outstanding, no-par	$ 150,000
Common shares, 180,000 shares outstanding, no-par	369,000

Contributed capital on common share retirement	110,000
Retained earnings	550,000

During the year, the company acquired and retired shares, while other shares were issued:

15 March	24,000 common shares bought and retired at $6 per share
16 March	3,000 preferred shares bought and retired at $27 per share
20 May	8,000 common shares bought and retired at $1 per share
25 May	600 preferred shares bought and retired at $24 per share
30 May	10,000 common shares issued at $12.32 per share
15 Nov.	4,000 common shares bought and retired at $14 per share

Required:

1. Give journal entries to record each share retirement transaction.
2. Calculate the closing balance in each account in shareholders' equity.

★★★ A14-7 Share Retirement:

On 1 January 20X5, BC Ventures Corp. reported the following in shareholders' equity:

Preferred shares, no-par value; $0.70, cumulative; authorized, unlimited shares; issued, 80,000 shares	$386,000
Common shares, no-par value; authorized, unlimited shares; issued, 80,000 shares	642,000
Contributed capital on retirement of common shares	14,000
Retained earnings	1,250,000
AOCI for foreign exchange gains on foreign subsidiary	38,000

During 20X5, certain shares were reacquired. In accordance with the regulations in BC Ventures' incorporating legislation, all reacquired shares were retired. Transactions were as follows:

15 January	Bought 7,000 preferred shares for $5.20 per share
12 February	Bought 2,000 common shares for $11 per share
25 February	Bought 4,000 preferred shares for $4.00 per share
26 April	Bought 5,000 preferred shares for $6.00 per share

16 July   Bought 8,000 common shares for $7.50 per share

Other transactions during the year:

30 July   Stock dividend on common shares, 5%, declared and distributed. The
                       board of directors agreed to capitalize the dividend at the market value of
                       $7.75 per share.

30 November   The board of directors declared a dividend adequate to pay $1 per share
                       to all common shareholders. This meant that the board also had to
                       declare the preferred dividend.

Required:

1. Prepare journal entries to reflect the above transactions. Show the split between common and preferred dividends in the dividend entries, as appropriate.
2. Prepare the shareholders' equity section of the SFP after reflecting the above transactions. Earnings were $308,200, and total comprehensive income was $351,000, reflecting earnings plus an additional gain of $42,800 on foreign exchange caused by a foreign subsidiary.

 connect

 A14-8 Treasury Stock:

On 1 January 20X1, Grey Corp. issued 375,000 no-par common shares at $4 per share. In 20X5, there were treasury stock transactions. On 15 January 20X5, the company purchased 4,200 of its own common shares at $3 per share to be held as treasury stock. On 1 March, 750 of the treasury shares were resold at $4.50. On 15 March, 500 shares were purchased for $1.42. On 31 March, 850 of the treasury shares were sold for $1.75. The remaining shares were cancelled and retired on 1 June. The balance in retained earnings was $962,500 prior to these transactions.

Required:

1. Provide all 20X5 entries.
2. Calculate the resulting balance in each of the shareholders' equity accounts.

A14-9 Treasury Stock:

At the end of 20X2, Provoe Products Ltd. had 222,000 common shares outstanding, with a recorded value in the common share account of $875,000. Retained earnings was $673,500.

During 20X3, the following transactions affecting shareholders' equity were recorded:

a. Split common shares 3-for-1.
b. Purchased 8,000 shares of treasury stock at $4.25 per share.
c. Purchased 6,000 shares of treasury stock at $5 per share.
d. Issued 5,000 shares of treasury stock at $9.25.

e. Issued 6,000 shares of treasury stock at $3.

f. Retired 500 shares of treasury stock.

g. Declared and paid a dividend of $0.25 per common share.

Required:

1. Give entries for each of the above transactions.
2. Give the resulting balances in each capital account. Earnings for 20X3 was $472,000.

★ ★ **A14-10 Treasury Stock:**

Wonder Ltd. has treasury stock transactions in 20X9 as follows:

a. Feb. 27	Purchased 140,000 common shares as treasury stock at $6.50 per share.
b. March 15	Purchased 64,000 common shares as treasury stock for $5.50 per share.
c. April 30	Reissued 100,000 shares of treasury stock for $4.25 per share.
d. May 16	Purchased 54,000 common shares as treasury stock for $6.05 per share.
e. Nov. 26	Reissued 268,000 shares of treasury stock for $4 per share.

At the end of 20X8, Wonder Ltd. had reported the following in shareholders' equity:

Common shares, no-par value; authorized, unlimited shares; issued, 5,800,000 shares, outstanding, 5,500,000 shares	21,117,000
Contributed capital on treasury stock transactions	133,600
Retained earnings	14,840,000
Treasury stock, 300,000 common shares	(1,260,000)

Required:

1. Prepare journal entries for the treasury stock transactions.
2. Calculate the balances in the equity accounts, after the effects of the transactions in requirement 1.

★ **A14-11 Dividends:**

In 20X3, Snowboard Ltd. had the following share capital outstanding:

Preferred shares, no-par value; $1.20 dividend: authorized, unlimited shares; issued, 100,000 shares	$1,250,000
Common shares, no-par value; authorized, unlimited shares; issued, 480,000 shares	642,000

No dividends were declared in 20X1 or 20X2, but $1,000,000 of dividends were declared in 20X3.

Required:

Calculate the amount of dividends that would be paid in 20X3 to each share class under the following separate cases:

Case A   Preferred shares are cumulative and nonparticipating.

Case B   Preferred shares are cumulative and participating with common shares after the common shares receive a $1 per share dividend. Participation is based on relative annual total base dividends.

★ ★ A14-12 Dividends:

Massive Corp. is authorized to issue unlimited $0.80 no-par preferred shares and unlimited no-par common shares. There are 15,000 preferred and 45,000 common shares outstanding. In a five-year period, annual dividends paid were $2,000, $8,000, $64,000, $10,000, and $180,000, respectively.

Required:

Calculate the amount of dividends that would be paid to each share class for each year under the following separate cases. Where applicable, the matching dividend per common share is $1.00.

Case A   Preferred shares are cumulative and nonparticipating.

Case B   Preferred shares are noncumulative and nonparticipating.

Case C   Preferred shares are noncumulative and fully participating. Participation is based on the relative number of shares outstanding.

Case D   Preferred shares are noncumulative and partially participating up to an additional $0.80 per share. Participation is based on relative annual total base dividends.

★ ★ A14-13 Dividends:

Western Horizons Ltd. has the following shares outstanding:

Common, no-par	54,000 shares
Preferred, no-par, $0.75	18,000 shares

The matching dividend, if applicable, is $1 per share.

Required:

Compute the amount of dividends payable in total and per share on the common and preferred shares for each separate case:

Case A   Preferred is cumulative and nonparticipating; dividends declared, $64,800. Dividends have not been paid for the last three years prior to this year.

Case B   Preferred is noncumulative and nonparticipating; no dividends have been paid for the last three years prior to this year; dividends declared, $40,500.

Case C   Preferred is cumulative and fully participating after the common shares receive a matching dividend; no dividends have been paid in the last two years prior to this year; dividends declared, $120,000. Participation is based on relative annual total base dividends.

Case D   Preferred is cumulative and partially participating up to an additional $0.90 after the common shares receive a matching dividend. Dividends have been paid in all prior years; dividends declared, $160,000. Participation is based on relative annual total base dividends.

 ## A14-14 Stock Dividend:

Gupta Corp. was authorized to issue unlimited common shares and had 452,000 common shares outstanding on 8 March 20X2, with a recorded value of $1,367,000. On this date, the board of directors declared a 5% stock dividend, valued at the fair value of shares, $4.50 per share.

Required:

Prepare journal entry(ies) for each of the following independent circumstances:

1. The stock dividend is declared and issued on 8 March, and all shares are distributed on this date.

2. The stock dividend is declared and issued on 8 March, resulting in the issuance of a number of whole shares but also entitlement to the sum of 1,600 shares as fractional shares. These shares were outstanding until 30 April, at which time 70% were redeemed for whole shares and 30% expired.

3. The stock dividend is declared and issued on 8 March, resulting in the issuance of a number of whole shares but also involving entitlement to the sum of 1,600 shares as fractional shares. Cash was distributed to shareholders in lieu of fractional shares.

4. The stock dividend is declared on 8 March, and distributed on 8 April. The dividend is recorded on 8 March. On distribution on 8 April, whole shares are issued as well as entitlement to the sum of 1,600 shares as fractional shares. These fractional shares were outstanding until 30 April, at which time 70% were redeemed for whole shares and 30% expired.

5. Comment on the differences between requirements 2 and 3. What might be the advantages and disadvantages of issuing cash instead of fractional shares?

 ## A14-15 Stock Dividend:

The records of Victoria Corp. showed the following balances on 1 November 20X5:

Share capital, no-par, 40,000 shares	$344,300
Retained earnings	592,100

On 5 November 20X5, the board of directors declared a stock dividend to the shareholders of record as of 20 December 20X5. The dividend was one additional share for each five shares already outstanding; issue date, 10

January 20X6. The appropriate market value of the shares was $12.50 per share. The annual accounting period ends 31 December. The stock dividend was recorded on the declaration date with a memo entry only.

Required:

1. Give entries in parallel columns for the stock dividend on the issue date assuming:

    Case A   Fair value is capitalized.

    Case B $10 per share is capitalized.

    Case C   Average paid in is capitalized.

2. Explain when each value is most likely to be used.

3. With respect to the stock dividend, what should be reported on the statement of financial position at 31 December 20X5?

4. Explain how the financial statements as of 31 December 20X5 would be different if the stock dividend were recognized on the declaration date.

 Solution

 connect

★ **A14-16 Stock Dividend and Stock Split:**

At the end of 20X6, Home Ltd. reported the following in shareholders' equity:

Common shares, no-par value; authorized, unlimited shares; issued, 14,400,000 shares	$ 18,800,000
Retained earnings	52,840,000
	$71,640,000

At this time, the shares were trading in the range of $4 to $6 per share on public stock markets. The company's board of directors is contemplating two alternative courses of action:

1. Declaring a 50% stock dividend, or

2. Executing a 3-for-2 stock split.

Required:

1. Prepare the shareholders' equity section for each alternative, assuming that market value is used to capitalize the stock dividend.

2. What would be the expected share price in each case?

3. Which alternative would shareholders prefer? Explain.

4. Which alternative would the company prefer? Explain.

A14-17 Stock Split:

Altitude Ltd. had the following shareholders' equity on 31 December 20X8:

$2 Preferred shares (37,500 shares issued and outstanding; cumulative, nonparticipating, and convertible into two common shares for each preferred share)	$525,000
Common shares (120,000 shares issued and outstanding)	324,000
Retained earnings	1,010,000
AOCI: OCI: unrealized gains from investments	80,000
Total shareholders' equity	$1,939,000

Earnings for 20X8 had been $216,000, and comprehensive income, which also included a $13,500 unrealized gain on an investment, was $229,500. Basic earnings per share was calculated as $1.18:

Net earnings	$216,000
Preferred dividend entitlement (37,500 shares × $2)	(75,000)
Earnings attributable to common	$ 141,000
Earnings per share ($141,000 ÷ 120,000 shares)	$ 1.18

During 20X8, the company paid the $2 per share preferred dividends and also paid $90,000, or $0.75 per share, in dividends to common shareholders. Dividends are reported in total and per share in the financial statements.

On 1 April 20X9, Altitude executed a 3-for-1 split of its common shares. All share contracts were revised to reflect this split. On 15 July 20X9, the company repurchased and retired 9,000 common shares at $11 per share.

Required:

1. Prepare the journal entry to record the 20X9 share repurchase.
2. Post-split, how many common shares would the holder of 4,000 preferred shares receive on conversion?
3. When the company prepares its comparative financial statements for 20X9, what amount will be reported for 20X8 earnings per share? What amount would be reported for 20X8 cash dividends per common share?

  A14-18 Stock Dividend and Stock Split:

At the end of the 20X4 fiscal year, the shareholders' equity section of the statement of financial position of Chomney Corp. was as follows:

Shareholders' Equity

Contributed Capital:

    Share capital:

Preferred shares, no-par value, $1.25, cumulative and nonparticipating, unlimited shares authorized, 40,000 shares issued and outstanding	$ 1,000,000
Common shares, no-par value, unlimited shares authorized, 366,000 shares issued and outstanding	2,675,000
Other contributed capital: common share retirement	45,900
Total contributed capital	3,720,900
Retained earnings	12,001,000
AOCI for unrealized exchange gain on translation of foreign subsidiary	90,500
Total Shareholders' Equity	$15,812,400

The board of directors was considering three alternatives:

1. A 200% stock dividend for common shares, to be recorded as a memo entry.
2. A 200% stock dividend to be recorded at the fair value of the common shares, or $11 per share.
3. A 3-for-1 common stock split.

Required:

1. Prepare the shareholders' equity section, in three columns, with each column reflecting one of the alternatives above.
2. Evaluate the alternatives, and indicate what course of action you would recommend to the board of directors.

 A14-19 Retained Earnings and Equity Accounts:

Below are selected accounts from O'Hara Oil Corp. at 31 December 20X1. The accounts have not been closed for the year but transactions have been correctly recorded.

Treasury stock, common	$ 106,000
Contributed capital on preferred share retirement	23,100
Fractional common share rights outstanding	9,200
Excess on common share retirement (shares retired for $401,000 while average issuance price was $316,000)	85,000
Increase in unrealized FVTOCI investment fair value in 20X1	24,000
20X1 earnings	890,400
Common shares	9,411,200
Class A preferred shares	2,500,000
Cash dividends, common shares	94,500

Change in accounting policy, net of tax (increases prior earnings)	64,900
AOCI re: FVTOCI investments, 1 January 20X1	44,700
Cash dividends, preferred shares	125,000
Retained earnings, 1 January 20X1	8,216,700
Stock dividend, common shares	116,500

Required:

1. Calculate comprehensive income.
2. Calculate the closing balance in retained earnings and the amount in AOCI re: FVTOCI investments.
3. Prepare the shareholders' equity section of the SFP as of 31 December 20X1.

 ## A14-20 Accumulated Other Comprehensive Income:

During 20X7, Greens Ltd. reported the following:

a. FVTOCI investments with a recorded fair value of $455,000 were sold for $500,500. The original cost of these investments had been $200,000 in 20X5. Accumulated gains are transferred to retained earnings but are not a component of income or comprehensive income.

b. An exchange gain of $150,000 was recorded on the translation of the financial statements of a foreign subsidiary; this exchange gain is not included in earnings but is an element of comprehensive income and AOCI.

c. Recorded earnings were $725,000.

d. Treasury stock, on the books for $350,000, was reissued for $330,000.

e. A second FVTOCI investment, held at year-end, had a fair value of $500,000 at the beginning of the year and $480,000 at the end of the year.

f. A stock dividend was recorded during the year, involving 146,000 shares to be issued, valued at $3.75 per share. Of these shares, 140,000 were issued in the form of full shares and 6,000 fractional shares for which cash was issued.

On 1 January 20X7, Greens reported the following in shareholders' equity:

Common shares	1,800,000
Retained earnings	3,000,000
Accumulated other comprehensive income re: FVTOCI investments	400,000
Accumulated other comprehensive income (loss) re: foreign currency	(600,000)
Treasury stock	(350,000)

Required:

1. Calculate 20X7 comprehensive income.
2. Calculate the balances in all equity accounts, reflecting 20X7 comprehensive income and the transactions that occurred during the year.
3. Explain the meaning of each AOCI account. What would make each account increase or decrease?

 A14-21 Statement of Changes in Equity, Comprehensive:

The following statement of changes in shareholders' equity summarizes various equity transactions that occurred during 20X2:

MORGAN CORPORATION

Changes in Shareholders' Equity for the Year Ended 31 December 20X2 (in thousands)

	Preferred Shares	Common Shares	Contributed Capital from Common Share Retirement	Retained Earnings	Total Equity
Balance at 1 January 20X2	$ 210	$500	$70	$ 910	$1,690
Net earnings and comprehensive income				330	330
Shares issued	360	380			740
Share issue costs				(15)	(15)
Share buyback	(80)			(26)	(106)
Share buyback		(41)	11		(30)
Stock dividend to shareholders		107		(107)	—
Cash dividends to shareholders				(34)	(34)
Balance at 31 December 20X2	$490	$946	$ 81	$1,058	$2,575

Required:

Journalize the transactions in the statement of shareholders' equity. For earnings, close the income summary to retained earnings.

 A14-22 Statement of Changes in Equity, Comprehensive:

Below is a partially completed statement of changes in equity for Torino Capital Ltd. (in thousands of dollars).

	Preferred Shares	Common Shares	Fractional Shares Outstanding	Retained Earnings	AOCI Foreign Exchange Gains of Foreign Subsidiary	Total Equity
Balance at 1 January 20X1	$3,000	$7,400	$240	$6,780	$451	$17,871
Comprehensive income, including earnings of $871 and foreign exchange on subsidiary, a gain of $39						
Common shares issued for cash of $788						
Preferred shares bought back; 10% of opening balance bought back for cash; paid $85 more in total than average issue price						
Cash dividends to shareholders; $170 to preferred and $367 to common						

Fractional shares turned in for common (80% of fractional rights); remainder are still outstanding	
Balance at 31 December 20X1	

Required:

Complete the statement of changes in equity to reflect the transactions and events described.

★ A14-23 **Statement of Changes in Equity, Comprehensive:**

Robinson Industries reported the following statement of shareholders' equity for the year ended 31 December 20X7:

	Common Share Capital	Preferred Share Capital	Other Contributed Capital (all sources)	Retained Earnings	AOCI: Unrealized Gains, Investments
Balance, January 1, 20X7	$ 5,992	$3,500	$ 1,202	$ 775	$48
Issuance of common shares for cash	7,650				
Retirement of common shares	(1,005)		(356)		
Costs associated with equity issue				(124)	
Stock dividend	247			(247)	
Comprehensive income				1,980	13

Retirement of preferred shares		(630)	(116)	(35)	
Balance, 31 December 20X7	$12,884	$2,870	$ 730	$2,349	$61

Required:

1. What is the nature of AOCI? Where does it appear in the financial statements?
2. Earnings were $1,980. How much is comprehensive income?
3. What amount was paid to retire common shares during the year?
4. What amount was paid to retire preferred shares during the period? Why is there a deduction from contributed capital and also from retained earnings?
5. Costs associated with share issuance have been deducted from retained earnings. What other alternative could the company have considered?
6. What is the nature of the stock dividend? What are the alternatives for recording such a dividend?

★ ★ A14-24 Statement of Changes in Equity, Comprehensive:

Clean Energy Ltd. began 20X2 with shareholders' equity as follows:

Preferred shares; $2 dividend, 120,000 shares issued and outstanding	$3,000,000
Common shares; 600,000 issued and 500,000 shares outstanding	3,750,000
Contributed capital on retirement of preferred shares	20,000
Retained earnings	1,085,000
AOCI: foreign exchange on foreign subsidiary	(160,000)
	$7,695,000
Treasury stock; 100,000 common shares	(1,100,000)
	$6,595,000

The company's tax rate is 40%. In 20X2, the company reported transactions that affected equity accounts:

1. Common shares, 2-for-1 stock split.
2. Common shares, 91,000 shares post-split, were repurchased and retired for $439,525.
3. All of the treasury shares were reissued for $1,087,700.

4. Clean reported earnings of $210,900, including an after-tax discontinued operation loss amount of $17,300. There was an after-tax foreign exchange gain of $65,500 related to the foreign subsidiary.

5. Cash dividends of $163,250 were paid. This represented the required dividend on the preferred shares plus some common share dividend.

6. After the dividend was paid, 30,000 preferred shares were repurchased and retired for $11.75 per share.

7. Share retirement costs, legal fees relating to both preferred and common shares, amounted to $66,500 for the year.

8. The company recorded an error correction during the year, resulting in a $45,000 pretax increase to prior year's earnings.

Required:

Complete a columnar statement of changes in equity that reflects the transactions and events described. Use one column for each individual equity account, and show preferred dividends separately from common dividends.

★ ★ A14-25 Transactions, Comprehensive:

Howard Corp. is a publicly owned company whose shares are traded on the TSX. At 31 December 20X4, Howard had unlimited shares of no-par value common shares authorized, of which 15,000,000 shares were issued. The shareholders' equity accounts at 31 December 20X4 had the following balances:

Common shares (15,000,000 shares)	$230,000,000
Retained earnings	50,000,000

During 20X5, Howard had the following transactions:

a. On 1 February, a distribution of 2,000,000 common shares was completed. The shares were sold for $18 per share.

b. On 15 February, Howard issued, at $110 per share, 100,000 of no-par value, $8, cumulative preferred shares.

c. On 1 March, Howard reacquired and retired 20,000 common shares for $14.50 per share.

d. On 15 March, Howard reacquired and retired 10,000 common shares for $20 per share.

e. On 31 March, Howard declared a semi-annual cash dividend on common shares of $0.10 per share, payable on 30 April 20X5, to shareholders of record on 10 April 20X5. (Record the dividend declaration *and* payment.) The preferred share dividend will be paid on schedule in October.

f. On 15 April, 18,000 common shares were acquired for $17.50 per share and held as treasury stock.

g. On 30 April, 12,500 of the treasury shares were resold for $19.25 per share.

h. On 31 May, when the market price of the common was $23 per share, Howard declared a 5% stock dividend distributable on 1 July 20X5, to common shareholders of record on 1 June 20X5. Treasury shares were not given the stock dividend. The stock dividend was recorded at market value only on distribution. The dividend resulted in fractional share rights issued, that, when exercised, would result in the issuance of 2,300 common shares.

i. On 6 July, Howard issued 300,000 common shares. The selling price was $25 per share.

j. On 30 September, Howard declared a semi-annual cash dividend on common shares of $0.10 per share and the yearly dividend on preferred shares, both payable on 30 October 20X5, to shareholders of record on 10 October 20X5. (Record the dividend declaration and payment.)

k. On 31 December, holders of fractional rights exercised those rights, resulting in the issuance of 1,850 shares. The remaining rights expired.

l. Earnings for 20X5 were $25 million.

Required:

Prepare journal entries to record the listed transactions. Round per-share amounts to two decimal places.

 A14-26 Transactions, Comprehensive:

The following transactions may change an account in shareholders' equity in some way:

a. Declare and issue a 2-for-1 stock split.

b. Record donated building.

c. Acquire treasury shares.

d. Record a decrease in the value (an unrealized loss) of FVTOCI investments carried at fair market value.

e. Declare dividends on preferred shares.

f. Declare a stock dividend, to be issued in four weeks' time.

g. Issue the stock dividend in (f), resulting in the issuance of common shares and fractional share rights.

h. Fractional shares issued in (g) are exchanged for common shares (75%) and the rest lapse (25%).

i. Retire common shares for cash at a price higher than the average issuance price to date. This is the first time common shares have been retired.

j. Reissue treasury shares for cash at a price higher than average acquisition cost. This is the first time treasury shares have been reissued.

k. After the transaction in (j), reissue treasury shares for cash at a price lower than average acquisition cost.

l. Record earnings for the year.

Required:

In the table below, indicate the effect of each transaction on the accounts listed. Use I = Increase, D = Decrease, and NE = No effect. The first one is done as an example.

Item	Share Capital	Fractional Share Rights	Other Contributed Capital	Retained Earnings	Reserve: Unrealized Gains on Investments	Treasury Stock
a.	NE	NE	NE	NE	NE	NE
b.						
c.						
d.						

e.						
f.						
g.						
h.						
i.						
j.						
k.						
l.						

★ ★ 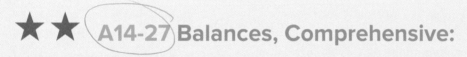 A14-27 Balances, Comprehensive:

Zu Corp. has the following items in shareholders' equity at 31 December 20X8:

Preferred shares, $0.60 cumulative dividend, participating with common shares after the common shares have received $0.30 per share, 15,000 shares authorized and 4,000 shares issued and outstanding. Participation is based on the relative annual total base dividends.	$ 360,000
Common shares, unlimited shares issued, 93,000 shares issued and 92,000 shares outstanding	1,080,000
Contributed capital on preferred share retirement	17,000
Retained earnings	4,356,900
Treasury stock, common, 1,000 shares	18,000

The following transactions and events happened in 20X9, in chronological order:

a. A cash dividend of $38,000 was declared and paid.
b. 4,000 additional common shares were issued for land. The land was valued at $50,000, while recent transactions in common shares indicated a share value of $75,000.
c. Treasury shares (common), 500 shares were bought at $12,500.
d. Preferred shares, 500 shares, were purchased and retired for $130 per share.
e. Treasury shares, 600 shares, were reissued at $15 per share.
f. A common stock dividend of 10% was issued. Treasury shares were considered ineligible for the stock dividend, by order of the board of directors. The stock dividend resulted in a number of whole shares issued, but 350 shares had to be issued in the form of fractional share rights, still outstanding at year-end. The dividend was valued at $40 per share.
g. Earnings for the year were $1,450,000.

Required:

1. From (a), specify the amount of cash dividend to the preferred shareholders, and the dividend to the common shareholders.
2. Calculate the final balance in each shareholders' equity account.
3. From (b), justify the value used to record the common shares issued.

 A14-28 Statement of Cash Flows:

The following data relates to Ottawa Ltd.:

31 December	20X5	20X4
Preferred shares, no-par	$ 520,000	$ 460,000
Common shares, no-par	8,438,350	6,840,000
Common share fractional rights	8,750	—
Contributed capital on preferred share retirement	29,000	22,000
Contributed capital on common share retirement	—	96,000
Retained earnings	3,867,000	3,911,500

Transactions during the year:

1. Preferred shares were issued for $100,000 during the year. Share issue costs of $2,000 were charged directly to retained earnings. Other preferred shares were retired.
2. On 31 December 20X4, there were 570,000 common shares outstanding.
3. A total of 20,000 common shares were retired on 2 January 20X5 for $18 per share.
4. There was a 10% stock dividend on 1 April 20X5. This dividend was capitalized at $17.50, the fair value of common shares. The stock dividend resulted in the issuance of fractional rights for 3,200 whole shares. Of these, 2,700 whole shares were subsequently issued and fractional rights for a remaining 500 shares are still outstanding at the end of the year.
5. Cash dividends were declared during the year.
6. Common shares were issued in June 20X5 for land. The transaction involved issuing 3,000 common shares for land valued at $52,000.
7. Common shares (46,000 shares) were issued for cash on 30 December 20X5.
8. Earnings were $1,200,000 in 20X5.

Required:

Prepare the financing activities section of the SCF, including dividends paid, based on the above information.

A14-29 Statement of Cash Flows:

Refer to the facts of A14-24.

Required:

Prepare the financing activities section of the SCF, including dividends paid.

 A14-30 Transactions, Statement of Cash Flows:

The following data is related to Cold Brook Resources Ltd.:

	20X9	20X8
Preferred shares, no-par	$ 2,000,000	$ 3,000,000
Common shares, no-par	45,000,000	36,000,000
Preferred shares subscribed	4,000,000	0
Common share fractional rights	0	574,000
Contributed capital on lapse of rights	114,800	0
Contributed capital on preferred share retirement	122,000	0
Retained earnings	8,005,000	5,940,000
Subscriptions receivable, preferred shares	(700,000)	0

During the year, the following transactions took place:

a. Earnings were $2,600,000.

b. Cash dividends were paid.

c. The common share fractional rights converted into common shares (80%), and the remainder (20%) lapsed.

d. Common shares plus $2 million cash were issued to acquire a patent that was valued at $6,500,000.

e. Contracts were signed to issue preferred shares with a total consideration of $4,000,000. The prospective shareholders paid $3,300,000 and will pay the balance within 12 months.

f. Preferred shares were retired for cash.

g. Additional common shares were issued for cash.

h. Retained earnings were reduced by $200,300 as the result of share issue costs.

Required:

1. Show the retained earnings T-account, beginning with the opening balance and going to the closing balance. Label all items that caused the change in the account.

2. Prepare the investing and financing sections of the SCF, in as much detail as possible with the information given. Dividends paid are included in financing activities.

Source: (Globe and money) © Vstock LLC/Getty Images RF; (Skyscrapers) © Arpad Benedek/Getty Images RF; (Canadian flag) © BjArn Kindler/Getty Images RF; (Tablet, pen, keyboard) © John Lamb/Getty Images RF.

CHAPTER 15

Financial Instruments: Complex Debt and Equity

INTRODUCTION

When accountants prepare financial statements, a major task is to classify and organize the accounts into categories. Unfortunately, some things are hard to classify. For example, Loblaw Companies Ltd. issued 9 million Second Preferred Shares—Series A, entitled to a 5.95% cumulative dividend. The company may redeem these shares for cash or convert these into common shares based on the prevailing share price at the time. In addition, these preferred shares are convertible by the holder after a certain date, into a number of common shares determined based on the prevailing market price at the time. Are these shares equity? These shares do not seem to be a permanent, residual equity interest since the company may redeem for cash or shares, and the number of shares on conversion is not fixed, but dependent on the price of the common shares at the time of conversion. Loblaw classifies these preferred shares as debt. Criteria will be reviewed in this chapter that help determine whether a security is debt or equity *in substance*.

Financial instruments that have elements of *both debt and equity* are called *compound financial instruments*. In this chapter, recognition and measurement of convertible debt will be used to illustrate accounting for compound financial instruments.

Another topic in this chapter is accounting for share-based payments, whether the contract is equity-settled or cash-settled, with the cash payment based on the value of shares. Share-based payments may be made to employees or provided to suppliers or to existing shareholders. The cost of share-based payments to employees (employee stock options) can be considerable. TD Bank, for example, has options for approximately 18.4 million shares outstanding, primarily with employees, which allow the purchase of shares at an average price in the range of $40.65 per share. Since market value is around $52 per share, the option holders are receiving something of value. Representational faithfulness dictates that this commitment, and its related cost, must be reflected in the financial statements.

This chapter also examines the use of derivative financial instruments to mitigate financial risk, specifically the use of hedges and swaps. The use of derivatives significantly alters the risk profile of a company, and they are recognized at fair value to ensure that the SFP reflects the complete financial position of the company.

FINANCIAL INSTRUMENTS—CLASSIFICATION
The Debt to Equity Continuum

Throughout most of the 20th century, the distinction between debt and equity financing instruments was clear. Debt financing was an amount borrowed, at some specific interest rate, payable at a fixed time in the future or at the option of the lender. Shareholders' equity was represented by share capital, plus residual interests accruing through retained earnings or capital transactions. The legal form of debt versus equity was unmistakable, and substance generally followed legal form.

Accountants traditionally relied on the legal nature of capital instruments for classification. If there was a share certificate, the instrument was accounted for as equity; if there was a loan contract or agreement, the instrument was accounted for as a liability.

However, there came to be many forms of financing where the legal description did not seem to correspond with the parties' rights and obligations. Financial markets support a continuum of investments, with features that range from pure debt to pure equity, with a lot of grey in the middle. Many financial instruments do not comfortably fit into either of these two simple categories.

For example, perpetual debt is a liability that pays annual interest, but the principal *never* has to be repaid. An **income bond** pays interest and principal, but interest is paid *only when the corporation has reported a certain level of earnings or operating cash flow* in the year. Then there are preferred **redeemable shares**, as reported by Loblaw, that may have to be retired for cash at a certain time.

Some **hybrid financial instruments** have elements of both debt and equity. They are also called **compound financial instruments**. **Convertible debt**, convertible into a fixed number of shares at the investor's option, is an example. The issuing company allows the investor to convert the principal portion of the bond into a specific number of common shares on a certain date at a set conversion price. The issuing company usually hopes that the bond will be converted to avoid paying out cash. Investors will convert if the shares are worth more money than the face value of the bond. Perhaps the company will avoid having to repay the principal, if share prices increase, but perhaps the company will have to repay the debt, if share prices are lower than the conversion price. This is an uncertain outcome and obviously hard to place into a pure debt or pure equity slot.

Classification by Substance

Reporting standards require that financial instruments must be classified as liability or equity in accordance with the *substance* of the contractual arrangement. If the financial instrument is part debt and part equity, it is a *compound financial instrument,* and *the component parts are classified separately.*

These requirements are an important application of the qualitative characteristic of *substance over form*: if it looks like a duck and it quacks like a duck, then it should be classified as a duck, even when it has a sign around its neck that says it is a moose! That is, classification depends on the nature of the instrument as debt or equity and not on its name or label.

Furthermore, payments to investors for the use of capital should be presented in accordance with the nature of the financial instrument as a liability or as equity. Payments that are associated with financial liabilities are an expense and should be presented in earnings, and payments associated with equity instruments should be presented in the statement of changes in equity. Gains and losses associated with debt retirement are reported in earnings. Gains and losses associated with equity are capital transactions and are *not* reported in earnings but, rather, affect equity accounts.

Tax Status Unaffected

It is important to remember that the accounting classification *will not change the tax classification of an investment vehicle* because the tax classification is established by the Canada Revenue Agency rulings. Thus, "interest" payments on instruments that legally are debt but in substance are equity will be tax deductible as "interest," *even if the interest is reported as a deduction from retained earnings.*[1]

---

1. There may be exceptions to interest being deductible for tax purposes depending on specific provisions of the Income Tax Act. In all cases, the accounting treatment of the financial instrument does not impact its tax treatment.

Similarly, if an "equity" item is classified as debt in the financial statements, and the "dividend" payment is reported as an expense in earnings, the "dividend" *will not be a tax-deductible expense.* The "dividend" in earnings will be adjusted in order to reconcile from accounting income to taxable income. This process is discussed in Chapter 16.

Debt versus Equity Classification Implications

Assume that a company raises $100,000 by issuing a financial instrument that will pay $6,000 per year to the investor. At the end of the fifth year, the company retires the financial instrument in a transaction in the open market, buying it back at market value of $109,500. The financial statements are affected by whether the instrument is classified as debt or equity. The impact of each classification can be summarized as follows:

Event	Liability Classification	Equity Classification
Issuance	Increases long-term liabilities	Increases shareholders' equity
Annual $6,000 payment	Increases interest expense; decreases earnings and thus decreases retained earnings	Reduces retained earnings as a dividend distribution; no impact on earnings
Annual $6,000 payment on SCF	In operating or financing section; company's choice of classification	In operating or financing section; company's choice of classification
Classification of $9,500 amount higher than book value at retirement	Recorded as a loss in earnings	Reduces shareholders' equity directly; no impact on earnings
$100,000 "repayment" of initial investment	Decreases long-term liabilities	Decreases shareholders' equity

There are two major differences between these alternative classifications:

1. Reported earnings is affected by interest expense and gains and losses on retirement when the classification is a liability. In contrast, these items bypass earnings if the classification is equity. For firms that jealously guard reported earnings and related trends, this distinction is important.

2. The classification of the element itself (i.e., as debt or equity) may be crucial to some corporations. The debt-to-equity ratio is often used in loan covenants to help control a major risk to lenders: the amount of debt outstanding. If debt-to-equity ratios are close to their contractually agreed maximums, then a new financial instrument issued and classified as equity is good news, indeed; one classified as a liability is not. The classification rules attempt to ensure that classification follows substance, not form, to limit the potential for manipulation.

Classification Factors

To classify a financial instrument, it is essential to look at the payment arrangements. A basic characteristic of debt is that *creditors have an enforceable legal right to receive payment.* In most ordinary debt arrangements, the debtor is obligated both to pay regular interest amounts and to repay the principal amount at a fixed and known time. For some debt instruments, there may be no fixed maturity date, such as demand loans or lines of credit from a financial institution. In these cases, the lenders have the option of demanding repayment. The crucial aspect of debt is that *the creditors can demand payment.* Equity investors, on the other hand, cannot demand payment; any payment of dividends and the redemption or repayment of the amount invested is a voluntary action of the company.

Therefore, to determine whether a financial instrument is debt or equity *in substance*, and whether component parts must be separated, the following factors must be considered:

Factor	Debt	Equity	Comment
Cash payment of the periodic return on capital (i.e., the cash "interest" or "dividend' payment)	Must be paid or Must be paid if the investor wishes	Paid if the company wishes	Any cash payment that is mandatory or is made at the investor's option is a liability.
Cash principal repayment	Must be paid or Must be paid if the investor wishes (i.e., at the investor's option)	Paid if the company wishes	Any cash payment that is mandatory or is made at the investor's option is a liability.
Unconditional right/ Ability to indefinitely defer cash payments by the (issuer) company	Cash payments cannot be deferred or Cash payments can be deferred for a limited period of time	Cash payments can be deferred forever if the company wishes	Classic dividends are payable only if the company declares them and thus can be deferred indefinitely by simply not declaring; they represent equity. *If deferral is only for a period of time, then the element is a liability.*
Cash payment dependent on the outcome of an uncertain future event beyond the control of both the investor and the (issuer) company	Future event possible or *controllable by (issuer) company or the investor*	Future event *abnormal* or *highly unlikely and uncontrollable*	If a financial instrument has to be repaid only on the dissolution of the company, this is deemed abnormal, and the element is equity. If the financial instrument must be repaid only if a covenant is violated, this is within the control of the company at some level, and the element is a liability.
Contract allows periodic return and/or the principal be settled in the (issuer) company's own shares; contract must specify how the number of shares to be issued is determined	Number of shares issued *is based on the market value of shares at the time of distribution*	Number of shares issued *is fixed by contract*	If the number of shares to be issued is fixed, then the risk of share price fluctuation rests with the investor, and *the element is equity.* If shares to be issued are calculated based on the share price on the date

Factor	Debt	Equity	Comment
			of payment, then the company has to issue shares with a cash value equal to the amount owing, and the element is a liability. In this latter case, risk of share price fluctuation rests with the issuer.

Classification Example—Retractable Preferred Shares

Most preferred shares have a call provision, whereby the corporation can call in the shares and redeem them at a given price *if the company wishes*. The call price is specified in the corporate articles governing that class of share. Preferred share *call provisions* give management more flexibility in managing the corporation's capital structure than would be the case without a call provision. These shares *do not have to be repaid*; as such, they are equity.

Some preferred shares include the provision that the shares *must* be redeemed on or before a specified date (**term preferred shares**) or an option to redeem that can be exercised *at the option of the shareholder* (**retractable shares**). When redemption is required or is at the option of the holder, then the mandatory final cash payout effectively makes the preferred shares a liability. The key is that cash repayment must either be contractually required or is at the option of the *investor*.

Effect of Escalation Clause

Sometimes, a preferred share issue will not have a direct or explicit requirement for the company to repay. Instead, the repayment obligation may be established indirectly through its terms and conditions. For example, suppose that a redeemable preferred share contract requires the company to triple the dividend rate after five years or to double the redemption price after five years. No prudent board of directors would leave the shares outstanding past year five at their significantly higher cost. The escalation clause clearly indicates that the shares will be redeemed before escalation. These shares are classified as debt.

Classification of Dividends

When preferred shares are classified as debt, *their dividends are reported as a financing expense*, a *deduction from earnings*, and are not reported as a direct reduction of retained earnings.

Recording dividends

Normally, dividends are a legal liability *only when declared,* and the classification of preferred shares as a liability does not alter this. Dividends on preferred shares are normally recorded as declared. However, if dividends are *mandatory*, then their status changes. Mandatory dividends are a liability. Dividends are recorded annually whether declared or not. For example, if dividends are mandatory *and must be fully paid in cash prior to redemption*, then dividends are accrued as time passes.

Required Redemption at a Premium

If preferred shares *must be redeemed at a value higher than book value*, the redemption premium should be accrued over the life of the shares using the effective interest method. For instance, assume that redeemable preferred shares were issued at $100 but have to be bought back for $110 at the end of five years. Each year, the company must accrue a portion of the $10 premium and expense it as a cost of financing.

Reporting Example

Brookfield Investment Corp Inc. is an investment holding company with total assets of just over $2.6 billion. The company reports approximately $1,057 million of redeemable preferred shares as a liability as these preferred shares are retractable at the option of the holder. Terms are described in the disclosure note as follows (emphasis added):

Selected Financial Statement Disclosures

6. RETRACTABLE PREFERRED SHARES

The company's Authorized Share Capital includes two classes of retractable preferred shares:

(i) unlimited Class 1 Senior Preferred shares issuable in series; and

(ii) unlimited Class 1 Junior Preferred shares issuable in series.

	December 31	December 31
(US$ millions, except number of shares)	2014	2013
5,986,595 Class 1 Senior Preferred Shares, Series A (2013 — 5,987,195)	$ 129	$ 141
17,999,718 Class 1 Junior Preferred Shares, Series A (2013 — 17,999,718)	558	558
17,200,000 Class 1 Junior Preferred Shares, Series B (2013 — 17,200,000)	370	405
	$ 1,057	$ 1,104

The retractable preferred shares are retractable at the option of the holder and, accordingly, are liabilities for accounting purposes.

The following rights and privileges apply to the outstanding Class 1 Senior Preferred shares:

(i) entitlement to cumulative quarterly dividends calculated on the issue price of C$25.00 per share at a fixed rate of 4.70% per annum; and

(ii) in the case of the Senior Preferred shares, Series A, redeemable at the option of the company or the holder at C$25.00 per share plus accrued and unpaid dividends thereon.

The following rights and privileges apply to the outstanding Class 1 Junior Preferred Series A shares:

(i) entitlement to non-cumulative quarterly dividends calculated on the issue price of $31.00 per share at 4%, as and when declared by the Board of Directors of the company; and

(ii) redeemable at the option of the company or the holder at any time at $31.00 per share plus declared and unpaid dividends thereon.

The following rights and privileges apply to the outstanding Class 1 Junior Preferred Series B shares:

(i) entitlement to cumulative quarterly dividends calculated on the issue price of C$25.00 per share at 4%, as and when declared by the Board of Directors of the company; and

(ii) redeemable at the option of the company or the holder at any time at C$25.00 per share plus declared and unpaid dividends thereon.

The dividend payments on the preferred shares of $29 million (2013 — $29 million) are classified as interest expense.

Source: Brookfield Investments Corporation, 2014 Annual Financial Statements, www.sedar.com, posted 31 March 2015.

Classification Example—Other Redeemable Shares

"Redeemable" does not automatically mean that shares are liabilities. Shares that are redeemable *at the company's option* are not a liability. The company cannot be forced to pay cash, since redemption is voluntary; redemptions that can be avoided do not create a liability. Also, any senior shares that are *convertible into common shares* are clearly equity.

Classification Example—Mutual Funds

In some open-ended mutual funds, all shares are redeemable in cash at the option of the investors, who also have the legal right to cash payouts for accumulated earnings. These entities accordingly have no equity at all, since all ownership interests have the characteristics of debt and are classified as liabilities.

Classification Example—Perpetual Debt

Perpetual debt provides the holder with a contractual right to receive cash interest, but the principal (1) never has to be repaid, (2) has to be repaid only in the indefinite future, or (3) has to be repaid only in highly unlikely situations, such as upon liquidation of the company. For example, the ING Group has outstanding perpetual debt of over €6.1 billion, at interest rates from 4.2% to 9%.

Reporting

Perpetual debt is reported entirely as a liability. This is a compound instrument with both debt and equity components, but the equity portion is valued at zero. All that remains is the liability. The principal amount of perpetual debt is equity in that it is an obligation due only on liquidation. What is the value of a payment that has a due date in the infinite future? *The present value of such an indefinite payment is zero.* However, the interest payments are a liability because they represent an obligation at fixed dates. The lender will be willing to pay for the interest stream, and it is the interest stream that generates loan proceeds. Only a liability is recorded, which is valued at the present value of the stream of future interest payments.

Classification Example—Compound Instrument: Convertible Debt

Convertible debt is a common example of a *compound instrument*, classified in the financial statements as part debt and part equity. These bonds often are issued by a corporation with the provision that they may be converted by the holder into shares (usually, common shares) at a specified price or ratio of exchange.

The conversion date might be the bond's maturity date, or at various points prior to maturity (e.g., for the last four years of the bond's life). There might be different conversion rights during different conversion windows. For example, an investor is entitled to 10 common shares for every $1,000 bond if converted within the first five years of a 15-year bond, 7.5 shares for conversion in the sixth through tenth year, but only five common shares during years 11 through 15.

The conversion ratio is expressed either in the number of shares per bond, or in a price per share. For example, a bond that is convertible into 20 common shares per $1,000 bond is the same as one that is convertible at a price of $50 ($1,000 ÷ $20).

For example, Paladin Energy Ltd. issued US$150 million of unsecured convertible bonds in March 2015. The bonds mature on 31 March 2020, and have a conversion price of US$0.356 per share, which means that 421,348,314 shares ($150 million ÷ $0.356) would be issued if the investors took shares instead of cash at maturity. The bonds also bear interest at 7%. Note that at the time of issue, Paladin's shares were trading at US$0.284 (C$0.36) and the company's effective interest rate was 12.37%. Generally, convertible bonds have coupon rates below the interest that would have been paid on nonconvertible debt. As the option to convert has value, bond holders are willing to accept a lower rate of interest. The issue of this bond was classified as $16 million (net of transaction costs) in equity with the remaining net proceeds recognized as a liability.

Characteristics of Convertible Debt

A key element of convertible bonds is that in issuing the bonds, management hopes that the conversion privilege will be attractive to the investors. That is, the investors will, in fact, convert to common shares, and therefore the company will never have to repay the principal amount of the bonds in cash.

Conversion of a bond becomes attractive when the market price of the share entitlement rises above the conversion price. For example, suppose that an investor has a $1,000 bond (purchased at par) that is convertible into 25 common shares (i.e., the conversion price is $40). If the market price of the common shares is $46, the investor can make a profit of $6 per share, less any transaction costs, by converting the bonds and then selling the shares on the open market:

Market value of shares obtained on conversion ($46 × 25)	$1,150
Less: cost of bond	1,000
Profit for investor from conversion	$ 150

The market recognizes this reality and, therefore, the market price of the bonds will increase to follow the conversion value of the shares. Therefore, once the market price of the shares rises above the conversion price, the bonds will sell at a price that is related to the value of the conversion privilege rather than at a price related to the merits of the debt instrument. In the eyes of the market, the bond ceases to trade as debt, and effectively is traded as equity.

Forced Conversion

A convertible debenture can often be called for *cash redemption* by the company prior to maturity. The point of the cash redemption option is that management can *force conversion* before maturity if the market price is higher than the conversion price of the shares. The company calls the bond for *cash redemption*, knowing that the shares are worth more, and the investor opts for the higher value of shares. By forcing early conversion, the company makes sure that the share conversion takes place and cash repayment will not be necessary.

Convertible Debt with a Floating Conversion Price per Share

Convertible debt may be issued where the *number of shares to be issued on conversion is not fixed by contract* but, rather, is based on the market value of the shares on the conversion date. If this is the case, the conversion option has *no intrinsic value to the investor* because the investor has no upside benefit. For example, if a $1,000,000 bond were convertible into shares at the market value of shares on the conversion date and this value was $80, then 12,500 shares would be issued. If the market value were $82, then 12,195 shares would be issued. *This type of bond has no equity component and is classified as all debt.*

The reason for this conclusion is that if the conversion price is not fixed, the risks and rewards of changing share prices stays with the company. The investor has no upside potential or downside risk. The bond will always trade in financial markets as a pure liability, with no option attached. Essentially, when the price is based on the fair value of the day of conversion, the investor could just as well take cash and use this cash to purchase shares in the market. The conversion option at a floating conversion price simply allows transaction costs to be minimized.

Accounting Treatment of Convertible Debt

A convertible bond with a fixed conversion price per share has elements of both debt and equity. The liability and the equity component are recognized separately when the bond is first recorded (as the Paladin example above demonstrated) and then are accounted for separately to maturity. Refer to the next two sections.

CONCEPT REVIEW

1. What is a compound financial instrument?
2. What classification factors must be considered to aid in classifying a financial instrument as debt or equity?
3. What is the distinguishing characteristic that causes retractable preferred shares to be reported as debt rather than as shareholders' equity?
4. Under what circumstances will the fair value of a convertible bond reflect the fair value of the shares that would be obtained on conversion?

CONVERTIBLE DEBT—CONVERSION AT THE INVESTOR'S OPTION

Convertible debt that is convertible at the option of the investor at a fixed conversion price is initially recognized as a compound instrument, where *proceeds from issuance are divided between the liability and the equity element. The equity element represents the value of the option on common shares. The debt element represents principal plus interest that are contractually required to be paid.*

Initial Recognition

Assume that Tollen Corp. sells $100,000 of 8% convertible bonds for $106,000 due in five years. The market interest rate on the day of issuance is 10%.[2] (Refer back to the Paladin example earlier that discussed the differences in interest rates.) Each $10,000 bond is convertible into 100 common shares on any interest date after the end of the second year from the date of issuance. Conversion is at the option of the investor. Also assume that it is appropriate to assign a value of $92,418 to the bond and $13,582 to the conversion privilege. (Measurement of these amounts will be analyzed in the next section.) The issuance will be recorded as follows:

Cash	106,000	
Bonds payable		92,418
Contributed capital: common share conversion rights		13,582

Alternatively, the discount on initial recognition can be separately recorded. A discount of $7,582 is recorded as the difference between the $92,418 net proceeds attributable to the bond and its $100,000 face value. The alternative entry is:

Cash	106,000	
Discount on bonds payable ($100,000 – $92,418)	7,582	
Bonds payable		100,000
Contributed capital: common share conversion rights		13,582

(The highlighted section is the only difference.)

2. As is discussed in a later section, this interest rate is established by determining an interest rate for nonconvertible debt with the same term and risk.

The account, *common share conversion rights*, is an equity account that will be reported as contributed capital. Using this approach, *the substance of the transaction* is recognized. Both a bond *and* an option were issued, and both are now reflected in the financial statements. The proceeds received for the equity portion of the instrument are reflected in equity. Accounting for the debt will reflect an effective interest rate.

Initial Recognition

Following on from the above example, assume that interest is paid annually. The effective interest rate method is used to amortize the bond discount. The entry for this interest payment is:

Interest expense (92,418 x 10%)	9,242	
Bonds payable		1,242
Cash ($100,000 x 8%)		8,000

Notice that the bonds payable amount will increase over the term of the bond to be the face value at maturity. Also note that there is no change in the contributed capital account as long as the bond remains outstanding and not converted. In later years, *the amount in that contributed capital account will either be transferred to share capital if and when converted or transferred to other contributed capital if the conversion rights lapse.*

Conversion

When convertible bonds are submitted for conversion, the first task is to update any accounts relating to bond premium or discount, accrued interest, and foreign exchange gains and losses on foreign currency–denominated debt. Following these routine adjustments, the balance of the liability account (and related unamortized premium or discount, if recognized seperately) that pertains to the converted bonds must be transferred to the share account. *As well, the proportionate balance of the contributed capital: common share conversion rights account must be transferred to the share equity account.*

The conversion is recorded using the **book value method**, and the book value, or carrying value, of the debt is simply transferred to equity. For example, assume that all of the $100,000 Tollen bonds payable are converted to 1,000 common shares on an interest date. Assume that on this date, the share price is $140 per share, and calculations show that $4,550 of discount remains unamortized after updating the discount account. The entry to record the conversion is:

Bonds payable	100,000	
Contributed capital: common share conversion rights	13,582	
Discount on bonds payable		4,550
Common shares		109,032

The market value of the common shares is not recorded. The value assigned to common shares ($109,032) is the carrying value of the bond ($100,000 − $4,550) plus the option value ($13,582).

Repayment at Maturity

If the market value of underlying shares is less than face value at maturity, investors will request repayment, and the conversion rights will expire. Since this happens *at maturity*, all discount or premium accounts will be zero. The option value remains in equity, but its description should be changed to indicate that the option is no longer outstanding. This is done in a reclassification entry. The entries on cash repayment of the Tollen bonds would be:

Bonds payable	100,000	
Cash		100,000
Contributed capital: common share conversion rights	13,582	
Contributed capital: lapse of rights		13,582

Repayment Prior to Maturity

If the bond is repaid prior to maturity, the amount paid for early retirement is allocated between the debt and equity components, using the **incremental method**. Any gain or loss on the liability retirement is recorded in earnings, while the retirement of equity results in adjustments to equity accounts, as illustrated in Chapter 14.

For example, return to the prior example of the Tollen bonds. Assume that the $100,000 Tollen bond is retired for $104,000 on an interest date prior to maturity. On this date, $4,550 of discount remains unamortized. Valuation models indicate that $97,000 of the $104,000 price paid represents the present value of the bond at current interest rates (for nonconvertible debt), and the remaining $7,000 relates to the equity portion. The entry to record the retirement is:

Bonds payable	100,000	
Contributed capital: common share conversion rights	13,582	
Loss on retirement of bonds [($100,000 − $4,550) − $97,000]	1,550	
Discount on bonds payable		4,550
Contributed capital: retirement of common share conversion rights ($13,582 − $7,000)		6,582
Cash		104,000

The loss on retirement of bonds is caused by the difference between the carrying value of the bonds ($95,450) and the portion of the retirement price assigned to debt ($97,000). The contributed capital amount is caused by the difference between the carrying value of the equity component ($13,582) and the portion of the retirement price assigned to equity ($7,000).

Measurement

When fair values must be estimated, the **fair-value hierarchy** is consulted.

In Level 1, there are quoted market prices for *this exact financial instrument* in an active market, and the result is objectively verifiable.

If the financial instrument is not actively traded, a Level 2 estimate might be made. In Level 2, observable values from similar financial instruments are used to imply value. Adjustments must be made for differences, such as credit risk, term, or conditions. For example, if the company's bonds do not trade in active markets, there are no separate objective prices provided by arm's-length market transactions. However, the fair value of another fairly similar bond might be verified. The second bond's fair value could be used as a reference point, adjusted for interest rate differentials, or credit rating, and so on. The resulting fair value is less reliable than a Level 1 directly observable value.

Finally, at Level 3 in the fair-value hierarchy, there are observable fair values, but multiple or significant adjustments have to be made to infer a fair value, including a company's own data or estimation of unobservable factors. The resulting fair value is used for reporting but is correspondingly less reliable.

Measurement of the fair value of debt versus equity components of convertible debt can be especially problematic because the component elements *do not separately trade* in financial markets. In the fair value hierarchy, this moves the valuation to at least a Level 2 estimate.

To value the *liability portion of the compound instrument,* the present value of the bond must be calculated. The interest rate used for discounting is the critical variable that must be measured. The conversion option is valued as the residual; that is, the issuance price less the present value of a comparable *nonconvertible* bond. This is called the **incremental method of valuation**.

For example, for the Tollen Corp. bond above, assume that the market interest rate for a similar, nonconvertible was established to be 10%. The present value of the cash flows of an 8%, five-year, $100,000 bond (assuming annual interest payments) at an effective interest rate of 10%, can be calculated as $92,418. This is a Level 2 estimation because the interest rate is estimated. Subtracting $92,418 from the net proceeds of $106,000 leaves $13,582 attributable to the conversion option.

The key to this method is *to establish an appropriate discount rate*, with reference to financial markets and established, observable prices. Ten percent should represent the market interest rate for a (nonconvertible) bond of similar term, security, and credit risk. This may be straightforward to establish, or not, depending on the activity in the bond market and the presence of similar companies.

Example

Assume that Easy Co. issues $1,000,000 of $1,000 bonds dated 1 January 20X2, due 31 December 20X4 (i.e., three years later), for $1,002,000. Interest at 6% is payable annually, and each bond is convertible at any time up to maturity into 250 common shares at a conversion price of $4. When the bonds are issued, the prevailing interest rate for similar debt without a conversion option is 9%.

Using the incremental method, the amount of the proceeds that is attributable to the liability is measured as the present value of the cash flows of principal and interest, using the market rate of interest of 9%:

Face value [$1,000,000 × (P/F, 9%, 3)]	$772,183
Interest [($1,000,000 × 6%) × (P/A, 9%, 3)]	151,877
Total liability component	$924,060

The issuance of the convertible bonds will be recorded as follows:

Cash	1,002,000	
Bonds payable		924,060
Contributed capital: common share conversion rights ($1,002,000 – $924,060)		77,940

Impact on Earnings

Interest expense is affected by the allocation of bond proceeds between debt and equity. In the entries above, a discount is recorded. The discount is amortized over the life of the bond, using the effective interest method, as illustrated in Chapter 12. Interest expense will decrease earnings.

Remember that the higher the value that is allocated to the option, the higher the discount. The higher the discount, the more interest expense is recognized, and the lower earnings will be. This effect may influence the valuation adopted by management when the bond proceeds are initially recorded. For example, if there is a corporate bias to maximize earnings, a valuation that minimizes the amount allocated to the common share conversion rights and the discount will likely be chosen.

Remember also that the amount allocated to the common share conversion rights remains in the contributed capital section of shareholders' equity permanently and never has an impact on earnings. The conversion rights account is *either folded into the common share account, if the option is exercised and the bonds are converted, or is part of other contributed capital, if the option is not exercised and the bonds are not converted.*

Convertible Debt with a Floating Conversion Price per Share

The previous example involved a bond with a fixed conversion price per share. If the conversion option was based on the market value of the common shares on the conversion date, then the option has no value to the investor. Such a convertible bond is classified entirely as debt.

CONCEPT REVIEW

1. Why might a convertible bond issued at a price above par result in a discount on bonds payable recorded on the books?
2. Where is the account *common share conversion rights* reported in the SFP? What happens to this account on bond conversion? Repayment?
3. What is the key valuation measurement in determining the amount of issuance proceeds from a convertible bond to be allocated to debt?

CONVERTIBLE DEBT—CONVERSION MANDATORY

The preceding discussion dealt exclusively with debt that is convertible at the investor's option. Corporations may also issue convertible debt that pays interest in cash, but principal *must be settled by issuance of a specific number of shares on maturity.* This is again a *compound financial instrument*; however, this time the obligation to pay cash interest is a liability, and the *entire* principal portion is equity. As long as shares can be forced on an investor *at a price set in advance,* (and therefore not at market value) a bond falls in this category. *If the company has the right to repay principal in cash or shares, the bond is still classified as "conversion mandatory."* This is because the company cannot be forced to pay cash.

Measurement

Using the *incremental method*, the liability portion of the compound instrument is valued based on present value of interest payments using an appropriate market yield rate, which reflects similar term, security, and credit risk. This is a Level 2 approximation of fair value. The equity portion of the bond is then the residual amount, the difference between issuance proceeds and the liability present value. Over the life of the bond, interest expense is recorded on the interest portion *only*, and cash payments are applied against the interest liability *only*, reducing it to zero by maturity. At maturity, the equity portion of the bond is transferred to share capital.

Example

Suppose that Gagnon Ltd. issues a $100,000, 6%, four-year debenture for $103,500, repayable at maturity through the issuance of a fixed number of common shares (fixed conversion price). Interest is payable annually, in cash. A similar bond that is not convertible carries an interest rate of 8%. Since conversion is mandatory, and the number of shares to be issued is fixed, principal is equity. The interest must be paid in cash, so it is a liability. The issuance price is disaggregated as follows:

Issuance proceeds	$103,500
Interest present value [$6,000 × (P/A, 8%, 4)]	19,873
Equity portion	$ 83,627

When the bond is issued, the entry will be:

Cash	103,500	
Interest liability on debenture		19,873
Share equity—debenture		83,627

Note how different this is from the treatment of a bond that is convertible at the investor's option. There, the only equity portion was an option amount, and principal and interest were both included in the liability amount. When conversion is mandatory, the bond has been cleanly split into the interest portion (a liability) and the principal portion (equity).

As time passes, interest will be accounted for by the effective interest method, calculated only on the *outstanding balance of the interest liability*. The carrying amount of the interest liability will be increased by 8% each year, and the $6,000 annual payment of interest will reduce the liability. At the end of the first year, Gagnon will make the following entries to record the interest expense and the annual payment:

Interest expense ($19,873 × 8%)	1,590	
Interest liability on debenture		1,590
Interest liability on debenture	6,000	
Cash		6,000

Note that the amount that is paid as "interest," the $6,000, is treated as the reduction of the liability. Interest expense is a far different number, based only on the recognized liability. The amortization of the interest liability over the four-year period is shown in Exhibit 15-1. At maturity, the interest liability will be zero by virtue of the payments made over the four years. The balance in the debenture equity account will be transferred to common share equity when the shares are issued at maturity:

Share equity—debenture	83,627	
Common shares		83,627

EXHIBIT 15-1

CONVERTIBLE DEBT—CONVERSION MANDATORY

Amortization of Interest Liability

Year	Beginning Balance of Interest Liability	Interest Expense at 8%	Payment	Ending Balance of Interest Liability
1	$19,873	$1,590	$6,000	$15,463
2	15,463	1,237	6,000	10,700
3	10,700	856	6,000	5,556
4	5,556	444	6,000	0

Interest Obligation Payment Variations

If the company *must* pay interest in cash, the interest portion of the issue proceeds is a liability, as seen above. If the company is permitted, at the company's option, to issue shares at their current fair value in full payment of interest, the interest is still a liability and is recorded as such. However, if the bond agreement allows the company to issue shares at a *fixed price* in payment of interest, then this interest portion of the debt is *equity*. Risk falls on the debenture holder when the price per share is set because the holder's ultimate benefit from interest payments will depend on the market value of the shares and is not on a fixed monetary amount. To summarize:

Bond Terms—Interest Arrangement	Classification
Interest that must be paid in cash	Debt (as above)
Interest that the company has the option of paying in a fixed number of shares or by using a fixed price per share	Equity; the entire bond is equity, since principal is also equity
Interest that the company has the option of paying in a variable number of shares, using current market prices to establish value	Debt (as above)

Debt Principal with a Floating Conversion Price per Share

Standard setters have determined that when the number of shares (price per share) required to settle the obligation is fixed, then the principal is equity, as illustrated above. If the number of shares is not fixed but, rather, is based on the current fair value of shares, the principal is a *financial liability* of the entity, and the bond is accounted for as a straightforward bond liability, as illustrated in Chapter 13. Remember that if the conversion price is the current share price, there is no transfer of risk, and the price risk stays with company.

CONCEPT REVIEW

1. If a bond must be converted to a fixed number of shares at maturity, how is the equity portion of the compound instrument measured?
2. If a bond must be converted to a fixed number of shares at maturity, will reported annual interest expense be higher or lower than the contractual interest paid?

STOCK OPTIONS

Stock options are financial instruments that give the holder the right, but not the obligation, to buy shares at a fixed price at a certain point in time, called the **exercise date**. When an option is first issued, it usually has an exercise price that is equal to or higher than the current market price of the shares. The option has an **intrinsic value** only when the current share price rises above the exercise price. An option term can be lengthy, and share prices can be volatile; so an option has a **fair value**, depending on market expectations about the *eventual share price on the exercise date*, combined with the time value of money.

Stock options are a form of **derivative instrument**. They are derivative because their value arises or is *derived* solely from the value of the primary common shares that the options can be used to buy. Derivative instruments are designed to transfer risk by setting the conditions of an exchange of financial instruments at a particular time at fixed terms.

Suppose that Mercurial Ltd. issues 10,000 stock options. Each option permits the holder to buy one Mercurial common share for $5 in four years' time. When the options are issued, the market price of Mercurial's shares is $4. These options are said to be **under water** or **out-of-the-money** when they are first issued because the exercise price ($5) is higher than the fair value of the shares ($4 per share). If the current market price of the shares rises to $8, the option then has an *intrinsic value* of $3. The option is also described as being **in-the-money** when it has an intrinsic value. However, the fair value of the option is higher than the intrinsic value since there is still time for the underlying share price to be higher than $8, making the option even more valuable. If the market price of the common shares is below $5 on the expiration date, the options will expire unexercised.

Logically, the fair value of the option is *the risk-adjusted present value of any expected positive difference between the underlying share price and the option exercise price on the day the options are exercised*. For the Mercurial options, the "perfect" valuation would be to predict the market price—accurately—in four years' time and discount the gain to today's dollars at an appropriate discount rate.

The fair value of stock options can be established by use of an option pricing model, such as the Black-Scholes or binomial pricing models. Option pricing models are complex mathematical formulas using inputs, including the exercise price in the option contract, length of the option, current market value of the underlying shares, volatility of of the underlying share price, expected dividends, and the risk-free interest rate.

When options trade in financial markets, option prices reflect Level 1 values; these fair values reflect the practical application of option pricing models. In other cases, if options are not traded or are thinly traded, option pricing models are the only valuation alternative available. Use of option pricing models to account for some options is contentious because these models were not developed to price long-term options. Furthermore, the results are a Level 2 or Level 3 measurement in the fair-value hierarchy and have no Level 1 measurement validity. That is, these options might never be separately traded and any suggested fair value is an educated guess. Standard setters feel, though, that it is better to be imprecise than to give up, and valuation based on these models is becoming increasingly entrenched in the financial reporting model.

Recording

Assume that a corporation issues 20,000 stock options allowing the holder(s) to acquire common shares at an acquisition price of $20 per share, which is the now-current market price of the common shares. The options expire in four years' time. The corporation receives $18,000 for the options. Valuation in this case is straightforward because there is a market transaction, which is presumably based on the investor's assessment of option pricing.

The relevant dates are the (1) announcement date; (2) issuance date, or grant date; (3) exercise date; and (4) expiration date. Consider the following entries:

Announcement date:		
Memorandum: 20,000 stock options approved, allowing purchase of 20,000 shares at $20 in four years' time.		
Issuance date; options sold for a total of $18,000:		
Cash	18,000	
Contributed capital: stock options outstanding		18,000

At exercise, assuming that the current market price of the common shares was $28, and all options were exercised:

Exercise date:		
Cash (20,000 shares × $20)	400,000	
Contributed capital: stock options outstanding	18,000	
Common shares		418,000

Alternatively, assuming that the current market price of common shares was $14, and all options expired:

Expiry date:		
Contributed capital: stock options outstanding	18,000	
Contributed capital, lapse of stock options		18,000

Note that the stock options outstanding account ends up in one of two places: *either folded into the common share account, if the options are exercised, or as part of other contributed capital, if the options are not exercised.* Both of these accounts are equity accounts, and both are elements of contributed capital.

Note also that *the current market value of the shares on the exercise date, $28, is not reflected in the entry that records exercise of the options.* Financial statement users would often like to judge the terms of the options, as approved by the board of directors. Details of all options are disclosed in the financial statements so that anyone can make these calculations.

RIGHTS

When a company issues new shares, the proportionate ownership of the existing shareholders is diluted. A rights offering is used in cases where the company gives existing shareholders the opportunity to purchase enough new shares to maintain their proportionate ownership. This is how it works.

Rexon Inc. is looking to raise $4 million in a new offering of shares. The company currently has 1,200,000 shares outstanding with a current price of $20 each. It has decided to issue a rights offering where each existing shareholder receives one right for each share owned. The right gives the shareholder the opportunity to buy a new share at a set subscription price and a set number of rights. Rexon has set the subscription price at $10 and therefore will issue 400,000 new shares ($4,000,000 /$10). Accordingly, it will take three rights (1,200,000/400,000) and $10 to buy one new share. It is now February 28 when the company makes the announcement; the date of record is March 15; the ex-rights date is March 13; and the rights expire on April 30. These dates are important. Shareholders owning the shares on the record date, March 15, are entitled to receive the rights. Two days prior to the record date, March 13, is the ex-rights date; if shares are purchased after this date, the shareholder is not entitled to receive the rights. On the ex-rights date, the right will now trade separately and have a separate value from the share, and the share price reduces by the value of each right.

For Rexon, the share price will decline by the value of the right on the **ex-rights date**. In this case, the rights are valued at $2.50 and the share price declines to $17.50. From the viewpoint of the shareholder, it costs 3 rights valued at $2.50 each (for a total of $7.50) plus $10 in cash which totals $17.50 to purchase one new share. The rights will be exercised only if the share price is at or above $17.50. If the share price dropped to $12 before April 30 (the expiry date), shareholders would not exercise their rights since it is cheaper to buy a share at $12 rather than exercise the rights and pay $10. This is a risk that companies take in making the rights offering and also is why the time to expiry for the rights is generally for a short period.

A shareholder receiving rights has four options: (1) exercise the rights and purchase new shares in proportion to the number currently owned; (2) purchase additional rights to buy additional shares in the company to increase the proportionate ownership; (3) sell the rights if the shareholder is not interested in investing more in the company (resulting in a reduction in proportionate ownership); and (4) let the rights elapse, which will result in losses for the shareholder if the rights have value.

From the company's point of view, there are no proceeds that have yet been received when the rights are issued. In actual fact, nothing has yet changed for the company. A memo entry is made in the books noting the number of rights issued. If the rights are exercised and new shares issued, at this point, the new shares issued are recognized. In the above example, assuming all rights are exercised, the journal entry will be:

Exercise date:		
Cash (400,000 shares × $10)	4,000,000	
Common shares		4,000,000

If the rights expire and are not exercised, this is documented in another memorandum.

Poison Pill Rights Not Recognized

Corporations trying to make themselves less attractive as a takeover target will sometimes issue rights that make it far more expensive for an outsider to gain control. These are known as **poison pill** rights. They are issued to existing shareholders for no consideration and are recorded by memorandum only because they have no fair value. If the rights were allowed to expire, a further memorandum entry would be recorded.

In the event of a hostile takeover bid, the existing shareholders *not involved* in the takeover bid and holding poison pill rights are allowed to buy shares at significantly reduced prices. This greatly increases the number of shares outstanding and severely dilutes the value of the shares held by the parties that back the takeover bid and are not able to exercise their own rights.

Poison pill rights are recorded only as a memo in the books until exercised. Disclosure is prominent, to scare off the wolves!

WARRANTS

Stock warrants can also be used for raising equity. **Warrants** allow the holder to purchase shares for a fixed price for a fixed period of time and are often issued as a *detachable contract* with another security (usually bonds). Warrants will trade separately from the bond to which they were originally attached and have a Level 1 fair value because of this separate market. Like options, warrants may be exercised to acquire additional shares from the corporation or allowed to lapse on the expiration date (if any). Warrants may also be issued separately for nominal amounts or attached to shares as part of a unit.

Warrants issued in conjunction with debt have three important characteristics that differentiate the "package" from regular convertible debt:

1. The warrants usually are *detachable*, which means that they can be bought and sold separately from the debt to which they were originally attached;
2. The warrants can be exercised without having to trade in or redeem the debt; and
3. The exercise of warrants results in cash paid for shares, which is not the case for convertible bonds.

On issuance, a portion of the bond price is allocated to the warrants for accounting purposes. The allocation is credited to a contributed capital (shareholders' equity) account, calculated based on the market values of the two securities on the date of issuance (a **proportional method**). The fair value of debt is based on present value at the market interest rate, and warrants are valued based on trading values as soon as they begin to trade.

Example

Embassy Corp. issues $100,000 of 8%, 10-year, nonconvertible bonds with detachable stock warrants. Nuvolari Corp. purchases the entire issue for 105 exclusive of accrued interest. Each $1,000 bond carries 10 warrants. Each warrant entitles Nuvolari to purchase one common share for $15. The bond issue therefore includes 1,000 warrants (100 bonds × 10 warrants per bond). Shortly after issuance, the warrants trade for $4 each ($4,000 in total) and the bonds trade at 103 ex-warrants (i.e., without warrants attached) ($103,000 in total).

These fair values total to $107,000, $2,000 higher than the $105,000 issuance price. This implies market inefficiencies or changed market conditions in the short gap between issuance and active trading. However, the $105,000 value is factual and must be accounted for using all information present. An allocation of the $105,000 issuance proceeds is therefore based proportionally on both market values:

Market value of bonds ($100,000 × 1.03)	$103,000
Market value of warrants ($4 × 1,000)	4,000
Total market value of bonds and warrants	$107,000
Allocation of proceeds to bonds [$105,000 × ($103,000 ÷ $107,000)]	$101,075
Allocation of proceeds to warrants [$105,000 × ($4,000 ÷ $107,000)]	3,925
Total proceeds allocated	$105,000

Issuance entry		
Cash	105,000	
Bonds payable		100,000
Premium on bonds payable ($101,075 − $100,000)		1,075
Contributed capital: detachable stock warrants		3,925

If all of the warrants are exercised when the market value of shares is $22:

Contributed capital: detachable stock warrants	3,925	
Cash ($15 × 1,000)	15,000	
Common shares		18,925

If the warrants expire because the share price falls below the exercise price:

Contributed capital: detachable stock warrants	3,925	
Contributed capital: lapse of warrants		3,925

The contributed capital account either rolls into the common share account on exercise, or remains in contributed capital with a different description on lapse. *This is the same pattern* as established for the contributed capital account created for the conversion option for bonds convertible at the investor's option and that used for options.

In cases where warrants have been issued alone or attached to shares, similar accounting entries as above would be required.

CONCEPT REVIEW

1. When does an option have an intrinsic value? How is this different from fair value?
2. When options are exercised, is the value assigned to the common shares issued equal to the fair value of the shares? Explain.
3. What are poison pill rights?
4. Past Ltd. issues common stock warrants as part of an issue of debentures. The exercise price for common shares under the warrants is higher than the market price of the common shares when the bonds are issued. Should any part of the proceeds of the bond issue be credited to shareholders' equity? Explain.

SHARE-BASED PAYMENTS

Share-based payments result from transactions in which an entity acquires or receives goods or services, in return for consideration in the form of the entity's shares or referenced to (based on) the price of the entity's shares. This includes transactions where share options are granted for goods and services. Long-term compensation to employees is a common example of a share-based transaction, but shares or options may also be used to compensate suppliers. These share-based arrangements may be **equity-settled plans** (the recipient receives shares) or **cash-settled plans** (the recipient receives cash based on the value of shares.) Alternatively, the arrangement may allow the recipient or the issuer to choose between cash and share considerations.

Share-based Payment to Nonemployees

Transactions involving equity-settled share-based payments with *nonemployees* are recognized when the service is rendered or the goods are received. Such transactions are valued at the fair value of the goods or services acquired. In the rare circumstances that fair value *cannot be measured*, then the fair value of the share-based instruments granted must be estimated and recorded.

Example

Assume that Terry Technologies Ltd. issues 500 no-par common shares to Vilt Holdings Ltd. for October 20X2 rent, which has been set in the lease agreement at $1,000 per month. The shares are currently trading at $2.10 per share. The entry is:

1 October 20X2		
Rent expense	1,000	
Common shares, no-par (500 shares)		1,000

The transaction is valued at the contractually set rent amount. The market value of the common shares is in the same range ($1,050; 500 shares × $2.10) but is not used to value the transaction. The board of directors, who must authorize this transaction, would consider this information, though, because they have a legislative duty to issue shares at fair value.

Example

Assume that GT Ltd. issues 250 stock options to Laura Brown as a director's fee. Each option entitles Brown to purchase one common share for $30. The options were issued on 1 March 20X2, expire on 31 December 20X2, and are exercised by Brown on 1 July 20X2 when the shares are trading for $36.50. Other directors were paid $800 cash. The entries to record issuance and exercise are:

1 March 20X2—issuance date		
Administrative expense (director's fees)	800	
Contributed capital: stock options outstanding		800
1 July 20X2—exercise date		
Cash (250 shares × $30)	7,500	
Contributed capital: stock options outstanding	800	
Common shares, no-par (250 shares)		8,300

The market value of the shares on the date the common shares were issued, $36.50, is not recognized. If the options were to expire, the entry would be:

Contributed capital: stock options outstanding	800	
Contributed capital: lapse of stock options		800

Note the pattern established: The contributed capital account either is folded into the common share account on exercise or remains in contributed capital with a different description on lapse.

Valuation

Valuation may not be as simple as presented in these examples. For example, if all GT directors[3] were compensated through options, no cash reference price would exist. Could the directors' fees of other companies be used as a reference price? There might be no comparable companies, or the companies might have different compensation practices. In the *fair value hierarchy,* adjustments to comparative amounts would move the fair value to Level 2 or perhaps Level 3 equivalents. In the rare circumstances that no fair value of the director's fees is obtainable, the stock option would be valued using an option pricing model—also a Level 2 or Level 3 equivalent.

Reporting Example

For example, read the following note from ESSA Pharma Inc. where the agent responsible for a private placement of shares was partially compensated through share warrants. These warrants were valued using the Black-Scholes model (an option pricing model) because the fair value of services received could not be determined.

> **Selected extracts from the Note 9**
>
> **9. SHAREHOLDERS' EQUITY**
>
> ....
>
> Private placements
>
> a) January 2015 Special Warrant Financing
>
> ......
>
> In connection with the 2015 Special Warrant financing, Bloom Burton & Co. and Roth Capital Partners, LLC, as Agents, and selling group members, received cash commissions equal to approximately US$706,800 and 257,018 broker warrants. Each broker warrant is exercisable to purchase one common share until January 16, 2017 at a price of US$2.75 per broker warrant. The warrants were valued at $334,396 using the Black-Scholes model with a risk-free interest rate of 0.87%, term of 2 years, volatility of 72.3%, and dividend rate of 0%, and have been recorded as a derivative liability (Note 8).
>
> Source: ESSA Pharma, Inc., 2015 Annual Financial Statements, www.sedar.com, posted 14 December 2015.

Cash-settled Payment to Nonemployees

Suppliers and other nonemployees might also be granted entitlements under a *cash-settled plan,* where they would be entitled to money rather than shares. In this case, a liability would be established and measurement would be adjusted annually. Cash-settled plans are illustrated for employees in the following section.

Share-based Payment to Employees

Share-based payments are a common form of long-term compensation granted to employees, senior management in particular. *Plans may be equity settled or cash settled.* There are many alternative structures, including **stock option plans**, **stock appreciation rights** (SARs), **phantom stock plans**, and **restricted share units**. The range of these alternatives reflects certain tax strategies and also the understanding that employees might prefer to have cash rather than company shares. It can be complicated, under insider trading rules, for managers to buy shares under an option plan and then sell them for cash.

Volatility in the underlying share price may make classic option programs unpopular. For instance, when share prices go down, instead of going up, employees may be disappointed and leave the company since the options have no value. When share prices shoot up, shareholders may be concerned with the generous returns granted to employees. For example, one executive of Potash Corp. of Saskatchewan was estimated to be holding options that were in-the-money to the tune of $300 million in 2014;[4] this is an extremely high level of compensation.

---

3. Directors are considered employees under the terms of IFRS 2.

4. "The payout goldmine that is Potash" by David Milstead, Globe and Mail, 11 April, 2014; accessed from: http://www.theglobeandmail.com/globe-investor/many-options-remain-for-outgoing-potash-corp-ceo/article17946220/ 6 January 2016.

Some of the more common long-term compensation arrangements are summarized in the table below:

Share-based Arrangement	Employee Receives	Description
Stock option	Shares	Employee has right to buy shares at a set price during a particular period.
SARs—cash-settled	Cash	Employee receives positive difference between set reference price of shares and (later) fair value of shares; share price is expected to increase over a period of time; value paid in cash.
SARs—equity-settled	Shares	As above, only value is distributed in shares.
SARs—employee option	Cash or perhaps shares (at the employee's choice)	As above, only value may be taken in cash or shares at the employee's choice.
SARs—employer option	Cash or perhaps shares (at the company's choice)	As above, only it is the company's choice as to whether cash or shares are distributed.
Phantom stock plan—cash	Cash	Employee receives cash award equal to the fair value of a certain number of shares at a certain point in time.
Phantom stock plan—employee option—cash or shares	Employee has choice of cash or shares; often higher value of shares is offered as incentive to take shares	Employee receives cash award equal to the fair value of a certain number of shares at a certain point in time. Payment is in cash or shares.
Restricted share units	Cash	Depending on terms, employee is awarded units and is paid cash after certain performance standards are met or time passes. Amount is based on the value of the *increase in underlying share value* or the *total value* of underlying shares.

Summary of Characteristics of Share-based Arrangements

The vesting period for share-based arrangements is important for accounting purposes. **Vesting** is achieved when the employee is entitled to the compensation, regardless of other conditions. Once vested, rights attached to the arrangement irrevocably pass to the recipient. For example, if an option vests after three years of employment and expires after 7 years, an individual who leaves the company in Year 4 would still be able to exercise the option, while one who left in Year 3 would **forfeit**, or give up, the option.

Accounting Patterns

Accounting for the share-based arrangements with employees can follow several patterns:

1. If the plan is *equity settled,* then the fair value is estimated *once, and once only,* when the share-based payments are granted; this value is accrued over the *vesting period*. Expected forfeiture rates are estimated annually and the amounts are adjusted to actual forfeiture rates each period and at the end of the vesting period (i.e., the plan is **trued up** annually, or brought to the correct final amount). If the plan vests immediately, the fair value is immediately recorded in full. Accrual increases an equity account and results in an expense that decreases earnings. The expense and equity accounts are recorded/adjusted annually for forfeitures only.

2. If the plan is *cash settled*, then the *fair value* is *recalculated annually*. Fair value is based on a valuation model, which would include certain factors, such as share price volatility, plan duration, and so on. The yearly accrual represents the current year amount plus a correction of the prior cumulative estimate, reflecting cumulative accrual over the vesting period. Expected forfeiture rates are estimated annually and the amounts are adjusted to actual forfeiture rates each period and at maturity. That is, a cash-settled plan is *trued up for both fair value and forfeiture* each year until paid. The initial accrual increases a liability account and results in an expense that decreases earnings. Each year, the fair value adjustment may increase or decrease the liability, resulting in an increase or decrease to the expense.

3. If the plan allows employees to choose between cash and shares at maturity, then the plan is a compound instrument. The equity portion is recorded as in (1), above, while the liability portion reflects the treatment in (2).

In summary:

Classification	Amount	Remeasure for	Elements	Comment
Equity-settled plan	Fair value set by option pricing model on date of grant, adjusted for forfeitures	Forfeitures	Expense and equity	Recorded over period to vesting; no adjustment of initial fair value estimate; Remeasured annually for estimated forfeitures
Cash-settled plan	Cash to be paid estimated at fair value each year-end, adjusted for forfeitures	Fair value and forfeitures	Expense and liability	Recorded over period to vesting; Remeasured annually for estimated fair value and forfeitures until paid
Compound instrument	Initial recognition of both liability and equity component	Equity—forfeitures only; Liability—fair value and forfeitures	Expense and equity and liability	Liability element measured as above; Equity element measured as above

Equity-settled Plans

Equity-settled plans all follow the same accounting pattern and will be demonstrated through employee stock option plans.

Employee Stock Options

Suppose that 20 employees are granted options for 250 shares each, a total of 5,000 common shares, at an exercise price of $15 per share that will be equity settled. The options *vest* immediately, meaning that the employees can exercise the options whether employment continues or not. The options expire after eight years; that is, there is an eight-year exercise window starting immediately.

The company must determine the fair value of the option *on the date it is granted*, using an option pricing model. Assume that this total value is $24,000 for all 5,000 options. Recognition of this amount is over the vesting period; it is recognized *all up front* if the options vest immediately or *over a period of years* if vesting spans more than one year. For this example, vesting is immediate, so the cost of the options is recognized as follows:

On the vesting date:		
Compensation expense	24,000	
Contributed capital: common share options outstanding		24,000

Now assume that the options do not vest until three years after they have been granted, and there is no risk of the employees forfeiting the options (i.e., all employees will stay with the company through the vesting period). In this case, one-third of the expense is recorded in each year:

Annual entry:		
Compensation expense ($24,000 ÷ 3)	8,000	
Contributed capital: common share options outstanding		8,000

Note that this amortization period is the *vesting period*, not the window during which the options can be exercised (five years) or the period from grant date to expiry date (eight years).

After this entry is made annually for three years, $24,000 of total compensation expense is recorded and there is a $24,000 balance in the contributed capital account. The $24,000 estimate is not revisited; this fair value is *not subsequently adjusted for changes in option pricing variables*.

When the options are exercised, the contributed capital amount is moved into the common share account along with cash paid:

At exercise:		
Cash (5,000 shares × $15)	75,000	
Contributed capital: common share options outstanding	24,000	
Common shares		99,000

Options may *lapse* because the exercise price is higher than the common share price and the options were not exercised before they expired. If the options lapse, the amount recorded as contributed capital remains, but its classification is changed to indicate that the options have expired:

If the options lapse:		
Contributed capital: common share options outstanding	24,000	
Contributed capital: share options expired		24,000

The ironic part of a "lapsed options" situation is that the company has recorded an expense for an option plan, which has turned out to be of no value to the employee. Expired options would have been *out-of-the-money* on the maturity date. However, the accounting valuation is based on the initial assessment of fair value on the date the options are granted. *The intrinsic value of the option on the exercise date, or the lack thereof, is not recognized in any circumstances.*

Measurement with forfeiture estimated

Forfeiture during the vesting period must be estimated annually, and the amounts *trued up* at the end of the vesting period. For example, assume that the company *initially* estimates that only 16 of the 20 employees covered by the option agreement illustrated above are expected to stay until vesting. Three leave in the first year, one in the second, and two in the third. By the end of the vesting period, six have forfeited and 14 receive options. Estimates of forfeitures are updated at the end of each period, and actual turnover is instructive in this estimate. Data are as follows:

Year	1	2	3
Estimates made by management:*			
Employees expected to remain until vesting	16 (80%)	14 (70%)	13 (65%)
Employees expected to forfeit	4 (20%)	6 (30%)	7 (35%)
Factual history:			
Employees actually forfeiting in the year (6 in total)	3	1	2
Employees actually receiving options (20 − 6)			14 (70%*)

*These estimates are prepared by the company annually.

The expense for each period is as follows:

Time Period	1	2	3
Fair value	$24,000	$24,000	$24,000
× *Cumulative* vested fraction	1/3	2/3	3/3
× Estimate of retention (above)	80%	70%	70%
= Required balance in the equity account at year-end	$ 6,400	$11,200	$16,800
Opening balance	0	6,400	11,200
Expense for the period (Debit expense, credit contributed capital)	$ 6,400	$ 4,800	$ 5,600

*Actual; 14/20

The annual expense is no longer an equal $8,000 amount, even though it is still based on the initial measure of $24,000 of fair value. Each year, the accrual is adjusted to the appropriate level of expected take-up, *on a cumulative basis*. In the first year, the expense of $6,400 is simply the $8,000 one-third fair value allocation multiplied by the expected 80% retention rate.

The Year 1 entry is:

Compensation expense	6,400	
Contributed capital: common share options outstanding		6,400

In the second year, however, the expected retention rate has declined to 70%. There is an annual expense of $8,000 multiplied by the new retention rate of 70% ($5,600) *combined with* an adjustment to the first-year expense to bring it down to the now-expected 70% retention rate (10% of $8,000, a recovery of $800.) The result is an expense of $4,800.

The Year 2 entry is:

Compensation expense	4,800	
Contributed capital: common share options outstanding		4,800

Fortunately, since cumulative adjustments are tedious, all adjustments are included on one line on the table shown above and do not have to be separately calculated. By the end of the third year, the equity account reflects the balance for the employees who actually receive vested options, and the cumulative expense is *trued up* at $16,800, or $24,000 ×14/20 employees.

Entry in Year 3 is:

Compensation expense	5,600	
Contributed capital: common share options outstanding		5,600

When the options are exercised or lapse, entries follow the pattern that has been established in prior examples.

ETHICAL ISSUES

Management must use *best estimates* in estimating compensation cost accruals. There are many estimates required by the option pricing models that are used to establish fair value. In addition, though, retention rates are critical. If retention rates decline, the expense is lower not only because the annual portion of the expense is lower but also because the cumulative correction reduces expense in the current year. The expense could even be a *recovery* if retention estimates are significantly lowered and the company is well into the vesting period. Evidence to support retention must be gathered, but trends may be difficult to predict, making this area high risk for manipulation and misstatement.

Reporting example

An example of accounting policies for share-based payments and stock option activity for PotashCorp follows.

Selected extracts from Disclosure Note 24

Note 24 Share-Based Compensation

The company had share-based compensation plans for certain employees and directors as part of their remuneration package, including 10 stock option plans, the performance unit incentive plan and the deferred share unit plan.

Accounting Policies	Accounting Estimates and Judgments
Grants under the company's share-based compensation plans are accounted for in accordance with the fair value-based method of accounting. For stock option plans that will settle through the issuance of equity, the fair value of stock options is determined on their grant date using a valuation model and recorded as compensation expense over the period that the stock options vest, with a corresponding increase to contributed surplus. Forfeitures are estimated throughout the vesting period based on past experience and future expectations, and adjusted upon actual option vesting. When stock options are exercised, the proceeds, together with the amount recorded in contributed surplus, are recorded in share capital. Share-based plans that are likely to settle in cash or other assets are accounted for as liabilities based on the fair value of the awards each period. The compensation expense is accrued over the vesting period of the award. Fluctuations in the fair value of the award will result in a change to the accrued compensation expense, which is recognized in the period in which the fluctuation occurs.	Determining the fair value of share-based compensation awards at the grant date requires judgment. The company uses the Black-Scholes-Merton option-pricing model to estimate the fair value of options granted under its equity-settled stock option plans as of each grant date. This pricing model requires judgment, which includes the items discussed in the weighted average assumptions table below and an estimate of the number of awards expected to be forfeited. The company used a Monte Carlo simulation model to estimate the fair value of its cash-settled performance unit incentive plan liability at each reporting period within the performance period. This required judgment, including making assumptions about the volatility of the company's stock price and the DAXglobal Agribusiness Index with dividends, as well as the correlation between those two amounts, over the three-year plan cycle. For those awards with performance conditions that determine the number of options or units to which employees will he entitled, measurement of compensation cost is based on the company's best estimate of the outcome of the performance conditions. If actual results differ significantly from these estimates, stock-based compensation expense and results of operations could be impacted. Prior to a Performance Option Plan award vesting, assumptions regarding vesting are made during the first three years based on the relevant actual and/or forecast financial results. Changes to vesting assumptions are reflected in earnings immediately. As at December 31, 2014, the 2012, 2013 and 2014 Performance Option Plans were expected to vest at 100 percent.

The following weighted average assumptions were used in arriving at the grant-date fair values associated with stock options for which compensation cost was recognized during 2014, 2013 and 2012:

		Year of Grant				
Assumption	Based On	2014	2013	2012	2011	2010
Exercise price per option	Quoted market closing price of common shares on the last trading day immediately preceding the date of the grant	$ 36.73	$ 43.80	$ 39.36	$ 52.26	$ 33.82
Expected annual dividend per share	Annualized dividend rate as of the date of grant	$ 1.40	$ 1.40	$ 0.56	$ 0.28	$ 0.13
Expected volatility	Historical volatility of the company's stock over a period commensurate with the expected life of the option	39%	50%	53%	52%	50%
Risk-free interest rate	Implied yield available on zero-coupon government issues with equivalent remaining term at the time of the grant	1.66%	1.06%	1.06%	2.29%	2.61%
Expected life of options in years	Historical experience	5.5	5.5	5.5	5.5	5.9

Supporting Information

As at December 31, 2014, the company had 12 share-based compensation plans (10 stock option plans, the deferred share unit plan and the performance unit incentive plan), which are described below (2013 - 11 plans, 2012 - 11 plans). The total compensation cost charged (recovered) against earnings for those plans was comprised of:

	2014	2013	2012
Stock option plans	$ 28	$ 27	$ 23
Deferred share unit plan	3	(2)	1
Performance unit incentive plan	(1)	(2)	4
	$ 30	$ 23	$ 28

Stock option plans

As at December 31, 2014, the outstanding number of performance options per plan that vest over three years and settle in shares were as follows:

2014	2013	2012	2011	2010	2009	2008	2007	2006	2005
3,144,600	1,899,000	1,444,100	1,073,600	1,069,500	1,488,675	1,128,750	2,983,600	3,433,050	3,244,960

In previous years, the company granted options under an Officers and Employees Plan (the last grant under which expired in 2013) and a Directors Plan (the last grant under which expired in 2012).

Under the terms of the plans, no additional options are issuable pursuant to the plans.

The exercise price is not less than the quoted market closing price of the company's common shares on the last trading day immediately preceding the date of the grant, and an option's maximum term is 10 years. In general, options granted under the Performance Option Plans will vest, if at all, according to a schedule based on the three-year average excess of the company's consolidated cash flow return on investment over the weighted average cost of capital.

The company issues new common shares to satisfy stock option exercises. Options granted to Canadian participants had an exercise price in Canadian dollars.

......

A summary of the status of the stock option plans as at December 31, 2014, 2013 and 2012 and changes during the years ending on those dates is as follows:

	Number of shares subject to option			Weighted average exercise price		
	2014	2013	2012	2014	2013	2012
Outstanding, beginning of year	20,332,335	23,164,444	27,649,074	$ 26.45	$22.32	$ 18.02
Granted	3,157,800	1,952,000	1,499,300	36.73	43.80	39.36
Exercised	(2,285,450)	(4,492,409)	(5,895,730)	(15.91)	(8.71)	(6.76)

Forfeited or cancelled	(294,850)	(291,700)	(88,200)	(50.94)	(45.33)	(50.26)
Expired	—	—	—	—	—	—
Outstanding, end of year	20,909,835	20,332,335	23,164,444	$ 28.01	$26.45	$ 22.32

The aggregate grant-date fair value of all options granted during 2014 was $29 (2013 - $30, 2012 - $24). The average share price during 2014 was $34.81 per share (2013 - $36.69 per share, 2012 - $42.54 per share).

The following table summarizes information about stock options outstanding as at December 31, 2014:

	Options Outstanding			Options Exercisable	
Range of Exercise Prices	Number	Weighted Average Remaining Life in Years	Weighted Average Exercise Price	Number	Weighted Average Exercise Price
$9.00 to $13.00	6,678,010	1	$ 10.53	6,678,010	$ 10.53
$19.00 to $21.00	2,983,600	2	20.61	2,983,600	20.61
$30.00 to $45.00	9,432,375	8	36.74	2,944,675	33.78
$52.00 to $67.00	1,815,850	4	59.14	1,815,850	59.14
	20,909,835	4	$ 28.01	14,422,135	$ 23.48

The foregoing options have expiry dates ranging from May 2015 to December 2024.

......

Other plans

The company offered a performance unit incentive plan ("MTIP") to senior executives and other key employees. The performance objectives under the plan were designed to further align the interests of executives and key employees with those of shareholders by linking the vesting of awards to the total return to shareholders over the three-year performance period ended December 31, 2014. Total shareholder return measures the capital appreciation in the company's common shares, including dividends paid over the performance period. Vesting of one-half of the awards was based on increases in the total shareholder return over the three-year performance period. Vesting of the remaining one-half of the awards was based on the extent to which the total shareholder return matched or exceeded that of the common shares of a pre-defined peer group index. None of the performance share units vested based on PotashCorp's performance during the three-year performance period ended December 31, 2014, and therefore no such units settled in cash at the end of such performance period. Compensation expense for this plan was recorded over the three-year performance cycle of the plan. The amount of compensation expense was adjusted each period over the cycle to reflect the current fair value of common shares and the number of shares estimated to vest.

The company offers a deferred share unit plan to non-employee directors, which allows each to choose to receive, in the form of deferred share units ("DSUs"), all or a percentage of the director's fees, which would otherwise be payable in cash. The plan also provides for discretionary grants of additional DSUs by the Board, a practice it discontinued on January 24, 2007 in connection with an increase in the annual retainer. Each DSU fully vests upon award, but is distributed only when the director has ceased to be a member of the Board. Vested units are settled in cash based on the common share price at that time. As at December 31, 2014, the total number of DSUs held by participating directors was 620,091 (2013 - 562,720, 2012 - 573,472).

Further information and a summary of the status of the MTIP units and outstanding DSUs as at December 31 are presented below:

	MTIP			DSUs		
	2014	2013	2012	2014	2013	2012
Cash used to settle units during the year	$ —	$ —	$ 17	$ —	$ 3	$ 2
Fair value of closing liability	—	1	4	22	19	23
Intrinsic value of closing liability		—	—	22	19	23

Source: PotashCorp, 2014 Annual Financial Statements, www.sedar.com, posted 25 February 2015.

Cash-settled Plans

Cash-settled plans all follow the same accounting pattern, and will be demonstrated through a cash-settled SARs plan.

Cash-settled SARs

Forty employees are awarded a total of 10,000 units of SARs at the beginning of 20X5. Each employee receives 250 units in a program that entitles him or her to a cash payment equal to the appreciation in share price over the life of the SARs contract. The employees will receive cash at the end of the 20X7 year, if still with the employer at that time. The cash to be distributed is calculated as the fair value of company shares in 20X7, less a $10 *reference price*, which the company has chosen because it is the fair value of company shares when the SARs were granted in 20X5. These terms are set by contract and are different for every SARs arrangement. Each of these SARs units has an *intrinsic value* at any point in time, which is the difference between $10 and the current market price of the shares. Each SARs unit also has a fair value, which is the *expected time-adjusted value of the SARs unit at maturity.* Fair value is not just intrinsic value.

Data are as follows:

End of Year	20X5	20X6	20X7
Intrinsic value:			
Market value per share	$ 18	$ 12	$ 19
Reference price per share	10	10	10
Intrinsic value per share	$ 8	$ 2	$ 9
Fair value:			
Estimated fair value per share *(provided by a valuation model)*	$ 8.70	$ 3.00	n/a
Total fair value (for 10,000 units)	$87,000	$30,000	n/a
Cash payout:			
Total intrinsic value ($9 × 10,000 units)			$90,000

No forfeitures are expected. The entries make an annual accrual *with an adjustment for the cumulative balance, referenced to the new fair value.* Unlike the share-settled pattern, these entries are based on a new fair value each period, and are trued up to intrinsic value when the cash payout is made. These calculations can be done with or without the structure of the table that was illustrated for options.

20X5 entry:		
Compensation expense [($87,000) × (1 year ÷ 3 years)]	29,000	
Long-term compensation liability		29,000

20X6 entry:		
Long-term compensation liability		
[($30,000) × (2 years ÷ 3 years) = $20,000 versus $29,000 recorded]	9,000	
Compensation expense (recovery)		9,000

20X7 entry; adjustment and employees paid cash:		
Compensation expense [($90,000 Intrinsic value) × (3 years ÷ 3 years)] = $90,000 versus $20,000 recorded	70,000	
Long-term compensation liability		70,000
Long-term compensation liability	90,000	
Cash		90,000

Compensation expense can be a recovery, as shown in the 20X6 entry. *Cumulative* compensation expense recorded cannot fall below zero. If the *fair value* of the SARs units falls to zero, the balance in the liability account is then zero, and compensation expense recorded to date is reversed.

Measurement with forfeiture estimated

Once expected forfeiture is incorporated, the calculations get one step more complicated, as illustrated below. The approach is the same as for options, but cash-settled plans *refer to a new fair value each period*, and so the approach is conceptually much different. Similar to the approach for options, forfeiture during the vesting period must be estimated annually, and the amounts *trued up* at the end of the vesting period to the real retention level *and the real cash cost*.

The cumulative actual level of forfeiture during the vesting period should be the base level of forfeiture rates but is also predictive evidence. In this example, the company initially estimates that 10 employees will leave and 30 will remain, for 75% retention. Seven actually leave, and 33 are paid under the SARs contract in 20X7, a retention level of 82.5%.

End of Year	20X5	20X6	20X7
Estimates made by management:*			
Employees expected to remain until vesting	30 (75%)	32 (80%)	n/a
Employees expected to forfeit	10 (25%)	8 (20%)	n/a
Factual history:			
Employees actually forfeiting in the year	6	1	0
Employees actually receiving SARs (40 − 7)			33 (82.5%)

*These estimates are prepared by the company annually.

The expense for each period is as follows:

End of Year	20X5	20X6	20X7
Fair value	$87,000	$30,000	$90,000
× *Cumulative* vesting fraction	1/3	2/3	3/3
× Estimate of retention (above)	75%	80%	82.5%*

End of Year	20X5	20X6	20X7
= Required balance in the liability account at year-end	$21,750	$16,000	$74,250
Opening balance	0	21,750	16,000
Expense for the period (recovery) (debit expense, credit liability, or the opposite for the recovery year)	$21,750	($ 5,750)	$58,250

*Actual; 33/40

Similar to the approach used for options, the annual expense is the combination of the new layer of expense and a correction of old estimates. This time, both the fair value and the retention rate are corrected, which makes compensation cost even more volatile. Annual entries are:

20X5 entry:		
Compensation expense	21,750	
Long-term compensation liability		21,750

20X6 entry:		
Long-term compensation liability	5,750	
Compensation expense (recovery)		5,750

At the end of 20X7, the liability is trued up, and money is paid to the 33 employees who are still with the company:

20X7 entry; adjustment and employees paid cash:		
Compensation expense	58,250	
Long-term compensation liability		58,250
Long-term compensation liability	74,250	
Cash (33 employees × 250 units × $9 intrinsic value)		74,250

Compound Plans

If a plan allows employees the choice of taking cash or shares at the exercise date, then the plan is a compound financial instrument and represents both a financial liability *and* an option on shares. The liability is valued on initial recognition, and a residual value is assigned to equity rights. Established patterns are then used to account for each element. Compound plans will be demonstrated through phantom stock plans.

Phantom Stock Plan with Employee Payment Option

Assume that an employee is awarded units in a phantom stock plan, where, after two years of employment, the employee is entitled to receive *either* 22,000 common shares *or* the right to a cash payment equal to the then-market value of 18,000 shares. The choice is up to the employee. This employee is expected to remain with the company for this period, so retention is not an issue. The shares are worth $8 each when the plan is established, at the beginning of Year 1, and share price increases to $9 and then $12 at the end of Years 1 and 2.

The equity portion is valued when the plan is established. At the beginning of Year 1, *valuation models* indicate that the fair value of the share alternative is $7 per share, or $154,000 ($7 × 22,000) in total. Initially, the cash alternative appears to be worth $144,000 ($8 × 18,000). Therefore, the option is valued at the residual, or $10,000 ($154,000 − $144,000.)

That is:

Equity alternative fair value, plan initiation, from valuation model	$154,000
Cash alternative fair value, plan initiation	144,000
Equity portion	$ 10,000

The equity portion is accrued over the two-year vesting period, or $5,000 per year. *The fair value of the option is recognized over the vesting period but is not subject to new estimates of fair value.*

The liability is revalued each period and is also recorded over the two-year vesting period. A valuation model is consulted, similar to a cash-based SARs plan. In this example, the intrinsic value of the shares is used as the best estimate of the fair value of the liability. Note that the first time recognition is required is at *the end of the first year*, at which time the entry is based on a calculation that relies on the end-of-year $9 share value, or a total of $162,000 ($9 × 18,000). *The initial value of $144,000 is not used for this period but was used to establish the $10,000 equity portion.*

If there were forfeitures expected, these would be *re-estimated each year for both elements.*

Year 1 entry:		
Compensation expense	86,000	
Contributed capital: common share options outstanding [($10,000) × (1 year ÷ 2 years)]		5,000
Long-term compensation liability [($162,000) × (1 year ÷ 2 years)]		81,000

The liability is then *trued up* to the cumulative value with a calculation at the end of Year 2, $216,000 ($12 ×18,000). If there were forfeitures expected, these would be re-established each year for both elements.

Year 2 entry:		
Compensation expense	140,000	
Contributed capital: common share options outstanding [($10,000) × (1 year ÷ 2 years)]		5,000
Long-term compensation liability [($216,000) × (2 year ÷ 2 years), less $81,000]		135,000

This second entry updates the accounts at the end of Year 2. The employee may then elect to receive shares:

Year 2 entry; employee receives shares:		
Contributed capital: common share options outstanding	10,000	
Long-term compensation liability	216,000	
Common shares		226,000

Alternatively, the employee may take cash:

Year 2 entry; employee receives cash, and the option expires:		
Contributed capital: common share options outstanding	10,000	
Contributed capital: share options expired		10,000
Long-term compensation liability	216,000	
Cash		216,000

These entries reflect the pattern for equity-settled plans in that the value of the option is recorded over time and then is either folded into common shares (issuance) or contributed capital (lapse). It also reflects the pattern for liability-settled plans in that the liability fair value is remeasured annually and trued up to annual estimates of fair value.

Additional Complications

Compensation plans are complex, and the accounting standards that govern their measurement, recognition, and disclosure are equally complex. There are rules that deal with performance conditions, market conditions, award restrictions, and changes after vesting, as well as rules that address indexed plans, combination plans, plan modifications, and so on. This section has looked at the overall patterns rather than the detailed rules for the many possible situations.

CONCEPT REVIEW

1. What do employees receive under a SARs compensation plan?
2. When there is a long-term compensation plan, under what circumstances is a liability recorded? A contributed capital account?
3. If a plan is equity settled, what will change if the fair value of the compensation contract increases? How would your response change if the plan were cash settled?

DERIVATIVES

General Nature of Derivatives

Corporations issue (or may buy) certain types of securities that are neither debt nor equity in themselves but that set terms and conditions for future exchanges. There are many types of such derivative instruments, which have value because of shifts in value of the underlying security or index. Stock options are one example. By themselves, stock options represent neither an obligation of the corporation nor a share interest in the corporation; their *value is derived* from the value of the underlying security (shares) that can be acquired by exercising the option.

Accounting standards define a *derivative* as a financial instrument that has three characteristics:

1. The value of the derivative changes in response to the change in the underlying primary instrument or index;
2. It requires no initial net investment, or a very small investment; and
3. It is settled at a future date.

There are three main types of derivatives:

1. Options;
2. Forward contracts; and
3. Futures contracts.

Options

An option is the right (but not an obligation) to buy or sell something in the future during a specified period. A **call option** is the right to buy something at a given price in the future, and a **put option** is the right to sell something at a given price in the future. Options may be for commodities or financial instruments. For example, a company may purchase a call option to buy 20,000 tonnes of coal at a given price at a given time. Alternatively, the company may be party to a put option to sell 1,000 shares of another company, now held as an investment, at a given price at a given time, if the company wishes.

Forward Contracts

A **forward contract** is an obligation to buy or sell something in the future at a specified price for a specified period. Both the price and the time period are specified, and there is no way to avoid the transaction. For example, if a company agrees to sell 12,000 share (now held as an investment) at $60 per share in 60 days, with no ability to avoid the transaction, this is a forward contract. If the transaction would take place only if the company wanted, then it would be an option.

Futures Contracts

A **futures contract** is also an obligation to buy or sell something in the future. Both the price and the time period are specified, and there is no way to avoid the transaction. Futures contracts differ from forward contracts, though, in that they are traded on stock exchanges, brokers act as collection and delivery agents, and the company usually has to put some money up front, which is collateral, in the form of a **margin**. For example, a company enters into a futures contract through a financial institution agreeing to buy US$1,000 for Cdn$1,200 in 60 days and is required to make an initial payment of $120, for the margin.

Embedded Derivatives

Some financial instruments are compound financial instruments and include both a **host contract** (which is not a derivative) and an **embedded derivative** contract. These are called **hybrid contracts**. The embedded derivative is not related to the economic risks and characteristics of the host contract and changes the cash flows of the contract over the life of the contract in some fashion, consistent with the presence of the derivative. If the derivative could be detached and transferred separately, it would be a *stand-alone derivative* and accounted for as such. *Embedded derivatives* cannot be detached from the host contract.

If the hybrid contract consists of a host contract that is a financial instrument, then the embedded derivative is not separately recognized. In this case, the entire contract is classified and recognized as a single financial instrument. If the host contract is not a financial asset or liability, the embedded derivative is separately recognized, valued at fair value and remeasured to fair value at each reporting date.

For example, assume that Brava Ltd. enters into a loan agreement, where the interest rate is changed each year, based on the price of silver. The host contract is the loan, and the embedded derivative is the adjustment of interest based on the silver commodity price. The entire contract is treated as a financial liability and classified as detailed in this chapter.

Accounting Recognition

Accounting standards require that companies:

- Recognize derivatives on the statement of financial position when the company becomes a party to the contract;
- Recognize the derivative instrument at fair value on initial recognition;
- At each reporting date, *remeasure* derivative assets or liabilities at their fair values; and
- Recognize gains and losses from the changed fair value, and gains and losses at settlement, in profit and loss in the period in which they arise, unless the derivative is designated as a hedge.

Although a derivative should be recorded when it is acquired (i.e., the company becomes a party to the contract), it often has no cost and a zero fair value at that time. Therefore, no entry is made. Adjustments to fair value are made on reporting dates and when the contract matures. The *fair value* of the derivative changes as underlying values change and is based on a valuation model that incorporates certain factors, such as duration, volatility, and risk. This change in fair value is recognized in net profit or loss.

Example

Assume that Bent Ltd. agrees to a forward contract to buy 4,000 shares of Resto Ltd. for $30 per share in 60 days. The current fair value of the shares is $30, so the initial fair value of this derivative is zero. This contract is not a hedge; accounting for hedges is explained below. There is no broker, and no margin payment is needed. The contract is recorded as a memorandum entry:

Memorandum entry: agreed to buy 4,000 Resto shares for $30 per share in 60 days.		

The shares of Resto are trading at $34 after 30 days, and the company has a gain because it can buy shares that are worth $136,000 for $120,000. The gain on the contract is recorded to reflect fair value.

Derivative instrument [($34 − $30) × 4,000]	16,000	
Gain on derivative instrument		16,000

When the shares are purchased, they have a fair value of $31 per share. A loss of $3 ($34 − $31) per share on the derivative contract is recorded, and then the contract is closed out:

Loss on derivative instrument	12,000	
Derivative instrument [($31 − $34) × 4,000]		12,000
Investment—Resto Ltd. shares ($31 × 4,000 shares)	124,000	
Cash ($30 × 4,000 shares)		120,000
Derivative instrument ($16,000 − $12,000)		4,000

Hedges

If an investor speculates in derivatives, the risk is *high* because derivatives essentially bet on future price changes. However, the usual purpose of derivatives in the corporate environment is to *reduce risk*. Derivatives often are used as **hedges**—as a way to offset a risk to which the company would otherwise be exposed. Hedged risks can include:

- Changes in foreign exchange rates because the company buys or sells in foreign currencies;
- Interest rates because the company has interest-bearing loans or interest-earning investments;
- Securities as the company has investments in other companies; and
- Commodities (e.g., fuel, grain, nickel, silver, gold) as the company either sells or uses these commodities.

For an item to be a hedge, the company must first *have risk* in an area and then put a hedge in place to *counter the risk*. That is, a loss on a primary instrument will offset a gain on a hedge instrument, and vice versa. The related gains and losses must be recognized in earnings concurrently.

Hedge accounting is complex and is a subject dealt with in advanced accounting courses. This discussion will focus on a brief look at the outcome in financial statements.

Hedge Example

Suppose that Clix Inc. sells goods to a U.S. customer. The selling price is stated in U.S. dollars. Assume that the amount of the sale is US$100,000 and that the U.S. dollar is worth Cdn$1.10 at the date of sale. Clix now has an account receivable (a primary financial asset) for US$100,000. On Clix's books, the receivable will be translated into Canadian dollars at the current exchange rate and reported at Cdn$110,000. Now, suppose that while Clix is waiting for the customer to pay, the exchange rate changes to US$1.00 = Cdn$1.02. The value of the receivable drops to Cdn$102,000; Clix has suffered a loss of $8,000 due to the exchange rate change.

Clix can protect itself from unpredictable exchange gains and losses by creating an offsetting financial liability for US$100,000. Any loss on the receivable will be exactly offset by a gain on the liability. It is possible that in the normal course of business, the company will incur U.S. dollar–denominated liabilities. For example, assume that Clix buys inventory from a U.S. supplier and agrees to pay in U.S. dollars. Even if the offset is not exactly $100,000, gains and losses will tend to cancel out.

That is:

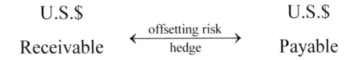

More commonly, however, a company will go to a financial institution and arrange a *forward contract*. As the result of such a contract, when the company receives US$100,000 from the customer, it will immediately turn the U.S. currency over to the bank. The bank agrees up front to the value (the price the bank will pay) for the U.S. dollars. For example, assume the *forward price* is $1.04 at the time Clix sold the goods to the US customer and Clix decides to enter into a forward contract with the bank. Clix is willing to "firm up" its future cash flow at $104,000. At maturity of the forward contract, Clix receives $104,000 from the bank and turns over US$100,000 collected from the customer.

A forward contract is a common type of hedge. The bank will charge a small fee for this service, but the contract is akin to an insurance policy—the expense of the contract will eliminate the risk of a large loss. The contract also eliminates the possibility of a gain. However, *most companies prefer to deal with known cash flows*. Hedging is widely practised by companies that have exchange risk as a result of a transaction or proposed transaction.

Criteria for Hedge Accounting

Hedge accounting is a set of accounting policies that dictate measurement and recognition of the hedge and its related transaction. *Hedge accounting* is voluntary and happens only after an element is designated as a hedge. The substance of a hedge is that the company is protected from gains or losses on the risk being hedged. Since there are so many ways to hedge, the designation of an accounting hedge is largely left to management. Under hedge accounting, hedges may be identified as *cash flow hedges* or *fair value hedges,* and accounting treatment is dictated by the classification. A financial statement element, such as a derivative, will qualify for hedge accounting when:

1. Both the hedged item and hedging instrument are eligible and qualify for hedge accounting (based on meeting certain);
2. Formal designation and documentation exist of the specific hedging relationship and the entity's reason for entering into the hedge; and
3. It is expected that the hedge will be highly effective, and the hedge is assessed each period.

Accounting Implications of Hedge Accounting

Once the element (for example, a derivative) has been designated as a hedge, accounting standards require that the gain or loss on a hedge be recorded in earnings *at the same time* that the gain or loss on the item being hedged is recognized. This simultaneous recognition of gains and losses allows for *offset*, and therefore the substance of the hedge is reflected in the financial statements.

Accounting mismatch

Sometimes it will happen that the primary financial statement element (the result of a transaction that creates exchange risk) is hedged by an item that does not generate accounting gains or losses. The *offset accounting treatment* must then be *created*. For example, assume that Clix forecasts that it will require US$300,000 in eight months' time for inventory purchases to be made. These are highly probable cash flows and so the company has entered into a forward contract to buy US$300,000. Clix designates the forward contract as a hedge of the future cash flows, since Clix plans to use the US$300,000 receipt on the forward contract to pay for the future purchases, and the timing of collection and payment coincide.

In this situation, the forward contract is recognized at fair value with the gain or losses having to be recognized. However, since the future cash flows have not yet occurred, there is no offsetting gain or loss on the hedged item to be recognized. This results in an accounting mismatch. If there is an $8,000 loss on the forward contract because of exchange rate change, there will be *no offsetting gain on the forecasted purchases because the payable is not recorded until the inventory is delivered.* The hedge is effective, but the accounting records do not reflect it. This is called an *accounting mismatch*. To fix this mismatch, the company can designate this as a cash flow hedge; therefore, the $8,000 loss on the forward contract is not recorded in earnings. Instead, it is recorded in *other comprehensive income (OCI)* and flows to an equity account, an accumulated OCI *reserve for hedging*. This remains as an element in shareholders' equity until the future transaction takes place at which time it is recycled to earnings.

In other circumstances, the hedged item may be on the books but valued at amortized cost and thus no gains and losses would be recorded to offset those of the primary financial instrument. To avoid this mismatch situation, the company may reclassify the hedged item as an element that will be carried at fair value, so that it will be measured at fair value, and generate recognized gains and losses for the purpose of offset.

However accomplished, the objective of hedge accounting is to *arrange valuation and recording so that the gains on one side will offset losses on the other side of the hedge relationship*, reflecting the economic reality of the hedge relationship.

CONCEPT REVIEW

1. Explain the difference between a derivative financial instrument and a primary financial instrument.
2. What is an embedded derivative?
3. How should an existing derivative financial liability be measured at each reporting date?

STATEMENT OF CASH FLOWS AND DISCLOSURE

Statement of Cash Flows (SCF)

The cash flows relating to complex financial instruments must be reported in the statement of cash flows (SCF) in a manner that is consistent with their substance. The net proceeds from the issuance of any financial instrument will be reported as a financing activity, with the nature of the instrument disclosed in the notes to the financial statements. If an instrument is a compound instrument that consists of both equity and liability components, then the individual components are reported *together* on the SCF—one line, not two, because one financial instrument was issued. Since conversions do not involve cash flow, they are not reported on the SCF. Non-cash transactions must be separately explained in the disclosure notes. Cash flows for interest and dividends may be presented in operating or financing sections, as determined by company policy.

As an example, consider the following liability and equity accounts of YTR Ltd.:

	20X5	20X4
	$	$
Term preferred shares (liability)	—	3,000,000
Convertible bonds payable (net of discount)	7,755,000	—
Contributed capital: common share conversion rights	457,000	—
Contributed capital: stock options outstanding	—	55,000
Common shares	13,800,000	13,645,000

Convertible bonds were issued in 20X5. Discount amortization in 20X5 was $15,000. The term preferred shares were redeemed during the year, at par. Stock options had been issued to a law firm for legal services performed in 20X4 and were exercised in 20X5. There were no other common share transactions. Interest expense is $525,000, and the company classifies interest paid as a separate line item in the operating activities section of the SCF.

As a result of these transactions, the SCF would report:

1. In financing, as a source of funds, proceeds on issuance of convertible bonds, $8,197,000. The bonds were originally allocated $7,740,000 of the original proceeds (i.e., $7,755,000 − $15,000; the amount of this year's amortization of this discount). In addition, proceeds of $457,000 were allocated to the contributed capital equity account, $7,740,000 + $457,000 = $8,197,000.

2. In financing, as a use of funds, redemption of preferred shares, $3,000,000.

3. In financing, as a source of funds, issuance of common shares, $100,000. The common shares account has actually increased by $155,000 (or $13,800,000 − $13,645,000). However, this represents not only the cash received on the sale of shares but also the stock options account, $55,000 that was transferred to common shares. Only the cash portion is shown on the SCF.

4. In operating activities, interest expense of $525,000 would be added back in operating activities and replaced with an outflow of $510,000 ($525,000 − $15,000) for interest paid.

The key to preparing an SCF is to reconstruct the changes to the various accounts, looking for cash flow. This cash flow is reportable. In operating activities, one must examine sources of revenue and expense that *do not reflect the underlying cash flow*. Discount and premium amortization and gains and losses from retirements must be adjusted.

Disclosure

The financial instruments described in this chapter are subject to common disclosure requirements. Financial instrument disclosure is extensive but should be limited to material areas to avoid overwhelming financial statement users. The objectives of disclosure are to ensure that information is available to *assess the significance of financial instruments for the company's financial position and performance,* the nature and extent of risks associated with financial instruments, and how those risks are managed. Some of the disclosures include:

1. The important components of each financial statement category (e.g., various loans);

2. Information related to fair value for liabilities. Methods used to assess fair value must be explained. When a financial instrument has been valued at fair value, detail about the change in fair value is required;

3. Information related to the legal terms of the financial instrument, including maturity dates, interest rates, collateral, and so on;

4. Various revenue and expense amounts and OCI reserve amounts that must be disclosed separately, including interest expense, changes in equity reserve accounts, and so on;

5. Information on exposure to various sources of risk, as appropriate. Risks might include credit risk, liquidity risk, and market risk. Objectives, policies, and processes for managing risk must be disclosed. Such disclosure is extensive, and includes both qualitative and quantitative elements; and

6. Accounting policy information required as a matter of course for all financial statement elements.

Critical to these general disclosure categories is the requirement that *financial instruments be completely described*. This would include the carrying amount, principal amount, amounts issued or retired, options issued and retired, maturity dates, share prices, early settlement options, futures contracts, forward contracts, scheduled future cash commitments, stated interest rate, effective interest rate, repricing dates, collateral, currency, payment dates, interest rates, security, conditions, changes in valuation allowances, and any breach of conditions or covenants.

To say that these disclosures are extensive is an understatement. The more complex the situation, the more extensive is the disclosure. The emphasis is on terms and conditions and also on analyzing the risk associated with recognized and unrecognized financial instruments.

Reporting Example

A portion of the financial risk management note for Andrew Peller Ltd. is shown in Exhibit 15-2. Note that the company identifies and evaluates various sources of financial risk, and its policy/process to manage these risks. This information deals with interest rate risk, credit risk, and liquidity risk. Note that interest rate derivatives may be used to hedge interest rate risk. Forward foreign exchange contracts are used to hedge foreign currency risk although the company has elected not to use hedge accounting for these derivatives. Liquidity risk is defined, risk management processes are described, and obligations are specifically classified as to timing.

EXHIBIT 15-2

ANDREW PELLER LIMITED

Financial Risk Management Disclosures

Selected extracts from Disclosure

Note 20. FINANCIAL INSTRUMENTS

Interest rate risk

The Company is exposed to interest rate risk as a result of cash balances, floating rate debt, and an interest rate swap. Of these risks, the Company's principal exposure is that increases in the floating interest rates on its debt, if unmitigated, could lead to decreases in cash flow and earnings, The Company's objective in managing interest rate risk is to achieve a balance between minimizing borrowing costs over the long term. ensuring that it meets borrowing covenants, and ensuring that it meets other expectations and requirements of investors. To meet these objectives, the Company's policy is to effectively fix the rates on long-term debt to match the duration of investments in long-lived assets and to use floating rate funding for short-term borrowing.

The Company has effectively fixed its interest rate on its long-term debt until April 2019 by entering into interest rate swaps. The interest rate swaps are measured at fair value. An unrealized loss of $1,169 (2014 - $1,052 gain) was recognized on the interest rate swaps, which is classified as net unrealized loss (gain) on derivative financial instruments in the consolidated statements of earnings.

The Company's short-term borrowings are funded using a floating interest rate and as such are sensitive to interest rate movements. As at March 31, 2015, with other variables unchanged, a 1% change in interest rates would impact the Company's net earnings by approximately $237 (2014 - $460), exclusive of the mark-to-market adjustments on the interest rate swaps.

Credit risk

Credit risk arises from cash and cash equivalents, derivative financial instruments and accounts receivable. The Company places its cash and cash equivalents with major Canadian financial institutions. Counterparties to derivative contracts are also major financial institutions.

Credit risk for trade receivables is monitored through established credit monitoring activities. Over 50% of the Company's accounts receivable balance relates to amounts owing from Canadian provincial liquor boards. Excluding accounts receivable from Canadian provincial liquor boards, the Company does not have a significant concentration of credit risk with any single counterparty or group of counterparties. Amounts owing from Canadian provincial liquor boards represent $13,504 (2014 - $12,515) of the total accounts receivable for which no allowance has been provided. Of the remaining non-provincial liquor board balances, $755 (2014 - $688) was over thirty days past due as at March 31, 2015. An allowance for doubtful accounts of $99 (2014 - $102) has been provided against these accounts receivable amounts, which the Company has determined to represent a reasonable estimate of amounts that may be uncollectible.

Sales to its largest customer, a provincial Crown corporation, were $49,068 (2014 - $46,410) during the year ended March 31, 2015. Sales to its second largest customer, a branch of a provincial government were $34,387 (2014 - $33,204) during the year.

An analysis of accounts receivable is as follows:

	2015	2014
Liquor boards	$ 13,504	$ 12,515
Non-liquor boards		
Current	9,380	8,355
Past due 0 - 30 days, due on delivery accounts	620	402
Past due 0 - 30 days	1,456	835
Past due 31 - 60 days	249	278
Past due > 60 days	506	410
Allowance for doubtful accounts	(99)	(102)
	$ 25,616	$22,693

The change in the allowance for doubtful accounts was as follows:

	2015	2014
Balance - Beginning of year	$ 102	$ 142
Provision for current year	54	68
Bad debts	(57)	(108)
Balance - End of year	$ 99	$ 102

Liquidity risk

The Company incurs obligations to deliver cash or other financial assets on future dates. Liquidity risk inherently arises from these obligations, which include requirements to repay debt, purchase grape inventory and make operating lease payments.

The Company manages liquidity risk by maintaining adequate cash and cash equivalent balances and by appropriately utilizing its operating line of credit. Company management continuously monitors and reviews both actual and forecasted cash flows and matches the maturity profile of financial assets and financial liabilities. Accounts payable are generally due within 30 days.

The following table outlines the Company's contractual undiscounted obligations. The Company analyzes contractual obligations for financial liabilities in conjunction with other commitments in managing liquidity risk. Contractual obligations include long-term debt, the expected payments under a swap agreement that fixes the Company's interest rate on long-term debt, operating leases and commitments on short-term forward foreign exchange contracts used to mitigate the currency risk on US dollar purchases as at March 31, 2015:

	<1 year	2 - 3 years	4 - 5 years	>5 years
Long-term debt	$ 56,952	$ 4,194	$ 8,212	$ 44,546	$ —
Leases and royalties	23,707	4,862	6,640	3,602	8,603
Pension obligations	5,306	987	1,413	858	2,048
Grape and bulk wine purchase contracts	317,176	74,636	89,782	53,656	99,102
	403,141	84,679	106,047	102,662	109,753
Interest rate swap	7,478	2,255	3,541	1,682	—
Foreign exchange forwards	35,937	35,937	—	—	—
Total contractual obligations	$446,556	$122,871	$109,588	$104,344	$109,793

The Company's obligations under its interest rate swap and foreign exchange forward contracts are stated above on a gross basis rather than net of the corresponding contractual benefits.

Foreign exchange risk

Certain of the Company's purchases are denominated in US dollars, euro or Australian dollars. Any increases or decreases to the foreign exchange rates could increase or decrease the Company's earnings. To mitigate the exposure to foreign exchange risk, the Company has entered into forward foreign currency contracts.

The Company's foreign exchange risk arises on the purchase of bulk wine and concentrate, which are made in US dollars and euro. The Company's strategy is to hedge approximately 50% to 80% of its annual foreign exchange requirements prior to or during the beginning of each fiscal quarter. As at March 31, 2015, the Company has forward foreign currency contracts to buy US$22,100 at rates ranging between $1.13 and $1.25, EUR3.500 at rates ranging between $1.38 and $1.44 and AU$4,000 at rates ranging between $0.94 and $0.97. These contracts mature at various dates to December 2015. After considering the offsetting impact of these forward contracts, a 1% increase or decrease to the exchange rate of the US dollar, the euro or the Australian dollar would impact the Company's net earnings by approximately $108 (2014 - $41), $16 (2014 - $133) or $69 (2014 - $64), respectively. The Company has elected to not use hedge accounting and as a result, has recognized $597 (2014 - $302 losses) of unrealized foreign exchange gains in the consolidated statements of earnings as a component of net unrealized gains on derivative financial instruments and has recorded the fair value of $697 in prepaid expenses and other assets in the consolidated balance sheets (2014 - $100).

Source: Andrew Peller Limited, 2015 Annual Financial Statements, www.sedar.com, posted 25 June 2015.

Looking Forward

Financial instrument standards, including hedging and derivatives, have recently been updated with the issue of IFRS 9. Although IFRS 9 must be adopted by entities with an annual period beginning on or after 1 January 2018, earlier adoption is permitted and this chapter reflects the new standards.

Accounting Standards for Private Enterprises

One might expect that a private company would have significantly different (simpler) capital structure and that complex financial instruments, including options and hedges, would be rare. However, uniquely tailored debt and equity instruments flourish in private companies, and foreign exchange contracts are common risk management tools. The accounting standards governing these elements are reasonably similar under IFRS and ASPE, but there are several important differences:

1. Private companies sometimes issue preferred shares, redeemable in cash at the shareholder's option as part of tax-planning structures (so-called *high-low shares*). However, the clear intent is to retain an equity investment and not to redeem for cash. Under ASPE, these shares are classified as equity, and recorded at par, stated, or assigned value. Conversely, *shareholder loans*, which many shareholders and lenders alike consider to be part of equity in a private company, are classified in the liability section regardless of intent.

2. Convertible debt must still be treated as a compound financial instrument, but the standard allows the company to record the equity element (the conversion option), at zero, which effectively makes the convertible debt entirely a liability.

Example

Return to the Tollen Corp. example, earlier in the chapter, where Tollen issues a $100,000 8% convertible bonds for $106,000. The market interest rate on the day of issuance is higher than 8%, but cannot be determined with certainty for this ASPE company. Each $10,000 bond is convertible into 100 common shares on any interest date after the end of the second year from the date of issuance. Conversion is at the option of the investor. Under IFRS, a value was assigned to the conversion rights, and there was a bond discount. Under ASPE, the company can elect to classify the bond entirely as debt, and there is a $6,000 premium:

Cash	106,000	
Bonds payable		100,000
Premium on bonds payable		6,000

Subsequent measurement of interest expense will include amortization of the premium, using either effective interest or straight-line approach, reducing the reported interest rate below 8% and not reflecting the expected higher market interest rate. This reporting is considered appropriate for ASPE companies due to the difficulty in measuring the appropriate yield rate and, thus, the value of the equity interest granted.

3. The stock-based compensation structure is largely the same, in that expense and equity elements are recognized for an equity-settled plan over the vesting period. Volatility measures used as an input for option pricing models are a challenge, since they are typically not observable for a private company. To alleviate this problem, ASPE allows a company to measure stock price volatility using a *calculated value* method. Following the calculated value method, the company would measure volatility using an industry-specific index or, if the industry were unique, a general stock price volatility index.

In addition, ASPE models allow a company to *account for forfeiture when it occurs; no estimates are made of forfeiture when making accruals*. The company can estimate forfeiture as per the IFRS standard, but it is not required.

Example

Return again to the example from earlier in the chapter where 20 employees are granted options for 250 shares each, a total of 5,000 common shares, at an exercise price of $15 per share. The options vest after three years and are estimated to have a fair value of $24,000. The company does not estimate forfeiture. Assume now that there is no forfeiture in the first year, four employees forfeit in Year 2, and one forfeits in Year 3:

First-year entry:		
Compensation expense ($24,000/3)	8,000	
Contributed capital: common share options outstanding		8,000
Second-year entries:		
Contributed capital: common share options outstanding	1,600	
Compensation expense (recovery) ($8,000 recorded to date × 4/20)		1,600
Compensation expense ($8,000 annual × 16/20 remaining)	6,400	
Contributed capital: common share options outstanding		6,400

Third-year entries:

Contributed capital: common share options outstanding	800	
Compensation expense (recovery) ($12,800 to date × 1/16)		800
Compensation expense ($8,000 annual × 15/20 remaining)	6,000	
Contributed capital: common share options outstanding		6,000

Using this approach, the cumulative balance recorded to date for the forfeit options is reversed when the forfeiture happens. (This is the $1,600 in the second year and the $800 in the third year, above.) In Years 2 and 3, two entries are used to highlight the reversal for the employees who forfeit in the year. The two entries may be combined in one entry; the end result is identical.

4. Standards established for share-based payments have a narrower scope, which may affect reporting of any such distributions to suppliers or others. In addition, measurement is often based on the fair value of the consideration given up or the fair value of what is received, *whichever is the more reliable measure*. IFRS measurements rest on the fair value of goods and services received, except in rare circumstances.

5. Hedge accounting follows a different approach, as does accounting for embedded derivatives. For example, since *other comprehensive income* does not exist under ASPE, standards cannot allow for recognition of cash flow hedge amounts in OCI with the cumulative amount set in an equity reserve. Hedge accounting is available, bypassing net income, only when the critical terms of the hedge match the hedged instrument.

6. Disclosures in all areas are less onerous under ASPE.

RELEVANT STANDARDS

CPA Canada Handbook, Part I (IFRS):

- IAS 32, Financial Instruments: Presentation
- IFRS 2, Share-Based Payment
- IFRS 7, Financial Instruments: Disclosures
- IFRS 9, Financial Instruments
- IFRS 13, Fair Value Measurement

CPA Canada Handbook, Part II (ASPE):

- Section 3856, Financial Instruments
- Section 3870, Stock-Based Compensation and Other Stock-Based Payments

SUMMARY OF KEY POINTS

1. Financial instruments must be classified as debt or equity in accordance with their substance, not necessarily their legal form. If there are two component parts to a financial instrument, the two components are separately recognized on issuance.

2. Annual payments associated with a financial instrument that is classified as debt are classified as an expense; annual payments associated with a financial instrument classified as an equity instrument are not an expense and are classified on the statement of changes in equity.

3. Classification factors for a liability include whether the company can be forced to pay cash for principal and/or interest, whether payments can be deferred indefinitely, whether payment is required only if a highly unlikely event outside management control occurs, and whether payments that can be made in shares have a fixed or variable value.

4. Bonds that are convertible into a fixed number of common shares at the *investor's* option embody two financial instruments: a liability and an option contract on common shares, each of which are recognized separately on issuance.

5. Bonds that are mandatorily redeemable into a fixed number of shares will be classified as a compound instrument: a liability as to their annual cash interest component, and the residual, which is assigned to equity.

6. Stock options of various kinds are recognized on issuance and recorded as an element of shareholders' equity. On issuance of the underlying shares, the options account is folded into the share account. If the options lapse, the options account becomes contributed capital.

7. Share-based payments to suppliers are recognized when goods and services are received and measured at the fair value of those goods or services.

8. Share-based payments to employees that are equity-settled result in recognition of an expense and an equity element. The options are valued using an option pricing model. Compensation is recognized over the vesting period, with forfeiture estimated; forfeitures are *trued up* annually but fair value is not re-estimated.

9. Share-based payments to employees that are cash-settled result in recognition of an expense and a liability, accrued over the vesting period. Fair value and forfeiture are estimated over this period, and both estimates are *trued up* annually.

10. Share-based payments to employees where the employee has the choice between cash and equity settlement are compound instruments, with both an equity and liability element recognized.

11. Derivatives are contracts that specify a future exchange at specified prices within a specified period. Derivatives include options, forward contracts, and futures contracts. They can be used to hedge various types of risk, including exchange risk.

12. Derivative contracts are recorded at fair value. Gains and losses from changes in fair value are reported in net profit or loss.

13. If a financial instrument is designated as a hedge, then gains or losses on the instrument will be recognized in earnings at the same time as gains or losses on the risk being hedged, so they offset each other. Under certain conditions, gains and losses on hedging items are recorded in other comprehensive income and accumulated in equity reserve accounts.

14. The cash inflows relating to issuance of financial instruments are classified on the SCF as financing transactions. Cash outflows are classified in a manner that is consistent with the substance of the payments, both for payments *on* capital (i.e., interest and dividends) and repayments *of* capital (i.e., principal and share buybacks).

15. A company must disclose extensive information with respect to accounting policies used for financial instruments, fair values, significance of financial instruments, and nature and extent of risks. Financial instruments must be fully described in the disclosure notes.

16. ASPE is different from IFRS in the way certain redeemable preferred shares are classified, in valuation of the equity component of a convertible bond, in the measurement of the fair value of stock options, and in the approach to forfeiture related to stock options. ASPE also has a narrower scope for share-based payments, a narrower scope for hedge accounting, and less required disclosure.

Key Terms

book value method

call option

cash-settled plan

compound financial instrument

convertible debt

derivative instruments

embedded derivative

equity-settled plans

exercise date

ex-rights date

fair value

fair-value hierarchy

forfeit

forward contract

futures contract

hedges

host contract

hybrid contracts

hybrid financial instrument

intrinsic value

in-the-money

income bond

incremental method of valuation

margin

out-of-the-money

perpetual debt

phantom stock plan

poison pill

proportional method

put option

redeemable shares

restricted share units

retractable shares

share-based payment

stock appreciation rights

stock options

stock option plan

stock warrants

term preferred shares

trued up

under water

vesting

warrants

Review Problem 15-1

On 1 January 20X1, Amershi Ltd. issues $1,000,000 face amount of 8%, five-year, convertible debentures. Interest is payable semi-annually on 30 June and 31 December. The debentures are convertible at the investor's option at the rate of 20 common shares for each $1,000 bond at any time after 31 December 20X3. The market rate of interest for nonconvertible bonds of similar risk and maturity is 10%. The net proceeds received by Amershi amounted to $1,250,000.

Required:

1. Record the issuance of the bonds on 1 January 20X1.

2. Prepare the journal entries for interest expense on 30 June 20X1 and 31 December 20X1. Amershi uses effective interest amortization for bond premium and discount.

3. Indicate how all amounts relating to the bonds will be shown on Amershi's statement of financial position and statement of comprehensive income for the year ending 31 December 20X1.

4. Assume that the holders of $300,000 face value bonds exercise their conversion privilege on 1 January 20X4, when the market value of the common shares is $65. Prepare the journal entry to record the conversion.

REVIEW PROBLEM 15-1—SOLUTION

1. The first step is to calculate the present value of the cash flows at the market rate of 10%, using semi-annual interest periods:

Principal [$1,000,000 × (P/A, 5%,10)]	$ 613,913
Interest [$40,000 × (P/F, 5%,10)]	308,869
	$922,782

Journal entry to record issuance

Cash	1,250,000	
Convertible Bonds payable		922,782
Contributed capital: common share conversion rights		327,218

2. Entries for interest expense during 20X1:

30 June 20X1

Interest expense ($922,782 × 5%)	46,139	
Convertible Bonds Payable		6,139
Cash		40,000

Liability balance: $922,782 + $6,139 = $928,921

31 December 20X1

Interest expense ($928,921 × 5%)	46,446	
Convertible Bonds payable		6,446
Cash		40,000

Liability balance is $928,921 + $6,446 = $935,367

3. Bond-related items on 20X1 financial statements:

Statement of comprehensive income

Interest expense	$ 92,585

Statement of financial position

Long-term debt	
Bonds payable	$935,367
Shareholders' equity	
Contributed capital: common share conversion rights	$ 327,218

4. Conversion of $300,000 face value bonds into 6,000 common shares on 1 January 20X4:

The present value of the converted bond on 1 January 20X4:

Principal [$300,000 × (P/A, 5%,4)]	$ 246,811
Interest [$12,000 × (P/F, 5%,4)]	42,551
	$289,362

Bonds payable	289,362	
Contributed capital: common share conversion rights ($327,218 × 3/10)	98,165	
Common shares		387,527

Review Problem 15-2

On 1 January 20X5, Bateau Inc. issued $10,000,000 face amount of 4%, 10-year, subordinated convertible debentures for $10,500,000 in a private placement. The debentures pay interest annually, in cash, on 31 December. At maturity, the principal must be paid through the issuance of 50 common shares for each $1,000 of the bonds' face value. A market rate of interest for financial instruments with similar risk, security, and term is 8%.

Required:

1. Record the issuance of the bonds on 1 January 20X5.
2. Record the interest expense and payment on the first interest date of 31 December 20X5.

REVIEW PROBLEM 15-2—SOLUTION

1. Interest:

These debentures pay interest annually, in cash; the present value of this cash flow is recorded by Bateau as a liability, using the market rate of interest:

$$\$400,000 \times (P/A, 8\%, 10) = \$2,684,032$$

Principal:

The bond must be settled through the issuance of common shares, so the remainder of the issuance price is equity:

Cash	10,500,000	
Interest liability—subordinated convertible debentures		2,684,032
Share equity—subordinated convertible debentures		7,815,968

2. *Entry to record interest expense on 31 December 20X5:*

Interest expense ($2,684,032 × 8%)	214,723	
Interest liability - subordinated convertible debentures		214,723

Entry to record interest payment on 31 December 20X5:

Interest liability - subordinated convertible debentures	400,000	
Cash ($10,000,000 × 4%)		400,000

CASE 15-1

ZEBO LTD.

"Amy, I need you to put your other projects on hold and do a little work on these financials for me."

With a sinking heart, you follow Jon Wong, your boss and special projects manager for Holdings Ltd, into his office. It is mid-January 20X3. You catch the pile of documents he tosses at you. The movie you were going to see tonight is now a dream—you have done "a little work" for Jon many times, and it is usually time consuming.

While Jon deals with several urgent phone calls, you flip through the documents and see that you have the draft SFP for Zebo, a subsidiary of Holdings (Exhibit 1). You also discover information on the retractable preferred shares of Zebo (Exhibit 2), several financing alternatives (Exhibit 3), stock option information (Exhibit 4) and an existing debt covenant arrangement (Exhibit 5).

EXHIBIT 1

ZEBO LIMITED

DRAFT Statement of Financial Position

As of 31 December (in thousands)

	20X2	20X1
Assets		
Current assets		
Cash	$ 2,200	$ 1,300
Accounts receivable, net	5,150	6,200

	20X2	20X1
Inventory	14,450	12,220
Prepaid expenses and deposits	1,120	1,340
	22,920	21,060
Property, plant, and equipment (net)	40,500	31,230
Goodwill	5,500	5,500
	$68,920	$57,790
Liabilities		
Current liabilities		
Operating loan	$ 16,200	$ 7,900
Accounts payable and accrued liabilities	7,900	8,300
Deferred revenue	1,050	1,210
Provisions	2,640	2,050
	27,790	19,460
Long-term liabilities		
Bonds payable, net	9,300	9,250
Deferred tax	3,210	3,960
Shareholders' equity		
Preferred share capital	2,700	2,700
Common share capital	18,320	18,320
Contributed capital—options	1,200	1,200
Retained earnings	5,840	2,495
Accumulated OCI—hedging	560	405
	28,620	25,120
	$68,920	$57,790

EXHIBIT 2

ZEBO LIMITED

Retractable Preferred Shares

On 7 March 20X2, the company's board of directors approved the cash redemption at par plus 10%, of all of the $2.7 million of mandatorily redeemable convertible preferred shares at 15 June 20X2. After this announcement, but before the cash redemption date, holders of $2.1 million of the preferred shares elected to convert their shares to common shares, according to the share agreement. These common shares had a fair value of $2.4 million at 15 June. The remaining $0.6 million preferred shares were redeemed for cash on 15 June 20X2.

EXHIBIT 3

ZEBO LIMITED

Financing Options

Objective: Raise $10 million on the bond market and retire $10 million in operating loans to reduce interest costs.

Note: Alternatives are priced to sell at par.

	Alternative 1	**Alternative 2**
Principal	$10 million	$10 million
Interest rate	4%, semi-annual payments	6%, semi-annual payments
Maturity date	Ten years	Ten years
Security	Second charge on tangible fixed assets	Second charge on tangible fixed assets
Other terms	Convertible to 500,000 shares at maturity at issuer's option	Convertible to common shares at market price per share at maturity at investor's option

EXHIBIT 4

ZEBO LIMITED

Stock Option Information, 20X2

Stock option activity in 20X2 is as follows:

(in millions)	Number of Options	Weighted Average Exercise Price
31 December 20X1	650	$27.76
Granted	22	$20.00
Exercised	(34)	$18.50
Forfeited	(42)	$30.00
31 December 20X2	596	$ 27.70

The Black-Scholes option pricing model is used to estimate the fair value of options granted under the equity incentive plan. Fair value is recognized over the vesting period and is adjusted for expected retention. Cumulative contributed capital related to share-based compensation should be $1,620 at the end of 20X2, *after all transactions*, but then adjusted for new retention levels (expected to be 92%). Options exercised in 20X2 are associated with $165 of accrued cumulative compensation.

Note: No entries have been made for exercise or compensation cost in 20X2.

EXHIBIT 5

ZEBO LIMITED

Operating Loan Covenants

As part of the operating loan arrangement, Zebo must satisfy the following covenants on an annual basis. Annual financial statements must be audited.

1. A ratio of Current Assets to Current Liabilities of not less than 1:1; and
2. A ratio of Total Liabilities to Tangible Net Worth of not greater than 1.5:1.

"Tangible Net Worth" means the total of equity less intangibles, deferred charges, leasehold improvements, deferred tax debits, and unsecured advances to related parties. For the purpose hereof, intangibles are assets lacking physical substance.

"Total Liabilities" means all liabilities, exclusive of deferred tax liabilities and postponed debt.

"Right, Amy. Thanks. These draft financials do not include the statement of changes in equity—I'm sure you can deal with that. Don't forget—we comply with IFRS! I also know the statements do not include two major areas—the retractable preferred transaction and all the stock option transactions. You have the information you need. Please get these things taken care of. Then I want you to take a look at the two financing alternatives we have on the table. We need this money to pay down the current debt of this company. Both the bond alternatives are much cheaper. We will be making a decision on these alternatives in the next week or two, and the transaction will happen next quarter. Let me know what you think, but back that up with numbers, will you? We will meet tomorrow."

"Sure, Jon." You glumly return to your desk. It might be a long night. No Bourne for you!

Required:

Prepare for your meeting with Jon tomorrow.

CASE 15-2

SIGNS AND DESIGNS

Signs and Designs Inc. (SDI) is a company operating in the advertising industry. SDL provides companies with designs for new signage and company logos. The company has a profit-sharing plan whereby 25% of the company's earnings before taxes are distributed to employees who have been with the company for the entire year. It is now late September 20X4, and Liam Zhang, the company's CFO, is currently preparing a draft of the company's financial statements for the year ended 31 December 20X4, to determine the amount of this bonus to be paid out to the employees. It has been decided at a recent board meeting that the company will enter into four unusual transactions during the period October to December. CEO Derrick Voshart has asked for a memo on the impact of these transactions on the bonus amount available for the employees. Extracts from the recent board meeting outlining the proposed transactions are provided in Exhibit 1. The net earnings for the year ended 31 December 20X4 and 20X5 are forecasted to be $850,000 before taxes and any impact of these proposed transactions.

EXHIBIT 1

SIGNS AND DESIGNS INC.

Extract from Board Meeting notes

To: Kelly

From: Liam Zhang

Re: Potential accounting issues—

The following transactions are proposed for the period October 1, to 31 December 20X4.

Convertible Debt

On 1 October, the company will issue convertible bonds with a face value of $700,000 and receive proceeds of $700,000. The bonds pay interest at 5%, semi-annually and are due 30 September 20X9. The company currently pays interest on similar debt with no conversion options at 8%. The bonds are repayable at maturity through the issuance of a fixed number of common shares.

Preferred Shares

On 1 November, the company will issue 10,000 preferred shares to a private investor for $100 each. The shares have a mandatory redemption price of $100 per share, and each year 1,000 shares must be redeemed, commencing in 20X7. The shares have a monthly dividend rate of $0.85, which is cumulative and must be paid on redemption.

Options Granted to a Supplier

On 1 December, the company will issue 100,000 options to a design consultant that the company has used periodically since 20X1. The options are for services provided by this consultant for the work done on a recent customer's advertising campaign. The options have an exercise price of $25 per share and will expire in 10 years from the date of issue. The options are exerciseable at the time of grant. The fair value of the options has been determined to be $1.25 per option. The value of the services provided are estimated to be $150,000.

Exchange Rate Hedge

On 1 August, SDL placed an order with a German supplier for a new machine that will cost €250,000. The order is expected to be received and paid for in February 20X5. To mitigate part of the exchange risk, the board is considering entering into a forward contract to receive €250,000 in February 20X5, when payment is due. Although the board has no idea of the value of this forward contract at the end of December, assume that the forward contract has a loss value of $35,000 at the end of 20X4 for the discussion of the impact of this transaction. Assume that the company will not apply hedge accounting to this forward contract.

Required:

You, Kelly, work for the CFO, who has asked you to review the notes and prepare a memo outlining accounting and reporting issues and alternatives for each of the four transactions proposed. Liam would like you to outline the impact on the statement of financial position and net profit or loss before tax for 20X4 and 20X5. (Prepare the journal entry to be recorded at the time of issue for each transaction.) This memo will be the basis for the meeting with Derrick Voshart.

CASE 15-3

TECHNO WIZARD LTD.

Omni Services Ltd., a Canadian public company, is a conglomerate involved in publication of newspapers, media services, and information technology consulting. It recently entered into an agreement to purchase Techno Wizard Ltd. (TWL), which operates a printing business in Manitoba. Omni assumed control on 1 November 20X7.

It is now 14 November 20X7, and Omni has just received the 31 October 20X7 financial statements of TWL. Omni is now concerned that the price to be paid is excessive and is looking for advice leading up to its preclosing negotiations, scheduled for next week. Accordingly, you have been approached, as an outside accounting advisor, for your advice and expert opinion. The purchase agreement is described in Exhibit 1 and financial statement extracts are in Exhibit 2.

EXHIBIT 1

PURCHASE AND SALE AGREEMENT EXTRACTS

Omni Services Ltd. (Purchaser) and Techno Wizard Ltd. (Vendor)

7.0   Purchase Price

7.1   The purchase price shall be $7.0 million Canadian ($15 per share) subject to adjustment, if any, (see section 7.3), to be established two weeks after the reporting date in section 7.4.

7.2   The purchase price shall be payable $2 million in cash plus $2 million in Omni shares on 1 November 20X7, with the balance paid in cash on 15 December 20X7. Issued shares are valued using quoted prices for Omni shares on the TSX on 1 November 20X7.

7.3   The purchase price will be increased dollar-for-dollar for any excess over $7 million obtained as the product of two times the assets less liabilities of TWL on the SFP dated 31 October 20X7. Assets and liabilities are to be calculated as defined under IFRS standards.

7.4   TWL will provide 31 October 20X7 financial statements before the reporting date of 21 November 20X7.

EXHIBIT 2

EXTRACTS FROM TECHNO WIZARD LTD. FINANCIAL STATEMENTS

31 October 20X7

Statement of Financial Position (in thousands)

Assets

Current Assets

Cash	$ 1,420
Receivables	2,690
Inventory	3,700
Prepaid expenses	290
	8,100

Non-current Assets

Capital assets, net	3,100
	$11,200

Liabilities

Current Liabilities

Bank indebtedness	$ 860
Accounts payable	2,100

Deferred revenue	1,740
	4,700

Non-current liabilities

Bonds payable	2,100
Deferred income tax	162
Other	230
	$ 7,192

Equity

Preferred shares	500
Print shop equity—bond	300
Contributed capital—share plan	320
Common shares	1,080
Retained earnings	1,808
	$ 4,008
	$11,200

Disclosure Notes Extracts

1. Foreign exchange losses are part of "prepaid expenses" in the amount of $160. All gains are included in earnings.

2. Bonds payable consists of $2.4 million face value of 10-year debentures issued on 1 December 20X6. The debentures were issued at par, and require annual interest of 3.5% payable each 31 May.

   Debentures of similar term and risk were issued by another company at par, carrying an interest rate of 8% within a month of this transaction.

   The debenture holders are entitled to the use of 1,000 hours of print shop capacity at any time after 1 June 20X7. Print shop usage is to be negotiated with a 30-day lead time, and TWL is responsible for all overhead and direct labour. Paper product used in printing is the responsibility of the debenture holder. No print shop capacity has been used to date under the agreement.

3. Included in accounts receivable is a $710 two-year delayed-payment arrangement set on 1 January 20X7. The customer will pay $710 on 31 December 20X8, plus 3% interest each 31 December. Interest rates for a comparable term are in the range of 7%. No interest has been accrued to date.

4. Preferred shares are held by the founding family of TWL and carry a cumulative dividend of 4% annually. Omni did not acquire these shares but has the right to redeem them for cash at book value.

5. Deferred revenue includes various advance payments made by customers under long-term contracts. Some contracts involve upfront fees that are recognized in revenue when received. Other contracts allow a final year of free service or stipulate that a renewal contract will include a free year of average usage covered under the expiring contract. The average length of a contract is three years.

6. TWL has a SARs plan that allows eight managers a cash payment based on the value of 10,000 shares each. The plan was set up in 20X6, and payment will be made in 20X8 for any increase in share value above $10 per share to any manager still employed with TWL at that time. Share value was to be determined using a formula, since TWL is not a public company. The valuation model used placed a value at $6 per unit as the expected payout when the plan was established in 20X6. To date, $320,000 of cost has been recognized. Two of the eight managers have left the firm, but all others are expected to continue through 20X8.

7. TWL has entered into a foreign currency exchange contract with respect to $200,000 of U.S. dollar long-term debt at 31 October 20X7. The company has recorded an asset and a gain of $76 in relation to this arrangement, based on its expectations regarding currency movements over the period to maturity.

Required:

Prepare a report that identifies potential issues. Include quantification of issues where possible.

TECHNICAL REVIEW

connect

TR15-1 Retractable Preferred Shares:

AZZY Ltd. issued preferred shares as part of a transfer of ownership under specified sections of the *Income Tax Act*. The company issued 400,000 shares, for a nominal dollar amount of $1 per share. The shares are retractable at $15 per share, anytime, at the holder's option. Dividends of $20,000 in total were paid on the dividends during the year. AZZY has net earnings before tax of $750,000 before the recognition of the dividend, total liabilities of $2,300,000, and total shareholders' equity of $5,800,000 before the recognition of the preferred share issue.

Required:

1. Assuming AZZY follows IFRS, what is the revised net earnings before tax, total liabilities, and shareholders' equity after these transactions?

2. Assuming AZZY follows ASPE, what is the revised net earnings before tax, total liabilities, and shareholders' equity after these transactions?

connect

TR15-2 Convertible Debt, Investor's Option:

Closed Tech Ltd. issued convertible bonds on 1 July 20X8. The 15-year, 5% $10,000,000 bonds pay interest semi-annually each 30 June and 31 December. At the investor's option, each $1,000 bond is convertible into 50 common shares on the bond's maturity date.

Bond market analysts indicated that if the bonds had not been convertible, they would likely have sold to yield 6%, and have raised $9,020,000. They were, in fact, issued for $10,350,000.

Required:

1. Provide the journal entry to record the initial issuance of the bond.
2. Provide the entry to record interest at 31 December 20X8.
3. Prove that the $9,020,000 reference price provides a yield of 6% by establishing the present value of the bond. Allow for rounding.

connect

TR15-3 Convertible Debt, Investor's Option:

SCIFI Ltd. issued convertible bonds on 1 February 20X6. The 5-year, 3% $8,000,000 bonds pay interest semi-annually each 31 January and 31 July. At the investor's option, each $1,000 bond is convertible into 50 common shares on the bond's maturity date. The company has a 31 January year-end.

Bond market analysts indicated that if the bonds had not been convertible, they would likely have sold to yield 6%. They were, in fact, issued for $8,750,000.

Required:

1. Provide the journal entry to record the initial issuance of the bond.
2. Provide the entry to record interest at 31 July 20X6 and 31 January 20X7.
3. Provide the journal entry, assuming that on 1 February 20X7, the bonds were converted to shares, when the share price was $32 per share.

connect

TR15-4 Convertible Debt, Mandatory Conversion:

Mecca Energy Corp. issued a convertible bond on 1 August 20X9. The 10-year, 4% $12,000,000 bond pays interest semi-annually each 31 July and 31 January. At maturity, each $1,000 bond is convertible into 120 common shares. The bond was issued for $12,500,000. Market interest rates were approximately 5%.

Required:

1. Provide the journal entry to record the initial issuance of the bond.
2. Assume instead that the bond was convertible into common shares at the maturity date into common shares based on the market value of common shares at that time. Repeat requirement 1. Explain.

connect

TR15-5 Options:

Pont Chemical Remediation Ltd. issued options in 20X6 allowing the holder to acquire 50,000 common shares in five years' time at an acquisition price of $20 per share. Using an option pricing model, the options are valued at $120,000. The options were issued for consulting and promotion work done, tasks that are not easily valued.

Required:

1. Provide the journal entry to record the transaction.
2. Assume that the options were exercised when the market price of common shares is $44. Provide the entry for exercise.
3. Alternately, assume that the options were allowed to lapse when the price of common shares is $16. Provide the entry for the lapse.

connect

TR15-6 Rights:

Locomotive Co. decided to raise new equity using a rights offering and on June 15 announced that it would issue one right for each share owned to existing shareholders. The company currently has 1,800,000 shares outstanding, which are priced at $45 per share. The subscription price is $30 and it will take four rights and the subscription price to purchase one share. On 30 June the 1,800,000 rights were issued. The rights expire on 31 July. During the ex-rights period (after 29 June), the value of one right is $3.00 and the share price is $42. By 31 July, 1,750,000 rights had been exercised and 50,000 rights expired.

Required:

1. Provide the journal entry to record the issue of the rights on 30 June.
2. Provide the journal entry to record the total transactions to the end of July for the exercise of the rights and the expiration of rights.

connect

TR15-7 Warrants:

Shurwood Ltd. issued 5,000,000 8%, 10-year, nonconvertible bonds with detachable warrants for $5,100,000. Shortly after issuance, the warrants trade for $300,000 in total, and the bonds were trading at 99, or $4,950,000, ex-warrants (i.e., without warrants attached).

Required:

1. Provide the journal entry to record the transactions.
2. Provide the journal entry to record the first payment of interest on the convertible bond assuming that the bonds pay interest annually.

connect

TR15-8 Share-based Compensation; Equity Settled:

Forgin Co. issued 500 common shares to We Can Advertize for advertising services. The shares currently are valued at $24 per share, and the advertising services rendered are valued at $11,000.

Required:

Provide the journal entry to be recorded with respect to issue of these shares.

connect

TR15-9 Share-based Compensation; Equity Settled:

Darling Petrol Corp. granted stock options to executives in early 20X1. The stock options vest over five years and expire after eight years. In total, the options allow the purchase of 400,000 shares at $2 per share. Option pricing models indicate that the options have a total fair value of $1,400,000. Estimates of retention are 82% at the end of 20X1 and 80% at the end of 20X2.

Required:

1. Provide the journal entries to be recorded with respect to the options at the end of 20X1 and 20X2.
2. What would the balance be in the equity account for stock options at the end of the fifth year if retention was at 80%?
3. Assume that actual retention was 80%, and the options were exercised at the end of the sixth year when the market price of common shares is $29. Provide the entry for exercise.
4. Alternatively, assume that retention was 80% but the options were allowed to lapse after eight years when the price of common shares is $1.25. Provide the entry for the lapse.

connect

TR15-10 Share-based Compensation; Cash Settled:

IT Solutions Ltd. has a cash-settled SARs program for employees. These employees will receive a cash payment after five years of service, calculated as the excess of share price over $7.50. In early 20X1, employees in total are granted 60,000 units in the program.

The fair value of one SARs unit is estimated at $1 at the end of 20X1, $3 at the end of 20X2, and $2 at the end of 20X3. Estimated retention is 90% at the end of 20X1, 88% at the end of 20X2, and 75% at the end of 20X3. The payment is made at the end of 20X5.

Required:

Provide the journal entry to be recorded with respect to the SARS program at the end of 20X1, 20X2, and 20X3.

★ A15-1 Classification; Impact of Debt versus Equity:

Laffoley Corp. needs to raise $10,000,000 to finance a planned capital expansion. The company has investigated two alternatives:

1. Issue $10 million of preferred shares at par. The shares can be redeemed at the company's option at the end of 12 years for a price estimated to be in the region of $11,000,000. Annual (cumulative) dividends would amount to $585,000.

2. Issue bonds, which the company can buy back on the open market at the end of 12 years; analysts estimate that it would cost $11,000,000 to reacquire the $10,000,000 issue. Annual interest would amount to $900,000.

Required:

1. Assume Laffoley's tax rate is 35%. What is the *after-tax* annual cost of the two alternatives?

2. Provide journal entries to record issuance, annual dividends, or interest (for one year only), and retirement of both the shares and debt.

3. Assume that earnings, before interest and tax, in Year 12 was $3,000,000. The tax rate was 35%. Calculate earnings if equity were outstanding in Year 12, and retired at the end of the year. Calculate earnings if debt were outstanding in Year 12 and retired at the end of the year.

★ A15-2 Classification:

Description of several financial instruments follows:

Case 1   Convertible subordinated bonds payable, entitled to annual cash interest at 5%, paid semi-annually. At maturity, the bonds may be settled at the investor's option through the issuance of common shares using an exchange price of $5 per share. Alternatively, the investor may choose to be repaid in cash.

Case 2   Convertible subordinated bonds payable, entitled to annual cash interest at 5%, paid semi-annually. At maturity, the bonds may be settled at the issuer's option through the issuance of common shares using an exchange price of $5 per share. Alternatively, the issuer may choose to repay principal in cash.

Case 3   Convertible subordinated bonds payable, entitled to annual cash interest at 5%, paid semi-annually. At maturity, the bonds may be settled at the issuer's option through the issuance of common shares using the current market price of the shares. Alternatively, the issuer may choose to repay principal in cash.

Case 4   Convertible subordinated bonds payable, entitled to annual cash interest at 5%, paid semi-annually. At maturity, the bonds may be settled at the investor's option through the issuance of common shares using the current market price of the shares. Alternatively, the investor may choose to be repaid in cash.

Case 5   Series F second preferred shares, carrying a fixed cumulative dividend of $1 per share. The shares must be redeemed by the company at a price of $50 per share, plus dividends in arrears, if any, on 31 December 20X1.

Required:

Classify each of the above items as a financial liability, equity instrument, or compound instrument (part debt and part equity).

 A15-3 Classification:

Description of several financial instruments follows:

Case 1 Class D Series 2 shares, carrying a dividend entitlement equal to $5 per share or an amount equal to common share dividends, whichever is higher, redeemable at the investor's option at $62 per share. The company may, at its option, redeem the shares with class A common shares instead of cash, valued at their current market value.

Case 2 Convertible subordinated bonds payable, entitled to annual cash interest at 3.2%. At maturity, the bonds will be settled through the issuance of shares using an exchange price of $14 per share. Interest may also be paid in shares valued at $14 per share at the company's option.

Case 3 Series F second preferred shares, carrying a fixed cumulative dividend of $1 per share. The shares must be redeemed by the company at a price of $21 per share, plus dividends in arrears, if any, in 20X4.

Case 4 Convertible subordinated debentures payable, entitled to annual interest at 3.2%. At maturity, the debentures may, at the company's option, be paid out in cash or converted into common shares using an exchange ratio governed by the market value of shares at the conversion date.

Case 5 Series C first preferred shares, carrying a fixed cumulative dividend of $1.25 per share per annum, redeemable at the company's option at $25 per share.

Case 6 Series II preferred shares, carrying a fixed cumulative dividend of $1.75 per share increasing to $6.10 in 20X8. The shares are redeemable at the company's option at a price of $28 per share until 31 December 20X7 and at a price of $62 thereafter.

Case 7 Convertible subordinated 6% notes payable. At maturity, the debentures may, at the company's option, be paid out in cash or converted into common shares at the set exchange price of $30 per share.

Required:

Classify each of the above items as a financial liability, equity instrument, or compound instrument (part debt and part equity).

 **A15-4 Classification:**

Value Production Corp. currently has a debt to equity ratio of 3.2-to-1, based on $16 million of debt and $5 million of equity. The company is looking to raise $2 million in new financing for an expansion plan. There is a debt covenant that requires the debt to equity ratio to be no higher than 3.5:1, and this is a major factor as the company looks at several financing alternatives.

Alternative 1: Issuance of $2 million of 5% preferred shares, redeemable in cash at the option of the investor.

Alternative 2: Issuance of $2 million of 6% preferred shares, redeemable in cash at the option of Value.

Alternative 3:   Issuance of $2 million of 7% secured bonds, convertible into common shares at the option of Value, with conversion based on the market price of common shares at the conversion date.

Alternative 4:   Issuance of $2 million of 6.5% unsecured bonds, convertible into common shares at the option of the investor, with conversion at $20 per share. This conversion option is estimated to be worth $250,000.

Required:

1. Calculate and comment on the relative annual cost of each alternative from Value's perspective. The company has a 35% tax rate. For the investor, what are the attractive elements of each investment?

2. Classify each alternative as debt or equity, and recalculate the debt to equity ratio.

3. Which alternative would you recommend to Value? Explain.

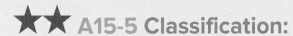 **A15-5 Classification:**

Glamour Mining Ltd. currently has a debt to equity ratio of 2.5-to-1, based on $80 million of debt and $32 million of equity. The company is looking to raise $16 million in new financing and must choose one of the following:

A. Convertible debt, unsecured, with a 7% interest rate, where conversion is mandatory in 25 years for 700,000 voting common shares. Interest is paid in cash annually.

B. Convertible debt, secured with company land and buildings, with a 6% interest rate, where conversion is at the investor's option in 25 years for 800,000 voting common shares. Interest is paid in cash annually. This conversion option is estimated to be worth $1,835,200.

C. Preferred shares, carrying an annual dividend of 5%, where the investor has the choice of cash repayment or 800,000 common shares in 25 years.

There is a debt covenant that requires the debt to equity ratio to be no higher than 3:1.

Required:

1. Calculate and comment on the relative annual cost of each alternative from the company's perspective. The company has a 35% tax rate. For the investor, what are the attractive elements of each investment?

2. Classify each alternative as debt or equity and recalculate the debt to equity ratio. Use 7% as a market yield rate if present value calculations are needed.

3. Which alternative would you recommend to Glamour? Explain.

 A15-6 Classification:

A description of several financial instruments follows:

Case A   Subordinated 8% debentures payable, interest payable semi-annually, due in the year 20X8. At maturity, the face value of the debentures may be converted, at the company's option, into common shares at the market price at that time. Interest may also be paid in shares using the market value of shares at the interest payment date.

Case B   Series B shares, nonvoting, annual $1.25 cumulative dividend, convertible at the investor's option into 10 common shares in 20X6.

Case C   Subordinated 4% debentures payable, interest payable in cash semi-annually, due in 20X9. At maturity, the face value of the debentures must be converted into common shares at a price of $22 per share.

Case D   Series C shares, nonvoting, annual $1.25 noncumulative dividend, redeemable at the investor's option for $29 per share at any time.

Case E   Subordinated bonds payable, bearing an interest rate of 5%, interest reset every five years with reference to market rates; principal due to be repaid only on the dissolution of the company, if ever, although may be repaid at the company's option on interest repricing dates.

Case F   Series B preferred shares, annual $6 cumulative dividend, convertible into four common shares for every $100 preferred share at the investor's option, redeemable at $32 per share at the company's option in 20X10.

Required:

Classify each financial instrument as debt, equity, or compound (part debt and part equity). Explain your reasoning.

★★ A15-7 Convertible Debt:

Marjorie Manufacturing Ltd. issued a convertible bond on 2 July 20X5. The $5 million bond pays annual interest of 8% each 30 June. Each $1,000 bond is convertible into 50 shares of common stock, at the investor's option, on 1 July 20X10 until 1 July 20X15, after which time each $1,000 bond may be converted into 45.6 shares until bond maturity on 30 June 20X20. Market analysts have indicated that had the bond not been convertible, it would have sold for $4,240,000, reflecting a market interest rate of 10% annually. In fact, it was issued for $5,325,000.

Required:

1. Provide the journal entry to record the initial issuance of the bond. Justify the amount allocated to the conversion privilege.

2. Verify the $4,240,000 price of the bond.

3. Calculate the interest expense that would be recorded in the first 12 months of the bond.

4. Would more or less interest expense have been recorded in requirement 3 if the conversion option were not recognized and the proceeds above par value ($325,000) were assigned to a premium account? Explain, but do not calculate.

★★ A15-8 Convertible Debt; Investor's Option:

Nero Solutions Co. issued an $800,000, 6%, three-year bond for $806,000. The bond pays interest annually, at each year-end. At maturity, the bond can be repaid in cash or converted to 60,000 common shares at the investor's option. The market interest rate for bonds of similar term and risk, but that are not convertible, is in the range of 7%.

Required:

1. Calculate the portion of the bond to be recorded as a liability.

2. Provide the entry to record issuance of the bond.

3. Provide the entries to record interest expense and the annual cash payment each year over the bond's three-year life.

4. Provide the entry to record the maturity of the bond, assuming that shares were issued.

5. Provide the entry to record the maturity of the bond, assuming that cash is paid.

6. Provide the entry to record early repayment of the bond, assuming that it was repaid in cash in an open market transaction after two complete years. Cash of $810,000 was paid, of which $802,000 related to the liability and $8,000 related to the conversion option.

★★ A15-9 Convertible Debt; Investor's Option:

Blue Cliff Ltd. issued subordinated bonds payable on 1 January 20X1, when the market interest rate was 6%. The company received $10,760,000 for the bonds. The bonds were $10,000,000 of 4% subordinated convertible debentures payable, with interest payable semi-annually. These bonds were convertible at the investor's option in 15 years' time into common shares of the company at the rate of 25 shares for each $1,000 bond issued.

Required:

1. At what price would the bonds be issued if they were not convertible?

2. Explain the method used to value the conversion option.

3. Provide the entry to record issuance of the bond on 1 January 20X1.

4. Provide the journal entry to record interest on 30 June 20X1. Use the effective interest method to record discount amortization.

5. Provide the entry to record bond conversion to common shares at maturity, on 31 December 20X10. Common shares had a fair value of $44 per share at this time.

6. Assume instead that the bond was repaid in cash at maturity. Provide all entries to record the repayment/bond maturity. If repayment is in cash, what fair value for common shares is implied?

★★★ A15-10 Convertible Debt; Three Cases:

The following cases are independent:

Case A

On 1 January 20X6, Wilson Products Ltd. issued a bond when market interest rates were 8%.

Bonds payable, $12,000,000, 6%, due in 20 years' time. The bonds pay interest semi-annually each 30 June and 31 December. The bonds were issued at 105. The bonds are mandatorily convertible into common shares at the fixed rate of 40 shares for each $200 bond at maturity. The company may, at its discretion, repay the bond for cash in lieu of shares.

Required:

Prepare the journal entry at 1 January 20X6, to record issuance of the bond. Also calculate interest expense for the year ended 31 December 20X6.

Case B

On 1 November 20X4, XBL Communications Ltd. issued a convertible bond that was convertible in 12 years' time into 500,000 common shares at the investor's option. The bond had a $7,000,000 par value, and 6% interest was paid semi-annually on 31 October and 30 April.

The bond sold for $7,900,000 when the market interest rate was 8%.

Required:

Provide entries on issuance and on 31 December 20X4, the fiscal year-end.

Case C

On the 31 August 20X1 SFP, Argon Mining Ltd. reported the following:

Debt

Convertible bond payable, 5%, due 31 August 20X4, convertible into 500,000 shares	$12,000,000	
Less: discount	(620,000)	
		$11,380,000

Equity

Contributed capital: common share conversion rights		$ 460,000

Interest is paid *annually* on 31 October, and the bonds were originally valued to yield 7%.

Required:

Provide entries on 31 August 20X2 to record the interest expense and payment. Assuming that conversion also occurs on this date, show the journal entry for conversion of the bonds to common shares on this date. The market price of common shares was $42 per share on 31 August 20X2.

★★★ A15-11 Convertible Debt; Investor Option versus Conversion Mandatory:

AMC Ltd. issued five-year, 5% bonds for their par value of $900,000 on 1 January 20X1. Interest is paid annually. The bonds are convertible to common shares at a rate of 50 common shares for every $1,000 bond.

Required:

1. Assume that the bonds were convertible at the investor's option and that the conversion option was valued at $73,800.
   a. Provide the journal entry on issuance.
   b. Calculate interest expense for each year of the bond's five-year life. Use an interest rate of 7% for this requirement.

    c. Provide the journal entry to record maturity of the bond assuming shareholders convert their bonds to common shares.

    d. Assume instead that the bonds were repaid for $940,000 after interest was paid in Year 3. Provide the journal entry for retirement, assuming $68,000 of the payment related to the option and the rest related to the bond.

2. Assume that the bonds were mandatorily convertible at maturity.

    a. Calculate the portion of the original proceeds relating to interest and the equity portion. Use a discount rate of 6%.

    b. Provide the journal entry on issuance.

    c. Explain the financial statement elements that change when the bond is converted at maturity.

A15-12 Convertible Debt; Mandatory Conversion:

Canada Resources Ltd. issued a 14-year, $15,000,000 debenture with an interest rate of 5%; cash interest is paid semi-annually. The market rate of interest for debt of similar size, risk, and term is 8%. The obligation can be satisfied at maturity either by cash or by issuing common shares valued at $19 per share, at the option of Canada Resources Ltd. The debenture was issued for $15,400,000.

Required:

1. Classify this debenture as debt, equity, or a compound instrument. Explain your reasoning.

2. Provide the entry to record issuance of the debenture.

3. What is the value of the liability amount(s) relating to the debenture that will be shown on the SFP at the end of the second year (after adjustments)?

4. Explain the financial statement elements that change when the bond is converted at maturity.

5. Suppose instead that the $15,000,000 debenture was convertible into common shares using a value of 105% of the average market value of common shares in the five trading days prior to conversion. Explain how this difference would affect your treatment of the debenture. Calculations are not necessary.

A15-13 Convertible Debt; Mandatory Conversion:

Twixt Corp. issued $5,000,000 of convertible bonds on 1 January for $4,790,000 cash. The bond had the following terms:

- Bonds mature in five years' time.
- Annual interest, 5%, is paid each 31 December.
- Bonds are convertible to 400,000 common shares at maturity or can be repaid in cash. This choice is up to Twixt Corp.

Current market interest rates are 6%.

Required:

1. Assign a value to the liability and the equity portions of the bond.
2. Provide the journal entry to record issuance of the bond.
3. Provide a schedule to show interest expense and amortization of the liability over the life of the bond.
4. What financial statement elements would be changed when common shares are issued at maturity? Explain.

★ A15-14 Share Options—Recognition:

Agmore Breakthrough Corp. is a small biotech company listed on the TSX. To conserve cash, the company frequently settles obligations through the issuance of options. Shares are now trading for $7 per share but have fluctuated between $5 and $21 in the last year. Selected transactions:

a. Issued options to the company lawyer for legal work done to date. These options allow purchase of 80,000 shares at $5 per share at any time over the next three years. The lawyer had billed $261,000, but the company felt it could have negotiated this down slightly—perhaps 15%—for cash payment.

b. Issued options that allow purchase of 300,000 common shares at $7 per share at any time over the next two years. The options were issued for $172,000 cash.

c. Issued options to a customer allowing the customer to receive 50,000 common shares in three years' time, for no cash cost. The options have been granted based on the long service relationship between the two companies, are fully vested, and are unconditional.

d. Options in (a) and (c) above were exercised when the shares were trading at $13 per share. Options in (b) later expired.

Required:

Provide journal entries to record the transactions listed above. Justify the values used, where possible.

 connect

★ A15-15 Share Options—Recognition:

Maritime Corp. is a junior mining company listed on the TSX. The common share price of Maritime fluctuates in value. Recent swings went from a high of $16 to a low of $0.30. Maritime issued stock options on 1 September 20X5 to a consultant, in exchange for a project completed over the last year. The consultant estimated her time was worth $37,000, but the company estimated that it could have had the necessary work done for about $31,000 cash. The options specified that 4,000 common shares could be bought for $0.20 per share at any time over the next 10 years. The market price of common shares was $1.50 on the day the options were issued. At the same time options were issued to the consultant, identical options were issued to the company lawyer for work done to date. An option pricing model valued each set of stock options at $35,000.

Required:

1. Provide journal entries to record issuance of the two sets of options. Justify values used.
2. Assume that two years after issuance, when the market price of the shares was $14, the consultant exercised her options. Provide the appropriate entry.
3. Assume that 10 years after issuance, when the market price of the shares was $0.10, the lawyer's options expired. Provide the entry, if any.

eXcel

★ ★★ A15-16 Share Options and Warrants:

On 31 December 20X2, the shareholders' equity section of Sersa Corp.'s statement of financial position was as follows:

Common shares, no-par, unlimited shares authorized, issued and outstanding, 4,543,400 shares	$16,876,400
Contributed capital: common share warrants outstanding, 12,300 warrants allowing purchase of three shares each at a price of $26 per share	110,000
Share options outstanding	161,000
Retained earnings	34,560,900
Total shareholders' equity	$51,708,300

There were 46,000 share options outstanding, issued for legal services, valued at $161,000. These allow purchase of one share each for $19 cash; the options are exercisable over several years.

Transactions during the year:

a. Options were issued to existing shareholders as a poison pill in the case of a hostile takeover. These options allow purchase of two shares for each existing share held at a price of $1 each, to be exercisable only under certain limited conditions.

b. Warrants outstanding at the beginning of the year were exercised in full. The market value of the shares was $40.

c. Some outstanding $19 share options were exercised and 10,000 shares were issued. Remaining share options were not exercised in the current year. The market value of the shares was $40.

d. Options were issued that allow purchase of a total of 2,000 shares at a price of $32 per share, beginning in 20X4. The options were issued for four months of 20X3 rent, which was set by contract at $4,000 per month.

e. Options were issued for proceeds of $45,000, allowing purchase of 40,000 shares at a price of $35 per share.

f. One-quarter of the options issued in (e), above, were exercised. The market value of the shares was $48.

Required:

1. Provide journal entries for each of the transactions listed above.

2. Prepare the shareholders' equity section of the statement of financial position, reflecting the transactions recorded in requirement 1.

3. What items would appear on the statement of cash flows in the financing activities section as a result of the changes in the equity accounts documented in requirement 2?

★ ★ A15-17 Share-based Compensation; Cash-Settled:

Just In Co. issues 500,000 SARs units to its eight-member top management group. These SARs allow the managers to receive a cash payment after holding the SARs for five years. The SARs vest on the payment date. The value of the SARs is calculated as the difference between the $34 per share fair market value of common shares on the date the SARs were issued and the fair market value on the date of payment. The company estimates that six of eight managers will remain with the company over the five-year period. This estimate remains unchanged over the first four years. One manager leaves after Year 2, one after Year 3, and one in Year 5, so that only five managers were paid at the end of Year 5.

The fair value of one SARs unit was estimated using a valuation model and was, at the end of Year 1, $4; Year 2, $1; Year 3, $2; Year 4, $17; and in Year 5, the actual market price of common shares was $53.

Required:

1. Why are SARs issued instead of common stock options?
2. How much compensation expense would be recorded in each of Years 1 to 5?
3. What would appear on the SFP at the end of each of Years 1 to 4?
4. What entry would be made on the maturity (payment) of the SARs?
5. Describe how the accounting for this compensation scheme would be different if the employees could choose between cash and shares at settlement.

★ A15-18 Share-based Compensation; Cash-Settled:

Pine Resources Ltd. has a SARs program for managers. These individuals receive a cash payment after four years of service, calculated as the excess of share price over $5. In early 20X1, individuals in the 25-member management team are granted a total of 100,000 SARs units. The payment is made at the end of 20X4. Data on estimated and actual retention are:

End of Year	20X1	20X2	20X3	20X4
Employees expected to remain until vesting	15 (60%)	20 (80%)	22 (88%)	n/a
Employees expected to forfeit	10 (40%)	5 (20%)	3 (12%)	n/a
Employees actually forfeiting in the year	2	0	1	1
Employees actually receiving SARs (25 − 4)				21 (84%)

The fair value of the entire 100,000 units was estimated to be $100,000 at the end of 20X1, $300,000 at the end of 20X2, and $120,000 at the end of 20X3. The actual share price was $7.40 at the end of 20X4.

Required:

1. Calculate compensation expense in each year of the SARs plan and the balance of the SARs liability at the end of each year.
2. What evidence suggests that the level of retention must be revised after 20X1 and 20X2?
3. Explain why compensation expense is volatile.

★★ A15-19 Share-based Compensation; Cash-Settled:

Pacific Trading Co. has a SARs program for managers. These individuals receive a cash payment after three years of service, calculated as the excess of share price over $10. In early 20X3, the 30 members of the management team in total are granted 25,000 units in the program. The payment is made at the end of 20X5. Data on estimated and actual retention are:

End of Year	20X3	20X4	20X5
Employees expected to remain until vesting	25 (83%)	24 (80%)	n/a
Employees expected to forfeit	5 (17%)	6 (20%)	n/a
Employees actually forfeiting in the year	1	4	3
Employees actually receiving SARs (30 − 8)			22 (73.3%)

The fair value of one SARs unit is estimated at $3 at the end of 20X3 and $12 at the end of 20X4. The actual share price is $19 at the end of 20X5.

Required:

1. Provide the entry to record compensation expense in each year of the SARs plan, including the entry for cash payment in 20X5.
2. What evidence suggests that the level of retention must be revised for 20X4?
3. Describe how the accounting for this compensation scheme would be different if the employees could choose between cash and shares at settlement.

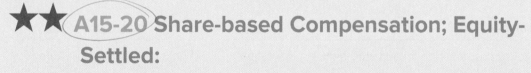

★★ A15-20 Share-based Compensation; Equity-Settled:

Wolmore Resources Ltd. is authorized to issue unlimited numbers of common shares, of which 40,500,000 have been issued at an average price of $22 per share. On 1 January 20X3, when shares were trading for $30 per share, the company granted stock options to each of its 42 senior executives. The stock options provide that each individual will be eligible to purchase, no earlier than 31 December 20X7, 3,000 common shares at a base option price of $30 per share. The options are nontransferable, vest on 31 December 20X7, and expire on 31 December 20X8. Option pricing models indicate that the options have a total value of $480,000. Estimates of retention are:

Year	20X3	20X4	20X5	20X6	20X7
Employees expected to remain until vesting	32 (76%)	30 (71%)	35 (83%)	34 (81%)	n/a
Employees expected to forfeit	10 (24%)	12 (29%)	7 (17%)	8 (19%)	n/a
Employees actually forfeiting in the year	0	5	2	0	0
Employees actually receiving options (42 − 7)					35 (83%)

Twenty-five individuals who received the options exercised on 31 December 20X7, when the share price was $54. The remaining individuals did not exercise the options. The share price fell to $24 in 20X8, and the remaining options lapsed.

Required:

1. Prepare the entries to record the granting of the options, annual expense, exercise, and lapse.
2. Why is the compensation expense not an equal amount each year? Be specific.
3. What intrinsic value was received when the options were exercised? Is this reflected in the financial statements? Explain.

 ## A15-21 Share-based Compensation:

Smith Minerals Ltd. had compensation plans in effect for senior managers that included two long-term compensation elements. SFP accounts at the end of 20X6 are:

Liability—SARs plan	$ 67,000

130,000 units are under SARs agreement, where the reference market price is $17 per common share, one share per SARs unit; valuation models indicate a fair value of $1.50 per SARs unit; the SARs have been outstanding for two years and must be held for a total of five years before vesting.

Contributed capital—employee share options outstanding	$314,000

123,000 shares are under option at an exercise price of $21. Common shares are now trading at $25. The options were valued using a binomial valuation model and determined to be worth $700,000. The options have been outstanding for three years and must be held for a total of five years before they can be exercised.

Retention levels were estimated to be 85% at the end of 20X6.

Required:

1. Describe the likely features of the two kinds of compensation plans above. Provide the calculation to support the balances recorded.
2. Assume no new compensation entitlements were offered in 20X7. At year-end, the common share price was $33 and the fair value of a SARs unit was estimated to be worth $1.70. Retention is now assumed to be 80%. Give the entries to record compensation expense related to the above plans.

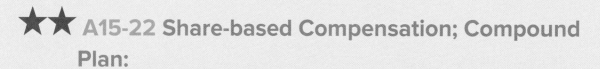 A15-22 Share-based Compensation; Compound Plan:

Five vice-presidents of Spinner Entertainment Ltd. are awarded units in a phantom stock plan at the beginning of 20X5. At the end of 20X7, after three years of employment, each vice president is entitled to receive *either:*

- 7,000 common shares; or
- Cash equal to the market value of 5,000 shares.

At the time of the grant, the shares had a market value of $25, and valuation models indicated that the share alternative was worth $27.50 per share. Based on this information, the equity portion of the plan was valued at $337,500 for accounting purposes. The share price was $21 at the end of 20X5, $27 at the end of 20X6, and $25 at the end of 20X7. The fair value of the cash alternative is to be based on the intrinsic value of the plan on each reporting date. All vice-presidents were expected to stay with the company, and all did. Four of the five executives elected to take cash in 20X7, and the remaining vice-president took shares.

Required:

1. Verify the $337,500 option value at the inception of the plan.
2. Prepare the entries to record the annual expense entries and disbursement in 20X5, 20X6, and 20X7.

 A15-23 Derivatives:

Moon Pacific Ltd. reported the following amounts on the 31 December 20X2 SFP (in thousands):

Assets		Liabilities	
Derivative asset	$1,455	Derivative obligation	$ 2,101
		Equity	
		Reserve: hedge gain	$ 134

Moon Pacific has material accounts receivable and purchase orders from customers that are denominated in euros. The company follows a policy of hedging all exchange exposure with futures contracts.

Required:

1. Explain the conditions that cause a derivative instrument to be an asset or a liability.
2. Explain the use of derivatives to hedge exchange exposure caused by U.S. dollar accounts receivable.

3. Are gains and losses from derivatives included in earnings? Explain.

4. What conditions must be met for hedge accounting to be invoked?

5. What is the most likely explanation for the presence of the $134 hedge reserve?

 A15-24 Derivatives:

Starco Corp. wishes to purchase 8,000 shares of Gertrom Ltd., a publicly traded company. Starco contracts to buy the shares from a related party, Unit Ltd., for $73 per share in 120 days' time. The fair value was $73 per share on this day. One month later, at year-end, the fair value of the Gertrom shares is $62 per share, and it is $68 per share at the end of 120 days. At that time, the shares are bought, and the contract is closed out.

Required:

1. Is this a forward contract or a futures contract? Explain.

2. What risk is the company hedging?

3. Prepare journal entries to record the inception of the contract, the change in its fair value at year-end, and its maturity.

connect

 A15-25 Derivatives:

Dauphinee DL Corp. plans to purchase 100,000 shares of Santos Technology Ltd., a publicly traded company. Dauphinee has signed a contract to acquire the shares from Holding Co. in 90 days, after certain approvals are obtained; these approvals are routine but time consuming. The agreed-upon price per share is $22.50, which is the fair value of the shares on the day the contract was signed. Santos shares have traded between $5 and $35 over the last year; the industry has been volatile. Sixty days after signing this agreement, it is Dauphinee's year-end, and Santos shares are trading for $28. At the time the contract matured, and the shares are purchased; the shares are trading for $16.

Required:

1. Is this a forward contract or a futures contract? Explain.

2. What risk is the company hedging?

3. Prepare journal entries to record the inception of the contract, the change in its fair value at year-end, and its maturity.

A15-26 ASPE; Classification:

Eldon Ltd. is a private company that complies with ASPE. Eldon issued the following financial instruments in 20X4:

1. *Convertible debentures* issued at 103. The debentures require interest to be paid semi-annually at a nominal rate of 7% per annum. The debentures are convertible by the holder at any time up to final maturity at a ratio of 10 common shares for each $1,000 principal amount.

2. *Shareholder loans*, 3%, due on demand, issued at par. The shareholders do not intend to request repayment unless the company is dissolved. This money was advanced as a loan but is considered equity by the shareholder and the lenders.

3. *Redeemable preferred shares* issued to Eldon's founding family. The shares carry an annual cash dividend at the rate of $12 per share and have a repurchase option at the choice of the investor. The shares were issued as a tax planning mechanism and are high/low shares.

Required:

With reference to ASPE, discuss the appropriate financial statement classification of each of these financial instruments.

 A15-27 ASPE; Convertible Debt:

On 1 January 20X7, Cedar Ltd. issues $7,600,000 face amount of 6%, eight-year, convertible debentures. Interest is payable annually on 31 December. The debentures are convertible at the investor's option at an exchange price of $8 per share. The market rate of interest for nonconvertible bonds of similar risk and maturity is 7%. The net proceeds received by Cedar amounted to $8,200,000.

Required:

1. Cedar is a public company. Record the issuance of the bonds on 1 January 20X7, and the journal entry for interest expense on 31 December 20X7. Cedar uses the effective interest amortization for bond premium and discount.

2. Cedar is a private company and complies with ASPE. Record the issuance of the bonds on 1 January 20X7 and the journal entry for interest expense on 31 December 20X7. Cedar uses straight-line interest amortization for bond premium and discount.

3. Comment on the differences between requirements 1 and 2. Comment on the impact on the financial statements, and suggest a justification for the ASPE treatment.

 A15-28 ASPE, Share-based Compensation; Equity-Settled:

Happy Ltd. has an executive stock option plan as follows: Each qualified manager will receive, on 1 January, an option for the computed number of common shares at a computed price. The number of option shares and the option price are determined by the board of directors, with advice from the compensation committee. The options are nontransferable. The vesting period is three years. Options can be exercised after they vest but expire six years after the date of issuance.

On 1 January 20X5, executives were granted options. An option pricing model was used to value the options, and a value of $690,000 was estimated. The options allow 200,000 shares to be issued for $4 per share. Retention estimates were 80% and 85% at the end of 20X5 and 20X6. In fact, the options were in-the-money on the vesting date, and 185,000 shares were issued at the end of 20X7 when the shares were trading for $12 per share. The remaining options were forfeit: 8,000 in 20X6 and 7,000 in 20X7. All forfeits were caused by turnover.

Required:

1. Happy is a public company. Record the entry for compensation associated with options at the end of 20X5, 20X6, and 20X7 and also the entries for share issuance under options.

2. Happy is a private company and complies with ASPE. Repeat requirement 1, including entries for forfeit options. The company does not estimate forfeiture in advance.

3. Comment on the differences between requirements 1 and 2. Comment on the impact on the financial statements, and suggest a justification for the ASPE treatment.

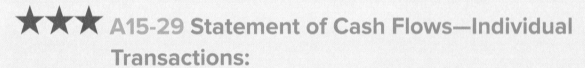

A15-29 Statement of Cash Flows—Individual Transactions:

The following cases are independent:

Case A

Information from the 31 December 20X7 SFP of Holdco Ltd.:

	20X7	20X6
Bonds payable	$2,600,000	$ —
Discount on bonds payable	121,680	—
Common stock conversion rights	361,400	—

Convertible bonds were issued during the year. Discount amortization was $7,280 in 20X7.

Case B

Information from the 31 December 20X7 SFP of Sellco Ltd.:

	20X7	20X6
Bonds payable	$ 2,400,000	$4,800,000
Discount on bonds payable	76,800	166,080
Common stock conversion rights	333,600	667,200
Common shares	8,160,000	3,408,000

One-half of the bonds converted to common shares during the period. Other common shares were issued for cash. Discount amortization during the year was $12,480.

Case C

Information from the 31 December 20X7 SFP of Buyco Ltd.:

	20X7	20X6
Stock options outstanding	$ 294,018	$ 389,400
Common shares	11,880,000	8,646,000

During the year, 13,200 stock options originally valued at a price of $7.26 were exercised, and 13,200 common shares were issued for the exercise price of $18,48. One million stock options, issued for nil consideration, allowing qualified shareholders to acquire common shares at one-tenth the then-current fair value in the event of hostile takeover, were also issued during the year. Other common shares were sold for cash.

Case D

Information from the 31 December 20X7 SFP of Bothco Ltd.:

	20X7	20X6
Bonds payable	$ —	$7,000,000
Discount on bonds payable	—	53,420
Common stock conversion rights	—	2,417,000
Contributed capital, lapse of conversion rights	2,417,000	—

Bonds payable matured in the year but were redeemed in cash at par and not converted.

Required:

For each case, list the appropriate items on the statement of cash flows caused by issuance, conversion, or derecognition of financial instruments. Do not include disclosure of interest or accounts related to interest expense (e.g., do not list discount amortization).

 **A15-30 Statement of Cash Flows—Comprehensive Equity:**

The following data are related to Eli Products Ltd.:

	20X9	20X8
Bonds payable, 7%	$10,000,000	$ 0
Discount on bonds payable	(690,000)	0
6% Preferred share liability, due 20X11	500,000	500,000
5% Preferred shares, no-par	2,600,000	2,600,000
Common shares, no-par	8,068,000	5,000,000
Contributed capital: common stock conversion rights	525,000	0
Contributed capital: common share retirement	150,000	0

Contributed capital: employee stock options outstanding	387,500	160,000
Contributed capital on treasury stock transactions	165,000	0
Retained earnings	7,005,000	6,940,000
Treasury stock, 5% preferred shares	(500,000)	0

During the year, the following transactions took place and have been correctly recorded:

a. Reported earnings and comprehensive income was $3,200,000. Cash dividends were paid at the end of the year.

b. Retained earnings was reduced by $175,000 as the result of share issue costs.

c. Earnings includes $400,000 of compensation expense recorded for options to employees and also an amount for the 6% preferred share dividends.

d. There was a common share stock dividend during the year that resulted in a reduction to retained earnings of $710,000.

e. Common shares with an average original issuance price of $500,000 were retired during the year.

f. 5% preferred shares with an original average book value of $900,000 were purchased as treasury shares early in the fiscal year. Half were resold almost immediately, and half were kept.

g. Additional common shares were issued for cash, as a stock dividend, and for the options in (i).

h. Convertible bonds were issued during the year. Discount amortization of $41,500 was recorded by the end of the year.

i. Employee stock options, along with $100,000 of cash, were exchanged for common shares during the year.

j. Any remaining change in accounts should be assumed to flow from a logical transaction.

Required:

1. List the items and amounts that caused the retained earnings account to change from its opening to closing balance. For the dividend through retained earnings, specify the amount to each share class.

2. List the items and amounts that caused the common share account to change from its opening to closing balance.

3. List the items that would appear in the financing activities section of the SCF. The company classifies dividends in the operating activities section.

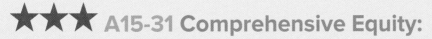 **A15-31 Comprehensive Equity:**

Acer Corp. reported the following balances at 1 January 20X1:

Interest liability—8% bond ($10,000,000 par value). Conversion into 76,000 common shares at maturity is mandatory	$ 4,997,000
Share equity—8% bond	5,102,000
Convertible $8, no-par preferred shares, 60,000 shares outstanding; convertible into 8 common shares for every 3 preferred shares outstanding	6,060,000
Class A no-par common shares, unlimited shares authorized, 915,000 issued and outstanding	32,940,000

Common share warrants, allowing purchase of 90,000 shares at $32.50	660,000
Contributed capital: employee share options outstanding*	160,000
Contributed capital on preferred share retirement	55,000
Retained earnings	116,300,000
Less: Treasury shares, 16,000 common shares	(512,000)

*Forty thousand common stock options are outstanding to certain employees allowing purchase of one share for every two options held at a price of $27.50 per share. These options are vested and expire in 20X4.

The following events took place in 20X1:

a. Common shares were issued to employees under the terms of existing outstanding share options. 16,000 options were exercised when the share market value was $45.

b. Options were issued in exchange for a piece of land, appraised at $75,000. The options allow purchase of 100,000 shares at $15 each in five years' time. The market value of the shares was $46 on this date. The option was valued at $81,000 using the Black-Scholes option pricing model.

c. 40,000 common shares were acquired and retired at a price of $47 each.

d. 10,000 common treasury shares were acquired at a price of $44 per share.

e. A cash dividend was declared and paid. The annual dividend for the preferred shares and $1 per share for the common shares were both declared and paid.

f. 24,000 preferred shares were converted to common shares.

g. The annual interest expense was accrued on the 8% bonds, using the effective rate of 7.8%. The annual payment was made.

h. Two-thirds of the common share warrants outstanding at the beginning of the year were exercised when the market value of the shares was $49.50; the remainder lapsed.

i. Options were granted to employees at the beginning of the year, allowing purchase of one share for every two options held at a price of $35. Fifty thousand options were issued. These options become vested at the beginning of 20X5. The fair value of the options was $720,000 and the retention rate for the employee groups covered was estimated at 90%.

j. 10,000 preferred shares were retired for $107 each.

k. 20,000 treasury shares were sold for $32 each.

l. A 10% stock dividend was declared and issued. Treasury shares were not eligible for the stock dividend. The board of directors decided that the stock dividend should be valued at $30 per share. Most of the dividend was issued in whole shares; however, 41,000 fractional shares allowing acquisition of 4,100 whole shares were issued.

Required:

1. Provide journal entries (or memo entries) for the events listed.
2. Calculate the closing balance in each of the listed accounts at 31 December 20X1, reflecting the entries in requirement 1. Earnings for the year were $6,200,000, including interest in (g) and stock option expense in (i).

Solution

CHAPTER 16

Corporate Income Tax

INTRODUCTION

Accounting for corporate income tax might seem rather straightforward. After all, the exact amount of income tax for each year is computed on the corporation's income tax return. However, income tax expense usually differs from income tax paid in a year; the outcome is that deferred income tax must be recognized on the statement of financial position (SFP), resulting from *interperiod income tax allocation*.

For example, Andrew Peller Ltd. reported 2014 pre-tax earnings of $19.2 million. The company paid $3.2 million to the government in income taxes, but the SCI shows income tax expense of $5.2 million. On Andrew Peller's SFP is a long-term *deferred income tax* liability of $15.8 million, which increased by $2 million in 2014. Why is this income tax a *deferred liability*?

The reason is that many individual assets (and liabilities) have different accounting treatment as compared to their tax treatment. These financial statement elements will have an *accounting carrying value* that differs from their *tax basis*. That difference will have an impact on the income tax that will be due in a future period when the asset is realized, used, or disposed. Accountants recognize the future tax consequences in the accounts as *deferred income tax*. Deferred income tax liabilities are not amounts that are actually owed to the government in the current period.

The subject of this chapter is the method of accounting for income tax, a subject that has been both complex and controversial. The major conceptual alternatives are summarized in Appendix 1 to this chapter, while the chapter provides coverage of the requirements of the standards that we now apply. A second aspect of income tax accounting pertains to the recognition of future benefits of tax loss carryforwards. This is the topic of discussion in Chapter 17.

One other aspect of accounting for income tax is the *investment tax credit*, a special tax provision intended to encourage certain types of capital investment by businesses. This specialized topic is discussed in Appendix 2 to this chapter.

One important note about the chapter title: only corporations are subject to income tax because only corporations are recognized as legal entities. The profits of partnerships and proprietorships are taxed as income of the owners. Income tax expense does not appear on the financial statements of either partnerships or proprietorships.

INCOME TAX PROVISION VERSUS EXPENSE

It is common in practice for companies to label income tax expense as the **provision for income tax**. This is a somewhat confusing label because we usually use "provision" to indicate an estimated liability, such as "Provision for Warranty Costs."

Companies use the term "provision" for income tax expense because when a company has a loss for tax purposes, the income statement entry for income tax may be a credit rather than a debit. Rather than switch the income statement label from "expense" to "recovery," companies use the vague term "provision" to fit all circumstances. IFRS does not apply the word "provision" to an income tax expense or recovery, but the term is used in practice.

In this book, to avoid confusion between the expense item and the tax liability, we will typically use the title "income tax expense," even when the expense is a credit (i.e., a recovery of previously paid income taxes).

INTERPERIOD TAX ALLOCATION—INTRODUCTION

Interperiod tax allocation deals with allocating tax expense to an appropriate year, regardless of when it is actually paid. A company adopts those accounting policies that management perceives will best satisfy the objectives of financial statement users and preparers. One broad objective of accounting standards and accounting policies is to measure earnings, which usually is the result of many accruals, interperiod allocations, and estimates. In contrast, the major objective of the *Income Tax Act* and Regulations is to generate revenue for the government.

Tax policy is complex. Because it is easier and more objective to assess tax when cash is flowing, *tax policy generally favours taxing revenues and expenses on the basis of cash flows* rather than coping with the results of accounting allocations. Of course, some tax policies use allocation, especially in the area of cost of goods sold and inventories, and depreciation and capital assets. In addition, the *Income Tax Act* exempts certain types of income from taxation and prohibits the deduction of certain types of expenses.

Differences between Taxable and Accounting Income

Both accounting income and taxable income are the net result of recognizing revenues and expenses (and gains and losses) of a period. Most items of revenue and expense are recognized in the same period for both accounting and tax purposes. But there are some significant differences. These differences can be categorized as:

- Permanent differences; or
- Temporary differences.

Permanent Differences

A **permanent difference** arises when a financial statement earnings element—a revenue, gain, expense, or loss—enters the computation of either taxable income or pre-tax accounting income but NEVER enters into the computation of the other. For example, dividend revenue received from another tax-paying Canadian corporation is included in accounting earnings but is NEVER included in taxable income. Such dividends are tax-exempt revenue. They are a non-reversing or *permanent* difference because they are not subject to taxation.

Similarly, a company may sell land that it has held for a long time. Since land is a capital asset, the gain from selling the land is known as a *capital gain* for tax purposes. The full amount of the gain will be recognized in earnings, but only 50% of a capital gain is included in taxable income. Therefore, the 50% of a capital gain that is *not* taxed is a permanent difference because it is in accounting earnings but NEVER in taxable income.

Certain types of expenses are NEVER deductible for tax purposes. A common example is golf club dues paid by a corporation. The *Income Tax Act* specifically identifies golf club dues as non-deductible for tax purposes, but they are a legitimate expense if the corporation believes they should be part of, say, a sales or marketing effort. Therefore, the difference between pre-tax accounting income and taxable income that arises from golf club dues is a permanent difference. Another example of a nondeductible expense is an interest or penalty assessed by the tax department because of a late tax instalment payment. The *Income Tax Act* does not allow this as a deduction, but it is an acceptable expense in accounting earnings.

There also may be deductions that are allowed in computing taxable income that have no equivalent for accounting income. In some years, for example, companies have been permitted to deduct tax depreciation, called *capital cost allowance*, or CCA, based on an amount higher than the cost basis of the assets (e.g., the CCA rate could be based on 150% of the specified asset's cost). Since accounting depreciation expense can never exceed 100% of an asset's cost, the excess CCA is a permanent difference.

Temporary Differences

A **temporary difference** arises when there is going to be the same total earnings and tax revenue or expense OVER TIME, but the pattern is different. As a result, the SFP tax basis of an asset or liability differs from its accounting carrying value over time.

Origination and Reversal

A temporary difference *originates* in the period in which it first enters the computation of either taxable income or accounting income and *reverses* in the subsequent period when that item enters into the computation of the other measure. An item can either:

- Be included in accounting income first and then included in taxable income in a subsequent period; or
- Enter into the calculation of taxable income first and then be included in accounting income in a later period.

A temporary difference can result from a revenue or expense, tied to a specific SFP item. For example, depreciation versus CCA is a common temporary difference, tied to the capital asset on the SFP.

An estimated warranty liability (provision) is accrued for accounting purposes when the company becomes obligated under a sales agreement. For income tax purposes, warranty costs are not allowed as a deduction until the warranty work is completed in the future (i.e., when cash is spent). Since the accounting expense and the tax expense will be equal over time, but are different in any given year, this is a temporary difference that is linked to the warranty provision. In the *originating year*, the accounting expense is not tax deductible. An accounting provision for a warranty obligation is recognized on the SFP. When warranty work is done and cash is spent, there is no additional accounting expense but the accounting provision is reduced. For tax purposes, though, there *is* an expense. This is the point that the tax treatment "catches up" with a tax deduction allowed.

To recap:

- A temporary difference is said to *originate* when the difference between accounting recognition and tax treatment first arises or when a recurring temporary difference *increases* the accumulated balance of temporary differences.
- A temporary difference is said to *reverse* when the accumulated temporary differences are *reduced* by the "catch-up" recognition for tax and accounting.

Examples

Exhibit 16-1 lists some of the more common types of permanent differences and temporary differences.

EXHIBIT 16-1

EXAMPLES OF PERMANENT AND TEMPORARY DIFFERENCES IN CANADA

Permanent Differences

- Dividends received by Canadian corporations from some other taxable Canadian corporations
- Equity in earnings of significantly influenced associate companies
- 50% of capital gains and losses

- Golf club dues
- 50% of meals and entertainment expenses
- Interest and penalties on taxes
- Political contributions

Temporary Differences

- Depreciation for accounting purposes; CCA for tax
- Amortization of capitalized development costs for accounting; immediate deduction for tax
- Amortization of capitalized interest for accounting; deducted when paid for tax
- Writedown (and writedown reversals) of investments, or tangible capital assets for accounting; loss recognized only when realized for tax
- Writedown (and writedown reversals) of inventories valued at the lower of cost and net realizable value for accounting; taxed when realized
- Instalment sales income recognized for accounting at time of sale; taxed when cash received
- Bad debt expenses recognized in year of sale for accounting; tax deductible when uncollectible
- Capital assets written up under the revaluation method; no taxable gain until asset class closed
- Fair value increases for investment properties or biological assets; gain taxable only when property is sold
- Warranty costs accrued for accounting in period of sale; tax deductible when paid
- Bond discount or premium, amortized for accounting but taxable expense or revenue only when the principal is settled at maturity

CONCEPT REVIEW

1. Explain why accounting income is different from taxable income.
2. What is a non-reversing or permanent difference? Give an example.
3. A company deducts warranty expense in 20X0 but pays warranty claims in 20X1. In what year does this temporary difference originate? In what year does it reverse?

CONCEPTUAL ISSUES IN INTERPERIOD TAX ALLOCATION

Choice of accounting policy for income tax accounting standards was an area of controversy for many years, and there have been many alternative policies adopted around the world at various points in time. Fortunately, this area has been stable for many years. Conceptually, there are three basic underlying policy issues:

1. The extent of allocation;
2. The measurement method; and
3. Discounting.

The standards require the following in these critical policy areas:

1. The extent of allocation	All temporary differences give rise to deferred income tax. This is called **comprehensive, or full, allocation.** Tax expense is based on tax payable combined with the effect of temporary differences.	ASPE *allows* use of the comprehensive method of tax allocation. However, ASPE *also allows* companies, if they choose, to NOT record deferred tax for ANY temporary differences. This is called the **taxes payable method** because tax expense is based only on tax payable.
2. The measurement method	Deferred tax amounts are measured using the best estimate of the tax rate that will be in effect when the temporary difference reverses; this must be an enacted tax rate. Future years' tax rates are used if they are enacted or substantially enacted. If there are no future rates enacted, the current year tax rate is used. If the enacted tax rate changes, deferred tax amounts must be updated to the new rate. This is called the **liability method**, or the *accrual method.*	
Discounting	Deferred tax amounts are not discounted.	

The second two issues are explained in more depth in Appendix 1 to this chapter.

Extent of Allocation

You can see that IFRS and ASPE may be very different when it comes to the *extent of allocation*, the first issue raised above. The *extent of allocation* refers to the range of temporary differences that give rise to deferred income tax.

Taxes Payable Method

The taxes payable method recognizes the amount of taxes assessed in each year as the income tax expense for that year:

> Taxes payable method: Income tax expense = current income tax payable
>
> *There are no deferred tax amounts recognized from any temporary difference.*

This method is also known as the **flow-through method** because the actual taxes paid "flow through" to earnings.

Advocates of the taxes payable method argue that:

- Income tax is an aggregate measure, applied to the overall operations of the company as a whole and it is artificial to disaggregate the income tax amount.
- The taxes payable method corresponds with the actual cash outflow for income tax. If cash flow prediction is a primary objective of financial reporting, the taxes payable method may be superior to earnings measured by using full allocation.

- Viewed in the aggregate, temporary differences in a stable or growing company typically reverse and originate each year, with new originating temporary differences replacing those that are reversing. As a result, these aggregated temporary differences are "permanent" and will never result in a real cash flow to decrease deferred income tax.
- The "future liability" that is created through tax allocation is not a genuine obligation—the government does not view the deferred tax "liability" as an amount owed to the government, and there certainly is no legal or constructive obligation to pay that amount.

Comprehensive Tax Allocation

The comprehensive tax allocation method recognizes both the current income tax payable and *the tax effect of all temporary differences that arise* when determining the income tax expense for that year:

> Comprehensive tax allocation method: Income tax expense = current income tax payable + the change in deferred tax balances
>
> *All temporary differences give rise to deferred tax amounts*

Those who support *comprehensive tax allocation* argue that:

- A future cash flow impact arises from all temporary differences, no matter how far in the future that impact occurs. Tax "saved" this year via an early tax deduction will have to be "paid" in a future year when the expense is recognized for accounting but cannot be deducted for tax.
- It is a serious violation of the recognition criteria to omit an inevitable deferred income tax amount. The SFP is incomplete without deferred income tax.
- While aggregate temporary differences may not decline, the individual temporary differences that make up the aggregate do, in fact, reverse, even if they are replaced by new temporary differences.

Example

The following example illustrates the taxes payable method and the comprehensive tax allocation method.

Suppose that Bowen Ltd. has pre-tax income in each of 20X1, 20X2, and 20X3 of $1,000,000. The first year's income includes a revenue amount of $400,000 that will not be collected until 20X3. As a result, there is a $400,000 account receivable on the books. There will be taxable revenue of $400,000, but not until the money is collected in 20X3. Since total accounting income and taxable income are the same over time, but the timing is different, this is a temporary difference related to the $400,000 accounts receivable. Bowen's income tax rate is 35%.

If Bowen gives no recognition to the temporary difference, and uses the taxes payable method:

- The company's taxable income will be $600,000 in 20X1, $1,000,000 in 20X2, and $1,400,000 in 20X3.
- Using the income tax rate of 35%, the taxes due for each period are $210,000 in 20X1, $350,000 in 20X2, and $490,000 in 20X3.

This information is summarized as follows:

	20X1	20X2	20X3
Income before taxes (accounting basis)	$ 1,000,000	$ 1,000,000	$ 1,000,000
20X1 accounting gain that is taxable in 20X3	− 400,000		+ 400,000
Taxable income	$ 600,000	$ 1,000,000	$ 1,400,000
Tax rate	× 35%	× 35%	× 35%
Income tax assessed for the year	$ 210,000	$ 350,000	$ 490,000

Under the *taxes payable method*, each year's full tax assessment *flows through* to tax expense and earnings:

	20X1	20X2	20X3
Earnings before income tax	$ 1,000,000	$ 1,000,000	$ 1,000,000
Income tax expense	210,000	350,000	490,000
Earnings	$ 790,000	$ 650,000	$ 510,000

In the view of most accountants, reporting on a taxes payable basis "distorts" earnings because the income tax relating to the $400,000 revenue is reported in 20X3, while the revenue itself is reported in 20X1. The corporation's reported earnings appear to decline significantly from 20X1 through 20X3, but the difference is due solely to the fact that income tax on part of the 20X1 revenue is included in income tax expense for 20X3.

When the *comprehensive tax allocation method* is used, the $400,000 temporary difference relating to the account receivable gives rise to a future (or *deferred*) income tax impact of $140,000 (i.e., $400,000 × 35%). The $140,000 income tax impact of the $400,000 revenue is recognized in the same period (for accounting purposes) as the revenue itself:

	20X1	20X2	20X3
Earnings before income tax	$1,000,000	$1,000,000	$1,000,000
Income tax expense:			
Current	210,000	350,000	490,000
Deferred	140,000	—	(140,000)
	350,000	350,000	350,000
Earnings	$ 650,000	$ 650,000	$ 650,000

The entry to record income tax expense in each year is:

20X1		
Income tax expense (I/S)	350,000	
Income tax payable (B/S)		210,000
Deferred income tax liability (B/S)		140,000

20X2		
Income tax expense (I/S)	350,000	
Income tax payable (B/S)		350,000
20X3		
Income tax expense (I/S)	350,000	
Deferred income tax liability (B/S)	140,000	
Income tax payable (B/S)		490,000

The deferred income tax liability originates in 20X1. It will be shown on the SFP at the end of 20X1 and 20X2, and then is *drawn down in* 20X3 when the temporary difference *reverses* and the tax is actually due. Note the distinction in terminology:

- A temporary difference *reverses*, while
- The deferred income tax liability/asset that relates to the temporary difference is *drawn down.*

Tax Rate to Use: The Liability Method

Accounting standards require use of the liability method to measure deferred income tax. This means that the tax rate that is expected to be in force in a future year is used to measure deferred tax. However, estimates of future rates are not acceptable. Only *enacted rates* are acceptable. This is to enhance reliability. Sometimes future tax rates are approved in advance, but sometimes not. As a result:

1. If a tax rate for a future year is *enacted, or substantially enacted* by the end of the current year, then the future rate is used. (*Substantially enacted* means that legislation has been drafted and presented in Council or Parliament, but has not yet been passed.)

2. If a tax rate for a future year is not enacted or substantially enacted by the end of the current year, then the *tax rate for the current year must be used as the most reliable surrogate* for a future tax rate.

In the example above, the tax rate was 35% for all years, so choice of a tax rate was not a problem.

CONCEPT REVIEW

1. Describe the taxes payable method of accounting for income tax expense.
2. Why does comprehensive tax allocation result in better income reporting?
3. What tax rate is used to measure a deferred tax amount in Year 1 that is expected to reverse in Year 4?

APPROACH TO INCOME TAX QUESTIONS

We will approach income tax questions in three steps:

Step 1—Calculate taxable income and income tax payable.

Step 2—Determine the change in deferred income tax accounts.

Step 3—Combine income tax payable with the change in deferred income tax accounts to determine tax expense for the year.

After finishing these three steps, we can determine the current-year presentation and account balances. Note that this approach is often called the *balance sheet approach*, as it is driven by balance sheet accounts—income tax payable and deferred income tax. This three-step approach provides a robust calculation methodology that also provides proof of balance sheet accounts.

We will look at a shortcut approach later in the chapter that can be used *only when tax rates have not changed*. However, be aware that corporate tax rates (federal and provincial) tend to change rather frequently.

Step 1—Calculate Taxable Income and Income Tax Payable

To calculate taxable income, first adjust accounting income for temporary and permanent differences. Such differences are typically identified in the data and must be sorted into permanent and temporary differences, and those items that are added back versus subtracted. Start with accounting income, and identify the differences.

- An expense now in earnings, but is not tax deductible, must be added back (e.g., depreciation, fines, golf club dues).
- A revenue now in earnings, but is not taxable, is subtracted (e.g., dividend revenue).
- An expense not in earnings, but allowable for tax purposes, is subtracted (e.g., CCA).
- A revenue that is taxable, but not in earnings this year, is added (e.g., collections of accounts receivable that are taxable this year but were revenue in a prior year, like our $400,000 20X3 taxable revenue in the prior example).

After calculating taxable income, multiply by the *current tax rate* to obtain income tax payable.

Example

The following facts pertain to accounting and taxable income for Mirage Ltd. in 20X1, Mirage's first year of operations:

- Earnings before taxes are $825,000.
- In determining pre-tax earnings, Mirage deducted the following expenses:
  - Political contribution of $10,000;
  - Golf club dues of $25,000;
  - Accrued estimated warranty expense of $150,000; and
  - Depreciation of $200,000 (Mirage owns capital assets of $1,600,000, which are being depreciated straight-line over eight years).
- For tax purposes, Mirage deducts the following expenses:
  - Actual warranty costs incurred of $100,000; and
  - Capital cost allowance (CCA) of $300,000.
- The 20X1 tax rate is 30%.

The golf club dues and political contribution are permanent differences because this expense is not deductible for tax purposes at any point in time. The warranty costs and CCA/depreciation are temporary differences, relating to the SFP accounts, provision for warranty liability and capital assets, respectively.

When accounting earnings are adjusted for permanent differences, the result is *accounting income subject to tax*. In this example, the result is $860,000. Temporary differences are then included, to yield taxable income of $810,000. Multiplying by the tax rate gives tax payable, $243,000.

Pre-tax accounting income		$825,000
Permanent differences		
Political contribution		+ 10,000
Golf club dues		+ 25,000
Accounting income subject to tax		860,000
Temporary differences		
Warranty expenses accrued, not tax deductible	+150,000	
Warranty costs incurred, tax deductible	−100,000	+ 50,000
Depreciation, not tax deductible	+200,000	
Capital cost allowance (CCA), tax deductible	−300,000	−100,000
Taxable income		$810,000
Tax rate		× 30%
Income tax payable		$243,000

Exhibit 16-2 summarizes the calculation of taxable income and extends the example for three years: 20X1, 20X2, and 20X3. Data is assumed for 20X2 and 20X3. In each year, but not in advance, Parliament legislated a reduction in tax rates to 28% for 20X2 and then to 27% for 20X3.

Each column shows the adjustments for permanent differences, then the two types of temporary differences: warranty costs and CCA/depreciation. Income tax payable is then calculated from taxable income using the tax rate of each year.

EXHIBIT 16-2			
MIRAGE LIMITED—CALCULATION OF TAXABLE INCOME			
	20X1	**20X2**	**20X3**
Net income, before tax	$825,000	$900,000	$725,000
Permanent differences			
Political contributions	+ 10,000	0	0
Golf club dues	+ 25,000	+ 25,000	+ 30,000
Accounting income subject to tax	860,000	925,000	755,000
Timing differences			
Warranty expense	+ 150,000	+200,000	+160,000
Warranty claims paid	− 100,000	−140,000	−230,000
Depreciation	+200,000	+200,000	+200,000
Capital cost allowance (CCA)	−300,000	−240,000	− 180,000
Taxable income	$810,000	$945,000	$705,000
Enacted tax rate	30%	28%	27%
Income tax payable	$243,000	$264,600	$190,350

If the *taxes payable method* is used, analysis stops at this point. Tax expense is equal to tax payable, and no other financial statement elements are created.

We will return to the Mirage example later.

Step 2—Determine the Change in Deferred Income Tax

Deferred income tax is caused when the carrying value (book value) of an asset or liability is different for tax versus accounting. The change in deferred income tax can be calculated in total, from all sources. However, a total calculation is not quite adequate because individual types of temporary differences will reverse in different years. Thus, to determine the change in deferred income tax from year to year, *we must calculate the required balance in deferred income tax for each source of temporary difference.* We will then compare this required closing balance to the existing balance and get the adjustment needed.

We will use a table for this calculation. The following example table has some data filled in for a hypothetical capital asset example, for Smith Co., which we will explain as we proceed. Assume that the enacted tax rates are 30% for Year 1 and 25% for Year 2; these rates are enacted in the year to which they pertain:

	[1]	[2]	[3]	[4]	[5]	[6]
				$\times\, t =$		
		Less:	$=$	Deferred Tax	Less:	
		Accounting	Year-End Temporary	Liability, Year-End	Opening	$=$
	Tax Basis	Basis	Difference	Balance	Balance	Adjustment
Year 1 (30% tax rate)						
Capital asset	$172,000	$190,000	$(18,000)	$(5,400)	0	$(5,400)
Year 2 (25% tax rate)						
Capital asset	$136,000	$160,000	$(24,000)	$(6,000)	$(5,400)	$ (600)

This table tracks:

- *Tax carrying value* (column 1);
- *Accounting carrying value* (column 2);
- The difference between column 1 and column 2 (column 3);
- The closing balance in deferred tax (column 4);
- The opening deferred tax balance (column 5); and
- The needed adjustment for each year (column 6).

Note that the year-end balance is in column 4 and the journal entry amount is in column 6.

Looking at the table, column by column:

Column 1—If there were a set of books kept for tax purposes, this would be the balance in the capital assets account. In this example, a capital asset was bought for $200,000 at the beginning of Year 1, and $28,000 of CCA was charged for tax purposes in Year 1. CCA, of course, is the tax equivalent of depreciation, so cost less accumulated CCA is $172,000. Looking vertically down this column, CCA was $36,000 in Year 2, bringing tax book value down to $136,000. These amounts are assets, so the numbers are not in parentheses.

Column 2—This is the net book value of capital assets on the books of the company. This $200,000 asset had $10,000 of depreciation in Year 1 and $30,000 in Year 2. Net book value is therefore $190,000 in Year 1 and $160,000 in Year 2. Again, the amounts are assets and are not in parentheses.

Column 3—Column 3 is calculated by subtracting column 2 from column 1. Note that the difference is negative because column 2 is the larger number; the column 3 amount is in parentheses because it is negative.

Column 4—Column 4 is calculated by multiplying column 3 by the enacted tax rate. This is $5,400 in Year 1 ($18,000 × 30%) and $6,000 in Year 2 ($24,000 × 25%). This is in parentheses; it keeps its character as a negative number, which means it will be a credit account. Column 4 is important—it is the *closing statement of financial position* balance of deferred income tax.

Column 5—Column 5 is the opening balance in the deferred income tax account. In Year 1, it is zero, assuming that this is the first year of the temporary difference. In subsequent years, the opening balance is the closing balance of the prior year. That is, the $5,400 closing balance in Year 1 is the opening balance in Year 2. In our case, the Year 2 opening balance was a credit and, thus, is in parentheses.

Column 6—This is the adjustment column, and is the difference between the desired year-end balance (4) and the opening balance (5). It can be either a debit or a credit. In our example, the credit balance grows each time, so additional credits, in parentheses, are needed. *These amounts are part of the journal entries prepared.*

Tax Rate to Use: The Liability Method

Accounting standards require use of the liability method to measure deferred income tax. This policy decision dictates the use of the current enacted tax rate, unless a future tax rate is enacted in advance. In this example, the tax rate changed from 30% in Year 1 to 25% in Year 2, but the rate change was enacted in Year 2. In Year 1, the 30% had to be used to measure deferred income tax. The Year 2 rate was used in Year 2.

Impact of the change in tax rate   Deferred tax is credited for $600 in Year 2. What has caused this $600 change? Two things are going on:

- The change in tax rate from 30% to 25%, applied to the beginning balance of the temporary difference, has caused a $900 decrease (debit) that affects the opening balance; and

- There is an increase in deferred tax caused by the new temporary difference of $6,000, multiplied by the current tax rate; this results in a credit of $1,500.

That is:

(1) $(18,000) × (−5)% rate change	$ 900
(2) $(6,000) × 25% tax rate for Year 2	(1,500)
	$ (600)

Observe that the table simply produces the $600 adjustment in Year 2, and thus automatically captures the two factors that affect the year-end closing balance of the deferred tax amount. Separate calculation of the impact of these two factors is not necessary but it has to be included in the disclosure notes, as we will discuss later.

The deferred tax table provides complete documentation of the sources of deferred income tax. Most columns are straightforward. The problematic columns are the first two—determining the tax basis and accounting basis of temporary differences.

Determining the Accounting Basis

Think about the common sources of temporary differences listed in the first column below, and note the related statement of financial position account that gives rise to each type of temporary difference:

Source of Temporary Difference	Related SFP Account
Depreciation and amortization	Net book value of capital assets, tangible and/or intangible
Inventory writedowns and reversals	Inventory
Fair-value adjustments	Investment property or biological assets
Revenue	Accounts receivable or deferred revenue
Warranty	Warranty provision

Source of Temporary Difference	Related SFP Account
Bond discount and premium amortization	Net bond liability
Revaluation surplus	Capital assets

Determining the Tax Basis

Determining the tax basis can be complicated. We have already seen that for capital assets, the notional "tax balance sheet" would show cost less accumulated CCA charged. Cost less accumulated CCA is referred to as *undepreciated capital cost*, or UCC. As another example, assume that inventory is written down from cost of $400,000 to net realizable value of $375,000 on the books. The accounting basis is $375,000, but the expense is not allowable for tax purposes until the inventory is sold, and therefore the inventory has a tax basis of $400,000.

With respect to assets:

- For monetary assets (i.e., receivables), the tax basis of a taxable asset is its accounting carrying value less any amount *that will be added to taxable income in future periods.*

- For non-monetary assets, the tax basis is the tax-deductible amount less all amounts *already deducted* in determining taxable income of the current and prior periods.

With respect to liabilities:

- For monetary liabilities, the tax basis is the accounting carrying value less any amount *that will be deductible for income tax in future periods.*

- For non-monetary liabilities (e.g., unearned revenue), the tax basis is its carrying amounts less any amount that *will not be taxable in future periods.*

An important aspect of these definitions of tax basis is that they all relate to future impacts on taxable income. That is, the tax bases are determined with respect to both the past and future impacts on taxable income.

Application

The following examples apply these rules to determine the tax basis of financial statement elements:

- Company A owns bonds of Company Z. Interest income of $15,000 is accrued by Company A on 31 December 20X5, which will be received on 28 February 20X6. Interest will be taxable income when the cash is received. That is, Company A reports $15,000 interest income in earnings for 20X5, but the interest will not be taxed until 20X6. The tax basis of the interest receivable is zero: the carrying value of $15,000 less the amount that will be taxable in the future, which is the full $15,000.

- Company B has capital assets. The tax basis of this non-monetary asset is the tax-deductible amount, its full cost, less accumulated tax deductions to date, or accumulated CCA.

- Company C has a $45,000 warranty liability. The accounting liability is established because an expense is charged on the books, some of which is paid in the period but $45,000 of which will be paid in the future. For tax purposes, warranty claims are deducted when paid—in the future. The tax basis is the accounting carrying value, $45,000, less amounts that will be deducted in the future, the whole $45,000. Therefore, the tax basis is *zero*.

- Company D has a $75,000 unearned revenue account. The cash was received, and is taxable, in this period. It will be recognized in earnings later, when earned. The tax basis is *zero*: the accounting carrying value of $75,000 less the amount already included in taxable income; it will therefore not be taxable again in the future.

You must carefully reason your way through these definitions, then do a reality check: *For asset and liability items other than capital assets, the tax basis is often zero.* If there is a non-zero tax basis for an account related to a temporary difference, check your logic carefully! A non-zero result is plausible but relatively rare other than for capital assets and asset writedowns.

Permanent Differences Do Not Create Deferred Income Tax

By definition, permanent differences do not create deferred income tax. However, there may be statement of financial position accounts that relate to permanent differences (e.g., prepaid golf club dues). If this is the case, the tax basis is equal to the accounting basis.

For example, suppose that a company has been fined $2,000 for a late income tax payment. The fine is not yet paid, and the company carries it as a current liability. Fines imposed by CRA are not deductible for income tax purposes. Therefore, the tax basis of the fine is $2,000.

Clearly, the fine is a permanent difference and will have no tax impact. The fine has already been included in accounting income, since it has been accrued. For a monetary liability, the rule is that the tax basis is the accounting value ($2,000) less the amount that will be deductible for tax purposes (zero), so the tax basis is $2,000.

Since the tax basis is equal to the accounting basis for permanent differences, deferred income taxes are always zero for these items, and we simply exclude them from the table.

The equation becomes more complicated when an asset is partially tax deductible. For example, certain intangible assets, such as purchased goodwill and purchased subscription lists, are classified as eligible capital property for tax purposes, and 75% of the cost is subject to CCA at a declining-balance rate of 7%. The other 25% of the cost is not tax-deductible and therefore is a permanent difference. The tax basis is determined separately for the two components that make up the accounting carrying value. The cost of these assets must be broken down, with 75% included in calculations of deferred income tax and 25% excluded.

Example

To illustrate the calculation of deferred income tax balances and adjustments, we will return to the Mirage Ltd. example.

At the end of 20X1, the tax bases and the accounting carrying values are as follows:

	Tax Basis dr. (cr.)	Carrying Value dr. (cr.)
Capital assets	$1,300,000	$1,400,000
Accrued warranty liability	0	(50,000)

The tax basis of the capital assets is the cost less accumulated CCA claimed: $1,600,000 − $300,000 = $1,300,000. Similarly, the carrying value of the capital assets is the cost less accumulated depreciation. Since 20X1 is the first year of operations and the year in which the assets were acquired, the carrying value is $1,600,000 − $200,000 = $1,400,000.

The carrying value of the warranty liability is the year-end balance in the accrual account: $150,000 − $100,000 = $50,000. The tax basis for a monetary liability is the accounting carrying value less the amounts that will be deducted for tax purposes in the future. Therefore, the tax basis of the warranty liability is $50,000 − $50,000 = $0.

These values are entered in the table in Exhibit 16-3, in columns 1 and 2. The difference between columns 1 and 2 is the temporary difference, shown in column 3. Columns 4 to 6 are completed by applying the tax rate, entering the zero opening balances for this first year of operation, and then subtracting.

EXHIBIT 16-3

MIRAGE LIMITED—DEFERRED INCOME TAX TABLE

	[1] Year-End Tax Basis dr. (cr.)	[2] Year-End Accounting Carrying Value dr. (cr.)	[3] = [1] − [2] Temporary Difference Deductible (Taxable)	[4] = [3] × t Deferred Tax Asset (Liability) at Year-End Rate	[5] = Previous Year Beginning Balance [4] dr. (cr.)	[6] = [4] − [5] Adjustment for Current Year dr. (cr.)
20X1—30%						
Capital assets	$ 1,300,000	$ 1,400,000	$ (100,000)	$ (30,000)	0	$ (30,000)
Accrued warranty liability	0	(50,000)	50,000	15,000	0	15,000
Total	$ 1,300,000	$ 1,350,000	$ (50,000)	$ (15,000)	0	$ (15,000)
20X2—28%						
Capital assets	$ 1,060,000	$ 1,200,000	$(140,000)	$ (39,200)	$(30,000)	$ (9,200)
Accrued warranty liability	0	(110,000)	110,000	30,800	15,000	15,800
Total	$ 1,060,000	$ 1,090,000	$ (30,000)	$ (8,400)	$ (15,000)	$ 6,600
20X3—27%						
Capital assets	$ 880,000	$ 1,000,000	$ (120,000)	$ (32,400)	$ (39,200)	$ 6,800
Accrued warranty liability	0	(40,000)	40,000	10,800	30,800	(20,000)
Total	$ 880,000	$ 960,000	$ (80,000)	$ (21,600)	$ (8,400)	$ (13,200)

In this example, the tax rates change each year and the tax rates are not enacted in advance. That is, the tax rate for each year is exacted in the year to which it pertains. Thus, the tax rate in the table cannot "look forward" to next year's tax rate.

Return to Exhibit 16-2, and note the facts assumed for 20X2 and 20X3. In 20X2, Mirage claims CCA of $240,000 and $140,000 in warranty costs on its tax return while recognizing $200,000 in depreciation and $200,000 in accrued warranty expense on its income statement. Return to Exhibit 16-3, and note the tax and accounting bases. The carrying value of the capital assets declines to $1,200,000, while the tax basis declines by the amount of the 20X2 CCA, to $1,060,000. The difference is $140,000. At the 20X2 tax rate of 28%, the balance of the deferred tax liability relating to the CCA/depreciation temporary difference is $140,000 × 28% = $39,200 credit at 20X2 year-end.

For the warranty liability, the temporary difference is $110,000 at the end of 20X2. That is, the opening warranty liability on the books was $50,000. This is increased by 20X2 expense of $200,000 and decreased by payments of $140,000. The accounting liability is $110,000 at the end of 20X2. The tax basis is still zero. At 28%, the balance in the deferred income tax asset is $30,800. Opening balances are carried down from the closing balances of 20X1, totalled, and the required adjustment calculated.

We must calculate the ending deferred tax balance relating to *each type* of temporary difference because this information is needed for disclosure, as we will illustrate shortly. However, it is not necessary to calculate the *adjustment* for each type of temporary difference; only the total adjustment of $6,600 need be calculated.

The year 20X3 continues, with the data included in calculating taxable income from Exhibit 16-2. CCA was $180,000, reducing the tax basis to $880,000. Depreciation was $200,000, and the accounting basis is now $1,000,000. The warranty liability on the books began at $110,000. It was increased by warranty expense of $160,000 and reduced by claims paid of $230,000 to end the year at $40,000. The tax basis is zero, since claims will be deducted when paid. Arithmetically, the row is extended, noting the tax rate is now 27%.

Impact of the change in tax rate The adjustment in Column 6 for each year is the result of two factors:

1. *The effect of the change in the tax rate on opening temporary differences.* For example, the 20X2 tax rate decreased by 2%. The total opening temporary difference was $50,000, and thus the decrease in the tax rate decreases deferred income tax liability by $1,000 (i.e., $50,000 × 2%).

2. *The effect of current-year temporary differences.* In 20X2, the total temporary difference was reduced from a liability of $50,000 to a liability of $30,000. The impact of this is to *reduce* deferred income tax liability by $5,600—that is, ($50,000 − $30,000) × 28%.

The $6,600 debit adjustment in the table is the result of both factors; $1,000 from the change in rate plus $5,600 from the change in cumulative temporary differences.

Step 3—Combine Income Tax Payable with the Change in Deferred Income Tax to Determine Tax Expense for the Year

Our final step is to combine the calculation of tax payable with the change in the deferred income tax accounts to produce tax expense. This can be done in a schedule but is easily summarized in a journal entry, where there is:

1. A credit to tax payable, from step 1;
2. A debit or credit to deferred income tax asset/liability from step 2; and
3. A debit to tax expense, to balance.

Example

Refer to the entries in Exhibit 16-4, based on the Mirage example. In each year, there is a credit to tax payable and a debit or credit to the deferred tax account, and tax expense is debited to balance the entry. The *balance* in the deferred income tax asset/liability account will be as follows in each year (per column 4 of the table):

Year	Year-End Balance Asset/(Liability)
20X1	(15,000)
20X2	(8,400)
20X3	(21,600)

In this example, the balance is a credit in each year, and thus a net liability will be shown as a noncurrent liability on the statement of financial position.

EXHIBIT 16-4

MIRAGE LIMITED—INCOME TAX JOURNAL ENTRIES

Income tax journal entry, 20X1

Income tax expense	258,000	
Deferred income tax asset/liability		15,000
Income tax payable (Exhibit 16-2)		243,000

Income tax journal entry, 20X2

Income tax expense	258,000	
Deferred income tax asset/liability	6,600	
Income tax payable (Exhibit 16-2)		264,600

Income tax journal entry, 20X3

Income tax expense	203,550	
Deferred income tax asset/liability		13,200
Income tax payable (Exhibit 16-2)		190,350

One account or two? You will see in the entries in Exhibit 16-4 that only one deferred tax account is used in the books. Refer to Exhibit 16-3, and then note that in 20X1, the $30,000 credit from capital assets and the $15,000 debit related to the warranty are included in one deferred tax account, a $15,000 credit in the entry in Exhibit 16-4.

In 20X2, the $9,200 credit from capital assets and the $15,800 debit related to the warranty from Exhibit 16-3 are netted for one debit of $6,600 in the entry. This corresponds to the SFP presentation of deferred income tax, as we will see below. Alternatively, separate deferred income tax accounts for each source of temporary can be recorded. Either approach is acceptable, but we will generally use one account. Netting is discussed further in a later section.

STATEMENT OF FINANCIAL POSITION ELEMENTS

Deferred Income Tax Liabilities

Deferred income tax liabilities are created when tax paid is less than accounting accrual-based income tax expense. This occurs when revenue is recognized on the books but is not taxable until a later period. An accounting asset, such as an account receivable, exists and its tax basis is zero. Deferred income tax liabilities are also created when tax expense deductions precede accounting expense deductions. For example, a declining-balance CCA results in higher expense in early years than straight-line accounting depreciation expense. As a result, UCC (undepreciated capital cost) is less than net book value. Deferred income tax liabilities result.

Deferred Income Tax Assets

Deferred income tax assets are created when tax is effectively prepaid. That is, tax on revenue is paid before the revenue is reflected on the income statement. For example, unearned revenue might appear on the accounting books, but deposits may be taxable when received. Tax is therefore paid before revenue is recognized for accounting purposes. A deferred tax asset is also created when expenses are on the accounting income statement before they are tax deductible, as for accrued warranty liabilities and the related expenses.

Asset Recognition Limit

There are special concerns when deferred income tax is a debit balance. As you know, assets must represent future economic benefits, and those benefits must be probable. Deferred income tax assets will be *realized* only when future years come to pass and those temporary differences reverse in taxable income. If the company is in financial distress, there may not be sufficient taxable income in future years to benefit from the deferred income tax assets—if there is no taxable income and thus no tax due, the company cannot realize the benefit of lower taxes. Therefore, deferred income tax assets on the balance sheet can be recognized only to the extent that their realization is probable. We will explore this issue in more depth in the next chapter.

Classification

The *deferred income tax account is always a noncurrent asset or a noncurrent liability.* The classification of deferred tax balances is not affected by the nature of the asset or liability that gave rise to the deferred tax (i.e., current or noncurrent) or the time frame within which the temporary differences will reverse.

Of course, income taxes currently payable (or receivable) must be shown separately as a current asset or liability. Current taxes receivable or payable cannot be combined with deferred income tax balances.

Netting

The deferred income taxes relating to all temporary differences are lumped together and netted as a single amount if *for the same taxable company and the same taxing government.*

Since consolidated financial statements include several taxable entities, consolidated statements often show both a deferred tax *asset* and a deferred tax *liability*. For example, the company might have a net deferred tax liability relating to the parent company but a net deferred tax asset relating to a subsidiary. In this case, two deferred tax accounts are included on the SFP.

Example

Return to the Mirage example, above, where the company reports a net $21,600 deferred income tax liability in 20X3, the net of deferred tax liability of $32,400 relating to capital assets, and a $10,800 deferred tax asset relating to a warranty provision. If these two deferred tax balances were in different legal companies, in different tax jurisdictions, they would not be netted.

Assume, instead, that the deferred tax liability was in a Canadian parent company and the deferred tax asset was in a Mexican subsidiary that is consolidated in the annual financial statements. In this case, the deferred tax liability would be presented as a $32,400 liability, and there would be a separate long-term deferred tax asset of $10,800 on the SFP.

CONCEPT REVIEW

1. What condition is necessary before a company can report a net deferred tax debit as an asset on its statement of financial position?
2. A corporation has two types of temporary differences. One type of temporary difference gives rise to a deferred tax liability, while the other gives rise to a deferred tax asset. Under what circumstances would the asset and liability be shown separately on the SFP?

DISCLOSURE

General Requirements

Income Tax Expense

The general recommendations for disclosure of the components of income tax expense are as follows:

- The amount of income tax expense (or benefit) on earnings from continuing operations must be reported separately in the SCI; income tax expense should not be combined with other items of expense.
- The amount of income tax expense that is attributable to (1) current income tax and (2) deferred income tax should be disclosed, either on the face of the statement or in the notes.
- Discontinued operations and each component of OCI are reported net of income tax, and the amounts of income tax expense that relate to each item should be disclosed. Also, any income tax relating to capital transactions (e.g., share repurchase) should be disclosed.
- The change in deferred income tax due to (1) changes in temporary differences and (2) tax rate changes (or imposition of new taxes) should be disclosed in the notes.

Example

These disclosure standards, applied to the Mirage example, would result in the following disclosure on the SCI:

	20X1	20X2	20X3
Income before income tax	$825,000	$900,000	$725,000
Income tax expense:			
Current	243,000	264,600	190,350
Deferred	15,000	(6,600)	13,200
	258,000	258,000	203,550
Net income	$567,000	$642,000	$521,450

This disclosure breaks income tax expense down into the portion that is paid during the year, and the portion that relates to deferred income tax. This breakdown could also be shown in the disclosure notes.

In the notes, Mirage would break down the annual change in the deferred tax liability into the amounts caused by (1) tax rate changes and (2) changes in temporary differences:

	20X1	20X2	20X3
Increase (decrease) in deferred tax liability due to:			
Change in income tax rate applied to opening balance*	—	$ (1,000)*	$ (300)**
Change in temporary differences	$15,000	(5,600)†	13,500††
Total change	$15,000	$(6,600)	$13,200

*$50,000 opening balance × 2% rate decrease = $(1,000)

**$30,000 opening balance × 1% rate decrease = $(300)

†$20,000 decrease in temporary differences × 28% = $(5,600)

††$50,000 increase in temporary differences × 27% = $13,500

Temporary Differences

Publicly accountable enterprises also are required to disclose the types of temporary differences. For *each type*, an entity should disclose the amount of deferred tax recognized in the deferred tax balance on the statement of financial position. Obviously, materiality becomes an issue. Some companies have many different kinds of temporary differences. Some of these are substantial, while others may be quite small. Usually, the smaller ones are combined into an "other" category rather than being separately disclosed in detail.

In addition, any tax assets that are NOT recognized because their use is uncertain must also be disclosed, along with any change in this unrecorded asset.

Exhibit 16-5 presents the disclosure given by Andrew Peller Ltd. The company reports net deferred income tax liabilities of $15,811 (all amounts in thousands of Canadian dollars) on the SFP (not repeated here). This deferred tax amount is broken down in the disclosure notes into deferred tax liabilities of $18,139 and deferred tax assets of $2,328. Major sources of temporary differences include property, plant and equipment, biological assets, and intangible assets. Note also that some of the deferred taxes relate to items in OCI.

EXHIBIT 16-5

ANDREW PELLER LIMITED—DISCLOSURE OF TEMPORARY DIFFERENCES

(amounts in thousands of Canadian dollars)

14. INCOME TAXES (extracts)

Deferred income taxes

The significant temporary differences giving rise to the deferred income tax liability are comprised of the following:

Deferred income tax liability

	Accelerated tax depreciation and deductions on property, plant and equipment	Biological assets	Accelerated tax deductions on intangible assets	Tax deductions on goodwill	Total
March 31, 2012	$ 6,720	$ 2,790	$ 2,584	$ 2,799	$ 14,893
Provision (recovery) in net earnings	1,310	279	(110)	160	1,639
March 31, 2013	$ 8,030	$ 3,069	$ 2,474	$ 2,959	$ 16,532

Provision (recovery) in net earnings	877	263	314	153	1,607
March 31, 2014	$ 8,907	$ 3,332	$ 2,788	$ 3,112	$ 18,139

Deferred income tax asset

	Loss carry-forwards	Fair value change on derivatives	Post-employment benefits	Other	Total
March 31, 2012	$ (151)	$ (812)	(1,675)	$ (217)	$ (2,855)
Provision (recovery) in net earnings	151	316	271	(286)	452
Recovery in comprehensive income	—	—	(248)	—	(248)
March 31, 2013	—	$ (496)	$ (1,652)	$ (503)	$ (2,651)
Provision (recovery) in net earnings	—	190	104	83	377
Recovery in other comprehensive income	—	—	(54)	—	(54)
March 31, 2014	$ —	$ (306)	$ (1,602)	$ (420)	$ (2,328)

Source: Andrew Peller Limited, 2014 annual financial statements, www.sedar.com, posted 24 June 2014.

Reconciliation of Effective Tax Rates

The tax status of the corporation may not be obvious to the financial statement users. The reason is that the income tax expense (including both current and deferred taxes) reported by the company on its financial statements may appear to bear little resemblance to the expected level of taxes under the prevailing statutory tax rate. There is no way for an individual investor or lender to know what factors caused the variation in the apparent tax rate for a public company.

Therefore, companies are required to provide a reconciliation between the statutory tax rate and the company's effective tax. The reconciliation can be either in percentages or in dollar terms.

As we have already seen, there are two general categories of causes for variations in the rate of tax:

1. Permanent differences, which cause items of income and/or expense to be reported in accounting income that is not included in taxable income, and
2. Differences in tax rates, due to:
   a. Different tax rates in different tax jurisdictions;
   b. Special taxes levied (and tax reductions permitted) by the taxation authorities; or
   c. Changes in tax rates relating to temporary differences that will reverse in future periods.

Temporary differences themselves are *not* a cause of effective tax *rate* variations. The "effective tax rate" is based on income tax expense and not on the amount of taxes a company actually paid. Therefore, deferred income tax expense is included in the apparent effective tax rate.

Exhibit 16-6 shows an example of the tax rate reconciliation for Andrew Peller. This company provides its reconciliation in dollars. The 2014 reconciliation begins by showing that the statutory rate that Andrew Peller normally would be expected to pay is 26.3%. However, the effective rate was increased by permanent differences and the cumulative effect of the change in the tax rate. These differences appear to increase Andrew Peller's effective tax rate to 27.1% ($5,223 ÷ $19,244 earnings before tax).

EXHIBIT 16-6

ANDREW PELLER EFFECTIVE TAX RATE DISCLOSURE

(amounts in thousands of Canadian dollars)

14. INCOME TAXES (extracts)

The Company's income tax expense consists of the following:

	2014	2013
Provision for income taxes at blended statutory rate of 26.30% (2013–25.70%)	$ 5,062	$ 5,305
Permanent differences and non-deductible items	385	335
Future income tax rate changes	193	285
Other	(417)	211
	$ 5,223	$ 6,136

The increase in the blended statutory rate applicable to the Company is primarily a result of an income tax rate increase in the province of British Columbia during the year.

Source: Andrew Peller Limited, 2014 annual financial statements, www.sedar.com, posted 24 June 2014.

Accountant's versus Analyst's Concepts of Effective Tax Rate

The definition of effective tax rate prescribed by accounting standards (e.g., 27.1% for Andrew Peller) includes deferred income tax. On the other hand, financial analysts usually view the effective tax rate as the amount of current taxes divided by pre-tax earnings. This is quite different from the effective tax rate as defined by accounting standards.

For example, Andrew Peller had 2014 pre-tax earnings of $19,244 thousand. The breakdown of income tax expense on the SCI shows $3,239 of current income tax, plus $1,984 of deferred income tax for a total provision of $5,223.

Under accounting standards, the effective tax rate is 27.1%, calculated (above) as $5,223 ÷ $19,244 = 27.1%. In contrast, financial analysts would ignore the deferred income taxes and focus on the amount actually due to the government for the year, calculated as follows:

$$\$3,239 \div \$19,244 = 16.8\%$$

Financial analysts (and banks) are sometimes interested in what the company has to pay in cash, not what it might have to pay sometime in the future when the temporary differences reverse. Financial statement disclosure is complete, so that these alternate measures can be calculated.

SHORTCUT APPROACH IF RATES HAVE NOT CHANGED

In some cases, a shorter computational approach may be used to account for income tax. This approach should be used *only if the income tax rate has not changed from the prior year*—if there is a change in tax rates, this simplified approach will give you the wrong answer. However, if the facts support the shortcut, it will save time.

The steps are as follows:

Step 1 — Calculate taxable income and income tax payable.

Step 2 — Determine the change in deferred income tax through a direct calculation.

Step 3 — Combine income tax payable with the change in deferred income tax to determine tax expense for the year.

Only Step 2 has changed. A table (such as that shown in Exhibit 16-3) need not be prepared. All that is needed is a direct calculation of the change in deferred income tax balances. Remember that the adjustment that flows from the table has two components—(1) a change to opening deferred income tax balances because of the tax rate change and (2) the current year increase. If the tax rate has not changed, there is no adjustment of opening deferred income tax balances, and the current-year increase (or decrease) is all that is needed. The balance in deferred income tax can be tracked with a simple T-account.

In Step 2, to determine the change in deferred income tax for the year, the calculation is:

Change in deferred income tax = the temporary difference during the year (accounting
revenue or expense less the tax revenue or expense) × tax rate.

To illustrate the shortcut method, we will calculate the tax amounts for KelCo. Facts are as follows:

	20X2	20X3	20X4
Income before income tax	$242,000	$934,000	$1,361,000
Depreciation	230,000	230,000	230,000
CCA	287,000	197,000	312,000

	20X2	20X3	20X4
Tax-free dividend revenue	—	75,000	—
Non-tax-deductible expenses	32,000	—	—
Tax rate	25%	25%	25%

The first step in the solution is to calculate taxable income and income tax payable for each year:

	20X2	20X3	20X4
Accounting income	$242,000	$934,000	$1,361,000
Permanent differences			
Dividend revenue	—	(75,000)	—
Non-tax-deductible expenses	32,000	—	—
Temporary differences			
Depreciation	230,000	230,000	230,000
CCA	(287,000)	(197,000)	(312,000)
Taxable income	217,000	892,000	1,279,000
Tax rate	25%	25%	25%
Income tax payable	$ 54,250	$223,000	$ 319,750

The second step is to determine the change in deferred income tax each year. There is only one source of deferred income tax, the depreciation/CCA on capital assets. In 20X2, CCA is $57,000 higher than depreciation ($287,000 − $230,000). This translates into a $14,250 (i.e., $57,000 × 25%) increase (credit) in a deferred income tax liability. This is the first year, so the balance in deferred income tax is also $14,250.

In 20X3, CCA is less than depreciation by $33,000 (i.e., $230,000 − $197,000). This will reduce the credit balance in the liability by $8,250: ($33,000 × 25%). The balance in deferred income tax liability is now $6,000: ($14,250 − $8,250). This $6,000 balance can be verified as the cumulative temporary differences multiplied by the tax rate. In this example, we have total depreciation over the two years of $460,000, versus $484,000 of CCA, for a $24,000 cumulative difference, multiplied by the tax rate of 25% to again give $6,000.

In 20X4, CCA is larger than depreciation, this time by $82,000: ($312,000 − $230,000). This will increase the deferred income tax liability by $20,500: ($82,000 × 25%). The balance in deferred income tax liability is now $26,500: ($6,000 + $20,500). This can also be verified as $796,000 of cumulative CCA minus $690,000 of cumulative depreciation = $106,000 × 25% = $26,500.

The last step is to prepare the tax entries, which determine the tax expense for the year:

20X2		
Income tax expense	68,500	
Deferred income tax ($287,000 − $230,000) × 25%		14,250
Income tax payable		54,250

20X3		
Income tax expense	214,750	
Deferred income tax ($230,000 − $197,000) × 25%	8,250	
Income tax payable		223,000
20X4		
Income tax expense	340,250	
Deferred income tax ($312,000 − $230,000) × 25%		20,500
Income tax payable		319,750

With this information, appropriate financial statement disclosure may be prepared.

Evaluation

This method is far more straightforward than having to complete a table! Remember, though, that it does not provide documentation to back up the deferred tax balance. And, of course, it will be accurate *only when the tax rate does not change.* In the Canadian business world, changing tax rates are a fact of life.

Actually, it is possible to use the shortcut method if the tax rate changes by also preparing a separate calculation of the effect of the tax rate change on the opening deferred income tax balance, and including this in the journal entry. However, the possibility for error starts to climb, and the table approach is far more reliable. The other significant advantage of the table approach is that the deferred income tax account is proven each year, with the difference between tax and accounting basis backing up the integrity of this account. It is important to have such proof for all financial statement elements.

STATEMENT OF CASH FLOWS

The impact of income tax accounting on the statement of cash flows is clear: All tax allocation amounts must be reversed out of transactions reported on the SCF. The SCF must include only the actual taxes paid. When a company uses the direct method of presenting cash flow from operating activities, the amount of tax paid (recovered) during the year is a deduction (addition).

When the indirect method of presentation is used for operating activities, the deferred tax liability (and/or asset) that has been charged (or credited) to earnings must be added back to (or subtracted from) earnings. That is, the change in deferred income tax is an add-back or deduction in operating activities. The change in income tax payable is another adjustment in operating activities.

Companies are required to disclose the amount of income taxes paid on the face of the statement of cash flows. The indirect approach described above does not accomplish this result because only the deferred tax add-back is displayed on the face of the statement. Therefore, companies that use the indirect approach typically add back income tax expense, and then show the income taxes paid as a separate item.

CONCEPT REVIEW

1. What breakdown of tax expense must be provided?
2. What is the purpose of the reconciliation of the effective tax rate?
3. What amounts relating to income tax should appear in the operating activities section of the statement of cash flows?

IS DEFERRED INCOME TAX A LIABILITY?

Many questions are raised with respect to the validity of deferred income tax as a liability or asset on the SFP. Deferred income tax is an allocation of an amount that arises largely from other allocations. It seems firmly grounded in revenue and expense recognition policies and practices, even though the FASB and IASB have painstakingly justified income tax allocation under the asset–liability definitional approach.

The most important question, however, is the validity of viewing deferred income tax credits as a true liability when they arise as the result of major recurring temporary differences. We observed earlier in this chapter that the major single cause of temporary differences is the difference between two allocations: depreciation for accounting versus CCA for tax. In *aggregate*, these temporary differences will not reverse as long as the company continues to invest in replacing its physical assets.

One important aspect of the liability definition is that *a liability represents an existing obligation*. But to whom is this obligation owed? Supporters of tax allocation argue that deferred income tax is similar to a warranty liability—the obligation is real, even though the specific parties to whom the liability will be fulfilled cannot be specifically identified. It is true that a warranty requires a cash outflow to as-yet-unknown parties. However, any income tax liability must be owed to specific known government jurisdictions. The other party is known precisely, but there is no current obligation for future taxes. The government does not have an offsetting asset.

The reality of having to pay out cash in the future as recurring temporary differences (e.g., depreciation–CCA differences) are reversed depends on the joint occurrence of two conditions:

1. The asset basis of the temporary differences (i.e., the capital assets being depreciated) must shrink before there can be a net reversal, precipitating an actual cash outflow; and

2. The company must be earning taxable income while the net reversals are occurring.

While it is *possible* for these two conditions to co-exist, co-existence is unlikely. Asset bases contract when old assets are not being replaced, and that usually happens when the company is in decline. If a company is in decline it is unlikely to be generating taxable income.

Accounting standards call for recognizing a contingent liability when a cash flow *probably* will be realized. It can be argued that, at best, deferred income tax liabilities relating to recurring temporary differences should be evaluated as a contingent liability because the conditions necessary to precipitate a cash flow are not likely to occur—the liability is neither likely to occur, nor is the amount of future cash flow measurable.

Looking Forward

Income taxes are not now on the agenda of either the IASB or the Canadian AcSB.

Accounting Standards for Private Enterprises

Accounting Method

Private enterprises may elect to use either the *taxes payable method* of accounting for income taxes or the *comprehensive allocation method* (liability method).

Under the taxes payable method, income tax expense is simply the amount of current income tax paid (or payable) to the government. There is no interperiod allocation of income taxes, and there are no deferred income tax amounts reported on the statement of financial position. This method was demonstrated earlier in the chapter.

Intraperiod allocation is still applied, however. Income tax expense must be allocated to:

- Earnings from continuing operations;
- Discontinued operations;
- Gains and losses recorded directly in retained earnings; and
- Capital transactions recorded directly in share capital.

The choice of accounting for income taxes is an all-or-nothing affair. A company cannot decide to use deferred income tax accounting for some types of temporary differences while using the taxes payable basis for other types.

Example

Refer back to the Mirage example earlier in the chapter. If the taxes payable method were used, the following entries would be recorded for income tax:

Income tax journal entry, 20X1

Income tax expense	243,000	
Income tax payable		243,000

Income tax journal entry, 20X2

Income tax expense	264,600	
Income tax payable		264,600

Income tax journal entry, 20X3

Income tax expense	190,350	
Income tax payable		190,350

These entries simply record the tax payable as an expense.

Terminology

The *CPA Canada Handbook*, *Part II* (ASPE), uses the term *future* income tax instead of *deferred* income tax. This is a carryover from the pre-2011 Canadian standard. However, there is no *requirement* to use that particular terminology—the two terms are used interchangeably. Many companies use "deferred" instead of "future."

Classification

ASPE requires companies to classify deferred/future income tax liabilities and assets as either current or long-term. This is in contrast to the IFRS approach, which establishes deferred tax as a noncurrent asset or liability.

Deferred tax amounts are classified as current or noncurrent *on the basis of the assets or liabilities that generated the temporary differences.* That is,

If the balance sheet account that causes the deferred tax is a current asset or a current liability (e.g., accounts receivable, warranty liability, unearned revenue)	The related deferred tax balance is a current asset or a current liability
If the balance sheet account that causes the deferred tax is a noncurrent asset or a noncurrent liability (e.g., property, plant and equipment, intangible assets, bonds payable, pension obligation)	The related deferred tax balance is a noncurrent asset or a noncurrent liability

For example, in the Mirage example used in this chapter, the deferred tax asset relating to the warranty temporary difference would be classified as a current asset because the deferred tax relates to a current liability. The deferred taxes related to capital assets would be classified as noncurrent. In 20X3, there would be (per Exhibit 16-3):

Current asset:

Deferred income tax $10,800

Non-current liability

Deferred income tax $32,400

A company would NOT have just one net deferred tax account, as is the case under IFRS. Instead, there could be two deferred tax amounts presented on the balance sheet: all current deferred tax accounts would be lumped together, and all noncurrent deferred tax accounts would be lumped together.

Disclosure

There is less disclosure required for private enterprises. In the accounting policies note, a company should disclose the fact that it is using the taxes payable method.

In addition, the company should reconcile its income tax expense to the average statutory income tax rate. This disclosure is similar to that described above for public companies. The reconciliation would include items such as:

- Large corporation tax;
- Nondeductible expenses;
- Nontaxable gains, including the nontaxable portion of capital gains; and
- The amount of deductible temporary differences for which a future tax asset has not been recorded.

RELEVANT STANDARDS

CPA Canada Handbook, Part I (IFRS):

- IAS 12, Income Taxes

CPA Canada Handbook, Part II (ASPE):

- Section 3465, Income Taxes

SUMMARY OF KEY POINTS

1. The amount of taxable income often differs from the amount of pre-tax net income reported for accounting purposes.

2. The difference between taxable income and accounting income arises from two types of sources: nonreversing or *permanent* differences and reversing or *temporary* differences.

3. Permanent differences are items of revenue, expense, gains, or losses that are reported for accounting purposes but never enter into the computation of taxable income. Permanent differences also include those items that enter into taxable income but are never included in accounting income.

4. Temporary differences arise when the tax basis of an asset or liability is different from its carrying value (i.e., its accounting basis) in the financial statements.

5. The objective of *comprehensive interperiod income tax allocation* (liability method) is to recognize the income tax effect of every item when that item is recognized in accounting earnings. The alternative to comprehensive allocation is the *taxes payable method*, which is a choice allowed under ASPE but is not permitted under IFRS.

6. When a temporary difference item of revenue, expense, gain, or loss first enters the calculation of *either* taxable income or accounting income, it is an *originating* temporary difference.

7. A temporary difference *reverses* when it is recognized in the other measure of income. For example, if an item is recognized first for tax purposes and later for accounting purposes, the temporary difference originates when the item is included in the tax calculation and reverses when the item is recognized for accounting.

8. Under the liability method of tax allocation, the tax effect is recorded at the currently enacted rate that will apply in the period that the temporary difference is expected to reverse. The current rate is used if no future years' tax rates are enacted or substantially enacted.

9. Under the liability method, the balance of deferred income tax assets and liabilities must be adjusted to reflect changes in the tax rate as they are enacted.

10. Accounting for income tax involves calculating tax payable, calculating the change in the deferred income tax accounts, and then combining both these elements to determine tax expense. Deferred income tax is calculated as the difference between the tax basis and the accounting carrying value of related balance sheet accounts, multiplied by the enacted tax rate.

11. Deferred income tax assets and liabilities are classified as one single netted noncurrent asset or noncurrent liability. However, deferred taxes relating to different taxing jurisdictions or different taxable entities cannot be offset against each other.

12. A reporting enterprise must explain in a note the difference between its effective tax rate and the statutory rate. In this context, the effective tax rate is the income tax expense (including deferred taxes) divided by the pre-tax net income. Entities must also disclose the sources of temporary differences.

13. The statement of cash flows must disclose the amounts of taxes actually paid or received for the year as part of cash flow from operations.

14. Private enterprises may choose to use the taxes payable method for income tax, in which case no deferred income tax is recorded, and tax expense equals tax paid.

Key Terms

comprehensive tax allocation

deferral method

flow-through method

interperiod tax allocation

liability method

permanent difference

provision for income tax

taxes payable method

temporary difference

Review Problem 16-1

The following information pertains to Suda Corp. at the end of 20X1:

	Tax Basis	Accounting Basis
Equipment	$400,000 UCC	$500,000
Capitalized development costs	0	$200,000

At the end of 20X1, Suda had a balance in its deferred income tax liability account of $105,000, pertaining to both the amounts above. There is a $35,000 liability related to equipment and a $70,000 liability related to the capitalized development costs. The enacted income tax rate (combined federal and provincial) at the end of 20X1 was 35%.

The following information pertains to the next three years:

	20X2	20X3	20X4
Income before tax	$200,000	$160,000	$100,000
New equipment acquired	—	100,000	—
Depreciation expense on equipment	65,000	70,000	75,000
CCA claimed	80,000	74,000	69,000

Amortization of development costs	40,000	50,000	45,000
Development costs incurred (deductible for tax purposes)	50,000	30,000	70,000
Income tax rate (enacted in each year; not enacted in advance)	35%	38%	38%

Required:

For each of 20X2, 20X3 and 20X4, calculate:

1. The income tax expense that would appear on Suda's income statement.
2. The balance of the deferred income tax liability or asset account(s) that would appear on Suda's statement of financial position.

REVIEW PROBLEM 16-1—SOLUTION

Calculation of taxable income and tax payable:

	20X2	20X3	20X4
Net income	$200,000	$160,000	$100,000
Plus depreciation on equipment	65,000	70,000	75,000
Less: CCA	(80,000)	(74,000)	(69,000)
Plus amortization of development costs	40,000	50,000	45,000
*Less:*Development costs incurred	(50,000)	(30,000)	(70,000)
Taxable income	$175,000	$176,000	$ 81,000
Tax rate	35%	38%	38%
Tax payable	$ 61,250	$ 66,880	$ 30,780

Calculation of tax basis and carrying value:

	Equipment		Development Costs	
	Tax Basis	Carrying Value	Tax Basis	Carrying Value
20X1 ending balances	$400,000	$500,000	0	$200,000
Additions	—	—		+ 50,000
CCA & depreciation/amortization	(80,000)	(65,000)		(40,000)
20X2 ending balances	320,000	435,000	0	210,000
Additions	+100,000	+100,000		+ 30,000
Depreciation/amortization	(74,000)	(70,000)		(50,000)
20X3 ending balances	346,000	465,000	0	190,000
Additions				+ 70,000
Depreciation/amortization	(69,000)	(75,000)		(45,000)
20X4 ending balances	$277,000	$390,000	0	$215,000

Calculation of changes in deferred income tax liability:

	Year-End Tax Basis dr. (cr.)	Carrying Value dr. (cr.)	Temporary Difference Deductible (taxable)	Deferred Tax Asset (Liability) at Yr.-End Rate	Less Beginning Balance dr. (cr.)	Adjustment for Current Year dr. (cr.)
20X2—35%						
Equipment	320,000	435,000	(115,000)	(40,250)	(35,000)	(5,250)
Development costs	0	210,000	(210,000)	(73,500)	(70,000)	(3,500)
				(113,750)		(8,750)
20X3—38%						
Equipment	346,000	465,000	(119,000)	(45,220)	(40,250)	(4,970)
Development costs	0	190,000	(190,000)	(72,200)	(73,500)	1,300
				(117,420)		(3,670)

	Year-End Tax Basis dr. (cr.)	Carrying Value dr. (cr.)	Temporary Difference Deductible (taxable)	Deferred Tax Asset (Liability) at Yr.-End Rate	Less Beginning Balance dr. (cr.)	Adjustment for Current Year dr. (cr.)
20X4—38%						
Equipment	277,000	390,000	(113,000)	(42,940)	(45,220)	2,280
Development costs	0	215,000	(215,000)	(81,700)	(72,200)	(9,500)
				(124,640)		(7,220)

Tax entries:

20X2

Tax expense	70,000	
Tax payable		61,250
Deferred income tax liability		8,750

20X3

Tax expense	70,550	
Deferred income tax liability		3,670
Tax payable		66,880

20X4

Tax expense	38,000	
Deferred income tax liability		7,220
Tax payable		30,780

1. *Income tax expense*

	20X2	20X3	20X4
Current	$ 61,250	$66,880	$ 30,780
Deferred	8,750	3,670	7,220
Income tax expense	$70,000	$70,550	$38,000

2. *Deferred income tax liability balance*

Per table, column [4] above. Each year's balance will be reported as a single long-term liability amount, as follows:

20X2	$ 113,750
20X3	$ 117,420
20X4	$124,640

CASE 16-1

WILSTAR PRODUCTS LTD.

Wen Chu is a senior account manager for a large Canadian bank. The bank is considering the possibility of syndicating a large debenture issue for Wilstar Products Ltd. (WPL), a manufacturer of auto parts. Wen has been given the task of analyzing WPL's financial performance. When the bank's account managers or analysts are reviewing any client's financial statements, the bank's policy is to remove the effects of income tax allocation in order to enhance the usefulness of the statements for analytical procedures such as evaluating return on investment, earnings, and debt/equity ratios. That is, all deferred tax amounts are eliminated.

Wen has assigned you, William MacDonald, an analyst, the task of evaluating WPL's financial statements both with and without the effect of deferred tax (DT). Wen also would like your comments on the likelihood of Wilstar's accumulated DT being reversed in the foreseeable future.

Condensed versions of Wilstar's SCI, SFP, and SCF are presented in Exhibits 1 to 3. Exhibit 4 shows an excerpt from Note 9 to the financial statements, on Income Taxes.

EXHIBIT 1
WILSTAR PRODUCTS LIMITED
Statement of Comprehensive Income (condensed)
(in millions of dollars)

	31 December 20X2	31 December 20X1
Revenue	$24,088	$ 20,129
Expenses		
Manufacturing costs	9,140	8,184

Operating, selling and general	4,897	4,417
Depreciation and amortization	904	668
Other expenses	4,690	4,108
	19,631	17,377
Earnings before income tax	4,457	2,752
Provision for income tax		
Current	23	55
Deferred	1,060	855
	1,083	910
Net earnings and comprehensive income	$3,374	$ 1,842

EXHIBIT 2

WILSTAR PRODUCTS LIMITED

Statement of Financial Position

(in millions of dollars)

	31 December 20X2	31 December 20X1
Assets		
Current assets		
Cash and cash equivalents	$ 677	$ 304
Accounts receivable	1,350	1,190
Inventories	2,689	1,606
Income taxes receivable	78	45

Total current assets	4,794	3,145
Property, plant and equipment, net	21,189	22,966
Deferred development and other	210	260
Total assets	$26,193	$26,371
Liabilities and Shareholders' Equity		
Current liabilities		
Short-term debt	$ 1,603	$ 1,049
Accounts payable and accrued liabilities	2,170	2,830
Total current liabilities	3,773	3,879
Long-term debt	6,385	8,995
Provisions and other	2,953	4,118
Deferred tax	4,224	3,013
	17,335	20,005
Shareholders' equity		
Share capital	860	851
Contributed surplus	400	400
Retained earnings	7,709	5,295
Accumulated other comprehensive income	(111)	(180)
Total shareholders' equity	8,858	6,366
Total liabilities and shareholders' equity	$26,193	$26,371

EXHIBIT 3

WILSTAR PRODUCTS LIMITED

Statement of Cash Flows (condensed)

(in millions of dollars)

	31 December 20X2	31 December 20X1
Cash flow from operating activities	$2,578	$2,146
Cash flow from (used in) investing activities	810	(1,113)
Cash flow used in financing activities	(3,015)	(754)
Increase in cash and cash equivalents	373	279
Cash and cash equivalents at beginning of year	304	25
Cash and cash equivalents at end of year	$ 677	$ 304

EXHIBIT 4

WILSTAR PRODUCTS LIMITED

Deferred Tax

(in millions of dollars)

	31 December 20X2	31 December 20X1
Deferred tax assets:		
Employee future benefits	$ 12	$ 7
Asset retirement obligations	32	19
Inventories	59	67
Employee future benefits	8	87
Asset retirement obligations	20	162
Other	99	96
	230	438

Deferred tax liabilities:		
Excess of book value of assets over tax values	(4,411)	(3,400)
Deferred maintenance shutdown costs	(43)	(51)
Deferred tax	$ (4,224)	$ (3,013)

Required:

Prepare a memo from William MacDonald to Wen Chu.

CASE 16-2

SOFTWARE INC.

Software Inc. (SI) is a private corporation formed in the 1990s. SI develops and sells software for many purposes; theft recovery, geomapping, data and device security, and IT asset management. To help motivate management, SI has a stock option plan.

To help fund continued software development, SI has a bank loan with a major bank. The bank requires annual audited financial statements and has a financial covenant that stipulates a minimum current ratio.

SI has an expected taxable loss of $10,000,000 in 20X9. For the last three years the company has had taxable profits of $2,000,000 in 20X6; $5,000,000 in 20X7, and $1,000,000 in 20X8. SI's taxable loss this year was due to intensive development of new software for security over personal data. SI anticipates sales of this product to be significant due to concerns over identity theft.

You have recently been hired to develop new accounting policies for SI's 31 December year-end. You have been asked by the owners to discuss alternatives and provide recommendations on the appropriate accounting policies for events below that have occurred during 20X9. Where possible, you have been asked to quantify the impact of the accounting policies. SI is seriously considering going public next year and would like to know how your recommendations would be different if it was a public company. The incremental borrowing rate for SI is 10%. The tax rates for the last few years were 20X6 (38%), 20X7 (39%), and both 20X8 and 20X9 (40%).

1. SI offers computer theft recovery and secure asset-tracking services. These services are provided for a period of one to five years. The customer pays a fee that includes software, monitoring, a warranty, and maintenance. The fee is due 30 days after installation of the software. Sales staff are paid a commission based on the number of service contracts they sell.
2. SI offers a warranty with its theft recovery software. If a computer equipped with the software is stolen and SI is unable to recover the stolen software using its software or delete data on the stolen computer, then the customer is eligible for a warranty of up to $1,000. To qualify, customers must file a police report. The amount of the warranty depends on the value of the stolen computer. Estimated warranty liabilities on the balance sheet at the end of 20X8 were $8 million. During 20X9, the estimated warranty costs based on a percentage of sales will be an additional $5 million. Actual warranty costs during 20X9 were $1 million.

3. SI currently uses the taxes payable method of accounting for income taxes. In 20X8, SI changed its method of accounting for software development from expensing to capitalizing as an intangible asset.

4. SI entered into a forward contract for the purchase of new equipment that the company is purchasing from Germany in 20X9 to protect itself against changes in the value of the euro. SI often enters into forward contracts, interest rate swaps, and foreign currency swaps to protect the company from risks. SI also has shares in a number of companies for the sole purposes of earning money. It has an investment department that manages this portfolio of investments. These investments are traded on a frequent basis.

5. SI has installed a series of satellite towers as part of its software-tracking services at a cost of $15 million. There is a regulatory obligation to dismantle these satellite towers in 20 years. The anticipated cost at that time is $2.5 million.

6. SI uses the Black-Scholes method for estimating its stock option expense. During 20X9, SI estimated an expense of $15 million using the following assumptions:

	20X8	20X9
Expected life of options	4	3
Expected stock price volatility	71%	60%
Risk free interest rate	4%	3%

Required:

Prepare the requested report.

TECHNICAL REVIEW

connect

TR16-1 Temporary versus Permanent Difference:

Listed below are a number of items that are required to adjust net income before income tax to taxable income.

Item	Add or Subtract
a. Golf club dues, $20,000	_____
b. Depreciation expense, $60,000	_____
c. Development costs incurred during year; capitalized for accounting purposes, $100,000	_____
d. Warranty costs accrued during year, $30,000	_____

e. Interest and penalty for late payment payroll taxes, $25,000 _____

f. CCA, $180,000 _____

g. Amortization of capitalized development costs, $10,000 _____

h. Costs incurred during year for warranty work completed, $22,000 _____

Required:

1. For each item, indicate if it will be added or subtracted from net income before income taxes.
2. For each item, indicate if it is a permanent difference or a temporary difference.

connect

TR16-2 Calculation of Taxes Payable:

Hendrie Inc. reported earnings before income taxes of $2,200,000 in 20X9. The tax rate for this year is 40%.

Required:

1. Use the information from TR16-1. Calculate taxable income.
2. What is the amount of income taxes payable?

connect

TR16-3 Taxable Income:

Lantz Ltd. reported earnings before income taxes of $540,000 in 20X5. The company had expensed $25,000 of golf club dues that were not tax deductible. There was tax-free dividend revenue of $10,000. Warranty expense was $40,000. Depreciation was $120,000, while CCA was $190,000. Warranty claims paid were $35,000. The tax rate for this year is 25%.

Required:

Calculate taxable income and income tax payable.

connect

TR16-4 CCA—Depreciation Differences:

Parry Corp. acquired new equipment for $1,200,000 in 20X6. For accounting purposes, the equipment will be depreciated over five years, straight-line, with a full year's depreciation in the first year. For income tax purposes, Parry can take CCA over the next three years of $120,000 in 20X6, $216,000 in 20X7, and $175,000 in 20X8. Parry's income tax rate is 34%.

Required:

For each 31 December 20X6 through 20X8, determine:

1. The tax basis for the equipment.
2. The accounting basis for the equipment.
3. The cumulative amount of the temporary difference relating to the equipment.
4. The balance of deferred income tax asset or liability that would be reported on the statement of financial position.
5. The amount of the deferred income tax adjustment.

connect

TR16-5 Accounts Receivable Temporary Difference:

Leonard Ltd. recorded revenue in 20X6 in the amount of $100,000. The amount will be collected from the customer in the amount of $40,000 in 20X7 and $60,000 in 20X8. The revenue will be taxable when the cash is received. Leonard's income tax rate is 22%.

Required:

For each 31 December 20X6 through 20X8, determine:

1. The tax basis for the account receivable.
2. The accounting basis for the account receivable.
3. The cumulative amount of the temporary difference relating to the account receivable.
4. The balance of deferred income tax asset or liability that would be reported on the statement of financial position.
5. The amount of the deferred income tax adjustment.

connect

TR16-6 Warranty Temporary Difference:

Zygote Ltd. recorded warranty expense of $125,000 in 20X6, $35,000 in 20X7, and $75,000 in 20X8. Warranty claims paid were $70,000 in 20X6, $55,000 in 20X7, and $90,000 in 20X8. Warranty amounts are tax deductible when the cash is paid. Zygote's income tax rate is 28%.

Required:

For each 31 December 20X6 through 20X8, determine:

1. The tax basis for the warranty liability.
2. The accounting basis for the warranty liability.
3. The cumulative amount of the temporary difference relating to the warranty liability.
4. The balance of deferred income tax asset or liability that would be reported on the statement of financial position.
5. The amount of the deferred income tax adjustment.

≡ connect

TR16-7 Temporary Differences:

The following is a list of temporary differences:

1. Depreciation versus CCA on equipment.
2. Money received from a customer prior to services being performed; cash is taxable when received.
3. An expense for warranty is recognized in the same period that revenue is recognized but is not tax deductible until it is paid in a later period.
4. Revenue is recognized in the books but the customer will not pay for two years. The amount is taxable when the cash is received.
5. Pension expense is recorded in the books over the working lives of the employees but amounts are not tax deductible until money is paid to the pension trustee in later years.

Required:

For each temporary difference above, identify the SFP account that is related.

≡ connect

TR16-8 Temporary Differences:

Listed below are six independent sources of deferred income tax. For each item, indicate whether the deferred income tax account from this source alone would be a debit or a credit.

Item	Debit or Credit
a. Accelerated amortization (CCA) for income tax and straight-line depreciation for accounting	_____
b. Estimated warranty costs: cash basis for income tax and accrual basis for accounting	_____
c. Sales revenue when payment is deferred: cash basis for tax purposes but recognized on delivery for accounting	_____
d. Development costs: cash basis for income tax and capitalization and amortization for accounting	_____
e. Unrealized loss: loss recognized only on later disposal of the asset for income tax but market value (LCM) recognized for accounting	_____
f. Rent revenue collected in advance: cash basis for income tax, accrual basis for accounting	_____

eXcel

TR16-9 Tax Expense, Change in Rates:

Cell Image Corp. reported a deferred tax liability of $120,000 in 20X5, caused by equipment with a UCC of $1,500,000 and net book value of $1,980,000. The tax rate was 25%. In 20X6, accounting earnings were $350,000, depreciation expense was $150,000, and CCA was $200,000. The tax rate is 35%.

Required:

1. Calculate tax payable.

2. Calculate the tax basis of the equipment.

3. Calculate the accounting basis of the equipment.

4. Calculate the amount of the deferred income tax adjustment.

5. Calculate the amount of the adjustment in requirement 4 that was caused by the (a) change in the tax rate and (b) new temporary difference.

6. Calculate tax expense for 20X6.

connect

TR16-10 Tax Expense, Change in Rates:

Marsh Corp. reported a deferred tax asset of $24,000 in 20X2, caused by a warranty liability of $80,000. The tax rate was 30%. In 20X3, accounting earnings were $200,000, warranty claims paid were $70,000, and warranty expense was $35,000. The tax rate is 22%.

Required:

1. Calculate tax payable.

2. Calculate the tax basis of the warranty liability.

3. Calculate the accounting basis of the warranty liability.

4. Calculate the amount of the deferred income tax adjustment.

5. Calculate the amount of the adjustment in requirement 4 that was caused by the (a) change in the tax rate and (b) new temporary difference.

6. Calculate tax expense for 20X3.

ASSIGNMENTS

★ A16-1 Income Tax Allocation—Two-Year Period:

Nalad Corp. provided the following data related to accounting and taxable income:

	20X8	20X9
Pre-tax accounting income (financial statements)	$400,000	$ 440,000
Taxable income (tax return)	240,000	600,000
Income tax rate	38%	38%

There are no existing temporary differences other than those reflected in these data. There are no permanent differences.

Required:

1. How much tax expense would be reported in each year if the taxes payable method was used? What is potentially misleading with this presentation of tax expense?
2. How much tax expense and deferred income tax would be reported using comprehensive tax allocation (liability method)? Why is the two-year total tax expense the same in requirements 1 and 2?

★ A16-2 Deferred Tax Balances:

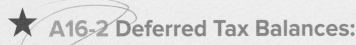

Olong Ltd. started operations in 20X6. The company provided the following information for its warranty balances for the past four years:

	20X6	20X7	20X8	20X9
Warranty costs accrued	25,000	20,000	27,500	40,000
Costs incurred—warranty work	22,500	17,500	30,000	27,500
Costs incurred—development costs	45,000	50,000	60,000	25,000
Amortization—development costs	0	9,000	19,000	25,000
Tax rate	40%	38%	38%	36%

Required:

1. What is the tax basis for development costs and the provision for warranty costs in each year?
2. What is the accounting basis for development costs and the provision for warranty costs in each year?
3. What is the deferred tax balance in each year?
4. Is the balance an asset or a liability?

A16-3 Income Tax Allocation:

The financial statements of Dakar Corp. for a four-year period reflected the following pre-tax amounts:

	20X4	20X5	20X6	20X7
Statement Profit and Loss (summarized)				
Revenues	$ 110,000	$ 124,000	$ 144,000	$ 164,000
Expenses other than depreciation	(80,000)	(92,000)	(95,000)	(128,000)
Depreciation expense (straight line)	(10,000)	(10,000)	(10,000)	(10,000)
Pre-tax accounting income	$ 20,000	$ 22,000	$ 39,000	$ 26,000
Statement of Financial Position (partial)				
Machine (four-year life, no residual value), at cost	$ 40,000	$ 40,000	$ 40,000	$ 40,000
Less: Accumulated depreciation	(10,000)	(20,000)	(30,000)	(40,000)
	$ 30,000	$ 20,000	$ 10,000	$ 0

Dakar has a tax rate of 40% each year and claimed CCA for income tax purposes as follows: 20X4, $16,000; 20X5, $12,000; 20X6, $8,000; and 20X7, $4,000. There were no deferred income tax balances at 1 January 20X4.

Required:

For each year, calculate the deferred income tax balance on the statement of financial position at the end of the year, and also net income.

 **A16-4 Cumulative CCA—Depreciation Differences:**

McQuinn Corp. started operations in 20X5. The company acquired equipment in the first year for a price of $180,000. The equipment will be depreciated for accounting purposes over three years on a straight-line basis (with a full year's depreciation in the year of acquisition). For determining income tax payable, the company can deduct one-half of the purchase cost as CCA in the first year, one-third in the second year, and one-sixth in the third year.

The company's 20X5 startup was successful, and in 20X6 the company bought identical equipment for $192,000. In 20X7, a third set of equipment was acquired for $198,000. The pattern of depreciation and CCA is proportionately the same for each acquisition. McQuinn's tax rate is 40%.

The company's management plans to continue the same level of investment for the foreseeable future, as long as the company remains profitable.

Required:

1. Determine the temporary difference relating to the tax versus accounting bases of the equipment (i.e., CCA versus accounting depreciation) for each year, 20X5 through 20X7. What is the accumulated balance of the temporary difference at the end of each year?

2. What is the balance of the deferred income tax account at the end of each year?

3. What will happen to the accumulated temporary differences and deferred income tax if McQuinn continues to maintain its current level of investment in equipment, replacing each asset as it comes to the end of its useful life?

4. What conditions will be necessary to cause the timing difference balance to decline in future years?

5. Under what conditions will reversal of the accumulated timing differences cause a cash outflow?

★ ★ A16-5 Cumulative Temporary Differences:

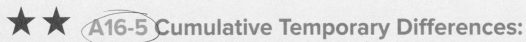

At the end of 20X8, Bent Angel Ltd.'s statement of financial position showed equipment at total cost of $2,000,000. The equipment was being amortized at 10% per year, straight-line, and was 40% depreciated at the end of 20X8. The income tax files showed UCC for the equipment of $550,000. The statement of financial position also showed an asset of $300,000 for unamortized development costs. The development costs had been incurred in previous years and all costs had been deducted for income tax purposes in those prior years.

In 20X9, the company acquired an additional $300,000 in equipment while scrapping equipment that originally cost $125,000. CCA claimed for 20X9 was $115,000. The company amortized $50,000 of the development cost asset.

The company pays income tax at a rate of 38%.

Required:

1. What are the accounting basis and the tax basis of the equipment and of the development cost asset at the end of each of 20X8 and 20X9?

2. What is the cumulative temporary difference for each item, and the balance of the deferred income tax account at the end of each year?

3. If the company maintains its capital asset base by reinvestment and renewal in future years, when will the deferred income tax balance begin to decline? Explain.

 connect

★ A16-6 Tax Calculations:

The following is selected information from the accounting records of Slow Inc. for 20X9 its first year of operations:

Earnings before income taxes	$490,000

In determining pre-tax accounting earnings, the following deductions were made:

a. Golf club dues	12,500
b. Accrued warranty costs	40,000
c. Depreciation	62,500

For tax purposes, the following deductions were made:

a. Warranty costs incurred	32,500
b. CCA	125,000

The capital assets, originally costing $625,000, are depreciated on a straight-line basis over 10 years, zero residual value, with a full year of depreciation taken in Year 1. The tax rate is 36%.

Required:

Prepare the journal entry to record income tax at the end of 20X9.

 A16-7 Tax Calculations:

The records of Boomer Corp., in its first year of operation, at the end of 20X8, provided the following data related to income taxes:

a. Golf club dues expense in 20X8, $10,000, properly recorded for accounting purposes but not tax deductible at any time.

b. Investment revenue in 20X8, $325,000, properly recorded for accounting purposes but not taxable at any time.

c. Estimated expense for warranty costs, $70,000; accrued for accounting purposes at the end of 20X8; to be reported for income tax purposes when paid. There were no warranty costs incurred in 20X8.

d. Gain on disposal of land, $240,000; recorded for accounting purposes at the end of 20X8; to be reported as a capital gain for income tax purposes when collected at the end of 20X10.

e. Costs incurred for development costs, $50,000; deducted for income tax purposes; recognized for accounting purposes as depreciated. There was no depreciation of development costs in 20X8.

f. Equipment purchased in 20X8, $1,500,000; depreciation $100,000 recorded for accounting purposes in 20X8; CCA of $150,000 was deducted for income tax purposes in 20X8.

Accounting earnings (from the SCI) for 20X8 was $1,200,000; the income tax rate is 38%. There were no deferred tax amounts as of the beginning of 20X8.

Required:

1. Are the individual differences listed above permanent differences or temporary differences? Explain why.

2. Prepare the journal entry to record income tax at the end of 20X8.

3. Show the amounts that will be reported on (a) the statement of financial position and (b) the statement of profit and loss for 20X8.

A16-8 Tax Calculations:

Penguin Corp. reported accounting earnings before taxes as follows: 20X6, $675,000; 20X7, $57,000. Taxable income for each year would have been the same as pre-tax accounting income except for the tax effects, arising for the first time in 20X6, of $7,200 in rent revenue, representing $1,200 per month rent revenue collected in advance on 1 October 20X6, for the six months ending 31 March 20X7. Rent revenue is taxable in the year collected. The tax rate for 20X6 and 20X7 is 25%, and the year-end for both accounting and tax purposes is 31 December. The rent revenue collected in advance is the only difference between accounting earnings and taxable income, and it is not repeated in October 20X7.

Required:

1. Is this a temporary difference? Why, or why not?
2. What is the accounting carrying value for the unearned rent at the end of 20X6? The tax basis? Explain.
3. Calculate taxable income and income tax payable, and prepare journal entries for each year-end.
4. Prepare a partial statement of profit and loss for each year, starting with pre-tax accounting earnings.
5. What amount of deferred income tax would be reported on the 20X6 and 20X7 statements of financial position?

 A16-9 Tax Calculations:

The pre-tax income statements for Moonstone Ltd. for two years (summarized) were as follows:

	20X8	20X9
Revenues	$264,000	$328,000
Expenses	180,000	236,000
Pre-tax income	$84,000	$ 92,000

For tax purposes, the following income tax differences existed:

a. Revenues on the 20X9 statement of profit and loss include $36,000 rent, which is taxable in 20X8 but was unearned at the end of 20X8 for accounting purposes.
b. Expenses on the 20X9 statement of profit and loss include political contributions of $12,000, which are not deductible for income tax purposes.
c. Expenses on the 20X8 statement of profit and loss include $20,800 of estimated warranty costs, which are not deductible for income tax purposes until 20X9.

Required:

1. What was the accounting carrying value and tax basis for unearned revenue and the warranty liability at the end of 20X8 and 20X9?
2. Compute (a) income tax payable, (b) deferred income tax, and (c) income tax expense for each period. Assume a tax rate of 30%.
3. Give the entry to record income taxes for each period.

4. Complete statements of profit and loss to include income taxes expense.

5. What amount of deferred income tax will be reported on the statement of financial position at each year-end?

 ## A16-10 Tax Calculations:

Fellows Inc. started operations on 1 January 20X8 and purchased $2,000,000 of equipment. The income tax rate was 40% in 20X8 and 38% in 20X9. The following is information related to 20X8 and 20X9:

	20X8	20X9
Accounting earnings before income tax	$550,000	$820,000
Golf club dues	10,000	12,000
Accrued warranty costs	50,000	120,000
Warranty costs	40,000	90,000
Depreciation expense on equipment	200,000	200,000
Capital cost allowance	300,000	250,000

Required:

1. Prepare all income tax journal entries for 20X8 and 20X9.
2. What are the deferred tax balances on the statement of financial position in 20X8 and 20X9?

 ## A16-11 Deferred Income Tax; Change in Tax Rates:

DCM Metals Ltd. has a 31 December year-end. The tax rate is 30% in 20X4, 35% in 20X5, and 42% in 20X6. The company reports earnings as follows:

20X4	$550,000
20X5	123,000
20X6	310,000

Taxable income and accounting income are identical except for a $300,000 revenue reported for accounting purposes in 20X4, with one-half reported in 20X5 and one-half in 20X6 for tax purposes. The revenue is related to a long-term account receivable, taxable only when collected.

Required:

Compute tax expense and deferred income tax on the statement of financial position for 20X4, 20X5, and 20X6.

 Solution

A16-12 Deferred Income Tax; Change in Tax Rates:

Stacy Corp. would have had identical income before tax on both its income tax returns and statements of profit and loss for the years 20X4 through 20X7, except for equipment that cost $120,000. The equipment has a four-year estimated life and no residual value. The equipment was depreciated for income tax purposes using the following amounts: 20X4, $48,000; 20X5, $36,000; 20X6, $24,000; and 20X7, $12,000. However, for accounting purposes, the straight-line method was used (i.e., $30,000 per year). The accounting and tax periods both end on 31 December. Income amounts before depreciation expense and income tax for each of the four years were as follows:

	20X4	20X5	20X6	20X7
Accounting earnings before tax and depreciation	$60,000	$80,000	$70,000	$70,000
Tax rate	30%	30%	40%	40%

Required:

1. Explain why this is a temporary difference.
2. Calculate the accounting carrying value and tax basis of the equipment at the end of each year.
3. Reconcile pre-tax accounting and taxable income, calculate income tax payable and tax expense, compute the balance in the deferred income tax account, and prepare journal entries for each year-end.

 A16-13 Deferred Income Tax; Change in Tax Rates:

Buck Co. has a deferred income tax liability in the amount of $192,000 at 31 December 20X7, relating to a $600,000 receivable. This sale was recorded for accounting purposes in 20X7 but is not taxable until the cash is collected. In 20X8, $400,000 is collected. Warranty expense in 20X8 included in the determination of pre-tax accounting income is $165,000, with the entire amount expected to be spent and deductible for tax purposes in 20X9. Pre-tax accounting earnings are $735,000 in 20X8. The tax rate is 28% in 20X8.

Required:

1. What was the tax rate in 20X7?
2. What is the accounting carrying value and the tax basis of both the account receivable and the warranty liability, at the end of 20X7 and 20X8?

3. Calculate taxable income and income tax payable, compute the balance in the deferred income tax accounts, and prepare the tax journal entry for year-end 20X8.

4. Of the deferred tax adjustment recorded in requirement 2, how much is caused by the change in the tax rate and how much is caused by new temporary differences?

5. Calculate the deferred income tax that would be reported on the statement of financial position at the end of 20X8.

★ ★ A16-14 Tax Calculations; Change in Tax Rates:

On 1 January 20X3, Highmark Corp. had the following deferred tax balances:

Deferred income tax asset related to warranty	$ 16,000
Deferred income tax liability related to capital assets	$120,000

On this date, the net book value of capital assets was $1,750,000 and UCC was $1,450,000. There was a warranty liability of $40,000.

In 20X3, accounting income was $170,000. This included non-tax-deductible expenses of $42,000, dividend revenue (non-taxable) of $12,000, depreciation of $75,000, and a warranty expense of $39,000. Warranty claims paid were $51,000 and CCA was $99,000.

Required:

Provide the journal entry to record tax expense in 20X3. The enacted tax rate was 41% in 20X3.

★ ★ A16-15 Tax Calculations—Tax Rate Change:

The records of Samuel Corp. provided the following data at the end of Years 1 through 4 relating to income tax allocation:

	Year 1	Year 2	Year 3	Year 4
Pre-tax accounting earnings	$87,000	$105,000	$120,000	$132,000
Taxable income (tax return)	42,000	120,000	135,000	147,000
Tax rate	26%	28%	30%	30%

The above amounts include only one temporary difference; no other changes occurred. At the end of Year 1, the company prepaid an expense of $45,000, which was then amortized for accounting purposes over Years 2–4 (straight-line). The full amount was included as a deduction in Year 1 for income tax purposes. Each year's tax rate was enacted in each specific year—that is, the Year 2 tax rate was enacted in Year 2 and so on.

Required:

1. Calculate income tax payable for each year.
2. Calculate income tax expense for each year.
3. Comment on the effect of cumulative temporary differences on income tax expense when the income tax rate changes.

 A16-16 Tax Rate Change; Enacted Tax Rates:

At the end of 20X6, Tap Ltd. had accumulated temporary differences of $500,000 arising from CCA/depreciation on capital assets. UCC was $2,500,000 and net book value of these assets was $3,000,000. The balance of the deferred income tax liability account was $150,000. Over the next three years, Tap reported the following:

	20X7	20X8	20X9
Accounting earnings, before income taxes	$200,000	$240,000	$300,000
Expenses not deductible for computing income tax	16,000	20,000	12,000
Depreciation expense	100,000	100,000	100,000
CCA	180,000	150,000	140,000

The tax rate was 30% for 20X6 and 20X7, 26% for 20X8, and 24% for 20X9.

Required:

1. Calculate income tax expense for each year, 20X7, 20X8, and 20X9. Assume that the rates for 20X8 and 20X9 were enacted in the year to which they pertain. Specify the amount of current income tax expense and deferred income tax expense for each year.
2. Calculate the amount of the change in deferred tax in each year that is caused by the change in the tax rate, versus the effect of new temporary differences.
3. Assume instead that the rates for 20X8 and 20X9 were both enacted in 20X7. Recalculate income tax expense in 20X7. State any additional assumptions that you make.

 A16-17 Tax Calculations:

Martin Ltd., in the first year of its operations, reported the following information regarding its operations:

a. Earnings before tax for the year was $2,500,000 and the tax rate was 38%.
b. Depreciation was $240,000, and CCA was $134,000. Net book value at year-end was $1,680,000, while UCC was $1,786,000.

c. The warranty program generated an estimated cost (expense) on the statement of profit and loss of $514,000 but the cash paid out was $348,000. The $166,000 liability resulting from this was shown as a current liability. On the income tax return, the cash paid is the amount deductible.

d. Golf club dues of $30,000 were included in the statement of profit and loss but were not allowed to be deducted for tax purposes.

In the second year of its operations, Martin Ltd. reported the following information:

a. Earnings before income tax for the year was $2,750,000, and the tax rate was 40%.

b. Depreciation was $240,000, and the CCA was $740,000. Net book value at year-end was $1,440,000, while UCC was $1,046,000.

c. The estimated costs of the warranty program were $574,000, and the cash paid out was $484,000. The liability had a balance of $256,000.

Required:

Prepare the journal entry to record income tax expense in the first and second years of operations. The second-year tax rate was not enacted until the second year.

(Source: [Adapted] © CGA-Canada. Reproduced with permission.)

★ ★ A16-18 Tax Calculations; Enacted Tax Rate Change:

In its first year of operations, Martha Enterprises Corp. reported the following information:

a. Income before income taxes was $620,000.

b. The company acquired capital assets costing $1,800,000; depreciation was $120,000, and CCA was $90,000.

c. The company recorded an expense of $125,000 for the one-year warranty on the company's products; cash disbursements amounted to $77,000.

d. The company incurred development costs of $75,000 that met the criteria for capitalization for accounting purposes. Development work was still ongoing at year-end. These costs could be immediately deducted for tax purposes.

e. The company made a political contribution of $20,000 and expensed this for accounting purposes.

f. The income tax rate was 28% and the year 2 tax rate was enacted, at 30%.

In the second year, the company reported the following:

a. Earnings before income tax were $1,600,000.

b. Depreciation was $120,000; CCA was $260,000.

c. The estimated warranty costs were $200,000, while the cash expenditure was $205,000.

d. Additional development costs of $150,000 were incurred to complete the project. For accounting purposes, amortization of $38,000 was recorded.

e. Golf club memberships for top executives cost $25,000; this was expensed for accounting purposes as a marketing expense.

Required:

1. Prepare the journal entries to record income tax expense for the first and second years of operation.
2. Explain the tax rate used to determine deferred income tax in the first year.

 A16-19 Tax Calculations; Rate Change:

Golf Inc., which began operations in 20X3, uses the same policies for financial accounting and tax purposes with the exception of warranty costs and franchise fee revenue. Information about the $60,000 of warranty expenses and $90,000 franchise revenue accrued for book purposes is provided below:

	20X3	20X4	20X5
Warranty cost for book purposes	$60,000	—	—
Warranty cost for tax purposes (claims paid)	15,000	$20,000	$25,000
Franchise fee revenue, book, on account	90,000	—	—
Franchise fee revenue, tax, cash received	9,000	51,000	30,000
Effective tax rate	38%	40%	45%
Earnings before tax	$75,000	$90,000	$80,000

Required:

Prepare journal entries to record taxes for 20X3 to 20X5. The tax rate for a given year is not enacted until that specific year.

(Source: [Adapted] © CGA-Canada. Reproduced with permission.)

 A16-20 Tax Calculations:

Diversified Ltd. (DI) is a public company that started operations in 20X4. It opened a number of locations across Canada. In fiscal 20X4, the company had earnings before tax of $290,000. The tax rate for 20X4 was 30%. DI has a 31 December year-end. The following occurred during 20X4.

a. DI purchased assets with an original cost of $780,000. The total depreciation for 20X4 was $52,000. For tax purposes, DI had $15,600 CCA deducted.

b. For sales during 20X4, DI recognized warranty expenses of $44,000. Actual warranty work completed during 20X4 was $30,000.

c. DI capitalized development costs of $200,000 for new product innovations. Amortization of this asset has not occurred yet, since the development work will continue in 20X5. These costs are deductible for tax purposes in the year.

d. DI contributed $5,000 to a local political campaign and expensed these costs during the year.

e. DI recognized revenues of $500,000 in 20X4. Only $440,000 of these revenues were collected and taxed during the year. The remainder will not be taxed until they are due and collected next year.

Required:

1. Provide the journal entry to record income tax expense during 20X4. Show all supporting calculations.
2. Identify the amount of income tax expense that is current and the amount that is deferred.
3. Identify the relevant amounts that will be shown on the December 31 year-end statement of financial position with respect to income tax.

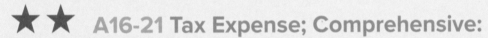

★ ★ A16-21 Tax Expense; Comprehensive:

At the end of 20X8, Anderson Corp., a public company, had the following balances:

Deferred income tax liability related to accounts receivable	$ (198,000)
Deferred income tax liability related to capital assets	(432,000)
Deferred income tax asset related to warranties	54,000
Deferred income tax liability, per SFP	$(576,000)

In 20X8, the company had reported $1,350,000 of taxable income. It also reported a $550,000 long-term receivable, taxable when collected. At the end of 20X8, capital assets had a net book value of $4,800,000 and a UCC balance of $3,600,000. Estimated warranty liabilities were $150,000.

In 20X9, Anderson reported accounting earnings of $2,250,000. Collections on the long-term receivable amounted to $420,000. There were non-deductible golf club dues of $32,000. Warranty expense was equal to claims paid. Depreciation was $200,000 and CCA was $300,000. The tax rate was 38%.

Required:

1. What was the tax rate in 20X8?
2. Prepare a journal entry to record tax expense in 20X9. Tax rates were enacted in the year to which they pertain.
3. Calculate the deferred income tax liability on the SFP at the end of 20X9.

★ ★ ★ A16-22 Tax Expense; Comprehensive:

Zhang Ltd. reported earnings before income tax of $560,000 in 20X9. The tax rate for 20X9 was 30% and was enacted during the year. The enacted tax rate at the end of the previous year was 28%.

At the end of 20X8, the balance sheet of Zhang included the net book value of equipment of $795,000, long-term accounts receivable of $120,000, and a warranty liability of $49,000. Long-term receivables represent taxable income when collected.

In 20X9, dividends (tax-free) received from taxable Canadian corporations were $16,000. Political contributions were $20,000. UCC was $480,000 at the beginning of the year. In 20X9, CCA was $50,000, and depreciation expense was $63,000.

During 20X9, long-term receivables of $40,000 were collected. There were no new long-term receivables. The warranty expense of $46,000 was equal to the warranty claims paid.

Required:

1. Calculate income tax expense for 20X9.
2. How much of the change in deferred income tax in 20X9 is caused by a change in the income tax rate, and how much is caused by temporary differences of the year?

★ ★ ★ A16-23 Tax Calculations; Comprehensive:

Crandall Corp. was formed in 20X1. Relevant information pertaining to 20X1, 20X2, and 20X3 is as follows:

	20X1	20X2	20X3
Earnings before income tax	$100,000	$100,000	$100,000
Accounting income includes the following:			
Depreciation (assets have a cost of $120,000)	10,000	10,000	12,000
Pension expense*	5,000	7,000	10,000
Warranty expense	3,000	3,000	3,000
Dividend income (nontaxable)	2,000	2,000	3,000
Taxable income includes the following:			
Capital cost allowance	25,000	15,000	7,000
Pension funding (amount paid)	7,000	8,000	9,000
Warranty costs paid	1,000	4,000	3,000
Tax rate—enacted in each year	40%	44%	48%

*Pension amounts are tax deductible when paid, not when expensed. Over the long term, payments will equal total expense. The tax basis for the pension will always be zero. For accounting purposes, there will be a statement of financial position asset account asset called "deferred pension cost" for the difference between the amount paid and the expense, since the amount paid is higher.

Required:

Prepare the journal entry to record income tax expense for each year.

 ## A16-24 Tax Calculations, Rate Change (ASPE):

Refer to the facts in A16-18.

Required:

Prepare the journal entries to record income tax expense for the first and second years of operation, assuming the company is a private company that uses the taxes payable method. Show all supporting calculations.

 ## A16-25 Tax Calculations (ASPE):

Refer to the case facts in A16-20.

Required:

Provide the journal entry to record income tax expense for 20X4, assuming the company is a private company that uses the taxes payable method. Show all supporting calculations.

 ## A16-26 Investment Tax Credit (Appendix):

Pegasus Printing began operations in 20X4 and has bought equipment for use in its printing operations in each of the last three years. This equipment qualifies for an investment tax credit of 14%. Information relating to the three years is shown below:

	20X4	20X5	20X6
Income before income tax	$165,000	$ 456,000	$468,000
Income tax rate	25%	25%	25%
Equipment eligible for ITC	$ 40,000	$689,000	$450,000
Estimated life of equipment	10 years	13 years	12 years

a. Income before tax includes non-deductible advertising expenditures of $20,000 each year.

b. Equipment is depreciated straight-line over its useful life for accounting purposes, assuming zero salvage value. A full year of depreciation is charged in the year of acquisition. CCA claims in 20X4 were $12,000; 20X5, $135,000; and 20X6, $216,000.

Required:

1. Calculate the depreciation expense in each of the three years, net of the investment tax credit amortization.

2. Calculate taxes payable in each of the three years. Note that depreciation added back is net depreciation, as calculated in requirement 1.

3. Calculate tax expense for each year, using Canadian standards (cost reduction) to account for the investment tax credit.

4. Calculate tax expense, using the flow-through approach for all tax amounts.

5. Why is the cost reduction approach preferable?

6. Show how capital assets, and the deferred investment tax credit, would be presented on the statement of financial position at the end of 20X4.

APPENDIX 1

CONCEPTUAL ISSUES IN INTERPERIOD TAX ALLOCATION

As the chapter points out, income tax accounting standards reflect policy choices in three major areas:

1. The extent of allocation;

2. The measurement method; and

3. Discounting.

Extent of Allocation

The extent of allocation issue is analyzed in the chapter material. It refers to the range of temporary differences to which interperiod tax allocation is applied. The two basic options are:

1. No allocation—the taxes payable method; and

2. Full allocation—the comprehensive tax allocation (liability) method.

An intermediate approach known as *partial allocation* was used in some countries in the past (notably, in the United Kingdom), but this method has largely been discarded. Partial allocation recognized some sources of temporary differences as deferred income tax, but disregarded others.

Measurement Method

The measurement method chosen dictates the tax rate that is used to measure deferred income tax. The tax rate could be:

1. The rate in effect at the time that the temporary difference *first arises* (the deferral method), or

2. The rate that is *expected to be in effect* when the temporary difference reverses (the liability, or accrual, method)

Deferral Method

The deferral method was used in Canadian and US GAAP in the past. This method records the future tax impact by using the corporation's effective average tax rate in the year that the temporary difference first arises, or *originates*. Advocates of the deferral method argue that interperiod income tax allocation is simply a method of moving expense from one period to another and that the best measure of that expense is the effect that it had in the year that the temporary difference originated. The implication of the deferral method is that the SFP credit (or debit) for deferred income taxes is simply a deferred credit (or deferred debit) and should not be accorded the status of a liability (or asset). Deferred income tax credits and debits on the SFP are simply a necessary result of improving income measurement. Conceptually, the focus is on the SCI.

Liability Method

In contrast, the liability method uses the tax rate that will be in effect in the year of *reversal*. Proponents of this view argue that ultimate realization of the amount of the temporary difference depends on the tax rates in effect when the temporary differences reverse, and thus the amounts to be realized bear no relationship to the tax rates in effect when they originated. Conceptually, the emphasis is on measurement of the future cash flow impact, and the future amount to be paid (or received, if there is a net tax benefit) is viewed as a liability (or asset). The focus, therefore, is on the SFP.

How can the tax rate in the year of reversal be projected? Prediction of future tax rates is a very tenuous proposition and might also tempt a company's management to use a high or low prediction that has a desired impact of increasing or decreasing net income. Therefore, the practical solution is that only *enacted* rates of tax will be used. If this year's tax rate is 30% and the tax rate for next year has already been enacted and is, say, 32%, then 32% is used to measure the balance in deferred income taxes.

Effect of Tax Rates

In a world of stable tax rates, there would be no difference between the two methods. But tax rates are not always stable. Tax rates in Canada are subject to annual adjustment by the governments (federal and provincial), including the use of surtaxes (i.e., an extra tax calculated as a percentage of the basic income tax at the statutory rate).

What happens when tax rates change? Under the deferral method, no consequence for tax allocation arises from a change in tax rates. In contrast, the liability method requires that the liability (or asset) be adjusted to reflect each year's *best estimate* of the future tax liability (asset) arising from temporary differences. Therefore, every time there is a change in the corporate tax rate, companies must increase or decrease the amount recorded for the deferred tax liability or asset. The offset to the adjustment is the income tax expense in the income statement.

Example

The following example illustrates the impact of changing income tax rates. The following facts are assumed:

- Earnings before income tax is $1,000,000 in each of 20X1, 20X2, and 20X3.
- A revenue of $400,000 is included in accounting income in 20X1 but is not subject to tax until 20X3.
- The income tax rate in 20X1 is 35%; during 20X2, the rate is reduced by act of Parliament to 32%, which remains in effect for both 20X2 and 20X3.

The calculation of income tax payable under this revised scenario is as follows:

	20X1	20X2	20X3
Earnings before tax (accounting basis)	$ 1,000,000	$1,000,000	$1,000,000
20X1 accounting revenue that is taxable in 20X3	− 400,000	_____	+ 400,000
Taxable income	$ 600,000	$1,000,000	$1,400,000
Tax rate	× 35%	× 32%	× 32%
Income tax payable	$ 210,000	$ 320,000	$ 448,000

Entries for the liability method are shown below.

20X1		
Income tax expense	350,000	
Income tax payable		210,000
Deferred income tax liability		140,000

In 20X2, using the liability method, the deferred income tax account must be adjusted to reflect the tax rate change. The temporary difference of $400,000 now will result in taxation of only $128,000 (i.e., the $400,000 temporary difference × 32%) instead of $140,000 ($400,000 × 35%). Therefore, we must reduce the balance of the deferred income tax liability by $12,000.

20X2		
Deferred income tax liability	12,000	
Income tax expense	308,000	
Income tax payable		320,000

The tax expense recorded is the net amount of the payable ($320,000) minus the reduction in deferred income tax ($12,000). The tax expense is now $308,000.

In 20X3, the temporary difference is *reversed* and the deferred tax liability is *drawn down* because the revenue enters taxable income.

20X3		
Income tax expense	320,000	
Deferred income tax liability	128,000	
Income tax payable		448,000

Discounting

A final conceptual issue is whether deferred income tax balances should be discounted to present value. If the future tax consequence of a temporary difference is a liability, then the time value of money can be taken into account. If a corporation delays paying large amounts of income tax by taking advantage of (completely legal) aspects of the *Income Tax Act* (such as large CCA deductions), then the deferred tax liability represents, in effect, an interest-free loan from the government. (Bear in mind, however, that the government does not view the amount as owing to it. The liability is an accounting construct, not a "real" liability; the government cannot demand payment.)

In general, accounting standards require that noncurrent monetary assets and liabilities be shown at their discounted present value. Non-interest-bearing loans normally are discounted at an imputed rate of interest. Therefore, many accountants argue that income tax assets and liabilities also should be discounted to measure these monetary assets and liabilities in a manner that is consistent with the measurement of other monetary items.

Despite the strength of the theoretical arguments in favour of discounting, practical problems get in the way. There are difficulties in determining the interest rate to be used in discounting, and the timing of reversals is particularly problematic, as they depend on accounting policy, management judgements, and prediction of future years' taxable income.

Largely as the result of the many estimates that must be made to apply discounting, discounting is not applied to interperiod tax allocation.

CONCEPT REVIEW

1. What is the essential difference between the deferral method and the liability method of tax allocation?
2. A company records a deferred income tax liability in 20X1. In 20X2, the income tax rate changes. In 20X4, the deferred tax liability is drawn down and disappears. In what year is the impact of the rate change recognized, using the liability method?
3. Why aren't deferred income tax amounts discounted as are other long-term liabilities?

SUMMARY OF KEY POINTS

1. Three policy issues that must be established in accounting standards with respect to accounting for income tax are the extent of allocation, the measurement method, and the possibility of discounting deferred tax balances.
2. In terms of the extent of allocation, the comprehensive tax allocation method requires that all temporary differences give rise to deferred income tax; the opposite end of the spectrum is the taxes payable method, where no deferred tax is recognized.

3. Deferred tax balances can be measured at the rate of accumulation, referred to as the deferral method, or the tax rate expected to be in effect when the deferred tax amount reverses, which is called the liability method. The liability method is used in accounting standards, and it requires that deferred tax balances be remeasured if the tax rate changes.

4. Deferred tax balances are not discounted, despite strong arguments that discounting would be appropriate.

APPENDIX 2

THE INVESTMENT TAX CREDIT

General Nature

A *tax credit* is a direct, dollar-for-dollar offset against income taxes that otherwise are payable. The advantage of a tax *credit* (instead of a tax *deduction* for the expenditures) is that the amount of the tax credit is not affected by the tax rate being paid by the corporation. For example, if a $100,000 expenditure qualifies for a 7% tax credit, the tax reduction will be $7,000 regardless of whether the corporation is paying taxes at 20%, 30%, 40%, or any other rate.[1]

The *Income Tax Act* provides for *investment tax credits* (*ITC*) for (1) qualifying research and experimental development expenditures and (2) specified types of expenditures for capital investment. The expenditures that qualify for the investment tax credit are matters of government policy and change from time to time. By giving a tax credit, the government can influence companies to increase investments in certain types of facilities and in selected geographic areas by effectively reducing their cost. Qualifying expenditures can vary on three dimensions:

1. Type of expenditure;
2. Type of corporation; and
3. Geographic region.

To realize the benefit of a tax credit, it usually is necessary for the qualifying corporation to have taxable income and to generate income tax payable. If there is not sufficient tax payable in the year of the qualifying expenditures, the tax credit can be carried back three years to trigger a refund and also carried forward to reduce tax to be paid in a subsequent year. Certain types of corporations may be eligible to receive the credit in cash, even if there is not enough tax due within the current and carryback periods to completely utilize the tax credit.

Accounting Treatment

In theory, there are two possible approaches to accounting for the investment tax credit (ITC):

1. The *flow-through approach*, whereby the ITC for which the corporation qualifies is reported as a direct reduction in the income tax expense for the year; or

2. The *cost-reduction approach,* in which the ITC is deducted from the expenditures that give rise to the ITC; the benefit of the ITC is thereby allocated to the years in which the expenditures are recognized as expenses.

International standards do not specifically discuss investment tax credits. However, *IAS* 20 does address the more general topic of government assistance, and tax credits clearly are a form of government assistance.

---

1. Depending on the type of capital expenditure and the location of the enterprise, the investment tax credit may range from 7% to 35%.

IAS 20 prescribes the *cost reduction approach*. The two categories of "cost" are:

- Costs recorded as expenses in the current period; and
- Costs that are recorded as assets.

The general approach for government grants, including ITCs, is to recognize them in profit or loss over the same periods in which the company recognizes the related costs as expenses. The following sections describe the accounting treatment for each type of cost.

Costs Reported as Current Expenses

The government often grants ITCs for research and development expenditures. Some of those expenditures will not qualify for capitalization as development costs and instead will be charged to expense in the period in which they are incurred.

Investment tax credits that relate to expenditures that are reported as expenses in the income statement are permitted to flow through to the income statement in the same period.

The ITC on current expenses may be reported in either of two ways:

1. As an item of "other income" in the profit and loss section of the statement of comprehensive income; or
2. As a reduction of (or offset against) the expense that gave rise to the ITC.

The second method may seem more consistent with the cost-reduction approach, but it is contrary to the general principle that revenues and expenses should not be shown net of taxes. Both treatments are acceptable under international standards.

Since the ITC will reduce the effective tax rate being paid by the corporation, a publicly accountable enterprise will treat the ITC as a tax rate reduction and will include it in its tax rate reconciliation.

Costs Capitalized

If the ITC qualifying expenditures are for a capital asset or are for development costs that can be capitalized and amortized, then the ITC itself is deferred and amortized on the same basis as the asset. This can be accomplished either by reducing the capitalized cost of the asset or by separately deferring and amortizing the ITC.

Investment tax credits related to the acquisition of assets would be either:

1. Deducted from the related assets with any amortization calculated on the net amount; or
2. Deferred and amortized to income on the same basis as the related assets.

The first option is to deduct the deferred ITC from the balance of the asset. The second approach is to recognize the ITC as *deferred income* on the balance sheet and then to amortize it along with the asset itself. The second approach seems more consistent with the cost-reduction theory than the first, but either may be used in practice.

For income tax purposes, the ITC is deducted from the tax basis of the asset.[2] The effect is as follows:

- For expenditures that are capitalized for accounting purposes but are deducted immediately for tax purposes (e.g., some development costs), a temporary difference is created because the cost (net of ITC) is being deducted immediately but is charged to income via amortization over several years; and
- For capital assets, the tax basis and the accounting basis start out the same (i.e., both reduced by the amount of the ITC benefit), but temporary differences arise from any differences between CCA and depreciation.

Exhibits 16A-1 and 16A-2 demonstrate the relevant accounting procedures. Exhibit 16A-1 contains the basic data and illustrates the journal entries used to record the qualifying expenditure and the ITC. Exhibit 16A-2 shows the impacts on the financial statements. The exhibits assume that the deferred ITC is deducted from the asset on the balance sheet.

EXHIBIT 16A-1

RECORDING THE INVESTMENT TAX CREDIT

Illustrative Data

1 May 20X5

Purchased eligible transportation equipment (30% CCA rate) costing $100,000, to be depreciated straight-line over 10 years, no residual value, with a half-year's depreciation in the year of acquisition for both accounting and tax purposes.

31 December 20X5

Pre-tax income (after depreciation on new equipment), $150,000 but before ITC amortization. Investment tax credit ($100,000 × 7%; not included in previous amounts), $7,000. The tax rate is 30%.

Entries for 20X5

a. *1 May—purchase qualified equipment*

Equipment	100,000	
Cash		100,000

b. *31 December—record ITC*

Income tax payable	7,000	
Deferred investment tax credit		7,000

c. *31 December—record depreciation expense*

Depreciation expense ($100,000 × 1/10 × ½)	5,000	
Accumulated depreciation		5,000

d. *31 December—record amortization of investment tax credit for 20X5*

Deferred investment tax credit ($7,000 × 1/10 × ½)   350

Amortization expense   350

e. *31 December—record income tax on 20X5 earnings**

Income tax expense   45,105

Deferred income tax liability
($13,950 − $4,650) × 30%   2,790

Income tax payable   42,315

*See Exhibit 16A-2 for the calculation of these amounts.

EXHIBIT 16A-2

REPORTING THE INVESTMENT TAX CREDIT

Calculation of Income Tax Expense

Tax and accounting cost of asset:	
Capital cost of equipment	$100,000
Less: Investment tax credit of 7%	7,000
Net capital cost	$ 93,000
Accounting income, after ITC amortization	$150,350
Depreciation [($100,000 × 1/10 × 1/2 year) − ($7,000 × 1/10 × ½)]	+ 4,650
CCA ($93,000 × 30% × ½ year*)	− 13,950
Taxable income	$ 141,050
Tax rate	× 30%
Current tax due before ITC	$ 42,315

Less: Investment tax credit ($100,000 × 7%)		7,000
Income tax payable (Journal entry of $7,000 dr. and $42,315 cr.)		$ 35,315
Current income tax		$ 42,315
Deferred income tax liability [($13,950 − $4,650) × 30%]		2,790
Income tax expense		$ 45,105

*Only a half-year's deduction for CCA is claimable in the first year, as is usual.

SCI Reporting, Year Ended 31 December 20X5

Depreciation expense ($5,000 − $350 amortization of ITC)		$ 4,650
Pre-tax income ($150,000 + $350)		$ 150,350
Income tax expense—current (from above)	$42,315	
—deferred (from above)	2,790	45,105
Net income		$105,245

SFP Reporting, 31 December 20X5

Equipment (at cost)		$100,000
Accumulated depreciation	$ 5,000	
Deferred investment tax credit ($7,000 − $350)	6,650	11,650
Reported carrying value		$ 88,350
Income tax payable (from above) ($42,315 − $7,000)		$ 35,315
Deferred income tax liability (from above)		$ 2,790

Disclosure of ITC and Other Government Grants

ITCs (and other types of government assistance) affect both the income/expense structure of the entity's operations and its cash flows. Therefore, the notes should disclose:

- The accounting policy and the method of presentation in the financial statements;
- The nature and extent of ITCs (and any government grants); and
- Any unfulfilled conditions or contingencies.

RELEVANT STANDARDS

CPA Canada Handbook, Part I (IASB):

- IAS 20, Accounting for Government Grants and Disclosure of Government Assistance

CPA Canada Handbook, Part II (ASPE):

- Section 3800, Government Assistance
- Section 3805, Investment Tax Credits

SUMMARY OF KEY POINTS

1. The investment tax credit (ITC) is a direct reduction of income taxes that is granted to enterprises that invest in certain types of assets or in research and development costs.

2. There are two possible approaches to accounting for ITCs: (1) the flow-through approach and (2) the cost reduction approach.

3. IFRS recommends using the cost reduction approach, wherein the ITC is deducted (either directly or indirectly) from the asset or expense that gave rise to the ITC.

4. ITCs on expenditures that are reported as current expenses can be shown as an item of "other income" or deducted from the investment expense.

5. When qualifying expenditures are made to acquire an asset (including capitalized development costs), the ITC can either be (1) deducted from the asset's carrying value, with depreciation based on the net amount or (2) deferred separately as "deferred income" and amortized on the same basis as the asset itself.

6. The nature and amount of ITCs should be disclosed in the notes, as well as the company's accounting policy for ITCs, the method of presentation, and any unfulfilled conditions or contingencies.

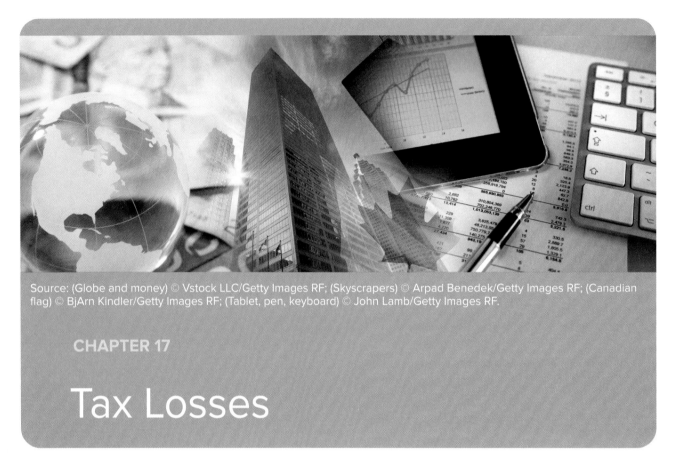

Source: (Globe and money) © Vstock LLC/Getty Images RF; (Skyscrapers) © Arpad Benedek/Getty Images RF; (Canadian flag) © BjArn Kindler/Getty Images RF; (Tablet, pen, keyboard) © John Lamb/Getty Images RF.

CHAPTER 17

Tax Losses

INTRODUCTION

When a corporation's taxable "income" is actually a loss, the corporation can use that loss to reduce past and future income tax otherwise payable. That might mean a refund for past years' tax paid, or the ability to earn income and not pay income tax in future years. Accounting for refunds of past tax paid is not complicated. Accounting for future tax benefits *is* complicated, though, because these future tax benefits will not be *realized* until future years, and might not be realized at all if there are no profits in future years. Should future tax benefits be *recognized as an asset* in the year of the loss, when they arise, or should recognition be delayed, until they are realized?

Alderon Iron Ore Corp. is a development-stage company that is advancing toward production of its Canadian properties located in western Labrador. To the end of 2014, the company had not commenced commercial production, and therefore had no revenue. Recognized assets were approximately $272 million, and reported operating losses in 2014 were approximately $12 million. No income tax recovery was recognized in earnings, meaning that the loss before tax *and* after tax were *both* $12 million. The tax benefit of the operating loss—the tax loss carryforward—was not recognized. Start-ups are risky business, with no guarantee of eventual success. However, the company has a substantial unrecognized asset—the ability to earn profits in the future and pay no tax because of the use of loss carryforwards. This is apparent only from the disclosure notes.

This chapter begins with an explanation of the income tax benefits that arise from a loss. Then we will discuss the issue of when and how to recognize those benefits.

RECOGNIZING THE TAX BENEFIT OF A LOSS

Accounting income is converted to taxable income by making appropriate adjustments for all temporary and permanent differences. This is true whether the accounting records report positive or negative earnings. Accounting income may become a taxable loss, and an accounting loss may become taxable income, depending on the nature of the permanent and temporary differences.

When a corporation prepares its tax return and finds it has a taxable loss, the corporation is entitled to offset the loss against past and future taxable income as follows:

- The loss can be *carried back* for three years for a refund of tax previously paid.

- Any remaining loss can be *carried forward* for up to 20 years to reduce tax that would otherwise be payable.

If the loss is not used through carryback or in the carryforward period, it expires and the benefit is lost.

Because of the potential to lose the benefit of a loss carryforward, a company may also reduce the temporary differences claimed for tax purposes. We will illustrate this with the most common temporary difference, which is CCA. A company may reduce the amount of CCA charged, in the loss year or in any of the three carryback years. This will either reduce the loss amount, or maximize the amount used as a carryback.

Loss Carryback

It is simple to account for the tax benefits of the tax **loss carryback**; the taxes recovered are recognized in earnings as a tax recovery in the loss year, and the refund receivable is shown on the SFP as a current asset. Recognition occurs in the period of the loss because there is no uncertainty about whether or not the company will actually realize the benefit. Accounting for loss carrybacks will be demonstrated in the next section.

Reduce and/or Refile Temporary Differences

The *Income Tax Act* imposes various restrictions on the amendment of prior years' returns, but strategically adjusting CCA is a fully legitimate way of either reducing a tax loss or using it up in prior and subsequent years. Recall that CCA is a voluntary deduction; CCA is limited to a maximum, but there is no minimum. A company will reduce its tax loss if it reduces or eliminates CCA in a loss year, and the lower the loss, the more likely that its tax benefits can be realized.

The key to this strategy is that CCA not claimed *is not lost*. If a company chooses not to claim CCA in a year, the undepreciated capital cost (UCC) remains higher—still adjusted for additions to and retirements from the class—but CCA on the undiminished balance remains available as a deduction in future years. If the UCC of taxable assets remains higher, this allows higher CCA in the future, or a lower recapture on sale of the assets. It can be sensible tax planning for an uncertain business enterprise.

If the strategy is adopted, then this will:

- Decrease the amount of the loss, if CCA is not claimed in the loss year.
- Increase taxable income in a prior year, if prior-year CCA is eliminated. A higher dollar value of loss is then needed as a carryback, and more of the loss is used in this fashion.
- Elimination of CCA in future years will increase the tax loss used as a carryforward.

CCA reduction will affect the balance in deferred tax. This will be demonstrated in the examples to follow.

Loss Carryforward

If the carrybacks do not fully utilize the loss, a recognition problem arises. Income taxes can be reduced in *future* periods as a result of the tax **loss carryforward**. Should the benefit of reduced future taxes be recognized in the period of the loss, or should it be recognized in the future, in the period during which the benefits are realized?

The definition of an asset in the conceptual framework specifies that an asset must have a future benefit. This benefit must be *probable*. The general principle, therefore, is that the tax benefits of tax losses should be recognized as an asset in the period of the loss, *to the extent that the benefits are probable*.

It can be difficult to assess the probability associated with a tax loss carryforward. In order to realize the benefit, the company must have enough taxable income during the carryforward period to use the loss carryforward. The carryforward benefit can be considered a contingent item—a benefit will be realized only *if* something happens in the future.

The amount of the tax benefit must also be measurable to qualify for recognition. If a company has a tax loss of $1 million and the tax rate is 35%, the potential benefit of the tax loss is that past and future income taxes will be reduced by $350,000 (i.e., $1 million × 35%). Enacted (or substantially enacted) tax rates are used for measurement. While changes in the tax rate may cause some variation, the amount of the benefit can be *measured* with reasonable assurance.

Opposition to loss carryforward recognition Some observers are troubled by the recognition of tax loss carryforward benefits before their realization. The principal concern is that future tax assets do not satisfy the basic definition of an asset. There has been no transaction that establishes the corporation's right to receive the future benefit; realization of the benefits is contingent on generating sufficient taxable income in the future. And, clearly, the government does not consider that it owes any money to the company.

The recognition of unrealized tax assets for tax loss carryforwards has the effect of reducing the apparent accounting loss. That is, the effect of an operating loss is softened by this practice and gives financial statement users the perception that the loss is "not as bad" as it really is, even though the benefit of a carryforward has not been realized and there may be no more than a marginal positive probability that the benefit will ever be realized.

Tax Loss versus Tax Benefits

To avoid confusion, it is necessary to keep track separately of the amount of the tax *loss* and the amount of the tax *benefit*. The **tax loss** is the final amount of taxable loss on the tax return. The **tax benefit** is the total present and future benefit that the company will be able to realize from the tax loss through a refund or reduction of income taxes paid or payable to governments. Basically, the tax benefit is equal to the tax loss multiplied by the tax rate. Put another way, *the tax loss is the gross amount, and the tax benefit is the tax savings.* Since tax rates can change, keeping track of the gross amount is essential for calculating the tax savings.

TAX LOSS CARRYBACKS

A tax loss carryback entitles the corporation to recover income tax actually paid in the previous three years. For example, assume that Fabian Corp. was established in 20X1. For the first four years, the company was moderately successful, but in the fifth year, Fabian suffered a tax loss of $500,000. Fabian's taxable income for the first five years was as follows:

Year	Taxable Income	Tax Rate	Income Tax Paid
20X1	$100,000	40%	$ 40,000
20X2	240,000	40	96,000
20X3	160,000	35	56,000
20X4	300,000	37	111,000
20X5	(500,000)	38	—

The loss will be carried back to the preceding three years to recover tax previously paid. Normally, the loss is carried back to the earliest (oldest) year first, and then applied to succeeding years until the loss is used up. The year 20X1 is outside the three-year carryback period, and therefore the loss can be carried back only as far as 20X2. The tax recovery will be as follows:

Year	Carryback	Tax Rate	Tax Recovery
20X2	$240,000	40%	$ 96,000
20X3	160,000	35	56,000
20X4	100,000	37	37,000
Totals	$500,000		$189,000

In this example, the carryback completely utilizes the 20X5 tax loss of $500,000. Note that the tax is recovered at the rate at which it was originally paid, since Fabian is recovering taxes previously paid. The tax rate in the year of the loss (i.e., 38% for 20X5) is irrelevant for determining the amount of tax recoverable via the carryback. Fabian will record the benefit of the carryback as follows:

Income tax receivable (SFP)	189,000	
Income tax expense (recovery) (SCI)		189,000

The *credit* to income tax expense reflects the fact that it is a recovery of taxes paid in earlier years. A company will usually label this amount as "provision for income tax" or "income tax recovery" on the SCI. If any part of the tax loss is attributable to discontinued operations, the recovery must be allocated to the relevant components of income, as we described in Chapter 3 for *intraperiod* allocation.

Choice of Carryback Year

In 20X3, the tax rate was 35%; in 20X4 it had increased to 37%. The company could maximize its recovery by applying more of the carryback to 20X4 instead of 20X3; there is no requirement in the *Income Tax Act* to apply the carryback sequentially. If the company follows a recovery maximization strategy, the carryback would be applied as follows:

Year	Carryback	Tax Rate	Tax Recovery
20X2	$240,000	40%	$ 96,000
20X4	260,000	37	96,200
Totals	$500,000		$192,200

Maximizing the carryback tax recovery is a viable strategy, but it is a bit of a gamble because if the company has a loss in 20X7, the 20X4 carryback potential will have already been used up, and the 20X3 tax is then out of reach because it is no longer within the allowable carryback period of three years. Therefore, companies usually apply the carryback sequentially, even if there may be an advantage of a higher income tax receivable if the carryback is applied nonsequentially to the years that had the highest tax rate.

TEMPORARY AND PERMANENT DIFFERENCES IN A LOSS YEAR

Step 1: Calculate Taxable Income (Loss)

The first step in doing a tax question is always to calculate taxable income. This involves adjusting accounting income for permanent and temporary differences. Temporary differences continue to originate and/or reverse regardless of whether the company is experiencing profits or losses. Permanent differences are likewise adjusted, whether accounting and/or taxable income are positive or negative. Indeed, it is quite possible for temporary differences and permanent differences to convert a pre-tax accounting profit to a tax loss.

Assume the following facts for Michelle Ltd. for the fiscal year ending 31 December 20X8:

- Net income before taxes of $90,000, after deducting depreciation expense of $150,000;
- CCA totalling $280,000 deducted on the tax return;
- Net book value of plant, and equipment of $1,700,000 and UCC of $1,200,000 on 1 January 20X8, a temporary difference of $500,000 that is reflected in an accumulated deferred income tax liability balance of $200,000 at 1 January 20X8;

- Nondeductible golf club dues of $10,000;
- Cumulative taxable income in the three-year carryback period of $360,000; and
- Tax rate of 40% in the current and all previous years.

Michelle's taxable income for 20X8 will be computed as follows:

Accounting income	$ 90,000
Permanent difference:	
Golf club dues	+ 10,000
Temporary difference:	
Depreciation	+ 150,000
CCA	−280,000
Taxable income (loss)	$ (30,000)

Step 2: Determine Deferred Income Tax

The next step is to determine the change to deferred income tax caused by current-year temporary differences and/or any change in the tax rate. Using a table:

	Year-End Tax Basis dr. (cr.)	Carrying Value dr. (cr.)	Temporary Difference Deductible (taxable)	Deferred Tax (Liability) at Year-End Rate	Less Beginning Balance dr. (cr.)	Adjustment for Current Year dr. (cr.)
20X8—40%						
P&E	920,000	1,550,000	(630,000)	(252,000)	(200,000)	(52,000)

Since the tax rate did not change this year, the shortcut approach could also be used. The difference between CCA and depreciation yields a temporary difference of ($130,000) (i.e., $150,000 − $280,000). This temporary difference increases the deferred income tax liability by $52,000 (i.e., $130,000 × 40%).

Step 3: Journal Entry

The third step is to prepare the journal entries. First, the effect of the tax loss must be determined. The $30,000 tax loss creates a tax benefit of $12,000 (at 40%). This amount is carried back to prior years. The prior-year tax returns are refiled, and a tax refund will be requested.

The tax entry accordingly records the change in deferred income tax, and income tax receivable, and the impact on income tax expense:

Income tax expense (SCI)	40,000	
Income tax receivable—carryback benefit (SFP)	12,000	
Deferred income tax liability—P&E (SFP)		52,000

The bottom section of the SCI will show:

Earnings before income tax	$90,000
Income tax expense (Note x)	40,000
Earnings	$50,000

Note x:

Deferred income tax	$52,000
Recovery of amounts paid in prior years	(12,000)
Income tax expense	$40,000

Tax Planning—Adjusting Temporary Differences

In the Michelle example above, the company reported a tax loss of $30,000, after claiming CCA of $280,000. Since the company had taxable income available in the carryback period against which the loss can be offset, this was logical: good tax strategy calls for taking the maximum allowable CCA in 20X8 in order to obtain a refund of taxes previously paid.

Suppose instead that the company did not have taxable income in the preceding three years and the prospect for earning positive income in the future was uncertain. Any loss not used as a carryback would have to be used as a carryforward and might expire unused. The tax loss would go to waste unless the company generates profits in the carryforward period.

Instead of reporting a tax loss, the company can simply reduce the amount of CCA that it deducts on its tax return for 20X8 by $30,000, from $280,000 to $250,000. CCA is an *optional* deduction; in any year, a company can deduct anywhere from zero to the maximum percentage allowed by tax regulations. A company will have a higher amount of UCC (and CCA) in *future years* if it claims less CCA in the *current year*. Companies make these decisions based on advice from their tax-planning advisors.

If Michelle follows this strategy, the tax loss is zero. The revised deferred tax table and the tax journal entry are as follows:

	Year-End Tax Basis dr. (cr.)	Carrying Value dr. (cr.)	Temporary Difference Deductible (taxable)	Deferred Tax (Liability) at Year-End Rate	Less Beginning Balance dr. (cr.)	Adjustment for Current Year dr. (cr.)
20X8—40%						
P&E	950,000	1,550,000	(600,000)	(240,000)	(200,000)	(40,000)

Note that UCC is now $950,000; only $250,000 of CCA was charged.

The tax entry accordingly records the change in deferred tax, and the impact on income tax expense:

Income tax expense (SCI)	40,000	
Deferred income tax liability—P&E (SFP)		40,000

The tax expense is still $40,000. Notice that only the SFP accounts are changed by the tax planning decision. Cash flow is different, though: in the prior example, Michelle had a $12,000 current tax refund receivable. Now, Michelle has only a lower deferred income tax liability. The cash flow benefits of refiling temporary differences are more long term.

CONCEPT REVIEW

1. How many years can a tax loss be carried back? How many years into the future can it be carried forward?
2. What is the difference between the tax loss in a particular year and the tax benefit of the loss?
3. Why do companies usually apply a loss carryback sequentially (i.e., to the earliest year first), even if the tax refund might be slightly larger if they applied it to the carryback year that had the highest tax rate?

TAX LOSS CARRYFORWARDS

In the Fabian Corp. example earlier in the chapter, the tax benefit of the $500,000 tax loss in 20X5 was fully realized through carryback. But suppose instead that the loss in 20X5 was $1,000,000. Then the carryback could utilize only $700,000 of the loss:

Year	Carryback	Tax Rate	Tax Recovery
20X2	$240,000	40%	$ 96,000
20X3	160,000	35	56,000
20X4	300,000	37	111,000
Totals	**$700,000**		**$263,000**

The tax benefit of $263,000 relating to $700,000 of the $1 million tax loss is realized through the carryback; the tax benefit is both *recognized* and *realized* in 20X5. After the carryback, there is a gross carryforward of $300,000 remaining. The tax benefit of the loss carryforward cannot be realized until future years, when the carryforward is applied against otherwise taxable income.

The accounting question is whether the future tax benefit of the carryforward can be *recognized* in 20X5, the period of the loss. If the benefit is recognized in the loss year, the benefit of the tax loss will decrease the reported accounting loss.

In the Fabian example, assume that the loss carryforward benefit can be recognized and the tax rate is 40%. The income tax recovery account is a credit entry in earnings, reducing the amount of the reported loss. Recognition will also create an asset on the SFP. The entry would be as follows:

Income tax receivable ($700,000 loss carryback × various tax rates) (SFP)	263,000	
Deferred income tax asset — carryforward benefit ($300,000 × 40%)(SFP)	120,000	
Income tax expense (recovery) (SCI)		383,000

Basic Probability Principle

The criterion for recognizing the future benefit *as an asset* is simply a matter of probability. If it is probable that the carryforward will be realized, then the benefit is recognized. On the other hand, if realization is unlikely, or not probable, then the potential benefit should not be recognized.

Conceptually, it is simple: If use is probable, recognize the asset. If use is not probable, do not recognize. In practice, determining the probability can be challenging and requires the use of professional judgement. There should be objective evidence as to the likelihood of realization.

Evidence of Probability

IAS 12 provides some guidelines to help management (and auditors) decide whether the probability threshold has been met over the 20-year carryforward period. Favourable evidence to support recognition includes the following:

- The company has an earnings history that indicates future taxable profits;

- The taxable loss was the result of an unusual event not likely reoccur (e.g., a long strike);

- The company has enough accumulated taxable temporary differences to absorb the unrealized loss as the temporary differences reverse; or

- The company has tax-planning opportunities that will create taxable profit in the carryforward period.

Another factor that can contribute to a positive probability assessment is the existence of contracts or back orders that are likely to generate more than enough taxable income to absorb the loss carryforward.

On the other hand, the probability criterion will *not* be met if:

- The company has a history of tax losses expiring without being used;

- A change in the company's economic prospects indicates that losses may continue for the next few years; and

- There are pending circumstances that, if not resolved in the company's favour, will impair the company's ability to operate profitably (e.g., significant patent infringement lawsuits or potential major environmental impacts caused by the company's operations).

When a company's management decides that the probability criterion for recognition of any part of the benefit of a tax loss carryforward has been met, the "nature of evidence supporting its recognition" must be disclosed in the notes.

Reassessment in Years Subsequent to the Loss Year

If a future tax benefit of a tax loss carryforward has been recognized as an asset, the asset is subject to review at each reporting date. If realization becomes not probable, the deferred income tax asset should be written off to income tax expense.

There is nothing unusual about this requirement; assets are generally subject to review and to writedown if their value has been impaired. If an asset is unlikely to recover its carrying value, either through use or through sale, it should be written down.

The tax asset may also be written up, or reinstated, in a subsequent year, if use becomes probable. *Previous years* are not restated because the chance is the result of an estimate, which rests on evidence in the current year. That is, changes in estimates are accounted for prospectively, not retrospectively.

Examples of Recognition Scenarios

We can illustrate the various basic recognition points using a simple illustration. Suppose that Parravano Ltd. has been in business for five years and incurs a loss of $500,000 in 20X5. The company has no temporary or permanent differences, and therefore the pre-tax accounting loss is the same as the loss for income tax purposes. The history of the company's earnings since the company began operations is as follows:

Year	Taxable Income (Loss)	Taxes Paid (Recovered)
20X1	$100,000	$40,000
20X2	(60,000) (used as a loss carryback)	(24,000)
20X3	140,000	56,000
20X4	30,000	12,000

The tax rate has been constant at 40% from 20X1 through 20X5.

In 20X5, Parravano incurs a loss of $500,000. A further loss of $100,000 occurs in 20X6. In 20X7, accounting earnings and taxable income are positive, at $900,000. There are no temporary or permanent differences.

In 20X5, Parravano can carry back $170,000 of the loss to recover taxes paid in 20X3 and 20X4, a total of $68,000. A carryforward of $330,000 remains, the potential tax benefit of which is $132,000 ($330,000 × 40%). In 20X6, the further loss increases the tax loss carryforward, by $100,000, to $430,000, the benefit of which is $172,000 ($430,000 × 40%). In 20X7, there is taxable income of $900,000, which is reduced by the $430,000 loss carryforward to $470,000 ($900,000 − $430,000). This results in income tax payable of $188,000 ($470,000 × 40%).

Recognition of the future benefits of the carryforward depends on management's conclusions regarding the likelihood of realizing the benefits.

The following scenarios illustrate recognition of the benefits of tax loss carryforwards under various possible assumptions concerning the likelihood of realization. The entries under each scenario are summarized in Exhibit 17-1.

EXHIBIT 17-1

TAX LOSS CARRYFORWARD BENEFIT ALTERNATIVE SCENARIOS

Scenario	Year			
1a. C/B + full recognition of 20X5 C/F benefit	**20X5**	IT rec.—C/B	68,000	
		DT asset—C/F	132,000	
		IT exp. (recovery)		200,000
1b. Full recognition of 20X6 C/F benefit	**20X6**	DT asset—C/F	40,000	
		IT exp. (recovery)		40,000
1c. Full recognition of all C/F benefit	**20X7**	IT exp	360,000	
		IT payable		188,000
		DT asset-C/F		172,000
2a. C/B, but no recognition of C/F benefit	**20X5**	IT rec.—C/B	68,000	
		IT exp. (recovery)		68,000
2b. Recognize full 20X5 + 20X6 C/F benefit	**20X6**	DT asset—C/F	172,000	
		IT exp. (recovery)		172,000

2c. Full recognition of all C/F benefit	**20X7**	IT exp	360,000	
		IT payable		188,000
		DT asset – C/F		172,000
3a. C/B but no recognition of C/F benefit	**20X5**	IT rec.—C/B	68,000	
		IT exp. (recovery)		68,000
3b. Partial recognition of C/F benefit	**20X6**	DT asset—C/F	80,000	
		IT exp. (recovery)		80,000
3c. Full recognition of all C/F benefit	**20X7**	IT exp	268,000	
		IT payable		188,000
		DT asset — C/F		80,000
4a. Same as scenario 1, above —full recognition	**20X5**	IT rec.—C/B	68,000	
		DT asset—C/F	132,000	
		IT exp. (recovery)		200,000
4b. Only $200,000 of total C/F benefit is now deemed probable	**20X6**	IT expense	52,000	
		DT asset—C/F		52,000
4c. Full recognition of all C/F benefit	**20X7**	IT exp	268,000	
		IT payable		188,000
		DT asset – C/F		80,000
5a. C/B, but no recognition of C/F benefit	**20X5**	IT rec.—C/B	68,000	
		IT exp. (recovery)		68,000
5b. No recognition of C/F benefit	**20X6**	No entry		
5c. Full recognition through realization of all C/F benefit	**20X7**	IT exp	188,000	
		IT payable		188,000

Legend:

C/B = carryback

C/F = carry forward

I/T = income tax

DT = deferred tax

Scenario 1: Assuming future realization is judged to be probable in each year of the losses. If the use of the tax loss carryforward is judged to be probable in 20X5 and again in 20X6, the potential $132,000 benefit (20X5) and then $40,000 (20X6) is recognized in the year of the loss. The total income tax expense (recovery) account on the 20X5 SCI is $200,000 (i.e., $68,000 + $132,000 = $200,000). The full potential tax benefit of the loss has been *recognized*, although only $68,000 will be *realized* in the current year. In 20X6, the $40,000 potential tax benefit of the $100,000 loss will also be recognized on the SCI.

In 20X7, tax expense is based on $900,000 of taxable income, the $172,000 deferred income tax asset from the loss carryforward is eliminated, and tax payable of $188,000 is recorded. The loss carryforward is realized.

Scenario 2: Assuming future realization is judged to be improbable in 20X5 but becomes probable in 20X6. Now, suppose instead that, due to Parravano's erratic earnings history, realization of the benefit of the carryforward is judged to be not probable. The entry to record the tax benefit in 20X5 would then be limited to the amount of tax recovered through the carryback, or $68,000.

In the following year, 20X6, Parravano has a loss for both accounting and tax purposes of $100,000. Since there is no available taxable income in the carryback period, the $100,000 tax loss will be carried forward. The loss is still available to reduce future taxable income. The company now has two carryforwards:

- $330,000 from 20X5, expiring 20 years from 20X5; and

- $100,000 from 20X6, expiring 20 years from 20X6.

The total carryforward is $430,000.

However, suppose that Parravano obtained a large contract late in 20X6. The 20X6 operating results do not yet reflect the profit that will be generated by the contract, but the contract is expected to boost earnings considerably in 20X7 and the next several years. Therefore, management decides when preparing the 20X6 financial statements that it is probable that the full benefit of tax loss carryforwards from both 20X5 and 20X6 will be realized within the carryforward period.

Assuming a continuing tax rate of 40%, the future tax benefit of the total $430,000 carryforward is $172,000. Since, in management's judgement, the probability criterion has now been satisfied, all of the future benefit is recorded as an asset.

When the future benefit of $172,000 is recognized in earnings, the 20X6 pre-tax loss of $100,000 will be converted into positive *earnings* of $72,000 simply as the result of recognizing the still-unrealized tax loss carryforward benefit:

Earnings (loss) before income tax	$(100,000)
Income tax expense (recovery)	(172,000)
Earnings	$ 72,000

In 20X7, tax expense is based on $900,000 of taxable income, the $172,000 deferred income tax asset from the loss carryforward is eliminated, and tax payable of $188,000 is recorded. The loss carryforward is again realized.

Scenario 3: Partial recognition. In scenario 2, we assumed that Parravano recognized all of the accumulated tax benefits in 20X6. It is possible, however, that management may decide that realization of only part of the benefit is probable. Suppose, for example, that Parravano management decided in 20X6 that the benefits from only $200,000 of the accumulated tax loss carryforwards was probably going to be realized in the future. This would result in a deferred income tax asset of $80,000 being recognized, along with a tax recovery on the SCI of $80,000. Refer to the entries in Exhibit 17-1.

The company still has a tax loss carryforward of $430,000, the benefit of which is $172,000. Of this amount, $80,000 of the benefit is recognized and $92,000 is not recognized.

Analyze the 20X7 entry in scenario 3. The credit to income tax payable is based on taxable income, and is still $188,000. The credit to the deferred income tax asset for the loss carryforward is limited to the amount that was recognized to the end of 20X6. As a result, tax expense is only $268,000 ($188,000 + $80,000). In scenario 2, this was $360,000. Why is tax expense $92,000 lower? This is the benefit of using the unrecorded loss carryforward. It is *recognized through a lower tax expense when it is realized in 20X7.*

The next example in the chapter will illustrate a two-entry approach for recording tax expense (recovery) in a year where there is use of an unrecorded loss carryforward.

Scenario 4: Reduction of previously recognized benefit. Like any other asset, the deferred income tax asset that arises from recognizing the future benefit of a tax loss carryforward must continue to have probable future benefit. If an asset no longer is likely to be recoverable or realizable, it must be written down to its probable future benefit. If the probable future benefit is zero, the asset must be completely written off. If the probable future benefit is greater than zero but less than the originally recorded amount, the balance should be reduced accordingly.

For example, return to the scenario 1 entry for 20X5, when Parravano recorded a $132,000 deferred income tax asset because of a loss carryforward in 20X5. At the end of 20X6, the total tax loss carryforward is $430,000, the benefit of which is $172,000.

At the end of 20X6, Parravano's management decides that, within the next 20 years, realization of only $200,000 of the tax loss carryforward is probable (this is a tax benefit of $200,000 × 40% = $80,000). The deferred income tax asset of $132,000 must be reduced to the $80,000 amount of probable recovery. This is a reduction of $52,000.

There is nothing final about the estimate of future recovery. The probability of realizing the benefit is evaluated at each reporting date until the carryforward expires. In future years within the carryforward period, Parravano may decide that realization of the full carryforward benefit has become probable. If that happens, then the deferred income tax asset can be increased to reflect the higher probable amount.

Again, the 20X7 entry is limited to the recognized deferred income tax amount plus the payable. The unrecorded $92,000 amount is *recognized through a lower tax expense when it is realized in 20X7.*

Scenario 5: Recognition on realization In this scenario, we assume that Parravano cannot meet the probability tests at the end of 20X5 or 20X6, and the benefit of the loss carryforward is recognized only when realized in 20X7. This is a common scenario, because the presence of operating losses often makes probability of future profits difficult to establish.

In 20X5, the only element that can be recognized is the $68,000 benefit of the loss carryback. In 20X6, there is no recognition and no entry. The loss carryforward exists as an unrecognized asset.

In 20X7, there is $900,000 of taxable income, reduced to $470,000 because of the loss carryforward. Tax expense would have been $360,000 ($900,000 × 40%) but is only $188,000 because of recognition of the $172,000 ($430,000 × 40%) previously unrecorded loss carryforward. All the benefit of the loss carryforward is recognized when realized. This is the latest possible recognition point.

A Final Reminder

In all these cases, at the end of 20X6, Parravano has a tax loss carryforward of $430,000, the expected benefit of which is $172,000. The issue under discussion is *whether that tax benefit can be* recognized as an asset before it is used. Recognized or not, the tax benefit exists.

Impact of Recognition Assumption on Earnings

The difference between these five scenarios is the estimated probability of realizing the loss carryforward benefits. *This will have an impact on the pattern of earnings.*

The earnings impacts of these different scenarios are summarized in Exhibit 17-2. Regardless of the decisions made, the total after-tax earnings for the three years combined is $180,000. This is the outcome because all the tax loss carryforward was used, or realized, by the end of 20X7.

EXHIBIT 17-2

COMPARISON OF EARNINGS UNDER
DIFFERENT RECOGNITION SCENARIOS

Scenario		20X5	20X6	20X7	Total
1	Income (loss) before income taxes	$(500,000)	$(100,000)	$900,000	
	Income tax expense (recovery)	(200,000)	(40,000)	360,000	
	Earnings (loss)	$(300,000)	$ (60,000)	$540,000	$ 180,000
2	Income (loss) before income taxes	$(500,000)	$(100,000)	$900,000	
	Income tax expense (recovery)	(68,000)	(172,000)	360,000	
	Earnings (loss)	$ (432,000)	$ 72,000	$540,000	$ 180,000
3	Income (loss) before income taxes	$(500,000)	$(100,000)	$900,000	
	Income tax expense (recovery)	(68,000)	(80,000)	268,000	
	Earnings (loss)	$(432,000)	$ (20,000)	$632,000	$ 180,000
4	Income (loss) before income taxes	$(500,000)	$(100,000)	$900,000	
	Income tax expense (recovery)	(200,000)	52,000	268,000	
	Earnings (loss)	$(300,000)	$(152,000)	$632,000	$ 180,000
5	Income (loss) before income taxes	$(500,000)	$(100,000)	$900,000	
	Income tax expense (recovery)	(68,000)	—	188,000	
	Earnings (loss)	$(432,000)	$(100,000)	$712,000	$ 180,000

However, *the earnings pattern is very different between the different scenarios.* Depending on management's realization estimates, the after-tax net loss in 20X5 varies from $(300,000) to $(432,000). In 20X6, the bottom line varies from a loss of $(152,000) to earnings of $72,000. In 20X7, earnings fluctuates from $540,000 to a high of $712,000. Earnings are higher in any year where *unrecorded loss carryforwards* are recognized. Remember, though, that recognition might be because the loss carryforward is actually used, or because the probability assessment for future use is favourable.

ETHICAL ISSUES

Earnings will be higher in a year where unrecorded loss carryforwards are newly assessed as probable, or if unrecorded loss carryforwards are realized. Since income tax is a material percentage of earnings, the impact on the bottom line is also material. This has implications for various contracts based on earnings, such as bonuses or return ratios or coverage ratios used in loan covenants. There can be temptation to let a "bad year" go very bad—take a bath—and leave loss carryforward unrecognized. After all, in a loss year, perhaps the bonus or covenant would be missed regardless of the tax asset recognition decision. This would then create an opportunity to arbitrarily create a positive trend in a subsequent year. Evidence to support probability must be carefully weighed.

CHOICE OF TAX RATE

Accounting standards require deferred income tax assets and liabilities to be recognized at the rate(s) that are expected to be in effect when the temporary differences reverse or the tax loss carryforward benefits are realized. In most instances, tax rates are not enacted for future years, and the current-year rate that is enacted at the reporting date is used for measurement. If a future tax rate is enacted or substantively enacted, the future benefits of tax loss carryforwards should be measured at the substantially enacted rates for those future years in which the benefits are expected to be realized. Refer to the discussion in Chapter 16.

Tax Rate Changes

Once a deferred income tax asset has been recorded for a tax loss carryforward, the balance of that account must be maintained at the tax rate that is expected to be in effect when the carryforward is utilized. As noted above, the **substantially enacted tax rate** will be used.

In scenario 1, above, Parravano recorded the full amount of the tax benefit from its $330,000 accumulated tax loss carryforwards in 20X5. Parravano will have a deferred income tax asset of $132,000, recorded at a 40% tax rate.

Suppose that the tax rate goes down to 38% before Parravano actually uses any of the carryforward. The asset will have to be revalued to $330,000 × 38%, or $125,400. If the carryforward benefit is the only component of Parravano's DT asset, the writedown would be recorded as follows:

Income tax expense ($132,000 − $125,400) (SCI)	6,600	
Deferred income tax asset—carryforward benefit (SFP)		6,600

If, instead, the tax rate goes up, the increase in the asset account will be *credited* to income tax expense(recovery).

CONCEPT REVIEW

1. What is the basic criterion for recognizing the benefit of a tax loss carryforward prior to its realization?
2. What tax rate should be used to recognize the future benefits of a tax loss carryforward?
3. Is it possible to recognize the future benefits of tax loss carryforwards in years subsequent to the loss year? If so, explain the necessary circumstances. If not, explain why not.
4. Once the future benefit of a tax loss carryforward has been recognized, does the asset always remain on the statement of financial position until the benefit has been realized?

BASIC ILLUSTRATION

To illustrate the recognition of tax loss carryforward benefits over a series of years, when the tax rates change, assume the following information for Dutoit Ltd.:

	20X1	20X2	20X3	20X4
Earnings before tax	$100,000	$(300,000)	$150,000	$250,000
Taxable income*	100,000	(300,000)	150,000	250,000
Tax rate	45%	40%	42%	43%

*Prior to including any tax loss carrybacks or carryforwards.

There are no temporary or permanent differences. The first year of operations for Dutoit was 20X1. Assume that the tax rate for each year is determined during that year. For example, we do not know in 20X2 that the tax rate for 20X3 will be 42%.

Assuming Realization Is Not Probable

We will first assume that at no point does management believe that the company will be able to realize the benefits of any unused tax loss carryforward. This is a pessimistic assumption, of course, but in an uncertain environment, management really may not know if the company will have a profitable year until it is well underway.

20X1   In 20X1, the income tax expense is simply the taxable income times the tax rate:

Income tax expense ($100,000 × 45%)	45,000	
Income tax payable		45,000

20X2   In 20X2, $100,000 of the loss can be carried back to 20X1, to recover the prior year's taxes paid:

Income tax receivable—carryback benefit	45,000	
Income tax expense (recovery)		45,000

Note that the tax rate used is 45%, based on the amount paid in the prior year. There is an unrecognized tax loss carryforward of $200,000.

20X3   Taxable income prior to deducting the tax loss carryforward is $150,000. The tax loss carryforward of $200,000 more than offsets the otherwise-taxable income for 20X3. No taxes will be due, and no income tax expense will be recorded or reported. There is a tax loss of $50,000 still unused.

For the sake of clarity, two entries can be made in a year where a loss carryforward is used. The first entry records income tax as though there were no loss carryforward:

Income tax expense ($150,000 × 42%)	63,000	
Income tax payable		63,000

Of course, the income tax payable does not have to be paid, so the second entry eliminates it, recording the use of the loss carryforward:

Income tax payable	63,000	
Income tax expense (recovery)		63,000

The SCI would reflect the offsetting effects of the two opposite income tax expenses on 20X3 earnings. The disclosure could be either on the face of the SCI or in the notes. If SCI presentation is used:

Earnings before income tax		$150,000
Income tax expense (recovery):		
Income tax on current year's earnings	$63,000	
Tax reduction from tax loss carryforward	(63,000)	—
Earnings		$150,000

20X4 In 20X4, there is $250,000 of taxable income, on which $250,000 × 43%, or $107,500, of tax would be payable. The remaining $50,000 carryforward is used, reducing the taxes otherwise due by $50,000 × 43%, or $21,500. The net amount owing is $86,000. Using two entries, for clarity:

Income tax expense	$107,500	
Income tax payable		$107,500
Income tax payable	21,500	
Income tax expense (recovery)		21,500

The breakdown of income tax expense may be included in the notes or on the SCI:

Earnings before income tax		$250,000
Income tax expense (recovery)		
Tax on current earnings	$107,500	
Recovered through loss carryforward	(21,500)	86,000
Earnings		$164,000

Note that in each year, the carryforward is applied against taxable income in that year at the current rate. *The tax rate in the year of the loss is irrelevant.*

Assuming Realization Is Probable

Now, let us re-examine the situation assuming instead that in 20X3, Dutoit's management judges that it is probable that the benefits of the remaining carryforward will be realized.

The entries in 20X1 and 20X2 will not change. In 20X3, however, $150,000 of the carryforward is used to reduce 20X3 taxable income to zero. The remaining $50,000 carryforward is also recognized. The benefit of the full $200,000 carryforward is *recognized*, even though the benefit of only $150,000 is *realized* in that year by applying it against the taxable income in that year. The entries for 20X3 now are:

Income tax expense	63,000	
Income tax payable (unchanged)		63,000
Deferred tax asset—carryforward benefit ($50,000 × 42%)	21,000	
Income tax payable	63,000	
Income tax expense (recovery)		84,000

Notice again the use of two entries for the tax effects. In the first entry, we record income tax assuming there is no loss carryforward. The second entry disposes of the loss carryforward. The balance in income tax payable is zero, the net of the two entries.

The full benefit of the $200,000 carryforward has been *recognized* in 20X3. Income tax expense is a net credit on the income statement of $21,000, the unrealized portion of the carryforward.

Earnings before income tax		$150,000
Income tax expense (recovery):		
Income tax on current earnings	$63,000	
Recovery from tax loss carryforward ($200,000 × 42%)	(84,000)	(21,000)
Earnings		$171,000

The SCI may simply show the $21,000 net recovery, but the detail must be disclosed in the notes.

In 20X4, the remaining $50,000 of tax loss carryforward is used, but it has already been *recognized*. The result, therefore, is that the balance of the deferred tax asset goes from $21,000 at the beginning of 20X4 to zero at the end of the year. The entries are:

Income tax expense	107,500	
Income tax payable ($250,000 × 43%)		107,500
Income tax payable ($50,000 × 43%)	21,500	
Deferred income tax asset—carryforward benefit		21,000
Income tax expense (recovery)		500

In the entry above, the credit to the deferred income tax asset is the $21,000 amount previously recorded. The change in the tax rate has made the loss carryforward worth an extra $500 ($50,000 × 1% = $500), which is credited to income tax expense.

EXTENDED ILLUSTRATION

In this illustration of accounting for the tax benefits of tax losses, we will assume that (1) the company has one type of temporary difference relating to equipment; (2) a loss arises in the second year; and (3) the income tax rate changes in the third and fourth years. The facts for Birchall Inc. are as follows:

- In 20X1, Birchall begins operations and acquires equipment costing $1 million.
- The equipment is being depreciated straight-line at 10% (i.e., at $100,000 per year), and the company's policy is to expense a full year's depreciation in the year of acquisition.
- Birchall claims CCA of $350,000 in 20X1, $200,000 in 20X2, $150,000 in 20X3, and $100,000 in 20X4.
- The tax rate is 40% in 20X1 and 20X2. During 20X3, Parliament increases the tax rate to 42%, applicable to 20X3 and following years, and, in 20X4, the rate is changed to 43%.
- Birchall's earnings before income tax for 20X1 through 20X4 are as follows:

20X1	$ 300,000
20X2	$(600,000) (loss)
20X3	$ 200,000
20X4	$ 600,000

The first step is to calculate taxable income, shown in Exhibit 17-3. In 20X1, taxable income is $50,000. At 40%, the current tax payable is $20,000.

EXHIBIT 17-3

EXTENDED ILLUSTRATION—CALCULATION OF TAXABLE INCOME AND INCOME TAX PAYABLE

	20X1	20X2	20X3	20X4
Tax Rate (t)	40%	40%	42%	43%
Accounting earnings (loss) subject to tax	$300,000	$(600,000)	$200,000	$600,000
Temporary difference:				
+ Depreciation	100,000	100,000	100,000	100,000
− CCA	(350,000)	(200,000)	(150,000)	(100,000)
Taxable income (loss) for current year	$50,000	$(700,000)	$150,000	$600,000
Income tax payable (before using any loss carryforward)	$ 20,000		$ 63,000	$258,000

Income tax expense	120,000	
Income tax payable		20,000
Deferred income tax liability—equipment		100,000

Next, the change in deferred income tax is calculated. This is done in table format, as shown in Exhibit 17-4. The initial cost of the equipment was $1,000,000. In 20X1, Birchall deducts CCA of $350,000 on its tax return and has depreciation expense of $100,000. As a result, the *tax basis* of the equipment at the end of 20X1 is $650,000 (i.e., $1,000,000 − $350,000) while the accounting carrying value is $900,000; a temporary difference of $250,000 exists. At the 40% enacted tax rate, the deferred tax liability for the equipment is $100,000. Combining these two elements gives Birchall's 20X1 income tax expense of $120,000:

EXHIBIT 17-4

EXTENDED ILLUSTRATION—DEFERRED TAX TABLE

	[1] Year-End Tax Basis dr. (cr.)	[2] Year-End Carrying Value dr. (cr.)	[3] = [1] − [2] Temporary Difference Deductible (Taxable)	[4] = [3] × t Deferred Tax Asset (Liability) at Yr.-End Rate	[5] = prev.[4] Less Beginning Balance dr. (cr.)	[6] = [4] − [5] Adjustment for Current Year dr. (cr.)
20X1						
[t = 40%]:						
Equipment	$650,000	$900,000	(250,000)	$(100,000)	0	$(100,000)
20X2						
[t = 40%]:						
Equipment	450,000	800,000	(350,000)	(140,000)	$(100,000)	(40,000)
20X3						
[t = 42%]:						
Equipment	300,000	700,000	(400,000)	(168,000)	(140,000)	(28,000)
20X4						
[t = 43%]:						
Equipment	200,000	600,000	(400,000)	(172,000)	(168,000)	(4,000)

In 20X2, Birchall has a loss. The accounting loss (pre-tax) is $600,000, but the loss for tax purposes is $700,000 after adding back depreciation and deducting CCA (see Exhibit 17-3). Of the tax loss, $50,000 can be carried back to 20X1 to claim a refund of the $20,000 paid in that year. The remaining $650,000 of the tax loss will be carried forward.

At the end of 20X2, the tax basis of the equipment declines to $450,000 (after the 20X2 CCA of $200,000), while the carrying value declines to $800,000 (after deducting another $100,000 of depreciation). The temporary difference relating to the equipment therefore is $350,000, resulting in a DT liability of $140,000 at the end of 20X2. The year-end DT liability adjustment is an increase of $40,000 over the previous year.

The 20X2 components related to the income tax can be summarized as follows:

- Tax loss is $700,000, of which $50,000 is carried back and $650,000 is carried forward.
- DT liability relating to equipment increases by $40,000.
- Birchall has a receivable for tax recovery (carryback) of $20,000.

From this point on, we must make assumptions about the probability of realizing the benefits of the $650,000 carryforward.

Situation 1: Assuming Realization Is Not Probable

20X2

If realization is *not* probable, the refund receivable and the change to DT are recorded, but the benefit of the loss carryforward is not recorded. This results in tax expense of $20,000, reflecting the net effect of a $40,000 increase to DT and a $20,000 loss carryback. Refer to Exhibit 17-5 for the journal entries in this sequence.

20X3

In 20X3, taxable income is $150,000, as is shown in the third numeric column of Exhibit 17-3. There is also a change in the DT liability caused by the CCA versus temporary difference, as calculated in Exhibit 17-4. The first 20X3 entry in Exhibit 17-5 records tax expense without the loss carryforward, and tax expense is $91,000.

Of course, the taxable income permits Birchall to use some of the tax loss carryforward to offset the otherwise taxable income. The second 20X3 entry in Exhibit 17-5 reduces tax payable by $63,000, and records the income tax recovery from the previously unrecognized loss carryforward. Remember, the entries to record income tax expense can be condensed into a single entry, but it may be more helpful to present them as two separate entries.

EXHIBIT 17-5

EXTENDED ILLUSTRATION—SITUATION 1 CARRYFORWARD

Realization Not Probable

Income Tax Journal Entries

Income tax journal entry, 20X1

Income tax expense	120,000	
Deferred income tax liability—equipment		100,000
Income tax payable		20,000

Income tax journal entry, 20X2

Income tax expense	20,000	
Income tax receivable—carryback benefit	20,000	
Deferred income tax liability—equipment		40,000

EXHIBIT 17-5

EXTENDED ILLUSTRATION—SITUATION 1 CARRYFORWARD

Realization Not Probable

Income Tax Journal Entries

Income tax journal entries, 20X3

Income tax expense	91,000	
Deferred income tax liability—equipment		28,000
Income tax payable ($150,000 × 0.42)		63,000
Income tax payable	63,000	
Income tax expense—carryforward benefit		63,000

Income tax journal entries, 20X4

Income tax expense	262,000	
Deferred income tax liability—equipment		4,000
Income tax payable ($600,000 × 0.43)		258,000
Income tax payable	215,000	
Income tax expense—carryforward benefit ($500,000 × 43%)		215,000

The result for 20X3 is that net income tax expense of only $28,000 is recognized. At the end of 20X3, Birchall has an unused gross tax loss carryforward of $500,000:

20X2 tax loss	$700,000
Carryback to 20X1	– 50,000
Carryforward used in 20X3	– 150,000
Remaining carryforward at end of 20X3	$500,000

20X4

For 20X4, taxable income is $600,000. In this year, CCA is equal to depreciation, and therefore there is no change in the amount of temporary difference relating to the equipment. However, there is a change in the tax rate, from 42% to 43%, and there is a change in the DT liability. The DT liability is $400,000 × 43% = $172,000, an increase of $4,000 over the 20X3 year-end DT liability.

Again, two entries are used to record income tax: the first, assuming there is no loss carryforward, and the second to incorporate the loss carryforward element. Tax expense is $262,000 in the first entry, and there is a $215,000 recovery in the second entry when the $500,000 loss carryforward is used. As the result of these entries, income tax expense reported in earnings is $47,000: ($262,000 − $215,000).

Situation 2: Assuming Realization Is Probable

20X1

There has been no change from the prior example. See Exhibit 17-6 for the deferred tax table and Exhibit 17-7 for a summary of the entries for this situation.

EXHIBIT 17-6

EXTENDED ILLUSTRATION—SITUATION 2 CARRYFORWARD

DEFERRED TAX TABLE

Realization Probable

	Year-End Tax Basis dr. (cr.)	Year-End Carrying Value dr. (cr.)	Temporary Difference Deductible (Taxable)	Deferred Tax Asset (Liability) at Yr.-End Rate	Less Beginning Balance dr. (cr.)	Adjustment for Current Year dr. (cr.)
20X1 *[t = 40%]*:						
Equipment	$650,000	$900,000	(250,000)	$(100,000)	0	$(100,000)
20X2 *[t = 40%]*:						
Equipment	450,000	800,000	(350,000)	(140,000)	$(100,000)	(40,000)
Carryforward benefit	n/a	n/a	650,000	260,000	0	260,000
				120,000		
20X3 *[t = 42%]*:						
Equipment	300,000	700,000	(400,000)	(168,000)	(140,000)	(28,000)
Carryforward benefit	n/a	n/a	500,000	210,000	260,000	(50,000)
				42,000		
20X4 *[t = 43%]*:						
Equipment	200,000	600,000	(400,000)	(172,000)	(168,000)	(4,000)
Carryforward benefit	n/a	n/a	0	0	210,000	(210,000)
				(172,000)		

EXHIBIT 17-7

EXTENDED ILLUSTRATION—SITUATION 2 CARRYFORWARD

Realization Probable
Income Tax Journal Entries

20X1

Income tax expense	120,000	
Deferred income tax liability—equipment		100,000
Income tax payable		20,000

20X2

Deferred income tax asset—carryforward benefit	260,000	
Income tax receivable—carryback benefit	20,000	
Deferred income tax liability—equipment		40,000
Income tax expense (recovery)		240,000

20X3

Income tax expense	91,000	
Deferred income tax liability—equipment		28,000
Income tax payable		63,000
Income tax payable ($150,000 × 42%)	63,000	
Deferred income tax asset—carryforward benefit		50,000
Income tax expense (recovery) [$650,000 × (42% − 40%)]		13,000

20X4

Income tax expense	262,000	
Deferred income tax liability—equipment		4,000
Income tax payable ($600,000 × 43%)		258,000
Income tax payable ($500,000 × 43%)	215,000	
Deferred income tax asset—carryforward benefit		210,000
Income tax expense (recovery) [$500,000 × (43% − 42%)]		5,000

20X2

If realization is probable, then a tax asset will be recognized for the carryforward. In 20X2, the future benefit of the carryforward of $650,000 is recognized at the then-enacted rate of 40%, and this creates a deferred income tax asset in the amount of $260,000.

One deferred income tax account or two? Notice in Exhibit 17-7 that we have two deferred income tax accounts—one for temporary differences, and one for the loss carryforward. On the SFP, these two accounts are netted. However, the journal entries are more clear if the loss carryforward account is kept as a separate asset, and that is the approach we will follow.

Once the loss carryforward asset is recognized, the tax expense (recovery) becomes a recovery of ($240,000), rather than an expense of $20,000, as in the first scenario. Refer to the entry in Exhibit 17-7 and notice:

1. Recognition of carryback benefits—the receivable of $20,000 (debit);
2. Recognition of the future benefits of the carryforward of $260,000 (debit); and
3. Change in the temporary difference for equipment of $40,000 (credit).

The balancing amount is the $240,000 income tax recovery for 20X2 that will be shown in earnings.

The loss carryforward can be included in the deferred income tax table, as shown in Exhibit 17-6. Refer to 20X2. The first two columns are left blank, and the *gross* tax loss carryforward is included as a positive number in column 3. Each year the *remaining* gross tax loss carryforward is entered in column 3 and the rest of the table is completed as usual. Equipment data is included in Exhibit 17-6 for the sake of completeness.

Note that column 4 shows the SFP position at year-end. The statement of financial position at the end of 20X2 will show a single amount, a noncurrent deferred income tax *asset* of $120,000:

DT asset—carryforward benefit	$260,000
DT liability—equipment	(140,000)
DT asset (noncurrent, net)	$120,000

20X3

In 20X3, there is initial taxable income of $150,000, after adjusting accounting income for the additional $50,000 temporary difference relating to equipment but before applying the tax loss carryforward. There is a net change in the DT relating to equipment of $28,000 (see Exhibit 17-6). Applying $150,000 of the tax loss carryforward against the $150,000 taxable income reduces the tax loss carryforward to $500,000 (column 3) and the recorded amount to $210,000 (column 4). This is an adjustment of $50,000 (column 6).

Exhibit 17-6 shows the two entries for this year, where tax expense is first recorded at $91,000. The second entry reflects the impact of the change in tax rates on the opening loss carryforward. Use of $150,000 of the loss carryforward clearly eliminates $63,000 of tax payable. This is the debit.

The table in Exhibit 17-6 tells us to credit the loss carryforward DT asset by $50,000, to arrive at the correct closing balance. To make the journal entry balance, a further $13,000 credit to tax expense is needed. This amount can be proven as the change in the tax rate (2%, or 42% − 40%) multiplied by the *opening* tax loss of $650,000. In other words, the tax loss carryforward is more valuable because the tax rate increased, and tax expense is credited as a result.

20X4

In 20X4, there is taxable income of $600,000, tax payable (before any loss carryforward is used) of $258,000, and an increase in the DT account of $4,000, as is shown in Exhibit 17-6. The entries reflect an initial $262,000 of tax expense and then a $5,000 recovery. The second entry eliminates the DT—loss carryforward asset, since it is all consumed. The $5,000 tax recovery is caused by the effect of the increase in tax rate on the opening tax loss carryforward.

On the SFP at the end of 20X4, only the DT relating to equipment remains, at a credit balance of $172,000: $400,000 accumulated temporary differences at a tax rate of 43%.

Comparison of Results

The earnings impact of the above situations is summarized in the partial SCIs shown in Exhibit 17-8. When realization is not probable, income tax expense in each year has no relationship to the pre-tax earnings, except in the first year. Instead, tax expense reflects the adjustments needed to show appropriate assets—or not.

EXHIBIT 17-8

COMPARISON OF EARNINGS RESULTS
NOT PROBABLE VERSUS PROBABLE REALIZATION OF TAX LOSS
CARRYFORWARD BENEFITS

	20X1	20X2	20X3	20X4
Not Probable (see Exhibit 17-5):				
Earnings (loss) before income tax	$300,000	$(600,000)	$200,000	$600,000
Less: Income tax expense (recovery)	120,000	20,000	28,000	47,000
Net income (loss)	$180,000	$(620,000)	$ 172,000	$553,000
Probable (see Exhibit 17-7):				
Earnings (loss) before income tax	$300,000	$(600,000)	$200,000	$600,000
Less: Income tax expense (recovery)	120,000	(240,000)	78,000	257,000
Net income (loss)	$180,000	$(360,000)	$122,000	$ 343,000

When the initial assessment of realization is probable, the full benefits of the tax loss are recognized in the year of the loss, thereby matching the benefits in the year that the loss arose. Of course, it may seem a little odd to be talking about the "benefits" of a loss. A loss itself is not beneficial, but at least it can have some favourable consequences if the company is able to utilize the tax loss carryforward to reduce taxes payable.

ETHICAL ISSUES

There is a certain appealing logic to the results when the benefit of a loss carryforward is reported in the loss year. For example, assume that a company had an accounting and taxable loss of $100,000 in 20X2 and then accounting and taxable income of $100,000 in 20X3. The tax rate is 40%. It seems appropriate reporting to show both years net of $40,000 tax and report an after-tax net loss of $60,000 in 20X2 and an after-tax net income of $60,000 in 20X3. It is understood that the $40,000 benefit of the loss carryforward can be recorded in 20X2 before it is realized in 20X3 as long as realization is probable.

However, what if realization is not probable? In this case, the 20X2 net loss would be reported as $100,000, and the benefit of the loss carryforward would be recorded in 20X3. This would result in net tax expense of zero in 20X3, and reported net income would be $100,000. While the $100,000 loss is greater in 20X2 than the after-tax $60,000 alternative, the $100,000 20X3 reported results are greater as well. Management may prefer the "bounce" and be prepared to take a "big bath" in 20X2.

The swing caused by recognition may be even more pronounced. For example, assume that the $100,000 loss in 20X2 is followed by two years of breakeven results. If the probability of loss carryforward use shifts to "probable" in one of these years, $40,000 of net income will be reported, reflecting recognition of the loss carryforward deferred income tax asset. In this case, a positive trend in earnings can be manufactured by reassessment of probability. Alternatively, two or three years of loss carryforward may be recognized in one particular year, increasing results materially.

The reporting decision is based on the probability of realization, and probability is assessed by management, with the decision reviewed by external auditors. Management has discretion over the probability estimates and thus the timing of recognition of tax assets. Management also has the ability to remeasure those benefits at any time within the 20-year carryforward period. Thus, the recognition of unrealized tax loss carryforwards can become an ethical challenge. Accounting standards provide some guidance for evaluating probability, but auditors must proceed with great caution, given the magnitude of tax expense.

Situation 3: Refiling CCA and LCF Not Probable

Now, we assume that realization of the loss carryforward is not probable, and there is risk that the loss carryforward will expire in the carryforward period. Accordingly, the company refiles its 20X1 tax return, eliminating the CCA charge. No CCA will be charged in 20X2, either, to keep tax losses at a minimal level and increase UCC.

20X1

There has been no change from the prior example. The decisions made were all in 20X2, and 20X1 in and of itself has not been changed. Refer to prior data, and Exhibit 17-6 for the deferred tax table. The 20X1 income tax entry:

Income tax expense	120,000	
Deferred income tax liability—equipment		100,000
Income tax payable		20,000

20X2

20X2 must reflect the impact of refiling 20X1, and also eliminating the 20X2 CCA claim. The recalculation of taxable income is as follows:

	20X1	20X2
Accounting earnings (loss) subject to tax	$300,000	$(600,000)
Temporary difference:		
+ Depreciation	100,000	100,000
− CCA	--- (1)---	----(2)--
Taxable income (loss) for current year	$400,000	$(500,000)

(1) Was $350,000 before refiling; now zero

(2) Was $200,000 in the prior example; now zero

Things to notice:

- The entry for 20X1 will not change, because the refiling was an action of 20X2, not 20X1.
- The company cannot increase its cash refund in 20X2; only taxes paid can be recovered.
- The tax loss used as a carryback is now $400,000, which causes the refund but also a debit to deferred taxes because of the refiling.
- There is a $100,000 loss carryforward, the benefit of which cannot be recorded because use is not probable.
- The deferred income table must change to reflect new UCC.

In the revised calculation of the change in deferred income tax, the beginning liability balance of $100,000 is unchanged from the prior example. UCC, however, reflects the refiling ($1,000,000 of original cost, with no CCA claimed in 20X1, as refiled, and no CCA in 20X2.) The result is a debit adjustment of $180,000, to bring the deferred income tax account to an $80,000 asset value. Note that deferred income tax is now an asset of $80,000; it must be probable that temporary differences will reverse in future years for this asset to be recorded. Otherwise, it fails the recognition test and is not recorded.

The $180,000 debit adjustment can also be proven with the shortcut method, because the tax rate has not changed. CCA eliminated from 20X1 was $350,000, and there are $100,000 of new depreciation/CCA differences in 20X2; $450,000 × 40% = $180,000.

DEFERRED TAX TABLE						
	Year-End Tax Basis dr. (cr.)	Year-End Carrying Value dr. (cr.)	Temporary Difference Deductible (Taxable)	Deferred Tax Asset (Liability) at Yr.-End Rate	Less Beginning Balance dr. (cr.)	Adjustment for Current Year dr. (cr.)
20X2 (40%)						
Equipment	$1,000,000	$800,000	200,000	$80,000	(100,000)	$180,000

The 20X2 journal entry:

Income tax receivable—carryback benefit (no change)	20,000	
Deferred income tax liability—equipment	180,000	
Income tax expense (recovery)		200,000

Remember also that there is a $100,000 loss carryforward, which is not recorded. Refiling and reducing CCA has reduced the loss carryforward from $650,000 to $100,000, and has changed the UCC from $450,000 at the end of 20X2 to $1,000,000.

DISCLOSURE

Income tax expense relating to continuing operations should be shown on the face of the SCI. The amount of income tax expense may include benefits from either carrybacks or carryforwards, but there is no requirement that those benefits be disclosed on the face of the SCI. Information on tax losses is confined to the disclosure notes and generally focused on *unrecognized* tax loss carryforwards rather than on amounts *realized* during the period. Disclosure is recommended for:

- The amount of benefit arising from a *previously unrecognized* tax loss that is used to either:
    1. Reduce current income tax expense by using the carryforward in the current period *if* it had not been recognized as a deferred income tax asset in prior periods; or
    2. Reduce current deferred income tax expense, such as by reducing CCA in prior periods and thereby reducing the amount of temporary differences relating to property, plant, and equipment (as well as the remaining tax loss carryforward).

- The amount of deferred income tax expense arising from the writedown or reversal of a previous writedown of deferred income tax assets.

- The amount and expiry date of *unused* tax losses for which no deferred income tax asset has been recognized in the SFP.

Companies usually do disclose the amounts of tax loss carrybacks and carryforwards that were used during the year, whether or not they had been previously recognized as a deferred income tax asset.

It is very difficult, and often impossible, for a reader to figure out whether an income tax recovery has been *realized* or merely *recognized*. Recourse to the notes, to the effective tax rate disclosure, and to the statement of cash flows may provide clues, but often the information relating to income tax assets and liabilities is so summarized that it may be impossible to figure out the details.

Disclosure Example

Alderon Iron Ore Corp. is a development-stage mining company with mine operations in Labrador. Commercial production has yet to begin, and no revenue has been reported to the end of 2014. It is easy to understand the presence of operating losses in these circumstances, and also easy to support the assessment of loss carryforward use as "not probable," given the considerable inherent uncertainties. Loss carryforwards exist, but an asset cannot be recognized.

The disclosure notes indicate that there is a $33.9 million unrecognized deferred income tax debit—a would-be asset—from various temporary differences, not just operating losses. Operating loss carryforwards ($18.2 million), mineral properties ($14.9 million), share-issue expenses ($0.6 million), and property, plant, and equipment ($0.1 million) all will generate future tax reduction or deductions. The benefit cannot be recognized because of the uncertainty of the operating environment. If recognized, operating losses alone would result in an asset of $18.2 million. This is the after-tax amount. The gross tax losses are $62.9 million. The disclosure note includes the dollar value of losses and expiry dates. At the point that these tax loss carryforwards are recognized or used, operating results will reflect the benefit.

EXHIBIT 17-9

ALDERON IRON ORE CORPORATION—DISCLOSURE OF DEFERRED INCOME TAX ASSETS

From the 2014 financial statements:

Note 21 Income taxes (extracts)

Significant components of the Company's unrecognized deferred income tax assets are summarized below.

EXHIBIT 17-9

ALDERON IRON ORE CORPORATION—DISCLOSURE OF DEFERRED INCOME TAX ASSETS

	Years ended December 31,		
	2014	2013	2012
	$	$	$
Temporary differences attributable to:			
Non-capital losses	18,237,500	15,134,000	11,486,000
Mineral properties	14,932,000	16,075,500	16,655,000
Share-issue expenses	554,750	862,000	1,228,000
Property, plant and equipment	111,500	102,250	35,000
Allowable capital losses	136,000	136,000	136,000
	33,971,750	32,309,750	29,540,000

As of December 31, 2014, the Company's unrecognized non-capital loss carryforwards expire as follows:

	$
2015	271,231
2027	289,664
2028	385,975
2029	81,027
2030	2,956,099
2031	7,672,864
2032	29,359,621
2033	13,052,010
2034	8,819,260
	62,887,751

Source: Alderon Iron Ore Corp., 2014 Audited Annual Financial Statements, pp. 34, 35, www.sedar.com, posted 27 March 2015.

INTERNATIONAL CONSISTENCY?

The primary purpose of international standards is to harmonize financial reporting across financial markets so that companies can report in financial markets other than that of their home country. Thus, it would appear that all international reporting would have to use the methods described in this chapter in order to conform to international standards.

While that may be true on the surface, the fact is that companies in some countries will be more conservative in their appraisal of realization probabilities, depending on the prevailing ethos in their home country. In a country that has very conservative accounting practices and a strong tradition of prudence in financial reporting (e.g., Germany and France), companies generally will view the probability of future recognition as being low. Thus, the future benefit of the carryforwards will not be recognized, even though they might have been recognized in similar circumstances if the reporting company were based in the United States or in Canada. The influence of the accounting and business environments of a company's home country can be very powerful.

Looking Forward

Income taxes are not currently on the agenda of either the IASB or the Canadian AcSB.

Accounting Standards for Private Enterprises

Accounting Method

Private companies can choose between the taxes payable method and the comprehensive allocation method of accounting for income taxes. If the choice is to use comprehensive income tax allocation, the coverage in this chapter applies in full.

Section 3465 uses the phrase "more likely than not" instead of "probable" for assessing recognition of tax loss carryforwards. There is no difference in meaning, however. *Likely*, *probable*, and *more likely than not* all have the same meaning.

Taxes Payable Method and Tax Loss Carryforwards

If an entity is using the taxes payable method, the company will not be able to recognize *deferred (future) tax assets* arising from tax loss carryforwards. Tax loss carryforwards will still be used to reduce income taxes in future years, but the benefit will be *recognized* only when *realized* via actual reductions in the company's tax bill when the carryforwards are used in future years. This is essentially the same sequence of recognition rules as are used when use of a tax loss carryforward is not probable.

Remember, the company's accounting method does not affect the carryforwards themselves or the way that a company can use them to reduce taxes.

RELEVANT STANDARDS

CPA Canada Handbook, Part I (IFRS):

- IAS 12, Income Taxes

CPA Canada Handbook, Part II (ASPE):

- Section 3465, Income Taxes

SUMMARY OF KEY POINTS

1. In Canada, tax losses may be carried back and offset against taxable income in three years previous to the loss year. The company is entitled to recover tax paid in those years. The tax recovery is based on the tax actually paid and not on the tax rate in the year of the loss.

2. If the three-year carryback does not completely use up the tax loss, a company is permitted to carry the remaining loss forward and apply it against taxable income over the next 20 years.

3. The future benefits of tax loss carryforwards should be recognized in the year of the loss if it is probable that the loss carryforward will be realized in future years.

4. The likelihood of realizing the tax benefits of a loss carryforward can be increased by reducing the corporation's claim for CCA on its tax return in the carryback and carryforward years.

5. Future benefits of unrecognized tax loss carryforwards may be recognized in years following the loss when realization occurs, or when relalization becomes probable.

6. Management reporting objectives may bias the probability assessment to allow loss carryforward recognition in particular years to emphasize an earnings recovery or other favourable trends.

Key Terms

loss carryback

loss carryforward

substantially enacted tax rate

tax benefit

tax loss

Review Problem 17-1

Dezso Development Ltd. is a Canadian-controlled public company. The company has a 31 December fiscal year-end. The company has a policy of using loss carrybacks in the earliest possible year. Data concerning the earnings of the company for 20X6 and 20X7 are as follows:

	20X6	20X7
Earnings (loss) before income taxes	$(90,000)	$30,000
Amounts included in income		
Investment income	$ 1,000	$ 2,000
Depreciation expense—equipment	30,000	30,000
Depreciation expense—development costs	20,000	22,000

	20X6	20X7
Amounts deducted for income tax		
Capital cost allowance	nil	35,000
Development expenditures	25,000	15,000
Income tax rate	38%	37%

Other information:

- Taxable income and the income tax rates for 20X2 through 20X5 are as follows:

Year	Taxable Income (loss)	Tax Rate
20X2	$ 7,000	40%
20X3	13,000	40
20X4	9,000	40
20X5	(12,000)	41

- At 31 December 20X5, equipment had net book value of $570,000, and UCC of $310,000.
- At 31 December 20X5, the SFP showed an unamortized balance of development costs of $200,000 under Other Assets.
- The investment income consists of dividends from taxable Canadian corporations.

Required:

1. For each of 20X6 and 20X7, prepare the journal entry or entries to record income tax expense. Assume that management judges that it is probable that the full benefit of any tax loss carryforward will be realized within the carryforward.

2. Show how the deferred tax amounts would appear on the 20X6 year-end SFP.

3. Suppose that in 20X7 management decided in 20X8 that it was probable that the company would use only $10,000 of the remaining gross tax loss carryforward.
   a. Show the entry that would be made to reduce the carryforward benefit.
   b. What impact would this entry have on the 20X8 financial statements for Dezso?

REVIEW PROBLEM —SOLUTION

1. (a) 20X6 Tax Expense

The taxable income or loss can be calculated as follows:

	20X6	20X7
Earnings (loss) before tax	$(90,000)	$30,000
Permanent difference: investment income	(1,000)	(2,000)

	20X6	20X7
Accounting income (loss) subject to tax	(91,000)	28,000
Depreciation	30,000	30,000
CCA	nil	(35,000)
Depreciation of development costs	20,000	22,000
Development cost expenditures	(25,000)	(15,000)
Taxable income (loss)	$(66,000)	$30,000

The 20X5 tax loss will have been carried back to 20X2 ($7,000) and 20X3 ($5,000). After the 20X5 tax loss has been carried back, there remains $17,000 taxable income in the carryback period for the 20X6 loss:

Year	Taxable Income	Used in 20X5	Available in 20X6	Tax Receivable at 40%
20X2	$ 7,000	$ (7,000)	—	—
20X3	13,000	(5,000)	$ 8,000	$3,200
20X4	9,000	—	9,000	3,600
20X5	(12,000)	12,000	—	—
			$17,000	$6,800

The gross carryforward that remains after the carryback is $66,000 − $17,000 = $49,000. Realization of these benefits is probable and the enacted tax rate is 38%, the carryforward benefit is $49,000 × 38% = $18,620.

The adjustments for the temporary differences for both years are summarized in the table below:

	Year-End Tax Basis dr. (cr.)	Year-End Carrying Value dr. (cr.)	Temporary Difference Deductible (Taxable)	Deferred Tax Asset (Liability) at Yr.-End Rate	Less Beginning Balance dr. (cr.)	Adjustment for Current Year dr. (cr.)
20X6 **[*t* = 38%]:**						
Equipment	310,000	540,000	(230,000)	$(87,400)	$(106,600)[(1)]	$19,200
Development costs	0	205,000[(3)]	(205,000)	(77,900)	(82,000)[(2)]	4,100
						23,300
Carryforward benefit	—	—	49,000	18,620	0	18,620

	Year-End Tax Basis dr. (cr.)	Year-End Carrying Value dr. (cr.)	Temporary Difference Deductible (Taxable)	Deferred Tax Asset (Liability) at Yr.-End Rate	Less Beginning Balance dr. (cr.)	Adjustment for Current Year dr. (cr.)
20X7 [$t = 37\%$]:						
Equipment	275,000	510,000	(235,000)	$(86,950)	$(87,400)	450
Development costs	0	198,000	(198,000)	(73,260)	(77,900)	4,640
						5,090
Carryforward benefit	—	—	19,000	7,030	18,620	(11,590)

[1]($570,000 − $310,000) × 0.41

[2]($200,000) × 0.41

[3]$200,000 + $25,000 − $20,000

Putting all of these elements together gives us the following 20X6 summary of income tax expense:

Income tax receivable—carryback benefit	6,800	
Deferred income tax asset—carryforward benefit	18,620	
Deferred income tax liability	23,300	
Income tax expense (recovery)		48,720

Notice again that we have used two deferred income tax accounts—one for the loss carryforward and one for temporary differences. On the SFP, these two accounts are netted/combined. However, the entries are easier to follow if the loss carryforward account is kept as a separate asset.

(b) 20X7 Tax Expense

The taxable income for 20X7 is $30,000, as calculated previously. No tax is due for 20X7 because there is an available tax loss carryforward of $49,000. After applying $30,000 of the carryforward against 20X7 taxable income, a carryforward of $19,000 remains. At the newly enacted tax rate of 37%, the DT asset related to the carryforward is $7,030. In recording the income tax expense for 20X7, the balance of the DT carryforward account must be reduced from its beginning balance of $18,620 (debit) to an ending balance of $7,030 (debit), a credit adjustment of $11,590.

The adjustments for all types of temporary differences are summarized in the preceding table. The entry to record income tax expense, exclusive of the loss carryforward, is:

Income tax expense	6,010	
Deferred income tax liability	5,090	
Income tax payable ($30,000 × 0.37)		11,100

The entry to record loss carryforward use:

Income tax expense[1]	490	
Income tax payable ($30,000 × 0.37)	11,100	
Deferred income tax asset—carryforward benefit (per table)		11,590

[1]This is the reduction in value of the opening tax loss because of a 1% decline in the tax rate; ($49,000 × 1%).

2. 20X6 SFP Presentation

All three of the 20X6 temporary differences are noncurrent. Therefore, they will be combined into a single net amount when the SFP is prepared. The net amount is:

DT asset—carryforward benefit	$18,620 (dr.)
DT liability—equipment	(87,400) (cr.)
DT liability—deferred development costs	(77,900) (cr.)
DT liability, noncurrent	$(146,680) (cr.)

3. (a) Adjustment to DT-carryforward benefit

The remaining carryforward at the beginning of 20X8 is $19,000, as determined in the answer to 1(b), above. At the enacted rate of 37% (assuming no change), the remaining carryforward benefit is $7,030 (i.e., $19,000 × 37%). An entry must be recorded to reduce the *reported* balance of the benefit to $3,700 (i.e., $10,000 × 37%), an adjustment of $3,330:

Income tax expense ($7,030 – $3,700)	3,330	
DT asset—loss carryforward benefit		3,330

(b) Financial Statement Impact

There will be two effects:

- Income tax expense will be increased by $3,330.
- The deferred income tax asset relating to the tax loss carryforward benefit will be reduced to $3,700 on the SFP.

Deferred income tax asset—carryforward benefit	$3,700

CASE 17-1

WATER TOURS LTD.

Water Tours Ltd. (WTL) is a small Canadian company incorporated under the *Canada Business Corporations Act*. The company was formed ten years ago but has only been marginally profitable. Recent severe losses have significantly reduced its equity base and made WTL the subject of close scrutiny by lenders. Secured creditors have requested audited statements for the first time in 20X3. Company management is convinced that the operation is viable. A description of operations is presented in Exhibit 1.

EXHIBIT 1

OPERATING INFORMATION

Water Tours Limited

WTL owns four ships, used for week-long cruises on rivers and along ocean shorelines, each with the capacity of 100 guests. WTL strives continually for quality service and customer comfort. WTL provides package cruises to singles, couples, and families. Packages include all accommodation, meals, beverages, and entertainment for a one-week period. Rooms are only available under these packages and cannot be booked for shorter visits.

WTL operates one boat on the Atlantic coast, one on the Pacific coast, and two in Southern Ontario. Each boat has a two-to-three-month busy season and less busy shoulder seasons. All boats shut down in the off-season.

Customers book in advance and make a deposit of 60% of the cruise fee at that time. If a customer cancels more than 30 days prior to the cruise date, 80% of the deposit is refunded. Fewer than 5% of customers cancel more than 30 days prior to the cruise. If a cancellation is made less than 30 days prior to the cruise, all the deposit is forfeit. The balance of the fee is paid as the customer checks in. At 31 December 20X3, prepayments totalled $500,000, down $150,000 from 31 December 20X2.

WTL advertises heavily during September to January in travel magazines catering to upper-income consumers. These expenditures have medium-term benefits—likely three to five years—in that they build the reputation and name recognition of the company. Promotional offers are given to travel agents when facilities are not fully booked 30 days in advance. Travel agents pay only for the cost of meals. WTL feels this is an effective form of advertising and promotion.

Every three years the "common areas" of each ship—lounges, restaurant, and reception rooms—are redecorated. This is done when the ships are closed for the off-season. Individual rooms are redecorated every five years, when the rooms are not in use (during off-season or shoulder season). Expenditures for room renovations were $400,000 a year in each of the past 10 years, but were $700,000 in 20X3. Common area renovations amounted to $600,000 in 20X1 and $750,000 in 20X2. There were none in 20X3.

During 20X3, WTL experienced a most unfortunate incident. One of the Southern Ontario ships was severely damaged by a storm. Fortunately, all clients were evacuated safely. The insurance carried by WTL paid for alternative accommodations and for a $3 million replacement value on the WTL ship. The new ship will be about 25% larger than the ship as it was when it was damaged and cost about $4,200,000. Meanwhile, the ship is not operating; some bookings were transferred to other WTL ships while others had to be refunded in full.

As a CPA in public practice, you have been appointed auditor. You have scheduled a meeting to discuss the 20X3 draft financial statements as prepared by WTL, with the WTL controller (see Exhibit 2 for extracts from these statements). You wish to discuss the appropriateness of accounting policies but you are aware that you must quantify, if possible, the earnings impact of your recommendations and be sensitive to WTL's financial position. WTL complies with ASPE but has been asked by lenders to use comprehensive tax allocation in the income tax area in order to preserve comparability with other entities.

EXHIBIT 2

FINANCIAL STATEMENT EXTRACTS

Water Tours Limited

Income Statement

31 December 20X3

Revenue		
Rooms		$6,375,700
Food and beverages		3,226,000
Gain on insurance proceeds		1,140,000
Total revenues		$10,741,700
Direct operating expenses		
Rooms		4,115,000
Foods and beverage		2,194,000
Operating		1,241,000
Depreciation and amortization		2,094,500
Total expenses		9,644,500
Operating income		1,097,200
Interest		289,200
Income before tax		808,000
Tax expense (recovery)		
Current	$351,500	
Deferred	150,000	
Provision for loss recovery	-351,500	
Total provision		150,000
Net income		$ 658,000

Notes to financial statement:
1. Revenue is recognized as cash is received.
2. The following expense are included in other operating expenses as paid:

EXHIBIT 2

FINANCIAL STATEMENT EXTRACTS

a) Advertising ($60,000 in 20X3, $58,000 in 20X2)

b) Renovation ($700,000 in 20X3, all for room renovations)

3. The gain in insurance proceeds was calculated as follows:

Net book value, destroyed property	$1,860,000
Proceeds	3,000,000
Gain	$1,140,000

The corporate income tax rate is 40%. For tax purposes, all the gain is a temporary difference. The $150,000 income statement expense for deferred income tax is net of $456,000 of deferred income tax related to this gain.

4. No accounting recognition is given to the "bargain" price given to travel agents.

5. Last year, housekeeping services in the Ontario resort were subcontracted to Housekeeping Services Ltd, a company owned by one of the shareholders of WTL. This was meant as a cost-cutting move, but actual expense of $76,200 was 10% higher than last year, when WTL did it themselves.

6. At the end of 20X3, there was a credit balance of $421,200 in deferred income tax on the balance sheet. There were also gross unrecorded loss carryfowards in the amount of $795,000. The tax rate is 40%.

Required:

Prepare a report dealing with accounting policy choice as a basis for the upcoming discussion. If changes in accounting policy are advised, your recommendations should include revised 20X3 earnings and also guidance on how to treat the changes in the financial statements.

CASE 17-2

SOCCER INC.

Soccer Inc. (SI) is a public corporation incorporated in 20X2. SI operates a professional soccer team and related activities. New bank financing was obtained in 20X9 for the construction of a new stadium. The bank requires annual audited financial statements and SI has a covenant with a maximum debt-to-equity ratio.

SI's players have an agreement with SI that entitles them to a bonus if SI exceeds net income of $25 million in the year. They agreed to this new bonus arrangement in 20X9 instead of a salary increase. Net income before any adjustments on 31 December 20X9 was $24 million. The players are upset, since the games have been well attended and they anticipated a substantial bonus payment. Management has stated that they have invested in the future, which will provide healthy bonuses in later years. Exhibit 1 includes the income statement.

EXHIBIT 1

STATEMENT OF COMPREHENSIVE INCOME

Soccer Incorporated

Income Statement

(unaudited)

Year Ended 31 Dec. 20X9 (in millions)

Revenues	$ 50	
Operating expenses	(22)	
Operating profit		28
Finance costs	(7)	
Finance income	3	
Net income		$24
Other Comprehensive Income		
Unrealized gain on investments recorded—FVTOCI	5	
Fair value changes on cash flow hedge	(1)	
Foreign exchange gain - subsidiary	2	
Actuarial gain pension plan	3	
Comprehensive Income		$33

You have been hired by the players to review the accounting policies for SI's 31 December year-end. Exhibit 2 provides the notes to the financial statements. You have been asked by the players to analyze the current accounting policies; discuss alternatives, where possible; and provide recommendations on the appropriate accounting policies for events that have occurred during 20X9. The incremental borrowing rate for SI is 10%. The tax rate for SI is 30%.

EXHIBIT 2

NOTES TO FINANCIAL STATEMENTS

1. Tickets can be purchased on-line through SI's new website or at the box office at the stadium. Customers using a credit card can purchase online tickets up to a year in advance. Revenue for on-line sales is recognized when the ticket is used. To increase sales of season tickets for the 20X10 season, when tickets are purchased, customers received a $50 gift card for use in the souvenir shop. Many customers used the gift card for holiday shopping in December. Revenue for season tickets is recognized as games are played.

2. SI provided 100,000 coupons for $2 off the game food combination at local grocery stores and pharmacies. The $200,000 was expensed as an advertising cost.

3. SI received a $100 million loan from the bank for the construction of the new stadium. Transaction costs of $2 million were expensed during the year as a finance cost. In 20X9, SI invested cash from the bank loan until needed for construction in shares of High Tech Inc. SI purchased 2% of the company's shares and will sell them when cash is needed over the next year and a half. These shares were classified as FVTOCI.

4. SI started construction of the new sports stadium in March 20X9. The estimated completion date was December 20X11. Costs capitalized in 20X9 were $15 million and included materials, labour, and variable overhead. Costs expensed in 20X9 were $2 million in interest. In July 20X9, a strike occurred that shut down construction for two months and will delay the opening of the new stadium.

5. SI issued $1,000,000 of term preferred shares to two of the SI owners. These shares have a cumulative dividend of 10% and a mandatory repayment date in 10 years. Any unpaid dividends must be repaid at that date. These shares were recorded on the statement of financial position as debt, and dividends were recorded as a finance cost.

6. SI issued common shares during the year. Share issue costs of $1 million were expensed as a financing cost.

7. SI has $10 million of unused tax losses. It has decided that the future is too uncertain to recognize the benefit of these losses. This industry has a history of strikes.

8. SI's uses the Black-Scholes model to determine fair value for stock options granted to the executive team. Since SI's shares are not frequently traded, it does not measure stock price volatility. SI's stock option plan vests annually over a five-year period. The entire stock option expense recognized in period stock option is granted. Forfeitures are recognized when they occur.

CASE 17-3

DOWNHILL SKI CO.

Downhill Ski Co. is experiencing financial difficulties. Earnings have been declining sharply over the past several years. The company has barely maintained profits over the last four years. In the current year, the company is expected to suffer a substantial loss for the first time in 10 years. A taxable loss will also be reported. The losses are expected to be significantly greater than the profits reported in the previous three years.

Downhill Ski is a manufacturer specializing in downhill racing skis and boots. The company supplies the Canadian ski team but competition from larger manufacturers has forced Downhill Ski to keep its prices low when its expenses have been increasing. Also, the popularity of snowboarding has had a negative impact on sales. However, it has been found that many older adults who switch to snowboarding go back to skiing.

North Johnston, the sales and marketing manager, left the company last year to join Rossignol, a large multinational company. Cathy Thomas, former ski champion, was hired earlier this year as the new sales and marketing manager.

The owner of Downhill Ski, Wendy Hogarth, is not overly concerned with the loss for the current year and has the following comments to make:

"With the hiring of Cathy Thomas as sales and marketing manager we will develop relationships with the national ski team and work on improving sponsorship of events. This should increase our sales.

"Downhill Ski is developing a new type of ski that is not on the market yet. Some of the national ski team members tested the prototype of the ski and were thrilled with its performance. We are sure sales of the new ski will give us solid sales. We have already lined up buyers across Canada and the United States for this ski. Our financial forecast for next year is to make a profit.

"We have a new large piece of equipment acquired at the end of last year. This manufacturing equipment is more efficient and will save us money on maintenance and repairs."

You have been hired by Wendy to provide accounting advice. She wants to know if she can recognize the loss this year as an asset on the statement of financial position. She would also like to know the impact on the financial statements of recognizing versus not recognizing the loss and if there are any tax-planning strategies the company should use in respect to recognition of the loss.

Required:

Write the report to Wendy.

TECHNICAL REVIEW

connect

TR17-1 Loss Carryback:

Burgher Ltd. had a taxable loss of $300,000 in 20X7. The tax rate in 20X7 is 32%. In the past three years, the company had the following taxable income and tax rates:

	20X4	20X5	20X6
Taxable income	$200,000	$120,000	$80,000
Tax rate	36%	38%	40%

There are no temporary differences other than those created by income tax losses.

Required:

1. What is the amount of refund that will be claimed in 20X7, taking the loss back to the oldest possible year, first? Provide the journal entry for income tax receivable in 20X7.
2. Is there a different pattern for claiming a refund that the company could use? Recalculate the refund and provide the journal entry under this assumption.

≡ connect

TR17-2 Loss Carryback/Carryforward:

Colavecchia Ltd. had a taxable loss of $1,500,000 in 20X8. The tax rate in 20X8 is 28%. In the past three years, the company had the following taxable income and tax rates:

	20X5	20X6	20X7
Taxable income	$420,000	$300,000	$210,000
Tax rate	25%	25%	25%

There are no temporary differences other than those created by income tax losses. The loss was triggered by a downturn in the economy.

Required:

1. What is the amount of refund that will be claimed in 20X8?
2. What is the amount of the loss carryforward?
3. Assuming that loss carryforward usage is probable, prepare a journal entry for income tax in 20X8.
4. Assuming that loss carryforward usage is not probable, prepare a journal entry for income tax in 20X8.

≡ connect

TR17-3 Loss Carryback/Carryforward, Change in Rate:

Petrilli Ltd. had a taxable loss of $3,500,000 in 20X8 and a further loss of $100,000 in 20X9. The tax rate in 20X8 was 32% and in 20X9, 33%. All rates are enacted in the year to which they pertain. In the three years before the losses, the company had the following taxable income and tax rates:

	20X5	20X6	20X7
Taxable income	$880,000	$950,000	$670,000
Tax rate	26%	28%	30%

There are no temporary differences other than those created by income tax losses. The company was struggling due to a competitor entering the market.

Required:

1. What is the amount of refund that will be claimed in 20X8?
2. What is the amount of the loss carryforward in 20X8?
3. Assuming that loss carryforward usage is probable in each year, prepare a journal entry for income tax in 20X8 and 20X9.
4. Assuming that loss carryforward usage is not probable in each year, prepare a journal entry for income tax in 20X8 and 20X9.

■ connect

TR17-4 Loss Carryback/Carryforward, Temporary Differences:

Lin Ltd. reported the following:

	20X7 (first year of operations)	20X8
Earnings (loss)	$90,000	($150,000)
Depreciation (assets have a cost of $210,000)	$20,000	$ 20,000
CCA	$35,000	$ 45,000
Non-deductible expenses	$ 10,000	$ 10,000
Tax rate	25%	25%

Required:

1. What is the amount of the taxable income or loss in each year?
2. How much is the tax refund to be claimed in 20X8?
3. How much is tax expense (recovery) in 20X8, assuming that use of the loss carryforward is not probable?

■ connect

TR17-5 Loss Carryback/Carryforward, Refile CCA:

Moon Ltd. reported the following:

	20X7 (first year of operations)	20X8
Earnings (loss)	$200,000	($310,000)
Depreciation (assets have a cost of $450,000)	40,000	40,000
CCA	80,000	120,000
Non-taxable revenue	30,000	10,000
Tax rate	25%	25%

Required:

1. What is the amount of the taxable income or loss in each year?
2. How much is the tax refund to be claimed in 20X8?

3. What is the amount of the loss carryforward at the end of 20X8?

4. Repeat requirements 1–3 based on the assumption that Moon decides to not claim CCA in 20X8 or 20X7. Why might the company choose this strategy?

■ connect

TR17-6 Loss Carryback/Carryforward, Refile CCA:

Jupiter Ltd. reported the following:

	20X7 (first year of operations)	20X8
Earnings (loss)	$100,000	($290,000)
Depreciation (assets have a cost of $1,000,000)	40,000	40,000
CCA	50,000	90,000
Non-tax-deductible expenses	20,000	20,000
Tax rate	20%	20%

Required:

1. What is the amount of the taxable income or loss in each year? What is the amount of the loss carryforward at the end of 20X8?

2. Prepare a journal entry for income tax for 20X8 assuming probability of loss carryforward use is low.

3. Repeat requirements 1 and 2 assuming that Jupiter decides to not claim CCA in 20X8 or 20X7. Why might the company choose this strategy?

■ connect

TR17-7 Benefits of Carryback and Carryforward:

Saturn Ltd. began operations in 20X3. For the first six years of operations, the company had the following pre-tax net earnings (loss):

Year	Taxable Income	Tax Rate
20X3	$ (120,000)	25%
20X4	720,000	30%
20X5	880,000	30%
20X6	(2,600,000)	30%
20X7	280,000	35%
20X8	1,000,000	35%

There have been no temporary differences between pre-tax accounting income and taxable income.

In all years, the probability of loss carryforward use was low.

Required:

For each year, prepare a journal entry or entries to record income tax expense (recovery).

≡ connect

TR17-8 Deferred Income Tax LCF Asset; Table:

Melinda Ltd. had a gross $100,000 loss carryforward at the end of 20X6. This gross loss carryforward increased to $140,000 at the end of 20X7. In 20X8, $50,000 of the LCF was used. The enacted tax rates, enacted in the year to which they pertain, were 25% in 20X6, 27% in 20X7, and 28% in 20X8.

Required:

1. For each year, show how the LCF would be reflected in a table that documents deferred income tax balances and adjustments.
2. Calculate the components of the change in the deferred tax account in 20X7.

≡ connect

TR17-9 LCF Use, Change in Rate:

Mercury Ltd. reported earnings of $75,000 in 20X9. The company has $55,000 of depreciation expense this year, and claimed CCA of $90,000. The tax rate was 25%. At the end of 20X8, there was a $10,000 loss carryforward reported in a deferred tax asset account valued at $2,200, and a deferred tax liability of $35,200 caused by capital assets with a net book value of $500,000 and UCC of $340,000.

Required:

What is the amount of income tax expense in 20X9? Prepare the income tax entry or entries.

≡ connect

TR17-10 LCF Use, Change in Rate:

Sol Ltd. reported earnings of $400,000 in 20X8. The company has $80,000 of depreciation expense this year, and claimed CCA of $120,000. The tax rate was 28%. At the end of 20X7, there was a $100,000 loss carryforward that was not recorded because use was considered less than probable. The company also reported a deferred tax liability of $60,000 caused by capital assets with a net book value of $1,200,000 and UCC of $900,000. The tax rate had been 20% in 20X7.

Required:

What is the amount of income tax expense in 20X8? Prepare the income tax entry or entries.

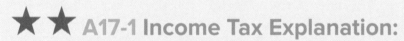

ASSIGNMENTS

 A17-1 Income Tax Explanation:

Kong Corp. reported the following items with respect to income tax in the 20X6 financial statements:

Deferred income tax asset	$ 10,400
Deferred income tax liability	328,400

The 20X6 statement of comprehensive income shows the following income tax expense:

Income tax expense:	
Current	$75,000
Deferred	68,500
Impact of loss carryforward	(75,000)
	$68,500

The disclosure notes indicate that there is an unrecognized loss carryforward in the amount of $406,400. No tax loss carryforwards have been recorded as assets. The tax rate is 40%.

Required:

1. Explain the components of the 20X6 income tax expense. Why is there income tax expense if there is a loss carryforward?

2. Give an example of a statement of financial position account that could have caused a deferred income tax asset and a deferred income tax liability. Why are these two accounts not netted on the SFP?

3. Why would the loss carryforward not have been recognized in its entirety in 20X6? What amounts and accounts would change if it could be recognized?

4. How much tax is currently payable? How much tax would have been payable if there had been no loss carryforward?

★ A17-2 Probable Test:

After utilizing any carrybacks, Nu Inc. had a taxable loss carryforward of $1 million in 20X9. The company is trying to determine if the "probable" condition has been met and if it should record a deferred income tax asset or not. For the past five years, Nu has had declining profits. The company has recently acquired one of its competitors, which had research in progress for a new product. Work has been completed on the project, and a patent was filed by the end of 20X9. Marketing studies show that this product, if successful, will have huge sales potential for a number of years. The company has initiated an advertising campaign to promote the product, which is expected to be launched 14 February 20X10. Unfortunately, in January 20X10 a lawsuit was launched, indicating patent infringement. Lawyers for Nu do not think there is merit in the lawsuit. The company plans to go ahead with the launch of the product. The tax rate for the company is 38%.

Required:

1. Is use of the tax loss carryforward probable? Provide support for both sides.
2. What is the amount that would be recorded as a deferred income tax asset if probable?
3. What is the impact of the tax losses if it is determined the probable condition has not been met? Could a deferred income tax asset be recorded in the future?

 connect

★ ★ A17-3 Loss Carryback/Carryforward:

Landmark Corp. started operations in 20X6. The statements of comprehensive income for the first four years of operations reflected the following pre-tax amounts:

	20X4	20X5	20X6	20X7
Pre-tax earnings (loss)	$100,000	$(240,000)	$20,000	$40,000

There are no temporary differences other than those created by income tax losses. Landmark has had a constant income tax rate of 38% for all four years.

Required:

1. Give entries to record income tax expense for each year, assuming that management has assessed that use of the loss carryforwards is probable.
2. Give entries to record income tax expense for each year, assuming that management has assessed that use of the loss carryforwards is not probable.
3. Give entries to record income tax expense for each year, assuming that management has assessed that use of the loss carryforwards is probable, but reassessment in 20X6 indicated that probability of use was unlikely.

★ A17-4 Loss Carryback; Entries and Reporting:

Halton Corp. reported pre-tax earnings from operations in 20X7 of $120,000 (the first year of operations). In 20X8, the corporation experienced a $70,000 pre-tax loss from operations. Future operations are highly uncertain. Assume an income tax rate of 40%. The company has no temporary differences.

Required:

1. Assess Halton's income tax situation for 20X7 and 20X8. How should Halton elect to handle the loss in 20X8?
2. Based on your assessments in requirement 1, give the 20X7 and 20X8 income tax entries.
3. Show how all tax-related items would be reported on the 20X7 and 20X8 statement of comprehensive income and statement of financial position.

A17-5 Recognition of Loss Carryforward:

Innis Corp. experienced an accounting and tax loss in 20X5. The benefit of the tax loss was realized in part by carryback. The remainder of the tax loss carryforward of $630,000 was not recognized because management felt that there was considerable doubt as to its eventual recognition. In 20X6, a further accounting and tax loss was recognized. This time, the tax loss was much smaller, $120,000, and the benefit of the tax loss carryforwards was still not recorded. In 20X7, the company recorded positive accounting earnings. The taxable income prior to using the loss carryforward was $240,000. There were no temporary differences. The tax rate was 35% in 20X7. The tax rate for 20X8 was 40%, enacted in 20X8.

Required:

1. Record 20X7 tax entries, assuming that the likelihood of using the remaining tax loss carryforwards is still not considered to be probable.
2. Assume that in 20X8 accounting and taxable income was $890,000. Record income tax.
3. Record 20X7 tax entries assuming that the probability of using the remaining tax loss carryforwards is considered probable for the first time.
4. Assume that accounting and taxable income in 20X8 was $890,000 but that the entries from requirement 3 were made. Record 20X8 income tax.

A17-6 Calculate a Loss Carryback and Its Benefit; Temporary Differences:

Tyler Toys Ltd. reported the following:

	20X3	20X4	20X5	20X6
Accounting earnings before tax	$10,000	$15,000	$(40,000)	$10,000
Depreciation expense (original cost of asset, $75,000)	6,000	6,000	6,000	6,000
Golf club dues	3,000	4,000	3,000	4,000
CCA (maximum available claim)	3,000	6,000	12,000	10,000
Tax rate—enacted in each year	20%	20%	30%	35%

Required:

1. Calculate taxable income each year, and tax payable. Tyler claims the maximum CCA each year.
2. How much of the loss could Tyler use as a tax loss carryback? How much tax refund will it receive? How much is the tax loss carryforward? How much is the tax benefit?

★ A17-7 Recording Temporary Differences; Loss; Rate Change:

Refer again to the data in A17-6.

Required:

1. Provide the journal entry to record the benefit of the tax loss in 20X5, assuming that the tax loss is first used as a tax loss carryback and the remainder is available as a tax loss carryforward. Be sure to adjust the deferred income tax account for the temporary difference between depreciation and CCA and also the change in tax rates.
2. What condition has to be met to record the loss in 20X5?

★ ★ A17-8 Calculate a Loss Carryback and Its Benefit; Temporary Differences:

Benata Ltd. started operations in 20X5 and purchased buildings and equipment with an original cost of $400,000. Benata reported the following information:

	20X5	20X6	20X7	20X8
Accounting earnings before tax	$150,000	$230,000	$310,000	$(460,000)
Golf club dues	15,000	15,000	20,000	15,000
Depreciation expense	45,000	45,000	45,000	45,000
CCA claimed	55,000	92,500	70,000	—
Warranty expense	25,000	41,000	57,000	29,000
Warranty costs incurred	22,000	32,000	55,000	23,000
Tax rate—enacted in each year	35%	37%	40%	40%

Required:

1. Prepare the journal entries for income taxes for each of the four years. Assume that the company is concerned that it might have another significant loss in 20X9.

2. Prepare the journal entries for income taxes for each of the four years, assuming that the company wants to maximize the amount it can recover from the tax carryback, it sees the loss in 20X8 as an isolated incident, and it anticipates large profits in the next few years.

3. Repeat requirements 1 and 2, assuming that the taxable loss in 20X8 was $950,000.

★ ★ A17-9 Loss Carryforward; Temporary Difference:

Cloud Corp. began operations in 20X8. In its first year, the company had a net operating loss before tax for accounting purposes of $200,000. Depreciation was $230,000, and CCA was $250,000. The company claimed CCA in 20X8. Warranty costs expensed in the period were $150,000, and actual warranty costs incurred were $120,000. In 20X9, Cloud had taxable income before the use of the tax loss carryforward of $480,000. This was after adding back $230,000 of depreciation and deducting $280,000 of CCA, and adding back $230,000 of warranty costs accrued and deducting $210,000 of warranty costs incurred. The income tax rate is 38% in both years. Capital assets had an original cost of $2,500,000 in 20X8.

Required:

1. Prepare a journal entry or entries to record income tax in 20X8 and 20X9, assuming that the likelihood of using the tax loss carryforward is assessed as probable in 20X8. Also prepare the SCI section showing earnings before income tax and income tax expense for 20X8 and 20X9.

2. Repeat requirement 1, assuming that the likelihood of using the tax loss carryforward is not probable. In addition, deferred income tax asset amounts do not meet recognition criteria and cannot be recorded.

3. Which assessment—probable or not probable—seems more logical in 20X8? Discuss.

★ ★ A17-10 Loss Carrybacks and Carryforwards; Rate Change:

Lu Ltd. has experienced the following accounting earnings and taxable income:

	Accounting Earnings	Taxable Income*	Tax Rate
20X4	($86,000)	($62,000)	36%
20X5	80,000	50,000	38
20X6	90,000	82,000	36
20X7	50,000	(88,000)	32

*Before applying any available tax loss carryforwards

The differences between accounting and taxable income are caused by differences between accounting and tax expenses that will not reverse (permanent differences). All tax rates are enacted in the year to which they relate.

Required:

1. Record income tax for 20X4 through 20X7 assuming that the future use of tax loss carryforwards is not considered to be probable.

2. Repeat requirement 1, assuming that the use of tax loss carryforwards is considered to be probable in the loss year.

 A17-11 Deferred Tax Asset Revaluation; Rate Change:

Lopez Ltd. reports the following asset on the statement of financial position at 31 December 20X8:

Deferred income tax asset, loss carryforward	$334,400

This asset reflects the benefit of a tax loss carryforward recorded in 20X7. It was not used in 20X8. The enacted tax rate was 38%. In 20X9, the enacted tax rate changed to 40%.

Required:

1. Record 20X9 tax entries if Lopez reported accounting and taxable income of $50,000 in 20X9. The use of the tax loss carryforward is still considered to be probable.

2. Record 20X9 tax entries if Lopez reported accounting and tax losses of $220,000 in 20X9. The use of the tax loss carryforward is still considered to be probable.

 A17-12 Loss Carryback/Carryforward; Temporary Difference:

Bogdan Ltd. shows the following on its 31 December 20X4 statement of financial position:

Deferred income tax liability	$870,000

All this income tax liability relates to the difference between the NBV and UCC of property, plant, and equipment. At 31 December 20X4, NBV is $9,630,000, and UCC is $7,455,000.

In 20X2, 20X3, and 20X4, the company had reported a total taxable income of $324,750 and paid taxes of $81,450.

In 20X5, Bogdan reported an accounting loss before tax of $480,000. Depreciation of $67,500 is included in this calculation. No CCA will be claimed in 20X5. The enacted tax rate was 40% in 20X5.

Required:

1. Calculate the tax loss in 20X5.

2. How much of the tax loss can be used as a loss carryback? What will be the benefit of this loss carryback?

3. How much of the loss is available as a tax loss carryforward? What is the benefit of this tax loss carryforward?

4. Under what circumstances can the benefit of the tax loss carryforward be recorded as an asset?

5. Record income tax for 20X5, assuming that the tax loss carryforward can be recorded.

6. Record income tax for 20X5, assuming that the tax loss carryforward cannot be recorded.

7. Assume that accounting and taxable income was $150,000 in 20X6 and the enacted tax rate was still 40%. Prepare the journal entry to record income tax in 20X6, assuming that the tax loss carryforward (a) was recorded in 20X5 as in requirement 5, and (b) was not recorded in 20X5 as in requirement 6.

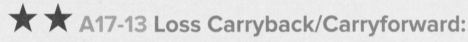

★ ★ A17-13 Loss Carryback/Carryforward:

Nueve Ltd. had the following pre-tax earnings and losses:

Year	Pre-Tax Earnings (Loss)	Tax Rate
20X3	$ 330,000	34%
20X4	165,000	34
20X5	540,000	34
20X6	660,000	36
20X7	(3,330,000)	36
20X8	375,000	36
20X9	915,000	40

The tax rates are those effective for the year indicated. The rates were enacted the year in which they became effective. Taxable income (loss) was equal to accounting earnings (loss) in each year.

Required:

1. Prepare the entry to record income tax expense for 20X7. At the end of 20X7, management estimates it is probable Nueve will utilize only $225,000 of the loss carryforward.

2. Prepare the entry to record income tax expense for 20X8 and 20X9. At the end of 20X8, management estimates it is probable Nueve will utilize the entire loss carryforward, not just the $225,000.

★ ★ ★ A17-14 Loss Carryback/Carryforward; Refiling; Entries:

Simeoni Ltd. began operations in 20X5 and reported the following information for the years 20X5 to 20X9:

	20X5	20X6	20X7	20X8	20X9
Pre-tax earnings	$80,000	$120,000	$50,000	$(550,000)	$110,000
Depreciation	25,000	25,000	30,000	30,000	30,000

Capital cost allowance	50,000	90,000	14,000	0	0
Golf club dues	2,000	2,000	2,000	2,000	2,000

The income tax rate is 40% in all years. Assume that Simeoni's only depreciable assets were purchased in 20X5 and cost $500,000.

Required:

1. Prepare the journal entries for income taxes for 20X8 and 20X9. In 20X8, it was determined by management that it was probable that the loss carryforwards would be realized.

2. What is the balance of deferred income tax at the end of 20X9? Show calculations.

3. Repeat requirements 1 and 2 with the assumption that management determined the tax loss carryforward would not be realized in 20X8. In addition, management decided to refile 20X5, 20X6, and 20X7 tax returns to eliminate CCA and use more of the loss as a loss carryback. The deferred tax asset caused by temporary differences can be recognized in 20X8. The probability of loss carryforward use did not change in 20X9, even though some of the loss carryforward was used.

★ ★ A17-15 Loss Carryback/Carryforward; Refile; Rate Change:

In the years 20X4 through 20X6, Leader Corp. reported a total of $450,000 of taxable income. The enacted tax rate during those years was 38%. At the end of 20X6, Leader reported a deferred income tax liability related to capital assets. The net book value of these assets was $800,000, while the UCC was $630,000 at the end of 20X6.

During 20X7, Leader recorded an accounting loss of $660,000 after depreciation expense of $50,000. No CCA was claimed in 20X7. In 20X7, the enacted rate changed to 40% for both 20X7 and 20X8.

In 20X8, Leader reported accounting earnings before tax of $520,000. Depreciation of $50,000 was equal to the CCA claim.

Required:

1. Determine after-tax earnings for 20X7 and 20X8, assuming that the loss carryforwards are most likely to be used in the carryforward period.

2. Repeat requirement 1, assuming that loss carryforward use is not likely.

3. Repeat requirement 1, assuming that loss carryforward use is not likely and 20X4–20X6 tax returns are refiled in 20X7 and a total of $160,000 of CCA is eliminated.

★ ★ A17-16 Loss Carryforward; Temporary Differences; Rate Change; Entries:

The Village Co. manufactures and sells television sets. The company recorded warranty expense of 2% of sales for accounting purposes. The following information is taken from the company's books:

(in thousands)	20X5	20X6	20X7	20X8	20X9
Sales	$3,000	$6,000	$8,000	$10,000	$15,000
Actual warranty claims paid	60	80	200	90	75
Accounting earnings (loss) before taxes	nil	(980)	nil	2,000	4,000
Depreciation	600	600	600	600	600
Capital cost allowance	600	nil	500	450	400
Dividend revenue (nontaxable)	nil	20	20	nil	nil

Net book value of depreciable assets at 31 December 20X5 is $7,600,000. Undepreciated capital cost at 31 December 20X5 is $5,600,000. There is a deferred income tax liability of $800,000 with respect to this temporary difference. There is no taxable income remaining to absorb loss carrybacks prior to 20X5.

The tax rate is 40% in 20X5 through 20X7 and increases to 45% for 20X8 and 20X9. Tax rates are enacted in the year to which they pertain. There are no other sources of temporary differences.

Required:

Give journal entries to record income taxes for 20X6 to 20X9, inclusive. Realization of the loss carryforward is considered to be probable in 20X6.

★ ★ A17-17 Loss Carryback/Carryforward; Temporary Differences; Rate Change:

On 1 January 20X7, Chang Inc. commenced business operations. At 31 December 20X9, the following information relates to Chang:

	20X7	20X8	20X9
Earnings (loss) before tax	$302,400	($453,600)	$720,000
Tax rate (enacted in each year)	30%	35%	40%
Depreciation expense (asset cost was $600,000)	50,000	50,000	50,000
Capital cost allowance	180,000	0	78,000
Dividends received (nontaxable)	38,400	60,000	60,000
Golf club dues	9,600	9,600	9,600

Required:

1. Prepare journal entries to record tax for 20X7, 20X8, and 20X9. Assume that the loss carryforward usage in 20X8 is considered to be probable.

2. Prepare journal entries to record tax for 20X7, 20X8, and 20X9. Assume that the loss carryforward usage in 20X8 is not considered to be probable but is considered to be probable in 20X9.

 A17-18 Loss Carryback/Carryforward; Temporary Differences; Rate Change:

On 1 January 20X4, Dart Inc. commenced business operations. The following information is available to you:

	20X4	20X5	20X6	20X7
Earnings (loss) before tax	$45,000	($300,000)	$45,000	$65,000
Tax rate (enacted in each year)	36%	36%	32%	30%
Depreciation (original cost of assets, $500,000)	25,000	25,000	25,000	25,000
Capital cost allowance	30,000	0	60,000	50,000
Rental revenue recognized*	30,000	—	—	—

*There is a rent receivable account at the end of 20X4, because rent revenue was earned in 20X4 but will not be collected until 20X6. This amount is not part of taxable income in 20X4, but will be taxable income in 20X6 when it is collected.

Required:

Prepare journal entries to record tax for 20X4, 20X5, 20X6, and 20X7. Assume that the tax loss carryforward usage in 20X5 is considered to be not probable but that in 20X6 the balance of probability shifts and in 20X6 the loss usage is considered to be probable.

★ ★ ★ A17-19 Loss Carryback/Carryforward; Rate Change; Comprehensive:

Dexter Ltd. began operations in 20X5 and reported the following information for the years 20X5 to 20X9:

	20X5	20X6	20X7	20X8	20X9
Pre-tax earnings	$ 8,000	$15,000	$ 9,000	$(95,000)	$ 6,000
Depreciation	10,000	10,000	10,000	10,000	10,000
CCA	10,000	18,000	14,000	0	0
Net book value	90,000	80,000	70,000	60,000	50,000
UCC	90,000	72,000	58,000	58,000	58,000

Required:

1. Prepare journal entries to record income taxes in each year, 20X5 through 20X9. Assume that realization of the tax loss carryforward benefits is probable and the tax rate is 40% in all years.

2. Repeat requirement 1, assuming that the tax rate is now 40% in 20X5 and 20X6, 43% in 20X7, 45% in 20X8, and 47% in 20X9. Tax rates are enacted in the year to which they pertain.

3. Return to the facts of requirement 1 (the tax rate is 40%). Repeat your journal entries for 20X8 and 20X9, assuming that use of the tax loss carryforward is deemed to be not probable in 20X8 but probable in 20X9.

★ ★ A17-20 Loss Carryback/Carryforward; Temporary Differences; Use in Subsequent Year:

Dynamic Ltd. reported the following 20X8 statement of profit and loss:

DYNAMIC LIMITED

Statement of Profit and Loss

For the Year Ended 31 December 20X8

Revenue	$ 1,560,000
Cost of goods sold	700,000
Depreciation	180,000
General and administrative expenses	50,000
Other	20,000
	950,000
Profit before tax	$ 610,000

Other information:

a. There is a $80,000 accrued rent receivable on the statement of financial position. This amount was included in rental income (revenue) this year but will not be taxed until next year. This is the first time such an accrual has been made.

b. The CCA claim for 20X8 is $301,000. At the beginning of 20X8, UCC was $2,165,000, while net book value was $2,916,000. The balance in the related deferred income tax liability was $300,400 (cr.).

c. Revenue includes dividends received of $50,000, which are not taxable at any time.

d. Other expenses include nondeductible political donations of $30,000.

e. The statement of financial position shows an asset account called "deferred income tax asset $30,000," which is the benefit of a $75,000 loss carryforward, recorded in 20X7.

Required:

Prepare the journal entry or entries to record tax in 20X8. Show all calculations. The tax rate is 40%.

(Source: [Adapted] © CGA-Canada. Reproduced with permission.)

★ ★ ★ A17-21 Loss Carryback/Carryforward; Comprehensive; Rate Change:

Loo Corp. was incorporated in 20X5. Details of the company's results are presented below:

	20X5	20X6	20X7
Earnings (loss) before tax	$ 60,000	($200,000)	$100,000
Depreciation expense	40,000	40,000	40,000
Capital cost allowance claimed	50,000	0	50,000

	20X5	20X6	20X7
Dividend income (nontaxable)	10,000	10,000	10,000
Tax rate	40%	40%	40%
Net book value, end of year	360,000	320,000	280,000
UCC, end of year	350,000	350,000	300,000

Required:

1. Prepare journal entries for tax for 20X5, 20X6, and 20X7. Assume that realization of the benefit of the loss carryforward is probable in 20X6.

2. Repeat requirement 1, assuming that the tax rate is 40% in 20X5 but is changed to 42% in 20X6 and to 44% in 20X7. All tax rates are enacted in the year in which they are effective.

3. Revert to the facts of requirement 1 (i.e., 40% tax rate in each year). Assume that the use of the unused tax loss carryforward is considered to be not probable in 20X6 and is still not probable in 20X7 other than the loss carryforward actually utilized in 20X7. Provide journal entries for 20X5, 20X6, and 20X7.

A17-22 Tax Losses; Intraperiod Allocation; Income Statement:

At the beginning of 20X4, Caprioli Tracking Corp. (CTC) had a deferred income tax liability on its statement of financial position of $60,000. The deferred income tax balance reflects the tax impact of gross accumulated temporary differences of $95,000 relating to CCA/depreciation and $55,000 relating to pension costs. The tax expense has been higher (i.e., CCA and pension funding have been higher) than the accounting expense (i.e., depreciation and pension expense). Over the past three years, taxes have been due and paid as follows:

Year	Taxable Income	Taxes Due
20X1	$60,000	$22,000
20X2	20,000	7,600
20X3	40,000	16,000
		$45,600

In 20X4, CTC suffered the first loss in its history due to a general economic turndown. The accounting loss amounted to $200,000 before taxes. In computing accounting earnings, CTC deducted depreciation of $10,000 per year. On its 20X4 tax return, CTC elected to take no CCA, and therefore the 20X4 loss for tax purposes was as follows:

Accounting income (loss)	$(200,000)
Depreciation	10,000
Pension expense (not deductible)	30,000
Pension funding (deductible)	(60,000)
Taxable income (loss)	$(220,000)

The income tax rate, which had gradually increased over several years to 40% in 20X3, remained at 40% for 20X4 taxable income. In 20X4, Parliament enacted legislation to reduce the income tax rate to 36% for 20X5 and the following years.

In management's judgement, it is probable that any tax loss carryforward will be fully utilized in the carryforward period.

Required:

Show the journal entry to record income taxes. Prepare the lower part of the CTC SCI for 20X4, starting with "earnings before income tax."

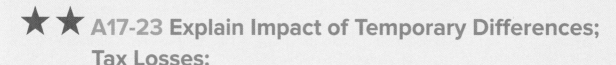

A17-23 Explain Impact of Temporary Differences; Tax Losses:

You are the new accountant for Evanoff Ltd. (EL). You have been asked to explain the impact of income tax on the financial statements for the year ended 31 December 20X5. You discover the following:

- EL's product development expenses of $2 million have been deferred, to be amortized over the anticipated product life of four years starting two years from now.
- EL had depreciation expense of $780,000 in 20X5 but claimed no CCA. In the past, CCA charges have been significantly higher than depreciation, resulting in a $460,000 deferred income tax liability on the statement of financial position.
- In 20X5, EL had a loss for tax purposes of $3 million. The company's tax rate is 40%, constant since incorporation 10 years ago.
- In the past several years, accounting and taxable income have been steady but unimpressive in the range of $250,000 to $450,000. EL is aware that management has to make significant strategic changes to combat disastrous operating results this year. In particular, EL is faced with the need to upgrade capital assets to remain competitive. However, raising money for this venture will be very difficult.

Required:

Explain the income tax impacts of the above, and describe how results would be reported on the company's financial statements.

(Source: ICAO, adapted. These materials are produced by permission of the Institute of Chartered Accountants of Ontario, and may not be further reproduced without the prior written permission of the Institute of Chartered Accountants of Ontario.)

★ ★ A17-24 Tax Losses; Temporary Differences:

The 20X6 records of Laredo Inc. show the following reconciliation of accounting and taxable income:

Earnings per the financial statements	$124,000
Plus (minus)	
Dividend revenue	(2,900)
CCA in excess of depreciation	(42,300)
Warranty payments in excess of expense	(500)
Non-tax-deductible expenses	2,900
Taxable income	$ 81,200

In 20X5, Laredo had reported an operating loss, the tax benefit of which was fully recognized in 20X5 through loss carryback and recognition of a deferred income tax asset.

Selected SFP accounts at the end of 20X5:

Income tax receivable		$ 16,400
Net book value of capital assets, after 20X5 depreciation of $41,000		618,000
Deferred income tax (asset: loss carryforward)		20,000
Warranty liability		1,000
Deferred income tax (regarding capital assets)	$48,000	
Deferred income taxes (regarding warranty amounts)	(320)	
Deferred income taxes—net liability		$47,380

UCC at the end of 20X5 was $468,000. Depreciation expense in 20X6 was $41,000. The enacted tax rate in 20X5 was 32%. The enacted tax rate in 20X6 was 38%.

Required:

1. Prepare the income tax entries for 20X6.
2. Present the lower portion of the 20X6 SCI.

A17-25 Tax Losses; Temporary Differences (ASPE):

Refer to case facts in A17-8.

Required:

Prepare the journal entries for income taxes for each of the four years. Assume the company uses the taxes payable method and that it is concerned it might have another significant loss in 20X9.

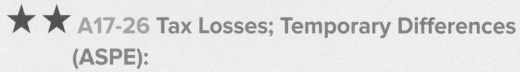

A17-26 Tax Losses; Temporary Differences (ASPE):

Refer to case facts in A17-17.

Required:

Prepare the journal entries for income taxes for 20X7, 20X8, and 20X9. Assume the company uses the taxes payable method.

A17-27 Loss Carryforward; Valuation Allowance (Appendix):

The pre-tax income of Barrows Ltd. for the first three years was as follows:

	20X6	20X7	20X8
Revenues	$276,000	$300,000	$325,000
Expenses	333,000	286,000	306,000
Earnings (loss) before income taxes	$ (57,000)	$ 14,000	$ 19,000

The company had no temporary differences in any of the three years. The income tax rate was constant at 36%.

In 20X6 and 20X7, the prospect for future earnings was highly uncertain. In 20X8, management decided that the future outlook for the company was quite good and that significant earnings would be generated in the near future.

Required:

1. Restate the above statements of comprehensive income to reflect income tax effects for each year.
2. Show any amounts relating to income taxes that would be reported on Barrows' statement of financial position in each of the three years.
3. Prepare journal entries to record income taxes in each year. The company's accountant has recommended using the valuation allowance approach to recording tax loss carryforward benefits.

★ ★ ★ A17-28 Loss Carryback/Carryforward; Valuation Allowance (Appendix):

The following information pertains to Towers Corp.:

- From 20X1 through 20X3, Towers had pre-tax income totalling $150,000.
- In 20X4, Towers had a pre-tax loss of $550,000.
- Earnings of each year is equal to taxable income.
- The income tax rate was 40% from 20X1 through 20X4.
- In 20X4, a rate of 38% was enacted for 20X5, and a rate of 36% was enacted for 20X6 and the following years.
- In 20X4, management predicted that the benefits of only $200,000 of the tax loss carryforward were probable of realization in the carryforward period. Management also estimated that pre-tax earnings for 20X5 would be no more than $60,000.
- Actual pre-tax earnings in 20X5 were $80,000. Management estimated that only $120,000 of the tax loss carryforward was probable of realization.
- Pre-tax 20X6 earnings were $100,000. Management decided that it was highly probable that the full benefit of the remaining tax loss carryforward would be realized.

Required:

Towers uses a valuation account for its deferred income tax assets. What are the balances in SFP deferred income tax related accounts for 20X4, 20X5, and 20X6?

APPENDIX 1

USING A VALUATION ALLOWANCE

In the examples in the chapter, we directly increased or decreased the balance of the deferred income tax asset caused by the loss carryforward. The account changes when probability shifts, when the tax rate changes, or when a loss originates or is used. An alternative approach is to record the full amount of the potential future benefit regardless of the probability assessment and then use a *valuation allowance* to adjust for the probability of realization. This is common in practice, because it helps track the available loss carryforward. Use of a valuation allowance will not affect the end-result elements reported on the financial statements; it is simply a bookkeeping method.

As an analogy, think of accounts receivable. The full amount of accounts receivable is always recorded in the accounts, and then an allowance for doubtful accounts is used to reduce the balance to its estimated realizable value. The same principle can be applied to potential tax benefits of tax loss carryforwards.

Illustrative entries for the valuation allowance approach are shown below, using the Parravano example from the chapter, and Scenario 3, where:

- In 20X5, there was $330,000 of loss carryforward and use was not probable,
- In 20X6 there was $100,000 of new loss carryforward and a total of $200,000 was deemed probable (at a tax rate of 40%, this is a benefit of $80,000), and
- In 20X7, there was $900,000 of taxable income and all loss carryforward is used.

We will use two entries in this illustration, where the first entry records the loss carryback, and the second entry adjusts the valuation allowance. In 20X5:

Income tax receivable—carryback benefit	68,000	
Deferred income tax asset—carryforward benefit[1]	132,000	
Income tax expense (recovery)		200,000
[1]$330,000 × 40%		

Since use of the loss carryforward is not probable in this scenario, a valuation allowance for the full $132,000 is needed:

Income tax expense (recovery)	132,000	
Valuation allowance—deferred income tax (DT) asset		132,000

When the company prepares an SFP for 20X5, the valuation allowance will completely offset the DT asset, and none of the asset will appear on the SFP. Tax expense nets out to $68,000.

In 20X6, none of the 20X5 loss carryforward is used, and the company has an additional loss carryforward of $100,000. The full future benefit of the loss carryforward is recorded:

Deferred income tax asset—carryforward benefit	40,000	
Income tax expense (recovery)		40,000

The deferred income tax asset and its related valuation account now appear in the books as follows:

Deferred income tax benefit relating to 20X5	$ 132,000
Deferred income tax benefit relating to 20X6	40,000
Total potential future benefits	172,000
Less: Valuation allowance	(132,000)
Balance prior to year-end 20X6 adjustment	$ 40,000

In this scenario, at the end of 20X6, management decides that $80,000 ($200,000 × 40%) is now probable. Therefore, the valuation allowance is reduced to $92,000 in order to permit the correct value of the asset (i.e., $80,000) to appear on the 20X6 SFP:

Valuation allowance—DT asset	40,000	
Income tax expense (recovery)		40,000

Only the net amount of $80,000 will be reported on the 20X6 SFP:

Deferred income tax asset—carryforward benefit	$ 172,000
Valuation allowance—DT asset	(92,000)
Balance reported on 31 December 20X6 statement of financial position	$ 80,000

In 20X7, the company has earnings and taxable income of $960,000, on which there would be tax of $360,000. The loss carryforward (and the DT loss carryforward) are used to reduce income tax payable to $188,000:

Income tax expense (recovery)	360,000	
Deferred income tax asset—carryforward benefit		172,000
Income tax payable		188,000

At this point, the valuation allowance is no longer needed:

Valuation allowance—DT asset	92,000	
Income tax expense (recovery)		92,000

After this entry, tax expense is $268,000 ($360,000 − $92,000). This is identical to the outcome in the chapter material.

Use of the Valuation Allowance Method

The valuation allowance method may seem more cumbersome than simply recognizing or not recognizing the deferred income tax asset represented by a tax loss carryforward. However, many companies prefer the valuation allowance method because it keeps track of the full tax loss carryforward benefits. They are comfortable with the valuation allowance method because it is consistent with the approach used for other financial statement elements, such as accounts receivable and inventory net realizable amount valuations.

Of course, one reason for its popularity is that U.S. standards *require* use of the valuation allowance method. Therefore, any Canadian companies that report in the United States necessarily will use a valuation allowance.

Bear in mind that a valuation allowance is simply a bookkeeping convenience. Using a valuation method is *not a choice of accounting policy* because it has no effect on the numbers reported in the financial statements. The amount of future tax benefit that is reported on the SFP and in profit or loss will not be affected by the bookkeeping method the company chooses.

IFRS versus ASPE

ASPE specifically refers to use of a valuation allowance in conjunction with tax loss carryforwards. In contrast, *IAS 12* makes no specific reference to valuation allowances. However, any company can use a valuation allowance instead of direct recognition.

Source: (Globe and money) © Vstock LLC/Getty Images RF; (Skyscrapers) © Arpad Benedek/Getty Images RF; (Canadian flag) © BjArn Kindler/Getty Images RF; (Tablet, pen, keyboard) © John Lamb/Getty Images RF.

CHAPTER 18

Leases

INTRODUCTION

Air Canada operated 200 aircraft in its operating fleet at the end of 2014, either as part of its mainline fleet or through Air Canada Rouge. Of these, only 91 aircraft are owned outright. Another 17 are under *finance leases*, 15 are owned by special purpose entities, and 77 are rented by Air Canada, under the terms of *operating leases*. The aircraft fleet is obviously a critical asset for a company like Air Canada. Equally obviously, there are different arrangements that can be put in place to gain use of aircraft. These arrangements have a significant impact on the financial statements of the company.

What is the difference between an operating lease and a finance lease?

Accounting for a rental agreement such as a lease may appear to be straightforward. After all, the lessee is paying rent to the lessor, so on the surface it would appear that the lessee simply recognizes rent expense, while the lessor reports rent revenue. However, things are not always what they seem.

The purpose of this chapter is to explain the circumstances under which a lease is treated as a form of financing, instead of a simple rental agreement, and how operating and financing leases should be reported by lessees under current accounting standards. An appendix to this chapter describes the more complex lessor accounting arrangements. In a second appendix to this chapter, we explain forthcoming changes in lease accounting that will have a profound impact on financial statements.

DEFINITION OF A LEASE

A **lease** s a rental contract that transfers the right to use an asset in return for the payment of rent. In the commonly used sense of the term, a lease is a fee-for-usage contract between an owner of property and a renter. The **lessor** owns the asset, and the **lessee** uses the asset. The lease specifies the terms under which the lessee has the right to use the owner's property and the compensation to be paid to the lessor in exchange.

Leased assets can include both real property and personal property. **Real property** means real estate: land and buildings. **Personal property** is any property that is not real property and includes both tangible assets (e.g., machinery, equipment, or transportation vehicles) and certain intangibles (e.g., patents).

THE LEASING CONTINUUM

Some leases are more or less standard contracts, but each lease is individual. Every lease requires separate negotiation, and the lease contract must be signed by both the lessor and the lessee.

In the process of negotiation, the parties reach agreement on many contractual terms, such as:

- The length of the lease (the *lease term*);
- The amount and timing of *lease payments*;
- Each party's responsibility for maintenance, insurance, and property taxes, if any;
- Cancellation terms, including payouts or the return of the leased asset at the end of the lease term;
- Upgrading responsibilities; and so on.

The leasing continuum goes from very short term leases (hourly or daily rental) to very long term leases (multi-year/ multi-decade rentals), with many lease terms in the middle. As the lease term lengthens, in relationship to an asset's economic life, more of the risks and rewards of ownership pass from the lessor to the lessee. Accordingly, the risk premium associated with the lease payments typically declines when the term lengthens.

For example, consider a car rental arrangement. If the term of the rental arrangements is for one month, the monthly rental is set on one scale that provides return to the lessor based on constant, but risky, re-rental of the unit. If the lease term is four years, and has a guaranteed buyout of the asset at the end of the fourth year, the average monthly rental rate is far lower because re-rental is no longer a risk factor. However, the total rent paid by the lessee is clearly higher with a four-year lease. This four-year lease provides return to the lessor based on a completely different risk profile. *At some point in the term and price continuum, the lessee essentially agrees to pay the full value of the car via the rent payments and final payout.*

To recognize the dividing line along this continuum, the accounting standards have used two classifications for leases:

- Finance leases, wherein the lessor transfers substantially all of the risks and rewards of ownership to the lessee; and
- Operating leases, wherein the lessor does *not* transfer substantially all of the risks and rewards of ownership to the lessee.

Note that an operating lease is not defined directly. *Essentially, an operating lease is a lease that does not fit the definition of a finance lease.* If it's not one, it has to be the other!

Accounting treatment for each of these two lease classifications is very, very different, in an effort to portray the substance of a lease agreement in the financial statements. Unfortunately, this has provided an incentive to structure leases as operating leases. Accountants must be able to exercise their professional judgement and discern *substance over form* so that financial statements are not misleading.

Operating Leases

A lessee enters into an **operating lease** to essentially obtain temporary use of an asset without having to buy it. This might be appropriate when there is no long-term need for an asset or when the lessee's business is volatile and there is no continuous need for the asset. The key to designating a lease as *operating* is not the actual length of the lease in time—it is the length of the lease *in relation to the asset's economic life*. An operating lease term covers a *relatively small proportion of the asset's economic life*.

Because an operating lease provides only a relatively short-term return to the lessor, the lessor bears the risk of ownership. If the lessee returns the asset after the rental period and the lessor cannot find another lessee, then the lessor incurs the costs not only of maintaining the asset but also of watching it sink slowly into obsolescence.

Finance Leases

At the other end of the leasing continuum, a finance lease gives the lessee substantially all of the benefits of ownership. The lessee also has to bear most of the risks of ownership. For example, the lessee is committed to the lease contract, even if the lessee has no further use for the asset.

When a lease transfers substantially all of the benefits and risks of ownership to the lessee, the lessee might as well have purchased the asset outright. Indeed, purchasing the asset would give more flexibility—there are no restrictions on what the owner does with an owned asset but a lease may well include restrictions.

We will return to the criteria that determine whether a lease is a finance lease later in the chapter. First, however, we will look at operating lease accounting.

OPERATING LEASES

Remember, an operating lease is *a lease that is not a finance lease*. Accounting for operating leases is not complicated; the lessee simply has rent expense over the life of the lease.

Rent Expense

The lessee makes periodic lease payments that are accounted for as operating expenses by the lessee. For example, assume that:

- Empire Equipment Ltd. (EEL) buys a crane on 6 January for $1,580,000. The crane has an estimated useful life of 10 years and an estimated residual value of $260,000.
- On 25 January, Builders Inc. enters into a 10-month lease contract with EEL for the use of the crane. The monthly rent is $20,000. The crane will be delivered to Builders Inc. on 1 February.
- EEL charges Builders Inc. a standard fee of $15,000 for the cost of the crane's assembly, disassembly, and transport cost.

Builders Inc. records the following entries:

25 January—inception of the lease:		
No entry		
1 February—payment of installation fee:		
Rent expense—crane*	15,000	
Cash		15,000
*May also be debited to prepaid expense and recognized over 10 months, as discussed below.		

Monthly entry—payment of monthly rent		
Rent expense—crane	20,000	
Cash		20,000

This monthly entry is made ten times, once per month. The crane itself does not appear on Builder Inc.'s books.

Dates

Note that there are two dates for the lease:

- The *inception of the lease*, which is the date at which the lessor and lessee commit to the principal provisions of the lease; this usually coincides with the signing of the lease agreement but could be earlier, such as in a *memorandum of agreement*; and

- The *commencement of the lease term*, which is the date upon which the lessee is entitled to use the asset.

For the lease above, the *inception* of the lease is 25 January, while the *commencement* of the lease term is 1 February.

The *date of inception* is the date when the accounting treatment of the lease as either an operating lease or a finance lease is determined. A substantial period of time can elapse between inception and commencement, such as when the asset must be constructed before the lease can commence (e.g., aircraft ordered under lease agreement that will not be delivered for several years). However, no formal entries are made in the accounting records until the lease commences.

Executory Costs

Many operating leases require the lessee to pay specified costs relating to the leased asset during the lease term. These are known as **executory costs**. In this example, the lessee is required to pay $15,000 for the lessor's delivery and construction of the crane. For the lessee, this is just part of the cost of renting the crane and is charged to rent expense. This amount might be treated as a prepaid expense, and then expensed over the life of the lease, but executory expenses for operating leases are usually expensed immediately because of the short lease term.

Uneven Payments

Sometimes the operating lease payments are uneven. For example, a lessee may be required to make an initial lump-sum payment *in addition to* the periodic rent payment.[1] If there is a large payment at the beginning (or inception) of the lease, the special payment is amortized over the period of time that the lessee is required to make lease payments. This period of time is called the **initial lease term**. The lease may be renewable, but since there is no obligation on the part of the lessee to renew the lease, the amortization period is limited to the initial term. For example, if a tenant pays $10,000 as an upfront fee on a five-year operating lease of storage facility, the $10,000 is accounted for as a prepaid expense and recognized in the amount of $2,000 per year.

An alternative arrangement that also occurs, particularly for office real estate rentals, is that the lessor will "forgive" lease payments for a specific, limited period of time at the beginning of the lease. For example, in a market that has excess supply, a lessor may attract a lessee by agreeing that lease payments will not begin until six months after the lease starts. These forgiven payments also are amortized over the initial term of the lease. The lessee must determine the total cash paid over the lease term, and expense the same amount each period, regardless of whether a payment is made that period.

For example, assume that F212 Ltd. leases space in an office building for five years for an annual rental of $100,000. Because the office rental market is "soft," the lessor agrees that F212 need not begin paying rent until the second year; the first year's rent is forgiven. The substance of this deal is that F212 agrees to pay a total of $400,000 for five years; this averages out to an effective rental rate of $80,000 per year. For the first year, there is no cash flow for rent, but F212 will record an expense of $80,000, which is offset by a deferred credit:

| Rent expense | 80,000 | |
| Deferred rent liability | | 80,000 |

For each of the next four years, the $80,000 will be adjusted to rent expense, thereby reducing rent expense from the cash outflow of $100,000 to the average annual expense of $80,000. The annual entry on F212's books will be:

---

1. When the rental contract is for real estate, such payments sometimes are known as *key money* and may be prohibited in some jurisdictions, particularly in those with rent controls on residential properties.

Rent expense	80,000	
Deferred rent liability	20,000	
Cash		100,000

The deferred rent will be reported as a liability on the SFP, allocated between short-term and long-term liabilities, and usually combined with other provisions. Discounting may also be appropriate.

A fundamental question remains: *When is a lease an operating lease?* To understand the distinction between an operating lease and a finance lease, we must examine the guidelines for designating a lease as a finance lease.

FINANCE LEASES

A **finance lease** is defined as *any lease that transfers substantially all of the risks and rewards of ownership from the lessor to the lessee.* The lessor agrees to purchase an asset and lease it immediately to a lessee for substantially all of the economic life of the asset. When that happens, the lessor is not interested in using the asset, even though the lessor will hold legal title. A finance lease is a form of financing because the lessee acquires essentially full benefits of the leased asset without actually having to buy it. The lessor is providing an asset to the lessee in return for a cash flow stream that enables the lessor to recover its investment in the asset as well as earn a reasonable rate of return on the investment. Finance leases are also referred to as **capital leases**.

Classification as a Finance Lease

The basis for designating a lease as a finance lease is judgemental: *Do the terms of the lease transfer substantially all of the benefits and risks of ownership from the lessor to the lessee?* However, the exercise of professional judgement requires criteria or guidelines. There are circumstances that individually or in combination indicate that substantially all of the risks and rewards of ownership are being passed to the lessee.

If *any one of the following guidelines is satisfied*, the lease should be classified as a finance lease:

1. *Is there reasonable certainty that the lessee will obtain ownership of the leased property at the end of the lease term?* This occurs (1) if the lease provides for automatic transfer of title to the lessee at the end of the lease, or (2) if the lessee is entitled to buy the asset at the end of the lease term at a price significantly lower than the expected fair value at that time (this is called a **bargain purchase option**).

2. *Will the lessee receive substantially all of the economic benefits expected to be derived through use of the leased property?* This normally is indicated by a lease term that covers most of the asset's economic life. Since the economic benefit of assets goes down over time (through deterioration and obsolescence), *substantially all* of the economic benefit can be derived during a lease term that falls short of the full physical life of the asset. Although not included in the standard, the normal rule of thumb is (in the range of) 75%.

3. *Will the lessor be assured of recovering substantially all of the investment in the leased property, plus a return on the investment, over the lease term?* This is determined by calculating the present value of the minimum net lease payments. Although not included in the standard, the normal rule of thumb is that the test is met if the present value is (in the range of) 90% or more of the fair value of the leased asset at the inception of the lease. The discount rate is the interest rate implicit in the lease, or, if this rate is not known by the lessee, the lessee's incremental borrowing rate.

4. *Is the leased asset so highly specialized that only the lessee can obtain the benefit without substantial modification?* This is particularly true of assets that are fixed in place and cannot be moved without incurring costs that probably would exceed the asset's remaining benefits. If the lessee is the only possible user of the asset, the lease is a finance lease.

No Bright Lines

The classification guidelines established by IFRS standards include some numeric suggestions—"in the range of 75% of economic life" for the term of the lease, and "in the range of 90% of fair value" when comparing discounted cash flow to fair value. It is important to understand that these are *not hard-and-fast limits*. Hard-and-fast limits are sometimes called **bright lines**, meaning that they are not negotiable. For example, if the present value of the minimum lease payments were 89.4% of fair value, and 90% was interpreted as a bright line, the test would not be met and the lease would not be a financing lease based on this guideline. Since the numeric limits are ranges, or suggestions, though, 89.4% might be interpreted as very close indeed to the judgemental spirit of the guideline and the lease might be classified as a financing lease. The 75% and 90% numbers are from FASB and ASPE standards, where they are interpreted as bright lines.

Definitions

The guidelines and this discussion use certain terms, which must be clearly defined.

- A bargain purchase option exists when there is a stated or determinable buyout price given in the lease that is sufficiently lower than the expected fair value of the leased asset at the option's exercise date to make it *probable that the lessee will exercise the option*. Even if the lessee does not really want the asset after the end of the lease term, it would be advantageous to exercise a bargain purchase option and then resell the asset at its higher fair value. While "bargain purchase option" is not an explicit term in the accounting standard, it is a useful shorthand expression that is well understood in practice.

- A **bargain renewal term** is one or more periods for which the *lessee* has the option of extending the lease at lease payments that are substantially less than would normally be expected for an asset of that age and type. "Bargain renewal term" is a term used in practice because it captures the essence of renewal terms that would strongly entice a lessee to renew.

- The **lease term** includes:
  - All terms prior to the exercise date of a bargain purchase option;
  - All bargain renewal terms; and
  - All renewal terms at the *lessor's* option.

- A **guaranteed residual value** is an amount that the lessee promises that the lessor can receive for the asset by selling it to a third party at the end of the lease term. If there is any deficiency in the sales proceeds when the lessor sells the asset, *the lessee must make up the difference*. The guaranteed residual value is decided when the lease contract is negotiated. A high guaranteed residual value will effectively reduce the periodic lease payments, while a low guarantee will increase the lease payments that a lessor will require to recover the lessor's investment in the asset.

- In contrast, the lessee may not guarantee the residual value, in which instance there is an **unguaranteed residual value**. This is the value that the lessor expects to realize on sale of the asset at the end of the lease term. The lessee has no liability for such an amount, and in fact would usually be unaware of the dollar amount. However, the size of the lessor's expected residual value will have a direct impact on the size of the lease payments.

- The lessee's **minimum net lease payments** are all payments that the lessee is required to make over the *lease term*, as described above (i.e., including bargain renewal terms), *net* of any operating or executory costs that are implicitly included in the lease payment, *plus* any guaranteed residual value. A bargain purchase option value (if any) also is included.

It is important to deduct operating costs from the lease payments to find the *net* lease payments. For example, if the lessor pays insurance on the asset, the lessor includes an estimate of the cost of insurance premiums when setting the lease payments. The insurance is not a cost of *acquiring* the asset; however, it is a cost of *using* the asset. Therefore, any operating costs that are implicitly included in the lease payments must be estimated and subtracted to find the amount of the payments that represent, in substance, the cost of acquiring the asset.

The lessee's minimum net lease payments also exclude any amounts for **contingent lease payments**, which are additional lease payments that are based on subsequent events, such as payments calculated on a percentage of a lessee's gross sales revenue.

- **Initial direct costs** are the costs incurred when negotiating and arranging a lease. For a lessor, these costs may include not only negotiations with the lessee but also negotiations with the vendor or manufacturer from whom the lessor will obtain the asset to be leased.
- The **implicit lease interest rate** is the interest rate that equates:
  - The minimum net lease payments, the initial direct costs, the residual value (whether guaranteed or not), and the tax cash flows; and
  - The fair value of the leased property at the beginning of the lease.

  This rate is calculated from the *lessor*'s point of view—the estimated cash flows *of the lessor* over the minimum lease term (as defined above).
- The lessee's **incremental borrowing rate (IBR)** is the interest rate that the lessee would have to pay to obtain financing through a financial institution to buy the asset.

Guaranteed versus Unguaranteed Residual Values

It is important to understand the different roles of guaranteed and unguaranteed residual values in finance lease accounting:

- A *guaranteed* residual value is part of the definition of *net lease payments* for both the lessee and the lessor.
- The lessee uses only the *guaranteed* residual value as part of its discounted cash flow because the lessee is committed to pay it if the lessor is not able to recover that amount by disposal of the asset at the end of the lease. An unguaranteed residual is excluded from net minimum lease payments for the lessee.

Discount Rate

The interest rate used for discounting the net lease payments is the *lessor's* interest rate implicit in the lease, *if known by the lessee*. When the lessee does not know the lessor's interest rate implicit in the lease, the lessee's incremental borrowing rate is used.

Sometimes, lending legislation requires that the lessee be informed of the interest rate implicit in the lease. In other cases, the rate is not disclosed. If the lessor does not disclose an implicit interest rate, the lessee usually would not be able to calculate it, because:

- The lessee will not know the lessor's direct costs of the lease;
- The lessee does not know the lessor's estimated unguaranteed residual value;
- The lessor takes into account the expected value of any contingent rent when negotiating the lease terms, but the lessor's estimate of these expected amounts is not known to the lessee; and
- The lessor normally calculates the lease payments with an eye to obtaining an *after-tax rate of return*, and the lessor's tax status is not known to the lessee.

Contingent Rent

Contingent rent is rent that depends on specified future events. Leases for retail space offer a common example of contingent rent—in addition to basic rent, the lessee (i.e., a retailer) usually agrees to pay a percentage of the store's gross sales to the lessor. Contingent rent may also be based on factors such as an asset's volume of use, on variations in the lessor's operating expenses (including property taxes) in connection with the lease, on price indices, or on market interest rates, to name a few.

Contingent rent is excluded from accounting lease calculations for both lessor and lessee. However, contingent rent arrangements are a very important part of decision analysis for both the lessor and the lessee. Indeed, some lease agreements, especially for retail space, depend on achieving a certain volume of activity; if that volume is not achieved, the lessor may have the right to terminate the lease.

Contingent rents are reported as operating expenses in the period that they are *incurred* rather than when they are *paid*. Sometimes this will require the lessee to accrue estimated contingent rent payments on a quarterly or monthly basis, even though the exact amount will not be known until after the end of the lease year.

Economic versus Useful Life

The **economic life** of an asset is the maximum number of years that it can be economically productive. The **useful life** to a particular company may be shorter. For example, desktop computers may be useful for six years, but a company may choose to keep its desktop computers no more than four years to stay up-to-date. The economic life is six years, while the useful life is four years. Useful life can never be longer than economic life.

Fair-Value Ceiling

In no case may an asset be recorded at higher than its fair value. Consider a simple example. Consider an equipment lease, where a lessee agrees to pay the lessor $100,000 at the end of each year for four years. The fair value of the equipment being leased is $300,000, and the asset has a four-year useful life. This is a financing lease because it covers the entire useful life of the equipment. The lessor's implicit rate of return is unknown, and therefore the lessee's IBR of 10% is used in present value calculations. At 10%, the present value of the lease payments is $316,987:

$$PV = \$100,000 \times (P/A, 10\%, 4) = \$316,987$$

 If the lessee uses its IBR, the book value of the asset will be higher than the fair value of the asset. In such a case, the lessee must:

1. Record the asset at its fair value, or $300,000; and
2. Increase the interest rate to a rate that discounts the lease payments to the $300,000 fair value of the asset. The equation is:

$$\$300,000 = \$100,000 \times (P/A, i, 4)$$

This must be solved for the value of i.

The interest rate that solves this equation is 12.6%. The implicit rate can be quickly calculated with a financial calculator or with an Excel spreadsheet. An explanation of present value calculations can be found on Connect.

An Informal Guideline

When interpreting the guidelines, the basic issue is whether, in substance, the risks and benefits have been transferred from the lessor to the lessee.

One criterion that is not explicitly cited by the standard setters but that is very useful in practice is to look at the *nature of the lessor*. The nature of the lessor may be important to determining whether the lease is a finance lease or an operating lease.

To fully realize the tax advantages that often are the driving force behind finance leases, a lessor must qualify as a lessor under the income tax regulations. That means that a lessor must derive at least 90% of its revenues from lease transactions. Any company that meets this criterion is a **financial intermediary**. Any lease that such a financial institution enters into can be assumed to be a finance lease, even if finance lease classification is not clear when the four finance lease guidelines have been applied.

For example, if the lessor is the leasing subsidiary of a financial institution, it should be clear that the lease is not an operating lease. Financial institutions have financial assets, not operating assets (except for their own tangible operating assets, of course) on their SFPs. The leasing division of a financial institution will not assume the risks of owning an asset, even though it has legal title to many thousands of them through lease contracts.

Land Leases

Land is a unique asset in that it has an indefinite useful life. Land would be expected to hold its value over its life, and be generally useful to a number of business operations. As a result, a land lease would always fail the guideline that deals with a comparison of the lease term with the life of the asset, portion of fair value represented by the lease payments, and specialized asset. Accordingly, *land leases are operating leases* unless title passes to the lessee.

CONCEPT REVIEW

1. What is the basic judgemental criterion that determines whether a lease is a finance lease?
2. List the four guidelines that help determine whether a lease is a finance lease. Are the numeric suggestions bright lines or general guidance?
3. When are operating lease rental payments expensed in periods other than in the period of payment?
4. Define the following terms:
   - Bargain renewal options;
   - Incremental borrowing rate; and
   - Lease term.
5. How can the nature of the lessor influence the lease classification?

ACCOUNTING FOR FINANCE LEASES—LESSEE

If a long-term lease qualifies as a finance lease for accounting purposes, the asset is recorded on the lessee's books as though it had been purchased and financed by instalment debt. An outline of the accounting treatment is described briefly below:

- The present value of the lease payments is determined by using the following:
    - The discount rate is the lessor's implicit rate, if known, and otherwise the lessee's IBR.
    - The cash flows to be discounted are the *net minimum* lease payments over the initial term, plus net lease payments for any bargain renewal terms, plus net lease payments for any term prior to a bargain purchase option, plus any renewal terms at the *lessor's* option, and plus any *guaranteed* residual value or any bargain purchase price.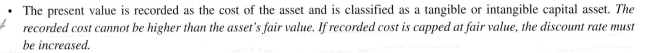

- The present value is recorded as the cost of the asset and is classified as a tangible or intangible capital asset. *The recorded cost cannot be higher than the asset's fair value. If recorded cost is capped at fair value, the discount rate must be increased.*
- The offsetting credit is to a *lease liability* account.
- Interest is accrued for each period, charged to interest expense, and credited to the lease liability account. Interest is based on the discount rate.
- Lease payments are debited to the lease liability account, reducing the liability.
- The asset is depreciated or amortized over its useful life using the company's normal depreciation or amortization policy for that type of asset. However, the depreciation or amortization period cannot exceed the lease term unless the lease contains a bargain purchase option or automatic transfer of title at the end of the lease. Otherwise, the asset will be depreciated or amortized over the lease term (including bargain renewal terms).
- Depreciation can be calculated to the nearest month, or an accounting convention, such as the half-year rule, may be used for simplicity.

Depreciation

The depreciation period is the period of time that the lessee will use the asset: its useful life to the company. This may be limited by the lease term and conditions. Consider the following cases:

	Case 1	Case 2	Case 3
Lease term, including bargain renewals	5 years	5 years	5 years
Economic life of the leased asset	8 years	8 years	4 years
Bargain purchase option included in lease contract	No	Yes	No
Choice of depreciation term	5 years	8 years	4 years

In Case 1, the asset will last 8 years, but the lessee has use of it for only 5 years, so depreciation is taken over 5 years. In Case 2, the lessee has a bargain purchase option and so will control the asset after the end of the lease term. Assuming that the lessee will continue to use it, the asset would be depreciated over 8 years. If not, it will have a shorter useful life and some estimated residual value on sale. In Case 3, the economic life is 4 years, and this is the maximum depreciation period.

In practice, Case 3 is highly unlikely—economic life is typically longer than the lease term. After all, why agree to pay for an asset after it has stopped being useful? However, things happen. Perhaps an asset becomes obsolete during its lease term, or the lessee changes the nature of its business and no longer needs that asset. In any case, the lessee may need to change the estimate of useful life for depreciation; these estimates are revisited annually.

The really important point is that the depreciation period can never be *longer* than the lease term unless the lessee will obtain title to the asset at the end of the lease, either automatically or by exercising a bargain purchase option.

Depreciation is based on the recorded asset value, minus any estimate of residual value at the end of its useful life. This residual value is either:

- The guaranteed residual value, if any; or
- A normal estimate of residual value at the end of the asset's life, if the lessee keeps/buys the asset at the end of the lease; or
- Zero, if the asset reverts to the lessor with an unguaranteed residual.

LEASES IN THE STATEMENT OF CASH FLOWS

Lease capitalization has an interesting impact on the statement of cash flows. If a lease is reported as an operating lease, the lease payments are deducted as an expense. Since the expense represents a cash flow, the impact of the lease payments stays in the cash flow from operations.

The only exception arises when the cash flows are uneven or differ from the pattern of rent expense recognition. If lease payments in a year are different from the amount expensed, the difference will be an adjustment to cash flow from operations because of the change in the prepaid or deferral account (if the indirect approach is used).

If a lease is capitalized, on the other hand, the effects on the statement of cash flows are quite different:

- Although the initial lease agreement is viewed, in substance, as a purchase, the transaction is not shown on the SCF as an investing activity or financing activity because it is a non-cash transaction—a lease obligation is exchanged for a leased asset. This non-cash transaction must be disclosed in the notes.
- Expenses relating to the leased asset are removed from earnings when determining cash flow from operations:

- Depreciation expense relating to the leased asset is added back to net income; and
- Interest expense is segregated on the statement of cash flows as part of interest expense relating to long-term obligations; the interest paid can be classified as either operating or financing.
- The principal repayment portion of the lease payments is shown as a financing activity (i.e., as a reduction of a liability).

The overall effect of lease capitalization is that the lessee can remove the lease payments from operating cash flow and reclassify them as financing activities.

FINANCE LEASE ILLUSTRATION—BASIC EXAMPLE

We will begin our illustration of accounting for finance leases with a fairly simple example that focuses on the most significant aspects of lease accounting.

Assume that Lessee Ltd. wishes to acquire equipment that has an expected economic life of eight years and a fair value of $66,000. Instead of buying the asset outright, the company enters into a lease with Borat Corp., a Canadian finance company that specializes in asset-based financing. The facts are shown in Exhibit 18-1.

EXHIBIT 18-1

LEASE TERMS—BASIC EXAMPLE

- The fair value of the asset is $66,000.
- The lease begins on 1 January 20X2.
- The initial lease term is three years.
- The economic life of the asset is eight years.
- Payments over the initial lease term are $20,000 per year, payable at the beginning of each lease year (i.e., on 1 January 20X2, 20X3, and 20X4).
- At the end of the initial lease term, the lease is renewable for another two years *at Lessee's option* for $5,000 per year. Assume that the normal rental cost of three-year-old equipment of this type is almost $10,000 per year.
- Lessee is responsible for insuring and maintaining the equipment.
- The asset reverts to the lessor at the end of the lease; the lease agreement contains no obligation for Lessee to *guarantee* the residual value. The lessee does not know the amount of the unguaranteed residual value.
- Lessee does not know the lessor's implicit rate of interest in the lease. Lessee's incremental borrowing rate is 8%.

In this example, the important elements for analysis are as follows:

- The *lease term* is five years—the initial lease term of three years plus the bargain renewal term of two years. Five years is 63% of the asset's estimated economic life of eight years.
- The *minimum net lease payments* are $20,000 for each of the first three years and $5,000 per year for the fourth and fifth years, for a total of $70,000. The present value of the minimum lease payments is $63,310:

PV = $20,000 (P/AD, 8%, 3) + $5,000 (P/AD, 8%, 2) (P/F, 8%, 3)

PV = $55,666 + $7,644

PV = $63,310

Note: P/AD means "present value of an annuity due," which is an annuity that requires payments at the *beginning of each period.* It is common for lease payments to be required at the beginning of each period. If payments were at the end of each period, the present value would be based on the "present value of an ordinary annuity," or (P/A).

Classification: Applying Lease Guidelines

Does this lease qualify for classification as a finance lease? Exhibit 18-2 applies the four finance lease classification guidelines to this example. *Only one guideline needs to be met for the lease to qualify as a finance lease.* The first and fourth guidelines clearly do not apply. Looking at the lease term relative to the asset's economic life, the lease covers *much* (5/8, or 63%) of the asset's economic life, but clearly not the full life. However, the lease clearly meets the third guideline, based on present value, because the present value is over 90% of the fair value at the inception of the lease. Lessee should classify the lease as a finance lease.

EXHIBIT 18-2

APPLYING THE FINANCE LEASE GUIDELINES—BASIC EXAMPLE

Guideline	Analysis
1. Does the lease transfer ownership to the lessee at the end of the lease, either automatically or by provision for a bargain purchase option?	**No.** The lease contains no purchase option and ownership of the asset will not transfer to the lessee at any time.
2. Is the lease term for the major part of the economic life of the asset?	**Perhaps.** The lease covers 5/8 of the asset's economic life, which is a majority of the years.
3. Does the PV of the minimum lease payments amount to substantially all of the asset's fair value?	**Yes.** The PV of minimum lease payments is 96% of the asset's fair value. ($63,310 ÷ $66,000)
4. Is the leased asset highly specialized to the lessee?	**No.** The lessor estimates a significant residual value, which would not be the case if the asset were highly specialized to the lessee's use.

Liability Amortization Table

A *liability amortization table* is useful in lease accounting. This amortization table is similar to the tables illustrated in Chapter 13 for long-term debt issued at a discount or premium. For leases, the payments are blended payments—part interest and part principal. The purpose of the table is to determine how much of each year's cash lease payment goes to (1) interest expense and (2) reduction of principal.

A liability amortization table for this lease example is shown in Exhibit 18-3. The beginning-of-year cash flows are placed in the fourth column, and the net lease present value (at 8%) is placed at the beginning of the second column ("outstanding balance").

The first payment is made at the commencement of the lease, 1 January 20X2. Since this is the first day of the lease, there has been no elapsed time and therefore no interest element. The table shows that this first payment is all principal.

On 1 January 20X3, the payment must be divided between interest and principal payment. Exhibit 18-3 shows that interest is $3,465 (i.e., $43,310 × 8%), which means that of the second $20,000 lease payment, $3,465 is charged to interest, and the remaining $16,535 of the lease payment will go to reducing the outstanding principal balance.

Notice for each payment, there is an allocation to interest based on the *opening liability balance,* and the *remainder is a principal reduction.* Principal outstanding is reduced to zero at the end of the payment stream. *The payment stream includes all five cash payments included in the discounting calculation.*

EXHIBIT 18-3

LEASE LIABILITY AMORTIZATION TABLE

1 January	Outstanding Balance	Interest at 8%	Net Lease Payment 1 January	Decrease in Balance	31 December Balance
20X2	$63,310	$ —	$20,000	$(20,000)	**$43,310**
20X3	43,310	3,465	20,000	(16,535)	**26,775**
20X4	26,775	2,142	20,000	(17,858)	**8,917**
20X5	8,917	713	5,000	(4,287)	**4,630**
20X6	4,630	370	5,000	(4,630)	**0**
Totals		$6,690	$70,000	$ (63,310)	

The lines of the table must be interpreted carefully—they represent lease payments, not fiscal years. For example, the top line of the table is related to the 1 January 20X2 payment. *Interest expense for 20X2, though, is $3,465* (from the 20X3 line). This is 8% of the liability of $43,310 that was outstanding from 2 January 20X2 to 31 December 20X2.

Proofs

At any point in time, the outstanding balance in the table is equal to the present value of the remaining payments. This is a convenient way to check a table as you progress, or to begin a table in mid-stream, if needed.

To illustrate, the opening balance in the table is $63,310:

PV = $20,000 (P/AD, 8%, 3) + $5,000 (P/AD, 8%, 2) (P/F, 8%, 3)

PV = $55,666 + $7,644

PV = $63,310

After two payments, the balance is now $26,775:

PV = $20,000(P/F, 8%, 1) + $5,000 (P/AD, 8%, 2) (P/F, 8%, 2)

PV = $18,519 + $8,256

PV = $26,775

After four payments, the balance is now $4,630:

PV = $5,000 (P/F, 8%, 1)

PV = $4,630

Note that the cash flows and interest rate used are not changed, but the payment stream may have changed from an annuity to a lump sum, and *n* changes, both of which reflect the actual cash flow pattern remaining.

Initial Recognition

The principal amount at the inception of the lease, 2 January 20X2, is the full present value of $63,310. (This is lower than fair value of $66,000—there is no fair value cap.) The lease will be recorded as follows:

Asset under finance lease	63,310	
Lease liability		63,310

The first lease payment is made on this date:

Lease liability	20,000	
Cash		20,000

Year-End Adjustments

The interest that has accrued through 20X2 must be recorded at year-end:

Interest expense	3,465	
Lease liability		3,465

Note that the credit is recorded to the lease liability account, which adds an element of accrued interest to the account. Accrued interest payable is an alternative account choice. We will use the lease liability account for interest accrual because subsequent entries are less complicated.

In addition, Lessee must depreciate the asset. The asset will be held and used by the company for five years, and it reverts back to the lessor at that time with an unguaranteed residual value. If we assume that Lessee's accounting policy for this type of asset is to depreciate it on the straight-line basis with a full year's depreciation taken in the first year, then the depreciation of the leased equipment on 31 December 20X2 will be $12,662 (i.e., $63,310 ÷ 5). There is no residual value because the amount is unguaranteed. The entry is:

Depreciation expense	12,662	
Accumulated depreciation-asset under lease		12,662

20X3 Entries

On 1 January 20X3, Lessee makes the second lease payment:

Lease liability	20,000	
Cash		20,000

Note that the 31 December 20X2 interest accrual is credited directly to the lease liability account. If the accrued interest had been credited to *accrued interest payable*, the debit in this entry would be broken down between interest payable and principal.

The interest that has accrued through 20X3 must be recorded at year-end; note that this is *from the 20X4 line* of the table:

Interest expense	2,142	
Lease liability		2,142

The depreciation entry is unchanged:

Depreciation expense	12,662	
Accumulated depreciation—asset under lease		12,662

Remaining Entries

Exhibit 18-4 shows all of Lessee's entries for the lease. The final column of the exhibit shows the accumulated balance of the total lease liability account. The year-end interest accruals increase the balance, while the lease payments reduce the balance. The final lease payment, on 1 January 20X6, reduces the balance to zero.

EXHIBIT 18-4			
LESSEE'S RECORDING OF FINANCE LEASE—BASIC EXAMPLE			

			Lease Liability
	Dr.	**Cr.**	**Balance**
1 January 20X2			
Asset under finance lease	63,310		
Lease liability		63,310	63,310
Lease liability	20,000		**43,310**
Cash		20,000	
31 December 20X2			
Interest expense	3,465		
Lease liability		3,465	46,775
Depreciation expense	12,662		
Accumulated depreciation—asset under lease		12,662	
1 January 20X3			
Lease liability	20,000		**26,775**
Cash		20,000	

	Dr.	Cr.	Lease Liability Balance
31 December 20X3			
Interest expense	2,142		
Lease liability		2,142	28,917
Depreciation expense	12,662		
Accumulated depreciation– asset under lease		12,662	
1 January 20X4			
Lease liability	20,000		**8,917**
Cash		20,000	
31 December 20X4			
Interest expense	713		
Lease liability		713	9,630
Depreciation expense	12,662		
Accumulated depreciation—asset under lease		12,662	
1 January 20X5			
Lease liability	5,000		**4,630**
Cash		5,000	
31 December 20X5			
Interest expense	370		
Lease liability		370	5,000
Depreciation expense	12,662		
Accumulated depreciation—asset under lease		12,662	
1 January 20X6			
Lease liability	5,000		**0**
Cash		5,000	
31 December 20X5			
Depreciation expense	12,662		
Accumulated depreciation—asset under lease		12,662	

Observe that the lease liability balance *after each lease payment* is exactly the same amount as shown in the final column (year-end balance) of Exhibit 18-3. These amounts are shown in bold type in both exhibits.

End of Lease Term

At the end of the lease term, when the asset is returned to the lessor, Lessee must write off the fully depreciated asset:

Accumulated depreciation—asset under lease	63,310	
Asset under finance lease		63,310

Financial Statement Impact—Lessee

Statement of Financial Position

At the end of 20X2, the outstanding principal balance in the lease liability account is $43,310 (before any accrued interest), as shown in both Exhibits 18-3 and 18-4. With interest, this is $46,775 at 31 December 20X2.

This liability is divided between the short-term portion and the long-term portion on the SFP. The short-term portion is:

1. Any interest accrual included in the liability balance; and
2. The principal portion of any payment made in the next fiscal period.

The reminder is long term, and will correspond to a table value.

In our example, the short-term portion is interest of $3,465 and the principal portion of the 20X3 payment, or $16,535. This is equal to $20,000. The long-term portion is $26,775, per the second line of the table in Exhibit 18-3. The SFP reflects the following:

Current liability	$20,000
Long-term liability	26,775
Total	$46,775

Although the full amount of the next payment, $20,000, is classified as current in this simple example, that situation will arise *only when the payment is due immediately after the reporting date.* That is, the current liability is not normally the full amount of the next payment due.

On the asset side, the leased equipment will be shown either separately (if material) or as a part of the general equipment account. Similarly, the accumulated depreciation will be shown either separately or combined with the accumulated depreciation of similar assets. If the leased asset and its accumulated depreciation are shown on the face of the SFP as part of property, plant, and equipment, the company must disclose the amounts pertaining to leased assets in a disclosure note.

As usual, of course, the equipment can be shown net of accumulated depreciation on the face of the SFP with the gross amount and accumulated depreciation shown in a note.

Statement of Comprehensive Income

The net earnings section of the SCI will include depreciation expense and interest expense. For 20X2, the amounts relating to the lease are:

Depreciation expense	$12,662
Interest expense	3,465

Each of these expenses can be combined with similar costs; the expenses relating to leased assets need not be reported separately. The interest expense for the lease will, however, be included with other long-term interest, which is reported separately from interest on short-term obligations.

Statement of Cash Flows

Points to note:

- At the inception of the lease, an asset and liability were recorded. This is a non-cash transaction and is excluded from the SCF. However, note disclosure of this non-cash transaction will be required.
- If the indirect approach to operating cash flow is used, depreciation expense ($12,662) will be added back as an adjustment to earnings to determine the cash flow from operations. Similarly, earnings includes $3,465 in interest expense that was not a cash outflow in 20X2 and the change to the current liability for interest will adjust for this.
- The amount of principal repayment ($20,000, at the beginning of 20X2) will be shown as a financing outflow.

Notes to Financial Statements

The notes should disclose the commitment for future finance lease payments, both in total and individually for each of the next five years. The payments due under all of the reporting enterprise's finance leases can be added together and reported in the aggregate, of course.

Deferred Income Taxes

In Canada, leases normally are taxed in accordance with their legal form. The tax deduction is the amount of lease payments made during the tax year. The fact that a lease may be accounted for as a finance lease does not change the tax treatment.

Therefore, leases that are accounted for as finance leases are generally taxed by CRA as an operating lease. This difference in treatment will give rise to a *temporary difference*. Accounting for deferred income taxes and temporary differences was explained in Chapter 16.

CONCEPT REVIEW

1. How is an annual lease payment split between principal and interest in a lease liability amortization table?
2. How would you prove the closing liability balance that was recorded after the fourth payment, in a six-payment lease liability amortization table?
3. How much of a lease liability is a current liability on the SFP?

Accounting by Lessees—Modified Example

The prior example was fairly simple because (1) the lease year coincided with the lessee's reporting year, (2) there was no guaranteed residual value, (3) the present value was less than the fair value, and (4) the lease included no provisions for operating costs. To explore lessee accounting a little more realistically, we will use an example that removes those simplifying assumptions.

The terms of the lease are given in Exhibit 18-5. In this example, the net lease payments are $180,000 per year—the $200,000 annual lease payment minus the annual insurance cost included therein. *Executory costs must be excluded from the discounted cash flows*. The present value of the lease includes both the net lease payments and the guaranteed residual value, even though the likelihood of having to pay that full guaranteed residual value is low. The present value calculation is:

PV = $180,000(P/AD, 8%, 5) + $75,000(P/F, 8%, 5)

PV = $776,183 + $51,044 = $827,227

EXHIBIT 18-5

LEASE TERMS—MODIFIED EXAMPLE

- The fair value of the equipment is $800,000 at the inception of the lease.
- The lease term is five years. The lease commences on 1 April 20X2.
- There is no renewal option.
- Annual lease payments are $200,000 per year. Payments are due at the beginning of each lease year.
- The lease payments include the cost of insurance, estimated at $20,000 per year; these are called executory costs and are annual operating costs that are paid by the lessor but built into annual lease payments.
- The lessee guarantees a residual value of $75,000; the lessor promises to exercise due diligence to get the highest residual value on the open market at the end of the lease.
- The lessee does not know the lessor's implicit rate of interest in the lease. The lessee's incremental borrowing rate is 8%.
- The lessee's fiscal year ends on 31 December.

Observe that the guaranteed residual value increases the present value by about 7%, even though the lessee may not have to pay all or any of this amount. This additional amount will affect the implicit interest cost implicit in the annual payments. The present value is higher than the asset's fair value of $800,000.

Fair-Value Cap and Initial Entry

The fair value of the leased asset is the upper limit of the amount that can be recorded as an asset and liability. In this example, the lessee's IBR yields a present value higher than the fair value. Therefore, the lessee must record the leased asset and liability initially at $800,000:

Asset under finance lease	800,000	
Lease liability		800,000

Implicit Interest Rate and Amortization Table

Because the fair-value cap was applied, the lessee must increase the interest rate applied to the lease payments. The interest rate must be the discount rate that equates the lease payments (plus residual value) to the $800,000 fair value.

$$\$800,000 = \$180,000(P/AD, i, 5) + \$75,000(P/F, i, 5)$$
$$i = 9.8034\%$$

This calculation has been done in Excel; implicit interest rates seldom work out to round numbers!

Exhibit 18-6 shows the amortization table for this lease liability, using the interest rate implicit in the lease. Notice that *the $75,000 guaranteed residual value has its own line*, and is treated like any other payment—part interest, part principal.

	EXHIBIT 18-6

LESSEE LIABILITY AMORTIZATION TABLE—MODIFIED EXAMPLE

Lease Year Ending 31 March	Outstanding Balance	Interest at 9.8034%	Net Lease Payment 31 March	Change (Decrease) in Balance	Ending Balance
20X2	$800,000	$ —	$180,000	$ (180,000)	**$620,000**
20X3	620,000	60,781	180,000	(119,219)	**500,781**
20X4	500,781	49,094	180,000	(130,906)	**369,875**
20X5	369,875	36,260	180,000	(143,740)	**226,135**
20X6	226,135	22,169	180,000	(157,831)	**68,304**
20X7	68,304	6,696	75,000	(68,304)	**0**
Totals		$175,000	$975,000	$(800,000)	

Annual Entries—20X2

Payment When the lessee makes the lease payment, the insurance cost is debited to an expense account. The amount may be debited to a prepaid expense asset account, but it will be adjusted at reporting dates regardless of the initial entry made. The entry for the initial payment on 1 April 20X2:

Insurance expense	20,000	
Lease liability	180,000	
Cash		200,000

The insurance expense debit is for the originally *estimated* amount and not for the actual amount, even if the lessor actually pays a different amount for insurance. The reason is that the estimate was used to determine the net lease payments, which then were discounted to find the present value. The only way that the liability accounting will work out is to stick to the predetermined *net lease* payments, even though the actual cost to the lessor may be different.

Interest

At the end of 20X2, the lessee must accrue interest. In this modified example, the lease year starts in April while the fiscal year starts in January. This is normal, of course—leases are not arranged for accountants' convenience at the beginning or end of a fiscal year.

The outstanding balance from 2 April to 31 December is $620,000. Interest for the full year is $60,781 (Exhibit 18-6), and for 9 months is $45,586. The entry on 31 December 20X2 is:

Interest expense ($60,781 × 9/12)	45,586	
Lease liability		45,586

After this interest accrual, the balance of the lease liability is $620,000 + $45,586 = $665,586.

Depreciation

The example contains a guaranteed residual value of $75,000. When determining the asset's depreciable cost, this guaranteed residual amount must be treated in exactly the same manner as a residual amount for an asset had been purchased rather than leased.

Accordingly, depreciation is based on $725,000 (i.e., $800,000 − $75,000). Annual depreciation will be $145,000 *per lease year.* Assuming that the company charges depreciation to the nearest month:

Depreciation expense ($145,000 × 9/12)	108,750	
Accumulated depreciation—asset under lease		108,750

Insurance Adjustment

Insurance must be allocated to the appropriate fiscal year:

Prepaid insurance ($20,000 × 3/12)	5,000	
Insurance expense		5,000

Annual Entries—20X3

Interest On 1 April 20X3, the interest expense must be updated, *completing the recording of the $60,781 interest related to the first 12 months of the lease:*

Interest expense ($60,781 × 3/12)	15,195	
Lease liability		15,195

Notice that there is no recalculation of the $60,781 interest amount, *because that would involve compounding.* Interest is determined for each 12-month period after a payment is made *and then allocated out per month until it is exhausted.* Specifically, our calculation is ($60,781 × 3/12), NOT (($620,000 + $45,586 = $665,586) (balance at the end of the prior fiscal year) × 9.8034% × 3/12.) The latter calculation is wrong because is recompounds/recalculates the liability balance and that is done only after a payment.

Payment The payment is recorded as before:

Insurance expense	20,000	
Lease liability	180,000	
Cash		200,000

Year-end adjustments The depreciation entry is recorded at the end of the reporting period, for a full year this time:

Depreciation expense	145,000	
Accumulated depreciation—asset under lease		145,000

The recorded insurance expense is $20,000, and the prepaid amount is unchanged from 20X2 at $5,000. These balances are correct and no further adjustment is needed.

Finally, interest must be recorded for the final 9 months of the year:

Interest expense ($49,094 × 9/12)	36,821	
Lease liability		36,821

Notice again that we use the amortization table interest amount, and pro-rate it for the appropriate number of months in the fiscal year.

Allocating Interest to Fiscal Years

It bears repeating: the lease liability amortization table is for the lease year, not for the fiscal year. The table shows 12 months of interest attached to a particular payment. Each of these amounts is fully recorded in the appropriate fiscal year. Exhibit 18-7 shows the interest allocation that will occur over the five-year lease term, which affects six fiscal periods because of the overlap between the lease year and fiscal year.

Disposal at End of Lease

At the end of the lease term, the lessee returns the leased asset to the lessor, which is responsible for selling it to a third party. The lessee has guaranteed that the lessor will receive $75,000 in this transaction.

First, depreciation and interest are recorded up-to-date.

The leased asset ($800,000) and its accumulated depreciation ($145,000 × 5 = $725,000) must be removed from the books. At this point, the liability has a carrying value of $75,000 ($68,304 + $6,696 of interest; see Exhibit 18-6), and it must also be removed from the books. The entry, if the lessor is successful in resale at $75,000:

Lease liability	75,000	
Accumulated depreciation—leased asset	725,000	
Asset under finance lease		800,000

Notice that the lessee returns an asset to the lessor with a net book value of $75,000, and cancels the $75,000 lease liability. *No cash changes hands.*

Assume now that at the end of the lease, the lessor is able to sell the asset to a third party for only $50,000. The lessee will have to pay the $25,000 difference between the guarantee and the actual value. This amount must be recorded as a loss because the lease has ended—there is no future benefit to be gained from this payment.

EXHIBIT 18-7

ALLOCATION OF INTEREST EXPENSE TO FISCAL YEARS

Lease Payment	Implicit Interest*		Interest Expense	Year-End
			Allocation for Accounting	
			Fiscal Year	
1 April 20X2	$ 0 =	$ 0 } =	$ 45,586	31 Dec. 20X2
		45,586 }		
1 April 20X3	60,781 =	15,195 } =	52,016	31 Dec. 20X3
		36,821 }		
1 April 20X4	49,094 =	12,273 } =	39,468	31 Dec. 20X4
		27,195 }		
1 April 20X5	36,260 =	9,065 } =	25,692	31 Dec. 20X5
		16,627 }		
1 April 20X6	22,169 =	5,542 } =	10,564	31 Dec. 20X6
		5,022 }		
1 April 20X7	6,696 =	1,674 =	1,674	31 Dec. 20X7
Total interest	$175,000	$175,000	$175,000	

*From Exhibit 18-6.

The entries to record the return of the asset to the lessor and this loss will be as follows:

Lease liability	75,000	
Accumulated depreciation—leased asset	725,000	
Loss on lease termination	25,000	
Asset under finance lease		800,000
Cash		25,000

Full Set of Entries

All of the journal entries to record both the leased asset and the lease liability over the entire five-year lease term are shown in Exhibit 18-8. The last column shows the lease liability balance at each date. The amounts highlighted in **blue** show the balance after each payment; these amounts match the ending lease-year balances shown on the amortization table in Exhibit 18-6. The amounts highlighted in **green** show the liability balance at the end of each fiscal year.

Current Portion

On the SFP, the total will be divided into current and long-term portions, as described earlier in the chapter. Consider the 31 December 20X3 liability balance of $537,602 (see Exhibit 18-8). The short-term portion is interest of $36,821 and the principal portion of the 20X4 payment, or $130,906 (refer to Exhibit 18-6 for the principal portion of the 20X4 payment). This is equal to $167,727. The long-term portion is $369,875, per the table in Exhibit 18-6. The SFP reflects the following:

Current liability	$ 167,727
Long-term liability	369,875
Total	$537,602

EXHIBIT 18-8

LESSEE'S RECORDING OF FINANCE LEASE—MODIFIED EXAMPLE

	Dr.	Cr.	Lease Liability Balance
1 April 20X2			
Asset under finance lease	800,000		
Lease liability		800,000	
Insurance expense	20,000		
Lease liability	180,000		620,000
Cash		200,000	
31 December 20X2			
Interest expense	45,586		
Lease liability		45,586	665,586
Depreciation expense (9 months)	108,750		
Accumulated depreciation		108,750	
Prepaid insurance	5,000		
Insurance expense		5,000	

	Dr.	Cr.	Lease Liability Balance
1 April 20X3			
Interest expense	15,195		
Lease liability		15,195	
Insurance expense	20,000		
Lease liability	180,000		500,781
Cash		200,000	
31 December 20X3			
Interest expense	36,821		
Lease liability		36,821	537,602
Depreciation expense	145,000		
Accumulated depreciation		145,000	
1 April 20X4			
Interest expense	12,273		
Lease liability		12,273	
Insurance expense	20,000		
Lease liability	180,000		369,875
Cash		200,000	
31 December 20X4			
Interest expense	27,195		
Lease liability		27,195	397,070
Depreciation expense	145,000		
Accumulated depreciation		145,000	
1 April 20X5			
Interest expense	9,065		
Lease liability		9,065	
Insurance expense	20,000		
Lease liability	180,000		226,135
Cash		200,000	

	Dr.	Cr.	Lease Liability Balance
31 December 20X5			
Interest expense	16,627		
Lease liability		16,627	242,762
Depreciation expense	145,000		
Accumulated depreciation		145,000	
1 April 20X6			
Interest expense	5,542		
Lease liability		5,542	
Insurance expense	20,000		
Lease liability	180,000		68,304
Cash		200,000	
31 December 20X6			
Interest expense	5,022		
Lease liability		5,022	73,326
Depreciation expense	145,000		
Accumulated depreciation		145,000	
1 April 20X7			
Interest expense	1,674		
Lease liability		1,674	
Depreciation expense (3 months)	36,250		
Accumulated depreciation		36,250	
Insurance expense	5,000		
Prepaid insurance		5,000	
Lease liability	75,000		0
Accumulated depreciation	725,000		
Loss on lease termination	25,000		
Asset under finance lease		800,000	
Cash (return of asset)		25,000	

CONCEPT REVIEW

1. Why are insurance and executory costs subtracted from annual lease payments before the present value is determined?
2. When lease payment dates do not coincide with the company's reporting periods, how is interest expense calculated?
3. How does a guaranteed residual value affect the lessee's accounting for the lease?

SALE AND LEASEBACK

A **sale and leaseback** is an arrangement whereby a company sells an asset to a lessor and simultaneously leases it back from the lessor. This is a linked set of two transactions:

1. The seller transfers title to the asset to the lessor for a certain price, and the lessor pays the cash proceeds to the seller;
2. Simultaneously, the seller becomes a lessee and leases the exact same asset back, signing a lease arrangement with a series of periodic payments to the lessor.

Sale and leaseback arrangements are most common for real property. A sale and leaseback gives *an immediate cash inflow to the seller*. The cash can be used to retire debt (particularly any outstanding debt on the asset, such as a mortgage or a collateral loan), used for operating purposes, or used for any other purpose that management wishes (e.g., paying a dividend). However, the seller is now committed to a series of periodic payments to the lessor—usually a financing lease over a long period.

Bear in mind that the *original cash proceeds need not be fair value*. The cash proceeds may be more or less than fair value, since the proceeds are in reality linked to repayment arrangements via the lease arrangement. The *cash proceeds often reflect the cash needs* of the vendor for other projects, combined with the lender's credit policies. However, an accounting gain or loss is determined by the relationship between (1) the proceeds and (2) the asset's net book value. Fair value might not come into it—it is quite possible for the sales price to be above or below fair value and trigger a gain or loss.

The seller must evaluate the lease and identify it as being either a finance lease or an operating lease. The criteria for this decision are exactly as described in earlier sections of this chapter.

Defer the Gain on a Finance Lease

The sale element of the transaction is initially recorded just like any other sale, with a gain or loss recorded for the difference between the net proceeds from the sale and the asset's net book value. However, accounting standards require that if the lease element of the sale-and-leaseback arrangement is a finance lease, *any gain or loss is deferred and amortized in proportion to the lease payments over the lease term*.

The objective of deferring the gain is to prevent earnings manipulation. Without this restriction, a company could sell property and then lease it back under a finance lease, thereby recognizing a gain in the period of the sale. In fact, what the company really would be doing is using the property as collateral for a loan that is in the form of a lease. Therefore, any gain (except as noted below for certain operating leases) must be deferred and amortized over the lease term.

Decision on the Gain on an Operating Lease

If the lease is an *operating lease*, the treatment of the gain or loss depends on the relationship between the selling price of the asset and its fair value at the date of sale:

- If the sale price is *equal* to the fair value, the gain or loss is recognized immediately.

- If the sale price is *greater* than fair value, the excess over fair value is deferred and amortized over the term that the asset is expected to be used (i.e., the lease term).

- If the sale price is *less* than the asset's fair value, any gain or loss is recognized in earnings immediately *unless* the lease payments are less than market lease terms, in which case the gain or loss is deferred and amortized over the lease term.

Recording a Sale and Leaseback

Assume that Vendeur Ltd. owns a building in central Montreal. Vendeur enters into an agreement with Bailleur Inc., whereby Vendeur sells the building—but not the land on which it sits—to Bailleur and simultaneously leases it back. The details are as follows:

- The original cost of the building was $10,000,000; it is 60% depreciated on Vendeur's books.

- Bailleur agrees to pay Vendeur $8,500,000 for the building, which is the fair value at the time of the sale.

- Bailleur agrees to lease the building to Vendeur for 20 years. The annual lease payment is $850,000, payable at the *end* of each lease year.

- There is no guaranteed residual value.

- Vendeur will pay all of the building's operating and maintenance costs, including property taxes and insurance.

- The effective date of the agreement is 1 January 20X1.

- Vendeur's incremental borrowing rate is 9%.

- Bailleur's interest rate implicit in the lease is computed after tax and is not disclosed to Vendeur.

- Vendeur uses straight-line depreciation for its buildings, with full-year depreciation in the year of acquisition.

The building has a net book value, after accumulated depreciation, of $4,000,000. Since the selling price is $8,500,000, Vendeur realizes a gain of $4,500,000 on the transaction. The treatment of the gain depends on *whether the lease qualifies as a finance lease or as an operating lease*.

Finance Lease

If the lease qualifies as a finance lease, the gain must be deferred and amortized over the lease term. Applying the four tests:

1. Is it likely that the lessee will obtain ownership of the leased property at the end of the lease? *No.* There is no transfer of title or bargain purchase option.

2. Will the lessee receive substantially all of the economic benefits of the building? *Uncertain.* The building was 60% depreciated at the time of the sale, indicating that it is not a new building. The 20-year lease term could well be a major part of the remaining economic life of the building.

3. Is the lessor assured of recovering the investment in the leased property, plus a return on the investment, over the lease term? *Probably, because the present value of the lease payments is $7,759,264 at 9%, which is more than 90% of the sales price of the building.*

4. Is the leased asset highly specialized to the lessee? *No, there is no indication to that effect.*

Since at least one of the guidelines for classifying the lease as a finance lease appears to be satisfied, the lease should be recorded as a finance lease. As a result, the gain must be deferred and amortized over the 20-year lease term.

The journal entry to record this sale on 1 January 20X1 is:

Cash	8,500,000	
Accumulated depreciation, building	6,000,000	
Building		10,000,000
Deferred gain on sale and leaseback of building		4,500,000

Using Vendeur's IBR of 9% yields a present value of the 20-year stream of end-of-year payments equal to $7,759,264. The lease is recorded as follows:

Building under finance lease	7,759,264	
Lease liability		7,759,264

At the end of 20X1, Vendeur will:

- Record the interest expense (at 9%);
- Pay the $850,000 annual lease payment to Bailleur;
- Depreciate the asset; and
- Amortize the deferred gain.

On 31 December 20X1, the interest expense and the lease payment will be recorded as follows:

Interest expense ($7,759,264 × 9%)	698,334	
Lease liability		698,334
Lease liability	850,000	
Cash		850,000

Vendeur uses straight-line depreciation with a full year's depreciation in the year of acquisition. Since the lease term is 20 years, the straight-line rate is 5%. The entry to record depreciation of the leased building will be as follows, assuming no residual value:

Depreciation expense, building under finance lease	387,963	
Accumulated depreciation, building under finance lease		387,963

Finally, the deferred gain on the sale must be amortized. The gain will be amortized over the lease term in proportion to the lease payments. Since the payments are straight-line over 20 years, the gain must similarly be amortized straight-line over 20 years:

Deferred gain on sale and leaseback of building	225,000	
Depreciation expense, leased building ($4,500,000 ÷ 20)		225,000

The amortization of the gain is *credited* to the depreciation expense charged for the asset. The reason is that the sale and leaseback transaction had the effect of taking a building with a $4,000,000 book value and re-recording it on Vendeur's books at $7,759,264, close to its fair value. By offsetting the gain against the asset depreciation, the depreciation expense is reduced to $162,963, which is closer to the amount the building depreciation would have been if it had not been sold.

Operating Lease

If the lease did not qualify as a finance lease, then by default it would be an operating lease. When the lease is an operating lease, the treatment of the gain or loss depends on the relationships between (1) the *carrying value* (or net book value) of the asset being sold, (2) the *fair value* of the asset sold, and (3) the *transaction price* assigned to the asset in the sale and leaseback:

- If the sale transaction is *at fair value*, any gain or loss would be recognized immediately and not deferred.
- If the sale transaction price is *above fair value*, the difference between carrying value and the transaction price would be treated in two segments:
  - The difference between carrying value and fair value would be recognized immediately as a gain or loss; and
  - The difference between fair value and the transaction price would be deferred and amortized over the period during which the asset is expected to be used.
- If the transaction price is *below fair value*, the difference between carrying value and fair value is recognized immediately, *except* when the lease has sub-market-rate lease payments that compensate the lessee for the loss. In that case, the difference between the transaction price and the carrying value is deferred and amortized over the period of expected use of the asset.

The first situation—a fair-value transaction—is highly likely to occur in arms-length transactions. Other types of deals are likely to occur only between related parties, thereby raising many questions concerning accounting manipulation and tax avoidance, as well as potential ethical issues.

Leases for Land plus Buildings

A single long-term lease may cover the lease of a building as well as the land it is on. When accounting for such a lease, accounting standards require that the minimum lease payments be allocated between the land and building on the basis of "relative *fair values of the leasehold interests* in the land element and buildings element of the lease." This statement is easily misunderstood. It does *not* mean that the fair values of the land and building are the basis for the allocation. Instead, it means the fair value of each asset's *benefits* are being transferred to the lessee.

Perhaps the simplest way of grasping this concept is look at the land first. Land does not normally lose its economic value over time. There is no need for the lessor to be compensated for land deterioration, provided that the land is not being polluted and thereby becoming less valuable during the lease term. The lessor simply needs to earn a return on the investment in the land.

Buildings are different. Over the course of a long lease term, there is bound to be significant deterioration in a building, as well as obsolescence. For example, old multi-floor industrial buildings are largely obsolete now. Modern production generally requires vast floor spaces on a single level. Thus, those old buildings end up either getting torn down, or (if they are in good locations), they are converted for residential use, which has far less value. A long-term lease for a building, therefore, must compensate the lessor for significant loss of economic value.

Once the lease cash flows have been allocated to land and buildings, each component is accounted for separately.

Land leases are finance leases only if title reverts to the lessor at the end of the lease term. Otherwise, *the land lease is reported as an operating lease,* since the lease does not cover the major part of the land's life (being infinite) nor does the land-related portion of the lease payments cover most of the land's value.

The building, however, may be reported as either an operating lease or a finance lease. The guidelines for that reporting decision are the same as we have discussed above.

If the land portion of the lease is immaterial, or if there is no basis on which to allocate the land and building portions, the lease can be accounted for as a whole without separate regard for the land portion.

LESSEE DISCLOSURE

Operating Leases

In the notes to the financial statements, lessees should give a general description of their significant leasing arrangements, including the basis on which contingent rent (if any) is determined and whether there are any renewal and/or purchase options. If any lessor has imposed financial restrictions on the lessee, such as limitations on additional debt or on dividend distributions, those should be disclosed.

Quantitatively, lessees should disclose lease payments recognized as expense in the current period, separated into (1) minimum lease payments and (2) contingent rents. Lessees should also disclose the company's obligation for operating lease payments (1) for the next year, (2) in total for the next four years, and (3) in total for all later years.

Finance Leases

Leased assets and the related lease obligations must be reported separately from "regular" assets and liabilities, either on the face of the SFP or in a disclosure note. This disclosure is required because the lessee does not have the same rights of ownership for a leased asset as compared to an owned asset, even though the lessee bears substantially all of the risks and benefits of ownership.

The current portion of the lease liability should be shown separately, as has been described earlier in this chapter.

Other disclosures are:

- A general description of the lessee's significant finance lease arrangements, including:
  - The basis for contingent rent, if any;
  - Any renewal terms, purchase options, or escalation clauses; and
  - Any financial restrictions imposed by the lessor, such as limits on dividend payments, additional debt, or additional leasing.
- The amount of any contingent rents recognized as expense during the period.
- For each class of leased asset, the net carrying value at the reporting date.
- The total of future minimum lease payments *and their present value* for:
  - The coming year;
  - Future years 2 through 5; and
  - All years (in aggregate) after year 5.
- A reconciliation between total future minimum lease payments and their present value.

Leases are financial instruments. Therefore, leases must conform to the general disclosure requirements for financial instruments, as discussed in Chapter 13.

Disclosure Example

An example of a finance lease disclosure note is shown in Exhibit 18-9. Air Canada has finance leases for two types of assets—aircraft and facilities. The company also has significant operating leases. Disclosure shows that the company is committed to total future payments of $397 million on the year-end 2014 finance leases. The present value of that commitment is $283 million. For operating leases, the total cash commitments are $1,633 million. This demonstrates that operating lease commitments are a significant element of the financial strategy.

EXHIBIT 18-9

EXTRACTS FROM AIR CANADA FINANCIAL STATEMENTS
LEASE ELEMENTS

(dollar amounts in millions)

4. PROPERTY AND EQUIPMENT

As at December 31, 2014, property and equipment included finance leased assets including 17 aircraft (2013 – 18) with a net book value of $145 (2013 – $150) and facilities with a net book value of $42 (2013 – $45).

8. LONG-TERM DEBT AND FINANCE LEASES

	Final Maturity	Weighted Average Interest Rate (%)	2014	2013
Long-term debt				
Finance lease obligations (f)	2015 – 2033	10.08	283	328

> (f) Finance leases, related to facilities and aircraft, total $283 ($73 and US$181) (2013 – $328 ($76 and US$237)). During 2014, the Corporation recorded interest expense on finance lease obligations of $32 (2013 – $46). The carrying value of aircraft and facilities under finance leases amounted to $145 and $42 respectively (2013 – $150 and $45).
>
> Air Canada has aircraft leasing transactions with a number of structured entities. Air Canada controls and consolidates leasing entities covering 22 aircraft as at December 31, 2014. This debt amount includes any guarantee by Air Canada in the residual value of the aircraft upon expiry of the lease. The related aircraft are charged as collateral against the debt by the owners thereof. The creditors under these leasing arrangements have recourse to Air Canada, as lessee, in the event of default or early termination of the lease.

Certain aircraft and other secured finance agreements contain collateral fair value tests. Under the tests, Air Canada may be required to provide additional collateral or prepay part of the financings. The maximum amount payable in 2015, assuming the collateral is worth nil, is $212 (US$183). The maximum amount payable declines over time in relation to the outstanding principal. Total collateral as at December 31, 2014 is $12 (US$11) (2013 – $5(US$5)) in the form of cash deposits, included in Deposits and other assets, has been provided under the fair value test for certain of these aircraft leases.

Cash interest paid on Long-term debt and finance leases in 2014 by the Corporation was $287 (2013 – $345).

Refer to Note 16 for the Corporation's principal and interest repayment requirements as at December 31, 2014.

16. COMMITMENTS

...

Operating Lease and Capital Commitments

The estimated aggregate cost of the future firm Boeing 787, Boeing 777 and Boeing 737 MAX aircraft deliveries and other capital purchase commitments as at December 31, 2014 approximates $8,256. US dollar amounts are converted using the December 31, 2014 closing rate of CDN$1.1601. The estimated aggregate cost of aircraft is based on delivery prices that include estimated escalation and, where applicable, deferred price delivery payment interest calculated based on the 90-day US LIBOR rate at December 31, 2014.

	2015	2016	2017	2018	2019	Thereafter	Total
Capital commitments	$ 1,067	$ 2,122	$ 1,598	$ 1,362	$ 1,066	$ 1,041	$ 8,256

As at December 31, 2014 the future minimum lease payments under existing operating leases of aircraft and other property amount to $1,633 using year end exchange rates.

	2015	2016	2017	2018	2019	Thereafter	Total
Aircraft	$ 313	$ 268	$ 238	$ 204	$ 172	$ 145	$ 1,340
Other property	46	32	28	23	13	151	293
Total	**$ 359**	**$ 300**	**$ 266**	**$ 227**	**$ 185**	**$ 296**	**$ 1,633**

Maturity Analysis

...

The following is a maturity analysis, based on contractual undiscounted cash flows, for financial liabilities. The analysis includes both the principal and interest component of the payment obligations on long-term debt and is based on interest rates and the applicable foreign exchange rate effective as at December 31, 2014.

	2015	2016	2017	2018	2019	Thereafter	Total
...							
Finance lease obligations	91	48	46	46	46	120	**397**

...

Source: Air Canada, 2014 Consolidated financial statements. www.sedar.com, posted 11 February, 2015.

LONG-TERM LEASES: PROS AND CONS

Transfer of Income Tax Benefits

The transfer of income tax benefits from the lessee to the lessor is often the driving force behind finance leases. The legal owner of an asset can deduct CCA. But if the owner is not able to use the CCA deduction or the full benefit of that deduction, the company would be better off having another party take title, get the tax advantages, and pass that on to the lessee through lower annual cash payments. Some examples of such a situation are:

- The owner is a nonprofit organization, such as a school, hospital, or charity.

- The owner is a for-profit business but either is losing money or is not earning enough to use the full amount of the available CCA.

- The owner is profitable but pays taxes at a lower rate than potential lessors.

If any of these conditions exist, then the CCA is more valuable to a lessor than to the potential user of the asset. Lessors calculate their return on investment on an after-tax basis, and lease industry competition forces the lessor to pass the benefit of any tax reduction on to the lessee in the form of lower lease payments. Therefore, the asset can often be leased for a cash flow present value that is less than the amount the lessee would pay to buy the asset.

Long-term leasing has several other potential advantages over buying an asset. However, the perceived advantages to the lessee also have offsetting disadvantages. For each factor, we will look at the apparent benefits first *(Pro)*, and then at the related disadvantages *(Con)*.

Off-Balance-Sheet Financing

Pro

If a company enters a long-term lease and that lease does not qualify as a finance lease for accounting purposes, the company effectively has obtained financing for an asset without having to show the asset (and any related liability) on its SFP. Airlines often enter into operating leases for a substantial proportion of their aircraft and vehicle fleet. Lessees may view **off-balance-sheet financing** as an advantage because they effectively incur debt that does not appear on the SFP. This may allow the company to meet debt covenants imposed by other lenders.

Con

The shorter the lease, the greater is the cost to the lessee. In shorter leases, more of the risk remains with the lessor. The lessor does not accept this risk out of generosity. The cost is passed back to the lessee in the form of higher annual lease payments and/or heavy cancellation penalties if the lessee does not renew. Therefore, a lessee may obtain off-balance-sheet financing, but at a real economic cost in higher expenses and operating cash flow expenditures.

100% Financing

Pro

Financial institutions will not lend a buyer the full amount of an asset purchase price. Normally, financing can be obtained for no more than 75% or 80% of the cost of the asset. In contrast, a lease can effectively provide full financing, since there is no substantial down payment to be made at the inception of the lease.

Con

This advantage exists only for assets that are readily transferable if the lessee defaults (e.g., automobiles, airplanes) and only to lessees that have high credit ratings. For other assets and less creditworthy lessees, the lessor covers the risk by forward-weighting the lease payments; that is, most of the cash flow for lease payments is in the early years of the lease. Also, since lease payments are payable at the beginning of each period, the first payment is, in effect, a down payment.

Protection against Obsolescence

Pro

The shorter the lease term, the easier it is for the lessee to stay up-to-date with the latest technology. If a new product or process becomes available, the lessee can refuse to renew the existing lease and move to the newer product. An alternative is for the lessor to provide upgrade privileges in the lease. For example, an existing leased photocopier may be replaced by a newer model, or a leased automobile may be "rolled over" to a new model every second or third year. Such lease arrangements help the lessee guard against obsolescence.

Con

Flexibility comes at a price. The risk of obsolescence falls on the lessor, and the lessor will compensate for the added risk by charging higher lease payments. Lessor-provided upgrades can help provide flexibility, but they lock the lessee into the lessor's product. As well, automatic upgrades are expensive. Many companies find it much less costly to skip a product generation unless it is crucial to be on the cutting edge of technology.

Protection against Interest Rate Changes

Pro

Lease payments are always determined on the basis of fixed interest rates, even when the lease contains escalation clauses or contingent payments. Therefore, a long-term or finance lease can protect the lessee from interest rate fluctuations.

Con

If the lessee's business fluctuates in response to economic conditions, it may be better to use variable-rate loans from financial institutions to finance the assets. When the economy is down, interest rates are down, thereby not locking the company into a high implicit interest rate.

CONCEPT REVIEW

1. What is meant by off-balance-sheet financing?
2. Who holds legal title to a leased asset?
3. How can a lease be used to transfer CCA tax benefits from the lessee to the lessor?

AVOIDING LEASE CAPITALIZATION

Accounting standards establish guidelines for determining a financing lease. Determined minds can devise creative contracts that appear to be capitalization-avoidance techniques. In fact, a whole industry is dedicated to devising ways of leasing assets to companies while avoiding the capitalization criteria. Four common methods of avoiding capitalization are discussed below.

Use Contingent Rent

Contingent rent is an amount that is dependent on future events, such as the sales volume for the retail occupant in a shopping mall. Contingent rent is not included in present value calculations when the lease is being evaluated as a possible finance lease. Therefore, the larger the amount of rental that can be made dependent on future events, the lower the minimum net lease payments will be.

Insert a Third Party

The true nature of a lease can be disguised by inserting a third party between the lessee and the lessor. The most common approach is for the lessee to form a separate company, the purpose of which is to lease assets to the operating company. The separate company enters into the formal lease agreement with the lessor, obligating itself to pay for the full cost of the asset over the lease term, and then enters into a year-by-year lease with the operating lessee.

Impose a Substantial Penalty for Non-Renewal

Corporations may lease major and crucial operating assets under lease agreements that provide for a year-by-year renewal (at the lessee's option) or for lease terms that are considerably shorter than the economic life of the asset. The lessor's offset for assuming higher risk is to insert very high cancellation or non-renewal penalties, which are not included in minimum lease payments. However, the substance of this contract must be discerned to classify it properly.

Side Letter

Corporations may lease assets on a year-by-year lease. They might simultaneously sign a *side letter* that commits them to renewal for a certain period. The lease on its own is an operating lease, but the term and thus the classification is far different when the side letter is also considered. If a corporation follows this approach, and *fails to disclose the presence of a side letter*, there is a *serious breach of ethics*. Fortunately, this once-popular approach is rarely encountered in today's environment.

ETHICAL ISSUES

The accounting standard for leases offers multiple opportunities for managers to commit actions to deliberately mislead financial statement users. The most obvious and widespread is the simple expedient of leasing long-term assets through a series of relatively short-term leases. Accounting standards were not intended to make lease capitalization an *option*. The intent was to *require* companies to report leases according to their substance.

In practice, though, managers often choose the reporting method for long-term leased assets and then negotiate the lease to accomplish that reporting goal. By carefully structuring lease provisions, management (with the encouragement of the leasing industry) can obtain long-term use of assets while still reporting the leases as operating leases.

For managers who are trying to meet short-term profit goals, this practice has two primary advantages. When leases are classified as operating leases:

- Both the leased assets and the related liabilities are kept off the balance sheet; and
- The lease-related expenses flowing into earnings will be lower in the early years of the lease contracts.

This is a practice known as "window dressing"—making the financial position of the company look better than it really is. Since the intent is to mislead financial statement readers, it is clearly an unethical practice.

Leasing also provides an opportunity for unethical behaviour through the use of related parties. Leasing through a related third party, such as through a company controlled by an officer or shareholder of the lessee, provides an opportunity for the third party to skim off profits through inflated lease payments. The requirements for consolidating *special purpose entities* are intended to keep a company from hiding leases off-balance-sheet, but this intent can be circumvented by unethical managers.

Finally, sale-and-leaseback arrangements provide an opportunity to manipulate earnings. This can be done by (1) either selling an entire asset and then leasing only part of it back, or (2) leasing it via a series of operating leases that permit the selling company to recognize gains from the transaction in net income.

Looking Forward

Standard setters' attempts to deal with *substance over form* for lease accounting has long been problematic. The challenge is that, while there is a continuum of lease terms in economic terms, there are only two (very different) approaches to lease accounting—*operating* leases and *finance* leases. The outcome is that *many shades of grey are classified as either black or white.* And unfortunately, a whole new industry sprouted, one that was dedicated to devising leases that were finance leases in substance but that avoided classification as such under the accounting standards.

Widespread dissatisfaction with lease accounting has led accounting standard setters to reconsider lease accounting. The approach has been to eliminate the operating-finance distinction and to treat all lease commitments in the same way, reporting them on the SFP at the present value of the lease commitment. This will result in capitalization of most leases. This approach is described in an appendix to this chapter.

The process has been much delayed, though; the current feeling is that revised lease accounting standard will not be implemented before 2019.

Accounting Standards for Private Enterprises

The leasing standard under ASPE is, in substance, the same as for IFRS. However, there are some differences. One difference is that ASPE uses the term *capital lease* rather than the IASB term *finance lease*. This is not a substantive difference because the terms *capital lease, finance lease,* and *financial lease* (the term used in the finance industry) all mean the same thing and are interchangeable.

Criteria for Lease Capitalization

The basic guidelines (or criteria) for classifying a lease as a capital lease are essentially the same under ASPE and IFRS except:

- ASPE does not have a guideline that addresses "specialized use asset"; this is the fourth guideline under IFRS and ASPE has only three guidelines.
- ASPE establishes quantitative *bright lines* that are only suggestions under IFRS:
  - When assessing the lease term as compared to the asset's economic life, the bright line is "usually 75% or more."
  - When assessing the present value of minimum lease payments as compared to the fair value of the asset, the bright line is "usually 90% or more."

Although the IFRS standard deliberately avoids specifying quantitative bright lines, those thresholds continue to be used in practice in most entities, public and private, because they provide a target of "reasonableness" that tends to promote consistency. Nevertheless, the intended overall guiding principle for capital/finance leases continues to be whether the lease transfers substantially all of the risks and rewards of ownership to the lessee.

Interest Rate for Discounting

Under IFRS, the discount rate is the lessor's rate implicit in the lease, if known, and otherwise the lessee's IBR. In contrast, ASPE requires that the *lower* of the two rates be used. If the lessor's implicit pretax rate of return is not known, the distinction may have little significance in general practice.

Leases of Land and Buildings

When a lease involves land *and* buildings, the lease payments are segregated between the land and buildings on the basis of the fair values of the underlying properties. This differs from IFRS, in which the allocation is based on the *fair values of the leasehold rights*, not on the land and buildings themselves.

Disclosure

The disclosure requirements are relatively modest under ASPE:

Operating leases For leases lasting more than one year, disclose the future minimum lease payments (1) for each of the next five years and (2) in total.

Capital Leases

For capital leases, the following should be disclosed:

- The total amount of payments required for each of the next five years;
- The interest rate, maturity date, and amount outstanding for capital leases;
- The aggregate amount of interest expense, disclosed either separately or as part of interest on long-term debt;
- Whether leases are secured (e.g., by other assets of the entity); and
- For the leased asset(s), the cost (i.e., initial discounted present value), the depreciation method being used, and the amount of accumulated depreciation.

Sale and Leaseback

The ASPE requirements for reporting any gain or loss arising from the sale in a sale and leaseback transactions differ from those of IFRS as follows:

- If the lease is a capital lease, any gain or loss from the sale transaction should be capitalized and amortized proportionate to the depreciation on the leased asset (i.e., *not* over the term of the lease as required by IFRS).
- If the asset's fair value is less than its carrying value at the time of the sale, the loss should be recognized immediately because the asset was impaired at the date of sale. This applies to operating leases as well as capital leases.
- If the lease is an operating lease, any gain or loss from the sale transaction should be capitalized and amortized proportionate to the rental payments over the lease term (i.e., *not* immediately recognized as allowed by IFRS under most circumstances).

RELEVANT STANDARDS

CPA Canada Handbook, Part I (IFRS):

- IAS 17, Leases

CPA Canada Handbook, Part II (ASPE):

- Section 3065, Leases

SUMMARY OF KEY POINTS

1. A lease is an agreement that conveys from a lessor to a lessee the right to use an asset for a contracted price per period.

2. A lease for a relatively short period of an asset's useful life that does not transfer substantially all of the asset's risks and benefits to the lessee is classified as an *operating lease*. Under an operating lease arrangement, rent payments are reported by the lessee as an expense as the asset is used.

3. A lease that transfers substantially all of the risks and benefits of ownership to the lessee is called a *finance lease*. One of four guidelines must be met for a lease to be a finance lease: (1) do the terms of the lease make it highly likely that title to the asset will transfer to the lessee at the end of the lease; (2) does the lessee have the use of the asset over the major part of its economic life; (3) is the lessee committing to lease payments that will return substantially all of the lessor's investment in the leased asset plus a return on the investment; or (4) is the asset so specialized for the lessee that it would have little benefit to others?

4. Finance leases are recorded by the lessee as though the asset had been purchased. The net minimum lease payments over the lease term are discounted, using the interest rate implicit in the lease, or, if this rate is unknown, at the lessee's incremental borrowing rate. The present value amount is recorded as both an asset and a liability. Once recorded, the asset and the liability are accounted for independently.

5. The asset is depreciated in accordance with the lessee's policy for other assets of that type except that the depreciation period must be evaluated as the period that the lessee will use the asset. This is limited to the minimum lease term (including bargain renewal terms) unless there is a bargain purchase option or other transfer of title to the lessee at the end of the lease term.

6. The lease liability is accounted for as an instalment loan with blended payments. Interest expense is calculated at the same rate as was used for discounting the payments; the excess of payments over interest expense reduces the outstanding liability balance.

7. The current portion of the lessee's lease liability consists of (1) accrued interest to the SFP date plus (2) the amount of principal that will be paid over the next year.

8. A sale and leaseback arrangement is an agreement in which the owner of an asset sells it to a lessor and simultaneously leases it back. The subsequent lease is accounted for as either finance or operating, as for other leases. For a finance lease, any gain or loss on the sale is deferred and amortized over the lease term. For an operating lease, the accounting treatment of the gain or loss depends on the relationship between the selling price of the asset and its fair value at the date of sale.

9. The amount of finance lease obligations and assets held under finance leases should be separately disclosed. Cash commitments under operating leases and under finance leases for the next year, for the next four years in total, and then the aggregate amount for all remaining years must also be disclosed.

10. Under ASPE, there are bright lines set for lease classification guidelines (75% of economic life and 90% of fair value). There is no guideline at all regarding specialized equipment. The discount rate used is the lower of the interest rate implicit in the lease, and the lessee's incremental borrowing rate.

Key Terms

bargain purchase option
bargain renewal terms
bright lines
capital lease
contingent lease payments
contingent rent
economic life
executory costs
finance lease
financial intermediary
guaranteed residual value
implicit lease interest rate
incremental borrowing rate (IBR)
initial direct costs
initial lease term

lease
lease term
lessee
lessor
minimum net lease payments
off-balance-sheet financing
operating lease
personal property
real property
sale and leaseback
unguaranteed residual value
useful life

Review Problem 18-1

Orion leased a computer to Lenox Silver Inc. on 1 April 20X5. The terms of the lease are as follows:

• Lease term (fixed and noncancellable)	3 years
• Estimated economic life of the computer	5 years
• Fair market value of the asset at lease inception	$5,000
• Bargain purchase offer	None
• Transfer of title	None

- Guaranteed residual value by lessee, 1 April 20X8 $1,000

- Lessee's normal depreciation method*   straight line

- Lessee's incremental borrowing rate   11%

- Executory costs included in lease payments   None

- Initial direct costs   None

- Annual lease payment, beginning of each lease year $1,620

- Lessor's implicit interest rate   10%

- Lessee's fiscal year-end   31 December

*Lenox Silver Inc. charges a half-year depreciation in the year of acquisition and a half-year in the year of disposition, regardless of the actual dates of acquisition and disposal.

Required:

1. Classify the lease from the perspective of the lessee.
2. Provide entries for the lease from 1 April 20X5 through 31 December 20X6.
3. Show how the leased asset and the lease obligation will be shown on the lessee's SFP at 31 December 20X6.
4. Suppose that at the end of the lease, the lessor tells the lessee to dispose of the asset, and to keep any proceeds in excess of the guaranteed residual value. Provide entries for the lessee on 1 April 20X8, assuming that the lessee sells the asset for $1,200 and remits the required $1,000 payment to the lessor.

REVIEW PROBLEM 18-1—SOLUTION

1. The lessor's implicit rate is known, and therefore is used as the discount rate. Discounting the minimum lease payments, including the guaranteed residual value of $1,000, yields:

    P = $1,620 (P/A due, 10%, 3) + $1,000(P/F, 10%, 3)
      = $4,432 + $751 = $5,183

    Clearly, the lease is a finance lease because the present value of the minimum lease payments, $5,183, is greater than the $5,000 fair value of the leased property.

2. The asset and the related liability must be capitalized. The capitalized value of the leased asset cannot be greater than the asset's fair value, and therefore the fair value of $5,000 must be used instead of the present value of $5,183. The entries at the inception of the lease will be:

    1 April 20X5—commencement of the lease

    Asset under finance lease   5,000

        Lease liability   5,000

1 April 20X5—first payment

Lease liability	1,620	
Cash		1,620

Since the lessee's IBR yields a present value that is higher than the fair value of the asset, it cannot be used for further accounting for the lease. Instead, the implicit rate *to the lessee* must be calculated by solving the following equation for i, the implicit interest rate:

$$\$5,000 = \$1,620 \ (P/A \ \text{due}, i, 3) + \$1,000 \ (P/F, i, 3)$$

By using a computer spreadsheet, or a financial calculator, we can find the implicit rate of 13.29%. This rate must then be used to accrue the interest and to record the components of the annual lease payments. The liability amortization table for the lease obligation is as follows:

Year	Beginning Balance	Interest Expense at 13.29%	Cash Payment	Reduction of Principal	Ending Balance
20X5	$5,000	$ 0	$1,620	$1,620	$3,380
20X6	3,380	449	1,620	1,171	2,209
20X7	2,209	294	1,620	1,326	883
20X8	883	117	1,000	883	0

The entries to record the depreciation, interest accrual, and payments through 31 December 20X6 are shown below.

31 December 20X5—adjusting entries

Depreciation expense	667	
Accumulated depreciation		667
[($5,000 − $1,000) ÷ 3 × 1/2 = $667]		
Interest expense	337	
Lease liability		337
[$449 × 9/12 = $337]		

1 April 20X6—interest accrual

Interest expense	112	
Lease liability		112
[$449 × 3/12 = $112]		

1 April 20X6—second payment

Lease liability	1,620	
Cash		1,620

31 December 20X6—adjusting entries

Depreciation expense	1,333	
Accumulated depreciation		1,333
[($5,000 − $1000) ÷ 3]		
Interest expense	221	
Lease liability		221
[$294 × 9/12]		

3. The lessee's SFP at 31 December 20X6 will include the following amounts:

Capital assets

Asset under finance lease	$ 5,000
Less accumulated depreciation	(2,000)
	$ 3,000

Current liabilities

Current portion of finance lease liability	$ 1,547

[$221 accrued interest at 31 December 20X6, plus $1,326 principal portion of the next payment]

Long-term liabilities

Obligation under finance lease	$ 883

4. 1 April 20X8—sale of asset

Cash (received from sale)	1,200	
Lease liability	1,000	
Accumulated depreciation	4,000	
Asset under finance lease		5,000
Cash (paid to lessor)		1,000
Gain on disposal of leased asset		200

This entry assumes that adjustments have already been made to (1) accrue the last of the interest and (2) record depreciation for 20X8.

CASES: CASE 18-1

PREMIUM BLINDS LTD.

Premium Blinds Ltd. specializes in the manufacture of custom and pre-finished blinds and drapes for windows and doors. The firm was founded by Bill Khadim, who retired 10 years ago and now lives in Orlando, Florida. When he retired, Bill assigned 60% of the shares of the corporation to Sara Khadim, his daughter. Much of Bill's retirement income comes from the dividends he receives on his remaining Premium Blinds shares. Premium Blinds is now run by Sara. There are no other shareholders.

The custom window covering industry has been a highly competitive industry for many years, challenged by overcapacity and by less expensive on-line options. Premium Blinds has generally been able to attain reasonable profit levels in most years by specializing in higher quality installations with select builders and window manufacturers across Canada. During lean years, Premium Blinds has been able to rely on its credit union, the Town Credit Union (TCU), for loan support. As a result, a close working relationship has developed between TCU and Premium Blinds.

In the spring of 20X2, Sara decided that the firm needed to acquire some new, technologically improved production equipment in order to stay up-to-date and to protect the company's already-thin profit margins. The equipment has a list price of $350,000, although Sara thought that it would be possible to bargain the price down to about $330,000.

After discussing the purchase with the credit union, Sara realized that the company had two options for acquiring the equipment. One option was to buy the equipment directly, with financing for 100% of the purchase price provided by means of a ten-year term loan from the credit union, to be repaid at $33,000 per year for ten years, with interest at 6% per annum due each year-end.

The second option was to lease the equipment from LeaseCorp, the leasing subsidiary of a major Canadian bank. LeaseCorp would buy the equipment on behalf of Premium Blinds and would then lease it to Premium for 10 years, with beginning-of-year lease payment of $36,000 per year. After the expiration of the initial lease term, Premium would have the option of continuing the lease by paying $1,000 per year for as long as Premium wishes to retain the equipment. Such equipment normally has a useful life of 15 to 20 years, although the later years of the useful life are marked by decreasing productivity due to continuing technological improvement in equipment design.

Premium's thin profit margins made it quite possible that the firm would not be able to get the quickest possible tax advantage from CCA on the new equipment if the firm bought the equipment directly. On the other hand, if LeaseCorp held title under a lease the lessor could use the depreciation to reduce its income taxes, and the tax benefits would be passed on to Premium Blinds in the form of an after-tax implicit interest rate of 4%, less than the 6% rate that Premium would have to pay on the term loan from the bank.

Before deciding on the financing method, Sara wants a report from her accountant, David Geroux, on the cash flow and financial reporting implications of the alternatives. She also wants David to make a recommendation on the most appropriate accounting policies to adopt should the lease option be chosen. Sara is hoping Premium will be acquired by a public company, as part of industry consolidation in the next year or two, and she does not want to take actions that might prove detrimental to the company's reported results.

Required:

Assume the role of David Geroux, and prepare a report to Sara Khadim.

CASE 18-2

BRING-IT-HOME INC.

Bring-It-Home Inc. (BIHI) is a Canadian corporation based and operating in Nova Scotia. BIHI's wide-ranging products and services are targeted at enhancing customers' quality of living, not only in their own homes but also within their communities. The company has enjoyed considerable growth due to the insight of its management team and creative talents of some key employees. BIHI is majority-owned by Flanagan's Inc., a Nova Scotia–based holding company. Flanagan's prepares its financial statements in accordance with International Financial Reporting Standards (IFRS), as does BIHI.

It is 15 February 20X5, and you, as a professional accountant with the accounting firm Mansbridge & Lang, have been asked by BIHI's president, Steve Power, to fill in as acting controller at BIHI. The current controller, Marcel Crosby, has gone on extended leave from BIHI for medical reasons. Mr. Crosby joined BIHI partway through the current fiscal year, replacing the former controller who moved to another province with her family.

The one constant in BIHI's accounting department has been the assistant controller, Rick McIlroy. Although Rick is not a professional accountant, he is very energetic and willing to work extra hours when needed. Rick feels that the head office staff's bonus based on pre-tax income is a nice perk and he wants to make sure he is doing his best to help out his co-workers.

Mr. Power wants you to review the draft condensed financial statement for 31 December 20X4 (Exhibit 1). You also have reviewed the accounting for certain transactions underlying the draft statement (Exhibit 2). If you feel that any adjustments are needed, you are to explain the reason(s) and draft any necessary adjusting journal entries. You should then prepare a revised statement of financial position.

EXHIBIT 1
BRING-IT-HOME INC.
Condensed Draft Financial Statement (*unaudited*) 31 December 20X4
(prepared by Rick McIlroy)

	31 December 20X4
Statement of Financial Position	
Current assets	$ 44,725
Greenhouse, net	81,000
Other property plant, and equipment (net)	143,365
Total assets	$269,090
Current liabilities	$ 8,250

Loan payable, government agency	90,000
Other long-term liabilities	67,000
Total liabilities	165,250
Common shares	7,000
Retained earnings	96,840
Total shareholders' equity	103,840
Total liabilities and shareholders' equity	$269,090

EXHIBIT 2

NOTES ON THE DRAFT FINANCIAL STATEMENTS

1. Bank Indebtedness

BIHI has a $60,000 long-term loan payable to Canadiana Bank. BIHI is to provide Canadiana with its audited financial statements, prepared in accordance with IFRS, within 90 days of its year-end. The loan bears interest at 10% and is callable if the company's debt to equity ratio exceeds 3:1.

The 10% interest rate Canadiana charged BIHI on its own creditworthiness exceeds the 7% that Flanagan normally pays on its bank loans because BIHI's parent company deals with an international consortium of banks and thus is able to negotiate a better rate than BIHI.

2. Lease

On 2 January 20X4, BIHI acquired equipment via a five-year lease that requires annual payments of $25,000, due at the beginning of each year. The first payment was made on 2 January 20X4 and was charged to rent expense. The present value of the five payments, based on the 10% rate implicit in the lease, was $104,250 while the fair value of the equipment at the inception of the lease was $132,000. Because the equipment was custom-made for BIHI's needs, there is no residual value at the end of the five-year lease. The lease covers only five of the equipment's estimated physical life of eight years and is, therefore, being recorded as an operating lease.

3. Community Vegetable Greenhouse

On 1 July 20X4, BIHI acquired ownership of a large community greenhouse through a provincial government lending agency. To facilitate acquisition of the greenhouse, BIHI signed an agreement that requires the company to pay $90,000 to the lending agency on 30 June 20X9. As well, BIHI must pay simple interest of 3% on the loan, or $2,700 per year, on each of 30 June 20X5 through 30 June 20X9.

Acquisition of the greenhouse qualified for federal government assistance as the greenhouse was located in an economically challenged area of the province. After signing the paperwork to acquire the greenhouse on 1 July 20X4, BIHI received $15,000 from a federal government agency. The company expects to use the greenhouse for five years after which it should be almost worthless. Rick diligently made the following related entries during the current fiscal year:

1 July 20X4		
Greenhouse	90,000	
Loan payable		90,000
To record acquisition of the greenhouse		
Cash	15,000	
Head office expenses		15,000
To record receipt of government grant		
31 December 20X4		
Depreciation expense	9,000	
Accumulated depreciation, greenhouse		9,000
To record six months of depreciation under the straight-line method		
Interest expense	1,350	
Interest payable		1,350
To accrue six months of interest owing		

4. Sales

Until late 20X4, BIHI had an arrangement with Crafty Cabinets Ltd. (Crafty) to design kitchen cabinets requested by BIHI's customers. Crafty manufactures the cabinets as specified by BIHI. BIHI asks Crafty to hold these products in its warehouse for delivery to BIHI or to BIHI's customers, as specified. There is a fixed schedule for delivery of the goods to BIHI or its customers. Crafty notifies BIHI of all shipments from Crafty to BIHI or any of BIHI's customers.

In December, Rick recorded sales of $10,000 and a related cost of goods sold of $7,360 for goods manufactured by Crafty for one of BIHI's customers, John Doyle. BIHI had ordered the goods on behalf of Doyle. In mid-December, John emailed BIHI and copied Crafty, asking that the goods not be shipped until January 20X5. John will still pay BIHI according to the original schedule and terms but, due to unforeseen circumstances, will not be available to receive the goods in December.

5. Patent

BIHI is interested in expanding its manufacturing of customized kitchen cabinets and counter tops. In mid-December 20X4, BIHI was approached by Skerwink Designs Ltd., which was were interested in swapping a parcel of land that would allow BIHI the space needed for expansion. The land was recorded at $12,000 on the books of Skerwink. In November, Skerwink had received an offer from another company to purchase this land for $14,400. BIHI's land was recorded at $15,125 and had recently been professionally appraised at $18,750. The exchange was completed on 29 December 20X4. Rick recorded the trade by capitalizing the new land at $18,750 and recording a gain on the trade of $3,625.

Required:

Prepare the information requested by Mr. Power. BIHI's combined federal and provincial tax rate is 20%.

(Judy Cumby; adapted)

CASE 18-3

WARMTH HOME COMFORT LTD.

Warmth Home Comfort Ltd. (WHCL) is a Canadian manufacturer of furnaces and air-conditioning units. The company was acquired by a group of 15 investors eight years ago. Three of the investors are senior managers with the company, including Jacob Kovacs, who is president and chief executive officer.

Over the years WHCL had been quite successful, but it has struggled in the face of increasing competition from overseas competitors. The owners believe that three years from now WHCL will be poised to be a major player in the Canadian and the U.S. heating and cooling markets and may consider going public. Summary financial statements are provided in Exhibit 1. Kovacs points out that the company's financial performance seems to be improving, given the smaller loss in 20X7 and the increasing revenues after two years of falling sales.

EXHIBIT 1		
WARMTH HOME COMFORT LIMITED		
Extracts from the Draft Financial Statements Balance Sheet		
As at December 31 (in thousands of dollars)		
	20X7 **(Unaudited)**	**20X6** **(Audited)**
Assets		
Current:		
Cash	$ 15	$ 100
Accounts receivable	875	587

Inventory	500	540
Other current assets	56	120
	1,446	1,347
Capital assets	2,606	2,256
Accumulated depreciation	(1,071)	(926)
	1,535	1,330
Total assets	$2,981	$2,677
Liabilities		
Current:		
Bank indebtedness	$ 450	$ 400
Accounts payable	581	395
Other current liabilities	118	100
	1,149	895
Long-term debt	825	525
	1,974	1,420
Shareholders' equity:		
Share capital	100	100
Retained earnings	907	1,157
	1,007	1,257
Total liabilities and shareholders' equity	$2,981	$2,677

Your firm has been auditor of WHCL since its first audit in 20X0. It is now January 20X8. This is the first year that you are in charge of the audit. Yesterday, you visited WHCL and met with key personnel to discuss the forthcoming audit engagement. You obtained the following information.

1. In early fiscal 20X7, the company increased its debt load significantly by borrowing $300,000 from Colo Investors Ltd. Excerpts from the loan agreement are as follows:

Warmth Home Comfort Ltd. (the borrower) covenants that:
a. A current ratio of 1.2 or higher will be maintained; and
b. The debt-to-equity ratio will not exceed 2:1. Debt is defined as all liabilities of the company.

2. In 20X1, WHCL introduced a new model of gas furnace that is popular with consumers because its reduced gas consumption results in lower heating bills. The furnace design has remained virtually unchanged since it was introduced. The furnaces are sold with 10-year warranties on parts and labour. Historically, claims have been minimal.

    In the summer of 20X7, several warranty claims were made against WHCL. Routine inspections by gas-company employees revealed cracked heat exchangers, which could leak gases that might cause health problems when mixed with warm air inside the house. Thirty claims were made, and WHCL paid for repairs. The cost of repairing each furnace was $150, which was expensed by WHCL.

    Jacob Kovacs believes that the furnaces were damaged because of poor installation by contractors. He cannot see more than an additional 40 or 50 units being damaged. The 30 repaired furnaces were manufactured in 20X5 and 20X6. Over 10,000 units of this model have been sold over the past seven years.

    Later, in a discussion with the chief engineer, you learn that she had examined the heat exchanger used in the gas-furnace model in question and saw no evidence of a design flaw. However, she expressed concern that the problem might be due to heavy use of the furnace. She noted that the 30 reported problems were in northern locations where the demands on the equipment are considerable. Between 1,500 and 2,000 furnaces were installed in houses in those locations.

3. In January 20X7, WHCL bid on and won a $1.05 million contract to supply heating and air conditioning equipment for a large commercial and residential project. Construction on the project began in March 20X7.

    The fixed-price contract calls for WHCL to start delivering and installing the equipment in early September 20X7. In addition, WHCL has agreed to pay a penalty if the project is delayed because WHCL is unable to meet the agreed-to timetable. A brief strike by its factory employees has caused production and delivery to lag about two weeks behind schedule, so WHCL is shipping units as soon as they are produced. According to the agreement, half of the equipment has to be shipped and installed at the project site by the end of February 20X8. Jacob Kovacs is confident that WHCL will be able to catch up to the promised timetable.

    In 20X7, WHCL recognized $350,000 of revenue based on the number of units shipped to year-end. WHCL has received $50,000 for the units that have been installed by year-end.

4. Starting in February 20X8, WHCL will begin offering customers the option of paying a monthly fee for the use of a furnace. At the end of a certain number of years, the customer can purchase the unit for a nominal amount or ask for a replacement furnace and continue with the monthly payments. WHCL will do all maintenance at no cost until a customer purchases the unit. This scheme is intended to help WHCL remain competitive. The terms for such arrangements have not been finalized, but Jacob Kovacs is confident that they will increase sales revenue. Jacob has asked for advice on how to account for this arrangement.

    Your partner asks you to prepare a memo for him outlining the accounting issues that came to your attention as a result of your visit, applying IFRS.

Required:

Prepare the memo.

(Source: The Canadian Institute of Chartered Accountants, © 2010)

connect

TR18-1 Lease Classification:

Information has been gathered for three leases:

Lease	A	B	C
Fair value of equipment	$240,000	$110,000	$230,000
Title passes	no	no	no
Bargain purchase option	no	no	no
Useful life of equipment	10 years	7 years	9 years
Lease term	3 years	5 years	8 years
PV of minimum lease payments	$ 94,400	$95,000	$ 230,000
Residual, guaranteed, end of term lease	no	no	$ 5,000
Residual, unguaranteed, end of term lease	unknown	unknown	no

Required:

None of the leased assets are specialized for the lessee. Classify each lease as an operating lease or a finance lease. Provide a rationale for each decision.

connect

TR18-2 Operating Lease:

Argyle Ltd. signed a 36-month lease to rent a computer system for $5,400 per month. The value of the computer equipment is $400,000. The lease will commence on 1 November 20X1. As encouragement to lease the system, the lessor waived the first six months' rent. The remaining 30 payments will be due at the beginning of each month, starting on 1 May 20X2. Argyle Ltd.'s fiscal year-end is 31 December.

Required:

Prepare summary journal entries for Argyle for 20X1 and 20X2.

connect

TR18-3 Present Value:

Information has been gathered for two leases:

LEASE A

- The fair value of the equipment is $800,000 at the inception of the lease.
- The lease term is five years, and there is a three-year renewal term at the option of the lessor.
- Annual lease payments are $145,000 per year for the first five years and $100,000 for the next three years. Payments are due at the beginning of each lease year.
- All lease payments include the cost of insurance, estimated at $15,000 per year.
- The lessee guarantees a residual value of $40,000 at the end of the eighth year.
- The lessee does not know the lessor's implicit rate of interest in the lease. The lessee's incremental borrowing rate is 8%.

LEASE B

- The fair value of the equipment is $700,000 at the inception of the lease.
- The lease term is five years.
- Annual lease payments are $145,000 per year. Payments are due at the beginning of each lease year.
- The lessee is permitted to purchase the asset for $18,000 at the end of the lease term. This is considered a bargain.
- The lease payments include the cost of insurance, estimated at $12,000 per year.
- The lessor's implicit rate of interest in the lease is 6%. The lessee's incremental borrowing rate is 8%.

Required:

Calculate the present value of the minimum lease payments for each lease.

connect

TR18-4 Lease Liability Amortization Table:

Peridis Inc. has entered into a contract with an asset-based finance company to acquire some specialized equipment. The lease payments are $20,000 per year for eight years, with payments commencing at the start of each lease year. . At the end of the lease, Peridis guarantees to either (1) acquire the equipment from the lessor for $10,000 or (2) pay for the lessor's cost of removing the equipment, which also is estimated at $10,000. Peridis's incremental borrowing rate for this amount and term is estimated to be 8%. Peridis's fiscal year ends on 31 December.

Required:

1. Determine the present value of the lease payments.
2. Prepare a liability amortization table for this lease for Peridis.
3. Assume that the lease starts on 1 January 20X1. How much interest expense will Peridis report for each of 20X1 and 20X2?
4. Assume instead that the lease starts on 1 October 20X1. How much interest should the company record for each of 20X1 and 20X2?

■ connect

TR18-5 Lease Liability Amortization Table:

The following lease liability amortization table was developed for Smith Company and Lease 34T:

LEASE LIABILITY AMORTIZATION TABLE

Lease Year	Outstanding Balance	Interest	Payment	Incr/(Decr) in balance	Ending Balance
Aug. 1 20X1	$40,000		$ 11,720	($11,720)	$28,280
Aug. 1 20X2	28,280	1,980	$ 11,720	(9,740)	18,540
Aug. 1 20X3	18,540	1,298	$ 11,720	(10,422)	8,117
Aug. 1 20X4	8,117	568	$ 4,490	(3,922)	4,196
Aug. 1 20X5	4,196	294	$ 4,490	(4,196)	(0)

Required:

1. Provide an independent proof of the $18,540 liability balance after the second payment.
2. Smith has a 31 December fiscal year-end. How much interest expense is recorded in 20X3?
3. What is the balance in the lease liability account at 31 December 20X3? How much of this is a current liability versus a long-term liability?

■ connect

TR18-6 Depreciation Period:

Information has been gathered for three finance lease assets that will be accounted for through straight-line depreciation:

	Lease 1	Lease 2	Lease 3
Initial lease term	6 years	6 years	5 years
Renewal option, lessor's option	n/a	3 years	n/a
Renewal term, lessee's option	n/a	n/a	4 years
Economic life of the leased asset	7 years	10 years	10 years
Bargain purchase option included in lease contract	Yes	No	No

Required:

For each leased asset, choose a depreciation period. Explain your choice.

connect

TR18-7 Finance Lease:

Niko Ltd. signed a lease for a five-year term that requires yearly, beginning-of-year payments of $104,000, including $9,600 of annual maintenance and property taxes. Niko guarantees a residual value of $26,500 at the end of the lease term, although both parties expect the asset to be sold as used equipment for approximately $35,000 at that time.

Required:

1. How much are Niko's minimum lease payments, before discounting, as defined for lease accounting purposes?
2. If Niko's IBR is 10%, what amount will Niko record as an asset?
3. How much will Niko record as an asset if the residual value is *unguaranteed*?
4. Suppose that the fair value of the leased asset is $375,000 at the inception of the lease. How would this fact affect the amount recorded for the leased asset and the interest rate?

connect

TR18-8 Finance Lease:

Return to the lease liability amortization table developed for Smith Co. and Lease 34T in TR 18-5. Each lease payment also includes $1,000 of estimated insurance. That is, the cash payment is $1,000 higher than that listed in the table. The asset reverts to the lessor at the end of the lease term, and the residual value is unguaranteed.

Required:

Provide journal entries for Smith for 20X1 and 20X2. Smith has a 31 December fiscal year-end. Smith uses straight-line depreciation for similar assets, with a half-year of deprecation recorded in the year of acquisition.

connect

TR18-9 Appendix A; Lessor:

On 1 January 20X1, Canada Leasing Inc. acquired an asset on behalf of Magnum Ltd. for $100,000. Canada Leasing and Magnum enter into a six-year lease for the asset, effective 1 January 20X1, with equal payments at the beginning of each lease year. Canada Leasing will earn 8% (before taxes) on the lease. Canada Leasing has a 31 December fiscal year-end.

Required:

1. Determine the amount of each lease payment.
2. Make the journal entries that would appear in Canada Leasing Inc.'s accounts for 20X1, 20X2, and 20X3, using the net method of recording.
3. Repeat requirement 2, but use the gross method of recording the lease.
4. What amount(s) relating to the lease will be shown on Canada Leasing Inc.'s SFP on 31 December 20X3?

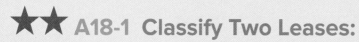

TR18-10 Appendix B; Lease Recognition:

On 1 March 20X4, Machine Manufacturing Co. leased a machine to Dry Goods through a three-year lease. The machine has an eight-year estimated useful life and no residual value at the end of the eighth year. The annual lease payments of $25,000 start on 1 March 20X4, and continue for three years. There is a guaranteed residual value of $18,000 at the end of the three-year lease term. The interest rate implicit in the lease is 8%, which is known. The incremental borrowing rate for Dry Goods is 6%. The accounting period ends on December 31.

Required:

1. Under the new lease standard, what amount will Dry Goods recognize as an asset on 1 March 20X4?
2. Is there any way to avoid recognition of the right-of-use asset for this lease?

ASSIGNMENTS

★★ A18-1 Classify Two Leases:

GBT Corp. has signed two leases in the past year. One lease is for handling equipment, the other for a truck.

HANDLING EQUIPMENT:

The handling equipment has a fair market value of $548,000. Lease payments are made each 2 January, the date the lease was signed. The lease is for four years and requires payments of $110,000 per year on each 2 January and can be renewed at the lessee's option for subsequent one-year terms up to three times, at a cost of $46,000 per year. At the end of any lease term, the equipment reverts to the lessor if GBT does not exercise its renewal option. Annual maintenance and insurance costs are paid by the lessor and are estimated to be $10,000 per year for the first four years and $6,000 per year thereafter. These costs are included in the lease payments. GBT estimates that the equipment has an economic life of eight to 10 years before it becomes obsolete.

TRUCK:

The truck has a list price of $270,000 but could be purchased with cash for 10% less. The truck lease runs for four years and has an annual lease payment of $40,000, due at the beginning of each year. The lease commences on 1 January. If the truck is used for more than 50,000 kilometres in any 12-month period, a payment of $0.50 per extra kilometre must be paid in addition to the annual rental. GBT is responsible for all operating and maintenance costs.

At the end of the four-year lease agreement, GBT may, at its option, renew the lease for an additional period; term and payments to be negotiated at that time.

GBT has an 8% incremental borrowing rate. The company uses straight-line depreciation for all of its tangible capital assets, using the half-year convention (i.e., a half-year depreciation in the first and last years). The truck has an estimated useful life of 10 years.

Required:

Classify each lease as a finance or operating lease. Justify your response.

 # A18-2 Terminology; Classification; Entries:

Plaid Ltd. has a 6% incremental borrowing rate. On 1 January 20X1, Plaid signed a lease agreement for a piece of equipment. The equipment has a fair value of $38,000 and a 12-year economic life. Other information is as follows:

- The noncancellable lease is for eight years.
- The lease payment is $4,800 annually, payable at the beginning of each lease year.
- Lease payments include $720 of maintenance expense annually.
- At the end of the lease term, the leased asset reverts to the lessor.

Other information:

- Plaid has a fiscal year that ends on 31 December.
- Plaid uses straight-line depreciation for similar fixed assets.

Required:

1. For this lease, provide the:
    a. Lease term;
    b. Guaranteed residual value;
    c. Unguaranteed residual value;
    d. Bargain purchase option; and
    e. Minimum net lease payment.
    If these amounts do not exist in the above lease, enter "none" as your response. State any assumptions.
2. Is this lease an operating lease or a finance lease for the lessee? Explain your reasoning.
3. Prepare the journal entries for the first year of the lease on Plaid's books.
4. Would your answer to requirement 2 change if the lease contained a guaranteed residual value of $10,000? Explain.

★ ★ A18-3 Terminology; Classification; Entries:

Canadian Leasing Inc. leased a piece of machinery to Ornamental Concrete Ltd., with the following terms:

- The lease is for five years; Ornamental cannot cancel the lease during this period.
- The lease payment is $79,600 per year. Included in this is $7,900 in estimated insurance costs.
- At the end of the five-year initial lease term, Ornamental can elect to renew the lease for one additional five-year term at a price of $29,500, including $2,500 of estimated insurance costs. Market rentals are approximately twice as expensive.
- At the end of the first or second lease term, the leased asset reverts to the lessor.
- Lease payments are due at the beginning of each lease year.

Other information:

- Ornamental could borrow money to buy this asset at an interest rate of 8%.
- The equipment has a fair market value of $430,000 at the beginning of the lease term and a useful life of approximately 12 years.
- The lease term corresponds to the fiscal year.
- Ornamental uses straight-line depreciation for all capital assets.

Required:

1. For this lease, provide the:
   a. Lease term;
   b. Guaranteed residual value;
   c. Unguaranteed residual value;
   d. Bargain purchase option;
   e. Bargain renewal terms;
   f. Minimum net lease payment; and
   g. Incremental borrowing rate.

   If these amounts do not exist in the above lease, enter "none" as your response. State any assumptions.
2. Is this lease an operating lease or a finance lease for the lessee? Why?
3. Prepare journal entries for the first year of the lease on Ornamental's books.

★ A18-4 Lease Classification and Operating Lease:

Lockhart Co. complies with IFRS reporting standards. Lockhart signed a lease for a truck on November 1, 20X1 that had the following terms:

- The lease payments are $34,700 per year, payable each November 1 for nine years. (However, the lease term is 12 years. See below)
- The lease payments include $2,100 for insurance expense.
- After the lease payment on November 1, Year 9, the lessee can keep the asset for free until November 1, 20X13.

- The asset will be returned to the lessor on November 1, 20X13, and the lessor will sell the asset. If the lessor does not receive at least $30,000, then Lockhart will make up the difference.
- The leased asset has a useful life of 20 years and a fair value of $400,000.
- The interest rate implicit in the lease is 6%. Lockhart has a normal borrowing rate of 7%.

Required:

1. Classify the lease as an operating lease or a finance lease.
2. Assume this is an operating lease and calculate the total rent expense for the year ended 31 December 20X1.

★ A18-5 Operating Lease; Lessee Inducement:

Legal Services Inc. leases space in an office complex and has recently signed a new, four-year lease, at the rate of $9,200 per month. However, the lessor offered six months "free" rent at the beginning of the lease as an inducement to sign the lease agreement.

The lease agreement was signed on 1 October 20X1; the lease will commence on 1 November 20X1. The company has a 31 December fiscal year-end. Rent is due on the first day of each month.

Required:

1. Prepare journal entries for the first, sixth, and seventh months of the lease. Assume that financial statements are prepared monthly.
2. What amounts would be shown on the company's SCI and SFP for this lease as of 31 December 20X2?

 connect

★ ★ A18-6 Finance Lease; Lessee Liability Amortization Table and Entries

On 31 December 20X0, Columbia Inc. entered into an agreement with Scotia Ltd. to lease equipment. Columbia Inc. will make four equal payments of $80,000 at the beginning of each lease year. Columbia Ltd. anticipates that the equipment will have a residual value of $64,000 at the end of the lease, net of removal costs. Columbia Inc. has the option of (1) paying $64,000 to retain the equipment or (2) allowing Scotia Ltd. to remove it.

Scotia Ltd.'s implicit interest rate in this lease is 7%. Columbia Inc.'s incremental borrowing rate is 8%. Columbia Inc. depreciates the leased equipment on a straight-line basis over four years. The lease commences on 1 January 20X1. Assume that the fair value of the equipment on the open market is greater than the present value of the lease payments.

Required:

1. Prepare a lease liability amortization table for this lease for Columbia Inc.
2. Prepare all entries that Columbia Inc. will record for this lease and the leased equipment for 20X1 and 20X2.

e**X**cel

★ ★ A18-7 Finance Lease:

On 2 January 20X4, Yvan Ltd., a public company, entered into a five-year equipment lease with Jeffery Leasing Inc. The lease calls for annual lease payments of $150,000, payable at the beginning of each lease year. Yvan's IBR is 7%. Yvan does not know the lessor's interest rate. The fair value of the equipment is $675,000. Yvan depreciates equipment on a straight-line basis, taking a full year's depreciation in the year of acquisition.

Required:

1. Prepare the lease liability amortization schedule for Yvan.

2. Prepare the journal entries relating to the leased asset and the lease liability for 20X4 and 20X5 for Yvan.

3. What amounts will appear on Yvan's statement of financial position, statement of comprehensive income, and statement of cash flows as of 31 December 20X4?

e**X**cel

★ ★ ★ A18-8 Finance Lease; Fair Value Cap:

On 31 December 20X1, Lessee Ltd. entered into a lease agreement by which Lessee leased a jutling machine for six years. Annual lease payments are $20,000, payable at the beginning of each lease year (31 December). At the end of the lease, possession of the machine will revert to the lessor. The normal economic life for this type of machine is 8 to 10 years.

At the time of the lease agreement, jutling machines could be purchased for approximately $90,000 cash. Equivalent financing for the machine could have been obtained from Lessee's bank at 14%.

Lessee's fiscal year coincides with the calendar year. Lessee uses straight-line depreciation for its jutling machines.

Required:

1. Prepare a lease liability amortization table for the lease, assuming that Lessee accounts for it as a finance lease.

2. Prepare all journal entries relating to the lease and the leased asset for 20X1, 20X2, and 20X3.

3. How would the amounts relating to the leased asset and lease liability be shown on Lessee's statement of financial position at 31 December 20X4?

4. Repeat requirement 2 assuming that the fair market value of the equipment was $77,273 at the inception of the lease.

 connect

★ ★ A18-9 Finance Lease:

Watson Co. entered into a financing lease for a truck on 1 April 20X2 that had the following terms:

- The lease payments are $12,500 per year, payable each 1 April for four years.
- The lease may be renewed at the option of the lessor for a further five years for $3,600 per year.
- The initial lease term payments include $1,200 for maintenance expenses, but there is no maintenance built into the second lease payment stream.
- There is a guaranteed residual value of $15,000 at the end of the first lease term and $5,000 at the end of the second lease term. (These are not bargain purchase options.)
- The leased asset has a useful life of ten years and a fair value of $70,000.
- The interest rate implicit in the lease is 7%.

Required:

1. The residual values are not bargain purchase options, as stated above. What evidence would be collected to support this conclusion?
2. The lessee doesn't own this truck. Why is it an asset on its SFP?
3. Calculate the present value of the minimum lease payments.
4. Prepare a lease liability amortization table for only the first four payments.
5. List the items that would appear in the lessee's SCI for the year ended 31 December 20X3.
6. What is the amount of the total lease liability on the balance sheet on 31 December 20X3? Split this amount into the current and long-term portions.

Jain Corp. has negotiated a lease for new machinery. The machinery has a fair value of $412,500 and an expected economic life of seven years. The lease has a five-year term. Annual rental is paid at the beginning of the lease year, in the amount of $78,225. Insurance and operating costs, approximately $15,000, are paid directly by Jain and are not included in the lease payments. At the end of the lease term, the machinery will revert to the lessor, which will sell it for an expected $56,250. If the lessor does not realize $56,250 in the sale, then Jain has agreed to make up the difference. Jain does not know the lessor's implicit interest rate.

Required:

1. Prepare a lease liability amortization table for the lease. Jain's IBR is 10%.
2. Assume that the lease was entered into on 1 January 20X2. Jain has a 31 December fiscal year-end. Prepare journal entries for the lease for 20X2, including depreciation.
3. Assume that at the end of the lease, the lessor is able to sell the asset for $45,000 and that Jain makes up the shortfall. Prepare Jain's entry to record the lease termination (after first recording interest to the date of the transaction).

Griffiths Ltd. has a five-year financing lease, and the following lease liability amortization table was prepared when the lease was originally signed, using an 8% interest rate. Note the presence of a guaranteed residual value at the end of the lease term.

SCHEDULE OF LEASE LIABILITY AMORTIZATION					
Lease Payment	Outstanding Balance	Interest	Payment	Incr./(Decr.) in Balance	Ending Balance
Opening; first	$59,000	--	$ 13,000	($13,000)	$46,000
second	46,000	$3,680	13,000	(9,320)	36,680
third	36,680	2,934	13,000	(10,066)	26,614
fourth	26,614	2,129	13,000	(10,871)	15,744
fifth	15,744	1,259	13,000	(11,741)	4,003
final	4,003	320	4,323	(4,003)	0

Required:

1. The lease was entered into on 1 March 20X5. Give the journal entries for 20X5, up to and including the 31 December 20X5 adjusting journal entries for the end of the fiscal year. The company uses the half-year rule for depreciation.

2. It is now 31 December 20X7. All payments have been made on schedule, and all entries have been made correctly. Calculate 20X7 total interest expense, and the amount that will appear on the 31 December 20X7 SFP with respect to the lease liability. Show the current and long-term amounts separately.

3. The residual value, guaranteed by Griffiths, was $4,323, and this was felt to be a valid estimate all during the lease life. However, at the end of the fifth lease year, the asset was sold for $2,700, and the appropriate amount was remitted to the lessor. Provide all journal entries that would be made on this date with respect to interest, depreciation, the sale and final payment to the lessor.

★ ★ A18-12 **Lessee Liability Amortization Table; Entries:**

Bombay Ltd. is expanding and needs more manufacturing equipment. The company has been offered a lease contract for equipment with a fair value of $260,000. The lease has a five-year term, with beginning-of-year payments. The lease is renewable for a further two years at the option of the lessee. Annual rental for the first term is $57,200, for the second, $23,000. The inception of the lease is 1 January, and payments are made each 1 January. The first term rental includes $5,200 for maintenance and insurance, the second, $3,000. Lease payments are close to market lease rates for both the first and second terms. At the end of the second term, Bombay can buy the asset for $1. The machinery has an expected life of 10 years. Bombay has an incremental borrowing rate of 10%. Bombay has been told that the interest rate implicit in the lease is 8%.

Required:

1. Prepare a lease liability amortization table for the lease.

2. Assume that the lease was entered into on 1 January 20X2. Bombay has a 31 December fiscal year-end. Prepare journal entries for the lease for 20X2, including any entries relating to the asset.

3. Prepare the entry or entries necessary on 31 December 20X9, assuming Bombay exercises the bargain purchase option.

★ ★ A18-13 Finance Lease:

Sondheim Ltd. entered into a finance lease with New Age Leasing Corp. The lease is for new specialized factory equipment that has a fair value of $3,200,000. The expected useful life of the equipment is 10 years, although its physical life is far greater. The initial lease term begins on 1 April 20X2 and runs for 10 years. Annual lease payments are $400,000, payable at the beginning of each lease year. After the initial lease term, Sondheim has the option of renewing the lease on a year-by-year basis for as long as Sondheim wishes. Since the equipment will be obsolete by that time, the renewal is set at $10,000 per year, which is expected to be a fair rental value for equipment of that age. Other information is as follows:

- The interest rate implicit in the lease is 7%; Sondheim's incremental borrowing rate is 6%.
- Sondheim will amortize the equipment on a straight-line basis over the lease term and has a 31 December fiscal year-end.

Required:

1. Prepare the journal entries relating to the lease liability and the leased equipment for Sondheim for 20X2, including all appropriate adjusting entries.
2. What amounts will appear on Sondheim's SFP and SCF for the year ended 31 December 20X2?

★ ★ ★ A18-14 Finance Lease; Lessee Reporting:

Videos-to-Go signed a lease for a vehicle that had an expected economic life of eight years and a fair value of $18,000. The lessor is the leasing subsidiary of a national car manufacturer. The terms of the lease are as follows:

- The lease term begins on 1 January 20X2 and runs for five years.
- The lease requires payments of $5,800 each 1 January, including $1,700 for maintenance and insurance costs.
- At the end of the lease term, the lease is renewable for three one-year periods, for $2,600 per year, including $2,100 for maintenance and insurance. The normal rental costs for a similar used vehicle would be approximately double this amount.
- At the end of any lease term, if Videos-to-Go does not renew the contract, the vehicle reverts to the lessor. The lessor may choose to leave the vehicle with Videos-to-Go if its value is low.

Videos-to-Go does not know the interest rate implicit in the lease from the lessor's perspective but has an incremental borrowing rate of 12%. Videos-to-Go has a 31 December year-end and uses straight-line depreciation for all assets.

Required:

1. Prepare a lease liability amortization schedule.
2. Prepare journal entries for 20X2 and 20X3.
3. Show how the lease would be reflected on the SFP, SCI, and SCF for 20X2 and 20X3. Segregate debt between its current and noncurrent components.
4. How much interest expense would be reported on the SCI in each year from 20X2 to 20X9 if Videos-to-Go has a 31 May fiscal year-end?

eXcel

★ ★ ★ A18-15 Finance Lease; Guaranteed Residual:

Lessee Ltd. agreed to a noncancellable lease for which the following information is available:

a. The asset is new at the inception of the lease term and is worth $160,000.

b. Lease term is four years, starting 1 January 20X1.

c. Estimated useful life of the leased asset is six years.

d. The residual value of the leased asset will be $30,000 at the end of the lease term. The residual value is guaranteed by Lessee.

e. The declining-balance depreciation method is used for the leased asset, at a rate of 30% per year.

f. Lessee's incremental borrowing rate is 10%.

g. Four annual lease payments will be made each 1 January during the lease term, and the first payment, due at inception of the lease term, is $43,130, including $5,500 of maintenance costs.

h. Lessee has a 31 December fiscal year-end.

Required:

1. Is this an operating lease or a finance lease? Explain.

2. Prepare a table showing how the lease liability reduces over the lease term.

3. Record the entries for 20X1.

4. Prepare the financial statement presentation of all lease-related accounts as they would appear in the financial statements of the lessee at 31 December 20X1.

★ ★ A18-16 Sale and Leaseback:

On 31 March 20X2, Supergrocery Inc. sold its major distribution facility, with a 30-year remaining life, to a real estate investment trust (REIT) for $9,000,000 cash. The facility had an original cost of $10,400,000 and accumulated depreciation of $3,600,000 on the date of sale.

Also on 31 March 20X2, Supergrocery signed a 20-year lease agreement with the REIT, leasing the property back. At the end of the 20-year lease term, legal title to the facility will be transferred to Supergrocery. Annual payments, beginning on 31 March 20X2, are $875,000. Maintenance and repair costs are the responsibility of Supergrocery. Supergrocery has an incremental borrowing rate of 9%. The company uses straight-line depreciation and has a 31 December year-end. Supergrocery records a part-year's depreciation on buildings, based on the date of acquisition.

Required:

1. Give the 20X2 entries that Supergrocery would make to record the sale and the lease.

2. Show how the SFP and SCI would reflect the transactions at the end of 20X2. Do not segregate statement of financial position items between current and noncurrent items.

★ ★ A18-17 Sale and Leaseback:

Central Purchasing Ltd. (CPL) owns the building it uses; it had an original cost of $825,000 and a net book value of $250,000 as of 1 January 20X2. On this date, the building was sold to a real estate investment trust (REIT) for $500,000, which also was the building's fair value, and simultaneously leased back to CPL.

The lease has a guaranteed, 12-year term and required payments on 31 December of each year. The payments are $76,500, and the lease allows the property to revert to the lessee at the end of the lease. CPL could have mortgaged this property under similar terms at an interest rate of 9%. The REIT will pay property taxes estimated to be $16,200 per year. These costs are included in the lease payment. CPL will pay maintenance and operating costs. The building is being depreciated straight-line, with an estimated remaining life of 16 years.

Required:

1. Prepare entries to record the sale and leaseback of the building.

2. Prepare year-end adjusting entries for 20X2.

3. Show how all amounts related to the sale and leaseback will be presented on the statement of financial position and statement of comprehensive income in 20X2.

★ ★ A18-18 Sale and Leaseback:

Sportco Ltd. is suffering temporary cash flow difficulties due to poor economic conditions. To raise sufficient finances to allow operations to continue until economic conditions improve, Sportco entered into an agreement with a major lease corporation, Leaseco. On 1 January 20X2, Sportco sold its largest manufacturing property to Leaseco at its fair market value, $1,750,000. The property had a net book value of $250,000 at the time of the sale.

Sportco, in turn, leased back the property from Leaseco for 15 years. The annual rent was $175,000, due each year starting on 1 January 20X2. Sportco can repurchase the property from Leaseco at the end of the lease term for $1. The land value is estimated to be 40% of the total fair market value of the property, while the building represents the other 60%. Sportco amortizes its buildings at a declining-balance rate of 10%.

Sportco's incremental borrowing rate is 7%. Its financial statements are prepared in accordance with generally accepted accounting principles.

Required:

How should Sportco account for this transaction in its financial statements for the year ending 31 December 20X2? Be specific, and explain the approach that you have chosen.

(Source: The Canadian Institute of Chartered Accountants, © 2010)

★ ★ A18-19 Statement of Cash Flows; Review:

Each of the following items must be considered in preparing a statement of cash flows for Phillie Fashions Inc. for the year ended 31 December 20X6:

1. Fixed assets that had a cost of $10,000 6½ years before and were being depreciated straight line on a 10-year basis, with no estimated scrap value, were sold for $3,125.

2. Phillie leased an asset in lieu of buying it. Phillie recognized an asset and liability of $25,400 at the end of the year. No interest or depreciation was recorded because the transaction took place at the end of the fiscal

year. The first lease payment of $7,000 was made at the end of the fiscal year, reducing the lease liability to $18,400.

3. During the year, goodwill of $5,000 was completely written off to expense.

4. During the year, 250 shares of common stock were issued for $32 per share.

5. Fixed asset depreciation amounted to $1,000 and patent amortization was $200.

6. Bonds payable with a par value of $12,000, on which there was an unamortized bond premium of $360, were redeemed at 103.

7. Phillie, as lessee, reported a net lease liability of $14,678 at the end of 20X6 in relation to equipment that had been leased since 20X4. In 20X5, the liability had been $15,766. The current portion of the liability was $2,410 each year.

Required:

For each item, state what would be included in the statement of cash flows, whether it is an inflow or outflow, and the amount(s). Assume that correct entries were made for all transactions as they took place and that the indirect method is to be used to disclose cash flow from operations. In your response, use a three-column format as follows:

Operating/Investing/Financing	Inflow/Outflow	Amount

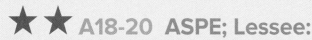 **A18-20 ASPE; Lessee:**

Refer to the information in A18-13. Assume that Sondheim is a private enterprise that has chosen to use ASPE.

Required:

1. Determine the present value of Sondheim's lease payments.

2. What amounts relating to the lease (and the leased asset) will Sondheim report in the company's statement of financial position and its statement of comprehensive income for the year ending 31 December 20X2?

3. If A18-13 has been solved, explain the relative impact of using ASPE, as compared with IFRS.

★ **A18-21 ASPE; Lessee:**

On 24 February 20X1, Ready Distributing Ltd., a private company, signed a lease for conveyor equipment. This is specialized equipment that can be used only in Ready's manufacturing plant. The fair value of the leased equipment is $500,000.

The lease will commence on 1 October 20X1. The lease is for four years with lease payments of $120,000 per year, due at the beginning of each year. The lessor does not require a residual value guarantee. The equipment's estimated economic life is 10 years.

Ready's incremental borrowing rate is a nominal 6% per annum, and the interest rate implicit in the lease is 7%.

Required:

Classify the lease under IFRS, and then under ASPE. Include an evaluation of all guidelines.

 **A18-22 ASPE; Lessee and Lessor:**

On 10 December 20X0, Noel Inc. entered into a six-year equipment lease with Williams Ltd. The terms of the lease are as follows:

- The lease will term begin on 1 January 20X1.
- The fair value of the equipment at the inception of the lease is $120,000. The equipment's expected useful life is six or seven years.
- Noel Inc.'s incremental borrowing rate is 11%.
- Lease payments are $25,000 per year, payable at the end of each lease year. That is, the first payment will be due by 31 December 20X1.
- Because of Noel Inc.'s shaky financial condition, Williams Ltd. determined the lease payments based on a 12% return, which is higher than Williams Ltd.'s normal return, Noel Inc. is aware of Williams Ltd.'s rate.

Both Noel and Williams apply ASPE accounting standards.

Required:

1. Should Noel account for this lease as a capital lease or an operating lease? Explain fully and evaluate all guidelines.
2. How should Williams report this lease? Explain fully.
3. What anomaly arises under ASPE when the lessor is bearing a higher-than-normal risk of default by the lessee?

 A18-23 Appendix A; Finance Lease; Lessor; Amortization Table; Gross and Net Method Entries

Refer to the information in A18-6.

Required:

1. Prepare an amortization table for this lease for the lessor.
2. Prepare all entries that the lessor will record for this lease over its full term, using the gross method. Assume that the lessee exercises the purchase option.
3. On the lessor's 31 December 20X2 SFP, what amount will appear for the net lease receivable?
4. Prepare all entries that the lessor will record for this lease for the first two years, using the net method.

A18-24 Appendix A; Finance Lease; Lessor:

Refer to the information in A18-7. Jeffrey Leasing Inc. is a public company. Jeffrey's implicit interest rate in the Yvan lease is 6%.

Required:

1. Prepare the lease net receivable amortization schedule for Jeffrey.
2. Prepare the journal entries relating to the lease for Jeffrey for 20X4 and 20X5, using the net method of recording the leased asset.
3. Repeat requirement 2, using the gross method.

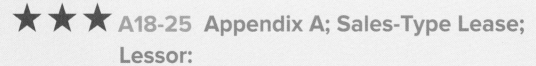

★ ★ ★ A18-25 Appendix A; Sales-Type Lease; Lessor:

Jordin is an equipment dealer that occasionally uses leasing as a means of selling its products. On 1 January 20X1, Jordin leased equipment to Easten Corp. The lease term was four years with annual lease payments of $5,769 to be paid on each 31 December. The equipment has an estimated zero residual value at the end of the lease term. The equipment was carried in Jordin's accounts at a cost of $15,000. Jordin expects to collect all rentals from Easten, and there were no material cost uncertainties at the inception of the lease. The implicit interest rate in the lease was 11%.

Required:

1. Why is this a sales-type lease for Jordin?
2. How much is the gross profit or loss recognized by Jordin? The finance revenue recognized over the life of the lease?
3. Assume that the implicit interest rate is 4% (not 11%). How much is the gross profit or loss recognized by Jordin? The finance revenue recognized over the life of the lease?
4. Give the entries made by Jordin (based on the 11% rate) at the inception of the lease. Use the gross method.
5. Based on requirement 4, show all lease-related accounts as they would appear in the SFP and SCI of the lessor at 31 December 20X1, for the year then ended. The lessor's SFP is unclassified.

★ ★ A18-26 Appendix A; Sales-Type Lease; Lessor:

On 14 June 20X1, Bruckner Corp. entered into an agreement to lease materials-handling equipment from Mahler Inc. The five-year lease commences on 1 July 20X1. Bruckner will pay lease payments of $100,000 at the beginning of each lease year. Bruckner also guarantees a residual value of $50,000.

Mahler is the manufacturer of the equipment Bruckner is leasing. The standard cost of manufacture is $350,000. The leased equipment normally sells for $480,000. When Mahler negotiates a lease with a customer, the company's expected rate of return varies with economic conditions and the cost of capital; currently, Mahler negotiates leases to obtain a return of 8%.

Required:

Prepare the appropriate entries for Mahler for 20X1 and 20X2 to record this lease, including the receipt of payments and the recognition of any revenue and expense. Mahler has a 31 December fiscal year-end.

★ A18-27 Appendix B; Equipment; Lessee:

On 18 December 20X1, Kushner Construction Ltd. leased a crane from Schultz Equipment Inc. for use in a building project. The lease is for three years. The lease commences on 1 January 20X2. Annual lease payments are $150,000, payable at the beginning of each year. In addition, Kushner must pay $45,000 for delivery and set-up of the crane and another $45,000 at the end of the lease term for deconstruction and removal of the crane. The lease is not renewable. Schultz will lease the crane to other construction companies after Kushner's project is finished. The crane has a fair value of $700,000 and a useful life of ten years. Kushner's incremental borrowing rate is 8%.

Required:

1. Classify the lease under the existing lease standard, and then under the new standard.
2. Using the new standard, calculate the amount that would be recorded as a right-of-use asset on 1 January 20X2.

★ A18-28 Appendix B; Equipment; Lessee:

Keener Construction Ltd. leased equipment from Dominion Leasing Inc. for use in a building project. The lease is for five years and Keener has a bargain purchase option of $5,000 at the end of the five-year term. The lease commences on 1 January 20X5. Annual lease payments are $100,000, payable at the beginning of each year. In addition, Keener must pay $30,000 for delivery and set-up of the equipment. The equipment has a fair value of $600,000 and a useful life of six years. Keener's incremental borrowing rate is 6%.

Required:

1. Classify the lease under the existing lease standard, and then under the new standard.
2. Using the new standard, calculate the amount that would be recorded as a right-of-use asset on 1 January 20X5.

★ A18-29 Appendix B; Building; Lessee:

Mackenzie Ltd. leased a building from Brooklong Inc. The lease term was four years; the annual rent was $60,000 due at the start of each lease year. The lease commenced on 1 January 20X1. The building has an expected useful life of 40 years. Mackenzie's incremental borrowing rate is 6%.

Required:

1. Classify the lease under the existing lease standard, and then under the new standard.
2. Using the new standard, calculate the amount that would be recorded as a right-of-use asset on 1 January 20X1.

★ A18-30 Appendix B; Equipment; Lessee:

Open Ltd. leased equipment from Hamilton Rent-It Inc. The lease term was three years; the annual rent was $40,000 due at the start of each lease year. Initial costs for installation were $20,000, paid by Open. The equipment has an expected useful life of eight years and a fair value of $250,000. The lease commenced on 1 January 20X4. Open's incremental borrowing rate is 5%.

Required:

1. Classify the lease under the existing lease standard, and then under the new standard.
2. Using the new standard, calculate the amount that would be recorded as a right-of-use asset on 1 January 20X4.

APPENDIX 1

LESSOR ACCOUNTING

Lessors: A Finance Industry

Lessors constitute a highly concentrated specialized industry. The specialized nature of leasing is the result of the provisions of the *Income Tax Act*. Only companies that derive at least 90% of their revenue from leasing are permitted to deduct CCA in excess of rental revenue—a crucial aspect of successful lessor activity. Often, lessors are subsidiaries of broader financial institutions, such as chartered banks or asset-based lending institutions. There are no separate publicly listed lessors in Canada.

Captive Finance Companies

A lessor may also be a finance subsidiary of a manufacturer that was set up to facilitate sales of the manufacturer's products. These subsidiaries are known as **captive leasing companies**. For example, private-company Daimler Chrysler Financial Services Inc. offers sales financing through its subsidiaries, Chrysler Financial Canada, Mercedes-Benz Credit Canada, and Truck Finance Canada.

A manufacturing company also may carry out leasing services by incorporating a special purpose entity (SPE) that is then consolidated into the parent company's financial statements.

Lessor accounting is very complex, and this overview is meant to lightly cover the major issues.

First, a lessor may have an operating lease or a finance lease. *The lessor uses the same classification criteria as the lessee,* although the interest rate used for discounting is always the interest rate implicit in the lease. If the lease is a finance lease, the lease may either be a straight finance lease or a sales-type lease.

LESSOR ACCOUNTING— OPERATING LEASES

Operating Lease—Lessor Accounting

A lease is an operating lease if it is not a finance lease. When the lease is an operating lease, the lessor receives the periodic rent payment and credits rental income or lease income. The lessor credits the cash receipts to an income account, such as *rent revenue* (or *other income* if leasing is not one of the company's mainstream business activities.) Returning to the crane rental example earlier in the chapter, the $20,000 monthly payment is recorded by Empire Equipment Ltd. (EEL), the lessor:

| Cash | 20,000 | |
| Rent revenue—crane | | 20,000 |

However, the lessor must acquire a piece of equipment before it can be leased out. The crane cost $1,580,000 to purchase and is expected to be useful for 10 years. The crane will appear on the lessor's SFP as "equipment available for lease" and will be depreciated over its estimated useful life.

In our example, the lessee also paid $15,000 for initial costs of having the crane moved and installed, ready for use. For the lessor, the payment is reimbursement for labour and transportation costs that the lessor incurs to make sure that the crane is handled and assembled safely. The lessor would have capitalized these costs to the crane asset account, and now cash received is credited to this account.

The lessor entries are summarized in Exhibit 18A-1. There are no special complications for this revenue stream.

EXHIBIT 18A-1

LESSOR ACCOUNTING OPERATING LEASES

Lessor Accounting—Empire Equipment Ltd.

6 January—purchase of crane:		
Equipment for available for lease	1,580,000	
Cash		1,580,000
January—installation costs (assumed):		
Equipment for available for lease	15,000	
Cash		15,000

1 February—receipt of installation fee:		
Cash	15,000	
Equipment for available for lease		15,000

Summary entry—receipt of rent:		
Cash	200,000	
Lease revenue ($20,000 × 10 months)		200,000

31 December—depreciation of crane		
Depreciation expense*	132,000	
Accumulated depreciation— crane		132,000

*$1,580,000 − $260,000 residual value, assumed ÷ 10 years = $132,000

LESSOR ACCOUNTING—FINANCE LEASES

A lease is a finance lease if it transfers the risks and rewards of ownership to the lessee. Meeting any one of the four guidelines explained in the chapter provides evidence of a finance lease.

Differences between Lessee's and Lessor's Net Cash Flows

The lessor will work with the same basic set of lease terms, except that the lessor must use the interest rate that is implicit in the lease. This is the rate of return that equates the present value of the lease payments, plus the present value of the tax savings, to the cost of acquiring the asset. Asset cost includes any direct costs incurred in negotiations and any incidental costs to acquire the asset (e.g., transportation, commissions, etc.). There are some aspects of the lease that do not apply to the lessee and that therefore differentiate the lessor's net cash flow from that of the lessee. The three most important differences are:

1. *The initial cost of the asset.* The lessor may obtain a more favourable price on the asset, often by bulk buying. For example, lessors that deal in aircraft leasing usually buy a large number of planes from the manufacturer and then lease them in smaller quantities to a several individual airlines. By bulk buying, the lessor can negotiate especially favourable prices that would not be available to individual airlines. Therefore, an asset's cost to the lessor may be significantly less than the asset's fair value as perceived by the lessee.

2. *Residual value.* The lessor may expect a significant residual value. For example, when an airplane's lease with a mainline carrier ends, the residual value of the plane may still be quite high because smaller carriers, charter airlines, and cargo lines will use older planes.

3. *Tax shield.* The lessor can gain a significant tax shield from the aircraft's depreciation. The early tax cash flow savings from deducting tax depreciation (CCA) will increase the after-tax cash flow from the lease, especially in the early years, greatly affecting the internal rate of return (IRR) on the lease.

We will not incorporate tax implications in this discussion, because it is a highly specialized topic.

Internal Rate of Return

The lessor accounts for the lease by the effective interest method. It may seem apparent that the lessor would automatically know the interest rate that it is charging the lessee. However, leases are *negotiated*, and since the lessor's cash flows will not be exact mirrors of the lessee's cash flow, the lessor's effective interest rate may not be obvious. Therefore, we must first determine the interest rate implicit in the lease, which represents the **internal rate of return** (**IRR**) that a lessor is earning (before tax) in this lease.

Return to the basic example in the chapter; we will now look at this lease from the perspective of Borat Corp, the lessor. The facts of the example are repeated here, in Exhibit 18A-2. Additional facts:

- Borat negotiated a purchase price of $60,000 for the asset, although the list price is higher, at $66,000. Additional direct costs amounted to $1,500.

- The expected unguaranteed residual value at the end of the lease term (i.e., five years), unknown to the lessee, is $4,300.

EXHIBIT 18A-2

LEASE TERMS—BASIC EXAMPLE

- The fair value of the asset is $66,000.
- The lease begins on 1 January 20X2.
- The initial lease term is three years.
- Payments over the initial lease term are $20,000 per year, payable at the beginning of each lease year (i.e., on 1 January 20X2, 20X3, and 20X4).
- At the end of the initial lease term, the lease is renewable for another two years *at Lessee's option* for $5,000 per year. Assume that the normal rental cost of three-year-old equipment of this type is almost $10,000 per year.
- Lessee is responsible for insuring and maintaining the equipment.
- The asset reverts to the lessor at the end of the lease; the lease agreement contains no obligation for Lessee to *guarantee* the residual value.
- Lessee does not know the lessor's implicit rate of interest in the lease. Lessee's incremental borrowing rate is 8%.

The lessor uses the estimate of residual value when determining the lease's implicit interest rate, regardless of whether it is guaranteed or unguaranteed by the lessee. The best estimate of residual value is used in the IRR calculation, whether it is guaranteed or unguaranteed.

To find the internal rate of return, we find the value of *i* in the following equation:

$$\$60,000 + \$1,500 = \$20,000\ (P/AD, i, 3) + \$5,000\ (P/AD, i, 2)\ (P/F, i, 3) + \$4,300(P/F, i, 5)$$

This equation can be solved by using or an Excel spreadsheet or a financial calculator.

The value of *i* that satisfies this equation is 14%. The lessor's rate of return is significantly higher than the 8% cost to Lessee. The higher rate is due to the lower purchase price that the lessor was able to negotiate, plus (to a lesser extent) the unguaranteed residual value. This phenomenon is what can make leasing quite attractive in the right circumstances.

FINANCE LEASE ACCOUNTING— LESSOR

The first type of lease we shall examine from the lessor's perspective is a finance lease.

Finance Lease Lessor Accounting—Net Lease Basis

Initial Recording

As we discussed previously, finance leasing companies are often financial institutions or financial intermediaries. Their business is to provide financing for an entity's asset acquisition, financing that is in the form of a lease rather than purchase financing, such as a direct loan. The lessor really does not want any physical assets—the lessor's assets are *financial* assets. Thus, when a lessor acquires an asset on behalf of a lessee, the asset is delivered directly to the lessee.

Instead of recording the physical asset, the lessor records the *net lease receivable*. The **net lease receivable** is the present value of the lease payment agreement, including the guaranteed or unguaranteed residual, discounted at the interest rate implicit in the lease. *It is also equal to the amount that the lessor spent (or owes) for the asset and associated direct costs.* After all, the lessor negotiates a lease agreement with the lessee that will enable the lessor to recover all of the investment in the leased asset as well as earn interest. The entry for Borat would appear as follows:

Net lease receivable	61,500	
Cash (and/or accounts payable)*		61,500
* This entry assumes that the asset is purchased simultaneously with the lease contract. If the leased asset were already on the books of the lessor, the asset would be credited instead of cash.		

After initially recording the lease, Borat will account for each lease payment as a combination of (1) interest income and (2) principal payments to reduce the outstanding lease receivable. This is the reverse of the lessee's lease liability, but the amounts usually will be different because the lessor has a somewhat different cash flow. A receivable amortization table will clarify the lessor's accounting.

Receivable Amortization Table

The receivable amortization table for Borat Corp. is shown in Exhibit 18A-3. This leaves $41,500 as the lease receivable throughout 20X2. At the end of 20X2, Borat must record the accrued interest, which is $41,500 × 14%, or $5,810, as indicated in the amortization table. The remaining amount of the payment, $14,190, reduces the net lease receivable. Again, remember that the table is for the lease year, not the fiscal year.

EXHIBIT 18A-3

LESSOR RECEIVABLE AMORTIZATION TABLE—BASIC EXAMPLE

1 January	Lease Receivable Before Payment	Interest at 14%	Payment Received, 1 January	Lease Receivable Change	Lease Receivable After Payment
20X2	$61,500	$ —	$20,000	$(20,000)	**$41,500**
20X3	41,500	5,810	20,000	(14,190)	**27,310**
20X4	27,310	3,823	20,000	(16,177)	**11,133**
20X5	11,133	1,559	5,000	(3,441)	**7,692**
20X6	7,692	1,077	5,000	(3,923)	**3,769**
20X7	3,769	531*	4,300	(3,769)	**0**
Totals		$12,800	$74,300	$(61,500)	

*Rounded up by $3 to balance.

Recording by the Net Method

The series of entries recorded by Borat is shown in Exhibit 18A-4. These entries are in some *respects the reverse of the lessee's entries*, except that Borat uses a different interest rate, has no depreciation, and accounts for the receipt of the residual value at the end of the lease.

	EXHIBIT 18A-4		

LESSOR RECORDING OF FINANCE LEASE—BASIC EXAMPLE			

	Dr.	Cr.	Net Lease Receivable Balance—Dr.
31 December 20X1			
Lease receivable	61,500		
Cash, accounts payable		61,500	$61,500
[Delivery of equipment and commencement of the lease]			
1 January 20X2			
Cash	20,000		
Lease receivable		20,000	**$41,500**
31 December 20X2			
Lease receivable	5,810		$ 47,310
Finance revenue—leases ($41,500 × 14%)		5,810	
1 January 20X3			
Cash	20,000		
Lease receivable		20,000	**$ 27,310**
31 December 20X3			
Lease receivable	3,823		$ 31,133
Finance revenue—leases ($27,310 × 14%)		3,823	
1 January 20X4			
Cash	20,000		
Lease receivable		20,000	**$ 11,133**

31 December 20X4			
Lease receivable	1,559		
Finance revenue—leases ($11,133 × 14%)		1,559	
1 January 20X5			
Cash	5,000		
Lease receivable		5,000	**$ 7,692**
31 December 20X5			
Lease receivable	1,077		$ 8,769
Finance revenue—leases ($7,692 × 14%)		1,077	
1 January 20X6			
Cash	5,000		
Lease receivable		5,000	**$ 3,769**
31 December 20X6			
Lease receivable	531		$ 4,300
Finance revenue—leases ($3,769 × 14%)		531	
1 January 20X7			
Cash	4,300		
Lease receivable*		4,300	**$ 0**
(to record the receipt of the residual value)			

*The actual value received would be recorded, not the estimate. Any gain or loss is reported in earnings.

The first two entries are to record the lease at its commencement and to record the first lease payment. At the end of 20X2, Borat must accrue the finance revenue earned on the principal balance of $41,500 that was outstanding throughout 20X2, computed by the implicit interest rate of 14%. The accrued revenue is debited to the lease receivable balance rather than being recorded as accrued finance revenue. Receipt of the 1 January 20X3 lease payment is then credited in its entirety to the lease receivable.

Throughout the life of the lease, Borat records the lease payments and accrues interest on the outstanding balance. The net lease receivable balances are shown in the final column of Exhibit 18A-4. The balances shown in boldface type are those at the end of the lease year, and correspond directly to the end-of-year balances shown in Exhibit 18A-2. The nonbolded amounts are the lease balances that will be shown on Borat's SFP at the end of each fiscal year.

Current—Noncurrent Distinction

Companies that negotiate leases are *financial intermediaries.* Financial institutions do not classify their assets on a current/noncurrent basis—the classification usually is in order of liquidity. Therefore, there is no need to determine the current balance of the net lease receivable on the SFP.

Finance Lease Lessor Accounting—Gross Lease Basis

It is easy to see that lessor accounting is essentially just the reverse of lessee accounting, *if* the **net lease basis** is used. However, lessors usually *record* their lease receivables on a **gross lease basis**. Under the gross lease basis, the lessor records a gross receivable, the *undiscounted* cash flows *offset by a contra account for unearned finance revenue.* At each reporting date, the lessor calculates the amount of finance revenue that has been earned for the reporting period, and recognizes a portion of the unearned finance revenue.

For *reporting*, the lessor will show only the net amount on the SFP. That is, the net asset is the remaining undiscounted lease payments minus the remaining unearned finance revenue. As a result, the gross method will be presented in an identical way as the net method on the SFP.

Example

Using the example above, the beginning net lease receivable consists of two amounts—(1) the total undiscounted cash flows that the lessor expects to receive, reduced by (2) the amount of interest that the lessor will recognize over the lease term:

Lease payments receivable	$70,000
Estimated residual value	4,300
Gross lease receivable (see Exhibit 18A-3)	74,300
Less: Unearned finance revenue (i.e., interest) (see Exhibit 18A-3)	12,800
Net lease receivable	$61,500

The initial entry for Borat would appear as follows:

Gross lease receivable	74,300	
Unearned finance revenue		12,800
Cash (and/or accounts payable)		61,500

Subsequent entries are as follows:

1 January 20X2		
Cash	20,000	
Lease receivable		20,000

31 December 20X2		
Unearned finance revenue	5,810	
Finance revenue		5,810

1 January 20X3		
Cash	20,000	
Lease receivable		20,000

Compare these to the entries for the net method in Exhibit 18A-4 and notice the use of the unearned revenue account in the gross method.

At the end of 20X2, the balance of the lease receivable, netted with unearned revenue, is:

Lease receivable ($74,300 − $20,000)	$54,300
Less unearned finance revenue ($12,800 − $5,810)	6,990
Net lease receivable	$ 47,310

This is the same amount shown in Exhibit 18A-4 as the net lease receivable on 31 December 20X2. After the second $20,000 lease payment is made, the net balance drops to $27,310, which also can be verified by referring to Exhibit 18A-3.

Why Use the Gross Method?

The gross and net methods yield the same results for the lessor's financial reporting. The net method is simpler and corresponds to the method normally used by lessees, and thus one might wonder why lessors prefer the gross method for recording.

Like many of the accounts shown on a SFP, the leases receivable account is a *control account*. The SFP amount is a total; underlying that total is a large number of individual leases. For good internal control, a control account must be readily reconciled to the underlying subsidiary records. For leases receivable, that means that the receivables for the individual leases can be added up to verify the balance in the control account. The gross method makes that reconciliation easier. The gross method has the additional advantage of separating the control account function (via the lease payments receivable) from the revenue recognition function (via the unearned finance revenue).

Lessors will have thousands, perhaps tens of thousands, of individual leases. Since the amounts in the lease payments receivable account are gross amounts, the balance can be verified by adding the remaining gross payments shown on all of the individual leases.

In contrast, under the net method it is necessary to compute the present value of each lease at a particular point of time to perform the reconciliation. Some of the leases may be in arrears, and the present values may not correspond with their planned amortization schedules. Reconciliation on the net method would be a major headache. Therefore, the gross method is used.

SALES-TYPE LEASE ACCOUNTING — LESSOR

A finance lease may be simply a finance lease, or it may be a sales-type lease.

Leases by Manufacturers and Dealers

Basic Nature

Manufacturers and dealers may use leasing as a way of making sales. We all are familiar with the automobile advertising that prominently features low interest rates for leasing cars, sometimes 0%. But automobiles are not the only products sold heavily via leases. Other examples include computer equipment, office equipment, many types of industrial equipment, and airplanes.

A **sales-type lease** is a finance lease that, from the lessor's point of view, represents the *sale of an item of inventory.* The real point of the lease arrangement is to "move" the product. IFRS refers to this as a **manufacturer's lease**, although such leases are used by dealers as well as by manufacturers.

The distinguishing features of a sales-type lease are:

1. The lessor is a manufacturer/dealer; and
2. The leased asset has a carrying value (cost) that is different than fair value.

For the *lessee's* financial reporting, it does not matter whether the lessor is the producer of the product or whether the lessor is simply a financial intermediary. For the *lessor's* financial reporting, however, a finance lease involves only finance revenue recognized over the lease term. A sales-type lease, on the other hand, is viewed as two distinct (but linked) transactions:

1. The sale of the product, with recognition of a profit or loss on the sale; and
2. The financing of the sale through a finance lease, with finance revenue recognized over the lease term.

The new aspect in the accounting for a sales-type lease, as compared to a finance lease, is the initial entry to recognize the lease. The *sale* is recorded at the fair value of the asset being sold, *cost of goods sold* is the carrying value of the asset, and accordingly, gross profit is recorded on the lease/sale. The lease itself is accounted for by recognizing the present value of the lease payments, either through the gross method or the net method, as you would see in a finance lease. *The lease payments and finance revenue are then accounted for exactly as for a finance lease.*

Example—Sales-Type Lease

Assume that on 31 December 20X1, Binary Corp. (BC), a computer manufacturer, leases a large computer to a local university for five years at $200,000 per year, payable at the beginning of each lease year. The normal cash sales price of the computer is $820,000. *This is also the present value of the lease payments receivable.* The computer cost BC $500,000 to build. The lease states that the computer will remain with the lessee at the end of the lease. Because of this, the lease is a finance lease.

The implicit interest rate that discounts the lease payments to the $820,000 fair value of the computer is 11.04%. Because the lessor is the manufacturer of the product and because the computer is carried on BC's books at a value that is less than fair value, the lease clearly is a sales-type lease.

The sale component of the transaction will be recorded as follows, using the net method for the lease payments receivable:

31 December 20X1		
Lease payments receivable	820,000	
Sales revenue		820,000
Cost of goods sold	500,000	
Computer inventory		500,000

If the gross method were used, the first entry would reflect a debit to the lease payment receivable account of $1,000,000 ($200,000 × 5 payments), and a credit to unearned revenue of $180,000.

The first payment (at the inception of the lease) will be recorded as:

31 December 20X1		
Cash	200,000	
Lease payments receivable		200,000

The SCI for 20X1 will include a gross profit of $320,000 relating to the lease transaction, which is the profit on the sale. The SFP on 31 December 20X1 will include a net lease receivable of $620,000.

In 20X2 and following years, the lease will be accounted for exactly as illustrated above for direct financing leases. Finance revenue (or interest revenue) will be accrued each reporting period at the rate of 11.04% on the net balance of the receivable. Payments will be credited directly to the lease payments receivable account. The SFP will include the *net* balance of the receivable.

Gross Profit versus Finance Revenue

In the example above, there is a total revenue/gain amount of $500,000 over the life of the lease ($1,000,000 ($200,000 × 5 payments) less the cost of $500,000). Setting the fair value at $820,000 means that $320,000 of this revenue/gain is recognized at the beginning of the lease as gross profit, and then the rest, $180,000, is finance revenue recognized slowly over the life of the lease.

But what if the fair value were $900,000? Then, the split would be $400,000 for gross profit, taken immediately, and $100,000 is finance revenue over the life of the lease. *The total is the same*, but the pattern is very different. *The fair value of the asset at the inception of the lease is the dividing line*—and is a very important number for this reason.

Determination of Fair Value

In practice, the fair value or "cash price" may not be obvious. The problem arises because many products that are sold via sales-type leases are subject to discounts or special deals wherein the actual price is less than the stated list price. In fact, the asset may never be sold outright—all sales may involve leases with various payment terms. What is the fair value of the asset when there are no reference transactions?

This value is often determined by taking the present value of the minimum lease payments. This is a reasonable way to approximate sales value. However, the discount rate must be one that reflects market lending conditions.

Another way to circle around this fair value is to determine if the discount rate is appropriate. For example, a common tactic in long-term automobile leasing is to advertise a very low rate of interest (e.g., 0.9%), a rate that clearly is below the market rate of interest. A super-low rate really represents a decrease in the price of the car. A potential lessee can see what price he or she is getting by discounting the lease payments at whatever rate the bank would be willing to finance the car (i.e., at the borrower's incremental borrowing rate).

This essentially is the solution offered by the accounting standard—the sales amount should be measured as the lower of:

- The selling price as recorded for outright sales; or
- The present value of the minimum lease payments accruing to the lessor, discounted at the market rate of interest.

The actual determination of the revenue split (and profit split) between the sale and the lease components of the transaction is a matter of considerable judgement. The split will affect (1) gross profit on the sale in the current period and (2) finance revenue in future periods. Management is likely to define the sales price in a way that best suits its reporting needs. If the statements are audited, the auditor must test the reasonableness of management's sales price definition.

CONCEPT REVIEW

1. What is the basic difference between a sales-type lease and a straightforward finance lease?
2. In a sales-type lease, why is it often difficult to determine objectively the sales price of the item being "sold"?

Disclosure for Lessors

Lessors with finance leases must disclose the following:

- A general description of the lessor's leasing arrangements;
- The aggregate future minimum lease payments receivable (i.e., the gross amount) and the total amount of unearned finance revenue, reconciled to the present value of leases as shown on the SFP;
- The gross lease payments and present value of future minimum lease payments for each of the following periods:

    − Within the next year;
    − The total for years two through five; and
    − Later than the fifth year, in total.

- Any contingent rentals that have been taken into earnings;
- The estimated amount of unguaranteed residual values; and
- The accumulated allowance for uncollectible lease payments.

Accounting Standards for Private Enterprises

Lessor Classification

Whereas IFRS uses the same criteria for both lessees and lessors, ASPE imposes additional requirements before the lessor can classify a lease as a capital lease:

- The lessor's credit risk relating to the lease and the lessee is normal and is compared with the collectibility of similar receivables; and
- The lessor's unreimbursable costs can be reasonably estimated.

Both of these additional requirements must be satisfied. If not, then the lease is reported as an operating lease rather than a capital lease.

An interesting result of this additional requirement is that the lease can end up being reported asymmetrically. If the lessee reports the lease as a finance lease while the lessor reports it as an operating lease, the asset will be reported on the SFP of *both* the lessee and the lessor.

If the criteria for capitalization are met, a lessor then must classify the lease as either a direct financing lease or as a sale-type lease. A direct financing lease is essentially the same as a finance lease under IFRS.

Initial Direct Costs

Under IFRS, the lessor's initial direct costs (e.g., commissions or legal fees) for finance leases are capitalized as part of the lessor's cash flow and amortized over the lease period. In contrast, ASPE says that the lessor's initial direct costs should be expensed, both for a direct financing lease and a sales-type lease. However, ASPE also requires that an equivalent amount of the unearned lease income be recognized. The net effect is that there is no difference in the impact on earnings.

For operating leases, initial direct costs are deferred and amortized over the lease term.

SUMMARY OF KEY POINTS

1. A lease that does not transfer substantially all of the asset's risks and benefits to the lessee is classified as an *operating lease*. Rent payments are reported by the lessor as rental revenue.

2. The interest rate used in lessor accounting for a finance lease is the rate implicit in the lease.

3. Finance leases are recorded by the lessor as an increase to a financial asset, lease payments receivable. This may be at the gross amount, with an unearned revenue contra account used. Alternatively, the asset may be recorded at its net amount. The net method and the gross method give the same results in the financial statements. Lessors normally use the gross method of recording finance leases to make it easier to reconcile the portfolio of leases to the summary amount in the SFP control account.

4. Annual payments received by the lessor reduce the lease receivable asset. Finance revenue is earned with the passage of time.

5. A lessor must classify a finance lease as either a straightforward finance lease or as a sales-type lease. A direct financing lease arises when a lessor acts purely as a financial intermediary. A sales-type lease arises when a manufacturer or dealer uses leasing as a means of selling a product, and the book value of the asset is not its fair value. A sales-type lease has two profit components for the lessor: (1) the profit or loss from the sale and (2) interest revenue from the lease financing.

6. Under ASPE, a lessor treats a lease as a capital lease if, in addition to transferring substantially all of the risks and rewards of ownership to the lessee, two other criteria are met: (1) the credit risk is normal and (2) all executory and operating costs included in the lease payments can be reasonably estimated.

Key Terms

gross lease basis

internal rate of return (IRR)

manufacturer's lease

net lease basis

net lease receivable

sales-type lease

Review Problem 18A-1

Orion leased a computer to the Lenox Silver Co. on 1 January 20X5. The terms of the lease and other related information are as follows:

- Lease term (fixed and noncancellable)   3 years
- Estimated economic life of the equipment   4 years
- Fair market value of the computer at lease inception $5,000
- Lessor's cost of asset $5,000
- Bargain purchase price   none
- Transfer of title   none
- Guaranteed residual value by lessee (excess to lessee) 1 January 20X8 $1,000
- Collectibility of rental payments   assured
- Annual rental (first payment 1 January 20X5) $1,620

Required:

1. Assuming this is a financing lease, provide entries for the lessor from 1 January 20X5 through 1 January 20X6, using the net method of recording.

2. Provide the lessor's journal entry at the termination of the lease on 1 January 20X8, assuming that the asset is sold by the lessee on that date for $1,200.

3. Prepare the entries at the commencement of the lease (i.e., 1 January 20X5), assuming that the gross method is used instead.

REVIEW PROBLEM 18A-1—SOLUTION

The lease is a finance lease because the lease term (three years) is a major part of the economic life of the asset. The lessor must account for the lease by using the interest rate implicit in the lease. The interest rate that discounts the lease cash flows to $5,000 is 13.29% (before tax) (solved by spreadsheet).

1. Lease entries, net method:

   1 January 20X5—commencement of lease

Lease receivable	5,000	
Cash, Inventory, etc.		5,000

   1 January 20X5—first payment

Cash	1,620	
Lease receivable		1,620

   31 December 20X5—interest accrual

Lease receivable	449	
Finance revenue		449

   ($5,000 − $1,620) × 13.29% = $449

   1 January 20X6—second payment

Cash	1,620	
Lease receivable		1,620

2. Termination of lease

   1 January 20X8—receipt of guaranteed residual value from lessee

Cash	1,000	
Lease receivable		1,000

   The fact that the lessee was able to sell the asset for $1,200 is irrelevant. The lessee keeps the extra $200.

3. Lease commencement, gross method:

   1 January 20X5—commencement of lease

Lease receivable [($1,620 × 3) + $1,000]	5,860	
Unearned finance revenue		860
Cash, Inventory, etc.		5,000

   1 January 20X5—first payment

Cash	1,620	
Lease receivable		1,620

APPENDIX 2

IFRS 16—LEASES

Overview

The issue of leasing has been under consideration by the IASB since 2006. There has been widespread dissatisfaction with the current operating/finance lease distinction. In particular, financial statement users (and many accountants) have been dissatisfied with preparers' practice of acquiring long-term use of major assets by entering into financing leases that are disguised as operating leases.

The IASB issued IFRS 16, *Leases*, in 2016, effective for years beginning on or after 1 January 2019. This standard has incorporated changes that have been under consideration for several years, although the IASB and FASB abandoned efforts to issue a harmonized standard for lease accounting.

The most significant feature of the proposed standard is that it will eliminate the distinction between an operating lease and a finance lease for the lessee. Instead, all leases will be reflected on the SFP of the lessee as "right-of-use" assets, accompanied by a related liability. The lessee may use an optional exemption for short-term and low-value assets, and simply expense rent paid over the lease term. For lessors, the emphasis is on accounting for the performance obligation, consistent with the approach adoption in IFRS 15, *Revenue from Contracts with Customers*. However, the classification for the lessor continue to rest on the transfer of the risks and rewards of ownership, with the same judgemental criteria applied. A lessor with a finance lease has either a financing lease or a sales-type lease.

We will focus on lessee accounting in this appendix, because this is the area in which the changes will have the greatest consequences.

LEASE IDENTIFICATION

Control

A contract is a lease if the contract conveys control over the use of an identified asset for a period of time in exchange for consideration. *Control gives the lessee the right to direct use of the asset and obtain substantially all the economic benefits from the use of the asset.*

Control is critical. For example, if a corporation contracts for a computer server to be used specifically and exclusively by that corporation, the contract is a lease because the corporation controls use of the server. In contrast, if the corporation contracts to use a server that also is used for other clients, the owner of the server controls the asset, or its *allocation of space*; this contract is not a lease but is simply a supply-of-services contract.

SHORT-TERM AND LOW-VALUE LEASES

A **short-term lease** is one that has a maximum term of no more than 12 months. "Short term" refers to the maximum term over which the lessee has made a binding commitment. The maximum term includes *any period of time that gives the lessee economic incentive to exercise renewal or purchase options.* Short-term leases include leases that have no financial commitment beyond a year but may be repeatedly renewed at market rates. Accordingly, the lease term does not include continuing monthly or annual rental renewals because the lessee has no binding commitment until the renewal actually happens. This might be typical in an annual rental contract for office space.

However, if the lessee has strong *economic incentive* to extend the term of a lease beyond 12 months, the lease automatically becomes a **long-term lease** for accounting purposes. Any lease that has onerous nonrenewal penalties built into the lease would be long term, as would a lease with a bargain renewal term or a bargain purchase option.

A **low-value lease** is one where the *underlying asset* has a low value when new. Items such as personal computers or pieces of office furniture are examples.

Accounting for Short-Term and Low-Value Leases

Lessees may avoid the requirement to record a value-in-use asset and related liability by taking advantage of an optional exemption in IFRS 16. This must be chosen for an *entire class of assets for short-term leases* (e.g., all construction equipment on short-term leases) but can be chosen on an asset-by-asset basis for low-value leases.

If the election is chosen, lessees will account for short-term leases by recognizing the lease payments as an expense, normally allocated on a straight-line basis. If another allocation scheme is more logical when considering the benefits received during the lease, then the pattern of benefit is used.

If lease payments do not have a straight-line pattern, the accounting treatment would include accruals or deferrals to affect the expense pattern. Otherwise, the lessee does not recognize any liability or asset relating to the lease contract. This is current practice for an operating lease.

LONG-TERM LEASES

Basic Approach

The basic rule is simple—at the commencement of a lease, the lessee recognizes two elements:

- A **right-of-use asset**; and
- A liability for the lease payments, including any initial direct costs *paid by the lessee.*

The two elements are measured at the present value of the cash flow stream. The discount rate is the pre-tax rate the lessor charges the lessee if it is readily determinable; this is the interest rate implicit in the lease. If this rate is not readily determinable, the present value is based on the lessee's incremental borrowing rate.

Lease payments included in the cash flow stream are the amounts set by contract. If these are inflation-adjusted, then the adjusted amounts (i.e., any amounts set with reference to an index) are included. Guaranteed residual amounts are also included.

Variable lease payments based on usage (mileage on a vehicle, for example) are expensed when they are incurred.

The right-of-use asset is also increased by any initial direct costs paid to enter into the lease, such as a commission paid to enter into the lease. The right-of-use asset also includes asset retirement obligations, measured at the present value of the expected payment.

After recognition, the asset and liability are accounted for separately. That is, over the term of the lease, the lessee will:

- Amortize or depreciate the asset as appropriate for that type of asset; and
- Account for the liability by the effective interest method.

This is the same as current accounting for finance leases except that *the judgemental criteria for lease classification have been removed.* Essentially, *all leases will be accounted for as finance leases,* as described in the main body of this chapter.

Definitions

The *lease term* is the noncancellable period during which the lessee may use the asset, plus:

1. Any periods covered by an extension option if exercise of that option is reasonably certain; and
2. Periods covered by a termination option, as long as the lessee is reasonably certain not to exercise that option.

For example, a lease might be for three years, but include a clause that allows the lessee to pay a termination fee and end the lease after the first year. As long as the lessee is reasonably certain to *not exercise* the termination option, the lease term is three years.

The lessee's *incremental borrowing rate* is the cost of borrowed funds for a similar term and similar security, consistent with existing lease standards.

Example of Right-of-Use Asset Approach

While the lease capitalization under IFRS 16 is identical to that shown in the chapter, one further example is provided as reinforcement.

Speedy Ltd., a courier company, leases a storage building for a five-year period at $10,000 per year, payable at the beginning of each year, starting on 2 January 20X1. Speedy is required to pay for adapting the building for its purposes, a cost of $5,000. The interest rate implicit in the lease is 6%.

The building has a 40-year life, and this lease would likely be an operating lease under existing rules. However, it does not qualify for an optional exemption under IFRS 16, because the term is longer than a year, and the underlying asset, a building, is not low value. Accordingly, Speedy must record the value-in-use asset.

The present value calculation is:

$$PV = \$5,000 + (\$10,000 \times (P/A, 6\%, 5)) = \$49,651$$

A liability amortization table must be completed, as shown in Exhibit 18B-1. Interest expense will total $5,349 over the life of the payment stream.

		EXHIBIT 18B-1		
		LESSEE AMORTIZATION TABLE—SPEEDY LTD.		
1 January	**Lease Liability Before Payment**	**Interest at 6%**	**Payments, 2 January**	**Lease Liability After Payment**
20X1	$49,651	$ —	$ 15,000	**$34,651**
20X2	34,651	2,079	10,000	**26,730**
20X3	26,730	1,604	10,000	**18,334**
20X4	18,334	1,100	10,000	**9,434**
20X5	9,434	566	10,000	**0**
Totals		$5,349	$55,000	

In addition, the asset must be depreciated. Straight-line depreciation is $9,930 ($49,651 ÷ 5).

At commencement, Speedy would record the lease as follows:

2 January 20X1—commencement of the lease		
Right-of-use asset under lease—delivery van	49,651	
Lease liability		49,651

2 January 20X1—first payment of $10,000 plus initial direct cost of $5,000		
Lease liability	15,000	
Cash		15,000

The lease liability declines to $34,651 after the initial payment. At the end of 20X1, interest will have accrued on that outstanding balance:

31 December 20X1—interest accrual		
Interest expense	2,079	
Lease liability		2,079
($34,651 × 6% = $2,079 per Exhibit 18B-1)		
31 December 20X1—asset depreciation		
Depreciation expense	9,930	
Accumulated depreciation		9,930

Reassessment of the Lease Liability

An important aspect of the new standard is that it specifically provides for the possibility that economic circumstances will change and either the lease payments or the discount rate will change. For example:

- Market factors concerning the leased asset (e.g., changing technology) may make a bargain purchase option or renewal option no longer favourable. The lessee can then remeasure the value imputed to the right-of-use asset by reassessing the lease without the additional purchase or renewal payments originally envisioned.

- Similarly, market interest rates may have changed so that the lessee no longer has incentive to exercise a purchase option or renewal option.

The lessee reports the amount of the change in a right-of-use asset (and liability) value due to circumstances in the reporting period, in earnings (i.e., a gain or loss will be reported).

To be specific, lease amounts are remeasured if:

1. The lease term changes; a revised discount rate as of the remeasurement date is applied;
2. The likelihood of exercising a purchase option changes: a revised discount rate is applied in this case, as well;
3. The amount to be paid under a guaranteed residual value changes; the discount rate is NOT changed in this case; and
4. The indexed amount of payments is reassessed; the discount rate is NOT changed in this case.

Sale and Leaseback

A transaction will be accounted for as a *sale and leaseback* only if a performance obligation is satisfied, using the framework established in IFRS 15, *Revenue from Contracts with Customers*.

If there is a sale, then the seller measures the right-of-use asset as the portion of the previous carrying value that relates to the right of use retained. That is, if only 30% of the building subject to a sale and leaseback is retained through a lease agreement, then 30% of the existing book value is retained. Any gain for the portion retained is not recognized. However, a gain is recognized based on the sale of the remaining 70%.

LESSOR ACCOUNTING

Lessor Classification of Leases

As stated in the current standard, a lessor classifies a lease as either an operating lease or a finance lease. A lease is a finance lease if it transfers substantially all the risks and rewards of ownership related to ownership of the underlying asset. Otherwise, the lease is an operating lease.

The transfer of risks and rewards is set out as in the current standard, with consideration given to transfer of title, the presence of a bargain purchase option, the length of the lease, the present value of the minimum lease payments as compared to fair value, and whether the leased assets are specialized for the lessee. If none of these conditions are met, the lease is an operating lease.

Inconsistency of Classification

The lessee uses one set of capitalization criteria, and the lessor uses another. This may result in assets subject to lease agreements appearing on *both* the lessee's SFP and the lessor's SFP. For example, the Speedy example shown above results in a right-of-use asset on Speedy's books. Because the asset has a long life, the lease terms are unlikely to qualify as a finance lease for the lessor, and the building will also be on the lessor's SFP.

Financial statement users will have to adapt to this new reality!

Lessor Accounting for Operating Leases

The lessor recognizes lease revenue in earnings over the term of the lease. The leased asset is depreciated as appropriate for its nature and intended life cycle. This is largely unchanged from the existing standard for operating leases.

Lessor Accounting for Finance Leases

Lessor accounting for finance leases is different in certain technical areas under IFRS 16, but is largely unchanged:

- A lessor recognizes an asset equal to the net investment (present value) of the lease, and recognizes finance revenue over the life of the lease using the effective interest method.
- If the lease is a sales-type lease, the lessor is a manufacturer or dealer, and will recognized gross profit at the inception of the lease in a manner that is consistent with outright sales of the asset.

Looking Forward

At the time of preparing this edition, the new standard has been released with a 2019 implementation date. However, the IASB has had a history of delayed implementation dates when standards have proven contentious, and also a history of amending new standards prior to implementation. Accordingly, the technical details may well shift. The new standard, though, is the result of many years of study and discussion by the IASB—and FASB—and is a clear indication of the future direction.

One thing is abundantly clear—for the lessee, more capitalization will be required. For any lease term longer than one year, all lease payments (plus the amounts of any end-of-lease payments and/or renewals) will be discounted to present value.

Stay tuned for future developments.

KEY TERMS

long-term lease	**right-of-use asset**
low-value lease	**short-term lease**

SUMMARY OF KEY POINTS

1. A new lease accounting standard has been released by the IASB, with implementation in 2019.

2. All leases are accounted for by the lessee as a right-of-use asset, and a liability. Lease term and payments include terms and amounts where the actions of the lessee are reasonably certain.

3. Short-term leases and low-value leases may be accounted for as operating leases. This is an optional decision on the part of the lessee that must be applied to all short-term assets of a given class, but can be applied to any individual asset if the underlying asset is low value.

4. A right-of use asset and related liability are measured at discounted cash flow. The discount rate is the interest rate implicit in the lease, if known, or the lessee's IBR.

5. Lessor accounting retains the operating versus financing criteria and classifications. Emphasis is on accounting for performance obligations.

Source: (Globe and money) © Vstock LLC/Getty Images RF; (Skyscrapers) © Arpad Benedek/Getty Images RF; (Canadian flag) © BjArn Kindler/Getty Images RF; (Tablet, pen, keyboard) © John Lamb/Getty Images RF.

CHAPTER 19

Post-Employment Benefits

INTRODUCTION

Many companies promise to provide their employees with benefits after they retire. The most common form of a *post-employment benefit* is a pension. However, a company may also provide other post-employment benefits, such as extended health care. These benefits are provided as compensation for employees' services during their working lives. Therefore, post-employment benefits are a form of deferred compensation, and the cost must be recognized during the employee's working life.

A pension may take the form of a *defined contribution plan*, where the employer's commitment and cost is limited to defined contributions. Alternatively, the plan might be a *defined benefit plan,* where the employer's commitment is to provide benefits, making the cost difficult to estimate because future events must be projected. Some of these projections are retention rates, mortality rates, retirement trends, and future interest rates. Accounting for defined benefit plans is complex.

To make matters more complicated, there are several different *actuarial cost methods* used to measure and allocate the annual cost of a defined benefit pension plan. Every actuarial cost method allocates the future estimated cost of pension benefits to the years of an employee's service in an effort to determine appropriate funding. Each actuarial cost method provides a different funding pattern. For those who want a better understanding of actuarial methodology, a supplemental unit on Connect illustrates the three basic actuarial methods.

Pension plans are big business and can affect an assessment of the solvency of the sponsoring company. For example, Air Canada reports total assets of $10.7 billion at the end of 2014, liabilities of $11.8 billion, and a shareholders' *deficit* of $1.1 billion. Included in the net pension and other benefit liabilities showing on the SFP is a net pension liability of $1.2 billion but the disclosure notes indicate that the pension plan itself has assets of $17.4 billion and obligations of $18.6 billion, making the pension plan larger than the book value of the entire employer company. The pension plan is underfunded by $1.2 billion.

This chapter focuses primarily on accounting for pension plans but includes an example of other post-employment benefits. The general structure of pension calculations and assumptions are analyzed, various components of pension expense are explored, and a spreadsheet is introduced that helps to organize the data. The extensive disclosure requirements for post-employment benefits are reviewed.

TYPES OF PENSION PLANS

Pension plans are typically *formal agreements* and part of contractual terms of employment. Pension plans may also be *legislative* or *industry based*, for example, if companies are required to contribute to national, provincial, or industry-specific plans. Pensions may also be represented by *constructive obligations,* based on informal practice. Informal practice gives rise to a constructive obligation when the company has no realistic choice but to pay employee benefits because of past practices or competitive forces.

There are two general types of pension plans:

1. Defined contribution plans; and
2. Defined benefit plans.

A **defined contribution plan** is one in which the employer makes agreed-upon (or *defined*) cash contributions to the plan each period, which are invested by a trustee on behalf of the employee. The employer has no legal or constructive liability to pay further contributions. For example, an employer may agree to contribute 6% of an employee's salary to a separate pension fund each year. The pension that the employee eventually receives as a result of those contributions is a function of the fund's investment success; the pension annuity is determined by the amount of accumulated contributions plus earnings on contributions at the time that the employee retires. The employee accepts both *actuarial risk* (benefits will be less than expected) and *investment risk* (assets invested will not completely fund the expected pension.)

A **defined benefit plan** is one in which the eventual *benefits* to the employee are stated in the pension plan. It is the employer's responsibility to fund this pension, and thus all risk stays with the employer. The benefits are normally calculated on the basis of the employee's salary at or near retirement and the length of her employment with the company. However, the defined benefit may also be a flat amount per year or a lump-sum benefit on retirement. The estimate of the present value of cumulative pension benefits, adjusted for expected life expectancy, turnover, and a myriad of other factors, is called the *defined benefit obligation* and is estimated by an actuary.

The essential difference between the two types of plans can be summarized as follows:

Type of Plan	Contributions	Benefits	Risk
Defined contribution	Fixed	Variable	Employee has risk of low pension benefits
Defined benefit	Variable	Fixed	Employer has risk of high pension contributions

Classification of a Pension Plan

Classification of a plan as defined contribution or defined benefit rests on the *economic substance* of the plan, based on its terms and conditions. If the benefit formula is based on *anything more than* the contributions and the investment history to date or if the employer guarantees some specific level of pension or plan earnings, then the plan is a *defined benefit plan.*

PENSION TERMS

Contributory versus Noncontributory

A **contributory pension plan** is one in which the *employee* makes contributions to the plan, in addition to those made by the employer. Both defined contribution plans and defined benefit plans can be contributory, which acts to enforce some level of retirement savings. The other alternative is that the pension plan is a **noncontributory pension plan**; in this case, the pension assets are contributed entirely by the employer.

Vesting

Pension plan benefits are said to be *vested* when the employee has the right to receive his or her pension entitlement even if he or she leaves the employer before retirement age. The pension is not actually paid until retirement, of course, but the funds in the pension plan are "earmarked" for that individual or rolled into the individual's RRSP. Some provinces require that benefits be immediately vested. Others require vesting after two years of service. Other jurisdictions apply the 10 + 45 rule; contributions become vested when the employee has worked for the same employer for 10 years *and* has reached age 45. Of course, employers may voluntarily commit themselves to faster vesting than legislation requires. Note that any contributions to a pension plan made by an *employee* are automatically vested.

Trustee

Most pension plans are trusteed, which means that there is an independent **trustee** that receives the pension contributions from the employer (and, if appropriate, from the employee), invests the contributions in accordance with provincial regulations and agreed-upon guidelines, and pays out benefits to pensioners. Trustees of pension funds are often financial institutions, such as trust companies and banks; a pension trustee is not an individual person. Most plans are trusteed because:

- Trusteeship is required for a plan to be registered; and
- From an accounting perspective, if a pension plan is not trusteed and instead is administered by the company, the company must report both the pension plan assets and the defined benefit obligation separately on its SFP because the assets are under the control of the company. When a plan is administered by a trustee, however, the plan assets are beyond control of the company's managers and accounting recognition is based on the net pension plan position.

Trusteeship does not absolve the employer of responsibility to ensure that a defined benefit pension plan is solvent and able to pay pension benefits when they come due.

Registered

Pension plans normally are **registered** with the pension commissioner in the province of jurisdiction. The commissioner's office is responsible for seeing that the pension plan abides by pension legislation, including requirements for funding, reporting, trusteeship, actuarial valuation, and control over surpluses.

An important benefit of registration is that it enables the company to deduct from taxable income amounts contributed to the plan. If the plan is not registered, the employer *cannot deduct the pension contributions;* tax deductions will come only when the pension is actually paid to the employee or when a pension annuity is purchased on behalf of the employee at the retirement date. Since pension contributions are material, this would delay the tax deduction for the company and would be highly undesirable!

Actuarial Cost Methods

Since defined benefit plans entitle the employee to a specified (or *defined*) pension, the challenge for the employer is to make payments into the plan that will eventually provide enough money to pay the pension.

The task of determining an appropriate funding amount is the task of the **actuary**. An *actuary* is an expert who calculates statistical risks, life expectancy, payout probabilities, and so on. Actuaries are typically employed by insurance agencies and other financial institutions. Actuarial science is a well-established profession, with a rigorous multi-stage qualification process.

There are several different methods of measuring and allocating the pension amounts, known as **actuarial cost methods**. Every actuarial cost method allocates the future estimated cost of such post-employment benefits to the years of an employee's service in an effort to determine appropriate funding. The actuarial cost methods must also determine the present value of the defined benefit obligation to employees at the measurement date.

Actuarial Gains and Losses

Actuarial gains and losses exist in defined benefit plans. There are two sources of actuarial gains and losses:

1. A change in the present value of the defined benefit obligation to employees, *resulting from the experience of the plan to date, as compared with predicted amounts.* This is a retrospective measurement, based on experience to date and is sometimes referred to as an *experience gain or loss.*

2. Changes in the present value of the defined benefit obligation to employees, *resulting from a change in an assumption about the future.*

For example, assume that employee turnover was projected to be 2% in 20X1. The actual turnover was 5%, which means that the cumulative defined benefit obligation to the end of the 20X1 is now lower and an experience gain is measured. However, the 5% turnover rate for 20X1 is also used as evidence to lower retention projections for the next 20 years. This causes a prospective remeasurement and a further actuarial gain.

Pension legislation usually requires an employer to have an **actuarial revaluation** done at least once every three years. The actuary looks at the actual performance factors since the preceding revaluation (causing experience gains and losses) and at factors affecting future outlook (causing further actuarial gains and losses), and restates the defined benefit obligation accordingly. If the defined benefit obligation increases as the result of a revaluation, a loss occurs; if the defined benefit obligation decreases, a gain occurs.

Plan Settlement and Curtailment

On occasion, an employer may end its legal liability under an existing defined benefit pension plan, or end a portion of the benefits under a plan. This is called a **pension plan settlement**; the obligation to the pensionable group is settled by transferring assets to a trustee, purchasing specified annuities for employees, or otherwise terminating the financial commitments of the employer.

A **pension plan curtailment** takes place when there is a significant reduction in the number of employees covered by a plan, or some significant element of future service that will no longer qualify for benefits. This may happen when a company closes down a division or otherwise restructures or downsizes operations. It may also happen when workers agree to a major change in benefits, perhaps to preserve competitiveness.

In these circumstances, there is likely to be a substantial gain. Other times, a curtailment or settlement agreement may include special pension benefits that will increase the company's obligation and thereby result in a loss. It depends on the situational variables. *The gain or loss is the sum of the change in the defined benefit obligation and the change in pension assets.*

CONCEPT REVIEW

1. Explain the difference between a defined contribution pension plan and a defined benefit pension plan.
2. Why is trusteeship critical when accounting for pensions?

3. What is the risk to an employee if pension rights are not vested?
4. Who makes contributions to the pension plan if it is noncontributory?
5. What is a curtailment?

DEFINED CONTRIBUTION PLANS

The trend over the last 30 years, both in Canada and around the world, has been for more and more private sector companies that grant pensions to do so through defined contribution plans. Many companies with defined benefit pension plans are curtailing these plans and/or enrolling new employees in defined contribution plans. Defined contribution plans have lower financial risk for the employer because the cost of the program is known with certainty.

Current Service Cost

Accounting for defined contribution pension plans is straightforward because the obligation for each period is determined by the contribution for that period. The required payment equals the expense. The employer's required contribution for services rendered during the period is known as the *current service cost* for the period. No actuarial assumptions are required, and there is accordingly no actuarial gain or loss from a change in assumptions.

Note that:

- The amount recorded is undiscounted unless the payment to the pension fund is delayed for more than 12 months after the end of the fiscal year. If discounting is required, the discount rate is based on the market yield of high-quality corporate bonds with similar term and currency as the pension payment stream.
- If there is an overpayment in a given year, the overpayment is recorded as a prepaid pension amount as long as the prepayment will lead to a reduction in future payments, or a cash refund, to the employer.

Example

Suppose that Enterprise Fourchu Limité (EFL) pays $60,000 into the pension plan at the end of 20X1 as required under its pension plan for 20X1 services rendered. The entry is:

Pension expense	60,000	
Cash		60,000

Be careful to expense only amounts relating to the *current* year's service; there may well be an agreement covering 20X2, but it would not be recorded as a liability in 20X1.

Example—Delayed Payment

Assume that EFL has instead agreed to pay $60,000 at the end of 20X1 and *also* agrees to make another payment of $40,000 *relating to employees' 20X1 services* at the end of 20X4. Assuming an interest rate of 6%, the present value of the future payment is $40,000 × (P/F, 6%, 3) = $33,585. The entry to record 20X1 pension expense will be:

Pension expense	93,585	
Cash		60,000
Defined contribution pension liability		33,585

The defined contribution pension liability must have interest at 6% recorded each year. Interest is always calculated using the same rate that was used in discounting the obligation in the first place. Interest is an expense in earnings. It may be part of pension expense or recorded as interest expense; presentation is up to the company. In our examples, we will include the amount in pension expense.

Note the $33,585 pension liability recognized by EFL in this example. In 20X2, EFL will record interest of $33,585 × 6% = $2,015. The liability will grow to $35,600 ($33,585 + $2,015) at the end of 20X2.

Example—Prepaid Amounts

For a third example, assume instead that EFL contributes $80,000 to a plan for 20X1, and then discovers that its 20X1 payroll was less than expected for the year and the contribution should have been only $60,000. If the excess $20,000 can be used toward the 20X2 required payment or can be obtained as a cash refund, then a prepaid pension asset (or account receivable) is recorded and pension expense is $60,000. The entry is:

Pension expense	60,000	
Prepaid pension asset	20,000	
Cash		80,000

If no relief is offered for the overpayment, then pension expense is $80,000, and no asset exists.

Past Service Cost

An employer with a defined contribution plan may make an additional payment to a pension fund in recognition of past years' service, in essence improving the plan for employees. This amount is expensed in the period in which the payment is made. No deferrals are permitted.

DEFINED BENEFIT PLANS—INTRODUCTION

A defined benefit plan is a post-retirement benefit plan where the financial risk remains with the employer, as we have seen. Before examining the accounting approach for such plans, we will analyze plan structure, variables to be estimated, and actuarial cost methods.

Note that in defined benefit pension plans, the pension paid to a retiree must be based on some specific formula. Pensions that are based on a specific percentage of final year's salary are called **final pay pension plans**. However, pension benefits could alternatively be based on:

- **Flat benefit** per year of service, with no entitlement related to salary;
- Career average pay—that is, an average of the employee's earnings over the entire time spent with the employer;
- The best year's earnings (which permits employees to phase out toward the end of their careers); or
- An average of the last three (or five) years' earnings.

For example, a company may provide that an employee will receive an annual pension that is equal to 2% of the employee's final year's salary for each year of service. If the employee is earning $100,000 in the year before retirement and has worked for the company for 35 years, the annual pension will be:

Annual pension annuity = $100,000 × 2% × 35 years = $70,000

Alternatively, the pension agreement may provide a flat benefit of a life annuity of $1,000 per year for every year of service, regardless of salary, in which case the annual pension is:

Annual pension annuity = $1,000 × 35 years = $35,000.

Defined Benefit Plans—Structure

A defined benefit pension plan consists of pension fund assets, placed with a trustee, and the post-employment defined benefit obligation to employees.

Pension Plan Assets

The assets of a pension fund are the assets held in a separate long-term employee benefit fund. This must be a separate legal entity. The sole purpose of the fund must be to pay employee benefits, and *the assets must not be available* to pay other liabilities of the employer, even if the employer is bankrupt.

Fund assets increase when the employer or the employee makes contributions to the fund, and when the assets generate return. The assets can decline if the plan generates a negative return. Assets also decline when benefits are paid to pensioners.

Assets are valued at *fair value*, the amount for which assets could be exchanged in a transaction between knowledgeable willing parties in an arms-length transaction. If fair values are not readily available, valuation models, such as adjusted reference prices or discounted cash flow, must be used to approximate fair value.

Defined Benefit Obligation

The **defined benefit obligation** of a pension plan to its members is measured as the *present value of expected future payments* resulting from employee service in current and prior periods. It is a cumulative amount that increases each year that the employee works and earns a higher pension. The obligation also increases annually for an interest component because of the time value of money. It can increase or decrease because of actuarial gains or losses: when experience to date is different from the original estimate and/or when there are changed future estimates regarding retention, mortality, future salary levels, adjustments to past service costs, and so on. The obligation will decrease when benefits are paid to retirees.

Net Defined Benefit Liability (Asset)

The **net defined benefit liability (asset)** is the net overall funded status of the pension plan: the pension plan assets netted with the defined benefit obligation. If the defined benefit obligation is $4,500,000, and the plan assets are $3,700,000, then the plan has a net defined benefit liability status of $800,000. If the assets were $4,800,000 and the defined benefit obligation was $4,500,000, then the plan has a net defined benefit asset status of $300,000.

Ceiling Test for a Net Defined Benefit Asset

If the pension plan assets are greater than the obligation, companies must evaluate an asset ceiling before declaring their asset status. The **asset ceiling** is a test to see if the "excess" assets in the plan *can be used to benefit the employer* in the future: This benefit must be in the form of a reduction of future contributions, or perhaps a cash refund. If the time span is greater than one year, the ceiling is a discounted value. Sometimes such future recoveries are realized through a **pension holiday**, whereby the employer in an overfunded plan is permitted to temporarily reduce or eliminate payments for the current service funding requirements.

Consider the example above, where assets were $4,800,000 and the defined benefit obligation was $4,500,000. These values are both present values. If future contributions could be reduced because the plan was overfunded, then the fund is genuinely in a $300,000 net asset position. If no such relief is permitted under the terms of the plan and/or pension legislation, then the asset ceiling is invoked, and the plan is recognized for reporting purposes at a zero net position.

Defined Benefit Plans—Variables to Be Estimated

Estimates must be made to calculate the defined benefit obligation, and the annual funding amount. *It is the actuary's responsibility to suggest the estimates necessary for the measurement of pension funding amounts and to make required calculations*; these are reviewed by the company to ensure they are appropriate.

ETHICAL ISSUES

The estimates used by management for pension measurements must be *unbiased* and *mutually compatible*. For example, since inflation rates and salary increases are related over the long run, it would make little sense to use a high estimated discount rate (which would include a high future inflation rate) while also assuming a very low rate of increase in salaries (which would imply a low future inflation rate).

There is always risk of bias in estimates, and there may be a corporate motive to minimize or maximize pension amounts. Unbiased estimates are neither imprudent nor excessively conservative. Care must be taken when looking at the quality of estimates; *best estimates* are required.

Major categories of assumptions can be described as follows:

1. Demographic assumptions—decisions that relate to the characteristics of the employees eligible for benefits:

    *   *Employee turnover, disability, and early retirement.* Vesting may not occur immediately in defined benefit plans. Therefore, it is usually necessary to estimate what proportion of employees will stay long enough for vesting to occur. It is also necessary to establish how many will qualify for disability benefits prior to retirement, or elect to take a reduced, early retirement.

    *   *Mortality rates.* Mortality determines the term of the eventual pension and is an important variable. Most plans provide minimum guarantees; the pensioner's estate receives a lump-sum payment if the pension is not paid for a certain number of years. A pension plan may specify **death benefits** or **survivor benefits** that give lump-sum or continuing benefits to a surviving spouse, partner, and/or child. The mortality rate and the extent of any trailing entitlements must be estimated. *Best estimates* assumptions in this category generally involve adjusting population mortality statistics for the characteristics of the specific employee group.

2. Financial assumptions—decisions that deal with economic variables:

    *   *Future salary increases.* Since pension benefits are often tied to the employee's future earnings, it is necessary to estimate (or *project*) future salary increases. Salary increases are related, in part, to inflation rates. Therefore, it is necessary to estimate future inflation rates. Other variables include supply and demand in the labour force, seniority, and promotion. Costs of other benefits, such as medical services, may also need to be projected.

    *   *Discount rates.* The discount rate is established with reference to market yield at the end of the fiscal year on high-quality corporate bonds. Again, inflation rates must be projected. Currency and term should be consistent with the pension obligation. If the market for these bonds is not deep, then the yield on government bonds is used as a reference point.

Defined Benefit Plans—Actuarial Cost Methods

Understanding *pension accounting* requires understanding *pension funding* because they interact. **Funding** is the manner in which the actuary, in consultation with the employer, sets the necessary contributions to the plan. The accounting measurements determine pension expense and do not have to be equal to funding. Similar factors and the same family of actuarial methods may be used for both—or not.

An actuary can prepare a valuation for funding purposes or for accounting purposes. If the actuarial valuation is prepared for accounting purposes, then the objectives are to determine the amount of the net defined benefit obligation and current service costs for accounting purposes as of the valuation date.

There are several actuarial cost methods that are used by the actuary. The three basic actuarial cost methods that can be used are described briefly as follows:

Method	Accounting Valuation for the Current Service Costs and Net Benefit Obligation
Accumulated benefit method	Calculates the cost of the plan to which an employee currently is entitled, based on the *actual* years of service to date and on the *current* salary. Future salary levels and cost escalation do not affect the amount of the employee future benefits.
Projected unit credit method (also known as the accrued benefit method pro-rated on service or as the benefit/ years of service method)	Allocates the cost of the plan over the periods that the employee works and earns the benefits. Each period of service entitles the employee to an additional unit of benefit that builds up over time. Estimates of future salary levels or cost escalation are included to estimate the current service costs.
Level contribution method	Projects both the *final salary* and the *total* years of service and then allocates the cost evenly over the years of service.

Clearly, the level contribution method involves *more projections*, and the accumulated benefit method involves *fewer projections*.

Actuarial Cost Methods Comparison

To illustrate the three actuarial cost methods, consider a basic illustration of a defined benefit pension. Assume that an employee named Chris begins working for Celebrities Ltd. at age 30. Assume the following:

- Chris's starting salary is $25,000 per year.
- The normal retirement age at Celebrities is 65.
- The pension plan provides that an employee will receive an annual pension of 2% of the final year's salary for each year of service.
- The pension is fully vested from the date of employment.

Some additional estimates are needed, which are provided by the actuary:

- The estimated life expectancy after retirement is 14 years.
- The expected return on the investment in pension plan assets will be 6%.
- Chris's salary will increase by a compound average annual rate of 3%.
- Chris will work for Celebrities for 35 years, until normal retirement age.

Comparison

The computation details for each of the three methods are explained in a supplemental unit on Connect. *These calculations (for a group of employees) are performed by the actuary; the accountant should understand the approach and the estimates to which the calculations are sensitive.* Exhibit 19-1 summarizes the current service cost allocation for Chris's pension under each of the actuarial cost methods at selected ages. Remember, a company may use any actuarial cost method to determine funding.

The allocation patterns are very different, and yet each method results in *full allocation of costs over the years of service.* The accumulated benefit method's annual cost will change as and when the employee's salary actually changes. The projected unit credit method includes estimates of future salary growth into the current cost estimates and results in annual costs initially higher than the accumulated benefits method. The level contribution method, as the name states, results in the same cost each year as it estimates at the onset what the total benefit cost will be and allocates this over the time to retirement.

| | EXHIBIT 19-1 | | |

COMPARISON OF CURRENT SERVICE COSTS USING DIFFERENT ACTUARIAL COST METHODS

	Allocated Costs under Each Method		
Chris's Age	**Accumulated Benefit**	**Projected Unit Credit**	**Level Contribution**
30	$ 679	$ 1,856	$4,227
35	1,207	2,484	4,227
40	2,111	3,324	4,227
45	3,645	4,448	4,227
50	6,228	5,953	4,227
55	10,551	7,966	4,227
60	17,748	10,660	4,227
64	26,786	13,458	4,227

Bear in mind that the above calculation is for just one employee, which is unrealistic. *A company's overall pension funding requirement is calculated for the employee group as a whole.* Employees just entering the workforce may have low pension amounts attributable to their service, which will offset the apparently dramatic increase in amounts for older employees. For an employee group as a whole, the relative difference in pension amounts between methods will level out *if the employee group is stable and has an even age composition.* However, the age and length-of-employment composition of employee groups are often unstable; there are usually more employees at the lower-experience levels of employment than at the senior levels.

Actuarial Valuation for Funding Purposes

Actuarial valuation reports may also be prepared for funding purposes using any of the three methods above. In some cases, actuarial funding valuations are required by legislation, regulations, or contractual agreements. However, in this case, the objective is to determine the amount that should be paid into the plan annually. If prepared for funding purposes, the amount of the funding will be equal to the annual costs as seen in Exhibit 19-1. As can be seen, there will be significant differences between the *pattern* of payments made to the trustee over an employee's working life depending on the actuarial cost valuation method used. In the case of the level contribution method, higher cash contributions are required in the early years of an employee's tenure with the company. This could be viewed as more fiscally conservative. Other actuarial cost methods require the bulk of funding to occur later in the employee's working life. All methods are acceptable for funding under pension legislation, and all are used in practice.

Sensitivity to Assumptions

The calculations are extremely sensitive to all basic assumptions within methods: turnover, early retirement and disability, mortality, salary increase, and discount rate. If the assumed rate of salary increase is changed from 3% to 4%, for example, all of the costs in the table above would *increase by almost 40%.* The discount rate sensitivity is also worthy of note. If the assumed discount rate were increased from 6% to 8% in the preceding example, the required contributions at age 35 would change as shown below for the three methods:

Interest Rate Assumed	At 6%	At 8%
Accumulated benefit method	$1,207	$ 635
Projected unit credit method	2,484	1,305
Level contribution method	4,227	2,470

This highlights the need to use appropriate assumptions. As previously stated, the accounting standard requires use of unbiased and mutually compatible assumptions.

Actuarial Cost Method for Accounting Measurement

Accounting standards require the use of the *projected unit credit method* for pension measurements. Companies are all required to use the same actuarial cost method to ensure that a common measurement tool is used, and thus comparability is preserved. Generally, this method is felt to best measure the cost of entitlements earned during the period, and standard setters have been consistent in their preference for this method.

Companies do not have to use this method for funding, however. Many do because it is costly to have the calculations done twice by the actuarial consultants. If the projected unit credit method is used for accounting and another method is used for funding, a long-term accrual—either an asset or a liability—will result.

CONCEPT REVIEW

1. What events or transactions cause pension fund assets to change?
2. Identify two major demographic assumptions that must be made to project the cost of a pension.
3. Name three actuarial cost methods, and specify what projections, if any, are involved for each one.
4. Which actuarial method is required for accounting measurements for a defined benefit plan?

DEFINED BENEFIT PLAN PENSION ACCOUNTING—THREE ELEMENTS

Accounting for a defined benefit pension plan requires measuring and recording three different elements:

1. **Service cost**, which is the total of current service cost, any past service cost, and any gain or loss on plan settlement or curtailment. This amount is expensed.

2. Net interest on the *net defined benefit liability* (i.e., net interest on the defined benefit obligation less pension plan assets). The net defined benefit liability is multiplied by the discount rate, and the resulting expense (or income) is included in earnings. If the plan is overfunded, the net status is an asset, and this is a revenue item.

3. **Remeasurements** of the *net defined benefit liability*, whether caused by actuarial gains or losses, a difference between the actual return on the plan assets' and the expected return applied in item 2, or other measurement issues. This amount is recorded in *other comprehensive income* (OCI) and *accumulated other comprehensive income* (accumulated OCI). *It is never recycled to earnings.* Amounts in accumulated OCI can be reassigned to retained earnings.

The following sections explain these three elements.

Element 1: Service Cost

Service cost is an expense. It comprises:

1. Current service cost;
2. Past service cost; and
3. A gain or loss on plan settlement or curtailment.

Current service cost (CSC) is the annual measurement of the cost of the pension earned for work done during the year. Accounting standards require that current service cost be measured using the *projected unit credit method.* The actuary determines this figure and provides it in an actuarial report. It is an *expected present value* calculation based on numerous assumptions, as we have seen.

Past service cost (PSC) is the actuarial present value of pension benefits granted (or reduced) in an amended (or brand new) pension plan *for years of service already rendered* by current employees. Changes caused by a *curtailment,* which is the significant reduction in the number of employees covered by a plan, are also included in PSC. PSC will increase service cost if benefits are increased and decrease service costs if benefits are decreased.

PSC may arise when a plan is first initiated. At that time, employees *may* be given pension entitlements for their employment period prior to the initiation of the plan. From time to time, a company will amend its pension plan, often to increase benefits but sometimes to decrease benefits. PSC is created whenever an existing plan is amended to change benefits *based on years of service to date.* This involves a retrospective change in the defined benefit obligation that relates to prior service.

PSC is not amortized, and is not expensed over any potential funding period. It is expensed in its entirety when granted.

The final element of service cost is any gain or loss caused by a plan settlement, a transaction that winds up a plan. The gain or loss on settlement is the difference between plan obligations and assets, recalculated to the date of settlement and reflecting the terms of the settlement. The gain or loss is fully expensed in the year it occurs.

Alternative Classification of Settlement, Curtailment, and Termination

A gain or loss on settlement or curtailment is normally part of service cost. If the plan settlement or curtailment arises when a company restructures or discontinues some aspect(s) of its operations, the costs would be presented separately in earnings, as *discontinued operations*, or as a *restructuring,* depending on the facts.

An employer sometimes offers special incentives to induce employees to retire, or to take early retirement. Enhanced retirement offers are called **termination benefits** and may include lump-sum payments, continuation of salary, and enhanced pension benefits. With respect to enhanced pension benefits, these special termination benefits are in addition to the benefits normally offered to employees. Therefore, the cost of providing these special benefits has not been included in the actuarial calculations for the employee group, either for funding or for accounting purposes. Consequently, special termination benefits require separate recognition of extra cost.

The costs of special termination benefits are accrued in the financial statements as an expense and a liability, once a company is demonstrably committed to the termination, as explained in Chapter 12. This commitment must take the form of a formal and detailed plan. The cost is recognized as a lump sum and a provision is recognized. Since the employees are leaving the company, amortization of the cost over future periods is not appropriate.

Example

Refer to Exhibit 19-2 for data for Walker Corp.; this example will be extended for the remaining two elements of pension accounting in the following sections.

EXHIBIT 19-2

PENSION EXAMPLE

Walker Corp.has a defined benefit pension plan. It is now 31 December 20X5. The following data apply to the plan:

Current service cost for 20X5, measured using the projected unit credit method	$ 456,200
New past service cost granted in 20X5; the increased amount in the defined benefit obligation required for this	910,000
Amount paid to pension fund trustee on 1 June 20X5	1,700,000
Actuarial gain in 20X5, caused by lower anticipated future retention rates; defined benefit obligation decreases	(124,000)
Actual earnings in the fund, reported by the pension fund trustee, including interest, dividends, and change in fair value	398,200
Benefits paid to pensioners from pension fund assets	134,800

Balances:

Defined benefit obligation, end of 20X4	$11,675,000
Pension plan assets, fair value, end of 20X4	10,010,000
SFP Net defined benefit liability, end of 20X4	$1,665,000 cr.
SFP Accumulated OCI, pension, end of 20X4	288,400 dr.
Retained earnings, end of 20X4	23,688,100 cr.
20X5 Earnings, prior to any pension expense	8,842,500 cr.

Service cost is a straightforward combination of current and past service cost. However, sifting through the data can be challenging! The calculation is as follows:

1. Current service cost, measured using the projected unit credit method	$ 456,200
2. Past service cost granted in 20X5	910,000
	$1,366,200

The entry to record service cost:

Pension expense	1,366,200	
Net defined benefit liability		1,366,200

The $1,700,000 contribution to the pension fund is also recorded. It is not an expense but affects the SFP pension account:

| Net defined benefit liability | 1,700,000 | |
| Cash | | 1,700,000 |

At the end of the day, the SFP account, labelled the net defined benefit liability, will be equal to the pension assets less the defined benefit obligation. If it has a credit balance, it is a liability and is reported as a long-term liability on the SFP. If it has a debit balance, it is an asset and is reported as a long-term asset. In this example, the account now has a credit balance of $1,331,200 (opening balance of $1,665,000 credit, plus $1,366,200, less $1,700,000), but more adjustments are to come. Remember that the net defined benefit liability is affected by all three elements of pension accounting: service costs; interest; and remeasurements. It is also affected by the funding amounts and the actual return on the plan assets.

In this example, the pension fund has paid $134,800 to pensioners during the year. This amount is not recorded by the employer; it reduces both the defined benefit obligation and the pension fund assets. It thus has no effect on the net position of the pension fund. *Payments to pensioners are not a component of pension expense.*

Element 2: Net Interest on the Net Defined Benefit Liability (Asset)

Net interest on the net defined benefit liability is a change caused by the passage of time. It is, in essence, the combination of expected investment earnings on pension plan assets and accrued interest on the defined benefit obligation, all at the same discount rate. *The discount rate is the yield rate on high-quality corporate bonds determined at the beginning of the year (i.e. the same rate used at the end of the previous year). Terms and currency must match the pension liability terms and currency.*

In order to calculate this interest amount, the discount rate is applied to the beginning balance of the net defined benefit liability (asset) adjusted for any contributions and benefit payments made during the year on a weighted average basis. The net interest calculation may be done by the actuary and provided in the actuarial report. In fact, the net interest comprises three components: interest expense on the pension obligation, interest income on the plan assets, and interest on the effect of the asset ceiling amount (if any).

The accounting standard also encourages use of shortcuts and approximations in calculations. The following steps are required:

1. Determine the defined benefit obligation at the beginning of the year.
2. Determine the fair value of pension plan assets at the beginning of the year.
3. Determine the net defined benefit liability or asset by combining #1 and #2.
4. Determine the weighted average period of time that contributions and payments were made.
5. Multiply the net position adjusted to the weighting of the contributions and by the appropriate discount rate. The appropriate discount rate is the yield rate on high-quality corporate bonds with matching term and currency.

The resulting expense (or revenue) item may be presented as part of pension expense or shown separately as a finance expense. This presentation decision is left to the company, and diversity is expected in practice. In our examples, we will include the amount in interest expense.

Example

Refer to Exhibit 19-2 for data for Walker Corp.; this example will now be used to demonstrate net interest. The market yield rate for high-quality corporate bonds of similar term and identical currency is 6% at the end of the year. On 1 June 20X5, the contribution of $1,700,000 was made to the plan assets. Since the pension payments to the pensioners were made evenly over the year, we assume, on a weighted average that these were paid on July 1 for simplicity.

Net interest:

Defined benefit obligation, beginning of the year	$ 11,675,000
Pension plan assets, fair value, end of 20X4	10,010,000
Net defined benefit liability (not an asset, so the ceiling test is not needed)	$ 1,665,000
Weighted average for the contributions (1,700,000 x 7/12 (June to Dec)	(991,667)
Weighted average balance outstanding	$ 673,333
Net interest, at 6% ($673,333)	$ 40,400

Remember that benefits paid to the pensioners do not impact the net defined benefit amount outstanding since they reduce both the obligation and the plan assets by the same amount.

Note that this $40,400 is made up of interest expense on the defined benefit obligation and interest income on the plan assets. *Each of these can be separately calculated as follows:*

Interest expense:

Defined benefit obligation, beginning of the year	$ 11,675,000
Weighted average for the benefit payments ($134,800 × 6/12 (July to Dec)	(67,400)
Weighted average balance outstanding	$ 11,607,600
Interest expense, at 6% ($11,607,600)	$ 696,456

Interest income:

Pension plan assets, fair value, end of 20X4	$10,010,000
Weighted average for the contributions ($1,700,000 × 7/12)	991,667
Weighted average for the benefit payments ($134,800 × 6/12)	(67,400)
Weighted average balance outstanding	$10,934,267
Interest income, at 6% ($10,934,267)	$ 656,056
Net interest expense ($696,456 – $656,056)	$ 40,400

The interest income of $656,056 is the *expected earnings on the pension fund assets*. The difference between this expected earnings and the actual earnings on the plan assets is recognized as a remeasurement, as discussed below.

The entry is made using the net amount:

Interest expense	40,400	
Net defined benefit liability		40,400

Asset Ceiling Example

Had the plan assets been $12,000,000, then the net defined benefit *asset* would have been $325,000 ($11,675,000 of obligation versus $12,000,000 of assets).

Net interest before the effect of the asset ceiling is calculated as follows:

Defined benefit obligation, beginning of the year	($11,675,000)
Pension plan assets, fair value, end of 20X4	12,000,000
Net defined benefit asset	$ 325,000
Weighted average for the contributions ($1,700,000 × 7/12 (June to Dec)	991,667
Weighted average balance outstanding	$ 1,316,667
Net interest income, at 6% ($1,316,667)	$ 79,000

The net interest income is $79,000 assuming there is no effect of a ceiling test.

If the ceiling test indicated that the highest net defined benefit asset value that could be recognized on the SFP was only $25,000 (and not $325,000), the impact of applying the asset ceiling test is a reduction of $300,000. In this case, the net interest income now has three components calculated as follows:

Interest expense	
Defined benefit obligation, beginning of the year	$ 11,675,000
Weighted average for the benefit payments ($134,800 × 6/12 (July to Dec)	(67,400)
Weighted average balance outstanding	$ 11,607,600
Interest expense, at 6% ($11,607,600)	$ 696,456
Interest income on plan assets:	
Pension plan assets, fair value, end of 20X4 ($12,000,000)	$ 12,000,000
Weighted average for the contributions ($1,700,000 × 7/12)	991,667
Weighted average for the benefit payments ($134,800 × 6/12)	(67,400)
Weighted average balance outstanding	$12,924,267
Interest income, at 6% ($12,924,267)	$ 775,456
Interest income on effect of asset ceiling	
Effect of the asset ceiling (balance at the beginning of the year)	$ 300,000

| Interest income on effect of asset ceiling ($300,000 × 6%) | $ | 18,000 |

Net interest income ($775,456 − $696,456 - $18,000) $ 61,000
Proof: ($25,000 + 991,667) x 6% = $61,000

The net interest income of $61,000 is made up of the net interest on the net defined benefit asset of $79,000 less interest on the effect of the asset ceiling of $18,000. This is recognized as follows:

| Net defined benefit asset | 61,000 | |
| Interest income | | 61,000 |

Element 3: Remeasurement of the Net Defined Benefit Liability (Asset)

Remeasurement of the net defined benefit liability (asset) is recorded in OCI. It is not **recycled** to earnings but may be reclassified to another equity account, such as retained earnings. Remeasurement has three components:

1. Actuarial gains and losses;
2. The difference between expected earnings on pension plan assets, included in element 2 above (for example, $757,456), and actual fund earnings or loss; and
3. The difference between the total change as dictated by the effect of invoking the asset ceiling rule and the interest income (included in element 2 above, for example, $18,000).

Actuarial Gains and Losses

Previous sections of this chapter have stressed that assumptions and estimates have a major impact on the measurement of pension amounts. An inevitable aspect of these estimates is that they will be wrong. Re-estimates will give rise to changes in the present value of the defined benefit obligation, changes that represent actuarial gains and losses. The two sources of changes in the present value of the defined benefit obligation are:

1. *Experience gains and losses* caused by actual experience that shows that *what has actually occurred* is different from the assumptions made; and
2. *Changes in assumptions:* increases or decreases to pension amounts caused by changes in the assumptions *about the future* that underlie calculation of the defined benefit obligation.

Actuarial gains and losses are calculated by the actuary.

The impact on the SFP is as follows:

- Actuarial losses increase the net defined benefit liability on the SFP and are recorded as a debit to OCI.
- Actuarial gains reduce the net defined benefit liability on the SFP and are recorded as a credit to OCI.

For example, if there was a $46,000 experience loss, the following entry would be made:

| OCI: pension | 46,000 | |
| Net defined benefit liability | | 46,000 |

The debit creates a negative (contra) accumulated element of shareholders' equity on the SFP that accumulates over time. The recorded amount each year is reported in OCI, and earnings are combined with this OCI adjustment to arrive at comprehensive income. For example, if net profit for this year was $100,000 in the example above, then comprehensive income would be $54,000 ($100,000 − $46,000) and an accumulated debit OCI reserve of $46,000 is reported on the SFP as part of equity.

Expected versus Actual Return on Pension Plan Assets

The expected return on plan assets is an estimate based on the corporate bond yield and will be incorrect, both over the long run and year-by-year. Actual return is reported by the fund trustee and includes all forms of return, including the change in fair value. Expected return is part of the net interest calculated in the second element of pension accounting, illustrated above. The difference between actual and expected return is calculated and recorded in accumulated OCI. That is, calculations may have assumed a 4% average return, but the actual return this year might have been +13% or −20%. This difference creates a remeasurement gain or loss, which is recorded in accumulated OCI.

For example, if the expected returns were $39,000, and actual investment performance was $60,000, there is an $21,000 experience gain, and the following entry would be made:

| Net defined benefit liability | 21,000 | |
| OCI: pension | | 21,000 |

The recorded OCI pension amounts are netted in one accumulated OCI pension account, whether they are positive or negative, and regardless of the cause in the pension analysis. That is, the accumulated OCI account for pensions includes all the required element 3 adjustments: actuarial gains and losses *and* expected versus actual return.

Example

Refer back to Exhibit 19-2 for data for Walker Corp.; this example will now be used to demonstrate actuarial gains and losses.

There is an actuarial gain during 20X5, caused by a change in assumptions. It is recorded as follows:

| Net defined benefit liability | 124,000 | |
| OCI: pension | | 124,000 |

The interest income related to the plan assets, representing the expected return at 6%, was calculated to be $656,056. This was recorded as part of the net interest expense; one component of the second element of pension accounting. Actual earnings were $398,200. The difference is a loss of $257,856 ($656,056 − $398,200). This is recorded:

| OCI: pension | 257,856 | |
| Net defined benefit liability | | 257,856 |

The net balance in the accumulated OCI account is now a debit of $422,256 ($288,400 dr. opening balance + $257,856 dr. − $124,000 cr.).

Effect of the Asset Ceiling

As we have seen, a net defined benefit asset balance sometimes exists and is subject to a validity check to ensure that this asset, representing a surplus, is not overvalued and *that the enterprise will obtain value from that surplus in the future.* There are complex rules and definitions in this area to establish the recoverable asset ceiling amount. In very simple terms, if a company has a net defined benefit asset and if it is limited by the asset ceiling, a loss amount is initially recorded to OCI as a result. Valuations are done yearly and may reverse if the ceiling is revalued.

For example, recall the earlier example, where the defined benefit obligation was $11,675,000 and the fair value of the pension assets was $12,000,000. Even though there is a net surplus of $325,000, invoking the asset ceiling resulted in a reduction of $300,000, capping the net defined benefit asset at $25,000. This then is the the net defined benefit asset recognized on the SFP. The initial adjustment of $300,000 is required as follows:

OCI: pension ($325,000 − 25,000 ceiling)	300,000	
Net defined benefit asset		300,000

Each year, the difference between the total change in the asset ceiling and the amount of interest income related to the asset ceiling will be recognized as a remeasurement. This is a complex area and more specific examples are beyond the scope of this chapter.

SFP Net Defined Benefit Liability (Asset) Recognition

When all pension adjustments are recorded, the *net defined benefit liability/asset* on the SFP will equal the difference between the plan assets and the defined benefit obligation at the end of the year (and any effect of the asset ceiling). That is, the net overfunded or underfunded status of the plan will be recorded as an asset (overfunded) or a liability (underfunded). This is a highly desirable reporting result because it reflects reality. The pension adjustments are summarized as follows:

Pension Element	Normal Effect on Net Defined Benefit Liability (SFP)	Comment
Contributions to the plan	Debit net defined benefit liability (credit cash)	
Service cost	Credit net defined benefit liability (debit expense)	Applies to current and past service, also plan settlements and curtailments.
Net interest cost	Credit net defined benefit liability (debit interest expense) (opposite if net position is an asset)	Calculated based on net balance of pension fund at the beginning of the year; adjusted for the weighted average period of time for contributions and payments made during the period. The expense may be classified as a pension expense or a financing expense, at the company's option.
Actuarial gains and losses	For a loss: Credit net defined benefit liability (debit accumulated OCI) For a gain: Debit net defined benefit liability (credit accumulated OCI)	Applies to actuarial gains and losses, the difference between plan assets' actual earnings and expected earnings, effect of asset ceiling test, and other remeasurement issues.

Example

Refer to Exhibit 19-2 for data for Walker Corp.; this example will now be used to demonstrate the net defined benefit liability on the SFP. The new balance of this account is a liability $1,505,456, calculated as follows:

Opening balance (given)	$1,665,000 cr.
Payment to pension fund trustee	1,700,000 dr.
Service cost	1,366,200 cr.
Net interest	40,400 cr.
Actuarial gains	124,000 dr.
Actuarial losses	257,856 cr.
Closing balance	$1,505,456 cr.

It is possible to derive the closing balances in the pension benefit obligation and pension fund assets. The net amount of these two accounts provides proof for the $1,505,456 net defined benefit liability account.

Defined benefit obligation	
Opening balance—credit	$11,675,000 cr.
Increase due to current service cost	456,200 cr.
Increase due to interest accrued (6% of opening balance)	696,456 cr.
Increase due to new past service granted	910,000 cr.
Decrease due to change in actuarial assumptions	124,000 dr.
Decrease due to pension benefits paid to pensioners	134,800 dr.
Closing balance	$13,478,856 cr.
Pension fund assets	
Opening balance—debit	$10,010,000 dr.
Increase due to actual investment income earned	398,200 dr.
Decrease due to pension benefits paid to pensioners	134,800 cr.
Increase due to contributions during the year	1,700,000 dr.
Closing balance	$11,973,400 dr.
Net defined benefit plan ($13,478,856 − $11,973,400)	$ 1,505,456 cr.

Reporting

The three elements that comprise pension accounting are now completely accounted for in the Walker example. Reporting is as follows, disregarding income tax considerations:

On the SCI:

Earnings (given, excluding pension expense and related interest expense)	$8,842,500 cr.
Interest expense	40,400 dr.
Pension expense ($1,366,200)	1,366,200 dr.
Earnings	$7,435,900 cr.
Other comprehensive income:	
OCI—Remeasurements for pension adjustments	
($257,856 dr. and $124,000 cr.)	133,856 dr.
Comprehensive income	$7,302,044 cr.

On the statement of changes in equity:

	Retained Earnings	Accumulated OCI, Pension
Opening balance (given)	$23,688,100 cr.	$288,400 dr.
Comprehensive income	7,435,900 cr.	133,856 dr.
Closing balance	$ 31,124,000 cr.	$422,256 dr.

On the SFP:

Long-term liability:	
Net defined benefit liability	$ 1,505,456 cr.
Equity:	
Retained earnings	31,124,000 cr.
Accumulated OCI, pension	422,256 dr.

Disposition of Accumulated OCI Amounts

Accumulated OCI may be reclassified into another equity account, most likely retained earnings. *Accumulated OCI amounts may not be included in earnings and thus are never recycled out of accumulated OCI as a revenue or an expense item.* If accumulated OCI is reclassified to retained earnings, the entry is straightforward. Refer again to the Walker example above. The cumulative balance in accumulated OCI is now a debit of $422,526. In cases where the company decides to reclassify to retained earnings, the journal entry is:

Retained earnings	422,256	
OCI: pension		422,256

EVALUATION

As demonstrated, the net defined benefit pension liability or asset on the SFP represents the *net status* of the pension plan (assuming no effect of the asset ceiling). That is:

	Defined benefit obligation (credit)	
Less:	Pension plan assets (debit)	
=	Net defined benefit asset/liability (debit or credit)	

Netting financial statement elements is usually not permitted in financial statements unless certain stringent conditions are met. In the case of a pension plan, the company has both *the legal right* and *the intent* to meet pension obligations through the use of segregated pension assets. Thus, netting is justified.

One troubling aspect of the current IFRS standard for pensions is the use of accumulated OCI for actuarial gains and losses, with no recycling to earnings. Such amounts are never recorded as an expense or revenue item and therefore are never reported in earnings. In particular, using a corporate borrowing yield rate to establish expected earnings for pension fund assets ensures that experience gains and losses will persist annually, since borrowing and investment yield rates diverge.

If the earnings figure is meant to reflect the company's results in dealing with business risks, then eliminating the continuing item of experience and other actuarial gains and losses from the calculation of pension expense is curious. The earnings figure is incomplete. Standard setters may have allowed this treatment on the basis that the standard at least deals with the SFP issue, without stirring up significant resistance among constituents. Note, however, that the U.S. FASB approach requires amounts to be (eventually) recycled out of OCI and into pension expense, so the IASB standard represents a step backward in creating harmonized standards.

ETHICAL ISSUES

The exclusion of actuarial gains and losses from earnings establishes some motive to shade initial estimates of fund earnings on the optimistic side, if earnings maximization is a reporting objective. Subsequent correction of these estimates, creating losses, will never impact earnings. Evaluation of reasonable estimates is particularly important in this context.

CONCEPT REVIEW

1. List the three elements that must be considered to account for a defined benefit pension plan.
2. What are the components of service cost?
3. How is net interest on the net defined benefit liability calculated?
4. What types of adjustments are recorded to accumulated OCI with respect to a defined benefit pension plan?
5. What entries affect the SFP account related to a defined benefit pension plan? What will this account equal, after all adjustments have been made?

SPREADSHEET APPROACH

One of the practical problems in pension accounting is simply keeping track of all of the different amounts that are involved, and a spreadsheet helps.

Example—First-Year Data

To begin the spreadsheet illustration, we will assume that the company, St. Mark Spas Ltd. (SMS), establishes a pension plan effective 1 January 20X1. The employees will receive pension entitlements for past years' service. The plan will be accounted for by the projected unit credit method, using unbiased assumptions. Additional information is obtained from the pension plan trustee and the actuary.

- The interest rate on corporate bonds with similar term and currency is 8%.
- At 1 January, 20X1, the present value of the defined benefit obligation for past service is $100,000 (at the 8% rate), which has not yet been recorded.
- Current service cost for the year 20X1 is $30,000, using the projected unit credit method.
- To adequately *fund* the current service cost and part of the past service cost, the company is required to make a cash contribution of $65,000 to the plan at the end of 20X1.

Element 1: Service cost for 20X1 is:

Current service cost	$ 30,000
PSC	100,000
Service cost, 20X1	$ 130,000

Element 2: Net interest cost for 20X1:

Defined benefit obligation, *beginning of the year*	$ 100,000
Pension fund assets, *beginning of the year*	0
Net defined benefit	$ 100,000
Net interest, 20X1, at 8%	$ 8,000

Since the contributions are made at the end of the year, there is no adjustment required for contributions made during the year for the net interest calculation.

Element 3: Not applicable for 20X1

Since $65,000 was paid to the pension fund trustee, there will be a $73,000 ($65,000 − $130,000 − $8,000) net defined benefit liability reported as a long-term liability at year-end.

Spreadsheet Organization

Exhibit 19-3 shows the pension accounting spreadsheet. Refer to this exhibit as the explanation proceeds, below. The columnar arrangement is as follows:

- The first two numerical columns keep track of the amount of the defined benefit obligation (credit) and the pension fund assets (debit). These are memorandum accounts and are not recorded directly on the company's books.
- The third column is used for summarizing pension expense, including both service cost and net interest cost. Once complete, pension expense is closed out to the (following) net defined benefit liability column, increasing the liability.
- Finally, there are two columns for the SFP accounts: the net defined benefit liability (or asset), and the accumulated OCI account.

EXHIBIT 19-3

PENSION ACCOUNTING SPREADSHEET

			SCI Account	SFP Account	SFP Account
	Defined Benefit Obligation Decrease/ (Increase)	Plan Assets Decrease/ (Increase)	Pension (Including Interest) Expense	Net Defined Benefit (Liability)/Asset	Accumulated OCI
20X1					
Initial PSC	$(100,000)		$ 100,000 dr.		
Current service cost	(30,000)		30,000 dr.		
Net interest on net pension	(8,000)		8,000 dr.		
			$ 138,000 dr.	$ (138,000) cr.	
Funding contribution		$ 65,000		65,000 dr.	
Ending balance	**$(138,000)cr.**	**$ 65,000 dr.**		**$ (73,000) cr.**	**—**

	Defined Benefit Obligation Decrease/ (Increase)	Plan Assets Decrease/ (Increase)	SCI Account Pension (Including Interest) Expense	SFP Account Net Defined Benefit (Liability)/Asset	SFP Account Accumulated OCI
20X2					
Current service cost	(35,000)		35,000 dr.		
Net interest on net pension	(11,040)	5,200	5,840 dr.		
Actuarial gain re: assets		2,000		2,000 dr.	(2,000) cr.
			$ 40,840 dr.	(40,840) cr.	
Funding contribution		68,000		68,000 dr.	
Ending balance	**$(184,040) cr.**	**$140,200 dr.**		**$ (43,840) cr.**	**$ (2,000) cr.**
20X3					
Current service cost	(32,000)		32,000 dr.		
Net interest on net pension	(14,723)	11,216	3,507 dr.		
Actuarial loss re: assets		(916)		(916) cr.	916 dr.
Actuarial revaluation	22,000			22,000 dr.	(22,000) cr.
			$ 35,507 dr.	(35,507) cr.	
Benefits paid	18,000	(18,000)			
Funding contribution		37,000		37,000 dr.	
Ending balance	**$(190,763)**	**$169,500**		**$ (21,263) cr.**	**$(23,084) cr.**

Note that when the spreadsheet is completed each period, *the first two columns cross-add to equal the fourth column*. That is, the *net defined benefit liability* (first two columns) is equal to the *SFP liability* account (fourth column). Brackets in the spreadsheet are used to denote credits. Unbracketed numbers are debits. Note for this example, the interest expense has been included with the pension expense. Note also, for this example, we are assuming that contributions and benefit payments are made at the end of the year, so there is no weighting required in calculating the net interest amount.

First Year

When the pension is initiated in 20X1, the $100,000 defined benefit obligation (credit, in brackets) and pension past service cost (debit) are entered.

Current service cost of $30,000 increases the defined benefit obligation (first column) and pension (and related interest) expense (third column), as does the $8,000 net interest on the net liability. The $65,000 funding contribution increases fund assets (second column) and is therefore recognized as a decrease to the net defined benefit liability account. Pension expense, once complete, is transferred to the net defined benefit liability account. The columns are then added. Note that the first two columns add to equal the fourth column at this point. This is the reconciliation of the SFP net defined benefit liability account and proves that the spreadsheet is complete.

The entries for amounts are as follows:

Pension expense ($100,000 + $30,000)	130,000	
Net defined benefit liability		130,000

Net defined benefit liability	65,000	
Cash		65,000

Pension (or Interest) expense	8,000	
Net defined benefit liability		8,000

Second Year

For 20X2, there will be another calculation of service cost. There now will be some earnings on the plan assets. SMS will receive a report from the pension plan trustee that explains the investment activity and investment results. Assume the following:

- Current service cost is $35,000.
- The *actual* return on the plan assets was $7,200 (a return of approximately 11% on the $65,000 in the plan at the *beginning* of 20X2).
- SMS contributes $68,000 cash to the plan at the end of 20X2, in accordance with the actuary's calculations for funding. (Again, this contribution has no impact on the calculation of net interest since it is made at the end of the year.)
- The fair value of the plan assets at the end of 20X2 is $140,200.

Element 1: Service cost for 20X2 is:

Current service cost	$ 35,000

Element 2: Net interest cost for 20X2:

Defined benefit obligation, beginning of the year	$ 138,000
Pension fund assets, beginning of the year	65,000

Net defined benefit liability	$ 73,000

Net interest, 20X2 at 8% (8% of the obligation ($138,000) is $11,040
and 8% of the asset ($65,000) is $5,200; $11,040 − $5,200 = $5,840)   **$ 5,840**

Element 3: The *expected* return on the plan assets for 20X2 was 8% of the beginning-of-year plan assets of $65,000, or $5,200. The actual return was $7,200. The extra return of $2,000 above the expected return is an *experience gain*, which is one type of actuarial gain and is recorded in OCI.

The entries for the 20X2 expenses, actuarial gain, and funding payment are as follows:

Pension expense	35,000	
Net defined benefit liability		35,000
Net defined benefit liability	68,000	
Cash		68,000
Interest expense (components are $11,040 less $5,200)	5,840	
Net defined benefit liability		5,840
Net defined benefit liability ($7,200 − $5,200)	2,000	
OCI: pension		2,000

Refer again to the spreadsheet in Exhibit 19-3. Find the following items:

- Service cost of $35,000 increases the defined benefit obligation and pension expense.
- Net interest on the net pension obligation of $5,840 increases pension (including interest) expense, and the two components of $11,040 (cr.) and $5,200 (dr.) are entered, increasing the defined benefit obligation and plan assets, respectively. See the row highlighted in yellow.
- The actuarial gain of $2,000 is entered in the pension fund asset column; this increases the return in column two to $7,200 ($5,200 expected plus the extra $2,000 of earnings). The $2,000 actuarial gain must be entered *twice more* in the spreadsheet; in the net defined benefit liability column and in accumulated OCI. It increases accumulated OCI because it is a gain, and decreases the net defined benefit liability account. See the row highlighted in blue.
- Funding contributions of $68,000 increase fund assets and are also entered as a debit in column four.
- To complete the spreadsheet, pension expense is totalled and entered as a credit in column four. The columns are totalled and cross-added. Again, the total of the first two columns equals the fourth column, the net defined benefit liability account.

Third Year

Assume the following additional facts for 20X3:

- Current service cost is $32,000, as calculated by the actuary;
- Actual return on the plan assets is $10,300;
- The first actuarial revaluation occurs. Due to changes in mortality assumptions, the defined benefit obligation is *decreased* by $22,000;

- Benefits of $18,000 are paid to retirees by the pension plan trustee (in this case, assumed to be paid at the end of the year so there is no impact on the interest calculation); and
- SMS contributes $37,000 cash to the plan at the end of 20X3.

Element 1: Service cost for 20X3 is:

Current service cost	$ 32,000

Element 2: Net interest cost for 20X3:

Defined benefit obligation, beginning of the year	$ 184,040
Pension fund assets, beginning of the year	140,200
Net defined benefit liability	$ 43,840
Net interest, 20X3 at 8% (8% of the obligation ($184,040) is $14,723 and 8% of the asset ($140,200) is $11,216; $14,723 − $11,216 = $3,507)	$ 3,507

Element 3: The *expected* return on plan assets for 20X3 was 8% of the beginning-of-year plan assets of $140,200, or $11,216. The actual return was $10,300. The shortfall of $916 below the expected return is an actuarial loss. There is also a $22,000 actuarial gain on the change in assumptions that triggered a recalculation of the pension benefit obligation.

The entries for the 20X3 expenses, actuarial gains and losses and funding payment are as follows:

Pension expense	32,000	
Net defined benefit liability		32,000
Net defined benefit liability	37,000	
Cash		37,000
Interest expense (components are $14,723 less $11,216)	3,507	
Net defined benefit liability		3,507
Net defined benefit liability	22,000	
OCI: pension		22,000
OCI: pension ($11,216 − $10,300)	916	
Net defined benefit asset/liability		916

Spreadsheet

Refer to Exhibit 19-3. The following items are entered on the spreadsheet:

- The current service cost of $32,000 is added to the pension benefit obligation and pension expense.
- Net interest on the net defined benefit obligation of $3,507 is added to pension (including interest) expense and the components of $14,723 interest on the obligation and $11,216 expected earnings on pension fund assets are included in the appropriate columns. See the row highlighted in yellow.

- The $916 ($11,216 − $10,300) shortfall in actual earnings is a deduction from pension assets; the combination of positive $11,216 and negative $916 in this column is equal to the actual earnings of $10,300. The $916 affects *both* the net defined benefit liability and accumulated OCI; since it is a loss, it is a debit in accumulated OCI and increases (credits) the SFP liability. See the row highlighted in blue.

- The $22,000 gain from the actuarial revaluation *reduces* the defined benefit obligation in the first column, and it also is entered *twice more*. It decreases the net defined benefit liability and is a credit in accumulated OCI because it is a gain. See the row highlighted in green.

- Benefits of $18,000 paid to retirees reduce pension plan assets and the defined benefit obligation but have no impact on financial statement accounts.

- Total pension expense is transferred to the net defined benefit pension asset/liability, in the fourth column.

- The funding contribution of $37,000 is added to the pension plan assets and is debited to the net defined benefit asset/liability.

Once more, the proof of accuracy is that the first two columns are equal to the fourth column. The pension is underfunded by $21,263, and this is the net defined benefit liability that appears on the SFP. The defined benefit obligation is $190,763, and pension fund assets are $169,500, a net of ($21,263).

Summary of Spreadsheet Adjustments

The following table provides a summary of spreadsheet items caused by pension elements:

Column	Normal Balance	Increase	Decrease	Either Increase or Decrease
Defined benefit obligation	Credit	• Current service cost • Interest on obligation • New past service cost	• Benefit payments to retirees	• Actuarial revaluation • Credit this column if liability increases and debit this column if liability decreases
Pension plan assets	Debit	• Annual funding contribution • Expected earnings (interest income)	• Benefit payments to retirees	• Actuarial gain or loss, the difference between expected and actual earnings • Credit if actual earnings are lower and debit if actual earnings are higher

Pension (including interest) expense[1]	Debit	• Service cost		• Net interest on net pension liability/asset
				  • Debit if net interest cost on net liability
				  • Credit if net interest revenue on net asset

Column	Normal Balance	Increase	Decrease	Either Increase or Decrease
Net defined benefit asset/ liability	Debit if an asset Credit if a liability			• Credit for the expense amount • Debit for the funding amount • Debit or credit for actuarial gains (debit) or losses (credit)
Accumulated OCI	Credit if accumulated gains Debit if accumulated losses			• Debit or credit for actuarial gains (credit) or losses (debit) • Debit or credit for the effect of the asset ceiling, if needed.

[1]Pension expense also includes gains and losses from nonroutine settlements.

CONCEPT REVIEW

1. How does expected return on pension plan assets affect pension expense?
2. What two spreadsheet accounts change for service costs?
3. What two spreadsheet accounts are changed by benefits paid to employees?
4. What three spreadsheet accounts are changed by newly arising actuarial losses?

OTHER POST-EMPLOYMENT BENEFITS

Post-employment benefits typically involve more than pensions. **Other post-employment benefits** (OPEBs) include supplementary health care, prescription drug plans, dental benefits, and various insurance plans for retirees. Because of universal health care in Canada, the cost of these benefits is less than in some other countries, such as the United States. However, the cost of OPEBs can still be substantial.

There are some practical differences between pensions and other post-employment benefits, summarized as follows:

	Pensions	Other Post-Employment Benefits
Use	Regular monthly payments with predictable or estimable increases until entitlements cease.	Sporadic use from employee to employee and unpredictable cost increases.
Beneficiary	Retired employee usually with some survivor rights.	Retired employee and family members, as specified in the plan.
Funding	Plans are typically registered; likely to be fully or mostly funded during the working life of the employee.	Plans are typically unregistered. Likely to be substantially unfunded because contributions to unregistered plans are not tax deductible for the employer.
Revaluations	Periodic as required by legislation.	Likely frequent, to reflect changed cost estimates.

The differences in usage of the plans, in particular, make cost estimation even more uncertain than the already-uncertain pension estimates. Nonetheless, the relevance of the information dictates that reliability be sacrificed, with appropriate disclosure of variables used.

Accounting standards require that OPEBs be accounted for in a similar manner as pensions. That is, the annual analysis includes three elements:

1. Service cost, both OPEB current service and past service, plus plan settlements and curtailments;
2. Net interest cost on the net OPEB plan liability or asset; and
3. Recognition of OPEB actuarial gains or losses in accumulated other comprehensive income.

From an accounting/economic perspective, the most significant difference between OPEB and pension situations is that there are unlikely to be segregated asset balances for OPEBs because these plans are rarely registered. For an unregistered plan, contributions are not tax deductible by the employer until eventual benefits are paid; accordingly, there is little incentive to fund these plans.

Example

Review the spreadsheet in Exhibit 19-4, which reflects the following data for 20X8:

Opening OPEB liability	$175,000	Contribution paid into OPEB asset fund	$22,000
Opening plan assets	$10,000	Benefits paid by OPEB fund to retirees during the period	$24,000
Actuarial revaluation during the period, OPEB liability increases because future health care costs are expected to rise	$16,000	Actual return on plan assets ($600 expected less $350 actuarial loss)	$250
Current service cost	$29,000	Yield for corporate bonds	6%

EXHIBIT 19-4

OBEB ACCOUNTING SPREADSHEET

	OPEB Obligation	OPEB Plan Assets	SCI Account OPEB Expense	SFP Account Net OPEB (Liability) Asset	SFP Account Accumulated OCI
20X8					
Opening	$(175,000)	$10,000		$(165,000) cr.*	
Current service cost	(29,000)		$29,000 dr.		
Net interest expense (6%)**	(10,500)	600	9,900 dr.		
			$38,900 dr.	(38,900) cr.	
Actuarial loss		(350)		(350) cr.	350 dr.
Actuarial loss	(16,000)			(16,000) cr.	16,000 dr.
Contribution		22,000		22,000 dr.	
Benefits paid	24,000	(24,000)			
Total	**$(206,500)**	**$ 8,250**		**$(198,250)***	**$16,350 dr.**

*For the opening balance. $175,000 obligation, less $10,000 fund assets. For the closing balance, $206,500 less $8,250.

** Interest is calculated based on the opening balance plus the weighted average time period for contributions or payments, similar to net interest on defined benefit pension plans. In the above case, for simplicity, assume that contributions and payments have been made at the end of the year and therefore do not impact the calculation of the net interest expense.

This spreadsheet follows the now-familiar pattern. Current service cost of $29,000 increases the obligation and the expense, as does the $9,900 net interest calculated on the opening net OPEB balance. That is, interest expense of $10,500 ($175,000 × 6%) on the OPEB obligation less expected interest income of $600 ($10,000 × 6%) on fund assets. The difference between expected return of $600 and actual return on $250 is a $350 actuarial loss recorded in assets, and also posted to accumulated OCI and the SFP net OPEB liability. The actuarial revaluation is a loss of $16,000, and is recorded in the OPEB obligation, SFP net OPEB liability, and accumulated OCI. Finally, cash paid to the fund increases the asset balance and affects the SFP liability account, and benefits paid reduce assets and the OPEB obligation.

STATEMENT OF CASH FLOWS

The cash flows relating to pensions and other OPEBs are almost certainly different from the accounting expense. On the statement of cash flows, the difference between expense and contributions to the fund is an adjustment in operating activities. Cash paid to the fund during the year is required disclosure in the pension note.

Example

Return to the Walker Corp. example earlier in the chapter. Recall that the reporting was as follows:

On the SCI:

Earnings (given, excluding pension expense and related interest expense)	$8,842,500 cr.
Interest expense	40,400 dr.
Pension expense	1,366,200 dr.
Earnings	$7,435,900 cr.
Other comprehensive income:	
OCI - Remeasurements for pension adjustments	
($257,856 dr. and $124,000 cr.)	133,856 dr.
Comprehensive income	$7,302,044 cr.

On the statement of changes in equity:

	Retained Earnings	Accumulated OCI, Pension
Opening balance (given)	$ 23,688,100 cr.	$288,400 dr.
Comprehensive income	7,435,900 cr.	133,856 dr.
Closing balance	$ 31,124,000 cr.	$422,256 dr.

On the SFP:

Long-term liability:	
Net defined benefit liability	$1,505,456 cr.
Equity:	
Retained earnings	31,124,000 cr.
Accumulated OCI, pension	422,256 dr.

On the SCF, the following items would be found:

In operating activities, earnings	$7,435,900
Changes in balance sheet accounts:	
Decrease in net defined benefit liability[1]	(293,400)

[1]Opening balance = $1,665,000 + $ 133,856 non-cash net actuarial losses = $1,798,856. The balance reported is $1,505,456, a further difference of $293,400. This is the remaining difference, and it is the difference between the $1,700,000 amount paid and the $1,366,200 pension expense and interest expense of $40,400, or $293,400. The amount paid is higher than the expense.

There are no other changes with respect to the pension reported on the SCF. Note that the change in accumulated OCI is a non-cash item, changing accumulated OCI and the net defined benefit liability. However, if the second element of pension expense is segregated and termed a financing expense ($40,400 in this case), it could be disclosed separately.

DISCLOSURE REQUIREMENTS

The disclosure requirements for post-employment benefits are unusually extensive. The financial statements themselves include the three elements relating to pensions and other post-employment benefits:

1. On the statement of comprehensive income, the amount of *expense* relating to providing post-employment benefits;
2. On the statement of comprehensive income, and the statement of financial position, the amount of *remeasurement* recorded (element 3 in our examples);
3. On the statement of financial position, the *net defined benefit asset or liability* that reflects the funded status of the pension plan; the defined benefit obligation netted with plan assets;
4. On the statement of cash flows, the change in the SFP pension liability *not* caused by accumulated OCI changes.

These amounts provide little direct information about the nature of post-employment benefits and the major underlying risks. Therefore, disclosure is the only viable way to assist users. Qualitative disclosure is required in three broad areas:

1. The characteristics of, and risks associated with, defined benefit plans;
2. Identification and explanation of recognized amounts and key assumptions used; and
3. A description of how such plans might affect the amount, timing, and uncertainty of future cash flows.

Selected Disclosures

A narrative description of the plan is required, along with the legislative and governance framework for the plan. Disclosure includes important information about changes in the plan, risks, and also measurements used for accounting. Measurement disclosures are extensive, and all calculations and assumptions must be disclosed. Assumptions may reflect biases and will affect comparability, and so they are especially important disclosures.

Some major items:

1. A reconciliation of relevant pension amounts to the SFP asset or liability account over the year (i.e., all components that explain the change in the first two spreadsheet columns, to equal the SFP asset or liability account);
2. Amount of expense recognized for the period, and the components of the expense;
3. Changes in reserves and other comprehensive income, with each component shown separately;
4. Numerical disclosure separating plan assets into various asset categories;
5. Actual return on plan assets during the year;

6. Information about funding commitments, including contributions to the plan for coming years and information about the maturity profile of the defined benefit obligation;

7. Significant actuarial assumptions used to measure the defined benefit obligation; and

8. Sensitivity analysis, including the effect of changing significant actuarial assumptions.

The extensive array of disclosures represents an attempt to converge the disclosures required in many jurisdictions.

Refer to Exhibit 19-5, which shows the line-by-line disclosure of the changes in the defined benefit obligation and pension fund assets. At the 2014 year-end, there is a defined benefit obligation of $48.7 million, and pension fund assets of $50.6 million. Other extensive disclosures by the company in this area have been omitted from Exhibit 19-5. For OPEBs, there is a $1.7 million obligation and no segregated assets, as is standard practice in this area. The listed items that cause change in the obligation and assets should be largely familiar from the spreadsheet examples. Note that references to disclosure notes have been deleted in the Exhibit 19-5 below.

EXHIBIT 19-5

INTERFOR CORPORATION

Partial Extracts from Disclosure Note 22, (part D)
Employee Future Benefits and Other Post-Retirement Plans

22. Employee future benefits and other post-retirement plan (continued):

(d) Defined benefit plans (continued):

The following summarizes the pension and other post-retirement obligations:

	Pension Benefits		Other Post-retirement Benefits	
	2014	2013	2014	2013
Defined benefit obligation:				
Beginning of year	$ 53,178	$ 54,812	$ 1,545	$ 1,833
Service cost	746	716	35	45
Employee contributions	369	342	-	-
Interest cost	2,430	2,272	72	78
Benefit payments	(2,839)	(3,222)	(70)	(87)
Past service cost (settlements)	(186)	-	-	(17)
Actuarial loss (gain) due to:				
Demographic assumptions	798	1,043	29	28
Financial assumptions	5,422	(3,390)	89	(1)
Experience adjustment	165	605	-	(334)
Settlements	(11,354)	-	-	-
End of year	$48,729	$53,178	$ 1,700	$ 1,545

Plan assets:

Beginning of year	$56,882	$51,897	$ -	$ -
Interest on plan assets	2,595	2,139	-	-
Employer contributions	1,263	1,471	70	87
Employee contributions	369	342	-	-
Benefit payments	(2,839)	(3,222)	(70)	(87)
Administration costs	(374)	(228)	-	-
Actuarial gain	4,395	4,483	-	-
Settlements	(11,716)	-	-	-
End of year	$50,575	$56,882	$ -	$ -

Asset ceiling:

Beginning of year	$ (700)	$ -	$ -	$ -
Interest effect	(32)	-	-	-
Impact of settlements	732	(700)	-	-
End of year	$ -	$ (700)	$ -	$ -

The following summarizes the balances recognized on the Statements of Financial Position:

	Pension Benefits		Other Post-retirement Benefits	
	2014	2013	2014	2013
Fair value of plan assets	$50,575	$56,882	$ -	$ -
Present value of unfunded obligations	393	414	1,700	1,545
Present value of funded obligations	48,336	52,764	-	-
Surplus (deficit)	1,846	3,704	(1,700)	(1,545)
Effect of asset ceiling limit	-	(700)	-	-
Accrued benefit (obligation)	$ 1,846	$3,004	$(1,700)	$ (1,545)

The following table shows the Company's net expense recognized in the Statement of Earnings and the actuarial (gains) losses recognized in Retained earnings through Other comprehensive income:

	Pension Benefits		Other Post-retirement Benefits	
	2014	2013	2014	2013
Statement of Earnings				
Production expense	$ 1,120	$ 944	$ 35	$ 28
Finance (income) costs	(133)	133	72	78
Restructuring costs	176	-	-	-
	$ 1,163	$ 1,077	$ 107	$ 106
Other comprehensive loss (income)				
Actuarial losses (gains)	$ 1,990	$(6,225)	$ 118	$ (307)
Effect of asset ceiling limit	(732)	700	-	-
	$ 1,258	$(5,525)	$ 118	$ (307)

The Company's accrued benefit assets (liabilities) are included in the Company's Statements of Financial Position as follows:

	Pension Benefits		Other Post-retirement Benefits	
	2014	2013	2014	2013
Employee future benefits asset	$ 2,520	$ 3,980	$ -	$ -
Trade accounts payable and provisions	(72)	(74)	(50)	(50)
Employee future benefits obligation	(602)	(902)	(1,650)	(1,495)
	$ 1,846	$3,004	$(1,700)	$(1,545)

[References to disclosure notes deleted.]

Source: Interfor Corporation, Annual Financial Statements, year ended December 31, 2014, www.sedar.com, posted 12 February 2015.

Looking Forward

Post-employment benefit issues are not now on the agenda of either the IASB or the Canadian AcSB. Both groups have had recent new standards in this area—effective 2013 (IFRS) and 2014 (ASPE). As a result, further changes in the near future are not be expected. However, this is an area where IASB and FASB standards are different, and pressure for harmonization may lead to change in the future.

FASB Approach to Accounting for Post-Employment Benefits

Under IASB rules, accumulated OCI amounts are never recognized in earnings. Accumulated OCI amounts may be transferred directly to retained earnings or another equity account. Under FASB rules, however, accumulated OCI amounts related to pensions are recycled to earnings; that is, actuarial amounts are recycled out of OCI and expensed over time.

This is a fundamental difference in the way accumulated OCI related to pensions is treated, and resolution of this difference will likely only come about after there is a conceptual framework that governs accumulated OCI. At the moment, this account is largely unstructured and is subject to some considerable inconsistencies in the hands of standard setters.

Accounting Standards for Private Enterprises

Defined Contribution Plans

Private companies with defined contribution plans follow the approach described previously in the chapter. There are no differences between ASPE and IFRS standards in this category.

Defined Benefit Plans

Private companies with defined benefit plans follow a simplified approach, reflecting the absence of OCI in ASPE reporting. To determine the year-end balance of the defined benefit obligation, companies have an accounting policy choice to use either:

- The *actuarial valuation prepared for accounting purposes* using the projected benefit method prorated on services, when future salary levels or cost escalation affect the amount of the employee future benefits; or using the accumulated benefits method when the pension is not dependent on future salary levels or escalation clauses; or
- The *actuarial valuation prepared for funding purposes.*

Pension expense for a defined benefit pension plan is equal to an amalgamation of four items: current service cost, finance cost, remeasurements and changes in the valuation allowance. Nothing is recorded in accumulated OCI.

Similar to IFRS in applying the asset ceiling test, when the defined benefit plan is in a net surplus position only the amount of future benefits can be recognized on the balance sheet. For example, if the net defined benefit surplus is $150,000 and the amount of future benefits available is only $120,000, there is a valuation allowance of $30,000 and only $120,000 net surplus can be recognized on the SFP. Any changes in this **valuation allowance** are recognized in current earnings as part of the pension expense.

Pension Expense   The components of pension expense for ASPE largely follow the IFRS pattern. These components are identified in the chart that follows:

ASPE Pension Expense Components	Comment
1. Current service cost	Measured based on the choice of actuarial valuation used (as described earlier).
2. Finance cost	Appropriate discount rate multiplied by the net defined benefit liability (asset) on the *opening balance sheet*. This net amount is the defined benefit obligation less plan assets at fair value. Note that this differs with IFRS, which requires adjustments be made for contributions and payments during the year. In addition, interest on the opening asset ceiling adjustment is also included in finance costs under IFRS. Under ASPE, the entire change of the valuation allowance is reflected in the pension cost (along with changes in the interest on the ceiling asset amount). The discount rate is the market interest rate on high-quality debt instruments with timing and amounts that match the pension outflows. If the plan could be settled by means of an insurance or annuity contract with a third party, the interest rate inherent in this arrangement can be used as a discount rate.
3a. Remeasurement: Actual versus expected return on plan assets	The difference between expected return on assets included in item 2 and actual return is included immediately in pension expense. This has the effect of recognizing *actual return* in pension expense. Actual returns may be volatile. Actual return includes annual payments, such as interest or dividends, and also the realized and unrealized gains and losses on the fair value of plan assets during the year.
3b. Remeasurement: Past service cost	Past service cost is the change in the defined benefit obligation caused by introduction, withdrawal, or amendment of plan benefits with reference to prior service. The amount is expensed immediately; no deferral or amortization is permitted.

ASPE Pension Expense Components	Comment
3c. Remeasurement: Actuarial gains and losses	Actuarial gains and losses are caused by revaluing the defined benefit obligation because of changes in assumptions. Actuarial gain and losses are immediately expensed. Under ASPE, nothing is recorded in accumulated OCI; this financial statement element does not exist in ASPE financial statements.
3d. Remeasurement: Other	Also included in pension expense are any changes caused by the presence of a valuation allowance, which is created when there is a net defined benefit *asset*, but there are limits on its use. Another cause of remeasurement are settlements and curtailments; if these latter elements are caused by restructuring or discontinued operations, any gain or loss is classified accordingly.

Comparison with IASB Rules   As compared with IFRS, the ASPE approach has much the same look and feel. An important aspect of this is that the balance sheet will reflect the net defined benefit liability or asset, which is the net status of the pension plan. The major difference between IFRS and ASPE is that there is no OCI classification. Amounts are expensed in the remeasurement (element 3) classification, rather than being classified to OCI. As compared with IFRS, the ASPE approach can be expected to cause some major volatility in net income when pension variables change.

Note that past service cost is classified as a *remeasurement* in ASPE and a *service cost* in IFRS; this is a classification difference with no implications for the treatment of past service cost; it is expensed in either scheme.

The disclosure required under ASPE for defined benefit plans is minimal requiring note disclosure on: description of the plans, the ending balance of the defined benefit obligation and plan assets, remeasurements, valuation allowance, date of most recent actuarial valuation report and any significant changes to the contractual commitments under the plans.

There are many, many minor differences between IFRS and ASPE, related to plan curtailment and settlement, multi-employer plans, disclosure, and the like.

Example   Refer to Exhibit 19-6 for data for Newmarket Ltd. Corporate borrowing rates for high-quality bonds are in the range of 6%. These bonds have a term similar to anticipated pension payments.

EXHIBIT 19-6

ASPE PENSION EXAMPLE

Balances:

Defined benefit obligation, end of 20X7	$2,472,900
Pension plan assets, fair value, end of 20X7	2,332,100

SFP Net defined benefit liability, end of 20X7 $140,800 cr.

Information relating to 20X8:

Current service cost for 20X8, measured using the projected benefit method	$ 76,800
New past service cost granted in 20X8; defined benefit obligation increases	110,700
Amount paid to pension fund trustee	98,000
Actuarial loss in 20X8, caused by anticipated longer lifespan of retirees; defined benefit obligation increases	109,400
Actual earnings in the fund, reported by the pension fund trustee, including interest, dividends, and change in fair value	45,500

Pension expense is calculated as follows:

1. Current service cost	$ 76,800
2. Interest cost ($140,800 × 6%), or [$2,472,900 × 6% ($148,374) – $2,332,100 × 6% ($139,926)]	8,448
3.a Remeasurement: Past service cost granted in 20X5	110,700
3.b Remeasurement: Actual versus expected return ($139,926 expected versus $45,500 actual)	94,426
3.c Remeasurement: Actuarial loss	109,400
	$ 399,774

The same total would be obtained by including interest on the entire defined benefit obligation, *actual return on assets*, and omitting *category 3b*:

1. Current service cost	$ 76,800
2.a Interest cost ($2,472,900 × 6%)	148,374
2.b Actual return	(45,500)
3.a Remeasurement: Past service cost granted in 20X8	110,700
3.b n/a	—
3.c Remeasurement: Actuarial loss	109,400
	$ 399,774

The entry to record pension expense:

| Pension expense | 399,774 | |
| Net defined benefit liability | | 399,774 |

The $98,000 contribution to the pension fund trustee is also recorded:

| Net defined benefit liability | 98,000 | |
| Cash | | 98,000 |

RELEVANT STANDARDS

CPA Canada Handbook, Part I (IFRS):

- IAS 19, Employee Benefits

CPA Canada Handbook, Part II (ASPE):

- Section 3462, Employee Future Benefits

SUMMARY OF KEY POINTS

1. In a defined contribution pension plan, the amounts to be paid into the pension plan fund are determined, and the eventual pension is a function of the amounts paid in plus the earnings accumulated in the pension fund. Risk rests with the employee. The annual expense is normally equal to the contribution made to the plan.

2. In a defined benefit pension plan, the retirement benefits are defined as a function of either years of service or employee earnings, or both. The employer is responsible for contributing enough into the fund that, combined with investment earnings, will pay the pension to which the employee is entitled. Risk rests with the employer.

3. Pension plans are contributory if the employee pays into the plan. An employee has ownership of pension assets when rights have vested. Vesting is governed by pension legislation and pension contracts.

4. An employer's annual contribution to a defined benefit pension plan is calculated using an actuarial cost method. Alternatives exist with respect to the variables that are projected and the funding patterns. The projected unit credit method must be used for external reporting. This actuarial cost method projects salary levels but does not project years of service.

5. Because of the long time span involved in pension estimates, pension amounts are sensitive to the underlying assumptions used. These include demographic and financial assumptions. Estimates that are unbiased and mutually compatible must be used for accounting purposes.

6. A defined benefit pension plan consists of pension plan assets, segregated in a separate legal entity and managed by a trustee, and a defined benefit obligation, measured using the projected unit credit method. The net of these two numbers is the net funded position and represents the net defined benefit liability or asset.

7. The SFP net defined benefit asset/liability account is equal to the net status of the pension plan. This is the overfunded or underfunded status of the plan–pension fund assets less the defined benefit obligation. The net defined benefit liability/asset is usually equal to the amount recognized on the SFP. However, in the case of a net defined benefit asset position, the amount of the asset recognized on the SFP is limited to a ceiling amount equal to the future benefits available to the company. This amount is determined by applying the asset ceiling test.

8. For a defined benefit pension plan, pension accounting involves examining three elements: (1) service cost measured using the projected unit credit actuarial cost method, (2) net interest on the net defined benefit liability or asset, and (3) remeasurements (through accumulated OCI) of the net defined benefit liability, including experience gains or losses and actuarial revaluations.

9. Service cost is an expense, and includes current service cost, past service cost, and gains and losses on plan settlements. Current service cost is an estimate of the cost of providing the pension entitlement that the employee has earned in the current year of employment. Past service cost is an estimate of the expected present value of retrospective pension entitlements relating to previous years' service when a new pension plan is instituted or when an existing plan is amended.

10. Net interest is an expense. It is measured by using the market yield for high-grade corporate bonds at the end of the last year—bonds with similar term and currency as the net benefit obligation. Interest is measured on the net pension liability or asset, which is the net amount of pension plan assets and the defined benefit obligation adjusted for contributions and payments made during the year. Net interest essentially has three elements: expected earnings on pension plan assets, accrued interest on the defined benefit obligation, and the interest impact on the effect of applying the asset ceiling test.

11. Remeasurements are included in accumulated OCI and are never recycled to earnings. Accumulated OCI amounts may be transferred to another equity amount, most likely retained earnings. Remeasurements include actuarial gains, which arise either because actual experience is different from expectations or because assumptions about the future are changed, or both. The difference between expected earnings on plan assets and actual return is a common source of remeasurement gain or loss. Changes in the amounts due to the effect of the asset ceiling test also impact OCI.

12. Benefits paid to retirees reduce the value of the plan assets and reduce the defined benefit obligation. Benefits paid do not enter directly into the calculation of pension expense.

13. A spreadsheet is a useful way to organize data needed for pension plan accounting. The spreadsheet tracks the defined benefit obligation, pension plan assets, pension expense, the SFP asset or liability pension account, and accumulated OCI.

14. Other post-employment benefits (OPEB) include supplementary medical and dental plans for retirees. These benefits are accounted for in a similar fashion as pensions, with the cost accrued over the working life of the employee.

15. Companies must provide extensive disclosures for pensions and OPEB with respect to accounting policies and measurement of estimates. Disclosures include all changes during the year for plan assets and the defined benefit obligation, with these two accounts reconciled to the recorded net defined benefit asset or liability.

16. Under ASPE, defined benefit pension plans are accounted for by expensing all elements of pension cost—service cost, interest cost, and remeasurements. There are no deferrals, and no items are recorded in accumulated OCI. There are some differences between ASPE and IFRS related to the calculations of current service, finance costs, and pension expenses.

Key Terms

accumulated benefit method	net defined benefit liability (asset)
actuarial cost methods	noncontributory pension plan
actuarial gains and losses	other post-employment benefits
actuarial revaluation	past service cost (PSC)
actuary	pension holiday
asset ceiling	pension plan curtailment
contributory pension plan	pension plan settlement
current service cost	projected unit credit method
death benefits	recycled to earnings
defined benefit obligation	remeasurements
defined benefit plan	registered
defined contribution plan	service cost
final pay pension plan	survivor benefits
flat benefit	termination benefits
funding	trustee
level contribution method	valuation allowance

Review Problem 19-1

The following data relate to a defined benefit pension plan:

Defined benefit obligation, 31 December 20X5	$25,000
Long-term interest rate on corporate bonds	10%
Past service cost from amendment dated 31 December 20X6, liability is reduced because benefits were reduced	$ (1,200)
Actuarial revaluation dated 31 December 20X6; increase to liability because of changed mortality assumptions	$ 600
Actual return on plan assets for 20X6	$ 2,100
Fair value of plan assets, 31 December 20X5	$ 16,000
Funding contribution at year-end 20X6	$ 4,000
Benefits paid to retirees in 20X6 throughout the year	$ 2,000
Current service cost for 20X6	$ 1,900

There is no balance in accumulated OCI on 31 December 20X5.

Required:

1. Calculate the SFP net defined benefit liability as of 31 December 20X5.
2. Compute the defined benefit obligation at 31 December 20X6 and the fair value of plan assets on the same date. Also calculate the net defined benefit position as at 31 December 20X6.
3. Analyze the three elements of pension accounting for 20X6: service cost, net interest, and remeasurements. Prepare entries for these elements and for the contribution made to the fund during 20X6.
4. Calculate the SFP net defined benefit liability as of 31 December 20X6, and prove that this represents the net defined benefit position.
5. Assume instead that this pension plan is sponsored by a private company and ASPE applies. Prepare all entries for 20X6. Calculate the SFP net defined benefit liability as of 31 December 20X6.

REVIEW PROBLEM 19-1—SOLUTION

1. Net defined benefit liability, 31 December 20X5

Defined benefit obligation, 31 December 20X5	$25,000 cr.
Pension plan assets, 31 December 20X5	16,000 dr.
Net defined benefit liability, 31 December 20X5	$ 9,000 cr.

2. Defined benefit obligation, 31 December 20X6

Obligation, 1 January 20X6	$25,000
Current service cost, 20X6	1,900
Interest (10% of opening balance + weighted average period of payments) ((25,000 - ((2,000) × 6/12)) × 10%	2,400
Past service cost amendment	(1,200)
Actuarial revaluation	600
Benefits paid	(2,000)
	$26,700 cr.

Fair value of plan assets, 31 December 20X6

Value at 1 January 20X6	$ 16,000
Actual return on plan assets	2,100
Funding contributions	4,000
Benefits paid	(2,000)
	$20,100 dr.

Net defined benefit liability, 31 December 20X6 ($26,700 – $20,100)	$ 6,600 cr.

3. Entries for three elements, and fund contribution

Service cost:

Pension expense ($1,900 − $1,200)	700	
Net defined benefit asset/liability		700

Net interest:

Pension expense ($9,000 × 10%)

(components are $2,400 − $1,600)	900	

   Interest expense: $((25,000 − ((2,000) × 6/12)) × 10\% = 2,400$

   Interest income: $((16,000 − ((2,000) × 6/12)) × 10\% = 1,500$

Net defined benefit asset/liability		900

Remeasurement:

Net defined benefit asset/liability

(Experience gain on assets: $2,100 − $1,500)	600	
OCI: pension		600
OCI: pension (Revaluation)	600	
Net defined benefit asset/liability		600

Contribution:

Net defined benefit asset/liability	4,000	
Cash		4,000

4. Net defined benefit liability, 31 December 20X6

($9,000 cr. Op. balance + $700 cr. + $900 cr. − $600 dr.   + $600 cr. − $4,000 dr.)   <u>$ 6,600</u> cr.

Proof: Equal to the net defined benefit as calculated in requirement 2

5. Pension expense, 20X6, under ASPE

Current service cost	$ 1,900
Finance cost ($9,000 × 10%), or $25,000 × 10% ($2,500) − $16,000 × 10% ($1,600)	900
Remeasurement: Past service cost; benefits reduced	(1,200)
Remeasurement: Actual versus expected return ($1,600 expected* versus $2,100 actual) (gain)	(500)
Remeasurement: Actuarial loss	600
	$ 1,700

*($16,000 × 10% no adjustment for benefit payments under APSE.

Entries:

Expense:

Pension expense	1,700	
Net defined benefit asset/liability		1,700

Contribution:

Net defined benefit asset/liability	4,000	
Cash		4,000
Net defined benefit liability, 31 December 20X6		$ 6,700 cr.

($9,000 cr. Op. balance + $1,700cr. − $4,000 dr.)

CASE 19-1

PROPULSION XT LTD.

Propulsion XT Ltd. (PXTL) is a manufacturer of personal and commercial transportation solutions, including train engines and train cars. The company is one of the largest private companies in Canada and complies with ASPE. A transition to IFRS has been discussed for some time but has never been implemented because of the more onerous disclosure requirements. The company does not prepare a classified balance sheet because inventories and unearned revenues would have to be split very arbitrarily into current and long-term amounts; there are many customer contracts outstanding that span multiple years. The company must comply with total debt to equity covenants for long-term debt arrangements, and there is an additional covenant on the maximum level of common share dividends.

The company reflects the $1,743 million unfunded status of its defined benefit pension plan as a long-term liability. The plan recorded large investment losses in 20X1, consistent with a sharp plunge in the stock market. Actuarial losses followed, caused by a decline in discount rates. Experience and actuarial losses are approximately $2,011 as at 31 December 20X5.

Both the audit committee and the risk management committee of the board of directors have pensions on the agenda. The audit committee of PXTL would like to more fully understand how the balance sheet would differ if IFRS standards were used. Restatement would be most helpful.

The risk management committee is concerned about the ongoing risk to PXTL of sponsoring this defined benefit plan. The committee would like to understand what leeway they have, if any, to reduce the underfunded status of the plan and annual expense, through re-examining the assumptions used. They are also wondering what the implication would be of switching to a defined contribution plan, as many companies in their industry have done. This might be a major issue in upcoming labour negotiations. Preliminary negotiations indicate that workers might be offered existing assets, plus $200 million, rolled to a separate trust in relation to existing claims. Premiums under a defined contribution plan are likely to be 120% of the $51 annual amount now transferred to the plan. Additional funding of $100 million per year, designed to address the underfunded status, would be eliminated.

You are an analyst in the financial reporting area, and you have been asked to redraft the financial statements and prepare a report that addresses the questions and alternatives raised to reflect IFRS for pension accounting. The report should include an explanation of your changes and any related concerns.

Required:

Prepare the suggested report.

EXHIBIT 1
PROPULSION XT LIMITED
Extracts from Balance Sheet
31 December 20X5
(in millions of dollars)

Liabilities	
Accounts payable and accrued liabilities	$ 5,540
Unearned revenue	2,126
Long-term debt	3,642
Net defined benefit liability	1,743

Deferred income tax		345
Derivative financial instruments		230
	$	13,626

Equity

Preferred shares		350
Common shares		1,235
Contributed surplus		116
Retained earnings		1,810
		3,511
	$	17,137

PROPULSION XT LIMITED

Pension Information

31 December 20X5

(in millions of dollars)

	31 December 20X5
Fair value of plan assets	$ 5,020
Defined benefit obligation	6,763
Funded status—deficit	$ 1,743

Weighted average assumptions:

Discount rate	5.25%
Rate of increase in future compensation	3.30%

Key assumptions: All future expected benefit payment cash flows at the measurement date are discounted at spot rates for AA corporate debt securities, as a surrogate for 30-year rates.

Sensitivity:

A 0.25% change in the discount rate would change the obligation by 3.4% and the pension expense by 7.5%.

A 0.25% change in future compensation expense would change the obligation by 0.2% and the pension expense by 1%.

CASE 19-2

CANDIDA LTD.

Candida Ltd. is a Canadian public company in the business of exploration, production, and marketing of natural gas. It also has power generation operations. Earnings in 20X5 were $2.4 billion, and total assets were $24.1 billion.

You have recently begun work in the finance and accounting department. Your immediate task is to analyze and report on the pension information (see Exhibit 1) included in the last annual report. Your supervisor provided this information with a request:

We have to prepare for an upcoming meeting of the audit committee. We have several new members of the committee, and the chairperson has suggested that we provide a brief report on Candida's pension issues to get everyone up to speed. It has been several years since we have discussed this issue in depth; this is the opportunity.

Your report should include an explanation of defined benefit versus contribution plans (we have both but are curtailing the former), and the financial statement elements that relate to each plan. It will be necessary to explain the nature of the defined benefit obligation for the defined benefit plans and the pension plan asset balances and relate these amounts to the $115 million net defined benefit liability we include on the statement of financial position. We are particularly concerned about our potential pension position for 20X6, the coming year. We will see an increase in compensation cost of about 5%, which will accordingly increase pension cost. On top of the large investment losses we experienced in 20X5, this may mean serious increases in pension amounts. Your report should review the accounting treatment of the investment loss but also project our 20X6 pension expense. Finally, since our pension expense is likely going to be problematic next year, you should identify some key assumptions that Candida can consider to help reduce pension expense.

EXHIBIT 1

CANDIDA LIMITED

Selected Pension Information (in millions)

Statement of Comprehensive Income	20X5	20X4	20X3
Total expense for defined contribution plans	$ 12	$ 9	$ 6
Total expense for defined benefit plans	$ 12	$ 6	$ 10
Statement of Financial Position			
Net defined benefit liability	$115	$75	$20
Accumulated OCI, pension	53	20	17

Disclosure Notes

For Defined Benefit Plans	20X5
Defined benefit obligation	$228
Fair value of plan assets	113

Current service cost was $7 in 20X5 and $3 in 20X4.

The company contributed $50 to all pension plans in total during 20X5.

Included in the above defined benefit obligation of $228 is $14 of unfunded benefit obligation related to the Company's other post-employment benefits.

Assumptions are as follows:	20X5	20X4
Corporate bond yield rate	6.0%	6.5%
Rate of compensation increase	4.75%	3.0%
Health care costs trend rate for next year	+10%	

Required:

Prepare the report.

CASE 19-3

SOLACE LTD.

Solace Ltd. (SL) is a grocery food distributor operating nationally throughout Canada. The CFO for the company died suddenly during the year and the payroll accountant was put in charge of recording all of the transactions related to the pension plan. The company has a December fiscal year-end. You have been recently hired as a new accounting analyst for the company, working for the new CFO. Both of you started work yesterday, on 7 January 20X8. The CFO has reviewed the draft year-end statements to determine if any year-end journal entries are required before the statements are forwarded to the auditors. In particular, he is concerned about some odd accounts and amounts related to the company's pension plan that appear on the statements. Exhibit 1 provides the extracts from the draft statements related to these accounts. Exhibit 2 provides the details of the pension plan and related transactions for the year.

EXHIBIT 1

SOLACE LIMITED

Selected Pension Information

Statement of Comprehensive Income	20X8
Pension expense	$ 203,500
Post-retirement benefits expense	$ 53,600
Statement of Financial Position	
Net defined benefit asset	$ 433,500 dr.
Other post-employment benefit liability	650,800 cr.
Accumulated OCI, pension	27,900 cr.

EXHIBIT 2

SOLACE LIMITED

Description of Pension Plan and 20X8 Transactions

1. The company has a defined benefit plan and an other post-employment benefits plan for its retirees.
2. At the end of 20X7, the pension accounts had the following balances:

Defined benefit obligation	$1,250,800
Fair value of plan assets	$1,684,300

3. The actuary determined the following information for 20X8:

   - Current service cost was 75,600 in 20X8.
   - The company paid $12,700 to the trustees of the plan on 1 August 20X8.
   - Pensioners were paid $82,300 during the year for their pensions.
   - There was a past service adjustment to the plan of $190,800 for 20X8 increasing the obligation.
   - The actuary has determined that the amount of the defined benefit obligation as at 31 December 20X8 is $1,597,200.
   - The corporate bond yield rate is 6%.
   - The asset ceiling test stipulates that any net surplus be no more than $116,900. There was no adjustment for the effect of the asset ceiling test required for 20X7.

4. The trustees of the plan reported that the fair market value of the plan assets as at 31 December 20X8 was $1,708,915.

5. The company also pays for post-employment benefits for its retirees related to health and medical insurance. During the year, the company paid $53,600 for these benefits on behalf of the retirees and the current service cost was $57,200. This is an unfunded plan, although the actuary has assessed the obligation to be $650,800 at the end of 20X7 and $625,100 at the end of 20X8.

6. The following journal entries were made to recognize the transactions related to the pension plan and the post-retirement benefits plan.

Pension expense	12,700	
Cash		12,700

To record the amount paid to the pension plan trustees during the year.

Post-retirement benefits expense	53,600	
Cash		53,600

To record the post-retirement benefits paid during the year.

Pension expense	190,800	
Retained earnings		190,800

Tor record the past service adjustment for the year.

The CFO has asked you to review the statements and related information to determine if the pension has been correctly measured and recorded. He has asked you to write a report, outlining what has been done incorrectly, if anything, along with any recommendations on journal entries to correct the accounting for the pension transactions during the year.

Required:

Prepare the report. (Note all of the balances were correct at the end of 20X7.)

TECHNICAL REVIEW

connect

TR19-1 Defined Contribution Plan:

Sotherlin Inc. has a defined contribution plan. It has agreed to pay $275,000 now at the end of 20X4 and another payment of $200,000 at the end of 20X6 for employees' services for 20X4. The current interest rate is 5%.

Required:

Prepare the journal entry for the pension expense for 20X4.

connect

TR19-2 Defined Benefit Plan; Assets and Defined Benefit Obligation:

The following data are to be used for TR19-2 to TR19-6. Goodday Ltd. has a defined benefit pension plan and a December 31 year-end. The following information relates to the plan:

Balances:

Defined benefit obligation, end of 20X7	$5,215,000
Pension plan assets, fair value, end of 20X7	4,810,000
SFP net defined benefit liability, end of 20X7	405,000 cr.
SFP accumulated OCI, pension, end of 20X7	69,200 dr.
Retained earnings, end of 20X7	8,601,400 cr.

20X8 earnings, prior to any pension expense	4,200,000 cr.
Current service cost for 20X8, measured using the projected unit credit method	601,900
New past service cost granted in 20X8, negative because benefits were reduced and the liability has declined	(356,000)
Contributions made to the pension plan assets paid at end of 20X8	450,000
Actuarial gain in 20X8, negative because caused by higher anticipated future mortality rates and the liability has declined	(106,000)
Actual earnings in the fund, reported by the pension fund trustee, including interest, dividends, and change in fair value	144,800
Benefits paid to pensioners from pension fund assets paid at end of 20X8	67,900
Interest rate on long-term corporate bonds, end of 20X8	5%

Required:

Calculate the balances of the defined benefit obligation and the pension plan assets at the end of 20X8. Use these values to calculate the SFP net defined benefit plan element for Goodday at the end of 20X8.

connect

TR19-3 Defined Benefit Plan; Element 1:

Refer to the data in TR19-2.

Required:

Calculate and record the first element of pension accounting for the defined benefit plan. That is, calculate service cost and prepare the entry to record service cost. Also record the payment to the pension fund trustee.

connect

TR19-4 Defined Benefit Plan; Element 2:

Refer to the data in TR19-2.

Required:

Calculate and record the second element of pension accounting for the defined benefit plan. That is, calculate net interest cost, and prepare the entry to record net interest cost. Calculate the two components of net interest: interest on the defined benefit obligation and expected earnings on fund assets.

connect

TR19-5 Defined Benefit Plan; Element 3:

Refer to the data in TR19-2 and your response to TR19-4.

Required:

Calculate and record the third element of pension accounting for the defined benefit plan. That is, calculate remeasurements and prepare the entry(ies) to record these remeasurement(s).

connect

TR19-6 Defined Benefit Plan; Reporting:

Refer to the data in TR19-2 and solutions to TR19-3 to TR19-5.

Required:

1. Show the presentation of earnings and comprehensive income, reflecting the entries made to record the three elements of pension accounting. Also prepare the statement of changes in equity for retained earnings and accumulated OCI, and list the pension-related SFP account.
2. Prove that the SFP balance is equal to the net defined benefit liability/asset for the pension plan.

connect

TR19-7 Impact of Asset Ceiling Test:

USLM Inc. has a defined benefit pension plan. At the end of the year 20X4, the pension fund assets were $7,670,000 and the defined benefit obligation was $7,250,000. Invoking the asset ceiling caps the net defined benefit asset at $315,000.

Required:

Prepare the journal entry to correctly recognize the net defined benefit asset.

connect

TR19-8 Net Interest with Asset Ceiling Amount:

Refer to the data in TR19-7 and related solution for the opening balances. For 20X5, the following information is provided. The market yield rate for high-quality corporate bonds of similar term and identical currency is 5.5% at the end of the year. On 1 April 20X5, the contribution of $560,000 was made to the plan assets. Pension payments to pensioners are made evenly over the year and totalled $230,000.

Required:

Calculate and record the second element of pension accounting for the defined benefit plan. That is, calculate net interest cost, and prepare the entry to record interest cost. Calculate the three components of net interest: interest on the defined benefit obligation, expected earnings on fund assets, and the interest on the effect of asset ceiling.

 connect

TR19-9 Net Interest When Contribution Made During the Year:

Refer to the data of TR19-2. Assume now that the contribution to the plan assets was made 1 September 20X8 and pension payments to pensioners were paid evenly throughout the year.

Required:

Using this new information, calculate and record the second element of pension accounting for the defined benefit plan. That is, calculate net interest cost, and prepare the entry to record interest cost. Calculate the two components of net interest: interest on the defined benefit obligation and expected earnings on fund assets.

 connect

TR19-10 ASPE—Calculation of Pension Expense:

Refer to the data provided in TR19-2. Assume that Goodday follows ASPE.

Required:

Calculate and record the pension expense for the year.

ASSIGNMENTS

★ A19-1 Pension Terms:

Complete the sentences below:

1. The actuarial cost method that must be used to determine current service cost is the _____.

2. A pension plan where the risk of the level of eventual pension payments rests with the employee is called _____.

3. A contributory pension plan is a plan in which _____.

4. The asset ceiling is a limiting factor in pension accounting when _____.

5. Pension plans are usually registered because _____.

6. The actuarial cost method that projects years of service, and final salary, is called the _____.

7. Past service cost will be a negative number (reduces the projected benefit liability) when
_____.

8. An experience gain or loss related to annual return on plan assets is the difference between _____
and _____.

9. The costs of pension benefit changes caused by _____ and _____ are often included in
discontinued operations rather than in pension expense.

10. The expected present value of future pension benefits, evaluated using present value and actuarial
expectations, including mortality, turnover, and the effects of current and future compensation levels, is called
_____.

11. Two examples of demographic assumptions that must be made to project pension variables are
_____ and _____.

 ## A19-2 Defined Contribution Plan:

Belfor Ltd. has a defined contribution pension plan for its employees. The plan is trusteed, and each year the
company makes an annual contribution, matching employee contributions to the plan to a certain maximum. The
funds are invested for the employees by the pension fund trustee using predetermined parameters.

The pension plan was established to target roughly 70% of final pay to employees as a pension, with survivor
benefits or a minimum 10-year payout. None of these targets is guaranteed. Calculations were done based on
mortality assumptions and an expected 6% yield. Contributions are re-evaluated every three years. Based on these
assumptions, TGY paid $375,000 to the fund in 20X7. At the end of 20X7, plan assets total $4,970,000.

Required:

1. What are the employees of TGY entitled to as a result of this pension? How is this different from a defined
benefit pension plan?

2. What difference would it make if the targets established above were guaranteed by the company?

3. What amount of pension expense would TGY report in 20X7?

4. If fund earnings were to be 8% in 20X8, instead of the 6% predicted, who would benefit? Explain.

 ## A19-3 Defined Contribution Plan:

A company has a contributory defined benefit pension plan covering all employees over the age of 30. An analyst
was quoted as saying:

> Defined benefit pension plans are really dead. Within 20 years, no companies in the
> private sector will be offering these plans—and the public sector is just daft if they
> don't follow suit. Why, in the first four months of this year, I know of dozens of
> companies that have frozen or closed their defined benefit plans. They allow new
> employees access to only defined contribution plans. Many of these companies just
> make end-of-year grants to employees directly into their personal RRSP accounts,
> and allow—force—the employees to make their own investment decisions. Of
> course, with employees more mobile between companies and less likely to stay
> with one employer all their lives, it can be attractive. Some people just like to get
> their hands on the money!

Required:

1. What factors associated with defined benefit plans have led to the trend toward defined contribution plans?

2. Evaluate the attractiveness of defined contribution plans for employees.

A19-4 Defined Contribution Plan:

Zio Ltd. established a defined contribution pension plan at the beginning of 20X9. The company will contribute 3% of each employee's salary annually. Total salaries in 20X9 were expected to be $7.3 million. Accordingly, Zio paid $219,000 into the fund. After the year-end, it was determined that actual salaries were $6.5 million. Interest rates are in the range of 6%.

Required:

1. Is pension expense $219,000 or a lesser number? Explain.

2. Assume instead that Zio has agreed to pay $165,000 into the fund at the end of 20X9. During 20X9, an employee left the company, forfeiting $35,000 of unvested pension benefits earmarked in the pension fund. Calculate the payment to the fund and the pension expense.

3. Assume instead that Zio agreed to pay $150,000 to the pension trustee in 20X9 but, because of cash flow issues, paid only $100,000. Zio agrees to pay the shortfall at the end of 20X11. In 20X10, the company makes a scheduled $150,000 payment to the pension fund for normal 20X10 pension entitlements. The same annual scheduled payment is made in 2011, plus the $50,000 arrears from 20X9. How much is pension expense and cash paid in each of 20X9, 20X10, and 20X11?

A19-5 Defined Benefit Plan; Variables:

TCGY Ltd. reports the following data for 20X8:

Plan assets, at fair value	
Balance, 1 January	$439,800
Balance, 31 December	$425,700
Defined benefit obligation	
Balance, 1 January	$ 601,790
Balance, 31 December	$720,500

The company has a contributory defined benefit pension plan covering all employees over the age of 30.

Required:

1. How much did the pension plan assets change during the year? Name three items that would cause plan assets to change.

2. How much did the defined benefit obligation increase during the year? Name five items that would cause this amount to change.

3. Compute the amount of the underfunded (overfunded) net position of the pension plan for accounting purposes at the beginning and the end of the year. Explain what these amounts mean.

★ A19-6 Defined Benefit Plan; Actuarial Cost Methods:

There are three major approaches to measure and allocate pension amounts to given fiscal years. These approaches are used by actuaries to determine funding amounts and by accountants to determine amounts to be recorded in financial statements. Holo Co. has a defined benefit pension plan that has been in existence for five years since 20X2. The company is reviewing its funding approach and has three different funding amounts for 20X7, each based on a different actuarial cost method:

#1 $5,000

#2 $2,500

#3 $3,900

Required:

1. Identify three actuarial cost methods, and specify the projections that differentiate these three methods.

2. Suggest which funding amount, above, is associated with which actuarial cost method. Explain.

3. Which actuarial cost method is required for external reporting? What will be the outcome if this method is not used for funding?

4. In each of the following circumstances, identify the funding method that Holo would likely find most appealing:

    a. Holo is experiencing a cash shortage and therefore is trying to conserve current cash balances.

    b. Holo would prefer to have cash payments stable from year to year.

    c. Holo would prefer to use a funding pattern that could also be used to measure the pension expense.

★ A19-7 Defined Benefit Plan; Actuarial Cost Methods:

Ivan Resources Corp. sponsors a defined benefit pension plan for its unionized labour force. The company disclosed the following in its annual financial statements:

(in thousands)	31 December 20X5
Fair value of plan assets	$422,400
Defined benefit obligation	590,200
Funded status—deficit	$167,800

The company is considering the impact that changes in assumptions will have on its pension situation. Specifically, the following:

a. Lower employee mortality rates

b. Higher than expected employee turnover

c. A rollback of wages by 3%

d. Higher borrowing rates

Required:

Separately for each suggested change in assumption, identify the impact on annual pension expense, the funded status of the pension, and accumulated OCI. Explain your conclusions.

Urban Life Ltd. sponsors a defined benefit pension plan for its employees. It is now the 20X9 fiscal year. An appropriate interest rate for long-term debt is 6%. Information with respect to the plan is as follows:

Fair value of plan assets, 31 December 20X8	$5,398,000
Defined benefit obligation, 31 December 20X8	6,499,000
Actual return on plan assets for 20X9	61,100
Past service cost from amendment dated 31 December 20X9, liability is reduced because benefits were reduced	(203,200)
Actuarial revaluation dated 31 December 20X9; liability is reduced because of changed mortality assumptions	(603,700)
Funding payment at year-end 20X9	450,000
Benefits paid to retirees during 20X9	105,000
Current service cost for 20X9	250,400

Required:

1. Calculate the SFP net defined benefit liability as of 31 December 20X8.
2. Calculate the net defined benefit liability as of 31 December 20X9 by calculating the defined benefit obligation and the fair value of plan assets at 31 December 20X9.
3. Analyze the three elements of pension accounting for 20X9: service cost, net interest, and remeasurements. Prepare entries, and also an entry for the contribution to the fund during 20X9.
4. Calculate the SFP net defined benefit liability as of 31 December 20X9, reflecting requirement 1 and the entries in requirement 3, and compare this with the net result in requirement 2.

★★ A19-9 IFRS—Defined Benefit Plan; Three Elements:

Micro Computers Inc. sponsors a defined benefit pension plan for its employees. It is now the 20X2 fiscal year. Long-term corporate borrowing rates for companies with this risk profile are 5%. Information with respect to the pension plan is as follows:

Current service cost for 20X2	$ 175,200
Fair value of plan assets, 31 December 20X1	1,936,000
Benefits paid to retirees during 20X2	214,900
Funding payment at 1 February 20X2	390,000
Defined benefit obligation, 31 December 20X1	2,870,000
Past service cost from amendment dated 31 December 20X2; liability is reduced because benefits were reduced	(116,500)
Actuarial revaluation dated 31 December 20X2; liability is increased because of changed salary increase assumptions	355,700
Actual return on plan assets for 20X2 (loss)	(104,800)

Required:

1. Calculate the SFP net defined benefit liability as of 31 December 20X1.
2. Calculate the net defined benefit liability as of 31 December 20X2 by calculating the defined benefit obligation and the fair value of plan assets at 31 December 20X2.
3. Analyze the three elements of pension accounting for 20X2: service cost, net interest, and remeasurements. Prepare entries, and also an entry for the contribution to the fund during 20X2.
4. Calculate the SFP net defined benefit liability as of 31 December 20X2, reflecting requirement 1 and the entries in requirement 3, and compare this with the net result in requirement 2.

eXcel

★★ A19-10 IFRS—Defined Benefit Plan; Three Elements:

The following data relate to a defined benefit pension plan:

Defined benefit obligation, 31 December 20X1	$106,000
Benefits paid to retirees in 20X2 during the year	14,000
Current service cost for 20X2	6,700
Actual return on plan assets for 20X2	3,200
Fair value of plan assets, 31 December 20X1	78,000
Funding payment 1, December 20X2	7,000
Past service cost from amendment dated 31 December 20X2; liability is increased because benefits were increased on a retrospective basis	3,700
Actuarial revaluation dated 31 December 20X2; decrease to liability because of changed mortality assumptions	(2,500)
Long-term interest rate on corporate bonds	7%

Required:

1. Calculate the SFP net defined benefit liability as of 31 December 20X1.

2. Compute the defined benefit obligation at 31 December 20X2 and the fair value of plan assets on the same date.

3. Analyze the three elements of pension accounting for 20X2: service cost, net interest, and remeasurements. Prepare entries and also an entry for the contribution to the fund during 20X2.

4. Calculate the SFP net defined benefit liability as of 31 December 20X2, and prove that this represents the net defined benefit position of the pension plan.

 A19-11 IFRS—Defined Benefit Plan; Three Elements:

The following data relate to a defined benefit pension plan:

Defined benefit obligation, 31 December 20X8	$ 496,000
Fair value of plan assets, 31 December 20X8	702,000
Impact of applying the asset ceiling test 31 December 20X8: Maximum surplus recoverable	$ 120,000

Past service cost from amendment dated 31 December 20X9; liability is increased because benefits were increased on a retrospective basis	56,000
Benefits paid to retirees in 20X9 throughout the year	7,200
Current service cost for 20X9	9,100
Funding payment 1 May 20X9	6,000
Actuarial revaluation dated 31 December 20X9; decrease to liability because of changed mortality assumptions	(12,000)
Actual return (loss) on plan assets for 20X9	(17,500)
Long-term yield on corporate bonds	5%
Impact of applying the asset ceiling test for 20X9: Maximum surplus recoverable	$125,000

Required:

1. Calculate the SFP net defined benefit asset as of 31 December 20X8. The asset ceiling does not limit the amount of the pension asset.
2. Compute the defined benefit obligation at 31 December 20X9 and the fair value of plan assets on the same date.
3. Analyze the three elements of pension accounting for 20X9: service cost, net interest, and remeasurements. Prepare entries and also an entry for the contribution to the fund during 20X9.
4. Calculate the SFP net defined benefit liability as of 31 December 20X9, and prove that this represents the net defined benefit position of the pension plan.

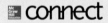

★★ A19-12 IFRS—Defined Benefit Plan; Three Elements:

Faste Ltd. has a defined benefit pension plan. The following information relates to this plan:

SFP net defined pension liability, 1 January 20X1	$793,500
Defined benefit pension obligation, 1 January 20X1	??
Actuarial loss on change in assumptions, arising during 20X1	115,000
Actual return on plan assets for 20X1	12,000
Fair value of plan assets, 1 January	344,000
Current service cost for 20X1	219,200
Plan contribution for 20X1 made on 1 March 20X1	424,000
Benefits paid in 20X1	57,500
Yield on long-term corporate bonds	4.5%
SFP Accumulated OCI, pension, 1 January 20X1	80,400 dr.
Retained earnings, 1 January 20X1	5,500,000 cr.
20X1 Earnings, prior to any pension expense	4,000,000 cr.

Required:

1. Compute the defined benefit obligation at 31 December 20X1 and the fair value of plan assets on the same date.
2. Analyze the three elements of pension accounting for 20X1: service cost, net interest, and remeasurements. Prepare entries and also an entry for the contribution to the fund during 20X1.
3. Calculate 20X1 earnings after pension expense is recorded. Ignore any income tax. Also calculate comprehensive income, the closing balance of retained earnings, accumulated OCI, and the SFP net defined benefit liability as of 31 December 20X1. Prove that the SFP liability account represents the net defined benefit position of the pension plan.

 A19-13 IFRS—Defined Benefit Plan; Three Elements:

Computer Imaging Ltd. (CIL) established a formal pension plan 10 years ago to provide retirement benefits for all employees. The plan is noncontributory and is funded through a trustee that invests all funds and pays all benefits as they become due. Vesting occurs when the employee reaches age 45 and has been employed by CIL ten years.

At the inception of the plan, past service cost (PSC) amounted to $300,000. The past service cost is being funded over ten years by level annual end-of-year payments calculated at 5%, which is a reasonable approximation of long-term borrowing rates (see actuarial report below for the funding amount). Each year, at the year-end, the company also funds an amount equal to current service cost less any new actuarial gains or plus any new actuarial losses on the pension obligation. The yield rate on corporate bonds with an appropriate currency and term is 6%.

At the beginning of 20X8, the defined benefit obligation was $1,400,200. The fair value of investments was $1,075,790, and the net defined benefit liability on the SFP was $324,410.

The independent actuary's biennial revaluation report follows:

COMPUTER IMAGING LIMITED

Noncontributory Defined Benefit Pension Plan

Actuarial Report, 31 December 20X8

Current service cost

Computed by the projected unit credit method		$ 85,375

Actuarial revaluation, effective 31 December 20X8

Experience gains for

Mortality	$ 7,875	
Employee turnover	12,625	
Decrease in defined benefit obligation due to increase in bond yield rate	49,500	
Net actuarial gains		$ 70,000

20X8 funding

Current service cost	$85,375	
Past service cost	38,853	
Less: Revaluation gains of 20X8	(70,000)	
Total cash contribution to plan		$ 54,228

Pension plan asset portfolio

Market value, 1 January 20X8	$1,075,790
Contributions	54,228
Portfolio performance, 20X8 Interest, dividends, and capital gains	151,685
Market value, 31 December 20X8	$ 1,281,703

Other information:

SFP Accumulated OCI, pension, 1 January 20X8	$ 100,900 dr.
Retained earnings, 1 January 20X8	$ 7,800,000 cr.
20X8 Earnings, prior to any pension expense	$5,850,000 cr.

Required:

1. Analyze the three elements of pension accounting for 20X8: service cost, net interest, and remeasurements. Prepare entries and also an entry for the contribution to the fund during 20X8.

2. Calculate 20X8 earnings after pension expense is recorded. Ignore any income tax. Also calculate comprehensive income, the closing balance of retained earnings, accumulated OCI, and the SFP net defined benefit liability as of 31 December 20X8. Prove that the SFP liability account represents the net defined benefit position of the pension fund.

 # A19-14 IFRS—Defined Benefit Plan; Three Elements:

In late 20X0, Security Sevices Ltd. established a defined benefit pension plan for its employees. At the inception of the plan, the actuary determined the present value of the defined benefit obligation relating to employees' past services to be $1 million, as of the beginning of 20X1. This amount vests over 10 years.

In each year following inception of the plan, the actuary measured the defined benefit obligation arising from employees' services in that year. These current service costs amounted to $80,000 in 20X1, $82,000 in 20X2, and $85,000 in 20X3. The costs were determined by using an actuarial cost method based on employees' projected earnings.

All actuarial obligations and funding payments were determined by assuming an interest rate of 6%, which was the long-term borrowing yield. In accordance with provincial legislation, the past service cost was to be funded over 15 years, the maximum period allowed. Current service costs were to be fully funded at the end of each year.

In 20X4, the actuary conducted the mandatory triennial revaluation. The revaluation revealed that the plan assets at the end of 20X3 were $712,500. The defined benefit obligation at the end of 20X3 was $1,249,800. There was a balance of accumulated OCI of $61,500 (debit) in relation to the pension at the end of 20X3. The actuary also determined that the current service cost for 20X4 was $87,500. There was an experience gain of $21,870 on the pension plan obligation, arising in 20X4, as a result of higher mortality rates. The actual plan earnings for 20X4 were $85,900. At the end of 20X4, there was a curtailment of the pension plan, resulting in a reduction in the pension obligation of $75,000 and a reduction in assets of $45,000. There were no benefits paid during the year.

Required:

Determine the amount of pension expense (including interest costs) for 20X4 and the change in accumulated OCI for the year.

★ ★ **A19-15 Defined Benefit Plan; Three Elements, Asset Ceiling:**

Morocco Corp. initiated a defined benefit pension plan on 1 January 20X5. The plan does not provide past service benefits for existing employees. The pension funding payment is made to the trustee on 31 December of each year. The following information is available for 20X5 and 20X6:

	20X5	20X6
Current service cost, measured as of the beginning of the year	$150,000	$145,000
Funding payment made at the end of the year	200,000	185,000
Net interest expense, as calculated by the actuary at 10%	15,000	11,000

Required:

1. Prepare the journal entries to record pension expense for 20X5 and 20X6. Net interest in 20X6 is the combination of interest on the defined benefit obligation and expected return on plan assets. Also record the funding payment. (Note that actual return is equal to expected return.)

2. What is the amount of the net defined benefit asset on the 31 December 20X6 statement of financial position? Prove that this is equal to the net position of fund assets and the defined benefit obligation.

3. What limits are there on the net defined benefit asset on the statement of financial position?

4. Prepare the necessary additional entry that would be made if there was an asset ceiling of $51,500 in 20X6. What would be the amount of the resulting net defined benefit asset on the 31 December 20X6 statement of financial position?

 connect

 e**X**cel

★ **A19-16 Pension Spreadsheet:**

Jones Manufacturing Inc. sponsored a defined benefit pension plan effective 1 January 20X7. The company uses the projected unit credit actuarial cost method for funding and accounting. Long-term corporate bonds have a yield of 4%. Employees were granted partial credit for past service. The past service obligation has been measured at $1,640,000 as of 1 January 20X7. The company will pay $200,000 (for past service) plus all current service cost to the pension plan trustee each 31 December beginning 31 December 20X7. This funding arrangement will continue for five years and then be re-evaluated.

Data for 20X7 and 20X8

	20X7	20X8
Current service cost	$117,000	$157,000
Actual return on fund assets	—	6,800
Decrease in defined benefit obligation at year-end due to change in assumptions	—	37,000
Payments to pensioners at end of year	—	41,400

Required:

Prepare a spreadsheet for 20X7 and 20X8 that determines pension expense and also the closing net defined benefit asset or liability account and accumulated OCI.

★ ★ A19-17 Pension Spreadsheet:

Maple Construction Corp. has a defined benefit pension plan. Information concerning the 20X7 and 20X8 fiscal years is presented below:

From the plan actuary:

- Current service cost in 20X7 is $430,000 and in 20X8 is $488,000.
- Defined benefit obligation is $4,975,000 at the beginning of 20X7.
- New past service cost in 20X8 is $45,000, a reduction in benefits.
- Accumulated OCI amounts are losses at the beginning of 20X7, amounting to $787,000.
- Benefits paid to retirees—at end of year, $235,000 in 20X7, and $295,000 in 20X8.
- Actuarial revaluation in 20X7 showed a $406,000 increase in the obligation due to changes in mortality. Revaluations take place every four years.

From the plan trustee:

- Plan assets at market value at the beginning of 20X7 were $3,705,000.
- 20X7 contributions at end of year were $510,000 and in 20X8, $525,000.
- Actual earnings were $276,000 in 20X7 and $80,000 in 20X8.

Other information:

- Yield on long-term debt, stable in 20X7 and 20X8, 6%.
- The opening net defined benefit liability on the SFP is the opening net amount of the defined benefit obligation and opening fund assets.

Required:

Prepare a spreadsheet for 20X7 and 20X8 that determines pension expense and also the closing net defined benefit asset or liability account and accumulated OCI.

★ ★ A19-18 Pension Spreadsheet:

Gurung Co. has a noncontributory, defined benefit pension plan adopted on 1 January 20X5. On 31 December 20X5, the following information is available:

For accounting purposes

- Interest rate used for pension amounts, 5%.
- Past service cost, granted as of 1 January 20X5, $200,000. This is also the defined benefit obligation on 1 January.
- Current service cost for 20X5, appropriately measured for accounting purposes, $67,000.

For funding purposes

- Funding was $99,500 in 20X5 for all pension amounts. The payment was made on 31 December.
- Actual earnings on fund assets, zero.

Required:

1. Prepare a pension spreadsheet that summarizes relevant pension data for 20X5.
2. Prepare a pension spreadsheet that summarizes relevant pension data for 20X6. The following facts relate to 20X6:

  - Current service cost for accounting was $96,000.
  - A plan amendment resulted in a past service cost of $40,000 being granted.
  - Total funding of the pension plan was $118,000, on 31 December 20X6.
  - Actual return on fund assets was $8,900.
  - An actuarial revaluation was done to reflect new information about expected turnover rates in the employee population. This resulted in a $35,000 increase in the defined benefit obligation, as of 31 December 20X6.

★ ★ A19-19 Pension Spreadsheet:

Solutions Ltd. sponsors a defined benefit pension plan for its employees. At the beginning of 20X3, there is an accrued SFP pension liability of $152,800, as follows:

Defined benefit obligation		$(509,100)
Plan assets (fair value)		356,300
Net defined benefit liability		$(152,800)

There are also actuarial losses of $72,700 in accumulated OCI with respect to the pension plan.

The following data relate to the operation of the plan for the years 20X3 and 20X4:

	20X3	20X4
Current service cost	49,000	$ 42,000
Yield rate on long-term corporate bonds	5%	5%
Actual return (loss) on plan assets	(17,000)	21,000
Annual funding contributions, at year-end	65,000	82,000
Benefits paid to retirees at end of year	45,500	106,000
Increase in defined benefit obligation due to changes in actuarial assumptions as of 31 December each year	86,000	34,000

Required:

Prepare a spreadsheet that summarizes relevant pension data for 20X3 and 20X4. As part of the spreadsheet, calculate pension expense, the net defined benefit accrued benefit asset/liability, and accumulated OCI for 20X3 and 20X4.

★ ★ 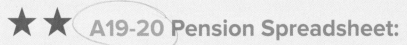 A19-20 Pension Spreadsheet:

Car Wash Ltd. began a pension fund in the year 20X3, effective 1 January 20X4. Terms of the pension plan follow:

- The yield rate on long-term high-grade corporate bonds is 5%.
- Employees will receive partial credit for past service. The past service obligation, valued using the projected unit credit actuarial cost method and a discount rate of 5%, is $416,000 as of 1 January 20X4.
- Past service cost will be funded over roughly 15 years. The initial payment, on 1 January 20X4, is $90,000. This will earn interest in 20X4. After that, another $90,000 will be added to the 31 December funding payment each year for past service, including the 31 December 20X4 payment. The amount of funding will be reviewed every five years to ensure its adequacy.
- Current service cost will be fully funded each 31 December, plus actuarial losses or minus actuarial gains of the year, if those actuarial gains or losses are related to the defined benefit obligation. Experience gains and losses related to the difference between actual and expected earnings on fund assets will not affect plan funding in the short run, as they are expected to offset over time.

Data for 20X4 and 20X5

	20X4	20X5
Current service cost	$51,000	$57,000
Funding amount, 1 January 20X4	90,000	
Funding amount, 31 December	??	??
Actual return on fund assets	1,000	16,800
Increase in defined benefit obligation at year-end due to change in assumptions	—	16,000

Required:

Prepare a spreadsheet for 20X4 and 20X5 that determines pension expense and also the closing net defined benefit asset or liability account and accumulated OCI.

★ ★ A19-21 Other Post-Employment Benefits:

Hruska Corp. provides post-employment benefits to its retirees for dental and supplementary health care. The following information relates to these benefits:

Benefit obligation, 1 January 20X6	$69,000
Current service cost for 20X6	16,000
SFP accrued net OPEB liability, 1 January, 20X6	11,000
Accumulated OCI, OPEBs, 1 January 20X6, loss	23,000
Fund assets, 1 January 20X6	58,000
Contributions to the benefit fund for 20X6 – paid 1 April	9,000
Benefit payments to retired employees for 20X6 evenly over year	12,000
Actual return on fund assets	350
Yield rate on long-term corporate bonds	7%

Required:

1. Compute the benefit obligation for post-employment benefits at 31 December 20X6 and plan assets at 31 December 20X6.
2. Compute the appropriate expense for post-employment benefits for the year ended 31 December 20X6.
3. Compute the closing balances on related SFP accounts at 31 December 20X6.

Note: The solution to this question is based on an optional spreadsheet.

 A19-22 Other Post-Employment Benefits:

Financial Metrics Ltd. provides life insurance and dental coverage to retirees. The yield rate on long-term debt is 5%. The following information relates to these benefits:

Fund assets, 1 January 20X2	0
Benefit obligation, 1 January 20X2	$1,282,000
Benefit payments to retired employees for 20X2 evenly over year	177,000
Service cost for 20X2	211,000
Accumulated OCI, OPEBs, 1 January 20X2, loss	186,000
Actuarial revaluation, performed at the end of 20X2; liability reduced due to change in mortality assumption	(300,000)
Contributions to the benefit fund for 20X2 at end of year	178,000
Actual return on fund assets	0

Required:

1. Compute the benefit obligation for post-employment benefits and plan assets at 31 December 20X2.
2. Compute the appropriate expense for post-employment benefits for the year ended 31 December 20X2.
3. Compute the closing balances in SFP accounts related to these benefits as at 31 December 20X2.

Note: The solution to this question is based on an optional spreadsheet.

 A19-23 Other Post-Employment Benefits; Spreadsheet:

Lin Developments Ltd. provides post-employment benefits to its retirees for supplementary health care, including prescription medication. Lin had an accumulated OCI loss amount related to OPEBs of $45,000 at the beginning of the year, an experience loss related primarily to unexpected cost increases in prescription medication.

Lin does not fund health care benefits to any great extent. As a result, there was only $21,500 in the fund asset account at the beginning of the year, while the estimated obligation for supplementary health care benefits was $566,300. Actual earnings of the fund this year were $600. At the end of the year, contributions of $46,400 were made to the fund and benefits paid out were $43,900. In the current year, actuarial estimates indicate that current service cost is $67,800, and there is a new actuarial loss of $35,000 related to further increases in health care costs.

Required:

Prepare a spreadsheet for the current year that determines the expense for post-employment benefits, accumulated OCI, and also the closing accrued asset or liability with respect to the benefits. Begin by calculating the opening SFP OPEB liability balance. The long-term bond yield rate is 5%.

 A19-24 Defined Benefit Plan; Disclosure:

Extracts from the pension disclosures of Blue Pony Ltd. are shown below.

Pension Benefits

The estimated present value of accrued plan benefits and the estimated market value of the net assets available to provide for these benefits are as follows:

	20X2	20X1
Plan assets, at fair value	$545	$484
Defined benefit obligation	612	575
Deficiency	$ (67)	$ (91)

Actuarial assumptions:

	20X2	20X1
Yield rate for defined benefit obligation	5.25%	5.3%
Weighted average rate of compensation increase for defined benefit obligation	3.50%	4.00%
Retention rate	84%	88%

Accumulated OCI:

	20X2	20X1
Opening; accumulated losses	$ 94	$91
Actuarial and experience losses	16	3
Closing	$110	$94

Required:

1. With respect to the actuarial assumptions listed, explain how each assumption would be developed. Indicate whether the trend in each assumption would lead to higher or lower pension expense.
2. Explain the amount that would be recorded as an SFP pension liability.
3. Explain the nature of amounts that are recorded in OCI. Are these amounts recycled to earnings?

★ A19-25 ASPE; Defined Benefit Plan:

Return to the facts of A19-8. Assume instead that this pension plan is sponsored by a private company and ASPE applies.

Required:

1. Prepare an entry to record pension expense and an entry to record the contribution to the pension fund for 20X9. *Note:* The solution to this assignment is based on one calculation of pension expense, followed by one entry for pension expense, rather than a series of entries for separate components.
2. Based on the entries in requirement 1, calculate the SFP net defined benefit liability as of 31 December 20X9, and prove this number based on the closing balances of the defined benefit liability and pension plan assets.

★ A19-26 ASPE; Defined Benefit Plan:

Return to the facts of A19-9. Assume instead that this pension plan is sponsored by a private company and ASPE applies.

Required:

1. Prepare an entry to record pension expense and an entry to record the contribution to the pension fund for 20X2. *Note:* The solution to this assignment is based on one calculation of pension expense, followed by one entry for pension expense, rather than a series of entries for separate components.
2. Based on the entries in requirement 1, calculate the SFP net defined benefit liability as of 31 December 20X2, and prove this number based on the closing balances of the defined benefit liability and pension plan assets.

★ A19-27 ASPE; Defined Benefit Plan:

Return to the facts of A19-10. Assume instead that this pension plan is sponsored by a private company and ASPE applies.

Required:

1. Prepare an entry to record pension expense and an entry to record the contribution to the pension fund for 20X2. *Note:* The solution to this assignment is based on one calculation of pension expense, followed by one entry for pension expense, rather than a series of entries for separate components.

2. Based on the entries in requirement 1, calculate the SFP net defined benefit liability as of 31 December 20X2, and prove this number based on the closing balances of the defined benefit liability and pension plan assets.

 A19-28 ASPE; Defined Benefit Plan:

Return to the facts of A19-11. Assume instead that this pension plan is sponsored by a private company and ASPE applies.

Required:

1. Prepare all entries for 20X9.
2. Based on the entries based on requirement 1, calculate the SFP net defined benefit liability as of 31 December 20X9, and prove this number based on the closing balances of the defined benefit liability and pension plan assets.

 A19-29 ASPE; Defined Benefit Plan:

Return to the facts of A19-16. Assume instead that this pension plan is sponsored by a private company and ASPE applies.

Required:

Prepare a spreadsheet containing all relevant pension information for 20X7 and 20X8.

★ ★ ★ A19-30 Comprehensive; Chapters 12, 13, 14, 15, 18, 19:

Oilfield Multiservices Ltd. (OML) offers oilfield operation services to the oil and gas industry in Alberta and Texas. OML owns no natural resource properties itself but assists in exploration activities through cementing and stimulation services. OML complies with ASPE. The company has prepared draft financial statements (Exhibit 1). However, some transactions during the year have not been properly reflected in the financial statements (Exhibit 2). Additional information on financial statement elements are provided in Exhibit 3. OML is required, as part of its bond agreement, to maintain a minimum level of retained earnings of $30 million, and a maximum debt-to-equity ratio of 1.5. In the debt-to-equity ratio, the numerator is "total liabilities." Since a number of the transactions that have not been processed affect debt and/or equity, the CFO is concerned that these key financial targets continue to be met.

EXHIBIT 1

OILFIELD MULTISERVICES LTD.—DRAFT FINANCIAL STATEMENTS FOR THE YEAR ENDED 31 DECEMBER 20X7 (IN THOUSANDS)

STATEMENT OF FINANCIAL POSITION

Assets

Cash		$ 14,960
Accounts receivable		30,497
Inventory		1,958
Prepaid expenses and deposits		930
Current assets		48,345
Fixed assets, net		78,441
Intangible assets		890
Suspense		8,338
Total assets		**$136,014**

Liabilities

Accounts payable and accrued liabilities		$ 19,511
Income tax payable		1,600
Current bank loan		12,100
Current liabilities		33,211
Lease liability		3,985
Long-term debt	30,000	
Premium	1,210	31,210
Deferred income tax		6,900
Defined benefit obligation		620
Total liabilities		75,926

Shareholders' equity

Preferred shares	5,100
Common shares	11,050
Contributed capital on common stock retirement	788
Stock options outstanding	450
Retained earnings	42,700
Total shareholders' equity	60,088
Total liabilities and shareholders' equity	**$136,014**

STATEMENT OF EARNINGS; YEAR ENDED 31 DECEMBER 20X7

Sales	**$146,560**
Expenses	
Operating	103,490
Selling, general, and administration	8,385
Interest	2,355
Depreciation	8,420
	122,650
Income before tax	23,910
Income tax	5,950
Net income	**$ 17,960**

STATEMENT OF RETAINED EARNINGS; YEAR ENDED 31 DECEMBER 20X7

Retained earnings, beginning of year	$ 27,965
Common share retirement	0
Dividends:	
Preferred dividends	0
Common share dividends	(3,225)

Stock dividends	0
Net income	17,960
Retained earnings, end of year	$ 42,700

EXHIBIT 2

OILFIELD MULTISERVICES LTD.—OUTSTANDING TRANSACTIONS

Note: Amounts are in thousands, except share volumes and per share amounts.

1. Preferred dividends were declared but not paid. They have not yet been recorded. They should be included in "Accounts payable and accrued liabilities."

2. On 1 October 20X7, 865,000 common shares were reacquired from a shareholder and retired. The $6,240 payment was debited to the "suspense" account, which now appears as an asset.

3. No premium amortization on the bond has been recorded for 20X7.

4. No adjustment has been made for compensation expense inherent in stock option plans.

5. The $2,098 payment made to the pension trustee was debited to the "suspense" account. No pension expense has been recorded in the 20X7 financial statements. The pension plan covers operating employees (85%) and administrative staff (15%).

6. A stock dividend of 10% was declared and distributed on 31 December on common shares. The Board of Directors agreed that this was to be capitalized at a value of $8 per share. The stock dividend has not yet been recorded.

7. The lease liability must be adjusted for interest and the current portion, which will be classified as part of the current liability "Current bank loan."

EXHIBIT 3

OILFIELD MULTISERVICES LTD.—ADDITIONAL INFORMATION

Note: Amounts are in thousands, except share volumes and per share amounts.

1. *Lease obligation*

   The lease obligation is the remaining portion of a 20-year capital lease with annual payments each 1 January of $612. The 1 January 20X7 payment was properly recorded. The interest rate used for lease capitalization was 7%. No interest has been recorded in 20X7, nor has the current portion of the lease liability been recorded.

2. *Share information*

   Preferred shares—$6 cumulative no-par preferred shares outstanding, 51,000 shares outstanding during the entire year in 20X7.

Common shares—No-par common shares outstanding at the beginning of 20X7, 6,210,000 shares. During the year, 865,000 shares were retired on 1 October, and a 10% stock dividend was declared and distributed on 31 December.

3. *Bonds payable*

Long-term debt consists of:

Bonds payable, 6 1/4%, due 30 June 20X21 $30,000

Premium amortization of $83 has yet to be recorded for the year.

4. *Outstanding stock options*

Stock options have been outstanding during 20X7 for 265,000 shares. These options are held by senior administrative employees. They may be exercised for the first time on 1 January 20X9, and the related cost is being amortized over four years. The options were originally valued at $900 using the binomial option pricing model.

5. *Pension information*

At the beginning of the year, the defined benefit pension plan had $9,096 in assets and $9,716 of defined benefit obligation. The actual return on assets was $435. Current service cost in 20X7 was $1,700 using the projected benefit actuarial cost method. A long-term interest rate of 6% was considered appropriate. Benefits paid to pensioners were $500 paid at the end of the year. There were no re-measurements or new past service during the year.

(Source: [Adapted] © CGA-Canada. Reproduced with permission.)

Required:

1. Provide journal entries to account for the information provided in Exhibits 2 and 3. None of the adjustments mentioned alters income tax expense, income tax payable, or future income tax. Round all adjustments to the nearest thousand. All amounts are given in thousands, except share volumes and per share amounts.

2. Prepare a revised statement of financial position, statement of comprehensive income, and statement of retained earnings.

3. Evaluate the key financial targets and suggest action for the coming year if there are concerns.

Source: (Globe and money) © Vstock LLC/Getty Images RF; (Skyscrapers) © Arpad Benedek/Getty Images RF; (Canadian flag) © BjArn Kindler/Getty Images RF; (Tablet, pen, keyboard) © John Lamb/Getty Images RF.

CHAPTER 20

Earnings per Share

INTRODUCTION

References to earnings data expressed as earnings per share (EPS) are common in the financial press. Public companies report their EPS numbers quarterly and use the statistic to benchmark results and communicate targets. For example, BCE Inc. reported 2014 basic EPS of $2.98 (and diluted EPS of $2.97). In comparison, 2013 EPS was $2.55 ($2.54 diluted). 2014 EPS was 16.9% higher than the previous year, which is slightly higher than net earnings growth of 13.8%. The difference in growth rates is due to a portion of the net earnings being allocated to the preferred shareholders and minority interest shareholders, and EPS being based on earnings available to the common shareholders. In addition, the number of shares outstanding increased by 2.3%.

All publicly listed enterprises must report earnings per share. EPS is calculated in order to indicate the proportionate per share interest in the company's earnings. An absolute increase in earnings is not, in itself, an adequate indicator because earnings may go up as a result of increased equity investment. For example, a company may issue more shares for cash. The increased investment should generate additional earnings for the company. For an individual shareholder, the real question is whether total net income increased enough to compensate for the increased number of shares outstanding. If the proportionate increase in earnings is higher than the proportionate increase in outstanding shares, then earnings attributable to each share will increase. Note that EPS is based on net income, not on comprehensive income.

This chapter demonstrates how to calculate earnings per share and its several subcomponents. We will deal first with basic EPS, which is defined as the profit or loss attributable to each outstanding share of common or "ordinary" shares. We will then deal with the intricacies of diluted EPS. Finally, we will explore the uses and limitations of earnings per share data.

EPS FIGURES

Public companies must report both basic EPS and diluted EPS on the statement of comprehensive income. EPS is calculated based on:

1. Profit or loss from continuing operations, if presented; and then
2. Profit or loss (including discontinued operations).

Basic earnings per share is calculated as profit or loss attributable to common shareholders (net profit or loss minus preferred share claims and other prior claims) divided by the weighted-average number of ordinary (common) shares outstanding. The per-share amount of discontinued operations on their own must also be disclosed, but this may be in a disclosure note rather than on the face of the SCI. If there are no discontinued operations, then only EPS based on profit and loss is reported.

Some companies have securities in their capital structure that commit the company to issue potentially significant amount of common or "ordinary" shares in the future. As we discussed extensively in Chapter 15, these commitments can cause substantial change in the corporation's capital structure. Examples include convertible securities, stock options, and contingent commitments to issue ordinary (common) shares.

Diluted earnings per share is calculated in order to provide a basis for forward predictions. Diluted EPS shows the maximum reduction to EPS that could occur if all dilutive potential ordinary shares were issued—that is, if all dilutive stock options were exercised, all contingently issuable shares were issued, and all dilutive convertible debt and convertible preferred shares were converted to common shares.

Like basic EPS, diluted EPS must be calculated both on (1) profit or loss from continuing operations, if presented, and then (2) profit or loss. Basic and diluted EPS on profit or loss from discontinued operations is also presented, either on the face of the statement or in the notes.

INTERPRETING EPS

EPS numbers can be used as follows:

- *Basic EPS.* This is an historical amount that is based on the actual number of shares outstanding during the earnings period. Current EPS can be compared with EPS numbers from prior years to see whether the company is earning more or less for its common shareholders. It is a common way to communicate earnings information to shareholders. Basic EPS may indicate a trend to assist in forecasting, but it essentially tells us what has happened in the past.

- *Diluted EPS.* This is a forward-looking measurement. Diluted EPS gives an indication of the potential future impact that conversions (and options) will have on the earnings attributable to common shares. Companies usually issue convertible securities with the hope and expectation that they will convert to common shares and become part of the permanent capital of the company. If the company is successful in its financing strategy, the convertible senior securities will be converted rather than repaid. Thus, diluted EPS is not just a hypothetical figure—it reflects an impact that is likely to occur if and when the conversion happen.

One important aspect of EPS numbers is that they mean nothing by themselves. Like all economic indices, they are meaningful only as part of a series. Trend over time is important. The EPS trend may be easier to interpret than the trend in earnings because EPS is adjusted for changes in capital structure. This removes the normal earnings expansion effect that arises through additional share capital and reinvested earnings.

By definition, discontinued operations will wind down and cease to be a factor in operating results. Therefore, EPS numbers based on earnings from continuing operations are more relevant for future projections than are EPS that includes discontinued operations.

When comparing companies, the absolute level of EPS is meaningless. The fact that one company has EPS of $4 per share while another has EPS of $28 per share does not demonstrate that the company with the higher number is more profitable. It all depends on the number of shares outstanding. Therefore, one company's EPS cannot be compared with another's. EPS numbers are meaningful only as part of the statistical series of that reporting company's historical and projected earnings per share.

Because EPS encapsulates a company's entire reported results for the year in a single number, EPS hides much more than it shows. If you place strong reliance on EPS as an indicator of a company's performance, you are blindly accepting management's selection of accounting policies, estimates, and measurements. EPS should be used only as a rough guide; it is no substitute for an informed analysis of the company's reporting practices.

ETHICAL ISSUES

EPS calculations are complex, and their meaning is sufficiently uncertain that many accountants believe the level of reliance on them is unwarranted. Using EPS as an important element in a company's goal structure can contribute to a short-term management attitude. This can lead to decisions that are detrimental to the long-term productivity and financial health of the company. For example, rather than investing cash in productive activities that enhance the company's earnings, management may engage in share buybacks in order to decrease the denominator of the EPS calculation, thereby increasing EPS. Indeed, managers have been known to issue debt to get cash for share buybacks, a strategy that increases leverage and thus exposes shareholders to greater risk.

Nevertheless, EPS computations continue to be reported by companies and anticipated by shareholders, analysts, and management. Knowledge of how EPS amounts are calculated is essential if intelligent use is to be made of the resulting figures.

BASIC EARNINGS PER SHARE

The basic EPS calculation is as follows:

$$\frac{\text{Net profit or loss available to ordinary shareholders}}{\text{Weighted-average number of ordinary shares outstanding}}$$

The following sections explain more fully both the numerator and denominator of the basic EPS calculation.

Ordinary (Common) Shares

EPS is calculated on the basis of ordinary shares. **Ordinary shares** are defined as equity instruments that are subordinate to all other classes of equity instruments. A company may also have **senior shares,** which are any shares that have claims with higher priority than ordinary shares. It is possible for a company to have more than one class of ordinary share, often with different voting rights. Typically, ordinary shares are common shares and senior shares are preferred shares.

If preferred shares participate fully in dividends with common shares, then they are not considered to be senior shares for the purpose of EPS calculation, regardless of whether the corporation calls them "preferred shares" or "senior shares."

Net Profit or Loss Available to Ordinary Shareholders

The numerator, *net profit or loss available to ordinary shareholders*, is net earnings of the company minus claims to earnings that take precedence over the ordinary share claim. The most usual prior claim to earnings is the dividend entitlement of senior (preferred) shares. The dividend rights of senior shares are deducted from earnings when calculating EPS as follows:

- For *noncumulative* senior shares, only those dividends actually declared during the period are subtracted in determining the EPS numerator.

- For *cumulative* senior shares, the annual dividend entitlement is subtracted from earnings *regardless of whether it has been declared for the year*; any future dividend distributions to ordinary shareholders can be made only after cumulative shares' dividends in arrears have been paid.

What happens if cumulative preferred share dividends are in arrears, and, say, three years' dividends are paid in Year 3 to clear up the arrears and bring the shares up to date? In Years 1 and 2, when no dividends were paid, the annual dividend entitlement would have been deducted from earnings in order to calculate basic EPS. In the third year, three years' dividends are paid, but *only the current-year dividend is deducted* when calculating basic EPS. It would be double counting (or double deducting!) to take Year 1 and Year 2 dividends off *again*.

So, for cumulative shares, the maximum deduction is one year's dividend. If shares are noncumulative, a deduction is made for any and all dividends declared in the period. This represents their maximum claim to earnings.

In Chapter 15, we discussed preferred shares that are classified as debt because they have fixed repayment terms, or other characteristics that, in substance, render the shares debt rather than equity. "Dividends" on these preferred shares are similar to interest and are deducted to arrive at earnings rather than as a deduction from retained earnings. *As a result, earnings will already be net of these preferred dividends.* Be sure to understand the starting point; preferred dividends are deducted only once!

Other Adjustments

While dividends on preferred shares are the most frequent adjustment to the earnings line in basic EPS, more adjustments may be needed. For example:

- If preferred shares are retired during the period, a "loss" will be recorded directly in shareholders' equity, if the price paid is higher than the average issuance price to date. This was described in Chapter 14. This loss is not included in net earnings but is included (subtracted) in the numerator of basic EPS.
- If there is a *capital charge* on a convertible bond that is recorded as a direct deduction from retained earnings, this amount is also subtracted in the numerator of basic EPS.

The important question is always *what are the earnings available to ordinary shareholders?* Increases or decreases to all equity accounts should be carefully reviewed before EPS is calculated.

Weighted Average Number of Shares

The denominator of the EPS calculation reflects the number of ordinary shares, *on a weighted average basis*, that were outstanding during the year. The denominator will include all classes of shares that have residual claim (last call) on dividends, whether or not they are called "ordinary" or "common" shares in the corporate or accounting records. The result is **weighted average ordinary shares (WAOS)** outstanding.

In this calculation, shares are weighted by the length of time they are outstanding during the period. If a corporation issues additional shares during the year, additional capital invested in the business should increase earnings proportionately. If the increase in outstanding shares does not result in a proportionate increase in earnings, then the company's use of that capital was inefficient and the new shares diluted the interests of the prior-existing shareholders.

Similarly, if the number of shares outstanding during the year is reduced through a share buy-back program, withdrawal of capital from the business can be expected to reduce earnings. The intent of the EPS calculation is to reflect the relative effect on earnings after including the change in shares outstanding.

Daily averaging is the most accurate method, and technically is required. However, *calculations done by full month are permitted* (8/12, 4/12, etc.), as an expedient and reasonable way to approximate the result that a more detailed daily analysis would provide. Calculations may have to be done more precisely if the approximation is not adequate in the circumstances. For example, if a new issue of shares doubles the number of shares outstanding, then rounding to the nearest month would be inappropriate.

Mandatorily Convertible Instruments

On occasion, a company will issue a limited-term convertible security (e.g., preferred shares or debt) that *must* be converted at the end of the term—conversion is not optional. This type of security usually arises in the context of venture capital. In order to raise capital during the early stages of a company's development or expansion, the company may issue preferred shares (or debentures) to an investor that contains a fairly generous dividend preference (or high interest). In return, the investor agrees to convert the preferred shares or debentures to ordinary (common) shares at the end of a specified period.

Since the additional **mandatorily convertible shares** will definitely be issued in the future (assuming the company survives to that point), those shares *must be included in basic EPS*. Since they already have been included in basic EPS, they are *not* again added in for the diluted EPS calculation—doing so would double-count them. The shares are included from the date that the company and the investor enter into the contract for the mandatorily convertible instrument.

Example

Assume that a company has 9,000,000 common shares outstanding at the beginning of the year. The fiscal year for this company is the calendar year. An additional 3,000,000 shares are issued on 1 September. There will have been 9,000,000 shares outstanding for the first eight months of the year, followed by 12,000,000 for the last four months. The weighted-average number of shares outstanding is 10,000,000. This can be calculated using a number of approaches. For example,

Method 1

9,000,000 shares outstanding for eight months: 9,000,000 × 8/12	= 6,000,000
12,000,000 shares outstanding for four months: 12,000,000 × 4/12	= 4,000,000
WAOS	= 10,000,000

Method 2	Number of Shares	×	Months Outstanding	=	Weighted No. of Shares
	9,000,000		8		72,000,000
	12,000,000		4		48,000,000
	Total				120,000,000

WAOS = 120,000,000 ÷ 12 months = 10,000,000

Method 3

9,000,000 shares outstanding for the full year: 9,000,000 × 12/12	= 9,000,000
3,000,000 shares outstanding for four months: 3,000,000 × 4/12	= 1,000,000
WAOS	= 10,000,000

Each of these methods generates the same correct answer and all are acceptable approaches. All illustrations in this chapter will use the first method.

ETHICAL ISSUES

The EPS calculation immediately incorporates the effect of a new issue of shares into the denominator. However, it is unrealistic to expect earnings (the numerator of EPS) to respond instantly to increased capital if the shares were issued to obtain capital for increasing productive capacity. Investing in production is highly worthwhile, but it takes a while to pay off. Until earnings rise in the future from the new investment, EPS is lower than before the share issue (hopefully temporarily) and management risks derision from investors who demand instant pay-off.

One situation in which EPS may not decline in response to a substantial new issue of ordinary shares is when the new shares are used to buy another company. This is called a **business combination** in accounting, but usually is called a **merger** in conversation. When new shares are used to acquire another company, the earnings of the acquired company appear in the buying company's earnings (and EPS) immediately, from the date of the acquisition.

Since EPS is the most-watched number by the majority of investors, many corporate mergers are motivated by managers' desire to demonstrate their success at increasing EPS. They can do this without making any additional investment in productive capital if the current earnings of the acquired company are high enough to offset the impact of the new shares on EPS. This is a practice known as **buying earnings**. Some company managers are quite adept at this; they often can manage to cover up declining internal profitability of the parent company through a "buying spree"—a series of acquisitions of other companies that creates the illusion of great growth and lots of "synergies" (that usually fail to materialize) but that often make no real contribution to the intrinsic earnings ability of the buying company.

For example, suppose that Edgar Ltd. has one million shares outstanding and net earnings of $10 million—an EPS of $10. Now, suppose Edgar found a profitable but relatively underpriced company, Monica Inc., which Edgar could acquire by giving Monica shareholders 100,000 Edgar shares in exchange for all of the Monica shares. Monica would then be a wholly owned subsidiary of Edgar. As such, Monica's earnings would be included in Edgar's consolidated earnings. Suppose that in the next year, Edgar continued to earn $10,000,000 and Monica earned $2,000,000. Edgar's consolidated earnings would rise to $12,000,000 while the outstanding shares would be 1,100,000. Thus, Edgar's EPS would rise to $10.91 simply because Edgar bought another company instead of increasing Edgar's own profitability or productivity.

Contingently Issuable Shares

Contingently issuable ordinary shares are ordinary shares that are issuable for little or no cash, upon the satisfaction of specific conditions in a contingent share agreement. For example, a company may agree to issue common shares to a stakeholder if a licence for a new product is granted or issue shares to the former shareholders of an acquisition target company if the acquired operation achieves a certain level of post-acquisition profit. Contingently issuable shares are included as outstanding in WAOS *from the date that the necessary conditions have been met.* This applies even if the shares are not issued until a later date.

For example, assume that Chairot Ltd. signed an agreement as part of a business acquisition that committed Chairot to issue 10,000 common shares for no cash consideration if the target company produced 500,000 units of a subassembly in the first quarter after acquisition. This goal was met at the end of March 20X0 and the shares were issued in July 20X0. For the purposes of WAOS calculation, the shares would be treated as though they were issued when the contingency was met, at the end of March 20X0.

Stock Splits and Stock Dividends

An entity may issue or reduce shares outstanding without a corresponding change in resources; that is, for no consideration. If shares are issued under such circumstances, they are sometimes called **bonus shares**. Two common examples of this situation are in the case of a **stock dividend** or a **stock split**. A stock dividend is a dividend payable by issuing shares of the company's own common stock. Such shares *are not weight-averaged.* Instead, the stock dividend or stock split is treated as though it had been in effect for the whole period. It is also *adjusted through all prior years* that are reported as comparative data. That is, dividend shares and split shares are treated as though they had always been outstanding.

Remember, when a stock dividend or split occurs, common share equity is not changed, nor is the composition of the broader capital structure affected (i.e., no change to long-term debt or other elements). There is no substantive change to the corporation's net asset structure. Splits and stock dividends do not bring new assets into the corporation and therefore cannot be expected to generate additional earnings. Earnings are simply split up into pieces of different size.

In order to ensure comparability of EPS, *all* reported prior years' EPS numbers are restated to reflect splits and stock dividends. In the case of a 2-for-1 split, all prior EPS figures will be divided by two because one share outstanding in previous years is equivalent to two shares outstanding after the split. The denominator of the fraction doubles, so the product is halved.

Example

The following example illustrates the calculation of WAOS when there are bonus shares.

- A corporation has 5,000 common shares outstanding on 1 January, the beginning of the fiscal year.
- On 31 March, the conversion privilege on convertible bonds is exercised by the bondholders, resulting in an additional 2,400 shares being issued.
- On 1 September, the shares are split 2-for-1.
- On 1 October, an additional 3,000 shares are issued for cash.

In this example, each share outstanding prior to 1 September is equivalent to two shares outstanding after that date. The denominator of the EPS calculation must be adjusted to reflect the shares outstanding at the end of the year, after the stock split. The discontinuity that occurs as the result of the stock split must be adjusted by multiplying the pre-September outstanding shares by the split factor (in this example, $\times$ **2**) as follows:

WAOS calculation:

1 January—31 March (pre-split)	$5,000 \times \textbf{2} \times 3/12$	2,500
1 April—31 August (pre-split)	$7,400 \times \textbf{2} \times 5/12$	6,167
1 September—30 September	$14,800 \times 1/12$	1,233
1 October—31 December	$17,800 \times 3/12$	4,450
WAOS		14,350

The 5,000 shares outstanding for the first three months are equivalent to 10,000 (5,000 $\times$ 2) shares after the split. Similarly, the 7,400 (5,000 + 2,400) shares are multiplied by two to arrive at 14,800 post-split shares. Shares issued after the date of the split are *not* multiplied by two because they are stated in post-split shares. Note the last share transaction that occurred after the split on 1 October; the shares outstanding for the period 1 October to 31 December are 17,800 (14,800 + 3,000) and the shares issued in October have not been doubled.

Post-Year-End Split or Dividend

If there is a stock dividend or stock split *after the end of the year* (in the next fiscal period), it is factored into the weighted-average calculation of the *current year (and all prior periods presented).* This applies to stock dividends and splits that take place before the financial statement is authorized for issue.

Assume a company's fiscal year ends on 31 December 20X5. Thirty thousand common shares have been outstanding for the entire period. On 15 January 20X6, before the financial statements are authorized for issue, the company executes a 1-for-3 reverse split. The 30,000 shares become 10,000 shares. This 10,000 figure will be used for EPS calculations, even though the reverse split happened after the end of the year. After all, by the time the financial statements are released, the shareholders will be holding their new, smaller shares, and all data should be applicable to this new capital arrangement.

Indirect Effects of a Split or Dividend

A stock split or stock dividend will change the terms of all outstanding share commitment contracts. That is, when there is a stock split or stock dividend, the number of shares into which each senior security is convertible is adjusted accordingly. For example, if a $1,000 bond was convertible into four common shares prior to a 2-for-1 split (i.e., a conversion price of

$250), then it will automatically be convertible into eight shares (a conversion price of $125) after the split. There is *always* an anti-dilution provision to protect the holders of convertible securities and options. Option contracts will also change, increasing the number of shares offered and decreasing the option price.

Example: Basic EPS

Exhibit 20-1 shows the computation of basic EPS in a situation involving a simple capital structure that has nonconvertible preferred shares. It is based on the following facts:

1. Capital structure:

Common shares, no-par, outstanding on 1 January	90,000 shares
Common shares, issued 1 May for cash	6,000 shares
Preferred shares, no-par, $1.20 (cumulative, nonconvertible) outstanding on 1 January	5,000 shares

2. Earnings data for the year ending 31 December:

Net earnings from continuing operations	$147,000
Discontinued operations, net of tax	30,000
Net earnings and comprehensive income	$177,000

Exhibit 20-1 presents the computation of the weighted-average number of common shares outstanding during the year. The numerator for basic EPS is adjusted for preferred dividends. Remember that earnings is *before* these dividends, and an adjustment is needed.

EXHIBIT 20-1			
BASIC EPS CALCULATION			
	Earnings Available to Common Shares	**Weighted Average Number of Shares**	**Earnings per Share**
Earnings:			
Net earnings from continuing operations	$147,000		
Less: Preferred dividend cumulative entitlement: 5,000 shares × $1.20	(6,000)		
Earnings available to common, continuing operations	$141,000		
Net earnings	$177,000		
Less: Preferred dividend cumulative entitlement: 5,000 shares × $1.20	(6,000)		

	Earnings Available to Common Shares	Weighted Average Number of Shares	Earnings per Share
Earnings available to common, net earnings	$171,000		
Shares outstanding:			
90,000 × 4/12		30,000	
96,000 × 8/12		64,000	
Weighted average		94,000	
Basic EPS:			
Earnings from continuing operations	$141,000	94,000	$1.50
Discontinued operations*	30,000	94,000	0.32
Net earnings	$171,000	94,000	$1.82

*This per share amount may be included in a disclosure note.

The two EPS figures of $1.50 and $1.82 must be reported on the face of the statement of comprehensive income. The $0.32 EPS figure for discontinued operations may be reported either on the statement of comprehensive income or in the disclosure notes.

Multiple Classes of Common Shares

As we saw in Chapter 14, Canadian corporations may have multiple classes of common, or ordinary, shares outstanding. These share classes *participate* in dividends. A primary reason for having two or more classes of common shares is to vary the voting rights between the different classes, normally in order to prevent the controlling shareholders from losing control to hostile investors. So-called "preferred shares" that participate fully in dividends also qualify as *ordinary shares*.

When evaluating a company with multiple classes of shares, it is important to evaluate their dividend privileges. If the dividend privileges are *different*, then EPS calculations must be done for each class. *If two or more classes share dividends equally, share for share, then they are all ordinary shares and are lumped together in the denominator of the EPS calculation.*

For example, assume that a corporation has two classes of ordinary voting shares, Class 1 and Class 2. The shares have equal dividend rights. If there were 100,000 Class 1 shares with 10 votes each and 400,000 Class 2 shares with one vote each outstanding throughout the year, then 500,000 shares would be used for WAOS. The *voting* differential does not matter for EPS; it is only the *dividend* differential that matters.

Unequal Dividend Entitlements

If the sharing of dividends is *unequal*, more than one basic EPS statistic will be calculated.

For example, assume that a corporation has net income of $280,000. The company also has 20,000 Class A shares and 80,000 Class B shares outstanding throughout the year. Class A shares receive three times the dividend declared on Class B shares. In this case, WAOS would amount to 140,000 shares—[(20,000 Class A shares × 3) plus 80,000 Class B shares]. Dividing $280,000 by 140,000 WAOS gives us $2 per share. Therefore, basic EPS is $6 per share ($2 per share × 3 times dividend entitlement) for Class A and $2 per share for Class B.

Complex/Unequal Dividend Entitlements

Dividend arrangements may provide a base dividend, followed by participation in any remaining dividends declared. For example, assume now that both Class A and Class B ordinary shares are entitled to receive a $1 per share dividend. After this amount, Class A shares are entitled to receive $2 per share in dividends for every $1 per share paid to Class B. Profit for the year was $220,000. As in the previous example, there were 20,000 Class A shares and 80,000 Class B shares outstanding throughout the year.

To keep it simple, also assume that there are no preferred shares, no shares issued or retired during the year, and no discontinued operations included in earnings.

To calculate basic EPS when the two share classes participate differently in dividend declarations, profit is assigned to the classes according to the base dividend, and then *all* of the remaining profit is allocated according to the sharing arrangement. This allocation is based on a ratio, which is a combination of the number of shares outstanding in each class and their relative dividend entitlement.

The result is two earnings pools, which are then divided by the number of shares for each respective pool. Finally, EPS for each pool is the additive sum of the base dividend and the entitlement to undistributed earnings. The calculations are as follows:

Step 1—Calculate earnings minus the base dividend

Profit is $220,000, and the base dividend is $100,000 [$1 × (20,000 Class A shares plus 80,000 Class B shares)]

Unallocated profit: $220,000 − $100,000 = $120,000

Step 2—Allocate undistributed earnings to the share classes

Class A receives $120,000 × 1/3[*] = $40,000

Class B receives $120,000 × 2/3[*] = $80,000

[*]Class A share dividend entitlement, in equivalent Class B shares = 40,000 [i.e., (20,000 ×2)[**]]

There are 80,000 Class B shares outstanding = 80,000

Fractions: A: 40 ÷ (40 + 80) = 1/3; B: 80 ÷ (40 + 80) = 2/3

[**]The 20,000 Class A shares are entitled to two times the Class B dividend.

Step 3—Determine per share amounts (from step 2)

Class A: $40,000 ÷ 20,000 shares = $2

Class B: $80,000 ÷ 80,000 shares = $1

Step 4—Add base dividend to the step 3 amounts

Class A: $1 + $2 = $3

Class B: $1 + $1 = $2

Basic EPS for each class reflects both the base dividend plus the dividend that would be received if *all earnings* were declared as dividends. If the number of shares outstanding had changed during the period, the denominator would be a weighted average for each class.

Declared or Not?

This example assumes that the base dividend was declared. If the dividend is not declared, but is *cumulative*, then nothing changes. However, if the base dividend is *not cumulative*, then it is lost if it is not declared, and excess dividends over the base in future years would follow the (step 2) residual allocation. Therefore, if the base is not cumulative and is not declared, step 1 would not be required in the EPS calculation. In the vast majority of cases, the base dividend is cumulative, so all steps are needed.

CONCEPT REVIEW

1. What type of corporation is required to disclose earnings per share amounts?
2. What is the formula for basic earnings per share?
3. How does earnings available to ordinary shares differ from net earnings?
4. Asquith Corp. has 2,000 common shares outstanding on 1 January 20X0, issues another 400 shares on 1 July 20X0, and declares a 2-for-1 stock split on 31 December 20X0. What is the weighted-average number of shares outstanding for the year? What is the impact of the stock split on prior years' EPS amounts?
5. List the steps in calculating basic EPS when there are multiple common share classes.

DILUTED EARNINGS PER SHARE

Real Dilution

Earnings dilution occurs when additional shares are issued without a proportionate increase in the level of total earnings. This happens when, after the new shares are issued, the denominator of the EPS ratio increases proportionately more than the numerator. Thus EPS declines, or is diluted. We discussed this phenomenon earlier in the chapter; a company that issues additional shares to finance new productive capacity will most likely suffer decreased EPS in that year and quite possibly in several future years, until the additional capacity is paying off through increased sales or greater efficiency, or both. Of course, dilution can also occur if new shares are issued to finance poor investments.

Stock market investors tend to be an impatient lot. A company that experiences dilution usually sees its share value drop. That is one reason that so many companies are "taken private" by major investors, private equity firms, or management buy-outs—after becoming a private enterprise, the owners can invest major new capital into improved productivity without being harassed by impatient shareholders and investment advisors. If the new investment is successful, then the private investors can convert the private enterprise into a public company once again. If the private investors sell their own shares, they of course make a profit, but they also are leaving the company in a much stronger position than it was. Everyone wins.

Diluted EPS

"Real" dilution is the result of issuing new shares without an instantly commensurate increase in earnings. Dilution also arises in the future, however, when investors and/or creditors exercise conversion options and/or stock options into ordinary shares. Since there is a predictable outcome based on current commitments, accounting standards require companies to quantify this future potential effect by computing not only basic EPS but also *fully diluted EPS*.

Diluted earnings per share is based on the *hypothetical situation* of complete share issuance for any contract that may entitle its holder to ordinary shares in the future. Diluted EPS is hypothetical in that it reflects the results of share transactions that have not taken place but are quite likely to take place in the future. It is often called a "what if?" number—that is, what happens *if and when the corporation satisfies all if its commitments to issue ordinary shares?*

Elements to Include

Diluted EPS reflects the earnings dilution that would result from future share transactions in the following circumstances:

- Dilutive options to purchase shares are exercised, *and*
- Dilutive convertible senior securities outstanding are converted to common shares, *and*
- Dilutive *contingently issuable ordinary shares* are issued, *and*
- Any shares actually issued *during the year* because of conversion of convertible senior securities, exercise of share options, or meeting the requirements of contingently issuable ordinary shares. In these case, the diluted EPS reflects the dilution as if these shares had been issued *at the beginning* of the fiscal year.

Convertible senior securities include debt and preferred shares, senior to common shares in their entitlement to interest or dividends. If these are convertible to common shares at some point in the future, they will enter into the calculation of diluted EPS. If these securities are converted to common shares during the year, they are included in the basic EPS. The diluted EPS reflects the impact if the securities had been converted at the beginning of the year.

A **stock option** gives the holder the right to acquire a share at a stated price. Options are widely used as a form of executive compensation or issued to suppliers as a form of payment. In addition to stock options, there are warrants that also give the right to acquire shares at a fixed price. In this chapter, the word "options" will be to encompass both options and warrants. If options are outstanding, they are considered when calculating diluted EPS. Similar to convertible securities, if exercised, the shares issued are included in the basic EPS and the diluted EPS is adjusted as if the shares had been issued at the beginning of the year.

As previously discussed, *contingently issuable ordinary shares* are ordinary shares that are issuable for little or no cash, upon the satisfaction of specific conditions in a contingent share agreement. If these agreements are in place, they will be a factor in diluted EPS. Again, if the conditions are met and shares have been issued during the year, these shares are included in the basic EPS. In this case, the diluted EPS is adjusted as if the shares had been issued at the beginning of the year.

Dilutive versus Anti-Dilutive

Diluted EPS is meant to be a worst-case scenario. **Dilutive** elements are those that, when included in EPS calculations, cause a decrease in earnings per share (or an increase in a loss per share). **Anti-dilutive** elements are those that cause earnings per share to increase (or a loss per share to decrease). If share agreements are anti-dilutive contracts, they are *excluded* from the calculation of diluted EPS. This is a realistic assumption—the investors holding anti-dilutive elements would have no reason to convert to ordinary shares because they would be worse off after converting.

Diluted EPS Calculation

To calculate diluted EPS, we start with basic EPS and make adjustments for the potential issuance of dilutive ordinary shares. Note that if the basic EPS is in a loss per share position, many of these items discussed below would increase the number of shares outstanding, thereby reducing the loss per share. As a result, these would be anti-dilutive and excluded from the diluted EPS calculation.

Adjustment for Dilutive Options

Options are dilutive when they are in-the-money. Options are said to be **in-the-money** *if the exercise price is lower than the market value of common shares.* For example, if an option contract specifies an exercise price of $34.50, and the share price is $50, then the options are in-the-money. If the share price is $20, the options are not in-the-money. *Options are included in diluted EPS calculations when dilutive, that is, only when they are in-the-money.* This reflects the fact that no sane investor would exercise an option if it were *not* in-the-money.

Treasury Stock Method

Dilution adjustments for options are based on the **treasury stock method**. When option holders exercise their options, they must pay the option price to the corporation. Under the treasury stock method, those proceeds are assumed to be used to reacquire and retire common shares at the average market price during the period.

For example, assume that 1,000 options are outstanding with an exercise price of $10. The average price of common shares during the year was $40, so these options are in-the-money. If the options were exercised, another 1,000 shares would be outstanding for the period, and the company would receive $10,000 (i.e., $10 × 1,000).

In diluted EPS calculations, it is assumed that this $10,000 is used to repurchase and retire other common shares, also at the beginning of the year. Ten thousand dollars would buy 250 shares ($10,000 ÷ $40). The *denominator* of diluted EPS would be increased by 1,000 shares issued and decreased by 250 shares retired. The net adjustment is an increase of 750 shares.

These 750 shares are sometimes referred to as *bonus shares*. This is based on the reasoning that the whole transaction can be viewed as $10,000 ($10 × 1,000) raised for 250 shares at full price ($10,000 total proceeds ÷ $40) and 750 shares issued for no consideration. The 750 bonus shares can be directly calculated as 1,000 × ($40 − $10) ÷ $40.

Note that options are dilutive when the number of shares issued is greater than the shares retired; this occurs *only when options are in-the-money.*

Adjustment for Contingently Issuable Shares

As previously described, contingently issuable shares involve little or no cash consideration and must be issued on the resolution of a specified contingency. If the contingency is resolved during the period and the shares become issuable, the shares are included in WAOS for basic EPS as of the date that the contingency was resolved. If not all of the necessary conditions have been satisfied, *the shares might have to be included when calculating diluted EPS.*

If the contingency period has ended, then there is nothing contingent—the outcome is known. Therefore, shares are included if the only unmet condition is that the date of the contingency period has not yet expired. Dilutive shares are included *based on the shares issuable as though the end of the reporting period were the end of the contingency period.* The shares are included in the denominator as of (1) the beginning of the reporting period or (2) the date of the contingent share agreement, whichever is later. Contingently issuable shares have no impact on earnings, and thus there is *no change to the numerator* of diluted EPS.

For example, assume that HyperForce Ltd. acquired GH Resources for $15 million early in 20X1. The purchase and sale agreement specified that if GH's core operations earned at least $4,000,000 per year for three years, the former shareholders of GH would be entitled to 100,000 ordinary shares in HyperForce. Assume the GH operation earned $5,800,000 during 20X1. If the contingency, earnings performance, were to have concluded at the end of 20X1 (i.e., been for one year only), the shares would be issuable. Therefore, the 100,000 common shares are included in the denominator of diluted EPS calculation for 20X1, backdated to the date in 20X1 when the acquisition became effective.

These shares are included in diluted EPS even though the agreement states that *three years* of earnings must be earned to satisfy the contingency. All that is required for inclusion in diluted EPS is that the necessary conditions are met *as if the contingency period ended at the end of 20X1.* If, on the other hand, the agreement was written to require *cumulative earnings of $12 million* before the shares were issuable, then the shares would not have been included in diluted EPS at the end of 20X1 because the condition had not yet been met.

Adjustment for Dilutive Senior Securities

Bond and preferred share adjustments are based on the **if-converted method**. Under this method, the numerator and denominator of the EPS ratio are adjusted as though *the securities had been converted at the beginning of the period (or at the date of issue, if later).*

The *numerator* of the EPS fraction is adjusted for dividends or after-tax interest that would have been saved if the bonds or preferred shares had been converted. In other words, how would the numerator be different if the convertible bonds did not exist? Interest expense would be eliminated. What if the preferred shares did not exist? No preferred dividends would have been paid. The effect to the denominator is straightforward in both cases. More shares would be outstanding!

Technicalities to note:

1. If there are a variety of conversion terms, perhaps depending on when the conversion were to take place, *the most dilutive alternative must be used.*

2. If convertible securities were issued during the year, the assumed conversion goes *back only to the date of issue,* not the beginning of the year.

3. If the conversion option lapsed during the year or if the security was redeemed or settled during the year, the conversion is still included (if dilutive) *up to the time at which it lapsed.*

Calculation Rules

To summarize the potential adjustments:

Element	Change to Numerator	Change to Denominator
Options—treasury stock method	None	1. Increase by shares issued 2. Decrease by shares retired
Contingently issuable shares	None	Increase by shares issued
Convertible bonds—if-converted method	Increase by after-tax interest avoided	Increase by shares issued
Convertible preferred shares—if-converted method	Increase by dividend claim avoided*	Increase by shares issued

*If there were any other items recorded in the financial statements, such as gains or losses on preferred share retirement, these items would have been adjusted when calculating the basic EPS numerator and also included in the numerator adjustment here.

Individual Effect

Note that convertible bonds and convertible preferred shares involve a change to the numerator *and* a change to the denominator. The **individual effect** of each convertible item is represented by this ratio. For instance, if there was $10,000 of after-tax interest on a bond that was convertible into 40,000 common shares, the individual effect would be $0.25 ($10,000 ÷ 40,000).

The *individual effect* must be calculated separately for each potentially dilutive element. It is the change to earnings entitlement divided by additional shares that would have to be issued, and it is used to establish dilution or anti-dilution and sequence for convertible senior securities.

Steps in Calculating Diluted EPS

The steps in calculating diluted EPS are listed in Exhibit 20-2. A flow chart of the process is shown in Exhibit 20-3. We will explain these steps in the example that follows; refer to the list as the example progresses.

EXHIBIT 20-2

STEPS IN CALCULATING DILUTED EPS

To Calculate Diluted EPS:

1. **Begin with the basic EPS numbers**, based on *earnings from continuing operations*. If there were no discontinued operations, begin with the only basic EPS number available, basic EPS based on net earnings.

2. If any options were **exercised** during the period, **determine if the options exercised were in-the-money**, and thus dilutive. **Adjust the denominator** as though these shares had been issued at the beginning of the period, using the **treasury stock method**.

3. **Identify options outstanding throughout the year**, the option price, and the average share price for the period. Determine if the options are in-the-money, and thus dilutive. **Adjust the denominator** as though these shares were issued at the beginning of the period, using the **treasury stock method**. If options were **issued during the year**, backdate only to the date of issue. Calculate a subtotal at this point.

4. If any contingently issuable shares were **issued** during the period, **adjust the denominator** as though these shares were issued at the beginning of the period. This moves the share issuance back to the beginning of the year.

5. **Identify contingently issuable shares outstanding at the end of the year**. Calculate the number of shares, if any, that would be issued if the contingency period were to end at the end of the current fiscal year. **Adjust the denominator** as though these shares were issued at the beginning of the period. *Calculate a subtotal at this point.*

6. **Identify any convertible senior debt or shares that actually converted** during the period. **Calculate the individual effect** of the converted securities, using the **if-converted method**. This adjustment moves the conversion back to the beginning of the year. The individual effect is after-tax interest or dividends divided by shares issued. Both the numerator and denominator reflect the number of months **before conversion** in the fiscal year.

7. **Identify the terms and conditions of convertible senior shares and debt outstanding throughout the year.** If there are various conversion alternatives at different dates, *use the most dilutive alternative*. If convertible securities were **issued during the year**, backdate only to the date of issue. **Calculate the individual effect** of the converted securities, using the if-converted method.

8. Compare the individual effects of the items identified in steps 6 and 7. **Rank the items,** from most dilutive (lowest individual effect) to least dilutive (highest individual effect).

9. Return to the subtotal taken in step 5. **Include the effects of actual and potential conversions** in cascading order, from most dilutive to least dilutive. Use the ranking from step 8. **Calculate a subtotal** after each item is added. Exclude anti-dilutive items.

10. Use the **lowest calculation** as diluted EPS.

11. **Repeat the process,** beginning with *basic EPS for net earnings*. Use exactly the same adjustments to the numerator and the denominator as in the first calculation. *No second test for anti-dilution is allowed.*

EXHIBIT 20-3

FLOW CHART OF STEPS FOR CALCULATING DILUTED EPS

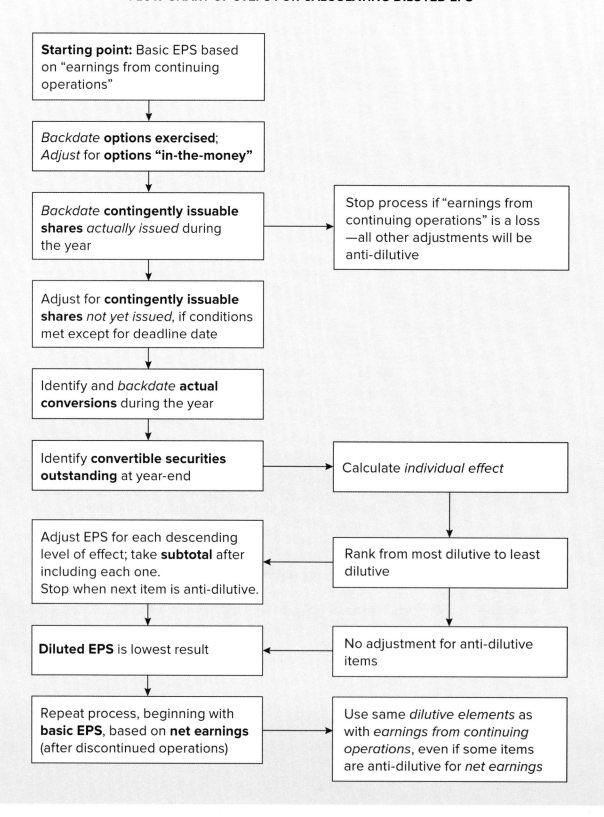

Diluted EPS Calculation: Example

Assume that a corporation has the following capital structure throughout all of 20X1:

- *Convertible debentures*: $1,000,000 maturity value; 10% interest paid annually; issued at par; convertible into 10 common shares for each $1,000 of bond maturity value at the option of the investor.

- *Convertible preferred shares*: 1,000 shares issued and outstanding; $150 annual per share dividend, cumulative; callable at $1,200 per share; convertible into common shares on a 5:1 basis until 20X5; convertible on a 10:1 basis thereafter.

- *Common shares*: 20,000 shares issued and outstanding all year.

Net earnings for 20X1 is $600,000 after income tax at a rate of 25%. There are no discontinued operations. There are no contingently issuable common shares. There are executive stock options outstanding all year, allowing purchase of 4,000 common shares at an exercise price of $50. The average market value of common shares during the period was $125. Interest expense recognized for the year for the convertible bond was $100,000; after-tax amount is $75,000 ($100,000 × (1 − 0.25)).

Refer to Exhibit 20-2 to follow the steps for computing diluted EPS. The calculations for this example are in Exhibit 20-4.

EXHIBIT 20-4			
BASIC AND DILUTED EPS CALCULATIONS			
	Earnings Available to Common Shares	**Weighted- Average Number of Shares**	**Earnings per Share**
Basic EPS:			
Earnings:			
Net earnings	$600,000		
Less: Preferred dividends: 1,000 shares × $150	(150,000)		
Net earnings available to common shareholders	450,000		
Shares outstanding		20,000	
Basic EPS	**$450,000**	**20,000**	**$22.50**
Diluted EPS:			
Data from basic EPS, above	$450,000	20,000	$22.50
Adjustments for assumed options exercise:			
Shares issued		4,000	
Shares retired		(1,600)	
Subtotal	$450,000	22,400	$20.09

Adjustments for debenture conversion:			
Interest avoided (after-tax equivalent)	75,000		
Additional common shares issued		10,000	
Subtotal	$525,000	32,400	$16.20
Adjustments for preferred share conversion:			
Dividends avoided	150,000		
Additional common shares issued		10,000	
Diluted EPS	**$675,000**	**42,400**	**$15.92**

Starting Point

The first step is to start with earnings before discontinued operations. Since this example has no discontinued operations, we can start with basic EPS of $22.50, as calculated at the top of Exhibit 20-4. Also, there are no shares issued under option contracts during the year, no contingently issuable common shares, and no actual conversions of senior securities during the period. Therefore, steps 2, 4, 5, 6, and 11 can be skipped. (A later comprehensive example will deal with these situations.)

Options

Outstanding options are the next thing to consider (step 3). The company has outstanding options to issue 4,000 common shares at $50. The $50 option price is less than the $125 average market price of shares during the period, and therefore these options are *in-the-money* and dilutive. They must be included in diluted EPS.

If these shares had been issued at the beginning of the period, another 4,000 shares would have been outstanding for the whole period, increasing the denominator by 4,000 shares. The total proceeds would have been $200,000 (i.e., 4,000 × $50).

In the diluted EPS calculation, we assume that the proceeds would have been used to retire other common shares at the market price: 1,600 shares ($200,000 ÷ $125). The denominator increases by 2,400 shares (4,000 − 1,600) and the numerator does not change. We also can make this 2,400 share calculation directly: 4,000 × ($125 − $50) ÷ $125 = 2,400.

Convertible Securities

In step 7, we calculate the individual effects of potential conversion of the two convertible securities. The numerator of the EPS fraction is adjusted by the amount of dividends or after-tax interest that will be saved if the senior securities are converted. The additional shares are added to the denominator.

Convertible Debentures

The debentures are convertible at the rate of 10 shares per $1,000. That works out to potential issuance of 10,000 additional shares ($1,000,000 / $1000 × 10) that would be added to the denominator of the EPS ratio. Bond interest on the debentures is $100,000 before tax, which is $75,000 after 25% tax.

The *individual effect* of this convertible bond is $7.50 ($75,000 ÷ 10,000). When compared with the basic EPS of $22.50, we can readily see that this is dilutive (i.e., $7.50 is lower than $22.50).

Convertible Preferred Shares

If the 1,000 shares of preferred shares had been converted at the beginning of the year, preferred dividends of $150,000 would have been avoided. Dividends are not tax deductible, and so we need no tax adjustment before adding this amount to the numerator.

The shares may be converted at the rate of 5:1 until the end of 20X5, and then the conversion ratio changes to 10:1. *The worst-case scenario, or more dilutive alternative, must be used in these calculations.* This is the 10:1 ratio. Thus, another 10,000 shares could potentially be issued. This gives us an *individual effect* of $15 (i.e., $150,000 ÷ 10,000 shares), which is dilutive in relation to basic EPS but is less dilutive than the *individual effect* of $7.50 for the bonds. This comparison is the step 8 ranking.

Ranking

Now for step 9. The bonds' individual effect of $7.50 is more dilutive than the preferred shares' individual effect of $15, and the effect of the most dilutive is taken first. After the dilutive effect of the bonds is taken into account, a subtotal is taken before the convertible preferred shares are considered. Inclusion of the bonds reduces diluted EPS to $16.20.

Next, the preferred shares' individual effect of $15 is compared with this new EPS subtotal of $16.20, which shows that the preferred shares still are dilutive. The dilutive effects of the preferred shares are then added in.

Step 10 is the final determination of diluted EPS—$15.92.

Reporting Diluted EPS

Diluted EPS is reported on the face of the statement of comprehensive income (or the statement of profit or loss if two statements are presented), given equal prominence with basic EPS. Even if the two numbers are identical, they must both be disclosed. In the above example, the company would report:

Basic EPS	$22.50
Diluted EPS	$15.92

Diluted EPS Cascade

In Exhibit 20-4, we illustrated the **diluted EPS cascade** of adjustments, going from the most dilutive to the least dilutive. Note that options that are in-the-money (and any contingently issuable ordinary shares) are always dilutive because they involve no increase to the numerator. That is why they are *always done first* in diluted EPS calculations.

The *individual effect* tells us which other elements are potentially dilutive, but only in relation to unadjusted basic EPS. However, that is just at the first stage. An apparently dilutive element may turn out to be anti-dilutive when it gets its turn to be considered. The convertible securities with the *lowest individual EPS effect* are the most dilutive, and are entered first. If inclusion of a later item causes EPS to *increase*, it is *anti-dilutive and excluded*.

For instance, suppose that a company has $100,000 net earnings available to common shareholders and 100,000 weighted-average ordinary shares. The company's basic EPS is $1. Two potentially dilutive securities are outstanding:

- Preferred shares, with a $45,000 dividend and a 100,000 share conversion entitlement ($0.45 individual effect); and
- Bonds, with after-tax interest of $68,000, and a share conversion entitlement of 75,000 shares ($0.91 individual effect).

Both elements look dilutive when compared to basic EPS of $1 but preferred shares are the more dilutive.

After the more dilutive preferred shares are included, diluted EPS is $0.73: ($100,000 + $45,000) ÷ (100,000 + 100,000). The bonds, with an individual effect of $0.91, are *no longer dilutive*. If they were included, diluted EPS would *increase* to $0.77: ($100,000 + $45,000 + $68,000) ÷ (100,000 + 100,000 + 75,000).

Diluted EPS is reported as $0.73, and the second security is omitted from the calculation. This is the cascade approach to diluted EPS calculations, and it results in diluted EPS being reported as the lowest possible number.

Interest Expense or Interest Paid?

There are many situations in which a bond is offered at a discount or premium. This is particularly true for convertible bonds when the coupon rate is usually less than the interest rate for a similar nonconvertible bond. When that happens, interest *expense* will include discount or premium amortization and will not coincide with amount of interest *paid*. In diluted EPS calculations, the adjustment to the numerator (i.e., earnings available to common shareholders) *must always be for interest expense*. A simple adjustment based on the nominal rate of interest will not work—discount or premium amortization must also be taken into account. Remember that we are adjusting earnings, and earnings reflect interest expense, not the amount of interest paid.

Actual Conversions During the Period

So far, we have illustrated diluted EPS giving effect to the year-end obligations to issue shares. Diluted EPS must also include calculations that reflect actual conversions, actual contingently issuable shares issued, and actual options exercised during the period. This adjustment is often called **backdating**: *adjusting the actual issuance as though it took place at the beginning of the period*. Backdating is done only if the result is dilutive.

The reason for backdating is to facilitate forward comparisons. In the years following the conversion, the full effects of the conversion will be reflected in basic EPS in that year, which will not be fully comparable with EPS in the year of the conversion because it included only a partial effect (i.e., following the date of actual conversion). Backdating puts actual conversions on the same footing as potential conversions, which are effectively backdated to the beginning of the fiscal period.

Steps 2, 4 and 6 in Exhibit 20-2 deal with backdating. The following examples demonstrate actual conversions of preferred shares, actual conversion of debt, and shares issued on the exercise of options.

Example 1—Converted Preferred Shares

Assume that a corporation has two classes of shares outstanding:

- Class A preferred shares, 600 shares issued and outstanding at the beginning of the year; annual dividend rate of $1,000 per share, cumulative, dividend paid at the end of each quarter; each share is convertible into 50 shares of Class B common.
- Class B common shares, 50,000 shares issued and outstanding at the beginning of the year.

Also assume that:

- There are no other senior securities.
- Net earnings for 20X1, the year of the conversion, is $2,175,000; there are no discontinued operations.
- All 600 shares of Class A are converted into 30,000 Class B shares on 1 October 20X1; dividends for the first three quarters of the year were fully paid.
- Options are outstanding to issue 10,000 common shares to senior executives for $1 per share; the average share price during the year was $8. No options were exercised during the period. These options were outstanding during the whole year.

Basic earnings per share for 20X1 is $30, as calculated at the top of Exhibit 20-5. Diluted EPS begins with this figure, and then includes the effect of options. (Step 3 as listed in Exhibit 20-2). This reduces EPS to $26.04. Note that the options effect could be directly calculated as a reduction to the denominator of 8,750 shares [10,000 × ($8 − $1) ÷ $8]. The result is the same.

EXHIBIT 20-5

BASIC AND DILUTED EPS CALCULATIONS

Actual Conversion of Preferred Shares

	Earnings Available to Common Shares	Weighted-Average Number of Shares	Earnings per Share
Basic EPS:			
Earnings:			
Net earnings	$ 2,175,000		
Less: Preferred dividends:			
600 shares × $250 per quarter × three quarters	(450,000		
Earnings available to common	$ 1,725,000		
Shares outstanding			
50,000 × 9/12		37,500	
[50,000 + (600 Class A × 50 Class B)] × 3/12		20,000	
Basic EPS	**$1,725,000**	**57,500**	**$30.00**
Diluted EPS			
Data from basic EPS, above	$ 1,725,000	57,500	
Adjustments for assumed options exercise:			
Shares issued		10,000	
Shares retired			
(10,000 × $1) ÷ $8		(1,250)	
Subtotal	$ 1,725,000	66,250	$26.04
Adjustments for converted shares:			
Dividends on converted shares:			
600 shares × $250 × three quarters	450,000		
Adjust shares for preceding three quarters:			
(600 Class A × 50 Class B) × 9/12		22,500	
Diluted EPS	**$2,175,000**	**88,750**	**$24.51**

In 20X1, all 600 Class A shares were converted into 30,000 Class B shares (at 50 Class B shares per Class A share). For basic EPS, these newly issued shares would be multiplied by the 3/12 of the year that they were outstanding and added to the *weighted-average* number of shares used in basic EPS. However, in future years there will be 30,000 additional Class B shares outstanding *all year*. Diluted EPS backdates the conversion (step 6). This is demonstrated in the highlighted section of Exhibit 20-5. There are two steps to the process of backdating:

- Profit available to common shareholders, the numerator, is adjusted for the dividends on the converted Class A shares that would not have been paid if the shares had converted at the beginning of the period. This is $450,000 ($250 per quarter × 600 shares × 3 quarters).

- The weighted-average number of shares is adjusted to reflect the full volume of additional Class B shares issued for the conversion, that is, 30,000 shares × 9/12, or 22,500 shares.

The *individual effect* of this conversion is $20 ($450,000 ÷ 22,500), which is dilutive in relation to the diluted EPS subtotal of $26.04. As a result, diluted EPS now drops to $24.51. Note that the total number of shares for the diluted EPS of 88,750 is the same as the original 50,000 Class B common shares plus the 30,000 shares issued on conversion for the preferred shares plus the net additional shares of 8,8750 for the exercise of the options.

Example 2—Converted Debt

Assume that a corporation has one class of shares outstanding but also has convertible bonds, some of which were converted during 20X1:

- 50,000 common shares are outstanding at the beginning of 20X1.

- Reported net profit for 20X1 is $3,000,000; there are no discontinued operations.

- The corporation has $40 million principal amount of 10-year, 6%, convertible debentures that were issued five years previously. All are still outstanding at the beginning of 20X1. Each $1,000 face value of bonds is convertible into two shares of common stock at the investor's option, and thus the full $40 million would be convertible into 80,000 shares.

- Interest is paid annually 31 December.

- The net proceeds from the bond issue amounted to $41 million. The present value of the liability cash flow at the date of issue was $32.3 million; the remaining $8.7 million was allocated to the conversion option. At the date of issuance, the market rate of interest for nonconvertible bonds of similar risk was 9%.

- On 30 June 20X1, one-quarter of the bonds are converted.

- The corporation's income tax rate is 25%.

Based on the convertible bond amortization schedule below, the interest expense (using an effective interest rate of 9%) in year 6 on the bonds is $3,179,918.

Date	Interest Paid	Interest Expense	Amortization	Principal
				32,298,811
Year 1	2,400,000	2,906,893	506,893	32,805,704
Year 2	2,400,000	2,952,513	552,513	33,358,217
Year 3	2,400,000	3,002,240	602,240	33,960,457
Year 4	2,400,000	3,056,441	656,441	34,616,898
Year 5	2,400,000	3,115,521	715,521	35,332,419

Date	Interest Paid	Interest Expense	Amortization	Principal
Year 6	2,400,000	3,179,918	779,918	36,112,337
Year 7	2,400,000	3,250,110	850,110	36,962,447
Year 8	2,400,000	3,326,620	926,620	37,889,067
Year 9	2,400,000	3,410,016	1,010,016	38,899,083
Year 10	2,400,000	3,500,917	1,100,917	40,000,000

The conversion of $10,000,000 principal amount of bonds results in an additional 20,000 shares issued. In the basic EPS calculation, the additional shares are outstanding for the second half of the year and are weighted proportionately in the denominator. On conversion, the amount of interest for year 6 would have been (based on the above schedule):

1 January to 30 June: $3,179,918 × 6/12 × 40/40 = $1,589,959

1 July to 31 December: $3,179,918 × 6/12 × 30/40 = $ 1,192,469

Total interest expense $2,782,428

The EPS numerator already includes, in earnings, a deduction for (pretax) interest of $1,589,959 on $40,000,000 for the first half of the year. After the conversion, the interest for the second half of the year will be an interest expense of $1,192,469 ($1,589,959 × 30/40) on the remaining $30,000,000 for the second half of the year following conversion. The calculation of basic EPS is shown at the top of Exhibit 20-6.

EXHIBIT 20-6

BASIC AND DILUTED EPS CALCULATIONS

Partial Actual Conversion of Debt

	Earnings Available to Common Shares	Weighted-Average Number of Shares	Earnings per Share
Basic EPS:			
Earnings:			
Net earnings	$3,000,000		
Earnings available to common	$3,000,000		

Shares outstanding:			
50,000 shares × 6/12		25,000	
70,000 shares × 6/12		35,000	
Basic EPS	**$3,000,000**	**60,000**	**$50.00**
Diluted EPS:			
Data from basic EPS, above	$3,000,000	60,000	
Adjustments for converted debt:			
Remove after-tax interest on converted debt for portion of year outstanding: $3,179,918 × 10/40 × 6/12 × (1.00 − 0.25)	298,117		
Adjust shares for first six months: 20,000 shares × 6/12		10,000	
Subtotal	$ 3,298,117	70,000	$ 47.12
Adjustment for remaining convertible debt:			
Remove after-tax interest on remaining debt: $3,179,918 × 30/40 × (1.00 − 0.25)	1,788,704		
Shares			
($30,000,000 ÷ $1,000) × 2 shares per bond		60,000	
Diluted EPS	**$5,086,821**	**130,000**	**$ 39.13**

To calculate diluted EPS, the conversion must be backdated to the beginning of the year (step 6). The effect of the remaining unconverted bonds must be included (step 9). Both of these adjustments are made *only if dilutive*.

For backdating, the EPS numerator must be reduced by the six months' interest actually expensed on the $10,000,000 principal amount of converted bonds. At a 25% income tax rate, the first six-months' interest on the converted bonds was:

Interest expense after-tax = 1,589,959 × 10/40 × (1.00 − .25) = 298,117

In general, the formula for computing the interest savings from conversion is:

Interest expense for the period × fraction of year *before* conversion × (1 − tax rate)

For example, if the bonds had been retired after four months of the fiscal year, four months of interest would be added back.

The highlighted section of Exhibit 20-6 shows the add-back of $298,117 after-tax interest expense, and the weighted-average number of shares is increased to reflect the full amount of shares issued on conversion. Shares are calculated as 20,000 shares × 6/12. The EPS *individual effect* is $29.81 (i.e., $298,117 ÷ 10,000), which is dilutive, relative to basic EPS of $50.

Finally, the assumed conversion of the remaining dilutive convertible bonds must be considered. The interest expense for these still-outstanding bonds is:

$$\text{After-tax interest expense} = \$3,179,918 \times 30/40\,(1.00 - 0.25) = 1,788,704$$

Shares to be issued would be 60,000 [($30,000,000 ÷ $1,000) × 2], and the *individual effect* of the bonds is $29.81 (i.e., $1,788,704 ÷ 60,000). These bonds are dilutive. The adjustment is included in Exhibit 20-6, resulting in final diluted EPS of $39.13.

Note that the individual effect of the converted bonds and the unconverted bonds is identical—it does not matter which is done first in the cascade. As a check, the total interest after-tax added back is equal to $2,086,821 ($298,117 + $1,788,704) which is the same as the actual after-tax amount of the total expense for the year ($2,782,428 × 0.75 = $2,086,821).

Example 3—Exercised Options

If options had been exercised during the period, we would need to make an adjustment to backdate these shares to the beginning of the period *if they were dilutive*. Again, the treasury stock method would be applied for that portion of the year.

For example, suppose that a holder exercised options for 10,000 shares at $1 per share on 1 November, for a total consideration of $10,000. The average share price for the first 10 months of the year was $9. When calculating basic EPS, these shares would be weight-averaged in the denominator for two months.

For diluted EPS, as in step 2, the shares must be backdated to the start of the year. The denominator is increased by a net of 7,407. This is calculated as follows: 10,000 shares issued on exercise of the options less 1,111 shares ($10,000 /$9) repurchased. This net number of shares of 8,889 is then adjusted for 10 months; i.e. 8,889 × 10/12 = 7,407. As always, the adjustment is made only if the options are in-the-money, and thus are dilutive.

Note that the $9 average market price used was the average for the first 10 months of the year, which is more applicable to this calculation than the average for the entire year.

CONCEPT REVIEW

1. What is the purpose of calculating diluted EPS?
2. Explain the difference between dilutive and anti-dilutive elements.
3. What is added to the numerator of diluted EPS for convertible bonds? For convertible preferred shares?
4. Assume basic EPS is $5. Two potentially dilutive elements exist, with an individual effect of $1 and $4.50, respectively. Under what circumstances would the $4.50 item be considered anti-dilutive?
5. How do actual conversions of senior securities affect the calculation of diluted EPS?
6. What assumption is made regarding the proceeds of option contracts when calculating diluted EPS? When are options dilutive?

COMPLICATING FACTORS

Convertible Securities and Options Issued During the Year

If convertible securities are issued during the year, the effect of a hypothetical conversion is backdated in the calculation of diluted EPS *only to the date of issue.* For example, suppose that DRV Corp. issued 8% convertible bonds payable on 1 November. When measuring interest expense, of course, only two months' interest would have been recorded. In calculating diluted EPS, two months' interest (not 12 months'!) is added to the numerator and two months of shares (not 12 months'!) are added to the denominator. That is, the bond is assumed to be converted on the date of issuance *if it was issued during the period.* Next year, when the bonds have been outstanding for a full year, the adjustments revert to normal—a full year.

The reason for not backdating new debt to the beginning of the year is that the additional capital introduced into the firm by issuing new debt has contributed to earnings only from the date of issue, not for the entire year. Remember that the numerator and denominator of the EPS ratio must always be consistent with each other.

Similarly, if options are issued during the year, they are backdated *only to the date of issuance* in diluted EPS calculations. Employee stock options are often issued at the end of a fiscal period, which means that they do not affect diluted EPS in their first year.

An illustration of this situation is included in the final example in the chapter.

Convertible Securities and Options Extinguished During the Year

What happens if a company has convertible securities or options during the year that are redeemed or settled in cash, or that expire during the year? Accounting standards specify that in that situation, the potential common shares, *if dilutive,* are included in the calculation of diluted EPS only up to the date of redemption, settlement, or expiry.

In practice, such securities or options would never be dilutive, and thus this is not something one really needs to worry about. If the holder of a convertible security accepts a cash repayment instead of converting, it is because the security is *not* in-the-money. If a security is in-the-money, issuers often call in the bonds for redemption in order to force holders to convert. This practice is called **forced conversion**.

The treatment of options is a little different. Suppose that options were outstanding until they expired on 30 September. The fact that they expired unexercised means that they were not in-the-money on the expiry date, but *theoretically* they may have been in-the-money earlier in the fiscal year. The options would be factored into diluted EPS for any period before 30 September during which they were in-the-money.

Reference Point for Diluted EPS

EPS on earnings from continuing operations always should be the yardstick used for assessing dilution versus anti-dilution. All decisions are made with this as the starting point. So, if an item is included for earnings from continuing operations, it is *also always included* for EPS based on net earnings.

For example, assume that earnings from continuing operations is $450,000. There is an after-tax loss from discontinued operations of $200,000, resulting in net earnings of $250,000. There are 10,000 common shares outstanding all year, and no preferred shares. Basic EPS is $45 based on earnings before the discontinued operation and $25 based on net earnings. Convertible debt, with after-tax interest of $70,000 and a share entitlement of 2,500 shares, is outstanding.

The individual dilutive effect of the convertible debt is $28 ($70,000 ÷ 2,500). This is dilutive to EPS calculated on earnings from continuing operations, but anti-dilutive to EPS calculated on net earnings. Nevertheless, the item must be included in diluted EPS for *both measures of diluted EPS.*

Diluted EPS will be as follows:

- For *earnings from continuing operations*: ($450,000 + $70,000) ÷ (10,000 + 2,500) = $41.60
- For *net earnings*: ($250,000 + $70,000) ÷ 12,500 = $25.60

Diluted EPS for net earnings, at $25.60, is higher than basic EPS of $25! But the bonds have to be included for both diluted EPS measures, since they were definitely dilutive for earnings from continuing operations.

Measuring Share Price

Average share price is used to determine whether options are in-the-money and to calculate the share adjustment for the denominator of diluted EPS. Accounting standards state that a simple average of weekly or monthly prices is usually appropriate. If prices fluctuate widely over the period being used, an average of the high and low point for the period will usually be a more representative value than the closing price. If shares are thinly traded, an average of bid and asked price may be appropriate. Using average share price is justified because profit (the numerator for EPS) is generated *over the period,* and the denominator should also reflect the entire year.

However, use of averages can be problematic. Assume that the share price on average was $40 for the period, but falls to $25 at the end of the fiscal year. Options are outstanding with a per-share price of $30. These options are in-the-money with respect to average share price, but not in relation to the closing price. If the closing market price is a good predictor of share price through the coming year, diluted EPS will imply an option exercise that would not be economically logical. Average share price is used.

Diluted EPS in a Loss Year

When a company has reported a loss from continuing operations, adding *anything* positive to the numerator and/or increasing the number of common shares outstanding will *reduce the loss per share* and be anti-dilutive. Thus, diluted EPS is equal to basic EPS in a loss year because all potentially dilutive items will be anti-dilutive.

What if a company reported a loss of $100,000 from continuing operations but a gain of $500,000 from discontinued operations? Net earnings would be positive, at $400,000. Dilutive securities and options *are still classified as anti-dilutive* because the dilution test is performed with reference to earnings from continuing operations. If it is dilutive—or anti-dilutive—to the top line, it must be classified consistently thereafter.

Bonds Convertible at the Issuer's Option

Convertible bonds may be convertible at the option of either the investor or the issuer. The examples shown above have dealt with convertible bonds that are convertible at the option of the investor. *If it is the company's option to issue shares or cash on the maturity date, the bonds still must be considered for diluted EPS calculations.* The company cannot avoid inclusion by claiming that it intends to repay the bond with cash rather than shares. If the result is dilutive, the bond is included in diluted EPS calculations.

FVTPL Liabilities

Most liabilities are carried at amortized cost. Some, however, are classified as fair value through profit or loss (FVTPL) financial instruments. A company may designate a liability as FVTPL on initial recognition for a variety of reasons, including the need to avoid a mismatch if a related, hedged asset must be valued at fair value; if the liabilities are managed with reference to their fair value; or to simplify valuation if there is an embedded derivative in the liability.

FVTPL liabilities are valued at fair value, and changes in fair value are recorded as a component of earnings. If these liabilities are convertible bonds, then in the calculation of diluted EPS, their effect on net earnings includes fair-value changes. Any gain or loss on the change in fair value that is included in net earnings must be adjusted on the numerator, after tax, and considered when evaluating whether the liability is dilutive or anti-dilutive.

CONCEPT REVIEW

1. What is the reference point for the dilution test?
2. When there is a difference between interest expense and interest paid, which number is used for convertible bonds in diluted EPS?
3. Why is diluted EPS generally equal to basic EPS in a loss year?

COMPREHENSIVE ILLUSTRATION

Having discussed all of the pieces of basic and diluted EPS, we'll now turn to a comprehensive illustration. Exhibit 20-7 contains the information for this example, and Exhibit 20-8 works through the EPS calculations.

EXHIBIT 20-7

FRM CORPORATION

Data for Comprehensive EPS Illustration

Year Ended 31 December 20X1

Capital Structure, 31 December 20X1:

Long-term debt:

12% first mortgage bonds, due 1 July 20X9	$1,300,000
10% unsecured debentures issued at par, due 31 July 20X7, convertible into Class A common shares at $50 at any time prior to maturity	$ 960,000
8% unsecured debentures issued at par, due 15 April 20X20, convertible into 12,000 Class A common shares on or after 31 December 20X12	$1,500,000

Share capital:

Preferred shares, dividend rate of $20 per share, cumulative and nonparticipating, convertible to Class B common shares at the rate of two shares of Class B for each share of preferred	5,000 shares
Class A common shares, one vote per share	104,800 shares
Class B common shares, 20 votes per share, sharing dividends equally with Class A common shares	10,000 shares

Options:

3,000 employee stock options issued on 31 December 20X0, each exchangeable for one Class A share as follows:

$30 per share prior to 1 January 20X4

$40 per share between 1 January 20X4 and 31 December 20X7

$55 per share between 1 January 20X8 and 31 December 20X10

The options expire at the close of business on 31 December 20X10

5,000 employee stock options, issued on 31 December 20X1, each exchangeable for one Class A share at a price of $25 per share prior to 31 December 20X11. The options expire at the close of business on 31 December 20X11.

Contingent shares:

FRM entered into a contingent share agreement in 20X0 when it acquired another company. FRM must issue 9,000 Class A shares in March of 20X4 if the acquired company's core operations earn $400,000 before tax each year from the acquisition date through 20X3. To date, earnings have surpassed this level.

Additional information:

- After-tax earnings for the year ended 31 December 20X1 were $1,200,000; this was after a $200,000 after-tax gain from discontinued operations.
- The income tax rate was 25%.
- The average market value of common shares during the period was $45.
- Dividends were paid quarterly on the preferred shares; there are no dividends in arrears.
- Dividends of $1 per quarter were declared on both Class A and Class B shares; the dividends were payable to shareholders of record at the end of each calendar quarter, and were paid five business days thereafter.
- On 1 October 20X1, 10% debentures with a principal amount of $240,000 were converted into 4,800 Class A shares (included in the outstanding shares listed above). At the beginning of the year, the total principal amount of the 10% debentures was $1,200,000.
- On 1 May 20X1, FRM issued $ 1,500,000 face value of 8% unsecured debentures, due 15 April 20X20, convertible into 12,000 Class A common shares on or after 31 December 20X12. The bonds were issued for $1,650,000, and $150,000 of the proceeds was classified in equity as the value of the conversion option.

EXHIBIT 20-8

FRM CORPORATION

Comprehensive EPS Illustration

(Based on Data in Exhibit 20-7)

	Earnings Available to Common Shares	Weighted-Average Number of Shares	Earnings per Share
Basic EPS:			
Earnings from continuing operations after tax	$1,000,000		
Less: Preferred dividends: 5,000 shares × $20	(100,000)		
Shares outstanding:			
Class A			
100,000 × 9/12		75,000	
104,800 × 3/12		26,200	
Class B 10,000 × 12/12		10,000	
Basic EPS	**$ 900,000**	**111,200**	**$ 8.09**
Individual effect ratios:			
Preferred shares (per share)	$ 20	2	$10.00
Actual conversion of 10% debenture			
Interest saved: ($240,000×10%)×(1.00−0.25)×9/12	13,500		
Additional shares: 4,800 × 9/12		3,600	3.75
10% debentures (remainder)			
Interest saved: ($960,000 × 10%) × (1.00 − 0.25)	72,000		
Additional shares: $960,000 ÷ $50		19,200	3.75
8% debentures			
Interest saved: ($1,500,000×8%)×(1.00−0.25)×8/12	60,000		
Additional shares: given 12,000 × 8/12		8,000	7.50

Diluted EPS:

Data from basic	$ 900,000	111,200	
Adjustment for assumed options exercise:			
Shares issued		3,000	
Shares retired		(2,000)	
Subtotal	900,000	112,200	$ 8.02
Adjustment for contingently issuable shares:		9,000	
Subtotal	900,000	121,200	$ 7.43
Actual conversion of 10% debenture:			
Interest saved	13,500		
Additional shares		3,600	
Subtotal	913,500	124,800	7.32
Adjustments for potential conversions:			
10% debenture:			
Interest avoided (after-tax equivalent)	72,000		
Additional shares		19,200	
Subtotal	985,500	144,000	6.84
8% debenture:			
Anti-dilutive since $7.50 is higher than $6.84		—	
Adjustment for preferred shares:			
Anti-dilutive since $10.00 is higher than $6.84		—	
Diluted EPS	**$ 985,500**	**144,000**	**$ 6.84**

This example uses data from FRM Corp., a public corporation. The company has a complex capital structure that includes bonds and three classes of shares. At the beginning of the year, one class of convertible bond was outstanding, and a second class of convertible bonds was issued during the year. The Class A shares are publicly traded and are listed on the TSX. Each Class A share has one vote. The Class B common shares have 20 votes each. Class B shares are closely held by the company's founding family, as are the preferred shares. Although Class A and Class B have different voting rights, in all other respects the two classes of common shares are equal, including the rights to dividends and to assets upon dissolution.

As we can see in Exhibit 20-7, two of the bond issues are convertible (into Class A), as are the preferred shares (into Class B). In addition, there are contingently issuable Class A shares and employee stock options outstanding that give the holder the right to acquire one Class A share for each option held.

Before beginning the calculations, it is important to take notice of any changes in the capital structure that occurred during the year. Exhibit 20-7 shows the capital structure at the *end* of the fiscal year, but the *additional information* states that there was a partial conversion of the 10% debentures on 1 October. That piece of information is important for two reasons:

1. Shares were outstanding for only *part* of the year, which means that the weighted-average number of shares outstanding must be calculated for basic EPS; *and*

2. If dilutive, the conversion must be backdated when calculating diluted EPS.

The 8% convertible bonds were issued on 1 May. This is important because when the bonds are considered for diluted EPS calculation, they will be backdated only to the date of issue, or 8/12 of the year. Also note that the second set of options was issued on 31 December 20X1, at the end of the fiscal year. When backdating, these options are also backdated to the day of issue, giving them a weight of 0/12. To simplify this complex example, it is assumed that the effective interest rate and the coupon rate are the same (although for convertible bonds this would rarely be the case in practice). Refer back to Exhibit 20-6 for an example where the effective interest rate is different from the coupon rate.

Basic EPS

The top section of Exhibit 20-8 presents the calculation of basic EPS. The starting point is earnings from continuing operations, which is then reduced by the preferred dividends. Class A and Class B share *equally* in dividends, and therefore they are added together for the denominator without adjustment. The weighted-average number of shares reflects the new shares issued on 1 October. Basic EPS is $8.09 for earnings from continuing operations. The EPS effect of the discontinued operation is $1.80 ($200,000 ÷ 111,200) and EPS for net earnings is $9.89 [($1,200,000 − $100,000) ÷ 111,200].

Diluted EPS

Diluted EPS must be calculated. The first item to evaluate is options, dilutive when the option price is less than market value. Refer back to the steps needed to calculate diluted EPS (see Exhibit 20-2). This is step 3; step 2 is not needed.

Only the first group of options, for 3,000 shares, must be evaluated. We should use the lowest option price of $30 because it is the most dilutive and is in-the-money. Exercising the options would raise additional capital of $90,000 (3,000 shares × $30). Retirement is calculated as $90,000 ÷ $45, or 2,000 shares. The net increase to the denominator is 1,000 shares (3,000 − 2,000). This can be directly calculated as [3,000 × ($45 − $30)] ÷ $45.

The second set of options was issued on 31 December 20X1. These options have no EPS effect because options are backdated only to the day of issue, which was the end of the current year. Now, let us move through the rest of the steps for this example.

Contingently Issued Shares

Step 4—contingently issued shares actually issued during the year—is not needed because no new shares were actually issued during the period as the result of satisfying a contingency.

Contingently Issuable Shares

Step 5 evaluates the 9,000 contingently issuable shares. These shares must be included in the denominator of diluted EPS because if the contingency period were to have ended at the end of 20X1, the shares would have to be issued because earnings targets have been met to date. There is no adjustment to the numerator for contingently issuable shares. These numbers are included in the calculation of diluted EPS, reducing the subtotal to $7.43.

Convertible Debt or Senior Shares

We now proceed to steps 6, 7, and 8 (refer to Exhibit 20-2). The highlighted section of Exhibit 20-8 shows the calculation of individual effects for the preferred shares and convertible debt:

- *Preferred shares.* Each share of the convertible preferred has a dividend of $20. Each is convertible into two shares of Class B common. The individual effect is $20 ÷ 2 = $10. This is clearly anti-dilutive to basic EPS of $8.09. Preferred shares will be excluded from the diluted EPS calculation. (Note that the individual effect calculation can be based on the outstanding preferred share issue as a whole or on a per-share basis; the result is the same.)

- *10% debenture, actual conversion.* The conversion occurred on 1 October 20X1. This conversion must be backdated for 9/12 of the year, back to 1 January. Both after-tax interest and the number of shares are adjusted. Additional interest would be $24,000 ($240,000 × 10%) for a year, but is $13,500 after being multiplied by (1 − 25% tax rate) and by 9/12 of the year. Shares issued were 4,800, as used in the basic calculation, but are backdated by multiplying by 9/12 of the year. The *individual effect* is $3.75.

- *10% debentures.* Interest on the $960,000 principal amount is $96,000. Since the interest is deductible for income tax purposes, the effect of the interest on net earnings is $72,000, that is, $96,000 × (1 − 0.25). At a conversion price of $50, the $960,000 bonds can be converted into 19,200 Class A common shares ($960,000 ÷ $50). The *individual effect* is $3.75.

- *8% debentures.* These debentures carry interest of $120,000 pretax or $90,000 after-tax. They are convertible into 12,000 Class A common shares. The *individual effect* is $7.50. Both the interest and issuable shares are backdated from 31 December to the date of issuance, 1 May of the current year. This is a factor of 8/12 for both the numerator and the denominator.

The Cascade

In steps 9 and 10 (see Exhibit 20-2), the securities are included in diluted EPS *in order of their dilutive effects:*

- First the 10% debentures, both the actual conversion and the assumed conversion. Their order does not matter, since their individual effects are the same. The subtotal is now $6.84.
- The 8% debentures, with an individual effect of $7.50, looked dilutive with respect to basic EPS of $8.09. However, they are anti-dilutive to the subtotal of $6.84. Thus they are excluded.
- The preferred shares, with an individual effect of $10, are also anti-dilutive and thus excluded.

The final result is diluted EPS of $6.84 for earnings from continuing operations.

EPS on Net Earnings

So far, we have been dealing only with earnings from continuing operations. We also need to determine EPS on net earnings, including discontinued operations; this is step 11. We make no further dilution tests at this stage; the calculations are based on the dilutions arising from EPS on continuing operations, as follows:

- Basic EPS on net earnings: ($1,200,000 − $100,000) ÷ 111,200 shares = $9.89
- Diluted EPS on net earnings: ($1,200,000 − $100,000 + $13,500 + $72,000) ÷ 144,000 shares = $8.23

Basic EPS for discontinued operations is $1.80 (i.e., $200,000 ÷ 111,200 shares), which increases basic EPS on net earnings to $9.89 (i.e., $8.09 + $1.80). Diluted EPS for discontinued operations is $1.39 (i.e., $200,000 ÷ 144,000 shares).

Reporting

EPS disclosure on the statement of comprehensive income would be as follows:

Earnings per share:	Basic	Diluted
Earnings from continuing operations	$8.09	$6.84
Discontinued operations	1.80	1.39
Net earnings	$9.89	$8.23

Basic and diluted ESP for both earnings from continuing operations and for net earnings must be shown on the face of the statement of comprehensive income. However, the individual effect of the discontinued operations may be disclosed in the notes instead of being shown on the face of the SCI.

RESTATEMENT OF EARNINGS PER SHARE

Reported EPS is rarely revised. Once earnings are reported, they are retrospectively restated (i.e., changed) only in three circumstances:

- An error is discovered that would change earnings and EPS in one or more prior years; or
- The entity makes a change in accounting policy, either voluntarily or due to a change in accounting standards; or
- The entity has declared a stock dividend or stock split during the fiscal year (or after the fiscal year but before the financial statements are issued); EPS is retrospectively restated to reflect the different amount of shares that are now outstanding—all prior years' EPS numbers would be reduced by 50% after a 2-for-1 stock split, for example.

These retrospective changes improve the comparability of the financial statements. Needless to say, restatement is accompanied by extensive disclosure to ensure that financial statement users are adequately informed.

Changes in estimates, the most common classification of accounting change, affect only the current year and future years and thus do not require restatement. We will look at the matter of corrections and restatements more intensively in the next chapter, Chapter 21.

SUBSEQUENT CHANGES IN SHARE CAPITAL

Companies have special disclosures required for *subsequent events*—transactions or events that take place in the period between the end of the fiscal period and the date that financial statements are authorized for issue. If there have been common share transactions in this period, then the effects of these share transactions must be disclosed. That is, if a subsequent event would significantly change the number of common shares or the potential common shares used in basic or diluted EPS, the transaction must be disclosed and described. Companies have a relatively short period after their fiscal year in which to report; they obviously have added incentive to report quickly, to reduce the reporting burden by keeping this time period short.

Examples of transactions that would have to be disclosed include issuing common shares for cash on the exercise of options, or for cash with the proceeds used to pay out other sources of financing. For example, if common shares were issued after the end of the fiscal year and the proceeds were used to retire preferred shares or debt, disclosure would be required. Issuance of new options or convertible securities would introduce a new element into diluted EPS (potential shares) and also qualify for disclosure.

REQUIRED DISCLOSURE

Financial statements should include the following:

1. Basic and diluted EPS must be disclosed on the face of the statement of comprehensive income for both net earnings from continuing operations and net earnings. Basic and diluted EPS must both be reported, even if they are exactly the same amount. Materiality cannot be invoked to avoid disclosing diluted EPS! The EPS effect of the discontinued operation must also be disclosed, but this can be either on the SCI or in a disclosure note.

2. A disclosure note must include:

   - The amounts used as the numerator and denominator for both basic and diluted EPS.
   - A reconciliation of the numerators of both basic and diluted EPS to the profit or loss numbers reported. This includes an explanation of adjustments to the numerator of diluted EPS for each individual effect by class of instrument.
   - A reconciliation of the denominators of both basic and diluted EPS to the number of common shares outstanding.
   - Details of securities excluded from the calculation of diluted EPS because they were anti-dilutive.
   - Details of share transactions, in the period after the end of the fiscal year but before the financial statements are authorized for issue, including stock dividends or splits.
   - Details of convertible securities, options, and any other share contracts issued in the period after the end of the fiscal year but before the financial statements are authorized for issue.

Reporting Example

BCE Inc., a telecommunications and media company, reported earnings per share on the company's 2014 income statements and related notes as shown in Exhibit 20-9.

BCE INC.

Consolidated Income Statements and Partial Extract from

Notes to Consolidated Financial Statements

Consolidated income statements

FOR THE YEAR ENDED DECEMBER 31 (IN MILLIONS OF CANADIAN DOLLARS, EXCEPT SHARE AMOUNTS)	NOTE	2014	2013
Operating revenues	5	21,042	20,400
Operating costs	5,6	(12,739)	(12,311)
Severance, acquisition and other costs	5,7	(216)	(406)
Depreciation	5,14	(2,880)	(2,734)
Amortization	5,15	(572)	(646)
Finance costs			
Interest expense	8	(929)	(931)
Interest on post-employment benefit obligations	22	(101)	(150)
Other income (expense)	9	42	(6)
Income taxes	10	(929)	(828)
Net earnings		2,718	2,388
Net earnings attributable to:			
Common shareholders		2,363	1,975
Preferred shareholders		137	131
Non-controlling interest	29	218	282

		2,718	2,388
Net earnings			

Net earnings per common share

Basic	11	2.98	2.55
Diluted	11	2.97	2.54
Average number of common shares outstanding – basic (millions)		793.7	775.8

Note 11 Earnings per share

The following table shows the components used in the calculation of basic and diluted earnings per common share for earnings attributable to common shareholders.

FOR THE YEAR ENDED DECEMBER 31	2014	2013
Net earnings attributable to common shareholders – basic	2,363	1,975
Dividends declared per common share (in dollars)	2.47	2.33
Weighted average number of common shares outstanding (in millions)		
Weighted average number of common shares outstanding – basic	793.7	775.8
Assumed exercise of stock options[1]	0.9	0.6
Weighted average number of common shares outstanding – diluted	794.6	776.4

(1) *The calculation of the assumed exercise of stock options includes the effect of the average unrecognized future compensation cost of dilutive options. It excludes options for which the exercise price is higher than the average market value of a BCE common share. The number of excluded options was 2,871,730 in 2014 and 2,621,806 in 2013.*

Source: BCE Inc. Audited Annual Financial Statements 2014, www.sedar.com, posted 11 March 2015.

BCE had no discontinued operations. The company shows how the net earnings are allocated between the common shareholders, preferred shareholders and non-controlling interest shareholders. For the calculation of the diluted EPS, only stock options that are dilutive are included in the denominator.

OTHER PER SHARE AMOUNTS

EPS is not the only per share statistic that may be presented in the audited financial statements. Companies are permitted to disclose per share numbers other than basic and diluted figures in the disclosure notes. For example, a specific subcomponent of earnings may be reported on a per-share basis. The denominator must be calculated using WAOS as per basic and diluted requirements, and the company must disclose the basis on which the numerator is determined, including whether it is before or after tax.

Companies sometimes publish a statistic called **cash flow per share**, based on a subtotal in the SCF. Some companies use cash flow from operating activities as the basis for this calculation, and some use an intermediate subtotal such as earnings adjusted for non-cash items (e.g., depreciation expense and unusual gains and losses). Inclusion of cash flow per share is permitted under international standards, subject to the calculation and disclosure requirements described above.

However, securities regulators in Canada generally prefer that such disclosures be presented less prominently than the EPS. Presentation in the disclosure notes is considered to be more appropriate than showing them on the statement of cash flows or the statement of comprehensive income.

Looking Forward

The current international EPS standard has been in effect since 2005. The IASB has no plans to revise it in the foreseeable future. Since EPS is a very commonly used metric, it makes sense not to meddle with it too often—frequent revisions would have a negative effect on its perceived usefulness. However, bear in mind that as accounting standards change (which they do fairly regularly), historical EPS figures may not really be comparable with current amounts due to changes in measurement methods that cannot be applied retrospectively to more than one or two prior periods.

Accounting Standards for Private Enterprises

Under ASPE, there is no standard for EPS. Private companies may voluntarily decide to present EPS data, if they believe that it would be useful to their financial statement users. Private companies with a larger shareholder group, such as co-operatives and employee-owned companies, might present EPS as a standard part of financial reporting. Private companies may look to IAS 33 for guidance, or they may design a statistic that meets their users' requirements. Disclosure of the calculation approach used is obviously important to improve understanding.

RELEVANT STANDARDS

CPA Canada Handbook, Part I (IFRS):

- IAS 33, Earnings per Share

CPA Canada Handbook, Part II (ASPE):

- None

SUMMARY OF KEY POINTS

1. Earnings per share provides information about the change in earnings as compared with changes (if any) in the common share base. Basic EPS is the basis for comparing the current period's earnings with that of prior periods, while diluted EPS gives an indication of the long-run impact that conversions and options could have on common earnings. Because it is computed on a *per share* basis, EPS removes the effect of increases in net earnings due to larger invested capital obtained through new share issues.

2. EPS figures are computed for (1) earnings from continuing operations (2) earnings from discontinued operations, and (3) net earnings.

3. Basic EPS is calculated by dividing net profit or loss available to common shareholders (e.g., earnings less preferred dividend claims) by the weighted-average number of shares outstanding. Comprehensive income is not used to determine EPS.

4. Weighted-average ordinary shares (WAOS) is used in the denominator of basic EPS. WAOS is calculated by weighting shares for the number of months they are outstanding. However, if there was a stock dividend or stock split during the reporting period, these additional ordinary shares are not weight-averaged but treated as though they have always been outstanding in the current and comparative period.

5. If there are multiple classes of common shares with different dividend entitlements, separate basic EPS statistics must be calculated to reflect their claims.

6. When a company has dilutive senior securities, contingently issuable shares or options, diluted EPS must be calculated. The steps to calculate diluted EPS are shown in Exhibit 20-2. For the purposes of calculating diluted EPS, elements are included at their most unfavourable (lowest) price. Potentially dilutive items are included in diluted EPS calculations in a cascade, beginning with the most dilutive.

7. Diluted EPS excludes the effects of any convertible securities or options contracts that are anti-dilutive. Anti-dilutive items have the effect of *increasing* EPS in relation to basic EPS from continuing operations.

8. When calculating diluted EPS, in-the-money options are assumed to be issued at the beginning of the fiscal period and proceeds used to retire shares at average market values. This is called the *treasury stock method*.

9. Contingently issuable shares are included in diluted EPS if the shares would be issuable if the contingency period were to end at the end of the current fiscal year.

10. Convertible bonds and preferred shares are included in diluted EPS calculations using the *if-converted method*, whereby after-tax interest and preferred dividends are adjusted in the numerator and common shares issued for the denominator. This reflects a hypothetical conversion to common shares at the beginning of the year. Note that it is the interest expense, including any amortization of discount or premiums, that is added back to net earnings.

11. Diluted EPS includes an adjustment that backdates actual conversions of senior securities (convertible debt and preferred shares) and shares issued under option contracts to the beginning of the fiscal period, if dilutive.

12. Securities and options issued during the period are backdated only to the date of issue. Dilutive conversion privileges and options that expired or were extinguished during the period are included for the period during which they were outstanding.

13. All potentially dilutive elements are anti-dilutive in a loss year because they would *decrease* a loss per share; this means that diluted EPS is equal to basic EPS in a loss year.

14. Both basic and diluted EPS figures are reported on the statement of comprehensive income. This is the case even if there is no potential dilution. A disclosure note must include calculation details, including reconciliation of earnings and WAOS data, and details of excluded anti-dilutive elements. The amount of EPS that is attributable to discontinued operations also should be disclosed, either on the face of the SCI or in the notes.

Key Terms

anti-dilutive	if-converted method
backdating	in-the-money
basic earnings per share	individual effect
bonus shares	mandatorily convertible shares
business combination	merger
buying earnings	ordinary shares
cash flow per share	senior shares
contingently issuable ordinary shares	stock dividend
convertible senior securities	stock option
diluted earnings per share	stock split
diluted EPS cascade	treasury stock method
dilutive	weighted average ordinary shares (WAOS)
earnings dilution	
forced conversion	

Review Problem 20-1

Ice King Products Inc. reported after-tax profit of $6.5 million in 20X5. Its capital structure included the following as of 31 December 20X5, the end of the company's fiscal year:

Long-term debt:

Bonds payable, due 20X11, 12%	$ 5,000,000
Bonds payable, due 20X14, $10,000,000 face value, 3% interest payable annually (effective interest rate is 7%), convertible into common shares at the rate of one share per $100 (Balance outstanding at 20X4 - $7,190,567)	$ 7,393,907

Shareholders' equity:

Preferred shares, $4.50, no-par, cumulative, convertible into common shares at the rate of two common shares for each preferred share, shares outstanding, 150,000

Preferred shares, $2.50, no-par, cumulative, convertible into common shares at the rate of one common share for each preferred share, shares outstanding, 400,000

Common shares, shares outstanding, 1,500,000

Options to purchase common shares (options have been outstanding all year):

Purchase price, $20; expire 20X11, 100,000 options

Purchase price, $52; expire 20X14, 200,000 options

Each option allows the purchase of one share.

Transactions during 20X5:

On 1 July, 400,000 common shares were issued on the conversion of 200,000 of the $4.50 preferred shares.

On 1 December, 100,000 common shares were issued for cash.

Additional information:

Average common share price, stable during the year, $40

Tax rate, 25%

Quarterly dividends were declared on 31 March, 30 June, 30 September, and 31 December

Required:

Calculate basic and diluted earnings per share for 20X5.

REVIEW PROBLEM 20-1—SOLUTION

	Earnings Available to Common Shares	Weighted- Average Number of Shares	Earnings per Share
Basic EPS:			
Net profit	$6,500,000		
Less: Dividends on $4.50 preferred:			
($4.50 ÷ 4) × 350,000 shares × 2 quarters	(787,500)		

	Earnings Available to Common Shares	Weighted-Average Number of Shares	Earnings per Share
($4.50 ÷ 4) × 150,000 shares × 2 quarters	(337,500)		
Less: Dividends on $2.50 preferred:			
400,000 shares × $2.50	(1,000,000)		
WAOS:			
1,000,000 shares × 6/12		500,000	
1,400,000 shares × 5/12		583,333	
1,500,000 shares × 1/12		125,000	
Basic EPS	**$4,375,000**	**1,208,333**	**$3.62**
Individual effect; dilution test			
3% Convertible Bonds:			
Interest, ($7,190,567 × 7%) × (1.00 − 0.25)	$ 377,505		
Shares, ($10,000,000 ÷ $100)		100,000	$3.78
$4.50 preferred actual conversion:			
Dividend adjustment:			
(4.50 ÷ 4) × 200,000 shares × 2 quarters	$ 450,000		
Additionalweighted-averageshares:400,000×6/12		200,000	$2.25
$4.50 preferred			
Dividends, $4.50 × 150,000 shares	$ 675,000		
Shares, 150,000 × 2 common shares		300,000	$2.25
$2.50 preferred			
Dividends, $2.50 × 400,000	$ 1,000,000		
Shares, 400,000 × 1 share		400,000	$2.50
Diluted EPS			
Basic EPS	$ 4,375,000	1,208,333	$3.62
$20 options—shares issued		100,000	
—shares retired (100,000 × $20) ÷ $40		(50,000)	

	Earnings Available to Common Shares	Weighted-Average Number of Shares	Earnings per Share
$52 options—excluded, $52 > $40			
Subtotal	$ 4,375,000	1,258,333	$3.48
$4.50 preferred actual conversion:			
Dividend adjustment:			
(4.50 ÷ 4) × 200,000 shares × 2 quarters	450,000		
Additional weighted average shares 400,000 × 6/12		200,000	
$4.50 preferred:			
Dividends, $4.50 × 150,000 shares	675,000		
Shares, 150,000 preferred × 2 common shares		300,000	
Subtotal	5,500,000	1,758,333	3.13
$2.50 preferred shares: dividends, $2.50 × 400,000	1,000,000	400,000	
Subtotal	$ 6,500,000	2,158,333	3.01
9% Bonds			
Bonds, with an individual effect of $3.78, are anti-dilutive as their inclusion would increase diluted EPS above $3.01.	—	—	
Diluted EPS	**$6,500,000**	**2,158,333**	**$3.01**

CASE 20-1

PHONUS LTD.

PhonUs Ltd. (PUL) is a Canadian public company involved in network technology for mobility telecommunications. This network technology allows super-fast data services to be offered through mobile platforms at a premium rate as a strategy to increase revenue per user for the carriers. PUL's customers are mobility carriers in many North, Central, and South American countries.

In 20X2, PUL reported basic earnings per share of $2.27 and diluted EPS of $2.10. The company forecasted EPS growth of approximately 12% for 20X3.

Unfortunately, 20X3 revenues were relatively flat through the first three quarters. PUL reported an EPS growth rate of 8% during the first three quarters, an increase that had been generated largely through cost reduction rather than revenue growth. Internal projections indicated that this lower growth rate in EPS would likely be reported for the overall year if immediate action was not taken. Exhibit 1 shows the projected annual 20X3 EPS figures, reflecting the 8% improvement from operations.

EXHIBIT 1

PROJECTED EPS—20X3

Basic EPS:

$$\frac{\text{Net income} - \text{Preferred dividends}}{\text{Weighted-average ordinary shares}} = \frac{\$50,621,900 - \$2,000,000}{19,765,500}$$

$$= \frac{\$48,621,900}{19,765,500}$$

$$= \underline{\$2.46}$$

Diluted EPS:

$$\frac{\text{Basic} + \textit{preferred} \text{ dividends}}{\text{Basic} + \text{common shares for preferred}} = \frac{(\$48,621,900 + \$2,000,000)}{(19,765,500 + 1,600,000)}$$

$$= \frac{(\$48,621,900 + \$2,000,000)}{(19,765,500 + 1,600,000) + (1,200,000 - 160,000)^*}$$

$$= \frac{\$50,621,900}{22,405,500}$$

$$= \underline{\$2.26}$$

*Shares under stock options − shares retired with option proceeds

---

Consequently, early in the fourth quarter, senior management began to discuss ways to "close the gap" between the 8% actual EPS growth rate and the 12% target. Mindful of the sluggish stock market share price, and with an eye on its own compensation and stock option packages, management expressed strong interest in making significant changes before the end of the 20X3 fiscal year.

PUL has 1.2 million common shares promised for future distribution under option contracts granted to senior management. Stock options are a substantial element of compensation. Additional options will be granted at the end of 20X3. The options granted will be at a price equal to the current share price and will vest immediately. They may be exercised in four years' time, as long as the manager is still with PUL. The number of shares granted under option depends on corporate performance and could range from zero to 500,000 shares.

A number of situations and/or opportunities that would potentially affect EPS for the year have been discussed internally. For example, management has proposed that 850,000 common shares be repurchased and retired in the fourth quarter. The required funding for this, $16,150,000, would have to be borrowed. Management is permitted to borrow up to $2 billion without further board of directors' approval; at the end of the third quarter, outstanding debt amounted to $1.8 billion. This buyback would be completed by 1 November. The interest rate on this new debt is estimated to be 6%.

PUL has idle land on the books at an historical cost of $695,000 that was purchased early in 20X3. The company is holding this land for capital appreciation and therefore is considering changing its accounting policy for this land to account for it using the fair-value method. The market value of this land is $1,180,000.

The company has an investment in bonds that is currently being held with the objective to receive the interest and principal payments and is classified as amortized cost. The current amortized cost of the bonds is $480,000 with an effective interest rate of 5%. The company has decided to reclassify this bond as FVOCI-Bonds. The fair market value of the bonds is estimated to be $530,000 by 31 December.

PUL has a major order for product that is complete, but the customer does not want it delivered until the first quarter of 20X4. The product is complete and the company has put it aside in its warehouse, separate from its other inventory that is available for sale. Because the product is complete and simply waiting for the customer to tell PUL when it can be shipped, PUL believes that it can be booked as revenue in the last quarter. The amount of revenue related to this sale is $2,500,000 and the related cost of goods sold is $1,950,000.

During October, the PUL board of directors of is expected to approve that the division operating in India, Bombay Telecom Limited (BTL), will be put up for sale. Operations are planned to cease on 15 November, and net losses with respect to this division are estimated to be $425,000 (before-tax) (currently included in the estimated net income). Since the company already has a few interested buyers, it expects that the division will be sold in the first quarter in 20X4. Based on preliminary estimates, the company expects a gain on disposal (after-tax) to be $320,000.

Required:

Prepare a report for management in which you explain the effects that the situations described above would have on basic earnings per share for the 20X3 fiscal year. Assume that PUL has a 25% marginal income tax rate. Also, point out any concerns that management should consider before undertaking these proposed solutions to the EPS situation.

CASE 20-2

DEXLUX LTD.

Dexlux Ltd. (DL) is a vertically integrated manufacturer and retailer of moderately priced high-fashion footwear, leather goods, and accessories. DL's common shares are listed on the Toronto Stock Exchange. DL has stores in over 180 major Canadian shopping malls and operates over 50 "boutiques" in larger retail stores. Until the current year, DL had three retail stores in the United States. In general, operating results in 20X9 have been disappointing, with lower same-store sales trends and higher costs across the board.

Exhibit 1 shows preliminary operating results for 20X9. Exhibit 2 shows details of accounting issues that must be resolved before the financial statements can be finalized. No accounting recognition has been given to stock options outstanding or granted during the year, as valuation estimates were not complete when the draft financial statements were prepared. This information has recently been obtained.

EXHIBIT 1
DEXLUX LIMITED
Draft Statement of Comprehensive Income
(in thousands of Canadian dollars)

For year ended 31 December	**20X9**
Revenue	
Sales	$164,960
Investment and other revenue	4,320
	169,280

Expenses

Cost of sales, selling, and administrative	142,860
Amortization	11,940
Closure costs, U.S. operations	1,450
Interest, net	2,230
	158,480
Operating earnings, before tax	10,800
Income tax	2,700
Net earnings and comprehensive income	$ 8,100

EXHIBIT 2

DEXLUX LIMITED

Additional Information

1. Outstanding share information:

	Number	Consideration (in thousands)
A. Multiple voting shares,		
31 December 20X8 and 20X9	1,580,000	Nominal
B. Subordinate voting shares		
Balance, 31 December 20X8	5,225,000	$23,890
Shares repurchased 20 March 20X9	(816,000)	(3,730)
Shares issued on exercise of stock options		
31 August 20X9	78,000	728
Balance, 31 December 20X9	4,487,000	$20,888

The multiple voting shares and subordinate voting shares have identical attributes except that the multiple voting shares entitle the holder to four votes per share and four times the dividend, if declared, on the subordinate voting shares. The multiple voting shares are held by the company founder and his family. Only the subordinated voting shares are publicly traded.

2. On 2 March 20X9, the company received permission from the Ontario Securities Commission for a Normal Course Issuer Bid that allows the company to repurchase up to 20% of its outstanding shares, or approximately 1,045,000 shares during the period from 2 March 20X9 to 2 March 20X10. The share transaction in March 20X9 was made pursuant to this bid agreement. Consideration of $6,840 (thousand) was paid for the shares, with the excess over average paid-in capital to date charged to retained earnings.

3. On 24 February 20X6, DL issued $40 million of convertible senior subordinated notes payable. The net proceeds after deducting offering expenses and underwriter's commissions were $37 million. The convertible debt was allocated between debt and equity elements, which are classified separately on the statement of financial position. The value of the debt element was based on the present value of the interest stream over the life of the note using an interest rate for a similar liability that did not have an associated conversion feature. The balance was recorded as equity.

The notes are convertible at DL's option at various dates between 20X14 and the maturity date of the note, 24 February 20X17. The conversion price is set at $15 per share until 20X15 and then changes to $10 per share. In 20X9, there is a charge for interest expense amounting to $1,780 and a $590 after-tax reduction to retained earnings, representing accretion on the equity amount. When calculating basic EPS, the $590 must be deducted from the numerator.

4. DL maintains a stock option plan for the benefit of directors, officers, and senior management. The granting of options and the related vesting period are at the discretion of the Board of Directors. The option price is set as the five-day average of the trading price of the subordinated voting shares prior to the effective date of the grant. Options granted vest 36 months after the date of issuance, and can be exercised from the vesting date until 10 years after the date of grant. Options are granted on 31 December in the year of grant. The fair value of options granted was as follows:

Year of Grant	Per Share Value	Share Entitlements Originally Granted
Prior to 20X6	$4.785	404,000
20X6	4.270	210,000
20X7	6.473	176,000
20X8	5.540	206,000
20X9	7.180	25,000

The status of outstanding options is as follows:

	Shares Under Option	Weighted-Average Exercise Price
Outstanding at the beginning of the year	695,000	$11.21
Granted, 31 December, 20X9	25,000	10.53
Exercised	(78,000)	6.62
Outstanding at the end of the year	642,000	11.10
Options exercisable at the end of the year	405,800	10.90

At the end of the year, the market price of subordinated voting shares was $11.25, and had been stable for most of the year. Any recorded compensation cost is a permanent difference for tax purposes and will not change recorded tax amounts.

5. In March 20X9, DL announced that it would close its U.S. retail operation, consisting of three retail stores. The stores had been a separate division of the company, reported separately with a dedicated retail manager. The stores were run using normal retail protocols established for other stores and relied on DL infrastructure. However, fashion trends appeared to be unique in these locations, and DL did not have adequate brand recognition to reach required sales targets. Two retail stores were closed at the end of March, with the third one closed at the end of April. Pre-tax information (in thousands) concerning these locations:

	20X9
Sales	$ 532
Operating loss	(467)
Writedown of capital assets	(1,045)
Lease and employee termination costs	(405)
Current assets	$ 23
Capital assets	—
Current liabilities	—

Required:

Analyze the accounting issues as identified, and prepare a revised draft statement of comprehensive income, including earnings per share.

CASE 20-3

DECATUR HOLDINGS LTD.

Decatur Holdings Ltd. (DHL) is a diversified Canadian company based in Winnipeg, Manitoba. DHL's primary business is the distribution and retailing of pharmaceutical and health care products. DHL's shares are traded on the Toronto Stock Exchange. Common shares traded in the $8–$14 range in 20X5. The primary holder of DDL's debt is the Amalgamated Public Sector Pension Plan. Extracts from DHL's draft 20X5 financial statements are shown in Exhibit 1; DHL's share capital disclosures are shown in Exhibit 2.

EXHIBIT 1

DECATUR HOLDINGS LIMITED

Extracts from Financial Statements

31 December 20X5

(in millions of Canadian dollars)	20X5 Draft	20X4
Statement of comprehensive income		
Revenue	$15,015	$14,065
Operating earnings	$ 468	$ 473
Earnings before capital gains	$ 388	$ 368
Capital gains	—	89
Income tax	(116)	(126)
Net earnings and comprehensive income	$ 272	$ 331
Statement of financial position		
Capital stock	$ 365.7	$ 257.7
Contributed surplus	2	0.1
Retained earnings	2,405	2,207

EXHIBIT 2

DECATUR HOLDINGS LIMITED

Share Capital Information
31 December 20X5

(in millions of Canadian dollars)	20X5 Draft	20X4
Preferred shares, par value $25 each, Series 2 cumulative, redeemable at the company's option, dividend 3%, convertible 2-for-1 into Class A shares, unlimited shares authorized, 1,680,000 shares outstanding (20X4, 2,600,000 shares)	$ 42	$ 65
Class A shares, with no par value, entitled to dividends on an equal per share basis with Class B shares, voting, one vote per share, unlimited shares authorized, 34,000,000 shares outstanding (20X4, 31,300,000 shares)	316.1	185.1
Class B shares, voting, three votes per share, unlimited shares authorized, 34,000,000 shares outstanding, sharing dividends equally with Class A, share per share	7.6	7.6

In January 20X5, 190,000 options were issued. Options allow the holders to purchase 190,000 Class A shares at nil cost beginning in 20X14 and expiring in 20X18 and 20X19.

In late March 20X5, 1,200,000 Class A shares were purchased for cancellation at a cost of $60 million. Other shares were issued for cash in July 20X5. In late December 20X5, 920,000 Series 2 preferred shares were purchased for cancellation at a cost of $25 million.

You are an accountant in the corporate reporting department of DHL. Financial statements are in the process of being finalized for the 20X5 fiscal year, which ended on 31 December 20X5. The audit committee will meet next week, with several accounting policy issues left to resolve. EPS calculations must also be completed.

DHL owns and operates distribution facilities in several locations across Canada. The company also operates a chain of retail health care stores. While the company operates stores in every province, DHL has the strongest presence in the western provinces. The company owns the real estate under all of its distribution centres and most of its stand-alone stores but also operates stores some in leased properties. When DHL stores are anchor tenants in small malls, DHL prefers to own the commercial real estate property and act as landlord to other tenants. Stores in large urban malls, however, are leased from the mall operator, which, in most cases, is Lincoln Property Investments Inc.

As an owner of 284 real estate parcels, DHL frequently engages in real estate transactions, frequently as seller when the company decides to close a store in an underperforming location. Each transaction results in a gain or loss, of course. DHL labels gains on sale of real estate as "capital gains" on the statement of comprehensive income. The term is not used in its income tax context; it is just DHL's term for gains and losses on sale.

In the late fall of 20X5, one major real estate property owned by DHL burned to the ground. DHL was the sole occupant of this building, which had a book value of $17 million. Inventory with a book value of $7.2 million was destroyed in the fire. A team of insurance adjustors is assessing the situation; the fire is thought to be electrical in origin. The fire investigators and the insurance adjustors have yet to file their reports.

DHL carries property and casualty insurance. Lawyers for DHL believe that DHL is entitled to insurance recovery for the fair value of the property destroyed. Consequently, DHL filed a claim for $32.2 million, of which $25 million is for the building, and $7.2 million for inventory. The expected payout is $31.2 million, after a $1 million deductable under the policy. Income tax triggered by the potential insurance proceeds is estimated to be $1.4 million in current taxes payable and another $0.7 million in deferred income tax. The property and inventory remain on DHL's books in the meantime.

Effective 31 December 20X5, DHL sold certain real estate properties to Sunne Real Estate Investment Trust (Sunne REIT). The properties had a book value of $239 million and were sold for $374 million gross cash proceeds. In addition, DHL received units in Sunne REIT estimated to be worth $50 million. There were brokerage and legal costs of $7 million associated with the sale. Income tax triggered by the sale amounted to $27 million in current taxes payable plus another $4 million in deferred income tax. The transfer has yet to be reflected in the 20X5 financial statements.

As part of the transaction with Sunne REIT, DHL entered into new lease agreements with respect to its occupancy in a portion of the real estate properties now owned by Sunne REIT. The leases have an expected total term of between 17 and 23 years; initial lease arrangements are established for five years, followed by renewal periods to the end of the term. Minimum rents range from $8 to $14 per square foot, plus a percentage of gross revenue, and there are planned base rental increases every five years.

DHL entered into a five-year referral contract during the year. Physiotherapy and chiropractic services represent a large and growing market in Canada, and pharmacists in DHL stores are often consulted by customers about appropriate action. Any retail customer who requests physiotherapy and chiropractic advice or services in a DHL store will be referred to Nature Force Ltd., a national chain that is the Canadian leader in such services. The agreement specifies that in the first year of the agreement, DHL will be paid the higher of $1 million or 30% of client billings resulting from referrals. Revenues in the second year are 30% of billings, with no minimum, and then the percentage reduces from 30% to 25%, then 20% and 15% over the remaining three years of the contact. After the first year, either side can end the agreement with 60 days' notice. An appropriate information system has been established to ascertain the extent of billings Nature Force realizes from the referrals, subject to external verification.

To date, Nature Force has not made any payment to DHL for Year 1 minimum payment because the amount is not due until the 12-month anniversary of the agreement, which occurs in October 20X3. No revenue has been recorded by DHL in the 20X5 financial statements. The pharmacists report that referrals have been "quite strong," although there are regional differences.

The company regularly calculates and disseminates information on basic and diluted EPS numbers, before and after capital gains and income tax. Company management prefers to focus on results before capital gains and income tax when communicating to shareholders, as gains from sale of real estate are sporadic, and business units have operating targets on a pretax basis. In 20X4, the company recorded earnings before capital gains and income tax of $5.60 per share, and diluted EPS before capital gains and income tax of $5.56. After capital gains and income tax, the numbers were $5.03 and $4.99.

Required:

In preparation for the coming audit committee meeting, prepare a report that includes analysis of the accounting issues inherent in the transactions above and any other reporting issues. Recalculate net earnings, if appropriate, and prepare EPS calculations for 20X5.

TECHNICAL REVIEW

■ connect

TR20-1 Basic EPS:

Angelo Ltd., a public company, had 600,000 common shares outstanding at the beginning of 20X4. On 1 March 20X4, Angelo purchased and retired 120,000 shares that had been owned by one of the company founders. On 30 June, the company issued 60,000 shares to a venture capital firm upon maturity of a $100,000 10% mandatorily convertible debenture. On 30 September, the company issued 120,000 new shares for cash. Angelo Ltd.'s after-tax 20X4 earnings amounted to $1,200,000.

Required:

Compute basic EPS.

■ connect

TR20-2 Basic and Diluted EPS:

Hominem Inc. has 100,000 common shares outstanding. Earnings from continuing operations amounted to $1,500,000 (after tax) for the year ended 31 December 20X4. Hominem's income tax rate is 25%. The company had no discontinued operations. At the end of 20X4, the market price of the company's common shares was $27. Hominem had these additional components in its capital structure at the end of the year:

- 15,000 cumulative preferred shares outstanding since 20X2; each share is entitled to an annual dividend of $20 per share and is convertible into five shares of common after 30 June 20X9.

- 4% debentures amounting to $500,000 were issued on 1 January 20X4. On this issue date, the bonds were recorded at $425,000. The debentures are convertible into 12 shares per $1,000. On 1 January 20X4, similar bonds with no conversion options had a market yield of 6%. Interest is payable annually.

- Outstanding options permitting the holder to buy 5,000 common shares in 20X6 or later for $35 per share.

Required:

1. Compute basic EPS.
2. Compute diluted EPS, using a cascade if appropriate.

connect

TR20-3 EPS with Loss from Discontinued Operations:

Refer to the information in T20-2. Assume that Hominem Inc. had a loss on discontinued operations of $1,000,000 (after tax).

Required:

Compute diluted EPS.

connect

TR20-4 Basic EPS:

CNZ Co. had 1,200,000 shares outstanding at the beginning of the year—1 June 20X8. During the year, the following transactions occurred:

1 August 20X8—5,000 share options with an exercise price of $35 per share, were exercised.

1 October 20X8—A 3:1 stock split was completed.

1 February 20X9—The company repurchased 500,000 shares for $20 each.

For the year ended 31 May 20X9, the company reported net earnings of $1,757,000.

Required:

Compute the basic EPS for the company for the year ended 31 May 20X9.

connect

TR20-5 Basic and Diluted EPS:

CH Holdings Inc. has net earnings of $5,456,000 for the year ended 31 December 20X5. It has convertible bonds currently outstanding with a face value of $8,500,000 and a book value of $7,871,852 at 1 January, 20X5. The bonds have a coupon interest of 2.5% payable semi-annually on 30 June and 31 December. The effective interest rate on similar bonds with no conversion option at the time of issue was 6.5%. The bonds have a conversion price of $40 per share. The weighted average number of shares outstanding for the year was 1,500,000. CH's income tax rate is 28%.

Required:

Compute the basic and diluted EPS for CH Holdings Inc.

connect

TR20-6 Basic and Diluted EPS:

Wilcorp Ltd. reported a loss of $610,000. There are 550,000 shares outstanding. The company has outstanding stock options for 100,000 common shares at $10 per share. The average common share price was $25 during the period.

Required:

1. Calculate the number of shares that would be added for the dilution on exercise of the options.
2. Calculate the basic EPS and diluted EPS.

connect

TR20-7 EPS—Complex Capital Structure:

Kouk Corp. has the following capital structure at the end of 20X7:

- 100,000 Class A shares carrying five votes per share.
- 100,000 Class B shares, carrying one vote per share.
- Dividends are shared on a 5:1 ratio—$5 to Class A for every dollar paid to Class B.

Additional information:

- Kouk Corp.'s tax rate is 20%.
- Net earnings amounted to $2,100,000 for 20X7; there were no discontinued operations.
- Kouk paid $1,200,000 in dividends at the end of 20X7.

Required:

1. Determine the amount of dividends that were paid to Class A and Class B shares, both in total and per share for each class.
2. Calculate basic EPS.

connect

TR20-8 Basic and Diluted EPS—Conversions:

During 20X1, Discolux Ltd. had two classes of shares outstanding:

- Class A preferred shares, 1,000 shares issued and outstanding at the beginning of the year; quarterly dividend rate of $200 per share, cumulative; each share is convertible into 40 shares of Class B common.
- Class B common shares, 141,000 shares issued and outstanding at the beginning of the year.

Also assume the following:

- Net income for the year is $3,000,000; there are no discontinued operations.

- 600 shares of Class A were converted into 24,000 Class B shares on 1 April 20X1; dividends for the first quarter of the year were paid on 30 March 20X1.
- Options to issue 10,000 common shares to senior executives for $3 per share were outstanding during the entire year. No options were exercised during the year. The average share price during the year was $10.

Required:

1. Determine the weighted-average number of shares outstanding during 20X1.
2. Determine basic EPS.
3. Determine diluted EPS.

connect

TR20-9 Basic and Diluted EPS:

Farmhill Ltd. had 1,400,300 common shares outstanding on 1 January 20X6, the beginning of its 20X6 fiscal year. During the year, on 1 May, the company issued 520,000 preferred shares convertible into common shares on a 1-for-1 basis. These preferred shares have a $0.75 annual cumulative dividend. The investors must convert the shares to common shares by 30 April 20X9. During the year, there were no conversions and the dividends were declared and paid on 30 November. The company reported net profit of $2,900,800 and total comprehensive income of $2,250,600 for the year ended 31 December 20X6.

Required:

Calculate the company's basic and diluted EPS for 20X6.

connect

TR20-10 Basic and Diluted EPS—Contingent Issuable Shares:

Kolanso Inc. had 870,000 common shares outstanding on 1 January 20X8. On 1 June, the company entered into an agreement to purchase the shares of Leroy Co. As part of this acquisition transaction, Kolanso agreed to issue 100,000 new common shares to the previous shareholders of Leroy if the company had total sales of $7.8 million for the first year. The goal was met at the end of December 20X8 and issued on 1 February 20X9. Also during the year, the company repurchased 30,000 shares on 1 December.

Required:

Calculate the company's weighted average number of shares outstanding for the basic EPS calculation for the year ended 31 December 20X8.

★ A20-1 Weighted-Average Common Shares:

The following cases are independent.

Case A   Jethrow Ltd. had 1,000,000 common shares outstanding on 1 January 20X2.

- On 27 February 200,000 shares were issued for $50 each.
- 300,000 shares were issued on 1 August.
- A 2-for-1 stock split was distributed on 30 August.

Case B   On 1 January 20X7, Doomsday Corp. had 200,000 nonvoting Series A shares and 600,000 Series B voting shares outstanding. Series A shares have a $2 per share cumulative dividend paid quarterly and are convertible into two Series B shares at any time after 31 December 20X9.

- On 1 October 20X7, 30,000 Series A shares were converted to B shares.
- On 1 December 20X7, 72,000 Series B shares were retired for cash.

Required:

For each case, calculate the number of weighted-average ordinary shares to use in the calculation of basic EPS. Assume a 31 December year-end.

★ A20-2 Weighted-Average Common Shares:

The following cases are independent:

Case A   Halifax Ltd. had 2,500,000 common shares outstanding on 1 January 20X8. On 1 March, 600,000 common shares were issued for cash. On 1 July, 300,000 common shares were repurchased and retired. On 1 November, 560,000 common shares were issued as a stock dividend.

Case B   Marvelex Ltd. had 6,000,000 common shares outstanding on 1 January 20X8. No shares were issued or retired during 20X8, which has a 31 December year-end. On 15 January 20X9, before the financial statements were finalized, a 1-for-4 reverse stock split took place.

Case C   Redux Ltd. had 2,860,000 common shares outstanding on 1 January 20X8. On 1 March, 286,000 common shares were issued as a 10% stock dividend. On 1 June, 200,000 common shares were repurchased and retired. On 1 November, 400,000 shares were issued as part of a contingent share agreement. The contingency had been met on 1 August 20X8, but the shares were not issued until 1 November 20X8.

Required:

For each case, calculate the weighted-average number of common shares to use in the calculation of basic EPS in 20X8.

★ A20-3 Dual Share Classes:

Murchie Ltd. earned $16,000,000 in 20X6 and paid dividends of $7,400,000. The company has two classes of voting shares. Class A shares have six votes per share, while Class B shares have one vote per share. Both participate in the distribution of net assets in the event of dissolution. There were 1,200,000 Class A shares outstanding all during 20X6, and 2,800,000 Class B shares.

Class A shares are entitled to dividends as declared, in the amount of $1.5 per share, before the Class B shares receive any dividends. After the Class A dividend, Class B shares will receive dividends as declared up to $2.00 per share. If any dividends are declared above this amount, both classes are to be allocated an identical per share dividend.

Required:

1. Determine basic EPS for each share class for 20X6.
2. Repeat requirement 1 assuming that there is no base dividend and dividends are split on a per-share basis between the two classes such that Class A shares receive 10 times the Class B entitlement per share.

★ A20-4 Dual Share Classes:

Darlington Industries Ltd. reported earnings of $1,000,000 in 20X6; no dividends were declared. Darlington has two classes of ordinary shares—Class A and Class B. The characteristics of the two classes of shares are as follows:

- 60,000 Class A shares and 750,000 Class B shares were outstanding throughout the year.
- Class A shares get 15 votes per share; Class B has one vote.
- If dividends are declared, Class A shares are entitled to a base dividend of $3 per share while Class B shares are entitled to a base dividend of $0.60 per share. Additional dividends beyond the base dividend are shared on an equal basis per share.

Required:

Calculate basic EPS for 20X6.

★ A20-5 Basic EPS:

At the end of 20X6, the records of Security Systems Corp. showed the following:

Bonds payable, 9%, nonconvertible	$450,000
Preferred shares:	
Class A, no-par, $0.80, nonconvertible, noncumulative, outstanding 80,000 shares	400,000
Class B, no-par, $0.90, nonconvertible, cumulative, outstanding 40,000 shares	700,000

Common shares, no-par, authorized unlimited shares:

Outstanding 1 January, 150,000 shares	$1,875,000
Retired shares 1 May, 40,000 shares	(453,834)
Issued a 200% stock dividend on 1 November, on outstanding shares	1,394,715
Retained earnings (no dividends declared)	2,130,000
Earnings from continuing operations, after income taxes	$164,250
Discontinued operations, net of tax	19,000
Net earnings	$183,250

Required:

Compute basic EPS. Show computations.

A20-6 Basic EPS for Three Years; Restatement:

Ramca Corp.'s accounting year ends on 31 December. During the three most recent years, its common shares outstanding changed as follows:

	20X7	20X6	20X5
Shares outstanding, 1 January	190,000	150,000	90,000
Shares sold, 1 April 20X5			60,000
25% stock dividend, 1 July 20X6		40,000	
2-for-1 stock split, 1 July 20X7	190,000		
Shares sold, 1 October 20X7	60,000		
Shares outstanding, 31 December	440,000	190,000	150,000
Net earnings and comprehensive income	$533,250	$406,600	$331,500

Required:

1. For purposes of calculating EPS at the end of each year, for each year independently, determine the weighted-average number of shares outstanding.
2. For purposes of calculating EPS at the end of 20X7, when comparative statements are being prepared on a three-year basis, determine the weighted-average number of shares outstanding for each year.
3. Compute EPS for each year based on computations in requirement 2. There were no preferred shares outstanding

eXcel

★ A20-7 Contingently Issuable Shares:

On 1 January 20X1, Barnhill Information Technologies reported 3,650,000 common shares outstanding. During the prior year, 20X0, the company had acquired Semere Systems, a supplier company, in a cash and share transaction. The purchase agreement included the following provisions:

1. Barnhill will issue an additional 250,000 common shares to the prior shareholders of Semere if the operating profit of the Semere business unit, as defined by agreement, was in excess of $1,000,000 for each of 20X0, 20X1, and 20X2;

2. Barnhill will issue an additional 100,000 shares to the prior shareholders of Semere if a new product under development by Semere is patented before year-end 20X4; and

3. Barnhill agreed to issue an additional 200,000 shares to the prior shareholders of Semere if a lawsuit outstanding in 20X0 against Semere were resolved for a net cost of less than $150,000, including legal fees.

In late March 20X1, the court dismissed the lawsuit against Semere. Consequently, 200,000 shares were issued to the prior shareholders of Semele on 31 October 20X1.

Barnhill reported earnings of $5,092,000 for 20X1. The Semere Systems business unit turned in strong operating results, with $1,500,000 profit earned, similar to its results in 20X0. The product under development had not advanced to the patent stage by the end of 20X1. Barnhill had no other share transactions in 20X1.

Required:

Calculate basic and diluted earnings per share figures for 20X1.

★ A20-8 Contingently Issuable Shares:

On 1 January 20X5, Aker Aviation Services Ltd. entered into an agreement to purchase Moore Fuels Ltd. The agreement included the following terms:

1. Aker agreed to issue an additional 3,000,000 shares to the prior shareholders of Moore if Aker retained 70% of the customers of Moore at the end of 20X7.

2. Aker agreed to issue 1,400,000 common shares to the prior shareholders of Moore if seven key employees remained with Aker through the end of 20X9.

3. Aker agreed to issue an additional 900,000 shares to the prior shareholders of Moore if four new retail fuel units were opened before the end of 20X8.

Aker had 13,200,000 common shares outstanding at the beginning of 20X6. Net earnings were $2,244,000 in 20X6. To date, customer retention was in the range of 75%, and the key employees have remained in Aker's employment. Three new retail outlets were opened in 20X5, and one in early February 20X6. Accordingly, 700,000 common shares were issued to the prior shareholders of Moore, but not until 31 August 20X6. Aker had no other share transactions in 20X6.

Required:

Calculate basic and diluted earnings per share figures for 20X6.

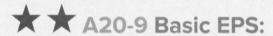

★ ★ A20-9 Basic EPS:

The Duckworth Ltd. 20X5 financial statements include the following:

Statement of comprehensive income

Year ended 31 December 20X5

Earnings from continuing operations	$ 3,336,000
Discontinued operations (net of tax)	432,000
Net earnings and comprehensive income	$ 3,768,000

Statement of financial position

31 December 20X5

Bonds payable, 5%, nonconvertible		$10,000,000
Preferred shares, no-par value, $0.90, nonconvertible, noncumulative, outstanding during year, 500,000 shares		10,000,000
Common shares, no-par value:		
Outstanding 1 Jan., 34,000,000 shares	$7,360,000	
Sold and issued 1 April, 3,240,000 shares	1,400,000	
Issued 10% stock dividend, 30 Sept., 3,724,000 shares	1,490,000	10,250,000
Retained earnings		7,910,000

The company declared and paid preferred dividends of $20,000 during the year and had an effective tax rate of 25%.

Required:

1. Compute basic EPS.
2. Repeat requirement 1, assuming that the preferred shares are cumulative.

★ ★ A20-10 EPS—Loss on Discontinued Operation:

The following information pertains to Archibald Acquisitions Ltd. (AAL) for the year ended 31 December 20X7:

a. AAL had 150,000 common shares outstanding at the end of 20X7. Of that number, 30,000 had been issued on 31 May 20X7. No dividends were issued to common shares during the year.

b. The company had 40,000 $15 cumulative nonparticipating preferred shares outstanding throughout 20X7. Dividends of $7 were declared and paid during the year. The preferred shares are convertible into two common shares for each preferred share at any time.

c. AAL had $1,500,000 in 5% convertible debentures outstanding throughout the period. The debentures are convertible into 30 common shares per $1,500 principal amount. The company paid $75,000 in interest and recorded interest expense of $112,000 during 20X7.

d. In December 20X7, the company recorded a loss of $800,000 (after income tax) on a discontinued operation.

e. AAL is subject to an income tax rate of 30%.

Required:

1. Determine 20X7 basic EPS and diluted EPS, both before and after discontinued operations, assuming after-tax earnings from continuing operations of $1,800,000.

2. Repeat the calculations of basic and diluted EPS, but assume instead that after-tax earnings from continuing operations were $700,000.

 connect

★ ★ A20-11 EPS—Loss on Discontinued Operation:

Bolshevik Ltd.'s statement of financial position at 31 December 20X2 reported the following:

Long-term notes payable, 6%, due in 20X9	4,000,000
Bonds payable, par value $10,000,000, 5%, each $1,000 of face value is convertible into 30 common shares; bonds mature in 20X13, net of discount	8,200,000
Common stock conversion rights	590,000
Common shares, voting, 950,000 shares outstanding	26,000,000

Additional information:

a. 50,000 common shares were issued at $50 on 1 July 20X2.

b. Common share options are outstanding, entitling holders to acquire 150,000 common shares at $9 per share.

c. Interest expense on the convertible bonds was $420,000 in 20X2.

d. Income tax rate is 25%.

e. The average common share price over the year was $11.

f. Earnings from continuing operations for 20X2 was $250,000, after tax; the company had a loss on a discontinued operation of $200,000, net of income tax effects.

Required:

Compute the EPS amount(s) that Bolshevik Ltd. should report for 20X2.

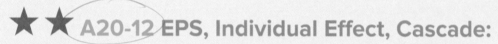

★ ★ A20-12 EPS, Individual Effect, Cascade:

The Birch Corp. has the following items in its capital structure at 31 December 20X7, the end of the fiscal year:

a. Options to purchase 400,000 common shares were outstanding for the entire period. The exercise price is $17.50 per share. The average common share price during the period was $40.

b. Preferred shares, $2 annual dividend, cumulative, no-par, convertible into common shares at the rate of five shares of common for each preferred share. Seven thousand shares were outstanding for the whole year.

c. $3 million par value of 7% debentures, outstanding for the entire year. Debentures are convertible into five common shares for each $100 bond. Interest expense of $285,000 was recognized during the year.

d. Preferred shares, $5 annual dividend, cumulative, no-par, convertible into common shares at the rate of three shares of common for each one preferred share. Four thousand shares were outstanding for the entire year. No dividends were declared in 20X7 on these shares.

e. $8 million par value of 5.5% debentures, outstanding for the entire year. Debentures are convertible into a total of 520,000 common shares. Interest expense of $660,000 was recognized during the year.

Required:

1. Calculate the individual effect for diluted EPS for each of the above items. The tax rate is 35%. For options, calculate shares issued and shares retired.

2. Assume Birch reported basic EPS from continuing operations items of $1.29 [($1,000,000 − $14,000 − $20,000) ÷ 750,000], discontinued operations gain of $1.00 ($750,000 ÷ 750,000) and EPS for net earnings of $2.29 [($1,750,000 − $14,000 − $20,000) ÷ 750,000]. Calculate diluted EPS, and show how it would be presented on the statement of comprehensive income.

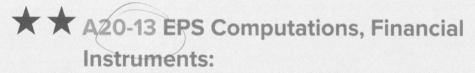

★ ★ A20-13 EPS Computations, Financial Instruments:

On 31 December 20X3, the capital structure of Victor Varieties Ltd. was as follows:

- $4,500,000 face value of 12% debentures, due 1 April 20X10, convertible into eight common shares per $1,000. Interest on the 12% debentures is paid on 1 April and 1 October of each year. On 2 April 20X3, 12% debentures with a face value of $1,500,000 had been converted. Interest expense on these bonds was $48,000 in 20X3. Interest expense on all the 12% bonds amounted to $432,000, including the $48,000.

- $3,000,000 face value of 12.4% debentures, due 30 June 20X15, convertible into eight common shares per $1,000 after 30 June 20X7. Interest expense related to these bonds was $450,000 in 20X3. Interest is paid on 30 June and 31 December of each year.

- 30,000 cumulative preferred shares issued and outstanding, $8 per share dividend, redeemable at the shareholder's option at $100 per share. These preferred shares are classified as debt. Dividends are reported as a financing expense in earnings.

- 100,000 options outstanding to senior management, exerciseable in 20X14. The options allow purchase of 100,000 at $25 per share. Average market price in 20X3 was $14.

- 60,000 common shares issued and outstanding.

Victor Varieties reported net earnings after tax of $600,000 for 20X3. The tax rate was 40%.

Required:

Compute EPS for 20X3.

★ ★ A20-14 Basic and Diluted EPS:

The following information relates to Willowdale Ltd.'s financial statements for the year ended 31 December 20X6:

a. On 1 January 20X6, Willowdale's capital structure consisted of the following:

- 450,000 common shares, issued for $5.75 million, were outstanding.
- 50,000 preferred shares bearing cumulative dividend rights of $5 per year.
- $1 million (par value) of 5% convertible bonds ($1,000 face value), with interest payable on 30 June and 31 December of each year. Each $1,000 bond is convertible into 65 common shares, at the option of the holder, at any time before 31 December 20X11. Interest expensed on the convertible bonds was $0,000.
- Outstanding options for 50,000 common shares at a price of $5 per share. The average market value of common shares during the period was $20.

b. On 30 September 20X6, Willowdale issued an additional 100,000 common shares for $1.5 million cash.

c. Willowdale reported earnings of $1.5 million for the year ended 31 December 20X6 net of tax of 25%.

Required:

Calculate the basic and diluted earnings per share figures for 20X6.

★ ★ A20-15 Basic and Diluted EPS:

At the end of 20X7, the records of Info Solutions Ltd. reflected the following:

Statement of financial position:

Bonds payable, 7%, $600,000 par value, issued 1 January 20X0; entirely converted to common shares on 1 December 20X7; each $1,000 bond was convertible to 110 common shares. Interest expensed on bonds $47,250	$ 0
Preferred shares, $0.50, convertible 2-for-1 into common shares, cumulative, nonparticipating; shares issued and outstanding during year, 30,000 shares	390,000

Common shares, no-par value, authorized unlimited shares; issued and outstanding throughout the period to 1 July 20X7, 150,000 shares. 300,000 shares were sold for cash on 1 July 20X7, additional shares were also issued on 1 December when bondholders converted	2,820,000
Common stock conversion rights, related to 10% bonds payable, above	0
Retained earnings (no dividends declared during year)	1,710,000

Statement of comprehensive income:

Net earnings (after $47,250 of interest expense to 1 December on convertible bonds, as above)	366,000

Average income tax rate, 30%.

Required:

Compute the required EPS amounts. Show computations, and round to two decimal places.

★★ A20-16 Individual Effects:

For the year ended 31 December 20X7, Daffy Daisy Donut Corp. (DDD) had earnings from continuing operations of $6,500,000 before taxes and a loss on discontinued operations of $2,520,000 before tax. DDD pays income tax at an average rate of 25%. DDD had the following items and occurrences regarding its capital structure in 20X7:

a. 600,000 common shares issued and outstanding during the entire year; the shares carry one vote each.

b. 7,000 preferred shares issued to a private equity firm on 1 July for cash. The shares carry a cumulative dividend of $15 per share per year. These preferred shares carry four votes per share. On 31 December 20X12, the preferred shares mandatorily convert to five shares of common for each share of preferred.

c. $90,000 in convertible bonds maturing in 20X13. The bonds are convertible into common shares at a conversion rate of $20 (that is, five shares per $100 or 50 shares per $1,000). Interest expense on the convertible bonds was $7,200 for the year.

d. 2,000 options issued to senior managers, exercisable for common shares at $22. The average market price of the common shares was $20 during 20X7.

Required:

1. Determine the individual effect on EPS for each any of the potentially dilutive items in DDD's capital structure.

2. Determine all earnings per share amounts that DDD should report in its financial statements for 20X7.

★ ★ A20-17 Individual Effects:

MacAfee Corp. has basic earnings per Class A common share of $2.61. MacAfee has a tax rate of 25%. The average share price during the year was $42. Review each of the following items:

a. Class B nonvoting cumulative $1 shares, 75,000 shares outstanding all year, convertible into Class A shares at the rate of four Class B shares for one Class A share. Dividends of $0.50 were declared this year and basic EPS properly reflects the dividend entitlement of these preferred shares.

b. Class A common stock options outstanding all year for 30,000 shares at a price of $65.

c. Class A common stock options outstanding all year for 30,000 shares at a price of $35.

d. Class A common stock options granted at the end of the fiscal year for 10,000 shares at $32 per share.

e. 12%, eight-year $5,000,000 convertible bonds outstanding all year, convertible into 18 Class A common shares for every $1,000 bond. A bond discount was recorded when the bond was originally issued and amortization of $43,750 was recorded on the discount this year. On issuance, $420,000 of common stock conversion rights were recorded in shareholders' equity.

f. 8%, 15-year, $9,000,000 convertible bonds outstanding all year, convertible into 24 Class A common shares for every $1,000 bond. A bond discount was recorded on issuance, and amortization of $19,200 was recorded on the discount this year. On issuance, $145,000 of common stock conversion rights were recorded in shareholders' equity.

Required:

Indicate whether each of the above items would be included or excluded in a calculation of diluted EPS, and why. The solution should include the individual effect of each item, as applicable. If the item is included, indicate the change to the numerator and denominator of diluted EPS.

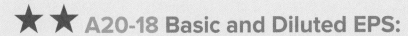

★ ★ A20-18 Basic and Diluted EPS:

The shareholders' equity of Cameron Corp. as of 31 December 20X6, the *end* of the current fiscal year, is as follows:

$1 cumulative preferred shares, no-par, convertible at the rate of 4-for-1; 350,000 shares outstanding	$ 9,150,000
Common shares, no-par; 3,500,000 shares outstanding	15,000,000
Common stock conversion rights	231,000
Retained earnings	30,600,000

Additional information:

• On 1 July 20X6, 150,000 preferred shares were converted to common shares at the rate of 4-for-1.

- During 20X6, Cameron had convertible subordinated debentures outstanding with a face value of $4,000,000. The debentures are due in 20X12, at which time they may be converted to common shares or repaid at the option of the holder. The conversion rate is 12 common shares for each $100 debenture. Interest expense of $175,000 was recorded in 20X6.

- The convertible preferred shares had been issued in 20X0. Quarterly dividends, on 31 March, 30 June, 30 September, and 31 December, have been regularly declared.

- The company's 20X6 net earnings were $2,289,000, after tax at 30%. Common shares traded for an average price of $18, stable in each quarter of the year.

- Cameron had certain employee stock options outstanding all year. The options were to purchase 600,000 common shares at a price of $14 per share. The options become exercisable in 20X13.

- Cameron had another 100,000 employee stock options outstanding on 1 January 20X6, at an exercise price of $22. They expired on 30 June 20X6.

Required:

Show the EPS presentation that Cameron would include on its 20X6 statement of comprehensive income.

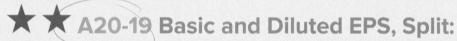

★ ★ A20-19 Basic and Diluted EPS, Split:

Accounting staff at Linfei Corp. have gathered the following information:

- Common shares outstanding on 31 December 20X4, 150,000.
- A 3-for-1 stock split was distributed on 1 April 20X4.
- 140,000 common shares were sold for cash of $50 per share on 1 July 20X4.
- Linfei purchased and retired 20,000 common shares on 1 October 20X4.
- 25,000 Series II options were issued in 20X1, originally allowing the holder to buy one share at $21 for every option held beginning in 20X8. Terms of the options were adjusted for the split in April. (The shares were tripled and the price reduced to one-third.)
- Linfei has $2,000,000 par-value convertible bonds outstanding. There is $346,000 in a common stock conversion rights account with respect to the bonds. Each $1,000 bond was originally convertible into 30 common shares. Terms were adjusted for the split in April. Interest expense on the bond, including discount amortization of $24,000, was $210,000 in 20X4. The bonds are convertible at any time before their maturity date in 20X18.
- Net profit in 20X4 was $430,000.
- The tax rate was 25% and the average common share price in 20X4, after being adjusted for the split, was $25.

Required:

Calculate all EPS disclosures for 20X4. Note that there were 150,000 common shares outstanding at the end of the fiscal period and calculations must work backward from this date.

★ ★ A20-20 Diluted EPS, Conversions:

Targeted Ltd. (TL) reports the following calculations for basic EPS, for the year ended 31 December 20X4:

Numerator:	Net earnings, $9,300,000, less preferred dividends of $1,188,000
Denominator:	Weighted-average ordinary shares outstanding, 3,120,000

Basic EPS: $2.60 ($8,112,000 ÷ 3,120,000)

Assume two different scenarios for Targeted Ltd—Case A versus Case B as shown below:

Case A   Assume that TL had 400,000 convertible preferred shares outstanding at the beginning of the year. Each share was entitled to a dividend of $2 per year, payable $0.50 each quarter. Each share is convertible into three common shares. After the third-quarter dividend was paid, 100,000 preferred shares converted to 300,000 common shares. The information above regarding dividends paid and the weighted-average ordinary shares outstanding properly reflects the conversion for the purposes of calculating basic EPS.

Case B   Assume instead that TL had nonconvertible preferred shares outstanding in 20X4, on which dividends of $1,188,000 were paid. Also assume that TL had convertible bonds outstanding at the beginning of 20X4. On 1 November, the entire bond issue was converted to 1,200,000 common shares, per the bond agreement. The information above regarding earnings properly reflects interest expense of $1,401,659 from 1 January to 1 November. The weighted-average ordinary share figure also reflects the appropriate common shares for the conversion. The tax rate is 25%. TL also had options outstanding at the end of the fiscal year, for 250,000 common shares at an option price of $17. The average common share price was $27 during the period.

Required:

Calculate diluted EPS for each of Case A and Case B, independently.

★ ★ A20-21 EPS, Cascade:

Ashante Sports Collections Ltd. (ASCL) ended 20X5 with 700,000 common shares outstanding, after issuing 200,000 common shares for cash on 31 December. The tax rate is 40%. There were no other common share transactions during the period. Net earnings were $1,300,000. The following elements are part of ASCL's capital structure:

a. ASCL had $5,000,000 (par value) of 6% bonds payable outstanding during the year. The bonds are convertible into 80 common shares for each $1,000 bond. Bond interest expense was $403,000 for the year.

b. ASCL had 40,000 options outstanding throughout 20X5 to purchase 120,000 common shares for $3 per share. The average share price during the year was $15. The options were not exercisable until 20X10.

c. ASCL had 70,000, $1.25 preferred shares outstanding. The shares were cumulative. No dividends were declared in 20X6. The shares were convertible into 50,000 common shares.

d. ASCL had a contingent share agreement outstanding to issue 50,000 common shares to the prior shareholders of a company that ASCL had acquired in 20X2. The shares become issuable if the acquired company's operations accumulate $5,000,000 of post-acquisition earnings before the end of 20X8. Earnings have been $3,500,000, to date, and the target is expected to be met in 20X7.

e. ASCL had $8,000,000 (par value) of 5% bonds payable, issued on 31 March 20X5. The bonds are convertible into 40 common shares for each $1,000 bond. Bond interest expense was $285,750 for the nine months of the year that the bond was outstanding.

Required:

Compute basic and diluted EPS for 20X5.

 ## A20-22 EPS, Cascade; Stock Split:

Bytol Corp had the following common share transactions and balances during 20X8:

1 January—160,000 shares outstanding

30 April—60,000 shares issued on conversion of $5,500,000 bonds payable

30 September—30,000 shares issued on conversion of preferred shares

1 December—3-for-1 stock split

Bytol reported net earnings of $998,000 in the year. The bond that converted on 30 April had been a 6%, five-year $5,500,000 convertible bond. It converted at maturity. There had originally been a bond discount recorded, with a remaining balance of $9,222 at the beginning of the year. There was also a $220,000 common stock conversion option recorded in equity with respect to this bond. This was transferred to the common share account on bond conversion. There were preferred shares outstanding, $4.00 cumulative shares, convertible 5-for-1 prior to the split and 15-for-1 after the split. The preferred dividend was payable quarterly (that is, $1.00 per quarter) and 5,000 of the total 20,000 outstanding preferred shares converted after the dividend paid on 30 September. The tax rate was 30%.

Required:

Calculate basic and diluted EPS for 20X8.

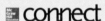

 ## A20-23 EPS—Stock Split, Discontinued Operations:

Sea Products Corp. (SPC) reported $6,080,000 of earnings from continuing operations for the 20X4 fiscal year, and an after-tax loss from discontinued operations of $7,610,000. Preferred dividends and a common dividend of $1 per share were declared in 20X4. The average common share price was $7 during the period (adjusted for the split; see below), and the tax rate was 35%.

SPC reported the following financial instruments as part of its capital structure at the end of 20X4:

1. 4,900,000 common shares outstanding. Of these, 2,450,000 had been issued as a 2-for-1 stock split on 1 October 20X4. The terms of all share contracts were adjusted to reflect the split, and adjusted values are given in the information that follows.

2. $5,000,000 of bonds payable, convertible into 120,000 common shares beginning in 20X12 at the option of the investor. The bonds are reported as a liability, with a discount, and as an element of equity. Interest paid this year was $240,000, and there was $50,600 of discount amortization recorded.

3. 600,000 preferred shares, with a $2 per share cumulative dividend. There had been 700,000 shares outstanding at the beginning of 20X3. In January, 100,000 shares, with an average issuance price of $625,000, were retired for $699,000.

4. Options outstanding: 150,000 shares at an option price of $10, exercisable beginning in 20X7; 500,000 shares at an option price of $5, exercisable beginning in 20X12; 200,000 shares at an option price of $4, exercisable beginning in 20X13.

Required:

Calculate required EPS disclosures.

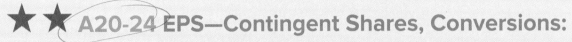

★ ★ A20-24 EPS—Contingent Shares, Conversions:

Information regarding Fujing Ltd:

- Common shares outstanding on 31 December 20X1: 80,000. The company had issued 30,000 shares under a contingent share agreement on 1 December 20X2. It had also issued 40,000 common shares when preferred shares converted on 30 September 20X2.
- The average price of common shares was $15.
- The 30,000 shares issued under a contingent share agreement were issued under an agreement with a previously acquired company. The agreement stated that if a lawsuit that had been filed against this acquired company (before it was acquired by Fujing) were to be dismissed in court action, then 30,000 shares would be issued. The court dismissed the lawsuit in late November, and shares were issued on 1 December.
- A second contingent share agreement related to profit levels of a target company. This contingent share agreement calls for an additional 60,000 common shares to be issued in 20X5 if 20X2, 20X3, and 20X4 earnings from the target company each reach a certain level. This level was attained in 20X2.
- Preferred shares, $2, cumulative: these shares were convertible 5-for-1. At the beginning of the year, 40,000 shares were outstanding and 10,000 shares converted on 30 September 20X2. The dividend is paid quarterly.
- Fujing Ltd. has $3,000,000 par value convertible bonds outstanding. There is $104,000 in a common stock conversion rights account with respect to the bonds. The bonds are convertible into 50,000 common shares. Interest paid on the bond was $180,000, and there was discount amortization of $17,000. The bonds are convertible at any time before their maturity date in 20X20.
- Net earnings in 20X2, $491,250.
- The tax rate was 25%.

Required:

Calculate basic and diluted EPS for 20X2.

★ ★ A20-25 Two-Year Basic EPS, Interpretation:

Huron Resources is a public oil field services company. Selected information follows:

	20X4	20X3
Bonds payable, 7%, due 20X16	$ 6,000,000	$ 6,000,000
Preferred shares, $3 dividend, noncumulative, 100,000 shares outstanding	$ 1,600,000	$ 1,600,000
Preferred shares, $2 dividend, cumulative, 50,000 shares outstanding. Redemption price $20 per share plus dividends in arrears, if any	$ 2,100,000	$ 2,100,000
Common shares, 900,000 shares outstanding at the end of 20X4 after 300,000 shares were issued for cash on 31 October 20X4; no share transactions in 20X3	$16,200,000	$10,700,000

Dividends declared during the year	$ 540,000	0
Net earnings and comprehensive income	$ 700,000	$ 400,000

Required:

1. Calculate basic EPS for 20X4 and 20X3.
2. Interpret the trend in basic EPS.
3. Repeat requirement 1, assuming that the shares issued in 20X4 were issued as a result of a stock dividend.

 A20-26 Two-Year Basic EPS, Interpretation:

Gannon Ltd. reported earnings as follows:

Year ended 31 December	20X2	20X1
Earnings from continuing operations (net of tax)	$496,500	509,500
Discontinued operations (net of tax)	(58,000)	38,500
Net earnings and comprehensive income	$438,500	$548,000

The capital structure of Gannon included the following:

31 December	20X2	20X1
Bonds payable, 7%, due 20X15	$2,500,000	$2,500,000
Class B Preferred shares, $0.50, cumulative, nonparticipating; shares issued and outstanding, 50,000 shares, issued 1 January 20X2	1,500,000	—
Class A Preferred shares, $1.50, noncumulative, nonparticipating; shares issued and outstanding, 70,000 shares	625,000	625,000
Common shares, no-par, authorized unlimited shares; issued and outstanding on 1 January 20X1, 75,000 shares. Retired for cash, on 1 November 20X1, 25,000 shares. Shares were	1,750,000	1,750,000

split 3-for-1 on 30 November 20X2. Outstanding 31 December 20X2, 150,000 shares.		
Retained earnings; no dividends declared in 20X2 or 20X1	1,285,000	846,500

Required:

1. Calculate 20X2 basic EPS, including the comparative 20X1 calculation.
2. Interpret the trend in basic EPS.

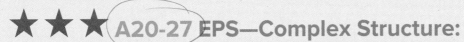

★ ★ ★ A20-27 EPS—Complex Structure:

MacDonald Corp. had the following securities outstanding at its fiscal year-end 31 December 20X7:

Long-term debt:	
Notes payable, 14%	$4,500,000
8% convertible debentures, par value $2,500,000, net of discount	2,410,000
9.5% convertible debentures, par value $2,500,000, net of discount	2,452,000
Equity:	
Preferred shares, $5 dividend, payable as $1.25 per quarter, no-par, cumulative convertible shares; authorized, 100,000 shares; issued, 30,000 shares	4,700,000
Common shares, no-par; authorized, 5,000,000 shares; issued, 600,000 shares	2,000,000
Common share conversion rights	189,000

Additional information:

a. 20X7 net earnings were $790,000. There were no discontinued operations.
b. Interest expense was $216,000 on the 8% debentures, and $250,000 on the 9.5% debentures.
c. Options to purchase 200,000 common shares at $11 per share beginning in 20X15 were outstanding throughout the year.

d. Additional options were issued on 1 May 20X7 to purchase 50,000 common shares at $27 per share in 20X9. The price per share becomes $25 in 20X10 and $20 in 20X11. These options expire at the end of 20X11.

e. The preferred shares are convertible into common shares at a rate of 9-for-1. They were issued on 1 October 20X7.

f. The 8% convertible debentures are convertible at the rate of seven shares for each $100 bond. The 9.5% convertible debentures are convertible at the rate of six shares for each $100 bond.

g. The tax rate is 30%; common shares traded for an average of $40 during the year.

h. No common shares were issued or retired during the year.

Required:

Calculate all EPS disclosures.

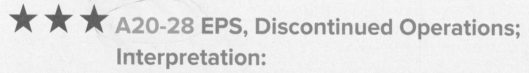

★ ★ ★ A20-28 EPS, Discontinued Operations; Interpretation:

Maria Corp. reported 20X6 earnings from continuing operations of $4,045,600 and a loss from discontinued operations of $1,355,600 after tax. The tax rate was 25%.

Maria reports the following information regarding its securities:

a. 400,000 $4 no-par cumulative preferred shares, issued 1 July 20X6. The shares are convertible into Class A common shares 6-for-1 at the option of the investor. The dividend was paid on a quarterly basis.

b. There are 175,000 $2.40 no-par cumulative preferred shares outstanding during 20X6. These shares were convertible into Class A common shares 4-for-1 at the option of the investor. All preferred shares converted to Class A common shares on 31 December 20X6 after the preferred dividend was paid.

c. There are $6,000,000 of convertible bonds payable outstanding during 20X6, convertible into Class A shares at the rate of 30 shares per $1,000 bond, at the option of the investor. This bond was recorded as a hybrid financial instrument. During the year, interest of $458,000 was paid; the company recorded interest expense of $562,000.

d. Maria had 2,300,000 Class A common shares outstanding at the beginning of the year. On 1 February, the company repurchased and retired 750,000 Class A common shares on the open market for $36 per share. Maria issued 50,000 common shares for $44 per share on 1 December.

At the beginning of the year, 200,000 options were outstanding, allowing senior management to purchase 200,000 Class A shares for $10 per share. On 1 September, 60,000 of these options were exercised, when the market value of the common shares was $38 per share. The average market value for the first eight months of the year was $30 per share. The remaining options are still outstanding and will expire in 20X10.

All preferred dividends, plus common dividends of $2 per share, were paid on schedule in 20X6.

At the end of 20X6, another 400,000 options, for 400,000 Class A shares at a price of $48, were issued to management. These options have an expiry date of 20X15. The average common share price for the entire year was $44 per share.

Required:

1. Calculate required EPS disclosures.
2. Interpret the EPS results

eXcel

★ ★ ★ A20-29 EPS—Complex Structure, Split:

At 31 December 20X1, Regina Realty Ltd. had the following items on the statement of financial position:

Preferred shares, Class A, nonvoting, cumulative, par $10, $0.50 dividend per share, redeemable at the investor's option at par in 20X11; 200,000 authorized, 30,000 issued	$ 300,000
Preferred shares, Class B, voting, cumulative, par $15, $0.90 dividend per share, redeemable at the company's option at par plus 20%; convertible at the rate of one preferred share to two Class A common shares; 200,000 authorized, 90,000 issued	$ 1,350,000
Common shares, Class A, voting with one vote per share; unlimited shares authorized, 500,000 shares issued	$ 5,357,000
Common shares, Class B, voting with ten votes per share; entitled to two times the dividends of a Class A common share, unlimited shares authorized, 50,000 shares issued	$ 587,000
Retained earnings	$2,966,000

The Class A preferred shares are redeemable in 20X11 at the investors' option and are classified as a liability. Dividends on these shares are reported as interest expense and have been deducted from earnings.

At 31 December 20X1, there were two common share Class A stock options outstanding:

- $10 per share exercise price and 60,000 shares, able to be exercised after 1 July 20X1 and expiring on 1 July 20X3.
- $9 per share exercise price and 88,000 shares, able to be exercised after 1 July 20X18 and expiring on 1 July 20X20.

During 20X2, the following occurred:

a. Net earnings was $1,140,000, correctly calculated.
b. Class A common shares were issued on 1 March 20X2 when the $10 options described above were fully exercised.
c. The tax rate was 40%.
d. The average Class A common share price during the period was $12, after giving effect to the stock split described in (f). The adjusted average for January and February was $14.
e. No dividends were declared or paid to any of the shareholders.
f. There was a 3-for-1 stock split of the Class A and Class B common shares on 1 November. All outstanding shares, option contracts, and conversion terms were adjusted accordingly. (That is, the number of shares increased and the price per share decreased.)

Required:

Prepare the earnings per share disclosure for the year ended 31 December 20X2 in good form.

(Source: The Canadian Institute of Chartered Accountants, © 2010.)

 **A20-30 EPS—Complex Structure:**

The following data relate to Freeman Inc.:

Year Ended 31 December 20X6	
From the statement of comprehensive income	
Net earnings and comprehensive income	$18,000,000
From the statement of financial position	
Long-term debt:	
10% convertible debentures, due 1 October 20X13	$ 9,000,000
Shareholders' equity	
Convertible, callable, voting preferred shares of no-par value, $0.20 cumulative dividend; authorized 600,000 shares; issued and outstanding 600,000 shares	10,600,000
Common shares, voting, no-par, authorized 5,000,000 shares; issued and outstanding, 3,320,000 shares	13,700,000
Common stock conversion rights	375,000

FROM THE DISCLOSURE NOTES:

- The $0.20 convertible preferred shares are callable by the company after 31 March 20X14, at $60 per share. Each share is convertible into one common share.
- Options to acquire 500,000 common shares at $53 per share were outstanding during 20X6.

Additional information:

a. Cash dividends of 12.5 cents per common share were declared and paid each quarter.

b. The 10% convertible debentures with a principal amount of $10,000,000 due 1 October 20X13 were issued 1 October 20X3. A discount was originally recorded, and discount amortization was $20,000 in the current year. Each $100 debenture is convertible into two common shares. On 31 December 20X6, ten thousand $100 debentures with a total face value of $1,000,000 were converted to common shares. Interest was paid to the date of conversion, but the newly issued common shares did not qualify for the 31 December common dividend.

c.   The 600,000 convertible preferred shares were issued for assets in a purchase transaction in 20X4. The dividend was declared and paid on 15 December 20X6. Each share is convertible into one common share.

d.   Options to buy 500,000 common shares at $53 per share for a period of five years were issued along with the convertible preferred shares mentioned in (c).

e.   At the end of 20X5, 3,300,000 common shares were outstanding. On 31 December 20X6, 20,000 shares were issued on the conversion of bonds.

f.   A tax rate of 40% is assumed.

g.   Common shares traded at an average market price of $75 during the year.

Required:

Calculate all EPS disclosures.

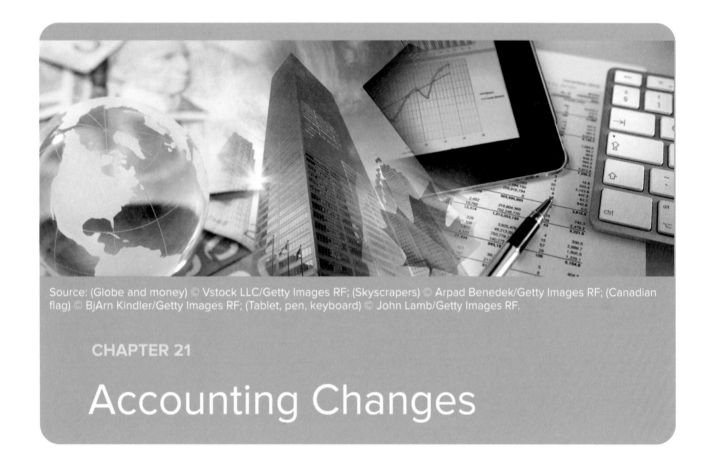

Source: (Globe and money) © Vstock LLC/Getty Images RF; (Skyscrapers) © Arpad Benedek/Getty Images RF; (Canadian flag) © BjArn Kindler/Getty Images RF; (Tablet, pen, keyboard) © John Lamb/Getty Images RF.

CHAPTER 21

Accounting Changes

INTRODUCTION

Between 2007 and 2009, Bombardier Inc. reported a total of nine changes in accounting policies. All of the changes were required by new or revised accounting standards. There were no accounting policy changes in 2010—that was a "quiet" year because Canadian publicly accountable enterprises were preparing for the changeover to IFRS in 2011. IFRS adoption necessitated a thorough revamping of accounting policies, and Bombardier devoted 20 pages of its 2011 note disclosures to the change and its effects. The change reduced the 2011 opening comparative shareholders' equity by 75%, from US$3,769 million to US$960 million. In the 2012 and 2014 financial statements, there were no policy changes, but there were seven in 2013. Obviously, understanding the financial statements and coming to meaningful conclusions based on year-to-year financial results is a challenge when accounting policies change regularly and have an important impact on earnings and net assets.

Accounting standards attempt to establish consistency of financial information in the face of inconsistent accounting policies by requiring retrospective application of accounting policy changes. That means full retroactive application of any new accounting policy; prior comparative financial statements must be restated and historical data series (e.g., earnings per share) must be restated as though the new policies have always been in effect.

While restatement is the ideal, it is often not possible. The data that are needed to restate previous year's earnings, EPS, and net assets simply may not be re-created in sufficient detail. As accounting has moved to encompass more fair-value reporting, restatement has become more complicated; a prior year estimated for value should be estimated only with the information available at that time. This is a challenge, since hindsight colours perceptions. Thus, many accounting changes *cannot* be fully reflected in prior years' restated statements and statistics.

This chapter will explore the ways that accounting policy changes are reported and the circumstances that govern each approach. As well, we will look at changes in estimates and corrections of errors, which are other types of accounting changes.

TYPES OF ACCOUNTING CHANGES

Some changes require adjustment to prior years' financial statements, or **retrospective restatement**, but other changes are applied on a prospective basis. It is important to understand the different types of accounting changes and the impact that each has on the financial statements of prior, current, and future years.

In particular, there are three types of accounting changes:

1. Change in accounting estimate;
2. Change in accounting policy; and
3. Correction of an error in prior years' financial statements.

We will discuss the nature of each of these types of changes in the following sections.

CHANGES IN ACCOUNTING ESTIMATES

Changes in accounting estimates are very common. Many financial statement elements require estimates of future values or events, and estimates are frequently changed. Examples of significant accounting estimates include the following:

- Uncollectible accounts receivable;
- Inventory obsolescence;
- Fair values of financial assets;
- Amount and probability of provisions; and
- Judgement concerning one or more of the criteria for capitalizing development costs.

A **change in accounting estimate** occurs when management decides that accounting measurements used in the past should be revised in light of new information or new circumstances. Changes can occur for several reasons:

- New, reliable information is available.
- Experience has provided insights into operating factors such as usage patterns or benefits.
- The company's economic environment has changed, requiring a re-evaluation of the assumptions underlying management's accounting estimates.
- Probabilities underlying accounting estimates have changed.
- There has been a shift in the nature of the company's business operations, so past estimates may need adjustment to fit current business strategies.

Accounting for Changes in Estimates

Changes in accounting estimates are part of the accounting routine. They reflect the environmental changes that affect an organization on a continuing basis rather than reflecting substantive changes in the *way* that accounting is being done. Therefore, changes in accounting estimates are accounted for *prospectively*, by applying them only in the current and future periods.

Prospective application means that the new or revised estimate is used in the current and future periods, until new evidence or circumstances indicate that the estimate needs to be changed again. *There is no revision of prior years' financial statements.*

One example is the estimates needed to apply a depreciation policy. There are many estimates required—(1) useful life, (2) residual value, and (3) pattern of asset usage. Any or all of these estimates may change over time as a company gains more experience with various types of assets or as changes in technology may alter the estimates. Prior years are not restated. The depreciation expense in the current period and future periods are based on the existing net book value and new estimates.

Change in Policy or Estimate?

Accounting estimates are changed very often, sometimes annually. Normally, the financial statement effect is less dramatic with a change in estimate as compared to a change in policy. Also, the application method is usually different—policy changes are applied retrospectively, while estimate changes are applied prospectively.

Therefore, it is important to distinguish between estimates and policies. When it is difficult to decide whether a change is a change in policy or estimate, *the change should be treated as a change in estimate*.

Example—Changes in Depreciation Method

Companies occasionally change their depreciation or amortization methods for long-term tangible and intangible assets. Classification of the change depends on the circumstances:

- If the change was made because of new information regarding management's estimate of the expected pattern of use, or other new information, then the *change is a change in estimate*. (e.g., benefits are now understood to be achieved evenly over the life of the asset and so the straight-line method is adopted, rather than the prior declining balance method; this is a change in estimate.)
- On the other hand, a company might change its depreciation method to conform to industry practice. This is not new information, and is accounted for as a *change in policy*. (e.g., the straight-line method is adopted, rather than the prior declining balance method, because straight-line is used by competitors; this is a change in policy.)

CONCEPT REVIEW

1. A company has accounts receivable of $200,000 and an allowance for doubtful accounts of $40,000. Bad debts have been estimated in the past at 25% of accounts receivable but now are estimated to be 15%. What kind of accounting change is this? How much is bad debt expense (recovery) this year?
2. Capital assets with a cost of $500,000 have been depreciated for three years, assuming a useful life of five years and no residual value. This year, revised estimates are a total of eight years of useful life with no residual value. What kind of accounting change is this? What is the amount of depreciation expense for this year?

CHANGES IN ACCOUNTING POLICIES

A **change in accounting policy** is a change in the way that a company accounts for a particular type of transaction or event, or for the resulting asset or liability. This is a change *from one policy to another for a given transaction or event*. It is not a new policy for a new transaction. Accounting policy changes can be mandatory or voluntary.

Mandatory Changes

A change is a **mandatory change** when standard setters issue a new accounting standard or revise an existing standard. GAAP-compliant companies must alter their policies to conform to the new recommendations.

Voluntary Changes

A change is a **voluntary change** when management switches from one acceptable method of accounting to another acceptable method. Voluntary accounting policy changes are allowed only if the new policy results in information that is both:

(1) *reliable;* and

(2) *more relevant* for financial statement users. The new policy is more relevant when the change gives the users of financial statements better information about the effects of transactions, events, or conditions on the entity's financial position, financial performance, or cash flows.

Clearly, information has to be *reliable* to be included in the financial statements. However, the new policy has to be *more relevant* than the old policy to be adopted. Standard setters do not provide guidance for judging the relevance of resulting information. Relevancy is subjective, so this will be a difficult judgement in some circumstances, particularly since it is *management* making assumptions about what will be more relevant to *users*.

A voluntary change in accounting policy may occur in response to changes in an entity's reporting circumstances, such as:

- A change in reporting objectives;
- A change in the way of doing business—for example, a shift to higher-risk business strategies that make the prediction of future outcomes more difficult and less reliable; or
- A desire to conform to industry practice.

One of the most common reasons for changing one or more accounting policies is a change in reporting objectives. For example, when the ownership of a company changes, the priority of objectives often changes or new objectives that previously did not exist suddenly become important. Examples of changes in ownership include the following:

- A company that previously was privately held may decide to issue shares on the public market and will discontinue use of private enterprise reporting standards and adopt IFRS instead.
- Control of the reporting enterprise may be acquired by another corporation in a business combination, and the acquired company may need to change its accounting policies to be consistent with those used by its new parent company.
- A new investor may purchase shares in a private company and have the power to specify that certain reporting objectives, such as cash flow prediction, are adopted.

Some changes are dictated by industry practice. Financial analysts tend not to be kind to companies that use one or more significant accounting policies that differ from general practice in that industry. Financial analysts prefer conformity, so that information is more useful for comparisons.

Early Adoption

Early adoption means that a company applies a new or revised standard prior to its mandatory effective date. Some new and revised standards permit or encourage early adoption.

IFRS 9, *Financial Instruments*, is an example of a new standard that permitted early adoption and prospective application. The mandatory effective date was set for fiscal periods beginning on or after 1 January 2018, with retrospective application. In addition, though, the standard explicitly stated that if the new standard were applied prior to 1 January 2012, the company "need not restate prior periods."

Other new standards prohibit early adoption. There are two main reasons for prohibiting early adoption:

- *To promote comparability.* If the change is substantial and may significantly affect users' intercompany comparisons, it is best if all companies make the change in the same year.
- *To give time to collect data.* Early adoption usually means that a company will not restate (or not be able to restate) its prior-period data. By prohibiting early adoption, standard setters remove any excuse for not restating at least the most recent one or two prior years.

A "New" Policy Is Not Always a "Change"

Adopting a *new accounting policy* must not be confused with a *change* in accounting policy. The following are not *changes* in accounting policy:

1. *Adopting an accounting policy for transactions or other events that differ in substance from those previously occurring.* An example would be a change in the method of generating revenue, such as by introducing instalment sales in addition to sales that require full payment. There is a substantive difference in the way that revenue will be realized, and this change may call for applying a different accounting policy for the new revenue stream as compared to that used for the existing revenue stream.

2. *Adopting a new accounting policy for transactions or other events that did not occur previously or were immaterial.* For example, a company may have been expensing all product development costs without applying the criteria for capitalization because such costs were immaterial. If development costs become significant, the company then will begin applying deferral criteria. This is adoption of an accounting policy and is new to the company but is not a *change* of accounting policy because a material amount of development costs had not previously been incurred.

When a company adopts an accounting policy for the first time due to new types of contracts, transactions, or events, the new policy must be added to the company's accounting policy disclosure note with an explanation of why a new policy has been adopted. Obviously, there would be no question of restatement, either because (1) that type of transaction or event has not arisen in prior periods or (2) the transaction or event has not been materially significant in prior years—any adjustment would also be immaterial.

Accounting for Changes in Policy

Changes in accounting policy are accounted for *retrospectively*, by applying them to all prior years. If information is not available for full retrospective treatment, the company has little choice but to apply prospective treatment, where the impact of the change is calculated as of the beginning of the current year, but no comparative financial statements are restated.

Use of Prospective Application

Prospective application of accounting policy changes is quite restricted. If a company does not have the information necessary to restate at least the prior year's results, *the change normally should be delayed for one year so that the necessary information can be accumulated to make a smooth transition.* That is one rationale for new accounting standards to become effective more than one year after they have been issued—the delay gives companies time to adjust their information collection process. Sometimes, however, standard setters believe that it is more important to make significant and meaningful changes quickly than to delay implementation until sufficient comparative information can be accumulated.

Voluntary changes always should be made only after sufficient information has been obtained to restate comparative numbers. Otherwise, users may suspect that the company is trying to hide something during a changeover without restatement.

ETHICAL ISSUES

Although information should be more relevant to users, an underlying motive for accounting changes may be management's desire to manage earnings. Management may wish to change accounting policies:

- To satisfy ratios specified in lending covenants;
- To meet the published expectations of financial analysts, feeding stock prices; or
- To maximize the value of stock options granted to management.

While these objectives may seem highly desirable to managers, they do not satisfy the requirement that new accounting policies must be *more relevant* to financial statement users. Both boards of directors and auditors must be alert to such "window dressing," which is exactly what the requirement for increased relevance is intended to discourage. All changes in accounting policy must be evaluated in an objective fashion before being approved by senior financial officers, the board of directors, and/or auditors.

CORRECTION OF AN ERROR IN PRIOR YEARS' FINANCIAL STATEMENTS

Prior-period errors are omissions or mistakes that were made in the application of accounting principles in one or more earlier periods. Mistakes can be mathematical errors, oversights, misinterpretations of fact, or intentional fraud. Errors relate to information that:

1. Was available when the prior-year financial statements were prepared; and
2. Could reasonably be expected to have been obtained and taken into account in the preparation and presentation of those prior financial statements.

An error correction is *not* an adjustment of an accounting estimate of a prior period. For example, suppose that in 20X1, a company uses past experience with existing products to estimate a warranty liability for a new product. In 20X2, that estimate turns out to be seriously inadequate. In 20X2, the company will adjust its warranty liability and the related 20X2 expense to reflect the new reality—a *change in accounting estimate*. However, if it turns out that the company's managers overlooked clear evidence that the liability would be significantly higher, and the evidence was available in 20X1, then the misstatement calls for an error correction.

Again, hindsight is not permitted to dictate error classification, but hindsight can be very illuminating when evaluating facts. Sometimes errors are quite clear cut and simple to fix:

- Management discovers that a portion of inventory at the beginning of the year was overlooked when the physical count was taken.
- The company sells through agents; the company failed to accrue commission liabilities that had not been paid at the end of the fiscal year.
- Routine repairs to equipment were capitalized instead of expensed.

However, errors are not always simple to identify.

Events Not Reportable as Errors

A vital aspect of errors is that they do not arise from a change in estimate or a change in policy. They are mistakes, whether accidental or intentional. Any item that is in error should have been recorded differently in the previous period given the accounting policies and accounting estimates at the time.

For example, a company may have followed a practice of capitalizing and amortizing development costs in earlier periods only to discover later that the company would receive no future benefit from the expenditures. The policy to capitalize and amortize may have been completely rational and justifiable on the evidence at the time, but later evidence alters the situation. The company would write off the development costs when it became clear that no future benefit would be derived, but that is a *change in estimate*, not an error.

Another example of an event that is *not* accounted for as an error correction is an income tax audit. The income tax reported for a year is considered to be an estimate until confirmed by a CRA audit. If, in 20X5, an audit results in $100,000 of extra tax paid, specifically relating to 20X2 and 20X3, restatement is not appropriate. Instead, 20X5 income tax expense is increased by $100,000.

Accounting for an Error Correction

The correction of an accounting error is accounted for retrospectively, with restatement. The error should not have happened, which means that the statements for one or more past periods were simply wrong. In many cases, the error will have reversed itself by the current period, requiring no adjustment to the *current period's* statements. Only comparative information in the published financial statements must be adjusted. In other cases, reversal is not complete and a correcting journal entry is needed.

For example, suppose that the inventory stored in a Cuban warehouse was accidentally not included in the ending inventory count for 20X1. As a result of this error, 20X1 ending inventory will be understated, cost of goods sold overstated, and earnings understated. The resulting understatement of beginning inventory in 20X2 will cause an understatement of cost of goods sold and an overstatement of earnings for 20X2. If the ending inventory for 20X2 is correctly stated (i.e., including the Cuban inventory), the cumulative error will "wash out" by the end of 20X2. The overstatement of 20X2 earnings will offset the understatement of 20X1 earnings—20X2 ending retained earnings will be correct.

If the error is discovered in 20X3, no adjustment needs to be made *on the books* because there are no misstated accounts (either SFP or SCI) for 20X3. But an error that self-corrects over time still causes misstatements for the earlier periods that were affected. The 20X1 and 20X2 comparative statements must be changed.

CONCEPT REVIEW

1. What criteria must be met for a voluntary change in accounting policy to be acceptable?
2. Because of an inability to estimate future revenue streams, development expenses were expensed. Future prospects are much more stable, and can now be estimated. Current-year development expenses are being considered, and will be capitalized. Is this a change in an estimate, an error correction, or a change in policy?

REPORTING ACCOUNTING CHANGES

General Methodology

Retrospective Application with Full Restatement

The basic approach to accounting for changes in policy is retrospective restatement. The process is as follows:

- The new accounting policy is applied to events and transactions from the date of origin of each event or transaction.
- The financial statements for each prior period that are presented for comparative purposes are restated to reflect the new policy.
- Opening retained earnings (or other component of share equity, as appropriate) for each comparative period is adjusted for the cumulative prior income effect.
- All summary financial information for earlier periods, such as earnings, total assets, earnings per share, and so on, are also restated. All reported financial results after the change look as though the new policy had always been in effect.

Retrospective application requires the company to restate balances as far back as possible. That means that at the date that the new policy is applied, the opening SFP balances should incorporate the effect of the new policy as though it had been applied throughout the life of the enterprise. Retrospective application of an accounting policy change is intended to make *current and future* financial information comparable with reported results for comparative prior periods. Earnings trends and other analytical data that are based on historical comparisons are not valid unless the same accounting policies are used throughout the time series. The qualitative criteria of *consistency* and *comparability* are enhanced by restatement, at least in the short run.

Retrospective Application with Partial Restatement

Often, it is impracticable to apply full retrospective restatement. Retrospective restatement is *impracticable* if:

- It is not possible or feasible to determine the effects of the new policy on previous period(s);
- Application would require assumptions about management's intent in prior period(s); or
- It is impossible to reliably know what the appropriate measurements and valuations would have been in the prior period(s).

If full restatement is impracticable, the next best approach is to *restate as far back as possible with the data available.* Sometimes, this is possible for the past five years (the normal period that companies publish comparative series of financial performance indicators). Sometimes, retrospective application is possible for only one year.

In a one-year restatement, this *partial restatement* usually means restating the opening balances of the prior and current years. The new policy is applied in full for both the current year, and one prior year. Thus, both the financial position and the earnings for the two years are based on the new standard, thereby facilitating comparison of the current year with the previous year.

Prospective Application

Even partial restatement is not always feasible. A company may not be able to measure the cumulative effect on opening SFP balances (or one year back.) If so, then prospective application may be used. Under *prospective application*, adjustments are made from the start of the current period. There is no adjustment to restate opening SFP balances.

Note, however, that changes in accounting policy may be delayed by a year or more to allow/force companies time to gather appropriate information to restate.

Comparability of Statistical Series—A Caution

The objective of retrospective restatement is, as explained above, to promote inter-year comparability. However, this works only in the short run. Long-run comparative series, such as net earnings, EPS, operating margin, and return on investment, are all compromised by frequent changes in accounting policies.

Many analysts try to work with a five-to-ten-year series of earnings, EPS, and return-on-investment ratios.It is impossible for a company to go back 10 years (or often even five years) and restate those statistics in any meaningful way. Frequent and significant changes in accounting standards have sharply reduced the feasibility of multiyear trend analysis.

One might argue that the nature of a business's operations has also been changing over time and thus the ingredients of earnings are ever-changing. While that may well be true, applying changing measurement to changing conditions just makes the statistical series even less meaningful. It is like constructing a price index that prices a different set of goods each year—it will yield a statistical series of prices, but comparisons will not have much meaning because the measurement method is not consistent: garbage in, garbage out.

RETROSPECTIVE APPLICATION

Now, let us go on to the application of a change in accounting policy.

Recording and Reporting Guidelines—Retrospective Application

The following guidelines apply to accounting policy changes that are applied by restating prior years. The same approach is used for correction of prior years' accounting errors.

In the following list, note that the first guideline refers to *recording* the change in the company's books, while the next four guidelines refer to *reporting* in the financial statements and disclosure notes.

For *recording* in the entity's accounts:

1. The *cumulative* impact of the change on the *beginning* balances of financial statement elements for the current year must be calculated. These changes are *recorded* in the accounts by means of a general journal entry. The cumulative impact of the accounting policy change on prior years' earnings is recorded as an adjustment to the beginning balance of retained earnings or accumulated OCI, depending on the type of adjustment required. *The current year is accounted for using the new policy.*

For financial statement *presentation*:

2. The information necessary to make the change *in the current and prior periods* must be obtained from the underlying accounting records.

3. Account balances that affect the prior years' comparative financial statements must be recalculated using the new policy, including all affected financial statement elements, whether assets, liabilities, revenue, expense, or equity accounts. The comparative statements must be changed (restated) to reflect the changed amounts in the full financial statements.

4. Summary comparative information (e.g., earnings per share, total assets, shareholders' equity) that are presented publicly, such as in the annual report, must be recalculated using the new policy.

5. Opening retained earnings is restated to remove the effect of the accounting change from prior earnings. Opening retained earnings *as restated* is shown as a subtotal. This is done for all comparative years. The amount of the adjustment will change in each comparative year because the *number of prior years* declines. (If the adjustment affected OCI, then the opening accumulated OCI amounts would require restatement and be shown as a subtotal.)

Reflecting retrospective restatement, all prior-period data are restated for financial reporting purposes. *However, the journal entry to record the cumulative effect of the change is made only in the current year.* Prior years' books have been closed—the cumulative adjustment must be made to opening retained earnings (or accumulated OCI) of the current year. Changes to the prior year financial statements are made when the financial statements are prepared.

Illustration

Exhibit 21-1 presents the data for an illustration of the retrospective approach with restatement. In this example, we assume that Sunset Corp. has decided to change its method of accounting for inventories from average cost (AC) to first-in, first-out (FIFO), in the fiscal year ending 31 December 20X5. To make the change, Sunset must not only recalculate its inventory balances for the end of 20X4 to determine earnings for 20X5 but also recalculate its inventory balances for the beginning of 20X4 to restate the comparative results for 20X4.

EXHIBIT 21-1

SUNSET CORPORATION DATA FOR CHANGE IN ACCOUNTING POLICY

Change from Average Cost to FIFO for Inventory

1. During 20X5, Sunset Corp. decides to change its inventory cost method from average cost (AC) to first-in, first-out (FIFO) for accounting purposes, effective for fiscal year 20X5. The company has always used FIFO for tax purposes, and this has been a source of temporary difference and thus deferred income tax, at the accumulation rate of 30%. The reporting year ends on 31 December, and the company's 20X5 income tax rate is 30%.

2. From its records, the company determines the following information relating to the change:

	20X5		20X4	
	FIFO	**AC**	**FIFO**	**AC**
Statement of Financial Position				
a. Beginning inventory	$ 60,000	$50,000	$47,000	$ 45,000
b. Ending inventory	80,000	65,000	60,000	50,000

	20X5		20X4	
	FIFO	**AC**	**FIFO**	**AC**
Statement of Changes in Equity; Retained Earnings column				
c. Retained earnings, beginning balance	$ 201,000			$ 92,000
d. Earnings (see below)				189,000
	210,000			
e. Dividends declared and paid	88,000			80,000
f. Retained earnings, ending balance	$323,000			$201,000
Statement of Comprehensive Income				
g. Earnings before income tax	300,000*			270,000
h. Income tax expense	90,000			81,000
i. Earnings and comprehensive income	$ 210,000			$189,000

*Reflects FIFO policy.

The first step in restatement is to determine which balances will be affected by the change. For a change in inventory method, the following balances will be affected in both 20X5 and 20X4:

- Beginning inventory;
- Ending inventory;
- Cost of goods sold;
- Income tax expense;
- Earnings;
- Deferred income tax; and
- Retained earnings.

The statement of comprehensive income, the statement of financial position, and the retained earnings section of the statement of changes in equity will all require restatement for 20X4.

In our inventory example, the following impacts of the accounting change must be calculated:

1. The cumulative effect on balances up to 1 January 20X5 (the year of the change);
2. The cumulative effect on balances up to 1 January 20X4; and
3. The specific impact on the accounts for the year 20X4, for comparative restatement purposes.

The new basis of accounting must then be used for the current year, 20X5. The calculations for Sunset are as follows, using the amounts presented in Exhibit 21-1.

Recording—Impact to 1 January 20X5

The journal entry to record the effects of the change in policy is based on the cumulative effect at the beginning of 20X5:

a. 20X5 opening inventory increases by $10,000—from $50,000 under AC to $60,000 under FIFO;
b. The increase in 20X5 opening inventory means an increase of $10,000 in 20X4 ending inventory;

c. The increase in 20X4 ending inventory means 20X4 cost of goods sold has changed, as well as income tax expense and therefore 20X4 earnings;

d. The $10,000 in retrospective additional 20X5 earnings flows is credited to retained earnings, after tax.

e. The company has had a deferred income tax balance caused by the use of FIFO for tax purposes but AC for reporting. This temporary difference will now be eliminated.

For reporting purposes, the cumulative increase belongs to retained earnings from prior years. The deferred income tax amount also relates to prior years' temporary differences. After tax (at 30%), the net increase in retained earnings is $7,000. The entry to restate prior years' earnings is:

Inventory	10,000	
Deferred tax (30% tax rate)		3,000
Retained earnings		7,000

This entry establishes the new accounting policy in the accounts as of the *beginning* of 20X5; all 20X5 entries will be made on the basis of the new FIFO accounting policy. No additional entries are necessary.

Reporting—Impact to 1 January 20X4

The cumulative impact of the change in policy for all years prior to 20X4 is captured in the change to 20X4 beginning inventory. The cost of goods sold adjustment is:

$47,000 (FIFO) – $45,000 (Average Cost) = $2,000; cumulative income is higher.

After income tax, with a 30% tax rate, the impact on accumulated earnings is:

$2,000 × (1 – 30%) = $1,400; cumulative income is higher.

This adjustment for pre-20X4 is not recorded as a separate journal entry in the books. The effect has already been captured in the cumulative retained earnings adjusting entry made in 20X5, as described just above. However, the $1,400 will be shown in the comparative financial statements.

Reporting—Effect on the Financial Statements of 20X4

Restatement of the 20X4 financial statements requires changing the beginning and ending inventory balance on the SFP and the cost of goods sold on the SCI. Changing the cost of goods sold also has an impact on income tax expense, and earnings. The change in earnings flows through to retained earnings and therefore to total shareholders' equity.

The ending 20X4 inventory under FIFO is $60,000, compared with the $50,000 originally reported in the 20X4 financial statements, as shown in Exhibit 21-1. Opening inventory is now $47,000, instead of $45,000. The effect on 20X4 earnings is as follows:

• FIFO has a higher beginning inventory, increasing cost of goods sold and lowering pretax earnings by $2,000.

• FIFO also has a higher ending inventory, lowering cost of the goods sold and increasing pretax earnings by $10,000.

• The net effect of the changes in the beginning and ending inventories is to increase 20X4 income before tax by $8,000—the $10,000 increase due to the impact on ending inventory minus the $2,000 decrease caused by the change in beginning inventory.

• The income tax rate is 30%; the increase in income tax expense from the change in policy is $2,400: $8,000 × 30%.

The changes to the 20X4 statements can be summarized as follows:

Statement of Comprehensive Income

Cost of goods sold decreases by $8,000 (credit).

Income tax expense increases by $2,400 (debit).

Earnings increases by $5,600 (credit).

Statement of Financial Position

Inventory (ending) increases by $10,000 (debit).

Deferred income tax changes by $3,000 (credit).

Retained earnings increases by $7,000 (credit).

Note that the changes in the SCI reflect the impact of the accounting policy change *only* for 20X4. The change in the SFP retained earnings account, however, reflects the *cumulative* impact of the changes up to the end of 20X4. The difference between the total adjustment of $7,000 and the 20X4-related adjustment is the amount related to periods *prior* to 20X4:

Total change in retained earnings	$7,000 credit
Less: Impact on the earnings and retained earnings for 20X4, as calculated above	5,600 credit
Impact on retained earnings prior to the beginning of 20X4	$1,400 credit

Restated Financial Statements

Exhibit 21-2 shows the relevant amounts from the 20X5 and restated 20X4 comparative statements. The figures in the statements are based on the amounts shown in Exhibit 21-1 except that the 20X4 statement amounts have been restated for the change to FIFO, based on the analysis above. The comparative 20X4 SFP includes inventory at FIFO instead of average cost.

EXHIBIT 21-2

SUNSET CORPORATION

Selected Amounts from Comparative Financial Statements Change from Average Cost to FIFO for Inventory—Retrospective Application

	20X5 (FIFO)	(Restated) 20X4 (FIFO)
Statement of Financial Position		
Ending inventory (FIFO)	$ 80,000	$ 60,000

Statement of Comprehensive Income—Earnings Section

Earnings before income tax	$300,000	$ 278,000[1]
Income tax expense	90,000	83,400[2]
Earnings and comprehensive income	$210,000	$ 194,600
Earnings per share (100,000 shares assumed)	$ 2.10	$ 1.95

Statement of Changes in Equity—Retained Earnings Section

Beginning balance, as previously reported	$201,000	$92,000
Add: Cumulative effect of inventory accounting policy change, net of tax of $3,000 in 20X5 (20X4—$600)	7,000	1,400
Beginning balance, restated	**208,000**	93,400
Add: Earnings (from above)	210,000	194,600
Deduct: Dividends declared	(88,000)	(80,000)
Ending balance	$330,000	**$208,000**

(1) $278,000 = $270,000 + $8,000 (decrease in 20X4 CGS due to accounting change)

(2) $83,400 = $81,000 + $2,400 (income tax expense for 20X4 due to accounting change)

Note to Financial Statements

During 20X5, the Corporation changed its accounting policy for inventory from average cost to first-in, first-out. As a result, restated 20X4 earnings increased by $5,600 (5.6¢ per share). The change increased 20X5 earnings by $3,500 (3.5¢ per share). The 20X4 statements have been restated to reflect the change in accounting policy.

The retained earnings statement shows an adjustment for *both* years instead of just the single adjustment of $7,000 that was recorded. The adjustment is based on the amount of adjustment for *prior* years. Remember that it is the *beginning* balances that are being adjusted. The pre-20X4 adjustment is effective at the beginning of 20X4; the restatement adjustment relating to 20X4 affects the beginning balance for 20X5.

Observe that the restated beginning balance for 20X5 agrees with the restated ending balance for 20X4, as it should. These amounts are **boldfaced** in Exhibit 21-2.

The disclosure note documents the impact of the change on each of 20X4 and 20X5. The 20X4 impact is apparent from the adjustments. The 20X5 impact, however, is derived from Exhibit 21-1. Under average cost, the increase in inventory for 20X5 would have been $15,000. Under FIFO, the increase is $20,000. FIFO causes an additional $5,000 of cost to flow into inventory rather than into cost of goods sold; the after-tax impact is $3,500 (i.e., $5,000 × 70%).

Deferred Tax or Income Tax Payable?

Usually, an accounting change impacts an existing temporary difference, and the tax impact of the change is recorded in deferred tax account. That is, the change is made for accounting purposes but not for tax purposes. For example, if the accounting value of, say, a warranty liability or equipment is changed, this changes the cumulative temporary differences to date, and deferred tax is adjusted. In other cases, tax returns are refiled, prior taxable income is affected, and the income tax amounts change an income tax payable or income tax receivable amount is recorded. Some helpful guidelines:

1. If the situation is an error correction, prior year tax returns must be refiled and income tax payable or receivable is recorded.

2. If the change relates to a pre-existing temporary difference (e.g., depreciation versus CCA), then deferred tax is the tax account changed.

3. There are some limited examples where a policy is changed for accounting purposes and for income tax purposes. However, prior year tax returns may not be changed because of a change in accounting policy. As a result, the current-year tax return would report the cumulative earnings impact of the change. In this case, income tax payable or receivable is recorded.

In the Sunset example, above, the change was made for accounting purposes, but FIFO was previously used for tax purposes, so there was no change to income tax payable. This is an example of the second case. When the entry was recorded in 20X5 to reflect the change, deferred tax was adjusted. This adjustment presumably reversed a pre-existing deferred tax balance relating to the difference between the accounting basis of the inventory and the tax basis.

Restating Statistical Series

Assume that Sunset issues a five-year summary of prior years' results, such as total revenue, cost of goods sold, net earnings, and EPS. To apply full restatement, Sunset must restate comparative information as well as restate the 20X4 financial statements. Revenue will not be affected by the change in inventory method, but CGS, net earnings, and EPS will be affected.

To restate the years prior to 20X4 (i.e., 20X0 through 20X3), Sunset must have the prior years' inventory data in its computer archives. These data can be retrieved to make the restatement. If inventory balances cannot be recreated, *partial restatement* (20X4 only), as illustrated, is all that is possible.

The adjustment to restate prior years will be quite straightforward as long as the inventory data are in sufficient detail to convert from average cost to FIFO. There is no need to go through a full CGS analysis. The impact on those statistical series can be measured by calculating the effect of the change in policy on opening and ending inventories for each of the preceding five years:

- An increase in *opening* inventory will increase the year's CGS and decrease net earnings and EPS; a decrease in opening inventory will have the opposite effects.

- An increase in *ending* inventory will decrease that year's CGS and increase net earnings and EPS; a decrease in ending inventory will have the opposite effects.

Remember that *full restatement* requires all historical series to be restated, not simply the one comparative prior year's financial statements.

CONCEPT REVIEW

1. A company changes from FIFO to average cost flow assumptions regarding inventory. At the beginning of the year of the change, the FIFO inventory was $120,000, while average cost was $105,000. If the tax rate is 30%, what is the amount of the cumulative adjustment to opening retained earnings?

2. Refer to the data in question 1. Does retained earnings increase or decrease?

PROSPECTIVE APPLICATION

If a company cannot restate its prior year's financial results due to a lack of sufficiently detailed information, the company can use prospective application. In this situation, the effect of the change is reported as far back as possible. Often, this means that the company makes a single catch-up adjustment in the year of the change, but prior years' comparative statements and summary information are not restated.

The prospective approach also is used for a change in accounting policy if it is permitted by a new accounting standard. The transition provisions in any new or revised accounting standard will say whether or not the prospective approach is permitted.

Guidelines

The following guidelines apply to accounting policy changes that are reported by using the prospective approach:

1. The cumulative impact of the change on all of the relevant beginning balances for the current year is computed and *recorded*, including the change in retained earnings (or accumulated OCI).
2. The cumulative impact of the change is reported in the financial statements as an adjustment to opening retained earnings (or accumulated OCI) for the current year.
3. Prior years' financial statements included for comparative purposes remain unchanged. All summary information reported for earlier years also remains unchanged.

Comparative Illustration

To illustrate the difference between retrospective and prospective application, assume the same facts as in the previous example for retrospective application (see Exhibit 21-1), *except* that Sunset Corp. does not have adequate information to determine the 20X4 beginning inventory on the FIFO basis.

If the opening 20X4 inventory at FIFO is not available, then it is not possible to restate the 20X4 financial statements; we can restate only the ending balance of 20X4 (which is the beginning balance of 20X5). The adjustment for 20X5 is exactly as was illustrated earlier:

Inventory	10,000	
Deferred tax (30% tax rate)		3,000
Retained earnings		7,000

Under prospective application, the $7,000 adjustment cannot be allocated between 20X4 and 20X5 retained earnings; the entire adjustment must be both *recorded* and *reported* in 20X5.

Selected comparative statement amounts are shown in Exhibit 21-3. *Note that there are no adjustments to the original 20X4 amounts.* Nevertheless, the year-end 20X5 amounts are identical to those in Exhibit 21-2 under retrospective application.

EXHIBIT 21-3

SUNSET CORPORATION

Selected Amounts from Comparative Financial Statements Change from Average Cost to FIFO for Inventory—Prospective Application

	20X5 (FIFO Basis)	20X4 (AC Basis)
Statement of Financial Position		
Ending inventory (FIFO)	$ 80,000	$ 50,000
Statement of Comprehensive Income—Earnings Section		
Earnings before income tax	$300,000	$270,000
Income tax expense	90,000	81,000
Earnings and comprehensive income	$210,000	$ 189,000
Earnings per share (100,000 shares assumed)	$ 2.10	$ 1.89
Statement of Changes in Equity—Retained Earnings Section		
Beginning balance, as previously reported	**$201,000**	$ 92,000
Add: Cumulative effect of inventory accounting policy change, net of tax of $3,000	7,000	—
Beginning balance, restated	208,000	92,000
Add: Earnings (from above)	210,000	189,000
Deduct: Dividends declared	(88,000)	(80,000)
Ending balance	$330,000	**$201,000**

Note to Financial Statements

During 20X5, the Corporation changed its accounting policy for inventory from average cost to first-in, first-out. Insufficient information was available to adjust 20X4 opening inventories to FIFO. As a result, 20X4 financial statements have not been restated. All relevant adjustments have been recorded in 20X5.

CONCEPT REVIEW

1. When is it appropriate to change deferred income tax, versus income tax payable, in an entry to record an accounting change?
2. What is time series data and how is it affected by a retrospective change in accounting policy?
3. What will remain unchanged if prospective application is applied?

ERROR CORRECTION—EXAMPLES

An example of disclosed error correction is shown in Exhibit 21-4. In the fourth quarter of 20X3, Joseph Ventures Inc. discovered an error in its reporting of marketable securities that had occurred at its 31 December 20X1 year-end. Exhibit 21-4 shows the company's disclosure of the correction.

EXHIBIT 21-4

JOSEPH VENTURES INC.

31 December 20X3

Example of Error Correction

Note J—Marketable securities

In the fourth quarter of 20X3, an error was discovered that understated marketable securities reported as investments at year-end 20X1. The fair value of marketable securities is adjusted at each reporting date and recorded as a fair value adjustment in the consolidated statement of comprehensive income. Accordingly, the error was corrected by restating the fair value of the securities by $22,717 at the start of 20X2 with a corresponding credit to 20X2 opening retained earnings. The adjustment resulted in a decrease in comparative earnings for 20X2 of $22,717, with no effect on the earnings for the year ended 31 December 20X3.

The error was that the fair value of these instruments was understated. The correction increases the fair value at the beginning of 20X2 by $22,717. This change increased the 20X1 comprehensive earnings by the same amount, which was offset by an offsetting decrease in the comparative earnings for 20X2. The earnings for 20X3 were unaffected because the error had self-corrected by adjustments to the securities' fair value in 20X2.

Counterbalancing Errors

Most changes flow through retained earnings at some point in time. If and when the impact of the change has "washed through," no entry for the change is needed. For example, assume that an amortizable asset with a cost of $15,000 and a useful life of three years was expensed when it was purchased in early 20X1 instead of being capitalized and amortized over its three-year life. If the error is discovered in late 20X2, the following adjustment must be made, assuming there is no income tax:

Amortization expense [20X2 ($15,000 ÷ 3)]	5,000	
Capital assets	15,000	
Accumulated amortization		10,000
Retained earnings		
($15,000 − $5,000 20X1 amortization)		10,000

However, if this error is discovered in 20X4, no entry is needed. The asset would have been fully amortized by the end of 20X3 and removed from the books. The $15,000 amortization that should have been recorded in 20X1, 20X2, and 20X3 is fully offset by the $15,000 expense erroneously recorded in 20X1. Both retained earnings and net assets are correct without any entries. The comparative figures must be adjusted for *reporting*, but such a restatement does not require any book entry for *recording*.

Example: Inventory Errors

Counterbalancing takes place in the course of one year for errors that are made in valuing inventory, since closing inventory for one year is opening inventory for the next year. Consider the data in Exhibit 21-5. Look first at the original data.

EXHIBIT 21-5				
COUNTERBALANCING INVENTORY ERRORS				
Income Statement:	*20X6—Original*	*20X6—Restated*	*20X5—Original*	*20X5—Restated*
Sales	$6,000,000	$ 6,000,000	$5,500,000	$5,500,000
Opening inventory	450,000	**425,000**	325,000	325,000
Purchases	3,520,000	3,520,000	3,400,000	3,400,000
Closing inventory	(345,000)	(345,000)	(450,000)	**(425,000)**
Cost of goods sold	3,625,000	**3,600,000**	3,275,000	**3,300,000**
Gross profit	$2,375,000	**$2,400,000**	$2,225,000	**$2,200,000**
Statement of Financial Position:				
Closing inventory	$ 345,000	$ 345,000	$ 450,000	**$ 425,000**
Retained earnings	$ 1,345,000	$ 1,345,000	$ 1,240,000	**$ 1,215,000**

What will change if the 20X5 closing inventory is found to be overstated by $25,000 in 20X7? That is, assume that the correct closing inventory for 20X5 is $425,000, not $450,000. Refer to the corrected numbers in **boldface** in Exhibit 21-5. The error has made 20X5 income, assets, and retained earnings too high by $25,000, and they are corrected downward. However, 20X6 income was too low by $25,000, and it is corrected upward. By the end of 20X6, retained earnings and inventory are correctly stated. No journal entry is needed in 20X7 for this correction, although *20X6 and 20X5 comparative financial statements must be changed.*

Impractibility

On rare occasion, restatement for error correction may be **impracticable**. This situation arises when the company does not have sufficient detail available in prior years to enable the company to restate prior years with sufficient accuracy. This may happen, for example, if fair values were incorrectly assigned to inventories (e.g., biological assets) or to investment properties over several years.

It may not always be feasible to determine the correct values in retrospect. When remeasuring the effect of the error in *all* prior years is impracticable, the error should be reported prospectively from the earliest date practicable, which usually will be the beginning of the year in which the error was discovered. If the error cannot be corrected even at the beginning of the current year, then no restatement of balances can be made and the correct accounting method and/or measurements must be applied completely prospectively.

CONCEPT REVIEW

1. A company expensed the acquisition of a $100,000 parcel of land three years ago. What SFP balances are incorrect, ignoring income tax? When would this situation self-correct?

2. An internal auditor has discovered that in the previous year, her company accidentally applied the estimation technique for doubtful accounts "upside-down," assigning the greatest risk of default to the newest accounts receivable and the lowest risk of default to the oldest

accounts. This resulted in a very large charge of $5 million for doubtful accounts in that year instead of the $1.5 million that a proper estimate would have yielded. In the current year, the technique was applied correctly and the appropriate adjustment was made to the allowance account. What action should the company take, if any, to correct this estimation error?

SUMMARY OF APPROACHES FOR ACCOUNTING CHANGES

Exhibit 21-6 shows the decision process for applying the three kinds of accounting changes. Exhibit 21-7 summarizes the treatment of cumulative effects and restatements. These two exhibits may be helpful when trying to conceptualize and remember the different approaches to accounting changes.

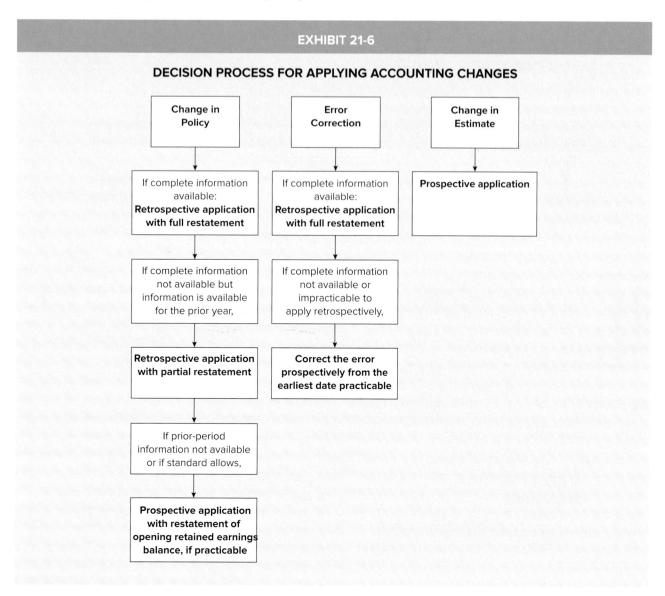

EXHIBIT 21-6

DECISION PROCESS FOR APPLYING ACCOUNTING CHANGES

Change in Policy	Error Correction	Change in Estimate
If complete information available: **Retrospective application with full restatement**	If complete information available: **Retrospective application with full restatement**	**Prospective application**
If complete information not available but information is available for the prior year,	If complete information not available or impracticable to apply retrospectively,	
Retrospective application with partial restatement	**Correct the error prospectively from the earliest date practicable**	
If prior-period information not available or if standard allows,		
Prospective application with restatement of opening retained earnings balance, if practicable		

EXHIBIT 21-7

SUMMARY OF ACCOUNTING CHANGES AND REPORTING APPROACHES

Type of Accounting Change	Accounting Approach	Restatement Methodology	
		Cumulative Adjustment Identified and Reported	Comparative Statements and Results of Prior Years
Accounting Estimate	Prospective	Cumulative adjustment not computed or reported	Prior years' results remain unchanged; new estimates applied only to accounting for current and future periods
Accounting Policy			
a. Complete information about impact in prior years is available	Retrospective with full restatement	Opening retained earnings retrospectively restated in all affected prior periods	Comparative prior years' results and statistical series restated to new policy

Provide three balance sheets (including an opening balance sheet for the prior year comparatives) |
| b. Not feasible to restate all prior years—sufficiently detailed information not available | Retrospective with partial restatement | Restated as far back as practicable, often only the previous year | One or more recent years restated; earlier years and statistical summaries unchanged |
| c. If (1) impracticable to determine cumulative effect at beginning of current period or (2) specifically permitted by a new accounting standard | Prospective without restatement | Current year's opening retained earnings adjusted for cumulative effect of the change, if known; if effect not known, then no adjustment | Prior years' results remain unchanged; new policy applied only to current and future events and transactions |

Accounting Error

a. Complete information about impact in prior years is available

Retrospective with full restatement

Opening retained earnings restated (if the error has not self-corrected)

Prior years' results restated to correct the error

Provide three balance sheets (including an opening balance sheet for the prior year comparatives)

b. Not feasible to restate all prior years—sufficiently detailed information not available

Retrospective with partial restatement

Restated as far back as practicable, usually only the previous year

One or more recent years restated; earlier years and statistical summaries unchanged

STATEMENT OF CASH FLOWS

Previous sections have shown that accounting changes affect the SFP, the retained earnings statement, and the SCI. It is not so obvious, however, that a new accounting policy may also affect the statement of cash flows. A change in accounting policy will not usually affect the net change in cash—the "bottom line" of the statement of cash flows. However, a new accounting policy may affect the classification of amounts in the statement of cash flows.

For example, a change from capitalizing to expensing of start-up costs will move the annual start-up cost from the investing section to the operations section. Cash inflow from operations will decrease because the expense is now included, while the cash outflow for investment in long-term assets (i.e., capitalized start-up costs) will also decrease. The long-term effect on the statement of cash flows, therefore, will be to shift the start-up costs from the *investing activities* section to the *operating activities* section of the statement of cash flows. The shift will decrease the apparent cash flow from operations, even though the overall cash flow is not affected.

Similarly, the *correction of prior-period errors* may affect the amounts shown in the statement of cash flows of prior periods if the error affects the amounts previously reported.

Changes in accounting estimates will not affect the classification of cash flows because such changes are applied prospectively. Changes in accounting estimates do not affect the method of reporting individual types of cash flows.

ETHICAL ISSUES

Accounting changes present something of an ethical minefield for the unwary professional accountant. Management is, quite properly, concerned about the perceptions of outsiders who use the financial statements. Managers can often feel tempted to alter accounting policies to mollify concerned statement users. However, the current standards on policy changes make it rather difficult for a company to make voluntary accounting policy changes, especially in a public company. Very few voluntary changes are observable in public companies. Private companies, however, have more opportunities to make policy changes because they are subject to less scrutiny and because they are less tightly constrained by a requirement for GAAP compliance.

Sometimes an accounting policy is changed effectively, though not technically, by a change in assumptions and estimates. For example, Canadian software companies usually followed the IFRS requirement that companies capitalize and amortize development costs if certain criteria are satisfied. In doing so, however, the companies found themselves penalized in the U.S. stock market because they did not treat all development costs as an expense, as required by U.S. GAAP. To make themselves more comparable with their U.S. competitors, many companies simply decided that the criteria for deferral were no longer being met and therefore that the costs should be expensed immediately. This was not a change in accounting policy *per se*, but it had the same effect by means of a declared change in assumptions.

That particular example is fairly innocent in that the change had the effect of not only lowering reported earnings but also improving investor perception of the transparency of financial reporting. The change did seem to provide more relevant information for the U.S. users, who felt that non-American standards were substandard and therefore discounted the companies' share value.

In other instances, however, voluntary policy changes may be driven primarily by management's desire to maximize earnings or to maximize its own compensation rather than by any demonstrable benefit to users. These changes lay a trap for the accountant who goes along with management's desires to manipulate earnings, and severe penalties may lie down the road.

Of course, we all are well aware of the subjectivity of accounting estimates. This subjectivity is unavoidable—it is the nature of estimates. But there is a fine line between reasonable estimates on one hand and earnings manipulation on the other hand. Manipulation leads to misstatement, and where the misstatement is deliberate, the accountant is guilty of fraud, even if the accountant is following instructions of his or her employer.

DISCLOSURE REQUIREMENTS

Change in Policy

When a company changes an accounting policy, the company should explain in the company's disclosure notes:

- The nature of the change;

- The amount of the adjustment for the current and prior period for each financial line item that is affected by the change;

- Revised basic and diluted EPS;

- An opening SFP for the (restated) comparative year (this is a third balance sheet, as compared to the two that are usually presented);

- The amount of adjustments for periods prior to those presented in the comparative statements, to the extent practicable; and

- If retrospective restatement is not applied or not applied fully, the reason(s) that retrospective application is wholly or partially impracticable should be explained, along with an a description of how and from when the change has been applied.

If the change is due to a new or revised accounting standard, the company should also disclose the title of the standard and its transition provisions.

If the change is *voluntary*, the company should explain why the new policy provides better and more useful (i.e., "reliable and more relevant") information for financial statement users.

Companies are required to disclose the impact, if any, of changes in accounting policy caused by issued but not yet effective standards.

Disclosures

When prospective application is used for changes in accounting policy, reporting requirements are reduced to the following disclosures:

1. The fact that the change has not been applied retrospectively, along with a description of how and from when the change has been applied;
2. The effect of the change on current and future financial statements; and
3. The reasons that retrospective application cannot be done.

Change in Estimates

Disclosure of changes in estimates is rare. Changes in estimates happen every year for many financial statement elements (allowance for doubtful account, warranty provisions) and these year-to-year changes are not separately disclosed. Most estimates are "year-by-year" in the sense that they must be made each year, and will fluctuate over time, depending on the company's business environment.

Technically, a company must disclose the *nature of the change* and *quantitative result of the change*, whether it affects the current period or a future period. In practice, the disclosure requirement only applies to estimates that are "fixed," such as the useful life estimates used for depreciation and amortization.

Error Correction

Disclosure requirements for errors include a description of the nature of the error, and the amount of the correction made to each financial statement element. The amount by which EPS has been restated must also be disclosed. If full retrospective treatment is impracticable, the circumstances must be explained. Finally, the amount of the correction to the earliest period presented must be disclosed.

Disclosure Example

Loblaw Companies Limited disclosed a voluntary accounting policy change in 2014. Refer to Exhibit 21-8. This change has been applied retrospectively, changing 2013, the comparative year. The disclosure note includes the impact on financial statements elements and earnings per share.

EXHIBIT 21-8

CHANGE IN ACCOUNTING POLICIES — DISCLOSURE EXAMPLE

Extract from Loblaw Companies Limited

Annual financial statements, 2014

Note 2

Accounting Standards Implemented in 2014 and Changes to Significant Accounting Policies

Vendor Allowances The timing of recognition of vendor allowances requires judgment to determine the point at which the Company has earned the allowance. In conjunction with the acquisition of Shoppers Drug Mart, management reviewed the timing of recognition of certain vendor allowances and has determined that it would be appropriate to align the policies of both companies. The Company has implemented the change retrospectively in 2014, as follows:

Consolidated Statement of Earnings and Comprehensive Income

Increase (Decrease)

(millions of Canadian dollars except where otherwise indicated)		2013
Cost of Merchandise Inventories Sold	$	5
Operating Income	$	(5)
Earnings Before Income Taxes	$	(5)
Income taxes		(2)
Net Earnings	$	(3)
Total Comprehensive Income	$	(3)
Net Earnings per Common Share ($)		
Basic	$	(0.01)
Diluted	$	(0.01)

Consolidated Balance Sheets Increase (Decrease) (millions of Canadian dollars)	As at December 28, 2013		As at December 30, 2012	
Accounts receivable	$	(39)	$	(32)
Inventories		13		11
Deferred Income Tax Assets		8		6
Total Equity Attributable to Shareholders of the Company	$	(18)	$	(15)

Source: Loblaw Companies Limited, 2014 annual financial statements, www.sedar.com, posted 26 February 2015.

ETHICAL ISSUES

Many changes in accounting estimates are disclosed, but many others are not. This is one of the "unknowns" that make financial statement analysis a challenge. Is the company using essentially the same estimates this year as it did in prior years? There is no way of knowing without inside information. Even for the estimates that are disclosed, it can be quite a challenge to sift through all of the changes and make sense of their implications.

This lack of transparency leads to a potential ethical concern. Since estimates underlie virtually every amount in the balance sheet, fairly subtle simultaneous changes in many estimates can have a significant impact on reported earnings. Individual changes may be immaterial, but the cumulative effect of many changes can be quite material.

For example, if a company's senior management wants to increase reported earnings, they may decrease the estimate of uncollectible receivables, prolong depreciation and amortization, take "the benefit of the doubt" about inventory items of dubious salability, use relatively lower estimates of accrued liabilities, and so forth.

The changes wrought by each individual change in estimate may be relatively minor, but if the changes increase EPS by a few cents to meet the company's earnings projections, it is a successful management strategy (although deficient in ethics). Remember that earnings is a residual number; if earnings is 10% of revenue, then changing estimates to reduce total reported expense by 1% will increase earnings by almost 10% when those expense reductions flow through to earnings. Variation in estimates is not trivial.

By definition, all estimates are just that—*estimates*, not known or verifiable amounts. There always is a feasible range of estimates. Managers and accountants should strive to base their judgements on reasonable estimates that do not push at the high or low limits of the feasible range.

Looking Forward

The IASB has no plans to revisit the topic of accounting changes.

Accounting Standards for Private Enterprises

The requirements for all types of accounting changes are essentially similar for ASPE versus IFRS. The ASPE standard has been harmonized with IFRS. However, several differences remain:

- IFRS requires disclosure of new standards that have been issued but not yet effective; the potential effect must be disclosed.

  In contrast, ASPE does not require disclosure of issued but not-yet-effective standards.

  - Like the IFRS standard, ASPE requires that any voluntary change in accounting policy meet the test of being reliable and more relevant. However, several changes in accounting policy are permissible without meeting this test. Examples include:

    _ Accounting for an investment in the shares of another company (where the policies might be consolidation, equity method, fair value, or the cost method, where choices for a given category exist under ASPE);

    – Accounting for development expenses; and

    – Accounting for income tax (where the policies might be taxes payable or future income tax, where choices exist under ASPE).

RELEVANT STANDARDS

CPA Canada Handbook, Part I (IFRS):

- IAS 8, Accounting Policies, Changes in Accounting Estimates and Errors

CPA Canada Handbook, Part II (ASPE):

- Section 1506, Accounting Changes

SUMMARY OF KEY POINTS

1. Changes in accounting *estimates* may be caused by new information or by recent experience that changes previous predictions or perceptions. Changes in accounting estimates must always be applied prospectively.

2. If there is doubt as to whether a change is a change in estimate or a change in policy, it should be assumed to be a change in estimate.

3. Changes in accounting policy may be *mandatory*, caused by a new or revised accounting standard.

4. Changes in accounting policy may be *voluntary*, but only if the change results in information that is both reliable and more relevant.

5. Changes in accounting policy must be accounted for *retrospectively*, with restatement of prior periods if practicable. Statistical series, such as earnings and return on equity, must also be restated to reflect the new policy.

6. If full restatement of prior periods is not practicable, then application should be retrospective as far back as possible, with an adjustment to retained earnings for any earlier cumulative effect of the change.

7. If restatement is impracticable, opening retained earnings for the current period should be adjusted for the cumulative effect of the policy change, if possible, and the effect of the change should be accounted for *prospectively* in the current period and future periods.

8. Some new or revised accounting standards permit early adoption. When early adoption is permitted, the IASB *may* permit prospective application for specific standards.

9. On occasion, a company discovers that there was an accounting error in a prior period. If the error was material, the error must be corrected in the comparative figures, even if it has self-corrected over the long run. If it is impracticable to restate, the error must be corrected prospectively.

10. Accounting changes do not typically affect underlying cash flows, but they can affect the amounts presented on prior years' statement of cash flows by changing the section in which the cash flows are reported.

11. Information must be disclosed to allow users to understand (1) the justification for an accounting change and (2) the effect of the accounting change.

Key Terms

change in accounting estimate

change in accounting policy

early adoption

impracticable

mandatory changes

prior-period errors

prospective application

retrospective application

retrospective restatement

voluntary changes

Review Problem 21-1

Each of the following situations is independent:

1. *Change in estimated useful life and residual value.* Phelps Co. purchases equipment on 1 January 20X6 for $36,000. The company uses the straight-line method of depreciation, taking a full year's depreciation in the year of acquisition. The equipment has an estimated residual value of $6,000 and an estimated useful life of three years. In 20X7, Phelps decides that the machine really has an original total life of four years and a residual value of $5,000.

   ### Required:

   How much is depreciation expense for 20X7?

2. *Retrospective change in accounting policy.* Rhein Inc. (a private enterprise) changes its method of accounting for long-term construction contracts from the percentage-of-completion method (PC) to the completed-contract method (CC) in 20X7. The years affected by the change, and incomes under both methods, appear below (ignore income tax):

Year	PC	CC
20X5	$400	$200
20X6	300	150
20X7	500	800

   ### Required:

   If the financial statements for 20X6 and 20X7 are shown comparatively, what is the amount of the accounting policy adjustment to the 1 January balance of retained earnings for 20X6 and 20X7?

3. *Error correction and retrospective adjustment.* Helms Ltd. purchases a delivery truck for $14,000 on 1 January 20X6. Helms expects to use the truck for only two years and then sell it for $4,000. The accountant is instructed to use straight-line depreciation with a full year of depreciation taken in the first year, but neglects to record any depreciation in 20X6. Rather, the accountant charges the entire cost to delivery expense in 20X6. The company's controller discovers the error late in 20X7.

   ### Required:

   Provide the 20X7 entries to record depreciation and the error correction, and indicate the amounts of the cumulative retrospective adjustment to opening retained earnings appearing in the 20X6 and 20X7 comparative retained earnings statements. Ignore income tax.

4. *Error correction, retrospective adjustment, and comparative statements.* On 1 July 20X7, a full year's insurance of $2,400, covering the period from 1 July 20X7 through 30 June 20X8, was paid and debited to insurance expense. Assume:

   - The company uses a calendar fiscal year.
   - Retained earnings at 1 January 20X7 is $20,000.
   - No adjusting entry for insurance is made on 31 December 20X7.
   - Reported earnings for 20X7 (in error) is $22,800.
   - Earnings for 20X8 is $30,000 (assuming that the error has not been discovered).

- Earnings for 20X9 is $40,000.
- There is no income tax.

Required:

a. List the effect of the error on relevant accounts, and earnings, in 20X7 and 20X8.

b. Prepare the entry to record the error if it was discovered in 20X7.

c. Prepare the entry to record the error if it was discovered in 20X8, and prepare the 20X7 and 20X8 comparative retained earnings statements. The amount is deemed material.

d. Prepare the entry (if needed) to record the error if discovered in 20X9.

REVIEW PROBLEM 21-1—SOLUTION

1. Book value, 1 January 20X7 = $36,000 − [($36,000 − $6,000) ×1/3] = $26,000

Depreciation for 20X7 = ($26,000 − $5,000) ×1/(4 − 1) = $7,000

2. The impact on the opening retained earnings is the cumulative difference in prior years' earnings under the two methods:

At 1 January 20X6: $200 dr. This is the $200 decline in 20X5 income from $400 under PC to $200 under CC.

At 1 January 20X7: $350 dr. Also a decline in income, for 20X5 and 20X6: ($400 + $300) − ($200 + $150).

3. The purchase should have been debited to equipment, but instead was debited to delivery expense, which has since been closed to retained earnings. Therefore, retained earnings must be reduced (credited) by the difference between the (correct) depreciation expense and the (incorrect) recorded delivery expense. The 20X7 entry to record the error correction is:

Equipment	14,000	
Retained earnings, error correction		9,000
Accumulated depreciation—equipment		5,000

    [20X6 depreciation = ($14,000 − $4,000) ×1/2 = $5,000]

In 20X7, depreciation expense is recorded for that year:

Depreciation expense	5,000	
Accumulated depreciation—equipment		5,000

The opening retained earnings adjustment would be $9,000 for 20X7. There is no adjustment to the opening retained earnings in 20X6, since the equipment did not exist prior to 20X6.

4.   **a.** *Effect of error if not discovered* (− means understated; + means overstated)

Item	20X7	20X8
Insurance expense	+$1,200	−$1,200
Ending prepaid insurance	− 1,200	No effect

Earnings	– 1,200	+ 1,200
Ending retained earnings	– 1,200	now correct

b. *If error discovered in 20X7:*

Prepaid insurance	1,200	
Insurance expense		1,200

c. *If error discovered in 20X8:*

Prepaid insurance	1,200	
Retained earnings, error correction		1,200

A second entry would be made to record 20X8 insurance expense:

Insurance expense	1,200	
Prepaid insurance		1,200

Comparative retained earnings statement:

	20X8	**20X7**
Retained earnings, 1 January, as previously reported	$42,800*	$20,000
Error correction	1,200	0†
Retained earnings, 1 January, restated	44,000	20,000
Earnings	28,800‡	24,000§
Retained earnings, 31 December	$72,800	$44,000

* This balance reflects erroneous 20X7 income: $42,800 = $20,000 + $22,800.

† No year prior to 20X7 was affected by the error.

‡ $30,000 erroneous income – $1,200 (20X8 income was overstated).

§ $22,800 + $1,200.

d. *If error discovered in 20X9:*

No entry is needed because the error has counterbalanced.

CASE 21-1

RICO CORP.

Rico Corp. manufactures exercise equipment for commercial health clubs and home gyms. The company was started 15 years ago, and, after initial start-up difficulties, now has an established reputation as an industry leader in high-quality and versatile exercise equipment. The company is owned by a group of investors who hope to either take the company public in the next five years or be an acquisition target of a larger public company. Accordingly, management is interested in steady growth in accounting income. Lending arrangements require audited financial statements.

It is now the end of the 20X4 fiscal year, and several issues have yet to be resolved. You, Denise LaTour, are a professional accountant with a role in the VP Finance office of Rico. You have been asked to prepare a report for the audit committee on these issues.

Inventory has always been valued using first-in, first-out cost flow assumption. It has been suggested that the company switch to average cost, in order to be comparable to industry norms. The cost of inventory would be 10% lower under average cost than under FIFO at the end of 20X4. It is not clear that the average cost of prior inventory balances could be ascertained.

With respect to accounts receivable, the company has always established an allowance for doubtful accounts, based on an assessment of aged accounts receivable. However, estimates of bad debts have not been accurate in the past. Accordingly, it has been suggested that the company switch to a direct write-off approach, where accounts would be written off only after collection initiatives were exhausted. Prior balances could be recreated, and the reliability of the bad debt expense would increase.

Rico's term financing with its bank involved an up-front fee. This was paid to the bank when the loan was initially negotiated, three years ago. The amount was expensed at that time. Now it has been suggested that the up-front fee should have been deferred as an asset, and expensed over the life of the loan on a straight-line basis. Prior balances could be re-created.

Required:

Assume the role of Denise LaTour and prepare a report dealing with the issues raised.

CASE 21-2

MTC

Philip Roth is just finishing his first week as chief financial officer of MTC. He was recruited from Atkins Consulting to replace the former CFO who had been relieved of his duties when major errors and shortfalls in certain inventory and trading accounts were discovered.

MTC is the current corporate name of an enterprise once known as Midlands Telephone Corp. Midlands had been providing landline telephone service to several central provinces for most of the 20th century and into the 21st century. The company had been reorganized in the early 1980s to separate its regulated telephone service from its more adventurous, nonregulated endeavours. The company had grown to a billion-dollar enterprise with investments in several fields, acquired largely through purchases of other going concerns. The core of MTC's earnings, however, remained in the telephone business.

Early this year, the company lost an appeal to the regulatory agency to protect its base market. The agency had ruled that MTC would no longer have a protected monopoly for landline telephone service in its service region but that other companies (including TV cable companies and wireless companies) could compete for local telephone service. MTC had an enormous asset base, built up over the years to generate the highest possible earnings. As is typical in regulated industries, the company had been permitted to set rates that would enable it to earn a set rate of return on its asset base—the larger the asset base, the higher the earnings. The company capitalized all betterments and replacements, and used the longest possible depreciation periods for its capital assets. With the advent of deregulation, the company would no longer be able to generate such an attractive rate of return on its assets, which raised questions in the financial press about the "overvaluation" of its capital asset base.

This regulatory ruling was only one of several blows that the company had suffered in recent months. A previous loss of protection in the long-distance telephone market had caused MTC's earnings to drop sharply, with the result that MTC had the first loss of its history in its telephone business last year. The loss was expected to be even larger in the current year.

To make matters worse, rumours began to circulate in the financial community that MTC was covering up huge losses in one of its nontelephone divisions, one that manufactured copper wire and electrical switching devices. Copper is a world-traded commodity that has a very volatile price, and most companies that use copper engage in hedging operations to protect themselves. MTC's board of directors hired Atkins Consulting to find out if there was any truth to the rumours, and, unfortunately, there was. Managers and traders in the division had been speculating heavily in copper, and had covered up massive trading losses over the past three years, some of which were hidden in fictitious inventory records. MTC's copper inventory (and other accounts) turned out to be overstated by over $100 million.

The company's employees were also becoming restive. In its latest labour negotiations, just completed last month for the telephone operations, the company had to promise redundancy protection for employees if the company was required to downsize its telephone operations. The company agreed not to lay off any employees with more than 15 years of service, although the company would have the right to place them in a "redundancy pool" to be redeployed anywhere else in the company that they might be useful. Employees who are laid off will be given a severance package amounting to two months' salary plus one month's additional salary for each year of service. The severance would not be given as a lump sum but would be paid to the individual over a one-year period following the departure. Furthermore, the new labour agreement provided that pension benefits for any laid-off employee would automatically vest, even if the employee had not reached the point at which the benefits would normally become vested. The remaining employees would benefit from a significant enhancement of their defined benefit pension plan; employees' benefits would increase by between 10% and 20%, depending on the length of service.

The company had just served notice to the first 1,200 of its employees that they would be laid off, but the board of directors expected that at least 5,000 employees would be laid off over the next two years.

Philip Roth was one of the consultants who uncovered the rogue copper trading. He had been hired as CFO of MTC to "clean up the mess" in the financial reporting and control areas. One of his first responsibilities was to recommend to the audit committee of the board of directors how the company should report the impacts of its recent changes in fortune in its financial statements for the current year. Although the company was only midway through the fiscal year, the board and CEO would have to discuss financial projections in a public forum, particularly with the investment analysts who closely followed the company's performance.

Required:

Assume that you are Philip Roth. Prepare a report to the audit committee.

TECHNICAL REVIEW

■ connect

TR21-1 Change of Policy:

Larry Corp. purchased a capital asset for $150,000 in early 20X3. Management estimated that the asset would have a 10-year life with an estimated residual value of $20,000 and would be depreciated on a straight-line basis with a full year's depreciation in the year of purchase. In 20X5, management decides to change the depreciation method to 10% declining balance. This is a change in policy because the change is motivated by a desire to conform to industry practice. The tax rate is 30%.

Required:

1. Calculate depreciation expense for 20X3–20X5, inclusive, using the old policy and then the new policy.
2. Calculate the effect of the change on opening 20X5, 20X4, and 20X3 retained earnings, if any.

■ connect

TR21-2 Change of Estimate:

Sarto Co. purchased a $350,000 asset on 1 January 20X2. In 20X6, the company changed the total useful life from 20 years to 14 years. The asset was originally expected to be sold for $50,000 at the end of its useful life, but that amount was also changed in 20X6 to $20,000. Sarto applies the straight-line method of depreciation to this asset, and had claimed a full year of depreciation in the year of acquisition.

Required:

Calculate 20X6 depreciation expense.

■ connect

TR21-3 Error Correction:

In 20X7, after the 20X6 annual financial statements had been issued, Marcella Stores Inc. discovered that a significant transposition error had been made in recording the ending inventory for 20X6. The inventory had been recorded as $1,401,000 when it should have been $1,104,000. The average income tax rate is 30%.

Required:

1. Explain how discovery of this error will affect Marcella's comparative financial statements and financial reporting for 20X7.
2. Prepare any journal entries that would be necessary in 20X7 to correct this error.
3. Suppose that the error in the 20X6 ending inventory was not discovered until 20X8. How, if at all, would this change your answers to requirements 1 and 2?

▣ connect

TR21-4 Error Correction:

Tianan Corp. acquired equipment in 20X1 for $200,000. Management instructed the accounting staff to depreciate the equipment on a 20% declining balance rate. In 20X3, as the year-end financial statements are being prepared, the chief accountant discovers that the equipment had been depreciated over the previous two years at 25% instead of 20%. Tianan's income tax rate is 30%.

Required:

1. Calculate the amounts of the adjustments that should be made to opening retained earnings in the comparative statements of changes in equity for each of 20X2 and 20X3.
2. Provide the 20X3 entries to record 20X3 depreciation and to correct the previous years' error.

▣ connect

TR21-5 Accounting Change:

Cleat Corp. changed its policy for accounting for certain staff training costs in 20X5. Previously, the costs were capitalized and amortized straight-line over three years, starting with the year of the expenditure. The new policy is to expense training costs as incurred. A total of $45,000 was spent in 20X3, $0 in 20X4, and $60,000 in 20X5. The 20X5 expense has not yet been recorded, but the $60,000 was capitalized to the intangible asset when the money was spent. The tax rate is 30%.

Required:

1. Is this a change in policy or an error correction? Explain.
2. Calculate the original and revised expense for 20X3–20X5, inclusive.
3. Provide the 20X5 entries to record 20X5 expense and to record the change.

▣ connect

TR21-6 Accounting Change:

New Corp Ltd. has been in operation for five years but only recently has become profitable. In 20X5, the company had significant accumulated tax loss carryforwards of $3,000,000 that were not recorded as assets because probability of use was considered low. In 20X6, management determined that the probability of loss carryforward usage shifted, and it is now probable that the benefit of losses will be realized in the carryforward period. The tax rate is 30%.

Required:

1. Is this a change in policy, an error correction, or a change in estimate? Explain.
2. Provide the 20X6 entry to record the benefit of the loss carryforwards.

■ connect

TR21-7 Change in Policy or Estimate:

North Ltd. purchased a building in 20X5 for $1,200,000. Straight-line depreciation was used, with a useful life of 40 years and a residual value of $200,000. A full year of depreciation was charged in 20X5.

In 20X8, the company decided to switch depreciation methods to declining balance, using a rate of 10%. The tax rate is 30%.

Required:

1. Assume this is a change in estimate, and calculate 20X8 depreciation expense.
2. Assume this is a change in policy, and calculate 20X8 depreciation expense and the cumulative effect of the change on 20X8 opening retained earnings.
3. Under what circumstances would a change in depreciation method be considered a change in estimate?

■ connect

TR21-8 Error Correction:

D Ltd. has an investment with an original cost of $100,000, purchased in 20X1. The investment was accounted for using the cost method in 20X1, 20X2, and 20X3. The investment had a fair value of $120,000 at the end of 20X1, $210,000 at the end of 20X2, and $160,000 at the end of 20X3. It is now the end of 20X4, and the investment has a fair value of $175,000. The company realizes at the end of 20X4 that it should have been accounting for the investment at fair value through other comprehensive income. There is no income tax.

Required:

1. Calculate the amounts of the adjustments that should be made to opening retained earnings in the comparative statements of changes in equity for each of 20X1, 20X2, 20X3, and 20X4.
2. Prepare appropriate 20X4 journal entries for this situation.

■ connect

TR21-9 Accounting Policy Change:

Brockton Ltd. began applying IFRS in 20X8. One of the necessary adjustments was to adjust past inventory records to remove warehousing expenses from the balances of the ending inventories for 20X5, 20X6, and 20X7, and restate earnings. The pre-adjustment inventory balances and the warehousing costs contained therein were as follows:

Year	Balance, 31 December	Warehousing Costs
20X7	$800,000	$ 30,000
20X6	680,000	18,000
20X5	720,000	25,000

Required:

1. Explain the impact this change will have on the company's earnings. Assume an income tax rate of 30%.
2. Prepare the adjusting entry (entries) that Brockton will need to make on its books in 20X8 to reflect the above information.

 connect

TR21-10 Accounting Policy Change:

Plastics Ltd. (PL) had been a public company for the past 15 years. However this year, 20X6, PL's senior management acquired 90% of the shares outstanding in public hands and, as permitted by securities legislation, forced the redemption of the remaining minority shares and took the company private. Management then sought to simplify some of PL's accounting policies for the benefit of its bankers and creditors, with greater transparency regarding cash flows. One of the changes management wished to make was to report product development expense on the basis of costs incurred rather than by capitalizing and amortizing those costs. The company's records contain the following information regarding the deferred development cost account:

Year	Beginning Balance	Costs Incurred	Amortization	Ending Balance
20X5	$35,584	$ 6,000	$8,317	$33,267
20X4	28,480	16,000	8,896	35,584
20X3	25,600	10,000	7,120	28,480
20X2	12,000	20,000	6,400	25,600
20X1	0	15,000	3,000	12,000

Required:

Determine the restatements that PL will need to make to net earnings for each year, 20X1 through 20X5, as well as the necessary 20X6 adjusting entry. PL's income tax rate is 30%.

ASSIGNMENTS

★ A21-1 Overview—Types of Accounting Changes:

Analyze each case and choose a letter code under each category (type and approach) to indicate the preferable accounting for each case.

Type of Change	Accounting Treatment
P = Policy	RFR = Retrospective with full restatement
E = Estimate	RPR = Retrospective with partial restatement
AE = Accounting error	PNR = Prospective with no restatement

(handwritten note: Pf stock Delen Paid Ealing E)

a. A private company changed from the percentage-of-completion method to completed-contract method for all contracts currently in process and for all new contracts. All prior balances can be reconstructed.

b. Changed the measurement method for asset retirement obligations to present value basis instead of undiscounted estimated costs.

c. Changed from FIFO to average cost for inventory to reduce accounting costs. Only the previous year's opening balance can be reconstructed.

d. Changed depreciation method from declining-balance to straight-line to conform with industry practice.

e. Discovered that a $400,000 acquisition of machinery two years ago had been debited to the land account.

f. Changed from cost method to revaluation method for capital assets; prior years' valuations are obtainable.

g. Wrote off development costs accumulated and capitalized in two previous years due to serious doubts about the project's viability.

h. Changed from historical cost to net realizable value for inventory valuation to comply with new accounting standards. The opening balance cannot be reconstructed.

i. Changed residual value of an intangible capital asset to zero based on new economic circumstances.

j. Discovered a transposition error in the previous year's opening inventory: $17,200; should have been $71,200.

 A21-2 Overview—Types of Accounting Changes:

Analyze each case and choose a letter code under each category (type and approach) to indicate the preferable accounting for each case.

Type	Approach
P = Policy	RWR = Retrospective with restatement
E = Estimate	RNR = Retrospective with no restatement
AE = Accounting error	P = Prospective

a. Used the instalment sales method in the past five years; an internal audit revealed that use of this method was intended to delay revenue recognition, even though the customers were highly creditworthy.

b. Incorrectly applied a 20% declining balance rate to equipment acquired three years previously when management had instructed that a 15% rate be used.

c. Changed the method of estimating bad debts accrued from a percentage-of-sales to an aging methodology.

d. Changed inventory cost method to exclude warehousing costs, as required by IFRS.

e. Discovered that a contract with a supplier had become an onerous contract in the previous year but the company had not recognized any associated loss.

f. Recognized an impairment of $1.5 million in a capital asset group. An impairment of $1 million became apparent two years previously but had not been recorded until this year.

g. Began capitalizing development costs because criteria for deferral were met this year for the first time; in the past, future markets had been too uncertain to justify capitalization.

h. Changed the depreciation method for delivery vehicles from straight-line to declining-balance.

i. Changed from straight-line to accelerated depreciation to reflect the company's changing technological environment.

j. Switched from FIFO to average cost for inventory to conform to parent company preferences. Opening balances for the current and previous two years can be reconstructed.

 A21-3 Overview—Types of Accounting Changes:

The following situations all involve a change in accounting. Assume the company is public unless specified otherwise.

a. A private company adopted percentage-of-completion for a long-term construction contract; all prior contracts were short term and used completed contract.

b. Arithmetic error was made in calculating the closing inventory for 20X1; it now is 20X3.

c. A tree farm changed its inventory valuation method from historical cost to net realizable value to comply with the requirements of IAS 41. Past NRVs cannot be determined.

d. Straight-line depreciation for the past three years has been calculated with no deduction for residual value because none was expected; management now believes a residual value of 10% of original cost is appropriate.

e. The unamortized balance of capitalized development costs is deemed worthless as a result of technological changes that occurred in the current year; all further development costs will be expensed.

f. Changed from revenue recognition at cash collection to revenue recognition at point of delivery because of a marked improvement in the creditworthiness of the customer.

g. Straight-line depreciation for the past three years has been calculated with no deduction for residual value because of an oversight.

h. A private company had been using full allocation for income taxes; the company changes to the taxes payable method for the current year.

i. Investment property was reported at fair value in prior years but the measurement method was discovered to be flawed. A more accurate method has been adopted for the current year.

Required:

For each of these situations, briefly explain:

1. The type of accounting change.
2. The appropriate method for reporting the change, including a discussion of how amounts, if any, are determined.
3. The effect of the change on the financial statements, if any.

A21-4 Change in Estimate:

The comparative statements of Nextext Ltd., an outdoor advertising company, showed the following information:

	20X7	20X6
Retained earnings 1 January 20X7	$4,528,000	$ 4,341,000
Earnings	607,000	467,000
Dividends	(300,000)	(280,000)
Retained earnings 31 December 20X7	$4,835,000	$4,528,000

In 20X8, it came to the attention of Nextest's newly hired financial vice-president that management had re-estimated the cost of removing roof-mounted billboards and restoring the roofs at the end of 20X7 but had made no adjustment in that year.

The cost estimates at the end of 20X7 had increased by close to 35%, from $425,000 to $575,000. The average remaining period of time before the roof leases expire (and the decommissioning costs are incurred) was eight years from the end of 20X7. Decommissioning costs (i.e., asset retirement obligations) are discounted at a rate of 6%.

Required:

1. Should the financial results for 20X7 be restated, or should the change in estimate be accounted for prospectively from 20X8? Explain fully.

2. Assume for the purposes of this requirement that 20X7 results should be restated. Prepare the journal entry (or entries) necessary to effect the restatement. Nextext's income tax rate is 32%.

★★ A21-5 Accounting Changes:

Ng Holdings Ltd. had its first audit in 20X4. Its preliminary income figure, before tax, was $786,000. The following items were discovered:

a. Ng issued a bond payable at the beginning of 20X1 and received par value for its $1,000,000 convertible bond. The bond is convertible at the option of the investor. A value of $84,000 should have been assigned to the conversion option and classified in shareholders' equity. Any discount on the bond should be amortized over its 15-year life, straight-line.

b. The company uses the aging method of estimating the required allowance for doubtful accounts. However, the method had been incorrectly applied in 20X4, with the result that the allowance was understated by $26,000 at the end of 20X4.

c. In April 20X4, a building site was swapped for another, similar property. No cash changed hands. The land had a book value of $233,000; the transaction was recorded at the appraised value of the property received, which was $325,000.

d. The company had accumulated tax loss carryforwards amounting to $400,000 at the end of 20X4, after the 20X4 tax returns were filed. None of the future tax benefit of these carryforwards had previously been recognized. In January 20X5, before the 20X4 financial statements were finalized, company managers realized that the loss carryforward would most likely be used in 20X5.

Required:

1. Classify each of the changes described above, and identify the correct accounting treatment.
2. Calculate revised 20X4 earnings. The tax rate is 25%.
3. If a retrospective adjustment to retained earnings is needed, calculate the retrospective adjustment. The tax rate is 25%.

 A21-6 Change in Estimated Useful Life:

Stacey Corp. has been depreciating equipment over a 10-year life on a straight-line basis. The equipment, which cost $24,000, was purchased on 1 January 20X1. It has an estimated residual value of $6,000. On the basis of experience since acquisition, management has decided in 20X5 to depreciate it over a total life of 14 years instead of 10 years, with no change in the estimated residual value. The change is to be effective on 1 January 20X5. The 20X5 financial statements are prepared on a comparative basis; 20X4 and 20X5 incomes before depreciation were $49,800 and $52,800, respectively. Disregard income tax considerations.

Required:

1. Identify the type of accounting change involved, and analyze the effects of the change. Which approach should be used—prospective without restatement, retrospective with partial restatement, or retrospective with full restatement? Explain.
2. Prepare the entry, or entries, to appropriately reflect the change (if any) and 20X5 depreciation in the accounts for 20X5, the year of the change.
3. Show how the accounting change, the equipment, and the related depreciation should be reported on the 20X5 financial statements, including comparative 20X4 results.

 A21-7 Change in Estimate:

Waves Corp., which has a calendar fiscal year, purchased its only depreciable capital asset on 1 January 20X3. Information related to the asset:

Original cost	$700,000
Estimated residual value	83,000
Depreciation method	Declining balance
Depreciation rate	25%

In 20X5, Waves decreased the estimated residual value to $30,000, and increased the depreciation rate to 40%. Both changes are the result of experience with the asset and revised expectations about the pattern of usage.

Additional information:

	20X5	20X4
Revenue	$3,320,000	$2,740,000
Expenses other than depreciation and tax	1,963,000	1,491,000
Gain (loss) from discontinued operations, before tax	55,000	—
Tax rate	30%	30%

Required:

1. Calculate the ending 20X5 balance of accumulated depreciation, and show the 20X5 entry/entries for depreciation.
2. Provide the condensed comparative statement of comprehensive income for 20X5, including disclosures related to the accounting change.

★ **A21-8 Error Correction:**

Dutta Ltd. signed an operating lease on 1 January 20X0. The lease was a 60-year term on a piece of land. The land reverts to the lessor at the end of the lease term. The lease requires annual payments, on each 1 January, of $50,000 for the first 15 years. Annual 1 January payments of $30,000 were required for the second 15 years, 1 January payments of $15,000 for the third 15 years, and 1 January payments of $5,000 for the final 15 years. The lease payments have all been made on schedule but have all been expensed as paid. That is, at the end of 20X4, the 20X0–20X4 rent has been paid and expensed, but the 20X4 books are still open. The lease should have been expensed evenly over the lease term, regardless of the payment scheme.

Required:

1. Provide the entry to correct the error.
2. Determine the amount by which pretax earnings must be adjusted in each prior year when Dutta prepares a five-year summary of financial results.

★ **A21-9 Error Correction:**

In 20X6, Dalia Corp., a calendar fiscal-year company, discovered that depreciation expense was erroneously overstated $52,000 in both 20X4 and 20X5 for financial reporting purposes. Net income in 20X6 is correct. The tax rate is 35%. The error was made only for financial reporting, affecting depreciation and deferred income tax accounts. CCA had been recorded correctly, and thus there will be no change in taxes payable.

Additional information:

	20X6	20X5
Beginning retained earnings	$437,000	$415,000
Earnings (includes error in 20X5)	82,000	92,000
Dividends declared	60,000	70,000

Required:

1. Record the entry in 20X6 to correct the error.
2. Prepare the comparative retained earnings section of the statement of changes in shareholders' equity for 20X5, reflecting the change.

 A21-10 Accounting Changes—Depreciable Assets:

Swift Corp. reports the following situations in 20X6 with respect to its high-tech manufacturing equipment:

a. Machine 1 was acquired at a cost of $1,106,000 in 20X3. The machine was depreciated on a straight-line basis over its expected seven-year life. At the end of 20X6, management decided that this machine should have been depreciated over a total useful life of 11 years. Salvage value, expected to be negligible, has not changed.

b. Machine 2 was acquired at a cost of $620,000 in 20X5. It was being depreciated on a declining-balance method using a rate of 40%. Salvage values were expected to be minimal. In 20X6, management decided that, based on the usage patterns seen to date, units-of-production would be a more appropriate method of depreciation. The machine is used sporadically and suffers from wear and tear only as used (i.e., obsolescence is not much of a factor in the loss of utility). Estimated units-of-production total 150,000, of which 70,000 units were produced in 20X5 and 25,000 units in 20X6.

c. Machine 3 was acquired in 20X3 at a cost of $423,000. Management discovered in 20X6 that the machine was expensed in 20X3, despite the fact that it had a useful life of 9 years, with a 10% salvage value. Straight-line depreciation should have been used for this asset.

For all depreciation methods, the company follows a policy of recording a full year of depreciation charged in the first year, but no depreciation is charged in the year of disposal.

Required:

1. Classify each of the changes described above, and identify the correct accounting treatment.
2. For each machine, calculate 20X6 depreciation.
3. If a retrospective adjustment is needed, calculate the retrospective adjustment in 20X6. The tax rate is 36%.

★★★ A21-11 Policy Change—Resource Exploration Costs:

Gunnard Ltd. was formed in 20X4 and has a 31 December year-end. Gunnard changed from successful efforts (SE) to full costing (FC) for its resource exploration costs in 20X5. SE is still used for tax purposes. The new majority shareholder preferred FC. Under FC, all exploration costs are deferred; under SE, only a portion are deferred. Under both approaches, the deferred cost balance is amortized yearly.

Had FC been used in 20X4, a total of $3,200,000 of costs originally written off under SE would have been capitalized. A total of $4,700,000 of such costs were incurred in 20X5. Gunnard discloses 20X4 and 20X5 results comparatively in its annual financial statements. The tax rate is 30% in both years.

	SE	FC
Amortization of resource development costs:		
20X4	$ 40,000	$ 240,000
20X5	200,000	850,000
Resource development costs expensed:		
20X4	$3,200,000	—
20X5	4,700,000	—

Additional information:

	20X5	20X4
Revenues	$7,100,000	$4,400,000
Expenses other than resource development costs, amortization, and income tax	2,050,000	720,000

Required:

1. Prepare a 20X5 comparative statement of comprehensive income using the old policy, successful efforts.
2. Prepare the 20X5 entry/entries for FC amortization and the accounting change. Assume that no amortization has been recorded by Gunnard to date in 20X5.
3. Prepare the comparative statements of comprehensive income under FC, and include disclosures related to the accounting change.
4. Prepare the comparative retained earnings section of the statement of changes in shareholders' equity for 20X5, reflecting the change.
5. How will the classification of development costs on the statement of cash flows change as a result of the new policy?

Solution

★★ A21-12 Error Correction—Lease:

In early 20X1 Picton Ltd., a public company, entered into a finance lease that required Picton to make $100,000 beginning-of-year payments for six years. The interest rate implicit in the lease was 7%; Picton's IBR was 6%. For accounting purposes, Picton calculated the present value of the lease at 6%, obtaining a value of $521,236. This amount was used in 20X1 and 20X2 to account for the lease liability and for straight-line depreciation of the asset under lease. In 20X3, the chief accountant discovered that the company should have used the lessor's rate implicit in the lease, as required by IFRS.

Required:

1. Determine the amounts relating to the lease that Picton included in its 20X1 and 20X2 SFP and SCI. The lease liability may be stated in total on the SFP; it is not necessary to subdivide the liability into current and long-term portions.
2. Determine the correct amounts that Picton should have reported.
3. Prepare journal entries necessary to retrospectively correct the errors. Assume a 20% income tax rate. The change relates temporary differences and thus deferred tax is affected.

★★ A21-13 Error Correction:

Excerpts from the 31 December financial statements of Tungston Ltd., before any corrections:

	20X7	20X6	20X5
SCI:			
Cost of goods sold	$395,000	$352,600	$338,400
SFP:			
Inventory	$ 17,250	$ 15,450	$ 9,850
Statement of changes in equity; retained earnings:			
Opening retained earnings	$ 165,500	$ 130,400	$105,750
Net income	104,700	45,600	35,150
Dividends	(10,500)	(10,500)	(10,500)
Closing retained earnings	$259,700	$ 165,500	$130,400

After these financial statements were prepared, but before they were issued for 20X7, a routine review revealed a major mathematical error in calculating 20X5 closing inventory. Instead of $9,850, closing inventory should have been $8,050. There is no income tax.

Required:

1. What entry is needed to correct the error in 20X7? Explain.
2. Restate all the above information, as appropriate, to retrospectively correct the error.
3. What disclosure of the error is needed?

 A21-14 Error Correction:

Purple Ltd. reported the following in its 31 December financial statements:

	20X9	20X8	20X7
Income statement			
Depreciation expense			
(for all capital assets)	$ 200,800	$ 183,200	$ 184,800
Balance sheet			
Capital assets (net)	$2,432,400	$2,295,200	$2,010,800
Retained earnings statement			
Opening retained earnings	$ 1,758,400	$ 1,811,600	$ 1,311,600
Net income (loss)	(271,400)	82,400	635,600
Dividends	(135,600)	(135,600)	(135,600)
Closing retained earnings	$ 1,351,400	$ 1,758,400	$ 1,811,600

After the draft 20X9 financial statements were prepared but before they were issued, Purple discovered that a capital asset was incorrectly accounted for in 20X5. A $400,000 capital asset was purchased early in 20X5, and it should have been depreciated on a straight-line basis over eight years with a $80,000 residual value. Instead, it was written off to expense.

The error was made on the books, but the capital asset was accounted for correctly for tax purposes. The tax rate was 25%.

Required:

1. What entry is needed to correct the error in 20X9? The 20X9 books are still open.
2. Restate all the above information, as appropriate, to retrospectively correct the error.
3. Describe the required disclosure of the error.

★★ A21-15 Error Correction—Lease:

On 4 July 20X2, Giovanni Inc. leased computer equipment through the leasing subsidiary of Giovanni's bank. The lease was for five years at $240,000 per year, payable at the beginning of each lease year. Giovanni recorded the initial lease payment as prepaid rent and amortized it to rent expense at the end of each month.

In April 20X4, the controller determined that the lease had been incorrectly reported as an operating lease; it should have been accounted for as a finance lease. The implicit interest rate in the lease was 6%.

Giovanni uses straight-line depreciation for equipment. The company's income tax rate is 25%. The change relates to temporary differences and thus deferred tax is affected.

Required:

1. What effect will this correction have on the financial statements for 20X2 and 20X3? Provide calculations. The lease liability may be stated in total on the SFP; it is not necessary to subdivide the liability into current and long-term portions.
2. Prepare the necessary journal entries to correct lease accounting as of 1 January 20X4.

★ A21-16 Policy Change—Investment:

Catherine Ltd. has an investment with an original cost of $400,000. The investment was accounted for using the cost method in 20X0, 20X1, and 20X2. This year, 20X3, the company must conform to new accounting standards and report the investment at fair value through OCI. Fair values were $390,000, $410,000, and $450,000 at the end of 20X0, 20X1, and 20X2, respectively. The investment had a fair value of $466,000 at the end of 20X3. The change is to be accounted for retrospectively with restatement of the prior-year's statements. The company will record the change in 20X3, and then adjust the investment account to fair value at the end of 20X3.

Note: The change affects the shareholders' equity account, *accumulated other comprehensive income—unrealized holding gains* (a separate component of accumulated other comprehensive income), instead of retained earnings.

Required:

Prepare appropriate journal entries for this situation. The income tax rate is 25%.

★★ A21-17 Retrospective Policy Change:

Armstrong Ltd. has used the average cost (AC) method to determine inventory values since the company was first formed in 20X3. In 20X7, the company decided to switch to the FIFO method, to conform to industry practice. Armstrong will still use average cost for tax purposes. The tax rate is 30%. The following data have been assembled:

	20X3	20X4	20X5	20X6	20X7
Earnings, as reported, after tax	$56,000*	$65,000*	$216,000*	$255,000*	$125,000**
Closing inventory, AC	35,000	45,000	56,000	91,000	116,000
Closing inventory, FIFO	41,000	57,000	52,000	84,000	130,000
Dividends	5,000	7,000	7,000	10,000	14,000

*Using the old policy, average cost

**Using the new policy, FIFO.

Required:

Prepare the comparative retained earnings section of the statement of changes in shareholders' equity for 20X7, reflecting the change in accounting policy.

 A21-18 Inventory Policy Change:

On 1 January 20X5, Teal Ltd. decided to change the inventory costing method used from average cost (AC) to FIFO to conform to industry practice. The annual reporting period ends on 31 December. The average income tax rate is 30%. The following related data were developed:

	AC Basis	FIFO Basis
Beginning inventory, 20X4	$ 6,000	$6,000
Ending inventory		
20X4	8,000	14,000
20X5	8,800	15,200
Earnings		
20X4: AC basis	16,000	
20X5: FIFO basis		16,400
Retained earnings		
20X4 beginning balance	24,000	
Dividends declared and paid		
20X4	12,800	
20X5		14,000

Required:

1. Identify the type of accounting change involved. Which approach should be used—prospective, retrospective without restatement, or retrospective with restatement? Explain.

2. Give the entry to record the effect of the change, assuming the change was made only for accounting purposes, not for income tax purposes.

3. Complete the following schedule:

	FIFO Basis	
	20X5	20X4
Statement of financial position		
Inventory	$	$
Retained earnings		
Statement of comprehensive income		
Earnings and comprehensive income		
Statement of changes in equity—retained earnings section		
Beginning balance, as previously reported		
Cumulative effect of accounting change		
Beginning balance restated		
Earnings		
Dividends declared and paid		
Ending balance		

★★ A21-19 Change in Policy; Error:

TXL Corp. has tentatively computed income before tax as $660,000 for 20X4. Retained earnings at the beginning of 20X4 had a balance of $3,600,000. Dividends of $270,000 were paid during 20X4. There were dividends payable of $60,000 at the end of 20X3 and $90,000 at the end of 20X4. The following information has been provided:

1. The company used FIFO for costing inventory in deriving net income of $660,000. It wishes to change to average cost to be comparable with other companies in the industry. Accordingly, the change in policy should be applied retrospectively. The comparable figures for ending inventory under the two methods are:

December 31	FIFO	Average Cost
20X1	$408,000	$420,000
20X2	450,000	435,000
20X3	480,000	462,000
20X4	486,000	510,000

2. In January 20X3, the company acquired some equipment for $3,000,000. At that time, it estimated the equipment would have an estimated useful life of 12 years and a salvage value of $360,000. In 20X3, the company received a government grant of $480,000, which assisted in purchasing the equipment. The grant was credited to income in error. The company has been depreciating the equipment on a straight-line basis and has already provided for depreciation for 20X4 without considering the government grant. Management realizes that the company must account for the government grant by crediting it directly to the equipment account and recording a lower amount of depreciation over time.

The income tax rate for the company is 30%. Assume that all of the stated items affect deferred income tax.

Required:

1. Prepare a schedule to show the calculation of the correct earnings for 20X4 in accordance with generally accepted accounting principles.
2. Prepare, in good form, the retained earnings section of TXL's statement of changes in equity for the year ended 31 December 20X4. Comparative figures need not be provided.

(Source: [Adapted] © CGA-Canada. Reproduced with permission.)

★★ **A21-20 Change in Accounting for Natural Resources:**

In 20X6, Black Oil Inc. changed its method of accounting for oil exploration costs from the successful efforts method (SE) to full costing (FC) for financial reporting because of a change in corporate reporting objectives. Black Oil has been in the oil exploration business since January 20X3; prior to that, the company was active in oil transportation. Pre-tax earnings under each method:

	SE	FC
20X3	$ 15,000	$ 45,000
20X4	66,000	75,000
20X5	75,000	105,000
20X6	120,000	180,000

Black Oil reports the result of years 20X4 through 20X6 in its 20X6 annual report and has a calendar fiscal year. The tax rate is 30%. The change is made for accounting purposes but not for tax purposes. Thus, the deferred income tax account is changed.

Additional information:

	20X3	20X4	20X5	20X6
Ending retained earnings (SE basis)	$54,000	$69,000	$93,000	n/a
Dividends declared	27,000	31,200	28,500	$36,000

Required:

1. Prepare the entry in 20X6 to record the accounting change. Use "natural resources" as the depletable asset account.
2. Prepare the retained earnings section of the comparative statement of changes in equity. Include three years: 20X6, 20X5, and 20X4.
3. Explain how the accounting policy change would affect the statement of cash flows.

 A21-21 Retrospective Policy Changes:

Linfei Ltd. has a 31 December year-end, and a tax rate of 25%. Management has asked you to respond to the following situations:

1. The company has always used the FIFO method of determining inventory costs; starting in 20X7, it will now use average cost. Opening and closing inventories for 20X7 under FIFO are $531,000 and $660,000, respectively. Opening and closing inventories under average cost are $420,000 and $520,000, respectively. Provide the journal entry to record the change.
2. Return to requirement 1. Additional information is as follows:

   - In 20X7, opening retained earnings was $873,000. Net income, before any adjustment due to the change in inventory method, was $320,000. Dividends were $47,000.
   - In 20X6, opening retained earnings was $802,000, net income was $113,000, and dividends were $42,000.
   - For 20X6, opening inventory was $480,000 under FIFO and $400,000 under average cost.

   Prepare a comparative retained earnings section of the statement of changes in equity, giving retrospective effect to the change in accounting policy.
3. Return to your retained earnings statement in requirement 2. Prepare a comparative retained earnings statement assuming that comparative balances could not be restated; that is, the only information you have to work with, in addition to the income, retained earnings, and dividend information, is that provided about opening and closing inventory balances in requirement 1.
4. An asset was acquired in 20X4 at a cost of $80,000. The salvage value of $8,000 was estimated. The asset has been depreciated on the declining-balance method at a rate of 20% in each of 20X4, 20X5, and 20X6. On 1 October of this year, 20X7, management decided to change depreciation methods and will now use the straight-line method. This change is made on the basis of usage information that indicates that the asset is used about the same amount in each year of life. The new estimates are a *total* life of 11 years and a salvage value of $5,000. Depreciation expense has not yet been recorded for 20X7. Provide the appropriate journal entry/entries.

★★★ **A21-22 Accounting Changes, Comprehensive:**

EC Construction Ltd. (EC) has 100,000 common shares outstanding in public hands. The balance of retained earnings at the beginning of 20X7 was $2,400,000. On 15 December 20X7 EC declared dividends of $3 per share payable on 5 January 20X8. Income before income tax was $600,000 based on the records of the company's accountant.

Additional information on selected transactions/events is provided below:

a. At the beginning of 20X6, EC purchased some equipment for $230,000 (salvage value of $30,000) that had a useful life of five years. The accountant used a 40% declining-balance method of depreciation but mistakenly deducted the salvage value in calculating depreciation expense in 20X6 and 20X7.

b. As a result of an income tax audit of 20X5 taxable income, $74,000 of expenses claimed as deductible expenses for tax purposes was disallowed by the CRA. This error cost the company $29,600 in additional tax. This amount was paid in 20X7 but has been debited to a prepaid expense account.

c. EC contracted to build an office building for RD Corp. The construction began in 20X6 and will be completed in 20X8. The contract has a price of $30 million. The following data (in millions of dollars) relate to the construction period to date:

	20X6	20X7
Costs incurred to date	$ 8	$13
Estimated costs to complete	12	7
Progress billings during the year	6	10
Cash collected on billings during the year	5	8

The accountant used the completed-contract method in accounting for this contract, which is not permitted for a public company.

d. On 1 January 20X7, EC purchased, as a long-term investment, 19% of the common shares of One Ltd. for $50,000. On that date, the fair value of identifiable assets of One was $220,000 and was equal to the book value of identifiable assets. Goodwill has not been impaired. No investment income has been recorded. One paid no dividends, but reported income of $25,000 in the year. EC has significant influence over One.

e. EC has an effective tax rate of 25%.

Required:

1. Calculate 20X7 earnings for EC.
2. Prepare the retained earnings section of the comparative statement of changes in equity. Comparative numbers need not be shown.

A21-23 ASPE—Change from IFRS to ASPE:

Wuhan Corp. is a Vancouver-based company that engages in a large volume of international activities. The company had a largely independent wholly owned subsidiary in Hong Kong. Wuhan had been publicly traded on the TSX-V until mid-20X6, when a wealthy Vancouver tycoon purchased all of Wuhan's outstanding shares through his private investment company. As Wuhan is no longer public but still needs to be audited, management decided to change its financial reporting from IFRS to Canadian ASPE effective in 20X6. Selected financial information (as reported under IFRS) is shown below (in thousands of Canadian dollars):

	20X3	20X4	20X5
Balances, 31 December:			
Retained earnings	$44,000	$45,000	$41,000
Deferred income tax liability	11,000	8,000	9,000
OCI—accumulated translation gain (loss)	5,300	6,800	4,800
OCI—accumulated pension remeasurement gain (loss)	(8,000)	(11,000)	(9,600)
Year's translation gain (loss) on subsidiary (OCI)	(2,700)	1,500	(2,000)
Year's actuarial gain (loss) on defined benefit pensions (OCI)	(1,500)	(3,000)	1,400
Earnings for the year	7,000	7,500	2,000
Dividends declared and paid during the year	5,000	5,000	6,000

Wuhan's management, with the consent of the new owner, has elected to change to the taxes payable method.

Required:

1. Explain the impacts that the change to ASPE will have on Wuhan's restated comparative financial statements for 20X4 and 20X5.
2. Calculate the restated earnings for 20X4 and 20X5.

 A21-24 ASPE—Rationale for Accounting Changes:

Arctic Charm Corp. is a privately owned Canadian company. The company experienced poor operating results in the years 20X0 to 20X3, and, in 20X3, it reorganized and refinanced its operations. Creditors were asked to accept partial payment; shareholders invested additional capital. As part of the restructuring, Arctic Charm accepted covenants imposed by Spenser Venture Capital Corp. Violation of these debt covenants would trigger a demand for immediate repayment of long-term debt and almost certainly mean that the company would be placed in receivership or bankruptcy. The covenants included minimum working capital requirements, and an upper limit on the overall debt-to-equity ratio.

The 20X4 pretax operating results were acceptable. The company wishes to make the following two accounting changes before issuing its financial statements for 20X4:

a. Change from comprehensive tax allocation to the taxes payable method.

b. Change depreciation policies from declining-balance to straight-line. Capital assets are fairly new but have been depreciated for three to five years under declining-balance rates. The company would adjust all capital asset balances to the amounts that would have existed had straight-line depreciation always been used. The company believes that straight-line depreciation is more indicative of the equipment's actual usage. The equipment is not subject to rapid technological obsolescence.

Arctic Charm's CFO met with officials from Spenser to obtain their consent to these changes. The officials accepted Arctic Charm's proposed changes as being in compliance with ASPE as required by the loan agreement.

Required:

Describe the impact of these changes on the financial statements and debt covenants. Consider the appropriateness of these changes in your response.

 A21-25 ASPE—Accounting Changes, Inventory, and Revenue:

Late in 20X6, the management of Richter Minerals Inc., a Canadian private company, decided to change the company's inventory valuation method and, concurrently, its revenue recognition method. Historically, the company had used an average cost basis for all inventories and had recognized revenue when minerals were shipped to customers. Now, effective with the year beginning 1 January 20X7, Richter will recognize revenue when the minerals have been refined and are ready for sale, at which point the inventory will be adjusted to net realizable value at the end of each reporting period. Richter's minerals are easily sold at any time on the world market via electronic trading. Richter's shareholders and principal lenders have approved the change in policy.

At the end of 20X6, Richter had inventory (at cost of production) totalling $70 million. Of that total, $20 million was of unrefined ore, and $50 million was refined minerals. At NRV, Richter's refined minerals inventory was $72 million. The 20X6 opening inventory contained refined minerals of $44 million at cost; using market price indices, Richter's management was able to determine that the 20X6 opening inventory was worth $60 million at NRV. Richter's 20X6 sales revenue was $250 million.

During 20X7, Richter recognized revenue of $360 million, on the new reporting basis. Ending inventory of refined minerals amounted to $82 million; production cost was $55 million.

The income tax rate was 25% in both years.

Required:

1. How much will this change affect the previously reported net income for 20X6?

2. Can this change be applied retrospectively with restatement? Explain the difficulties that management might encounter when restating years prior to 20X6.

3. Prepare any journal entries that are necessary to record the change in accounting policies.

 **A21-26 ASPE—Change Regarding Construction Contracts:**

KLB Corp., a private company, has used the completed-contract method to account for its long-term construction contracts since its inception in 20X3. On 1 January 20X7, management decided to change to the percentage-of-completion method to better reflect operating activities and conform to industry norms. Completed contract was used for income tax purposes and will continue to be used for income tax purposes in the future. The income tax rate is 25%. The following information has been assembled:

Year Ended 31 December	20X3	20X4	20X5	20X6	20X7
Net income, as reported	$100,000	$120,000	$150,000	$140,000	160,000*
CC income, included in above	0	60,000	0	120,000	0
PC income, as calculated	40,000	65,000	50,000	40,000	75,000
Opening retained earnings	0	90,000	190,000	320,000	440,000
Dividends	10,000	20,000	20,000	20,000	20,000
Closing retained earnings	90,000	190,000	320,000	440,000	580,000

*Includes PC income, not CC income, in earnings.

Required:

1. Identify the type of accounting change involved. Which approach should be used—retrospective with full restatement, retrospective with limited restatement, or prospective without restatement? Explain.

2. Give the entry to appropriately reflect the accounting change in 20X7, the year of the change.

3. Restate the 20X7 retained earnings section of the statement of changes in equity, including the 20X6 comparative figures.

4. Assume that only the opening balance in 20X7 can be restated and that the cumulative effect cannot be allocated to individual years. Recast the 20X7 comparative retained earnings section of the statements of changes in equity accordingly.

5. Assume that no balances can be restated. Should the change be made in 20X7? Explain.

Source: (Globe and money) © Vstock LLC/Getty Images RF; (Skyscrapers) © Arpad Benedek/Getty Images RF; (Canadian flag) © BjArn Kindler/Getty Images RF; (Tablet, pen, keyboard) © John Lamb/Getty Images RF.

CHAPTER 22

Financial Statement Analysis

INTRODUCTION

Between 2012 and 2013, Air Canada increased revenue by 2%, while net earnings increased by 101%; from a loss of $136 million to a net profit of $10 million. Between 2013 and 2014, revenue increased by 7.2% and net earnings by 950%! That sounds really impressive, but the percentages depend partially on the starting point—the denominator. What happened? Well, we can make some guesses—the company's revenues are mainly in Canadian dollars while its aircraft purchases, aircraft lease payments, and fuel costs are all in U.S. dollars. On the financing side, Air Canada has long-term debt, denominated in both Canadian and U.S. dollars, to finance its assets. Changing fuel prices, exchange rates, and interest rates can add a lot of volatility to the company's net profits.

If you were a major lender to Air Canada, or an investor, how would you go about analyzing the company's asset and liability structure, its earnings performance, its return on assets and equity, and its ability to service its debt load? If you were an employee representative, how would you appraise a company's ability to increase wages or to meet pension funding obligations?

Financial statement analysis is a broad and complex field. Entire books (and whole university courses) are devoted to financial statement analysis. In this chapter, we touch only on the more general aspects of financial analysis. Any aspiring accountant should understand how to take financial statements apart and analyze their significance.

The emphasis in the chapter is on basic analytical techniques. However, it often is necessary to recast a company's financial statements in order to make them more useful for the analyst's specific needs. The appendix to this chapter contains an example of recasting. The example has been adapted from a real company (although disguised).

OVERVIEW OF STATEMENT ANALYSIS

Financial statement analysis can be broken down into the following steps:

1. *Determine why the analysis is being done and clarify the decision focus.* What questions does the analyst hope to answer by completing the analysis? A lender will have concerns different from an equity investor or supplier.

2. *Gather all available data.* This would include not only the most recent financial statements but also information on the company's business, its industry and competitors, and the economy. A complete analysis may be done only with an understanding of the environment within which the company conducts business.

3. *Apply the appropriate analytical techniques.* There is a large variety of ratios and other analytical tools to use; given the decision being made and the context, the "right" analytical tools must be chosen.

4. *Analyze and interpret the results.* This is the most important step of any financial statement analysis. It is easy to perform the calculations; it is much more difficult to understand how the results will impact the decisions being made.

We will now look at each of these steps in some detail.

Clarify the Decision Focus

The starting point is to be clear about the decision to be made as a result of the financial statement analysis. A sample of possible decisions includes:

1. Equity investment decisions;
2. Lending decisions;
3. Contractual decisions, such as accepting employment, negotiating collective agreements, or entering into a joint venture; and
4. Regulatory decisions, including the need for rate or price increases, or the impact of past regulatory decisions.

Each of these decisions will require a different approach to the analysis and a different set of priorities. For example, a prospective investor in common shares will be concerned primarily with the long-term profitability of the company while a trade creditor will be primarily interested in short-term liquidity. This difference in emphasis is illustrated by the fact that many creditors will continue to extend credit to a company with declining profitability in which no rational investor would buy shares.

There also is a difference between looking at a company as a new, prospective stakeholder or as an existing stakeholder who needs to decide whether to continue the relationship or to bail out. A prospective stakeholder (e.g., an investor, creditor, or contractor) is concerned about the future safety and profitability of a contemplated investment or contract. In contrast, an existing stakeholder is concerned with the financial and/or operational ramifications of terminating an existing investment or contract.

Therefore, it is crucial to know the nature of the decision in question.

This chapter describes several different techniques for analysis, but most of the discussion is devoted to traditional ratio analysis. It is possible to compute dozens of financial statement ratios, but an analyst should first determine what decisions need to be made and then select the relevant ratios that will assist with this assessment.

Gather the Data

Different types of data will be required to prepare and analyze ratios. The company's financial statements and notes are only the starting point. An analyst must also obtain an understanding of the company and the industry in which the company operates. Information that the analyst requires about the company itself might include:

• The mix of products and services sold;
• The geographic areas in which the company sells its products/services;
• Assets that are leased versus owned;
• Businesses acquired in the past few years;
• The company's strategy for growth; and
• Major shareholders.

The above information is vital to understanding profitability and efficiency ratios discussed later in the chapter.

The Environment

Company analysis must always be a forward-looking process interpreted within a broader context of:

- The general economic environment;
- The economic and competitive climate of the country or region in which the company operates; and
- The structure and outlook of the industry in which the company competes.

The company's financial outlook must be assessed in respect of the future trends of the industry and how competitors will react. Investors will also need to evaluate the market price of the company's shares. For lenders, the company's future must be evaluated with respect to its ability to service its debt without straining its current operations and its competitiveness.

We will give examples of how the environment impacts specific ratios later in the chapter.

The Financial Statements

The most important piece of data is the financial statements, including the notes, auditor's report, and other additional information. However, before the statements can be used for calculating ratios, the analyst should review the accounting policies used, in conjunction with the auditor's report, to ensure the statements are in a format that is useful. Later in this chapter, we look at examples of recasting that might be required to make the statements more useful for analysis.

Examine the Auditor's Report

A public company must have an unqualified audit opinion to be traded on major stock exchanges. In cases where a private company has used non-GAAP accounting policies, the auditor will have to qualify their opinion. A qualification in an **auditor's report** should not *necessarily* be cause for concern. A company may choose to use accounting policies that are more in accordance with the interests of the primary users than IFRS or ASPE would be.

Normally, an auditor will attempt to quantify the impact (i.e., on net income) of a deviation from GAAP and will either report the impact in the auditor's report or refer the reader to a financial statement note that discusses the deviation.

If a private company does not have an audit, a public accountant may nevertheless be retained for a **review engagement**, in which a full audit is not performed but a review of the financial statements for general consistency with GAAP (or with a disclosed basis of accounting) and for appropriate presentation is completed. Banks often rely on these review engagement reports as assurance that the company's accounting practices are worthy of belief and that the financial statements are therefore plausible.

Examine Accounting Policies

We have stressed throughout this book that managers' accounting policy choices are governed by the objectives of financial reporting in the particular circumstance.

The financial reporting objectives adopted by a company may not correspond with a specific user's preferred objectives. Therefore, the first task of an analyst is to determine the reporting objectives that are implicit in the financial statements. If the implicit objectives do not correspond with the user's objectives, then adjustments to the financial statements will probably be needed before they are of maximum use. Discerning the implicit objectives often is easier said than done.

Notes to Financial Statements

To the extent that they exist, most of the clues to the implicit reporting objectives can be found in the notes to the financial statements.

The first note to financial statements is the accounting policy note in which the company describes the GAAP that is being followed and its accounting policy choices. In Canada, it will be important for the analyst to know which GAAP has been used: IFRS, ASPE, or Accounting Standards for Not-for-profit Organizations (*Part III* of the *CPA Canada Handbook*) or accounting standards for the public sector (used by universities, governments, etc.)

An analyst looks in the notes to gain an understanding of how assets, liabilities, revenue, and expenses have been recognized. Exhibit 22-1 highlights examples of the type of information that an analyst would look for in reviewing the notes for each of the related statements.

EXHIBIT 22-1		

INFORMATION TO GATHER FROM THE NOTES

Statement of Comprehensive Income	Statement of Financial Position	Statement of Cash Flows
What type of revenue recognition policy is being used: one that recognizes revenue early or more on a deferred basis?	What inventory costing policies are being used: FIFO, average cost?	If earnings (with depreciation/amortization added back) are significantly and repeatedly larger than operating cash flows, the company may be maximizing net income.
Are costs immediately expensed or capitalized and amortized in later periods?	Are accounts receivables securitized? Should the securitization be shown on the SFP as a form of financing?	If operating cash flow is significantly larger than earnings, the company may be very conservative in its accounting practices, reporting minimum net earnings (e.g., by anticipating future expenditures through current provisions), or may be trying to minimize its current tax bill.
Is revenue being deferred but all operating costs being expensed as incurred? (Note that this might b done to achieve income minimization.)	What models are used for long-term assets—cost, fair value, or the revaluation model?	Does the cash flow from operations exclude important operating expenses (e.g., development costs) that management has capitalized and shifted to the investing section?
Are there any nonrecurring gains included in operating revenues?	What depreciation/ amortization policies are used for the long-term assets?	How much of the investing cash flow is for replacement to maintain the level of current operations versus growth expenditures for expanding operations?
What is the extent of nonrecurring losses and where are these reported?	Are there significant off-balance sheet assets and liabilities due to operating leases being used?	

Recast the Financial Statements

Based on the results of her review of the company's financial statements and notes, an analyst may need to recast the financial statements to suit her needs before applying analytical approaches. Examples of situations that suggest a needed restatement include:

- The SCI is revised to remove nonrecurring gains and losses.
- The SCI and SFP are revised to remove the effects of deferred income tax liabilities and assets.
- The SCI and SFP are revised to reflect a different policy on capitalization of certain costs:
  - Capitalized costs are shifted to the SCI in the year they occurred and depreciation/amortization is removed; or
  - Expenditures charged directly to the SCI are removed and capitalized instead with depreciation/amortization added.
- Loans to and from shareholders are reclassified as shareholders' equity.
- The securitization of accounts receivable is classified as debt on the SFP rather than as a sale of receivables (see Chapter 7).
- The estimated present value of assets under operating leases is added to property, plant, and equipment, and to liabilities to "put back on the balance sheet" the assets being used and the related obligations. (See Chapter 18.)

In recasting the statement to reflect different accounting policies, it is important to remember to adjust for both sides of the transactions. For example, deleting deferred income tax expense must be accompanied by adding the balance of the deferred income tax liability to retained earnings and not by simply *ignoring* the balance.

An illustration of recasting financial statements is presented in the Appendix to this chapter.

Apply the Appropriate Techniques

Once the focus of the analyst's decision is clarified and the data has been gathered, the analyst then selects the appropriate ratios to use for her review. The key word here is "appropriate." As there are a large number of analytical tools to choose from, the analyst should select only those that will aid in her decision. Many ratios overlap in the input data and results. In this chapter, we have selected some of the more common analytical tools that are used in practice. There are many more ratios that analysts use, some of which are specific to certain industries. For example, in the retail industry, sales-per-square-foot is a key ratio that is used to assess how effectively and efficiently retail floor space is used. Later in the chapter, we will see how the techniques are applied.

Analyze and Interpret the Results

Ratios do not give answers; they give clues about what is going on in the company. Analysts take these clues and make conclusions by putting together their knowledge of the company, the industry, and their experience. But ratios are useless unless they can be compared with something else. Below, we examine comparisons that can be made along with some precautions to be taken.

Comparative Information

There are two bases for comparison: (1) cross-sectional and (2) longitudinal.

Cross-sectional comparison analyzes a company in relation to other companies in the same year. Comparisons of this type frequently appear in business articles that compare the recent performance of one company with its competitors. Cross-sectional comparison is very useful, but caution must be exercised that similar measurements (i.e., ratios) are being used. If the comparison companies used significantly different accounting policies then no comparison can be valid unless the companies have all been adjusted to reflect similar accounting policies. Comparison of the return on assets for a company that owns all of its capital assets with one that uses operating leases for its capital assets will be invalid. Similar business models are also important for a proper comparison.

For example, in the grocery retail industry, some companies operate a franchise model, while others own their retail outlets directly. Let us look at an example. Company A operates a franchise model. All of its retail outlets are operated by franchisees who are independent entrepreneurs. Company A, the franchisor, sells product to the franchisees and owns large distribution centres from which the inventory is shipped. Revenue consists of franchise fees and sales of product to the franchisees. In this situation, the sales are all credit sales with terms requiring payment within 21 days. Inventory is held for fewer than 5 days in the distribution centres before it is shipped to the stores. In comparison, Company B operates a business model where it owns all of its own retail outlets. Revenue represents sales to the end consumers with no credit terms available. Inventory consists of product that is in distribution centres and in the stores. Although inventory is held for fewer than 5 days in the distribution centre, it has an average holding period of 18 days in the stores.

Given these operating policies, Company A and Company B will have different ratios for days in inventory and days in receivable. An analyst who did not properly gather data on these companies and did not understand these differences in the business models would end up making incorrect conclusions when comparing these ratios. In addition, ratios such as return on assets and debt to assets will differ between the two companies depending on the nature of assets owned or leased.

Longitudinal comparisons look at a company over time, comparing this year's performance with earlier years. A comparison is often made to other companies or to general economic returns during the same time span. Care must be taken that the company has not changed significantly in the past few years. Consider a company that has made several acquisitions or has changed its strategy and product mix. In these situations, year-over-year comparisons would not be relevant or helpful.

Some databases facilitate both types of comparison on an industry basis. These industry comparisons can be helpful but must be used with a great deal of caution. Industry statistics are constructed without attention to underlying reporting, accounting policy, or business model differences, and therefore it seldom is clear whether the comparisons are truly valid. In addition, it is tempting to decide that one company is a good investment because its profitability ratios are better than its competitors. It may well be, however, that the entire industry is sick, and that the company being analyzed is perhaps less sick.

Remember, ratio analysis can be useful, but can also be very misleading if inappropriate comparisons are made.

Other Limitations to Ratio Analysis

Other than choosing the right "comparables" and ensuring consistent accounting policies, there are other limitations for ratio analysis:

- *Universality.* Ratios with the same name can be calculated using different inputs. For example, some analysts calculate a debt to equity ratio using only market values, not book values. Others may use only interest-bearing long-term debt, while others may use total liabilities. There is no "right" calculation. The analyst will choose the inputs she wishes to use based on the information she is trying to obtain. The caution here is for the analyst to determine her own ratios and not rely on the calculations performed by others.

- *Size.* Ratios calculate relationships between one number and another and by definition remove the effect of size. For example, take two companies that manufacture the same product. Company A has sales of $500 million and gross profit of $175 million resulting in a gross profit margin of 35% ($175/$500). Company B has sales of only $7,000,000, and gross profit of $2,100,000, with a gross profit margin of 30% ($2,100/$7,000). Although Company A is more than 70 times larger than Company B, we still do the comparison. The key question here is, could Company A have a better gross profit margin simply because it is larger? The answer is maybe. If there are economies of scale and Company A can purchase inputs cheaper (e.g., due to volume discounts) and have lower unit manufacturing costs, then size does matter. In comparing these companies, the impact of size would be considered.

There are also some potential drawbacks to using ratios:

- Ratios are meaningful only if there is a clear understanding of the purpose of each relationship.
- Ratios are only as valid as the data from which they are derived.
- Ratios require a basis for comparison.
- Ratios are a clue to areas needing investigation—they rarely, if ever, supply answers.

Throughout this book, we have emphasized that different accounting policy decisions and different accounting estimates can yield dramatically different reported results. If the basic financial data are subject to variability, then ratios calculated from that data are unreliable.

Indeed, managers may deliberately select accounting policies and estimates with the intent of affecting certain ratios; we have repeatedly referred to this motivation throughout the book. For example, the decision to lease major operating assets through an operating lease rather than a finance lease often is motivated by management's desire to keep the implicit debt off the balance sheet. In using ratios, therefore, the rule most certainly must be, *analyst be wary*!

We are now ready to look at how ratios are calculated and used in practice.

RATIO ANALYSIS

Once the statements have been adjusted to suit the needs of the analyst (i.e., to facilitate making the decision at hand), the statements may be subject to numerical analysis or "number crunching." The basic tool of numerical analysis is ratios. A ratio is simply one number divided by another. Given the amount of numbers in a set of financial statements, especially over a series of years, an incredible number of ratios could be computed. The trick to avoiding overwork (and total confusion) is to identify which ratios have meaning for the analyst's purpose, and then focus just on those few instead of computing every possible ratio.

To demonstrate how these analytical techniques are applied and analyzed, we will be examining the same set of financial statements throughout the chapter. Exhibit 22-2 provides the statement of financial position and the statement of comprehensive income for our company, Grocery Retailer Inc. (GRI). GRI operates across Canada and has 630 owned retail outlets with total sales of $13 billion. It competes in the grocery retail sector, and competitors include smaller, locally owned stores, similar size domestic competitors, and larger global competitors. Some competitors use a franchise approach; others corporately own their retail outlets; and some even have a mix of both types of operating strategies. Since food is a staple product and the industry is mature, sales are constant, with low year-over-year growth rates due to inflation. Intense competition and changing customer preferences play a large role in companies gaining or losing market share. In this type of industry, growth primarily comes from acquisitions. Costs are impacted by fuel prices, labour relations, regulatory requirements, and logistics. During 20X6, GRI acquired another company that retails specialty products to a new customer group. The bulk of the acquisition price was for property, plant, equipment, and intangible assets. GRI also owns investment property that is accounted for using the fair-value model. Rental income and related costs were immaterial and included in revenue for the year.

EXHIBIT 22-2			
GROCERY RETAILER INC. FINANCIAL STATEMENTS			
Statement of Comprehensive Income for Years Ended 31 December, 20X6, 20X5, and 20X4			
(in millions of dollars)			
	20X6 $	20X5 $	20X4 $
Sales	13,000	12,400	12,230
Cost of goods sold	10,400	10,150	10,020
Gross profit	2,600	2,250	2,210
Expenses			
Electricity and natural gas	120	110	110
Rent, taxes, and occupancy costs	270	250	240
Wages and benefits	710	645	690
Depreciation and amortization	260	260	270
Change in fair value of investment properties	10	5	—
Other	280	260	300
Total expenses	1,650	1,530	1,610

	20X6 $	20X5 $	20X4 $
Operating income	950	720	600
Finance costs	120	130	150
Earnings before income taxes	830	590	450
Income taxes	210	150	130
Net earnings	620	440	320
Other comprehensive income			
Actuarial gains (losses)	(70)	(40)	20
Comprehensive income	550	400	340

Statement of Financial Position as at December 31, 20X6, 20X5, and 20X4

(in millions of dollars)

	20X6 $	20X5 $	20X4 $
ASSETS			
Current assets			
Cash and cash equivalents	70	100	90
Accounts receivable	350	300	320
Inventories	1,050	720	760
Prepaid expenses	10	10	10
	1,480	1,130	1,180
Noncurrent assets			
Property, plant and equipment	4,150	3,370	3,450
Investment properties	50	30	10
Intangible assets	1,250	650	670
Goodwill	900	700	700
Total assets	7,830	5,880	6,010

	20X6 $	20X5 $	20X4 $
LIABILITIES AND EQUITY			
Current liabilities			
Bank loans	340	380	400
Accounts payable and accrued liabilities	1,400	1,100	980
Provisions	230	20	30
Current portion of long term debt	280	280	280
	2,250	1,780	1,690
Noncurrent liabilities			
Long term debt	2,700	1,750	1,850
Defined benefit liabilities	150	120	130
Deferred taxes	130	110	80
Other liabilities	120	10	10
	5,350	3,770	3,760
Equity			
Common shares	680	680	980
Retained earnings	1,970	1,530	1,390
Accumulated other comprehensive income	(170)	(100)	(120)
Total shareholders' equity	2,480	2,110	2,250
Total liabilities and equity	7,830	5,880	6,010

Note 1—Dividends of $180 million were paid each year.

Note 2—During 2015, there was a direct transfer from AOCI to retained earnings of $60 million, reducing retained earnings. In addition, due to the repurchase of shares, there was a reduction in the retained earnings of $60 million.

Note 3—Finance costs for 2016 includes interest on short-term debt of $15 million and interest on long-term debt of $105 million. For 2015, interest on short-term debt and long-term debt was $17 million and $113 million, respectively.

Note 4—The income tax rate for 2016 and 2015 was 25.3% and 25.4% respectively.

Note 5—The cash flow from operations was $1,010 million and $870 million for 2016 and 2015, respectively.

Common-Size Analysis

Common-size analysis or *vertical analysis* takes each item on a financial statement and computes it as a percentage of a fixed base. On the SFP, the base is usually total assets. On the SCI, each line item would be calculated as a percentage of net sales. Vertical analysis is the simplest of a broader set of techniques known as *decomposition analysis*; the more complex approaches to decomposition analysis will not be discussed in this text.

Vertical (common-size) analysis is useful for seeing the relative composition of the SFP or SCI. Analysts sometimes use these numbers for comparisons with industry norms or other competitors. For example, an analyst may want to compare the *gross margin* of one company with another by comparing the relative proportion of sales that is consumed by cost of goods sold. Similarly, an analyst may look at common-size numbers to see if a company's inventory is too large, in comparison with total assets, relative to others in the industry.

Managers sometimes are sensitive to the uses that analysts make of vertical analysis and adopt accounting policies accordingly. For example, managers who are aware that analysts look closely at the relative proportion of cost of goods sold may elect accounting policies that treat many manufacturing overhead costs as inventory costs rather than as period costs, allowing some costs to be deferred to a future year as part of inventory. This results in a lower cost of goods sold relative to sales because fewer costs are immediately expensed and the gross margin percentage appears to be higher.

Exhibit 22-3 shows the vertical analysis for GRI. On the SCI, sales are set at 100% and all other numbers are calculated as a proportion of sales.[1] This analysis shows that the cost of goods sold as a percentage of sales has declined from 81.9% to 80%. This would be seen as an improvement but the analyst would have to investigate what caused this to happen. Although most other costs have remained relatively constant over the three years, wages and income taxes have increased, while finance costs have decreased as a percentage of revenues. On the SFP, total assets is set at 100% and all other numbers are computed as a percentage of total assets. The analysis of the SFP indicates a lot more variation over the period with almost all elements on the statement changing as a percentage of total assets. Some of the more notable changes include declines in cash and property, plant, and equipment; and increases in inventory, intangible assets, and long-term debt. The next step would be for the analyst to try to determine the cause of these changes and the impact on his decision. We will gather more information on this as we examine specific ratios.

EXHIBIT 22-3			

VERTICAL ANALYSIS OF GRI

Grocery Retailer Inc. Statement of Comprehensive Income for Years Ended 31 December 20X6, 20X5, and 20X4

	20X6 $	20X5 $	20X4 $
Sales	100.0%	100.0%	100.0%
Cost of goods sold	80.0%	81.9%	81.9%
Gross profit	20.0%	18.1%	18.1%
Expenses			
Electricity and natural gas	0.9%	0.9%	0.9%
Rent, taxes, and occupancy costs	2.1%	2.0%	2.0%

1. The calculations for vertical and horizontal analysis are easy to do in a computer spreadsheet, since in each case the process is simply dividing all cells by a constant. The tedious part is entering the data in the worksheet in the first place.

	20X6 $	20X5 $	20X4 $
Wages and benefits	5.5%	5.2%	5.6%
Depreciation and amortization	2.0%	2.1%	2.2%
Change in fair value of investment properties	0.1%	0.0%	0.0%
Other	2.2%	2.1%	2.5%
Total expenses	12.8%	12.3%	13.2%
Operating income	7.2%	5.8%	4.9%
Finance costs	0.9%	1.0%	1.2%
Earnings before income taxes	6.3%	4.8%	3.7%
Income taxes	1.6%	1.2%	1.1%
Net earnings	4.7%	3.6%	2.6%
Other comprehensive income			
Actuarial gains/losses	−0.5%	−0.3%	0.2%
Comprehensive income	4.2%	3.3%	2.8%

Note: There might be slight differences due to rounding.

Grocery Retailer Inc. Statement of Financial Position as at 31 December 20X6, 20X5, and 20X4

	20X6 $	20X5 $	20X4 $
ASSETS			
Current assets			
Cash and cash equivalents	0.9%	1.7%	1.5%
Accounts receivable	4.5%	5.1%	5.3%
Inventories	13.4%	12.2%	12.6%
Prepaid expenses	0.1%	0.2%	0.2%
	18.9%	19.2%	19.6%
Noncurrent assets			
Property, plant and equipment	53.0%	57.3%	57.4%
Investment properties	0.6%	0.5%	0.2%

	20X6 $	20X5 $	20X4 $
Intangible assets	16.0%	11.1%	11.2%
Goodwill	11.5%	11.9%	11.6%
Total assets	100.0%	100.0%	100.0%
LIABILITIES AND EQUITY			
Current liabilities			
Bank loans	4.3%	6.5%	6.7%
Accounts payable	17.9%	18.7%	16.3%
Provisions	2.9%	0.3%	0.5%
Current portion of long term debt	3.6%	4.8%	4.7%
	28.7%	30.3%	28.2%
Noncurrent liabilities			
Long term debt	34.5%	29.8%	30.8%
Defined benefit liabilities	1.9%	2.0%	2.1%
Deferred taxes	1.7%	1.8%	1.3%
Other liabilities	1.5%	0.2%	0.2%
	68.3%	64.1%	62.6%
Equity			
Common shares	8.7%	11.6%	16.3%
Retained earnings	25.2%	26.0%	23.1%
Accumulated other comprehensive income	−2.2%	−1.7%	−2.0%
Total shareholders' equity	31.7%	35.9%	37.4%
Total liabilities and equity	100.0%	100.0%	100.0%

Trend Analysis

Trend analysis or **horizontal analysis** looks at how the individual items on a financial statement have changed over time. The base year selected is set to 100 and other years' amounts are recomputed relative to the base amount. Obvious calculations include the trend of sales over time and the trend of net income over time. Analysts may construct special measures, such as EBIT (earnings before interest and taxes) or EBITDA (earnings before interest, taxes, depreciation, and amortization), and perform trend analysis on those measures. If the trend of sales is stronger than the trend of earnings, then the company is experiencing declining earnings relative to sales, even though earnings are increasing in absolute terms. That may be either good or bad (as will be explained in the following sections), depending on other factors in the analysis.

Horizontal analysis is best used when the nature of the company's operations is relatively stable, with few changes in lines of business and without significant business combinations. Otherwise, it is difficult to discern whether significant changes in SFP and SCI amounts are the result of continuing business or of entering and leaving new lines of business.

Exhibit 22-4 shows the trend analysis for GRI. The base year is 20X4 and each item on the statement is calculated as a percentage of the base year. One thing to note about horizontal analysis is that you cannot add up the percentages in a given year to derive any totals. On examining the SCI, we see that sales increased 6% from 20X4 to 20X6. However, net earnings increased by 94%. Part of this difference is the lower cost of goods sold, as we saw earlier. Although some costs increased more than the 6%, wages and benefits, depreciation, and finance costs all were less, contributing to the higher net income. The SFP analysis shows that most items grew more than 6%. Inventories, investment properties, and intangibles grew significantly as did many of the liabilities. One caution about using percentages is the absolute dollar amount of the starting base. Look at the investment properties, which grew 500% from 20X4 to 20X6. However, the base in 20X4 was only $10 million, and the absolute growth was only $40 million to a closing amount of $50 million.

EXHIBIT 22-4

TREND ANALYSIS FOR GRI

Grocery Retailer Inc. Statement of Comprehensive Income for Years Ended 31 December 20X6, 20X5, and 20X4

	20X6 $	20X5 $	20X4 $
Sales	106.3%	101.4%	100.0%
Cost of goods sold	103.8%	101.3%	100.0%
Gross profit	117.6%	101.8%	100.0%
Expenses			
Electricity and natural gas	109.1%	100.0%	100.0%
Rent, taxes, and occupancy costs	112.5%	104.2%	100.0%
Wages and benefits	102.9%	93.5%	100.0%
Depreciation and amortization	96.3%	96.3%	100.0%
Other	93.3%	86.7%	100.0%
Total expenses	102.5%	95.0%	100.0%
Operating income	158.3%	120.0%	100.0%
Finance costs	80.0%	86.7%	100.0%
Earnings before income taxes	184.4%	131.1%	100.0%
Income taxes	161.5%	115.4%	100.0%
Net earnings	193.8%	137.5%	100.0%
Other comprehensive income			

	20X6 $	20X5 $	20X4 $
Actuarial gains/losses	−350.0%	−200.0%	100.0%
Comprehensive income	161.8%	117.6%	100.0%

Grocery Retailer Inc. Statement of Financial Position as at December 31, 20X6, 20X5, and 20X4

	2016 $	2015 $	2014 $
ASSETS			
Current assets			
Cash and cash equivalents	77.8%	111.1%	100.0%
Accounts receivable	109.4%	93.8%	100.0%
Inventories	138.2%	94.7%	100.0%
Prepaid expenses	100.0%	100.0%	100.0%
	125.4%	95.8%	100.0%
Noncurrent assets			
Property, plant and equipment	120.3%	97.7%	100.0%
Investment properties	500.0%	300.0%	100.0%
Intangible assets	186.6%	97.0%	100.0%
Goodwill	128.6%	100.0%	100.0%
Total assets	130.3%	97.8%	100.0%
LIABILITIES AND EQUITY			
Current liabilities			
Bank loans	85.0%	95.0%	100.0%
Accounts payable	142.9%	112.2%	100.0%
Provisions	766.7%	66.7%	100.0%
Current portion of long term debt	100.0%	100.0%	100.0%
	133.1%	105.3%	100.0%
Noncurrent liabilities			

	2016 $	2015 $	2014 $
Long term debt	145.9%	94.6%	100.0%
Defined benefit liabilities	115.4%	92.3%	100.0%
Deferred taxes	162.5%	137.5%	100.0%
Other liabilities	1200.0%	100.0%	100.0%
	142.3%	100.3%	100.0%
Equity			
Common shares	69.4%	69.4%	100.0%
Retained earnings	141.7%	110.1%	100.0%
Accumulated other comprehensive income	141.7%	83.3%	100.0%
Total shareholders' equity	110.2%	93.8%	100.0%
Total liabilities and equity	130.3%	97.8%	100.0%

As we see, common-size and trend analyses are providing clues and indicators that will require further investigation by the analyst.

CONCEPT REVIEW

1. Why is it crucial to approach financial statement analysis with a clear understanding of the decision focus?
2. How can an analyst find out what accounting policies a company is using? What type of information should the analyst look for in the notes?
3. Why would a financial analyst want to recast a company's financial statements before performing ratio analysis or other analytical techniques?
4. What is the difference between *vertical* analysis and *horizontal* analysis of financial statement components?
5. What type of data, other than financial statements, is required to complete the analysis of a company?

Ratio Analysis

Common-size (vertical) and trend (horizontal) analysis are systematic computations of index ratios, but the term **ratio analysis** is most commonly applied to a large family of ratios that compare the *proportional relationship* between two different account amounts in a single year's financial statements. Common-size ratios are strictly within a single financial statement, but other ratio analyses can be either between amounts within a single statement or between amounts in two different statements.

There are literally dozens of ratios that can be computed from a single year's financial statements. The important task for an analyst is to focus on the ratios that have primary meaning for the decision at hand. There are many ways of grouping ratios, but those that will be discussed in the following pages are grouped as follows:

- Profitability ratios measure the company's ability to generate a return on invested capital;
- Efficiency ratios measure how well the company manages its assets;
- Solvency ratios measure the company's ability to meet its debt commitments; and
- Liquidity ratios measure the company's ability to pay obligations coming due in the next 12 months.

Profitability Ratios

It is common for the press and individual investors to talk about the return on sales that a company is earning, such as "Canadian Tire had 2014 earnings of $639 million on revenues of $12,463 million, a return of 5.1%."

Statements like this suggest that the most important profit relationship is between profit and revenue. However, the driving force in a capitalistic enterprise is to earn a return *on invested capital.* If you are going to put money into a savings account, you normally will want to put it in the bank that will give you the largest interest rate. You want to know how much you will make on your investment, *in percentage terms.* You will compare *rates* of interest, not absolute amounts, because the quantity of dollars that you have in your savings account will vary over time.

The same principle is true for all investments. An enterprise's profitability is measured by the rate of return that it earns on its invested capital and not by the absolute dollar profit that it generates. A billion dollars in profit is high if it was earned on an investment of only $2 or $3 billion. But if it was the return on a $50 billion investment, then the investment is yielding only 2% ($1/$50); a very poor return, indeed.

Similarly, companies may proudly cite sharply increased profit figures, perhaps up 40% or even 100% over the preceding year, and attribute this increase to the managers' fiscal and business acumen. But if a 50% increase in profit was accompanied by a 100% increase in invested capital, then the return on investment has gone down, not up. For example, a company increased its profits from $4 million in 20X2 to $6 million in 20X3, representing a 50% increase. However, the total amount invested in the company increased from $40 million to $100 million resulting in a return of 10% ($4/$40) in 20X2, but only 6% ($6/$100) in 20X3.

Sometimes an increase in absolute profit is due to an acquisition of another company; the current year's earnings are a reflection of combined performance for *both* companies, whereas the previous year's results included only the parent company. The return on the current combined company has to be compared to the return on the sum of both companies in the previous year to get any meaningful comparison. Extending this to the example above—suppose that the company acquired another company for $60 million, causing the investment to increase from $40 million to $100 million. If the acquired business should have generated a 10% yield similar to the parent company, then the combined profit in 20X3 should have also been $10 million and not $6 million.

Profitability ratios fall into two categories. *Profitability on sales (return on sales profitability) ratios* assist in providing information on how much of each dollar of revenue is retained for profits (similar to the vertical analysis discussed above). *Return on investment profitability ratios* determine the yields on different types of investments. These ratios consist of a numerator from the SCI and a denominator from the SFP.

Types of Profitability Ratios

Some of the common return-on-sales profitability ratios are:

- Gross profit margin:

$$\frac{\text{Gross profit}}{\text{Total revenue}}$$

This ratio examines how much of the revenue is used to cover the cost of the goods and how much is left over to cover the other operating costs of the company.

- Operating margin:

$$\frac{\text{Net income + Interest expense + Income taxes (i.e., EBIT)}}{\text{Total revenue}}$$

This is a commonly used ratio. It tells us how much the company earns on each dollar (or euro, yuan, yen, peso, etc.) of revenue. Since the numerator is EBIT, it removes the effects of financing and income taxes and makes it easier to compare profitability between companies that use different proportions of debt versus equity and are subject to different tax rates.

However, both of these ratios should never be used in isolation as they give us only information on costs incurred and no indication of the return on *investment* that the company is achieving. Operating margin must be used in conjunction with asset turnover, a ratio that we discuss in the next section (and which is illustrated in Exhibit 22-5).

EXHIBIT 22-5

SUMMARY OF PROFITABILITY RATIOS

Ratio Name	Computation	Significance and Difficulties
Gross profit margin	$$\frac{\text{Gross profit}}{\text{Total revenue}}$$	Indicates the gross profit margin earned on each dollar of sales. Should be used in conjunction with *operating margin* and *asset turnover*.
Operating margin	$$\frac{\text{Net income + Interest expense + Income taxes}}{\text{Total revenue}}$$	Indicates the profit margin (before taxes) earned on each dollar of sales. Should be used in conjunction with asset turnover.
Return on total long-term capital, after tax	$$\frac{\text{Net income + [Interest expense on long-term debt} \times (1-t)]}{\text{Average long-term debt + Average shareholder's equity}}$$	Measures the return on long-term interest-bearing debt and equity.

Ratio Name	Computation	Significance and Difficulties
Return on total assets, before tax	$$\frac{\text{Net income} + \text{Total interest expense} + \text{Total income taxes}}{\text{Average total assets}}$$	Indicates the overall return that the company is earning on its asset investment on a before-tax basis.
Return on total assets, after tax	$$\frac{\text{Net income} + [\text{Total interest expense} \times (1 - t)]}{\text{Average total assets}}$$	Indicates the overall return that the company is earning on its asset investment on an after-tax basis.
Return on equity	$$\frac{\text{Net income}}{\text{Average total shareholder's equity}}$$	Shows the historical after-tax return to all shareholders for the period.
Return on common shareholders' equity	$$\frac{\text{Net income} - \text{Preferred dividends}}{\text{Average total shareholders'equity} - \text{Average preferred share equity}}$$	Shows the historical after-tax return to just the common shareholders for the period.

For the return-on-investment profitability ratios, the analyst has to view the investment from the appropriate standpoint for her decision. A common shareholder will be interested primarily in **return on common share equity**; a preferred shareholder will be interested in the return on total shareholders' equity; and a bond holder will be interested in the return on long-term capital (i.e., shareholders' equity plus long-term debt, often called **total capitalization**). All analysts will be interested in the underlying **return on total assets**. These are some of the possible denominators for a profitability ratio.

The numerator of any profitability ratio will reflect a return *over time* because it is derived from the SCI. In contrast, the denominator will reflect SFP values at a *point in time*. To make the numerator and denominator consistent, the denominator should be calculated as the *average* over the year.[2] Ideally, the denominator should be based on an average of monthly or quarterly investments, but a simpler and more common approach is to average the SFP numbers at the beginning and end of the year being analyzed. However, if there were major changes in the investment during the year (e.g., the acquisition of another company in the first quarter of the year), then a weighted average should be estimated.

The numerator of any ratio must be consistent with its denominator in substance as well as on the time dimension. The return to common shareholders is measured not by net earnings, but by *earnings available to common shareholders* (which basically is net earnings less preferred share dividends, as explained in Chapter 20).

Common profitability ratios are discussed below.

- Return on total long-term capital, after tax:

$$\frac{\text{Net income} + [\text{Interest expense on long-term debt} \times (1 - t)]}{\text{Average long-term debt} + \text{Average total shareholder's equity}}$$

---

2. Note that this may differ between analysts. For example, some analysts may use the beginning balance of the investment only, rather than an average for the period.

The **return on long-term capital** measures the return on all types of capital invested in the company—both the equity and the interest-bearing debt. It must be calculated by dividing total capitalization into a profit measure that adds back the effects of financing. Since interest expense is included in net income and since interest also affects income tax, the numerator must remove the effects of interest on long-term debt by adding back the after-tax interest expense (by multiplying interest by $1 - t$, where t = average tax rate for the corporation).

- Return on total assets (ROA), before tax:

Return on *total assets* can be measured by dividing total assets into EBIT.

$$\frac{\text{Net income} + \text{Total interest expense} + \text{Income tax expense}}{\text{Average total assets}}$$

- Return on total assets (ROA), after tax:

Return on *total assets* after tax can be measured by dividing total assets into net earnings before interest:

$$\frac{\text{Net income} + \left[\text{Total interest expense} \times (1 - t)\right]}{\text{Average total assets}}$$

This ratio measures the return on the total investment made in assets. A higher ratio indicates a better return. However, the analyst should also examine why this is occurring. For example, does the company lease many of its assets, which cause the assets to be reported off-balance-sheet? Even when assets are reflected on the SFP, their values are hard to assess. Are the assets valued at historical cost or fair value? If the assets are old and the profitability is compared with a company that has newer assets, the company with the older assets appear to be more profitable because its asset base cost is less (due to cheaper historical costs) and is more fully depreciated. The net income figure will reflect lower relative depreciation expenses, due to the relatively lower cost of older assets. The apparent profitability in such a company can be quite misleading; if new investments were made, the same return would not be earned. This higher ROA is likely not sustainable in the long run.

An analyst may elect to use ROA before tax, if taxes are volatile year-over-year, or she is comparing to competitors that have different income tax rates. Some analysts attempt to adjust for differing relative accumulated depreciation by basing the measurement on EBITDA, earnings before interest, taxes, depreciation, and amortization.[3]

- Return on equity (ROE):

$$\text{Return on equity} = \frac{\text{Net income}}{\text{Average shareholder's equity}}$$

This ratio measures the return that the company has been able to earn on the shareholders' equity. Net income already includes interest expense (and its tax benefit). If we wanted to examine the return to the common shareholders only, then we would have to subtract the preferred dividends from the net income in the numerator to arrive at the amount of earnings left after all other claims are deducted and adjust the denominator to be average common shareholders' equity.

---

3. In the airline industry, aircraft rental payments usually are also added back, so the measure becomes EBITDAR: earnings before interest, tax, depreciation, amortization, and aircraft rental.

It is very useful to compare this ratio with the return on assets. If financial leverage is positive, the return on shareholder's equity will be higher than the return on assets. However, if after-tax interest on debt is higher than the return on assets, this ratio will be lower than the return on assets and may be negative.

Whatever profitability ratio(s) is (are) used, the effects of accounting policies (and of operating policies, where these create off-balance-sheet assets and liabilities) must be considered. Pay particular attention to assets that are reported at fair values versus historical costs as this will impact all of the investment profitability ratios. Asset balances may be volatile as fair values change year-over-year; the same volatility will also impact the closing balances in shareholders' equity.

Lessons to Remember When Evaluating Profitability

The moral of this tale is:

- Profitability ratios must have a measure of investment in the denominator (based on the statement of financial position) and a measure of profitability in the numerator (based on the income statement, excluding other comprehensive income).
- The denominator and the numerator must be logically consistent.
- Both the denominator and the numerator are the product of many accounting policy choices and even more accounting estimates by management.
- Both components of the ratio may need adjustment both for accounting policies and for off-balance-sheet financing and investment.

Profitability ratios are summarized in Exhibit 22-5.

Profitability ratios do have one clear advantage over other measures of profitability (e.g., earnings per share or total net income). The advantage is that since profitability is expressed as a *percentage of investment* (except for operating margin and gross profit margin), it is possible to separate true increased profitability from normal growth. Most profitable companies pay out only a portion of their earnings as dividends. Some companies pay no dividends at all. The earnings retained by the company are reinvested in operations; since shareholders' equity increases, so must the net assets of the company. Since there is more invested capital, the company will have to generate a larger net income to maintain the same return on invested capital. This is normal growth.

The proper test of managerial competence is not whether management has been able to increase EPS or net income; in a profitable industry and good economic times, managers have to be truly incompetent *not* to enjoy increased profits. The proper test is whether management has been able to maintain or, preferably, increase the rate of return on the increasing investment base.

Using Total Comprehensive Income

As the accounting standards move to recognize more items in other comprehensive income, there is some debate as to whether or not profitability ratios should use total comprehensive income (which includes OCI) as the numerator instead of net income. Supporters for using total comprehensive income suggest that because some items will never recycle back to profit or loss, any profitability measures should include these gains and losses. Items that will never recycle include gains and losses arising from revaluations, actuarial adjustments, and fair-value changes for investments classified as FVOCI-Equity. Once again, it will be up to the analyst to decide the level of inputs for profitability to be measured.

Components of Profitability Ratios

The previous section discussed several overall measures of profitability. A key to profitability analysis, however, involves breaking profitability down to its basic components. For example, any company's return on total assets can be dissected into two components: asset turnover and operating margin. Recall that return on assets before-tax is calculated as follows:

$$\textit{Return on assets before tax} = \frac{\text{Earnings before interest and taxes (EBIT)}}{\text{Average total assets}}$$

This can be disaggregated into two other ratios:

1. EBIT ÷ Total revenue = *Operating margin*
2. Total revenue ÷ Average total assets = *Asset turnover*

Operating margin multiplied by asset turnover equals return on assets:

$$\frac{\text{EBIT}}{\text{Total revenue}} \times \frac{\text{Total revenue}}{\text{Average total assets}} = \frac{\text{EBIT}}{\text{Average total assets}}$$

Earlier, we pointed out that earnings as a proportion of revenues (i.e., **operating margin**) by itself is not a useful measure of profitability because it ignores the amount of investment that was employed to generate that level of sales and income. A valid and often successful strategy for a company is to increase its sales volume (i.e., its *asset turnover*) by cutting its profit margin. Although the profit margin goes down, the return on assets will rise if the increase in sales volume is enough to make up for the reduced profit margin.

Other companies may use a strategy of increasing the operating margin, even at the risk of a possible loss of sales volume. If the operating margin is very small, such as 4%, only a 2% increase in price will increase the operating margin by 50% (i.e., from 4% of sales to 6% of sales). The company will be better off unless sales volume drops by 33%; that will depend on the price elasticity of demand. In a highly competitive market, a small increase in price could easily cost the company more by a drop in sales volume than it gains in margin.

The point is that *judging profitability by using only the operating margin is always wrong*. Operating margin does not reflect the level of investment, and overall profitability can be judged only in relation to investment.

Exhibit 22-6 calculates profitability ratios for GRI and summarizes the findings.

EXHIBIT 22-6

PROFITABILITY RATIOS FOR GRI

Ratio	20X6	20X5	Discussion
Gross profit margin	2,600/13,000 = 20%	2,250/12,400 = 18.1%	The gross profit margin has improved. The question is why? The analyst would look to see whether or not selling prices had increased and/or costs of goods sold declined over the year due to cheaper products/costs.
Operating margin	950/13,000 = 7.3%	720/12,400 = 5.8%	The operating margin has also improved by 1.5%. However, we know

Ratio	20X6	20X5	Discussion
			1.9% (20% – 18.1%) of this came from the gross profit margin. This means that other operating costs actually increased. From the common size and trend analysis, we saw that wages and benefits increased over the year.
Return on total long-term capital	620 + 105 (1 – 0.253)/[(2,700 + 1,750 + 2,480 + 2,110)/2] = 698/4,520 = 15.4% *Interest on long-term debt.	440 + 113 (1 – 0.254)/[(1,750 + 1,800 + 2,110 + 2,250)/2] = 524/3,955 = 13.2% *Interest on long-term debt.	The return on total long-term capital also increased from 13.2% to 15.4%, or 2.2%. This is an improvement. Although the absolute dollar value of the long-term debt increased, the company appears to have invested the new debt in assets that produce a higher return.
Return on assets, after tax	620 + 120 (1 – 0.253)/[(7,830 + 5,880)/2] = 10.3%	440 + 130 (1 – 0.254)[(5,880 + 6,010)/2] = 9.0%	This ratio has also improved. GRI has made a significant increase in total assets, but the return has improved with this investment.
Return on equity	620/[(2,480 + 2,110)/2] = 27%	440/[(2,110 + 2,250)/2] = 20.2%	This also shows improvement for the year, increasing about 6.8%.

Putting these ratios together, what conclusions can be reached? We see that earnings for GRI increased primarily due to a reduction in the costs of goods sold. We also know that the company acquired another company that resulted in increases in its tangible and intangible assets. The company uses the fair-value method for reporting its investment property and the amount of the fair-value change added about 1% to the operating profit. We also have to see if the company has entered into any new operating leases that are reported off the balance sheet. Since the new business acquired is a specialty business, it may be that this business earns a higher margin, which would explain the increases in all of the profitability ratios. Before this analysis is complete, we need to compare to competitors to see if the returns were consistent with, above, or below peers in the same industry.

Efficiency Ratios

The objective of **efficiency ratios** is to analyze certain aspects of operational efficiency. Efficiency ratios are also known as **turnover ratios** because the two most commonly cited efficiency ratios are *accounts receivable turnover* and *inventory turnover.*

Accounts Receivable Turnover

This ratio is intended to measure the average length of time it takes to collect accounts receivable. The turnover ratio is determined by dividing sales revenue by average accounts receivable.

$$\text{Accounts receivable turnover} = \text{Revenue} \div \text{Average accounts receivable}$$

If the ratio is 4:1, for example, it indicates that, on average, the accounts receivable "turns over" four times a year, which implies that the average collection period is one quarter of a year, or three months.

This ratio is translated into a parallel ratio called the **average collection period of accounts receivable** by dividing the accounts receivable turnover into 365 days; a turnover of four yields an apparent collection period of 91(365/4) days.

The numerator should include only sales on account, but an external analyst of a retail enterprise may have no way of knowing how much of the revenue was on account. In these cases, total revenue is used. In some industries, however, it is rare to have cash sales and therefore the total sales can safely be assumed to represent credit sales on account.

The **accounts receivable turnover ratio** is difficult to interpret. Presumably, a short collection period (a high turnover ratio) is better than a long one because it indicates that the company is able to realize cash from its sales in a shorter period of time. It also implies that there are very few long-outstanding accounts that may prove to be uncollectible. This might be true for companies in industries where there is a widespread customer base and essentially equal terms given by each company to its customers.

However, one is quite likely to encounter companies that have special relationships with major customers. The major customers may effectively dictate payment terms. For example, a company that derives most of its revenue from government contracts may show a very slow turnover, and yet the collectability of the accounts is assured despite the "age" of the accounts.

Another problem for an external analyst is that the accounts receivable shown on the SFP may not be typical throughout the year. The fiscal year of a business may be established on the basis of the *natural business year* and the report date may be the lowest period of activity in a seasonal business. The accounts receivable may be at their lowest level for the whole year. Bankers who use the turnover ratio may insist on monthly data. However, an even more likely scenario for such analysts is to request an **accounts receivable aging schedule**, in which the receivables are categorized by the length of time they have been outstanding (e.g., less than 30 days, 31–60 days, 61–90 days, and more than 90 days). Any special payment terms (such as extra-long payments for related companies) are specifically indicated.[4] Disclosure notes on credit risk included in the financial statements often provide this information for external users who do not have access to internal documents.

Because of the problems cited above, an analyst may be more interested in the *trend* of the ratio, as an indicator of whether the collection period is stable or getting longer or shorter. If the ratio changes year to year, it will not be easy for an external analyst to determine the cause of the change and whether the change is good or bad. Additional information, such as the type of customers and the economic trends, may be required to complete this analysis.

Inventory Turnover

The **inventory turnover ratio** indicates the relationship between the cost of goods sold and the average inventory balance:

$$\text{Inventory turnover} = \text{Cost of goods sold} \div \text{Average inventory}$$

---

4. Some companies give different payment terms to different customers. In that case, aging schedules are usually based on the due date of payment and reflect the number of days past due.

A high turnover ratio is often presumed to be better than a low ratio because a high ratio suggests that less investment in inventory is needed to generate sales. A low ratio, on the other hand, suggests that there may be excessive quantities of inventory on hand or that there are a lot of slow-moving or unsellable items in inventory.

The objective of inventory management is to maintain *optimum* inventory levels rather than *minimum* inventory levels. Maintaining too low an inventory may result in items not being available for sale when the customer requests them, and therefore sales are lost. Furthermore, with the advent of just-in-time inventory systems in many businesses, suppliers are sometimes left with the burden of maintaining inventories. This means that a supplier's finished goods inventory may be higher than in earlier years, and yet the ability to sell that inventory may be virtually guaranteed through the supplier arrangements. Therefore, a low inventory turnover may not necessarily be bad, and a high turnover may not necessarily be ideal.

The inventory turnover ratio can be converted to **days in inventory** by dividing 365 days by the turnover. A turnover of 12 times indicates that the inventory is on hand for approximately 30 days. This ratio will be impacted by the nature of the inventory and how long the process takes to convert raw materials into finished goods. Consider a winery, where wine is aged for years before it is ready for sale and therefore a significantly higher days in inventory (lower turnover ratio) is expected.

Accounts Payables Turnover

This ratio is intended to indicate how long the company takes to pay its suppliers and is calculated as below:

Accounts Payables turnover = Cost of goods sold ÷ Average accounts payables

Similar to the above ratios, the **days in payables** can be determined by taking 365 days and dividing by the payables turnover ratio. This is a difficult ratio to interpret because on the one hand, the company should take as long as possible to pay its suppliers. This will free up cash to be used internally and give the company "free credit" from the supplier. On the other hand, if the company takes too long to pay its suppliers, this will jeopardize supplier relationships and force suppliers to require cash on delivery or refuse to ship to the company. How many days a company can take to pay its suppliers will often depend on how much "power" it has to dictate payment terms. For example, if the company represents a large percentage of the supplier's sales, then it is likely that the company will be able to take longer to pay.

For this ratio to be as accurate as possible, only costs that are included in accounts payable should be used. Cost of goods sold may include depreciation, wages, and other costs not in payables. Ideally, total purchases and other supplier costs should be used in place of cost of goods sold. However, this information is rarely available in the eternal reports and so cost of goods sold is used as an approximation.

Asset Turnover

As we have seen, **asset turnover** is a major component of return on assets. It measures the sales dollars generated by all of the assets. The higher this ratio, the more efficient the company is at using its assets in its sales effort. This ratio is calculated as follows:

Total asset turnover = Total Revenue/Average Total assets

This ratio is impacted by the type of assets used by the company, the measurement bases used (i.e., fair value or historical cost), and whether or not there are substantial off-balance-sheet assets due to the use of operating leases.

The principal efficiency ratios are summarized in Exhibit 22-7. Exhibit 22-8 shows the calculations of the efficiency ratios for GRI.

EXHIBIT 22-7

SUMMARY OF EFFICIENCY RATIOS

Ratio Name	Computation	Significance and Difficulties
Accounts receivable turnover	$$\frac{\text{Sales revenue (on credit)}}{\text{Average trade accounts receivable}}$$	Indicates efficiency of trade accounts receivable collection but is difficult to interpret without knowledge of the customer base. Average year-end accounts receivable balances may not be representative of seasonal variation.
Average collection period of accounts receivable	$$\frac{365 \text{ (days)}}{\text{Accounts receivable turnover}}$$	Converts the accounts receivable turnover into the average collection period, in days. Has the same measurement problems as does the turnover ratio.
Inventory turnover	$$\frac{\text{Cost of goods sold}}{\text{Average inventory}}$$	Yields the number of times that the inventory "turns over" during a year. A low ratio may indicate possible overstocking, if valid comparative information is available. Year-end average inventory balances may not be representative of seasonal variation.
Average days in inventory	$$\frac{365 \text{ (days)}}{\text{Inventory turnover}}$$	Converts the inventory turnover into the average days in inventory. Has the same measurement problems as does the turnover ratio.
Accounts payable turnover	$$\frac{\text{Cost of goods sold}}{\text{Average accounts payable}}$$	Yields the number of times that the accounts payables "turn over" during a year. A low ratio may indicate the company is taking too long to pay its suppliers. Year-end average payable balances may not be representative of seasonal variation.

Ratio Name	Computation	Significance and Difficulties
Average days in payables	$$\frac{365 \text{ (days)}}{\text{Accounts payable turnover}}$$	Converts the payables turnover into the average days in payables. Has the same measurement problems as does the turnover ratio.
Asset turnover	$$\frac{\text{Total revenue}}{\text{Average total assets}}$$	Shows the level of sales that are being generated per dollar of investment in assets. This is one component of return on assets, and should be used in conjunction with operating margin (see Exhibit 22-5).

EXHIBIT 22-8

EFFICIENCY RATIOS FOR GRI

Ratio	20X6	20X5	Discussion
Accounts receivable turnover	13,000/[(350 + 300)/2] = 40 times	12,400/[(300 + 320)/2] = 40 times	See discussion for average collection period below.
Average collection period of accounts receivable	365/40 = 9 days	365/40 = 9 days	The collection period for the accounts receivable remained consistent at 9 days. The reason this is very low is that a large portion of the sales will be cash sales and therefore paid immediately. Ideally, we would want to use just credit sales in this ratio, but this amount is not known. Without knowing the amount of credit sales, this ratio may not be useful for companies with significant cash sales.
Inventory turnover	10,400/[(1,050 + 720)/2] = 11.8 times	10,150/[(720 + 760)/2] = 13.7 times	See discussion below for days in inventory.
Days in inventory	365/11.8 = 31 days	365/13.7 = 27 days	The number of days that inventory is held has increased by 4 days from 27 to 31 days. Does the company have a different product mix now? What happens to the inventory that is spoiled, and are there any holding costs?

Ratio	20X6	20X5	Discussion
Accounts payable turnover	10,400/[(1,400 + 1,100)/2] = 8.3 times	10,150/[(1,100 + 980)/2] = 9.8 times	See discussion below for days in account payable.
Days in accounts payable	365/8.3 = 44 days	365/9.8 = 37 days	GRI is taking about 44 days to pay its suppliers, and this has actually increased by 7 days over the year. Is this consistent within the industry? How many suppliers does the company deal with, and does GRI have some power with its suppliers to delay payments, or will this jeopardize supplier relationships?
Total asset turnover	13,000/[(7,830 + 5,880)/2] = 1.9 times	12,400/[(5,880 + 6,010)/2] = 2.1 times	The asset turnover ratio has worsened over the year. The company has increased its investment in assets by 33%, but revenues have increased by only 5%. Why have the assets increased, and what are the types of assets that have increased?

Since ratios should never be analyzed in isolation, what do these efficiency ratios tell us? We can see that GRI is holding inventory longer. The asset turnover ratio has also worsened. We know that the company purchased another company during the year. This could cause the mix of inventory products to change, causing the turnover ratios to decline. However, we also saw under the profitability ratios that all ratios had improved, indicating that although there was an increase in the level of investment in various asset accounts, the company was earning higher profits from this investment. Additional information would be required to understand the inventory turnover results.

Solvency Ratios

The basic objective of **solvency ratios** is to assess the ability of the company to make both the interest and principal payments on its long-term obligations. These ratios stress the long-term financial and operating structure of the company. They can be further classified as follows:

- **Leverage ratios**, which measure the relative amount of the company's financing that was obtained through debt (versus equity); and
- **Debt service ratios**, which test the ability of the company to generate sufficient cash flow from operations to pay the required payments for debt interest and principal.

Solvency ratios interact with profitability ratios because a company's long-run solvency is in doubt if the company cannot generate enough profit to not only service the debt but also earn an adequate return for shareholders.

Leverage Ratios

Leverage is the extent to which a company uses interest-bearing obligations to finance its assets. In public companies, the focus is on long-term debt (including retractable preferred shares, if any). For analysis of a private company, the focus is on interest-bearing debt, primarily bank debt, perhaps both short term and long term; loans from shareholders are not included but are reclassified as owners' equity.[5]

---

5. The concept of leverage is discussed more extensively in financial management texts.

The concept of **leverage** is that if a company can earn a rate of return on its assets that is higher than the rate it has to pay on debt, the surplus return (i.e., above the rate of interest on borrowings) will flow through to benefit the shareholders in the form of higher earnings per share. Of course, if a company earns *less* on its investment than the rate of interest, the shareholders' interests will suffer; this is known as **negative leverage**. The return on total assets, before tax (EBIT ÷ total assets) can be directly compared with the average interest rate on debt to see if leverage is positive or negative. The margin by which the return on assets exceeds the average interest rate is the **margin of safety**; the smaller the margin, the greater is the risk of negative leverage. Therefore, leverage plays an important role in the assessment of profitability because it affects the distribution of the earnings to the different providers of capital. Leverage also is a measure of solvency because it is one measure of risk.

If a company has a large amount of debt relative to its shareholders' equity, the company is said to be *highly levered* (or *highly leveraged*). Leverage increases the volatility of the residual earnings to the shareholders because the interest must always be paid, regardless of the amount of earnings. For example, a company has the following results:

(in thousands of dollars)	20X3 $	20X2 $	20X1 $
Operating income before interest and taxes	2,000	1,000	1,500
Interest	(500)	(500)	(500)
Taxes	(450)	(150)	(300)
Net profit or loss	1,050	350	700

From the above table, we see that operating income decreased by 33% in 20X2 and increased by 100% in 20X3. However, the net profit or loss left for the shareholders decreased by 50% in 20X2 and increased by 200% in 20X3. The interest is fixed at $500 in all three years and as a result the fluctuations in earnings are amplified.

Some companies try to lessen this risk by entering into variable-rate loans instead of fixed-rate loans. If the company's earnings are responsive to the general economy, and if interest rates tend to decrease when the economy slows, then a decrease in earnings might be at least partially matched by a decrease in interest rates. Some companies that have substantial fixed-rate obligations can effectively convert these to variable-rate obligations by entering into interest rate swaps.

The most basic measure of leverage is the **total debt to equity ratio**.

Debt to equity = Total debt* ÷ Total Shareholders' equity

*Total debt refers to all short-term and long-term interest-bearing debt.

The numerator, in its simplest form, is the total interest-bearing debt including short-term debt, current portion of long-term debt, and long-term debt. The denominator is the total shareholders' equity (excluding retractable preferred shares, which are classified as debt, but including shareholders' loans, if any).

This is one ratio where the numerator and denominator can be defined in a number of ways, depending on the nature of the company and the objectives of the analyst. When the ratio is computed for assessing solvency (and risk of insolvency), all monetary obligations, both short term and long term, are normally included (Non-monetary items such as deferred income taxes, unearned revenues, and other miscellaneous deferred credits are excluded).

There are many other adjustments that could be added to the numerator including:

- Estimated present value of operating lease obligations on assets essential to operations;
- All other monetary obligations, including trade accounts payable; and
- Liabilities related to pension obligations and long-term provisions (environmental and decommissioning liabilities, for example).

The key point here is that there is no one correct method to calculate this ratio and many variations are used in practice depending on the objectives of the analyst.

Variants to the basic debt to equity ratio use some measure of *invested capital* as the denominator, which includes both debt and equity. These ratios answer the question: *How much of the company's invested capital has been financed using debt?* These ratios can be defined as follows (in their simplest form):

Debt to total capitalization = Total debt* ÷ (Total debt* + Shareholders' equity)

Debt to total assets   = (Total debt*) ÷ Total assets

*Total debt refers to all short-term and long-term interest-bearing debt.

As is the case with the basic debt to equity ratio, the numerator and denominator for the above ratios may vary somewhat, depending on the point of view of the analyst, and be adjusted for inclusions and exclusions as noted earlier. Also note how the debt to equity ratio relates to the debt to total capitalization ratio. The value for a debt to equity ratio will be higher than for a debt to total assets ratio. A debt to equity ratio of 1:1 will be a debt to total capitalization ratio of 1:2. This arithmetic may seem obvious, but since all of these types of ratios are commonly referred to as debt to equity ratios, it is important to be clear on the definition of the ratio used in discussions.

The debt to equity ratio (and its variants) is a measure of **financial risk**. Because leverage increases the volatility of earnings, the increase in return to shareholders is a result of an increase in financial risk. A high debt to equity ratio is safest when a company has a high and steady level of earnings, particularly when the company can control its return on assets. High levels of financial risk can be most safely used in companies that have low levels of *operating risk*. **Operating risk** is the responsiveness of a company's earnings to fluctuations in its level of revenue. The more volatile operating earnings are, the less a company should rely on financial leverage.

For example, leverage is high in the financial services sector and in regulated public utilities. In financial institutions, the interest being paid on debt and the interest charged to borrowers are both responsive to money market conditions. As long as the debt portfolio is matched (in maturities) to the asset portfolio, net earnings can be relatively stable. In public utilities, rates are set to achieve a rate of return on assets that has been approved by the regulators; the permitted rate of return on assets is too low to attract share equity, but by levering up the earnings through lower-rate debt, utilities can provide an adequate return to attract share capital. In contrast, biotech companies that have a very high operating risk with volatile earnings and cash flows will likely have little or no leverage.

Debt Service Ratios

Debt service ratios measure the company's ability to pay its interest and principal obligations. If a company has too much debt, its cash flows generated from operations may be insufficient to cover the required payments.

A traditional ratio used in solvency analysis is the **times-interest-earned ratio**, or interest coverage ratio, which is the ratio of interest expense to earnings before interest and taxes (EBIT). This is believed to indicate the relative amount by which earnings can decrease before there is not enough to pay the interest. In reality, the interest would be paid, since failure to do so risks throwing the company into receivership and possibly bankruptcy.

Times-interest-earned = (Net income + Interest Expense + Tax) ÷ (Interest Expense)

Since interest expense is tax deductible, the numerator of the ratio normally is EBIT. Again, it may be appropriate to use net earnings adjusted for accounting policies, as described in earlier sections. Also, the numerator and denominator should include interest on all indebtedness, long term and short term, plus interest on finance leases. Default on any component of interest can have dire consequences. Remember that finance costs on the SCI may include gains and losses as well as interest costs; this ratio requires only interest expenses.

If a times-interest-earned ratio is approaching 1:1, the company already is suffering negative financial leverage. It is possible to estimate the number of times by which EBIT must exceed interest expense to avoid negative leverage. To avoid negative leverage, a company must earn an overall rate on its total capitalization that is at least equal to the interest being charged on the debt. Therefore, if the amount of shareholders' equity is three times the amount of debt, EBIT should be at least four times the total interest expense (i.e., the earnings on one part debt *plus* three parts owners' equity).

A broader debt-service ratio is **times-debt-service-earned ratio**. This ratio goes well beyond the times-interest-earned ratio to look not only at the amount of interest that must be paid, but also at the amount of principal payments that must be made. The times-interest-earned ratio implicitly assumes that debt can be refinanced, which may be a valid assumption in prosperous times. But if the company's fortunes decline, the financial markets freeze up, or interest rates soar, it may be difficult to obtain new financing to "roll over" the debt. The debt-service ratio attempts to look at the ability of a company to *service* its overall debt load.

Times-debt-service-earned = (Cash flow from operations + Interest expense + Tax) ÷

(Interest + Finance lease payments + [Projected annual principal payments ÷ (1 − t)])

The numerator of this ratio is *cash*, not earnings. The starting point is the cash flow from operations as reported on the statement of cash flows. This amount should be adjusted by adding back interest paid when it is included in operating activities. Interest is tax deductible, and therefore the current income tax paid should also be added back to the cash flow from operations—$C_{op}BIT$ instead of EBIT.

The denominator should include not only interest paid but also the cash outflows for principal repayments and finance lease payments. The denominator is not always easy to measure and requires a careful reading of the notes. The cash flows relating to debt and finance leases for the next year are disclosed in the notes to the financial statements.

Taxes raise a particular problem because interest is deductible for tax purposes, while principal payments are not. Since principal payments have to be paid in after-tax dollars, it takes a higher pre-tax cash flow from operations to generate enough cash to repay principal. On the other hand, finance lease payments usually are deductible in full, including both the capital portion and the implicit interest expense, thereby adding an additional complication. The easiest way around this problem is to divide the non-tax-deductible cash flows by 1 minus the company's average tax rate: $1 − t$. This converts the principal payments to pre-tax equivalents and then all amounts in the ratio are comparable.

Common solvency ratios are summarized in Exhibit 22-9.

EXHIBIT 22-9

SUMMARY OF SOLVENCY RATIOS

Note: Below, "Total debt" refers to interest-bearing short-term and long-term debt. (In other cases, "Total debt" may refer to all liabilities. Similarly, "Long-term debt" may refer to just the long-term interest-bearing debt or all long-term liabilities.)

Ratio Name	Computation	Significance and Difficulties
Debt to equity	$\dfrac{\text{Total debt}}{\text{Total shareholders' equity}}$	Indicates the relative proportions by which the company is financed with total debt regardless of whether short term or long term. May vary if the level of short-term debt changes year by year. Inclusions may be necessary, as described earlier.

Ratio Name	Computation	Significance and Difficulties
Long-term debt to equity	$$\frac{\text{Long-term debt}}{\text{Total shareholders' equity}}$$	Indicates the relative proportions by which "permanent" investment is financed through long-term debt versus shareholders' equity.
Total debt-to-total-capitalization	$$\frac{\text{Total debt}}{\text{Total debt + Total shareholders' equity}}$$	Indicates the proportion of total capital that is financed through debt.
Long-term debt-to-total-capitalization	$$\frac{\text{Long-term debt}}{\text{Long-term debt + Shareholders' equity}}$$	Indicates the proportion of long-term capital that is financed through debt.
Debt to total assets	$$\frac{\text{Total debt}}{\text{Total assets}}$$	Indicates the proportion by which assets are financed through debt.
Times-interest-earned	$$\frac{\text{Net income + Interest expense + Tax}}{\text{Interest expense}}$$	Indicates the ability of the company to withstand a downturn in earnings and still be able to earn enough to pay interest (and avoid default). Reflects accounting earnings rather than cash flow.
Times-debt-service-earned	$$\frac{\text{Cash flow from operations + Interest + Tax}}{\text{Interest + Finance lease payments +}\ [\text{(Projected annual principal payments)} \div (1 - t)]}$$	Indicates the ability of the company to service its debt, including leases, from its pre-tax operating cash flow. Operating cash flow must include changes in current monetary items.

Exhibit 22-10 shows the calculations of the solvency ratios for GRI.

EXHIBIT 22-10

SOLVENCY RATIOS FOR GRI

Ratio	20X6	20X5	Discussion
Debt to equity	(340 + 280 + 2,700)/2,480 = 1.3 times	(380 + 280 + 1,750)/2,110 = 1.14 times	Debt has increased so the company has more total debt than in 2015.
Long-term debt to equity	2,700/2,480 = 1.1 times	1,750/2,110 = 0.83 times	Most of the increase in debt was in long-term debt.
Total debt-to-capitalization	(340 + 280 + 2,700)/(340 + 280 + 2,700 + 2,480) = 0.57	(380 + 280 + 1,750)/(380 + 280 + 1,750 + 2,110) = 0.53	As a result of the higher debt, we see that the proportion of debt used to finance the company has increased from 53% to 57%.
Total debt-to-assets	(340 + 280 + 2,700)/7,830 = 0.42	(380 + 280 + 1,750)/5,880 = 0.41	Even though debt increased significantly, there was little change in this ratio. This indicates that the debt was used for investment in assets.
Times-interest-earned	(620 + 120 + 210)/120 = 7.9 times	(440 + 130 + 150)/130 = 5.5 times	Even though the debt has increased, the company's ability to finance the debt has actually improved due to increases in its net earnings year-over-year. We do see that the finance costs were lower in 20X6 compared with 20X5, even though the debt was higher. This could be due to lower rates negotiated on the debt, and the timing of when the new debt was actually issued.
Times debt-service-earned	(1,010 + 120 + 210)/[120 + (280/(1 − 0.253))] = 2.7 times	(870 + 130 + 150)/[130 + (280/(1 − 0.254))] = 3.1 times	Even though there is a significant increase in the amount of debt, the company still generates enough operating cash flows to cover the annual payments required to service the debt (although the ratio has declined). It appears that the new debt has no annual repayments required and will be repaid at maturity.

Overall, we see that the company's level of debt increased, as well as its asset base. This indicates that the debt was used primarily to finance the purchase of the new assets. Even though there is more debt, the increased earnings and cash flows indicate the company still has the ability to service the debt on an annual basis.

Liquidity Ratios

The general objective of **liquidity ratios** is to test the company's ability to meet its short-term financial obligations. Therefore, the focus is on the composition of current assets and current liabilities.

Current Ratio

The grandparent of all ratios is the **current ratio**. Use of this ratio has been traced back almost 100 years. It is a simple ratio to calculate:

$$\text{Current ratio} = \text{Current assets} \div \text{Current liabilities}$$

The current assets are the "reservoir" of assets from which the current liabilities will be paid. Therefore, this ratio suggests the margin of safety for creditors. A common rule of thumb is that current assets should be twice the current liabilities; the ratio should be 2:1. But like all rules of thumb, a ratio of 2:1 may not be appropriate for a particular company or a particular industry. If cash flows are steady and reliable, then there is no need for such a high ratio. On the other hand, a volatile cash inflow may require a higher average ratio to provide a margin of safety so that the company can continue to pay its payroll and other immediate cash expenses.

If the current ratio is used as a measure of liquidity, then the components of current assets must be "liquid" or realizable in the short run. Current assets include inventory and prepaid expenses. Prepaid expenses obviously are not convertible into cash, but they do indicate expenses that have already been paid and will not require an additional cash outflow in the next period.

Inventories are a bigger problem. If the inventories are readily sellable, then it is appropriate to include them as a liquid asset. However, inventories may include supplies and spare parts that are not sold but used instead. Careful analysis of the disclosure note for the inventories is required to assess which inventory amounts are liquid and should be included in the ratio. If inventories are an important component of current assets, increasing inventory levels can be a danger sign since the longer inventories are held, the higher the risk of obsolescence.

Current liabilities may include unearned revenue. As with prepaid expenses, unearned revenue represents past cash flow. It does not represent a cash obligation of the company in the same way that accounts and notes payable do.

Quick Ratio

The **quick ratio** is also called the **acid-test ratio**. It is intended to overcome the deficiencies of the current ratio by excluding inventories and other nonmonetary current assets. Generally, cash and cash equivalents, short-term marketable securities, and accounts receivable are the monetary current assets to include. To be consistent, nonmonetary current liabilities (e.g., unearned revenue and other deferred credits) should also be excluded. Therefore, the ratio is determined as follows:

$$\text{Quick ratio} = \text{Monetary current assets} \div \text{Monetary current liabilities}$$

A ratio of less than 1:1 is generally undesirable. However, a low ratio is no cause for concern if the company's operating cash flow is steady and reliable. As with solvency ratios, liquidity ratios can be effectively interpreted only in reference to the *operating risk* and *financial risk* of the company. If cash inflows are stable, a low liquidity ratio should not be a cause for concern. But if operating cash flows are very volatile, even a high liquidity ratio should not make the analyst complacent. Cash can vanish from a high-risk operation very quickly.

Cash Conversion Cycle

A measure known as the **cash conversion cycle** also gives us some idea of liquidity and how long cash is tied up in financing the accounts receivable and inventories. It is actually a combination of some earlier ratios as follows:

$$\text{Cash conversion cycle} = \text{Average days in inventory} + \text{Average collection period for accounts receivable} - \text{Average days in payables}$$

The cash conversion cycle starts with a company's investment in inventory. At the time, the inventory is sold (after the holding period of days in inventory), an accounts receivable will result. The payable to the supplier must be paid, and finally cash is collected from the accounts receivable and the cycle begins again. If the cash conversion cycle is positive, then a company must finance these numbers of days. If the cash conversion cycle is negative, this implies that the company has the use of cash before the suppliers must be paid. Consider the following two examples:

	Days in Inventory	Average Collections Period for Accounts Receivable	Average Days in Payable	Cash Conversion Cycle
Company A	10	30	45	−5
Company B	30	30	45	15

In both cases the suppliers are paid in 45 days and receivables are collected in 30 days. However, in the case of Company A, the days in inventory is only 10 days, which results in a negative cash cycle. Company B has 30 days for inventory, resulting in a positive cash conversion cycle. These results indicate that Company A likely has short-term investments on hand (for investing the excess cash on a short-term basis), and Company B may have to borrow short-term debt to finance the 15 days.

Defensive-Interval Ratio

The current ratio and the quick ratio are static ratios in that they look at only the ability of the company to pay its short-term obligations with the short-term assets that exist at the SFP report date. Both ratios are flawed because they do not consider the rate at which expenditures are incurred. An alternative ratio is one that tests the number of days that the company could operate if the cash inflow were cut off, such as by a strike or an emergency shutdown. While many expenses are eliminated in a shutdown, others continue. For a company to survive a shutdown, it has to be able to pay its continuing operating costs. The intent of the **defensive-interval ratio** is to see how many days the company could pay its continuing expenses in the absence of an inflow of cash from operating revenue. The basic form of the ratio is as follows:

$$\frac{\text{Monetary current assets}}{\text{Annual operating expenditures} \div 365}$$

The difficulty with this ratio is in deciding what should be in the numerator and what should be in the denominator. The numerator clearly should be restricted to monetary assets (e.g., cash and cash equivalents, accounts receivable, and short-term investments).

The denominator would include only those cash expenses that will continue in the event of a shutdown. Many labour costs would be eliminated in a shutdown, as would acquisitions of new inventories and supplies. The problem for the external analyst, however, is that the financial statements seldom give enough detail to permit this analysis. Therefore, external analysts usually use short-term monetary assets (without deduction for monetary liabilities) as the numerator and operating expenses less non-cash charges (e.g., depreciation and amortization) in the denominator. The name of the ratio, by the way, comes from the concept of the short-term monetary assets as being *defensive assets*.

Common liquidity ratios are summarized in Exhibit 22-11.

EXHIBIT 22-11

SUMMARY OF LIQUIDITY RATIOS

Ratio Name	Computation	Significance and Difficulties
Current	$\dfrac{\text{Current assets}}{\text{Current liabilities}}$	Indicates ability to pay liabilities with current assets but includes inventories, prepaid expenses, and other deferred assets and liabilities.
Quick (acid-test)	$\dfrac{\text{Monetary current assets}}{\text{Monetary current liabilities}}$	A more refined test than the current ratio because it excludes nonmonetary assets and liabilities.
Cash conversion cycle	Average days in inventory + Average collection period for accounts receivable – Average days in payables	A measure of how long cash is "tied up" in working capital and not available for use. How long it takes to convert working capital investments into cash.
Defensive interval	$\dfrac{\text{Monetary current assets}}{\text{Projected daily operating expenditures}}$	Indicates the approximate number of days that the company can continue to operate with the currently available liquid assets. Denominator is very difficult to estimate by an external analyst.

Exhibit 22-12 shows the calculations of the liquidity ratios for GRI.

EXHIBIT 22-12

LIQUIDITY RATIOS FOR GRI

Ratio	20X6	20X5	Discussion
Current ratio	1,480/2,250 = 0.66	1,130/1,780 = 0.63	The current ratio has slightly increased, but it is still significantly below 1 (and even more below 2:1). Is this cause for concern? Likely not, since in this industry, most of the sales are cash sales and cash will be coming in daily and at a steady rate to cover the current obligations.

Ratio	20X6	20X5	Discussion
Quick ratio	(70 + 350)/ 2,250 = 0.19	(100 + 300)/ 1,780 = 0.22	The quick ratio is very low, but the same issues discussed above are still relevant.
Cash conversion cycle	31 + 9 − 44 = −4 days (From Exhibit 22-8)	27 + 9 − 37 = −1 days (From Exhibit 22-8)	The cash conversion cycle has improved. Although inventory days increased by 4 days, the company also lengthened its payment terms by 7 days. As long as the suppliers are in agreement with this, there should not be any concerns.
Defensive Interval	[(70 + 350)/(10,400 + 120 + 270 + 710 + 280)/365] = 13 days (See Notes 1 and 2)	[(100 + 300)/(10,150 + 110 + 250 + 645 + 260)/365] = 13 days (See Notes 1 and 2)	There has been no change in this, although it is very low.

Note 1—GRI has both cash sales and credit sales. The cash sales have an immediate collection period. If we calculated a weighted average of the cash and credit sales amounts, we would arrive at a better indicator for cash collection on sales.

Note 2—As discussed earlier, the specific numbers to use for the denominator and numerator are difficult to determine for external analysts. For GRI, we have estimated projected daily operating expenditures, using the sum of cash expenditures from the SCI as follows:

(COGS) + (Electricity + natural gas) + (Rent, taxes and occupancy costs) + (Other)/365 days

Assessment of GRI's liquidity ratios indicates that the current ratio, quick ratio, and defensive interval measures are all very low. However, the cash conversion cycle is negative, indicating that excess cash is generated from the operations, and this is primarily due to most of its sales being cash sales. As a result, cash will steadily come in to pay for current obligations and liquidity should not suffer.

Consolidated Statements

Most Canadian corporations operate through a series of subsidiaries. This is true even of quite small companies. One small chain of three restaurants, for example, may have each restaurant set up as a separate corporation. A company that operates in more than one province almost certainly will have at least one subsidiary in each province. Therefore, the analyst must be aware of just what she is analyzing: an individual corporation or a corporate group?

IFRS requires that the primary set of statements for a public company with subsidiaries be the *consolidated* financial statements, wherein all of the assets, liabilities, revenues, and expenses of all of the companies in the group are combined. The statements will give no clue as to which items belong to which legal corporate entity within the corporate group. If the company is a private corporation using ASPE, consolidated statements are optional and not a requirement.

An investor who is considering purchasing the shares of a corporation usually will want to see statements that show the full resources under control of the corporation, including those held by subsidiaries. The prospective investor is investing in the *economic entity*, and the consolidated statements are the appropriate basis of analysis.

A creditor or lender is in a different position, however. A creditor or lender holds an obligation only of the *separate legal entity*, not of the corporate group. Therefore, creditors or lenders must be careful to analyze the separate-entity statements of the specific corporation to which they are extending credit or granting loans.

The consolidated statements can give a very misleading view; lenders have been burnt in the past by lending money to a parent company on the basis of consolidated statements only to discover later that all of the cash flow is in the operating subsidiaries. Lenders may demand cross-company guarantees of debt, but trade creditors usually cannot demand such a guarantee. Cross-company guarantees may not be very effective anyway, since they are usually subordinated, and there may be legal impediments to their enforcement when they cross borders, especially national borders.

Therefore, financial statement analysis must be performed on the statements that are appropriate for the decision being made. Generally speaking, equity investors will use consolidated statements while creditors and lenders should use unconsolidated statements for their primary analysis.

Multi-Industry Corporations

Many corporations engage in several lines of business. These corporations may be either publicly or privately owned. Because they have a broad spectrum of activities, they cannot be classified as being in a specific industry. Industry comparisons are a common aspect of financial statement analysis, particularly of ratio analysis. The inability to slot many corporations into a specific industry classification may create a problem for the analyst for finding appropriate comparisons.

At the level of profitability analysis, the rate of return *on investment* should vary only by risk. The competition for capital is economy-wide and worldwide, so an investor should expect the same return on an investment *at a given level of risk* no matter what industry or industries a company is in.

Risk

Assessment is also a function of risk and return—while companies in a certain industry often have similar capital structures because of an underlying commonality of operating risk, there also are significant differences between companies in an industry. Industry classification is not an adequate definition of risk. For example, there is a relatively low risk level inherent in the operations of established mobile phone companies in contrast to the high risk borne by new entrants to the market.

The key is *risk*; the analyst must be able to evaluate the risks to the company and its ability to survive downturns and benefit from upturns. Industry analysis is useful because the general *market risk* is broadly similar to all of the players in that market. When a company's participation in several different markets is summarized in annual financial statements, it is impossible to tell just what the company's exposure to different risks is in different markets. Therefore, public companies are required to provide **segment reporting** as supplementary information in their annual financial statements. The volume of activity is reported both by industry and by geographic region.

Segment reporting gives the analyst a better idea of the company's exposure to the risks inherent in different industries and in different parts of the world. However, it is not feasible to perform ratio analysis at the same level of detail as for the company as a whole because the numbers included in the segment data are distinctly "fuzzy." The revenues include revenues between segments at transfer prices; the costs include allocated amounts with no useful disclosure of the nature of the allocations, and the operating profits therefore are the net result of two approximations. Segment disclosures certainly are better than no disclosures at all, often include limited information. For example, assets and liabilities may not be reported by segment.

Conclusion

The following are some concluding observations on ratio analysis:

- The apparent simplicity of ratio analysis is deceptive; ratios are only as good as the underlying data.
- The analyst must take care to analyze the correct set of financial statements: consolidated or separate legal entity.
- Financial statements often have to be adjusted to suit the analyst's needs before meaningful ratio analysis can be performed.
- Industry comparisons can be helpful, but there is no assurance that the industry averages are "right" or are based on similar accounting policies and measurements.
- Assessments of investment profitability, solvency, and liquidity are not really industry dependent, but they do depend to some extent on an analysis of risk for each line of business.
- There is no point in computing masses of ratios; it is more important to identify one or two key ratios in each category that are relevant to the analyst's decision needs and concentrate on those.

- Given the many estimates and approximations underlying both the numerator and denominator of *all* ratios, it is absurd to calculate them to more than two significant digits; computing to three or more digits gives ratios an appearance of precision that is completely unwarranted.
- Be careful in using ratios that have been calculated by others. As we have seen, ratios can have many variations where different analysts use different numbers in both the numerator and the denominator. Remember the variations of the debt to equity ratio that were available, depending on what was included and excluded in determining its components.

Finally, ratios can be very helpful when understood and used properly. Ratios provide clues and indicators; it is up to the analyst to use her expertise in analyzing all of the ratio results on an integrated basis to make the final conclusions.

CONCEPT REVIEW

1. What is the essential relationship between the numerator and denominator of any effective investment profitability ratio?
2. Is it necessarily a good thing for efficiency ratios to be very high?
3. Why do some analysts prefer to use debt-service ratios, such as times-debt-service-earned ratio, rather than the more common times-interest-earned ratio?
4. Why should creditors and lenders be wary of basing their analyses on consolidated financial statements?

OTHER ANALYTICAL TECHNIQUES

In addition to basic ratio analysis, other more sophisticated analytical techniques can be applied to the amounts in the financial statements or to the ratios themselves. These techniques include the following:

- *Time-series analysis.* The purpose of time-series analysis is to predict the future values of the ratios. Time-series analysis can be applied to cross-sectional ratios themselves or to the underlying financial data. The data can be used "raw" or can be subjected to transformations, such as logarithmic transformation.
- *Residual analysis.* This is a time-series analysis based on the differences between computed ratios and industry (or economy) averages. The intent is to identify the extent to which changes in a company's ratios are common to the industry (or economy) as a whole. Such an analysis may help to discover when a company is performing better or worse than other companies over a period of time.
- *Statistical multivariate ratio analysis.* In this approach, ratios are not analyzed one by one but fitted into a statistical model in an attempt to predict some type of outcome, such as impending bankruptcy.

An implicit assumption of these approaches is that the underlying *economic processes* that generate the numbers and ratios are stable. Furthermore, there is an implicit assumption that the underlying *measurement methods* (i.e., accounting policies and accounting estimates) also are stable and remain unchanged over the period of analysis and into the period being predicted. Neither assumption should automatically be taken as correct in a rapidly changing economic environment, especially in light of the dozens of changes in accounting standards over the past decade. This book will not delve further into these sophisticated statistical approaches.

Looking Forward

Accounting Standards for Private Enterprises

 Analytical techniques described above can be used on any financial statements, regardless of the underlying accounting standards followed. In all cases, the analyst must first be aware if the statements are prepared under IFRS or ASPE and make adjustments in the ratios, accordingly.

SUMMARY OF KEY POINTS

1. There are four main steps to completing financial statement analysis: understanding the objective of the analysis; gathering the data required; calculating the ratios; and analyzing the results.

2. The auditor's report (if any) should be reviewed with an eye to opinion qualifications and to comments regarding accounting policies, if any. The auditor's report serves only as assurance that accounting policies meet current accounting standards.

3. The essential first step in statement analysis is to fully understand the financial statements. The statements cannot be meaningfully analyzed unless they are viewed within the framework of management's reporting objectives and accounting policies.

4. Clues to the accounting policies used by management are found in the notes to the financial statements. The policy note may give only general information, but the notes relating to individual financial statement components may provide more useful information.

5. The accounting policies used by management may not be the most suitable for the purpose of the analyst's decision needs. The analyst may find it useful to recast the financial statements using different policies, such as by removing the effects of nonrecurring gains and losses from net income, or by treating as expense certain expenditures that the company has capitalized.

6. When the analyst recasts a company's financial statements, there may not be adequate information provided in the notes for an accurate restatement. Approximations often are necessary.

7. *Vertical analysis* (or *common-size analysis*) involves calculating financial statement components as a percentage of the total, such as SFP amounts as a percentage of total assets and SCI components as a percentage of total revenue.

8. Vertical analysis is useful for removing the effects of absolute changes in amounts; changes in the relative composition of SFP and SCI components may become more readily apparent.

9. *Horizontal analysis* (or *trend analysis*) involves calculating individual financial statement components over several years as an index number, with a base year set at 100. Horizontal analysis is used to determine the relative change in amounts between years.

10. *Ratio analysis* compares the proportional relationship between different items within a single year's financial statements. Often, it is necessary to adjust the numerator and denominator of a ratio by excluding or reclassifying certain components.

11. *Return on sales profitability ratios* measure how dollars of revenue are spent in costs required to earn those revenues. *Investment profitability ratios* are those that compare a measure of earnings (the numerator) with a measure of investment (the denominator). It is essential that the numerator and denominator be logically consistent.

12. *Efficiency ratios* attempt to measure selected aspects of the company's operations, such as inventory turnover or the accounts receivable collection period. Efficiency ratios must be used with great caution by an external analyst because the SFP amounts may not be typical of the balances throughout the period.

13. *Solvency ratios* reflect the ability of the company to meet its long-term obligations. Static solvency ratios include various forms of the debt to equity ratio; flow ratios examine the ability of the company to meet its debt financing obligations through its cash flows from operations.

14. *Liquidity ratios* test the company's ability to cover its short-term obligations with its existing current assets.

15. All ratios are based on accounting numbers that are the result of the company's accounting policies and which include the effects of many estimates made by management. Despite the fact that ratios can be computed to many decimals, they really are very approximate measures that must be interpreted with extreme caution.

Key Terms

accounts receivable aging schedule

accounts receivable turnover ratio

acid-test ratio

asset turnover

auditor's report

average collection period of accounts receivable

cash conversion cycle

cross-sectional comparison

current ratio

days in inventory

days in payables

debt service ratios

debt to equity

debt-to-total assets

debt-to-total-capitalization

defensive-interval ratio

efficiency ratios

financial risk

horizontal analysis

inventory turnover ratio

leverage

leverage ratios

liquidity ratios

longitudinal comparisons

margin of safety

negative leverage

operating margin

operating risk

profitability ratios

quick ratio

ratio analysis

return on common share equity

return on long-term capital

return on total assets

review engagement

segment reporting

solvency ratios

times-debt-service-earned ratio

times-interest-earned ratio

total capitalization

total debt-to-equity ratio

turnover ratios

vertical (common-size) analysis

Review Problem 22-1

Below are the financial statements of Gold Mining Inc. (GMI) for the years ended 20X1 to 20X3.

GOLD MINING INC.

Statement of Financial Position as at December 31

(in millions of Canadian dollars)

	20X3	20X2	20X1
	$	$	$
Cash and cash equivalents	281	404	758
Accounts receivable	560	519	311
Inventory	487	509	304
Prepaid expenses	80	25	15
	1,408	1,457	1,388
Property, plant, and equipment	6,342	6,010	4,385
Mineral property costs	1,894	1,940	1,569
Total assets	9,644	9,407	7,342
Liabilities			
Accounts payable and accrued liabilities	403	465	325
Taxes payable	105	69	22
Total current liabilities	508	534	347
Long-term debt	1,775	2,408	1,249
Deferred income taxes	689	481	357
Asset retirement obligations	383	267	180
Total liabilities	3,355	3,690	2,133
Shareholders' equity			
Share capital	3,050	2,945	2,902
Retained earnings	3,239	2,772	2,307
Total shareholder's equity	6,289	5,717	5,209
Total liabilities and shareholder's equity	9,644	9,407	7,342

GOLD MINING INC.

Statement of Comprehensive Income for the Years Ended December 31

(in millions of Canadian dollars)

	20X3	20X2	20X1
	$	$	$
Total net sales	4,240	4,232	2,616
Operating expenses			
Operating costs	1,659	1,726	936
Distribution costs	401	395	328
Royalty costs	275	279	242
Depreciation	510	502	305
Total operating costs (Cost of goods sold)	2,845	2,902	1,811
Profit from mining operations	1,395	1,330	805
Other expenses			
General and administration	223	210	189
Interest expense	179	115	130
Other	36	32	39
Total other expenses	438	357	358
Net earnings before taxes	957	973	447
Income taxes	240	244	112
Comprehensive income for the year	717	729	335

Required:

Calculate the following ratios for Gold Mining Inc. for 20X3 and 20X2:

- Operating margin
- Return on total long-term capital, after tax
- Return on assets, after tax
- Return on equity
- Average collection period of accounts receivable
- Average days in inventory
- Average days in payables
- Debt to equity

- Debt to total assets
- Times interest earned
- Current ratio
- Quick ratio

Comment on what the ratios reveal; that is, has the ratio improved or worsened from 20X2 to 20X3, and is there cause for concern? What additional information would you need to complete your analysis?

REVIEW PROBLEM 22-1 SOLUTION

	20X3	20X2	Discussion
Operating margin	(1,395 – 223 – 36)/4,240 = 26.8%	(1,330 – 210 – 32)/4,232 = 25.7%	Slight increase in margin
Return on total long-term capital, after tax	717 + 179 (1 – 0.25)/[(1,775 + 2,408 + 6,289 + 5,717)/2] = 10.5%	729 + 115 (1 – 0.25)/[(2,408 + 1,249 + 5,717 + 5,209)/2] = 11.2%	Decrease in return on capital
Return on assets, after tax	717 + 179 (1 – 0.25)/[(9,644 + 9,407)/2] = 8.9%	729 + 115 (1 – 0.25)/[(9,407 + 7,342)/2] = 9.7%	Decrease in return on assets
Return on equity	717/[(6,289 + 5,717)/2] = 11.9%	729/[(5,717 + 5,209)/2] = 13.3%	Decrease in return on equity
Average collection period of accounts receivable	365/[4,240/(560 + 519)/2] = 46 days	365/[4,232/(519 + 311)/2] = 36 days	Significant increase and cause for concern
Average days in inventory	365/[2,845/(487 + 509)/2] = 64 days	365/[2,902/(509 + 304)/2] = 51 days	Significant increase and cause for concern
Average days in payables	365/[(2,845 – 510*)/(403 + 465/2)] = 68 days	365/[(2,902 – 502*)/(465 + 325)/2] = 60 days	Significant increase and cause for concern
Debt to equity	1,775/6,289 = 0.28	2,408/5,717 = 0.42	Large reduction due to substantial increase in equity and reduction in debt
Debt to total assets	1,775/9,644 = 0.18	2,408/9,407 = 0.26	Large reduction due to reduction in debt
Times interest earned	(717 + 179 + 240)/179 = 6.3 times	(729 + 115 + 244)/115 = 9.5 times	Decreased due to decline in profits, but an increase in interest expense

	20X3	20X2	Discussion
Current ratio	1,408/508 = 2.8	1,457/534 = 2.7	Very slight improvement; no cause for concern
Quick ratio	(281 + 560)/508 = 1.7	(404 + 519)/534 = 1.7	Relatively stable year-over-year The only concern here is that the average collection period for receivables has increased, which may impact bad debts and decrease the true liquidity of this asset

Note 1—Tax rate is estimated as 25% (240/957) for 20X3 and 25% (244/973) for 20X2.

*Depreciation is subtracted, since this is not a cash cost and would not be part of payables.

Overall, the margins and profits have declined in 20X3 compared with 20X2. This has caused the profitability ratios to worsen. However, the solvency ratios have improved due to an increase in equity (due to a share capital issue) and a reduction in debt. Although the times-interest-earned has increased, with the reduction in debt, this may decline in the coming year. The most critical areas of concern are the efficiency ratios. The company's accounts receivable days collection period has increased 10 days, along with the company's days in inventory, which has increased 13 days. We see that the company is dragging its payables out to 68 days, likely to compensate for the amount of additional cash tied up in receivables and inventories. The current ratio and quick ratio have remained stable over the two-year period.

Examples of additional information required include:

- First of all, in the mining industry, we need to understand what the price of gold has done over the two-year period and how this impacts revenues.
- Why have the operating margins declined? This could be due to lower selling prices and/or higher operating costs. In the case of GMI, why might operating costs have increased?
- Why has the average days in inventory increased? Is this an industry trend indicating that supply is greater than demand? Or has GMI been producing too much inventory and is unable to sell it for some entity-specific reason?
- Why has the average days for collection of receivables increased? Is this a trend in the industry? Has GMI changed its mix of customers and/or credit terms?
- What is the average days in payables for competitors? GMI's days have increased significantly and may hinder its relationships with suppliers.
- What is the leverage of competitors in the industry? GMI has reduced its leverage with an issue of equity and a reduction of debt. Why was this action taken by the company?

CASE 22-1

PLASTICS MOULDING CO.

Plastics Moulding Co. (PMC) is a plastics company that operates in Canada. PMC manufactures plastic bottles for customers in North America. The company is publicly traded and follows IFRS. PMC has recently renewed its bank loan and the bank requested stricter covenants due to a reduction in lower forecasted revenues and earnings. The new covenants for 20X13 are as follows:

- Total liabilities (all liabilities excluding deferred taxes) to equity to be a maximum of 1.0.
- Times-interest-earned to be a minimum of 5.0 times.
- Current ratio to be a minimum of 1.0.

The company also has stock options outstanding that can be exercised only once profitability ratios meet certain targets. For the executive management team, these targets are as follows:

- Return-on assets-to be greater than 6%.
- Net income as a percentage of revenue to be no less than 10%.

It is now early December 20X13, and the accounting department has just completed its expected results for 20X13.

PMC recently hired a new financial analyst, Eric Forman, who has been examining the company's accounting policies. Eric would like to make some changes in some of these policies, as he believes that the changes will provide more relevant information to PMC's users. You are the CFO and Eric has come to you with some of his ideas. For you to be able to make this decision, you have asked Eric to explain the changes for 20X13 and what they would have been in 20X12 reports, if these new accounting policies were adopted.

Below is the summary of Eric's memo:

1. PMC should adopt the revaluation model for its land. The land was purchased about 30 years ago and has a cost of $50 million for 20X13 and 20X12. Eric has been able to determine that the fair value of the land at the end of 20X13, 20X12, and 20X11 to be $450 million, $400 million, and $425 million, respectively.

2. PMC currently uses the cost model for its investment properties. Eric suggests that the company adopt the fair-value model for investment properties. During 20X13 and 20X12, the company recognized depreciation of $24.9 million and $32 million, respectively (included in Other operating expenses). The fair value of all of the investment properties is estimated to be $850 million, $880 million, and $790 million for 20X13, 20X12, and 20X11, respectively.

3. The bonds receivable are currently recognized at amortized cost. Eric would like to classify these at FVTPL as the selling price has been increasing on these bonds, and it has been mentioned that PMC might sell once the price reaches a certain level. The bonds' fair market value was $195.2 million for 20X11; was $205.2 million in 20X12; and is estimated to be $210.2 million in 20X13.

As CFO, you have decided that the financial statements for 20X12 and forecasted 20X13 should be recast showing the impact of adopting the three proposed accounting policy changes. The memo to the board will have to include these restatements and a summary of the impact on the loan covenants and the share option targets. The memo should also discuss any possible volatility that these accounting policies may introduce on PMC's financial statements and ratios. A final recommendation will be required as to whether or not the company should adopt any of these changes. (The impact on deferred taxes is to be included using a rate of 30%.)

Required:

Prepare the memo for the board.

Below are the current financial statements of PMC.

Additional information:

Total assets for 20X11 were $2,904.6 million. Of this amount, the land was $50 million, investment property was $630 million, and the bonds receivable were $163 million.

EXHIBIT 1		

PLASTICS MOULDING CO.

Consolidated Statement of Financial Position 31 December

	20X13	20X12
(in millions of Canadian dollars)	**Forecasted**	**Actual**
Assets		
Current assets:		
Cash and cash equivalents	$ 17.1	$ 88.8
Short-term investments	45.8	75.9
Accounts receivable	373.1	378.2
Inventories	136.3	130.9
	572.3	673.8
Long-term bond receivables	165.2	165.2
Property, plant, and equipment	1,245.7	1,165.7
Investment properties	625.9	650.8
Intangible assets	171.7	163.4
Goodwill	369.1	375.5
Total assets	$3,149.9	$3,194.4
Liabilities and shareholders' equity		
Current liabilities:		
Accounts payable and accrued liabilities	$ 514.5	$ 609.6
Long-term debt due within one year	55.8	87.9
	570.3	697.5
Long-term debt	987.6	962.7
Deferred income taxes	98.4	106.1
	1,656.3	1,766.3
Shareholders' equity		
Capital shares	190.5	186.8
Retained earnings	1,303.1	1,241.3
	1,493.6	1,428.1
Total liabilities and shareholders' equity	$3,149.9	$3,194.4

Consolidated Statement of Comprehensive Income

Years Ended 31 December

(in millions of Canadian dollars)	20X13 Forecasted	20X12 Actual
Revenue	$ 1,116.7	$ 1,127.6
Cost of sales	718.0	690.7
Other operating expenses	190.9	194.8
	908.9	885.5
Earnings before interest and taxes	207.8	242.1
Interest income	11.0	13.0
Interest on long-term debt	(41.4)	(35.7)
Earnings before taxes	177.4	219.4
Income tax at 30%	53.2	65.8
Net earnings and comprehensive income	$ 124.2	$ 153.6

CASE 22-2

ALONGOS HOLDING CO.

Alongos Holding Co. (AHC) is owned by Edward and Mary Alongo. The company holds a variety of investments and currently follows ASPE for reporting purposes. Edward Alongo is considering changing to IFRS but he would like to understand the implications of adopting IFRS. He is particularly concerned about the impact these changes will have on some key ratios; in particular, return on assets after tax, return on equity after tax, and total debt to equity. The bank requires that the long-term debt to equity not be higher than 0.7.

Edward has come to you to request your assistance. He has asked that you calculate the ratios for the most recent ASPE statements (provided in Exhibit 1). He has also asked that you restate the 20X4 financial statements on the basis that IFRS is adopted and recalculate the ratios based on these restated amounts. The net earnings for 20X4 was $520,000 after tax. The company has an income tax rate of 30%. Although the company follows the future income tax method, there were no future income taxes at the end of 20X4. Recently you met with Edward and took notes on accounts that would be impacted with the changeover to IFRS. A summary of your notes are in Exhibit 2.

EXHIBIT 1

ALONGOS HOLDING COMPANY
BALANCE SHEET

(all amounts in thousands of Canadian dollars)	20X4
Current assets	
Cash and cash equivalents	$ 175
Marketable securities	720
	895
Bonds receivable	2,000
Investment in preferred shares	3,800
Investment in SODA	1,200
Vacant land	1,950
Total assets	$ 9,845
Current liabilities	
Accounts payable and accrued expenses	$ 320
Long-term bank loans	3,500
Total liabilities	3,820
Shareholders' equity	
Preferred shares	2,800
Common shares	1,500
Retained earnings	1,725
	6,025
Total liabilities and shareholders' equity	$9,845

EXHIBIT 2

ALONGOS HOLDING COMPANY
PROPOSED CHANGES TO ACCOUNTS

Summary of notes about proposed changes on adoption of IFRS
1. The bonds receivable have a face value of $2 million. The bonds mature in 10 years, and bear interest at 8%, payable quarterly. Current market yield on similar risk bonds is 10%. The bonds

are currently recorded at amortized cost and will be classified as FVTPL on adoption of IFRS. At the end of 20X3, the bonds had a market yield of 9%.

2. The investment preferred shares represents 40,000 shares with a stated dividend rate of $5.10 per share. The shares are currently at cost. This investment will be classified as FVOCI on adoption of IFRS. The shares have a current market value of $85 per share. At the end of 20X3, the market value per share was $80.

3. Investment in SODA is an equity investment purchased during 20X4, in which the company holds 30% voting ownership and has significant influence. The company currently recognizes this at cost. The investee, SODA, reported a net loss of $250,000 for 20X4. The investment has a current book value of $1,200,000 and a market value of $3,500,000.

4. The vacant land is being held for capital appreciation purposes. The land is currently recognized at historical cost. The land was recently appraised at a market value of $2,600,000. At the end of 20X3, the land had a market value of $2,750,000.

5. The preferred shares were issued as part of estate tax planning for the Alongos completed in 20X2. The shares are retractable for $2,800,000 at the holder's option at any time.

Required:

Prepare the memo for Edward showing the revised statements under IFRS and the revised ratios. Provide reconciliations of revised retained earnings, AOCI, and deferred income taxes.

CASE 22-3

FOREST INDUSTRY

You are evaluating two public companies in the forest industry. Both companies follow IFRS and are integrated companies that own or lease timber properties (biological assets), harvest trees, and make building supplies and paper products. This industry is very volatile. The profiles are as follows:

Canamora Forest Products Inc.

Canamora Forest Products Inc. (CFP) is a leading Canadian-integrated forest products company. The company employs approximately 6,800 people. The company has extensive production facilities in British Columbia and Alberta, and a lumber remanufacturing plant in the United States. The company is a major producer and supplier of lumber and bleached kraft pulp. It also produces semi-bleached and unbleached kraft pulp, bleached and unbleached kraft paper, plywood, remanufactured lumber products, hardboard panelling, and a range of specialized wood products, including baled fibre and fibremat. Products are sold in global markets.

Fallsview Building Materials Ltd.

Fallsview is a North American–based producer of building materials, including oriented strand board, medium-density fibreboard, hardwood plywood, lumber, I-joists, specialty papers, and pulp. The company is also the United Kingdom's largest producer of wood-based panels, including particleboard and value-added products. The company employs over 2,600 people in North America and 1,000 in the United Kingdom.

You have obtained some limited industry norms that relate to years prior to those presented for the two companies; industry norms are difficult to establish for the current years.

Selected ratios for the forest industry in Canada:

	20X5	20X4	20X3
Long-term interest-bearing debt-to-equity (%)	0.81	0.68	0.72
Operating profit margin	15.8	13.4	7.7
Return on assets (using year-end balance for denominator)	7.6	6	0.7
Return on equity (using year-end balance for denominator)	17.4	12.5	1.5
Current ratio	2.1	2.1	1.9

Summarized financial data for each company is shown in Exhibit 1. A standard financial statement analysis form is included.

EXHIBIT 1

COMPARATIVE FINANCIAL STATEMENTS (IN MILLIONS)

Statements of Financial Position

	Fallsview		Canamora	
	20X6	20X5	20X6	20X5
Assets				
Cash and cash equivalents	$ 208	$ 17	$ 20	$ 67
Temporary investments	24	—	—	—
Accounts receivable	304	321	267	242
Inventory	325	381	515	530
Total current assets	861	719	802	839
Property, plant, and equipment	1,469	1,518	1,984	1,903
Biological assets	230	190	27	22
Total assets	$2,560	$2,427	$ 2,813	$2,764
Liabilities				
Current liabilities				
Accounts payable	$ 480	$ 364	$ 323	$ 316
Current portion of long-term debt	53	49	4	15
Total current liabilities	533	413	327	331
Long-term debt	556	384	1,077	921
Other liabilities	170	65	96	97

	Fallsview		Canamora	
	20X6	**20X5**	**20X6**	**20X5**
Deferred income tax	147	363	38	112
	873	812	1,211	1,130
Total liabilities	1,406	1,225	1,538	1,461
Shareholders' equity				
Preferred shares	—	—	60	60
Common shares	657	657	889	880
Retained earnings	497	545	326	363
	1,154	1,202	1,275	1,303
Total liabilities and equity	$2,560	$2,427	$ 2,813	$2,764

STATEMENTS OF COMPREHENSIVE INCOME

	Fallsview		Canamora	
	20X6	**20X5**	**20X6**	**20X5**
Net sales	$1,986	$2,265	$2,066	$2,134
Costs and expenses				
Manufacturing/product costs	1,809	1,642	1,803	1,730
Change in fair value of biological assets	(50)	(20)	(10)	(8)
Depreciation and depletion	106	113	148	144
Selling and administration	58	67	90	90
	1,923	1,802	2,031	1,956
Operating income	**63**	**463**	**35**	**178**
Interest expense	64	60	52	40
Other (income) expense	(9)	(6)	(62)	25
Income before income tax	8	409	45	113
Income tax expense (recovery)	(18)	84	26	(34)
Net income and comprehensive income	$ 26	$ 325	$ 19	$ 147
Dividends				
Preferred	—	—	$ 2	$ 2
Common	$ 74	$ 25	$ 54	$ 50

(Source: [Adapted] © CGA-Canada. Reproduced with permission.)

The companies both have unqualified audit reports and have similar accounting policies except for the following:

1. Fallsview uses FIFO while Canamora uses weighted-average cost for inventory.
2. Both companies use a combination of straight-line and units-of-production depreciation methods for property, plant, and equipment, but Fallsview uses useful lives that are approximately 25% longer than those used by Canamora.

Required:

Provide an analysis that compares Fallsview and Canamora from the perspective of:

1. A potential short-term creditor.
2. A potential common stock investor.

Assume a tax rate of 30% for both companies.

TECHNICAL REVIEW

connect

TR22-1 Profitability Ratios:

Riyers Inc. has the following selected information for its years ended June 30:

	20X3	20X2	20X1
Gross sales	$567,800	$650,700	$589,200
Gross profit	$359,700	$422,950	389,460
Interest expense	$66,000	$75,000	$90,000
Income taxes (at 28%)	$56,000	$45,000	$35,000
Net earnings	$217,000	$160,600	$127,100

Required:

Calculate the gross profit margin and operating margin for each of the three years. Comment on the trend. What additional information would an analyst require to properly understand this trend?

connect

TR22-2 Profitability Ratios:

Refer to the information provided in TR22-1 along with the selected additional information below.

	20X3	20X2	20X1
Total assets	$1,782,000	$1,593,000	$1,498,000
Long-term debt	$862,000	$912,000	$1,120,000
Shareholders' equity	$678,000	$356,000	202,000

Required:

Calculate the return on total long-term capital, after tax; return on total assets, after tax; and return on equity for 20X2 and 20X3. Comment on the trend. Assume all of the interest expense relates to interest on long-term debt.

connect

TR22-3 Accounts Receivable Turnover:

PWX Inc. has the following information for its years ended June 30:

	20X3	20X2	20X1
Gross sales	$567,800	$650,700	$589,200
Accounts receivable	$62,500	$67,500	$53,200

Required:

Calculate the accounts receivable turnover and average collection period for 20X3 and 20X2. Comment on the trend. What additional information would an analyst require to properly understand this trend?

connect

TR22-4 Inventory Turnover:

Maddox Steel Co. had an inventory turnover of 9 in 20X3 and 7 in 20X4.

Required:

Interpret these figures and comment on the trend. What is the company's average days in inventory?

■ connect

TR22-5 Return on Assets Before Tax:

Below is selected information for XTM Inc. for the years ended December 31:

	20X9	20X8	20X7
Revenue	$12,700,200	$10,520,000	$8,900,500
EBIT	$1,040,000	$956,000	$875,000
Total assets	$16,800,000	$17,300,000	$18,600,000

Required:

Calculate the return on assets before tax for 20X9 and 20X8. Discuss what the ratios reveal about the company.

■ connect

TR22-6 Cash Conversion Cycle:

Selected data is provided below for KLS Co.:

	20X5	20X4	20X3
Revenue	$12,700,200	$10,520,000	$8,900,500
Cost of goods sold	$10,922,000	$8,940,000	$7,743,000
Accounts receivable	$1,220,000	$1,070,000	$975,400
Inventories	$1,690,300	$1,326,800	$909,000
Accounts payable	$1,346,000	$1,090,600	$997,000

Required:

Calculate the cash conversion cycle for 20X5 and 20X4. Is it likely that the company has short-term investments or requires short-term bank financing?

■ connect

TR22-7 Current Ratio and Quick Ratio:

Selected accounts from the SFP of SMI Ltd. at 31 December 20X8 and 20X7 are provided below:

(in thousands of dollars)	20X8	20X7
Current assets		
Cash and cash equivalents	$ 17,100	$ 88,900
Short-term investments	65,700	75,900
Accounts receivable	373,900	370,100
Inventories	156,900	126,700
Prepaid expenses	156,700	45,100
Total current assets	$770,300	$706,700
Total current liabilities	$451,000	$425,000

Required:

Calculate the current ratio and quick ratio for SMI for 20X8 and 20X7. Comment on what the ratios reveal.

■ connect

TR22-8 Time-Interest-Earned Ratio:

Refer to the information provided in TR22-1 and in TR22-2.

Required:

Calculate the times-interest-earned and the long-term debt-to-total capitalization ratios for 20X1, 20X2, and 20X3. Comment on what the ratios reveal.

■ connect

TR22-9 Times-Debt-Service-Earned:

SmartCo. has the following selected information for 20X6 and 20X7:

	20X7	20X6
Interest expense	$ 39,600	$ 36,700
Income taxes	$204,500	$ 147,900
Cash flow from operations	$572,600	$608,200
Finance lease payments	$285,000	$436,000
Principal repayments	$ 160,000	$ 190,000

The company pays taxes at the rate of 28%.

Required:

Calculate the times-debt-service-earned ratio for 20X6 and 20X7. Comment on what the ratio means and the trend from 20X6 to 20X7.

connect

TR22-10   Debt to Equity Ratio:

Selected accounts from the SFP of ARM Co. at 31 August 20X3 and 20X2:

(in thousands of dollars)	20X8	20X7
Short-term bank loans	6,790	5,800
Current portion of long-term debt	560	720
Long-term debt	89,700	92,000
Total shareholders' equity	75,900	93,400

Required:

Calculate the debt to equity ratio for ARM. What has happened to the leverage of the company, and why?

ASSIGNMENTS

eXcel

   A22-1 Horizontal and Vertical Analysis—Income Statement:

Buslines Inc.'s income statement (condensed) for two years is shown below:

31 December	20X4	20X5
Gross sales	$550,000	$606,000
Sales returns	(10,000)	(6,000)
	540,000	600,000
Cost of goods sold	(170,000)	(280,000)
Gross margin	370,000	320,000
Expenses		
Selling expenses	180,600	170,700
Administrative expenses	125,600	106,000
Restructuring	10,800	8,000
Interest	5,400	6,000
Income tax expense	14,400	7,300
	336,800	298,000
Net income and comprehensive income	$ 33,200	$ 22,000

Required:

1. Prepare vertical percentage analysis of the income statement. Round to the nearest percent. Comment on any particularly notable changes from 20X4 to 20X5.
2. Prepare a horizontal percentage analysis of the income statement. Use a single-step format. Round to the nearest percent. Comment on any significant changes from 20X4 to 20X5.

 A22-2 Horizontal and Vertical Analysis—SFP:

Bryant Co.'s statement of financial position (condensed and unclassified) for two years is shown below:

31 December	20X4	20X5
Cash	$ 60,000	$ 80,000
Accounts receivable (net)	120,000	116,000
Inventory (FIFO)	144,000	192,000
Prepaid expenses	8,000	4,000
Funds and investments (at cost)	60,000	88,000
Property, plant, and equipment	560,000	664,000

31 December	20X4	20X5
Accumulated depreciation	(104,000)	(196,000)
Intangible assets	12,000	60,000
Total	$860,000	$1,008,000
Accounts payable	$ 160,000	$ 100,000
Other current liabilities	40,000	40,000
Long-term mortgage payable	200,000	172,000
Common shares, no-par	340,000	520,000
Retained earnings	120,000	176,000
Total	$860,000	$1,008,000

Required:

1. Prepare a comparative SFP in good form, including vertical percentage analysis. Round to the nearest percent.
2. Prepare a horizontal percentage analysis of the comparative SFP in good form. Round to the nearest percent.

★★ A22-3 Vertical and Horizontal Analyses—SFP:

The SFP for Bold Chocolates Ltd. is as follows:

	31 December		
Statement of Financial Position	20X5	20X4	20X3
Cash	$ 116,000	$ 30,000	$ 95,000
Marketable securities	420,000	570,000	430,000
Receivables, net	650,000	510,000	550,000
Inventory	1,725,000	1,494,000	934,000
Property, plant, and equipment	7,644,000	5,239,000	4,039,000
Less: Accumulated depreciation	(1,951,000)	(1,461,000)	(1,176,000)

	31 December		
Statement of Financial Position	**20X5**	**20X4**	**20X3**
Intangible capital assets	378,000	405,000	350,000
	$8,982,000	$6,787,000	$5,222,000
Current liabilities	$ 379,000	$ 258,000	$ 579,000
Debentures payable	1,978,000	1,822,000	800,000
Common shares	3,151,000	2,100,000	2,100,000
Retained earnings	3,474,000	2,607,000	1,743,000
	$8,982,000	$6,787,000	$5,222,000

Required:

1. Prepare a comparative vertical percentage analysis. Round to the nearest percent.
2. Prepare a horizontal percentage analysis of the comparative SFP. Round to the nearest percent.
3. What conclusions can you reach about the changes in the company's asset and liability structure between 20X3 and 20X5?

 A22-4   Ratio Interpretation:

Simon Inc. had the following events occur during the year. Simon follows IFRS.

1. Simon has a fleet of trucks. It was recently decided that the company would replace old trucks with new finance leases rather than buying trucks as it had in the past using borrowed funds.
2. The company repurchased shares during the year, at prices lower than issue prices.
3. The company has bond investments that have been classified as FVOCI-Bonds. The bonds had increased in value since they had been purchased five years ago. However, during the year, the investments were sold for less than current book value but greater than original cost.

Required:

For each of the above transactions, discuss the implication on the company's debt to equity ratio, return on assets, and operating profit margin. (Treat each event in isolation.)

A22-5   Ratio Interpretation:

Sweets Inc., a candy manufacturer that follows IFRS, had the following events occur during the year:

1. Sweets decided to increase the number of years in depreciating its property and equipment from 30 to 40 years for the property, and from 10 to 15 years for its equipment. The company uses the straight-line depreciation method.

2. Sweets has taken on a new customer that will result in a 25% increase in sales. However, to obtain this contract, Sweets had to agree to extend credit terms to 45 days. For all other customers, credit terms have been consistently 30 days.

3. In the current year, Sweets determined that tax loss carryforward benefits were now probable and set up the benefit in the current year. The benefits were significant and represented more than 30% of net income.

Required:

For each of the above changes, discuss the implication on the company's debt-to-total assets, days in receivable, current ratio, and operating margin. Treat each change in isolation.

 connect

 A22-6 Ratio Interpretation:

Trimaz Co. has the following selected information from its financial statements:

(in thousands of dollars)	20X9	20X8
Revenues	2,330	1,805
Cost of goods sold	1,860	1,238
Accounts receivable	330	275
Inventories	230	225
Accounts payable	281	275

Required:

1. Calculate the cash conversion cycle for 20X9 and 20X8. (Use closing balances, rather than average balances, in the calculations.)

2. The company would like to improve its cash conversion cycle by three days by changing its days in inventory for 20X9. What would the revised inventory balance have to be to accomplish this reduction?

★★ **A22-7 Ratio Interpretation:**

Wilcox Ltd. has total assets of $35,000,000, and manufactures fine hand tools. Selected financial ratios for Wilcox and industry averages are as follows:

	Wilcox			Industry Average
	20X5	20X4	20X3	
Current ratio	2.41	2.12	2.04	2.28
Quick ratio	1.11	1.10	1.05	1.22
Inventory turnover	2.62	2.78	2.90	3.50
Return on equity	0.16	0.14	0.15	0.11
Debt-to-equity ratio	1.44	1.37	1.41	0.95
Return on assets	.12	.11	.11	.10
Asset turnover	3.14	3.01	3.00	3.70
Operating margin	.06	.05	.05	.05

Required:

Referring to the information presented above:

1. Identify two financial ratios of particular interest to:
   a. A financial institution that provides an operating line of credit for daily cash management needs. The line of credit is secured with a charge on inventory.
   b. A supplier, about to decide whether to sell to Wilcox on credit.
   c. An investment banker, consulting with Wilcox on a potential public offering of common shares.
2. Discuss what these financial ratios reveal about Wilcox.

 A22-8 Vertical and Horizontal Analyses:

Four-year comparative statements of comprehensive income and SFP for Firenza Products Inc. (FPI) are shown below. FPI has been undergoing an extensive restructuring in which the company has discontinued or sold several divisions in order to concentrate on its core business. As a result, the size of the company has decreased considerably.

Statement of Comprehensive Income				
Years ended 31 December	**20X8**	**20X7**	**20X6**	**20X5**
Net sales	$ 284.1	$ 949.6	$1,388.8	$2,153.9
Cost of products sold	369.2	793.5	1,045.9	1,649.0
Depreciation and amortization	38.4	94.8	88.7	146.9
Selling and administrative	46.4	49.0	53.4	82.7

Statement of Comprehensive Income

Years ended 31 December	20X8	20X7	20X6	20X5
Operating earnings (loss)	(169.9)	12.3	200.8	275.3
Interest expense	(1.7)	(14.8)	(16.2)	(40.5)
Other income (expense)	32.6	(0.5)	(5.3)	34.8
Earnings (loss) from continuing operations before income tax	(139.0)	(3.0)	179.3	269.6
Income tax (recovery)	(46.9)	(2.6)	79.7	115.4
Earnings (loss) from continuing operations	(92.1)	(0.4)	99.6	154.2
Earnings (loss) from discontinued operations	390.7	119.9	54.8	—
Net earnings and comprehensive income	$ 298.6	$ 119.5	$ 154.4	$ 154.2

Condensed Statement of Financial Position

31 December	20X8	20X7	20X6	20X5
Assets				
Current assets	$ 957.7	$ 407.6	$ 126.2	$ 197.7
Assets of discontinued operations	—	647.4	1,262.9	—
Investments and other	90.6	36.3	65.8	97.8
Property, plant, and equipment	1,289.2	1,286.5	1,318.2	2,200.3
Net assets	$2,337.5	$2,377.8	$2,773.1	$2,495.8
Liabilities and shareholders' equity				
Current liabilities	$ 736.5	$ 329.0	$ 157.3	$ 131.3
Liabilities of discontinued operations	—	174.5	438.3	—
Long-term debt	—	—	75.0	227.6
Deferred income taxes	161.8	202.8	136.7	190.0
Common shares	250.0	250.0	250.0	250.0
Retained earnings	1,189.2	1,421.5	1,539.6	1,488.1
Preferred shares issued by subsidiaries	—	—	—	34.3
Noncontrolling interest	—	—	176.2	174.5
Total liabilities and shareholders' equity	$2,337.5	$2,377.8	$2,773.1	$2,495.8

Required:

1. Prepare a vertical analysis of both the SCI and the SFP.
2. Prepare a horizontal analysis of the SCI and SFP. Use 20X5 as the base year.
3. What conclusions about the company and its financial practices can you discern from your analysis?

 A22-9   Ratio Interpretation:

The following ratios are available for a three-year period for Woolfrey Ltd.:

	20X6	20X7	20X8
Current ratio	1.7	1.8	1.9
Quick ratio	1.1	0.9	1.0
Average collection period of accounts receivable	51 days	57 days	66 days
Inventory turnover	4.5	4.0	3.3
Debt to total assets	51%	46%	41%
Long-term debt to shareholders' equity	52%	57%	62%
Sales as a percentage of 20X6 sales	100%	103%	107%
Gross profit percentage	36%	35%	35%
Operating margin	7%	7%	7%
Return on total assets	8%	8%	8%
Return on shareholders' equity	14%	13%	13%

Required:

1. Explain why the current ratio is increasing while the quick ratio is decreasing.
2. Comment on the company's use of financial leverage.

★★ A22-10 Compute and Explain Profitability Ratios:

The 20X5 comparative financial statements for Wilson Corp. reported the following selected information:

	20X3	20X4	20X5
Sales revenue	$17,000,000	$18,500,000	$19,250,000
Net income	160,000	180,000	112,500
Interest expense, long-term debt	15,000	18,000	27,000
Income tax expense	60,000	90,000	90,000
Long-term debt	1,100,000	1,600,000	1,350,000
Shareholders' equity, common and preferred*	2,300,000	2,275,000	2,090,000
Total assets	5,250,000	5,250,000	5,700,000
Preferred share dividends	19,000	15,000	18,000
Income tax rate	30%	27%	25%

*Preferred shares, $150,000 in all years.

Required:

1. Based on the above financial data, compute the following ratios for 20X4 and 20X5:
   a. Return on total assets, before tax
   b. Return on total assets, after tax
   c. Return on long-term capital, before tax
   d. Return on long-term capital, after tax
   e. Return on common shareholders' equity
   f. Operating margin
   g. Asset turnover
2. As an investor in the common shares of Wilson, which ratio would you prefer as a primary measure of profitability? Why?
3. Explain any significant trends that appear to be developing.

★★ A22-11 Ratio Analysis:

The table below shows selected information reported by a Canadian retailer during a five-year period:

(in millions of dollars, except EPS)	20X5	20X4	20X3	20X2	20X1
Gross operating revenue	$ 8,687	$ 9,121	$ 8,606	$ 8,253	$ 7,714
Operating expenses	7,788	8,200	7,694	7,416	6,896
Depreciation and amortization	248	226	207	192	185
Interest expense	147	123	63	76	84
Income taxes	144	168	200	201	190
Net earnings	335	375	412	355	330
Current assets	5,113	3,979	3,138	2,541	2,973
Inventories	934	917	779	667	675
Property and equipment (net)	3,180	3,199	3,284	2,881	2,744
Total assets	8,790	7,784	6,765	5,805	5,956
Current liabilities	2,564	2,000	2,114	1,664	1,821
Long-term debt (excl. current)	1,102	1,374	1,342	1,168	1,171
Shareholders' equity	3,687	3,565	3,108	2,785	2,511
Basic EPS	$ 4.10	$4.60	$ 5.05	$ 4.35	$ 4.04
No. of common shares at year-end (000s)	78,178	78,178	78,048	78,047	78,033
No. of retail outlets	1,216	1,207	1,168	1,130	1,112

Required:

Based on the data above, analyze the changes that have occurred over this five-year period in terms of profitability and solvency.

 ## A22-12 Ratio Analysis; Liquidity and Efficiency:

The condensed financial information given below was taken from the annual financial statements of Conter Corp.:

	20X3	20X4	20X5
Current assets (including inventory)	$840,000	$1,008,000	$1,176,000
Current liabilities	630,000	672,000	588,000
Cash sales	1,360,000	1,276,000	2,444,000

	20X3	20X4	20X5
Credit sales	1,840,000	2,176,000	2,050,000
Cost of goods sold	2,352,000	2,457,000	2,520,000
Inventory (ending)	604,000	688,000	520,000
Accounts receivable	252,000	268,800	256,200
Total assets (net)	5,200,000	6,040,000	6,880,000
Projected daily operating expenditures	12,600	13,020	12,180

Required:

1. Based on the above data, calculate the following ratios for 20X4 and 20X5. Briefly explain the significance of each ratio listed. Use the following format:

Ratio	20X4	20X5	Significance
Current			
Quick			
Defensive interval			
Asset turnover			
Accounts receivable turnover			
Average collection period of accounts receivable			
Inventory turnover			

2. Evaluate the overall results of the ratios, including trends.

 connect

★★ A22-13 Compute and Summarize Significance of Ratios:

Fader Corp.'s 20X4 and 20X5 SFP and 20X5 SCI are as follows (in millions of dollars, except per share amounts):

Condensed Statement of Financial Position

31 December	20X5	20X4
ASSETS		
Cash	$ 11	$ 20
Investments (short-term)	3	4
Accounts receivable (net of allowance)	23	19
Inventory (FIFO)	31	37
Prepaid expenses	4	3
Investments, long-term	31	31
Property, plant, and equipment (net of accumulated depreciation of $29 (20X4), $37 (20X5)	81	72
Total assets	$184	$186
LIABILITIES AND SHAREHOLDERS' EQUITY		
Accounts payable	$ 22	$ 10
Accrued liabilities	2	2
Notes payable, long-term	41	45
Common shares, no par (60,000 shares outstanding)	76	76
Retained earnings (including 20X4 and 20X5 income)	43	53
Totals	$184	$186

Statement of Comprehensive Income, 20X5

Sales revenue (1/3 were credit sales)	$153
Investment revenue	4
Cost of goods sold	(70)
Distribution expense	(20)
Administrative expense (includes $8 of depreciation)	(15)
Interest expense	(4)
Income tax expense (the tax rate is 40%)	(20)
Net income and comprehensive income	$ 28

Additional information:

Cash flow from operations	$ 22

Required:

Compute the 20X5 ratios that measure:

a. Profitability (after tax only)
b. Efficiency
c. Solvency
d. Liquidity

For each category, use a format similar to the following (example given for 20X4):

Ratio	Formula	Computation	Significance
Current ratio	$\dfrac{\text{Current assets}}{\text{Current liabilities}}$	$83 ÷ $12 = 6.9	Short-term liquidity; adequacy of working capital

 A22-14 Selected Ratios:

The 20X9 condensed SCI and the 20X9 and 20X8 condensed SFP for Georgian Ltd. are shown below. All sales are on credit. The company's income tax rate is 28%.

Condensed Statement of Comprehensive Income

Year ended 31 December 20X9

Sales revenue (all on credit)	$40,000
Cost of goods sold	22,500
Gross profit	17,500
Operating expenses	12,100
Operating income	5,400
Interest expense	1,500
Income before income taxes	3,900
Income tax expense	1,100
Net income and comprehensive income	$ 2,800

Condensed Statement of Financial Position

31 December	20X9	20X8
Cash	$ 5,500	$ 7,500
Accounts receivable (net)	13,500	14,500
Inventory	8,000	6,000
Plant and equipment	40,000	38,000
Accumulated depreciation	(18,000)	(22,500)
Land	35,000	30,500
Total	$84,000	$74,000
Accounts payable	$ 5,800	$ 6,000
Long-term notes payable	13,700	10,000
Common shares	20,000	15,000
Retained earnings	44,500	43,000
Total	$84,000	$74,000

Required:

Compute the following ratios for 20X9:

a. Return on assets after taxes
b. Times interest earned
c. Gross profit margin
d. Return on shareholders' equity
e. Days in inventory
f. Accounts receivable turnover

(Source: [Adapted] © CGA-Canada. Reproduced with permission.)

 A22-15 Profitability and Solvency Ratios, Competing Companies:

Abacus Ltd. and Zandi Corp. are competing businesses. Abacus owns all of its operating assets, financed largely by secured loans. Zandi leases its operating assets from a major industrial leasing company. The 20X2 SCIs and SFPs for the two companies are shown below.

Statements of Comprehensive Income

Year ended 31 December 20X2	Abacus	Zandi
Sales revenue	$540,000	$270,000
Direct costs of providing services	300,000	150,000
Depreciation	100,000	10,000
Other expenses	60,000	87,000
Total operating expenses	460,000	247,000
Net operating earnings	80,000	23,000
Interest expense	24,000	—
Earnings before income taxes	56,000	23,000
Provision for income taxes	17,000	7,000
Net earnings and comprehensive income	$ 39,000	$ 16,000

Statements of Financial Position

31 December 20X2	Abacus	Zandi
Current assets	$260,000	$130,000
Property, plant, and equipment	1,000,000	50,000
Accumulated depreciation	(600,000)	(30,000)
Total assets	660,000	$150,000
Current liabilities	$ 120,000	$ 60,000
Long-term liabilities	360,000	—
Common shares	100,000	50,000
Retained earnings	80,000	40,000
Total liabilities and shareholders' equity	$660,000	$150,000

Required:

1. Compute the following ratios for both companies (for convenience, use 20X2 year-end balance sheet amounts instead of averages):
   a. Operating margin
   b. Asset turnover

   c. Return on assets

   d. Return on shareholders' equity

   e. Total debt-to-shareholder's equity

2. Evaluate the two companies, based on the ratios you have calculated. Which company do you think is more profitable?

 A22-16 Competing Companies, Continuation:

Refer to the information in A22-15; Zandi's financial statements contain the following note disclosure:

Commitments:

The Company has commitments for operating lease payments for the next five years as follows:

20X3	$103,000
20X4	89,000
20X5	75,000
20X6	55,000
20X7	40,000

Required:

Determine how this additional information would affect the ratios for Zandi that are required in A22-15. Assume that the disclosed lease payments are due at the end of each year and that Zandi's incremental borrowing rate is 6%. Ignore any income tax impact.

 A22-17 Ratio Analysis—Segmented Information:

Clothing Stores Inc. has operating segments defined by geographic regions. Below is the information that was provided in the notes related to these segments:

(in millions of Canadian dollars)	Canada	United States	Europe
Revenues	2,389	5,860	1,458
Gross margin	824	1,558	508
Operating expenses	(502)	(1,348)	(335)
Depreciation and amortization included in operating expenses	50	120	38
Total assets	3,289	7,500	1,490
Total liabilities	1,570	5,720	450

Required:

1. What ratios can be calculated using the above information?
2. What do these ratios reveal? Why might differences arise in these ratios?

 A22-18 Leverage—Sell Share Capital versus Debt, Analysis:

Alpha Ltd. is considering building a second plant at a cost of $4,700,000. Management has two alternatives to obtain the funds: (1) sell additional common shares or (2) issue $4,700,000, five-year bonds payable at 9% interest. Management believes that the bonds can be sold at par for $4,700,000 and the shares at $65 per share. The statements (before the new financing) show the following selected information:

Average net income for past several years (net of tax)	400,000
Long-term liabilities	$1,600,000
Common shares, no par (40,000 shares)	3,200,000
Retained earnings	1,300,000

The average income tax rate is 25%. Dividends per share have been $5 per share per year. Expected increase in pre-tax income (excluding interest expense) from the new plant is $950,000 per year.

Required:

1. Prepare an analysis to show, for each financing alternative,
   a. Expected total net income after the addition;
   b. After-tax cash flows from the company to prospective owners of the new capital; and
   c. The (leverage) advantage or disadvantage to the present shareholders of issuing the bonds to obtain the financing, as represented by comparing return-on-assets to return-on-equity.
2. What are the principal arguments for and against issuing the bonds, as opposed to selling the common shares?

 A22-19 Comparative Analysis:

Frank Smythe, the owner of Cuppola Ltd., has asked you to compare the operations and financial position of his company with those of Ling Ltd., a large company in the same business and a company that Frank Smythe considers representative of the industry.

	Cuppola Limited		Ling Limited	
	20X1	**20X0**	**20X1**	**20X0**
Statements of Financial Position				
Assets				
Cash	$ 100,000	$ 20,000	$ 100,000	$ 125,000
Accounts receivable	70,000	60,000	800,000	750,000

	Cuppola Limited		Ling Limited	
	20X1	20X0	20X1	20X0
Inventories	230,000	190,000	2,400,000	1,825,000
	400,000	270,000	3,300,000	2,700,000
Property, plant, and equipment	500,000	500,000	5,300,000	5,000,000
Accumulated depreciation	(300,000)	(270,000)	(2,600,000)	(2,300,000)
Goodwill	—	—	500,000	500,000
	200,000	230,000	3,200,000	3,200,000
	$ 600,000	$ 500,000	$6,500,000	$5,900,000
Liabilities and shareholders' equity				
Bank indebtedness	$ 40,000	$ 30,000	$ 500,000	$ 300,000
Trade accounts payable	135,000	100,000	1,300,000	650,000
Current portion of long-term debt	20,000	20,000	300,000	300,000
	195,000	150,000	2,100,000	1,250,000
Long-term debt	30,000	50,000	1,400,000	1,700,000
	225,000	200,000	3,500,000	2,950,000
Shares issued and outstanding				
—preferred	—	—	500,000	500,000
—common	50,000	50,000	1,500,000	1,500,000
Retained earnings	325,000	250,000	1,000,000	950,000
	375,000	300,000	3,000,000	2,950,000
	$ 600,000	$ 500,000	$6,500,000	$5,900,000

	Cuppola Limited		Ling Limited	
	20X1	**20X0**	**20X1**	**20X0**
Statements of Comprehensive Income				
Sales	$1,300,000	$1,000,000	$9,000,000	$7,500,000
Cost of sales	(936,000)	(700,000)	(6,120,000)	(5,250,000)
Expenses, including income tax	(266,500)	(250,000)	(2,100,000)	(1,800,000)
Net income and comprehensive income	$ 97,500	$ 50,000	$ 780,000	$ 450,000

Required:

Compare the operations and financial positions of the two companies, supporting your comments with useful ratios and percentages.

 A22-20 Investment Analysis:

Sandy Panchaud has come to you for some independent financial advice. He is considering investing some of his money in an operating company, and he wants to know which of the two alternatives he has identified is the better investment. They are both in the same industry, and Mr. Panchaud feels he could buy either for book value. The most recent statements for each company are provided below:

	Company A	Company B
Statements of Comprehensive Income		
Sales	$2,797,000	$2,454,000
Cost of goods sold	1,790,000	1,594,000
Gross margin	1,007,000	860,000
Operating expenses	807,000	663,000
Operating income	200,000	197,000
Interest expense	70,000	43,000
Income before income tax	130,000	154,000
Income tax expense	52,000	62,000
Net income and comprehensive income	$ 78,000	$ 92,000

	Company A	Company B
Statements of Financial Position		
Cash	$ 66,000	$ 27,000
Accounts receivable (net)	241,000	262,000
Merchandise inventory	87,000	110,000
Prepaid expenses	12,000	7,000
Plant and equipment (net)	792,000	704,000
	$ 1,198,000	$ 1,110,000
Accounts payable and accrued liabilities	$ 191,000	$ 173,000
Long-term debt	635,000	310,000
Common shares	50,000	200,000
Retained earnings	322,000	427,000
	$ 1,198,000	$ 1,110,000

Required:

Prepare a response to Mr. Panchaud. Your response should include an appropriate selection of ratios and a common-size (vertical analysis) income statement.

 A22-21 Recasting, Selected Ratios (Appendix):

A loan officer for the Dominion Bank of Alberta wishes to recast her client's financial statements so that they reflect income tax expense on a taxes payable basis. The tax rate is 30%. One of her clients is Frobisher Bay Corp. (FBC). FBC's condensed year-end 20X4 statements are shown below:

Statement of Comprehensive Income

Year ended 31 December 20X4

Sales revenue	$660,000
Cost of goods sold	360,000
Depreciation expense	72,000
Interest expense	12,000
Other expenses	96,000
	540,000

Earnings before income tax	120,000
Income tax:	
—current	14,400
—deferred	21,600
	36,000
Net earnings and comprehensive income	$ 84,000

Statement of Financial Position

31 December 20X4

Current assets	$ 144,000
Capital assets:	
—Tangible (net)	624,000
—Identifiable intangible	168,000
Total assets	$936,000
Current liabilities:	
Accounts payable	96,000
Accrued liabilities	24,000
	120,000
Long-term debt	384,000
Deferred income tax	192,000
Total liabilities	696,000
Common shares	60,000
Retained earnings	180,000
Total shareholders' equity	240,000
Total liabilities and shareholders' equity	$936,000

Required:

1. Recast FBC's statements.
2. Compute the following ratios, both before and after recasting the statements:
   a. Operating margin.
   b. Return on total assets (after tax).
   c. Total liabilities to shareholders' equity.

 connect

★★ A22-22 Integrative Problem, ASPE:

The following information is available for Davison Ltd., a private company, for the year ended 31 December 20X6:

Balance Sheet 31 December

	($ thousands)	
	20X6	20X5
Cash	$1,720	$1,110
Marketable securities	450	550
Receivables, net	1,150	1,170
Inventory	2,575	2,110
Property, plant, and equipment	3,984	3,396
Less: Accumulated amortization	(1,650)	(1,487)
Intangible assets	555	417
Goodwill	135	135
	$8,919	$ 7,401
Current liabilities	$2,190	$ 1,900
Convertible bond payable	833	834
Future income taxes	619	585
Preferred shares	500	500
Common stock conversion rights	166	166
Common shares	2,150	1,700
Retained earnings	2,461	1,716

Balance Sheet 31 December

	($ thousands)	
	20X6	**20X5**
	$8,919	$ 7,401

Statement of Earnings

Year ended 31 December	**20X6**
Sales (on account)	$10,450
Cost of goods sold	7,619
	2,831
Operating expenses	1,548
	1,283
Income tax	385
Net income	$ 898

Additional information:

- The company has a $1,000,000, 10% bond outstanding. Each $1,000 bond is convertible into 50 common shares at the investor's option. The bond proceeds were split between the debt and equity when the bond was issued. In 20X6, interest expense of $98 per bond was recognized.
- The tax rate is 30%.
- In 20X6, stock options were outstanding to key employees, allowing them to buy 40,000 common shares for $16 per share at any time after 1 January 20X18. The common shares were recently valued to be $20 for 20X6.
- 420,000 common shares were outstanding on 31 December 20X6; 40,000 of those shares had been issued for cash on 1 February 20X6.
- Preferred shares are cumulative and have a dividend of $4 per share; 10,000 shares are outstanding. Each share can be converted into four common shares at any time.
- Davidson Ltd. declared and paid dividends totalling $25,000 in 20X6.

Required:

Calculate the following ratios for 20X6 based on the financial statements above:

a. Debt to equity (total debt)
b. Inventory turnover
c. Quick ratio
d. Return on assets (after tax)
e. Return on common shareholders' equity

f.   Accounts receivable turnover (all sales are on account)

g.   Asset turnover

h.   Return on long-term capital, after tax

i.   Operating margin

APPENDIX 1

RECASTING FINANCIAL STATEMENTS— DEMONSTRATION CASE

Introduction

This chapter has emphasized that it may be necessary for an analyst to recast a company's financial statements before any ratio analysis is undertaken. To illustrate the task of restatement, we have chosen the financial statements of a Canadian company, QDO Ltd. (not the real name). We will restate these financial statements to reflect different accounting policy choices. After the restatement, we will compare the results of ratio analysis before and after restatement.

The Company

QDO is a publicly traded software development company following IFRS. Its primary line of business is the design and development of large-scale custom software for specific large clients. Clients include several of the provinces, one Canadian bank, and two international insurance companies. Between 20X5 and 20X8, gross revenue tripled and net income increased from $262,725 to over $2 million. Operating margin, based on the published financial statements, increased from 0.26% in 20X5 to 7% in 20X8. The company's consolidated statement of comprehensive income for the most recent four years is shown in Exhibit 22A-1; the consolidated statement of financial position is shown in Exhibit 22A-2; the consolidated statement of cash flows is shown in Exhibit 22A-3.

EXHIBIT 22A-1

QDO LIMITED

Consolidated Statement of Comprehensive Income

For the Years Ended 31 December

(in thousands of Canadian dollars)	20X8	20X7	20X6	20X5
Gross revenue	$29,276	$19,305	$ 14,317	$10,231
Less: Cost of goods sold	4,497	2,519	1,519	1,407

(in thousands of Canadian dollars)	20X8	20X7	20X6	20X5
Gross profit	24,779	16,786	12,798	8,824
Expenses				
Operating and administrative	22,390	15,108	11,718	8,323
Depreciation and amortization—PPE	203	49	22	6
Finance leases	143	85	23	1
Software development costs	513	67	—	—
Total expenses	23,249	15,309	11,763	8,330
Operating profit	1,530	1,477	1,035	494
Finance income (interest on cash deposits)	1,265	—	—	—
Finance costs	(164)	(224)	(238)	(95)
Income before income tax	2,631	1,253	797	399
Income tax expense (recovery)	569	(199)	(3)	137
Net profit or loss and comprehensive income	$ 2,062	$ 1,452	$ 800	$ 262

EXHIBIT 22A-2

QDO LIMITED

Consolidated Statement of Financial Position

As at 31 December

(in thousands of Canadian dollars)	20X8	20X7	20X6	20X5
ASSETS				
Current assets				
Cash and cash equivalents	$ 8,716	$ —	$ —	$ —
Accounts receivable	6,459	4,658	5,112	2,370
Work in progress	7,451	2,780	—	—
Hardware inventory	569	—	—	—
Prepaid expenses and supplies inventory	1,151	470	126	123
	24,346	7,908	5,238	2,493

(in thousands of Canadian dollars)	20X8	20X7	20X6	20X5
Property, plant, and equipment				
Leasehold improvements	852	317	278	16
Furniture, fixtures, and computer equipment	624	121	138	16
Assets under finance lease	1,374	817	359	156
	2,850	1,255	775	188
Less: Accumulated depreciation	(293)	(90)	(38)	(11)
	2,557	1,165	737	177
Other assets				
Software development costs	15,233	5,157	1,580	112
Deferred income taxes	—	355	409	409
	15,233	5,512	1,989	521
Total assets	$42,136	$14,585	$7,964	$3,191
LIABILITIES AND SHAREHOLDERS' EQUITY				
Current liabilities				
Bank and other loans	$ 2,806	$ 3,371	$2,653	$ 900
Accounts payable and accrued liabilities	7,054	3,550	2,131	918
Deferred revenue	530	461	183	140
Current portion of finance lease obligations	281	161	85	23
	10,671	7,543	5,052	1,981
Noncurrent liabilities				
Finance lease obligations	1,488	1,101	662	134
Deferred income taxes	214	—	104	104
Total liabilities	12,373	8,644	5,818	2,219
Shareholders' equity				
Share capital	26,994	3,989	1,090	497
Retained earnings	2,769	1,952	1,056	475
	29,763	5,941	2,146	972
Total liabilities and shareholders' equity	$42,136	$14,585	$7,964	$3,191

EXHIBIT 22A-3

QDO LIMITED

Consolidated Statement of Cash Flows

For the Years Ended 31 December

(in thousands of Canadian dollars)	20X8	20X7	20X6	20X5
Operations				
Net profit or loss for the year	$ 2,062	$1,452	$ 800	$ 262
Add: Non-cash items				
Deferred income taxes	569	(50)	—	50
Depreciation and amortization	859	200	45	7
Deferred lease rent credits	—	82	142	—
Finance income	(1,265)			
Finance costs	164	224	238	95
Income taxes (recovery)	0	(149)	(3)	87
Net change in working capital items	(3,619)	(579)	(1,315)	(261)
	(1,230)	1,180	(93)	240
Interest paid	(178)	(230)	(257)	(105)
Interest received	1,202			
Income taxes paid	(150)	10	(90)	(110)
Cash provided by (used for) operating activities	(356)	960	(440)	25
Investment				
Investment in software products	(10,588)	(3,645)	(1,469)	(110)
Purchase of fixed assets	(1,034)	(36)	(162)	(89)
Proceeds from disposal of fixed assets	—	—	—	160
Cash provided by (used for) investment activities	(11,622)	(3,681)	(1,631)	(39)
Financing				
Net issue (repayments) of bank and other loans	(565)	718	1,753	(164)
Repayments of finance lease obligations	(325)	(161)	(55)	(24)
Issue of shares	21,858	2,525	2,138	244
Loss on sale of repurchased shares	(46)	—	—	—

(in thousands of Canadian dollars)	20X8	20X7	20X6	20X5
Dividends declared	(14)	(295)	(176)	(33)
Shares purchased and cancelled	(214)	(66)	(1,589)	(9)
Cash provided by (used for) financing activities	20,694	2,721	2,071	14
Increase (decrease) in cash during year	$ 8,716	$ 0	$ 0	$ 0
Cash and cash equivalents, beginning of year	0	0	0	0
Cash and cash equivalents, end of year	$ 8,716	$ 0	$ 0	$ 0

In 20X7, the company's managers decided to develop some of its large-scale custom software designs into off-the-shelf turn-key proprietary products that would be adaptable to any prospective user. In addition, the company launched an ambitious sales expansion plan, establishing offices in 11 Canadian cities and 10 U.S. cities, plus one in Singapore. To help finance the expansion, the company raised approximately $22 million through a public issue of common shares early in 20X8. The company also increased its line of credit with a Canadian bank to $5 million.

The product development expenditures for the proprietary products were accounted for in accordance with accounting standards. Since, in management's judgement, all of the criteria for capitalization were satisfied, it was acceptable to capitalize the development expenditures. It is now 20X9. Over the first three months of the year, the company has completely used the cash and cash equivalents that are shown on the year-end 20X8 SFP and is near the limit on its line of credit. The company's CEO has approached the Canadian bank with a proposal to further extend the company's line of credit to enable the company to continue development of its proprietary software and to support the costs of the new sales offices until the offices become self-sufficient.

Task

You are an analyst for the Canadian bank. The bank's credit committee is interested in the sustainable operating cash flow of QDO. Investment in software development is considered by the bank to be an ongoing operating activity, crucial to the success of the company. Therefore, the chair of the Credit Committee has asked you to recast QDO's 20X7 and 20X8 financial statements as follows:

- Development costs incurred in each year should be shown as a current expense.
- All deferred income tax amounts should be reversed out of the statements.

Once the statements have been restated, the credit committee would like you to calculate a few ratios that relate to the company's ability to sustain increased borrowing. Specifically, the requested ratios are:

1. Return on total assets, before tax;
2. Total liabilities-to-shareholders' equity; and
3. Times-interest-earned.

Nonrecurring items of revenue or expense should be eliminated before calculating any ratios based on net income. The ratios should be calculated both on the original financial statements and on the restated amounts.

Additional Information

The following information is extracted from QDO's disclosure notes:

1. **Summary of significant accounting policies**

   (c)   Software product costs

   Costs, including an allocation of interest and overhead, which relate to the development and acquisition of computer-based systems, where the systems are expected to be sold in substantially the same form in the future, are capitalized. It is the Company's policy to charge these costs to profit or loss, commencing in the year of development completion, based on projected-unit-sales over a period of no longer than three years or when it is determined that the costs will not be recovered from related future revenues.

5. **Software product costs**

   The following is an analysis of software product costs:

	20X8	20X7
Net balance, beginning of year	$ 5,157,271	$ 1,579,174
Additions during the year	10,588,218	3,644,763
Less: Amortization for the year	(512,711)	(66,666)
Net Balance, end of year	$15,232,778	$5,157,271

Demonstration Case—Solution

Approach

The assignment from the credit committee is to recast the statements by making two changes:

- The accounting policy for development costs should be changed from capitalization to immediate expensing.
- The effects of income tax allocation are to be removed so that the statements reflect only the current income tax due.

To make these changes, we need to take the following steps:

1. *Statement of comprehensive income*

   - Add expenditures on development costs to expenses.
   - Remove amortization expense relating to development costs from expenses (to avoid double-counting).
   - Remove deferred income tax expense, if any.

2. *Statement of financial position*

   - Remove development costs from assets.
   - Reclassify deferred income tax balances—move from other assets and noncurrent liabilities to retained earnings.
   - Restate retained earnings.

3. *Statement of cash flows*

   - Reclassify development expenditures—move from investing activities to operations.
   - Remove development cost amortization addbacks.
   - Remove deferred income tax addbacks.

Statement of Comprehensive Income

The SCI shows "software development costs" of $513 for 20X8 and $67 for 20X7. These numbers tie in to Note 5, which shows the same amounts as amortization. Therefore, these amounts must be removed from the SCI. Expenditures on development costs of $10,588,218 for 20X8 and $3,644,763 for 20X7 are shown in Note 5. These must be added to expenses in the recast SCIs.

Since the bank wants to see the effects of using a "flow-through" approach for income tax, the deferred income tax expense must be removed. The 20X7 SFP shows an asset balance for deferred income taxes of $355. In 20X8, the balance is a liability of $214. The net change, therefore, is a credit of $569 on the SFP. To balance, the company must have charged $569 in deferred income tax to the income statement. This amount can be verified by referring to the statement of cash flows, which shows a non-cash addback of $569 for deferred income taxes. This is also the total amount of income tax expense shown in the income statement. The company had no current taxes due in 20X8.

For 20X7, the statement of cash flows shows a *negative* addback for deferred income tax of $50. This indicates that the amount was a *credit* to income. This can be verified by looking at the change in the net balance of deferred income taxes on the SFP. At the end of 20X6, there were two deferred income tax balances, a liability for $104 and an asset of $409, for a net debit balance of $305. In 20X7, the company recorded a net deferred income tax credit to income of $50. The net change can be reconciled in the form of a general journal entry:

Change in Deferred Tax Amounts, Year-End 20X6 to Year-End 20X7

Deferred income tax liability ($104 – $0)	104	
Deferred income tax asset ($409 – $355)		54
Income tax expense, deferred		50

The SFP effect of this change is to eliminate the liability balance of $104 and reduce the asset balance from $409 to $355.

In summary, the adjustments to net income for 20X8 and 20X7 are as follows:

	20X8	20X7
Net income, as reported	$ 2,062	$ 1,452
Plus: Amortization of software development costs	513	67
Less: Expenditures on software development costs	(10,588)	(3,645)
Plus (less): Deferred income tax expense (credit)	569	(50)
Restated net income (loss)	$ (7,444)	$(2,176)

These adjustments obviously will change retained earnings for both year-ends. However, there are two other adjustments that must be made to the 20X7 *beginning* balance of retained earnings:

1. The SFP at year-end 20X6 shows software development costs as an asset of $1,580. Using the bank's preferred policy of expensing development costs, these costs should have been charged to operations when incurred. Reclassifying this amount means removing it as an asset and charging it against year-end 20X6 retained earnings.

2. The change to flow-through reporting of income tax expense requires that the balances of the deferred tax balances at the beginning of 20X7 (i.e., at year-end 20X6) be eliminated. The net balance at the end of 20X6 is $409 asset minus $104 liability, for a further net reduction in retained earnings of $305.

Therefore, the 20X7 beginning retained earnings must be restated to a deficit of $829:

	20X6
Ending retained earnings, as reported	$ 1,056
Adjustment to reclassify capitalized software development costs	(1,580)
Adjustment to eliminate deferred income tax balances	(305)
Restated retained earnings (deficit), 31 December 20X6	$ (829)

The adjustments shown above for 20X6 retained earnings and for 20X7 and 20X8 net income can be used to restate the SFP and the SCI. The restated SCIs are shown in Exhibit 22A-4.

EXHIBIT 22A-4

QDO LIMITED

Consolidated Statement of Comprehensive Income

Years Ended 31 December

	As Reported		Restated	
(in thousands of Canadian dollars)	20X8	20X7	20X8	20X7
Gross revenue	$29,276	$19,305	$29,276	$ 19,305
Less: Cost of goods sold	4,497	2,519	4,497	2,519
Gross profit	24,779	16,786	24,779	16,786
Expenses				
Operating and administrative	22,390	15,108	22,390	15,108
Depreciation and amortization—PPE	203	49	203	49
Finance leases	143	85	143	85
Software development costs	513	67	10,588	3,645
Total expenses	23,249	15,309	33,324	18,887
Operating profit	1,530	1,477	(8,545)	(2,101)
Finance income (interest on cash deposits)	1,265	—	1,265	—

(in thousands of Canadian dollars)	As Reported 20X8	As Reported 20X7	Restated 20X8	Restated 20X7
Finance costs	(164)	(224)	(164)	(224)
Income before income tax	2,631	1,253	(7,444)	(2,325)
Income tax expense (recovery)	569	(199)	0	(149)
Net profit or loss and comprehensive income	$ 2,062	$ 1,452	$ (7,444)	$ (2,176)

Statement of Financial Position

Adjustments to the restated SFPs shown in Exhibit 22A-5 are:

- The asset amounts shown for software development costs in the original SFPs are both removed.
- The deferred income tax balances are removed.
- The retained earnings is restated for the two above adjustments:

	20X8	20X7
Original balance in retained earnings	$2,769	1,952
Remove the software development costs balance	(15,233)	(5,157)
Remove the deferred income taxes balance	214	(355)
Restated balance in retained earnings	(12,250)	(3,560)

EXHIBIT 22A-5

QDO LIMITED

Consolidated Statement of Financial Position

Years Ended 31 December

(in thousands of Canadian dollars)	As Reported 20X8	As Reported 20X7	Restated 20X8	Restated 20X7
ASSETS				
Current assets				
Cash and cash equivalents	$ 8,716	$ —	$ 8,716	$ —
Accounts receivable	6,459	4,658	6,459	4,658

(in thousands of Canadian dollars)	As Reported		Restated	
	20X8	**20X7**	**20X8**	**20X7**
Work in progress	7,451	2,780	7,451	2,780
Hardware inventory	569	—	569	—
Prepaid expenses and supplies inventory	1,151	470	1,151	470
	24,346	7,908	24,346	7,908
Property, plant, and equipment				
Leasehold improvements	852	317	852	317
Furniture, fixtures, and computer equipment	624	121	624	121
Assets under finance lease	1,374	817	1,374	817
	2,850	1,255	2,850	1,255
Less: Accumulated depreciation	(293)	(90)	(293)	(90)
	2,557	1,165	2,557	1,165
Other assets				
Software development costs	15,233	5,157	—	—
Deferred income taxes	—	355	—	—
	15,233	5,512	—	—
Total assets	$42,136	$14,585	$26,903	$ 9,073
LIABILITIES AND SHAREHOLDERS' EQUITY				
Current liabilities				
Bank and other loans	$ 2,806	$ 3,371	$ 2,806	$ 3,371
Accounts payable and accrued liabilities	7,054	3,550	7,054	3,550
Deferred revenue	530	461	530	461
Current portion of finance lease obligations	281	161	281	161
	10,671	7,543	10,671	7,543
Noncurrent liabilities				
Finance lease obligations	1,488	1,101	1,488	1,101
Deferred income taxes	214	—	—	—
Total liabilities	12,373	8,644	12,159	8,644

(in thousands of Canadian dollars)	As Reported		Restated	
	20X8	20X7	20X8	20X7
Shareholders' equity				
Share capital	26,994	3,989	26,994	3,989
Retained earnings (deficit)	2,769	1,952	(12,250)	(3,560)
	29,763	5,941	14,744	429
	$42,136	$14,585	$26,903	$ 9,073

Statement of Cash Flows

On the statement of cash flows, the operations section begins with the restated net income for each year. The two amounts of amortization must be adjusted by the amounts of amortization included in the original statements but now eliminated in the restatement. Also, the addback for deferred income taxes is eliminated.

In the investment section, investment in software products must be eliminated. The total cash flows for each year do not change, of course, but the subtotals for operating and investment change considerably. The restated statement of cash flows are shown in Exhibit 22A-6.

EXHIBIT 22A-6

QDO LIMITED

Consolidated Statement of Cash Flows

Years Ended 31 December

(in thousands of Canadian dollars)	As Reported		Restated	
	20X8	20X7	20X8	20X7
Operations				
Net profit or loss for the year	$ 2,062	$ 1,452	$ (7,444)	$(2,176)
Add: Non-cash items				
Deferred income taxes	569	(50)	—	—
Depreciation and amortization	859	200	346	133
Deferred lease rent credits	—	82	—	82
Finance income	(1,265)		(1,265)	
Finance costs	164	224	164	224
Income taxes (recovery)	0	(149)	0	(149)

	As Reported		Restated	
(in thousands of Canadian dollars)	**20X8**	**20X7**	**20X8**	**20X7**
Net change in working capital items	(3,619)	(579)	(3,619)	(579)
	(1,230)	1,180	(11,818)	(2,465)
Interest paid	(178)	(230)	(178)	(230)
Interest received	1,202		1,202	
Income taxes paid	(150)	10	(150)	10
Cash provided by (used for) operating activities	(356)	960	(10,944)	(2,685)
Investment				
Investment in software products	(10,588)	(3,645)	—	—
Purchase of fixed assets	(1,034)	(36)	(1,034)	(36)
Proceeds from disposal of fixed assets	—	—	—	—
Cash provided by (used for) investment activities	(11,622)	(3,681)	(1,034)	(36)
Financing				
Net issue (repayments) of bank and other loans	(565)	718	(565)	718
Repayments of finance lease obligations	(325)	(161)	(325)	(161)
Issue of shares	21,858	2,525	21,858	2,525
Loss on sale of repurchased shares	(46)	—	(46)	—
Dividends declared	(14)	(295)	(14)	(295)
Shares purchased and cancelled	(214)	(66)	(214)	(66)
Cash provided by (used for) financing activities	20,694	2,721	20,694	2,721
Increase (decrease) in cash during year	$ 8,716	$ 0	$ 8,716	$ 0
Cash and cash equivalents, beginning of year	0	0	0	0
Cash and cash equivalents, end of year	$ 8,716	$ 0	$ 8,716	$ 0

Ratios

It is obvious that changing the development cost accounting has a major impact on QDO's financial statements. Instead of showing a profit, the restated amounts indicate a substantial loss. Assets are significantly reduced and retained earnings go into a deficit position.

The operating loss situation in 20X8 is actually even worse than stated, when nonrecurring items are considered, as requested. Net income for the most recent year includes investment income of $1,265,000. This investment income is the result of temporary investment of the proceeds of the common share issue. The case states that all of the cash and short-term investments were used in operations (and development) early in 20X9. Since there are no investments, there will be no investment income in 20X9. Removing the nonrecurring income increases the 20X8 loss:

	As Reported	Restated
Net income (loss)	$2,062	$ (7,444)
Less: Non-recurring investment income	(1,265)	(1,265)
Income (loss) on continuing operations	$ 797	$(8,709)

The ratios requested, before and after restatement, are as follows:

1. Return on total assets, before tax, 20X8:

$$\frac{\text{Net income} + \text{Interest expense} + \text{Income tax expense}}{\text{Total assets (average)}}$$

Before restatement:

($2,062 + $164 + $569) ÷ [($14,585 + $42,136) ÷ 2] = $2,795 ÷ $28,361 = **9.9%**

After restatement:

(−$8,709 + $164) ÷ [($9,073 + $26,903) ÷2] = − $8,545 ÷ $17,988 = **−47.5%**

2. Total liabilities to shareholders' equity:

$$\frac{\text{Total liabilities}}{\text{Shareholders' equity}}$$

Before restatement: $12,373 ÷ $29,763 = **42%**

After restatement: $12,159 ÷$14,744 = **82%**

Times-interest-earned:

$$\frac{\text{Net income} + \text{Interest expense} + \text{Income tax expense}}{\text{Interest expense}}$$

Before restatement: ($2,062 + $164 + $569) ÷$164 = $2,795 ÷ $164 = **17.0**

After restatement: (−$8,709 + $164) ÷$164 = −$8,545 ÷ $164 = **−52.1**

Conclusion

This case demonstrates not only the process that must be followed for restatements but also the importance of ensuring that the financial statements reflect accounting policies that are consistent with the decisions to be made. If the bank looked at the financial condition of the company only as shown in the published statements, it would receive a much different picture of the financial health and profitability of the company than is presented in the recast statements. Changing the underlying reporting objective to cash flow prediction results in using accounting policies that give a much more negative view of the company.

The moral of this story? It is foolish to undertake any ratio analysis without first examining the appropriateness of the underlying financial accounting policies of the company!

STATEMENT OF CASH FLOWS

COMPREHENSIVE ILLUSTRATION

The statement of cash flows (SCF) was the subject of Chapter 5. Subsequent chapters have reviewed the impact of various transactions and accounting policies on the SCF, when topics were covered. This appendix summarizes that material and reviews a comprehensive SCF example.

The SCF has three main sections—operating, investing, and financing activities. The *operating activities* section deals with cash generated, or used, from the primary revenue-producing activities of the enterprise, and the related expenditures. The operating activities section has two formats: the *indirect method*, which involves a reconciliation of earnings to cash flow, and the less common *direct method*, which shows cash inflows from customers, and cash outflows to suppliers, employees, and so on. When the indirect method of presentation is used, the adjustments for non-cash items are typically presented first, with a subtotal, and then the adjustments for changes in statement of financial position (SFP) elements are included, providing a two-step method of presentation.

The *investing activities* section deals with cash flows related to long-term assets (fixed assets), investments, and other long-term assets, both purchase and sale. The *financing activities* section includes cash flows from or for borrowing, and transactions with shareholders.

Cash consists of cash balances, cash-equivalent investments with initial term of under 90 days, less bank overdrafts if those overdrafts regularly fluctuate during the period. Cash on the SCF must be reconciled to the balances reported on the SFP.

Cash paid for dividends must be shown separately. It may be included in financing activities or in operating activities, at the company's choice.

Cash flow for/from income tax must be shown separately. This can be accomplished on the SCF, but some companies use supplementary disclosure to convey this information. Taxes related to non-operating activities will be classified in operating activities or financing activities, depending on the nature of the taxes paid. For example, a tax related to a dividend payment to shareholders would be classified in the same section as the dividend cash flow.

Cash received for dividend or interest income, and cash paid for interest must also be shown separately. Again, this can be accomplished on the SCF, but supplementary disclosure may also be used.

Non-cash transactions are omitted from the SCF.

Offsetting (e.g., offsetting loan repayments with new loans) is not permitted.

The reporting standard allows some *policy choice* for classification:

- Cash paid for interest on borrowings can be classified in operating activities or in financing activities.
- Cash paid to shareholders for dividends may be classified in operating activities or in financing activities.
- Cash interest received and cash dividends received by an investor may be classified in operating activities or in investing activities.

The major points to remember about the SCF are summarized in Exhibit A-1.

EXHIBIT A-1

STATEMENT OF CASH FLOWS

Cash	• Cash is defined as cash plus cash-equivalent temporary investments (e.g., money market certificates; maximum original 90-day term) less bank overdrafts that regularly fluctuate.
Comprehensive income	• Begin SCF operating activities (indirect method) with earnings, not comprehensive income. Elements of OCI usually are non-cash items, but if they involve cash, they are classified according to their nature.
Discontinued operations	• Begin SCF operating activities (indirect method) with earnings before discontinued operations. • Show cash flow impact of discontinued operation separately in appropriate section.
Income tax	• Cash paid or received for income tax is usually classified in operating activities. Cash paid or received for income tax must be separately disclosed. • If tax relates to a capital transaction (e.g., tax triggered by a dividend payment to shareholders), then it is included with that capital transaction in another section of the SCF. • The change in deferred income tax is a non-cash item and is an element in determining the amount paid.
SFP elements related to revenues and expenses	• Adjust earnings for the change in SFP elements items that relate to revenue or expense items. (e.g., accounts receivable and payable, inventory, prepaids, etc.) • If a SFP element item does not relate to earnings (e.g., dividends payable), adjust for the change in the appropriate section (e.g., financing).
Investments	• Purchase price is an outflow under investing activities; proceeds of sale are an inflow. • Recognized changes in fair value of FVTPL investments are non-cash items in earnings and are adjusted in the operating activities sections of the SCF. If the investment is a FVTOCI investment, changes in fair value are recorded to OCI, and are non-cash items that are excluded from the SCF. • Cash inflow from interest or dividends may be classified in operating activities or in investing activities. Cash inflow must be separately disclosed in either case.

	• Investment revenue based on the equity method is backed out of earnings; dividends received from an associate are included in operating (or investing) activities.
Property, plant and equipment	• Purchase price (if cash) is an outflow under investing activities; proceeds of sale are an inflow.
	• Non-cash transactions (e.g., swaps) excluded from the SCF. Transactions that are partially cash and partially non-cash are included on the SCF at the cash amount.
	• Depreciation is added back in operating activities as a non-cash expense.
	• Gains and losses on retirement are adjusted in operating activities.
	• Impairment writedowns are added back in operating activities. Impairment reversals are deducted.
Identifiable intangible assets	• Purchase price (if cash) is an outflow under investing activities; proceeds of sale are an inflow.
	• Amortization is added back in operating activities.
	• Impairment writedowns are added back as a non-cash charge in operating activities. Impairment reversals are deducted.
Goodwill	• Part of a larger purchase of a business unit; purchase price (if cash) is an outflow under investing activities; proceeds of sale are an inflow.
	• Impairment writedowns are added back in operating activities.
Borrowing	• Amount borrowed is an inflow under financing activities; repayments are outflows.
	• Netting new and old loans is not permitted.
	• Interest paid may be classified in operating activities or in financing activities. Cash outflow must be separately disclosed in either case.
	• Amortization of discount is a non-cash item and is an element in determining the amount of interest paid.
	• Gains and losses on retirement are adjusted in operating activities.
Equity	• Cash investment by shareholders is an inflow under financing activities.
	• Amount paid to retire shares is an outflow under financing activities.
	• The difference between the amount paid to retire shares and the average issuance price changes equity accounts and is not listed separately on the SCF.

Dividends	• Dividends paid may be classified in operating activities or in financing activities.
	• Stock dividends and splits are not cash flows and do not appear on the SCF.
Complex financial instruments	• Amount borrowed/invested is an inflow under financing activities; repayments are outflows.
	• If a hybrid instrument is issued, only one cash inflow is recorded on the SCF for both elements.
	• Amortization of discount is adjusted in operating activities and is an element of determining the amount of interest paid.
	• Conversion of a financial instrument into common shares is a non-cash transaction and is excluded from the SCF.
	• Gains and losses on retirement that are included in earnings are adjusted in operating activities.
Stock options	• Expense is adjusted in operating activities; added back as a non-cash transaction.
	• Cash received for shares issued under options, if any, is recorded as an inflow in financing activities. The value of options recorded in common shares upon exercise is a non-cash transaction and is not recorded on the SCF.
	• If options are recorded on the receipt of non-cash assets, the transaction is a non-cash transaction and is excluded from the SCF.
Leases	• Increase in assets and liabilities because of a new finance lease for the lessee is a non-cash transaction and excluded from the SCF.
	• Reduction in lease liability principal because of a payment is an outflow under financing activities.
	• Depreciation on leased assets is added back in operating activities.
	• Interest is classified and disclosed as per borrowing section.
Pensions	• Change in accrued benefit pension obligation on the SFP recorded in AOCI is non-cash and not included on the SCF.
	• Other change in the accrued benefit pension obligation on the SFP is adjusted in operating activities.
	• Amount paid to pension trustee is adjusted in operating activities.

COMPREHENSIVE SCF EXAMPLE

The data for a comprehensive example is found in Exhibit A-2 and includes the financial statements and additional information concerning critical transactions. To analyze the data, the changes in the transactions will be translated into journal entries, then entered into the T-accounts that support the SCF. The information may also be analyzed through journal entries alone or in a worksheet. All analysis approaches will produce the same SCF.

EXHIBIT A-2

HUM ENTERPRISES LIMITED

The records of Hum Enterprises Limited show the following:

Statement of Earnings, for the Year Ended 31 December 20X8

Sales		$1,402,300
Cost of goods sold		631,100
Gross profit		771,200
Operating expenses and other:		
Depreciation expense	$ 43,200	
Selling expenses	107,900	
Administrative expenses	119,900	
Interest expense	35,300	
Other expenses	43,200	
Investment revenue	(1,400)	
Loss on sale of machinery	16,000	
Total expenses		364,100
Earnings before income tax		407,100
Income tax expense		174,000
Earnings		$ 233,100

SCI, for the Year Ended 31 December 20X8

Earnings	$ 233,100
Plus: Increase in fair value, FVTOCI investment	44,300
Less: Realized gain on sale of FVTOCI investment	(2,800)
Less: Actuarial loss on defined benefit pension	(20,000)
Comprehensive income	$254,600

Statement of Changes in Equity, for the Year Ended 31 December 20X8

	Common Shares	CSCR	CC: Options	Retained Earnings	AOCI: Pension	AOCI: Investments
Opening balance	$ 930,000	$83,300	$60,000	$209,000	$ (44,000)	$22,000
Comprehensive income:						
Earnings				233,100		
Pension and FVTOCI adjustments					(20,000)	44,300
FVTOCI transfer on realization				2,800		(2,800)
Dividends				(75,500)		
Share issuance; machinery	261,100					
Share issuance; bond	735,500	(83,300)				
Share issuance; options	51,400		(14,000)			
Options amounts expensed			24,000			
Share retirement	(478,000)			(121,200)		
Closing balance	$1,500,000	$ 0	$70,000	$248,200	$(64,000)	$63,500

Statement of Financial Position, Year Ended

December 31	20X8	20X7
Assets:		
Cash	$ 40,000	$ 29,200
FVTOCI investments	226,300	70,700
Accounts receivable (net)	112,500	147,200
Inventory	179,100	187,300
Prepaid rent	4,700	—
Land	276,000	204,000
Machinery	1,899,000	1,743,900
Accumulated depreciation	(801,600)	(839,000)

December 31	20X8	20X7
Goodwill	890,400	890,400
Total	$2,826,400	$2,433,700
Liabilities and shareholders' equity:		
Accounts payable	$ 139,000	$ 215,200
Salaries payable	46,100	45,500
Taxes payable	21,000	29,000
Bonds payable; 6%	—	652,200
Bonds payable; 7.2%	600,000	—
Discount on 7.2% bonds payable	(11,200)	—
Deferred income tax	148,900	184,800
Accrued pension liability	64,900	46,700
Common shares, no-par	1,500,000	930,000
Common stock conversion rights	—	83,300
Contributed capital: stock options	70,000	60,000
Retained earnings	248,200	209,000
AOCI: pension	(64,000)	(44,000)
AOCI: investments	63,500	22,000
Total	$2,826,400	$2,433,700

Analysis of selected accounts and transactions:

1. Issued additional 7.2% bonds payable for cash, $588,000.
2. Cash dividends were declared and paid.
3. A FVTOCI investment with an original cost of $47,200 was sold for $50,000 cash at the beginning of 20X8. This investment had a carrying value of $50,000 (fair value) at that time. Realized gains are transferred to retained earnings. FVTOCI investments with a cost of $161,300 were acquired during the year.
4. There is a stock option plan for senior administrative staff, accounted for using the fair-value method. Stock options with a book value of $14,000 were exchanged, along with $37,400 cash, for common shares in 20X8. The remaining increase in the stock options account is explained by additional compensation expense recorded.
5. The 6% bond payable was converted into common shares at the beginning of the fiscal year.
6. Land was acquired for cash.
7. Machinery with an original cost of $106,000 and a net book value of $25,400 was sold for a loss of $16,000. Additional machinery for other activities was acquired for common shares.
8. Common shares with an average original issue price of $478,000 were retired for $599,200.
9. The accrued pension liability was increased by $20,000 due to an actuarial revaluation and $1,800 because of the difference between funding and pension expense.

The entries that follow *re-create* the transactions for the year, reflecting (in summary) the company's entries for the year. The entries must be sufficient to change the opening balance to the closing balance, per the financial statements provided. In the re-creation of entries, the SCF amounts are represented by cash or operating activities items in an entry.

As a first step, earnings is entered as an increase to retained earnings and the first item in the operating activities sections:

a. *Cash: operating activities,* net earnings	233,100	
Retained earnings		233,100

Next, the changes in all non-cash working capital accounts that relate to revenue and expense items are adjusted to the operating activities section:

b. Cash: operating activities—decrease in accounts receivable	34,700	
Accounts receivable		34,700
c. *Cash: operating activities*—decrease in inventory	8,200	
Inventory		8,200
d. Prepaid rent	4,700	
Cash: operating activities—increase in prepaid rent		4,700
e. Accounts payable	76,200	
Cash: operating activities—decrease in accounts payable		76,200
f. *Cash: operating activities*—increase in salaries payable	600	
Salaries payable		600
g. Taxes payable	8,000	
Cash: operating activities—decrease in taxes payable		8,000

The obvious non-cash expenses are adjusted:

h. *Cash: operating activities*—depreciation expense	43,200	
Accumulated depreciation		43,200
i. Deferred income tax	35,900	
Cash: operating activities—deferred income tax		35,900

j.	Cash: operating activities—discount amortization	800	
	Discount on bonds payable		
	($12,000 – $11,200)		800

The original discount on the bond was $12,000 ($600,000 – $588,000). The discount appears as $11,200 on the SFP, implying discount amortization of $800 during the period.

The accrued pension liability increased by $20,000 this period, caused by an actuarial revaluation that was recorded in AOCI. The amount does not change cash flow and is not recorded on the SCF. The remaining $1,800 change in the accrued pension liability is caused by the difference between pension expense and pension funding, and is shown in the operating section of the SCF:

k.	AOCI—pension	20,000	
	Accrued pension liability		20,000
l.	Accrued pension liability	1,800	
	Cash: operating activities—pension liability		1,800

Remaining non-cash items, and gains and losses on various transactions, will be adjusted as other accounts are analyzed.

FVTOCI investments were purchased during the period:

m.	FVTOCI investments	161,300	
	Cash: investing activities—purchased FVTOCI investments		161,300

A FVTOCI investment was sold for $50,000 cash, as the question states. The investment has a carrying value of $50,000 at the time of sale. The investment had been written up from cost of $47,200 to fair value through the recognition of an unrealized gain in accumulated other comprehensive income. This unrealized holding gain is reclassified to retained earnings when any actual sale takes place.

n.	Cash: investing activities—sale of FVTOCI investments (fair value)	50,000	
	FVTOCI investments		50,000
	Accumulated other comprehensive income: investments ($50,000 – $47,200)	2,800	
	Retained earnings		2,800

The remaining change in the investments account and accumulated other comprehensive income is explained by the revaluation of FVTOCI investments to fair value at year-end. There is no effect on the SCF.

o. FVTOCI investments ($70,700 – $50,000 + $161,300 = $182,000 vs. $226,300)	44,300	
Accumulated other comprehensive income: investments ($22,000 – $2,800 = $19,200 vs. $63,500)		44,300

Land was purchased during the period:

p. Land ($204,000 – $276,000)	72,000	
Cash: investing activities—purchase of land		72,000

Machinery was sold:

q. *Cash: investing activities*—sale of machinery ($25,400 – $16,000)	9,400	
Accumulated depreciation ($106,000 – $25,400)	80,600	
Cash: operating activities—loss on sale on machinery (as reported)	16,000	
Machinery		106,000

The accumulated depreciation account has been increased by current-year depreciation expense and decreased by the accumulated depreciation on the machinery sold. These two entries completely explain the change in the accumulated depreciation account.

Machinery was acquired for common shares. This transaction is assumed to explain the remaining change in the machinery account. The acquisition is a non-cash transaction that is not reflected on the SCF:

r. Machinery ($1,899,000 – ($1,743,900 – $106,000))	261,100	
Common shares		261,100

Bonds were converted into common shares, which explains the decrease in the 6% bond and the common stock conversion rights account. Again, this is a non-cash transaction that does not appear on the SCF.

s. Bonds payable, 6%	652,200	
Common stock conversion rights	83,300	
Common shares		735,500

Bonds were also issued in 20X8:

t. *Cash: financing activities*—issuance of bond	588,000	
Discount on bonds payable	12,000	
Bonds payable, 7.2%		600,000

The original discount was $12,000; it has already been amortized by $800, and thus the closing balance of $11,200 is fully explained in the entries.

Common shares were retired, at a price higher than average issuance price. The difference is a direct debit to retained earnings:

u. Common shares	478,000	
Retained earnings	121,200	
Cash: financing activities—retirement of common shares		599,200

Common shares were issued under the terms of stock options, which results in a cash inflow to the company:

v. *Cash: financing activities*—issued common shares	37,400	
Contributed capital: stock options	14,000	
Common stock		51,400

The common stock account has had many changes, but the entries now explain all the changes. The opening balance was $930,000, decreased by $478,000 because of the retirement and increased by common shares issued for machinery, $261,100; common shares issued on bond conversion, $735,500; and shares issued under option terms, $51,400. This equals the closing balance of $1,500,000.

Stock options were also recorded as compensation expense, which is a non-cash expense:

w. *Cash: operating activities*—non-cash compensation expense	24,000	
Contributed capital: stock options ($60,000 – $14,000 = $46,000 vs. $70,000)		24,000

Finally, there were cash dividends:

x. Retained earning ($209,000 + $233,100 + $2,800 – $121,200 = $323,700 – $248,200)	75,500	
Cash: financing activities—dividends		75,500

HUM ENTERPRISES LIMITED

T-Account Analysis

Cash

Opening	29,200		
Operating Activities			
a) Net earnings	233,100	d) Increase in prepaid rent	4,700
b) Decrease in accounts receivable	34,700	e) Decrease in accounts payable	76,200
c) Decrease in inventory	8,200	g) Decrease in taxes payable	8,000
f) Increase in salaries payable	600	i) Decrease in deferred tax	35,900
h) Depreciation expense	43,200	l) Decrease in pension liability	1,800
j) Discount amortization	800		
q) Loss on sale of machinery	16,000		
w) Compensation expense	24,000		
Investing Activities			
n) Sold FVTOCI investments	50,000	m) Purchased FVTOCI investments	161,300
q) Sold machinery	9,400	p) Purchased land	72,000

Financing Activities

t) Issued bond	588,000	599,200
v) Issued shares	37,400	75,500
		u) Retired shares
		x) Dividends
Closing	40,000	

FVTOCI Investments

Op.	70,700		
m)	161,300	n)	50,000
o)	44,300		
Cl.	226,300		

Common shares

		Op.	930,000
		r)	261,100
		s)	735,500
		v)	51,400
u)	478,000		
		Cl.	1,500,000

Salaries payable

		Op.	45,500
		f)	600
		Cl.	46,100

Land

Op.	204,000		
p)	72,000		
Cl.	276,000		

AOCI: pension

		Op.	44,000
		k)	20,000
		Cl.	64,000

Discount on bonds payable

Op.	—		
t)	12,000	j)	800
Cl.	11,200		

Accounts payable

		Op.	215,200
e)	76,200		
		Cl.	139,000

Accounts receivable (net)

Op.	147,200		
		b)	34,700
Cl.	112,500		

CSCR

		Op.	83,300
s)	83,300		
		Cl.	—

Bonds payable. 7.2%

		Op.	—
		t)	600,000
		Cl.	600,000

Machinery

Op.	1,743,900		
r)	261,100	q)	106,000
Cl.	1,899,000		

AOCI: investments

		Op.	22,000
n)	2,800	o)	44,300
		Cl.	63,500

Inventory

Op. 187,300	c) 8,200
Cl. 179,100	

Accumulated depreciation

	Op. 839,000
q) 80,600	h) 43,200
	Cl. 801,600

Deferred income tax

	Op. 184,800
i) 35,900	
	Cl. 148,900

Taxes payable

	Op. 29,000
g) 8,000	
	Cl. 21,000

Goodwill

Op. 890,400	
Cl. 890,400	

Bonds payable, 6%

	Op. 652,200
s) 652,200	
Cl. —	

CC: stock options

	Op. 60,000
v) 14,000	w) 24,000
	Cl. 70,000

Prepaid rent

Op. —	
d) 4,700	
Cl. 4,700	

Retained earnings

	Op. 209,000
u) 121,200	a) 233,100
x) 75,500	n) 2,800
	Cl. 248,200

Accrued pension liability

	Op. 46,700
l) 1,800	k) 20,000
	Cl. 64,900

These entries retrace the effects of all transactions, isolating their impact on the SCF. The next step is to post them to T-accounts (Exhibit A-3), and then prepare the SCF itself (Exhibit A-4). Exhibit A-4 reflects the two-step indirect method to present the operating activities. Separate note disclosure is used to disclose cash flow for interest, income tax, and cash received for dividends and/or interest. (Note that these cash flows may be shown on the face of the SCF, but there is variation in practice, and we will begin with this simple presentation that is supplemented with note disclosure.) Dividends paid to shareholders are classified in financing activities.

EXHIBIT A-4

HUM ENTERPRISES LIMITED

Statement of Cash Flows

Year Ended 31 December 20X8

Cash provided by (used in) operating activities

Earnings	$233,100
Add (deduct) items not involving cash:	
Depreciation	43,200
Decrease in deferred income tax	(35,900)
Compensation expense re: stock options	24,000
Amortization of discount on long-term debt	800
Loss on sale of machinery	16,000
	281,200
Changes in non-cash balance sheet accounts:	
Accounts receivable decrease	34,700
Inventory decrease	8,200
Prepaid rent increase	(4,700)
Accounts payable decrease	(76,200)
Salaries payable increase	600
Taxes payable decrease	(8,000)
Decrease in accrued pension liability	(1,800)
	$234,000

Cash provided by (used in) investing activities

Investments purchased	(161,300)
Sale of investments	50,000
Sale of machinery	9,400
Land purchased	(72,000)
	(173,900)

Cash provided by (used in) financing activities

Bonds issued	588,000
Common shares retired	(599,200)
Common shares issued	37,400
Cash dividend paid	(75,500)
	(49,300)
Increase in cash and cash equivalents	10,800
Cash, beginning of year	29,200
Cash, end of year	$ 40,000

Supplementary information:

Note disclosure of non-cash transactions:
1. Machinery was acquired for common shares $261,100.
2. The 6% bond converted to common shares during the year. The bond carrying value of $652,200 and common stock conversion rights of $83,300 were transferred to common shares, resulting in an increase in common shares of $735,500.
3. Shares were issued for $51,400, of which $14,000 was cash; the balance was related to stock options.

Cash flows for interest and/or dividends received, interest paid, and income tax paid:
1. Cash received for interest and/or dividends was $1,400.
2. Cash paid for interest was $34,500 ($35,300 − $800 discount amortization).
3. Cash paid for income tax was $217,900 ($174,000 + $8,000 + $35,900).

Direct Method of Presentation for Operating Activities

The operating activities section for Hum Enterprises has been restated, using the direct method of presentation, in Exhibit A-5. The operating activities section now reflects cash received from customers and cash paid for various revenue and expense items. If a revenue or expense line item does not involve cash (e.g., depreciation) or does not reflect the actual cash flow (e.g., gains and losses on sale), it is excluded from the operating activities section.

EXHIBIT A-5

HUM ENTERPRISES LIMITED

Statement of Cash Flows

Direct Presentation of Operating Activities

Year Ended 31 December 20X8

Operating Activities—Direct Method	
Cash from customers ($1,402,300 + $34,700)	$1,437,000
Cash from investment revenue ($1,400)	1,400
Cash paid to suppliers (– $631,100 + $8,200 – $76,200)	(699,100)
Cash paid for salaries and other expenses (– $107,900 – $119,900 – $43,200 – $1,800 + $24,000 – $4,700 + $600)	(252,900)
Cash paid for interest (– $35,300 + $800)	(34,500)
Cash paid for income tax (– $174,000 – $8,000 – $35,900)	(217,900)
	$ 234,000

Note: Other sections of the SCF are identical.

To prepare the direct method disclosure, begin with the revenue or expense line item. For example, revenues imply an inflow of $1,402,300 in this example, which is sales revenue. Next, any adjustment from the indirect method reconciliation is included. In our case, this is a decrease in accounts receivable, increasing cash collected, by $34,700, so the cash collected is $1,437,000. For the expenses, the beginning point is an outflow, the expense reported. For example, interest expense was $35,300, implying a ($35,300) outflow of this amount. The indirect method included an add-back (positive amount) of amortization of the discount of $800. When the negative and positive are combined, the outflow for interest is ($34,500). All adjustments used with the indirect method must be incorporated for the direct method and will eliminate the non-cash income statement lines.

Alternative Classification

The SCF for Hum Enterprises has been restated in Exhibit A-6. This presentation shows cash paid for income tax on the face of the SCF in operating activities. It also uses the alternative classification of interest or dividends received (in investing activities) and interest paid (in financing activities). Note the highlighted items in the exhibit. The operating activities section now shows adjustments for the recognized revenue or expenses, essentially backing them all out of earnings. This is achieved by subtracting investment revenue and adding back income tax expense and interest expense. The operating activities section also omits all adjustments (i.e., bond discount amortization, deferred tax, change in tax payable) related to these line items. Cash flow for these items is now separately listed, as for income tax, or it is listed in the alternative classification—an inflow of interest or dividends in the investing activities section, and cash paid for interest (the expense combined with the discount amortization) in financing activities. Because these items are now listed separately on the SCF, supplementary disclosure for their cash flow amount is no longer needed. Other supplementary information, for non-cash transactions, has not changed and is not repeated.

Remember also that dividends paid may be classified in financing activities or in operating activities.

EXHIBIT A-6

HUM ENTERPRISES LIMITED

Statement of Cash Flows

Alternative Presentation of Cash Flows: Income Tax,

Interest Paid, and Dividend/Interest Received

Year Ended 31 December 20X8

Cash provided by (used in) operating activities

Earnings	$233,100
Add (deduct) items not involving cash and nonoperating items:	
Depreciation	43,200
Compensation expense re: stock options	24,000
Loss on sale of machinery	16,000
Income tax expense	174,000
Interest expense	35,300
Investment income	(1,400)
	524,200
Changes in non-cash balance sheet accounts:	
Accounts receivable decrease	34,700
Inventory decrease	8,200
Prepaid rent increase	(4,700)
Accounts payable decrease	(76,200)
Salaries payable increase	600
Decrease in accrued pension liability	(1,800)
	485,000

Cash paid for income tax (– $174,000 – $8,000 – $35,900)		(217,900)
		$ 267,100

Cash provided by (used in) investing activities

Investments purchased	(161,300)	
Sale of investments	50,000	
Interest/dividends received	1,400	
Sale of machinery	9,400	
Land purchased	(72,000)	
		(172,500)

Cash provided by (used in) financing activities

Bonds issued	588,000	
Interest paid	(34,500)	
Common shares retired	(599,200)	
Common shares issued	37,400	
Cash dividend paid	(75,500)	
		(83,800)
Increase in cash and cash equivalents		10,800
Cash, beginning of year		29,200
Cash, end of year		$ 40,000

CONCEPT REVIEW

1. What are the three categories of cash flows that are reported on a company's SCF?
2. What classification alternatives are permitted for dividends paid, cash from investment revenue, and interest paid?

3. What items must be adjusted to convert earnings to cash from operating activities?

4. How does the direct method of presentation differ from the indirect method in the operating activities section of the SCF?

5. Is a bond conversion included on the SCF? Explain.

6. What is reported on the SCF for the sale of a FVTOCI investment? Explain.

Looking Forward

SCF issues are not now on the agenda of either the IASB or the Canadian AcSB.

Accounting Standards for Private Enterprises

As stated in Chapter 5, a statement of cash flows is required under accounting standards for private enterprises (ASPE) as part of a set of complete financial statements. The ASPE requirements for this statement are very similar to the IFRS presentation requirements, with the following differences:

1. Dividends paid must be classified as a financing activity.

2. Interest received and paid and dividends received must be classified in operating activities. There is no choice of alternative classification.

3. There is no requirement to disclose separately the cash flow for interest paid, dividends and interest received, and cash paid for income tax.

RELEVANT STANDARDS

CPA Canada Handbook, Part I (IFRS):

- IAS 7, Statement of Cash Flows

CPA Canada Handbook, Part II (ASPE):

- Section 1540, Cash Flow Statement

SUMMARY OF KEY POINTS

1. The SCF classifies cash flows from operating activities, cash flows relating to investing activities, and cash flows relating to financing activities. In each category, cash flow includes both inflows and outflows.

2. Operating cash flows are related to the main revenue-producing activities of the business and are connected to the earnings process. Investing cash flows describe long-term asset acquisitions and the proceeds from sale of long-term assets. Financing cash flows describe the sources of debt and equity financing and repayments of liabilities and equities, excluding liabilities directly relating to operations, such as accounts payable.

3. The reporting basis for the SCF is the net cash position. The net cash position includes cash plus cash-equivalent investments, less bank overdrafts. Cash equivalents include short-term liquid investments that are held for current needs and that bear little risk of change in value (maximum 90-day term).

4. The SCF implications of major SFP elements have been summarized in Exhibit A-1.

5. Cash from operating activities can be presented though the indirect method or the direct method. When the indirect method is used, it is common to use a two-step approach where, first, non-cash and nonoperating items are added back, and then changes in SFP accounts related to revenue and expense are adjusted.

6. Gross cash flows are reported. Transactions are not offset, or netted, against other flows in the same category.

7. Cash paid for income tax, cash paid for interest, and cash received for interest or dividends must all be separately disclosed. This can be accomplished through add-backs and deductions using the indirect presentation method in operating activities. Some companies use supplementary note disclosure for this information.

8. Interest paid may be classified as an operating outflow or a financing outflow. The same two choices are available for dividends paid. Interest and dividends received may be classified as operating activities or investing activities.

TECHNICAL REVIEW

Note: In all assignment questions, unless directed otherwise, assume that dividends paid are financing activities, and assume that interest paid and received, and dividends received, are operating transactions.

connect

TRApp2-1 SCF—Cash from Operating Activities:

Selected accounts from the SFP of Iraj Ltd. at 31 December 20X5 and 20X4 are presented below, in thousands. Iraj reported earnings of $900 in 20X5, and depreciation expense was $165. Bonds of $150 par value were issued during the period for $135 and a discount of $15 was originally recorded.

As at 31 December	20X5	20X4
Accounts receivable	$450	$630
Inventory	375	260

As at 31 December	20X5	20X4
Accounts payable	225	285
Interest payable	60	20
Deferred income tax liability	210	150
Bonds payable	750	600
Discount on bonds payable	(33)	(35)

Required:

1. Prepare the operating activities section of the SCF, using the indirect approach and the two-step presentation method.
2. Calculate cash paid for interest and income tax, assuming that interest expense is $135 and income tax expense is $180.

connect

TRApp2-2 SCF—Cash from Operating Activities, Direct Method:

Continuing from TRApp2-1, the SCI for Iraj Ltd. follows:

Statement of Comprehensive Income, for the Year Ended 31 December, 20X5 (in thousands):		
Sales		$3,750
Cost of goods sold		1,500
Gross profit		2,250
Depreciation expense	$165	
Selling and administrative expenses	870	
Interest expense	135	1,170
Earnings before income tax		1,080
Income tax expense		180
Earnings and comprehensive income		$ 900

Required:

Using the SCI and the facts from TRApp2-1, prepare the operating section of the SCF. Cash paid for interest is included in the financing activities sections.

■ connect

TRApp2-3 SCF—Investing Activities:

Selected accounts from the SFP of Rad Ltd. at 31 December 20X5 and 20X4 are presented below. Equipment with an original cost of $200,000 and net book value of $20,000 was sold for $48,000. Other equipment was sold for cash. FVTPL investments with a carrying value of $60,000 were sold for $60,000. There were no other purchases or sale of investments.

As at 31 December	20X5	20X4
Assets		
FVTOCI investments	$ 600,000	$ 480,000
FVTPL investments	1,200,000	800,000
Equipment	2,120,000	1,600,000
Accumulated depreciation, equipment	(1,080,000)	(920,000)

Required:

List the items that would be included in the SCF from these accounts for 20X5. Include the appropriate section (operating, investing, or financing).

■ connect

TRApp2-4 SCF—Financing Activities:

Selected accounts from the SFP of Bonang Corp. at 31 December 20X5 and 20X4 are presented below (in thousands). Bonang reported earnings of $1,500 in 20X5. Bonds payable were retired during the year at 105. Discount amortization for the year was $30. A financing lease with a present value of $540 was recorded in 20X5; payments had been made under the lease contract by the end of the fiscal year.

As at 31 December	20X5	20X4
Bonds payable, 7%	$1,350	$2,100
Discount on bonds payable	(90)	(210)

As at 31 December	20X5	20X4
Lease liability	495	—
Common shares	900	690
Retained earnings	1,830	1,620

Required:

List the items that would be included in the SCF from these accounts for 20X5. Include the appropriate section (operating, investing, or financing). List the non-cash item disclosure. Make logical assumptions about unexplained changes in accounts.

connect

TRApp2-5 SCF—Transactions from Equity:

The statement of changes in equity, from the financial statements of Forte Corp., for the year ended 31 December 20X1, is as follows (in thousands):

	Common Shares	Contributed Capital: Options	Retained Earnings	AOCI: Pension	AOCI: Investments
Opening balance	$1,000	$220	$6,500	$(1,200)	$300
Comprehensive income			500	(100)	200
Transfer on realization			50		(50)
Cash dividends			(120)		
Stock dividend	440		(440)		
Share issuance; options	140	(60)			
Options recorded		90			
Share retirement	(30)		(210)		
Closing balance	$1,550	$250	$6,280	$(1,300)	$450

Required:

List the items that would be included in the SCF from these accounts for 20X1. Include the appropriate section (operating, investing, or financing). List the non-cash item disclosure. Assume that FVTOCI investments were sold for $75; carrying value was $75 on this date, but the original cost had been $25. The realized gain was transferred to retained earnings.

ASSIGNMENTS

Note: In all assignment questions, unless directed otherwise, assume that dividends paid are financing activities, and assume that interest paid and received and dividends received are operating transactions.

★★★ AApp2-1 Statement of Cash Flows:

The financial statements of Hardy Ltd. for the 20X1 fiscal year follow (in thousands):

Statement of Comprehensive Income, for the Year Ended 31 December 20X1:

Sales	$19,100
Cost of goods sold	12,500
Gross profit	6,600
Depreciation expense	860
Selling and administrative expenses	1,450
Goodwill impairment	2,000
Interest expense	440
Loss on sale of fixed assets	370
Earnings before income tax	1,480
Income tax expense	200
Earnings and comprehensive income	$ 1,280

Statement of Changes in Equity, for the Year Ended 31 December 20X1:

	Common Shares	Preferred Shares	Cont'd Capital: Options	Cont'd Capital: Preferred Share Retirement	Retained Earnings
Opening balance	$1,450	$1,200	$320	400	$1,950
Comprehensive income					1,280
Dividends—cash					(75)
Dividends—stock	200				(200)
Share issuance; fixed assets	710				

	Common Shares	Preferred Shares	Cont'd Capital: Options	Cont'd Capital: Preferred Share Retirement	Retained Earnings
Share issuance; options	50		(45)		
Options recorded			100		
Share retirement		(600)		100	
Share retirement	(400)				(180)
Closing balance	$2,010	$ 600	$375	$500	$2,775

Statement of Financial Position, Year Ended

December 31	20X1	20X0
Assets:		
Cash	$ 145	$ 200
Accounts receivable (net)	1,600	720
Inventory	1,615	820
Fixed assets	9,820	7,560
Accumulated depreciation	(4,120)	(3,500)
Goodwill	—	2,000
Total	$9,060	$7,800
Liabilities and shareholders' equity:		
Accounts payable and accrued liabilities	$ 625	$ 560
Income taxes payable	30	40
Notes payable	130	25
Bonds payable	700	700
Discount on bonds payable	(30)	(45)
Deferred income tax	1,345	1,200
Common shares, no-par	2,010	1,450
Preferred shares, no-par	600	1,200
Contributed capital: stock options	375	320
Contributed capital: preferred share retirement	500	400
Retained earnings	2,775	1,950
Total	$9,060	$7,800

Additional information:

1. There is a stock option plan for executives, on which $100 of expense was recorded. Options were exercised during the year.
2. Machinery was acquired in exchange for common shares during the year. Other fixed assets were acquired for cash.
3. Fixed assets with an original cost of $900 and a net book value of $660 were sold at a loss of $370.
4. Assume unexplained changes in accounts are from normal transactions.

Required:

1. Prepare the SCF, using the two-step indirect method in the operating activities section. Include a list of required note disclosure for non-cash transactions. Omit the separate disclosure of cash flow for interest, investment income, and income tax.
2. Explain the company's cash transactions for the year, based on the SCF.

 **AApp2-2 Statement of Cash Flows:**

The following data are provided regarding Tema Corp.:

Statement of Earnings and Comprehensive Income

For the Year Ended 31 December 20X8

Revenues		
Sales	$760,000	
Interest and dividends	30,500	
Gain on sale of land	7,000	
		$ 797,500
Expenses and losses		
Cost of goods sold	$350,000	
Selling expenses	40,200	
Depreciation expense	19,600	
Interest expense	8,300	
Loss on sale of fixed assets	2,100	
Income tax expense	113,200	533,400
Earnings and comprehensive income		$ 264,100

Statement of Financial Position

As at 31 December 20X8	20X8	20X7
Assets		
Cash and cash equivalents	$83,200	$53,100
Accounts receivable	209,000	240,000
Inventory	182,100	175,000
Land	—	8,900
Fixed assets (net)	814,200	695,000
	$1,288,500	$1,172,000
Liabilities and shareholders' equity		
Accounts payable	$89,900	$ 104,300
Income tax payable	75,700	47,100
Cash dividends payable	16,000	—
Bonds payable	200,000	—
Less: Unamortized discount	(44,000)	—
Preferred shares	90,000	50,000
Common shares	395,000	350,000
Common stock conversion rights	30,000	—
Retained earnings	435,900	620,600
	$1,288,500	$1,172,000

Additional information:

1. Fixed assets with an original cost of $45,200 were sold for $17,100. Land was also sold for cash.
2. A stock dividend valued at $25,000 was issued in June 20X8.
3. Fixed assets valued at $40,000 were acquired for preferred shares during the year.
4. Convertible bonds were issued for cash in January 20X8.
5. The bond discount was amortized by $4,000 during the year.
6. Assume other changes to SFP accounts represented normal events.

Required:

Prepare the SCF for the year ended 31 December 20X8. Use the indirect method for operations. Include a list of required note disclosure for non-cash transactions. Omit the separate disclosure of cash flow for interest, investment income, and income tax.

 **AApp2-3 Statement of Cash Flows:**

The following financial information is available for Drake Inc. for the 20X3 fiscal year:

Statement of Financial Position

As at 31 December	20X3	20X2
Cash	$ 10,000	$ 40,000
Accounts receivable	265,000	160,000
FVTPL investments	220,000	260,000
Inventory	701,000	602,000
Land	330,000	410,000
Building	1,040,000	1,120,000
Accumulated depreciation, building	(470,000)	(380,000)
Machinery	1,080,000	875,000
Accumulated depreciation, machinery	(219,000)	(212,000)
Goodwill	50,000	110,000
	$3,007,000	$2,985,000
Current liabilities	$42,000	$80,000
Bonds payable	1,000,000	1,000,000
Discount on bonds	(10,000)	(15,000)
Deferred income tax	34,000	76,000
Preferred shares	1,048,000	843,000
Common stock conversion rights	190,000	190,000
Common shares	565,000	500,000
Retained earnings	138,000	311,000
	$3,007,000	$2,985,000

Statement of Earnings and Comprehensive Income

For the Year Ended 31 December 20X3

Sales	$2,684,000
Cost of goods sold	2,103,000
Gross profit	581,000
Depreciation	
Building	110,000
Machinery	75,000
Goodwill impairment	60,000
Interest	115,000
Other expenses	311,000
Investment loss: decrease in fair value of FVTPL investments	40,000
Gain on sale of land	(22,000)
Loss on sale of machine	27,000
	716,000
Earnings (loss) before income tax	(135,000)
Income tax recovery	54,000
Earnings (loss) and comprehensive loss	$ (81,000)

Additional information:

1. No FVTPL investments were purchased or sold. These investments are not cash equivalents.
2. A partially depreciated building was sold for an amount equal to its net book value.
3. Cash of $40,000 was received on the sale of a machine whose original cost was $135,000. Other machinery was purchased for cash.
4. Preferred shares were issued for cash on 1 March 20X3. Dividends of $60,000 were paid on these shares in 20X3.
5. On 1 September 20X3, 25,000 common shares were purchased and retired. The shares had an average issuance price of $55,000 and were repurchased for $57,000. On 1 November 20X3, 65,000 common shares were issued in exchange for machinery valued at $120,000.
6. Bonds payable are convertible to common shares at the rate of 17 common shares per $1,000 bond after 1 July 20X5 at the investor's option.

Required:

Prepare the SCF, in good form. Include a list of required note disclosure for non-cash transactions. Use the direct method for cash flows from operating activities.

 ★ ★ ★ **AApp2-4 Statement of Cash Flows:**

The financial statements of CWL Corp. for the 20X7 fiscal year follow (in thousands):

Statement of Comprehensive Income, for the Year Ended 31 December 20X7:

Sales	$5,100
Cost of goods sold	2,900
Gross profit	2,200
Depreciation expense	450
Selling and administrative expenses	970
Interest expense	345
Gain on sale of fixed assets	(140)
Earnings before income tax	575
Income tax expense	310
Earnings and comprehensive income	$ 265

Statement of Changes in Equity, for the Year Ended 31 December 20X7:

	Common Shares	Preferred Shares	Cont'd Capital: Options	Common Stock Conversion Rights	Cont'd Capital: Preferred Share Retirement	Retained Earnings
Opening balance	$ 3,100	$500	$220	$500	200	$1,400
Comprehensive income						265
Dividends—cash						(135)
Share issuance; options	200		(10)			
Options recorded			60			
Bond conversion	1,400			(500)		
Share retirement		(100)			(200)	(75)
Share retirement	(105)					(315)
Closing balance	$4,595	$400	$270	$ 0	$ 0	$ 1,140

Statement of Financial Position, Year Ended

December 31	20X7	20X6
Assets:		
Cash and cash equivalents	$ 650	$ 890
Accounts receivable (net)	1,340	1,420
Inventory	2,295	2,170
Fixed assets	7,160	7,300
Accumulated depreciation	(2,040)	(2,900)
Total	$9,405	$8,880
Liabilities and shareholders' equity:		
Accounts payable and accrued liabilities	$ 540	$ 610
Income taxes payable	130	250
Notes payable	1,840	400
Bonds payable	—	1,000
Discount on bonds payable	—	(120)
Deferred income tax	490	820
Common shares, no-par	4,595	3,100
Preferred shares, no-par	400	500
Contributed capital: stock options	270	220
Common stock conversion rights, convertible bond	—	500
Contributed capital: preferred share retirement	—	200
Retained earnings	1,140	1,400
Total	$9,405	$8,880

Additional information:

1. There is a stock option plan for executives, on which $60 of expense was recorded. Options were exercised during the year.
2. The bond payable was convertible and was converted during the year after discount amortization of $20 had been recorded.
3. Fixed assets with an original cost of $1,650 and a net book value of $340 were sold at a gain of $140.
4. Assume unexplained changes in accounts are from normal transactions.

Required:

1. Prepare the statement of cash flows, using the two-step indirect method. Include a list of required note disclosure for non-cash transactions.
2. Prepare the separate disclosure of cash flow for interest paid, and income tax.
3. Repeat the operating activities section of the SCF, using the direct method of presentation.

★ ★ ★ AApp2-5 Statement of Cash Flows:

The financial statements of Flin Ltd. for the 20X2 fiscal year follow (in thousands):

Statement of Earnings, for the Year Ended 31 December, 20X2:

Sales	$102,300
Cost of goods sold	85,600
Gross profit	16,700
Depreciation expense	4,620
Selling and administrative expenses	7,850
Investment revenue	(650)
Interest expense	440
Loss on impairment of goodwill	3,900
Earnings before income tax	540
Income tax expense	110
Earnings	$ 430

SCI, for the Year Ended 31 December 20X2:

Earnings	$430
Less: Actuarial revaluation of projected benefit obligation	(400)
Comprehensive income	$ 30

Statement of Changes in Equity, for the Year Ended 31 December 20X2:

	Common Shares	CC: Options	Common Stock Conversion Rights	Retained Earnings	AOCI: Pension
Opening balance	$10,500	$850	$350	$8,700	$ (1,100)
Comprehensive income				430	(400)

	Common Shares	CC: Options	Common Stock Conversion Rights	Retained Earnings	AOCI: Pension
Stock dividends	350			(350)	
Share issuance; bond conversion	980		(350)		
Share issuance; options	200	(185)			
Options recorded		215			
Share retirement	(100)			(620)	
Closing balance	$11,930	$880	$ 0	$8,160	$(1,500)

Statement of Financial Position, Year Ended

December 31	20X2	20X1
Assets:		
Cash	$ 665	$ 1,770
FVTPL investments	1,460	1,400
Accounts receivable (net)	5,050	6,330
Inventory	19,980	11,900
Fixed assets	41,125	38,800
Accumulated depreciation	(28,320)	(23,700)
Goodwill	3,760	7,660
Total	$43,720	$44,160
Liabilities and shareholders' equity:		
Accounts payable and accrued liabilities	$13,950	$13,900
Income taxes payable	65	40
Long-term debt	5,970	6,500
Bonds payable	—	700
Discount on bonds payable	—	(80)
Accrued pension liability	3,650	3,100
Deferred income tax	615	700
Common shares, no-par	11,930	10,500

December 31	20X2	20X1
Contributed capital: stock options	880	850
Common stock conversion rights	—	350
Retained earnings	8,160	8,700
AOCI: pension	(1,500)	(1,100)
Total	$43,720	$44,160

Additional information:

1. The bond was convertible to common shares and was converted during the period after $10 of discount amortization had been recorded.

2. During the year, FVTPL investments had a $430 increase in value, included in earnings in the investment revenue category. Dividend revenue is also included in investment revenue. FVTPL investments were sold at $900 (their carrying value) and other FVTPL investments were purchased.

3. A fixed asset was acquired for $400 during the year, with the vendor issuing a long-term note for the full purchase price. Other fixed assets were acquired for cash.

4. There is a stock option plan for executives, on which $215 of expense was recorded. Options were exercised during the year.

5. Assume unexplained changes in accounts are from normal transactions.

Required:

1. Prepare the statement of cash flows, using the two-step indirect method. Include a list of required note disclosure for non-cash transactions. Omit the separate disclosure of cash flow for interest, investment income, and income tax.

2. Repeat requirement 1, assuming that cash flow for tax is shown separately in operating activities, cash flow for interest is classified in financing activities, and cash flow for investment income is included in investing activities.

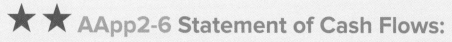 **AApp2-6 Statement of Cash Flows:**

Presented below are selected financial statements of Alfa Co. for the 20X4 fiscal year:

Statement of Financial Position		
As at 31 December	20X4	20X3
Assets		
Cash	$ 5,200	$ 44,000
FVTOCI investments	8,000	16,000

Accounts receivable (net)	230,400	192,000
Inventories	360,400	316,000
Land	27,000	64,000
Fixed assets (net)	274,000	264,000
Total assets	$905,000	$ 896,000

Liabilities and shareholders' equity

Bank overdraft	$ 88,600	$ 71,500
Accounts payable	91,700	93,000
Wages payable	26,000	24,000
Income tax payable	30,000	—
Cash dividends payable	6,000	—
Bonds payable, 10%	200,000	240,000
Convertible bonds payable	19,000	30,000
Discount on convertible bonds payable	(1,700)	(3,000)
Common share conversion rights	950	1,500
Common shares (no par)	277,450	277,000
Retained earnings	161,000	150,000
AOCI: investments	6,000	12,000
Total liabilities and equities	$905,000	$ 896,000

Statement of Earnings and Comprehensive Income

Year Ended 31 December 20X4

Sales		$1,260,000
Investment revenue: interest and dividends on FVTOCI investments		5,600
Total revenues		$1,265,600
Cost of sales	$ 948,000	
Wages expense	124,000	
Interest expense	16,600	
Depreciation expense	28,000	
Other expenses	75,000	

Loss on sale of land	5,000	1,196,600
Earnings before income tax		$ 69,000
Income tax		30,000
Earnings		$ 39,000
Change in value of FVTOCI investments		6,000
Comprehensive income		$ 45,000

The following additional data have been provided:

- Early in the year, FVTOCI investments were sold for their fair value of $16,000. The realized increase in fair value, $12,000, was transferred to retained earnings. Other investments were purchased for $2,000, and their fair value has increased by year-end.

- Equipment costing $43,000 was purchased during 20X4, and used equipment was sold at its book value of $5,000.

- The 10% bonds are being retired at the rate of $40,000 per year and were retired at par value. A portion of the convertible bonds was exchanged for common shares during 20X4. The discount was amortized by $200 during the year.

- The company spent $17,000 to reacquire and retire its own common shares. These shares had an average issue price of $10,000.

- Alfa declared cash dividends during 20X4.

Required:

1. Prepare the statement of cash flows, in good form. Use the indirect method to present the operating activities section. Also prepare separate disclosure of cash flow for dividends and interest received, interest paid, and income tax. Include a list of required note disclosure for non-cash transactions.

2. Provide an assessment of the company's cash transactions based on your SCF.

(Source: (Adapted) © CGA-Canada. Reproduced with permission.)

Solution

connect

★ ★ ★ AApp2-7 Statement of Cash Flows:

Presented below are the financial statements of Moose Co. for the year ending 31 December 20X3:

Statement of Financial Position

31 December	20X3	20X2
Assets		
Cash	$ 150,000	$ 145,000
Accounts receivable (net)	105,000	70,000
Inventories	230,000	210,000
Land	162,500	100,000
Plant and equipment (net)	245,000	266,500
Patents	15,000	16,500
	$907,500	$808,000
Liabilities and equities		
Accounts payable	$ 192,600	$ 133,700
Wages payable	36,400	45,000
Interest payable	6,700	15,800
Income tax payable	16,900	4,200
Deferred income tax liability	170,000	150,000
Bonds payable	65,000	100,000
Discount on bonds payable	(4,000)	(10,000)
Accrued pension liability	126,700	122,500
Common shares (no par)	191,500	182,000
Contributed capital on retirement of common shares	16,000	—
Retained earnings	101,000	73,000
AOCI: pension	(11,300)	(8,200)
	$907,500	$808,000

Statement of Earnings and Comprehensive Income

Year Ended 31 December 20X3

Sales	$800,000
Cost of sales	480,000
Gross margin	320,000

Expenses

Wages expense	$ 185,000	
Depreciation expense	10,000	
Amortization of patents	1,500	
Interest expense	18,000	
Gain on retirement of bonds	(10,000)	
Miscellaneous expense	3,500	
Loss on sale of equipment	2,000	210,000
Income before income tax		110,000
Income tax		49,500
Earnings		$ 60,500
Revaluation of pension liability		(3,100)
Comprehensive income		$ 57,400

Additional information:

- Common shares issued and outstanding at 31 December 20X2 were 42,000.
- In March, the company issued a 10% stock dividend to shareholders of record on 16 February 20X3, valued at market price per share of $7.
- In April, Moose issued common stock for land, valued at $20,000. Other shares were issued for cash.
- The company sold equipment costing $26,500, with a net book value of $11,500.
- On 31 October 20X3, Moose declared and paid a cash dividend to common shareholders.
- Common shares with an average issuance price of $90,000 were retired for cash in December 20X3.
- Discount amortization was $2,500 during the year. A portion of the bond payable was redeemed for cash.

Required:

1. Prepare a statement of cash flows in good form. Use the indirect method to present the operating activities section. Include separate disclosure of cash paid for interest and income tax paid in the operating activities section.
2. Provide an assessment of the company's cash transactions based on requirement 1.

(Source: [Adapted] © CGA-Canada. Reproduced with permission.)

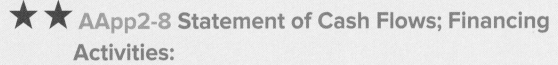 **AApp2-8 Statement of Cash Flows; Financing Activities:**

Information for Fortune Ltd. follows:

SFP extracts:	31 Dec. 20X5	31 Dec. 20X4
8% bonds payable	$ —	$2,000,000
Plus: Premium	—	45,600
	—	2,045,600
Convertible 6% bonds payable	3,000,000	—
Less: Discount	(57,000)	—
	2,943,000	—
Preferred shares	520,000	400,000
Common shares (500,000 shares as of 1 January 20X5)	8,678,000	6,800,000
Common share conversion rights	210,000	—
Contributed capital on common share retirement	—	52,000
$8.00 stock options outstanding	80,000	—
$11.50 stock warrants outstanding	400,000	605,000
Retained earnings	9,754,000	8,950,000

Additional information:

1. The 8% bonds payable were redeemed for cash at the beginning of the year at a redemption price of 102. There was no premium amortization prior to the redemption.

2. Convertible 6% bonds were issued during the period. Discount amortization of $3,000 was recorded in 20X5 after issuance.

3. On 1 January 20X5, 20,000 common shares were retired for $410,000.

4. Stock options, allowing purchase of 10,000 common shares at $8.00 each in 20X9, were issued for land on 1 October 20X5.

5. Earnings and comprehensive income for the period, $1,450,000.

6. Some of the $11.50 options outstanding at the beginning of the year were exercised. This resulted in the issuance of 100,000 common shares at $11.50 each.

7. Additional common shares were issued for cash and cash dividends were declared and paid.

Required:

Prepare the financing activities section of the statement of cash flows, in good form, for the year ended 31 December 20X5. The change in accounts is explained by the "other information" and/or by a logical transaction.

connect

★ ★ ★ AApp2-9 Statement of Cash Flows:

The financial statements of Clarion Ltd. for the 20X5 fiscal year follow (in thousands):

Statement of Earnings, for the Year Ended 31 December 20X5:

Sales	$3,620
Cost of goods sold	1,200
Gross profit	2,420
Depreciation and amortization expense	1,570
Selling and administrative expenses	750
Investment revenue	(240)
Interest expense	140
Gain on sale of fixed assets	(70)
Earnings before income tax	270
Income tax expense	80
Earnings	$ 190

SCI, for the Year Ended 31 December 20X5:

Earnings	$ 190
Plus: Increase in fair value, FVTOCI investment	310
Less: Realized gain on sale of FVTOCI investment	(160)
Comprehensive income	$ 340

Statement of Changes in Equity, for the Year Ended 31 December 20X5:

	Common Shares	CC: Options	Retained Earnings	AOCI: Investments
Opening balance	$2,700	$450	$3,900	$690
Comprehensive income			190	310
FVTOCI transfer on realization			160	(160)
Cash dividends			(100)	

	Common Shares	CC: Options	Retained Earnings	AOCI: Investments
Share issuance; patent	430			
Share issuance; options	150	(125)		
Options recorded		75		
Share retirement	(300)		(220)	
Closing balance	$2,980	$400	$3,930	$840

Statement of Financial Position, Year Ended

December 31	20X5	20X4
Assets:		
Cash	$ 75	$ 30
FVTPL investments	310	300
FVTOCI investments	1,900	1,200
Accounts receivable (net)	2,035	1,615
Inventory	1,480	2,100
Fixed assets	9,400	8,800
Accumulated depreciation	(4,250)	(3,200)
Patent (net)	390	—
Total	$11,340	$10,845
Liabilities and shareholders' equity:		
Accounts payable and accrued liabilities	$ 1,350	$ 1,800
Income taxes payable	15	40
Lease liability	540	—
Bonds payable	1,000	1,000

December 31	20X5	20X4
Discount on bonds payable	(30)	(35)
Deferred income tax	315	300
Common shares	2,980	2,700
Contributed capital: stock options	400	450
Retained earnings	3,930	3,900
AOCI: investments	840	690
Total	$11,340	$10,845

Additional information:

1. FVTOCI investments with an original cost of $300 were sold during the year. Their carrying value and fair value was $460. Unrealized gains were transferred to retained earnings when realized. Other FVTOCI investments with a cost of $850 were acquired during the year.

2. All the $10 change in the FVTPL investment account relates to unrealized changes in fair value of the investments, included in investment income. Investment income also includes $230 interest and dividend revenue on all investments and thus has totalled $240.

3. A financing lease for heavy machinery, with a present value of $600, was recorded in 20X5. Payments were made on the lease contract. The leased assets are included in fixed assets on the SFP.

4. There is a stock option plan for executives, on which $75 of expense was recorded. Options were exercised during the year.

5. A patent was acquired in exchange for common shares. Patent amortization expense of $40 is included in depreciation and amortization expense.

6. Fixed assets with an original cost of $700 and a net book value of $120 were sold for $290.

7. Assume unexplained changes in accounts are from normal transactions.

Required:

1. Prepare the statement of cash flows, using the two-step indirect method. Include a list of required note disclosure for non-cash transactions. Omit the separate disclosure of cash flow for interest, investment income, and income tax.

2. Explain the company's cash transactions for the year, based on the SCF.

3. Repeat the operating activities section of the SCF, using the direct method of presentation.

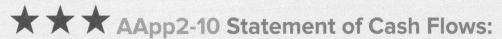 **AApp2-10 Statement of Cash Flows:**

The financial statements of Simon Corp. for the 20X9 fiscal year follow (in thousands):

Statement of Earnings, for the Year Ended 31 December, 20X9:

Sales	$26,800
Cost of goods sold	14,700
Gross profit	12,100
Depreciation	2,290
Selling and administrative expenses	4,250
Investment revenue	(640)
Interest expense	1,980
Gain on sale of fixed assets	(320)
Earnings before income tax	4,540
Income tax expense	2,080
Earnings	$ 2,460

SCI, for the Year Ended 31 December 20X9:

Earnings	$ 2,460
Plus: Increase in fair value, FVTOCI investment	70
Less: Realized gain on sale of FVTOCI investment	(200)
Less: Actuarial revaluation of projected benefit obligation	(560)
Comprehensive income	$ 1,770

Statement of Changes in Equity, for the Year Ended 31 December 20X9:

	Common Shares	CC: Options	Retained Earnings	AOCI: Investments	AOCI: Pension
Opening balance	$ 1,100	$350	$23,900	$360	(2,470)
Comprehensive income			2,460	70	(560)
FVTOCI transfer on realization			200	(200)	

	Common Shares	CC: Options	Retained Earnings	AOCI: Investments	AOCI: Pension
Dividends—cash			(225)		
Dividends—stock	450		(450)		
Share issuance; options	300	(270)			
Options recorded		175			
Share retirement	(20)		(320)		
Closing balance	$1,830	$255	$25,565	$230	$(3,030)

Statement of Financial Position, Year Ended

December 31	20X9	20X8
Assets:		
Cash	$ 1,155	$ 2,650
FVTPL investments	3,690	3,300
FVTOCI investments	250	430
Accounts receivable (net)	11,950	11,870
Inventory	7,910	7,310
Fixed assets	39,400	38,500
Accumulated depreciation	(14,700)	(13,950)
Goodwill	16,845	16,845
Total	$66,500	$66,955
Liabilities and shareholders' equity:		
Accounts payable and accrued liabilities	$ 7,240	$ 6,990
Income taxes payable	650	685

December 31	20X9	20X8
Short-term bank debt	3,905	8,405
Lease liability	1,060	—
Bonds payable	20,000	20,000
Discount on bonds payable	(225)	(285)
Deferred income tax	4,070	3,720
Accrued pension liability	4,950	4,200
Common shares, no-par	1,830	1,100
Contributed capital: stock options	255	350
Retained earnings	25,565	23,900
AOCI: investments	230	360
AOCI: pension	(3,030)	(2,470)
Total	$66,500	$66,955

Additional information:

1. FVTOCI investments with an original cost of $50 and carrying (fair) value of $250 were sold during the year. Unrealized gains were transferred to retained earnings when realized. No FVTOCI investments were acquired during the year.

2. In the FVTPL category, there were no purchases or sales during the year. Investment income includes the recognized change in fair value.

3. A financing lease for earth-moving equipment, with a present value of $1,200, was recorded in 20X9. Payments were made on the lease contract. The leased assets are included in fixed assets on the SFP.

4. There is a stock option plan for executives, on which $175 of expense was recorded. Options were exercised during the year.

5. Fixed assets with an original cost of $4,240 and a net book value of $2,700 were sold for cash.

6. Assume unexplained changes in accounts are from normal transactions.

Required:

1. Prepare the statement of cash flows, using the two-step indirect method. Include a list of required note disclosure for non-cash transactions.

2. Prepare the separate disclosure of cash flow for interest, interest received, and income tax paid.

3. Repeat the operating activities section of the SCF, using the direct method of presentation.

COMPOUND INTEREST TABLES AND FORMULAE

Table I-1: Present value of 1: (P/F, *i*, *n*)

$$P/F = \frac{1}{(1+i)^n}$$

n	2%	2.5%	3%	4%	5%	6%	7%	8%	9%	10%	11%	12%	14%	15%
1	0.98039	0.97561	0.97087	0.96154	0.95238	0.94340	0.93458	0.92593	0.91743	0.90909	0.90090	0.89286	0.87719	0.86957
2	0.96117	0.95181	0.94260	0.92456	0.90703	0.89000	0.87344	0.85734	0.84168	0.82645	0.81162	0.79719	0.76947	0.75614
3	0.94232	0.92860	0.91514	0.88900	0.86384	0.83962	0.81630	0.79383	0.77218	0.75131	0.73119	0.71178	0.67497	0.65752
4	0.92385	0.90595	0.88849	0.85480	0.82270	0.79209	0.76290	0.73503	0.70843	0.68301	0.65873	0.63552	0.59208	0.57175
5	0.90573	0.88385	0.86261	0.82193	0.78353	0.74726	0.71299	0.68058	0.64993	0.62092	0.59345	0.56743	0.51937	0.49718
6	0.88797	0.86230	0.83748	0.79031	0.74622	0.70496	0.66634	0.63017	0.59627	0.56447	0.53464	0.50663	0.45559	0.43233
7	0.87056	0.84127	0.81309	0.75992	0.71068	0.66506	0.62275	0.58349	0.54703	0.51316	0.48166	0.45235	0.39964	0.37594
8	0.85349	0.82075	0.78941	0.73069	0.67684	0.62741	0.58201	0.54027	0.50187	0.46651	0.43393	0.40388	0.35056	0.32690
9	0.83676	0.80073	0.76642	0.70259	0.64461	0.59190	0.54393	0.50025	0.46043	0.42410	0.39092	0.36061	0.30751	0.28426
10	0.82035	0.78120	0.74409	0.67556	0.61391	0.55839	0.50835	0.46319	0.42241	0.38554	0.35218	0.32197	0.26974	0.24718
11	0.80426	0.76214	0.72242	0.64958	0.58468	0.52679	0.47509	0.42888	0.38753	0.35049	0.31728	0.28748	0.23662	0.21494
12	0.78849	0.74356	0.70138	0.62460	0.55684	0.49697	0.44401	0.39711	0.35553	0.31863	0.28584	0.25668	0.20756	0.18691
13	0.77303	0.72542	0.68095	0.60057	0.53032	0.46884	0.41496	0.36770	0.32618	0.28966	0.25751	0.22917	0.18207	0.16253
14	0.75788	0.70773	0.66112	0.57748	0.50507	0.44230	0.38782	0.34046	0.29925	0.26333	0.23199	0.20462	0.15971	0.14133
15	0.74301	0.69047	0.64186	0.55526	0.48102	0.41727	0.36245	0.31524	0.27454	0.23939	0.20900	0.18270	0.14010	0.12289
16	0.72845	0.67362	0.62317	0.53391	0.45811	0.39365	0.33873	0.29189	0.25187	0.21763	0.18829	0.16312	0.12289	0.10686
17	0.71416	0.65720	0.60502	0.51337	0.43630	0.37136	0.31657	0.27027	0.23107	0.19784	0.16963	0.14564	0.10780	0.09293
18	0.70016	0.64117	0.58739	0.49363	0.41552	0.35034	0.29586	0.25025	0.21199	0.17986	0.15282	0.13004	0.09456	0.08081
19	0.68643	0.62553	0.57029	0.47464	0.39573	0.33051	0.27651	0.23171	0.19449	0.16361	0.13768	0.11611	0.08295	0.07027
20	0.67297	0.61027	0.55368	0.45639	0.37689	0.31180	0.25842	0.21455	0.17843	0.14864	0.12403	0.10367	0.07276	0.06110
21	0.65978	0.59539	0.53755	0.43883	0.35894	0.29416	0.24151	0.19866	0.16370	0.13513	0.11174	0.09256	0.06383	0.05313
22	0.64684	0.58086	0.52189	0.42196	0.34185	0.27751	0.22571	0.18394	0.15018	0.12285	0.10067	0.08264	0.05599	0.04620
23	0.63416	0.56670	0.50669	0.40573	0.32557	0.26180	0.21095	0.17032	0.13778	0.11168	0.09069	0.07379	0.04911	0.04017

24	0.62172	0.55288	0.49193	0.39012	0.31007	0.24698	0.19715	0.15770	0.12640	0.10153	0.08170	0.06588	0.04308	0.03493
25	0.60953	0.53939	0.47761	0.37512	0.29530	0.23300	0.18425	0.14602	0.11597	0.09230	0.07361	0.05882	0.03779	0.03038
26	0.59758	0.52623	0.46369	0.36069	0.28124	0.21981	0.17220	0.13520	0.10639	0.08391	0.06631	0.05252	0.03315	0.02642
27	0.58586	0.51340	0.45019	0.34682	0.26785	0.20737	0.16093	0.12519	0.09761	0.07628	0.05974	0.04689	0.02908	0.02297
28	0.57437	0.50088	0.43708	0.33348	0.25509	0.19563	0.15040	0.11591	0.08955	0.06934	0.05382	0.04187	0.02551	0.01997
29	0.56311	0.48866	0.42435	0.32065	0.24295	0.18456	0.14056	0.10733	0.08215	0.06304	0.04849	0.03738	0.02237	0.01737
30	0.55207	0.47674	0.41199	0.30832	0.23138	0.17411	0.13137	0.09938	0.07537	0.05731	0.04368	0.03338	0.01963	0.01510
31	0.54125	0.46511	0.39999	0.29646	0.22036	0.16425	0.12277	0.09202	0.06915	0.05210	0.03935	0.02980	0.01722	0.01313
32	0.53063	0.45377	0.38834	0.28506	0.20987	0.15496	0.11474	0.08520	0.06344	0.04736	0.03545	0.02661	0.01510	0.01142
33	0.52023	0.44270	0.37703	0.27409	0.19987	0.14619	0.10723	0.07889	0.05820	0.04306	0.03194	0.02376	0.01325	0.00993
34	0.51003	0.43191	0.36604	0.26355	0.19035	0.13791	0.10022	0.07305	0.05339	0.03914	0.02878	0.02121	0.01162	0.00864
35	0.50003	0.42137	0.35538	0.25342	0.18129	0.13011	0.09366	0.06763	0.04899	0.03558	0.02592	0.01894	0.01019	0.00751
36	0.49022	0.41109	0.34503	0.24367	0.17266	0.12274	0.08754	0.06262	0.04494	0.03235	0.02335	0.01691	0.00894	0.00653
37	0.48061	0.40107	0.33498	0.23430	0.16444	0.11579	0.08181	0.05799	0.04123	0.02941	0.02104	0.01510	0.00784	0.00568
38	0.47119	0.39128	0.32523	0.22529	0.15661	0.10924	0.07646	0.05369	0.03783	0.02673	0.01896	0.01348	0.00688	0.00494
39	0.46195	0.38174	0.31575	0.21662	0.14915	0.10306	0.07146	0.04971	0.03470	0.02430	0.01708	0.01204	0.00604	0.00429
40	0.45289	0.37243	0.30656	0.20829	0.14205	0.09722	0.06678	0.04603	0.03184	0.02209	0.01538	0.01075	0.00529	0.00373
45	0.41020	0.32917	0.26444	0.17120	0.11130	0.07265	0.04761	0.03133	0.02069	0.01372	0.00913	0.00610	0.00275	0.00186
50	0.37153	0.29094	0.22811	0.14071	0.08720	0.05429	0.03395	0.02132	0.01345	0.00852	0.00542	0.00346	0.00143	0.00092

Table I-2: Present value of an ordinary annuity of n payments of 1: (P/A, i, n)

$$P/A = \frac{1 - \frac{1}{(1 + i)^n}}{i}$$

n	2%	2.5%	3%	4%	5%	6%	7%	8%	9%	10%	11%	12%	14%	15%
1	0.98039	0.97561	0.97087	0.96154	0.95238	0.94340	0.93458	0.92593	0.91743	0.90909	0.90090	0.89286	0.87719	0.86957
2	1.94156	1.92742	1.91347	1.88609	1.85941	1.83339	1.80802	1.78326	1.75911	1.73554	1.71252	1.69005	1.64666	1.62571
3	2.88388	2.85602	2.82861	2.77509	2.72325	2.67301	2.62432	2.57710	2.53129	2.48685	2.44371	2.40183	2.32163	2.28323
4	3.80773	3.76197	3.71710	3.62990	3.54595	3.46511	3.38721	3.31213	3.23972	3.16987	3.10245	3.03735	2.91371	2.85498
5	4.71346	4.64583	4.57971	4.45182	4.32948	4.21236	4.10020	3.99271	3.88965	3.79079	3.69590	3.60478	3.43308	3.35216
6	5.60143	5.50813	5.41719	5.24214	5.07569	4.91732	4.76654	4.62288	4.48592	4.35526	4.23054	4.11141	3.88867	3.78448
7	6.47199	6.34939	6.23028	6.00205	5.78637	5.58238	5.38929	5.20637	5.03295	4.86842	4.71220	4.56376	4.28830	4.16042
8	7.32548	7.17014	7.01969	6.73274	6.46321	6.20979	5.97130	5.74664	5.53482	5.33493	5.14612	4.96764	4.63886	4.48732
9	8.16224	7.97087	7.78611	7.43533	7.10782	6.80169	6.51523	6.24689	5.99525	5.75902	5.53705	5.32825	4.94637	4.77158
10	8.98259	8.75206	8.53020	8.11090	7.72173	7.36009	7.02358	6.71008	6.41766	6.14457	5.88923	5.65022	5.21612	5.01877
11	9.78685	9.51421	9.25262	8.76048	8.30641	7.88687	7.49867	7.13896	6.80519	6.49506	6.20652	5.93770	5.45273	5.23371
12	10.57534	10.25776	9.95400	9.38507	8.86325	8.38384	7.94269	7.53608	7.16073	6.81369	6.49236	6.19437	5.66029	5.42062
13	11.34837	10.98318	10.63496	9.98565	9.39357	8.85268	8.35765	7.90378	7.48690	7.10336	6.74987	6.42355	5.84236	5.58315
14	12.10625	11.69091	11.29607	10.56312	9.89864	9.29498	8.74547	8.24424	7.78615	7.36669	6.98187	6.62817	6.00207	5.72448
15	12.84926	12.38138	11.93794	11.11839	10.37966	9.71225	9.10791	8.55948	8.06069	7.60608	7.19087	6.81086	6.14217	5.84737
16	13.57771	13.05500	12.56110	11.65230	10.83777	10.10590	9.44665	8.85137	8.31256	7.82371	7.37916	6.97399	6.26506	5.95423
17	14.29187	13.71220	13.16612	12.16567	11.27407	10.47726	9.76322	9.12164	8.54363	8.02155	7.54879	7.11963	6.37286	6.04716
18	14.99203	14.35336	13.75351	12.65930	11.68959	10.82760	10.05909	9.37189	8.75563	8.20141	7.70162	7.24967	6.46742	6.12797
19	15.67846	14.97889	14.32380	13.13394	12.08532	11.15812	10.33560	9.60360	8.95011	8.36492	7.83929	7.36578	6.55037	6.19823

20	6.25933	6.62313	7.46944	7.96333	8.51356	9.12855	9.81815	10.59401	11.46992	12.46221	13.59033	14.87747	15.58916	16.35143
21	6.31246	6.68696	7.56200	8.07507	8.64869	9.29224	10.01680	10.83553	11.76408	12.82115	14.02916	15.41502	16.18455	17.01121
22	6.35866	6.74294	7.64465	8.17574	8.77154	9.44243	10.20074	11.06124	12.04158	13.16300	14.45112	15.93692	16.76541	17.65805
23	6.39884	6.79206	7.71843	8.26643	8.88322	9.58021	10.37106	11.27219	12.30338	13.48857	14.85684	16.44361	17.33211	18.29220
24	6.43377	6.83514	7.78432	8.34814	8.98474	9.70661	10.52876	11.46933	12.55036	13.79864	15.24696	16.93554	17.88499	18.91393
25	6.46415	6.87293	7.84314	8.42174	9.07704	9.82258	10.67478	11.65358	12.78336	14.09394	15.62208	17.41315	18.42438	19.52346
26	6.49056	6.90608	7.89566	8.48806	9.16095	9.92897	10.80998	11.82578	13.00317	14.37519	15.98277	17.87684	18.95061	20.12104
27	6.51353	6.93515	7.94255	8.54780	9.23722	10.02658	10.93516	11.98671	13.21053	14.64303	16.32959	18.32703	19.46401	20.70690
28	6.53351	6.96066	7.98442	8.60162	9.30657	10.11613	11.05108	12.13711	13.40616	14.89813	16.66306	18.76411	19.96489	21.28127
29	6.55088	6.98304	8.02181	8.65011	9.36961	10.19828	11.15841	12.27767	13.59072	15.14107	16.98371	19.18845	20.45355	21.84438
30	6.56598	7.00266	8.05518	8.69379	9.42691	10.27365	11.25778	12.40904	13.76483	15.37245	17.29203	19.60044	20.93029	22.39646
31	6.57911	7.01988	8.08499	8.73315	9.47901	10.34280	11.34980	12.53181	13.92909	15.59281	17.58849	20.00043	21.39541	22.93770
32	6.59053	7.03498	8.11159	8.76860	9.52638	10.40624	11.43500	12.64656	14.08404	15.80268	17.87355	20.38877	21.84918	23.46833
33	6.60046	7.04823	8.13535	8.80054	9.56943	10.46444	11.51389	12.75379	14.23023	16.00255	18.14765	20.76579	22.29188	23.98856
34	6.60910	7.05985	8.15656	8.82932	9.60857	10.51784	11.58693	12.85401	14.36814	16.19290	18.41120	21.13184	22.72379	24.49859
35	6.61661	7.07005	8.17550	8.85524	9.64416	10.56682	11.65457	12.94767	14.49825	16.37419	18.66461	21.48722	23.14516	24.99862
36	6.62314	7.07899	8.19241	8.87859	9.67651	10.61176	11.71719	13.03521	14.62099	16.54685	18.90828	21.83225	23.55625	25.48884
37	6.62881	7.08683	8.20751	8.89963	9.70592	10.65299	11.77518	13.11702	14.73678	16.71129	19.14258	22.16724	23.95732	25.96945
38	6.63375	7.09371	8.22099	8.91859	9.73265	10.69082	11.82887	13.19347	14.84602	16.86789	19.36786	22.49246	24.34860	26.44064
39	6.63805	7.09975	8.23303	8.93567	9.75696	10.72552	11.87858	13.26493	14.94907	17.01704	19.58448	22.80822	24.73034	26.90259
40	6.64178	7.10504	8.24378	8.95105	9.77905	10.75736	11.92461	13.33171	15.04630	17.15909	19.79277	23.11477	25.10278	27.35548
45	6.65429	7.12322	8.28252	9.00791	9.86281	10.88120	12.10840	13.60552	15.45583	17.77407	20.72004	24.51871	26.83302	29.49016
50	6.66051	7.13266	8.30450	9.04165	9.91481	10.96168	12.23348	13.80075	15.76186	18.25593	21.48218	25.72976	28.36231	31.42361

Table I-3: Present value of an annuity due of n payments of 1: (P/AD, i, n)

$$P/AD = \left[\frac{1 - \dfrac{1}{(1+i)^n}}{i} \right] \times (1+i)$$

n	2%	2.5%	3%	4%	5%	6%	7%	8%	9%	10%	11%	12%	14%	15%
1	1.00000	1.00000	1.00000	1.00000	1.00000	1.00000	1.00000	1.00000	1.00000	1.00000	1.00000	1.00000	1.00000	1.00000
2	1.98039	1.97561	1.97087	1.96154	1.95238	1.94340	1.93458	1.92593	1.91743	1.90909	1.90090	1.89286	1.87719	1.86957
3	2.94156	2.92742	2.91347	2.88609	2.85941	2.83339	2.80302	2.78326	2.75911	2.73554	2.71252	2.69005	2.64666	2.62571
4	3.88388	3.85602	3.82861	3.77509	3.72325	3.67301	3.62432	3.57710	3.53129	3.48685	3.44371	3.40183	3.32163	3.28323
5	4.80773	4.76197	4.71710	4.62990	4.54595	4.46511	4.38721	4.31213	4.23972	4.16987	4.10245	4.03735	3.91371	3.85498
6	5.71346	5.64583	5.57971	5.45182	5.32948	5.21236	5.10020	4.99271	4.88965	4.79079	4.69590	4.60478	4.43308	4.35216
7	6.60143	6.50813	6.41719	6.24214	6.07569	5.91732	5.76654	5.62288	5.48592	5.35526	5.23054	5.11141	4.88867	4.78448
8	7.47199	7.34939	7.23028	7.00205	6.78637	6.58238	6.38929	6.20637	6.03295	5.86842	5.71220	5.56376	5.28830	5.16042
9	8.32548	8.17014	8.01969	7.73274	7.46321	7.20979	6.97130	6.74664	6.53482	6.33493	6.14612	5.96764	5.63886	5.48732
10	9.16224	8.97087	8.78611	8.43533	8.10732	7.80169	7.51523	7.24689	6.99525	6.75902	6.53705	6.32825	5.94637	5.77158
11	9.98259	9.75206	9.53020	9.11090	8.72173	8.36009	8.02358	7.71008	7.41766	7.14457	6.88923	6.65022	6.21612	6.01877
12	10.78685	10.51421	10.25262	9.76048	9.3064164	8.886878	8.49867	8.13896	7.80519	7.49506	7.20652	6.93770	6.45273	6.23371
13	11.57534	11.25776	10.95400	10.38507	9.86325	9.38384	8.94269	8.53608	8.16073	7.81369	7.49236	7.19437	6.66029	6.42062
14	12.34837	11.98318	11.63496	10.98565	10.39357	9.85268	9.35765	8.90378	8.48690	8.10336	7.74987	7.42355	6.84236	6.58315
15	13.10625	12.69091	12.29607	11.56312	10.89864	10.29498	9.74547	9.24424	8.78615	8.36669	7.98187	7.62817	7.00207	6.72448
16	13.84926	13.38138	12.93794	12.11839	11.37966	10.71225	10.10791	9.55948	9.06069	8.60608	8.19087	7.81086	7.14217	6.84737
17	14.57771	14.05500	13.56110	12.65230	11.83777	11.10590	10.44665	9.85137	9.31256	8.82371	8.37916	7.97399	7.26506	6.95423
18	15.29187	14.71220	14.16612	13.16567	12.27407	11.47726	10.76322	10.12164	9.54363	9.02155	8.54879	8.11963	7.3726	7.04716
19	15.99203	15.35336	14.75351	13.65930	12.68959	11.82760	11.05909	10.37189	9.75563	9.20141	8.70162	8.24967	7.46742	7.12797

20	16.67846	15.97889	15.32380	14.13394	13.08532	12.15812	11.33560	10.60360	9.95011	9.36492	8.83929	8.36578	7.55037	7.19823
21	17.35143	16.58916	15.87747	14.59033	13.46221	12.46992	11.59401	10.81815	10.12855	9.51356	8.96333	8.46944	7.62313	7.25933
22	18.01121	17.18455	16.41502	15.02916	13.82115	12.76408	11.83553	11.01680	10.29224	9.64869	9.07507	8.56200	7.68696	7.31246
23	18.65805	17.76541	16.93692	15.45112	14.16300	13.04158	12.06124	11.20074	10.44243	9.77154	9.17574	8.64465	7.74294	7.35866
24	19.29220	18.33211	17.44361	15.85684	14.48857	13.30338	12.27219	11.37106	10.58021	9.88322	9.26643	8.71843	7.79206	7.39884
25	19.91393	18.88499	17.93554	16.24696	14.79864	13.55036	12.46933	11.52876	10.70661	9.98474	9.34814	8.78432	7.83514	7.43377
26	20.52346	19.42438	18.41315	16.62208	15.09394	13.78336	12.65358	11.67478	10.82258	10.07704	9.42174	8.84314	7.87293	7.46415
27	21.12104	19.95061	18.87684	16.98277	15.37519	14.00317	12.82578	11.80998	10.92897	10.16095	9.48806	8.89566	7.90608	7.49056
28	21.70690	20.46401	19.32703	17.32959	15.64303	14.21053	12.98671	11.98516	11.02658	10.23722	9.54780	8.94255	7.93515	7.51353
29	22.28127	20.96489	19.76411	17.66306	15.89813	14.40616	13.13711	12.05108	11.11613	10.30657	9.60162	8.98442	7.96066	7.53351
30	22.84438	21.45355	20.18845	17.98371	16.14107	14.59072	13.27767	12.15841	11.19828	10.36961	9.65011	9.02181	7.98304	7.55088
31	23.39646	21.93029	20.60044	18.29203	16.37245	14.76483	13.40904	12.25778	11.27365	10.42691	9.69379	9.05518	8.00266	7.56598
32	23.93770	22.39541	21.00043	18.58849	16.59281	14.92909	13.53181	12.34980	11.34280	10.47901	9.73315	9.08499	8.01988	7.57911
33	24.46833	22.34918	21.38877	18.87355	16.80268	15.08404	13.64656	12.43500	11.40624	10.52638	9.76860	9.11159	8.03498	7.59053
34	24.98856	23.29188	21.76579	19.14765	17.00255	15.23023	13.75379	12.51389	11.46444	10.56943	9.80054	9.13535	8.04823	7.60046
35	25.49859	23.72379	22.13184	19.41120	17.19290	15.36814	13.85401	12.58693	11.51784	10.60857	9.82932	9.15656	8.05985	7.60910
36	25.99862	24.14516	22.48722	19.66461	17.37419	15.493257	13.94767	12.65457	11.56682	10.64416	9.85524	9.17550	8.07005	7.61661
37	26.48884	24.55625	22.83225	19.90828	17.54685	15.620997	14.03521	12.71719	11.61176	10.67651	9.87859	9.19241	8.07899	7.62314
38	26.96945	24.95732	23.16724	20.14258	17.71129	15.73673	14.11702	12.77518	11.65299	10.70592	9.89963	9.20751	8.08683	7.62881
39	27.44064	25.34860	23.49246	20.36786	17.86789	15.34602	14.19347	12.82837	11.69082	10.73265	9.91859	9.22099	8.09371	7.63375
40	27.90259	25.73034	23.80822	20.58448	18.01704	15.94907	14.26493	12.87853	11.72552	10.75696	9.93567	9.23303	8.09975	7.63805
45	30.07996	27.50385	25.25427	21.54884	18.66277	16.38318	14.55791	13.07707	11.86051	10.84909	9.99878	9.27642	8.12047	7.65244
50	32.05208	29.07137	26.50166	22.34147	19.16872	16.70757	14.76680	13.21216	11.94823	10.90630	10.03624	9.30104	8.13123	7.65959

INDEX